Sears List of
Subject Headings

Sears List of Subject Headings

14th Edition

Edited by

MARTHA T. MOONEY

New York

The H. W. Wilson Company

1991

Printed in the United States of America
95 94 93 92 91   5 4 3 2 1

Library of Congress Cataloging-in-Publication Data

Sears, Minnie Earl, 1873-1933.
    Sears list of subject headings. — 14th ed. / edited by Martha T. Mooney.
        p.   cm.
    Includes bibliographical references.
    ISBN 0-8242-0803-X : $42.00
    1. Subject headings.   I. Mooney, Martha T.   II. Title.
    Z695.S43   1991   91-10290
                                                                CIP

Table of Contents

Preface

History and Scope. Minnie Earl Sears prepared the first edition of this work in response to demands for a list of subject headings that was more suitable to the needs of the small library than the existing A.L.A. and Library of Congress lists. Published in 1923, the *List of Subject Headings for Small Libraries* was based on the headings used by nine small libraries that were known to be well cataloged. However, Minnie Sears early recognized the need for uniformity, and she followed the form of the Library of Congress subject headings with few exceptions. This decision was important and foresighted because it allowed a library to add Library of Congress headings as needed when not provided by the Sears List and to graduate to the full use of Library of Congress headings when collections grew too large for a limited subject headings list.

Minnie Sears used only *See* and "refer from" references in the first edition. In the second edition (1926) she added *See also* references at the request of teachers of cataloging who were using the List as a textbook. To make the List more useful as a textbook she wrote a chapter on "Practical Suggestions for the Beginner in Subject Heading Work" for the third edition (1933).

Isabel Stevenson Monro edited the fourth (1939) and fifth (1944) editions. A new feature of the fourth edition was the inclusion of Dewey Decimal Classification numbers as applied in the *Standard Catalog for Public Libraries*. The new subjects added to the List were based on those used in the Standard Catalog Series and on the catalog cards issued by The H.W. Wilson Company. Therefore, the original subtitle "Compiled from Lists used in Nine Representative Small Libraries" was dropped. Another new feature was the printing in italics of those subdivisions that had a general application.

The sixth (1950), seventh (1954), and eighth (1959) editions were prepared by Bertha M. Frick. In recognition of the pioneering and fundamental contributions made by Minnie Sears the title was changed to *Sears List of Subject Headings* with the sixth edition. Since the List was being used by medium-sized libraries as well as small ones, the phrase "for Small Libraries" was deleted from the title. The symbols *x* and *xx* were substituted for the "Refer from (see ref.)" and "Refer from (see also ref.)" phrases to conform to the format adopted by the Library of Congress.

The ninth edition (1965), the first to be prepared by Barbara M. Westby, continued the policies of the earlier editions, with one major exception. The Dewey Decimal Classification numbers were dropped by the publisher. Many users of Sears had called attention to the inconsistency of including classification numbers and at the same time instructing the cataloger to consult the Dewey Decimal Classification for numbers. Moreover, it was the expressed opinion of these users that the inclusion of numbers often led to a misuse of the publication owing to a misunderstanding of the relationship between subject headings and classification. The tenth edition (1972) also omitted the Dewey numbers, but they were reintroduced in the eleventh edition (1977), largely in response to the needs of librarians in many medium and small-sized libraries who had been left with little or no assistance in the classification of their collections.

With the eleventh edition, the "Practical Suggestions for the Beginner in Subject Heading Work" was retitled "Principles of the Sears List of Subject Headings" to emphasize "principles" and a section dealing with nonbook materials was added. The "Principles" have been substantially revised for this edition.

The thirteenth edition (1986), prepared by Carmen Rovira and Caroline Reyes, was the first to be created as an online database and to take advantage of computer validation capabilities. It also responded to changing theory in subject analysis occasioned by the development of online public access catalogs.

Addition of New Headings. The selection of new terms for the present edition covers many areas and reflects the continuing interest in health and environment, computer science, space technology, changing family relationships, minorities, consumerism, business and management, among others.

The headings added to this edition were suggested by librarians representing various sizes and types of libraries, by commercial vendors of bibliographic records, and by the catalogers and indexers at The H.W. Wilson Company who are responsible for the headings in the Standard Catalog Series, *Book Review Digest,* and such periodical indexes as *Readers' Guide to Periodical Literature.* In addition, *Library of Congress Subject Headings,* 13th edition, and the *Hennepin County Library Cataloging Bulletin* were consulted.

In accord with a suggestion of the Cataloging of Children's Materials Committee of A.L.A., the headings from *Subject Headings for Children's Literature* (Library of Congress) were incorporated into the Sears List with the thirteenth edition. Some of the headings were not included specifically because they fell into the category of headings that can be added to Sears as needed; others were omitted because they already existed in Sears in a slightly different form. Since the Sears List is intended for both adult and juvenile collections, two similar headings for the same subject could not be used. Therefore, when Library of Congress has chosen different headings for adult and juvenile approaches to the same subject, a choice was made for Sears. In cases where the Sears List uses the adult form, the cataloger of children's materials may prefer to use the form found in *Subject Headings for Children's Literature.*

No list can hope to keep completely abreast of the information explosion, nor can it provide for every idea, object, process, and relationship. By referring to the patterns established and examples provided, the cataloger can add new headings as needed. Guides for the wording of new headings may be found in the works themselves as well as in periodical literature and indexes. Although daily newspaper terminology may be too colloquial for use as headings, it does provide a clue to the way in which a user may ask for materials, and also suggests terms to be used as cross-references.

Revision of Headings. At the same time as new headings are added to the List, revision and updating of existing headings continues. Some terms have been changed to reflect current usage: **Drug addiction** replaces the old-fashioned **Narcotic habit;** the layman's **Litigation** replaces **Actions and defenses.** Some have been simplified: **Blues music** replaces **Blues (Songs, etc.); Information systems** replaces **Information storage and retrieval systems; Steel industry** and **Iron industry** replace the earlier **Steel industry and trade, Iron industry and trade,** etc. Others of decreasing interest, such as **Smallpox** and **Chemurgy,** have been removed.

In recent years the Library of Congress has increased the rate of revision and modernization of some of its long-standing subject headings. This edition of Sears, like the previous ones, has incorporated many of the changes, such as **Draft** instead of **Military service, Compulsory; RNA** instead of **Ribonucleic acid; Sexually transmitted diseases** instead of **Venereal diseases;** and **Silent films** instead of **Motion pictures, Silent.**

Form of Headings. The successive editors of the Sears List have followed the policy established by Minnie Earl Sears to use the Library of Congress form of subject headings with some modifications for current terminology and spelling. Further modifications, introduced to meet the needs of smaller collections, include the simplification of phrasing (e.g. **Asylum** for Asylum, Right of) and, in some cases, the broadening of a heading. Thus closely related headings have been combined to create one Sears heading from two Library of Congress headings (e.g. **Generic drugs** for Generic drugs and Drugs—Generic substitution; **Poisons and poisoning** for Poisons and Poisoning). Other compound headings, which the Library of Congress has divided into separate terms (**Acrobats and acrobatics; Anarchism and anarchists**) have been kept intact in Sears, on the assumption that they were sufficient for the needs of small and medium-sized libraries.

Beginning with the thirteenth edition of Sears, the direct form of entry has been preferred to the inverted form, both in new headings and in the revision of those already established, on the theory that most library users search for multiple-word terms in the order in which they occur naturally in the language. That effort continues in this edition with such new headings as **Frozen embryos, Hate crimes, Rap music.** Representative revisions to direct order include such changes as those from **Automobiles, Compact** and **Automobiles, Foreign** to **Compact automobiles** and **Foreign automobiles; Insurance, Life** to **Life insurance; Teachers, Interchange of** to **Teacher exchange.** The congestion under **Education** has been eased by changing the wording of different types of education to the direct form, for example, **Compulsory education, Preschool education, Secondary education,** etc. Similarly, the inversions at **Africa** have been replaced with direct order forms, so that **North Africa** now replaces **Africa, North,** etc.

Subdivisions. A common criterion of any list concerns the specificity of its headings. The degree or level of specificity required for a collection depends on its size, its function, its nature, and the group of users it serves. Practicality rather than theory should determine the degree of specificity, and a balanced blend of theory and practice has been the philosophy of Sears. In a small collection the use of too many specific headings can result in the scattering of like materials. Sears, by example or directive, suggests over 200 classes of headings that may be added by the cataloger when more specific subject headings are needed.

The use of subdivisions also affects specificity. Two "key" headings (**English language** and **United States**) with subdivisions applicable to a similar class of headings were provided in the first edition. The number of "Key" headings, intended as patterns for subdivision practice, has steadily increased. The "key" for individual presidents, provided in the ninth edition, was deleted in the tenth edition in favor of an expansion of the subdivisions applicable to presidents individually and collectively under **Presidents—United States.** Most of the subdivisions under **World War, 1914-1918** were omitted with the tenth edition because they also appeared under **World War, 1939-1945.** The latter heading is the "key" for all wars. For a list of "key" headings see p 27.

The patent usefulness of the list of "Free-Floating Subdivisions," established by the Library of Congress, prompted the editors of the thirteenth edition of Sears to revise and extend the "List of Subdivisions" that had appeared in the twelfth edition, merging the two lists from that edition into one and adding other subdivisions that appear under one or two headings, but could obviously be useful under other subjects. Most of these subdivisions also appear in the main list as general *See* references, with instructions and examples of how they can be applied to different subjects. The general references increase considerably the coverage of the List and its usefulness, and their number has been expanded in this edition.

Some subdivisions have also been revised. Some of these revisions reflect recent changes in Library of Congress subdivisions. *Collections* replaces *Collected works.* The clarity of *Anecdotes; Humor;* and *Cartoons and caricatures* will be appreciated over *Anecdotes, facetiae, satire, etc.;* and *Humor, caricatures, etc.,* which appeared formerly. In others cases the Sears List has further simplified Library of Congress modifications for application in smaller libraries; for example, the possibilities for descriptive and geographical materials about specific places are now simply, *Description; Geography;* and *Historical geography,* instead of the five earlier choices of *Description; Description and geography; Description and travel; Geography;* and *Historical geography. Discovery and exploration* and *Exploration* have been merged into the single subdivision *Exploration.*

Scope Notes. The use of scope notes or definitions of the headings used has once more been increased, sometimes to clarify the meaning of unfamiliar words, or to point out the differences in coverage of related terms. Scope notes have now been provided for headings for regions of Africa. It is hoped this will offer practical aid to small libraries lacking extensive reference works on that continent.

Classification. The classification numbers in this edition of Sears are taken from the twelfth edition of the *Abridged Dewey Decimal Classification and Relative Index,* published by Forest Press. In most cases only one number is assigned to a subject heading. There are instances, however, when a given subject is susceptible to more than one point of view, and one number is consequently inadequate for the subject heading, for example: **Food additives 641.4; 664.** In the Relative Index these numbers represent the viewpoints of home and commercial processing, respectively. Classification numbers are not assigned to some very general subject headings, e.g. **Charters, Exhibitions, Gifts, Hallmarks, Identification,** and **National characteristics.** These headings cannot be classified unless a specific application is identified.

Few of the numbers selected from the twelfth edition of "Abridged Dewey" are carried out more than four places beyond the decimal point. Except for libraries with large collections, where more detailed numbers may be required, the numbers in this edition of Sears should be adequate. The need for more detailed classification can often be satisfied by the addition of form and geographic subdivisions, as given in the Dewey schedules. To demonstrate the building of these numbers, the Dewey number has been carried out when an example of a form or geographic subdivision is provided in the List, e.g. **Antiques—United States** is given the Dewey number **745.10973.** A library preferring broad classification might elect to use the number found at the unsubdivided **Antiques,** that is, **745.1.** Libraries for whom even relatively brief numbers are too long should consult the section entitled "Close and Broad Classification" (p 24) in the Introduction to the Dewey volume.

The alphabetic notations of B for biographical material, E for easy materials, and Fic for works of fiction are occasionally provided in lieu of, or in addition to, Dewey classification numbers for the benefit of libraries using such notation in shelving these materials.

Style, Filing, Etc. For spelling and definition the editor consulted *Webster's Third New International Dictionary of the English Language, Unabridged* (1961) and *Webster's Ninth New Collegiate Dictionary* (1985). *Random House Dictionary of the English Language,* 2nd ed. Unabridged (1987) was used for technical terms and some other terms not present in either *Webster's.* In an effort to make the List more useful with online public access catalogs, the use of the hyphen has been restricted to proper nouns or to topical terms where the absence of a hyphen could alter the meaning. Capitalization and the forms of corporate entries and geographic names used as examples are based on the *Anglo-American Cataloguing Rules,* Second edition, 1988 revision.

Since the thirteenth edition of Sears, the filing of entries has followed the *ALA Filing Rules* (1980) without the exception made in previous editions—that is, all headings are interfiled regardless of any punctuation. Headings with parenthetical modifiers and phrase headings appear intermingled with those with dashes and commas (headings with subdivisions and inverted headings). Although this straight alphabetical arrangement may appear to be less logical than the one used before, the increasing use of automation in all types of libraries and the wish to adhere to standard rules prompted the editors to make this change.

Every heading in the List that may be used as a subject heading is printed in boldface type whether it is in the main file, in a *See also* paragraph, in a "refer from" reference, or is an example for an explanation. If a term is not printed in boldface, it is not used as a heading.

The List of *See also, x,* and *xx* references follows the customary format. (It is contemplated that subsequent editions of the List will adopt the symbols identifying broader, narrower, and related terms that are used in many thesauri and were recently introduced in the *Library of Congress Subject Headings.)* For a full explanation of cross-referencing see p 15-20.

Acknowledgments. The editor wishes to acknowledge with gratitude the contributions to this edition of the individual catalogers, reference librarians, and vendors of cataloging services who responded generously and thoughtfully to requests for suggestions for headings to be added to the List. Special appreciation is owed to Joseph Miller, Cataloger, *Book Review Digest,* who revised the classification to conform to the twelfth abridged edition of Dewey. John Comaromi, Editor, Dewey Decimal Classification, made valuable comments on earlier versions of the "Principles," and Gregory R. New, Assistant Editor, Dewey Decimal Classification, provided patient explanation and advice on the application of numbers from the twelfth abridged Dewey. Last, but not least, thanks are extended to the editors and catalogers of The H.W. Wilson Company, especially to Barbara Jo Riviello, Acting Editor of *Book Review Digest;* to Patricia Kuhr, Editor, Subject Authority Files; and to Ann Case, Associate Director of Indexing Services, for specific suggestions, constructive criticism, and editorial assistance.

The classification numbers have been reproduced from the *Dewey Decimal Classification Abridged Edition 12,* published in 1990, by permission of Forest Press, a division of OCLC Online Computer Library Center, owner of copyright.

This Preface incorporates some sections of the text for the Preface of the previous edition, written by Barbara M. Westby and revised by Caroline Reyes and Carmen Rovira, especially when it refers to the history of the earlier editions of the work and the guidelines followed by the earlier editors beginning with Minnie Earl Sears. The editor hopes that this fact emphasizes the continuity, and at the same time the flexibility, of an enterprise which started more than six decades ago, and which has tried to keep up with the changes in library techniques and in the world in which we live. The editor invites comments from users of this volume. All suggestions will be valued and given thoughtful consideration.

Martha Mooney

March 1991

Principles of the Sears List of Subject Headings

This chapter considers some principles and practices of subject cataloging that should be understood before an attempt is made to assign subject headings to library materials. Most of the illustrations refer to the Sears List of Subject Headings but the principles are applicable to other lists of subject headings as well, including the one issued by the Library of Congress on which the headings in this List are based.

Purpose of Subject Cataloging. The purpose of subject cataloging is to list under one uniform word or phrase all of the materials on a given subject that a library has in its collection. A subject is the topic treated in a book, videotape, or other work. A subject heading is the word or phrase used in the library catalog to express this topic. A subject entry is usually displayed at the top of the catalog record, above the main entry, regardless of the format of the catalog (card, book, microform, or online).

Library materials are given subject entries in the catalog in order to show what information the library has on a given subject, just as author entries are made to show the works that the library has by a given author. Properly made, the subject entry is a very important supplement to the reference tools in the library because it may enable the reader or librarian to identify rapidly and surely the material needed to provide information about a topic. Subject entries are sometimes also useful in locating a particular book. Ordinarily one consults the author entry for a specific work, but, if there is uncertainty about the author's name, one may find the individual piece more readily by searching under subject. Smith's *Basic Mathematics* would be difficult to find quickly if one did not know the author's first name and had to consult all the entries in the catalog under Smith. What if the author's name were really spelled Smyth? In either case, the book could be discovered under the subject **Mathematics.**

A printed list of subject headings, such as the Sears List, incorporates the thought and experience of many minds representing various types of libraries. By using the List as a base for establishing headings, the cataloger has a standard on which to rely. Consistency in both the level of specificity and the form of subject headings is attained by working from an accepted list where the choice among possible wordings has been made and recorded. By following the patterns of headings printed in the List, the cataloger will also be able to add new headings that will be compatible.

Determining the Subject of the Work. The first step in subject cataloging is to ascertain the true subject of the material and the purpose for which it was produced. Sometimes this is readily determined, e.g. **Butterflies** is obviously the subject of the book titled *Butterfly Book*. In others cases, the subject is not so easy to discern because it may be a complex one or the author may not express it in a manner clear to someone unfamiliar with the subject. The subject of a work cannot always be determined from the title alone. The title information is often uninformative or misleading and undue dependence on it can result in error. A book entitled *Great Masters in Art* immediately suggests the subject **Artists,** but closer examination reveals the book to be about painters specifically, not artists in general. Therefore, the more exact subject is **Painters,** not **Artists.** Another illustration is "Fundamentals of Instrumentation," part 1 of a *Manual of Instrumentation.* This title may suggest a treatise on musical instruments or music, but actually it is a book about engineering instruments.

The steps to follow in determining the subject of a work are the same whether one is considering its value for a reader, classifying it, or assigning subject headings to it. After reading the title page of a book to be cataloged, examine the table of contents, and skim the preface and introduction. Then, if the subject of the book is still not clear, examine the text carefully and read parts of it, if necessary. For nonbook materials examine the container, the label, any accompanying guides, etc., and view or listen to the contents if possible. The cataloger will be in a position to determine the subject of the item in hand *only* after this preliminary examination has been made. If the meaning of a subject is not clearly understood, one should consult reference sources, not only an unabridged dictionary and general encyclopedias, but also specialized reference books as well. Only when the cataloger has decided on the subject content of the work and *identified it with explicit words,* can the Sears List be used to advantage. The cataloger's own phrasing of the subject must next be adapted to the terminology of the List. The library catalog will be more useful if the cataloger considers materials from the reader's point of view. The reader's profile depends on age, background, education, occupation and geographical location, and takes into account the type of library—school, public, university, or special—as well. When examining a work the cataloger should ask "If I wanted material on this subject, under what words would I look in the catalog?" Then the List is consulted to insure uniformity in choice and form of the words. Local terminology may be used as references to the words in the List. In choosing these words, that is, assigning the proper subject headings, there are certain principles that should be followed. These are considered in the next five sections.

Specific and Direct Entry. Appreciation of the principle of specific entry is fundamental both in using and in making a modern subject catalog. The rule of specific and direct entry is to enter a work directly under the most specific term, i.e. subject heading, which accurately and precisely represents its content. This term serves as a succinct abstract of the work. If a reader wants information about bridges, the direct approach is to consult the catalog under the heading **Bridges,** not under the large topic **Engineering,** or even the more restricted field, **Civil engineering.** In other words, make direct entry under **Bridges,** not indirectly under **Engineering—Civil Engineering—Bridges.** Or, consider the principle of specific entry from the cataloger's point of view. If one is examining a work about penguins, it is not sufficient to regard it as belonging under the subject **Birds,** or even under **Water birds.** It must be entered directly under the most specific heading that expresses the content, that is, **Penguins.** If the work were entered under **Birds,** a reader would have to look through many entries in order to find information on penguins. Having found the most specific entry that will fit the item, the cataloger should not then make subject entries under both the specific and the general subject headings. A work with the title *Birds of the Ocean* should not be entered under both **Birds** and **Water birds** but only under **Water birds.** To eliminate this duplication, a network of *See also* references directs the reader from the broader subject headings to the more specific ones, e.g. **Birds.** *See also* . . . **Water birds;** and names of specific birds. . . . In many cases the most specific entry may be a general subject, e.g. *Song Birds of the World* will have the subject heading **Birds.** The specific term, as can be seen, refers to the exact word or phrase that summarizes the subject of the book for the user of the catalog. The level of specificity depends on the size of the library, the nature of its collection, its function, and its clientele. The heading should be as specific as possible for the topic it is intended to cover.

If the name of a specific subject is not found in the List, the name of the larger group to which it belongs should be consulted. For example, in assigning subject headings to a work discussing elm and ash trees, the cataloger would find neither **Elm** nor **Ash** listed. However, under the broader subject, **Trees,** the following directions are given: "Names of all trees are not included in this List but are to be added as needed, in the singular form, e.g. **Oak;** etc." The cataloger thus has the authority to use the two headings, **Elm** and **Ash.** (Further directions for adding headings can be found on p 26.)

Common Usage. The word or words used to express a subject must represent common usage. In American libraries this means current American spelling and terminology: **Labor** not Labour; **Color** not Colour; **Elevators** not Lifts. In British libraries these choices would be reversed. Foreign terms are not used unless they have been incorporated into the English language, e.g. Laissez faire. By the same token contemporary words are to be used: **Home economics** not Domestic economy. Today a more current term might be Homemaking, or Household management, but changing a heading is not always possible or advisable. There may be too many entries to change or, as in the case of **Home economics,** the term is still being used and newer usage may not have stabilized.

A general rule is to use a popular or common, rather than a scientific or technical, name where there is a choice. Subject headings are chosen to fit the needs of the people who are likely to use the catalog. A reader in a small public library will look under **Birds,** not Ornithology, or **Fishes,** not Ichthyology. In a scientific library Ornithology and Ichthyology might be more appropriate. After deciding on the common name as entry word, the cataloger should make a reference from the scientific name to the form used. Such references will be discussed later. A term in common usage and expressed in the language of the user will be understood by that person and will pass the test of comprehensibility.

Uniformity. Another very important factor to be considered is that of uniformity. One uniform term must be selected from several synonyms and this term must be applied consistently to all works on the topic. China, Chinaware, and Porcelain are all entered under **Porcelain.** This example also illustrates the fact that the subject heading must be inclusive and cover the topic. The heading chosen must be unambiguous. If several meanings attach to one word, that word must be qualified: **Masks (Facial); Masks (Plays); Masks (Sculpture).** When variant spellings are in use, one must be selected and uniformly applied: **Sulphur** not Sulfur.

A decision must be made whether the form of the heading is to be in a singular or plural form. Plural is the most prevalent but in practice both are used. Abstract ideas are usually stated in the singular. A concept or action is singular (**Theater**) whereas objects and things are plural (**Theaters**). The names of fruit trees are stated in the singular so that they can represent either the fruit or the tree. In this case, singular is more inclusive than the plural. In other cases, plural will have the broader coverage (**Art; Arts**).

Some descriptive phrases also carry different connotations, e.g. Arab, Arabian, and Arabic. Their use in headings appears to be inconsistent, but they are used in the following ways: Arab relating to the people; Arabian referring to the geographical area; and Arabic for the language, script, or literature. These subject headings should be consistent, with distinction being made between ethnic, geographical, and linguistic terms.

Materials should be considered in categories. The word or phrase chosen as a subject must fit not only the items being cataloged but also apply to a group of items on the same subject. The cataloger must consider not only the one piece in hand but also the other book and nonbook materials that discuss the same subject, albeit under different titles, in order to select a subject heading that will serve the entire group in the catalog with relation to other groups. In cataloging *Everybody's Cook Book* the inexperienced cataloger might think first of Cookbooks as the term that will give the best description. But there are two others works that belong in the same group: *How's and Why's of Cooking* and *Cooking for Profit*. These contain not only recipes but also other material on cooking. **Cookery** fits the three closely related items better than Cookbooks and it also fits well with the related subject **Cookery for the sick.** Terminology for a subject must be uniform to fit many similar works.

Form Headings. In addition to the subject headings that interpret the content of various materials, there are headings of another kind, usually known as form headings, or form subject headings, that have the same appearance as topical subject headings but refer to the literary or artistic form of a work and not to its subject matter, e.g. **Essays, Poetry, Fiction, Hymns, Songs,** etc. Literary form headings are usually used for collections rather than for works of an individual. For example, the form heading **Essays** is used not for works of an individual author but for collections of essays by authors of different nationalities. If the collection includes essays only by American authors, then the more specific heading **American essays** would be used. While the use of form entries for works of individual authors might be helpful, the result in most libraries is not considered to be worth the effort. The proliferation of entries would be an extra cost and would increase the size of the catalog unnecessarily. Materials of this type are generally classified and arranged on the shelves according to their literary forms, and the reader often has access to the shelves or to the shelf list. Ordinarily individual works of literature are remembered in association with an author, and a reader consults the author or title entry in the catalog for such works. Subject access to such materials is already available in reference sources such as *Short Story Index, Essay and General Literature Index,* etc.

For a work about the essay as a literary form, e.g. the appreciation of the essay or how to write it, the heading **Essay** represents a true subject and not a form heading. The distinction between form headings and topical subject headings can sometimes be made by using the singular form for the topical heading and the plural for the form heading, e.g. **Short story; Short stories.** But the peculiarities of language do not always permit this. For example, the heading **English poetry** is used for a book about English poetry, but in order to show that a book is a collection of poetry by several English authors, the subdivision *Collections* must be added, i.e. **English poetry—Collections.**

In addition to the literary form headings there are some other useful form headings that are determined by the general format of the material and the purpose of the work, e.g. **Almanacs; Encyclopedias and dictionaries; Gazetteers.**

Classification and Subject Headings. The cataloger should recognize a fundamental difference between classification and subject headings for the dictionary catalog. In a system of classification, which determines the arrangement of works on the shelves and groups together materials on one subject, a work can obviously stand in only one place. But in a catalog, entries representing the work can appear, if necessary, under more than one subject. The cataloger does not have to decide on one subject to the exclusion of all others, but can make the work useful with entries for as many different points of view as there are distinct subjects in the work (usually, however, not more than three). Classification is used to gather in one numerical place on the shelf works that give similar treatment to a subject. Subject headings gather in one alphabetical place in a catalog all treatments of a subject regardless of shelf location. An item may have more than one subject heading but can have only one class number.

Theoretically, there is no limit to the number of subject entries that could be made for one work, but practically, such a policy not only would be expensive but also inefficient for the user of the catalog. For many works, a single subject heading will represent the contents accurately. A book such as *Guide to the Trees* is fully and specifically covered by the subject heading **Trees.** Frequently two are necessary as in the title *Field Book of Trees and Shrubs,* to which one would assign both **Trees** and **Shrubs.**

Occasionally three are required to do justice to the work. More than three should be considered very carefully. The need for more than three may be due to the cataloger's inability to identify precisely the single heading that would cover all the topics in the work. Similarly, a subject heading should not be assigned for a topic that comprises less than one third of a work.

The practice may be stated as follows: As many as three specific subject headings in a given area may be assigned, but if a work treats of more than three, then the next larger inclusive heading is adopted and the specific headings are omitted. A work about lemons and limes would be entered under **Lemon** and **Lime**. If the work also included material on oranges, a third entry with the heading **Orange** would be made for the catalog. But if the work discusses grapefruit and citron as well, the only subject heading assigned would be **Citrus fruit.**

Do not assign both a general heading and one of its specific aspects to the same work. In the example cited above, the material may have discussed the orange in somewhat more detail than the other fruits, but **Citrus fruit** and **Orange** would not be assigned simultaneously.

The cataloger is now aware of another difference between classification and subject cataloging, and one particularly significant for small libraries: classification is frequently by broader subjects and so is less precise than the subject entries for the catalog. Material on floriculture in general as well as on types and specific kinds of flowers as garden plants are classed together in **635.9**. A book on flower gardening, one on perennial gardening, and one on rose gardening will all three be classified in one number in a library, while in the catalog each book will have its own specific subject heading: **Flower gardening; Perennials; Rose.**

It is well to remember this essential difference in the two processes; otherwise, the rule for classifying by broad subject in a small library (large libraries are not considered here) may cause confusion when the librarian assigns subject headings that must be specific in order to achieve maximum usefulness.

The cataloger has learned that subject headings are used for materials that have definite, definable subjects. However, there are a few works in which the subject is so indefinite that it is better not to assign a heading. A work could be a collection of materials produced by several individuals on a variety of subjects or one person's meandering thoughts and ideas. If a cataloger cannot find a definite subject, the reader may not find the item under a makeshift or general heading. Do not use vague terms. They are a disservice to the reader. One cataloger assigned the heading **Human behavior** while another assigned the word **Happiness** to a book titled *Appreciation*. In reality neither was correct. The book was a personal account of one of the sources of the author's pleasure in life and had no specific subject.

Now that certain principles of assigning subject headings are understood, the cataloger should consider the structure of subject headings.

Grammar of Subject Headings. (1) *Single Noun.* The simplest form of subject heading consists of a single noun and is the ideal type when the language supplies it. Such terms are not only the simplest in form but often the easiest to comprehend. Most of the large fields of knowledge can be expressed by single words (**Art; Agriculture; Education; Religion**) as can many specific objects (**Apple; Chairs; Pottery; Trees; Violin**). But many words have synonyms from which a choice has to be made, and conversely, a word may have two or more quite different meanings. For others there is a choice in spelling. A further consideration is the use of the singular or plural form. For example, in the case of **Pottery,** other words that might be used are: Crockery; Dishes; Earthenware; Faience; Fayence; Stoneware. In the Sears List, the term chosen is **Pottery** and references are made from other terms. On the other hand, the word Date may mean a fruit, an historical period, or a social engagement; File may refer to an arrangement of material or a tool; Forging may mean counterfeiting or metalwork; Bridge may refer to a game, a dental prosthesis, or an engineering structure. In the case of Bridge, using the plural removes the possibility of the game but the singular form requires qualification: **Bridge (Game)**. Also the plural **Bridges (Dentistry)** must be distinguished from the engineering structure.

Whenever identical words with different meanings are used in the catalog one of them must be qualified, that is, defined more specifically. In the example of the book on lemons and limes, neither heading is listed in Sears but may be added when needed, as instructed under both **Fruit** and **Citrus fruit**. However, in adding Lime to the List the cataloger finds **Lime** used in relation to **Cement**. The plural Limes should not be used because Sears states that the name of all fruit should be in the singular form. The cataloger would therefore add a qualifier to Lime, i.e. **Lime (Fruit)**. Since **Seals (Animals)** and **Seals (Numismatics)** are already in the List, any subject that must be added to the List but uses the same word must be defined, e.g. **Seals (Christmas, etc.)** or **Seals (Law)**.

Whether to use the singular or the plural or both sometimes depends on the peculiarities of the language since the two forms may express quite different concepts. In many cases, the singular connotes the general, and the plural the specific aspects. Or stated another way, the singular expresses abstract ideas and the plural refers to things. Thus, **Theater** means the art while **Theaters** refers to the buildings. The same parallel exists in the terms, **Essay** and **Essays**, **Short story** and **Short stories**. In all these cases, both forms are necessary, but in general if only one form is required, the plural should be adopted. However, the singular form has been chosen for the names of most fruits and nuts so that the more general term (**Apple; Pecan;** etc.) can be used to include works that consider the fruit or the tree or both.

(2) *Compound Headings.* Using two nouns joined by "and" usually groups together under one heading closely related material that cannot be separated easily in concept and that is usually treated together (**Bow and arrow; Cities and towns; Publishers and publishing**), or two different subjects that are treated in their relation to each other (**Aeronautics and civilization; Religion and science; Television and children**), or two subjects that are opposites but are usually discussed together (**Belief and doubt; Good and evil; Joy and sorrow**).

A problem in forming such headings is word order. There is no rule to cover all situations although catalogers have been prone to follow the alphabetic when there is no common usage. Whichever order is chosen, reference must be made from the opposite order.

The current trend toward simplification of subject access—influenced by the development of electronic information retrieval systems—argues for limiting compound headings when possible. Subject headings that treat the relationship between two broad subjects from the perspective of each, as with **Religion and science**, are clear exceptions to this.

(3) *Adjective with Noun.* Often a specific concept is best expressed by qualifying the noun with an adjective (**American literature; Electric engineering; Tropical fish**). In the past the expression was frequently inverted (**Psychology, Religious; Art, Municipal**). The reasons for inversion were two-fold: 1) an assumption was made that the searcher would think first of the noun; or 2) the noun was placed first in order to keep all aspects of a broad subject together. These assumptions have been questioned in recent years and a program of gradual revision of such headings to direct order in natural language is continuing.

In the case of inverted headings that still await revision, a reference from a direct order version usually sends the user to the inverted heading. When such a heading is a model for establishing similar headings, the cataloger should follow the inverted model until the pattern heading is revised in some future edition of the List. It should be noted that some adjective noun phrases were never inverted because the noun had no significance without the adjective, e.g. **International relations**.

(4) *Phrase Headings.* Some concepts that involve two areas of knowledge can be expressed only by more or less complex phrases. These are the least satisfactory headings as they offer the greatest variation in wording, are often the longest, and may not be thought of readily by either the maker or the user of the catalog—but the English language seems to offer no more compact terminology. Examples are **Applications for positions; Bible as literature; Freedom of information.**

Subdivisions. A means by which the scope of the List can be enlarged far beyond the actual headings printed is through the use of subdivisions of headings. The principle of specific entry can be achieved in some cases only by subdividing a general subject:

Birds	**Food**	**Music**
Birds—Eggs and nests	**Food—Analysis**	**Music—Acoustics and**
Birds—Migration	**Food—Fiber content**	**physics**
Birds—Protection	**Food—Sodium content**	**Music—Theory**

In each of the subjects above, the subdivisions are appropriate and characteristic of it; those used under one are not applicable to the other two listed here. However the subdivision *Analysis* would be applicable to a number of other topics besides **Food,** such as **Blood; Coal; Plants;** etc. Some terms or phrases used as subdivisions are applicable to so many different topics that the subdivisions are not printed under all possible headings. Some are referred to in their alphabetic places with directions for their use. They vary in kind and in value to an individual library.

(1) *Subdivisions by Physical Form.* Some materials present a subject not in expository or narrative form but as lists, outlines, or tables; or, graphically as maps, pictures, or filmstrips. The work may be a directory of chemists, a bibliography of children's literature, a dictionary of psychology, a collection of geological maps, a Bible picture book. In such cases, it is important to show the user of the catalog that they are not works *about* chemists, or children's literature, or psychology, or geology, or the Bible, respectively. If the reader wants a bibliography or dictionary or maps or pictures, etc., it is equally important to be able to locate this directly without having to read through all the entries under the main heading. Standard terms known as "form divisions" are the most common subdivisions and may be used whenever appropriate. Since they show what the material *is*, rather than what it is *about,* they are as necessary for a small library as for a large one. Following are examples of form divisions:

Bibliography	*Gazetteers*	*Pictorial works*
Catalogs	*Handbooks, manuals, etc.*	*Portraits*
Dictionaries	*Indexes*	*Registers*
Directories	*Maps*	*Statistics*

Some of these terms are also used alone as actual subject headings, but as subdivisions they are usually called form headings. In either case, each of these terms is listed in its alphabetic place in the List with directions for use; for example:

Bibliography
    See also **Archives** . . . also names of persons, places, and subjects with the subdivision *Bibliography,* e.g. **Shakespeare, William, 1564-1616—Bibliography; United States—Bibliography; Agriculture—Bibliography;** etc.

Comparable statements are included under each of the other form headings. Applying these directions to the types of materials mentioned above, the headings created would be:

Chemists—Directories	**Geology—Maps**
Children's literature—Bibliography	**Bible—Pictorial works**
Psychology—Dictionaries	

None of these heading-subdivision combinations is printed in the List unless it has been cited as an example, as is the case with **Agriculture—Bibliography** in the reference under **Bibliography**. The *See* or *See also* under the form heading is to be interpreted as authorization for use. Only when a heading has been established and added can the words *See* or *See also* be taken literally.

Form subdivision is particularly valuable under headings for the large fields of knowledge that are represented by many entries in the catalog. The cataloger must be guided by the character of the content, not by the title. Many works whose titles begin with such expressions as "Outline of," "Handbook of," "Manual of" are in fact comprehensive works. For example, Wells' *Outline of History* and Rose's *Handbook of Latin Literature* are comprehensive, lengthy treatises and to use the form divisions that the titles suggest would be inaccurate and ridiculous. Other so-titled "Outlines" or "Manuals" or "Handbooks" may prove to be bibliographies, dictionaries, or statistics of the subject.

(2) *Subdivisions That Show Special Aspects or Topics.* A subject may be presented from a particular point of view. The work may be a history of the subject (the most common of the special aspects) or it may deal with the philosophy of the subject, research in the field, the laws about it, or how to study and teach it. These concepts applied to general subjects are expressed by such headings as the following:

Education—History	**Radio—Law and legislation**
Religion—Philosophy	**Mathematics—Study and teaching**
Aeronautics—Research	

(3) *Subdivisions That Show Chronology.* In any catalog, large or small, there will be many works on American history. If they are all entered under the general heading, the library user must look through many entries to find a specific era. However, with chronological subdivisions corresponding to generally accepted periods of a country's history or to the spans of time most frequently treated in materials, a search can be narrowed to **United States—History—1945-1953**, etc. If a chronological era has been given a specific name, this is included in the heading with dates. The current trend is to use dates in preference to names. This facilitates filing both in the manual and machine modes. In fact, the computer needs very explicit instructions in order to create a chronological file and to ignore a word or phrase preceding a date. Therefore, the Subject Analysis Committee of the A.L.A. Cataloging and Classification Section recommended that dates precede phrases, e.g. **United States—History—1775-1783, Revolution.** It recommended further that century subdivisions be defined to insure correct numerical filing position, i.e. that 19th century be changed to **1800-1899 (19th century);** and that indefinite subdivisions be written as filed, i.e. that To 1500 be changed to **0-1500.** These recommendations were adopted in the twelfth edition of Sears.

The List includes period subdivisions only for those countries for which a library is apt to acquire so many works about their history (United States, Great Britain, France, Germany, Italy and a few others) that it is necessary to separate them into groups according to the period treated, or for contemporary events that have produced a considerable amount of literature, e.g. **Lebanon—History—1982-1984, Israeli intervention.** Although some countries have a longer history than any of these, period subdivisions of history are not needed because the library acquires so little material about them. Regardless of the period treated all the material would be assigned the general heading, e.g. **India—History.**

Some of the topical and form subdivisions that are applicable to a considerable number of subjects are listed in their alphabetic places in the List and are also gathered together in the List of Commonly Used Subdivisions on p 29. History subdivisions, however, are different for each country and so cannot be listed in one place. (The cataloger may wish to consult *LC Period Subdivisions under Names of Places,* 4th ed. 1990.)

(4) *Subdivisions That Show Place.* Subdivision by names of places is discussed below under Geographic Names: Subject Subdivided by Place.

Geographic Names. Many works limit the discussion of an otherwise general subject to a specific country, state, city, or other region. This is such a common practice that the List has provided directions for many subjects that may be so treated. Other subjects not so identified can be subdivided by the cataloger if this is needed or is desirable. Suggested reference sources to be used in researching and establishing geographic names are the most current editions of *The Columbia-Lippincott Gazeteer of the World, National Geographic Atlas of the World, Statesman's Year-book, Times Atlas of the World,* and *Webster's New Geographical Dictionary.*

(1) *Subject Subdivided by Place.* Various subject headings, especially in the fields of science, technology, and economics, are followed by a parenthetic statement giving permission to subdivide the heading geographically, such as: "**Agriculture** (May subdiv. geog.)." In application this means that if the work in hand deals with agriculture in general, only the heading **Agriculture** is used; but if it deals with agriculture in Iowa or in France, for example, then the cataloger may assign the heading **Agriculture—Iowa** or **Agriculture—France.**

The unit used as a subdivision may be the name of a country, state, city, or other political or geographic area, depending on the nature of the subject and its treatment in the work. There are, however, some topics that would not apply to cities, in which case the note will read: "(May subdiv. geog. country or state)."

If the subject is in the field of art or music, the wording varies slightly since one thinks of Spanish art, for example (rather than art in Spain), or German music (rather than music in Germany). The List reads "**Art** (May subdiv. geog. adjective form, e.g. **Art, Greek**)" and "**Music** (May subdiv. geog. adjective form, e.g. **Music, American**)." From these directions the work on Spanish art would be assigned the heading **Art, Spanish** and that on German music, **Music, German.**

Observe that the parenthetic note is permissive, not mandatory. If the library has only a few works on a subject for which geographic treatment is suggested, perhaps it would be easier for the user of the catalog to find these under the main heading without geographic subdivision. Some small libraries limit the use of geographic subdivision to countries other than the United States and to nationalities other than American since most of their material will be concerned with the United States. The Sears List historically has never distinguished between French art or Art in France (which is not necessarily French). Should a library have sufficient material to warrant such a distinction, **Art—France** could be established in addition to **Art, French,** which is suggested. One of the fundamentals of cataloging is to use one's judgment based on the materials at hand and the purpose and needs of the library. Therefore, if a library prefers geographic subdivisions for subjects that are not so indicated in Sears, the library should feel free to add them.

Geographic subdivisions can be either direct or indirect. The Sears List prefers direct subdivision as the most useful to the reader. In the direct form the name of the place discussed in the work is used as the subdivision, e.g. **Theater—Paris (France)** or **Agriculture—Iowa.** The indirect form of subdivision interposes the name of the country (the larger geographic area) between the subject and the smaller area that is covered in the work, e.g. Theater—France—Paris and Agriculture—United States—Iowa.

(2) *Names of Places Subdivided by Subject.* A different procedure is followed for most topics in the fields of history, geography, and politics which are treated from a regional point of view. In works discussing the history of California, a census of Peru, the government of Italy, the boundaries of Bolivia, the population of Paris, or the climate of Alaska, the area treated is the unique factor and its name with the appropriate topical subdivision is the most specific heading for the work. Directions for formulating such headings are given under appropriate subjects, for example:

Census

  See also names of countries, cities, etc., with the subdivision *Census*, e.g.
  United States—Census; etc.

The *See also* is to be interpreted as a direction for formulating a heading for the specific area needed and, when entered in the catalog, is also a guide to the reader. Similar directions appear under **Boundaries; Climate; Population;** etc., which, applied to the topics cited above, would result in the headings:

California—History	**Bolivia—Boundaries**
Peru—Census	**Paris (France)—Population**
Italy—Politics and government	**Alaska—Climate**

The name of any country, state, city, or other area could have been used if needed. However, some topics are applicable to countries only (e.g. *Commercial policy; Diplomatic and consular service*); others are used only under names of cities (e.g. *Suburbs and environs*). Instructions for application are explicit, e.g. Foreign policy. *See* names of countries with the subdivision *Foreign relations*, e.g. **United States—Foreign relations;** etc.

A list of suggested subject subdivisions that may be used under the name of any city is given in the List under **Chicago (Ill.);** those that may be used under the name of any state are listed under **Ohio;** while those that may be used under the name of any country or region, except for chronological subdivisions, are given under **United States.** Since each country's history is unique, its periods of history are individual.

Local materials are an exception to these rules for establishing headings for geographic names. If the library wishes to keep all of the hometown area materials together, then the discussion regarding subject subdivided by place can be ignored, and all materials entered under the name of the locality with all aspects as subdivisions.

Note that there are no definite rules on subdividing by place or by subject. In general, subject headings in the field of science, technology, economics, education, and the arts are subdivided by place, while aspects of history, geography, and politics are subdivisions under place. In many of the social sciences, the aspect of the subject that is most important or has the primary focus is the criterion for decision. When one reads about social life and customs, one asks where the social life exists, e.g. **United States—Social life and customs.** However, one aspect of social life today is the **Single parent family.** This is the subject of interest and one asks secondarily where the family is located. (Note that **Single parent family** is not subdivided by place in Sears as it is in the Library of Congress Subject Headings, but if a library has much material on the subject it might be advisable, and is permissible, to do so.)

In summary, the cataloger would enter under place and subdivide by subject those topics whose predominant interest is focused on area or people, such as history, geography, or government. One would enter under subject and subdivide by place those topics that are primarily of interest for the subject matter regardless of place. In the field of the social sciences the decision must be made in each instance on the element of predominance because no general rule applies.

Some headings in the subject areas of biography, language, and literature require subdivisions relevant to their areas, but others do not. Since knowing when not to subdivide is as important as when to use subdivision, the editor has treated these areas in some detail.

Biography. Works in the field of biography fall into two categories: those in which biography as a form of writing is discussed, a relatively small class covered adequately by the subject heading **Biography (as a literary form);** and lives of persons, a very large class that must be considered in two groups—individual biography and collective biography.

(1) *Individual Biography.* Usually the only subject heading needed for the life of an individual is the name of the person, established in the same way as an author entry. If the work is an autobiography, some catalogers do not make a subject entry for it since the author and the subject are the same. However, since readers have been trained to look under subject entries it seems reasonable to make both an author and a subject heading, especially if there are many other entries as author, or if there are subject entries by other authors, or if the library has a divided catalog.

Occasionally a biography will include so much material about the field in which the individual was working that a second subject heading is required in addition to the personal name. A life of Mary Baker Eddy, for example, may include a valuable account of the development of Christian Science that would require the subject heading, **Christian Science—History.** It must be emphasized that such additional subject headings should be used *only* when there is a substantial amount of material included and when the book tells more about a person's work than his personal life. They are not used simply because the biographee was prominent in the field.

There are a few individuals about whom there is a large amount of material that is other than biographical, such as works about their writings or other activities. In such cases, subdivisions are added to the person's name to separate various aspects treated, among them *Biography.* Two such examples are Jesus Christ and William Shakespeare. The List includes these names with subdivisions appropriate to material written about them. The subdivisions listed under Shakespeare may also be used, if needed, under the names of other individuals about whom there is a large amount of varied literature, for example, Dante and Leonardo da Vinci. Subdivisions listed under **Presidents—United States** are to be used where appropriate under the name of any president, or other rulers, if applicable. It must be noted that this represents the exceptional, not the usual, treatment. For most individual biographies only the name is needed.

(2) *Collective Biography.* This term refers usually to works containing more than three biographies, for if there are no more than three, each subject will be given a heading, consisting of the person's name, as in individual biography. (Some catalogers will treat even larger collections as a group of individual biographies. If they do this, they are analyzing the work, i.e., they are making analytic entries.) There are several varieties of collective biography, each requiring a separate kind of treatment.

General. Collections of biographies not limited to any area or to any class of people are assigned the heading **Biography.** Sometimes the work includes many individuals, such as *International Who's Who;* sometimes a small group, such as *Ten Biographies of Famous Men and Women.*

Local Biography. Very common are the biographies devoted to persons of a particular area, such as *Who's Who in Asia, Who's Who in Latin America, Dictionary of American Biography, Eminent Californians, Leaders in London;* or to ethnic groups, such as *Prominent Jews.* In such works the subject heading is the name of the area or ethnic group with the subdivision *Biography:*

Asia—Biography	**California—Biography**
Latin America—Biography	**London (England)—Biography**
United States—Biography	**Jews—Biography**

If there are many entries under any such heading, the literary works (i.e., those designed for continuous reading) may be separated from the reference works, which list a large number of names in alphabetic order, by adding to the heading for the latter the subdivision *Dictionaries.* The heading for such a work as *Who's Who in America* may be, therefore, **United States—Biography— Dictionaries.**

Classes of Persons. Collective biographies that are devoted to lives of persons of a particular occupation or profession are entered under the term applied to its members, such as **Artists; Authors; Engineers; Librarians; Musicians; Poets; Radiologists; Scientists;** etc., with the subdivision *Biography.*

In a field where there is no adequate term to express its members, or when the name of the class or group refers to the subject in general, not to individuals, the heading used for the specific field is subdivided by the term *Biography:*

Catholic Church—Biography   **United States—History—1861-1865,**
Religions—Biography   **Civil War—Biography**
                                                              Women—Biography

Observe that the headings for areas, classes, and groups are used for collective biographies only and not for the life of an individual artist, author, woman, etc. However, a general reference to names of individuals should be made under the class names, for example: "Artists. See also names of individual artists."

In concluding this discussion on subdivision, another fact should be noted: a subdivided subject can be further subdivided, more than once if necessary. As seen in an example above, **United States—Biography—Dictionaries** was the subject for *Who's Who in America.* For a bibliography of the history of education in the United States, the heading would be **Education—United States—History—Bibliography.** The general pattern of order for multiple subdivisions under topical headings is topic—place—chronology—form, although considerable variation exists.

Language and Literature. These fields are closely related, but they differ considerably in the amount of material published and in their treatment in the catalog. Any general library has proportionately a large number of works on literature, often its largest field of interest, and a comparatively small number of works on language. In both areas, but more particularly in language, the major interest is not in the general treatment but in the national aspect, that is, French language or English literature, German grammar or Italian drama, Spanish dictionaries or Hebrew poetry, etc.

Language. The subject heading for a general work about a specific language is the direct phrase: **English language; French language; German language.** If the work deals with a particular aspect or form of that language, terms representing them are used as subdivisions of the name of the language. Examples are:

English language—Etymology   **German language—Grammar**
French language—Dictionaries   **Spanish language—Terms and phrases**

Many of the general form and topical subdivisions discussed previously will be needed under names of languages, for example, **Italian language—History.**

Names of some languages are included in this List (and others are to be added as needed) but customarily no subdivisions are listed except under **English language.** This serves as a guide or "key" to the subdivisions that may be used under the name of any language.

Literature. The field of literature includes two classes of material that must be distinguished carefully: (1) works about literature, a relatively small group; (2) examples of literature, that is *belles lettres,* or the literature itself, a very large group. In the first we are dealing with actual subjects; in the second with literary forms, not subjects.

(1) *Works about Literature.* The subject headings for works about the various literary forms are their specific names, e.g. **Drama; Essay; Fiction; Poetry.** Works about the major literary forms of national literatures are entered under the direct phrase, e.g. **Irish drama; Italian poetry; Russian fiction.** Specific aspects or forms are expressed by subdivisions, as for other subjects; e.g. **Drama—Technique; English literature—Dictionaries; Short story—Congresses; American literature—History and criticism.** It should be noted that the subdivision *History and criticism* is always used in its entirety and corresponds to the subdivision *History* used with other than literature, motion pictures, and music subjects.

Names of some national literatures are included in the List (and others are to be added as needed) but a suggested list of subdivisions that may be used under them appears only under **English literature,** which thus serves as the "key" to subdivisions that may be used under the name of any national literature. The major literary forms may be used for any national literature by substituting its name for the word "English."

(2) *Examples of Literature, i.e. Belles Lettres.* This large class of material must be separated into two categories whose treatment is entirely different.

Individual Authors. In general, the literary works of individual authors receive no subject entry. Literature is known by author and title and readers usually want a specific novel, or a certain play, or poetry by a specific author—material that can be located in the catalog by author and title entries.

Collections of Several Authors. Collections consisting of works of several authors are usually entered in the catalog under the title of the collection. Therefore, as an aid to their location in the catalog, these materials are given a heading that represents the form of literature included in the collection. Since such headings are used also for topical treatment of the subject, distinction must be made between the headings for works *describing* a particular literary form and *examples* of it. The singular form is used as a topical subject heading. If it has an acceptable plural, this can be used to represent the form heading for collections, but if there is no true plural then the subdivision *Collections* is added to the name of the literary form:

Subject Heading	Form Heading for Collections
Essay	Essays; American essays; etc.
Parody	Parodies
Short story	Short stories
Drama	Drama—Collections
French drama	French drama—Collections
Fiction	Fiction—Collections
Russian fiction	Russian fiction—Collections
Literature	Literature—Collections
German literature	German literature—Collections
Poetry	Poetry—Collections
Japanese poetry	Japanese poetry—Collections

Minor literary forms, such as ballads, fables, fairy tales, parodies, satire, sermons, short stories, and tales, are not listed under the national adjective. If national treatment is needed, the adjective is added after the name of the form, e.g. **Satire, English.** These headings are used not only for collections by several authors but also for works of individual authors and for works about such forms. This departure in treatment from that given to the major literary forms is occasioned by the small number of books involved. If the number of books for any of them is large, the heading may be subdivided to separate the works about them from the literature itself, e.g. **Satire, English—History and criticism.**

Note that catalogers frequently give novels, poems and plays based on historical events or lives of famous persons a subject entry. Such headings must be distinquished from the headings that are assigned to factual accounts by adding the subdivision *Drama; Fiction;* or *Poetry,* as the case may be:

> **Slavery—United States—Drama**
> **Lincoln, Abraham, 1809-1865—Fiction**
> **Bunker Hill (Boston, Mass.), Battle of, 1775—Poetry**

Nonbook Materials. The assignment of subject headings for audiovisual and special instructional materials should follow the same principles that are applied to books. The heading most specifically describing the contents of the material should be used, and the same headings should be applied to book and nonbook materials alike. This is especially important if the catalog integrates all media. One integrated catalog would seem to be preferable because this would bring all materials on one subject together regardless of format. In the last edition of the List many of the subjects and subdivisions that included the word book were changed to make them applicable to all materials. Among the exceptions remaining are the subject **School yearbooks** and the subdivision *Handbooks, manuals, etc.*

Because nonbook materials often concentrate on very small aspects of larger subjects, the cataloger may not find in the List the specific heading that should be used. In such instances the cataloger should be generous in adding new subjects (see p 21-22). It may also be necessary to use a form heading for the format of the material, as well as a subject heading for the content. **Biographical films,** for example, could be created as a subject if needed to describe a specific type of film.

Subject headings for nonbook materials should not include form subdivisions to describe physical format, i.e. motion pictures, slides, sound recordings, music, etc. Some libraries may choose to maintain a separate catalog for each format; others may choose to list all materials in an omnimedia catalog. For libraries using omnimedia catalogs, AACR2 provides the option of using general materials designations (GMD), which are placed at the end of the title proper and alert users to the general class to which an item belongs. The appropriate GMD is selected from either the North American list or the British list. Additional information on this aspect of descriptive cataloging can be found in the *Anglo-American Cataloguing Rules,* 2nd edition, 1988 revision, and in *Common-sense Cataloging.*

Terminology. The subject headings for established fields of knowledge and for concrete objects are simple to comprehend, but terms for new or abstract ideas may offer some difficulty. By looking through the *See also* references under a given heading, or noting the *See* references to it, a cataloger may often determine how the term is used.

Sometimes two or more terms may seem to cover the same subject, unless the exact meaning and limitations of each is appreciated. Many headings in the List are accompanied by a scope note explaining their application as as aid to differentiating among related subjects. For example, the headings **Alcoholism; Drinking of alcoholic beverages; Liquor industry; Prohibition; Temperance** overlap to a certain degree, but because of distinctions in their definition one should not use all of them for any one book. By means of the scope notes included with these terms, it is understood that **Alcoholism** is used for medical materials, including works on drunkenness; **Drinking of alcoholic beverages** includes works on drinking in its social aspects and as a social problem; **Liquor industry** is used for works on the liquor industry and trade; **Prohibition** for works dealing with the legal prohibition of liquor traffic and liquor manufacture; and **Temperance** is used for general works on the temperance question and the temperance movement.

A cataloger must consult the library's own catalog in order to see how a subject heading has been used. Printed catalogs such as the *Cumulative Book Index* and the

"Standard Catalog Series" are also of value in order to see what kind of works are included under a given subject. Other cataloging aids are the *Weekly Record* and its monthly and annual cumulations, the *American Book Publishing Record, Subject Guide to Books in Print,* and the *National Union Catalog: Books* fiche. The *Readers' Guide to Periodical Literature* and other indexes are also useful. Aid in interpreting the scope and meaning of a subject heading may also be obtained by looking up its classification number or numbers in the *Dewey Decimal Classification.* There the topic can be studied in its relation to other topics, a development usually impossible to see directly in an alphabetic arrangement.

Each cataloger will have individual problems in interpretation of subjects. Whenever a decision has been made on the scope of a term about which there has been doubt, a definition or explanation should be recorded for future use. Such notes are a necessity for catalogers and they may be helpful also to users of the catalog. Whenever it is felt that such an explanation would be of general value, it may be entered in the catalog and filed preceding the entries under the subject heading. Of course, the wording may have to be adapted slightly from that in the List, which is addressed to catalogers.

References. After an item has been assigned a subject heading, attention must be directed to insuring that the reader who is searching for this material will not fail to find it because of insufficient references to the proper heading. The following is a summary of the types, methods of formulation, and use of references.

(1) *Specific "See" References.* These refer the reader from terms or phrases not used as subject headings to terms or phrases that are used. They are, therefore, absolutely essential to the success of the catalog. The reader must be directed from variant spellings and terminology to the one word or phrase that has been selected to represent the subject. While a subject heading may be used on as many entries as the library has works on the subject, the *See* reference is made only once. For example, the first time the heading **Agriculture** is used, the cataloger (following the suggestion in the x paragraph under **Agiculture** in the List) will make an entry for the catalog that reads: "Farming. See Agriculture." This will not be made again, no matter how many times the heading **Agriculture** is used, and no work will ever be assigned the word Farming as a heading. (For those familiar with the symbols for indicating cross-references found in many thesauri, note that x is the equivalent of UF or Used For and *See* is the equivalent of USE.)

See references are made

(1)   from synonyms or from terms so nearly synonymous that they would cover the same kind of material, e.g. **Instructional materials centers** requires a reference from School media centers

(2)   from the second part of compound headings, e.g. **Desertion and nonsupport** requires a reference from Nonsupport

(3)   from the direct form of an inverted heading, e.g. **Chemistry, Technical** requires a reference from Technical chemistry

(4)   from an inverted heading to direct order when a user might search under the noun, e.g. **Adult education** requires a reference from Education, Adult

(5)   from variant spellings to the spelling used, e.g. **Color** requires a reference from Colour

(6)   from opposites when they are included without being specifically mentioned, e.g. **Temperance** requires a reference from Intemperance

(7)   from the singular to the plural when the two forms would not file together in the catalog, e.g. **Mice** requires a reference from Mouse; **Cats** requires a reference from Cat. (Note the long list of headings between the singular and the plural of each of these two words.)

(2) *Specific "See also" References.* The *See* references are concerned mainly with terminology, guiding the reader from words he may think of to those actually used for subject headings. But the *See also* references are concerned entirely with leading the reader from headings where he has found information to other headings that list materials on related or more specific aspects of the subject. Consequently such references cannot be made without knowing whether the library has material under the other subjects.

As a rule, *See also* references are made from the general or broader subject to more specific or narrower parts of it, and not ordinarily from the specific to the general. For example, "Science. See also Mathematics," but not the other way around. Proceeding one step at a time to the next more specific topic would result in: "Mathematics. See also Arithmetic"; and "Arithmetic. See also Business arithmetic." *See also* references are also made between related or associated subjects of more or less equal specificity, for example, "Weather. See also Climate." (In thesaurus notation, a *See also* reference to a narrower term is indicated by NT and to a related term by RT.)

See also "refer from" references are much more difficult than *See* references both to make and to understand, and their value is not so unquestioned. They have been included freely under headings (in the *xx* paragraph) in the List but only knowledge of the library's collection can determine whether any of these suggestions should be followed. For example, a work that discusses both wages and prices will be entered in the catalog under **Wages** and under **Prices.** The List suggests the reference, "Wages. See also Prices," but it should not be made if the only material that is to be found in the catalog under **Prices** is this work which is already listed under **Wages.** (The *xx* is equivalent to the symbol BT, for a broader term, and RT, for a related term, in thesaurus usage.)

(3) *General References.* In addition to specific references, there are general *See* and *See also* references which, instead of referring to many individual headings, serve as blanket references to all headings of a particular group. Some references are a combination of specific and general. It is the general references that give the cataloger directions for adding specific headings that are not printed in the List, as explained previously. Their use and value in the public catalog are somewhat different. The most common types of general references are ones to the following:

(1) Common names of different species of a class, e.g.

> **Flowers**
> *See also* **Annuals (Plants)** . . . also names of flowers, e.g. **Roses;** etc.

(2) Names of individual persons, e.g.

> **Artists**
> *See also* **Architects** . . . also names of individual artists

(3) Names of particular institutions, buildings, societies, etc., e.g.

> **Abbeys**
> *See also* **Cathedrals** . . . also names of individual abbeys, e.g. **Westminster Abbey;** etc.

> **Labor unions**
> *See also* **Arbitration, Industrial** . . . also names of types of unions and name of individual labor unions, e.g. **Librarians' unions; United Steelworkers of America;** etc.

(4) Names of particular geographic features, e.g.

Mountains
See also **Mountaineering** . . . also names of mountain ranges, e.g **Rocky Mountains;** etc., and names of mountains, e.g. **Elk Mountain (Wyo.);** etc.

(5) Names of places subdivided by subject, e.g.

Population
See also **Birth control** . . . also names of countries, cities, etc., with the subdivision *Population,* e.g. **United States—Population; Chicago (Ill.)—Population;** etc.

(6) Form divisions, e.g.

Glossaries. *See* **Encyclopedias and dictionaries;** and names of languages or subjects with the subdivision *Dictionaries,* e.g. **English language— Dictionaries; Chemistry—Dictionaries;** etc.

(7) National literatures, e.g.

Literature
See also **Authorship** . . . also names of literatures, e.g. **English literature; French literature;** etc., and subjects and themes in literature, e.g. **Bible in literature;** . . . **Symbolism in literature; Women in literature;** etc.

It is apparent that the general references in the List save an enormous amount of space both in the List and the library catalog. If all the headings for which directions are given were formulated they would be innumerable. In an individual library relatively fewer of these headings are used so that it may be preferable to formulate specific references when specific headings are added, particularly if there are only a few in the class. That is, if the cataloger uses the headings **Azaleas; Parakeets; Pineapple** (none of which is in the printed List), these names would be added to the *See also* references under the respective groups represented. To take one example, assuming that the headings **Fruit; Berries;** and **Citrus fruit** had been used for materials in the library, the reference in the List and in the catalog would now read: "**Fruit.** *See also* **Berries; Citrus fruit; Pineapple.**"

However, when there is a long list of specific headings, catalogers disagree on the policy of adding them to the reference. For example, the heading **Artists** in the List reads: "*See also* . . . names of individual artists." Some catalogers, in preparing this reference for the catalog, would omit the phrase, "names of individual artists," and instead, add the names of all the artists that have been used as subject headings in the library's catalog; other catalogers expect the reader to recall the individual, and the reference is left as printed. Each library must determine its practice on the basis of the number of specific references that would be needed. Under headings where the individual names may not be numerous or well-known, it is feasible for the cataloger and useful to the reader to list the names rather than to rely on the general reference. However, in the example in the preceding paragraph, the cataloger would be well advised to make the reference as follows: "**Fruit.** *See also* types of fruit, e.g. **Berries; Citrus fruit;** etc; and names of fruits, e.g. **Pineapple;** etc."

The cataloger should note that under a *See* reference there is never a subject entry for a work, while under *See also* references there are always entries. Reading the reference structure in the List always poses a problem for beginners as does the making of the references for the library catalog. Below is a heading from the List and its reading:

> **Birds** (May subdiv. geog.)   **598**
> >Names of all birds are not included in this
> >list but are to be added as needed,
> >in the plural form, e.g. **Canaries;**
> >**Robins;** etc.
> >*See also* classes of birds, e.g. **Birds of prey;**
> >**Cage birds; Game and game birds;**
> >**State birds; Water birds;** etc., and
> >names of specific birds, e.g.
> >**Canaries; Peacocks; Robins;** etc.
> >*x* Bird; Ornithology
> >*xx* **Vertebrates; Zoology**

Note that the *See also* references read in direct order from top to bottom: **Birds.** *See also* **Birds of Prey; Cage birds; Game and game birds;** . . . The *See* references read in the reverse order, from bottom to top, that is, from the word opposite the *x* up to the heading: Bird. *See* **Birds.** Ornithology. *See* **Birds.** *See also* "refer from" references also read from the bottom to the top, that is, from the word opposite the *xx* up to the heading: **Vertebrates.** *See also* **Birds.** Zoology. *See also* **Birds.**

To maintain a subject authority file on cards rather than checking in the book as described on p 24-25, the cataloger would make cards for those subjects (including the printed instructions and scope notes) used from the List.

The set of cards on the next page illustrates one type of display.

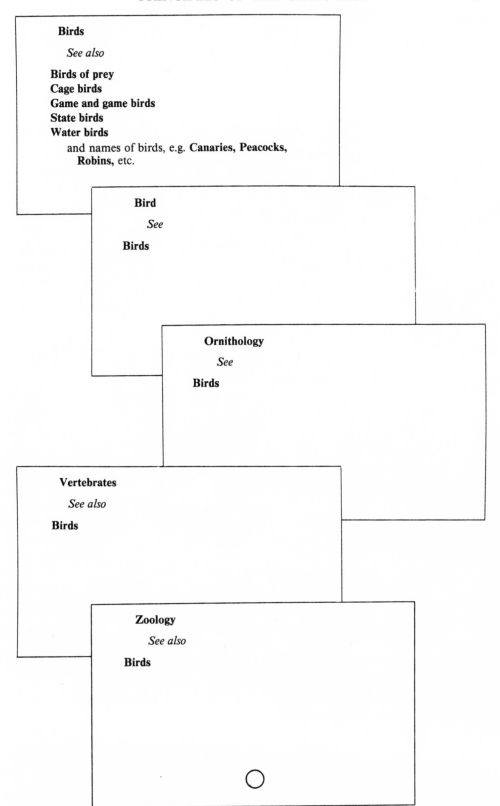

Birds

See also

Birds of prey
Cage birds
Game and game birds
State birds
Water birds
 and names of birds, e.g. **Canaries, Peacocks,**
  Robins, etc.

Bird

See

Birds

Ornithology

See

Birds

Vertebrates

See also

Birds

Zoology

See also

Birds

The directions and scope notes printed in the List for the guidance of the cataloger should be modified for the catalog if the cataloger feels that a note is needed for the public. Following is an example of a rewording:

As it appears in the List for the cataloger:

> **Space ships   629.45**
>> Use for materials limited to space vehicles with people on board. Comprehensive materials on spacecraft are entered under **Space vehicles.**
>> *See also* **Orbital rendezvous (Space flight);** **Rocket planes**
>> *xx*   **Astronautics; Life support systems (Space environment); Rocketry; Space vehicles**

As it appears in the catalog for the reader:

Space ships

Here are listed materials limited to space vehicles with people on board.

Comprehensive materials on spacecraft are entered under **Space vehicles.**

New Terminology for Existing Subjects. The English language is changing constantly so that from time to time new terms appear for subjects that are not new. Through the years many changes have had to be made: **Child welfare** was formerly *Children—Charities, protection, etc.;* **Radio advertising** started out as *Radio broadcasting—Business applications; House decoration* was in use before the present **Interior design;** *Profession, Choice of* before **Vocational guidance;** and *Space vehicles, Reusable* before **Space shuttles.**

It is impossible for the subject headings to reflect all the newest language usage, particularly in fields whose terminology fluctuates frequently. A term that is current today may soon be superseded by another, or a term considered passé may return to favor. But at least new terms can be represented in the catalog by *See* references to the heading used.

Of course, if a heading is found to be incorrect or obsolete, or suddenly assumes a pejorative or biased connotation, changes must be made. The adoption of a term means changing not only all the old entries to the new form but also the various references to and from it. It is impossible to state at what stage in the development of the language such changes should be made. Each heading must be considered individually. If change is desirable but the number of entries to be revised is prohibitive, one can accomplish the change by *See also* references. Using one of the aforementioned changes as an example, the cataloger would make the following entry substituting for (date) the calendar year in which the change is made:

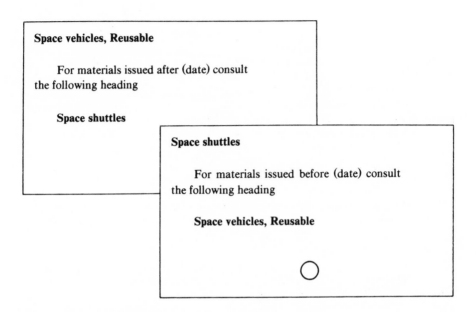

These references could also assume the following format for a card catalog. A guide card that protrudes above the other cards in the tray is more readily seen by the user of the catalog.

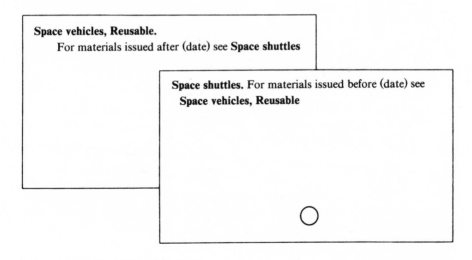

New Subjects. No printed list of subject headings can be entirely up to date. There are constantly new ideas, new inventions, or new countries being created. Headings for these new topics of current interest will have to be added by the cataloger as needed. They should be constructed in the same way as headings for related topics and as the cataloger has been shown in this text.

First aid is supplied by the periodical indexes, such as the *Readers' Guide to Periodical Literature, Applied Science & Technology Index,* etc., since their editors must assign subject headings to material as soon as it is published. As the new subject develops, some change in the heading may be made in succeeding issues of the index. By the time a book is written about a new subject, the terminology may have changed and become stabilized since the first periodical index article appeared. Therefore, bibliographies of new works such as *Booklist, Cumulative Book Index,* and *Book Review Digest* are valuable aids. The Library of Congress issues *LC Subject Headings Weekly List* and includes new "subject headings of current interest" in its quarterly *Cataloging Service Bulletin.* The *Weekly Record* publishes Library of Congress cataloging information which is cumulated in monthly and annual issues of the *American Book Publishing Record.* Through the Cataloging in Publication program the Library of Congress cataloging information will usually appear on the verso of the title page in books of those publishers cooperating in the program.

It is not always possible to decide at once on the permanent form for a new subject heading, but the cataloger cannot always wait for the subject to develop before giving headings to new material. Tentative headings can be assigned and used until the terminology becomes standardized. A list of these tentative headings should be kept (it will never be long) so that they can be reconsidered later and either adopted permanently or changed, as the case may be, and added to the List. One must be sure, of course, that the new term is not merely a new name or a colloquialism for a subject already in the catalog.

Recording Headings and References. The cataloger should keep a list of subject headings used and references made for them. This may be kept on cards and filed in the catalog department or a copy of the Sears List may be checked whenever a heading is used for the first time. Additions to the List should be entered and references should be recorded as needed. Detailed directions for checking the List and a sample page illustrating them will be found on p 24-25.

Bibliography

Akers, Susan Grey. *Akers' Simple Library Cataloging.* 7th ed. Completely revised and rewritten by Arthur Curley and Jana Varlejs. Metuchen, N.J.: Scarecrow Press, 1984. (Chapter 2)

American Library Association. Filing Committee. *ALA Filing Rules.* Chicago: American Library Association, 1980.

Bakewell, K. G. B. *A Manual on Cataloging Practice.* New York: Pergamon Press, 1972. (Chapter 5)

Bernhardt, Frances S. *Introduction to Library Technical Services.* New York: The H. W. Wilson Co., 1979. (pp. 155-174)

Chan, Lois Mai. *Cataloging and Classification: an Introduction.* New York: McGraw-Hill, 1981.

Chan, Lois Mai. *Library of Congress Subject Headings: Principles and Application.* 2nd ed. Littleton, Colo.: Libraries Unlimited, 1986.

Clack, Doris H. *Authority Control: Principles, Applications, and Instructions.* Chicago: American Library Association, 1990.

Coates, E. J. *Subject Catalogues: Headings and Structure.* London: Library Association, 1960.

Dewey, Harry. *An Introduction to Library Cataloging and Classification.* 4th ed. rev. and enl. Madison, Wis.: Capital Press, 1957. (Chapters 10-13 and 15)

Dewey, Melvil. *Abridged Dewey Decimal Classification and Relative Index.* 12th ed. Edited by John P. Comaromi, et al. Albany, N.Y.: Forest Press, 1990.

Dunkin, Paul S. *Cataloging U. S. A.* Chicago: American Library Association, 1969. (Chapter 5)

Eaton, Thelma. *Cataloging and Classification: an Introductory Manual.* 4th ed. Ann Arbor, Mich.: Edwards Brothers, 1967. (Chapters 5-6)

Elrod, J. McRee. *Choice of Subject Headings.* [programmed text] 3rd ed. Metuchen, N.J.: Scarecrow Press, 1980.

Foskett, A. C. *The Subject Approach to Information.* 4th ed. Hamden, Conn.: Linnet Books, 1982.

Frarey, Carlyle James. "Subject Headings." In *The State of the Library Art,* vol. 1, part 2, edited by Ralph R. Shaw. New Brunswick, N.J.: Graduate School of Library Service, Rutgers, The State University, 1960.

Harris, Jessica Lee. *Subject Analysis: Computer Implications of Rigorous Definition.* Metuchen, N.J.: Scarecrow Press, 1970.

Haycock, Ken, and Lynne Lighthall. *Sears List of Subject Headings: Canadian Companion.* 3rd ed. New York: The H. W. Wilson Co., 1987.

Haykin, David Judson. *Subject Headings: a Practical Guide.* Washington: U.S. Government Printing Office, 1951. Reprint. New York: Gordon Press, 1978.

Hennepin County Library. *HCL Cataloging Bulletin.* Edina, Minn.

Lancaster, F. W. *Vocabulary Control for Information Retrieval.* 2nd ed. Arlington, Va.: Information Resources Press, 1986.

Library Literature: an Index to Library and Information Science. New York: The H. W. Wilson Co., 1921-

Library of Congress. Subject Cataloging Division. *Subject Cataloging Manual: Subject Headings.* 3rd ed. Washington, D.C.: Library of Congress, 1988-

Mann, Margaret. *Introduction to Cataloging and the Classification of Books.* 2nd ed. Chicago: American Library Association, 1943. (Chapters 9-10)

Miksa, Francis L. *The Subject in the Dictionary Catalog from Cutter to the Present.* Chicago: American Library Association, 1983.

Miller, Rosalind E. and Jane C. Terwillegar. *Commonsense Cataloging: a Cataloger's Manual.* 4th ed. rev. New York: The H. W. Wilson Co., 1990. (Chapters 7-9)

Pettee, Julia. *Subject Headings: the History and Theory of the Alphabetical Subject Approach to Books.* New York: The H. W. Wilson Co., 1946.

Sears, Minnie Earl. *Sears: Lista de encabezamientos de materia.* Traducción y adaptación de la *12a edición en inglés, editada por Barbara M. Westby* por Carmen Rovira. New York: The H. W. Wilson Co., 1984. A Spanish translation by Carmen Rovira of the 12th edition of Sears, including the "Principles" section.

Tauber, Maurice Falcolm. *Technical Services in Libraries; Acquisitions, Cataloging, Classification, Binding, Photographic Reproduction, and Circulation Operations.* New York: Columbia University Press, 1954. (Chapters 10-11)

Taylor, Arlene G. *Cataloging with Copy: a Decision-Maker's Handbook.* 2nd ed. Englewood, Colo.: Libraries Unlimited, 1988. (pp. 135-169)

Theory of Subject Analysis: a Sourcebook. Edited by Lois Mai Chan, Phyllis A. Richmond, and Elaine Svenonius. Littleton, Colo.: Libraries Unlimited, 1985.

Wynar, Bohdan S. *Introduction to Cataloging and Classification.* 7th ed. by Arlene G. Taylor. Littleton, Colo.: Libraries Unlimited, 1985.

CHECKING AND ADDING HEADINGS

See Sample Page opposite

1. *Check the subject heading used.* When the subject heading **Birds** is used for the first time, the cataloger places a check mark in front of it.

2. *Make and check "See" references to the heading.* The x terms under **Birds** are considered and the cataloger decides to make a reference from Bird and from Ornithology as suggested. Cards are made for the catalog reading: "Bird. See Birds" and "Ornithology. See Birds." The terms Birds and Ornithology are checked both in their alphabetic places in the List and in the x references under **Birds.**

3. *Make and check "See also refer from" and "See also" references to the heading.* The xx headings given under **Birds** are examined to see whether they have been used in the catalog. The heading **Vertebrates** has a check mark beside it showing that it has been used. The cataloger decides to place a reference in the catalog reading: "Vertebrates. See also Birds." It is recorded in the List:

   > under **Birds,** in the xx paragraph, **Vertebrates** is checked
   > under **Vertebrates,** in the *See also* paragraph, **Birds** is checked

   For purposes of this explanation, the assumption is made that **Zoology** has not yet been used.

4. *Adding headings to the List.* The library acquires material about ostriches. The term is not in the List but the directions given in the note under **Birds** tell the cataloger that the heading **Ostriches** may be added. It is written in the margin in its alphabetic place and checked. To the public catalog is added the reference: "Birds. See also Ostriches." It is recorded in the List:

   > under **Birds,** to the *See also* paragraph is added, **Ostriches,** and checked
   > under **Ostriches,** is added, xx **Birds,** and checked

   The library acquires material on birds in Maine. Following the permission given with the heading **Birds,** "(May subdiv. geog.)," the cataloger uses the heading, **Birds—Maine,** writing it in the margin in its alphabetic place and checking it. Since the library has very little material about this region, it is decided to make a reference for the catalog reading, "Maine—Birds. See Birds—Maine." This reference is added also to the List and traced under the new heading by adding x Maine—Birds.

5. *Canceled subjects* If all entries for a subject are withdrawn from the catalog, turn to the subject heading in the List, find what references have been made and remove them (if they are unique references) or cancel the heading (if the references are valid for other headings). At the same time, erase or cross off the check marks in the List to show that the subject and its references are not now used.

SAMPLE PAGE OF CHECKING

Abbreviated entries taken from various pages of the Sears List. A check (✔) indicates that the heading or reference has been used in the library's catalog. The marginal notes show how subjects may be added when needed.

✔
Birds (May subdiv. geog.) **598**
> Names of all birds are not included in this List but are to be added as needed, in the plural form, e.g. **Canaries; Robins;** etc.
> *See also* classes of birds, e.g. **Birds of prey; Cage birds; Game and game birds; State birds; Water birds;** etc.; and names of specific birds, e.g. **Canaries; Peacocks; Robins;** etc.
> *x* Bird; Ornithology
> *xx* **Vertebrates; Zoology**

✔ *Ostriches*

Birds in literature 809
> *See also* **Bible—Natural history**
> *xx* **Nature in literature**
Birds—Marking. *See* **Birdbanding**

✔ *Birds—Maine*
x Maine—Birds

Mail systems, Electronic. *See* **Electronic mail systems**
Mainstreaming in education 371.9

✔ *Maine—Birds. See Birds—Maine*

Ornamental plants 635.9; 715
> *x* Plants, Ornamental
> *xx* **Flower gardening; Landscape gardening; Plants, Cultivated; Shrubs**
✔ Ornithology. *See* **Birds**
Orphan drugs 615
> Use for materials on drugs that appear to be useful for the treatment of rare disorders but owing to their limited commercial value have difficulty in finding funding for research and marketing.
> *x* Drugs, Orphan; Nonprofitable drugs
> *xx* **Drugs**

Osteopathy 615.5
> *See also* **Chiropractic; Massage**
> *xx* **Alternative medicine; Massage**
Ostrogoths. *See* **Teutonic peoples**

✔ *Ostriches*
xx Birds

Versification 808.1
> *See also* **Poetry; Rhyme**
> *x* English language—Versification; Meter; Prosody
✔ *xx* **Authorship; Poetics; Rhythm**
Vertebrates 596 ✔
> *See also* **Amphibians; Birds; Fishes; Mammals; Reptiles**
> *xx* **Animals; Zoology**

HEADINGS TO BE ADDED BY THE CATALOGER

It is neither possible nor necessary to enter all proper and common nouns in a subject heading list such as Sears. If a specific name is not included in the List, the cataloger must establish a heading for it, using available reference sources. Headings may be created for the kinds of names cited below. Note that wherever the List reads, "*See also* [or *See*] names of . . .," the specific name may be added even though it is not represented among these categories.

A. PROPER NAMES

    1. Names of persons

    2. Names of families

    3. Names of places

        a. Political units: countries, states, cities, provinces, counties, etc.

        b. Groups of states or countries: e.g. **Southern States; Baltic States;** etc.

        c. Geographic features: mountain ranges and individual mountains; island groups and individual islands; river valleys and individual rivers; regions; oceans; lakes; etc.

    4. Names of nationalities

    5. Names of national languages and literatures

    6. Names of wars and battles

    7. Names of treaties

    8. Names of Indian peoples

    9. Names of corporate bodies

        a. Names of associations, societies, clubs, etc.

        b. Names of institutions: colleges, libraries, hospitals, etc.

        c. Names of religious denominations

        d. Names of government bodies

        e. Names of hotels, retail stores, ships, etc.

B. COMMON NAMES

    1. Names from such categories as:

animals	fruits	sports
birds	games	tools
fishes	musical	trees
flowers	instruments	vegetables
foods	nuts	

    2. Names of diseases

    3. Names of organs and regions of the body

    4. Names of chemicals

    5. Names of minerals

"KEY" HEADINGS

To enable the cataloger to see the full display of possible subdivisions that may be used with some of the more popular categories, the editor has provided certain headings in the List to serve as models or "keys." Note that the subdivisions under the "Keys" are illustrative, not exclusive.

Persons:

Presidents—United States (to illustrate subdivisions that may be used under presidents, prime ministers and other rulers)

Shakespeare, William, 1564-1616 (to illustrate subdivisions that may be used under any voluminous author)

Peoples:

Indians of North America (to illustrate subdivisions that may be used under names of peoples and linguistic families)

Places:

United States; Ohio; Chicago (Ill.) (to illustrate subdivisions—except for historical periods—under geographic names)

Languages and Literatures:

English language (to illustrate subdivisions that may be used with any language)

English literature (to illustrate subdivisions that may be used with any literature)

Wars:

World War, 1939-1945 (to illustrate subdivisions that may be used under any war or battle)

LIST OF COMMONLY USED SUBDIVISIONS

In addition to the subdivisions listed under the "keys" mentioned on the preceding page, a large number of form or topical subdivisions may be used under subjects as needed. These subdivisions are also known as "free-floating subdivisions."

The following list is not all-inclusive. The subdivisions that appear under the "key" headings are not repeated here, except when they may also be used under other subjects.

Accidents
Accounting
Administration
Air conditioning
Alcohol use
Analysis
Anatomy
Anecdotes
Antiquities
Assassination
Atlases
Attitudes
Audiovisual aids
Automation
Behavior
Bibliography
Bio-bibliography
Biography
Books and reading
Buildings
Care
Care and hygiene
Cartoons and caricatures
Case studies
Catalogs
Censorship
Chemotherapy
Chronology
Citizen participation
Civil rights
Collectibles
Collection and preservation
Collections
Collectors and collecting
Colonies
Color
Communication systems
Competitions
Composition
Computer assisted instruction

Computer programs
Concordances
Congresses
Conservation and restoration
Contracts and specifications
Control
Correspondence
Corrupt practices
Costs
Costume
Curricula
Data processing
Desertions
Design
Design and construction
Designs and plans
Dictionaries
Diet therapy
Directories
Discography
Diseases
Diseases and pests
Documentation
Drama
Drug use
Economic aspects
Economic conditions
Education
Employment
Entrance requirements
Environmental aspects
Equipment and supplies
Estimates
Examinations
Exhibitions
Experiments
Fiction
Filmography
Finance
Fires and fire prevention

Folklore
Food
Fuel consumption
Genetic aspects
Geographical distribution
Government policy
Growth
Guidebooks
Handbooks, manuals, etc.
Health and hygiene
Heating and ventilation
Historiography
History (for all works except
  literature, film, and music)
History and criticism (for literature,
  film, and music)
Home care
Housing
Humor
Identification
In-service training
Indexes
Industrial applications
Insignia
Inspection
Institutional care
Integration
Intellectual life
International cooperation
Jargon
Kings, queens, rulers, etc.
Labeling
Labor productivity
Laboratory manuals
Language
Law and legislation
Lighting
Maintenance and repair
Malpractice
Management
Maps
Marketing
Materials
Mathematical models
Mathematics
Measurement
Medals, badges, decorations, etc.
Medical care
Methodology
Miscellanea
Models
Moral and religious aspects
Museums

Noise
Nursing
Nutrition
Officials and employees
Origin
Outlines, syllabi, etc.
Patterns
Periodicals
Philosophy
Photographs from space
Physiological effect
Pictorial works
Poetry
Political activity
Portraits
Practice
Preservation
Prevention
Prices
Problems, exercises, etc.
Production standards
Professional ethics
Programmed instruction
Prophecies
Protection
Protests, demonstrations, etc.
Psychological aspects
Psychology
Public opinion
Quality control
Quotations
Rating
Reading materials
Recreation
Recruiting
Recycling
Registers
Rehabilitation
Religion
Religious life
Remodeling
Repairing
Research
Reviews
Safety appliances
Safety measures
Security measures
Segregation
Sexual behavior
Social aspects
Social conditions
Social life and customs
Societies
Songs and music
Sources

Statistics
Stories, plots, etc.
Study and teaching
Suffrage
Surgery
Tables
Taxation
Technique
Telephone directories
Terminology
Testing

Texts
Therapeutic use
Thermodynamics
Tournaments
Toxicology
Training
Transplantation
Transportation
Vocational guidance
Voyages and travels

SYMBOLS USED

  x See from

  xx See also from

(May subdiv. geog.) Heading may be subdivided by name of place

See p 15-20 for further explanation of cross-reference practice.

Sears List of Subject Headings

3-D photography. *See* **Three dimensional photography**

3 mile limit. *See* **Territorial waters**

3D photography. *See* **Three dimensional photography**

4-H clubs 630.6
 x Boys' agricultural clubs; Four-H clubs; Girls' agricultural clubs
 xx **Agriculture—Societies; Boys' clubs; Girls' clubs**

4th of July. *See* **Fourth of July**

17 year locusts. *See* **Cicadas**

100 years' war. *See* **Hundred Years' War, 1339-1453**

200 mile limit. *See* **Territorial waters**

1200-1299 (13th century). *See* **Thirteenth century**

1300-1399 (14th century). *See* **Fourteenth century**

1400-1499 (15th century). *See* **Fifteenth century**

1500-1599 (16th century). *See* **Sixteenth century**

1600-1699 (17th century). *See* **Seventeenth century**

1700-1799 (18th century). *See* **Eighteenth century**

1800-1899 (19th century). *See* **Nineteenth century**

1900-1999 (20th century). *See* **Twentieth century**

2000-2099 (21st century). *See* **Twenty-first century**

A.B.C.'s. *See* **Alphabet**

A.B.M.'s. *See* **Antimissile missiles**

A-bomb victims. *See* **Atomic bomb victims**

A.C.O.A.s. *See* **Adult children of alcoholics**

A.D.C. *See* **Child welfare**

A.I.D.S. (Disease). *See* **AIDS (Disease)**

A.T.V.'s. *See* **All terrain vehicles**

Abacus 513.028
 xx **Calculators**

Abandoned children 362.7
 See also **Orphans**
 x Children, Abandoned
 xx **Child welfare; Children; Orphans**

Abandoned towns. *See* **Cities and towns, Ruined, extinct, etc.; Ghost towns**

Abandonment of family. *See* **Desertion and non-support**

Abbeys 271; 726
 See also **Cathedrals; Convents; Monasteries;** also names of individual abbeys, e.g. **Westminster Abbey;** etc.
 xx **Church architecture; Church history; Convents; Monasteries**

Abbreviations 411; 413; 421, etc.; 423, etc.
 See also **Acronyms; Ciphers; Code names; Shorthand; Signs and symbols**
 x Contractions; Symbols
 xx **Ciphers; Shorthand; Signs and symbols; Writing**

ABCs. *See* **Alphabet**

Abduction. *See* **Kidnapping**

Ability   153.9

    See also types of ability, e.g. **Creative ability;**
        Executive ability; Leadership; Musical abil-
        ity; etc.

    xx **Success**

Ability grouping in education   371.2

    See also **Nongraded schools**

    x Grouping by ability

    xx **Grading and marking (Education)**

Ability—Testing   153.9; 371.2

    x Aptitude testing

    xx **Educational tests and measurements; Mental
        tests**

ABMs.   *See* **Antimissile missiles**

Abnormal children.   *See* **Exceptional children;
    Handicapped children**

Abnormal growth.   *See* **Growth disorders**

Abnormal psychology.   *See* **Psychology, Pathologi-
    cal**

Abnormalities, Human.   *See* **Birth defects**

Abolition of capital punishment.   *See* **Capital pun-
    ishment**

Abolition of slavery.   *See* **Abolitionists; Slavery**

Abolitionists   326; 920

    x Abolition of slavery

    xx **Slavery—United States**

Abominable snowman.   *See* **Yeti**

Aborigines.   *See* **Ethnology**

Aborigines, Australian.   *See* **Australian aborigines**

Abortion   179; 344; 363.4; 618.8

    x Fetal death; Pregnancy, Termination of; Ter-
        mination of pregnancy

    xx **Birth control**

Abortion—Catholic Church   241

    xx **Catholic Church**

**Abortion—Moral and religious aspects   179; 241;
    291.5**

    See also **Pro-choice movement; Pro-life move-
        ment**

Abortion rights movement.   *See* **Pro-choice move-
    ment**

Abortion, Spontaneous.   *See* **Miscarriage**

Abrasives   553.6

Absence from school.   *See* **School attendance**

Absenteeism (Labor)   331.25; 658.3

    See also **Employee morale**

    x Employee absenteeism; Labor absenteeism

    xx **Hours of labor; Personnel management**

Absenteeism (School).   *See* **School attendance**

Abstinence.   *See* **Fasting; Temperance**

Abstract art.   *See* **Art, Abstract**

Abuse of animals.   *See* **Animal welfare**

Abuse of children.   *See* **Child abuse**

Abuse of husbands.   *See* **Husband abuse**

Abuse of persons.   *See* **Offenses against the person**

Abuse of substances.   *See* **Substance abuse**

Abuse of the elderly.   *See* **Elderly abuse**

Abuse of wives.   *See* **Wife abuse**

Abuse, Verbal.   *See* **Invective**

Abused aged.   *See* **Elderly abuse**

Abused wives.   *See* **Abused women**

Abused women   362.82

    See also **Wife abuse; Wives**

Abused women—*Continued*

    x Abused wives; Battered wives; Battered
        women

    xx **Victims of crime; Wife abuse; Wives; Women**

Academic achievement   370.1; 371.2

    x Achievement, Academic; Educational
        achievement; Scholastic achievement

    xx **Success**

Academic advising.   *See* **Educational counseling**

Academic degrees   378.2

    x College degrees; Degrees, Academic; Doctors'
        degrees; Honorary degrees; University de-
        grees

    xx **Colleges and universities**

Academic dissertations.   *See* **Dissertations, Aca-
    demic**

Academic freedom   371.1; 378.1

    Use for materials on the freedom of the mem-
        bers of the academic community to carry on
        their functions, including the right to teach,
        publish, learn, communicate, conduct re-
        search, etc.

    See also **Church and education**

    x Educational freedom; Freedom, Academic;
        Freedom of teaching; Teaching, Freedom of

    xx **Censorship; Church and education; Civil
        rights; Freedom; Intellectual freedom; Tol-
        eration**

Academic libraries   027.7

    x College and university libraries; Libraries,
        College; Libraries, University; University li-
        braries

    xx **Colleges and universities; Libraries**

Accelerated reading.   *See* **Rapid reading**

Accident insurance   368.3

    See also **Workers' compensation**

    x Disability insurance; Insurance, Accident; In-
        surance, Disability

    xx **Casualty insurance**

Accidents   363.1

    See also

Disasters	**Home accidents**
Explosions	**Poisons and poisoning**
Fires	**Shipwrecks**
First aid	**Traffic accidents**
Hazardous occupations	**Wounds and injuries**

    also subjects with the subdivision *Accidents,* e.g.
        **Aeronautics—Accidents; Railroads—
        Accidents;** etc.

    x Emergencies; Injuries

    xx **Disasters; First aid**

Accidents—Prevention   363.1; 658.3

    See also **Safety appliances; Safety education;** also
        subjects with the subdivision *Safety appli-
        ances* or *Safety measures,* e.g. **Aeronau-
        tics—Safety measures; Railroads—Safety
        appliances;** etc.

    x Prevention of accidents; Safety measures

    xx **Safety appliances; Safety education**

Accidents, Spacecraft.   *See* **Astronautics—Accidents**

Acclimatization.   *See* **Adaptation (Biology); Man—
    Influence of environment; Plant introduction**

Accompaniment, Musical.   *See* **Musical accompani-
    ment**

Accountability. *See* **Liability (Law)**
Accountants   657.092; 920
>   *x* Bookkeepers; Certified public accountants
Accounting   657
>   *See also* **Auditing; Bookkeeping; Cost account-
>   ing;** also names of industries, professions,
>   etc. with the subdivision *Accounting,* e.g.
>   **Corporations—Accounting;** etc.
>   *x* Finançial accounting
>   *xx* **Auditing; Bookkeeping; Business; Business
>   arithmetic; Business education**
Accounting machines. *See* **Calculators**
Accounts, Collecting of. *See* **Collecting of accounts**
Acculturation   303.48
>   *See also* **East and West; Ethnic relations; Inter-
>   cultural education; Race relations; Socializa-
>   tion**
>   *x* Culture contact
>   *xx* **Anthropology; Civilization; Culture; East and
>   West; Ethnology**
Acetate silk. *See* **Rayon**
Achievement, Academic. *See* **Academic achieve-
>   ment**
Achievement tests. *See* **Examinations**
Acid precipitation. *See* **Acid rain**
Acid rain   363.73; 628.5
>   *x* Acid precipitation; Rain, Acid
>   *xx* **Air pollution; Rain; Water pollution**
Acids   546; 661
>   Names of all acids are not included in this List
>   but are to be added as needed, e.g. **Carbolic
>   acid;** etc.
>   *See also* names of acids, e.g. **Carbolic acid;** etc.
>   *xx* **Chemicals; Chemistry**
Acne   616.5
>   *x* Blackheads (Acne); Pimples (Acne)
>   *xx* **Skin—Diseases**
ACOAs. *See* **Adult children of alcoholics**
Acoustics. *See* **Architectural acoustics; Hearing;
>   Music—Acoustics and physics; Sound**
Acquired immune deficiency syndrome. *See* **AIDS
>   (Disease)**
Acquisition of corporations. *See* **Corporate mergers
>   and acquisitions**
Acquisitions (Libraries). *See* **Libraries—
>   Acquisitions**
Acrobats and acrobatics   791.3; 796.47
>   *See also* **Gymnastics; Stunt men and women;** also
>   names of acrobatic feats, e.g. **Tumbling;**
>   etc.
>   *xx* **Circus; Gymnastics**
Acronyms   411; 421, etc.
>   *x* English language—Acronyms; Initialisms
>   *xx* **Abbreviations; Code names**
Acting   791.4; 792
>   Use for general materials on the art and tech-
>   nique of acting in any medium (stage, televi-
>   sion, etc.), on the presentation of plays, and
>   on acting as a profession. Materials limited
>   to the presentation of plays are entered un-
>   der **Amateur theater** or **Theater—
>   Production and direction.** Materials about
>   members of the profession are entered un-
>   der **Actors.**

Acting—*Continued*

    See also **Actors; Drama in education; Mime; Pageants; Pantomimes; Theater**

    x Dramatic art; Histrionics; Stage

    xx **Actors; Amateur theater; Drama; Drama in education; Public speaking; Theater**

Acting—Costume. *See* **Costume**

Action, Social. *See* **Social action**

Actions and defenses. *See* **Litigation**

Activism, Social. *See* **Social action**

Activities curriculum. *See* **Creative activities**

Activity schools. *See* **Education—Experimental methods**

Actors (May subdiv. geog. adjective form, e.g. **Actors, American;** etc.) **791.4; 792; 920**

    See also **Acting; Black actors; Comedians; Theater;** also names of individual female and male actors

    x Actors and Actresses; Actresses; Men actors; Motion picture actors; Stage; Television actors; Women actors

    xx **Acting; Celebrities; Entertainers; Theater**

Actors, American 791.4; 792; 920

    x Actors and Actresses, American; American actors; United States—Actors

Actors and Actresses. *See* **Actors**

Actors and Actresses, American. *See* **Actors, American**

Actors, Black. *See* **Black actors**

Actresses. *See* **Actors**

Acupressure 615.8

    x Finger pressure therapy; Myotherapy

    xx **Acupuncture; Alternative medicine; Massage**

Acupuncture 615.8

    See also **Acupressure**

    xx **Alternative medicine; Medicine**

Adages. *See* **Proverbs**

Adaptability (Psychology). *See* **Adjustment (Psychology)**

Adaptation (Biology) 574.5; 581.5; 591.5

    See also **Man—Influence of environment**

    x Acclimatization

    xx **Biology; Ecology; Evolution; Genetics; Variation (Biology)**

Adaptation (Psychology). *See* **Adjustment (Psychology)**

Adaptations. *See* **Film adaptations; Television adaptations;** and names of authors or individual works entered under title with the subdivision *Adaptations* for criticism and interpretation of literary, cinematic, video, or television adaptations, e.g., **Beowulf—Adaptations; Shakespeare, William—Adaptations;** etc.

Adaptations, Film. *See* **Film adaptations**

Adaptations, Television. *See* **Television adaptations**

Addiction. *See* **Substance abuse;** and types of addiction, e.g. **Alcoholism; Drug addiction;** etc.

Addiction to alcohol. *See* **Alcoholism**

Addiction to drugs. *See* **Drug abuse**

Addiction to exercise. *See* **Exercise addiction**

Addiction to gambling. *See* **Compulsive gambling**
Addiction to hard drugs. *See* **Drug addiction**
Addiction to substances. *See* **Substance abuse**
Addiction to work. *See* **Workaholism**
Addictive behavior. *See* **Compulsive behavior; Substance abuse;** and types of addictions and compulsive behaviors, e.g. **Alcoholism; Drug addiction; Compulsive gambling; Workaholism;** etc.
Addicts, Drug. *See* **Drug addicts**
Adding machines. *See* **Calculators**
Additives, Food. *See* **Food additives**
Addresses. *See* **Lectures and lecturing; Speeches, addresses, etc.**
Adhesives   620.1; 668; 691
  See also names of adhesives, e.g. **Cement; Glue; Mortar;** etc.
Adjustment (Psychology)   155.2
  x Adaptability (Psychology); Adaptation (Psychology); Coping behavior; Maladjustment (Psychology)
  xx **Psychology**
Adjustment, Social. *See* **Social adjustment**
Administration. *See* **Civil service; Management; Political science; Public administration; State, The;** and types of institutions and names of individual institutions with the subdivision *Administration,* e.g. **Libraries—Administration; Schools—Administration;** etc.; and names of countries, cities, etc., with the subdivision *Politics and government,* e.g. **United States—Politics and government;** etc.
Administration of criminal justice. *See* **Criminal justice, Administration of**
Administration of justice. *See* **Justice, Administration of**
Administrative ability. *See* **Executive ability**
Administrative agencies—Reorganization. *See* **United States—Executive departments—Reorganization**
Administrative law   342
  See also **Civil service; Constitutional law; Local government; Ombudsman; Public administration**
  x Law, Administrative
  xx **Constitutional law; Law; Public administration**
Administrators and executors. *See* **Executors and administrators**
Admirals   359.092; 920
  xx **Military personnel; Navies**
Admissions applications. *See* **College applications**
Admissions essays. *See* **College applications**
Adolescence   155.5; 305.23
  Use for materials on the process or the state of growing up. See note at **Youth.**
  x Age; Teen age; Teenagers—Development
Adolescence—Psychology. *See* **Adolescent psychology**
Adolescent fathers. *See* **Teenage fathers**
Adolescent mothers. *See* **Teenage mothers**
Adolescent pregnancy. *See* **Teenage pregnancy**
Adolescent prostitution. *See* **Juvenile prostitution**

Adolescent psychiatry   616.89
> *x* Psychiatry, Adolescent; Teenagers, Psychiatry
> of
> *xx* **Psychiatry**

Adolescent psychology   155.5
> *x* Adolescence—Psychology; Psychology, Ado-
> lescent; Teenagers—Psychology
> *xx* **Psychology**

Adolescents.   *See* **Teenagers**

Adopted children   306.87; 362.82
> *See also* **Orphans**
> *x* Children, Adopted
> *xx* **Adoptees; Adoption; Orphans**

Adoptees   346.01; 362.7
> Use for materials on anyone formally adopted as
> a dependent.
> *See also* **Adopted children; Birthparents**
> *x* Adult adoptees
> *xx* **Adoption; Birthparents**

Adoption   346.01; 362.7
> *See also* **Adopted children; Adoptees; Foster
> home care; Interracial adoption**
> *x* Child placing; Children—Adoption; Chil-
> dren—Placing out
> *xx* **Foster home care**

Adoption—Corrupt practices   364.1
> *x* Black market children; Infants, Sale of; Sale of
> infants; Selling of infants
> *xx* **Criminal law**

Adoption, Interracial.   *See* **Interracial adoption**

Adult adoptees.   *See* **Adoptees**

Adult children of alcoholics   362.29
> *x* A.C.O.A.s; ACOAs; Alcoholics' adult children
> *xx* **Alcoholics; Alcoholism; Children of alcoholics;
> Parent and child**

Adult education   374
> *See also* **Agricultural extension work; Continuing
> education; Evening and continuation schools;
> Prisoners—Education**
> *x* Education, Adult; Education of adults; Life-
> long education
> *xx* **Continuing education; Education; Evening and
> continuation schools; Higher education;
> Secondary education; University extension**

Adulteration of food.   *See* **Food adulteration and inspection**

Adultery   176; 306.73; 363.4
> *x* Extramarital relationships; Infidelity, Marital;
> Marital infidelity
> *xx* **Sexual ethics**

Adults and children.   *See* **Children and adults**

Adults, Runaway.   *See* **Runaway adults**

Adventure and adventurers   904; 904.092; 910.4; 920
> *See also*

Discoveries (in geography)	**Sea stories**
Escapes	**Seafaring life**
Explorers	**Shipwrecks**
Frontier and pioneer life	**Underwater exploration**
Heroes and heroines	**Voyages and travels**

> *xx* **Voyages and travels**

Adventure and adventurers—Fiction   E; Fic
> *x* Adventure stories

Adventure stories.   *See* **Adventure and adventurers—Fiction**

Advertisement writing. *See* **Advertising copy**
Advertising 659.1
    May be subdivided by topic, e.g. **Advertising—
      Libraries;** etc.
    See also

Commercial art	**Public relations**
Coupons (Retail trade)	**Publicity**
Electric signs	**Radio advertising**
Mail-order business	**Selling**
Marketing	**Show windows**
Packaging	**Sign painting**
Posters	**Signs and signboards**
Printing—Specimens	**Television advertising**
Propaganda	

  xx **Business; Propaganda; Public relations; Pub-
    licity; Retail trade; Selling**
Advertising and children 659.1
  xx **Children**
Advertising art. *See* **Commercial art**
Advertising copy 659.13
  x Advertisement writing; Copy writing
  xx **Authorship**
Advertising, Fraudulent. *See* **Deceptive advertising**
Advertising layout and typography 659.13
  xx **Printing; Type and type founding**
Advertising—Libraries 021.7
  x Libraries—Advertising; Library advertising
Advertising, Newspaper. *See* **Newspaper advertis-
  ing**
Advertising—Newspapers 659.1
    Use for materials discussing advertising of news-
      papers. Materials discussing advertising in
      newspapers are entered under **Newspaper
      advertising.**
  x Newspapers—Advertising
Advertising, Pictorial. *See* **Commercial art; Posters**
Advertising, Radio. *See* **Radio advertising**
Advertising, Television. *See* **Television advertising**
Advisors. *See* **Consultants**
Aerial bombs. *See* **Bombs**
Aerial navigation. *See* **Navigation (Aeronautics)**
Aerial photography 778.3
    Use for materials on photography from air-
      planes, balloons, high buildings, etc.
  See also **Remote sensing**
  x Photography, Aerial
  xx **Photography**
Aerial reconnaissance 355.4; 358.4
  x Reconnaissance, Aerial
  xx **Aeronautics, Military; Remote sensing**
Aerial rockets. *See* **Rockets (Aeronautics)**
Aerial spraying and dusting. *See* **Aeronautics in ag-
  riculture**
Aerobatic flying. *See* **Stunt flying**
Aerobatics. *See* **Stunt flying**
Aerobics 613.7
  x Dancing, Aerobic; Exercises, Aerobic
  xx **Dancing; Exercise; Respiration**
Aerobiology. *See* **Air—Microbiology**
Aerodromes. *See* **Airports**
Aerodynamics 533; 629.132
  See also **Aeronautics; Ground cushion phenom-
  ena**

Aerodynamics—*Continued*
> *x* Streamlining
> *xx* **Aeronautics; Air; Dynamics; Pneumatics**

Aerodynamics, Supersonic   629.132
> *See also* **Aerothermodynamics**
> *x* High speed aerodynamics; Speed, Supersonic;
> Supersonic aerodynamics
> *xx* **High speed aeronautics**

Aeronautical instruments   629.135
> *See also* **Airplanes—Electric equipment; Instrument flying;** also names of specific instruments, e.g. **Gyroscope;** etc.
> *x* Airplanes—Instruments; Instruments, Aeronautical
> *xx* **Scientific apparatus and instruments**

Aeronautical sports   797.5
> *See also* names of specific sports, e.g. **Airplane racing; Skydiving;** etc.
> *xx* **Aeronautics; Sports**

Aeronautics   629.13
> Use for materials on the scientific aspects of aircraft and their construction and operation; or for materials dealing collectively with various types of aircraft.
> *See also*

Aerodynamics	**Kites**
Aeronautical sports	**Lasers in aeronautics**
Airplanes	**Meteorology in aeronautics**
Airships	**tics**
Astronautics	**Navigation (Aeronautics)**
Balloons	**Parachutes**
Flight	**Radio in aeronautics**
Gliders (Aeronautics)	**Rocketry**
Helicopters	**Rockets (Aeronautics)**
High speed aeronautics	**Unidentified flying objects**

> *x* Aviation; Locomotion
> *xx* **Aerodynamics; Airships; Balloons; Engineering; Flight**

Aeronautics—Accidents   363.12; 629.13
> *See also* **Survival (after airplane accidents, shipwrecks, etc.)**
> *x* Air crashes; Airplane accidents; Airplane collisions; Airplanes—Accidents
> *xx* **Accidents**

Aeronautics and civilization   306
> *See also* **Astronautics and civilization**
> *x* Civilization and aeronautics
> *xx* **Civilization**

Aeronautics, Commercial   387.7
> *See also* **Air mail service; Airlines; Airplane industry**
> *x* Air cargo; Air freight; Air transport; Commercial aeronautics; Commercial aviation
> *xx* **Freight and freightage; Transportation**

Aeronautics, Commercial—Chartering   387.7
> *x* Air charters; Airlines—Chartering; Airplanes—Chartering; Charter flights

Aeronautics, Commercial—Hijacking. *See* **Hijacking of airplanes**

Aeronautics—Flights   387.7; 629.13
> *See also* **Space flight**
> *x* Aeronautics—Voyages; Flights around the world; Transatlantic flights
> *xx* **Voyages and travels**

Aeronautics, High speed.　*See* **High speed aeronautics**

Aeronautics in agriculture　631.3

> Use same pattern for aeronautics in other fields of endeavor.

> *See also* **Insect pests**

> *x* Aerial spraying and dusting; Airplanes in agriculture; Crop dusting; Crop spraying

> *xx* **Agricultural pests; Agriculture; Insect pests; Spraying and dusting**

Aeronautics—Medical aspects.　*See* **Aviation medicine**

Aeronautics, Meteorology in.　*See* **Meteorology in aeronautics**

Aeronautics, Military　358.4

> *See also*

Aerial reconnaissance	**Air raid shelters**
Air bases	**Aircraft carriers**
Air defenses	**Airplanes, Military**
Air power	**Parachute troops**

> also names of wars with the subdivision *Aerial operations,* e.g. **World War, 1939-1945—Aerial operations;** etc.

> *x* Aeronautics, Naval; Air raids—Protective measures; Air warfare; Military aeronautics; Naval aeronautics

> *xx* **Armaments; Military art and science; War**

Aeronautics, Naval.　*See* **Aeronautics, Military**

Aeronautics—Navigation.　*See* **Navigation (Aeronautics)**

Aeronautics—Piloting.　*See* **Airplanes—Piloting**

Aeronautics, Radio in.　*See* **Radio in aeronautics**

Aeronautics—Safety measures　387.7; 629.134

> *xx* **Accidents—Prevention**

Aeronautics—Study and teaching　629.1307

> *See also* **Airplanes—Piloting**

> *x* Flight training

Aeronautics—Voyages.　*See* **Aeronautics—Flights**

Aeroplanes.　*See* **Airplanes**

Aeroponics　631.5

> *x* Agriculture, Soilless; Gardening in space; Plants—Soilless culture; Soilless agriculture; Space gardening

> *xx* **Horticulture**

Aerosol sniffing.　*See* **Solvent abuse**

Aerosols　541.3; 551.5; 660

> *xx* **Air pollution**

Aerospace industries　338.4

> *See also* **Airplane industry**

> *x* Aircraft production

Aerospace law.　*See* **Space law**

Aerospace medicine.　*See* **Aviation medicine; Space medicine**

Aerothermodynamics　629.132; 629.4

> *x* Thermoaerodynamics

> *xx* **Aerodynamics, Supersonic; Astronautics; High speed aeronautics; Thermodynamics**

Aesthetics　111; 701; 801

> *See also*

Art appreciation	**Rhythm**
Color	**Romanticism**
Criticism	**Sculpture**
Painting	**Values**
Poetry	

Aesthetics—*Continued*
    x Beauty; Esthetics; Taste (Aesthetics)
    xx **Art**
Affection. *See* **Friendship; Love**
Affirmative action programs 331.13; 658.3
    xx **Discrimination in employment; Personnel management**
Affliction. *See* **Joy and sorrow**
Africa 960
    See also **Africans; Pan-Africanism**
Africa, Central. *See* **Central Africa**
Africa, East. *See* **East Africa**
Africa, Eastern. *See* **East Africa**
Africa, French-speaking Equatorial. *See* **French-speaking Equatorial Africa**
Africa, French-speaking West. *See* **French-speaking West Africa**
Africa—History 960
Africa—History—1960- 960.3
Africa, North. *See* **North Africa**
Africa, Northeast. *See* **Northeast Africa**
Africa, Northwest. *See* **Northwest Africa**
Africa, South. *See* **South Africa**
Africa, Southern. *See* **Southern Africa**
Africa—Study and teaching 960.07
    x African studies
    xx **Area studies**
Africa, Sub-Saharan. *See* **Sub-Saharan Africa**
Africa, West. *See* **West Africa**
African Americans. *See* **Blacks**
African civilization. *See* **Civilization, African**
African literature (English) 820
    x English literature—African authors
African relations. *See* **Pan-Africanism**
African songs. *See* **Songs, African**
African studies. *See* **Africa—Study and teaching**
Africans 305.896
    See also **Blacks—Africa**
    xx **Africa**
Afrikaaners. *See* **Afrikaners**
Afrikaners 305.83
    x Afrikaaners; Boers; South African Dutch; South Africans, Afrikaans-speaking
Afro-Americans. *See* **Blacks**
After dinner speeches 808.5; 808.85
    See also **Toasts**
    xx **Speeches, addresses, etc.; Toasts**
After school day care. *See* **After school programs**
After school programs 362.7; 372.12
    x After school day care
    xx **Student activities**
Afterlife. *See* **Future life**
Age. *See* **Adolescence; Middle age; Old age**
Age and employment 331.3
    See also **Age discrimination; Career changes; Children—Employment; Teenagers—Employment; Youth—Employment**
    x Employment and age
    xx **Age discrimination; Discrimination in employment; Middle age; Old age**
Age discrimination 305.2
    See also **Age and employment**
    xx **Age and employment; Discrimination**
Age, Drinking. *See* **Drinking age**

Age—Physiological effect. *See* **Aging**

Aged. *See* **Elderly**

Ageing. *See* **Aging**

Agent Orange 363.17; 615.9
> *xx* **Herbicides**

Agents, Sales. *See* **Sales personnel**

Aggregates. *See* **Set theory**

Aggressive behavior. *See* **Aggressiveness (Psychology)**

Aggressiveness (Psychology) 152.4; 155.2
> *See also* **Assertiveness (Psychology); Violence**
> *x* Aggressive behavior
> *xx* **Human behavior; Psychology**

Aging 574.3; 612.6
> *See also* **Male climacteric; Menopause**
> *x* Age—Physiological effect; Ageing; Senescence
> *xx* **Elderly; Gerontology; Longevity; Middle age; Old age**

Agnosticism 149; 211
> *See also* **Atheism; Belief and doubt; Positivism; Rationalism; Skepticism**
> *xx* **Atheism; Belief and doubt; Faith; Free thought; God; Positivism; Rationalism; Religion; Skepticism; Truth**

Agrarian question. *See* **Agriculture—Economic aspects; Agriculture—Government policy; Land tenure**

Agrarian reform. *See* **Land reform**

Agreements. *See* **Contracts**

Agribusiness 338.1
> *x* Corporate farming; Corporations—Farming operations; Farm corporations; Farming corporations
> *xx* **Agricultural industries; Agriculture—Economic aspects**

Agricultural bacteriology 630.2
> *See also* **Soils—Bacteriology;** also names of crops, etc., with the subdivision *Diseases and pests,* e.g. **Fruit—Diseases and pests;** etc.
> *x* Bacteriology, Agricultural; Diseases and pests
> *xx* **Soils—Bacteriology**

Agricultural botany. *See* **Botany, Economic**

Agricultural chemicals 631.8; 668
> *See also* **Fertilizers and manures;** also types of chemicals, e.g. **Herbicides; Insecticides; Pesticides;** etc.; and names of individual chemicals
> *xx* **Agricultural chemistry; Chemicals**

Agricultural chemistry 630.2
> *See also* **Agricultural chemicals; Soils**
> *x* Chemistry, Agricultural
> *xx* **Chemistry; Soils**

Agricultural clubs. *See* **Agriculture—Societies**

Agricultural cooperation. *See* **Agriculture, Cooperative**

Agricultural credit 332.7
> *x* Credit, Agricultural; Farm credit; Rural credit
> *xx* **Agriculture—Economic aspects; Banks and banking; Credit; Mortgages**

Agricultural economics. *See* **Agriculture—Economic aspects**

Agricultural education. *See* **Agriculture—Study and teaching**

Agricultural engineering   630

See also **Drainage; Electricity in agriculture; Irrigation**

x Agricultural mechanics; Farm mechanics

xx **Agricultural machinery; Engineering; Farm engines**

Agricultural experiment stations   630.7

See also **Agricultural extension work**

x Experimental farms; Farms, Experimental

xx **Agriculture—Government policy; Agriculture—Research; Agriculture—Study and teaching**

Agricultural extension work (May subdiv. geog.)   **630.7**

See also **Agriculture—Study and teaching; Community development; County agricultural agents**

x Extension work, Agricultural

xx **Adult education; Agricultural experiment stations; Agriculture—Government policy; Agriculture—Study and teaching; Community development**

Agricultural industries   338.1

See also **Agribusiness**

xx **Agriculture—Economic aspects**

Agricultural laborers   331.7

See also **Migrant labor; Peasantry**

x Farm laborers

xx **Labor; Peasantry**

Agricultural machinery   631.3

See also **Agricultural engineering; Electricity in agriculture; Farm engines;** also names of farm machinery, e.g. **Harvesting machinery; Plows; Tractors;** etc.

x Agricultural tools; Farm implements; Farm machinery; Farm mechanics; Implements, utensils, etc.

xx **Machinery; Tools**

Agricultural mechanics. *See* **Agricultural engineering**

Agricultural pests   632

See also **Aeronautics in agriculture; Fungi; Insect pests; Pests—Control; Plant diseases; Spraying and dusting; Weeds;** also names of crops, etc., with the subdivision *Diseases and pests,* e.g. **Fruit—Diseases and pests;** etc.

x Diseases and pests; Garden pests

xx **Insect pests; Pests; Zoology, Economic**

Agricultural pests—Biological control. *See* **Pests—Biological control**

Agricultural policy. *See* **Agriculture—Government policy**

Agricultural products. *See* **Farm produce**

Agricultural research. *See* **Agriculture—Research**

Agricultural societies. *See* **Agriculture—Societies**

Agricultural tools. *See* **Agricultural machinery**

Agriculture (May subdiv. geog.)   **630**

See also

Aeronautics in agriculture	**Dairying**
Aquaculture	**Domestic animals**
Botany, Economic	**Dry farming**
Crop rotation	**Family farms**

Agriculture—*Continued*
    Farmers
    Farms
    Food supply
    Forests and forestry
    Fruit culture
    Gardening
    Horticulture

    Land tenure
    Land use
    Organiculture
    Pastures
    Plant breeding
    Reclamation of land
    Soils

    also names of agricultural products, e.g. **Corn;**
        etc.; and headings beginning with the words
        Agricultural and **Farm**
    x Agronomy; Farming; Planting
    xx **Food supply; Life sciences**
Agriculture and state. *See* **Agriculture—**
    Government policy
Agriculture—Bibliography 016.63
    xx **Bibliography**
Agriculture, Cooperative 334
    Use for materials dealing with cooperation in the
        production and disposal of agricultural
        products.
    x Agricultural cooperation; Collective farms;
        Cooperative agriculture; Farmers' coopera-
        tives
    xx **Cooperation**
Agriculture—Documentation 025
    xx **Documentation**
Agriculture—Economic aspects 338.1
    See also **Agribusiness; Agricultural credit; Agri-**
        cultural industries; Farm management; Farm
        produce—Marketing; Land tenure
    x Agrarian question; Agricultural economics
    xx **Economics; Farm management; Farm pro-**
        duce—Marketing
Agriculture—Government policy 338.9
    See also **Agricultural experiment stations; Agri-**
        cultural extension work; Land reform
    x Agrarian question; Agricultural policy; Agri-
        culture and state; State and agriculture
    xx **Industry—Government policy; Land reform**
Agriculture—Research 630.7
    See also **Agricultural experiment stations**
    x Agricultural research
    xx **Research**
Agriculture—Societies 630.6
    See also names of agricultural societies, e.g.
        4-H clubs; Grange; etc.
    x Agricultural clubs; Agricultural societies;
        Boys' agricultural clubs; Girls' agricultural
        clubs
    xx **Country life; Societies**
Agriculture, Soilless. *See* **Aeroponics; Hydroponics**
Agriculture—Statistics 338.1; 630.2
    x Crop reports
    xx **Statistics**
Agriculture—Study and teaching 630.7
    See also **Agricultural experiment stations; Agri-**
        cultural extension work; County agricultural
        agents
    x Agricultural education
    xx **Agricultural extension work; Vocational edu-**
        cation
Agriculture—Tenant farming. *See* **Farm tenancy**

Agriculture—Tropics 630.913
   xx **Tropics**
Agriculture—United States 630.973
   x United States—Agriculture
Agronomy. *See* **Agriculture**
Ague. *See* **Malaria**
AI (Artificial intelligence). *See* **Artificial intelligence**
Aid to dependent children. *See* **Child welfare**
Aid to developing areas. *See* **Economic assistance; Technical assistance**
AIDS (Disease) 616.97
   x A.I.D.S. (Disease); Acquired immune deficiency syndrome; HIV disease
   xx **Communicable diseases; Diseases; Sexually transmitted diseases**
AIDS (Disease)—Prevention 616.97
   See also **Safe sex in AIDS prevention; Sexual hygiene**
   xx **Sexual hygiene**
Air 533; 546
   Use for materials dealing with air as an element and with its chemical and physical properties. Materials on the body of air surrounding the earth are entered under **Atmosphere.**
   See also **Aerodynamics; Atmosphere; Ventilation**
   xx **Atmosphere; Meteorology**
Air bases 358.4
   x Air stations, Military; Air stations, Naval; Military air bases; Naval air bases
   xx **Aeronautics, Military; Airports**
Air bearing lift. *See* **Ground cushion phenomena**
Air bearing vehicles. *See* **Ground effect machines**
Air cargo. *See* **Aeronautics, Commercial**
Air carriers. *See* **Airlines**
Air charters. *See* **Aeronautics, Commercial—Chartering**
Air, Compressed. *See* **Compressed air**
Air conditioning 644; 697.9
   See also **Refrigeration; Ventilation;** also subjects with the subdivision *Air conditioning,* e.g. **Automobiles—Air conditioning;** etc.
   xx **Refrigeration; Ventilation**
Air crashes. *See* **Aeronautics—Accidents**
Air cushion vehicles. *See* **Ground effect machines**
Air defenses 363.3
   Use for materials on civilian defense against air attack. Materials on military defense against air raids are entered under **Aeronautics, Military.** General materials on civilian defense are entered under **Civil defense.**
   See also **Air raid shelters; Ballistic missile early warning system; Poisonous gases—War use; Radar defense networks**
   x Air raids—Protective measures; Air warfare; Defenses, Air
   xx **Aeronautics, Military; Civil defense**
Air freight. *See* **Aeronautics, Commercial**
Air hostesses. *See* **Airlines—Flight attendants**
Air lines. *See* **Airlines**
Air mail service 383
   xx **Aeronautics, Commercial; Postal service**

Air—Microbiology   576
>   *x* Aerobiology
>   *xx* **Microbiology**

Air, Moisture of.   *See* **Humidity**

Air navigation.   *See* **Navigation (Aeronautics)**

Air pilots   629.13; 920
>   *See also* **Astronauts; Women air pilots**
>   *x* Airplanes—Pilots; Aviators; Pilots, Airplane;
>   Test pilots

Air piracy.   *See* **Hijacking of airplanes**

Air planes.   *See* **Airplanes**

Air pollution (May subdiv. geog.)   363.73; 628.5
>   *See also* **Acid rain; Aerosols**
>   *x* Atmosphere—Pollution; Pollution of air
>   *xx* **Environmental health; Pollution**

Air pollution—Measurement   363.73; 628.5
>   *xx* **Measurement**

Air pollution—United States   363.73; 628.5
>   *x* United States—Air pollution

Air ports.   *See* **Airports**

Air power   358.4
>   *xx* **Aeronautics, Military**

Air raid shelters   363.3
>   *x* Blast shelters; Bomb shelters; Fallout shelters;
>   Nuclear bomb shelters; Public shelters;
>   Shelters, Air raid
>   *xx* **Aeronautics, Military; Air defenses; Civil de-
>   fense**

Air raids—Protective measures.   *See* **Aeronautics,
     Military; Air defenses**

Air rights law.   *See* **Airspace law**

Air routes.   *See* **Airways**

Air-ships.   *See* **Airships**

Air space law.   *See* **Airspace law**

Air stations, Military.   *See* **Air bases**

Air stations, Naval.   *See* **Air bases**

Air stewardesses.   *See* **Airlines—Flight attendants**

Air stewards.   *See* **Airlines—Flight attendants**

Air surfing.   *See* **Gliding and soaring**

Air terminals.   *See* **Airports**

Air traffic control   387.7
>   *x* Airports—Traffic control

Air transport.   *See* **Aeronautics, Commercial**

Air warfare.   *See* **Aeronautics, Military; Air de-
     fenses; Airplanes, Military; Chemical war-
     fare;** and names of wars with the subdivi-
     sion *Aerial operations,* e.g. **World War,
     1939-1945—Aerial operations;** etc.

Aircraft.   *See* **Airplanes; Airships; Gliders (Aero-
     nautics); Helicopters**

Aircraft carriers   359.3; 623
>   *x* Airplane carriers; Carriers, Aircraft
>   *xx* **Aeronautics, Military; Warships**

Aircraft production.   *See* **Aerospace industries; Air-
     plane industry**

Airdromes.   *See* **Airports**

Airlines   387.7
>   Use for materials dealing with systems of aerial
>   transportation and with companies engaged
>   in this business. Materials dealing with the
>   routes along which the planes are flown are
>   entered under **Airways.**
>   *See also* **Airways**

Airlines—*Continued*
  x Air carriers; Air lines
  xx **Aeronautics, Commercial; Airways**
Airlines—**Chartering.** *See* **Aeronautics, Commercial**—**Chartering**
Airlines—**Flight attendants 387.7**
  x Air hostesses; Air stewardesses; Air stewards; Airlines—Hostesses; Airplane hostesses; Flight attendants; Hostesses, Airline; Stewardesses, Airline; Stewards, Airline
Airlines—**Hijacking.** *See* **Hijacking of airplanes**
Airlines—**Hostesses.** *See* **Airlines**—**Flight attendants**
Airplane accidents. *See* **Aeronautics**—**Accidents**
Airplane carriers. *See* **Aircraft carriers**
Airplane collisions. *See* **Aeronautics**—**Accidents**
Airplane engines. *See* **Airplanes**—**Engines**
Airplane hijacking. *See* **Hijacking of airplanes**
Airplane hostesses. *See* **Airlines**—**Flight attendants**
Airplane industry 338.4; 387.7
  x Aircraft production
  xx **Aeronautics, Commercial; Aerospace industries**
Airplane racing 797.5
  x Airplanes—Racing
  xx **Aeronautical sports**
Airplane spotting. *See* **Airplanes**—**Identification**
Airplanes 387.7; 629.133
  See also **Gliders (Aeronautics); Propellers, Aerial;** also types of airplanes and special makes of airplanes, e.g. **Bombers; Helicopters; Vertically rising airplanes;** etc.
  x Aeroplanes; Air planes; Aircraft; Biplanes; Monoplanes
  xx **Aeronautics**
Airplanes—**Accidents.** *See* **Aeronautics**—**Accidents**
Airplanes—**Chartering.** *See* **Aeronautics, Commercial**—**Chartering**
Airplanes—**Design and construction 629.134**
Airplanes—**Electric equipment 629.135**
  x Airplanes—Instruments
  xx **Aeronautical instruments**
Airplanes—**Engines 629.134**
  See also **Jet propulsion**
  x Airplane engines; Airplanes—Motors
  xx **Engines; Gas and oil engines**
Airplanes—**Flight testing.** *See* **Airplanes**—**Testing**
Airplanes—**Hijacking.** *See* **Hijacking of airplanes**
Airplanes—**Identification 623.7; 629.133**
  x Airplane spotting; Airplanes—Recognition
  xx **Identification**
Airplanes in agriculture. *See* **Aeronautics in agriculture**
Airplanes—**Inspection 387.7; 629.134**
Airplanes—**Instruments.** *See* **Aeronautical instruments; Airplanes**—**Electric equipment**
Airplanes, Jet propelled. *See* **Jet planes**
Airplanes—**Maintenance and repair 629.134**
  x Airplanes—Repair
Airplanes—**Materials 629.134**
Airplanes, Military 623.7
  See also types of military airplanes, e.g. **Bombers;** etc.

Airplanes, Military—*Continued*
  x Air warfare; Airplanes, Naval; Military air-
    planes; Naval airplanes
  xx **Aeronautics, Military**
Airplanes—Models 629.133
  x Model airplanes; Paper airplanes
  xx **Machinery—Models; Models and model mak-
    ing**
Airplanes—Motors. *See* **Airplanes—Engines**
Airplanes, Naval. *See* **Airplanes, Military**
Airplanes—Noise 629.132
  xx **Noise; Noise pollution**
Airplanes—Operation. *See* **Airplanes—Piloting**
Airplanes—Piloting 629.132
  Use for materials on instruction in the mechan-
    ics of flying.
  See also **Instrument flying; Stunt flying;** also
    types and names of airplanes with the subdi-
    vision *Piloting,* e.g. **Helicopters—Piloting;**
    etc.
  x Aeronautics—Piloting; Airplanes—Operation;
    Flight training
  xx **Aeronautics—Study and teaching; Navigation
    (Aeronautics)**
Airplanes—Pilots. *See* **Air pilots**
Airplanes—Propellers. *See* **Propellers, Aerial**
Airplanes—Racing. *See* **Airplane racing**
Airplanes—Recognition. *See* **Airplanes—
    Identification**
Airplanes—Repair. *See* **Airplanes—Maintenance
    and repair**
Airplanes, Rocket propelled. *See* **Rocket planes**
Airplanes—Testing 629.134
  x Airplanes—Flight testing; Test pilots
Airplanes, Vertically rising. *See* **Vertically rising
    airplanes**
Airports (May subdiv. geog.) **629.136**
  See also **Air bases; Heliports;** also names of indi-
    vidual airports
  x Aerodromes; Air ports; Air terminals; Air-
    dromes
Airports—Traffic control. *See* **Air traffic control**
Airships 629.133
  Use for materials on self-propelled aircraft that
    are lighter than air and that can be steered.
  See also **Aeronautics; Balloons**
  x Air-ships; Aircraft; Balloons, Dirigible;
    Blimps; Dirigible balloons; Zeppelins
  xx **Aeronautics**
Airspace law 341.4
  x Air rights law; Air space law
  xx **Space law**
Airways 387.7
  Use for materials dealing with routes along
    which planes are flown and where aids to
    navigation are maintained, such as landing
    fields, beacons, etc. Materials dealing with
    the companies engaged in aerial transporta-
    tion are entered under **Airlines.**
  See also **Airlines**
  x Air routes
  xx **Airlines**
Alaska Highway (Alaska and Canada) 388.1; 979.8

Alchemy   540.1

Use for materials on the medieval chemical science that sought to transmute baser metals into gold. Modern materials on the transmutation of metals are entered under **Transmutation (Chemistry).**

See also **Transmutation (Chemistry)**

x Hermetic art and philosophy; Metals, Transmutation of; Philosophers' stone; Transmutation of metals

xx **Chemistry; Occultism; Superstition**

Alcohol   547; 661

See also **Alcoholic beverages; Alcoholism; Distillation; Liquor industry; Liquors and liqueurs**

x Intoxicants

xx **Distillation; Stimulants**

Alcohol and employees.   *See* **Employees—Alcohol use**

Alcohol and teenagers.   *See* **Teenagers—Alcohol use**

Alcohol and youth.   *See* **Youth—Alcohol use**

Alcohol as fuel   662

See also names of alcohol fuels, e.g. **Gasohol;** etc.

x Alcohol fuel; Ethanol; Ethyl alcohol fuel

xx **Biomass energy; Fuel**

Alcohol consumption.   *See* **Drinking of alcoholic beverages**

Alcohol, Denatured   661

x Alcohol, Industrial; Denatured alcohol; Industrial alcohol

Alcohol fuel.   *See* **Alcohol as fuel**

Alcohol in the workplace.   *See* **Employees—Alcohol use**

Alcohol, Industrial.   *See* **Alcohol, Denatured**

Alcohol—Physiological effect   615

xx **Alcoholism; Temperance**

Alcohol use.   *See* classes of people with the subdivision *Alcohol use,* e.g. **Employees—Alcohol use; Youth—Alcohol use;** etc.

Alcoholic beverage consumption.   *See* **Drinking of alcoholic beverages**

Alcoholic beverages   641.2

See also **Drinking of alcoholic beverages; Liquors and liqueurs; Wine and wine making**

x Drinks; Intoxicants

xx **Alcohol; Beverages**

Alcoholics   362.29; 616.86

See also **Adult children of alcoholics; Children of alcoholics**

x Drunkards; Inebriates

xx **Alcoholism**

Alcoholics' adult children.   *See* **Adult children of alcoholics**

Alcoholics' children.   *See* **Children of alcoholics**

Alcoholism   362.29; 616.86

Use chiefly for medical materials, including works on drunkenness, dipsomania, etc.

See also **Adult children of alcoholics; Alcohol—Physiological effect; Alcoholics; Children of alcoholics; Drinking of alcoholic beverages; Temperance;** also classes of people with the subdivision *Alcohol use,* e.g. **Employees—**

Alcoholism—*Continued*
> **Alcohol use; Youth—Alcohol use;** etc.
> *x* Addiction to alcohol; Dipsomania; Drinking
> problem; Drunkenness; Intemperance; In-
> toxication; Liquor problem; Problem drink-
> ing
> *xx* **Alcohol; Drinking of alcoholic beverages;**
> **Drug abuse; Substance abuse; Temperance**

Alfalfa   633.3
> *xx* **Hay**

Algae   561; 589.3
> *x* Sea mosses; Seaweeds
> *xx* **Marine plants**

Algebra   512
> *See also* **Graph theory; Group theory; Loga-**
> **rithms; Number theory; Probabilities**
> *xx* **Mathematical analysis; Mathematics**

Algebra, Boolean   511
> *x* Boolean algebra
> *xx* **Group theory; Logic, Symbolic and mathemat-**
> **ical; Set theory**

Algebras, Linear   512
> *See also* **Topology**
> *x* Linear algebras
> *xx* **Mathematical analysis; Topology**

Alienation (Social psychology)   302.5
> *x* Estrangement (Social psychology); Rebels (So-
> cial psychology); Social alienation
> *xx* **Social psychology**

Aliens   323.6
> *See also* **Citizenship; Illegal aliens; Naturaliza-**
> **tion; Refugees;** also headings such as **Mexi-**
> **cans—United States;** etc.
> *x* Foreigners; Noncitizens; Nonnationals
> *xx* **Citizenship; Immigration and emigration; In-**
> **ternational law; Naturalization**

Aliens from outer space.   *See* **Extraterrestrial be-**
ings
Aliens, Illegal.   *See* **Illegal aliens**
Alkoran.   *See* **Koran**
All Fools' Day.   *See* **April Fools' Day**
All Hallows' Eve.   *See* **Halloween**

All terrain vehicles   629.22
> *See also* types of vehicles, e.g. **Snowmobiles;**
> etc.
> *x* A.T.V.'s; ATVs
> *xx* **Vehicles**

Allegories   808.88; 810.8, etc.
> Use for collections of allegories.
> *See also* **Fables; Parables**
> *xx* **Fiction; Parables; Symbolism in literature**

Allegory   704.9; 808
> Use for materials on allegory as a literary form
> as well as for allegory in the fine and deco-
> rative arts.

Allergy   616.97
> *See also* **Hay fever**
> *xx* **Immunity**

Alleys.   *See* **Streets**

Allied health personnel   610.69
> *See also* types of personnel, e.g. **Emergency**
> **medical technicians; Medical technologists;**
> **Nurse practitioners;** etc.
> *x* Paramedical personnel

Alligators   597.98
> *xx* **Crocodiles**

Allocation of time.   *See* **Time management**

Allowances, Children's.   *See* **Children's allowances**

Alloys   669
> *See also* **Brass; Metallurgy; Pewter;** also names of alloys, e.g. **Aluminum alloys;** etc.
> *xx* **Chemistry, Technical; Metallurgy; Metals; Solder and soldering**

Allusions   031.02; 803

Almanacs   030
> *See also* **Calendars; Chronology; Nautical almanacs**
> *x* Annuals
> *xx* **Calendars; Chronology**

Alphabet   411
> Use for materials dealing with the series of characters that form the elements of a written language and for materials teaching children the ABCs. Materials dealing with the styles of alphabets used by artists, etc., are entered under **Alphabets.**
> *See also* **Alphabets; Writing**
> *x* A.B.C.'s; ABCs; Alphabet books; Letters of the alphabet
> *xx* **Writing**

Alphabet books.   *See* **Alphabet**

Alphabetizing.   *See* **Files and filing**

Alphabets   745.6
> See note under **Alphabet.**
> *See also* **Illumination of books and manuscripts; Initials; Lettering; Monograms**
> *xx* **Alphabet; Initials; Lettering; Sign painting**

Alpine animals   591.909
> *x* Mountain animals
> *xx* **Animals; Wildlife**

Alpine plants   581.909; 635.9
> *x* Mountain plants
> *xx* **Plants**

Alternate energy resources.   *See* **Renewable energy resources**

Alternate work sites.   *See* **Telecommuting**

Alternating current machinery.   *See* **Electric machinery—Alternating current**

Alternating currents.   *See* **Electric currents, Alternating**

Alternative energy resources.   *See* **Renewable energy resources**

Alternative lifestyle. *See* **Counter culture; Lifestyles**

Alternative medicine   610; 613; 615.5
> *See also* **Health self-care; Homeopathy; Naturopathy; Osteopathy;** also types of alternative medicine, e.g. **Acupressure; Acupuncture; Chiropractic; Holistic medicine;** etc.
> *x* Therapeutic systems
> *xx* **Medicine**

Alternative press.   *See* **Underground press**

Alternative schools.   *See* **Experimental schools**

Alternative universities.   *See* **Free universities**

Alternative work schedules.   *See* **Hours of labor; Part-time employment**

Altitude, Influence of.   *See* **Man—Influence of environment**

Altruists.   *See* **Philanthropists**

Aluminum   669; 673

    See also **Aluminum foil**

    xx **Metals**

Aluminum alloys   669; 673

    xx **Alloys**

Aluminum foil   673

    xx **Aluminum; Packaging**

Aluminum—Recycling   628.4; 673

    xx **Recycling (Waste, etc.)**

Alzheimer's disease   616.8

    xx **Brain—Diseases**

Amateur films   778.5; 791.43

    See also **Camcorders; Motion picture cameras**

    x Amateur motion pictures; Films, Amateur; Home movies; Home video movies; Motion pictures, Amateur; Personal films

    xx **Camcorders; Motion picture cameras; Motion picture photography**

Amateur motion pictures.   *See* **Amateur films**

Amateur radio stations   621.3841

    x Ham radio stations; Radio stations, Amateur

    xx **Shortwave radio**

Amateur theater   792

    Use for materials on the production of plays, skits, recitations, etc., by nonprofessional groups. Collections of plays for such groups are entered under **American drama—Collections; Drama—Collections**; and similar subjects.

    See also

Acting	**One act plays**
Charades	**Pantomimes**
Children's plays	**Readers' theater**
College and school drama	**Shadow pantomimes and**
Drama in education	**plays**
Little theater movement	

    x Play production; Private theater; Theater, Amateur

    xx **Amusements; Drama in education; Theater**

Ambassadors.   *See* **Diplomats**

Amendments, Equal rights.   *See* **Equal rights amendments**

America   970

    Use for general materials on the Western Hemisphere.

    See also **Central America; Latin America; North America; South America**; also names of separate countries of these areas

America—Antiquities   970.01

America—Discovery and exploration.   *See* **America—Exploration**

America—Exploration   970.01

    See also **Northwest Passage; United States—Exploring expeditions; West (U.S.)—Exploration**

    x America—Discovery and exploration; Canada—Exploration; Conquistadores; North America—Exploration; South America—Exploration; United States—Discovery and exploration; United States—Exploration

    xx **Discoveries (in geography)**

America—History   970

    x American history

America—Politics and government 970
    See also **Pan-Americanism**
    xx **Pan-Americanism**
American actors. *See* **Actors, American**
American architecture. *See* **Architecture, American**
American art. *See* **Art, American**
American artificial satellites. *See* **Artificial satel-**
    lites, American
American artists. *See* **Artists, American**
American arts. *See* **Arts, American**
American authors. *See* **Authors, American**
American ballads. *See* **Ballads, American**
American Bicentennial. *See* **American Revolution**
    Bicentennial, 1776-1976
American bison. *See* **Bison**
American characteristics. *See* **National characteris-**
    tics, American
American Civil War. *See* **United States—**
    History—1861-1865, Civil War
American civilization. *See* **Civilization, American;**
    United States—Civilization
American colleges. *See* **Colleges and universities—**
    United States
American colonies. *See* **United States—History—**
    1600-1775, Colonial period
American color prints. *See* **Color prints, American**
American composers. *See* **Composers, American**
American Constitution. *See* **United States—**
    Constitution
American decoration and ornament. *See* **Decora-**
    tion and ornament, American
American drama 812
    xx **American literature; Drama**
American drama—Collected works. *See* **American**
    drama—Collections
American drama—Collections 812.008
    x American drama—Collected works
    xx **Drama—Collections**
American drama—History and criticism 812.009
    xx **Drama—History and criticism**
American dramatists. *See* **Dramatists, American**
American drawing. *See* **Drawing, American**
American economic assistance. *See* **Economic as-**
    sistance, American
American engraving. *See* **Engraving, American**
American environmental policy. *See* **Environ-**
    ment—Government policy—United States
American espionage. *See* **Espionage, American**
American essays 814; 814.008
    xx **American literature; Essays**
American ethics. *See* **Ethics, American**
American exploring expeditions. *See* **United**
    States—Exploring expeditions
American fiction 813; Fic
    x Fiction, American
    xx **American literature; Fiction**
American films. *See* **Motion pictures—United**
    States
American flag. *See* **Flags—United States**
American folk art. *See* **Folk art, American**
American folk dancing. *See* **Folk dancing, Ameri-**
    can
American folk music. *See* **Folk music—United**
    States

American folk songs. *See* **Folk songs—United States**

American furniture. *See* **Furniture, American**

American government. *See* **United States—Politics and government**

American graphic arts. *See* **Graphic arts, American**

American historians. *See* **Historians, American**

American history. *See* **America—History; United States—History**

American hostages. *See* **Hostages, American**

American illustrators. *See* **Illustrators, American**

American Indians. *See* **Indians; Indians of Central America; Indians of Mexico; Indians of North America; Indians of South America; Indians of the West Indies**

American labor unions. *See* **Labor unions—United States**

American letters 816; 816.008
> *xx* **American literature; Letters**

American literature (May subdiv. geog. by the names of states or regions, e.g. **American literature—Massachusetts; American literature—Southern States.**) **810**

> May be subdivided by the topical subdivisions and literary forms used under **English literature.**

> *See also*

American drama	**American wit and humor**
American essays	**Authors, American**
American fiction	**Ballads, American**
American letters	**Speeches, addresses, etc.,**
American prose literature	**American**

> also various forms of American literature, e.g. **American poetry; Satire, American**

> *x* United States—Literature

American literature—American Indian authors 810.8; 810.9

> Use same pattern for materials on literatures and literary forms written by other ethnic groups or classes of authors, such as women authors.

> Use for materials on literature written in the English language by American Indian authors. Literature written in an Indian language is entered under **Indians of North America—Literature.**

> *x* Indian literature (American)

American literature—Black authors 810.8; 810.9

> Use same pattern for other literary forms, e.g. **American poetry—Black authors;** etc.

> *See also* **Harlem Renaissance**

> *x* Black literature (American)

American literature—Collected works. *See* **American literature—Collections**

American literature—Collections 810.8

> Use for collections of both poetry and prose by several American authors. Collections consisting of prose only are entered under **American prose literature;** collections of poetry are entered under **American poetry—Collections.**

> *x* American literature—Collected works

American literature—Massachusetts 810

American literature—Southern States   810
   x Southern literature
American literature—Women authors   810.8; 810.9
   xx **Women authors**
American Loyalists   973.3
   x Loyalists, American; Tories, American
   xx **United States—History—1775-1783, Revolution**
American military assistance.   *See* **Military assistance, American**
American motion pictures.   *See* **Motion pictures—United States**
American music.   *See* **Music, American**
American musicians.   *See* **Musicians, American**
American national characteristics.   *See* **National characteristics, American**
American national songs.   *See* **National songs, American**
American newspapers   071
   xx **Newspapers**
American novelists.   *See* **Novelists, American**
American orations.   *See* **Speeches, addresses, etc., American**
American painters.   *See* **Painters, American**
American painting.   *See* **Painting, American**
American periodicals   051
   xx **Periodicals**
American personal names.   *See* **Personal names—United States**
American philosophers.   *See* **Philosophers, American**
American philosophy.   *See* **Philosophy, American**
American poetry   811
   xx **American literature; Poetry**
American poetry—Black authors   811
   x Black poetry (American)
American poetry—Collected works.   *See* **American poetry—Collections**
American poetry—Collections   811.008
   x American poetry—Collected works
   xx **Poetry—Collections**
American poetry—History and criticism   811.009
   xx **Poetry—History and criticism**
American poets.   *See* **Poets, American**
American politicians.   *See* **Politicians—United States**
American politics.   *See* **United States—Politics and government**
American pottery.   *See* **Pottery, American**
American prints.   *See* **Prints, American**
American prisoners of war.   *See* **Prisoners of war, American**
American propaganda.   *See* **Propaganda, American**
American prose literature   818
   Use for collections of prose writings by several American authors that may include a variety of literary forms, such as essays, fiction, orations, etc. May also be used for general materials about such prose writings.
   x Prose literature, American
   xx **American literature**
American Revolution.   *See* **United States—History—1775-1783, Revolution**

American Revolution Bicentennial, 1776-1976   973.3
> *x* American Bicentennial; Bicentennial celebra-
> tions—United States—1976; United
> States—Bicentennial celebrations; United
> States—History—1775-1783, Revolution—
> Centennial celebrations, etc.
> *xx* **United States—Centennial celebrations, etc.**

American Revolution Bicentennial, 1776-1976—
> **Collectibles   973.3075**
> *xx* **Collectors and collecting**

American satire.   *See* **Satire, American**

American science.   *See* **Science—United States**

American sculptors.   *See* **Sculptors, American**

American sculpture.   *See* **Sculpture, American**

American songs.   *See* **Songs, American**

American-Spanish War, 1898.   *See* **United States—**
> **History—1898, War of 1898**

American speeches.   *See* **Speeches, addresses, etc.,**
> **American**

American technical assistance.   *See* **Technical assis-**
> **tance, American**

American teenagers.   *See* **Teenagers—United States**

American travelers.   *See* **Travelers, American**

American wit and humor   817; 817.008; 817.009
> Use for collections of several authors. May be
> used also for materials about American wit
> and humor.
> *xx* **American literature; Wit and humor**

American youth.   *See* **Youth—United States**

Americana   069; 745.1; 973
> *xx* **Antiques—United States; Collectors and col-
> lecting; United States—Civilization; United
> States—History; United States—Popular
> culture**

Americanisms   427
> Use for materials dealing with the usage of
> words and expressions peculiar to the
> United States.
> *x* English language—Americanisms
> *xx* **English language—Dialects**

Americanization   305.813; 306.0973
> *See also* **Naturalization; United States—Foreign
> population; United States—Immigration and
> emigration**

Americans (May subdiv. geog. except U.S.)
> **305.813; 920; 973**
> Use for materials on citizens of the United
> States.
> *xx* **Ethnology—United States; United States**

Americans—Greece   305.813

Amerindians.   *See* **Indians; Indians of Central
> America; Indians of Mexico; Indians of
> North America; Indians of South America;
> Indians of the West Indies**

Amish   289.7
> *xx* **Mennonites**

Ammunition   623.4
> *See also* **Gunpowder;** also types of ammunition,
> e.g. **Bombs;** etc.
> *xx* **Armaments; Explosives; Gunpowder; Projec-
> tiles**

Amnesty   364.6
> *See also* **Pardon**
> *xx* **Pardon**

Amniocentesis 618.3
>*xx* **Prenatal diagnosis**

Amphetamines 615
>*See also* names of amphetamines, e.g. **Methamphetamine;** etc.
>*x* Pep pills
>*xx* **Stimulants**

Amphibians 567; 597
>*See also* names of amphibians, e.g. **Frogs; Salamanders;** etc.
>*x* Batrachia
>*xx* **Vertebrates**

Amplifiers (Electronics) 621.3815
>*See also* special types of amplifiers, e.g. **Transistor amplifiers; Masers;** etc.
>*xx* **Electronics**

Amplifiers, Transistor. *See* **Transistor amplifiers**

Amusement parks 791.06
>*See also* names of specific parks, e.g. **Walt Disney World (Fla.);** etc.
>*x* Carnivals (Circus); Theme parks
>*xx* **Parks**

Amusements (May subdiv. geog.) **790**
>Use for general materials on various kinds of entertainment and pastimes. All types of amusements are not included in this List but are to be added as needed.
>*See also*

Amateur theater	**Magic**
Charades	**Mathematical recreations**
Church entertainments	**Motion pictures**
Circus	**Play**
Concerts	**Puzzles**
Creative activities	**Recreation**
Dancing	**Riddles**
Entertaining	**Scientific recreations**
Fortune telling	**Shadow pictures**
Games	**Sports**
Hobbies	**Theater**
Indoor games	**Toys**
Juggling	**Vaudeville**
Literary recreations	**Ventriloquism**

>*x* Entertainments; Pastimes
>*xx* **Entertaining; Games; Indoor games; Play; Recreation; Sports**

Anabolic steroids. *See* **Steroids**

Anaesthetics. *See* **Anesthetics**

Analysis (Chemistry). *See* **Chemistry, Analytic;** and names of substances with the subdivision *Analysis,* e.g. **Food—Analysis;** etc.

Analysis (Mathematics). *See* **Calculus; Mathematical analysis**

Analysis, Microscopic. *See* **Metallography; Microscope and microscopy**

Analysis of food. *See* **Food adulteration and inspection; Food—Analysis**

Analysis situs. *See* **Topology**

Analysis, Spectrum. *See* **Spectrum analysis**

Analytical chemistry. *See* **Chemistry, Analytic**

Analytical geometry. *See* **Geometry, Analytic**

Anarchism and anarchists 320.5; 335
>*See also* **Terrorism**
>*xx* **Freedom; Political crimes and offenses; Political science**

Anatomical gifts. *See* **Donation of organs, tissues, etc.**

Anatomy 574.4; 611

    See also **Anatomy, Comparative; Bones; Human anatomy; Musculoskeletal system; Nervous system; Physiology;** also subjects with the subdivision *Anatomy,* e.g. **Birds—Anatomy; Botany—Anatomy;** etc.

    x Morphology

    xx **Biology; Medicine; Physiology**

Anatomy, Artistic 704.9; 743

    See also **Figure drawing; Figure painting**

    x Artistic anatomy; Human anatomy in art; Human figure in art

    xx **Art; Drawing; Nude in art**

Anatomy, Comparative 574.4; 591.4

    See also **Man—Origin**

    x Comparative anatomy; Morphology

    xx **Anatomy; Evolution; Man—Origin; Zoology**

Anatomy, Dental. *See* **Teeth**

Anatomy, Human. *See* **Human anatomy**

Anatomy of plants. *See* **Botany—Anatomy**

Anatomy, Vegetable. *See* **Botany—Anatomy**

Ancestor worship 291.2; 291.3

    x Dead, Worship of the

    xx **Cults; Religion**

Ancestry. *See* **Genealogy; Heredity**

Ancient architecture. *See* **Architecture, Ancient**

Ancient art. *See* **Art, Ancient**

Ancient civilization. *See* **Civilization, Ancient**

Ancient geography. *See* **Geography, Ancient**

Ancient Greece—Description. *See* **Greece—Description—0-323**

Ancient history. *See* **History, Ancient**

Ancient philosophy. *See* **Philosophy, Ancient**

Androgyny 155.3; 305.3

    Use for materials on the integration of male and female characteristics, including biological traits, personality traits, behavior, roles, etc.

    See also **Sex differences (Psychology); Sex role**

    x Unisexuality

    xx **Sex (Biology); Sex differences (Psychology); Sex role; Sexual behavior**

Androids. *See* **Robots**

Anecdotes 808.88; 818.008, etc.

    See also **Wit and humor;** also subjects with the subdivision *Anecdotes,* e.g. **Music—Anecdotes;** etc.

    x Facetiae; Stories

    xx **Wit and humor**

Anesthetics 615

    See also **Cocaine**

    x Anaesthetics

    xx **Materia medica; Pain; Surgery**

Angels 235

    x Spirits

    xx **Heaven**

Angina pectoris. *See* **Heart—Diseases**

Anglican Church. *See* **Church of England**

Angling. *See* **Fishing**

Anglo-French intervention in Egypt, 1956. *See* **Sinai Campaign, 1956**

Anglo-Saxon language   429

   x English language—0-1100; English language—
Old English, ca.450-1100; Old English language

Anglo-Saxon literature   829

   x English literature—0-1100; English literature—Old English, ca. 450-1100; Old English literature

Anglo-Saxons   305.82; 941.01

   x Saxons

   xx **Great Britain—History—0-1066; Teutonic
peoples**

Animal abuse. *See* **Animal welfare**

Animal attacks   591.6

   x Attacks by animals

   xx **Dangerous animals**

Animal babies. *See* **Animals—Infancy**

Animal behavior. *See* **Animals—Behavior**

Animal camouflage. *See* **Camouflage (Biology)**

Animal communication   591.59

   x Animal language; Animal sounds; Animals—
Language; Animals—Sounds; Communication among animals

Animal courtship   591.56

   x Animals—Courtship; Courtship (Animal behavior); Courtship of animals; Mate selection in animals; Mating behavior

   xx **Animals—Behavior; Sexual behavior in animals**

Animal defenses   591.57

   See also **Camouflage (Biology)**

   x Defense mechanisms (Zoology); Self-defense
in animals; Self-protection in animals

   xx **Animals—Behavior**

Animal drawing. *See* **Animal painting and illustration**

Animal embryos, Frozen. *See* **Frozen embryos**

Animal experimentation   619

   See also **Animal welfare; Vivisection**

   x Experimentation on animals; Laboratory animal experimentation

   xx **Animal welfare; Research**

Animal exploitation. *See* **Animal welfare**

Animal-facilitated therapy. *See* **Pet therapy**

Animal food   641.3

   Use for materials on human food of animal origin. Materials on the food and food habits
of animals are entered under **Animals—
Food.**

   x Animals as food; Animals, Edible

   xx **Food**

Animal homes. *See* **Animals—Habitations**

Animal husbandry. *See* **Livestock**

Animal industry. *See* **Domestic animals; Livestock**

Animal instinct. *See* **Instinct**

Animal intelligence   591.51

   See also **Animals—Behavior; Instinct; Learning,
Psychology of; Psychology, Comparative;**
also names of animals with the subdivision
Psychology, e.g. **Dogs—Psychology;** etc.

   x Animal psychology; Intelligence of animals

   xx **Animals—Behavior; Instinct; Psychology,
Comparative**

Animal kingdom. *See* **Zoology**

Animal language. *See* **Animal communication**
Animal liberation movement. *See* **Animal rights movements**
Animal light. *See* **Bioluminescence**
Animal locomotion   591.1
> *x* Animals—Movements; Locomotion; Movements of animals
Animal lore. *See* **Animals—Folklore; Animals in literature; Mythical animals; Natural history**
Animal magnetism. *See* **Hypnotism**
Animal migration. *See* **Animals—Migration**
Animal oils. *See* **Oils and fats**
Animal painting and illustration   704.9; 743; 758
> Use for materials on the art and methods of painting and drawing animals. Materials about representations of animals in works of art (painting, sculpture, etc.), or reproductions of them, are entered under **Animals in art.** Materials consisting of photographs or illustrations of animals are entered under **Animals—Pictorial works.**
> *See also* **Animals in art; Animals—Pictorial works; Photography of animals**
> *x* Animal drawing
> *xx* **Animals in art; Animals—Pictorial works; Painting; Photography of animals**
Animal parasites. *See* **Parasites**
Animal photography. *See* **Photography of animals**
Animal physiology. *See* **Zoology**
Animal pictures. *See* **Animals—Pictorial works**
Animal pounds. *See* **Animal shelters**
Animal products. *See* names of special products, e.g. **Hides and skins; Ivory; Wool;** etc.
Animal psychology. *See* **Animal intelligence; Psychology, Comparative**
Animal rights   179
> Use for materials on the inherent rights of animals. For materials on the protection and treatment of animals, use **Animal welfare.**
> *See also* **Animal rights movements; Animal welfare**
> *x* Animals' rights; Rights of animals
> *xx* **Animal rights movements; Animal welfare**
Animal rights movements   179
> Use for materials on any of the politically diverse movements engaged in animal rights or animal welfare support activities.
> *See also* **Animal rights; Animal welfare**
> *x* Animal liberation movement; Animal welfare movement; Antivivisection movement
> *xx* **Animal rights; Animal welfare**
Animal shelters   179; 636.08
> *x* Animal pounds; Shelters, Animal
> *xx* **Animal welfare**
Animal signs. *See* **Animal tracks**
Animal sounds. *See* **Animal communication**
Animal stories. *See* **Animals—Fiction**
Animal tracks   591
> *x* Animal signs; Tracks of animals
> *xx* **Tracking and trailing**
Animal training. *See* **Animals—Training**
Animal welfare   179
> Use for materials on the protection and treat-

Animal welfare—*Continued*
>ment of animals. Materials on the inherent
>rights of animals are entered under **Animal
>rights.**
>
>*See also* **Animal experimentation; Animal rights;
>Animal rights movements; Animal shelters**
>
>*x* Abuse of animals; Animal abuse; Animal ex-
>ploitation; Animals, Cruelty to; Animals—
>Mistreatment; Animals—Protection; Ani-
>mals—Treatment; Cruelty to animals; Hu-
>mane treatment of animals; Laboratory
>animal welfare; Prevention of cruelty to an-
>imals; Protection of animals
>
>*xx* **Animal experimentation; Animal rights; Ani-
>mal rights movements**

Animal welfare movement. *See* **Animal rights
movements**

Animals (May subdiv. geog.)   **591**
>Use for descriptive and nonsystematic or non-
>technical material.
>
>Subdivisions used under this heading may be
>used under names of orders and classes of
>the animal kingdom and under names of in-
>dividual animals.
>
>*See also*

Alpine animals	**Pets**
Dangerous animals	**Poisonous animals**
Desert animals	**Prehistoric animals**
Domestic animals	**Rare animals**
Forest animals	**Stream animals**
Freshwater animals	**Swamp animals**
Furbearing animals	**Wildlife**
Game and game birds	**Working animals**
Jungle animals	**Zoology**
Marine animals	**Zoos**
Natural history	

>also names of orders and classes of the animal
>kingdom, e.g. **Vertebrates; Mammals; Pri-
>mates;** etc.; and names of individual ani-
>mals, e.g. **Monkeys;** etc.
>
>*x* Beasts; Fauna; Wild animals
>
>*xx* **Zoology**

Animals and the handicapped   636.088
>*See also* **Guide dogs; Hearing ear dogs; Pet ther-
>apy**
>
>*x* Handi-animals; Handicapped and animals;
>Pets and the handicapped; Service dogs
>
>*xx* **Animals—Training**

Animals, Aquatic. *See* **Freshwater animals; Marine
animals**

Animals as food. *See* **Animal food**

Animals—Behavior   591.51
>*See also* **Animal courtship; Animal defenses; Ani-
>mal intelligence; Animals—Food; Instinct;
>Nature study; Tracking and trailing;** also
>types of specific behavior, e.g. **Animals—
>Hibernation; Animals—Migration; Sexual
>behavior in animals;** etc.; and names of ani-
>mals with the subdivision *Behavior,* e.g.
>**Primates—Behavior; Monkeys—Behavior;**
>etc.
>
>*x* Animal behavior; Animals—Habits and be-
>havior; Behavior; Habits of animals
>
>*xx* **Animal intelligence; Nature study**

Animals—Camouflage. *See* **Camouflage (Biology)**

Animals—Color 591.19; 591.57

 xx **Color**

Animals—Courtship. *See* **Animal courtship**

Animals, Cruelty to. *See* **Animal welfare**

Animals—Diseases 591.2; 636.089

 See also names of animals with the subdivision
  Diseases, e.g. **Cattle—Diseases;** etc.

 x Diseases of animals; Domestic animals—
  Diseases

 xx **Diseases; Veterinary medicine**

Animals, Domestic. *See* **Domestic animals**

Animals, Edible. *See* **Animal food**

Animals, Extinct. *See* **Extinct animals**

Animals—Fiction Fic

 See note under **Animals in literature.**

 See also **Animals in literature;** also names of animals with the subdivision *Fiction,* e.g.
  Dogs—Fiction; etc.

 x Animal stories; Animals—Stories

 xx **Animals in literature; Fables; Fiction**

Animals, Fictitious. *See* **Mythical animals**

Animals—Filmography 016.591

Animals—Folklore 398.24

 See also **Dragons; Monsters; Mythical animals**

 x Animal lore

 xx **Folklore; Mythical animals**

Animals—Food 591.53

 Use for materials on the food and food habits of
  animals. Materials on human food of animal origin are entered under **Animal food.**

 See also **Carnivores; Food chains (Ecology);** also
  names of animals with the subdivision
  Food, e.g. **Fishes—Food;** etc.

 x Feeding behavior in animals

 xx **Animals—Behavior; Food**

Animals, Fossil. *See* **Fossils**

Animals, Freshwater. *See* **Freshwater animals**

Animals—Geographical distribution. *See* **Biogeography**

Animals—Habitations 591.52

 x Animal homes; Habitations of animals;
  Houses of animals

Animals—Habits and behavior. *See* **Animals—
  Behavior**

Animals—Hibernation 591.54

 x Hibernation of animals

 xx **Animals—Behavior**

Animals, Imaginary. *See* **Mythical animals**

Animals in art 704.9

 Use for materials about representations of animals in works of art (painting, sculpture,
  etc.) or reproductions of them. Materials on
  the art and methods of painting and drawing animals are entered under **Animal
  painting and illustration.** Materials consisting of photographs or illustrations of animals are entered under **Animals—Pictorial
  works.**

 See also **Animal painting and illustration; Animals—Pictorial works**

 xx **Animal painting and illustration; Animals—
  Pictorial works; Art**

Animals in literature 809

Use for materials on the theme of animals in literature. Poems or stories about animals are entered under **Animals—Poetry; Animals—Fiction.**

See also **Animals—Fiction; Animals—Poetry; Bible—Natural history;** also phrase headings of specific animals in literature, e.g. **Dogs in literature;** etc.

x Animal lore

xx **Animals—Fiction; Animals—Poetry; Nature in literature**

Animals in motion pictures 791.43

xx **Motion pictures**

Animals in police work 363.2; 636.088

xx **Police; Working animals**

Animals—Infancy 591.3

x Animal babies; Baby animals

Animals—Language. *See* **Animal communication**

Animals, Marine. *See* **Marine animals**

Animals—Migration 591.52

See also names of animals with the subdivision *Migration,* e.g. **Birds—Migration;** etc.

x Animal migration; Migration of animals

xx **Animals—Behavior**

Animals—Mistreatment. *See* **Animal welfare**

Animals—Movements. *See* **Animal locomotion**

Animals, Mythical. *See* **Mythical animals**

Animals—Petting zoos. *See* **Petting zoos**

Animals—Photography. *See* **Photography of animals**

Animals—Pictorial works 591.022; 743; 778.9

Use for popular materials containing chiefly pictures and photographs of animals.

See note under **Animal painting and illustration.**

See also **Animal painting and illustration; Animals in art; Photography of animals**

x Animal pictures

xx **Animal painting and illustration; Animals in art; Photography of animals**

Animals—Poetry 808.81; 811, etc.; 811.008, etc.

See note under **Animals in literature.**

See also **Animals in literature**

xx **Animals in literature; Poetry**

Animals, Prehistoric. *See* **Prehistoric animals**

Animals—Protection. *See* **Animal welfare**

Animals, Rare. *See* **Rare animals**

Animals' rights. *See* **Animal rights**

Animals, Sea. *See* **Marine animals**

Animals—Sexual behavior. *See* **Sexual behavior in animals**

Animals—Sounds. *See* **Animal communication**

Animals—Stories. *See* **Animals—Fiction**

Animals—Temperature. *See* **Body temperature**

Animals—Training 636.088

See also **Animals and the handicapped;** also names of animals with the subdivision *Training,* e.g. **Dogs—Training; Horses—Training;** etc.

x Animal training; Training of animals

xx **Circus**

Animals—Treatment. *See* **Animal welfare**

Animals—United States 591.973

    x United States—Animals; Zoology—United States

Animals, Useful and harmful. *See* **Zoology, Economic**

Animals, Visiting. *See* **Pet therapy**

Animals—War use 355.4

    See also **Dogs—War use**

    x War use of animals

    xx **Working animals**

Animals, Working. *See* **Working animals**

Animated cartoons. *See* **Animated films**

Animated films 741.5; 791.43

    See also **Animation (Cinematography)**

    x Animated cartoons; Motion picture cartoons

    xx **Animation (Cinematography); Cartoons and caricatures**

Animation (Cinematography) 741.5; 778.5

    See also **Animated films**

    xx **Animated films**

Anniversaries. *See* **Holidays;** and names of special days, e.g. **Fourth of July;** etc.

Annual income. *See* **Wages—Annual wage**

Annual wage plans. *See* **Wages—Annual wage**

Annuals. *See* **Almanacs; Calendars;** and subjects with the subdivision *Periodicals,* e.g. **Engineering—Periodicals;** etc.

Annuals (Plants) 582; 635.9

    xx **Flower gardening; Flowers; Plants, Cultivated**

Annuities 368.3

    See also **Life insurance; Pensions**

    xx **Investments; Life insurance; Retirement income**

Annulment of marriage. *See* **Marriage—Annulment**

Anonyms. *See* **Pseudonyms**

Anorexia nervosa 616.85

    x Self-starvation; Starvation, Self-imposed

    xx **Eating disorders**

Answers to questions. *See* **Questions and answers**

Ant. *See* **Ants**

Antarctic expeditions. *See* names of expeditions, e.g. **Byrd Antarctic Expedition;** etc.

Antarctic regions 998

    See also **South Pole**

    x Antarctica

    xx **Earth; Polar regions; South Pole**

Antarctica. *See* **Antarctic regions**

Antenuptial contracts. *See* **Marriage contracts**

Anthems, National. *See* **National songs**

Anthracite coal. *See* **Coal**

Anthropogeography 304.2; 572.9

    See also **Geopolitics; Man—Influence of environment**

    x Geographical distribution of people; Geography, Social

    xx **Anthropology; Ethnology; Geography; Geopolitics; History; Human ecology; Immigration and emigration**

Anthropology 301; 573

    See also

Acculturation	**Anthropometry**
Anthropogeography	**Archeology**

Anthropology—*Continued*

    Civilization   **Man**
    Ethnology   **National characteristics**
    Ethnopsychology   **Physical anthropology**
    Eugenics   **Social change**
    Language and languages

         also names of races and peoples, e.g. **Semitic
            peoples; Navajo Indians;** etc.; and names of
            countries, cities, etc., with the subdivision
            Race relations, e.g. **United States—Race
            relations;** etc.

    x Human race
    xx **Civilization; Ethnology; Man**

Anthropology, Physical. *See* **Physical anthropology**

Anthropometry 573

    See also **Fingerprints**
    x Skeletal remains
    xx **Anthropology; Ethnology; Man**

Anti-abortion movement. *See* **Pro-life movement**

Anti-Americanism. *See* **United States—Foreign
    opinion**

Anti-apartheid movement (May subdiv. geog.) **172;
    320.5; 323.1**

    See also **Apartheid**
    xx **Apartheid; Civil rights; Social movements;
         South Africa—Race relations**

Anti-poverty programs. *See* **Economic assistance,
    Domestic**

Anti-Reformation. *See* **Reformation**

Antiabortion movement. *See* **Pro-life movement**

Antiamericanism. *See* **United States—Foreign
    opinion**

Antiballistic missiles. *See* **Antimissile missiles**

Antibiotics 615

    See also names of specific antibiotics, e.g. **Peni-
         cillin;** etc.
    xx **Chemotherapy**

Antibusing. *See* **Busing (School integration)**

Anticommunist movements 322.4

    x Underground, Anticommunist
    xx **Communism**

Anticorrosive paint. *See* **Corrosion and anticorro-
    sives**

Antimissile missiles 623.4

    x A.B.M.'s; ABMs; Antiballistic missiles
    xx **Guided missiles**

Antinuclear movement (May subdiv. geog.) **172;
    333.791; 355**

    See also **Nuclear power plants**
    x Nuclear freeze movement
    xx **Arms control; Nuclear power plants; Nuclear
         weapons; Social movements**

Antipathies. *See* **Prejudices**

Antipoverty programs. *See* **Economic assistance,
    Domestic**

Antiques (May subdiv. geog.) **745.1**

    See also **Art objects; Collectors and collecting**
    xx **Antiquities; Decoration and ornament; Decora-
         tive arts**

Antiques—United States 745.10973

    See also **Americana**
    x United States—Antiques

Antiquities   930.1

Use for materials about the relics or monuments of ancient times. Assign the heading for the name of an ancient city or town for materials about the relics or monuments of that place.

See also **Antiques; Archeology; Bible— Antiquities; Christian antiquities; Classical antiquities; Prehistoric man;** also names of ancient cities, e.g. **Delphi (Ancient city);** also names of groups of people extant in modern times and names of cities (except ancient cities), countries, regions, etc., with the subdivision *Antiquities,* e.g. **Indians of North America—Antiquities; United States—Antiquities;** etc.

x Archeological specimens

xx **Archeology**

Antiquities, Biblical.   *See* **Bible—Antiquities**

Antiquities, Christian.   *See* **Christian antiquities**

Antiquities, Classical.   *See* **Classical antiquities**

Antiquities—Collection and preservation   069

x Preservation of antiquities

xx **Collectors and collecting**

Antiquities, Ecclesiastical.   *See* **Christian antiquities**

Antiquity of man.   *See* **Man—Origin**

Antireformation.   *See* **Reformation**

Antisemitism   305.892

See also **Holocaust, Jewish (1933-1945); Jews— Persecutions**

xx **Jews and Gentiles; Prejudices**

Antiseptics   615

See also **Disinfection and disinfectants**

xx **Disinfection and disinfectants; Surgery; Therapeutics**

Antislavery.   *See* **Slavery**

Antitrust law   343

x Trusts, Industrial—Law and legislation

xx **Commercial law; Trusts, Industrial**

Antivivisection movement.   *See* **Animal rights movements**

Antiwar movements.   *See* names of wars with the subdivision *Protests, demonstrations, etc.,* e.g. **World War, 1939-1945—Protests, demonstrations, etc.;** etc.

Antonyms.   *See* names of languages with the subdivision *Synonyms and antonyms,* e.g. **English language—Synonyms and antonyms;** etc.

Ants   595.7

x Ant; Hymenoptera

xx **Insects**

Anxiety.   *See* **Fear; Stress (Psychology); Worry**

Apartheid   320.5

Use for materials on the economic, political, and social policies of the government of South Africa designed to segregate racial groups in South Africa and Namibia.

See also **Anti-apartheid movement**

x Separate development (Race relations)

xx **Anti-apartheid movement; Segregation; South Africa—Race relations**

Apartment houses   647; 728
>   *See also* **Condominiums**
>   *x* Flats
>   *xx* **Architecture, Domestic; Houses; Housing;
>   Landlord and tenant**

Apiculture.   *See* **Bees**

Apollo project   629.45
>   *See also* headings beginning with **Lunar** and
>   **Moon**
>   *x* Project Apollo
>   *xx* **Life support systems (Space environment); Or-
>   bital rendezvous (Space flight); Space flight
>   to the moon**

Apologetics   239
>   *See also* **Natural theology; Religion and science**
>   *x* Christianity—Apologetic works; Christiani-
>   ty—Evidences; Evidences of Christianity;
>   Fundamental theology

Apostles   225; 920
>   *x* Disciples, Twelve
>   *xx* **Christian saints; Church history—30(ca.)-600,
>   Early church**

Apostles' Creed   238
>   *xx* **Creeds**

Apostolic Church.   *See* **Church history—30(ca.)-
>   600, Early church**

Apparatus, Chemical.   *See* **Chemical apparatus**

Apparatus, Electric.   *See* **Electric apparatus and ap-
>   pliances**

Apparatus, Electronic.   *See* **Electronic apparatus
>   and appliances**

Apparatus, Scientific.   *See* **Scientific apparatus and
>   instruments**

Apparitions   133.1
>   *See also* **Demonology; Ghosts; Hallucinations
>   and illusions; Miracles; Spiritualism; Vi-
>   sions**
>   *x* Phantoms; Specters; Spirits
>   *xx* **Demonology; Ghosts; Hallucinations and illu-
>   sions; Parapsychology; Spiritualism; Super-
>   stition; Visions**

Apperception   153.7
>   *See also* **Attention; Consciousness; Knowledge,
>   Theory of; Number concept; Perception**
>   *xx* **Educational psychology; Knowledge, Theory
>   of; Perception; Psychology**

Appetite disorders.   *See* **Eating disorders**

Apple   583; 634; 641.3
>   *xx* **Fruit; Trees**

Appliances, Electric.   *See* **Electric apparatus and ap-
>   pliances; Household appliances, Electric**

Appliances, Electronic.   *See* **Electronic apparatus
>   and appliances**

Applications for college.   *See* **College applications**

Applications for positions   331.12
>   *See also* **Interviewing; Résumés (Employment)**
>   *x* Employment applications; Employment refer-
>   ences; Job applications; Letters of recom-
>   mendation; Recommendations for positions
>   *xx* **Job hunting; Personnel management**

Applied arts.   *See* **Decorative arts**

Applied mechanics   621
>   Use for materials on the application of the prin-

69

Applied mechanics—*Continued*
ciples of mechanics to engineering structure
other than machinery. Materials on the application of the principles of mechanics to
the design, construction and operation of
machinery are entered under **Mechanical
engineering.**
x Mechanics, Applied
Applied psychology. *See* **Psychology, Applied**
Applied science. *See* **Technology**
Apportionment (Election law) 324; 328.3; 342
x Legislative reapportionment; Reapportionment (Election law)
xx **Representative government and representation**
Appraisal. *See* **Assessment; Valuation**
Appraisal of books. *See* **Books and reading; Books
and reading—Best books; Books—Reviews;
Criticism; Literature—History and criticism**
Appreciation of art. *See* **Art appreciation**
Appreciation of music. *See* **Music—Analysis, ap-
preciation**
Apprentices 331.5
See also **Employees—Training**
xx **Children—Employment; Employees—
Training; Labor; Technical education**
Approximate computation 372.7; 513.2
x Arithmetic—Estimation; Computation, Ap-
proximate; Estimation (Mathematics)
xx **Numerical analysis**
April Fools' Day 394.2
x All Fools' Day
xx **Manners and customs**
Aptitude testing. *See* **Ability—Testing**
Aquaculture 639
See also **Fish culture**
x Aquiculture; Freshwater aquaculture; Mariculture; Marine aquaculture; Ocean farming;
Sea farming
xx **Agriculture; Food supply; Marine resources**
Aquanauts 627.092; 920
x Oceanauts
xx **Undersea research stations; Underwater exploration**
Aquarian Age movement. *See* **New Age movement**
Aquariums 597.0074; 639.3
See also **Fish culture; Goldfish; Marine aquari-
ums; also names of specific aquariums**
xx **Fish culture; Fishes; Freshwater animals;
Freshwater biology; Freshwater plants; In-
door gardening; Natural history**
Aquariums, Saltwater. *See* **Marine aquariums**
Aquatic animals. *See* **Freshwater animals; Marine
animals**
Aquatic birds. *See* **Water birds**
Aquatic plants. *See* **Freshwater plants; Marine
plants**
Aquatic sports. *See* **Water sports**
Aqueducts 628.1
x Conduits; Water conduits
xx **Civil engineering; Hydraulic structures; Water
supply**
Aquiculture. *See* **Aquaculture**
Arab civilization. *See* **Civilization, Arab**

Arab countries 956
> Use for materials dealing collectively with the Arabic-speaking countries of Asia and Africa, or of Asia only. For materials on the region consisting of Asia west of Pakistan, northeastern Africa, and occasionally Greece and Pakistan, use **Middle East.**

  xx **Islamic countries; Middle East**
Arab countries—Politics and government 956
> *See also* **Pan-Arabism**

Arab-Israel War, 1948-1949. *See* **Israel-Arab War, 1948-1949**
Arab-Israel War, 1956. *See* **Sinai Campaign, 1956**
Arab-Israel War, 1967. *See* **Israel-Arab War, 1967**
Arab-Israel War, 1973. *See* **Israel-Arab War, 1973**
Arab-Jewish relations. *See* **Jewish-Arab relations**
Arab refugees. *See* **Refugees, Arab**
Arabia. *See* **Arabian Peninsula**
Arabian Peninsula 953
> *x* Arabia
> *xx* **Peninsulas**

Arabs 305.892; 909
> *See also* names of specific Arab peoples, e.g. **Bedouins; Moors;** etc.

Arabs—Palestine. *See* **Palestinian Arabs**
Arachnida. *See* **Spiders; Ticks**
Arbitration and award 347
> Use for materials on the settlement of civil disputes by arbitration instead of a court trial.
> *See also* **Litigation**
> *x* Awards (Law); Mediation
> *xx* **Commercial law; Courts; Litigation**

Arbitration, Industrial 331.89
> *See also* **Collective bargaining; Strikes and lockouts**
> *x* Conciliation, Industrial; Industrial arbitration; Industrial conciliation; Labor arbitration; Labor negotiations; Mediation, Industrial; Trade agreements (Labor)
> *xx* **Collective bargaining; Industrial relations; Labor; Labor disputes; Labor unions; Negotiation; Strikes and lockouts**

Arbitration, International 341.5
> *See also* **Arms control; League of Nations; Peace; United Nations**
> *x* International arbitration; International mediation; Mediation, International
> *xx* **Arms control; International cooperation; International law; International relations; Peace; Security, International; Treaties**

Arboriculture. *See* **Forests and forestry; Fruit culture; Trees**
Arc light. *See* **Electric lighting**
Arc welding. *See* **Electric welding**
Archaeology. *See* **Archeology**
Archeological specimens. *See* **Antiquities**
Archeologists 920; 930.1092
> *xx* **Historians**

Archeology (May subdiv. geog.) **930.1**
> Use for materials on the discipline of archeology. For materials about the relics or monuments of ancient times, use **Antiquities.**

Archeology—*Continued*
> *See also*

Antiquities
Architecture, Ancient
Arms and armor
Bible—Antiquities
Brasses
Bronze Age
Bronzes
Christian antiquities
Christian art and symbolism
Cities and towns, Ruined, extinct, etc.
Classical antiquities
Cliff dwellers and cliff dwellings
Ethnology
Excavations (Archeology)
Funeral rites and ceremonies
Gems
Heraldry
Historic sites
Inscriptions
Iron Age
Mounds and mound builders
Mummies
Numismatics
Obelisks
Pottery
Prehistoric man
Pyramids
Radiocarbon dating
Religious art and symbolism
Rock drawings, paintings, and engravings
Stone Age
Stone implements
Temples
Tombs

> also names of ancient cities, e.g. **Delphi (Ancient city)**; also names of groups of people and names of cities (except ancient cities), countries, regions, etc. with the subdivision *Antiquities,* e.g. **Indians of North America—Antiquities; United States—Antiquities;** etc.

> *x* Archaeology; Prehistory; Ruins
> *xx* **Anthropology; Antiquities; Art; Bronze Age; Civilization; Classical antiquities; Ethnology; History; History, Ancient; Iron Age; Stone Age**

Archeology, Biblical. *See* **Bible—Antiquities**
Archeology, Christian. *See* **Christian antiquities**
Archeology, Classical. *See* **Classical antiquities**
Archery 799.3
> *See also* **Bow and arrow**
> *xx* **Bow and arrow; Martial arts; Shooting**
Architects 720.92; 920
> *xx* **Artists**
Architectural acoustics 690; 729
> *See also* **Soundproofing**
> *x* Acoustics
> *xx* **Sound**
Architectural decoration and ornament. *See* **Decoration and ornament, Architectural**
Architectural design. *See* **Architecture—Details**
Architectural designs. *See* **Architecture—Designs and plans**
Architectural details. *See* **Architecture—Details**
Architectural drawing 720.28
> *See also* **Architecture—Designs and plans; Architecture—Details**
> *x* Drawing, Architectural; Plans
> *xx* **Drawing; Mechanical drawing**
Architectural engineering. *See* **Building; Building, Iron and steel; Strains and stresses; Strength of materials; Structures, Theory of**
Architectural metalwork 721
> *x* Metalwork, Architectural
> *xx* **Metalwork**

Architectural perspective. *See* **Perspective**

Architecture (May subdiv. geog. adjective form, e.g. **Architecture, Greek;** etc.) **720**

All types of architecture and buildings are not included in this List but are to be added as needed.

See also

Building	**Naval architecture**
Building materials	**Obelisks**
Castles	**Palaces**
Cathedrals	**Public buildings**
Church architecture	**School buildings**
Concrete construction	**Skyscrapers**
Decoration and ornament, Architectural	**Spires**
Farm buildings	**Strains and stresses**
Historic buildings	**Strength of materials**
Indians of North America—Architecture	**Structural engineering**
Industrial buildings	**Synagogues**
Library architecture	**Temples**
Monuments	**Theaters**
Mosques	**Tombs**
	Underground architecture

also styles of architecture, e.g. **Architecture, Byzantine;** etc.; and types of buildings; and headings beginning with the word **Architectural**

x Construction

xx **Art; Building**

Architecture, American   720.973

x American architecture; United States—Architecture

Architecture, Ancient   722

See also **Architecture, Greek; Architecture, Roman; Pyramids; Temples**

x Ancient architecture

xx **Archeology**

Architecture and the handicapped   720

x Barrier free design; Handicapped and architecture

Architecture, Asian   720.95

See also **Mosques; Temples**

x Asian architecture; Oriental architecture

Architecture, Baroque   724

x Baroque architecture

Architecture, Byzantine   723

x Byzantine architecture

xx **Architecture**

Architecture, Church. *See* **Church architecture**

Architecture, Colonial   724

See also **Historic buildings—United States**

x Colonial architecture

Architecture—Composition, proportion, etc.   720; 729

x Architecture—Proportion; Proportion (Architecture)

xx **Composition (Art)**

Architecture—Conservation and restoration   690; 720.28

See also **Buildings—Maintenance and repair**

x Architecture—Restoration; Buildings, Restoration of; Conservation of buildings; Preservation of buildings; Restoration of buildings

Architecture—Conservation and
    restoration—*Continued*
    xx **Buildings—Maintenance and repair**
Architecture—Decoration and ornament. *See* **Dec-**
    oration and ornament, Architectural
Architecture—Designs and plans 720.28; 729
    See also **Architecture, Domestic—Designs and**
        plans
    x Architectural designs; Architecture—Plans;
        Designs, Architectural
    xx **Architectural drawing**
Architecture—Details 721; 729
    See also

Chimneys	**Foundations**
Doors	**Roofs**
Fireplaces	**Windows**
Floors	**Woodwork**

    x Architectural design; Architectural details; De-
        sign, Architectural; Details, Architectural
    xx **Architectural drawing**
Architecture, Domestic 728
    See also **Apartment houses; Farm buildings;**
        House construction; Houses; Prefabricated
        houses; Solar homes
    x Architecture, Rural; Country houses; Domes-
        tic architecture; Dwellings; Habitations,
        Human; Residences; Rural architecture;
        Suburban homes; Summer homes; Villas
Architecture, Domestic—Designs and plans 728
    x Home designs; House plans
    xx **Architecture—Designs and plans**
Architecture, Ecclesiastical. *See* **Church architec-**
    ture
Architecture, Gothic 723
    See also **Cathedrals; Church architecture**
    x Gothic architecture
    xx **Cathedrals; Christian antiquities; Church ar-**
        chitecture
Architecture, Greek 722
    x Greek architecture
    xx **Architecture, Ancient**
Architecture, Medieval 723
    See also **Architecture, Romanesque; Castles; Ca-**
        thedrals
    x Medieval architecture
    xx **Middle Ages**
Architecture, Modern 724
    x Modern architecture
Architecture, Modern—1600-1799 (17th and 18th
    centuries) 724
Architecture, Modern—1800-1899 (19th century)
    724
Architecture, Modern—1900-1999 (20th century)
    724
Architecture, Naval. *See* **Naval architecture; Ship-**
    building
Architecture—Plans. *See* **Architecture—Designs**
    and plans
Architecture—Proportion. *See* **Architecture—**
    Composition, proportion, etc.
Architecture, Renaissance 724
    xx **Renaissance**

Architecture—Restoration. *See* **Architecture—Conservation and restoration**

Architecture, Roman   722
   x Roman architecture
   xx **Architecture, Ancient**

Architecture, Romanesque   723
   x Romanesque architecture
   xx **Architecture, Medieval**

Architecture, Rural. *See* **Architecture, Domestic; Farm buildings**

Archives (May subdiv. geog.)   **026; 027**
   See also **Charters; Libraries; Manuscripts**
   x Documents; Government records—Preservation; Historical records—Preservation; Preservation of historical records; Public records—Preservation; Records—Preservation
   xx **Bibliography; Charters; Documentation; History—Sources; Information services; Libraries**

Archives—United States   026; 027; 353.0071
   x United States—Archives

Arctic expeditions. *See* names of expeditions.

Arctic regions   919.8; 998
   See also **North Pole; Northeast Passage; Northwest Passage**
   x Far north
   xx **Earth; North Pole; Polar regions**

Ardennes, Battle of the, 1944-1945   940.54
   x Bastogne, Battle of; Battle of the Bulge; Bulge, Battle of the
   xx **World War, 1939-1945—Campaigns**

Area studies   940-990
   Use for general materials on area studies.
   See also areas, countries with the subdivision *Study and teaching,* e.g. **Africa—Study and teaching;** etc.
   x Foreign area studies
   xx **Education**

Arena theater   725; 792
   x Round stage; Theater-in-the-round
   xx **Theater**

Argentine rummy. *See* **Canasta (Game)**

Argumentation. *See* **Debates and debating; Logic**

Aristocracy   305.5
   See also **Democracy; Nobility; Upper classes**
   xx **Democracy; Equality; Nobility; Political science; Social classes; Sociology**

Arithmetic   513
   See also

Average	**Numeration**
Business arithmetic	**Percentage**
Calculators	**Ratio and proportion**
Cube root	**Square root**
Fractions	

   also names of specific arithmetic operations, e.g. **Multiplication; Subtraction;** etc.
   x Computation (Mathematics)
   xx **Mathematics; Set theory**

Arithmetic, Commercial. *See* **Business arithmetic**

Arithmetic—Estimation. *See* **Approximate computation**

Arithmetic, Mental   513
   x Mental arithmetic; Oral arithmetic

Arithmetic—Study and teaching 372.7; 513.07
> *See also* **Counting; Mathematical readiness; Number games**

Arithmetical readiness. *See* **Mathematical readiness**

Armada, 1588. *See* **Spanish Armada, 1588**

Armaments 355.8
> Use for materials on military strength, including military personnel, munitions, natural resources and industrial war potential. Materials on the implements of war and the industries producing them are entered under the heading **Munitions.** Materials on the armament of a particular country are entered under the name of the country with the subdivision *Defenses,* e.g. **United States—Defenses;** etc.

> *See also*

Aeronautics, Military	**Arms race**
Ammunition	**Industrial mobilization**
Armed forces	**Munitions**
Armies	**Navies**
Arms control	**Ordnance**

> *xx* **Military art and science**

Armaments race. *See* **Arms race**

Armed forces 343; 355
> *See also* **Armies; Military personnel; Military service, Voluntary; Navies;** also specific branches of the armed forces under names of countries, e.g. **United States. Army;** etc.; and names of countries, regions, and international organizations with the subdivision *Armed forces,* e.g. **United States—Armed forces; United Nations—Armed forces;** etc.
> *x* Armed services
> *xx* **Armaments; Military art and science**

Armed services. *See* **Armed forces**

Armies 355.3
> *See also* **Arms control; Draft; Military art and science; Navies; Soldiers; War; World War, 1939-1945—Human resources;** also names of countries with the subhead *Army,* e.g. **United States. Army;** etc.; and headings beginning with the word **Military**
> *x* Army; Military forces; Military power
> *xx* **Armaments; Armed forces; Military art and science; Military personnel; Navies; Strategy; War**

Armies—Medical care 355.3
> *See also* **Medicine, Military; Military health;** also names of wars with the subdivision *Health aspects* or *Medical care,* e.g. **World War, 1939-1945—Health aspects; World War, 1939-1945—Medical care;** etc.
> *xx* **Medicine, Military; Military health**

Armistice Day. *See* **Veterans Day**

Armistices. *See* names of wars with the subdivision *Armistices,* e.g. **World War, 1939-1945—Armistices;** etc.

Armor. *See* **Arms and armor**

Armored cars (Tanks). *See* **Tanks (Military science)**

Arms aid. *See* **Military assistance**

Arms and armor   355.8; 623.4; 739.7
>   *See also* **Firearms; Ordnance; Rifles**
>   *x* Armor; Weapons and weaponry
>   *xx* **Archeology; Costume; Military art and science**

Arms, Coats of.   *See* **Heraldry**

Arms control   327.1; 341.7
>   *See also* **Antinuclear movement; Arbitration, International; Arms race; Peace; Sea power; Security, International**
>   *x* Disarmament; Limitation of armament; Military power; Non-proliferation of nuclear weapons; Nuclear test ban; Nuclear weapons and disarmament
>   *xx* **Arbitration, International; Armaments; Armies; International relations; Military art and science; Navies; Peace; Sea power; Security, International; War**

Arms proliferation.   *See* **Arms race**

Arms race   355
>   Use for materials on the competitive buildup and improvement of the military power of two or more nations or blocs.
>   *x* Armaments race; Arms proliferation; Proliferation of arms
>   *xx* **Armaments; Arms control; Munitions**

Arms sales.   *See* **Military assistance; Munitions**

Army.   *See* **Armies; Military art and science;** and names of countries with the subhead *Army,* e.g. **United States. Army;** etc.

Army desertion.   *See* **Military desertion**

Army life.   *See* **Soldiers;** and names of armies with the subdivision *Military life,* e.g. **United States. Army—Military life;** etc.

Army posts.   *See* **Military posts**

Army schools.   *See* **Military education**

Army tests.   *See* **United States. Army—Examinations**

Army vehicles.   *See* **Vehicles, Military**

Aromatic plant products.   *See* **Essences and essential oils**

Arrow.   *See* **Bow and arrow**

Art (May subdiv. geog. adjective form, e.g. **Art, Greek;** etc.)   700
>   Subdivisions listed under this heading may be used under other art media where applicable.
>   Names of all types of art are not included in this List but are to be added as needed.
>   Materials on special themes in art are entered under phrase headings of the type [subject] in art, e.g. **Animals in art.**

>   • *See also*

Aesthetics	**Collectors and collecting**
Anatomy, Artistic	**Commercial art**
Archeology	**Composition (Art)**
Architecture	**Decoration and ornament**
Art objects	**Decorative arts**
Arts and crafts movement	**Drawing**
Brasses	**Engraving**
Bronzes	**Etching**
Christian art and symbolism	**Folk art**
Collage	**Forgery of works of art**
	Futurism (Art)

Art—*Continued*
- Gems
- Graphic arts
- Illumination of books and manuscripts
- Illustration of books
- Indians of North America—Art
- Interior design
- Nude in art
- Painting
- Photography, Artistic
- Pictures
- Portraits
- Religious art and symbolism
- Rock drawings, paintings, and engravings
- Sculpture
- Surrealism
- Symbolism
- Video art
- World War, 1939-1945—Art and the war

also subjects and themes in art, e.g. **Animals in art; Blacks in art; Children in art; Plants in art; Women in art;** etc.

 x Iconography
 xx **Civilization; Humanities**
Art, Abstract   709.04
 See also **Cubism**
 x Abstract art; Art, Geometric; Art, Nonobjective; Art, Organic; Geometric art; Nonobjective art; Organic art; Painting, Abstract
 xx **Art, Modern—1900-1999 (20th century)**
Art, American   709.73
 See also **Folk art, American**
 x American art; United States—Art
Art—Analysis, interpretation, appreciation.   *See* **Art appreciation; Art criticism; Art—Study and teaching**
Art, Ancient   709.01
 See also **Classical antiquities**
 x Ancient art
Art and mythology   704.9
 Use same pattern for art and other subjects.
 x Mythology in art
 xx **Art and religion; Mythology**
Art and religion   704.9
 See also **Art and mythology; Religious art and symbolism**
 x Religion and art
 xx **Art and society; Religious art and symbolism**
Art and society   701
 See also **Art and religion; Art patronage; Folk art**
 x Society and art
Art, Applied.   *See* **Industrial design**
Art appreciation   701
 x Appreciation of art; Art—Analysis, interpretation, appreciation
 xx **Aesthetics; Art criticism**
Art, Asian   709.5
 x Art, Oriental; Asian art; Oriental art
Art, Baroque   709.03
 x Baroque art
Art, Black. *See* **Black art**
Art, Buddhist   709.17
 x Buddhist art
Art, Byzantine   709.02
 x Byzantine art
 xx **Art, Medieval**
Art, Christian.   *See* **Christian art and symbolism**
Art, Classical.   *See* **Art, Greek; Art, Roman**
Art collections.   *See* **Art—Museums**

Art collections, Private. *See* names of original own-
　　ers of private collections with the subdivi-
　　sion *Art collections.*
Art, Commercial. *See* **Commercial art**
Art—Composition. *See* **Composition (Art)**
Art, Computer. *See* **Computer art**
Art criticism　701
　　See also **Art appreciation**
　　x Art—Analysis, interpretation, appreciation
　　xx **Criticism**
Art, Decorative. *See* **Decoration and ornament**
Art, Ecclesiastical. *See* **Christian art and symbolism**
Art education. *See* **Art—Study and teaching**
Art, Electronic. *See* **Computer art; Video art**
Art, Erotic. *See* **Erotic art**
Art—Exhibitions　707.4
　　xx **Exhibitions**
Art forgeries. *See* **Forgery of works of art**
Art galleries. *See* **Art—Museums**
Art, Geometric. *See* **Art, Abstract**
Art, Graphic. *See* **Graphic arts**
Art, Greek　709.38; 709.495
　　x Art, Classical; Classical art; Greek art
　　xx **Classical antiquities**
Art—History　709
　　xx **History**
Art in advertising. *See* **Commercial art**
Art in motion. *See* **Kinetic art**
Art, Indian. *See* **Indians of North America—Art**
Art industries and trade. *See* **Decorative arts**
Art, Islamic　709.1
　　x Art, Mohammedan; Islamic art; Moham-
　　medan art; Moslem art
Art, Kinetic. *See* **Kinetic art**
Art, Medieval　709.02
　　See also **Art, Byzantine; Art, Romanesque; Illu-
　　mination of books and manuscripts**
　　x Medieval art; Religious art
　　xx **Civilization, Medieval; Middle Ages**
Art metalwork　739; 745.56
　　See also kinds of art metalwork, e.g. **Bronzes;
　　Goldwork; Jewelry; Silverwork;** etc.
　　x Decorative metalwork; Metalwork, Art
　　xx **Decorative arts; Metalwork**
Art, Modern　709.03
　　x Modern art
Art, Modern—1800-1899 (19th century)　709.03
　　See also **Impressionism (Art); Postimpressionism
　　(Art)**
Art, Modern—1900-1999 (20th century)　709.04
　　See also names of modern art, e.g. **Art, Ab-
　　stract; Computer art; Earthworks (Art); Ki-
　　netic art; Video art;** etc.
　　x Contemporary art
Art, Mohammedan. *See* **Art, Islamic**
Art, Municipal　711
　　See also **City planning; Public buildings**
　　x Civic art; Municipal art; Municipal improve-
　　ments
　　xx **Cities and towns; City planning**
Art—Museums　708
　　x Art collections; Art galleries; Collections of
　　art, painting, etc.; Galleries, Art; Picture

Art—Museums—*Continued*
   galleries
 xx **Museums**
Art, Nonobjective. *See* **Art, Abstract**
Art objects 700; 745
  Use for general materials about decorative arti-
   cles of artistic merit such as snuff boxes,
   brasses, pottery, needlework, glassware, etc.
   Materials on old decorative objects having
   historical or financial value are entered under **Antiques.**
  See also classes of art objects, e.g. **Furniture;**
   Pottery; etc.
 xx **Antiques; Art; Decoration and ornament; Dec-**
   orative arts
Art objects, Forgery of. *See* **Forgery of works of art**
Art, Organic. *See* **Art, Abstract**
Art, Oriental. *See* **Art, Asian**
Art patronage 700
  Use for materials dealing with patronage of the
   arts by individuals or corporations. Materi-
   als on government support of the arts are
   entered under **Arts—Government policy.**
  See also **Arts—Government policy**
 x Art patrons; Business patronage of the arts;
   Corporate patronage of the arts; Corpora-
   tions—Art patronage; Funding for the arts;
   Patronage of the arts; Private funding of the
   arts
 xx **Art and society; Arts—Government policy**
Art patrons. *See* **Art patronage**
Art, Prehistoric 709.01
  See also **Rock drawings, paintings, and engrav-**
   ings
 x Prehistoric art
Art—Prices 707.5
 xx **Prices**
Art, Renaissance 709.02
 xx **Renaissance**
Art robberies. *See* **Art thefts**
Art, Roman 709.37
 x Art, Classical; Classical art; Roman art
 xx **Classical antiquities**
Art, Romanesque 709.02
  See also **Painting, Romanesque**
 x Romanesque art
 xx **Art, Medieval**
Art schools. *See* **Art—Study and teaching**
Art—Study and teaching 707
 x Art—Analysis, interpretation, appreciation;
   Art education; Art schools
 xx **Study skills**
Art—Technique 702.8
Art thefts 364.1
 x Art robberies; Thefts, Art
Art, Video. *See* **Video art**
Artesian wells. *See* **Wells**
Arthritis 616.7; 618.97
 xx **Gout; Rheumatism**
Arthur, King—Romances. *See* **Arthurian romances**
Arthurian romances 398.22; 808.8; 809
  See also **Grail**
 x Arthur, King—Romances; Knights of the

Arthurian romances—*Continued*
    Round Table
    xx **Grail; Romances**
Articles of war. *See* **Military law**
Articulation (Education)   371.2
    Use for materials that discuss the integration of
        various elements of the school system so as
        to provide for continuous progress by the
        student. This may be the adjustments and
        relationships between different levels (e.g.
        elementary and secondary schools, high
        school and college); the integration between
        subjects (e.g. humanities and social studies);
        or the relationship between the school's pro-
        gram and outside factors (e.g. church,
        scouts, welfare agencies).
    x Integration in education
    xx **Education—Curricula; Schools—
        Administration**
Artificial flies   688.7; 799.1
    See also **Fly casting**
    x Fishing flies; Flies, Artificial
    xx **Fishing**
Artificial flowers   745.59
    x Flowers, Artificial
Artificial foods   641.3; 664
    x Food, Artificial; Synthetic foods
    xx **Food; Synthetic products**
Artificial fuels. *See* **Synthetic fuels**
Artificial heart   617.4
    xx **Artificial organs; Heart**
Artificial insemination   636.08
    Use for general materials and materials on artifi-
        cial insemination of livestock, etc. Materials
        limited to artificial insemination in humans
        are entered under **Artificial insemination,
        Human.**
    x Impregnation, Artificial; Insemination, Artifi-
        cial
    xx **Reproduction**
Artificial insemination, Human   176; 346.01; 618.1
    xx **Sexual ethics**
Artificial intelligence   006.3
    x AI (Artificial intelligence); Electronic brains;
        Intelligence, Artificial; Machine intelligence
    xx **Bionics; Electronic data processing**
Artificial islands. *See* **Drilling platforms**
Artificial limbs   617.5
    x Extremities, Artificial; Limbs, Artificial; Pros-
        thesis
Artificial organs   617.9
    See also names of artificial organs, e.g. **Artifi-
        cial heart;** etc.
    x Organs, Artificial; Prosthesis
Artificial respiration   617.1
    x Pulmonary resuscitation; Respiration, Artifi-
        cial; Resuscitation, Pulmonary
    xx **First aid**   ˙
Artificial satellites (May subdiv. geog. adjective
        form)   **629.43; 629.46**
    See also types of satellites, e.g. **Meteorological
        satellites; Space stations; Space vehicles;**
        etc.; also names of specific satellites, e.g.

Artificial satellites—*Continued*
> **Explorer (Artificial satellite);** etc.
> *x* Orbiting vehicles; Satellites, Artificial
> *xx* **Astronautics; Space vehicles**

Artificial satellites, American   629.43; 629.46
> *x* American artificial satellites; United States—
> Artificial satellites

Artificial satellites—Control systems   629.46
**Artificial satellites in telecommunication   384.5;
621.382**
> *See also* names of specific satellites or projects,
> e.g. **Telstar project;** etc.
> *x* Communication satellites; Communications
> relay satellites; Global satellite communica-
> tions systems; Satellite communication sys-
> tems
> *xx* **Telecommunication**

Artificial satellites—Launching   629.43
> *x* Launching of satellites
> *xx* **Rockets (Aeronautics)**

Artificial satellites—Law and legislation.   *See* **Space
law**

Artificial satellites—Orbits   629.4
> *xx* **Astrodynamics**

Artificial satellites, Russian.   *See* **Artificial satellites, Soviet**

Artificial satellites, Soviet   629.43; 629.46
> *x* Artificial satellites, Russian; Soviet artificial
> satellites; Sputniks

Artificial satellites—Tracking   629.43
> *x* Tracking of satellites

Artificial silk.   *See* **Rayon**

Artificial sweeteners.   *See* **Sugar substitutes**

Artificial weather control.   *See* **Weather control**

Artillery   355.8; 623.4
> *See also* **Ordnance**

Artistic anatomy.   *See* **Anatomy, Artistic**

Artistic photography.   *See* **Photography, Artistic**

Artists (May subdiv. geog. adjective form)   **700.92;
709.2; 920**
> *See also*

Architects	**Illustrators**
Black artists	**Painters**
Child artists	**Potters**
Engravers	**Sculptors**
Etchers	**Women artists**

> also names of individual artists
> *xx* **Painters**

Artists, American   709.2; 920
> *x* American artists; United States—Artists

Artists, Black.   *See* **Black artists**

Artists' materials   741.2; 751.2
> *x* Drawing materials; Painters' materials

Arts (May subdiv. geog. adjective form)   **700**
> Use for materials on the arts in general, includ-
> ing the visual arts, literature, and the per-
> forming arts. Materials on the visual arts
> only (architecture, painting, etc.) are entered
> under **Art.**
> *See also* **Visual literacy**
> *x* Arts, Fine; Fine arts

Arts, American   709.73
> *x* American arts

Arts and crafts movement   745
　　　Use for materials on the movement that pro-
　　　　　moted craftsmanship and a reform of ap-
　　　　　plied design or decorative arts. Originating
　　　　　in England in the second half of the 19th
　　　　　century under the influence of William Mor-
　　　　　ris and spreading to the United States, Ger-
　　　　　many, and Austria, the movement grew as a
　　　　　response to the Industrial Revolution and
　　　　　incorporated ideas of socialism and the
　　　　　moral need for integrating beauty with the
　　　　　accessories of daily life.
　　　See also **Handicraft**
　　　x Crafts (Arts)
　　　xx **Art; Decoration and ornament; Decorative
　　　　　arts; Folk art; Handicraft**
Arts and state.   *See* **Arts—Government policy**
Arts, Applied.   *See* **Decorative arts**
Arts, Decorative.   *See* **Decoration and ornament;
　　　Decorative arts; Interior design**
Arts, Fine.   *See* **Arts**
Arts—Government policy   351.85; 700
　　　See also **Art patronage**
　　　x Arts and state; Funding for the arts; State and
　　　　　the arts; State encouragement of the arts
　　　xx **Art patronage**
Arts, Graphic.   *See* **Graphic arts**
Arts, Minor.   *See* **Decorative arts**
Arts, Useful.   *See* **Industrial arts; Technology**
Asbestos   620.1; 666; 691
　　　xx **Geology, Economic**
Asceticism   248; 291.4
　　　xx **Fanaticism; Fasting; Religious orders**
Asia   950
　　　See also areas of Asia, e.g. **East Asia; Middle
　　　　　East; Southeast Asia;** etc.
　　　x East; Orient
Asia, East.   *See* **East Asia**
Asia—Politics and government   950
Asia, Southeast.   *See* **Southeast Asia**
Asian architecture.   *See* **Architecture, Asian**
Asian art.   *See* **Art, Asian**
Asian civilization.   *See* **Civilization, Asian**
Asphyxiating gases.   *See* **Poisonous gases**
Assassination   364.1
　　　See also **Terrorism;** also names of persons and
　　　　　groups with the subdivision *Assassination,*
　　　　　e.g. **Presidents—United States—
　　　　　Assassination;** etc.
　　　xx **Crime; Homicide; Offenses against the person;
　　　　　Political crimes and offenses**
Assault, Criminal.   *See* **Rape**
Assembly programs, School.   *See* **School assembly
　　　programs**
Assembly, Right of.   *See* **Freedom of assembly**
Assertive behavior.   *See* **Assertiveness (Psychology)**
Assertiveness (Psychology)   155.2; 158.2
　　　See also **Self-confidence**
　　　x Assertive behavior
　　　xx **Aggressiveness (Psychology); Psychology;
　　　　　Self-confidence**
Assessment   336.2
　　　Use for general materials only. Materials on the

Assessment—*Continued*

> assessment of a given locality are entered under **Taxation** followed by the appropriate geographical subdivision.
> *See also* **Taxation; Valuation**
> *x* Appraisal
> *xx* **Taxation**

Assessments, Political. *See* **Campaign funds**

Assistance in emergencies. *See* **Helping behavior**

Assistance to developing areas. *See* **Economic assistance; Technical assistance**

Association, Freedom of. *See* **Freedom of association**

Associations   060; 302.3; 366

> *See also* **Clubs; Community life; Cooperation; Social group work; Societies; Voluntarism;** also names of types of associations, e.g. **Trade and professional associations;** etc.; and subjects with the subdivision *Societies,* e.g. **Agriculture—Societies;** etc.; and names of specific associations
> *x* Organizations; Voluntary associations
> *xx* **Societies; Voluntarism**

Associations, International. *See* **International agencies**

Astrobiology. *See* **Life on other planets; Space biology**

Astrodynamics   521; 629.4

> *See also* **Artificial satellites—Orbits; Astronautics; Navigation (Astronautics); Space flight**
> *xx* **Astronautics; Dynamics; Space flight**

Astrogeology   559.9

> *See also* **Lunar geology;** also names of planets with the subdivision *Geology,* e.g. **Mars (Planet)—Geology;** etc.
> *xx* **Geology**

Astrology   133.5

> *See also* **Horoscopes**
> *x* Hermetic art and philosophy
> *xx* **Astronomy; Divination; Fortune telling; Occultism; Prophecies (Occult sciences); Stars; Superstition**

Astronautical accidents. *See* **Astronautics—Accidents**

Astronautical communication systems. *See* **Astronautics—Communication systems**

Astronautical instruments   629.4

> *See also* **Astronautics—Communication systems**
> *x* Instruments, Astronautical; Space vehicles—Instruments
> *xx* **Astronautics—Communication systems; Navigation (Astronautics); Space optics**

Astronautics (May subdiv. geog.)   **629.4**

> *See also*

Aerothermodynamics	**Space flight**
Artificial satellites	**Space flight to the moon**
Astrodynamics	**Space sciences**
Interplanetary voyages	**Space ships**
Navigation (Astronautics)	**Space stations**
Outer space	**Space vehicles**
Rocketry	**Unidentified flying objects**

> *xx* **Aeronautics; Astrodynamics; Space sciences; Space vehicles**

Astronautics—Accidents   363.12; 629.4
    x Accidents, Spacecraft; Astronautical accidents; Space ships—Accidents; Space vehicles—Accidents
Astronautics and civilization   306.4
    See also **Space colonies; Space law**
    x Civilization and astronautics; Outer space and civilization; Space age; Space power
    xx **Aeronautics and civilization; Civilization**
Astronautics—Communication systems   629.47
    See also **Astronautical instruments; Radio in astronautics; Television in astronautics**
    x Astronautical communication systems; Space communication
    xx **Astronautical instruments; Interstellar communication; Telecommunication**
Astronautics—International cooperation   629.4
    x International space cooperation
    xx **International cooperation**
Astronautics—Law and legislation.   *See* **Space law**
Astronautics, Photography in.   *See* **Space photography**
Astronautics—United States   629.40973
    See also **Project Voyager**
    x United States—Astronautics
Astronauts   629.450092; 920
    See also **Space vehicles—Piloting**
    x Cosmonauts; Space ships—Pilots
    xx **Air pilots; Space flight**
Astronauts—Clothing   629.47
    x Pressure suits; Space suits
    xx **Life support systems (Space environment)**
Astronauts—Food   629.47
    x Meals for astronauts; Menus for space flight
    xx **Astronauts—Nutrition**
Astronauts—Nutrition   629.47
    See also **Astronauts—Food**
    x Space nutrition
    xx **Nutrition**
Astronavigation.   *See* **Navigation (Astronautics)**
Astronomers   520.92; 920
    xx **Scientists**
Astronomical instruments   522
    See also **Astronomical photography;** also names of instruments, e.g. **Telescope;** etc.
    x Instruments, Astronomical
    xx **Scientific apparatus and instruments; Space optics**
Astronomical observatories   522
    x Observatories, Astronomical
Astronomical photography   522
    x Astrophotography; Photography, Astronomical
    xx **Astronomical instruments; Photography**
Astronomical physics.   *See* **Astrophysics**
Astronomy   520
    See also

Astrology	**Eclipses, Lunar**
Astrophysics	**Eclipses, Solar**
Bible—Astronomy	**Galaxies**
Black holes (Astronomy)	**Life on other planets**
Chronology	**Meteorites**
Comets	**Meteors**

Astronomy—*Continued*

Moon
Nautical astronomy
Outer space
Planetariums
Planets
Pulsars
Quasars
Radio astronomy
Seasons
Sky
Solar system
Space environment
Space sciences
Spectrum analysis
Stars
Sun
Tides
Zodiac

 x Constellations
 xx **Science; Space sciences; Stars; Universe**
Astronomy—Atlases. *See* **Stars—Atlases**
Astronomy—Mathematics 520.1
 xx **Mathematics**
Astronomy, Nautical. *See* **Nautical astronomy**
Astrophotography. *See* **Astronomical photography**
Astrophysics 523.01
 See also **Black holes (Astronomy); Spectrum**
  analysis
 x Astronomical physics; Physics, Astronomical
 xx **Astronomy; Physics; Stars**
Astros (Baseball team). *See* **Houston Astros (Base-ball team)**
Asylum 341.4
 See also **Political refugees; Sanctuary movement**
 x Asylum, Right of; Political asylum; Right of
  asylum; Sanctuary (Law)
 xx **International law**
Asylum, Right of. *See* **Asylum**
Asylums. *See* **Institutional care;** and classes of
 people with the subdivision *Institutional*
 care, e.g. **Blind—Institutional care; Deaf—**
 Institutional care; Mentally ill—
 Institutional care; etc.
At-home employment. *See* **Home business; Tele-commuting**
Atheism 211
 See also **Agnosticism; Deism; Rationalism; Skep-ticism; Theism**
 xx **Agnosticism; Deism; Faith; God; Rationalism;**
  Religion; Secularism; Theism; Theology
Athletes 796.092; 920
 See also **Black athletes**
Athletes, Black. *See* **Black athletes**
Athletes—Drug use 362.29; 796
 See also **Steroids**
 xx **Drugs and sports; Steroids**
Athletic coaching. *See* **Coaching (Athletics)**
Athletic medicine. *See* **Sports medicine**
Athletics 796
 See also **Coaching (Athletics); Martial arts;**
  Olympic games; Physical education; Sports;
  also names of specific athletic activities, e.g.
  Boxing; Gymnastics; Rowing; Track athlet-ics; Weight lifting; etc.
 x College athletics; Intercollegiate athletics
 xx **Physical education; Sports**
Atlantic cable. *See* **Cables, Submarine**
Atlantic Ocean 910.9163
 xx **Ocean**
Atlantic States 974; 975
 x Eastern Seaboard; Middle Atlantic States;

Atlantic States—*Continued*
     South Atlantic States
  xx **United States**
Atlas (Missile)   **623.4; 629.47**
  xx **Ballistic missiles; Intercontinental ballistic missiles**
Atlases   **912**
    Use as a form heading for geographical atlases of world coverage. General materials about maps and their history are entered under **Maps.**
    See also **Bible—Geography;** also names of scientific and technical subjects with the form subdivision *Atlases,* e.g. **Human anatomy—Atlases; Stars—Atlases;** etc.; and countries, cities, etc. with the subdivision *Maps,* e.g. **United States—Maps; Chicago (Ill.)—Maps;** etc.
  x Geographical atlases
  xx **Geography; Maps**
Atlases, Astronomical.   *See* **Stars—Atlases**
Atlases, Historical **911**
  x Geography, Historical—Maps; Historical atlases; Historical geography; History—Atlases; Maps, Historical
Atmosphere   **551.5**
    Use for materials on the body of air surrounding the earth as distinguished from the upper rarefied air. Materials dealing with air as an element and with its chemical and physical properties are entered under **Air.**
  See also **Air; Gaia hypothesis; Meteorology; Sky**
  xx **Air; Earth; Meteorology**
Atmosphere—Pollution.   *See* **Air pollution**
Atmosphere, Upper.   *See* **Upper atmosphere**
Atmospheric greenhouse effect.   *See* **Greenhouse effect**
Atmospheric humidity.   *See* **Humidity**
Atolls.   *See* **Coral reefs and islands**
Atom smashing.   *See* **Cyclotron**
Atomic bomb   **623.4**
  See also **Hydrogen bomb; Radioactive fallout**
  xx **Bombs; Hydrogen bomb; Nuclear warfare; Nuclear weapons**
Atomic bomb—Physiological effect   **616.9**
  See also **Radiation—Physiological effect**
  xx **Radiation—Physiological effect**
Atomic bomb—Testing   **623.4**
Atomic bomb victims   **940.54**
    Use for materials on the victims of atomic bomb warfare.
  x A-bomb victims; Victims of atomic bombings
Atomic energy.   *See* **Nuclear energy**
Atomic industry.   *See* **Nuclear industry**
Atomic medicine.   *See* **Nuclear medicine**
Atomic nuclei.   *See* **Nuclear physics**
Atomic piles.   *See* **Nuclear reactors**
Atomic power.   *See* **Nuclear energy**
Atomic power plants.   *See* **Nuclear power plants**
Atomic powered vehicles.   *See* **Nuclear propulsion**
Atomic submarines.   *See* **Nuclear submarines**
Atomic theory   **539.7; 541.2**
  See also **Nuclear energy; Quantum theory**

Atomic theory—*Continued*

   xx **Chemistry, Physical and theoretical; Quantum theory**

Atomic warfare. *See* **Nuclear warfare**

Atomic weapons. *See* **Nuclear weapons**

Atoms   539; 541

   See also **Cyclotron; Electrons; Nuclear physics; Transmutation (Chemistry)**

   xx **Chemistry, Physical and theoretical; Neutrons; Protons**

Atonement—Christianity   232; 234

   x Jesus Christ—Atonement; Vicarious atonement

   xx **Christianity; Jesus Christ; Sacrifice; Salvation**

Atonement, Day of. *See* **Yom Kippur**

Atonement—Judaism   296.3

   xx **Judaism**

Atrocities   909; 930-990

   See also **Massacres; Persecution**

   xx **Crime; Cruelty**

Atrocities, Military. *See* names of wars with the subdivision *Atrocities,* e.g. **World War, 1939-1945—Atrocities;** etc.; and names of specific atrocities

Attacks by animals. *See* **Animal attacks**

Attendance, School. *See* **School attendance**

Attention   153.1; 153.7

   See also **Listening**

   x Concentration

   xx **Apperception; Educational psychology; Listening; Memory; Psychology; Thought and thinking**

Attitude (Psychology)   152.4

   See also **Conformity; Job satisfaction; Prejudices; Public opinion; Racism; Sexism;** also names of groups of people with the subdivision *Attitudes,* e.g. **Teenagers—Attitudes;** etc.

   x Frustration

   xx **Emotions; Psychology; Public opinion; Social psychology**

Attorneys. *See* **Lawyers**

ATVs. *See* **All terrain vehicles**

Auction bridge. *See* **Bridge (Game)**

Auctions   658.8

   x Sales, Auction

Audio amplifiers, Transistor. *See* **Transistor amplifiers**

Audio cassettes. *See* **Sound recordings**

Audiodisc players. *See* **Compact disc players**

Audiotapes. *See* **Sound recordings**

Audiovisual education   371.3

   See also **Audiovisual materials; Motion pictures in education; Radio in education; Television in education;** also subjects with the subdivision *Audiovisual aids,* e.g. **Library education—Audiovisual aids;** etc.

   x Visual instruction

   xx **Education**

Audiovisual materials   025.17; 371.3

   See also **Manipulative materials;** also names of specific materials, e.g. **Filmstrips; Motion pictures; Sound recordings; Videodiscs; Videotapes;** etc.; and subjects with the subdivi-

Audiovisual materials—*Continued*
      sion *Audiovisual aids,* e.g. **Library education—Audiovisual aids;** etc.
    x Multimedia materials; Nonbook materials; Nonprint materials
    xx **Audiovisual education; Teaching—Aids and devices**
Audiovisual materials centers. *See* **Instructional materials centers**
Auditing   657
    See also **Accounting**
    xx **Accounting; Bookkeeping**
Aurora borealis. *See* **Auroras**
Auroras   538
    x Aurora borealis; Northern lights; Polar lights
    xx **Geophysics; Meteorology**
Australian aborigines   305.89
    x Aborigines, Australian; Australians (Native people)
Australians (Native people). *See* **Australian aborigines**
Author and publisher. *See* **Authors and publishers**
Authoring programs for computer assisted instruction. *See* **Computer assisted instruction—Authoring programs**
Authoritarianism. *See* **Fascism; Totalitarianism**
Authors (May subdiv. geog. adjective form, e.g. **Authors, English;** etc.)   809; 920
    See also **Black authors; Child authors; Literature—Bio-bibliography; Literature—History and criticism; Pseudonyms; Women authors;** also classes of writers, e.g. **Dramatists; Novelists; Poets;** etc.; and names of individual authors
    x Writers
    xx **Books; Literature—Bio-bibliography; Literature—History and criticism**
Authors, American   810.9; 920
    x American authors; United States—Authors
    xx **American literature**
Authors and publishers   070.5
    Use for materials on the relations between author and publisher.
    See also **Copyright**
    x Author and publisher; Publishers and authors
    xx **Authorship; Contracts; Copyright; Publishers and publishing**
Authors, Black. *See* **Black authors**
Authors—Correspondence   92; B
Authors, English   820.9; 920
    See also **English literature—Bio-bibliography**
    x English authors
    xx **English literature**
Authors—Homes and haunts. *See* **Literary landmarks**
Authorship   808
    Use for general materials dealing with the means of becoming an author. Materials concerning the composition of special types of literature are entered under more specific headings such as **Fiction—Technique; Love stories—Technique; Short story;** etc.

Authorship—*Continued*

See also

Advertising copy	**Love stories—Technique**
Authors and publishers	**Plots (Drama, fiction, etc.)**
Biography (as a literary form)	**Radio authorship**
	Report writing
Copyright	**Short story**
Creative writing	**Technical writing**
Drama—Technique	**Television authorship**
Fiction—Technique	**Versification**
Journalism	

   x Writing (Authorship)

   xx **Literature**

Authorship—Handbooks, manuals, etc. 808

   See also **Printing—Style manuals**

   xx **Printing—Style manuals**

Autism 616.89; 618.92

   xx **Child psychiatry**

Auto courts. *See* **Hotels, motels, etc.**

Autobiographies 920

   Use for collections of autobiographies.

   See also subjects with the subdivision *Biography* or *Correspondence,* e.g. **Women—Biography; Authors—Correspondence;** etc.; and names of events and wars with the subdivision *Personal narratives,* e.g. **World War, 1939-1945—Personal narratives;** etc.

   x Diaries; Memoirs; Personal narratives

   xx **Biography**

Autobiography (as a literary form). *See* **Biography (as a literary form)**

Autobiography—Technique. *See* **Biography (as a literary form)**

Autocodes. *See* **Programming languages (Computers)**

Autographs 929.8

   See also **Manuscripts**

   xx **Biography; Manuscripts; Writing**

Automata. *See* **Robots**

Automated genetic engineering. *See* **Genetic engineering, Automated**

Automated information networks. *See* **Information networks**

Automatic computers. *See* **Computers**

Automatic control. *See* **Automation; Cybernetics; Electric controllers; Servomechanisms**

Automatic data processing. *See* **Electronic data processing**

Automatic drafting. *See* **Computer graphics**

Automatic drawing. *See* **Computer graphics**

Automatic information retrieval. *See* **Information systems**

Automatic programming languages. *See* **Programming languages (Computers)**

Automatic speech recognition 006.4

   x Mechanical speech recognition; Speech recognition, Automatic

   xx **Speech processing systems; Voice**

Automatic teaching. *See* **Teaching machines**

Automation 629.8; 670.42

   See also **Feedback control systems; Servomechanisms; Systems engineering; Telecommuting;** also subjects with the subdivision

Automation—*Continued*
  Automation, e.g. **Libraries—Automation;** etc.
  x Automatic control; Computer control; Machinery, Automatic
  xx **Machinery in industry**
Automobile accidents. *See* **Traffic accidents**
Automobile driver education. *See* **Automobile drivers—Education**
Automobile drivers   629.28
  x Automobile driving; Automobiles—Driving; Drivers, Automobile
Automobile drivers—Education   629.28
  x Automobile driver education; Driver education
  xx **Education**
Automobile driving. *See* **Automobile drivers**
Automobile engines. *See* **Automobiles—Engines**
Automobile guides. *See* **Automobiles—Road guides**
Automobile industry   338.4; 388.3
Automobile insurance   368.5
  x Insurance, Automobile; No fault automobile insurance
  xx **Insurance**
Automobile parts. *See* **Automobiles—Parts**
Automobile pools. *See* **Car pools**
Automobile racing   796.7
  See also **Karts and karting;** also names of types of automobile races and names of specific races
  x Automobiles—Racing
Automobile repairs. *See* **Automobiles—Maintenance and repair**
Automobile touring. *See* **Automobiles—Touring**
Automobile trailers. *See* **Automobiles—Trailers**
Automobile transmission. *See* **Automobiles—Transmission devices**
Automobile trucks. *See* **Trucks**
Automobiles   388.3; 629.222
  See also **Buses; Sports cars; Trucks;** also names of specific makes and models of automobiles, e.g. **Ford automobile;** etc.
  x Cars (Automobiles); Locomotion; Motor cars
  xx **Transportation, Highway; Vehicles**
Automobiles—Accidents. *See* **Traffic accidents**
Automobiles—Air conditioning   629.2
  xx **Air conditioning**
Automobiles—Brakes   629.2
  xx **Brakes**
Automobiles, Compact. *See* **Compact automobiles**
Automobiles—Design and construction   629.222
Automobiles, Diesel. *See* **Diesel automobiles**
Automobiles—Driving. *See* **Automobile drivers**
Automobiles, Electric. *See* **Electric automobiles**
Automobiles—Electric equipment   629.25
  x Electric equipment of automobiles
Automobiles—Engines   629.25
  See also **Diesel automobiles; Electric automobiles**
  x Automobile engines; Automobiles—Motors
  xx **Diesel automobiles; Electric automobiles; Engines; Gas and oil engines**
Automobiles, Foreign. *See* **Foreign automobiles**
Automobiles—Fuel consumption   629.28
  xx **Energy consumption; Fuel**

Automobiles—Gearing. *See* **Automobiles—
Transmission devices**
Automobiles—Law and legislation   343.09
See also **Traffic regulations**
xx **Law; Legislation; Traffic regulations**
Automobiles—Maintenance and repair   629.28
See also **Automobiles—Restoration**
x Automobile repairs; Automobiles—Repairing
xx **Repairing**
Automobiles—Models   629.22
x Model cars
xx **Machinery—Models**
Automobiles—Motors. *See* **Automobiles—Engines**
Automobiles—Parts   629.28
x Automobile parts
Automobiles—Pollution control devices   629.25
x Pollution control devices (Motor vehicles)
xx **Pollution control industry**
Automobiles—Pools. *See* **Car pools**
Automobiles—Racing. *See* **Automobile racing**
Automobiles—Repairing. *See* **Automobiles—
Maintenance and repair**
Automobiles—Restoration   629.28
x Restoration of automobiles
xx **Automobiles—Maintenance and repair**
Automobiles—Road guides   912
See also **Road maps**
x Automobile guides
xx **Maps; Road maps**
Automobiles—Service stations   629.28
x Filling stations; Gas stations; Service stations,
Automobile
Automobiles—Touring   796.7
x Automobile touring; Motoring
xx **Travel**
Automobiles—Trailers   629.226
See also **Travel trailers and campers**
x Automobile trailers; Trailers
Automobiles—Transmission devices   629.2
x Automobile transmission; Automobiles—
Gearing; Transmissions, Automobile
xx **Gearing**
Autosuggestion. *See* **Hypnotism; Mental suggestion**
Autumn   508; 525
x Fall
xx **Seasons**
Avant-garde churches. *See* **Noninstitutional
churches**
Avant-garde films. *See* **Experimental films**
Avant-garde theater. *See* **Experimental theater**
Avenues. *See* **Streets**
Average   519.5
xx **Arithmetic; Probabilities; Statistics**
Aviation. *See* **Aeronautics**
Aviation medicine   616.9
See also **Jet lag; Space medicine**
x Aeronautics—Medical aspects; Aerospace
medicine; Medicine, Aviation
xx **Medicine; Space medicine**
Aviators. *See* **Air pilots**
Avocations. *See* **Hobbies**
Awakening, Religious. *See* **Religious awakening**
Awards. *See* **Rewards (Prizes, etc.);** and names of
awards

Awards (Law). *See* **Arbitration and award**
Awards, Literary. *See* **Literary prizes**
Axiology. *See* **Values**
Aztecs   972.004
   xx **Indians of Mexico**
B-52 bomber   623.7
   xx **Bombers**
Babies. *See* **Infants**
Baby animals. *See* **Animals—Infancy**
Baby care. *See* **Infants—Care**
Baby sitters. *See* **Babysitters**
Baby sitting. *See* **Babysitting**
Babysitters   649
   x Baby sitters; Sitters (Babysitters)
Babysitting   649
   x Baby sitting
   xx **Child care; Infants—Care**
Bacilli. *See* **Bacteriology; Germ theory of disease**
Back packing. *See* **Backpacking**
Backpacking   796.5
   x Back packing; Pack transportation
   xx **Camping; Hiking**
Bacon-Shakespeare controversy. *See* **Shakespeare,**
     William, 1564-1616—Authorship
Bacon's Rebellion, 1676   973.2
   xx **United States—History—1600-1775, Colonial**
     period
Bacteria. *See* **Bacteriology**
Bacterial warfare. *See* **Biological warfare**
Bacteriology   589.9
   See also **Disinfection and disinfectants; Fermen-**
     tation; Germ theory of disease; Immunity;
     Microorganisms; also subjects with the sub-
     division *Bacteriology,* e.g. **Cheese—**
     Bacteriology; etc.
   x Bacilli; Bacteria; Disease germs; Germs; Mi-
     crobes
   xx **Communicable diseases; Fermentation; Fungi;**
     Germ theory of disease; Medicine; Microbi-
     ology; Microorganisms; Parasites; Pathol-
     ogy
Bacteriology, Agricultural. *See* **Agricultural bacteri-**
     ology
Badges of honor. *See* **Decorations of honor; Insig-**
     nia; Medals
Bahai Faith   297
   x Bahaism
   xx **Islam; Religions**
Bahaism. *See* **Bahai Faith**
Baking   641.7
   See also names of baked products, e.g. **Bread;**
     Cake; Pastry; etc.
   xx **Cookery**
Balance of nature. *See* **Ecology**
Balance of payments   382
   See also **Balance of trade**
   xx **Balance of trade; International economic rela-**
     tions
Balance of power   327.1
   x Power politics
Balance of trade   382
   See also **Balance of payments**
   x Trade, Balance of

Balance of trade—*Continued*

    xx **Balance of payments; Commerce; Economics; Free trade and protection; Tariff**

Ball bearings. *See* **Bearings (Machinery)**

Ball games **796.3**

    See also names of games, e.g. **Baseball; Basketball; Soccer;** etc.; and names of competitions

    xx **Games**

Ballads **808.1; 808.81; 811, etc.**

    Use for collections of ballads and for materials about ballads. Materials dealing with the folk tunes associated with these ballads, and collections that include both words and music are entered under **Folk songs.**

    See also **Folk songs**

    xx **Folk songs; Literature; Poetry; Songs**

Ballads, American **811, etc.**

    x American ballads; United States—Ballads

    xx **American literature**

Ballet **792.8**

    See also **Pantomimes**

    xx **Dancing; Drama; Opera; Performing arts; Theater**

Ballet dancers **792.8092; 920**

    xx **Dancers**

Ballet, Water. *See* **Synchronized swimming**

Ballets **792.8**

Ballets—Stories, plots, etc. **792.8**

    xx **Plots (Drama, fiction, etc.)**

Ballistic missile early warning system **358.1; 621.3848**

    x BMEWS; Early warning system, Ballistic missile

    xx **Air defenses; Radar defense networks**

Ballistic missiles **358.1; 623.4**

    Use for materials on high-altitude, high-speed atomic missiles that are self-propelled and guided in the first stage of flight only and later have a natural and uncontrolled trajectory.

    See also types of ballistic missiles, e.g. **Intercontinental ballistic missiles;** etc.; also names of specific missiles, e.g. **Atlas (Missile);** etc.

    x Missiles, Ballistic

    xx **Guided missiles; Nuclear weapons; Rockets (Aeronautics)**

Balloons **623.7; 629.133**

    See also **Aeronautics**

    xx **Aeronautics; Airships**

Balloons, Dirigible. *See* **Airships**

Ballot. *See* **Elections**

Band music **784**

    xx **Instrumental music; Military music**

Bandages and bandaging **616.02**

    xx **First aid**

Bandits. *See* **Robbers and outlaws**

Bandmasters. *See* **Conductors (Music)**

Bands (Music) **784**

    See also **Conducting; Drum majoring; Instrumentation and orchestration; Orchestra; Wind instruments;** also names of types of bands

Bands (Music)—*Continued*
      and specific bands
  xx **Conducting; Orchestra; Wind instruments**
Bank credit cards.   *See* **Credit cards**
Bank debit cards.   *See* **Debit cards**
Bank failures   332.1
  x Failure of banks
  xx **Bankruptcy; Banks and banking; Business**
      failures
Banking.   *See* **Banks and banking**
Bankruptcy   332.7; 336.3; 346
  See also **Bank failures**
  x Business mortality; Failure in business; Insol-
      vency
  xx **Business failures; Commercial law; Debtor**
      and creditor; Finance
Banks and banking (May subdiv. geog.)   **332.1**
  See also

Agricultural credit	**Investment trusts**
Bank failures	**Investments**
Consumer credit	**Money**
Credit	**Negotiable instruments**
Federal Reserve banks	**Savings and loan associa-**
Foreign exchange	**tions**
Interest (Economics)	**Trust companies**

    also names of individual banks
  x Banking; Savings banks
  xx **Business; Capital; Commerce; Credit; Finance;**
      Money; Trust companies
Banks and banking, Cooperative   334
  See also **Credit unions**
  x Cooperative banks; People's banks
  xx **Cooperation; Cooperative societies; Personal**
      loans
Banks and banking—Credit cards.   *See* **Credit cards**
Banks and banking—Data processing   332.10285
  xx **Electronic data processing**
Banks and banking—Debit cards.   *See* **Debit cards**
Banks and banking—United States   332.10973
  x United States—Banks and banking
Banned books.   *See* **Books—Censorship**
Banners.   *See* **Flags**
Banquets.   *See* **Dinners and dining**
Baptism   234; 265
  See also **Regeneration (Theology)**
  x Christening; Immersion, Baptismal
  xx **Rites and ceremonies; Sacraments; Theology**
Baptists   286; 920
  See also **Mennonites**
Bar.   *See* **Lawyers**
Barbary corsairs.   *See* **Pirates**
Barbary States.   *See* **North Africa**
Barbecue cookery   641.7
  x Cookery, Barbecue; Grill cookery
  xx **Outdoor cookery**
Bargaining.   *See* **Negotiation**
Barns   631.2; 728
  xx **Farm buildings**
Barometer.   *See* **Barometers**
Barometers   551.5; 681
  x Barometer
  xx **Meteorological instruments**
Baronage.   *See* **Nobility**
Baroque architecture.   *See* **Architecture, Baroque**

Baroque art. *See* **Art, Baroque**
Barrier free design. *See* **Architecture and the handi-
    capped**
Barristers. *See* **Lawyers**
Barrows. *See* **Mounds and mound builders**
Bars and restaurants. *See* **Restaurants, bars, etc.**
Barter   332
    x Exchange, Barter
    xx **Commerce; Economics; Money; Subsistence
        economy; Underground economy**
Basal readers   372.4; 418
    Use for readers providing controlled vocabulary
        in a series of books to be read sequentially;
        and for materials about basal readers.
    x English language—Basal readers
    xx **Reading materials**
Baseball   796.357
    See also **Little league baseball; Softball**
    xx **Ball games; College sports; Sports**
Baseball clubs   796.357
    See also names of individual baseball clubs, e.g.
        Houston Astros (Baseball team); etc.
Basements   721
    x Cellars
    xx **Foundations; Underground architecture**
Bases (Chemistry)   546; 661
    xx **Chemistry**
Bashfulness   152.4
    x Shyness
    xx **Emotions**
Basic education   370.11
    x Basic skills education; Fundamental education
    xx **Education**
Basic life skills. *See* **Life skills**
Basic rights. *See* **Civil rights; Human rights**
Basic skills education. *See* **Basic education**
Basket making   746.41
    xx **Weaving**
Basketball   796.323
    xx **Ball games; College sports; Sports**
Bastardy. *See* **Illegitimacy**
Bastogne, Battle of. *See* **Ardennes, Battle of the,
    1944-1945**
Bat. *See* **Bats**
Baths   613; 615.8
    See also **Hydrotherapy**
    xx **Cleanliness; Hydrotherapy; Hygiene; Physical
        therapy**
Bathyscaphe   623.8
    xx **Oceanography—Research; Submersibles**
Batik   746.6
    xx **Dyes and dyeing**
Baton twirling   791.6
    See also **Drum majoring**
    xx **Drum majoring**
Batrachia. *See* **Amphibians**
Bats   599.4
    x Bat
    xx **Mammals**
Battered children. *See* **Child abuse**
Battered elderly. *See* **Elderly abuse**
Battered husbands. *See* **Husband abuse**
Battered men. *See* **Husband abuse**
Battered wives. *See* **Abused women**

Battered women. *See* **Abused women**

Batteries, Electric. *See* **Electric batteries; Storage batteries**

Batteries, Solar. *See* **Solar batteries**

Battering of wives. *See* **Wife abuse**

Battle of the Bulge. *See* **Ardennes, Battle of the, 1944-1945**

Battle ships. *See* **Warships**

Battle songs. *See* **War songs**

Battles   355.4; 909; 930-990
> Names of all battles are not included in this List but are to be added as needed, e.g. **Ardennes, Battle of the, 1944-1945;** etc.
> *See also* **Naval battles;** also names of wars with the subdivision *Campaigns,* e.g. **United States—History—1861-1865, Civil War—Campaigns; World War, 1939-1945—Campaigns;** etc.; and names of individual battles, e.g. **Ardennes, Battle of the, 1944-1945;** etc.
> *x* Fighting; Sieges
> *xx* **Military art and science; Military history; Naval battles; War**

Battleships. *See* **Warships**

Bay of Pigs invasion. *See* **Cuba—History—1961, Invasion**

Bazaars. *See* **Fairs**

Beaches   551.4
> *xx* **Seashore**

Beadwork   746.5
> *xx* **Crocheting; Embroidery; Weaving**

Bearings (Machinery)   621.8
> *See also* **Lubrication and lubricants**
> *x* Ball bearings; Journals (Machinery)
> *xx* **Lubrication and lubricants; Machinery**

Beasts. *See* **Animals; Domestic animals**

Beat generation. *See* **Bohemianism**

Beatniks. *See* **Bohemianism**

Beautification of landscape. *See* **Landscape protection**

Beauty. *See* **Aesthetics**

Beauty, Personal. *See* **Personal grooming**

Beauty shops   646.7
> *See also* **Cosmetics**

Beavers   599.32
> *xx* **Freshwater animals; Furbearing animals**

Bed and breakfast accommodations. *See* **Hotels, motels, etc.**

Bedouins   305.892; 909
> *xx* **Arabs**

Bedspreads   746.9
> *x* Coverlets
> *xx* **Interior design**

Bedtime   E
> *See also* **Lullabies**
> *x* Getting ready for bed
> *xx* **Night; Sleep**

Bee. *See* **Bees**

Beef   641.3; 664
> *xx* **Meat**

Beef cattle   636.2
> *See also* names of breeds of beef cattle, e.g. **Hereford cattle;** etc.

Beef cattle—*Continued*

    x Steers

    xx **Cattle**

Bees 595.79; 638

    See also **Honey**

    x Apiculture; Bee; Hymenoptera

    xx **Honey; Insects**

Begging 362.5

    See also **Tramps**

    x Mendicancy; Panhandling

    xx **Tramps**

Beginning reading materials. *See* **Easy reading materials**

Behavior. *See* **Animals—Behavior; Human behavior**

Behavior, Compulsive. *See* **Compulsive behavior**

Behavior genetics 155.7

    x Psychogenetics

    xx **Genetics; Psychology**

Behavior, Helping. *See* **Helping behavior**

Behavior modification 153.8

    See also **Brainwashing**

    xx **Human behavior; Learning, Psychology of; Psychology, Applied**

Behavior problems (Children). *See* **Emotionally disturbed children**

Behavior, Sexual. *See* **Sexual behavior**

Behaviorism 150.19

    Use for materials on the conception of psychology that claims that the proper subject matter of psychology is the objectively observable actions of organisms and not the study of mental phenomena.

    xx **Human behavior; Psychology; Psychophysiology**

Beijing Massacre, 1989. *See* **China—History—1989, Tiananmen Square Incident**

Belief and doubt 121

    Use for materials on belief and doubt from the philosophical standpoint. Materials on religious belief and doubt are entered under **Faith.**

    See also **Agnosticism; Rationalism; Skepticism; Truth**

    x Certainty; Doubt

    xx **Agnosticism; Emotions; Knowledge, Theory of; Philosophy; Rationalism; Religion; Skepticism**

Bell System Telstar satellite. *See* **Telstar project**

Belles lettres. *See* **Literature**

Bells 786.8

    x Carillons; Chimes; Church bells

Belts and belting 621.8

    See also **Power transmission**

    x Chain belting

    xx **Machinery; Power transmission**

Beneficial insects 591.6

    See also **Insect pests;** also names of beneficial insects, e.g. **Silkworms;** etc.

    x Economic entomology; Entomology, Economic; Helpful insects; Insects, Injurious and beneficial; Useful insects

    xx **Insect pests; Insects; Zoology, Economic**

Benevolent institutions. *See* **Institutional care**

Beowulf—Adaptations   829
Bequests.   *See* **Gifts; Inheritance and succession;
    Wills**
Bereavement   155.9; 248.8
    See also **Sympathy**
    xx **Death; Sympathy**
Bermuda Triangle   001.9
    x Devil's Triangle; Graveyard of the Atlantic
Berries   634
    Names of all berries are not included in this List
        but are to be added as needed in the plural
        form, e.g. **Strawberries;** etc.
    See also names of berries, e.g. **Strawberries;**
        etc.
    xx **Fruit; Fruit culture**
Best books.   *See* **Books and reading—Best books**
Best sellers (Books)   028; 070.5
    x Books—Best sellers
    xx **Book industries; Books and reading**
Betting.   *See* **Gambling**
Bevel gearing.   *See* **Gearing**
Beverages   613; 641.2; 641.8; 663
    See also names of types of beverages, e.g. **Alco-
        holic beverages; Liquors and liqueurs;** etc.;
        also names of specific beverages, e.g. **Cocoa;
        Coffee;** etc.
    x Drinks
    xx **Diet; Food**
Bias attacks.   *See* **Hate crimes**
Bias crimes.   *See* **Hate crimes**
Bias (Psychology).   *See* **Prejudices**
Bible   220
    The subject subdivisions under **Bible** may be
        used also for any part of the Bible, under
        the same form of entry as for the texts of
        such parts, e.g. **Bible. O.T.—Biography; Bi-
        ble. O.T. Pentateuch—Commentaries; Bible.
        O.T. Psalms—History; Bible. N.T. Gos-
        pels—Inspiration;** etc.
    x Holy Scriptures; Scriptures, Holy
    xx **Hebrew literature; History, Ancient; Jewish
        literature; Sacred books**
Bible and science   220.8
    x Bible—Science; Science and the Bible
    xx **Religion and science**
Bible—Animals.   *See* **Bible—Natural history**
Bible—Antiquities   220.9
    See also **Christian antiquities**
    x Antiquities, Biblical; Archeology, Biblical;
        Biblical archeology
    xx **Antiquities; Archeology**
Bible as literature   809
    See also **Bible—Criticism, interpretation, etc.;
        Bible—Parables; Religious literature**
    x Bible—Language, style, etc.; Bible—Literary
        character
    xx **Religious literature**
Bible—Astronomy   220.8
    xx **Astronomy**
Bible—Biography   220.9
    See also **Women in the Bible**
    x Biblical characters
Bible—Birds.   *See* **Bible—Natural history**
Bible—Botany.   *See* **Bible—Natural history**

Bible—Catechisms, question books   238
   x Bible—Question books
   xx **Bible—Study; Catechisms**
Bible—Chronology   220.9
   Use for materials on the dates of events related
     in the Bible and their correlation with the
     dates of general history.
   x Bible—History of biblical events—
     Chronology; Chronology, Biblical
Bible classes.   *See* **Bible—Study; Summer schools,**
     Religious; Sunday schools
Bible—Commentaries   220.7
   x Bible—Interpretation; Commentaries, Biblical
Bible—Concordances   220.4; 220.5
   x Bible—Indexes; Concordances
   xx **Bible—Dictionaries**
Bible—Criticism, interpretation, etc.   220.6
   x Bible—Exegesis; Bible—Hermeneutics; Bi-
     ble—Interpretation; Exegesis, Biblical; Her-
     meneutics, Biblical; Higher criticism
   xx **Bible as literature; Criticism**
Bible—Dictionaries   220.3
   See also **Bible—Concordances**
   x Bible—Indexes
Bible—Drama   808.2; 808.82; 812, etc.
   See also **Mysteries and miracle plays**
   x Bible plays; Plays, Bible
   xx **Religious drama**
Bible—Evidences, authority, etc.   220.1
   x Evidences of the Bible
   xx **Free thought**
Bible—Exegesis.   *See* **Bible—Criticism, interpreta-**
   tion, etc.
Bible—Fiction.   *See* **Bible—History of biblical**
   events—Fiction
Bible—Flowers.   *See* **Bible—Natural history**
Bible—Gardens.   *See* **Bible—Natural history**
Bible—Geography   220.9
   x Bible—Maps; Geography, Biblical
   xx **Atlases**
Bible—Hermeneutics.   *See* **Bible—Criticism, inter-**
   pretation, etc.
Bible—History   220.9
   Use for materials on the origin, authorship and
     composition of the Bible as a book. Materi-
     als dealing with historical events as de-
     scribed in the Bible are entered under **Bi-**
     ble—History of biblical events.
Bible—History of biblical events   220.9
   See note under **Bible—History.**
   x History, Biblical
Bible—History of biblical events—Chronology.   *See*
   Bible—Chronology
Bible—History of biblical events—Fiction   Fic
   See note under **Bible stories.**
   x Bible—Fiction
Bible—Illustrations.   *See* **Bible—Pictorial works**
Bible in literature   809
   Use for materials that discuss the Bible as a
     theme in literature. An additional subject
     heading may be necessary for the name of
     the literature or the name of the author dis-
     cussed.

Bible in literature—*Continued*

See also **Religion in literature**

xx **Literature; Religion in literature**

Bible in the schools. *See* **Religion in the public schools**

Bible—Indexes. *See* **Bible—Concordances; Bible—Dictionaries**

Bible—Inspiration   220.1

x Inspiration, Biblical

Bible—Interpretation. *See* **Bible—Commentaries; Bible—Criticism, interpretation, etc.**

Bible—Introductions. *See* **Bible—Study**

Bible—Language, style, etc. *See* **Bible as literature**

Bible—Literary character. *See* **Bible as literature**

Bible—Maps. *See* **Bible—Geography**

Bible—Miracles. *See* **Miracles**

Bible. N.T.   225

Use same subject subdivisions as those given under **Bible.** They may be used also for groups of books (e.g. **Bible. N.T. Gospels;** etc.) and for single books (e.g. **Bible. N.T. Matthew;** etc.)

x New Testament

Bible. N.T.—Miracles. *See* **Miracles—Christianity**

Bible—Natural history   220.8

x Bible—Animals; Bible—Birds; Bible—Botany; Bible—Flowers; Bible—Gardens; Bible—Plants; Bible—Zoology; Botany of the Bible; Natural history, Biblical; Zoology of the Bible

xx **Animals in literature; Birds in literature**

Bible. O.T.   221

Use same subject subdivisions as those given under **Bible.** They may be used also for groups of books (e.g. **Bible. O.T. Pentateuch;** etc.) and for single books (e.g. **Bible. N.T. Psalms;** etc.)

x Old Testament

Bible—Parables   226.8

See also **Jesus Christ—Parables**

xx **Bible as literature; Parables**

Bible—Pictorial works   220.022

x Bible—Illustrations

xx **Christian art and symbolism; Jesus Christ—Art**

Bible—Plants. *See* **Bible—Natural history**

Bible plays. *See* **Bible—Drama; Mysteries and miracle plays**

Bible—Prophecies   220.1

See also **Jesus Christ—Prophecies**

x Prophecies (Bible)

Bible—Psychology   220.8

x Psychology, Biblical

Bible—Question books. *See* **Bible—Catechisms, question books**

Bible—Reading   220.5

Bible—Science. *See* **Bible and science**

Bible stories   220.9

Use for materials that retell or adapt stories from the Bible. May also be used for materials about Bible stories. Fiction in which characters and settings are taken from the

Bible stories—*Continued*

>Bible is entered under **Bible—History of biblical events—Fiction.**

  x Stories

Bible—Study 220.07

>*See also* **Bible—Catechisms, question books**

  x Bible classes; Bible—Introductions

  xx **Christian education; Sunday schools**

Bible—Use 220.6

>Use for materials that show how the Bible is used as a guide to living, to cultivation of a spiritual life, and to problems of doctrine.

Bible—Versions 220.4; 220.5

>Use for history of versions, including materials on both the Old Testament and the New Testament.

Bible—Women. *See* **Women in the Bible**

Bible—Zoology. *See* **Bible—Natural history**

Biblical archeology. *See* **Bible—Antiquities**

Biblical characters. *See* **Bible—Biography**

Bibliographic control 025.3

>*See also* **Cataloging; Indexing; Information systems; MARC system**

  x Universal bibliographic control

  xx **Documentation**

Bibliographic data in machine readable form. *See* **Machine readable bibliographic data**

Bibliography 010

>*See also*

Archives	**Indexing**
Bookbinding	**Information systems**
Books	**Library science**
Cataloging	**Manuscripts**
Classification—Books	**Printing**
Indexes	**Serial publications**

>also names of persons, places, and subjects with the subdivision *Bibliography,* e.g. **Shakespeare, William, 1564-1616—Bibliography; United States—Bibliography; Agriculture—Bibliography;** etc.

  xx **Books; Cataloging; Documentation; Library science**

Bibliography—Best books. *See* **Books and reading—Best books**

Bibliography—Bilingual books. *See* **Bilingual books**

Bibliography—Editions 016

>*See also* **Paperback books; Rare books**

  x Bibliography—Reprints; Editions; Reprints

Bibliography—First editions 016

  x Books—First editions; First editions

Bibliography—Reprints. *See* **Bibliography—Editions**

Bibliomania. *See* **Book collecting**

Bibliophily. *See* **Book collecting**

Bicentennial celebrations—United States—1976. *See* **American Revolution Bicentennial, 1776-1976**

Biculturalism (May subdiv. geog.) **306.4**

  xx **Civilization; Culture**

Biculturalism—United States 306.4

  x United States—Biculturalism

Bicycle racing   796.6
>   *x* Racing
>   *xx* **Bicycles and bicycling**

Bicycles and bicycling   629.227; 796.6
>   *See also* **Bicycle racing; Minibikes; Motorcycles; Tricycles**
>   *x* Biking; Cycling

Big band music.   *See* **Dance music**

Big bang theory.   *See* **Universe**

Big books   372.4; E
>   Use as a form heading for books produced in an oversize format, usually with patterned and predictable language, and intended for use in shared-reading learning experiences. May also be used for materials about big books.
>   *See also* **Large print books**
>   *x* Enlarged texts for shared reading; Oversized books for shared reading; Shared reading books
>   *xx* **Children's literature; Large print books; Reading materials**

Big foot.   *See* **Sasquatch**

Bigfoot.   *See* **Sasquatch**

Bigotry.   *See* **Prejudices; Toleration**

Bigotry-motivated crimes.   *See* **Hate crimes**

Biking.   *See* **Bicycles and bicycling**

Bilingual books (May subdiv. by languages)
>   *x* Bibliography—Bilingual books
>   *xx* **Books**

Bilingual books—English-Spanish

Bilingual education   370.19; 371.97
>   *x* Education, Bilingual
>   *xx* **Bilingualism; Intercultural education**

Bilingualism (May subdiv. geog.)   400
>   *See also* **Bilingual education**
>   *xx* **Language and languages**

Bilingualism—United States   420
>   *x* United States—Bilingualism

Billboards.   *See* **Signs and signboards**

Bills and notes.   *See* **Negotiable instruments**

Bills of credit.   *See* **Credit; Negotiable instruments; Paper money**

Bills of fare.   *See* **Menus**

Bimetallism.   *See* **Gold; Monetary policy; Silver**

Binary system (Mathematics)   513.5
>   *x* Pair system
>   *xx* **Mathematics; Numeration**

Binding of books.   *See* **Bookbinding**

Binge eating behavior.   *See* **Bulimia**

Binge-purge behavior.   *See* **Bulimia**

Bio-bibliography.   *See* names of persons, subjects and names of countries, cities, etc. with the subdivision *Bio-bibliography,* e.g. **English literature—Bio-bibliography; United States—Bio-bibliography;** etc.

Bioastronautics.   *See* **Space biology; Space medicine**

Biochemistry   574.19
>   *See also* **Clinical chemistry; Metabolism; Molecular biology; Proteins; Steroids**
>   *x* Biological chemistry; Chemistry, Biological; Chemistry, Physiological; Physiological chemistry
>   *xx* **Biology; Chemistry; Medicine**

Bioconversion.   *See* **Biomass energy**

Bioethics 174

See also **Medical ethics; Transplantation of organs, tissues, etc.—Moral and religious aspects**

x Biological ethics; Biology—Ethics; Biomedical ethics; Ethics, Biological; Life sciences ethics

xx **Social ethics**

Biofeedback training 152.1

x Visceral learning

xx **Feedback (Psychology); Learning, Psychology of; Mind and body; Psychotherapy**

Biogeography 574.9

See also **Plants—Geographical distribution;** also names of plants and animals with the subdivision *Geographical distribution,* e.g. **Fishes—Geographical distribution;** etc.

x Animals—Geographical distribution; Distribution of animals and plants; Geographical distribution of animals and plants; Paleobiogeography; Zoogeography

xx **Ecology; Geography; Natural history**

Biographical dictionaries. See **Biography—Dictionaries**

Biography 920

Use for collections of biographies not limited to one country or to one class of people. Materials dealing with the writing of biography are entered under **Biography (as a literary form).**

See also

Autobiographies	**Men—Biography**
Autographs	**Musicians—Biography**
Celebrities	**Obituaries**
Chicago (Ill.)—Biography	**Portraits**
Epitaphs	**Religions—Biography**
Genealogy	**United States—Biography**
Heraldry	**Women—Biography**

also subjects with the subdivision *Biography* or *Correspondence;* and names of events and wars with the subdivision *Personal narratives,* e.g. **World War, 1939-1945—Personal narratives;** etc.

x Memoirs; Personal narratives

xx **Genealogy; History**

Biography (as a literary form) 809

Use for materials dealing with the writing of biography.

x Autobiography (as a literary form); Autobiography—Technique; Biography—Technique

xx **Authorship; Literature**

Biography—Dictionaries 920.02

Use for collections of biographies that are not limited to one class of people and that are arranged in dictionary form.

See also names of countries with the subdivision *Biography—Dictionaries,* e.g. **United States—Biography—Dictionaries;** etc.

x Biographical dictionaries; Dictionaries, Biographical

xx **Encyclopedias and dictionaries**

Biography—Technique. See **Biography (as a literary form)**

Biological anthropology. See **Physical anthropology**

Biological chemistry. *See* **Biochemistry**
Biological clocks. *See* **Biological rhythms**
Biological control of pests. *See* **Pests—Biological control**
Biological ethics. *See* **Bioethics**
Biological oceanography. *See* **Marine biology; Marine ecology**
Biological parents. *See* **Birthparents**
Biological physics. *See* **Biophysics**
Biological rhythms   574.1
>   *See also* **Jet lag**
>   *x* Biological clocks; Biology—Periodicity; Biorhythms
>   *xx* **Periodicity**
Biological warfare   358; 623.4
>   *x* Bacterial warfare; Germ warfare
>   *xx* **Communicable diseases; Military art and science; Tactics**
Biologists   574.092; 920
>   *xx* **Naturalists**
Biology   574
>   *See also*

Adaptation (Biology)	**Heredity**
Anatomy	**Life (Biology)**
Biochemistry	**Marine biology**
Biomathematics	**Microbiology**
Biophysics	**Natural history**
Botany	**Physiology**
Cells	**Protoplasm**
Cryobiology	**Radiobiology**
Death	**Reproduction**
Embryology	**Sex (Biology)**
Evolution	**Space biology**
Freshwater biology	**Variation (Biology)**
Gaia hypothesis	**Zoology**
Genetics	

>   *x* Morphology
>   *xx* **Evolution; Life (Biology); Life sciences; Natural history; Science**
Biology—Ecology. *See* **Ecology**
Biology, Economic. *See* **Botany, Economic; Zoology, Economic**
Biology—Ethics. *See* **Bioethics**
Biology, Marine. *See* **Marine biology**
Biology, Molecular. *See* **Molecular biology**
Biology—Periodicity. *See* **Biological rhythms**
Biology—Social aspects. *See* **Sociobiology**
Bioluminescence   574.19
>   *x* Animal light; Light production in animals; Luminescence, Animal
>   *xx* **Phosphorescence**
Biomass energy   333.95
>   Use for materials on the production of energy from a composition of living matter and organic waste.
>   *See also* names of matter as fuels, e.g. **Alcohol as fuel; Waste products as fuel;** etc.
>   *x* Bioconversion; Energy, Biomass; Energy conversion, Microbial; Microbial energy conversion
>   *xx* **Energy resources; Fuel; Waste products as fuel**
Biomass energy industries   338.2; 338.4
Biomathematics   574.01
>   *xx* **Biology; Mathematics**

Biomechanics. *See* **Human engineering**

Biomedical ethics. *See* **Bioethics**

Bionics   003

    Use for materials on the science of technological systems that function in the manner of living systems.

    See also **Artificial intelligence; Optical data processing**

    xx **Biophysics; Cybernetics; Systems engineering**

Biophysics   574.19

    See also **Bionics; Molecular biology; Radiobiology**

    x Biological physics; Molecular physiology; Physics, Biological; Physiology, Molecular

    xx **Biology; Physics**

Biorhythms. *See* **Biological rhythms**

Biosciences. *See* **Life sciences**

Biosociology. *See* **Sociobiology**

Biotechnology   620.8; 660

    Use for materials on the application of living organisms or their biological systems or processes to the manufacture of products.

    See also **Genetic engineering**

    xx **Chemical engineering; Genetic engineering; Microbiology**

Biplanes. *See* **Airplanes**

Bird. *See* **Birds**

Bird decoys (Hunting). *See* **Decoys (Hunting)**

Bird houses   690

Bird photography. *See* **Photography of birds**

Bird repelling devices. *See* **Scarecrows**

Bird song   598.259

    x Birds—Song

Bird watching   598.07

Birdbanding   598.07

    x Birds—Banding; Birds—Marking

Birds (May subdiv. geog.)   **598**

    Names of all birds are not included in this List but are to be added as needed, in the plural form, e.g. **Canaries; Robins;** etc.

    See also classes of birds, e.g. **Birds of prey; Cage birds; Game and game birds; State birds; Water birds;** etc.; and names of specific birds, e.g. **Canaries; Peacocks; Robins;** etc.

    x Bird; Ornithology

    xx **Vertebrates; Zoology**

Birds—Anatomy   598

    xx **Anatomy**

Birds, Aquatic. *See* **Water birds**

Birds—Banding. *See* **Birdbanding**

Birds—Behavior   598.251

    x Birds—Habits and behavior

Birds—Collection and preservation   579

    xx **Collectors and collecting; Taxidermy; Zoological specimens—Collection and preservation**

Birds—Color   598.257

    xx **Color**

Birds' eggs. *See* **Birds—Eggs and nests**

Birds—Eggs and nests   598.256

    x Birds' eggs; Birds' nests; Nests

    xx **Eggs**

Birds—Flight   598

Birds—Habits and behavior. *See* **Birds—Behavior**

Birds in literature   809
　　See also **Bible—Natural history**
　　xx **Nature in literature**
Birds—Marking.   *See* **Birdbanding**
Birds—Migration   598.252
　　x Migration of birds
　　xx **Animals—Migration**
Birds' nests.   *See* **Birds—Eggs and nests**
Birds of prey   598.9
　　See also names of birds of prey, e.g. **Eagles;**
　　　　etc.
　　xx **Birds**
Birds—Photography.   *See* **Photography of birds**
Birds—Protection   333.95; 639.9
　　See also **Game protection**
　　x Protection of birds
　　xx **Game protection; Wildlife conservation**
Birds—Song.   *See* **Bird song**
Birds—United States   598.2973
　　x United States—Birds
Birth.   *See* **Childbirth**
Birth control   176; 350.81; 363.9; 613.9
　　See also **Abortion; Birthrate; Childlessness;**
　　　　Family size; Fertility, Human; Sterilization
　　　　(Birth control)
　　x Conception—Prevention; Contraception;
　　　　Family planning; Fertility control; Planned
　　　　parenthood
　　xx **Birthrate; Eugenics; Family size; Fertility,**
　　　　Human; Population; Sexual ethics; Sexual
　　　　hygiene
Birth control—Moral and religious aspects   176;
　　　　241; 261.8
　　See also **Pro-choice movement; Pro-life move-**
　　　　ment
　　xx **Ethics**
Birth defects   616
　　See also **Growth disorders; Monsters**
　　x Abnormalities, Human; Birth injuries; Defor-
　　　　mities; Human abnormalities; Infants—
　　　　Birth defects; Malformations, Congenital
　　xx **Growth disorders; Medical genetics; Mon-**
　　　　sters; Pathology
Birth injuries.   *See* **Birth defects**
Birth, Multiple.   *See* **Multiple birth**
Birth order   306.87
　　x Firstborn child; Middle child; Oldest child;
　　　　Sibling sequence; Youngest child
　　xx **Children; Family**
Birth rate.   *See* **Birthrate**
Birth records.   *See* **Registers of births, etc.**
Birthdays   392
　　x Days
Birthparents   306.874
　　Use for materials on natural, i.e. biological, par-
　　　　ents who relinquished their children for
　　　　adoption.
　　See also **Adoptees**
　　x Biological parents; Natural parents; Parents,
　　　　Biological
　　xx **Adoptees**
Birthrate   304.6
　　See also **Birth control; Fertility, Human; Popula-**
　　　　tion

107

Birthrate—*Continued*

    x Birth rate

    xx **Birth control; Population**

Births, Registers of. *See* **Registers of births, etc.**

Bison 599.73; 636.2

    x American bison; Buffalo, American

    xx **Endangered species**

Bituminous coal. *See* **Coal**

Black actors 791.4; 792; 920

    x Actors, Black; Black actors and actresses;
        Black actresses; Black men actors

    xx **Actors**

Black actors and actresses. *See* **Black actors**

Black actresses. *See* **Black actors**

Black Africa. *See* **Sub-Saharan Africa**

Black Americans. *See* **Blacks**

Black art 704

    See note under **Blacks in art.**

    See also **Black artists; Harlem Renaissance**

    x Art, Black; Blacks—Art

    xx **Black artists**

Black art (Magic). *See* **Witchcraft**

Black artists 709.2; 920

    Use same pattern for Blacks in other occupa-
        tions and professions, e.g. **Black librarians;**
        etc.

    See also **Black art**

    x Artists, Black

    xx **Artists; Black art**

Black athletes 796.092; 920

    x Athletes, Black

    xx **Athletes**

Black authors 809; 920

    See also individual literatures and forms of lit-
        erature with the subdivision *Black authors,*
        e.g. **American literature—Black authors;**
        American poetry—Black authors; etc.

    x Authors, Black

    xx **Authors**

Black business people 338.092; 658.0092; 920

    x Business people, Black

    xx **Blacks—Employment; Business people**

Black children 305.23

    x Blacks—Children; Children, Black

    xx **Children**

Black death. *See* **Plague**

Black folk songs. *See* **Black songs**

Black folklore. *See* **Blacks—Folklore**

Black Friars. *See* **Dominicans (Religious order)**

Black Hawk War, 1832 973.5

    xx **Indians of North America—Wars; United**
        States—History—1815-1861

Black holes (Astronomy) 523.8

    x Frozen stars

    xx **Astronomy; Astrophysics; Stars**

Black lead. *See* **Graphite**

Black librarians 020.92; 920

    x Librarians, Black

    xx **Librarians**

Black literature (American). *See* **American litera-**
        ture—Black authors

Black magic (Witchcraft). *See* **Witchcraft**

Black market children. *See* **Adoption—Corrupt
practices**
Black men actors. *See* **Black actors**
Black music   780.089
See also **Black songs; Blacks—Songs and music;
Blues music; Gospel music; Harlem Renaissance; Rap music**
x Music, Black
xx **Blacks—Songs and music**
Black musicians   780.92; 920
x Musicians, Black
Black Muslims   297
x Muslims, Black; Nation of Islam
xx **Black nationalism; Blacks—Religion; Muslims—United States; United States—Race
relations**
Black nationalism   320.5
See also **Black Muslims**
x Black separatism; Nationalism, Black; Separatism, Black
xx **Blacks—Political activity; Blacks—Race identity**
Black poetry (American). *See* **American poetry—
Black authors**
Black power   322.4
xx **Blacks—Civil rights; Blacks—Economic conditions; Blacks—Political activity**
Black separatism. *See* **Black nationalism**
Black songs   782.42
See also **Blacks—Songs and music; Spirituals
(Songs)**
x Black folk songs; Folk songs, Black (Ameri-
can)
xx **Black music; Blacks—Songs and music; Mu-
sic, American; Songs; Songs, American;
Spirituals (Songs)**
Black suffrage. *See* **Blacks—Suffrage**
Black women   305.48
x Women, Black
xx **Women**
Blackboard drawing. *See* **Chalk talks; Crayon
drawing**
Blackheads (Acne). *See* **Acne**
Blackouts, Electric power. *See* **Electric power fail-
ures**
Blackouts in war. *See* **Civil defense**
Blacks (May subdiv. geog.)   **305.896**
Use for materials dealing collectively with
Blacks in the United States or with Blacks
in geographic areas outside the United
States.
Geographic subdivisions may be used for mate-
rials limited in scope to a particular area of
the United States, e.g. **Blacks—Arkansas;
Blacks—Chicago (Ill.); Blacks—Southern
States.** Geographic subdivisions may also
be used for materials dealing with Blacks in
other regions, countries, etc., e.g. **Blacks—
Africa; Blacks—France;** etc.
See also **Libraries and Blacks; Slavery—United
States**
x African Americans; Afro-Americans; Black
Americans; Blacks—United States; Negroes
xx **Ethnology; Slavery—United States**

Blacks—Africa   305.896; 960
  xx **Africans**
Blacks and libraries.   *See* **Libraries and Blacks**
Blacks—Arkansas   305.896; 976.7
Blacks—Art.   *See* **Black art**
Blacks—Biography   920
Blacks—Chicago (Ill.)   305.896; 977.3
Blacks—Children.   *See* **Black children**
Blacks—Civil rights   323.1; 342
  See also **Black power**
  x Demonstrations for Black civil rights—
      United States; Freedom marches—United
      States; Marches for Black civil rights—
      United States
  xx **Blacks—Political activity; Civil rights**
Blacks—Economic conditions   330.973
  See also **Black power**
  xx **Economic conditions**
Blacks—Education   370.19
  See also **School integration; Segregation in edu-
      cation**
  xx **Education**
Blacks—Employment   331.6
  See also **Black business people**
  x Blacks—Occupations
  xx **Discrimination in employment; Employment**
Blacks—Folklore   398.2
  x Black folklore; Folklore, Black
  xx **Folklore**
Blacks—France   305.896; 944
Blacks—Housing   307.3; 363.5
  x Housing, Black
  xx **Housing**
Blacks in art   704.9
  Use for materials on Blacks depicted in works of
      art. Materials on the attainments of Blacks
      in the area of art are entered under **Black
      artists.** Materials on works of art by Black
      artists are entered under **Black art.**
  xx **Art**
Blacks in literature   809
  Use for materials on the theme of Blacks in
      works of literature. Materials on the attain-
      ments of Blacks in the area of literature are
      entered under **Black authors.** Materials on
      works of literature by Black authors are en-
      tered under individual literatures and forms
      of literature with the subdivision *Black au-
      thors,* e.g. **American literature—Black au-
      thors; American poetry—Black authors;** etc.
  xx **Characters and characteristics in literature;
      Literature**
Blacks in motion pictures   791.43
  Use for materials on the depiction of Blacks in
      motion pictures. Materials on female or
      male Black actors are entered under **Black
      actors.** Materials discussing all aspects of
      Blacks' involvement in motion pictures are
      entered under **Blacks in the motion picture
      industry.**
  xx **Motion pictures**
Blacks in the motion picture industry   791.43092
  See note under **Blacks in motion pictures.**
  xx **Motion picture industry**

Blacks—Integration 305.896
    See also **School integration**
    x Integration, Racial
Blacks—Intellectual life 305.896
    x Intellectual life
Blacks—Occupations. *See* **Blacks—Employment**
Blacks—Political activity 322.4; 324
    See also **Black nationalism; Black power;**
        Blacks—Civil rights
Blacks—Race identity 305.896
    See also **Black nationalism**
    x Negritude
    xx **Race awareness**
Blacks—Religion 270.089; 299; 305.896
    See also **Black Muslims**
    xx **Religion**
Blacks—Segregation 305.896
    See also **Segregation in education**
    xx **Segregation**
Blacks—Social conditions 305.896
    xx **Social conditions**
Blacks—Social life and customs 305.896
Blacks—Songs and music 780.89
    See also **Black music; Black songs**
    xx **Black music; Black songs**
Blacks—Southern States 305.896; 975
Blacks—Suffrage 324.6
    x Black suffrage
    xx **Suffrage**
Blacks—United States. *See* **Blacks**
Blacksmithing 682
    See also **Forging; Welding**
    x Farriering; Horseshoeing
    xx **Forging; Ironwork**
Blast furnaces 669
    xx **Furnaces; Smelting**
Blast shelters. *See* **Air raid shelters**
Bleaching 667
    See also **Dyes and dyeing**
    xx **Chemistry, Technical; Cleaning; Dyes and**
        dyeing; Textile industry
Blended family. *See* **Stepfamily**
Blessed Virgin Mary. *See* **Mary, Blessed Virgin,**
    Saint
Blimps. *See* **Airships**
Blind 362.4
    xx **Physically handicapped; Vision disorders**
Blind—Books and reading 011.63; 027.6; 028
    See also **Large print books; Talking books**
    x Books for the blind; Braille books
Blind, Dogs for the. *See* **Guide dogs**
Blind—Education 371.91
    x Blind—Rehabilitation; Education of the blind
    xx **Vocational education; Vocational guidance**
Blind—Institutional care 362.4
    xx **Institutional care**
Blind—Rehabilitation. *See* **Blind—Education**
Blizzards 551.55
    xx **Storms**
Block grants. *See* **Grants-in-aid**
Block printing. *See* **Color prints; Linoleum block**
    printing; Textile printing; Wood engraving;
    Woodcuts
Block signal systems. *See* **Railroads—Signaling**

Blood 591.1; 612.1
> *xx* **Physiology**

Blood—Circulation 591.1; 612.1
> *See also* **Blood pressure; Cardiovascular system**
> *x* Circulation of the blood
> *xx* **Blood pressure; Cardiovascular system; Heart**

Blood—Diseases 616.1
> *See also* names of blood diseases, e.g. **Leukemia;** etc.
> *x* Diseases of the blood

Blood groups 612.1
> *See also* **Blood—Transfusion**
> *x* Rh factor
> *xx* **Heredity**

Blood pressure 612.1
> *See also* **Blood—Circulation; Hypertension**
> *xx* **Blood—Circulation**

Blood—Transfusion 615
> *xx* **Blood groups**

Blowing the whistle. *See* **Whistle blowing**
Blowouts, Oil well. *See* **Oil wells—Blowouts**
Blue collar workers. *See* **Labor**
Blue prints. *See* **Blueprints**

Blueprints 604.2; 692
> *x* Blue prints

Blues music 781.643; 782.42164
> *See also* **Jazz music**
> *x* Blues (Songs, etc.)
> *xx* **Black music; Folk music—United States; Jazz music; Popular music**

Blues (Songs, etc.). *See* **Blues music**
BMEWS. *See* **Ballistic missile early warning system**
Board sailing. *See* **Windsurfing**
Boarding houses. *See* **Hotels, motels, etc.**
Boarding schools. *See* **Private schools**
Boards of education. *See* **School boards**
Boards of health. *See* **Health boards**
Boards of trade. *See* **Chambers of commerce**
Boat building. *See* **Boatbuilding**

Boat racing 797.1
> *See also* names of races
> *x* Motorboat racing; Racing; Yacht racing
> *xx* **Boats and boating**

Boatbuilding 623.8
> *See also* **Shipbuilding; Yachts and yachting**
> *x* Boat building
> *xx* **Boats and boating; Naval architecture; Shipbuilding**

Boating. *See* **Boats and boating**

Boats and boating 797.1
> *See also*

Boat racing	**Motorboats**
Boatbuilding	**Rowing**
Canoes and canoeing	**Sailing**
Catamarans	**Ships**
Houseboats	**Steamboats**
Iceboats	**Submarines**
Marinas	**Yachts and yachting**

> *x* Boating; Locomotion
> *xx* **Sailing; Ships; Water sports**

Boats, Submarine. *See* **Submarines; Submersibles**
Body and mind. *See* **Mind and body**
Body building. *See* **Bodybuilding**

Body care. *See* **Hygiene**
Body heat. *See* **Body temperature**
Body, Human. *See* **Human anatomy; Physiology**
Body language   153.6; 302.2
   xx **Nonverbal communication**
Body temperature   591.1; 612
    See also **Fever**
     x Animals—Temperature; Body heat; Tempera-
       ture, Animal and human; Temperature,
       Body
   xx **Diagnosis; Fever; Physiology**
Body weight control. *See* **Reducing**
Bodybuilding   646.7
    See also **Weight lifting**
    x Body building; Physique
   xx **Exercise; Physical fitness; Weight lifting**
Bodybuilding (Weight lifting). *See* **Weight lifting**
Boers. *See* **Afrikaners**
Bogs. *See* **Marshes**
Bohemianism   306
    See also **Hippies**
    x Beat generation; Beatniks
   xx **Collective settlements; Counter culture; Man-
     ners and customs**
Bolshevism. *See* **Communism**
Bomb shelters. *See* **Air raid shelters**
Bombers   358.4; 623.7
    See also names of bombers, e.g. **B-52 bomber;**
     etc.
   xx **Airplanes; Airplanes, Military**
Bombs   623.4
    Use for materials on bombs in general and those
     to be launched from aircraft.
    See also names of types of bombs, e.g. **Atomic
     bomb; Guided missiles; Hydrogen bomb; In-
     cendiary bombs; Neutron bombs;** etc.
    x Aerial bombs
   xx **Ammunition; Ordnance; Projectiles**
Bombs, Flying. *See* **Guided missiles**
Bombs, Incendiary. *See* **Incendiary bombs**
Bonds   332.63
    See also **Junk bonds; Public debts; Stocks**
   xx **Finance; Investments; Negotiable instruments;
     Public debts; Securities; Stock exchange;
     Stocks**
Bonds—Rating   332.63
   xx **Performance standards**
Bones   596; 611; 612.7
    See also **Fractures; Skeleton**
    x Osteology
   xx **Anatomy; Musculoskeletal system; Physiol-
     ogy; Skeleton**
Bonsai   635.9
    x Kamuti
   xx **Dwarf trees**
Bonus, Soldiers'. *See* **Pensions, Military**
Book awards. *See* **Literary prizes;** and names of
     awards, e.g. **Caldecott Medal books; New-
     bery Medal books;** etc.
Book buying (Libraries). *See* **Libraries—
     Acquisitions**
Book catalogs. *See* **Catalogs, Book**

Book collecting   002.075
   x Bibliomania; Bibliophily
   xx **Book selection; Collectors and collecting**
Book fairs.   *See* **Book industries—Exhibitions**
Book illustration.   *See* **Illustration of books**
Book industries   686
   See also **Best sellers (Books); Bookbinding;**
      Booksellers and bookselling; Paper industry;
      Printing; Publishers and publishing
   x Book industries and trade; Book trade
   xx **Paper industry; Publishers and publishing**
Book industries and trade.   *See* **Book industries**
Book industries—Exhibitions   070.5074; 686.074
   See also **Printing—Exhibitions**
   x Book fairs; Book trade—Exhibitions; Books—
      Exhibitions
   xx **Printing—Exhibitions**
Book lending.   *See* **Library circulation**
Book numbers, Publishers' standard.   *See* **Publish-**
      ers' standard book numbers
Book plates.   *See* **Bookplates**
Book prices.   *See* **Books—Prices**
Book prizes.   *See* **Literary prizes;** and names of
      prizes, e.g. **Caldecott Medal books; New-**
      bery Medal books; etc.
Book rarities.   *See* **Rare books**
Book reviews.   *See* **Books—Reviews**
Book sales.   *See* **Books—Prices**
Book selection   025.2
   Use for materials that discuss the principles of
      book appraisal and how to select books for
      libraries. Lists of recommended books are
      entered under **Books and reading—Best**
      books.
   See also **Book collecting; Books and reading—**
      Best books
   x Books—Appraisal; Books—Selection; Choice
      of books
   xx **Books and reading—Best books; Libraries—**
      Acquisitions; Libraries—Collection develop-
      ment
Book trade.   *See* **Book industries; Booksellers and**
      bookselling; Publishers and publishing
Book trade—Exhibitions.   *See* **Book industries—**
      Exhibitions
Book week, National.   *See* **National book week**
Bookbinding   025.7; 095; 686.3
   x Binding of books
   xx **Bibliography; Book industries; Industrial arts;**
      Leather industry
Bookkeepers.   *See* **Accountants**
Bookkeeping   657
   See also **Accounting; Auditing; Cost accounting;**
      Office equipment and supplies; also names
      of industries, professions, etc. with the sub-
      division *Accounting,* e.g. **Corporations—**
      Accounting; etc.
   xx **Accounting; Business; Business arithmetic;**
      Business education
Bookmobiles   027.4
   xx **Library extension**
Bookplates   025.7
   x Book plates; Ex libris

Books   002
   See also

Authors	**Libraries**
Bibliography	**Literature**
Bilingual books	**Manuscripts**
Cataloging	**Paperback books**
Chapbooks	**Printing**
Illumination of books and	**Publishers and publishing**
manuscripts	**Serial publications**
Illustration of books	

    also headings beginning with the word **Book**

  xx **Bibliography; Literature; Printing; Publishers**
     and publishing; Serial publications

Books and reading   028
    Use for general materials on reading for infor-
      mation and culture, advice to readers, and
      surveys of reading habits.
    See also **Best sellers (Books); Books—Reviews;**
      Libraries; Literature; National book week;
      Reference books; also names of individuals
      and classes of people with the subdivision
      Books and reading, e.g. **Blind—Books and**
      reading; etc.
   x Appraisal of books; Books—Appraisal; Choice
     of books; Evaluation of literature; Litera-
     ture—Evaluation; Reading interests
  xx **Communication; Education; Reading**

Books and reading—Best books   010
    Use for lists of recommended books.
    See also **Book selection**
   x Appraisal of books; Best books; Bibliogra-
     phy—Best books; Books—Appraisal;
     Choice of books; Evaluation of literature;
     Literature—Evaluation
  xx **Book selection; Reference books**

Books and reading for children. *See* **Children—**
     Books and reading

Books—Appraisal. *See* **Book selection; Books and**
     reading; Books and reading—Best books;
     Books—Reviews; Criticism; Literature—
     History and criticism

Books—Best sellers. *See* **Best sellers (Books)**

Books—Catalogs. *See* **Catalogs, Book; Catalogs,**
     Booksellers'; Catalogs, Publishers'

Books—Censorship   025.2; 323.44
   x Banned books; Index librorum prohibitorum;
     Prohibited books
  xx **Censorship; Freedom of the press**

Books—Copyright. *See* **Copyright—Books**

Books—Exhibitions. *See* **Book industries—**
     Exhibitions; Printing—Exhibitions

Books, Filmed. *See* **Film adaptations**

Books—First editions. *See* **Bibliography—First**
     editions

Books for children. *See* **Children's literature**

Books for sight saving. *See* **Large print books**

Books for the blind. *See* **Blind—Books and reading**

Books—Large print. *See* **Large print books**

Books, Paperback. *See* **Paperback books**

Books—Preservation. *See* **Library resources—**
     Conservation and restoration

Books—Prices   002.075
   x Book prices; Book sales; Manuscripts—Prices
  xx **Booksellers and bookselling; Prices**

Books, Rare. *See* **Rare books**
Books—Reviews   028.1; 808
>   *x* Appraisal of books; Book reviews; Books—
>   Appraisal; Evaluation of literature; Litera-
>   ture—Evaluation
>   *xx* **Books and reading; Criticism**
Books, Sacred. *See* **Sacred books**
Books—Selection. *See* **Book selection**
Books, Talking. *See* **Talking books**
Booksellers and bookselling   070.5; 381; 658.8
>   *See also* **Books—Prices; Catalogs, Booksellers';**
>   **Publishers and publishing**
>   *x* Book trade
>   *xx* **Book industries; Publishers and publishing;**
>   **Sales personnel; Selling**
Booksellers' catalogs. *See* **Catalogs, Booksellers'**
Boolean algebra. *See* **Algebra, Boolean**
Boots. *See* **Shoes**
Border life. *See* **Frontier and pioneer life**
Borders (Geography). *See* **Boundaries**
Boring   622
>   Use for materials on the operation of cutting
>   holes in earth or rock. Materials dealing
>   with workshop operations in metal, wood,
>   etc., are entered under **Drilling and boring.**
>   *See also* **Wells**
>   *x* Drilling and boring (Earth and rocks); Shaft
>   sinking; Well boring
>   *xx* **Hydraulic engineering; Mining engineering;**
>   **Natural gas; Petroleum; Tunnels; Water**
>   **supply engineering; Wells**
Boring (Metal, wood, etc.). *See* **Drilling and boring**
Born again Christians. *See* **Regeneration (Chris-**
>   **tianity)**
Borrowing money. *See* **Loans**
Boss rule. *See* **Corruption in politics**
Botanical chemistry   581.1
>   *See also* **Plants—Analysis**
>   *x* Chemistry, Botanical; Plant chemistry
>   *xx* **Chemistry**
Botanical gardens   580.74
>   *See also* names of botanical gardens
>   *xx* **Gardens; Parks**
Botanical specimens—Collection and
>   preservation. *See* **Plants—Collection and**
>   **preservation**
Botanists   581.092; 920
>   *xx* **Naturalists**
Botany   581
>   *See also*

Bulbs	**Plants, Fossil**
Flower gardening	**Seeds**
Flowers	**Shrubs**
Fruit	**Trees**
Grafting	**Variation (Biology)**
Leaves	**Vegetables**
Plant physiology	**Weeds**
Plants	

>   *x* Flora; Vegetable kingdom

>   *xx* **Biology; Natural history; Nature study; Sci-**
>   **ence**
Botany, Agricultural. *See* **Botany, Economic**

Botany—Anatomy   581.4
   x Anatomy of plants; Anatomy, Vegetable; Bot-
       any—Structure; Morphology; Plant anat-
       omy; Plants—Anatomy; Structural botany;
       Vegetable anatomy
  xx **Anatomy**
Botany—Ecology   581.5
   See also **Desert plants**
   x Plants—Ecology; Symbiosis
   xx **Ecology; Forest influences**
Botany, Economic   581.6
   See also

Cotton	**Plant conservation**
Edible plants	**Plant introduction**
Forest products	**Poisonous plants**
Grain	**Weeds**
Grasses	

   x Agricultural botany; Biology, Economic; Bot-
       any, Agricultural; Economic botany; Plants,
       Useful
   xx **Agriculture**
Botany, Fossil.   *See* **Plants, Fossil**
Botany, Medical   581.6
   x Drug plants; Herbal medicine; Herbals;
       Herbs, Medical; Medical botany; Medicinal
       plants; Plants, Medicinal
   xx **Medicine; Pharmacy**
Botany—Nomenclature.   *See* **Botany—**
      Terminology; Plant names, Popular
Botany of the Bible.   *See* **Bible—Natural history**
Botany—Pathology.   *See* **Plant diseases**
Botany—Physiology.   *See* **Plant physiology**
Botany—Structure.   *See* **Botany—Anatomy**
Botany—Terminology   581.01
   Use for materials on the scientific names of
      plants, etc. Materials on popular names are
      entered under **Plant names, Popular.**
   See also **Plant names, Popular**
   x Botany—Nomenclature; Plant names, Scien-
      tific
   xx **Plant names, Popular**
Botany—United States.   *See* **Plants—United States**
Boulder Dam (Ariz. and Nev.).   *See* **Hoover Dam**
      (Ariz. and Nev.)
Boulevards.   *See* **Streets**
Boundaries   320.1; 341.4
   See also **Geopolitics;** also names of wars with the
      subdivision *Territorial questions,* e.g.
      World War, 1939-1945—Territorial ques-
      tions; etc.; and names of countries, cities,
      etc. with the subdivision *Boundaries,* e.g.
      United States—Boundaries; etc.
   x Borders (Geography); Frontiers; Geography,
      Political; Political boundaries; Political ge-
      ography
   xx **Geography; Geopolitics; International law; In-**
      ternational relations
Bounties.   *See* **Subsidies**
Bourgeoisie.   *See* **Middle classes**
Bow and arrow   799.3
   See also **Archery**
   x Arrow
   xx **Archery**
Bowed instruments.   *See* **Stringed instruments**

Bowling   794.6; 796.31
   x Tenpins
Boxes   688.8; 745.593
   x Boxes, Ornamental; Boxes, Wooden; Contain-
      ers, Box; Crates
   xx **Packaging**
Boxes—Collectors and collecting   745.593
Boxes, Ornamental.   *See* **Boxes**
Boxes, Wooden.   *See* **Boxes**
Boxing   796.8
   x Fighting; Prize fighting; Pugilism; Sparring
   xx **Athletics; Self-defense**
Boy Scouts (May subdiv. geog.)   369.43
   x Cub Scouts
   xx **Boys' clubs; Scouts and scouting**
Boycott   327.1; 331.89; 338.6; 341.5
   xx **Passive resistance**
Boys   155.43; 305.23
   See also **Children; Fathers and sons; Mothers
      and sons; Teenagers; Young men**
   xx **Children; Teenagers; Young men**
Boys' agricultural clubs.   *See* **4-H clubs; Agricul-
      ture—Societies; Boys' clubs**
Boys' clubs   369.42
   See also **4-H clubs; Boy Scouts**
   x Boys' agricultural clubs; Boys—Societies
   xx **Clubs; Men—Societies; Social settlements;
      Societies**
Boys—Employment.   *See* **Children—Employment**
Boys—Societies.   *See* **Boys' clubs**
Boys, Teenage.   *See* **Teenagers**
Boys' towns.   *See* **Children—Institutional care**
Brahmanism   294.5
   See also **Caste; Hinduism**
   xx **Buddhism; Hinduism; Religions**
Braille books.   *See* **Blind—Books and reading**
Brain   596; 611; 612.8
   See also

Dreams	**Nervous system**
Head	**Phrenology**
Memory	**Psychology**
Mind and body	**Sleep**

   xx **Head; Nervous system**
Brain damaged children   618.92
   xx **Exceptional children; Handicapped children**
Brain death   616.07
   x Irreversible coma
   xx **Death**
Brain—Diseases   616.8
   See also **Alzheimer's disease; Cerebral palsy**
Brain, Electronic.   *See* **Computers**
Brain opioids.   *See* **Endorphins**
Brain storming.   *See* **Problem solving, Group**
Brainwashing   153.8
   Use for materials on the forcible indoctrination
      of an individual or group in order to alter
      basic political, social, religious, or moral be-
      liefs.
   x Deprogramming; Forced indoctrination; In-
      doctrination, Forced; Mind control;
      Thought control; Will
   xx **Behavior modification; Learning, Psychology
      of; Mental suggestion; Psychological war-
      fare**

Brakes 625.2; 629.2

> *See also* subjects with the subdivision *Brakes,*
> e.g. **Automobiles—Brakes;** etc.
>
> *xx* **Railroads—Safety appliances**

Branch stores. *See* **Chain stores**

Brand name products 380.1; 658.8

> *See also* **Trademarks**
>
> *x* Products, Brand name
>
> *xx* **Commercial products; Manufactures; Trade-**
> **marks**

Brass 669; 673

> *See also* **Brasses**
>
> *xx* **Alloys; Founding; Zinc**

Brass instruments. *See* **Wind instruments**

Brasses 739.5

> *x* Monumental brasses; Sepulchral brasses
>
> *xx* **Archeology; Art; Brass; Inscriptions; Sculp-**
> **ture; Tombs**

Bravery. *See* **Courage**

Brazilian literature 869

> May use same subdivisions and names of liter-
> ary forms as for **English literature.**
>
> *See also* **Portuguese literature**
>
> *xx* **Latin American literature; Portuguese litera-**
> **ture**

Brazing. *See* **Solder and soldering**

Bread 641.8; 664

> *xx* **Baking; Cookery; Food**

Breadstuffs. *See* **Flour; Grain; Wheat**

Break dancing 793.3

> *xx* **Dancing**

Breakers. *See* **Ocean waves**

Breakfast cereals. *See* **Prepared cereals**

Breakfasts 642

> *x* Meals
>
> *xx* **Caterers and catering; Cookery; Menus**

Breast feeding 649

> *x* Nursing (Infant feeding)
>
> *xx* **Infants—Nutrition**

Breathing. *See* **Respiration**

Breeder reactors. *See* **Nuclear reactors**

Breeding 581.1; 631.5; 636.08

> *See also* **Domestic animals; Genetics; Heredity;**
> **Mendel's law; Plant breeding;** also subdivi-
> sion *Breeding* under particular animals, e.g.
> **Dogs—Breeding; Horses—Breeding; Live-**
> **stock—Breeding;** etc.
>
> *x* Selection, Artificial
>
> *xx* **Genetics**

Breeding behavior. *See* **Sexual behavior in animals**

Bricklaying 693

> *See also* **Masonry**
>
> *xx* **Bricks; Building; Masonry**

Bricks 666; 691

> *See also* **Bricklaying; Tiles**
>
> *xx* **Building materials; Clay; Clay industries**

Bridal customs. *See* **Marriage customs and rites**

Bridge (Game) 795.4

> *x* Auction bridge; Contract bridge; Duplicate
> bridge
>
> *xx* **Card games**

Bridges (May subdiv. geog. by countries, states, cities, etc., and by rivers) **624; 725**

Bridges—*Continued*

    See also names of bridges, e.g. **Golden Gate Bridge (San Francisco, Calif.);** etc.

    x Suspension bridges; Viaducts

    xx **Building, Iron and steel; Civil engineering; Masonry; Transportation**

Bridges—Chicago (Ill.)   624

    x Chicago (Ill.)—Bridges

Bridges—Hudson River (N.Y.).   *See* **Bridges— Hudson River (N.Y. and N.J.)**

Bridges—Hudson River (N.Y. and N.J.)   624

    x Bridges—Hudson River (N.Y.); Hudson River (N.Y. and N.J.)—Bridges

Brigands.   *See* **Robbers and outlaws**

Bright children.   *See* **Gifted children**

British Commonwealth of Nations.   *See* **Commonwealth of Nations**

British Dominions.   *See* **Commonwealth of Nations**

British Empire.   *See* **Great Britain—Colonies**

Broadcast journalism   070.4

    See also **Journalism**

    x News broadcasting; Radio journalism; Radio news; Television journalism; Television news

    xx **Broadcasting; Journalism; Press**

Broadcasting   384.5

    See also **Broadcast journalism; Minorities in broadcasting; Radio broadcasting; Television broadcasting**

    xx **Telecommunication**

Bronze Age   930.1

    See also **Archeology; Iron Age**

    x Prehistory

    xx **Archeology; Iron Age; Prehistoric man**

Bronzes   739.5

    xx **Archeology; Art; Art metalwork; Decoration and ornament; Metalwork; Sculpture**

Brothers and sisters   155.44; 306.875

    See also **Twins**

    x Siblings; Sisters and brothers

    xx **Family; Twins**

Brownouts.   *See* **Electric power failures**

Brutality.   *See* **Cruelty**

Bubonic plague.   *See* **Plague**

Buccaneers.   *See* **Pirates**

Buddhism   294.3

    See also **Brahmanism; Zen Buddhism**

    xx **Religions**

Buddhist art.   *See* **Art, Buddhist**

Budget (May subdiv. geog.)   **351.72**

    Use for materials on the budget or reports on the appropriations and expenditures of a government.

    See also **Finance**

    xx **Finance**

Budget—United States   353.0072

    See also **United States—Appropriations and expenditures**

    x Federal budget; United States—Budget

Budgets, Business   658.15

    x Business—Budget

    xx **Business**

Budgets, Household   640

   x Domestic finance; Family budget; Finance,
       Household; Home economics—Accounting;
       Household budget; Household finances

   xx Cost of living; Personal finance

Budgets, Personal.   *See* **Personal finance**

Buffalo, American.   *See* **Bison**

Buffing.   *See* **Grinding and polishing**

Bugging, Electronic.   *See* **Eavesdropping**

Building   690

   See also

Architecture	**Foundations**
Bricklaying	**House construction**
Carpentry	**Masonry**
Chimneys	**Roofs**
Concrete construction	**Sanitary engineering**
Doors	**Strength of materials**
Engineering	**Walls**
Floors	**Windows**

   x Architectural engineering; Construction

   **xx Architecture; Carpentry; Houses; Structural
      engineering; Structures, Theory of; Technol-
      ogy**

Building and earthquakes.   *See* **Buildings—
   Earthquake effects**

Building and loan associations.   *See* **Savings and
   loan associations**

Building, Concrete.   *See* **Concrete construction**

Building contracts.   *See* **Building—Contracts and
   specifications**

Building—Contracts and specifications   692

   x Building contracts; Building—Specifications

   xx Contracts

Building—Estimates   692

Building failures   690; 721

   xx Structural failures

Building, House.   *See* **House construction**

Building, Iron and steel   693

   See also **Bridges; Roofs; Skyscrapers; Steel,
      Structural; Strength of materials; Structures,
      Theory of**

   x Architectural engineering; Iron and steel
      building; Steel construction

   xx Iron; Steel; Steel, Structural

Building materials   691

   All types of building materials are not included
      in this List but are to be added as needed.

   See also

Bricks	**Strength of materials**
Cement	**Structural engineering**
Concrete	**Stucco**
Glass construction	**Terra cotta**
Reinforced concrete	**Tiles**
Steel, Structural	**Wood**
Stone	

   x Structural materials

   **xx Architecture; Engineering; Materials;
      Strength of materials**

Building repair.   *See* **Buildings—Maintenance and
   repair**

Building—Repair and reconstruction.   *See* **Buildings—Maintenance and repair**

Building security.   *See* **Burglary protection**

Building—Specifications. *See* **Building—Contracts and specifications**

Buildings (May subdiv. geog.) 690; 720
    See also **Historic buildings;** also names of types of buildings and construction, e.g. **Farm buildings; Industrial buildings; Prefabricated buildings; School buildings;** etc.; also names of institutions with the subdivision *Buildings,* e.g. **Colleges and universities—Buildings;** etc.; and names of specific buildings

Buildings, College. *See* **Colleges and universities—Buildings**

Buildings—Earthquake effects 693.8
    Use for materials on the design and construction of buildings to withstand earthquakes.
    x Building and earthquakes; Earthquakes and building
    xx **Earthquakes**

Buildings, Farm. *See* **Farm buildings**

Buildings, Historic. *See* **Historic buildings**

Buildings, Industrial. *See* **Industrial buildings**

Buildings, Library. *See* **Library architecture**

Buildings—Maintenance and repair 690
    See also **Architecture—Conservation and restoration; Houses—Maintenance and repair**
    x Building repair; Building—Repair and reconstruction; Maintenance and repair
    xx **Architecture—Conservation and restoration; Repairing**

Buildings, Office. *See* **Office buildings**

Buildings, Prefabricated. *See* **Prefabricated buildings**

Buildings, Public. *See* **Public buildings;** and names of cities, states, etc. with the subdivision *Public buildings,* e.g. **Chicago (Ill.)—Public buildings;** etc.; and names of countries with the subdivision *Public buildings* for that government's public buildings located within the country, as well as for embassies, consulates, and other public buildings of that country in foreign locations, e.g. **United States—Public buildings;** etc.

Buildings—Remodeling 643; 690
    x Remodeling of buildings

Buildings, Restoration of. *See* **Architecture—Conservation and restoration**

Buildings, School. *See* **School buildings**

Buildings—Security. *See* **Burglary protection**

Built-in furniture 684.1; 749
    x Furniture, Built-in
    xx **Furniture**

Bulbs 584; 635.9
    xx **Botany; Flower gardening; Gardening**

Bulge, Battle of the. *See* **Ardennes, Battle of the, 1944-1945**

Bulimarexia. *See* **Bulimia**

Bulimia 616.85
    x Binge eating behavior; Binge-purge behavior; Bulimarexia; Bulimia nervosa; Gorge-purge syndrome
    xx **Eating disorders**

Bulimia nervosa. *See* **Bulimia**

Bulletin boards   021.7; 371.3
   See also **Computer bulletin boards**
   xx **Teaching—Aids and devices**
Bullets. *See* **Projectiles**
Bullfights   791.8
   x Fighting
Bullion. *See* **Gold; Money; Silver**
Bunker Hill (Boston, Mass.), Battle of, 1775—Poetry
     811
   xx **Poetry**
Bunnies. *See* **Rabbits**
Bunny rabbits. *See* **Rabbits**
Bureaucracy   302.3
   See also **Civil service**
   xx **Civil service; Political science; Public adminis-**
     tration
Burglar alarms   621.389
   xx **Burglary protection; Electric apparatus and**
     appliances
Burglars. *See* **Robbers and outlaws**
Burglary protection   621.389; 643
   See also types of protective devices, e.g. **Bur-**
     glar alarms; Locks and keys; etc.; also types
     of buildings with the subdivision *Security*
     measures, e.g. **Nuclear power plants—**
     Security measures; etc.
   x Building security; Buildings—Security; Protec-
     tion against burglary; Residential security
Burial. *See* **Catacombs; Cemeteries; Cremation;**
     Cryonics; Epitaphs; Funeral rites and cere-
     monies; Mounds and mound builders; Mum-
     mies; Tombs
Burial statistics. *See* **Mortality; Registers of births,**
     etc.; Vital statistics; and names of coun-
     tries, cities, etc. with the subdivision
     Statistics, e.g. **United States—Statistics;**
     etc.
Buried cities. *See* **Cities and towns, Ruined, extinct,**
     etc.
Buried treasure   622; 910.4
   x Hidden treasure; Sunken treasure; Treasure
     trove
Burn out (Psychology)   158.7
   x Burnout syndrome
   xx **Job satisfaction; Job stress; Mental health;**
     Motivation (Psychology); Occupational
     health and safety; Stress (Psychology)
Burnout syndrome. *See* **Burn out (Psychology)**
Burying grounds. *See* **Cemeteries**
Buses   388.4; 629.222
   x Motor buses
   xx **Automobiles; Local transit; Transportation,**
     Highway
Bush survival. *See* **Wilderness survival**
Business   650
   See also

Accounting	**Commercial law**
Advertising	**Competition**
Banks and banking	**Corporations**
Bookkeeping	**Credit**
Budgets, Business	**Customer relations**
Business failures	**Department stores**
Business people	**Economic conditions**

Business—*Continued*

Efficiency, Industrial	Markets
Electronic spreadsheets	Merchants
Entrepreneurship	Occupations
Home business	Office management
Industrial management	Profit
Instalment plan	Real estate business
Mail-order business	Selling
Manufactures	Small business
Marketing	Trust companies

   x Trade

   xx **Commerce; Economics; Industrial management**

Business administration. *See* **Industrial management**

Business and government. *See* **Industry—Government policy**

Business and politics 322

   x Business—Political activity; Politics and business

   xx **Politics, Practical**

Business arithmetic 650.01

   See also **Accounting; Bookkeeping; Interest (Economics)**

   x Arithmetic, Commercial; Commercial arithmetic

   xx **Arithmetic**

Business—Budget. *See* **Budgets, Business**

Business colleges. *See* **Business schools**

Business combinations. *See* **Conglomerate corporations; Trusts, Industrial**

Business correspondence. *See* **Business letters**

Business cycles 338.5

   See also **Economic forecasting;** also names of types of business cycles, e.g. **Depressions, Economic;** etc.

   x Business depressions; Cycles, Business; Economic cycles; Stabilization in industry

   xx **Economic conditions**

Business depressions. *See* **Business cycles; Depressions, Economic; Economic conditions**

Business education 650.07

   Use for materials on how to teach business and for descriptions of business operations.

   See also

Accounting	Keyboarding (Electronics)
Bookkeeping	Secretaries
Commercial law	Shorthand
Handwriting	Typewriting

   x Business—Study and teaching; Clerical work—Training; Commercial education; Education, Business; Office work—Training

   xx **Education**

Business English. *See* **English language—Business English**

Business enterprises, International. *See* **Multinational corporations**

Business enterprises—Management. *See* **Entrepreneurship; Industrial management**

Business entertaining 395; 658

   xx **Entertaining; Public relations**

Business ethics 174

   See also **Competition; Deceptive advertising; Success**

Business ethics—*Continued*

   x Ethics, Business

   xx **Ethics; Professional ethics**

Business failures   **338; 658**

   See also **Bank failures; Bankruptcy**

   x Business mortality; Failure in business

   xx **Business; Industry**

Business forecasting   **338.5**

   xx **Economic forecasting; Forecasting**

Business—Information services   **658.4**

   xx **Information services**

Business—International aspects. *See* **Multinational corporations**

Business Japanese. *See* **Japanese language— Business Japanese**

Business language. *See* names of languages with unique language subdivisions, e.g. **English language—Business English; Japanese language—Business Japanese;** etc.

Business law. *See* **Commercial law**

Business letters   **651.7**

   See also **English language—Business English; Japanese language—Business Japanese**

   x Business correspondence; Commercial correspondence; Correspondence

   xx **English language—Business English; Japanese language—Business Japanese; Letter writing**

Business libraries   **026**

   Use for materials on libraries with a subject focus in business. Materials on libraries located within companies, firms, or private businesses, and covering any subject area, are entered under **Corporate libraries.**

   x Libraries, Business

   xx **Special libraries**

Business machines. *See* **Office equipment and supplies**

Business mortality. *See* **Bankruptcy; Business failures**

Business patronage of the arts. *See* **Art patronage**

Business people   **338.092; 658.0092; 920**

   See also **Black business people; Businessmen; Businesswomen; Capitalists and financiers; Entrepreneurs; Merchants**

   x Businesspeople

   xx **Business; Commerce; Industry**

Business people, Black. *See* **Black business people**

Business—Political activity. *See* **Business and politics**

Business schools   **650.071**

   x Business colleges; Colleges, Business; Schools, Business

   xx **Schools**

Business secrets. *See* **Trade secrets**

Business, Small. *See* **Small business**

Business—Study and teaching. *See* **Business education**

Businessmen   **338.092; 658.0092; 920**

   x Men in business

   xx **Business people**

Businesspeople. *See* **Business people**

Businesswomen 338.092; 658.0092; 920
  x Women in business
  xx **Business people**
Busing (School integration) 344; 370.19
  x Antibusing; Racial balance in schools; School
    busing; Student busing
  xx **School children—Transportation; School inte-
    gration; Segregation in education**
Butter 637; 641.3
  See also **Margarine**
  xx **Dairy products; Milk**
Butter, Artificial. *See* **Margarine**
Butterflies 595.7
  See also **Caterpillars; Moths**
  x Cocoons; Lepidoptera
  xx **Insects; Moths**
Buttons 687
  xx **Clothing and dress**
Buy American policy. *See* **Buy national policy—
  United States**
Buy national policy (May subdiv. geog.) 351.71;
    352.1
  Use for materials on the requirement that the
    government procure goods produced within
    the nation.
  xx **Commercial policy; Government purchasing**
Buy national policy—United States 353.0071
  x Buy American policy
Buyers' guides. *See* **Consumer education; Shopping**
Buying 351.71; 352.1; 658.7
  Use for materials on buying by government
    agencies and by commercial and industrial
    enterprises. Materials on buying by the con-
    sumer are entered under **Consumer educa-
    tion; Shopping.** See notes under these head-
    ings.
  See also **Consumer education; Government pur-
    chasing; Instalment plan; Shopping**
  x Purchasing
  xx **Consumer education; Industrial management;
    Shopping**
Buyouts, Corporate. *See* **Corporate mergers and ac-
  quisitions**
Buyouts, Leveraged. *See* **Leveraged buyouts**
By-products. *See* **Waste products**
Byrd Antarctic Expedition 919.8
Byzantine architecture. *See* **Architecture, Byzantine**
Byzantine art. *See* **Art, Byzantine**
Byzantine Empire 949.5
  x Eastern Empire
C.A.T.V. *See* **Cable television**
C.B. radio. *See* **Citizens band radio**
C.O.A.s. *See* **Children of alcoholics**
C.R.T.'s. *See* **Cathode ray tubes**
Cabala 135; 296.1
  See also **Symbolism of numbers**
  x Cabbala; Kabbala
  xx **Hebrew literature; Jewish literature; Judaism;
    Mysticism; Occultism; Symbolism of num-
    bers**
Cabbala. *See* **Cabala**
Cabinet officers 351.004; 353.04; 920
  See also **Prime ministers**
  x Ministers of state

Cabinet work   684.1
　　　Use for materials dealing with the making and finishing of fine woodwork, such as furniture or interior details. Materials dealing with the construction of a wooden building or the wooden portion of any building are entered under **Carpentry.**
　　See also **Veneers and veneering; Woodwork**
　　xx **Carpentry; Furniture; Woodwork**
Cabins.　*See* **Log cabins and houses**
Cable codes.　*See* **Cipher and telegraph codes**
Cable railroads   385; 625.5
　　See also **Street railroads**
　　x Funicular railroads; Railroads, Cable
　　xx **Street railroads**
Cable television   384.55
　　See also **Home Box Office**
　　x C.A.T.V.; CATV; Community antenna television; Pay television, Cable; Television, Cable
　　xx **Television broadcasting**
Cables   384.6; 621.319; 624.1
　　xx **Power transmission; Rope**
Cables, Submarine   384.1; 384.6
　　x Atlantic cable; Ocean cables; Pacific cable; Submarine cables; Submarine telegraph; Telegraph, Submarine
　　xx **Telecommunication; Telegraph**
Cactus   583; 635.9
　　xx **Desert plants**
CAD.　*See* **Computer aided design**
Cafeterias.　*See* **Restaurants, bars, etc.**
Cage birds   636.6
　　See also names of cage birds, e.g. **Canaries;** etc.
　　xx **Birds**
Cake   641.8; 664
　　xx **Baking; Cookery**
Cake decorating   641.8
　　xx **Confectionery**
Calculating machines.　*See* **Calculators**
Calculators   510.28; 651.8; 681
　　　Use for materials on present-day calculators or on calculators and mechanical computers made before 1945. Materials on modern electronic computers developed after 1945 are entered under **Computers.**
　　See also **Abacus; Computers; Cybernetics; Slide rule**
　　x Accounting machines; Adding machines; Calculating machines; Pocket calculators
　　xx **Arithmetic; Computers; Office equipment and supplies**
Calculus   515
　　x Analysis (Mathematics)
　　xx **Mathematical analysis; Mathematics**
Caldecott Medal books   028.5
　　xx **Children's literature; Illustration of books; Literary prizes**
Calendars   529
　　See also **Almanacs; Devotional calendars; Months; Week**
　　x Annuals
　　xx **Almanacs; Time**

California—Gold discoveries 979.4
    x Gold rush
Calisthenics. *See* **Gymnastics; Physical education**
Calligraphy 745.6
    xx **Decorative arts; Handwriting; Writing**
Calves. *See* **Cattle**
Calvinism 284
    See also **Congregationalism; Predestination; Puritans**
    xx **Congregationalism; Puritans; Reformation**
Cambistry. *See* **Foreign exchange; Weights and measures**
Camcorders 621.388; 778.59
    See also **Amateur films; Videotape recorders and recording**
    x Home video cameras; Video cameras, Home
    xx **Amateur films; Cameras; Home video systems; Videotape recorders and recording**
Camels 599.73; 636.2
    x Dromedaries
    xx **Desert animals**
Cameras 681; 771.3
    See also names of types of cameras and of individual makes of cameras, e.g. **Camcorders; Motion picture cameras; Kodak camera;** etc.
    xx **Photography; Photography—Equipment and supplies**
Camouflage (Biology) 591.57
    x Animal camouflage; Animals—Camouflage
    xx **Animal defenses**
Camouflage (Military science) 355.4; 623
    xx **Military art and science; Naval art and science**
Camp cooking. *See* **Outdoor cookery**
Camp Fire Girls 369.47
    xx **Girls' clubs**
Camp sites. *See* **Campgrounds**
Campaign funds (May subdiv. geog.) 324.7
    x Assessments, Political; Elections—Finance; Political assessments; Political parties—Finance
    xx **Corruption in politics; Elections; Politics, Practical**
Campaign funds—United States 324.7
    x Elections—United States—Finance; United States—Campaign funds
Campaign literature (May subdiv. by date and party) 324.2
    xx **Politics, Practical**
Campaigns, Political. *See* **Politics, Practical**
Campaigns, Presidential—United States. *See* **Presidents—United States—Election**
Campers and trailers. *See* **Travel trailers and campers**
Campgrounds 796.54
    See also **Trailer parks**
    x Camp sites
Camping 796.54
    See note under **Camps.**
    See also **Backpacking; Outdoor cookery; Outdoor life; Tents; Travel trailers and campers; Wilderness survival**
    xx **Outdoor life; Outdoor recreation**

Camps   796.54
> Use for materials on camps with a definite pro-
> gram of activities. Materials on the tech-
> nique of camping are entered under **Camp-
> ing.**

> *x* Summer camps

Camps (Military)   355.7
> *See also* **Concentration camps**
> *x* Military camps
> *xx* **Military art and science**

Campus disorders. *See* **College students—Political
activity**

Canada   971
> *See also* **Northwest, Canadian;** also names of in-
> dividual provinces and territories

Canada—English-French relations   305.811; 306.4
> *See also* **Québec (Province)—History—
> Autonomy and independence movements**
> *x* Canada—French-English relations

Canada—Exploration. *See* **America—Exploration**

Canada—French-English relations. *See* **Canada—
English-French relations**

Canada—History—0-1763 (New France)   971.01
> *x* New France—History

Canada—History—1763-1791   971.02

**Canada—History—1800-1899 (19th century)
971.03-971.05**

**Canada—History—1900-1999 (20th century)
971.06**

Canada—History—1914-1945   971.06

Canada—History—1945-   971.06

Canada, Northwest. *See* **Northwest, Canadian**

Canadian Indians. *See* **Indians of North America—
Canada**

Canadian Invasion, 1775-1776   973.3
> *xx* **United States—History—1775-1783, Revolu-
> tion**

Canadian literature   810; C810
> May use same subdivision and names of literary
> forms as for **English literature.**
> *See also* **French Canadian literature**
> *xx* **Literature**

Canadian literature, French. *See* **French Canadian
literature**

Canadian Northwest. *See* **Northwest, Canadian**

Canadians   305.811; 971
> *See also* **French Canadians**

Canals (May subdiv. geog.)   386; 627
> *See also* **Inland navigation;** also names of canals,
> e.g. **Panama Canal;** etc.
> *xx* **Civil engineering; Hydraulic structures; Inland
> navigation; Transportation; Waterways**

Canaries   598.8; 636.6
> *xx* **Birds; Cage birds**

Canasta (Game)   795.4
> *x* Argentine rummy
> *xx* **Card games**

Cancer   616.99
> *See also* **Leukemia**
> *x* Carcinoma; Malignant tumors
> *xx* **Tumors**

Cancer—Chemotherapy   616.99
> *xx* **Chemotherapy**

Cancer—Diet therapy 616.99
  xx **Diet therapy**
Cancer—Genetic aspects 616.99
  xx **Medical genetics**
Cancer—Nursing 610.73
  xx **Nursing**
Cancer—Surgery 616.99
  xx **Surgery**
Candles 621.32; 745.593
  xx **Lighting**
Candy. *See* **Confectionery**
Caning of chairs. *See* **Chair caning**
Cannabis. *See* **Marijuana**
Canned goods. *See* **Canning and preserving**
Cannibalism 291.3; 394
  xx **Ethnology; Human behavior**
Canning and preserving 641.4; 664
    See also names of foods with the subdivision
      Preservation, e.g. **Fruit—Preservation; Veg-**
      etables—Preservation; etc.
    x Canned goods; Food, Canned; Pickling; Pre-
      serving
    xx **Chemistry, Technical; Cookery; Food—**
      Preservation
Cannon. *See* **Ordnance**
Canoes and canoeing 797.1
  xx **Boats and boating; Water sports**
Canon law. *See* **Ecclesiastical law**
Cantatas 782.2
  xx **Choral music; Vocal music**
Canvas embroidery. *See* **Needlepoint**
Capital 332
    See also **Banks and banking; Capitalism; Interest**
      (Economics); Investments; Profit; Trusts, In-
      dustrial; Wealth
    xx **Capitalism; Economics; Finance; Income;**
      Money; Wealth
Capital and labor. *See* **Industrial relations**
Capital punishment (May subdiv. geog.) **179; 364.6**
    x Abolition of capital punishment; Death pen-
      alty; Executions; Hanging
    xx **Crime; Criminal law; Homicide; Punishment**
Capital punishment—United States 364.6
    x United States—Capital punishment
Capitalism 330.12
    See also **Capital; Entrepreneurship; Socialism**
    xx **Capital; Economics; Labor; Profit; Socialism;**
      Trusts, Industrial
Capitalists and financiers 332.092; 920
    See also **Millionaires**
    x Financiers
    xx **Business people; Wealth**
Capitalization (Finance). *See* **Corporations—**
      Finance; Railroads—Finance; Securities;
      Valuation
Capitals (Cities)
    Use for materials on the capital cities of several
      countries or states.
Capitols 725
Car pools 388.3
    x Automobile pools; Automobiles—Pools; Car-
      pools; Ride sharing; Van pools
    xx **Traffic engineering; Transportation**
Car wheels. *See* **Wheels**

Carbines. *See* **Rifles**
Carbolic acid   **547; 661**
  xx **Acids; Chemicals**
Carbon   **546; 547; 661; 662**
  See also **Charcoal; Coal; Diamonds; Graphite**
Carbon 14 dating. *See* **Radiocarbon dating**
Carbon dioxide greenhouse effect. *See* **Greenhouse**
    effect
Carburetors   **621.43**
  xx **Gas and oil engines**
Carcinoma. *See* **Cancer**
Card catalogs. *See* **Catalogs, Card**
Card games   **795.4**
  See also **Card tricks; Tarot;** also names of card
    games, e.g. **Bridge (Game); Canasta**
    (Game); etc.
  x Cards, Playing; Playing cards
  xx **Gambling; Games**
Card tricks   **795.4**
  xx **Card games; Magic; Tricks**
Cardiac diseases. *See* **Heart—Diseases**
Cardiac resuscitation   **616.1; 616.02**
  x Heart resuscitation; Resuscitation, Heart
  xx **First aid**
Cardinals   **262; 920**
  xx **Catholic Church—Clergy**
Cardiovascular system   **612.1**
  See also **Blood—Circulation; Heart**
  x Circulatory system; Vascular system
  xx **Blood—Circulation**
Cards, Debit. *See* **Debit cards**
Cards, Greeting. *See* **Greeting cards**
Cards, Playing. *See* **Card games**
Care and hygiene. *See* parts of the body with the
    subdivision *Care and hygiene,* e.g. **Foot—**
    Care and hygiene; Skin—Care and hygiene;
    etc.
Care, Medical. *See* **Medical care**
Care of children. *See* **Child care**
Care of persons. *See* classes of dependent persons
    with the subdivisions *Care* or *Home care*
    or *Institutional care,* e.g. **Infants—Care;**
    Elderly—Home care; Elderly—Institutional
    care; Mentally ill—Institutional care; etc.
Care of the dying. *See* **Terminal care**
Career changes   **331.7; 371.4**
  x Changing careers; Mid-career changes
  xx **Age and employment; Vocational guidance**
Career counseling. *See* **Vocational guidance**
Career development. *See* **Personnel management;**
    Vocational guidance
Career education. *See* **Vocational education**
Career guidance. *See* **Vocational guidance**
Careers. *See* **Occupations; Professions**
Caricatures. *See* **Cartoons and caricatures**
Carillons. *See* **Bells**
Carnivals. *See* **Festivals**
Carnivals (Circus). *See* **Amusement parks**
Carnivores   **599.74**
  See also names of carnivorous animals
  x Meat-eating animals
  xx **Animals—Food; Mammals**

Carols 782.28

    x Christmas carols; Easter carols

    xx **Christmas—Poetry; Church music; Folk songs; Hymns; Religious poetry; Songs; Vocal music**

Carpentry 694

    Use for materials dealing with the construction of a wooden building or the wooden portion of any building. Materials dealing with the making and finishing of fine woodwork, such as furniture or interior details, are entered under **Cabinet work.**

    See also

Building	**Roofs**
Cabinet work	**Turning**
Doors	**Walls**
Floors	**Woodwork**

    xx **Building; Woodwork**

Carpentry—Tools 694

    See also names of tools, e.g. **Saws;** etc.

    xx **Tools**

Carpetbag rule. *See* **Reconstruction (1865-1876)**

Carpets 645; 677; 746.7

    Use for materials on heavy woven or felted fabrics used as floor coverings, usually covering large areas. Materials on one-piece floor coverings, such as woven fabrics, animal skins, etc., are entered under **Rugs.**

    See also **Rugs; Weaving**

    xx **Decoration and ornament; Interior design; Rugs; Textile industry; Weaving**

Carpools. *See* **Car pools**

Carriages and carts 388.3; 688.6

    x Carts; Coaches, Stage; Stagecoaches; Wagons

Carriers, Aircraft. *See* **Aircraft carriers**

Cars, Armored (Tanks). *See* **Tanks (Military science)**

Cars (Automobiles). *See* **Automobiles**

Cartels. *See* **Trusts, Industrial**

Cartography. *See* **Charts; Map drawing; Maps**

Cartoons and caricatures 741.5

    Use for general collections of pictorial humor and for materials about caricatures and cartoons.

    See also **Animated films; Comic books, strips, etc.;** also subjects with the subdivision *Cartoons and caricatures,* e.g. **Computers—Cartoons and caricatures; World War, 1939-1945—Cartoons and caricatures;** etc.

    x Caricatures; Humorous pictures; Illustrations, Humorous; Pictures, Humorous

    xx **Comic books, strips, etc.; Pictures; Portraits**

Carts. *See* **Carriages and carts**

Carts (Midget cars). *See* **Karts and karting**

Carving (Arts). *See* kinds of carving, e.g. **Wood carving;** etc.

Carving (Meat, etc.) 642

    xx **Dinners and dining**

Carving, Wood. *See* **Wood carving**

Case studies. *See* subjects with the subdivision *Case studies,* e.g. **Juvenile delinquency—Case studies;** etc.

Case work, Social. *See* **Social case work**

Cassette books. *See* **Talking books**

Cassette recorders and recording. *See* **Magnetic recorders and recording**

Cassette tape recordings, Video. *See* **Videotapes**

Cassette tapes, Audio. *See* **Sound recordings**

Castaways. *See* **Survival (after airplane accidents, shipwrecks, etc.)**

Caste   294.5; 305.5; 323.3
> *See also* **Social classes**
> *xx* **Brahmanism; Hinduism; Manners and customs**

Casting. *See* **Founding; Plaster casts**

Castles (May subdiv. geog.)   728.8
> *x* Chateaux
> *xx* **Architecture; Architecture, Medieval**

Casts, Plaster. *See* **Plaster casts**

Casualty insurance   368.5
> *See also* **Accident insurance**
> *x* Insurance, Casualty
> *xx* **Insurance**

Cat. *See* **Cats**

CAT (Computerized axial tomography). *See* **Tomography**

CAT scan. *See* **Tomography**

Catacombs   393; 726
> *See also* **Church history—30(ca.)-600, Early church**
> *x* Burial
> *xx* **Cemeteries; Christian antiquities; Christian art and symbolism; Church history—30(ca.) -600, Early church; Tombs**

Cataloging   025.3
> May be subdivided by topic, e.g. **Cataloging—Music;** etc.
> *See also* **Bibliography; Classification—Books; Indexing; Machine readable bibliographic data; Subject headings**
> *x* Cataloguing
> *xx* **Bibliographic control; Bibliography; Books; Documentation; Indexing; Library science; Library technical processes**

Cataloging data in machine readable form. *See* **Machine readable bibliographic data**

Cataloging—Data processing   025.3

Cataloging—Music   025.3
> Use same form for the cataloging of other types of materials.
> *x* Music—Cataloging

Catalogs. *See* **Catalogs, Booksellers'; Catalogs, Publishers'; Library catalogs;** and subjects with the subdivision *Catalogs,* e.g. **Motion pictures—Catalogs;** etc.

Catalogs, Book   017; 025.3
> *x* Book catalogs; Books—Catalogs; Catalogs in book form
> *xx* **Library catalogs**

Catalogs, Booksellers'   017
> *x* Books—Catalogs; Booksellers' catalogs; Catalogs
> *xx* **Booksellers and bookselling**

Catalogs, Card   025.3
> *x* Card catalogs
> *xx* **Library catalogs**

Catalogs, Classified   017; 025.3
> *See also* **Classification—Books**
>> *x* Catalogs, Systematic; Classed catalogs; Classi-
>> fied catalogs
> *xx* **Classification—Books; Library catalogs**

Catalogs, COM.   *See* **Library catalogs on microfilm**
Catalogs in book form.   *See* **Catalogs, Book**
Catalogs, Library.   *See* **Library catalogs**
Catalogs on microfilm.   *See* **Library catalogs on mi-
crofilm**
Catalogs, Online.   *See* **Online catalogs**

Catalogs, Publishers'   015
>> *x* Books—Catalogs; Catalogs; Publishers' cata-
>> logs
> *xx* **Publishers and publishing**

Catalogs, Subject   016; 017
> *See also* **Subject headings**
> *xx* **Library catalogs**

Catalogs, Systematic.   *See* **Catalogs, Classified**
Cataloguing.   *See* **Cataloging**

Catalysis   541.3
> *See also* **Catalytic RNA**
> *xx* **Catalytic RNA; Chemistry, Physical and theo-
> retical**

Catalytic ribonucleic acid.   *See* **Catalytic RNA**

Catalytic RNA   574.87
> *See also* **Catalysis**
>> *x* Catalytic ribonucleic acid; Ribozymes; RNA,
>> Catalytic
> *xx* **Catalysis; Enzymes; RNA**

Catamarans   797.1
> *xx* **Boats and boating**

Catastrophes.   *See* **Disasters**

Catechisms   238; 268; 291.2
> *See also* **Bible—Catechisms, question books;
> Creeds**
> *xx* **Christian education; Creeds; Theology—Study
> and teaching**

Caterers and catering   642
> *See also* **Breakfasts; Desserts; Dinners and din-
> ing; Luncheons; Menus**
> *xx* **Cookery; Food service; Menus**

Caterpillars   595.78
> *x* Cocoons
> *xx* **Butterflies; Moths**

Cathedrals (May subdiv. geog.)   726
> *See also* **Architecture, Gothic;** also names of in-
> dividual cathedrals
> *xx* **Abbeys; Architecture; Architecture, Gothic;
> Architecture, Medieval; Christian art and
> symbolism; Church architecture; Churches**

Cathedrals—United States   726
> *x* United States—Cathedrals

Cathode ray tubes   537.5; 621.3815
> *x* C.R.T.'s; CRTs
> *xx* **Vacuum tubes**

Catholic Church (May subdiv. geog.)   282
> *See also* **Inquisition; Papacy;** also subjects with
> the subdivision *Catholic Church,* e.g. **Abor-
> tion—Catholic Church;** etc.
> *x* Roman Catholic Church
> *xx* **Christianity**

Catholic Church—Charities   361.7
> *xx* **Charities**

Catholic Church—Clergy 253

    See also **Cardinals; Ex-priests**

    xx **Clergy; Priests**

Catholic Church—Converts. *See* **Catholic converts**

Catholic Church—Foreign relations. *See* **Catholic Church—Relations (Diplomatic)**

Catholic Church—Liturgy 264

    Use for materials on the forms of prayers, rituals, and ceremonies used in the official public worship of the Catholic Church.

    xx **Liturgies; Rites and ceremonies**

Catholic Church—Missions 266

    xx **Missions, Christian**

Catholic Church—Relations (May subdiv. by church or religion) 282

    Use for materials on relations between the Catholic Church and other churches and religions.

Catholic Church—Relations (Diplomatic) (May subdiv. geog. by appropriate political jurisdiction) 282; 327.456; 945.6

    Use for materials on the dealings and relations between the Catholic Church and political jurisdictions.

    x Catholic Church—Foreign relations; Vatican City—Foreign relations

    xx **International relations**

Catholic Church—United States 282

    x United States—Catholic Church

Catholic converts 282

    x Catholic Church—Converts; Converts, Catholic; Converts to Catholicism

    xx **Converts**

Catholic ex-nuns. *See* **Ex-nuns**

Catholic ex-priests. *See* **Ex-priests**

Catholic laity. *See* **Laity—Catholic Church**

Catholic literature 282; 808; 809

    x Index librorum prohibitorum

    xx **Christian literature; Literature; Religious literature**

Catholics (May subdiv. geog.) 305.6

Catholics—United States 282; 305.6

    x United States—Catholics

Cats 599.74; 636.8

    See also names of specific breeds

    x Cat; Kittens

    xx **Domestic animals; Pets**

Cattle 599.73; 636.2

    Use for materials on domesticated bovine animals, usually kept on a farm or a ranch.

    See also **Beef cattle; Dairy cattle; Dairying; Pastures**

    x Calves; Cows

    xx **Dairying; Domestic animals; Livestock**

Cattle brands 636.2

Cattle—Diseases 636.2

    x Cows—Diseases

    xx **Animals—Diseases; Veterinary medicine**

CATV. *See* **Cable television**

Cave drawings 743; 759.01

    See also **Rock drawings, paintings, and engravings**

    xx **Mural painting and decoration; Picture writ-**

Cave drawings—*Continued*
ing; **Rock drawings, paintings, and engravings**
Cave dwellers   573.3; 930.1
xx **Prehistoric man**
Caves   551.4; 796.5
x Grottoes; Speleology
CB radio.   *See* **Citizens band radio**
CD-I technology   004.5
x CDI technology; Compact disc interactive technology; Interactive CD technology
xx **Compact discs; Optical storage devices**
CD players.   *See* **Compact disc players**
CD-ROM   004.5
x CDROM; Compact disc read-only memory
xx **Compact discs; Optical storage devices**
CDI technology.   *See* **CD-I technology**
CDROM.   *See* **CD-ROM**
CDs (Compact discs).   *See* **Compact discs**
Celebrities   920
See also types of celebrities, e.g. **Actors**; etc.
x Famous people; Public figures
xx **Biography**
Celery   635; 641.3
xx **Vegetables**
Celibacy   176; 253; 306.73
xx **Clergy; Religious life; Religious orders**
Cellars.   *See* **Basements**
Cello.   *See* **Violoncello**
Cells   574.87; 581.87; 591.87
See also **DNA; Embryology; Protoplasm; Protozoa**
x Cytology
xx **Biology; Embryology; Physiology; Protoplasm; Reproduction**
Cells, Electric.   *See* **Electric batteries**
Celtic legends.   *See* **Legends, Celtic**
Celts   305.891; 936.4
See also **Druids and Druidism**
x Gaels
xx **France—History—0-1328; Great Britain—History—0-1066**
Cement   620.1; 666; 691
See also **Concrete; Pavements**
x Hydraulic cement
xx **Adhesives; Building materials; Ceramics; Concrete; Lime; Masonry; Plaster and plastering**
Cemeteries (May subdiv. geog.)   393; 718
See also **Catacombs; Epitaphs; Tombs**; also names of cemeteries
x Burial; Burying grounds; Churchyards; Graves; Graveyards
xx **Public health; Sanitation; Tombs**
Censorship   303.3; 363.3
Use for general materials on the limitation of freedom of expression in various fields.
See also **Academic freedom; Free speech; Freedom of information; Freedom of the press**; also subjects with the subdivision *Censorship*, e.g. **Books—Censorship; Motion pictures—Censorship; Television—Censorship**; etc.
xx **Freedom of information; Intellectual freedom**

Census   304.6; 310; 351.81
    See also names of countries, cities, etc., with the
        subdivision *Census,* e.g. **United States—
        Census;** etc.
    xx **Population; Statistics; Vital statistics**
Centers for the performing arts   725; 790.2
    See also **Theaters;** also names of individual cen-
        ters
    xx **Performing arts**
Central Africa   967
    Use for materials dealing collectively with the
        region of Africa that includes what are now
        the Central African Republic, Equatorial
        Guinea, Gabon, Zaire, and the Congo.
    See also **French-speaking Equatorial Africa**
    x Africa, Central
Central America   972.8
    xx **America**
Central cities. *See* **Inner cities**
Central Europe   943
    Use for materials on the area included in the ba-
        sins of the Danube, Elbe and Rhine rivers.
    x Europe, Central
Central States. *See* **Middle West**
Centralization of schools. *See* **Schools—
    Centralization**
Centralized processing (Libraries). *See* **Library
    technical processes**
Ceramic industries   338.4
    See also **Clay industries;** also types of ceramic
        industries, e.g. **Glass manufacture;** etc.
Ceramic materials   620.1; 666; 738.1
    See also names of individual materials, e.g.
        Clay; etc.
Ceramics   666
    Use for materials on the technology of fired
        earth products or clay products intended for
        industrial use. Earthenware, chinaware, and
        porcelain are entered under **Pottery** and
        Porcelain.
    See also **Cement; Glass; Glazes; Pottery; Tiles**
    xx **Decorative arts**
Cereals. *See* **Grain**
Cereals, Prepared. *See* **Prepared cereals**
Cerebral palsy   616.8
    x Palsy, Cerebral; Paralysis, Cerebral; Paralysis,
        Spastic; Spastic paralysis
    xx **Brain—Diseases**
Ceremonies. *See* **Etiquette; Manners and customs;
    Rites and ceremonies**
Certainty. *See* **Belief and doubt; Probabilities;
    Truth**
Certified public accountants. *See* **Accountants**
Chain belting. *See* **Belts and belting**
Chain stores   658.8
    x Branch stores; Stores
    xx **Retail trade**
Chair caning   684.1
    x Caning of chairs
Chairs   645; 684.1; 749
    xx **Furniture**
Chalk talks   741.2
    x Blackboard drawing

Challenger (Space shuttle) 629.44
  xx **Space shuttles**
Chamber music 785
  xx **Instrumental music; Music; Orchestral music**
Chamber theater. *See* **Readers' theater**
Chambers of commerce 380.106; 381.06
  x Boards of trade; Trade, Boards of
  xx **Commerce**
Change of life in men. *See* **Male climacteric**
Change of life in women. *See* **Menopause**
Change of sex. *See* **Transsexuality**
Change, Social. *See* **Social change**
Changing careers. *See* **Career changes**
Chanties. *See* **Sea songs**
Chants (Plain, Gregorian, etc.) 782.32
  x Gregorian chant; Plain chant; Plainsong
  xx **Church music**
Chanukah. *See* **Hanukkah**
Chaos (Science) 003
  x Chaotic behavior in systems
  xx **Dynamics; Science; System theory**
Chaotic behavior in systems. *See* **Chaos (Science)**
Chapbooks 398
  See also **Comic books, strips, etc.**
  x Jestbooks
  xx **Books; Comic books, strips, etc.; Folklore; Literature; Pamphlets; Periodicals; Wit and humor**
Chaplains 253
  See also names of bodies or institutions having chaplains, with the subdivision *Chaplains,* e.g. **United States. Army—Chaplains;** etc.
  xx **Clergy**
Character 155.2
  See also **Human behavior; Temperament**
  xx **Personality; Temperament**
Character assassination. *See* **Libel and slander**
Character education. *See* **Moral education**
Characteristics, National. *See* **National characteristics**
Characters and characteristics in literature 809; 810.9, etc.
  See also **Blacks in literature; Children in literature; Drama—Technique; Plots (Drama, fiction, etc.); Women in literature;** also names of prominent authors with the subdivision *Characters,* e.g. **Shakespeare, William, 1564-1616—Characters;** etc.; and names of individual characters in literature
  x Literary characters
  xx **Literature**
Charades 793.2
  xx **Amateur theater; Amusements; Literary recreations; Riddles**
Charcoal 662
  xx **Carbon; Fuel**
Charitable institutions. *See* **Charities; Institutional care; Orphanages;** and classes of people with the subdivision *Institutional care,* e.g. **Blind—Institutional care; Deaf—Institutional care; Mentally ill—Institutional care;** etc.
Charities (May subdiv. geog.) 361.7; 361.8
  Use for materials on privately supported welfare activities. Materials on tax supported welfare activities are entered under **Public welfare.** Materials on the methods employed in welfare work, public or private, are entered under **Social work.**

Charities—*Continued*
    See also

Charities, Medical	**Institutional care**
Charity organization	**Orphanages**
Child care centers	**Public welfare**
Child welfare	**Social settlements**
Disaster relief	**Unemployed**
Endowments	**Voluntarism**
Food relief	

      also names of appropriate corporate bodies with
          the subdivision *Charities,* e.g. **Catholic**
          Church—Charities; etc.; and names of wars
          with the subdivision *Civilian relief,* e.g.
          World War, 1939-1945—Civilian relief; etc.
   x Charitable institutions; Endowed charities;
       Homes (Institutions); Institutions, Charita-
       ble and philanthropic; Philanthropy; Poor
       relief; Social welfare; Welfare agencies; Wel-
       fare work
  xx **Charity organization; Endowments; Poverty;**
       Public welfare; Social problems; Social
       work; Voluntarism
Charities, Legal. *See* **Legal aid**
Charities, Medical 362.1
    See also **Hospitals; Institutional care**
    x Medical charities; Socialized medicine
    xx **Charities; Medical care; Medicine, State; Pub-**
       lic health
Charities, Public. *See* **Public welfare**
Charity 177
    See also **Love (Theology)**
    xx **Ethics; Human behavior**
Charity organization 361
    See also **Charities**
    x Philanthropy
    xx **Charities**
Charlatans. *See* **Impostors and imposture**
Charms 133.4
    x Spells; Talismans
    xx **Demonology; Folklore; Superstition; Witch-**
       craft
Charter flights. *See* **Aeronautics, Commercial—**
       Chartering
Charters
    See also **Archives; Manuscripts**
    x Documents
    xx **Archives; History—Sources; Manuscripts**
Chartography. *See* **Charts; Map drawing; Maps**
Charts 912
    See also **Maps**
    x Cartography; Chartography
    xx **Maps**
Chateaux. *See* **Castles**
Chattel mortgages. *See* **Mortgages**
Cheating in sports. *See* **Sports—Corrupt practices**
Checkers 794.2
    x Draughts
Cheers and cheerleading 371.8; 791.6
Cheese 637; 641.3
    xx **Dairy products; Milk**
Cheese—Bacteriology 637
    xx **Bacteriology**
Chemical analysis. *See* **Chemistry, Analytic;** and

Chemical analysis—*Continued*
    names of substances with the subdivision
    Analysis, e.g. **Water—Analysis;** etc.
Chemical apparatus   542
    x Apparatus, Chemical; Chemistry—Apparatus
    xx **Scientific apparatus and instruments**
Chemical elements   546
    See also **Periodic law;** also names of elements,
        e.g. **Hydrogen;** etc.
    x Elements, Chemical
Chemical engineering   660
    See also **Biotechnology; Chemistry, Technical;
        Metallurgy**
    x Chemistry, Industrial; Industrial chemistry
    xx **Chemistry, Technical; Engineering; Metal-
        lurgy**
Chemical equations   540
    x Equations, Chemical
    xx **Chemical reactions**
Chemical geology. *See* **Geochemistry**
Chemical industries. *See* **Chemical industry**
Chemical industry   338.4; 660
    Use for materials about industries that produce
        chemicals or are based on chemical pro-
        cesses.
    See also types of industries, e.g. **Plastics indus-
        try;** etc.
    x Chemical industries; Chemistry, Industrial;
        Industrial chemistry
    xx **Chemicals; Chemistry, Technical**
Chemical landfills. *See* **Hazardous waste sites**
Chemical pollution. *See* **Pollution**
Chemical reactions   541.3
    See also **Chemical equations**
    x Reactions, Chemical
Chemical societies. *See* **Chemistry—Societies**
Chemical technology. *See* **Chemistry, Technical**
Chemical warfare   358
    See also **Incendiary weapons; Poisonous gases—
        War use;** also names of wars with the subdi-
        vision *Chemical warfare,* e.g. **World War,
        1939-1945—Chemical warfare;** etc.
    x Air warfare
    xx **Military art and science; War**
Chemicals   540; 661
    Use for general materials on chemicals, includ-
        ing their manufacture. See note under
        Chemical industry.
    See also **Chemical industry; Chemistry, Techni-
        cal;** also groups of chemicals, e.g. **Acids;
        Agricultural chemicals; Petrochemicals;**
        etc.; and names of individual chemicals, e.g.
        Carbolic acid; etc.
    xx **Chemistry, Technical**
Chemiculture. *See* **Hydroponics**
Chemistry   540
    See also

Acids	**Chemistry, Inorganic**
Agricultural chemistry	**Chemistry, Organic**
Alchemy	**Chemistry, Physical and**
Bases (Chemistry)	**theoretical**
Biochemistry	**Color**
Botanical chemistry	**Combustion**

140

Chemistry—*Continued*

Explosives	Pharmacy
Fermentation	Photographic chemistry
Fire	Poisons and poisoning
Geochemistry	Space chemistry
Microchemistry	Spectrum analysis
Pharmaceutical chemistry	

    also headings beginning with the word **Chemical**

  xx **Science**

Chemistry, Agricultural. *See* **Agricultural chemistry**

Chemistry, Analytic 543

  See also names of substances with the subdivision *Analysis,* e.g. **Water—Analysis;** etc.

  x Analysis (Chemistry); Analytical chemistry; Chemical analysis; Qualitative analysis; Quantitative analysis

Chemistry—Apparatus. *See* **Chemical apparatus**

Chemistry, Biological. *See* **Biochemistry**

Chemistry, Botanical. *See* **Botanical chemistry**

Chemistry, Diagnostic. *See* **Clinical chemistry**

Chemistry—Dictionaries 540.3

  xx **Encyclopedias and dictionaries**

Chemistry—Experiments 540; 542

  xx **Science—Experiments**

Chemistry, Industrial. *See* **Chemical engineering; Chemical industry; Chemistry, Technical**

Chemistry, Inorganic 546

  See also **Metals**

  x Inorganic chemistry

  xx **Chemistry**

Chemistry—Laboratory manuals 540.78

Chemistry, Medical. *See* **Clinical chemistry**

Chemistry, Medical and pharmaceutical. *See* **Clinical chemistry; Pharmaceutical chemistry**

Chemistry of food. *See* **Food—Analysis; Food—Composition**

Chemistry, Organic 547

  x Organic chemistry

  xx **Chemistry**

Chemistry, Organic—Synthesis 547

  See also **Plastics; Polymers and polymerization; Synthetic products**

  x Chemistry, Synthetic; Synthetic chemistry

  xx **Plastics**

Chemistry, Pharmaceutical. *See* **Pharmaceutical chemistry**

Chemistry, Photographic. *See* **Photographic chemistry**

Chemistry, Physical and theoretical 541

  See also

Atomic theory	Periodic law
Atoms	Polymers and polymerization
Catalysis	
Colloids	Quantum theory
Crystallography	Radiochemistry
Electrochemistry	Solids
Molecules	Thermodynamics
Nuclear physics	

  x Physical chemistry; Theoretical chemistry

  xx **Chemistry; Nuclear physics; Physics; Quantum theory**

Chemistry, Physiological. *See* **Biochemistry**

Chemistry—Problems, exercises, etc. 540.76

Chemistry—Societies 540.6
  x Chemical societies
Chemistry, Synthetic. *See* **Chemistry, Organic—**
    Synthesis
Chemistry, Technical 660
    See also

Alloys	**Electrochemistry**
Bleaching	**Food—Analysis**
Canning and preserving	**Gums and resins**
Chemical engineering	**Synthetic products**
Chemical industry	**Tanning**
Chemicals	**Textile chemistry**
Corrosion and anticorro-	**Waste products**
sives	

    also names of specific industries and products,
        e.g. **Clay industries; Dyes and dyeing;** etc.
    x Chemical technology; Chemistry, Industrial;
        Industrial chemistry; Technical chemistry
    xx **Chemical engineering; Chemicals; Metallurgy;**
        Technology
Chemistry, Textile. *See* **Textile chemistry**
Chemists 540.92; 920
    xx Scientists
Chemotherapy 615.5
    See also **Antibiotics;** also names of diseases with
        the subdivision *Chemotherapy,* e.g. **Can-**
        cer—Chemotherapy; etc.
    x Drug therapy; Pharmacotherapy
    xx **Pharmacology**
Chess 794.1
    xx **Games**
Chicago (Ill.) 917.73; 977.3
    Subdivisions have been given under this subject
        to serve as a guide to the subdivisions that
        may be used under the name of any city.
        They are examples of the application of di-
        rections given in the general references un-
        der various headings throughout the List.
        References are given only for those headings
        that are cited specifically under the general
        references. The subdivisions under **United**
        States may be consulted as a guide for for-
        mulating other references that may be
        needed.
Chicago (Ill.)—**Antiquities** 977.3
Chicago (Ill.)—**Bibliography** 015.773; 016.9773
Chicago (Ill.)—**Bio-bibliography** 012
Chicago (Ill.)—**Biography** 920.0773
    xx **Biography**
Chicago (Ill.)—**Biography—Portraits** 920.0773
Chicago (Ill.)—**Boundaries** 352.0773; 977.3
Chicago (Ill.)—Bridges. *See* **Bridges—Chicago (Ill.)**
Chicago (Ill.)—**Census** 317.73
Chicago (Ill.)—**Civil defense** 363.3
    xx **Civil defense**
Chicago (Ill.)—**Climate** 551.69773
Chicago (Ill.)—**Commerce** 381
Chicago (Ill.)—**Description** 917.73
Chicago (Ill.)—**Description—Guidebooks** 917.73
    x Chicago (Ill.)—Guidebooks; Guidebooks
Chicago (Ill.)—Description—Maps. *See* **Chicago**
    (Ill.)—Maps

Chicago (Ill.)—Description—Views 917.73
    x Chicago (Ill.)—Pictures; Chicago (Ill.)—
        Views; Scenery
    xx **Pictures; Views**
Chicago (Ill.)—Directories 917.730025
    Use for lists of names and addresses. Lists of
        names without addresses are entered under
        Chicago (Ill.)—Registers.
    See also **Chicago (Ill.)—Registers**
    xx **Chicago (Ill.)—Registers**
Chicago (Ill.)—Directories—Telephone. *See* **Chi-
    cago (Ill.)—Telephone directories**
Chicago (Ill.)—Economic conditions 330.9773
Chicago (Ill.)—Foreign population 305.8; 325.773
    x Foreign population; Population, Foreign
Chicago (Ill.)—Government. *See* **Chicago (Ill.)—
    Politics and government**
Chicago (Ill.)—Government publications 015.773
Chicago (Ill.)—Guidebooks. *See* **Chicago (Ill.)—
    Description—Guidebooks**
Chicago (Ill.)—Historic buildings. *See* **Historic
    buildings—Chicago (Ill.)**
Chicago (Ill.)—History 977.3
Chicago (Ill.)—History—Societies 977.3006
Chicago (Ill.)—Industries 338.09773
    x Chicago (Ill.)—Manufactures
    xx **Manufactures**
Chicago (Ill.)—Intellectual life 001.2; 977.3
Chicago (Ill.)—Manufactures. *See* **Chicago (Ill.)—
    Industries**
Chicago (Ill.)—Maps 912.773
    x Chicago (Ill.)—Description—Maps
    xx **Maps; Road maps**
Chicago (Ill.)—Moral conditions 977.3
Chicago (Ill.)—Occupations 331.7
    xx **Occupations**
Chicago (Ill.)—Officials and employees 352.09773
    x Officials
    xx **Civil service**
Chicago (Ill.)—Pictures. *See* **Chicago (Ill.)—
    Description—Views**
Chicago (Ill.)—Poetry 811; 811.008, etc.
    xx **Poetry**
Chicago (Ill.)—Politics and government 977.3
    x Chicago (Ill.)—Government; Politics
    xx **Municipal government**
Chicago (Ill.)—Popular culture 977.3
Chicago (Ill.)—Population 304.609773
    xx **Population**
Chicago (Ill.)—Protests, demonstrations, etc. *See*
    **Protests, demonstrations, etc.—Chicago
    (Ill.)**
Chicago (Ill.)—Public buildings 725.09773
    x Public buildings—Chicago (Ill.)
    xx **City planning**
Chicago (Ill.)—Public works 352.7
    xx **City planning; Public works**
Chicago (Ill.)—Race relations 305.8009773
    xx **Race relations**
Chicago (Ill.)—Registers 917.730025
    Use for lists of names without addresses. Lists of
        names that include addresses are entered
        under **Chicago (Ill.)—Directories.**

Chicago (Ill.)—Registers—*Continued*
    See also **Chicago (Ill.)—Directories**
    xx **Chicago (Ill.)—Directories**
Chicago (Ill.)—Social conditions   977.3
    xx **Social conditions**
Chicago (Ill.)—Social life and customs   977.3
Chicago (Ill.)—Social policy   361.6; 977.3
Chicago (Ill.)—Statistics   317.73
    xx **Statistics**
Chicago (Ill.)—Streets. *See* **Streets—Chicago (Ill.)**
**Chicago (Ill.)—Suburbs and environs   307.7609773;
    977.3**
    See also **Chicago metropolitan area (Ill.)**
    xx **Suburban life**
Chicago (Ill.)—Telephone directories   917.730025
    x Chicago (Ill.)—Directories—Telephone
Chicago (Ill.)—Urban renewal. *See* **Urban renew-
    al—Chicago (Ill.)**
Chicago (Ill.)—Views. *See* **Chicago (Ill.)—
    Description—Views**
Chicago metropolitan area (Ill.)   307.7609773; 977.3
    xx **Chicago (Ill.)—Suburbs and environs; Metro-
      politan areas**
**Chicago metropolitan area (Ill.)—Politics and govern-
    ment   977.3**
    xx **Metropolitan government**
Chicanos. *See* **Mexican Americans**
Chicken pox. *See* **Chickenpox**
Chickenpox   616.9
    x Chicken pox
    xx **Diseases; Viruses**
Chief justices. *See* **Judges**
Child abuse   362.7
    See also **Child molesting; Juvenile prostitution**
    x Abuse of children; Battered children; Child
      battering; Child neglect; Children—Abuse;
      Children, Cruelty to; Cruelty to children
    xx **Child rearing; Child welfare; Family violence;
      Parent and child**
Child abuse, Sex. *See* **Child molesting**
Child and father. *See* **Father and child**
Child and grandparent. *See* **Grandparent and child**
Child and mother. *See* **Mother and child**
Child and parent. *See* **Parent and child**
Child artists   704; 709.2; 920
    Use for materials on children as artists and on
      works of art by children.
    See also **Finger painting**
    x Children as artists
    xx **Artists; Gifted children**
Child authors   809; 920
    Use for materials on children as authors and dis-
      cussions of children's literary works. For
      works written by children, use **Children's
      writings.**
    x Children as authors
    xx **Authors; Gifted children**
Child battering. *See* **Child abuse**
Child birth. *See* **Childbirth**
Child care   649
    See also **Babysitting; Child rearing; Infants—
      Care**
    x Care of children; Children—Care; Children—
      Care and hygiene; Children, Care of

Child care centers   362.7

See also **Nursery schools**

   x Children—Day care; Children's day care centers; Day care centers; Day nurseries; Nurseries, Day

   xx **Charities; Child welfare; Children—Institutional care; Nursery schools**

Child custody   306.89; 346.01; 362.7

See also **Parental kidnapping**

   x Children—Custody; Custody of children; Joint custody of children; Parental custody; Shared custody

   xx **Divorce mediation; Parent and child**

Child development   155.4; 305.23; 612.6

See also **Child psychology; Child rearing; Children—Growth; Home instruction**

   x Child study; Children—Development

   xx **Child rearing; Children; Home instruction**

Child labor. *See* **Children—Employment; Teenagers—Employment; Youth—Employment**

Child molesting   362.7; 364.1

   x Child abuse, Sex; Child sex abuse; Children—Molesting; Molesting of children

   xx **Child abuse; Incest; Sex crimes; Sexual harassment**

Child neglect. *See* **Child abuse**

Child placing. *See* **Adoption; Foster home care**

Child prostitution. *See* **Juvenile prostitution**

Child psychiatry   616.89; 618.92

See also **Autism; Child psychology; Mentally handicapped children; Mentally ill children**

   x Children—Mental health; Pediatric psychiatry; Psychiatry, Child

   xx **Psychiatry**

Child psychology   155.4

See also **Child rearing; Children and adults; Educational psychology; Learning, Psychology of; Mental tests; Separation anxiety in children**

   x Child study; Children—Psychology; Psychology, Child

   xx **Child development; Child psychiatry; Child rearing; Educational psychology; Psychology**

Child raising. *See* **Child rearing**

Child rearing   392; 649

Use for materials on the principles and techniques of raising children. Materials on the psychological and social interaction between parents and their minor children are entered under **Parent and child**. Materials on the skills, attributes, and attitudes needed for parenthood are entered under **Parenting.**

See also

Child abuse	**Home instruction**
Child development	**Parenting**
Child psychology	**Socialization**
Children's allowances	**Toilet training**

   x Child raising; Children—Management; Children—Training; Discipline of children; Training of children

   xx **Child care; Child development; Child psychology; Children and adults; Home instruction; Parent and child; Parenting**

Child sex abuse. *See* **Child molesting**
Child snatching by parents. *See* **Parental kidnapping**
Child study. *See* **Child development; Child psychology**
Child support 306.89; 346.01; 362.7
    x Support of children
    xx **Child welfare; Desertion and nonsupport; Divorce mediation**
Child welfare 362.7
    Use for materials on the aid, support, and protection of children, by the state or by private welfare organizations.
    See also

Abandoned children	**Foster home care**
Child abuse	**Juvenile delinquency**
Child care centers	**Mothers' pensions**
Child support	**Orphanages**
Children—Employment	**Playgrounds**
Children—Institutional care	**Unmarried fathers**
	Unmarried mothers
Children's hospitals	

    x A.D.C.; Aid to dependent children; Children—Charities, protection, etc.; Protection of children
    xx **Charities; Children's hospitals; Juvenile delinquency; Mothers' pensions; Orphanages; Public welfare**
Childbirth 612.6; 618.2
    See also **Multiple birth; Natural childbirth; Pregnancy**
    x Birth; Child birth; Labor (Childbirth); Midwifery; Obstetrics
    xx **Pregnancy**
Childbirth, Natural. *See* **Natural childbirth**
Childhood diseases. *See* **Children—Diseases**
Childlessness 306.85
    See also **Infertility**
    xx **Birth control; Children; Family size; Fertility, Human; Marriage**
Childnapping. *See* **Parental kidnapping**
Children (May subdiv. geog.) 305.23
    Use for materials on people from birth through age twelve. Materials limited to the first two years of a child's life are entered under **Infants.**
    See also

Abandoned children	**Infants**
Advertising and children	**Kindergarten**
Birth order	**Missing children**
Black children	**Motion pictures and children**
Boys	
Child development	**Only child**
Childlessness	**Orphans**
Computers and children	**Play**
Exceptional children	**Playgrounds**
Girls	**Runaway children**
Handicapped children	**School children**
Heredity	**Television and children**
Indians of North America—Children	**World War, 1939-1945—Children**

    x Preschool children
    xx **Boys; Family; Girls; Infants**
Children, Abandoned. *See* **Abandoned children**

Children, Abnormal. *See* **Exceptional children; Handicapped children**

Children—Abuse. *See* **Child abuse**

Children, Adopted. *See* **Adopted children**

Children—Adoption. *See* **Adoption**

Children and adults   305.23; 362.7; 649

   See also **Child rearing; Children and strangers; Conflict of generations; Grandparent and child; Parent and child; Teacher-student relationships**

   x Adults and children

   xx **Child psychology**

Children and grandparents. *See* **Grandparent and child**

Children and motion pictures. *See* **Motion pictures and children**

Children and prostitution. *See* **Juvenile prostitution**

Children and strangers   362.7

   x Infants and strangers; Strangers and children

   xx **Children and adults**

Children and television. *See* **Television and children**

Children as artists. *See* **Child artists**

Children as authors. *See* **Child authors**

Children as consumers. *See* **Young consumers**

Children, Black. *See* **Black children**

Children—Books and reading   011.62; 028.5

   Use for materials on the reading interests of children, as well as for lists of books for children. Collections of works published for children are entered under **Children's literature.** For collections of works written by children use **Children's writings.** Materials on works written by children and materials about children as authors are entered under **Child authors.**

   x Books and reading for children; Reading interests of children

Children—Care. *See* **Child care**

Children—Care and hygiene. *See* **Child care; Children—Health and hygiene**

Children, Care of. *See* **Child care**

Children—Charities, protection, etc. *See* **Child welfare**

Children—Civil rights   323.3; 342

Children—Clothing. *See* **Children's clothing**

Children—Costume   391

   Use for descriptive and historical materials on children's costume among various nations and at different periods. Materials dealing with children's clothing from a practical standpoint are entered under **Children's clothing.**

   xx **Costume**

Children, Crippled. *See* **Physically handicapped children**

Children, Cruelty to. *See* **Child abuse**

Children—Custody. *See* **Child custody**

Children—Day care. *See* **Child care centers**

Children, Delinquent. *See* **Juvenile delinquency**

Children—Development. *See* **Child development**

Children—Diseases   618.92

   See also **Children—Health and hygiene; Chil-**

Children—Diseases—*Continued*
 dren's hospitals; also names of diseases, e.g.
 Chickenpox; etc.
 x Childhood diseases; Children's diseases; Diseases of children; Medicine, Pediatric; Pediatrics
 xx **Children—Health and hygiene; Children's
 hospitals; Diseases**
Children—Education. *See* **Elementary education;
 Preschool education**
Children, Emotionally disturbed. *See* **Emotionally
 disturbed children**
Children—Employment (May subdiv. geog.) **331.3**
 See also **Apprentices; Hours of labor; Moneymaking projects for children**
 x Boys—Employment; Child labor; Employment of children; Girls—Employment;
 Working children
 xx **Age and employment; Child welfare; Compul-
 sory education; Hours of labor; Labor; La-
 bor supply; School attendance; Social prob-
 lems**
Children—Employment—United States 331.3
 x United States—Children—Employment
Children, Exceptional. *See* **Exceptional children**
Children—Food 641.5
 See also **School children—Food**
 x Children's food
 xx **Children—Nutrition**
Children, Gifted. *See* **Gifted children**
Children—Growth 155.4; 612.6
 xx **Child development**
Children—Health and hygiene 613
 See also **Children—Diseases; Children—
 Nutrition; Children's hospitals; Health edu-
 cation; School hygiene; School nurses**
 x Children—Care and hygiene; Children—
 Hygiene; Pediatrics
 xx **Children—Diseases**
Children—Hospitals. *See* **Children's hospitals**
Children—Hygiene. *See* **Children—Health and hy-
 giene**
Children, Hyperactive. *See* **Hyperactive children**
Children, Illegitimate. *See* **Illegitimacy**
Children in art 704.9
 Use for materials on children depicted in works
 of art. Materials on children as artists are
 entered under **Child artists.**
 xx **Art**
Children in literature 809
 Use for materials on the theme of children in
 works of literature. For works written by
 children use **Children's writings.** Materials
 about children as authors and about works
 written by children are entered under **Child
 authors.**
 xx **Characters and characteristics in literature**
Children—Institutional care 362.7
 See also **Child care centers; Foster home care;
 Orphanages; Reformatories**
 x Boys' towns; Children's homes; Homes (Institutions)
 xx **Child welfare; Foster home care; Institutional
 care**

148

Children—Language   155.4; 372.6
  xx **Language and languages**
Children, Latchkey.   *See* **Latchkey children**
Children—Management.   *See* **Child rearing**
Children—Mental health.   *See* **Child psychiatry**
Children—Molesting.   *See* **Child molesting**
Children—Nutrition   613.2083; 641.1083; 649
  See also **Children—Food**
  xx **Children—Health and hygiene; Nutrition**
Children of alcoholics   362.29
  See also **Adult children of alcoholics**
  x Alcoholics' children; C.O.A.s; COAs
  xx **Alcoholics; Alcoholism; Parent and child**
Children of divorced parents   306.874; 646.7
  See also **Parenting, Part-time**
  xx **Divorce; Parent and child; Parenting, Part-time; Single parent family**
Children of drug addicts   362.29
  x Children of narcotic addicts; Cocaine babies; Crack babies; Drug addicts' children; Drug addicts' infants
  xx **Drug addiction; Drug addicts; Parent and child**
Children of immigrants   305.23
  x First generation children
  xx **Immigration and emigration; Parent and child**
Children of narcotic addicts.   *See* **Children of drug addicts**
Children of single parents.   *See* **Single parent family**
Children of working parents   306.874; 362.7
  See also **Latchkey children**
  x Working parents, Children of
  xx **Parent and child**
Children—Placing out.   *See* **Adoption; Foster home care**
Children—Psychology.   *See* **Child psychology**
Children, Retarded.   *See* **Mentally handicapped children; Slow learning children**
Children—Socialization.   *See* **Socialization**
Children—Training.   *See* **Child rearing**
Children—United States   305.230973
  x United States—Children
Children's allowances   332.024; 649
  See also **Moneymaking projects for children**
  x Allowances, Children's
  xx **Child rearing; Money; Moneymaking projects for children; Personal finance**
Children's books.   *See* **Children's literature**
Children's clothing   646.4; 649
  See note under **Children—Costume.**
  x Children—Clothing
  xx **Clothing and dress**
Children's courts.   *See* **Juvenile courts**
Children's day care centers.   *See* **Child care centers**
Children's diseases.   *See* **Children—Diseases**
Children's food.   *See* **Children—Food**
Children's homes.   *See* **Children—Institutional care**
Children's hospitals   362.1
  See also **Child welfare; Children—Diseases**
  x Children—Hospitals
  xx **Child welfare; Children—Diseases; Children—Health and hygiene; Hospitals; Public welfare**

Children's libraries   027.62

>*See also* **Children's literature; Elementary school libraries; Libraries and schools; Young adults' library services**
>
>*x* Libraries and children; Libraries, Children's; Library services to children
>
>*xx* **Children's literature; Elementary school libraries; Libraries and schools; School libraries; Young adults' library services**

Children's literature   808.8; 810.8, etc.

>Use for collections of works published for children. Materials on the reading interests of children, as well as lists of books for children, are entered under **Children—Books and reading.** For works written by children, use **Children's writings.** Materials about works written by children and materials about children as authors are entered under **Child authors.**
>
>*See also*

Big books	**Libraries and schools**
Caldecott Medal books	**Newbery Medal books**
Children's libraries	**Picture books for children**
Children's plays	**Plot-your-own stories**
Children's poetry	**Reading materials**
Easy reading materials	**Storytelling**
Fairy tales	

>*x* Books for children; Children's books; Children's stories; Juvenile literature
>
>*xx* **Children's libraries; Libraries and schools; Literature; School libraries**

Children's literature—History and criticism   809

Children's moneymaking projects.   *See* **Moneymaking projects for children**

Children's parties   395; 793.2

>*xx* **Games; Parties**

Children's plays   808.82; 809.3; 812, etc.; 812.008, etc.; 812.009, etc.

>Use for collections of plays for children by one or more authors and for materials about children's plays.
>
>*x* Plays for children; School plays
>
>*xx* **Amateur theater; Children's literature; Drama; Drama—Collections; Theater**

Children's poetry   808.81; 809.1; 811, etc.; 811.008, etc.; 811.009, etc.

>Use for collections of poetry for children by one or more authors and for materials about children's poetry. For poetry written by children use **Children's writings.** Materials about poetry written by children are entered under **Child authors.**
>
>*See also* **Children's songs; Lullabies; Nonsense verses; Nursery rhymes; Tongue twisters**
>
>*x* Poetry for children
>
>*xx* **Children's literature; Poetry; Poetry—Collections**

Children's reading.   *See* **Reading**

Children's songs   782.42

>*See also* **Lullabies; Nursery rhymes**
>
>*x* Songs for children
>
>*xx* **Children's poetry; School songbooks; Songs**

Children's stories.   *See* **Children's literature; Fairy tales**

Children's writings   808.8; 810.8, etc.
  Use for collections of literary works or individual literary works written by children. Discussions about children's literary works and materials on children as authors are entered under **Child authors.** Collections of works published for children are entered under **Children's literature.**
  See also **College and school journalism**
  x School prose; School verse
  xx **College and school journalism**
Chimes. *See* **Bells**
Chimneys   697; 721
  x Smoke stacks
  xx **Architecture—Details; Building; Fireplaces; Heating; Ventilation**
China   951
  Use as a heading or as a geographic subdivision for works discussing mainland China or the People's Republic of China, regardless of time period. Materials discussing the post-1948 Republic of China or the island of Taiwan are entered under **Taiwan,** regardless of time period.
  Appropriate period subdivisions may be added as needed.
  x China (People's Republic of China); People's Republic of China
China—History   951
China—History—1912-1949   951.04
China—History—1949-   951.05
China—History—1949-1976   951.05
China—History—1976-   951.05
China—History—1989, Tiananmen Square Incident   951.05
  x Beijing Massacre, 1989; Tiananmen Square Incident, China, 1989; Tiananmen Square Massacre, China; Tien-an men Incident, China, 1989; Tien-an men Massacre, 1989
China painting   738.1
  x Porcelain painting
  xx **Decoration and ornament; Painting; Porcelain**
China (People's Republic of China). *See* **China**
China (Porcelain). *See* **Porcelain**
China (Republic of China, 1949-). *See* **Taiwan**
Chinaware. *See* **Porcelain**
Chinese Americans   305.895
Chinese satellite countries. *See* **Communist countries**
Chipmunks   599.32
  xx **Squirrels**
Chiropody. *See* **Podiatry**
Chiropractic   615.5
  See also **Naturopathy**
  xx **Alternative medicine; Massage; Medicine; Naturopathy; Osteopathy**
Chivalry   394
  See also **Civilization, Medieval; Crusades; Feudalism; Heraldry; Knights and knighthood; Romances**
  xx **Civilization, Medieval; Crusades; Feudalism; Heraldry; Knights and knighthood; Manners and customs; Middle Ages**
Chivalry—Romances. *See* **Romances**

Chocolate 641.3
> *See also* **Cocoa**
> *xx* **Cocoa**

Choice, Freedom of. *See* **Free will and determinism**
Choice of books. *See* **Book selection; Books and reading; Books and reading—Best books**
Choice of college. *See* **College choice**
Choice of profession, occupation, vocation, etc. *See* **Vocational guidance**

Choice (Psychology) 153.8
> *See also* **Decision making**
> *xx* **Decision making; Psychology**

Choirs (Music) 782.5
> *See also* **Choral conducting; Choral music; Choral societies; Singing**
> *xx* **Choral conducting; Choral music; Choral societies; Church music; Singing**

Cholesterol content of food. *See* **Food—Cholesterol content**

Choose-your-own story plots. *See* **Plot-your-own stories**

Choral conducting 782.5
> See note under **Conducting.**
> *See also* **Choirs (Music); Choral music; Conductors (Music)**
> *x* Conducting, Choral
> *xx* **Choirs (Music); Choral music; Conducting; Conductors (Music)**

Choral music 782.5
> *See also* **Cantatas; Choirs (Music); Choral conducting; Choral societies**
> *x* Music, Choral
> *xx* **Choirs (Music); Choral conducting; Choral societies; Church music; Vocal music**

Choral societies 782.506
> *See also* **Choirs (Music); Choral music**
> *x* Singing societies
> *xx* **Choirs (Music); Choral music; Societies**

Choral speaking 808.5
> *x* Speaking choirs; Unison speaking

Christ. *See* **Jesus Christ**
Christening. *See* **Baptism**

Christian antiquities 225.9; 270; 930.1
> *See also* **Architecture, Gothic; Catacombs; Christian art and symbolism; Church architecture; Church furniture**
> *x* Antiquities, Christian; Antiquities, Ecclesiastical; Archeology, Christian; Christians—Antiquities; Church antiquities; Ecclesiastical antiquities
> *xx* **Antiquities; Archeology; Bible—Antiquities; Christian art and symbolism**

Christian art and symbolism 246
> *See also*

Bible—Pictorial works	**Illumination of books and**
Catacombs	**manuscripts**
Cathedrals	**Jesus Christ—Art**
Christian antiquities	**Mary, Blessed Virgin,**
Church architecture	**Saint—Art**
Church furniture	**Symbolism of numbers**

> *x* Art, Christian; Art, Ecclesiastical; Christian symbolism; Ecclesiastical art; Iconography; Sacred art

Christian art and symbolism—*Continued*

 xx **Archeology; Art; Christian antiquities; Jesus Christ—Art; Religious art and symbolism; Symbolism**

Christian biography. *See* **Christianity—Biography**

Christian civilization. *See* **Civilization, Christian**

Christian devotional calendars. *See* **Devotional calendars**

Christian doctrine. *See* **Doctrinal theology**

Christian education 268

 See note under **Church and education.**

 See also **Bible—Study; Catechisms; Church and education; Fundamentalism and education; Theology—Study and teaching**

 x Education, Christian

 xx **Christian life; Fundamentalism and education; Religious education; Theology—Study and teaching**

Christian ethics 241

 Use same form for ethics of other religious groups, e.g. **Jewish ethics;** etc.

 See also **Christian life; Christianity and economics; Conscience; Psychology, Pastoral; Sin**

 x Christian moral theology; Ethics, Christian; Moral theology, Christian

 xx **Christian life; Ethics**

Christian life 248.4

 See also **Christian education; Christian ethics; Conversion; Revivals**

 x Life, Christian; Religious life (Christian)

 xx **Christian ethics**

Christian literature 200

 See also **Catholic literature; Devotional literature**

 xx **Religious literature**

Christian literature—30(ca.)-600, Early. *See* **Early Christian literature**

Christian literature, Early. *See* **Early Christian literature**

Christian ministry. *See* **Ministry, Christian**

Christian missions. *See* **Missions, Christian**

Christian moral theology. *See* **Christian ethics**

Christian names. *See* **Personal names**

Christian new birth. *See* **Regeneration (Christianity)**

Christian regeneration. *See* **Regeneration (Christianity)**

Christian saints 270; 920

 See also **Apostles**

 xx **Saints**

Christian Science 289.5

 See also **Mental healing; Spiritual healing**

 x Church of Christ, Scientist; Divine healing; Mind cure

 xx **Medicine and religion; Mental healing; Spiritual healing**

Christian sociology. *See* **Sociology, Christian**

Christian symbolism. *See* **Christian art and symbolism**

Christian unity 262; 270.8

 Use for materials on the worldwide movement towards bringing all Christian faiths into cooperation, fellowship and eventually one organization.

Christian unity—*Continued*

    See also **Community churches; Interfaith relations**

    x Church unity; Ecumenical movement

    xx **Church**

Christianity 200

    See also

Atonement—Christianity	**Miracles—Christianity**
Civilization, Christian	**Missions, Christian**
Councils and synods	**Protestantism**
Deism	**Reformation**
God—Christianity	**Theology**
Jesus Christ	

    also names of Christian churches and sects, e.g. **Catholic Church; Huguenots;** etc. and headings beginning with the words **Christian** and **Church**

    xx **Church; Deism; God—Christianity; Jesus Christ; Religions; Theism; Theology**

Christianity and economics 261.8

    Use same form for Christianity and other subjects.

    See also **Church and labor**

    x Economics and Christianity

    xx **Christian ethics; Church and labor; Communism and religion; Economics; Sociology, Christian**

Christianity and other religions 261.2

    See also **Paganism**

    x Christianity—Relations; Comparative religion

Christianity and politics 261.7; 322

    x Politics and Christianity

    xx **Church—Government policy; Religion and politics**

Christianity and war. *See* **War and religion**

Christianity—Apologetic works. *See* **Apologetics**

Christianity—Biography 920

    x Christian biography; Ecclesiastical biography; Religious biography

    xx **Religions—Biography**

Christianity—Evidences. *See* **Apologetics**

Christianity—History. *See* **Church history**

Christianity—Origin. *See* **Church history—30(ca.)-600, Early church**

Christianity—Philosophy 201

    x Theology—Philosophy

Christianity—Psychology 201; 253.5; 261.5

    xx **Psychology, Religious**

Christianity—Relations. *See* **Christianity and other religions**

Christians—Antiquities. *See* **Christian antiquities**

Christians—Persecutions. *See* **Persecution**

Christmas (May subdiv. geog.) 263; 394.2

    See also **Christmas entertainments; Jesus Christ—Nativity; Santa Claus**

    xx **Fasts and feasts; Holidays; Jesus Christ—Nativity**

Christmas cards. *See* **Greeting cards**

Christmas carols. *See* **Carols**

Christmas decorations 394.2; 745.594

    See also **Christmas trees**

    x Christmas ornaments

Christmas—Drama 394.2; 792; 808.82; 812, etc.; 812.008, etc.

   x Christmas plays; Plays, Christmas

   xx **Christmas entertainments; Religious drama**

Christmas entertainments 394.2; 791

   See also **Christmas—Drama**

   x Entertainments

   xx **Christmas**

Christmas ornaments. *See* **Christmas decorations**

Christmas plays. *See* **Christmas—Drama**

Christmas—Poetry 808.81; 811.008, etc.

   See also **Carols**

   xx **Poetry—Collections**

Christmas tree growing 635.9

   x Growing of Christmas trees

   xx **Forests and forestry; Trees**

Christmas trees 394.2; 745.594

   xx **Christmas decorations; Evergreens; Trees**

Christmas—United States 394.2

   x United States—Christmas

Christology. *See* **Jesus Christ**

Chromosome mapping. *See* **Genetic mapping**

Chromosomes 574.8

   See also **Genetic recombination**

   xx **Genetics; Heredity**

Chronology 529

   Use for materials on the science that deals with measuring time by regular divisions and that assigns proper dates to events.

   See also **Almanacs; Day; Months; Night; Week;** also subjects with the subdivision *Chronology,* e.g. **Bible—Chronology; Indians of North America—Chronology;** etc.

   x Hours (Time)

   xx **Almanacs; Astronomy; History; Time**

Chronology, Biblical. *See* **Bible—Chronology**

Chronology, Historical 902

   Use for materials in which events are arranged by date.

   See also names of countries, cities, etc., with the subdivision *History—Chronology,* e.g. **United States—History—Chronology;** etc.

   x Dates, Historical; Historical chronology; History—Chronology

Church 260

   See also **Christian unity; Christianity**

   xx **Christianity; Theology**

Church and education 261; 377

   Use same form for the church and other subjects.

   Use for materials on the relation of the church to education in general, and for materials on the history of the part that the church has taken in secular education. Materials on church supported and controlled elementary and secondary schools are entered under **Church schools.** Materials on the instruction of religion in schools and private life are entered under **Religious education,** and on Christian religion under **Christian education.**

   See also **Academic freedom; Fundamentalism and education; Religion in the public schools;**

Church and education—*Continued*
  Theology—Study and teaching
 x Education and church; Education and religion; Religion and education
 xx **Academic freedom; Christian education; Church—Government policy; Education; Theology—Study and teaching**
Church and labor **261.8**
 See also **Christianity and economics**
 x Labor and the church
 xx **Christianity and economics; Labor**
Church and race relations **261.8**
 x Integrated churches; Race relations and the church
Church and social problems **261.8**
 Use for materials dealing with the practical treatment of social problems from the point of view of the church. For materials on social theory from a Christian point of view use **Sociology, Christian.**
 See also **Church work; Liberation theology; Sanctuary movement; Sociology, Christian**
 x Religion and social problems; Social problems and the church
 xx **Church work**
Church and state. *See* **Church—Government policy**
Church and war. *See* **War and religion**
Church antiquities. *See* **Christian antiquities**
Church, Apostolic. *See* **Church history—30(ca.)-600, Early church**
Church architecture **726**
 See also **Abbeys; Architecture, Gothic; Cathedrals; Churches; Mosques; Spires; Temples**
 x Architecture, Church; Architecture, Ecclesiastical; Ecclesiastical architecture; Religious art
 xx **Architecture; Architecture, Gothic; Christian antiquities; Christian art and symbolism; Churches**
Church attendance. *See* **Public worship**
Church bells. *See* **Bells**
Church councils. *See* **Councils and synods**
Church denominations. *See* **Sects;** and names of particular denominations and sects, e.g. **Presbyterian Church;** etc.
Church entertainments **259**
 x Church sociables; Entertainments; Socials
 xx **Amusements; Church work**
Church festivals. *See* **Fasts and feasts**
Church finance **254.8**
 See also **Tithes**
 x Finance, Church
 xx **Finance**
Church furniture **247; 726**
 x Ecclesiastical furniture
 xx **Christian antiquities; Christian art and symbolism; Furniture**
Church—Government policy (May subdiv. geog.)
  261.7; 322
 See also **Christianity and politics; Church and education; Ecclesiastical law; Freedom of conscience; Freedom of religion; Popes—Temporal power; Religion in the public**

Church—Government policy—*Continued*
> schools
>> *x* Church and state; Religion and state; State
>> and church; State church
>> *xx* **Freedom of religion; Popes—Temporal power**

Church—Government policy—United States 322
> *x* United States—Church—Government policy

Church history 270
> Use for materials dealing with the development
> of Christianity and church organization.
> *See also*

Abbeys	**Persecution**
Councils and synods	**Popes**
Creeds	**Protestant churches**
Jews	**Protestantism**
Martyrs	**Reformation**
Miracles—Christianity	**Revivals**
Missions, Christian	**Sects**
Papacy	

> also names of countries, states, etc. with the sub-
> division *Church history,* e.g. **United
> States—Church history;** etc.; names of de-
> nominations, sects, churches, etc.; and head-
> ings beginning with the word **Christian**
> *x* Christianity—History; Ecclesiastical history;
> History, Church; Religious history
> *xx* **History**

Church history—30(ca.)-600, Early church 209;
> **270.1; 270.2**
> *See also* **Apostles; Catacombs; Early Christian
> literature; Gnosticism**
> *x* Apostolic Church; Christianity—Origin;
> Church, Apostolic; Early church history;
> Primitive Christianity
> *xx* **Catacombs; Early Christian literature**

Church history—600-1500, Middle Ages
> **270.2-270.5**
> *See also* **Crusades; Inquisition; Popes—Temporal
> power**
> *x* Medieval church history
> *xx* **Middle Ages**

Church history—1500- , Modern period
> **270.5-270.8**
> *x* Modern church history

Church history—1517-1648, Reformation. *See*
> **Reformation**

Church law. *See* **Ecclesiastical law**

Church libraries 027.6
> *x* Libraries, Church; Parish libraries
> *xx* **Libraries**

Church music 781.71
> *See also*

Carols	**Gospel music**
Chants (Plain, Gregorian,	**Hymns**
etc.)	**Liturgies**
Choirs (Music)	**Oratorios**
Choral music	**Organ music**

> *x* Music, Sacred; Psalmody; Religious music;
> Sacred music
> *xx* **Devotional exercises; Hymns; Music**

Church of Christ, Scientist. *See* **Christian Science**

Church of England (May subdiv. geog.) 283
> *x* Anglican Church; England, Church of

Church of England—United States   283
>   Use for materials on the Episcopal Church in the
>   United States prior to 1789. Materials on
>   the Episcopal Church in the United States
>   after 1789 are entered under **Episcopal
>   Church.**
>   *See also* **Episcopal Church; Puritans**
>   *x* United States—Church of England
>   *xx* **Episcopal Church; Puritans**

Church of Jesus Christ of Latter-day Saints   289.3
>   *x* Latter-day Saints; Mormon Church
>   *xx* **Mormons**

Church schools   377
>   See note under **Church and education.**
>   *See also* **Fundamentalism and education**
>   *x* Denominational schools; Nonpublic schools;
>   Parochial schools; Schools, Parochial
>   *xx* **Fundamentalism and education; Private
>   schools; Schools**

Church service books.   *See* **Liturgies**

Church settlements.   *See* **Social settlements**

Church sociables.   *See* **Church entertainments**

Church unity.   *See* **Christian unity**

Church work   250
>   *See also*

Church and social problems	**Missions, Christian**
Church entertainments	**Psychology, Pastoral**
Evangelistic work	**Revivals**
Lay ministry	**Rural churches**
	Sunday schools

>   *xx* **Church and social problems; Pastoral work**

Church work, Rural.   *See* **Rural churches**

Church work with the sick   362.1
>   Use same form for church work with other
>   groups of people.
>   *xx* **Sick**

Church work with youth   259
>   *xx* **Youth**

Churches (May subdiv. geog.)   **280**
>   Use for general descriptive and historical materi-
>   als on churches which cannot be entered un-
>   der **Church architecture.**
>   *See also* **Cathedrals; Church architecture;** also
>   names of individual churches
>   *xx* **Church architecture**

Churches, Avant-garde.   *See* **Noninstitutional
    churches**

Churches, Community.   *See* **Community churches**

Churches, Country.   *See* **Rural churches**

Churches, Noninstitutional.   *See* **Noninstitutional
    churches**

Churches, Rural.   *See* **Rural churches**

Churches, Undenominational.   *See* **Community
    churches**

Churches—United States   277.3; 280.0973
>   *x* United States—Churches

Churchyards.   *See* **Cemeteries**

Cicadas   595.7; 632
>   *x* 17 year locusts; Locusts, Seventeen-year; Sev-
>   enteen-year locusts

Cigarettes   679
>   *xx* **Smoking**

Cigars   679
>   *xx* **Smoking**

Cinema. *See* **Motion pictures**
Cinematography. *See* **Motion picture photography**
Cipher and telegraph codes   384.1
    x Cable codes; Codes, Telegraph; Morse code;
        Telegraph codes
    xx **Telegraph**
Ciphers   652
    See also **Abbreviations; Cryptography; Writing**
    x Codes; Contractions
    xx **Abbreviations; Cryptography; Signs and sym-
        bols; Writing**
Ciphers (Lettering). *See* **Monograms**
Circuits, Electric. *See* **Electric circuits**
Circulation of library materials. *See* **Library circu-
        lation**
Circulation of the blood. *See* **Blood—Circulation**
Circulatory system. *See* **Cardiovascular system**
Circumnavigation. *See* **Voyages around the world**
Circus   791.3
    See also **Acrobats and acrobatics; Animals—
        Training; Clowns**
    xx **Amusements**
Cities and towns (May subdiv. geog.)   **307.76**
    Use for general materials on cities and towns.
        For materials on large cities and their sur-
        rounding areas use **Metropolitan areas.**
        General materials on the government of cit-
        ies are entered under **Municipal govern-
        ment;** general materials on local govern-
        ment other than that of cities are entered
        under **Local government.**
    See also

Art, Municipal	**Sociology, Urban**
City life	**Streets**
Inner cities	**Tenement houses**
Markets	**Urbanization**
Parks	**Villages**

    also headings beginning with the word **Munici-
        pal;** and names of individual cities and
        towns
    x Municipalities; Towns; Urban areas
    xx **Local government; Municipal government; So-
        ciology; Sociology, Urban**
Cities and towns—Civic improvement   307.3; 352.9
    See also **City planning; Community centers**
    x Civic improvement; Municipal improvements
Cities and towns—Growth   307.76
    See also **Metropolitan areas**
    x Cities and towns, Movement to; Urban devel-
        opment
    xx **Migration, Internal; Population; Vital statis-
        tics**
Cities and towns—Lighting. *See* **Streets—Lighting**
Cities and towns, Movement to. *See* **Cities and
        towns—Growth; Urbanization**
Cities and towns—Planning. *See* **City planning**
Cities and towns, Ruined, extinct, etc.   930
    See also **Excavations (Archeology); Ghost towns**
    x Abandoned towns; Buried cities; Extinct cit-
        ies; Ruins; Sunken cities
    xx **Archeology; Ghost towns**
Cities and towns—United States   307.760973; 973
    x United States—Cities and towns
Cities, Imaginary. *See* **Geographical myths**

Citizen participation. *See* appropriate subjects with
the subdivision *Citizen participation,* e.g.
City planning—United States—Citizen par-
ticipation; etc.
Citizens band radio   621.3845
x C.B. radio; CB radio; Citizens radio service
xx **Shortwave radio**
Citizen's defender. *See* **Ombudsman**
Citizens radio service. *See* **Citizens band radio**
Citizenship   172; 323.6
See also **Aliens; Naturalization; Patriotism; Suf-**
frage
x Civics; Foreigners; Franchise; Nationality
(Citizenship)
xx **Aliens; Constitutional law; Naturalization; Po-**
litical ethics; Political science; Social ethics
Citrus fruit   634
Names of fruits are not included in this List but
are to be added as needed, in the singular
form, e.g. **Orange;** etc.
See also names of citrus fruits, e.g. **Orange;**
etc.
xx **Fruit**
City and town life. *See* **City life**
City-federal relations. *See* **Federal-city relations**
City government. *See* **Municipal government**
City life   307.76
See also **Community life**
x City and town life; Town life; Urban life
xx **Cities and towns; Community life; Sociology,**
Urban
City manager. *See* **Municipal government by city**
manager
City planning (May subdiv. geog.)   **307.1; 352.9; 711**
See also

Art, Municipal	**Community development**
Chicago (Ill.)—Public	**Housing**
buildings	**Social surveys**
Chicago (Ill.)—Public	**Urban renewal**
works	**Zoning**

x Cities and towns—Planning; Municipal planning; Planning, City; Town planning; Urban
planning
xx **Art, Municipal; Cities and towns—Civic im-**
provement; Community development; Hous-
ing; Regional planning; Tenement houses;
Urban renewal
City planning—United States   307; 352.9; 711
x United States—City planning
City planning—United States—Citizen participation
307.1
xx **Social action**
City planning—Zone system. *See* **Zoning**
City-state relations. *See* **State-local relations**
City traffic   388.3
x Local traffic; Street traffic; Traffic, City; Ur-
ban traffic
xx **Streets; Traffic engineering**
City transit. *See* **Local transit**
Civic art. *See* **Art, Municipal**
Civic improvement. *See* **Cities and towns—Civic**
improvement
Civic involvement. *See* appropriate subjects with

160

Civic involvement—*Continued*
the subdivision *Citizen participation,* e.g.
City planning—United States—Citizen participation; etc.

Civics.   *See* **Citizenship; Political science; United States—Politics and government**

Civil defense   363.3
See note under **Air defenses.**
See also **Air defenses; Air raid shelters; Disaster relief; Rescue work; Survival skills;** also names of countries, cities, etc., with the subdivision *Civil defense,* e.g. **Chicago (Ill.)—Civil defense; United States—Civil defense;;** etc.; and individual wars with the subdivision *Evacuation of civilians,* e.g. **World War, 1939-1945—Evacuation of civilians;** etc.
x Blackouts in war; Civilian defense; Defense, Civil
xx **Disaster relief; Military art and science**

Civil disobedience.   *See* **Government, Resistance to; Passive resistance**

Civil disorders.   *See* **Riots**

Civil engineering   624
See also

Aqueducts	**Public works**
Bridges	**Railroad engineering**
Canals	**Reclamation of land**
Dams	**Rivers**
Drainage	**Roads**
Dredging	**Sanitary engineering**
Excavation	**Steel, Structural**
Foundations	**Streets**
Harbors	**Strength of materials**
Highway engineering	**Structural engineering**
Hydraulic engineering	**Subways**
Irrigation	**Surveying**
Marine engineering	**Tunnels**
Masonry	**Walls**
Mechanical engineering	**Water supply**
Military engineering	**Water supply engineering**
Mining engineering	

xx **Engineering**

Civil government.   *See* **Political science; United States—Politics and government**

Civil law suits.   *See* **Litigation**

Civil liberty.   *See* **Freedom**

Civil rights   323; 342
Use for materials on citizens' rights as established by law and protected by constitution. For materials on the rights of persons regardless of their legal, socioeconomic or cultural status and as recognized by the international community, use **Human rights.**
See also

Academic freedom	**Freedom of association**
Anti-apartheid movement	**Freedom of information**
Discrimination	**Freedom of movement**
Free speech	**Freedom of religion**
Freedom	**Freedom of the press**
Freedom of assembly	**Right of privacy**

also names of groups of people with the subdivision *Civil rights,* e.g. **Blacks—Civil rights;**

Civil rights—*Continued*

     Men—Civil rights; Women—Civil rights; etc.

  x Basic rights; Constitutional rights; Fundamental rights; Rights, Civil

  xx **Constitutional law; Discrimination; Freedom; Human rights; Political science**

Civil rights (International law). *See* **Human rights**

Civil service (May subdiv. geog.)   **350.6**

     Use for general materials on the history and development of public service. Materials on public personnel administration, including the duties of civil service employees, their salaries, pensions, etc., are entered under the name of the country, state or city with the subdivision *Officials and employees.*

     See also **Bureaucracy;** also names of countries, cities, etc., with the subdivision *Officials and employees,* e.g. **Chicago (Ill.)— Officials and employees;** etc.

  x Administration; Employees and officials; Government employees; Government service; Municipal employees; Office, Tenure of; Officials; Tenure of office

  xx **Administrative law; Bureaucracy; Political science; Public administration**

Civil service—Examinations   **351.3**

  xx **Examinations**

Civil service—United States   **353.006**

     See also **United States—Officials and employees**

  x United States—Civil service

  xx **United States—Officials and employees**

Civil War—England. *See* **Great Britain— History—1642-1660, Civil War and Commonwealth**

Civil War—United States. *See* **United States— History—1861-1865, Civil War**

Civilian defense. *See* **Civil defense**

Civilian evacuation. *See* **World War, 1939-1945— Evacuation of civilians**

Civilization   **306; 909**

     Use for materials dealing with civilization in general and with the development of social customs, art, industry, religion, etc., of several countries or peoples. Materials confined to the civilization of one country are entered under the name of the country with the subdivision *Civilization.* Materials on peoples whose culture spread beyond their own boundaries are entered under such headings as **Civilization, Asian; Civilization, Greek; Civilization, Occidental; Civilization, Scandinavian;** etc. Add as needed.

     See also

Acculturation	**Culture**
Aeronautics and civilization	**Education**
Anthropology	**Ethnology**
Archeology	**Industry**
Art	**Inventions**
Astronautics and civilization	**Learning and scholarship**
Biculturalism	**Manners and customs**
	Nonliterate folk society
	Popular culture

Civilization—*Continued*

    Progress

    Religions

    Science and civilization

    Technology and civilization

    War and civilization

    also names of countries, states, etc., with the subdivision *Civilization,* e.g. **United States—Civilization;** etc.

    xx **Anthropology; Culture; Ethnology; History; History—Philosophy; Progress; Sociology**

Civilization, African   306.096; 960

    x African civilization

Civilization, American   306.097; 306.098; 970; 980

    Use for general materials on the civilization of the Western Hemisphere or of Latin America, and for materials on ancient American civilization, including that of the Mayas, Aztecs, etc. Materials limited to the civilization of the United States are entered under **United States—Civilization.**

    x American civilization

Civilization, Ancient   306.093; 930

    See also **Prehistoric man**

    x Ancient civilization

    xx **History, Ancient**

Civilization and aeronautics. *See* **Aeronautics and civilization**

Civilization and astronautics. *See* **Astronautics and civilization**

Civilization and computers. *See* **Computers and civilization**

Civilization and science. *See* **Science and civilization**

Civilization and technology. *See* **Technology and civilization**

Civilization and war. *See* **War and civilization**

Civilization, Arab   306.0917; 909

    x Arab civilization

Civilization, Asian   306.095; 950

    x Asian civilization; Civilization, Oriental; Oriental civilization

    xx **East and West**

Civilization, Christian   200.9; 909

    x Christian civilization

    xx **Christianity**

Civilization, Greek   938

    Use same form for materials dealing with the culture of people not confined to one country, e.g. **Civilization, Arab; Civilization, Occidental;** etc.

    See also **Hellenism**

    x Greece—Civilization; Greek civilization

Civilization, Jewish. *See* **Jews—Civilization**

Civilization, Medieval   909.07

    See also **Art, Medieval; Chivalry; Feudalism; Middle Ages; Monasticism**

    x Medieval civilization

    xx **Chivalry; Middle Ages; Middle Ages—History; Renaissance**

Civilization, Modern   306.09; 909

    Use for materials covering the period after 1453.

    See also **History, Modern; Renaissance**

    x Modern civilization

    xx **History, Modern**

Civilization, Modern—1950-   306.09; 909.82

Civilization, Occidental   306.09; 909
  x Occidental civilization; Western civilization
  xx **East and West**
Civilization, Oriental.   *See* **Civilization, Asian**
Civilization, Scandinavian   948
  x Scandinavian civilization
Clairvoyance   133.8
  See also **Divination; Fortune telling; Telepathy**
  xx **Divination; Extrasensory perception; Fortune
      telling; Occultism; Parapsychology; Spiritu-
      alism; Telepathy**
Clans   306.85; 941.1
  See also **Tartans;** also names of families
  x Highland clans; Scottish clans
  xx **Family; Feudalism**
Class conflict.   *See* **Social conflict**
Class consciousness   305.5
  xx **Social classes; Social psychology**
Class distinction.   *See* **Social classes**
Class struggle.   *See* **Social conflict**
Classed catalogs.   *See* **Catalogs, Classified**
Classes (Mathematics).   *See* **Set theory**
Classical antiquities   937; 938
  See also **Archeology; Art, Greek; Art, Roman;
      Greece—Antiquities; Mythology, Classical;**
      also names of ancient cities of Greek and
      Roman antiquity e.g. **Delphi (Ancient city);**
      also names of groups of people extant in
      modern times and names of cities (except
      ancient cities), countries, regions, etc., with
      the subdivision *Antiquities,* e.g. **Great Brit-
      ain—Antiquities; Rome—Antiquities;** etc.
  x Antiquities, Classical; Archeology, Classical;
      Classical archeology; Greek antiquities; Ro-
      man antiquities
  xx **Antiquities; Archeology; Art, Ancient**
Classical antiquities—Dictionaries.   *See* **Classical
      dictionaries**
Classical archeology.   *See* **Classical antiquities**
Classical art.   *See* **Art, Greek; Art, Roman**
Classical biography.   *See* **Greece—Biography;
      Rome—Biography**
Classical dictionaries   937.003; 938.003
  x Classical antiquities—Dictionaries; Dictionar-
      ies, Classical
  xx **Encyclopedias and dictionaries; History, An-
      cient**
Classical education   370.11
  See also **Colleges and universities; Humanism;
      Humanities**
  x Education, Classical
  xx **Colleges and universities; Education; Higher
      education; Humanism; Humanities**
Classical geography.   *See* **Geography, Ancient;
      Greece—Historical geography; Rome—
      Geography**
Classical languages.   *See* **Greek language; Latin lan-
      guage**
Classical literature   870; 880
  See also **Greek literature; Latin literature**
  x Literature, Classical
  xx **Greek literature; Latin literature; Literature**
Classical mythology.   *See* **Mythology, Classical**

164

Classification—Books 025.4
> Use same form for classification of other library materials.
>
> *See also* **Catalogs, Classified; Dewey Decimal Classification**
>
> *x* Libraries—Classification; Library classification
>
> *xx* **Bibliography; Cataloging; Catalogs, Classified; Documentation; Library science; Library technical processes; Subject headings**

Classification, Dewey Decimal. *See* **Dewey Decimal Classification**

Classified catalogs. *See* **Catalogs, Classified**

Classroom management 371.1
> *xx* **School discipline; Teaching**

Clay 553.6; 666; 738.1
> *See also* **Bricks; Modeling**
> *xx* **Ceramic materials; Soils**

Clay industries 338.4; 666
> *See also* **Bricks; Pottery; Tiles**
> *xx* **Ceramic industries**

Clay modeling. *See* **Modeling**

Cleaning 648; 667
> *See also*

Bleaching	**House cleaning**
Cleaning compounds	**Laundry**
Dry cleaning	**Soap**
Dyes and dyeing	**Street cleaning**

Cleaning compounds 648; 667
> *See also* **Detergents, Synthetic; Soap**
> *xx* **Cleaning**

Cleanliness 391; 613; 646.7; E
> *See also* **Baths; Hygiene; Sanitation**
> *x* Messiness; Neatness

Clearing of land. *See* **Reclamation of land**

Clergy 253
> *See also* **Celibacy; Chaplains; Priests; Rabbis;** also church denominations with the subdivision *Clergy,* e.g. **Catholic Church—Clergy;** etc.
>
> *x* Curates; Ministers of the gospel; Pastors; Preachers; Rectors
>
> *xx* **Pastoral work**

Clergy—Office. *See* **Ministry**

Clergy—Political activity 253; 261.7

Clerical employees. *See* **Office employees**

Clerical work—Training. *See* **Business education**

Clerks. *See* **Office employees**

Clerks (Retail trade). *See* **Sales personnel**

Cliff dwellers and cliff dwellings 979
> *xx* **Archeology; Indians of North America**

Climacteric, Female. *See* **Menopause**

Climacteric, Male. *See* **Male climacteric**

Climate 551.6
> Use for materials on climate as it relates to man and to plant and animal life, including the effects of changes of climate. Materials limited to the climate of a particular region are entered under the name of the place with the subdivision *Climate.* Materials on the state of the atmosphere at a given time and place with respect to heat or cold, wetness or dryness, calm or storm, are entered under

Climate—*Continued*

    Weather. Scientific materials on the atmosphere, especially weather factors, are entered under **Meteorology.**

    See also **Forest influences; Greenhouse effect; Meteorology; Rain; Seasons; Weather;** also names of countries, cities, etc., with the subdivision *Climate,* e.g. **United States—Climate;** etc.

    x Climatology

    xx **Earth sciences; Meteorology; Physical geography; Weather**

Climate and forests. *See* **Forest influences**

Climatology. *See* **Climate**

Climbing plants 582.1; 635.9

    x Vines

    xx **Gardening; Plants**

Clinical chemistry 616.07

    Use for materials on the chemical diagnosis of disease and health monitoring.

    x Chemistry, Diagnostic; Chemistry, Medical; Chemistry, Medical and pharmaceutical; Diagnostic chemistry; Medical chemistry

    xx **Biochemistry; Diagnosis**

Clinical genetics. *See* **Medical genetics**

Clinical magnetic resonance imaging. *See* **Magnetic resonance imaging**

Clinics. *See* **Medical practice**

Clipper ships 387.2; 623.8

    xx **Ships**

Clippings (Books, newspapers, etc.) 025.17

    x Newspaper clippings; Press clippings

    xx **Newspapers**

Clocks and watches 681.1

    See also **Sundials**

    x Horology; Watches

    xx **Time**

Clog dancing 793.3

    xx **Tap dancing**

Cloisters. *See* **Convents; Monasteries**

Clones and cloning 174; 575.1; 660

    See also **Molecular cloning**

    x DNA cloning

    xx **Genetic engineering**

Cloning, Molecular. *See* **Molecular cloning**

Closed caption television 384.55

    xx **Deaf; Television**

Closed caption video recordings 384.55

    x Video recordings, Closed caption; Video recordings for the hearing impaired

    xx **Deaf; Videodiscs; Videotapes**

Closed-circuit television 384.55

    See also **Television in education**

    x Television, Closed-circuit

    xx **Intercommunication systems; Microwave communication systems; Television; Television in education**

Closed shop. *See* **Open and closed shop**

Cloth. *See* **Fabrics**

Clothes. *See* **Clothing and dress**

Clothiers. *See* **Clothing trade**

Clothing and dress 646

    Use for materials dealing with clothing from a practical standpoint including the art of dress. Descriptive and historical materials on the costume of particular countries, or periods, or peoples, and materials on fancy dress and theatrical costumes are entered under **Costume.** Materials describing the prevailing mode or style of dress are entered under **Fashion.**

Clothing and dress—*Continued*
    See also

Children's clothing	**Fashion**
Costume	**Men's clothing**
Dress accessories	**Tailoring**
Dressmaking	**Women's clothing**

        also names of articles of clothing and accessories, e.g. **Buttons; Hats; Hosiery; Leather garments; Shoes;** etc.
      x Clothes; Dress; Garments
      xx **Costume; Fashion; Manners and customs**
Clothing and dress—Dry cleaning. *See* **Dry cleaning**
Clothing and dress—**Repairing 646.2**
Clothing, Leather. *See* **Leather garments**
Clothing, Men's. *See* **Men's clothing**
Clothing trade 338.4; 687
    See also **Tailoring**
    x Clothiers
Cloud seeding. *See* **Weather control**
Clouds 551.57
    xx **Meteorology**
Clowns 791.3; 791.3092; 920
    xx **Circus; Entertainers**
Clubs 367
    See also **Boys' clubs; Girls' clubs; Men— Societies; Social group work; Societies; Women—Societies**
    xx **Associations; Societies**
Coaches, Stage. *See* **Carriages and carts**
Coaching. *See* **Horsemanship**
Coaching (Athletics) 796.07
    See also names of sports with the subdivision *Coaching,* e.g. **Football—Coaching;** etc.
    x Athletic coaching; Sports coaching
    xx **Athletics; College sports; Physical education; School sports; Sports**
Coal 553.2
    See also **Coal mines and mining**
    x Anthracite coal; Bituminous coal
    xx **Carbon; Fuel; Geology, Economic**
Coal gas. *See* **Gas**
Coal gasification 665.7
    x Gasification of coal
Coal liquefaction 622
    x Liquefaction of coal
Coal miners 622; 920
    xx **Miners**
Coal mines and mining 622
    See also **Mining engineering**
    xx **Coal; Mines and mineral resources**
Coal oil. *See* **Petroleum**
Coal tar products 547.8; 661
    See also **Gas; Oils and fats**
    xx **Gas; Petroleum**
COAs. *See* **Children of alcoholics**
Coast pilot guides. *See* **Pilot guides**
Coastal signals. *See* **Signals and signaling**
Coats of arms. *See* **Heraldry**
Cocaine 362.29; 615
    See also **Crack (Drug)**
    x Intoxicants
    xx **Anesthetics; Narcotics; Psychotropic drugs; Stimulants**

Cocaine babies. *See* **Children of drug addicts**
Cocoa   633.7; 641.3
 See also **Chocolate**
 xx **Beverages; Chocolate**
Cocoons. *See* **Butterflies; Caterpillars; Moths;**
 Silkworms
Code deciphering. *See* **Cryptography**
Code enciphering. *See* **Cryptography**
Code names   423
 See also **Acronyms**
 xx **Abbreviations; Names**
Codes. *See* **Ciphers**
Codes, Penal. *See* **Criminal law**
Codes, Telegraph. *See* **Cipher and telegraph codes**
Coeducation   376
 See also **Education; Men—Education; Women—**
 Education
 xx **Colleges and universities; Education; Men—**
 Education; Women—Education
Coffee   633.7; 641.8
 xx **Beverages**
Coffee houses. *See* **Coffeehouses**
Coffee shops. *See* **Restaurants, bars, etc.**
Coffeehouses   647.95
 Use for materials on public places that specialize
  in serving coffee and other refreshments and
  that sometimes provide informal entertain-
  ment or serve as a place where small groups
  meet. Materials on coffee shops, that is,
  small inexpensive restaurants, indepen-
  dently operated or part of a hotel, where
  light refreshments or regular meals are
  served, are entered under **Restaurants, bars,**
  etc.
 x Coffee houses
 xx **Restaurants, bars, etc.**
Cog wheels. *See* **Gearing**
Cognition. *See* **Knowledge, Theory of**
Cohabitation. *See* **Unmarried couples**
Coiffure. *See* **Hair and hairdressing**
Coin collecting. *See* **Coins**
Coinage   332.4
 Use for materials on the processing and history
  of metal money. Lists of coins and materials
  about coins and coin collecting are entered
  under **Coins.**
 See also **Counterfeits and counterfeiting; Gold;**
  Mints; Monetary policy; Money; Silver
 xx **Gold; Mints; Money; Silver**
Coinage of words. *See* **Words, New**
Coins   737.4
 Use for lists of coins, materials about coins and
  coin collecting. Materials on coins from the
  point of view of art and archeology are entered under **Numismatics;** materials on the
  processing of metal money are entered under **Coinage.**
 See also **Numismatics**
 x Coin collecting
 xx **Money; Numismatics**
Cold   536; 551.5; 551.6
 See also **Cryobiology; Ice; Low temperatures**
 xx **Low temperatures**

Cold (Disease)   616.2
See also **Influenza**
x Common cold
xx **Communicable diseases; Diseases**
Cold—Physiological effect   613
xx **Cryobiology**
Cold storage   641.4; 664
See also **Compressed air; Refrigeration**
xx **Food—Preservation; Meat industry; Refrigeration**
Cold—Therapeutic use   615.8
See also **Cryosurgery**
x Cryotherapy
Cold war. *See* **Psychological warfare; World politics—1945-1965**
Collaborationists. *See* **Treason**
Collage   702.8; 751.4
xx **Art**
Collapse of structures. *See* **Structural failures**
Collected works. *See* **Storytelling—Collections;** and form headings that represent collections of works of several authors, e.g. **American essays; Essays; Parodies; Short stories;** etc.; and names of literatures and literary forms with the subdivision *Collections,* e.g. **English literature—Collections; Poetry—Collections;** etc.
Collectibles. *See* names of events with the subdivision *Collectibles,* e.g. **American Revolution Bicentennial, 1776-1976—Collectibles;** etc.; and names of objects collected with the subdivision *Collectors and collecting,* e.g. **Boxes—Collectors and collecting; Postage stamps—Collectors and collecting;** etc.
Collecting. *See* **Collectors and collecting**
Collecting of accounts   658.8
x Accounts, Collecting of
xx **Commercial law; Credit; Debtor and creditor**
Collection and preservation. *See* antiquities and types of natural objects, including animal specimens and plant specimens, with the subdivision *Collection and preservation* for materials on methods of collecting and preserving those objects.
Collection development (Libraries). *See* **Libraries—Collection development**
Collections of art, painting, etc. *See* **Art—Museums;** and names of original owners of private collections with the subdivision *Art collections;* and names of galleries and museums.
Collections of literature. *See* **Literature—Collections; Storytelling—Collections;** and form headings that represent collections of works of several authors, e.g. **American essays; Essays; Parodies; Short stories;** etc.; and names of literatures and literary forms with the subdivision *Collections,* e.g. **English literature—Collections; Poetry—Collections;** etc.
Collections of natural specimens. *See* **Zoological specimens—Collection and preservation;** and names of natural specimens

Collections of natural specimens—*Continued*
with the subdivision *Collection and preservation,* e.g. **Birds—Collection and preservation;** etc.

Collections of objects. *See* **Collectors and collecting;** and names of events with the subdivision *Collectibles,* e.g. **American Revolution Bicentennial, 1776-1976—Collectibles;** etc.; and types of objects collected, excluding natural objects, with the subdivision *Collectors and collecting,* e.g. **Boxes—Collectors and collecting; Postage stamps—Collectors and collecting;** etc.

Collective bargaining   331.89; 658.3
May be subdivided by groups of professional and nonprofessional workers, e.g. **Collective bargaining—Librarians;** etc.

See also **Arbitration, Industrial; Labor contract; Labor unions; Participative management; Strikes and lockouts**

x Labor negotiations

xx **Arbitration, Industrial; Industrial relations; Labor; Labor contract; Labor disputes; Labor unions; Negotiation; Participative management; Strikes and lockouts**

Collective bargaining—Librarians   331.89
x Librarians—Collective bargaining; Libraries—Collective bargaining

Collective farms. *See* **Agriculture, Cooperative**

Collective labor agreements. *See* **Labor contract**

Collective security. *See* **Security, International**

Collective settlements (May subdiv. geog.)   **307.77; 335**
See also **Bohemianism; Counter culture;** also names of individual communes

x Communal living; Communes; Cooperative living; Group living

xx **Counter culture**

Collective settlements—Israel   307.77
x Israel—Collective settlements; Kibbutz

Collective settlements—United States   307.77
x United States—Collective settlements

Collectivism. *See* **Communism; Socialism**

Collectors and collecting   790.1
See also **Americana; Book collecting;** also types of objects collected, excluding natural objects, with the subdivision *Collectors and collecting,* e.g. **Postage stamps—Collectors and collecting; Postcards—Collectors and collecting;** etc.; names of original owners of private art collections with the subdivision *Art collections;* names of events with the subdivision *Collectibles,* e.g. **American Revolution Bicentennial, 1776-1976—Collectibles;** etc.; and antiquities and types of natural objects with the subdivision *Collection and preservation,* e.g. **Antiquities—Collection and preservation; Birds—Collection and preservation; Plants—Collection and preservation; Zoological specimens—Collection and preservation;** etc.

x Collecting; Collections of objects

xx **Antiques; Art; Hobbies**

Collects. *See* **Prayers**

College admissions essays. *See* **College applications**

College and school drama **371.8; 792**
> Use for materials about college and school drama. Collections of plays for production in colleges and schools are entered under **College and school drama—Collections.**
>
> *See also* **Drama in education**
>
> *x* College drama; School drama; Theatricals, College
>
> *xx* **Amateur theater; Drama; Drama in education; Student activities**

College and school drama—Collected works. *See* **College and school drama—Collections**

College and school drama—Collections **808.82; 812.008, etc.**
> *x* College and school drama—Collected works; College plays; Plays, College; School plays
>
> *xx* **Drama—Collections**

College and school journalism **371.8**
> *See also* **Children's writings**
>
> *x* College journalism; College periodicals; School journalism; School newspapers
>
> *xx* **Children's writings; Journalism; Student activities**

College and university libraries. *See* **Academic libraries**

College applications **378.1**
> *See also* **Colleges and universities—Entrance requirements**
>
> *x* Admissions applications; Admissions essays; Applications for college; College admissions essays; Colleges and universities—Applications
>
> *xx* **Colleges and universities—Entrance requirements**

College athletics. *See* **Athletics; College sports**

College choice **378.1**
> *x* Choice of college; Colleges and universities—Selection
>
> *xx* **Colleges and universities**

College costs **378.3**
> *x* Tuition
>
> *xx* **Colleges and universities—Finance**

College degrees. *See* **Academic degrees**

College drama. *See* **College and school drama**

College dropouts. *See* **Dropouts**

College entrance examinations. *See* **Colleges and universities—Entrance examinations**

College entrance requirements. *See* **Colleges and universities—Entrance requirements;** and names of individual colleges and universities with the subdivision *Entrance requirements*

College fraternities. *See* **Fraternities and sororities**

College graduates **331.11; 378; 650.1**
> *See also* **College students**
>
> *x* Graduates, College; University graduates
>
> *xx* **College students; Professions**

College journalism. *See* **College and school journalism**

College life. *See* **College students**

College periodicals. *See* **College and school journalism**

College plays. *See* **College and school drama—Collections**

College songs. *See* **Students' songs**

College sororities. *See* **Fraternities and sororities**

College sports 371.8; 796
> *See also* **Coaching (Athletics)**; also names of individual sports, e.g. **Baseball; Basketball; Football; Rowing; Soccer; Track athletics;** etc.
> *x* College athletics; Intercollegiate athletics; Varsity sports
> *xx* **School sports; Sports**

College students 371.8; 378
> *See also* **College graduates**
> *x* College life; Colleges and universities—Students; Undergraduates; University students
> *xx* **College graduates; Students**

College students, Foreign. *See* **Foreign students**

College students—Political activity 371.8; 378
> *x* Campus disorders
> *xx* **Politics, Practical**

College students—Sexual behavior 371.8; 378
> *xx* **Sexual behavior**

College teachers. *See* **Colleges and universities—Faculty; Educators; Teachers**

College yearbooks. *See* **School yearbooks**

Colleges and universities (May subdiv. geog.) 378
> *See also*

Academic degrees	**Free universities**
Academic libraries	**Higher education**
Classical education	**Junior colleges**
Coeducation	**Scholarships, fellowships,**
College choice	**etc.**
Commencements	**Teachers colleges**
Dissertations, Academic	**University extension**
Fraternities and sororities	

> also headings beginning with the word **College** and names of individual institutions
> *x* Universities
> *xx* **Classical education; Education; Higher education; Professional education; Schools**

Colleges and universities—Applications. *See* **College applications**

Colleges and universities—Buildings 727
> *x* Buildings, College
> *xx* **Buildings**

Colleges and universities—Curricula 378.1
> *x* Core curriculum; Courses of study; Curricula (Courses of study); Schools—Curricula; Study, Courses of
> *xx* **Education—Curricula**

Colleges and universities—Entrance examinations 378.1
> *See also* **Graduate record examination; Scholastic aptitude test**
> *x* College entrance examinations; Entrance examinations for colleges
> *xx* **Educational tests and measurements; Examinations**

Colleges and universities—Entrance requirements 378.1
> *See also* **College applications**; also names of indi-

**Colleges and universities—Entrance
         requirements—***Continued*
         vidual colleges and universities with the
         subdivision *Entrance requirements*
  x College entrance requirements; Entrance re-
         quirements for colleges and universities
  xx **College applications; Examinations; Free uni-
         versities**
Colleges and universities—Faculty   378.1
  x College teachers; Faculty (Education)
Colleges and universities—Finance   378
  See also **College costs; Federal aid to education**
  x Tuition
Colleges and universities—Insignia   378.2
  xx **Insignia**
Colleges and universities, Nonformal.   *See* **Free
         universities**
Colleges and universities—Selection.   *See* **College
         choice**
Colleges and universities—Students.   *See* **College
         students**
Colleges and universities—United States   378.73
  x American colleges; United States—Colleges
         and universities; United States—
         Universities
Colleges, Business.   *See* **Business schools**
Collies   636.7
  xx **Dogs**
Collisions, Railroad.   *See* **Railroads—Accidents**
Colloids   541.3; 547.1
  xx **Chemistry, Physical and theoretical**
Colonial architecture.   *See* **Architecture, Colonial**
Colonial furniture (U.S.).   *See* **Furniture, American**
Colonial history (U.S.).   *See* **United States—
         History—1600-1775, Colonial period**
Colonialism.   *See* **Colonies; Imperialism**
Colonies   321; 325
         Use for materials on general colonial policy. Ma-
         terials on the policy of settling immigrants
         or nationals in unoccupied areas are entered
         under **Colonization.** Materials on migration
         from one country to another are entered un-
         der **Immigration and emigration.** Materials
         on the movement of population within a
         country for permanent settlement are en-
         tered under **Migration, Internal.** Materials
         discussing collectively the colonies ruled by
         a country are entered under the name of the
         country with the subdivision *Colonies,* e.g.
         Great Britain—Colonies; etc.
  See also **Colonization; Immigration and emigra-
         tion; Land settlement; National liberation
         movements; Penal colonies;** also names of
         countries with the subdivision *Colonies,*
         e.g. **Great Britain—Colonies; United
         States—Colonies;** etc.
  x Colonialism; Dependencies
  xx **Colonization; Imperialism**
Colonies, Space.   *See* **Space colonies**
Colonization   325
         See note under **Colonies.**
  See also **Colonies; Immigration and emigration;
         Migration, Internal; Penal colonies;** also

Colonization—*Continued*

    names of countries with the subdivision *Immigration and emigration,* e.g. **United States—Immigration and emigration;** etc.

    x Dependencies

    xx **Colonies; History; Immigration and emigration; Imperialism; Land settlement**

Color   **535.6; 701; 752**

    See also **Dyes and dyeing;** also subjects with the subdivision *Color,* e.g. **Animals—Color; Birds—Color; Man—Color** etc.; and names of individual colors, e.g. **Red;** etc.

    x Colour

    xx **Aesthetics; Chemistry; Light; Optics; Painting; Photometry**

Color blindness   **617.7**

    xx **Color sense; Vision disorders**

Color etchings. *See* **Color prints**

Color photography   **778.6**

    x Color slides; Photography, Color

    xx **Photography**

Color printing   **686.2**

    Use for materials on typographic printing in color. Materials on pictures printed in color from engraved metal, wood or stone are entered under **Color prints.**

    See also **Illustration of books; Lithography; Silk screen printing**

    xx **Printing**

Color prints (May subdiv. geog. adjective form)   **769**

    See note under **Color printing.**

    See also **Linoleum block printing**

    x Block printing; Color etchings; Painting—Color reproductions

Color prints, American   **769.973**

    x American color prints

Color prints, Japanese   **769.952**

    x Japanese color prints; Japanese prints

Color—Psychological aspects   **152.14**

    x Psychology of color

    xx **Color sense; Psychology**

Color sense   **152.14**

    See also **Color blindness; Color—Psychological aspects**

    xx **Psychophysiology; Senses and sensation; Vision**

Color slides. *See* **Color photography; Slides (Photography)**

Color television   **621.388**

    x Television, Color

    xx **Television**

Colorado River—Hoover Dam. *See* **Hoover Dam (Ariz. and Nev.)**

Coloring books   **372.5; E**

    x Painting books

    xx **Picture books for children**

Colour. *See* **Color**

Columnists. *See* **Journalists**

COM catalogs. *See* **Library catalogs on microfilm**

Combinations in restraint of trade. *See* **Restraint of trade**

Combinations, Industrial. *See* **Trusts, Industrial**

Combustion   541.3; 621.402
> *See also* **Fire; Fuel; Heat**
> *x* Spontaneous combustion
> *xx* **Chemistry; Fire; Heat**

Comedians   791; 792.2; 920
> *See also* **Fools and jesters**
> *xx* **Actors; Entertainers**

Comedy   792.2
> *x* Comic literature
> *xx* **Drama; Wit and humor**

Comets   523.6
> *See also* **Halley's comet**
> *xx* **Astronomy; Solar system**

Comic books, strips, etc.   741.5
> Use for materials on printed comic strips, i.e.
> groups of cartoons in narrative sequence,
> and magazines consisting of comic strips,
> etc.
> *See also* **Cartoons and caricatures; Chapbooks;**
> also names of comic books, comic strips,
> and comic strip characters
> *x* Comic strips; Funnies; Humorous pictures
> *xx* **Cartoons and caricatures; Chapbooks**

Comic literature.   *See* **Comedy; Parody; Satire**
Comic opera.   *See* **Opera; Operetta**
Comic strips.   *See* **Comic books, strips, etc.**
Commandments, Ten.   *See* **Ten commandments**

Commencements   371.2
> *x* Graduation
> *xx* **Colleges and universities; High schools;**
> **School assembly programs**

Commentaries, Biblical.   *See* **Bible—Commentaries**

Commerce   380.1
> Use for general materials on foreign and domes-
> tic commerce. Materials limited to com-
> merce between states are entered under **In-**
> **terstate commerce.**
> *See also*

Balance of trade	**Merchants**
Banks and banking	**Monopolies**
Barter	**Multinational corporations**
Business	**Prices**
Business people	**Profit sharing**
Chambers of commerce	**Restraint of trade**
Competition	**Retail trade**
Contracts	**Stock exchange**
Cooperation	**Stocks**
Exchange	**Tariff**
Free trade and protection	**Trade routes**
Geography, Commercial	**Trademarks**
Interstate commerce	**Transportation**
Marine insurance	**Trusts, Industrial**
Markets	

> also names of countries, cities, etc. with the sub-
> division *Commerce,* e.g. **United States—**
> **Commerce;** etc.; names of articles of com-
> merce, e.g. **Cotton;** etc.; and headings be-
> ginning with the word **Commercial**
> *x* Distribution (Economics); Exports; Foreign
> trade; Imports; International trade; Trade
> *xx* **Economics; Exchange; Finance; Transporta-**
> **tion**

Commerce, Interstate.   *See* **Interstate commerce**

Commercial aeronautics. *See* **Aeronautics, Commercial**

Commercial arithmetic. *See* **Business arithmetic**

Commercial art   741.6

> Use for general materials on the application of art to business, i.e. in advertising layout, fashion design, lettering, etc.
>
> *See also* **Fashion design; Posters; Textile design**
>
> *x* Advertising art; Advertising, Pictorial; Art, Commercial; Art in advertising
>
> *xx* **Advertising; Art; Drawing**

Commercial aviation. *See* **Aeronautics, Commercial**

Commercial correspondence. *See* **Business letters**

Commercial education. *See* **Business education**

Commercial employees. *See* **Office employees**

Commercial endeavors in space. *See* **Space industrialization**

Commercial geography. *See* **Geography, Commercial**

Commercial law   346

> *See also*

Antitrust law	**Insider trading**
Arbitration and award	**Landlord and tenant**
Bankruptcy	**Maritime law**
Collecting of accounts	**Mortgages**
Contracts	**Negotiable instruments**
Corporation law	**Restraint of trade**
Debtor and creditor	**Unfair competition**

> *x* Business law; Law, Business; Law, Commercial; Mercantile law
>
> *xx* **Business; Business education; Law; Maritime law**

Commercial paper. *See* **Negotiable instruments**

Commercial photography   778

> *See also* **Photojournalism**
>
> *x* Photography, Commercial
>
> *xx* **Photography**

Commercial policy   380.1; 381.3; 382

> Use for general materials on the various regulations by which governments seek to protect and increase the commerce of a country, such as subsidies, tariffs, free ports, etc.
>
> *See also* **Buy national policy; Commercial products; Free trade and protection; Tariff;** also names of countries with the subdivision *Commercial policy,* e.g. **United States—Commercial policy;** etc.
>
> *x* Government regulation of commerce; Reciprocity; Trade barriers; World economics
>
> *xx* **Economic policy; International economic relations**

Commercial products   380.1

> *See also*

Brand name products	**Manufactures**
Forest products	**Marine resources**
Generic products	**Raw materials**
Geography, Commercial	**Substitute products**

> also names of individual products
>
> *x* Consumer goods; Consumer products; Merchandise; Products, Commercial
>
> *xx* **Commercial policy**

Commercial products recall. *See* **Product recall**

Commercial products—Safety measures. *See* **Product safety**

Commercial secrets. *See* **Trade secrets**

Commercials, Radio. *See* **Radio advertising**

Commercials, Television. *See* **Television advertising**

Commission government. *See* **Municipal government by commission**

Commission government with city manager. *See* **Municipal government by city manager**

Common cold. *See* **Cold (Disease)**

Common law marriage. *See* **Unmarried couples**

Common market. *See* **European Economic Community**

Common schools. *See* **Public schools**

Commonwealth of England. *See* **Great Britain—History—1642-1660, Civil War and Commonwealth**

Commonwealth of Nations   909

> Use for materials dealing collectively with Great Britain and the self-governing dominions.
>
> *See also* **Great Britain—Colonies**
>
> *x* British Commonwealth of Nations; British Dominions; Dominions, British
>
> *xx* **Great Britain; Great Britain—Colonies**

Commonwealth, The. *See* **Political science; Republics; State, The**

Communal living. *See* **Collective settlements**

Communes. *See* **Collective settlements**

Communicable diseases   614.4; 616.9

> *See also*

Bacteriology	**Immunity**
Biological warfare	**Insects as carriers of disease**
Disinfection and disinfectants	
Epidemics	**Sexually transmitted diseases**
Fumigation	**Vaccination**
Germ theory of disease	

> also names of communicable diseases, e.g. **AIDS (Disease); Cold (Disease); Influenza;** etc.
>
> *x* Contagion and contagious diseases; Contagious diseases; Diseases, Communicable; Diseases, Contagious; Diseases, Infectious; Infection and infectious diseases; Quarantine
>
> *xx* **Diseases; Epidemics; Immunity; Public health**

Communicable diseases—Prevention   614.4

Communication   302.2

> Use for general materials on communication in its broadest sense, including the use of the spoken and written word, signs, symbols, or behavior.
>
> *See also*

Books and reading	**Mass media**
Cybernetics	**Nonverbal communication**
Deaf—Means of communication	**Popular culture**
	Postal service
Information science	**Signals and signaling**
Language and languages	**Telecommunication**
Language arts	**Writing**

> *x* Mass communication

Communication among animals. *See* **Animal communication**

177

Communication arts. *See* **Language arts**

Communication satellites. *See* **Artificial satellites in telecommunication**

Communication systems. *See* subjects with the subdivision *Communication systems,* e.g. **Astronautics—Communication systems;** etc.

Communication systems, Computer. *See* **Computer networks**

Communications relay satellites. *See* **Artificial satellites in telecommunication**

Communion. *See* **Lord's Supper**

Communism (May subdiv. geog.)   320.5; 321.9; 324.1; 335.43

See also **Anticommunist movements; Dialectical materialism; Socialism**

x Bolshevism; Collectivism; Marxism

xx **Cooperation; Individualism; Labor; Political science; Socialism; Sociology; Totalitarianism**

Communism and literature   335.4; 809; 810.9, etc.

Use same pattern for communism and other subjects, e.g. **Communism and religion;** etc.

x Literature and communism

Communism and religion   261.7; 335.4

See also **Christianity and economics**

x Religion and communism

Communism—Soviet Union   320.5; 335.430947; 947.084

x Russian communism; Soviet Union—Communism

Communism—United States   320.5; 335.43; 973

x United States—Communism

Communist countries   909; 947

x Chinese satellite countries; Iron curtain countries; People's democracies; Russian satellite countries; Soviet bloc

Communities, Space. *See* **Space colonies**

Community and libraries. *See* **Libraries and community**

Community and school   370.19

Use for materials on ways in which the community at large, as distinct from government, may aid the school program.

See also **Parents' and teachers' associations**

x School and community

xx **Community life**

Community antenna television. *See* **Cable television**

Community based residences. *See* **Group homes**

Community centers   374; 790.06

See also **Playgrounds**

x Play centers; Recreation centers; School buildings as recreation centers; Schools as social centers

xx **Cities and towns—Civic improvement; Community life; Community organization; Playgrounds; Recreation; Social problems; Social settlements**

Community chests. *See* **Fund raising**

Community churches   254

Use for materials on local churches that have no denominational affiliations.

x Churches, Community; Churches, Undenomi-

Community churches—*Continued*
>national; Nondenominational churches;
>Undenominational churches; Union
>churches

xx **Christian unity**
Community colleges. *See* **Junior colleges**
Community councils. *See* **Community organization**
Community development (May subdiv. geog.) **307.1;
361.6**
>*See also* **Agricultural extension work; City plan-
>ning; Technical assistance**
>*x* Neighborhood development
>*xx* **Agricultural extension work; City planning;
>Economic assistance, Domestic; Social
>change; Technical assistance; Urban re-
>newal; Villages**

Community health services   362.1
>*xx* **Community services; Public health**
Community life   307
>*See also* **City life; Community and school; Com-
>munity centers; Community organization**
>*x* Neighborhood
>*xx* **Associations; City life**
Community organization   307
>*See also* **Community centers; Local government;
>Urban renewal**
>*x* Community councils
>*xx* **Community life; Social work; Urban renewal**
Community schools. *See* **Schools**
Community services   361.7; 361.8
>*See also* types of services, e.g. **Community
>health services;** etc.
Community songbooks. *See* **Songbooks**
Community surveys. *See* **Social surveys**
Community theater. *See* **Little theater movement**
Compact automobiles   629.222
>*See also* names of specific makes and models
>*x* Automobiles, Compact; Compact cars
Compact cars. *See* **Compact automobiles**
Compact disc interactive technology. *See* **CD-I
technology**
Compact disc players   621.389
>*x* Audiodisc players; CD players; Digital audio
>disc players; Disc players, Compact; Laser
>disc players; Players, Compact disc
>*xx* **Phonograph; Sound—Recording and reproduc-
>ing**
Compact disc read-only memory. *See* **CD-ROM**
Compact discs   621.389; 780.26
>*See also* **CD-I technology; CD-ROM**
>*x* CDs (Compact discs); Compact disks; Digital
>compact discs; Discs, Compact
>*xx* **Optical storage devices; Sound recordings**
Compact discs, Audio. *See* **Sound recordings**
Compact disks. *See* **Compact discs**
Companies. *See* **Corporations**
Companies, Trust. *See* **Trust companies**
Companion-animal partnership. *See* **Pet therapy**
Company libraries. *See* **Corporate libraries**
Company symbols. *See* **Trademarks**
Comparative anatomy. *See* **Anatomy, Comparative**
Comparative government   320.3
>*See also* names of countries, cities, etc., with the

Comparative government—*Continued*
> subdivision *Politics and government,* e.g.
> **United States—Politics and government;**
> etc.
> *x* Government, Comparative
> *xx* **Political science**

Comparative librarianship   020.9
> *x* Librarianship, Comparative
> *xx* **International education; Library science**

Comparative linguistics. *See* **Language and languages; Philology, Comparative**

Comparative literature. *See* **Literature, Comparative**

Comparative philology. *See* **Philology, Comparative**

Comparative physiology. *See* **Physiology, Comparative**

Comparative psychology. *See* **Psychology, Comparative**

Comparative religion. *See* **Christianity and other religions; Religions**

Comparison (English grammar). *See* **English language—Comparison**

Comparison of cultures. *See* **Cross cultural studies**

Compass   538; 623.8
> *x* Magnetic needle; Mariner's compass
> *xx* **Magnetism; Navigation**

Compassion. *See* **Sympathy**

Compensation. *See* **Pensions; Wages; Workers' compensation**

Compensatory spending. *See* **Deficit financing**

Competencies, Functional. *See* **Life skills**

Competition   338.6
> *See also* **Monopolies; Trusts, Industrial**
> *xx* **Business; Business ethics; Commerce; Monopolies; Trusts, Industrial**

Competition, Unfair. *See* **Unfair competition**

Competitions. *See* **Contests; Rewards (Prizes, etc.);** and subjects with the subdivision *Competitions,* e.g. **Literature—Competitions;** etc.

Complaints against police. *See* **Police—Complaints against**

Composers (May subdiv. geog. adjective form)
> **780.92; 920**
> *x* Songwriters
> *xx* **Musicians**

Composers, American   780.92; 920
> *x* American composers; United States—Composers

Composition (Art)   701
> *See also* **Architecture—Composition, proportion, etc.; Painting**
> *x* Art—Composition
> *xx* **Art; Painting**

Composition (Music)   781.3
> *See also* **Counterpoint; Fugue; Harmony; Instrumentation and orchestration; Musical accompaniment; Popular music—Writing and publishing**
> *x* Music—Composition; Musical composition; Song writing
> *xx* **Music; Music—Study and teaching; Music—Theory**

Composition of natural substances. *See* natural
substances of unfixed composition, such as
soils, plants, animals, farm products, with
the subdivision *Composition* for the results
of chemical analyses of those substances,
e.g. **Food—Composition;** etc.
Composition (Printing). *See* **Typesetting**
Composition (Rhetoric). *See* **Rhetoric;** and names
of languages with the subdivision
Composition and exercises, e.g. **English
language—Composition and exercises;** etc.
Compost   631.8
  xx **Fertilizers and manures; Soils**
Comprehensive health care organizations. *See*
  Health maintenance organizations
Compressed air   621.5
  x Air, Compressed; Pneumatic transmission
  xx **Cold storage; Foundations; Pneumatics; Power
  (Mechanics)**
Compressed work week. *See* **Hours of labor**
Compulsion (Psychology). *See* **Compulsive behav-
  ior**
Compulsive behavior   616.85
  See also **Workaholism;** also types of compulsive
  behavior, e.g. **Compulsive gambling; Exer-
  cise addiction;** etc.
  x Addictive behavior; Behavior, Compulsive;
  Compulsion (Psychology)
  xx **Psychology, Pathological**
Compulsive exercising. *See* **Exercise addiction**
Compulsive gambling   616.85
  x Addiction to gambling; Gambling, Compul-
  sive
  xx **Compulsive behavior; Gambling**
Compulsive working. *See* **Workaholism**
Compulsory education   379.2
  See also **Children—Employment; Evening and
  continuation schools; School attendance**
  x Compulsory school attendance; Education,
  Compulsory
  xx **School attendance**
Compulsory labor. *See* **Convict labor; Peonage;
  Slavery**
Compulsory military service. *See* **Draft**
Compulsory school attendance. *See* **Compulsory
  education; School attendance**
Computation, Approximate. *See* **Approximate
  computation**
Computation (Mathematics). *See* **Arithmetic**
Computer aided design   620
  x CAD; Computer assisted design; Drafting, Automatic
  xx **Computers; Engineering**
Computer art   700; 760
  Use for materials on works of art, mostly drawings and graphics, created or produced with
  the aid of digital computing or plotting devices.
  x Art, Computer; Art, Electronic; Computer
  drawing; Drawing, Computer; Drawing,
  Electronic; Electronic art; Electronic drawing
  xx **Art, Modern—1900-1999 (20th century);
  Computer graphics; Computers**

Computer assisted design. *See* **Computer aided design**

Computer assisted instruction   371.3

Use for materials on automated instruction in which a student interacts directly with a computer.

See also subjects with the subdivision *Computer assisted instruction,* e.g. **Mathematics—Computer assisted instruction;** etc.

x Computer teaching; Computers—Educational use; Education—Automation; Education—Data processing; Teaching, Computer; Teaching—Data processing

xx **Electronic data processing; Programmed instruction**

Computer assisted instruction—Authoring programs 371.3

Use for materials on computer programs that allow the user with comparatively little expertise to design customized computer programs for educational purposes.

x Authoring programs for computer assisted instruction; Computer authoring programs

xx **Computer programs**

Computer authoring programs. *See* **Computer assisted instruction—Authoring programs**

Computer awareness. *See* **Computer literacy**

Computer-based information systems. *See* **Information systems; Management information systems**

Computer bulletin boards   004.6; 384.3

Use for works on computer services that function as a community bulletin board and allow a remote caller to dial a central calling place to enter and receive messages, access bulletins or notices, etc.

x Electronic bulletin boards

xx **Bulletin boards; Computer networks; Electronic data processing; Electronic mail systems; Online data processing**

Computer communication systems. *See* **Computer networks**

Computer control. *See* **Automation**

Computer crimes   364.1

See also **Computer viruses; Right of privacy**

x Computer fraud; Fraud, Computer

xx **Crime; Right of privacy**

Computer drawing. *See* **Computer art**

Computer fraud. *See* **Computer crimes**

Computer games   794.8

Use for materials on games played on a computer.

xx **Electronic toys; Games**

Computer graphics   006.6

Use for materials on the technique for producing line drawings, particularly engineering drawings, by the use of digital computing and plotting devices. Representations may be online or hardcopy. Materials on the use of computer graphics to create artistic designs, drawings, or other works of art are entered under **Computer art.**

See also **Computer art**

182

Computer graphics—*Continued*

   x Automatic drafting; Automatic drawing;
Drafting, Automatic; Drawing, Automatic;
Drawing, Electronic; Electronic drawing;
Graphics, Computer

   xx **Electronic data processing**

Computer hardware. *See* **Computer peripherals**

Computer input-output equipment. *See* **Computer peripherals**

Computer interfaces **004.6; 621.39**

   Use for materials on equipment and techniques
linking computers to peripheral devices or
to other computers.

   x Interfaces, Computer

   xx **Computer peripherals**

Computer jargon. *See* **Computer science—Dictionaries**

Computer keyboarding. *See* **Keyboarding (Electronics)**

Computer keyboards. *See* **Keyboards (Electronics)**

Computer literacy **004**

   Use for materials on the awareness of or knowledge about computers as well as for materials on the ability to use and understand
computers, including their applications and
social implications.

   x Computer awareness; Literacy, Computer

   xx **Computers; Computers and civilization; Literacy**

Computer memory systems. *See* **Computer storage devices**

Computer music **786.7**

   See also **Computer sound processing**

   x Music, Computer

   xx **Computer sound processing; Electronic music; Music**

Computer networks **004.6; 384.3**

   Use for materials on computer systems consisting of two or more interconnected computing units.

   See also **Computer bulletin boards**

   x Communication systems, Computer; Computer communication systems; Data networks, Computer; Networks, Computer;
Teleprocessing networks

   xx **Data transmission systems; Electronic data
processing; Information networks; Telecommunication**

Computer operating systems **005.4**

   x Computers—Operating systems; Operating
systems (Computers)

   xx **Computer systems**

Computer peripherals **004.7; 621.39**

   See also **Computer interfaces; Computer storage
devices;** also names of types of computer peripherals, e.g. **Computer terminals; Keyboards (Electronics); Video display terminals;** etc.

   x Computer hardware; Computer input-output
equipment; Input equipment (Computers);
Output equipment (Computers)

   xx **Computer systems**

Computer program languages. *See* **Programming
languages (Computers)**

Computer programming. *See* **Programming (Computers)**

Computer programs 005.3

See note under **Computer software.**

See also **Computer assisted instruction— Authoring programs; Electronic spreadsheets; Utilities (Computer programs);** also subjects with the subdivision *Computer programs,* e.g. **Oceanography—Computer programs;** etc.; also names of computer programs

x Programs, Computer

xx **Computer software; Programming (Computers)**

Computer science 004

Use for materials discussing collectively the disciplines that deal with the general theory and application of computers.

See also **Electronic data processing**

xx **Electronic data processing; Science**

Computer science—Dictionaries 004.03

x Computer jargon; Computer terms; Computers—Dictionaries; Computers—Jargon; Jargon, Computer

Computer software 005.3; 651.8

Use for general materials on computer programs along with documentation such as manuals, diagrams and operating instructions, etc. Materials limited to computer programs are entered under **Computer programs.**

See also **Computer programs; Computer software industry; Computer viruses; Computers; Programming (Computers); Programming languages (Computers)**

x Software, Computer

xx **Computer systems; Computers; Programming (Computers)**

Computer software industry 338.4

xx **Computer software**

Computer sound processing 006.5

See also **Computer music; Speech processing systems**

x Sound processing, Computer

xx **Computer music; Computers; Sound; Speech processing systems**

Computer speech processing systems. *See* **Speech processing systems**

Computer storage devices 004.5; 621.39

See also **Optical storage devices**

x Computer memory systems; Computers—Memory systems; Computers—Storage devices; Direct access storage devices (Data processing); Random access memories (Data processing); Random access storage devices (Data processing); Rotating memory devices (Data processing); Storage devices, Computer

xx **Computer peripherals**

Computer stored cataloging data. *See* **Machine readable bibliographic data**

Computer systems 004

Use for materials on computers, their peripheral devices, and their operating systems.

See also **Computer operating systems; Computer**

184

Computer systems—*Continued*
    peripherals; Computer software; Computers
  xx **Electronic data processing**
Computer teaching. *See* **Computer assisted instruction**
Computer terminals   004.7; 621.39
  See also **Video display terminals**
  x Terminals, Computer
  xx **Computer peripherals**
Computer terms. *See* **Computer science— Dictionaries**
Computer utility programs. *See* **Utilities (Computer programs)**
Computer viruses   005.8
  x Computer worms; Software viruses; Viruses, Computer; Worms, Computer
  xx **Computer crimes; Computer software**
Computer worms. *See* **Computer viruses**
Computerized tomography. *See* **Tomography**
Computers   004; 338.4; 621.39
    Use for materials on modern electronic computers developed after 1945. Materials on present-day calculators and on calculating machines and mechanical computers made before 1945 are entered under **Calculators.**

  See also

Calculators	ing
Computer aided design	**Electronic data processing**
Computer art	**Home computers**
Computer literacy	**Information systems**
Computer software	**Supercomputers**
Computer sound process-	

    also names of types of computers and of specific computers, e.g. **Microcomputers; Minicomputers; IBM 7090 (Computer);** etc.; and also headings beginning with the word **Computer.**
  x Automatic computers; Brain, Electronic; Computers, Electronic; Computing machines (Electronic); Electronic brains; Electronic calculating machines; Electronic computers; Mechanical brains
  xx **Calculators; Computer software; Computer systems; Cybernetics; Electronic apparatus and appliances**
Computers and children   004.01
  xx **Children**
Computers and civilization   004.01; 303.4
  See also **Computer literacy**
  x Civilization and computers
  xx **Technology and civilization**
Computers—Cartoons and caricatures   338.4; 621.39; 741.5
  xx **Cartoons and caricatures**
Computers—Dictionaries. *See* **Computer science— Dictionaries**
Computers—Educational use. *See* **Computer assisted instruction**
Computers, Electronic. *See* **Computers**
Computers—Jargon. *See* **Computer science— Dictionaries**
Computers—Memory systems. *See* **Computer storage devices**

Computers—Operating systems. *See* **Computer operating systems**

Computers, Portable. *See* **Portable computers**

Computers—Programming. *See* **Programming (Computers)**

Computers—Storage devices. *See* **Computer storage devices**

Computers—Utility programs. *See* **Utilities (Computer programs)**

Computing machines (Electronic). *See* **Computers**

Con artists. *See* **Swindlers and swindling**

Con game. *See* **Swindlers and swindling**

Concentration. *See* **Attention**

Concentration camps   365

> *See also* **Prisoners of war;** also names of individual camps; and names of wars with the subdivision *Prisoners and prisons,* e.g. **World War, 1939-1945—Prisoners and prisons;** etc.
>
> *x* Internment camps
>
> *xx* **Camps (Military); Political crimes and offenses; Prisoners of war**

Concept formation. *See* **Concept learning**

Concept learning   153.2; 370.15

> Use for materials on the process of discovering the distinguishing features of particular concepts and the ensuing ability to use the concepts appropriately.
>
> *x* Concept formation; Learning, Concept
>
> *xx* **Concepts; Learning, Psychology of**

Conception—Prevention. *See* **Birth control**

Concepts   153.2

> *See also* **Concept learning;** also types of concepts and images, e.g. **Size and shape;** etc.
>
> *xx* **Perception**

Concerto   784.18

> *xx* **Musical form**

Concertos   784.18

> *xx* **Musical form; Orchestral music**

Concerts   780.78

> *See also* **Music festivals**
>
> *xx* **Amusements; Music**

Conchology. *See* **Shells**

Conciliation, Industrial. *See* **Arbitration, Industrial**

Concordances. *See* **Bible—Concordances;** and names of authors with the subdivision *Concordances,* e.g. **Shakespeare, William, 1564-1616—Concordances;** etc.

Concrete   691; 693

> *See also* **Cement; Pavements; Reinforced concrete**
>
> *xx* **Building materials; Cement; Foundations; Masonry; Plaster and plastering**

Concrete construction   693

> *x* Building, Concrete; Construction, Concrete
>
> *xx* **Architecture; Building**

Concrete, Reinforced. *See* **Reinforced concrete**

Concrete—Testing   620.1

> *xx* **Strength of materials**

Condemnation of land. *See* **Eminent domain**

Condensers (Electricity)   621.31

> *x* Electric condensers
>
> *xx* **Induction coils**

Condensers (Steam)   621.1

> *xx* **Steam engines**

Condominium timesharing. *See* **Timesharing (Real estate)**

Condominiums   346.04; 643

   See also **Timesharing (Real estate)**

   xx **Apartment houses**

Conduct of life. *See* **Human behavior**

Conducting   781.45

   Use for materials on orchestral conducting or a combination of orchestral and choral conducting. Materials limited to choral conducting are entered under **Choral conducting.**

   See also **Bands (Music); Choral conducting; Conductors (Music); Orchestra**

   xx **Bands (Music); Conductors (Music); Music—Study and teaching; Orchestra**

Conducting, Choral. *See* **Choral conducting**

Conductors, Electric. *See* **Electric conductors**

Conductors (Music)   784.2092; 920

   See also **Choral conducting; Conducting**

   x Bandmasters; Music conductors

   xx **Choral conducting; Conducting; Musicians; Orchestra**

Conduits. *See* **Aqueducts**

Confectionery   641.8; 664

   See also **Cake decorating**

   x Candy

   xx **Cookery; Ice cream, ices, etc.**

Confederacies. *See* **Federal government**

Confederate States of America   973.7

   xx **United States—History—1861-1865, Civil War**

Confederation of American colonies. *See* **United States—History—1783-1809**

Conference calls (Teleconferencing). *See* **Teleconferencing**

Conferences. *See* **Congresses and conventions**

Conferences, Parent-teacher. *See* **Parent-teacher conferences**

Confessions of faith. *See* **Creeds**

Confidence game. *See* **Swindlers and swindling**

Confidence, Self. *See* **Self-confidence**

Configuration (Psychology). *See* **Gestalt psychology**

Conflict, Ethnic. *See* **Ethnic relations**

Conflict of cultures. *See* **Culture conflict**

Conflict of generations   306.874

   See also **Parent and child**

   x Generation gap

   xx **Children and adults; Human relations; Parent and child; Social conflict**

Conflict of interests   351.9

   See also **Corruption in politics; Misconduct in office**

   xx **Political ethics**

Conflict, Social. *See* **Social conflict**

Conformity   153.8; 302.5

   See also **Dissent; Individuality; Social values**

   x Nonconformity; Social conformity

   xx **Attitude (Psychology); Freedom; Individuality**

Confucianism   181; 299

   xx **Religions**

Congenital diseases. *See* **Medical genetics**

Conglomerate corporations 338.8

   x Business combinations; Corporations, Conglomerate; Diversified corporations

   xx **Corporate mergers and acquisitions; Corporations**

Congregationalism 285.8

   See also **Calvinism; Puritans; Society of Friends; Unitarianism**

   xx **Calvinism; Puritans**

Congress (U.S.). *See* **United States. Congress**

Congresses and conventions 060

   See also **International organization; Treaties;** also names of specific congresses; and subjects with the subdivision *Congresses,* e.g. **World War, 1939-1945—Congresses;** etc.

   x Conferences; Conventions (Congresses); International conferences

   xx **Intellectual cooperation; International cooperation**

Congressional investigations. *See* **Governmental investigations**

Conjuring. *See* **Magic**

Conquistadores. *See* **America—Exploration**

Conscience 170; 241

   See also **Freedom of conscience**

   xx **Christian ethics; Duty; Ethics**

Conscientious objectors 343; 355.2

   See also **Draft resisters; Pacifism;** also names of wars with the subdivision *Conscientious objectors,* e.g. **World War, 1939-1945—Conscientious objectors;** etc.

   xx **Draft resisters; Freedom of conscience; Pacifism; War and religion**

Consciousness 126; 153

   See also **Gestalt psychology; Individuality; Knowledge, Theory of; Personality; Self; Subconsciousness**

   xx **Apperception; Mind and body; Perception; Psychology; Subconsciousness**

Consciousness expanding drugs. *See* **Hallucinogens**

Conscription, Military. *See* **Draft**

Conservation of buildings. *See* **Architecture—Conservation and restoration**

Conservation of energy. *See* **Energy conservation; Force and energy**

Conservation of forests. *See* **Forests and forestry**

Conservation of natural resources 333.7; 639.9

   See also **Energy conservation; National parks and reserves; Nature conservation; Plant conservation; Soil conservation; Wildlife conservation**

   x Preservation of natural resources; Resource management

   xx **Environment—Government policy; Environmental protection; Natural resources**

Conservation of nature. *See* **Nature conservation**

Conservation of plants. *See* **Plant conservation**

Conservation of power resources. *See* **Energy conservation**

Conservation of the soil. *See* **Soil conservation**

Conservation of water. *See* **Water conservation**

Conservation of wildlife. *See* **Wildlife conservation**

Conservation of works of art, books, etc. *See* sub-

Conservation of works of art, books, etc—*Continued*
   jects with the subdivision *Conservation and restoration,* e.g. **Library resources— Conservation and restoration; Painting— Conservation and restoration;** etc.
Conservatism   320.5
   See also **Right and left (Political science)**
   xx **Right and left (Political science)**
Consolation.   *See* **Sympathy**
Consolidation and merger of corporations.   *See* **Corporate mergers and acquisitions**
Consolidation of schools.   *See* **Schools— Centralization**
Consortia, Library.   *See* **Library cooperation; Library information networks**
Constellations.   *See* **Astronomy; Stars**
Constitution (U.S.).   *See* **United States— Constitution**
Constitutional history   342
   See also **Democracy; Monarchy; Political science; Representative government and representation; Republics;** also names of countries, states, etc. with the subdivision *Constitutional history,* e.g. **United States— Constitutional history;** etc.
   x Constitutional law—History; History, Constitutional
   xx **Constitutions; History; Political science**
Constitutional law   342
   Use for materials discussing constitutions or constitutional law in general. For general collections of texts of constitutions use **Constitutions.** Collections of texts of state constitutions are entered under **State constitutions.**
   See also

Administrative law
Citizenship
Civil rights
Constitutions
Democracy
Eminent domain
Executive power
Federal government
Injunctions
Legislation
Legislative bodies
Monarchy
Political science
Proportional representation
Referendum
Representative government and representation
Republics
Separation of powers
Suffrage

   also names of countries with the subdivision *Constitutional law,* e.g. **United States— Constitutional law;** etc.
   x Law, Constitutional
   xx **Administrative law; Constitutions; Law; Political science**
Constitutional law—History.   *See* **Constitutional history**
Constitutional rights.   *See* **Civil rights**
Constitutions   342
   Use for general collections of texts of constitutions. For collections of texts of state constitutions, use **State constitutions.** Materials discussing constitutions or constitutional law in general are entered under **Constitutional law.**

Constitutions—*Continued*

> *See also* **Constitutional history; Constitutional law; Equal rights amendments; State constitutions;** also names of corporate bodies, countries, states, provinces, etc., with the subdivision *Constitution,* e.g. **United States—Constitution;** etc.
>
> *xx* **Constitutional law; Political science; Representative government and representation**

Constitutions, State. *See* **State constitutions**

Construction. *See* **Architecture; Building; Engineering**

Construction, Concrete. *See* **Concrete construction**

Construction, House. *See* **House construction**

Construction of roads. *See* **Roads**

Consulates. *See* **Diplomatic and consular service**

Consuls. *See* **Diplomats**

Consultants

> *See also* types of consultants, e.g. **Educational consultants;** etc.
>
> *x* Advisors
>
> *xx* **Counseling**

Consultative management. *See* **Participative management**

Consumer behavior. *See* **Consumers**

Consumer credit   332.7

> *See also* **Credit cards; Credit unions; Instalment plan; Personal loans**
>
> *x* Credit, Consumer
>
> *xx* **Banks and banking; Credit; Credit unions; Personal finance**

Consumer education   640.73

> Use for materials on the selection and efficient use of consumer goods and services and on methods of educating consumers. Materials on the decision-making processes, external factors, and individual characteristics of consumers that determine their purchasing behavior are entered under **Consumers.** Materials on the economic theory of consumption are entered under **Consumption (Economics).**
>
> *See also* **Buying; Shopping**
>
> *x* Buyers' guides; Consumers' guides; Shoppers' guides
>
> *xx* **Buying; Home economics; Shopping**

Consumer goods. *See* **Commercial products; Manufactures**

Consumer loans. *See* **Personal loans**

Consumer organizations. *See* **Cooperative societies**

Consumer price indexes   338.5

> *x* Cost of living indexes; Price indexes, Consumer
>
> *xx* **Cost of living; Prices**

Consumer products. *See* **Commercial products; Manufactures**

Consumer protection   343; 381.3

> Use for materials on governmental and private activities that guard the consumer against dangers to his health, safety, or economic well-being.
>
> *See also* **Drugs—Adulteration and analysis; Food adulteration and inspection; Product recall;**

Consumer protection—*Continued*
     Product safety
  x Consumerism
Consumerism. *See* **Consumer protection**
Consumers   640.73; 658.8
    Use for materials on consumer behavior.
    See also **Young consumers**
  x Consumer behavior
  xx **Shopping**
Consumers' cooperative societies. *See* **Cooperative societies**
Consumers' guides. *See* **Consumer education**
Consumption (Economics)   339.4
    See note under **Consumer education.**
    See also **Prices**
  xx **Economics**
Consumption of alcoholic beverages. *See* **Drinking of alcoholic beverages**
Consumption of energy. *See* **Energy consumption**
Contact lenses   617.7
  xx **Eyeglasses; Lenses**
Contagion and contagious diseases. *See* **Communicable diseases**
Contagious diseases. *See* **Communicable diseases**
Containers, Box. *See* **Boxes**
Contaminated food. *See* **Food contamination**
Contamination of environment. *See* **Pollution**
Contemporary art. *See* **Art, Modern—1900-1999 (20th century)**
Contests   001.4; 790.1
    See also **Rewards (Prizes, etc.);** also types of contests and names of specific contests, e.g. **Olympic games;** and subjects with the subdivision *Competitions* or *Tournaments,* e.g. **Literature—Competitions; Tennis—Tournaments;** etc.
  x Competitions
  xx **Rewards (Prizes, etc.)**
Continental drift   551.1
    See also **Plate tectonics**
  x Drifting of continents
  xx **Continents; Geology; Plate tectonics**
Continental shelf   551.4
    See also **Territorial waters**
  xx **Geology; Territorial waters**
Continents   551.4
    See also **Continental drift**
Continuation schools. *See* **Evening and continuation schools**
Continuing education   374
    See also **Adult education; Evening and continuation schools**
  x Education, Continuing; Lifelong education; Permanent education; Recurrent education
  xx **Adult education; Education**
Contra-Iran Affair, 1985-. *See* **Iran-Contra Affair, 1985-**
Contraband trade. *See* **Smuggling**
Contraception. *See* **Birth control**
Contract bridge. *See* **Bridge (Game)**
Contract labor   331.5
    See also **Convict labor; Peonage; Slavery**
  x Indentured servants
  xx **Labor; Peonage**

Contractions. *See* **Abbreviations; Ciphers**
Contracts   346

> *See also* **Authors and publishers; Liability (Law);** also types of contracts, e.g. **Labor contract; Mortgages; Negotiable instruments;** etc.; and subjects with the subdivision *Contracts and specifications,* e.g. **Building—Contracts and specifications;** etc.
> *x* Agreements
> *xx* **Commerce; Commercial law**

Control. *See* types of control, e.g. **Flood control; Weather control;** etc. and animals, plants, or crops with the subdivision *Control,* e.g. **Pests—Control;** etc.
Control of self. *See* **Self-control**
Conundrums. *See* **Riddles**
Convenience cookery. *See* **Quick and easy cookery**
Convenience foods   641.3; 664

> Use for materials on prepackaged foods that are easy to prepare for eating.
> *x* Fast foods
> *xx* **Food**

Conventions (Congresses). *See* **Congresses and conventions**
Conventions, Political. *See* **Political conventions**
Convents   271; 726

> *See also* **Abbeys; Monasteries; Religious orders for women**
> *x* Cloisters; Nunneries
> *xx* **Abbeys; Monasteries**

Conversation   808.56

> *x* Discussion; Table talk; Talking
> *xx* **Language and languages**

Conversation in foreign languages. *See* **Languages, Modern—Conversations and phrases;** and names of foreign languages with the subdivision *Conversations and phrases,* e.g. **French language—Conversations and phrases;** etc.
Conversion   248.2; 291.4

> *See also* **Converts; Grace (Theology); Regeneration (Theology)**
> *xx* **Christian life; Evangelistic work; Regeneration (Theology); Theology**

Conversion of saline water. *See* **Sea water conversion**
Conversion of waste products. *See* **Recycling (Waste, etc.); Salvage (Waste, etc.)**
Converts   248.2

> Use for materials on converts from one religion or denomination to another. If needed, add headings for persons affiliating with a particular denomination or religion, e.g. **Catholic converts;** etc.
> *See also* **Catholic converts**
> *xx* **Conversion**

Converts, Catholic. *See* **Catholic converts**
Converts to Catholicism. *See* **Catholic converts**
Conveying machinery   621.8

> *See also* **Hoisting machinery**
> *x* Conveyors
> *xx* **Hoisting machinery; Machinery; Materials handling**

Conveyors. *See* **Conveying machinery**

Convict labor 331.5; 365

    See also **Peonage; Prisons**

    x Compulsory labor; Convicts; Forced labor;
        Prison labor

    xx **Contract labor; Criminals; Labor; Peonage;**
        Prisons

Convicts. *See* **Convict labor; Criminals; Penal colonies; Prisoners**

Cook books. *See* **Cookery**

Cookbooks. *See* **Cookery**

Cookery 641.5

    Use for general materials on cookery, including
        American cookery. If limited to a particular
        area in the U.S. may use geog. subdiv., e.g.
        Cookery—Ohio; Cookery—Southern States;
        etc. For materials on foreign cookery, use
        geog. subdiv. adjective form, e.g. **Cookery,
        French;** etc. For types of cookery, use direct
        form, e.g. **Microwave cookery; Outdoor
        cookery;** etc.

    See also

Baking	**Food**
Bread	**Luncheons**
Breakfasts	**Menus**
Cake	**Microwave cookery**
Canning and preserving	**Outdoor cookery**
Caterers and catering	**Pastry**
Confectionery	**Quantity cookery**
Cookery for the sick	**Quick and easy cookery**
Desserts	**Salads**
Diet	**Sandwiches**
Dinners and dining	**Soups**
Flavoring essences	**Vegetarian cookery**

    x Cook books; Cookbooks; Cooking; Food preparation; Gastronomy; Recipes

    xx **Diet; Dinners and dining; Food; Home economics**

Cookery, Barbecue. *See* **Barbecue cookery**

Cookery for institutions. *See* **Food service**

Cookery for large numbers. *See* **Quantity cookery**

Cookery for the sick 641.5

    See also **Diet therapy;** also names of diets, e.g.
        Salt free diet; etc.

    x Food for invalids; Invalid cookery

    xx **Cookery; Diet in disease; Nursing; Sick**

Cookery, French 641.5944

    x French cookery

Cookery, Microwave. *See* **Microwave cookery**

Cookery—Natural foods 641.5

    Use same form for materials on the cookery of
        other foods or types of food.

    See also **Natural foods**

    x Natural food cookery

    xx **Natural foods**

Cookery—Ohio 641.59771

    x Ohio—Cookery

Cookery, Outdoor. *See* **Outdoor cookery**

Cookery, Quantity. *See* **Quantity cookery**

Cookery—Southern States 641.5975

    x Southern States—Cookery

Cookery—Vegetables 641.6

    xx **Vegetables; Vegetarian cookery**

Cookery, Vegetarian. *See* **Vegetarian cookery**

Cooking. *See* **Cookery**

Cooking utensils. *See* **Household equipment and supplies**

Cooling appliances. *See* **Refrigeration**

Cooperation   334

Use for general materials on the theory and history of cooperation and the cooperative movement. Materials dealing specifically with cooperative enterprises are entered under **Cooperative societies.**

See also

Agriculture, Cooperative	**Labor unions**
Banks and banking, Cooperative	**Profit sharing**
Communism	**Savings and loan associations**
Cooperative societies	**Socialism**
International cooperation	

x Cooperative distribution; Distribution, Cooperative; Rochdale system

xx **Associations; Commerce; Economics; Profit sharing**

Cooperation, Intellectual. *See* **Intellectual cooperation**

Cooperation, International. *See* **International cooperation**

Cooperation, Library. *See* **Library cooperation**

Cooperative agriculture. *See* **Agriculture, Cooperative**

Cooperative banks. *See* **Banks and banking, Cooperative**

Cooperative building associations. *See* **Savings and loan associations**

Cooperative distribution. *See* **Cooperation; Cooperative societies**

Cooperative living. *See* **Collective settlements**

Cooperative societies   334; 658.8

See note under **Cooperation.**

See also types of cooperative societies, e.g. **Banks and banking, Cooperative; Credit unions; Savings and loan associations;** etc.

x Consumer organizations; Consumers' cooperative societies; Cooperative distribution; Cooperative stores; Distribution, Cooperative; Societies, Cooperative; Stores

xx **Cooperation; Corporations; Societies**

Cooperative stores. *See* **Cooperative societies**

Coping behavior. *See* **Adjustment (Psychology); Life skills**

Copper engraving. *See* **Engraving**

Copperwork   673; 739.5

xx **Metalwork**

Copy writing. *See* **Advertising copy**

Copybooks. *See* **Handwriting**

Copying processes and machines   686.4

See also names of specific processes, e.g. **Xerography;** etc.

x Duplicating processes; Photocopying machines; Reproduction processes; Reprography

Copyright   341.7; 346.04

May be subdivided by topic, e.g. **Copyright—Books;** etc.

See also **Authors and publishers; Fair use (Copyright); Publishers and publishing**

Copyright—*Continued*

    x Intellectual property; International copyright; Literary property; Property, Literary

    xx **Authors and publishers; Authorship; Publishers and publishing**

Copyright—Books 341.7; 346.04

    x Books—Copyright

Coral reefs and islands 551.4

    x Atolls

    xx **Geology; Islands**

Corals 563; 593.6

    xx **Invertebrates; Marine animals**

Cordials (Liquor). *See* **Liquors and liqueurs**

Core curriculum. *See* **Colleges and universities—Curricula; Education—Curricula;** and types of education and schools with the subdivision *Curricula,* e.g. **Library education—Curricula;** etc.

Corn 633.1; 633.2

    x Maize

    xx **Agriculture; Forage plants; Grain**

Corn—Therapeutic use 615.5

    xx **Diet therapy; Therapeutics**

Coronary heart diseases. *See* **Heart—Diseases**

Corporate acquisitions. *See* **Corporate mergers and acquisitions**

Corporate farming. *See* **Agribusiness**

Corporate libraries 027.6

    See note under **Business libraries.**

    x Company libraries; Industrial libraries; Libraries, Company; Libraries, Corporate; Libraries, Industrial

    xx **Special libraries**

Corporate mergers. *See* **Corporate mergers and acquisitions**

Corporate mergers and acquisitions 338.8; 658.1

    See also **Conglomerate corporations; Leveraged buyouts**

    x Acquisition of corporations; Buyouts, Corporate; Consolidation and merger of corporations; Corporate acquisitions; Corporate mergers; Corporate takeovers; Industrial mergers; Merger of corporations; Takeovers, Corporate

    xx **Corporations**

Corporate patronage of the arts. *See* **Art patronage**

Corporate symbols. *See* **Trademarks**

Corporate takeovers. *See* **Corporate mergers and acquisitions**

Corporation law 346

    See also **Public service commissions; Public utilities; Trusts, Industrial**

    x Law, Corporation

    xx **Commercial law; Corporations; Law; Monopolies; Public utilities**

Corporations 338.7; 658.1

    See also

Conglomerate corporations	**Municipal ownership**
Cooperative societies	**Public service commissions**
Corporate mergers and acquisitions	
Corporation law	**Public utilities**
Government ownership	**Trust companies**
Multinational corporations	**Trusts, Industrial**

Corporations—*Continued*

   x Companies

   xx **Business; Public utilities; Stocks; Trusts, Industrial**

Corporations—Accounting   657; 658.15

   xx **Accounting; Bookkeeping**

Corporations—Art patronage. *See* **Art patronage**

Corporations, Conglomerate. *See* **Conglomerate corporations**

Corporations—Farming operations. *See* **Agribusiness**

Corporations—Finance   658.15

   x Capitalization (Finance)

Corporations, International. *See* **Multinational corporations**

Corporations—Management. *See* **Industrial management**

Corporations, Multinational. *See* **Multinational corporations**

Corpulence. *See* **Obesity**

Correctional institutions (May subdiv. geog.)   **365**

   See also **Halfway houses;** also types of correctional institutions, e.g. **Prisons; Reformatories;** etc.

   x Penal institutions

Correctional services. *See* **Corrections**

Corrections   364.6

   Use for materials on the rehabilitation and treatment of offenders through parole, penal custody, probation programs, and the administration of such programs.

   See also **Parole; Probation; Punishment**

   x Correctional services; Criminals—Rehabilitation programs; Penology

   xx **Criminal justice, Administration of**

Correspondence. *See* **Business letters; Letter writing; Letters;** and subjects with the subdivision *Correspondence,* e.g. **Authors—Correspondence;** etc.

Correspondence schools and courses   374

   x Home education; Home study courses; Self-instruction

   xx **Education; Technical education; University extension**

Corrosion and anticorrosives   620.1

   See also **Paint**

   x Anticorrosive paint; Rust; Rustless coatings

   xx **Chemistry, Technical; Paint**

Corrupt practices. *See* subjects with the subdivision *Corrupt practices,* e.g. **Adoption—Corrupt practices; Sports—Corrupt practices;** etc.

Corruption in politics   324; 351.9; 352

   See also **Campaign funds; Iran-Contra Affair, 1985-; Lobbying and lobbyists; Misconduct in office; Whistle blowing;** also names of specific incidents, e.g. **Watergate Affair, 1972-1974;** etc.

   x Boss rule; Graft in politics; Political corruption; Political scandals; Politics—Corrupt practices; Spoils system

   xx **Conflict of interests; Lobbying and lobbyists; Misconduct in office; Political crimes and offenses; Political ethics; Politics, Practical**

Corruption in sports. *See* **Sports—Corrupt practices**

Corruption, Police. *See* **Police—Corrupt practices**

Corsairs. *See* **Pirates**

Cosmetic surgery. *See* **Plastic surgery**

Cosmetics   646.7; 668
> *See also* **Makeup, Theatrical; Perfumes**
> *x* Makeup (Cosmetics); Toilet preparations
> *xx* **Beauty shops; Costume**

Cosmic chemistry. *See* **Space chemistry**

Cosmic rays   539.7
> *x* Millikan rays
> *xx* **Nuclear physics; Radiation; Radioactivity; Space environment**

Cosmobiology. *See* **Space biology**

Cosmochemistry. *See* **Space chemistry**

Cosmogony. *See* **Universe**

Cosmogony, Biblical. *See* **Creation**

Cosmography. *See* **Universe**

Cosmology. *See* **Universe**

Cosmology, Biblical. *See* **Creation**

Cosmonauts. *See* **Astronauts**

Cost accounting   657
> *See also* **Efficiency, Industrial**
> *xx* **Accounting; Bookkeeping**

Cost of living   339.4
> *See also* **Budgets, Household; Consumer price indexes; Prices; Saving and thrift; Subsistence economy; Wages**
> *x* Food, Cost of; Household finances; Living, Cost of
> *xx* **Economics; Home economics; Labor; Prices; Saving and thrift; Social conditions; Standard of living; Wages**

Cost of living indexes. *See* **Consumer price indexes**

Cost of medical care. *See* **Medical care—Costs**

Costs. *See* subjects with the subdivision *Costs,* e.g. **Medical care—Costs;** etc.

Costume (May subdiv. geog.)   **391**
> Use for descriptive and historical materials on the costume of particular countries, or periods, or peoples, and for materials on fancy dress and theatrical costumes. Materials dealing with clothing from a practical standpoint, including the art of dress, are entered under **Clothing and dress.** Materials describing the prevailing mode or style of dress are entered under **Fashion.** For materials on the traditional costume and adornment of native peoples of the western hemisphere, assign the name of the native people with the subdivision *Costume and adornment,* e.g. **Indians of North America—Costume and adornment;** etc.
>
> *See also*

Arms and armor	**Hats**
Clothing and dress	**Makeup, Theatrical**
Cosmetics	**Millinery**
Fans	**Uniforms, Military**
Fashion	**Wigs**

> also classes of people with the subdivision *Costume,* e.g. **Children—Costume;** etc.
> *x* Acting—Costume; Fancy dress; Style in dress;

Costume—*Continued*

Theatrical costume

xx **Clothing and dress; Decorative arts; Ethnology; Fashion; Manners and customs**

Costume design. *See* **Fashion design**

Costume jewelry. *See* **Jewelry**

Costume, Military. *See* **Uniforms, Military**

Cottage industry. *See* **Home business**

Cottage industry, Electronic. *See* **Telecommuting**

Cottages. *See* **Houses**

Cotton 633.5; 677

xx **Botany, Economic; Commerce; Fibers; Yarn**

Cotton manufacture 677

xx **Textile industry**

Councils and synods 262

See also names of special councils and synods, e.g. **Vatican Council (2nd : 1962-1965);** etc.

x Church councils; Ecumenical councils; Synods

xx **Christianity; Church history**

Counseling 361.3; 371.4

Use for materials dealing with the principles or practices used in various types of guidance work—student, employment, veterans, personnel.

See also

Consultants	**Peer counseling**
Crisis centers	**School counseling**
Drug abuse counseling	**Social case work**
Interviewing	**Vocational guidance**

also types of counseling, e.g. **Educational counseling; Health counseling; Hotlines (Telephone counseling); Marriage counseling;** etc.; and classes of persons with the subdivision *Counseling of,* e.g. **Elderly—Counseling of;** etc.

x Guidance

xx **Helping behavior; Interviewing; Personnel management; Psychology, Applied; Social case work; Welfare work in industry**

Counter culture 306

See also **Alternative lifestyle; Bohemianism; Collective settlements**

x Counterculture; Nonconformity; Subculture

xx **Collective settlements; Lifestyles; Social conditions**

Counter-Reformation. *See* **Reformation**

Counterculture. *See* **Counter culture**

Counterespionage. *See* **Intelligence service**

Counterfeits and counterfeiting 332; 364.1

See also **Credit card crimes**

xx **Coinage; Crime; Forgery; Impostors and imposture; Money; Swindlers and swindling**

Counterintelligence. *See* **Intelligence service**

Counterpoint 781.2

See also **Fugue**

xx **Composition (Music); Music—Theory**

Counterreformation. *See* **Reformation**

Counting 513.2; E

Use for materials on counting, including counting books, etc. Materials on the systems of numeration and the theory of numeration are entered under **Numeration.** Materials on the psychology of numeration are entered under **Number concept.**

Counting—*Continued*

    See also **Number games; Numeration**

    x Counting books

    xx **Arithmetic—Study and teaching; Numeration**

Counting books. *See* **Counting**

Country and western music. *See* **Country music**

Country churches. *See* **Rural churches**

Country houses. *See* **Architecture, Domestic**

Country life (May subdiv. geog.) **307.72; 630**

    Use for descriptive, popular and literary materials on living in the country. Materials dealing with social organization and conditions in rural communities are entered under **Sociology, Rural.**

    See also **Agriculture—Societies; Farm life; Farmers; Mountain life; Outdoor life; Sociology, Rural**

    x Rural life

    xx **Outdoor life; Sociology, Rural**

Country life—United States **307.72; 630**

    x United States—Country life

Country music **781.642**

    x Country and western music; Hillbilly music; Western and country music

    xx **Folk music—United States; Popular music**

Country schools. *See* **Rural schools**

County agricultural agents **630.7**

    xx **Agricultural extension work; Agriculture—Study and teaching**

County government **352**

    x County officers

    xx **Local government**

County libraries **027.4**

    x Libraries, County

    xx **Library extension; Public libraries; Regional libraries**

County officers. *See* **County government**

County planning. *See* **Regional planning**

Couples, Married. *See* **Married people**

Coupons (Retail trade) **659**

    xx **Advertising**

Coups d'état. *See* **Revolutions**

Courage **179**

    See also **Fear; Heroes and heroines; Morale**

    x Bravery; Heroism

    xx **Heroes and heroines; Human behavior**

Courses of study. *See* **Colleges and universities—Curricula; Education—Curricula;** and types of education and schools with the subdivision *Curricula,* e.g. **Library education—Curricula;** etc.

Court fools. *See* **Fools and jesters**

Court life. *See* **Courts and courtiers**

Court martial. *See* **Courts martial and courts of inquiry**

Courtesy **177; 395**

    x Manners; Politeness

    xx **Etiquette; Human behavior**

Courtiers. *See* **Courts and courtiers**

Courting. *See* **Dating (Social customs)**

Courts (May subdiv. geog.) **347**

    See also **Arbitration and award; Courts martial and courts of inquiry; Criminal procedure;**

Courts—*Continued*
>   **Judges; Jury; Justice, Administration of; Juvenile courts**
>   *x* Judiciary
>   *xx* **Judges; Justice, Administration of; Law**

Courts and courtiers 390; 929.7
>   *See also* **Fools and jesters; Kings, queens, rulers, etc.**
>   *x* Court life; Courtiers
>   *xx* **Kings, queens, rulers, etc.; Manners and customs**

Courts martial and courts of inquiry 343
>   *See also* **Military law**
>   *x* Court martial; Military courts
>   *xx* **Courts; Military law; Trials**

Courts—United States 347.73
>   *x* Federal courts; United States—Courts

Courtship. *See* **Dating (Social customs)**

Courtship (Animal behavior). *See* **Animal courtship**

Courtship of animals. *See* **Animal courtship**

Covens. *See* **Witches**

Coverlets. *See* **Bedspreads; Quilts**

Cowboys. *See* **Cowhands**

Cowgirls. *See* **Cowhands**

Cowhands 390; 636.20092; 978
>   *See also* **Rodeos**
>   *x* Cowboys; Cowgirls; Gauchos
>   *xx* **Frontier and pioneer life; Ranch life**

Cowhands—Songs and music 782.42
>   *xx* **Music; Songs**

Cows. *See* **Cattle**

Cows—Diseases. *See* **Cattle—Diseases**

Crabs 565; 595.3
>   *xx* **Crustacea; Shellfish**

Crack babies. *See* **Children of drug addicts**

Crack cocaine. *See* **Crack (Drug)**

Crack (Drug) 362.29; 615
>   *x* Crack cocaine
>   *xx* **Cocaine**

Cradle songs. *See* **Lullabies**

Craft festivals. *See* **Craft shows**

Craft shows 745
>   *x* Craft festivals; Shows, Craft
>   *xx* **Exhibitions; Festivals; Handicraft**

Crafts (Arts). *See* **Arts and crafts movement; Handicraft**

Cranes, derricks, etc. 621.8
>   *x* Derricks
>   *xx* **Hoisting machinery**

Cranks. *See* **Eccentrics and eccentricities**

Crates. *See* **Boxes**

Crayon drawing 741.2
>   *See also* **Pastel drawing**
>   *x* Blackboard drawing
>   *xx* **Drawing; Pastel drawing; Portrait painting**

Creation 213; 231.7
>   *See also* **Earth; Evolution; God; Man; Mythology; Theology; Universe**
>   *x* Cosmogony, Biblical; Cosmology, Biblical
>   *xx* **Earth; Evolution; God; Man; Natural theology; Religion and science; Universe**

Creation (Literary, artistic, etc.) 153.3
  See also **Creative ability; Creative writing**
  x Inspiration
  xx **Creative ability; Genius; Imagination; Intellect; Inventions**
Creation—Study and teaching 213; 231.7
  See also **Evolution—Study and teaching; Fundamentalism and education**
  x Creationism
  xx **Evolution—Study and teaching; Fundamentalism and education**
Creationism. *See* **Creation—Study and teaching**
Creative ability 153.3; 701; 801
  See also **Creation (Literary, artistic, etc.); Creative thinking**
  x Creativity
  xx **Ability; Creation (Literary, artistic, etc.); Creative thinking**
Creative activities 372.5
  Use for materials on play or work activities for children that initiate new interests, facilitate the seeing of new relationships in thinking and learning, and result in some form of expressional art, i.e. painting, cooking, drama, etc.
  x Activities curriculum
  xx **Amusements; Elementary education; Handicraft; Kindergarten**
Creative movement. *See* **Movement education**
Creative thinking 153.4
  See also **Creative ability**
  xx **Creative ability**
Creative writing 808
  x Writing (Authorship)
  xx **Authorship; Creation (Literary, artistic, etc.); Language arts**
Creativity. *See* **Creative ability**
Creatures, Imaginary. *See* **Mythical animals**
Credibility. *See* **Truthfulness and falsehood**
Credit 332.7
  See also

  Agricultural credit   **Instalment plan**
  Banks and banking   **Loans**
  Collecting of accounts   **Mortgages**
  Consumer credit   **Negotiable instruments**
  Debtor and creditor   **Public debts**
  x Bills of credit; Letters of credit
  xx **Banks and banking; Business; Debtor and creditor; Economics; Finance; Money**
Credit, Agricultural. *See* **Agricultural credit**
Credit card crimes 364.1
  x Fraud, Credit card
  xx **Counterfeits and counterfeiting; Swindlers and swindling**
Credit cards 332.7
  x Bank credit cards; Banks and banking—Credit cards
  xx **Consumer credit**
Credit, Consumer. *See* **Consumer credit**
Credit unions 334
  Use for materials on cooperative associations that make small loans to its members at low interest rates.

Credit unions—*Continued*

    See also **Consumer credit**

    xx **Banks and banking, Cooperative; Consumer credit; Cooperative societies; Loans; Personal loans**

Creeds   238

    See also **Apostles' Creed; Catechisms; Nicene Creed**

    x Confessions of faith; Faith, Confessions of

    xx **Catechisms; Church history; Theology**

Cremation   393; 614

    See also **Funeral rites and ceremonies**

    x Burial; Incineration; Mortuary customs

    xx **Funeral rites and ceremonies; Public health; Sanitation**

Creoles   305.84; 972.9; 976

Crests.   *See* **Heraldry**

Crewelwork   746.44

    xx **Embroidery**

Crime (May subdiv. geog.)   **364**

    All types of crime are not included in this List but are to be added as needed.

    See also

Assassination	**son**
Atrocities	**Organized crime**
Capital punishment	**Parole**
Computer crimes	**Police**
Counterfeits and counterfeiting	**Prisons**
	Prostitution
Crime prevention	**Punishment**
Crimes without victims	**Racketeering**
Criminal law	**Reformatories**
Criminals	**Riots**
Drugs and crime	**Sex crimes**
Forgery	**Smuggling**
Hate crimes	**Swindlers and swindling**
Homicide	**Treason**
Justice, Administration of	**Trials**
Juvenile delinquency	**Victims of crime**
Lynching	**Vigilance committees**
Offenses against the per-	**White collar crimes**

    x Crimes; Criminology; Felony; Vice

    xx **Criminal justice, Administration of; Justice, Administration of; Police; Prisons; Punishment; Social ethics; Social problems; Trials**

Crime and drugs.   *See* **Drugs and crime**

Crime and narcotics.   *See* **Drugs and crime**

Crime-drug relationship.   *See* **Drugs and crime**

Crime prevention   364.4

    See also **Criminal psychology**

    x Prevention of crime

    xx **Crime**

Crime syndicates.   *See* **Organized crime; Racketeering**

Crime—United States   364.973

    x United States—Crime

Crime victims.   *See* **Victims of crime**

Crimean War, 1853-1856   947

    x Great Britain—History—1853-1856, Crimean War; Russo-Turkish War, 1853-1856

Crimes.   *See* **Crime**

Crimes against public safety.   *See* **Offenses against public safety**

Crimes against the person. *See* **Offenses against the person**

Crimes, Military. *See* **Military offenses**

Crimes of hate. *See* **Hate crimes**

Crimes, Political. *See* **Political crimes and offenses**

Crimes, Sex. *See* **Sex crimes**

Crimes, White collar. *See* **White collar crimes**

Crimes without victims   364.1

> *See also* names of crimes, e.g. **Drug abuse; Gambling;** etc.
>
> *x* Non-victim crimes; Nonvictim crimes; Victimless crimes
>
> *xx* **Crime; Criminal law**

Criminal assault. *See* **Rape**

Criminal investigation   363.2

> *See also*

Criminals—Identification	**Medical jurisprudence**
Detectives	**Missing children**
Eavesdropping	**Missing persons**
Fingerprints	**Police**
Lie detectors and detection	**Wiretapping**

> *xx* **Detectives; Police**

Criminal justice, Administration of   345

> *See also* **Corrections; Crime; Pardon; Parole; Prisons; Punishment**
>
> *x* Administration of criminal justice
>
> *xx* **Criminal law**

Criminal law   345

> *See also*

Adoption—Corrupt practices	**Military offenses**
	Misconduct in office
Capital punishment	**Offenses against public safety**
Crimes without victims	
Criminal justice, Administration of	**Offenses against the person**
Criminal procedure	**Poisons and poisoning**
Insanity defense	**Probation**
Jury	**Punishment**
Kidnapping	**Trials**
Medical jurisprudence	**Vigilance committees**

> also names of crimes, e.g. **Homicide;** etc.
>
> *x* Codes, Penal; Law, Criminal; Misdemeanors (Law); Penal codes; Penal law
>
> *xx* **Crime; Criminal procedure; Law; Prisons; Punishment**

Criminal procedure   345

> *See also* **Criminal law**
>
> *xx* **Courts; Criminal law**

Criminal psychology   364.3

> *See also* **Psychology, Pathological**
>
> *x* Psychology, Criminal
>
> *xx* **Crime prevention; Psychology, Pathological**

Criminals   364.3; 364.6

> *See also* **Convict labor; Penal colonies; Pirates; Prisoners; Robbers and outlaws; Swindlers and swindling**
>
> *x* Convicts; Delinquents; Gangs; Reform of criminals
>
> *xx* **Crime**

Criminals and drugs. *See* **Criminals—Drug use**

Criminals and narcotics. *See* **Criminals—Drug use**

Criminals—Drug use   362.2; 364.3

> *See also* **Drugs and crime**

Criminals—Drug use—*Continued*
  x Criminals and drugs; Criminals and narcotics; Drugs and criminals; Narcotics and criminals
  xx **Drugs and crime**
Criminals—Identification 363.2
  See also **Fingerprints**
  xx **Criminal investigation; Identification**
Criminals—Rehabilitation programs. *See* **Corrections**
Criminology. *See* **Crime**
Crippled children. *See* **Physically handicapped children**
Crippled people. *See* **Physically handicapped**
Crisis centers 361.3; 362
  See also types of crisis centers, e.g. **Hotlines (Telephone counseling)**; etc.
  x Crisis intervention centers
  xx **Counseling; Hotlines (Telephone counseling); Social work**
Crisis counseling. *See* **Hotlines (Telephone counseling)**
Crisis intervention centers. *See* **Crisis centers**
Crisis intervention telephone service. *See* **Hotlines (Telephone counseling)**
Crisis management 658.4
  xx **Management; Problem solving**
Critical thinking 153.4; 160
  Use for materials on thinking that is based on the careful evaluation of premises and evidence and that comes to conclusions as objectively as possible through the consideration of all pertinent factors and the use of logical procedures.
  xx **Decision making; Logic; Problem solving; Reasoning; Thought and thinking**
Criticism 801
  Use for materials on the history, principles, methods, etc. of criticism in general and of literary criticism in particular. Criticism in a specific field is entered under the subject in variant forms as listed below. Criticism of the work of an individual author, artist, composer, etc. is entered under his/her name as subject; only in the case of voluminous authors is it necessary to add the subdivision *Criticism, interpretation, etc.* Criticism of a single work is entered under the person's name followed by the title of the work.
  See also **Art criticism; Bible—Criticism, interpretation, etc.; Books—Reviews; Dramatic criticism; Shakespeare, William, 1564-1616—Criticism, interpretation, etc.; Style, Literary;** also literature, film, and music subjects with the subdivision *History and criticism,* e.g. **English literature—History and criticism; English poetry—History and criticism; Music—History and criticism;** etc.
  x Appraisal of books; Books—Appraisal; Evaluation of literature; Literary criticism; Literature—Evaluation

204

Criticism—*Continued*
  xx **Aesthetics; Literature; Literature—History and criticism; Rhetoric; Style, Literary**
Cro-Magnons 573.3
  x Cromagnons
  xx **Prehistoric man**
Crocheting 746.43
  See also **Beadwork; Lace and lace making**
Crockery. *See* **Pottery**
Crocodiles 597.98
  See also **Alligators**
  xx **Reptiles**
Cromagnons. *See* **Cro-Magnons**
Crop dusting. *See* **Aeronautics in agriculture**
Crop reports. *See* **Agriculture—Statistics**
Crop rotation 631.5
  x Crops, Rotation of; Rotation of crops
  xx **Agriculture**
Crop spraying. *See* **Aeronautics in agriculture**
Crops. *See* **Farm produce**
Crops, Rotation of. *See* **Crop rotation**
Cross cultural conflict. *See* **Culture conflict**
Cross cultural psychology. *See* **Ethnopsychology**
Cross cultural studies 155.8; 306
  Use for materials on the systematic comparison of sociological, psychological, anthropological, etc., aspects of two or more cultural groups, either within the same country or in different countries.
  x Comparison of cultures; Intercultural studies; Transcultural studies
  xx **Culture; Social sciences**
Cross-examination. *See* **Witnesses**
Crossword puzzles 793.73
  xx **Puzzles; Word games**
Crowds 302.3
  See also **Protests, demonstrations, etc.; Riot control; Social psychology**
  x Mobs
  xx **Riots; Social psychology**
CRT display terminals. *See* **Video display terminals**
CRTs. *See* **Cathode ray tubes**
Crucifixion of Christ. *See* **Jesus Christ—Crucifixion**
Crude oil. *See* **Petroleum**
Cruelty 179
  See also **Atrocities**
  x Brutality
  xx **Ethics**
Cruelty to animals. *See* **Animal welfare**
Cruelty to children. *See* **Child abuse**
Cruises. *See* **Ocean travel**
Crusades 909.07
  See also **Chivalry**
  xx **Chivalry; Church history—600-1500, Middle Ages; Middle Ages—History**
Crustacea 565; 595.3
  See also names of shellfish, e.g. **Crabs; Lobsters;** etc.
  xx **Invertebrates; Shellfish**
Cryobiology 574.19
  See also **Cold—Physiological effect; Frozen embryos**

Cryobiology—*Continued*
　　x Freezing; Low temperature biology
　　xx **Biology; Cold; Low temperatures**
Cryogenic internment. *See* **Cryonics**
Cryogenic surgery. *See* **Cryosurgery**
Cryogenics. *See* **Low temperatures**
Cryonics　621.5
　　x Burial; Cryogenic internment; Freezing of human bodies; Human cold storage
Cryosurgery　617
　　x Cryogenic surgery
　　xx **Cold—Therapeutic use; Surgery**
Cryotherapy. *See* **Cold—Therapeutic use**
Cryptography　652
　　See also **Ciphers**
　　x Code deciphering; Code enciphering; Secret writing
　　xx **Ciphers; Signs and symbols; Writing**
Crystal gazing. *See* **Divination**
Crystalline rocks. *See* **Rocks**
Crystallization. *See* **Crystallography**
Crystallography　548
　　See also **Mineralogy**
　　x Crystallization; Crystals
　　xx **Chemistry, Physical and theoretical; Petrology; Rocks; Science**
Crystals. *See* **Crystallography**
CT (Computerized tomography). *See* **Tomography**
Cub Scouts. *See* **Boy Scouts**
Cuba　972.91
　　xx **Islands**
Cuba—History　972.91
Cuba—History—1958-1959, Revolution　972.9106
Cuba—History—1959-　972.9106
Cuba—History—1961, Invasion　972.9106
　　x Bay of Pigs invasion; Operation Pluto; Pluto operation
Cube root　513.2
　　xx **Arithmetic**
Cubic measurement. *See* **Volume (Cubic content)**
Cubism　709.04; 759.06
　　See also **Postimpressionism (Art)**
　　xx **Art, Abstract; Painting; Postimpressionism (Art)**
Cults　291.9
　　See also **Ancestor worship; New Age movement; Sects**
　　x Religious cults
　　xx **Religions; Sects**
Cultural anthropology. *See* **Ethnology**
Cultural change. *See* **Social change**
Cultural exchange programs. *See* **Exchange of persons programs**
Cultural relations　306; 341.7
　　See also **Exchange of persons programs**
　　x Intercultural relations
　　xx **Intellectual cooperation; International cooperation; International relations**
Culturally deprived. *See* **Socially handicapped**
Culturally deprived children. *See* **Socially handicapped children**
Culturally handicapped. *See* **Socially handicapped**

Culturally handicapped children. *See* **Socially handicapped children**

Culture 306; 909
> Use for general discussions of refinement in manners, taste, etc. and the intellectual content of civilization. Materials limited to the culture of individual nations are entered under names of countries with the subdivisions *Civilization* or *Social life and customs.*

> *See also*

Acculturation	**Humanism**
Biculturalism	**Learning and scholarship**
Civilization	**Popular culture**
Cross cultural studies	**Self-culture**
Education	

> *x* Intellectual life

> *xx* **Civilization; Education; Learning and scholarship**

Culture conflict 155.8; 306
> *x* Conflict of cultures; Cross cultural conflict; Culture shock; Future shock

> *xx* **Ethnic relations; Ethnopsychology; Race relations**

Culture contact. *See* **Acculturation**

Culture, Popular. *See* **Popular culture**

Culture shock. *See* **Culture conflict**

Curates. *See* **Clergy**

Curiosities and wonders 030
> *See also* **Eccentrics and eccentricities; Monsters; World records;** also subjects with the subdivision *Miscellanea,* e.g. **Medicine—Miscellanea;** etc.

> *x* Enigmas; Facts, Miscellaneous; Miscellaneous facts; Oddities; Trivia; Wonders

Currency. *See* **Money**

Currency devaluation. *See* **Monetary policy**

Current events 907
> Use for materials on the study and teaching of current events. Periodicals and yearbooks devoted to the events themselves are entered under **History—Periodicals.**

> *xx* **History, Modern—Study and teaching**

Currents, Alternating. *See* **Electric currents, Alternating**

Currents, Electric. *See* **Electric currents**

Currents, Ocean. *See* **Ocean currents**

Curricula (Courses of study). *See* **Education—Curricula;** and types of education and schools with the subdivision *Curricula,* e.g. **Library education—Curricula; Colleges and universities—Curricula;** etc.

Curriculum materials centers. *See* **Instructional materials centers**

Curtains. *See* **Drapery**

Custody kidnapping. *See* **Parental kidnapping**

Custody of children. *See* **Child custody**

Custom duties. *See* **Tariff**

Customer relations 658.8
> *See also* **Customer service**

> *xx* **Business; Public relations**

Customer service 658.8
> *x* Service, Customer; Service (in industry); Ser-

Customer service—*Continued*
   vices, Customer; Technical service
   xx **Customer relations**
Customs, Social. *See* **Manners and customs;** and
   names of ethnic groups, countries, cities,
   etc., with the subdivision *Social life and cus-*
   toms, e.g. **Indians of North America—**
   Social life and customs; Jews—Social life
   and customs; United States—Social life and
   customs; etc.
Customs (Tariff). *See* **Tariff**
Cybernetics   003
   See also **Bionics; Computers; System analysis;**
      Systems engineering
   x Automatic control; Mechanical brains
   xx **Calculators; Communication; Electronics; Sys-**
      tem theory
Cycles. *See* **Periodicity**
Cycles, Business. *See* **Business cycles**
Cycles, Motor. *See* **Motorcycles**
Cycling. *See* **Bicycles and bicycling; Motorcycles;**
   Tricycles
Cyclones   551.55
   Materials on the cyclonic storms of the West In-
      dies are entered under **Hurricanes.** Storms
      of the China Seas and the Philippines are
      entered under **Typhoons.**
   See also **Hurricanes**
   xx **Meteorology; Storms; Winds**
Cyclopedias. *See* **Encyclopedias and dictionaries**
Cyclotron   539.7; 621.48
   x Atom smashing; Magnetic resonance accelera-
      tor
   xx **Atoms; Nuclear physics; Transmutation**
      (Chemistry)
Cytology. *See* **Cells**
Czechoslovakia   943.7
Czechoslovakia—History—1918-1968   943.7
Czechoslovakia—History—1968- ,
   Intervention. *See* **Czechoslovakia—**
   History—1968-1989
Czechoslovakia—History—1968-1989   943.704
   x Czechoslovakia—History—1968- , Interven-
      tion; Russian intervention in Czechoslova-
      kia; Soviet intervention in Czechoslovakia
Czechoslovakia—History—1989-   943.704
D.D.T. (Insecticide)   668
   x DDT (Insecticide); Dichloro-diphenyl-
      trichloroethane
   xx **Insecticides**
D Day. *See* **Normandy (France), Attack on, 1944**
D.N.A. *See* **DNA**
Daily readings (Spiritual exercises). *See* **Devotional**
   calendars
Dairies. *See* **Dairying**
Dairy cattle   636.2
   See also names of breeds of dairy cattle, e.g.
      Holstein-Friesian cattle; etc.
   x Milch cattle
   xx **Cattle; Dairying**
Dairy farming. *See* **Dairying**
Dairy products   637; 641.3
   See also **Dairying;** also names of dairy products,

Dairy products—*Continued*
       e.g. **Butter; Cheese; Milk;** etc.
    x Products, Dairy
    xx **Dairying**
Dairying (May subdiv. geog.)   **636.2; 637**
    Use for materials on the production and market-
       ing of milk, usually cows' milk and its prod-
       ucts and for general materials on the care of
       dairy cattle, their breeding, feeding, manage-
       ment, and milking.
    See also **Cattle; Dairy cattle; Dairy products;**
      Milk
    x Dairies; Dairy farming
    xx **Agriculture; Cattle; Dairy products; Home eco-**
      nomics; Livestock
Dams   **627**
    See also names of dams, e.g. **Hoover Dam**
      (Ariz. and Nev.); etc.
    xx **Civil engineering; Flood control; Hydraulic**
      structures; Irrigation; Rivers; Water power;
      Water supply
Dance. *See* **Dancing**
Dance music   **781.5; 784.18**
    See also **Jazz music; Popular music; Rock music**
    x Big band music
    xx **Dancing; Instrumental music; Music**
Dancers   **792.8092; 793.3092; 920**
    See also types of dancers, e.g. **Ballet dancers;**
      etc.
    xx **Entertainers**
Dancing (May subdiv. geog.)   **792.8; 793.3**
    See also **Aerobics; Dance music;** also types of
      dances and dancing, e.g. **Ballet; Break danc-**
      ing; Folk dancing; Modern dance; Tap danc-
      ing; etc.
    x Dance
    xx **Amusements; Etiquette; Performing arts**
Dancing, Aerobic. *See* **Aerobics**
Dancing—United States   **792.80973; 793.30973**
    See also **Folk dancing, American**
    x United States—Dancing
Dangerous animals   **591.6**
    See also **Animal attacks; Poisonous animals**
    xx **Animals; Wildlife**
Dangerous materials. *See* **Hazardous substances**
Dangerous occupations. *See* **Hazardous occupa-**
    tions
Danish language   **439.8**
    May be subdivided like **English language.**
    xx **Norwegian language; Scandinavian languages**
Danish literature   **839.8**
    May use same subdivisions and names of liter-
      ary forms as for **English literature.**
    xx **Scandinavian literature**
Dark Ages. *See* **Middle Ages**
Darkroom technique in photography. *See* **Photog-**
    raphy—Processing
Darwinism. *See* **Evolution**
Data base management. *See* **Database management**
Data networks, Computer. *See* **Computer networks**
Data processing. *See* **Electronic data processing;**
    Information systems; and subjects with the
    subdivision *Data processing,* e.g. **Banks**
    and banking—Data processing; etc.

Data processing, Electronic—Keyboarding. *See*
   Keyboarding (Electronics)
Data storage and retrieval systems. *See* **Informa-
   tion systems**
Data transmission systems   004.6; 621.38; 621.39
   See also
   Computer networks   **works**
   Electronic mail systems   **Teletext systems**
   Facsimile transmission   **Video telephone**
   Information networks   **Videotex systems**
   Library information net-
      x Transmission of data
      xx **Electronic data processing; Tele-
         communication**
Database management   005.74
      x Data base management; Systems, Database
         management
      xx **Electronic data processing; Information sys-
         tems**
**Database management—Computer programs
      005.75**
Date etiquette. *See* **Dating (Social customs)**
Dates, Historical. *See* **Chronology, Historical**
Dating, Radiocarbon. *See* **Radiocarbon dating**
Dating (Social customs)   306.73; 392; 646.7
      See also **Love**
      x Courting; Courtship; Date etiquette
      xx **Etiquette; Love; Manners and customs**
Daughters and fathers. *See* **Fathers and daughters**
Daughters and mothers. *See* **Mothers and daugh-
   ters**
Day   529
      See also **Night**
      xx **Chronology; Night; Time**
Day care centers. *See* **Child care centers**
Day dreams. *See* **Fantasy**
Day nurseries. *See* **Child care centers**
Day of Atonement. *See* **Yom Kippur**
Days. *See* **Birthdays; Fasts and feasts; Festivals;
         Holidays;** and names of special days, e.g.
         Christmas; Memorial Day; etc.
DDT (Insecticide). *See* **D.D.T. (Insecticide)**
Dead Sea scrolls   221.4; 229; 296.1
      x Qumran texts
Dead, Worship of the. *See* **Ancestor worship**
Deaf   362.4
      See also **Closed caption television; Closed caption
         video recordings; Hearing ear dogs**
      x Hearing impaired
      xx **Physically handicapped**
Deaf, Dogs for. *See* **Hearing ear dogs**
Deaf—Education   371.91
      x Education of the deaf
      xx **Education; Vocational education; Vocational
         guidance**
Deaf—Institutional care   362.4
      x Asylums; Charitable institutions; Homes (In-
         stitutions)
Deaf—Means of communication   362.4; 419
      Use for general materials on communication in
         the broadest sense by people who are deaf.
         For materials on language systems based on
         hand gestures, use **Sign language.**

Deaf—Means of communication—*Continued*
　　See also **Nonverbal communication; Sign language**
　　　x Finger alphabet; Lip reading
　　　xx **Communication; Nonverbal communication; Sign language**
Deaf—Sign language. *See* **Sign language**
Deafness 362.4; 617.8
　　See also **Ear; Hearing; Hearing aids**
　　xx **Hearing**
Death 128; 236; 306.9
　　See also

Bereavement	**Longevity**
Brain death	**Mortality**
Future life	**Right to die**
Heaven	**Terminal care**
Hell	**Terminally ill**

　　xx **Biology; Eschatology; Life; Mortality; Terminal care; Terminally ill**
Death masks. *See* **Masks (Sculpture)**
Death, Mercy. *See* **Euthanasia**
Death notices. *See* **Obituaries**
Death penalty. *See* **Capital punishment**
Death rate. *See* **Mortality; Vital statistics**
Death, Right of. *See* **Right to die**
Death with dignity. *See* **Right to die**
Deaths, Registers of. *See* **Registers of births, etc.**
Debates and debating 808.53
　　See also **Discussion groups; Parliamentary practice; Radio addresses, debates, etc.**
　　x Argumentation; Discussion; Speaking
　　xx **Public speaking; Rhetoric**
Debit cards 332.1
　　x Bank debit cards; Banks and banking—Debit cards; Cards, Debit
Debris, Space. *See* **Space debris**
Debtor and creditor 332.7; 346
　　Use for economic and statistical materials about debt as well as for legal materials involving debtor and creditor.
　　See also **Bankruptcy; Collecting of accounts; Credit**
　　xx **Commercial law; Credit**
Debts, Government. *See* **Public debts**
Debts, Public. *See* **Public debts**
Decalogue. *See* **Ten commandments**
Deceit. *See* **Fraud**
Decentralization of schools. *See* **Schools—Decentralization**
Deceptive advertising 343
　　x Advertising, Fraudulent; False advertising; Fraudulent advertising; Misleading advertising; Misrepresentation in advertising; Truth in advertising
　　xx **Business ethics**
Decimal system 389; 513.5
　　xx **Numeration; Weights and measures**
Decision making 153.8; 302.3; 658.4
　　See also **Choice (Psychology); Critical thinking; Problem solving**
　　xx **Choice (Psychology); Game theory; Problem solving**
Decks (Domestic architecture). *See* **Patios**

Declamations, Musical. *See* **Monologues with music**

Declaration of independence (U.S.). *See* **United States—Declaration of independence**

Decoration and ornament (May subdiv. geog. adjective form, e.g. **Decoration and ornament, American;** etc.) **745.4**

Use for materials dealing with the forms and styles of decoration in various fields of fine arts or applied art; the history of such styles of ornament, such as Empire, Louis XV, etc.; and with the various manifestations in different countries or periods, such as Chinese or Renaissance. Materials limited to the decoration of houses are entered under **Interior design.** Consider also **Decorative arts** and **Handicraft.**

See also

Antiques	**Ironwork**
Art objects	**Jewelry**
Arts and crafts movement	**Leather work**
Bronzes	**Lettering**
Carpets	**Metalwork**
China painting	**Monograms**
Decoupage	**Mosaics**
Design	**Mural painting and deco-**
Egg decoration	**ration**
Embroidery	**Needlework**
Enamel and enameling	**Painting**
Flower arrangement	**Plants in art**
Furniture	**Pottery**
Garden ornaments and fur-	**Sculpture**
niture	**Show windows**
Gems	**Stencil work**
Glass painting and stain-	**Stucco**
ing	**Table setting and decora-**
Holiday decorations	**tion**
Illumination of books and	**Tapestry**
manuscripts	**Terra cotta**
Illustration of books	**Textile design**
Interior design	**Wood carving**

x Art, Decorative; Arts, Decorative; Decorative art; Decorative design; Decorative painting; Design, Decorative; Ornament; Painting, Decorative

xx **Art; Decorative arts**

Decoration and ornament, American 745.4

x American decoration and ornament; United States—Decoration and ornament

Decoration and ornament, Architectural 729

x Architectural decoration and ornament; Architecture—Decoration and ornament

xx **Architecture**

Decoration Day. *See* **Memorial Day**

Decoration, Interior. *See* **Interior design**

Decorations, Holiday. *See* **Holiday decorations**

Decorations of honor 355.1; 929.8

See also **Heraldry; Insignia; Medals;** also names of medals

x Badges of honor; Emblems

xx **Heraldry; Insignia; Medals**

Decorative art. *See* **Decoration and ornament**

Decorative arts (May subdiv. geog.) **745**

Use for general materials on the various applied art forms having some utilitarian as well as decorative purpose, including furniture, woodwork, silverware, glassware, ceramics, needlework, the decoration of buildings, etc. Consider also **Decoration and ornament** and **Handicraft.**

Decorative arts—*Continued*

   See also

Antiques	**Glassware**
Art metalwork	**Interior design**
Art objects	**Jewelry**
Arts and crafts movement	**Lacquer and lacquering**
Calligraphy	**Leather work**
Ceramics	**Mosaics**
Costume	**Needlework**
Decoration and ornament	**Porcelain**
Decoupage	**Pottery**
Enamel and enameling	**Rugs**
Fabrics	**Silverware**
Folk art	**Tapestry**
Furniture	**Woodwork**

   x Applied arts; Art industries and trade; Arts, Applied; Arts, Decorative; Arts, Minor; Minor arts

   xx **Art; Folk art**

Decorative arts—United States   745.0973

   x United States—Decorative arts

Decorative design. *See* **Decoration and ornament**

Decorative metalwork. *See* **Art metalwork**

Decorative painting. *See* **Decoration and ornament**

Decoupage   745.54

   xx **Decoration and ornament; Decorative arts; Paper crafts**

Decoys (Hunting)   745.593; 799.2

   x Bird decoys (Hunting)

   xx **Hunting; Shooting**

Deduction (Logic). *See* **Logic**

Deep diving vehicles. *See* **Submersibles**

Deep sea diving. *See* **Diving, Submarine**

Deep sea drilling (Petroleum). *See* **Oil well drilling, Submarine**

Deep sea engineering. *See* **Ocean engineering**

Deep sea mining. *See* **Ocean mining**

Deep-sea Photography. *See* **Underwater photography**

Deep sea technology. *See* **Oceanography**

Deep sea vehicles. *See* **Submersibles**

Deep submergence vehicles. *See* **Submersibles**

Deer   599.73

   See also **Reindeer**

   x Fawns

   xx **Game and game birds**

Defamation. *See* **Libel and slander**

Defective speech. *See* **Speech disorders**

Defective vision. *See* **Vision disorders**

Defectors   325; 327.12

   x Defectors, Political; Political defectors; Turncoats

   xx **Political refugees**

Defectors, Military. *See* **Military desertion**

Defectors, Political. *See* **Defectors**

Defense, Civil. *See* **Civil defense**

Defense (Law). *See* **Litigation**

Defense mechanisms (Zoology). *See* **Animal defenses**

Defense policy. *See* **Military policy**

Defenses, Air. *See* **Air defenses**

Defenses, National. *See* **Industrial mobilization;** and names of countries with the subdivision

Defenses, National—*Continued*

    Defenses, e.g. **United States—Defenses;**
    etc.

Defenses, Radar. *See* **Radar defense networks**

Deficit financing (May subdiv. geog.) **336.3**

    See also **Public debts**

    x Compensatory spending; Deficit spending

    xx **Finance; Public debts**

Deficit spending. *See* **Deficit financing**

Defoliants. *See* **Herbicides**

Deformities. *See* **Birth defects**

Degrees, Academic. *See* **Academic degrees**

Degrees of latitude and longitude. *See* **Geodesy;**
    Latitude; Longitude

Dehydrated foods. *See* **Dried foods**

Dehydrated milk. *See* **Dried milk**

Deism 211

    See also **Atheism; Christianity; Free thought;**
      God; Positivism; Rationalism; Theism

    xx **Atheism; Christianity; God; Rationalism; Reli-**
      gion; Theism; Theology

Deities. *See* **Gods and goddesses**

Dejection. *See* **Depression, Mental**

Delinquency, Juvenile. *See* **Juvenile delinquency**

Delinquents. *See* **Criminals; Juvenile delinquency**

Delphi (Ancient city) 938

    xx **Greece—Antiquities**

Delusions. *See* **Hallucinations and illusions; Super-**
    stition; Witchcraft

Demineralization of salt water. *See* **Sea water con-**
    version

Democracy 321.4; 321.8

    See also

Aristocracy	**Referendum**
Equality	**Representative government**
Federal government	**and representation**
Freedom	**Republics**
Monarchy	**Suffrage**

    x Popular government; Self-government

    xx **Aristocracy; Constitutional history; Constitu-**
      tional law; Equality; Federal government;
      Monarchy; Political science; Representative
      government and representation; Republics

Democratic Party (U.S.) 324.2736

    xx **Political parties**

Demoniac possession 133.4

    See also **Devil; Exorcism**

    xx **Devil; Exorcism**

Demonology 133.4

    See also **Apparitions; Charms; Devil; Exorcism;**
      Occultism; Superstition; Witchcraft

    x Evil spirits; Spirits

    xx **Apparitions; Devil; Exorcism; Ghosts; Occult-**
      ism; Superstition; Witchcraft

Demonstrations for Black civil rights—United
    States. *See* **Blacks—Civil rights**

Demonstrations (Protest). *See* **Protests, demonstra-**
    tions, etc.

Demountable houses. *See* **Prefabricated houses**

Denationalization. *See* **Privatization**

Denatured alcohol. *See* **Alcohol, Denatured**

Denominational schools. *See* **Church schools**

Denominations, Religious. *See* **Sects;** and names

Denominations, Religious—*Continued*
      of particular denominations and sects, e.g.
      Presbyterian Church; etc.
Dentistry 617.6
   See also **Teeth**
   x Medicine, Dental
   xx **Teeth**
Deoxyribonucleic acid. *See* **DNA**
Department stores 658.8
   See also **Selling**
   x Stores
   xx **Business; Retail trade**
Dependencies. *See* **Colonies; Colonization**
Depression, Mental 616.85
   See also **Manic-depressive psychoses**
   x Dejection; Depressive psychoses; Melancho-
      lia; Mental depression; Mentally depressed
   xx **Manic-depressive psychoses; Neuroses; Psy-
      chology, Pathological**
Depressions, Economic 338.5
   x Business depressions; Economic depressions;
      Panics, Economic; Recessions, Economic
   xx **Business cycles; Economics**
Depressive psychoses. *See* **Depression, Mental**
Deprogramming. *See* **Brainwashing**
Derailments. *See* **Railroads—Accidents**
Dermatitis. *See* **Skin—Diseases**
Derricks. *See* **Cranes, derricks, etc.**
Desalination of water. *See* **Sea water conversion**
Desalting of water. *See* **Sea water conversion**
Descent. *See* **Genealogy; Heredity**
Description. *See* names of cities (except ancient
      cities), countries, states, and regions with
      the subdivision *Description,* e.g. **Chicago
      (Ill.)—Description; United States—
      Description;** etc., for descriptive materials
      and accounts of travel, including the history
      of travel, in those places; and names of
      places with the subdivision *Geography* for
      broad geographical materials about a spe-
      cific place, e.g. **United States—Geography;**
      etc.; also names of ancient cities or towns,
      without further subdivision, for general de-
      scriptive materials on those places, e.g. **Del-
      phi (Ancient city);** etc.
Descriptive geometry. *See* **Geometry, Descriptive**
Desegregated schools. *See* **School integration**
Desegregation. *See* **Segregation**
Desegregation in education. *See* **School integration**
Desert animals 591.52
   See also names of desert animals, e.g. **Camels;**
      etc.
   xx **Animals; Deserts; Wildlife**
Desert plants 581.5
   See also names of desert plants, e.g. **Cactus;**
      etc.
   xx **Botany—Ecology; Deserts; Plants**
Desert Shield Operation. *See* **Persian Gulf War,
      1991-**
Desert Storm Operation. *See* **Persian Gulf War,
      1991-**
Desertion. *See* **Desertion and nonsupport; Military
      desertion; Runaway adults**

Desertion and nonsupport   306.88; 346.01
> *See also* **Child support; Runaway adults**
> *x* Abandonment of family; Desertion; Nonsupport
> *xx* **Divorce; Domestic relations**

Desertion, Military.   *See* **Military desertion**

Deserts   551.4
> *See also* **Desert animals; Desert plants**

Design   745.4
> Use for materials on the theory of design.
> *See also* **Fashion design; Interior design; Pattern making; Textile design;** also topical headings with the subdivision *Design,* if a phrase heading for the concept has not been established, or where the subdivision *Design and construction* would not be appropriate, e.g. **Quilts—Design.** etc.
> *xx* **Decoration and ornament; Pattern making**

Design and construction.   *See* types of structures, machines, equipment, etc., with the subdivision *Design and construction,* for materials on their engineering and construction, e.g. **Airplanes—Design and construction; Automobiles—Design and construction;** etc. Also see types of tests and examinations with the subdivision *Design and construction,* for materials on methods of designing and constructing tests.

Design, Architectural.   *See* **Architecture—Details**

Design, Decorative.   *See* **Decoration and ornament**

Design, Industrial.   *See* **Industrial design**

Design, Interior.   *See* **Interior design**

Design, System.   *See* **System design**

Designed genetic change.   *See* **Genetic engineering**

Designer drugs   362.29; 615
> Use for materials on illicit drugs manufactured by altering the molecular structure of existing drugs to mimic the effects of the classical narcotics, stimulants, and hallucinogens.
> *See also* names of individual designer drugs, e.g. **Ice (Drug);** etc.
> *x* Drugs, Designer; Drugs of abuse, Synthetic; Synthetic drugs of abuse
> *xx* **Drugs**

Designs and plans.   *See* architectural and landscape headings with the subdivision *Designs and plans,* for materials containing architectural or landscape architecture drawings, e.g. **Architecture, Domestic—Designs and plans.** etc.

Designs, Architectural.   *See* **Architecture—Designs and plans**

Designs, Floral.   *See* **Flower arrangement**

Desktop publishing   070.5; 686.2
> Use for materials on the utilization of a personal computer, and writing, graphics, and page layout software to produce printed material for publication.
> *xx* **Electronic publishing**

Desoxyribonucleic acid.   *See* **DNA**

Desserts   641.8
> *See also* names of desserts, e.g. **Ice cream, ices, etc.;** etc.

Desserts—*Continued*

    xx **Caterers and catering; Cookery; Dinners and dining**

Destiny. *See* **Fate and fatalism**

Destitution. *See* **Poverty**

Destruction of Jews (1933-1945). *See* **Holocaust, Jewish (1933-1945)**

Destructive insects. *See* **Insect pests**

Details, Architectural. *See* **Architecture—Details**

Detective stories. *See* **Mystery and detective stories**

Detectives 351.74; 363.2; 920

    See also **Criminal investigation; Police; Secret service**

    xx **Criminal investigation; Police; Secret service**

Detergent pollution of rivers, lakes, etc. 363.73; 628.1

    x Water—Detergent pollution

    xx **Detergents, Synthetic; Water pollution**

Detergents, Synthetic 668

    See also **Detergent pollution of rivers, lakes, etc.**

    x Synthetic detergents

    xx **Cleaning compounds; Soap**

Determinism and indeterminism. *See* **Free will and determinism**

Deuterium oxide 546

    x Heavy water; Water—Heavy water

Devaluation of currency. *See* **Monetary policy**

Developing countries 330.9

    Use for comprehensive materials on those countries having relatively low per capita incomes in comparison with North American and Western European countries.

    This heading may be subdivided by those topical subdivisions used under countries, regions, etc., and may be used as a geographic subdivision e.g. **Education—Developing countries;** etc.

    See also **Economic assistance; States, New; Technical assistance**

    x Fourth World; Less developed countries; Third World; Underdeveloped areas

    xx **Economic assistance; Economic conditions; Industrialization; Technical assistance**

Developing countries—Commerce 338.91; 382

Development. *See* **Embryology; Evolution; Growth disorders; Modernization**

Deviation, Sexual. *See* **Sexual deviation**

Devices (Heraldry). *See* **Heraldry; Insignia**

Devil 235

    See also **Demoniac possession; Demonology**

    x Satan

    xx **Demoniac possession; Demonology**

Devil's Triangle. *See* **Bermuda Triangle**

Devotion. *See* **Prayer; Worship**

Devotional calendars 242

    x Christian devotional calendars; Daily readings (Spiritual exercises); Devotional exercises (Daily readings)

    xx **Calendars; Devotional literature**

Devotional exercises 242; 248.3

    Use for general materials on acts of private prayer and private worship and for materials on religious practices other than the cor-

Devotional exercises—*Continued*
porate worship of a congregation. Materials on the religious literature used as aids in devotional exercises are entered under **Devotional literature.**
See also **Church music; Meditation; Prayer**
x Devotions; Family devotions; Family prayers; Theology, Devotional
xx **Prayer; Worship**
Devotional exercises (Daily readings). *See* **Devotional calendars**
Devotional literature 242
See note under **Devotional exercises.**
See also **Devotional calendars; Hymns; Liturgies; Meditations**
xx **Christian literature; Literature**
Devotions. *See* **Devotional exercises**
Dewey Decimal Classification 025.4
x Classification, Dewey Decimal
xx **Classification—Books**
Diagnosis 616
See also **Body temperature; Clinical chemistry; Pain; Pathology; Prenatal diagnosis**
x Medical diagnosis; Symptoms
xx **Medicine; Pathology**
Diagnostic chemistry. *See* **Clinical chemistry**
Diagnostic magnetic resonance imaging. *See* **Magnetic resonance imaging**
Diagrams, Statistical. *See* **Statistics—Graphic methods**
Dialectical materialism 335.4
x Historical materialism
xx **Communism; Socialism**
Dialectics. *See* **Logic**
Dialects. *See* names of languages with the subdivision *Dialects,* e.g. **English language—Dialects;** etc.
Diamonds 553
xx **Carbon; Precious stones**
Diaries. *See* **Autobiographies**
Dichloro-diphenyl-trichloroethane. *See* **D.D.T. (Insecticide)**
Dictators 321.9092; 920
xx **Heads of state; Kings, queens, rulers, etc.; Totalitarianism**
Dictionaries. *See* **Encyclopedias and dictionaries**
Dictionaries, Biographical. *See* **Biography—Dictionaries**
Dictionaries, Classical. *See* **Classical dictionaries**
Dictionaries, Machine readable. *See* **Machine readable dictionaries**
Dictionaries, Multilingual. *See* **Polyglot dictionaries**
Dictionaries, Picture. *See* **Picture dictionaries**
Dictionaries, Polyglot. *See* **Polyglot dictionaries**
Dies (Metalworking) 621.9; 671.2
xx **Metalwork**
Diesel automobiles 629.222
See also **Automobiles—Engines**
x Automobiles, Diesel; Diesel cars
xx **Automobiles—Engines**
Diesel cars. *See* **Diesel automobiles**
Diesel engines 621.43
xx **Engines; Gas and oil engines**

Diet   613.2
> *See also*

Beverages	**Menus**
Cookery	**Nutrition**
Dietetic foods	**Reducing**
Digestion	**School children—Food**
Eating customs	**Vegetarianism**

> also names of diets, e.g. **Salt free diet;** etc.
> *x* Dietetics
> *xx* **Cookery; Digestion; Health; Hygiene; Nutrition; Reducing**

Diet in disease   613.2; 616.3
> *See also* **Cookery for the sick; Diet therapy;** also names of diets, e.g. **Salt free diet;** etc.
> *x* Dieting
> *xx* **Therapeutics**

Diet—Therapeutic use.   *See* **Diet therapy**

Diet therapy   615.8
> *See also* names of diseases with the subdivision *Diet therapy,* e.g. **Cancer—Diet therapy;** etc.; also names of food with the subdivision *Therapeutic use,* e.g. **Corn—Therapeutic use;** etc.
> *x* Diet—Therapeutic use; Invalid cookery
> *xx* **Cookery for the sick; Diet in disease; Therapeutics**

Dietary fiber.   *See* **Food—Fiber content**

Dietetic foods   641.3; 664
> *x* Food, Dietetic
> *xx* **Diet; Food**

Dietetics.   *See* **Diet**

Dieting.   *See* **Diet in disease; Reducing**

Diets, Reducing.   *See* **Reducing**

Digestion   574.1; 612.3
> *See also* **Diet; Food; Indigestion; Nutrition**
> *xx* **Diet; Nutrition; Physiology; Stomach**

Digital audio disc players.   *See* **Compact disc players**

Digital circuits.   *See* **Digital electronics**

Digital compact discs.   *See* **Compact discs**

Digital electronics   621.381
> *x* Digital circuits
> *xx* **Electronics**

Dimension, Fourth.   *See* **Fourth dimension**

Diners.   *See* **Restaurants, bars, etc.**

Dining.   *See* **Dinners and dining**

Dinners and dining   642
> *See also* **Carving (Meat, etc.); Cookery; Desserts; Food; Menus**
> *x* Banquets; Dining; Eating; Gastronomy; Meals
> *xx* **Caterers and catering; Cookery; Entertaining; Etiquette; Food; Menus**

Dinosaurs   567.9
> *xx* **Prehistoric animals; Reptiles, Fossil**

Dioptrics.   *See* **Refraction**

Diphtheria   616.9
> *xx* **Diseases**

Diplomacy   327.2; 341.3
> *See also* **Diplomatic and consular service; Diplomats; Treaties;** also names of countries with the subdivision *Foreign relations,* e.g. **United States—Foreign relations;** etc.
> *xx* **Diplomatic and consular service; International relations**

Diplomatic and consular service 341.3

    See also **Diplomacy; Diplomats;** also names of countries with the subdivision *Diplomatic and consular service,* e.g. **United States— Diplomatic and consular service;** etc.

    x Consulates; Embassies; Foreign service; Legations

    xx **Diplomacy; Diplomats; International relations**

Diplomats 327.2092; 920

    See also **Diplomatic and consular service; Statesmen**

    x Ambassadors; Consuls; Ministers (Diplomatic agents)

    xx **Diplomacy; Diplomatic and consular service; International relations; Politicians; Statesmen**

Dipsomania. *See* **Alcoholism**

Diptera. *See* **Flies; Mosquitoes**

Direct access storage devices (Data processing). *See* **Computer storage devices**

Direct current machinery. *See* **Electric machinery—Direct current**

Direct legislation. *See* **Referendum**

Direct primaries. *See* **Primaries**

Direct selling 658.8

    See also **Mail-order business; Peddlers and peddling; Telemarketing**

    xx **Marketing; Retail trade; Selling**

Direct taxation. *See* **Income tax; Taxation**

Direction (Motion pictures). *See* **Motion pictures— Production and direction**

Direction sense 152.1; 796.5

    See also **Navigation; Orienteering**

    x Orientation; Sense of direction

    xx **Hiking; Orienteering**

Direction (Theater). *See* **Theater—Production and direction**

Directories 910.25

    Use for materials about directories and for bibliographies of directories.

    See also subjects and names of countries, cities, etc., with the subdivision *Directories,* e.g. **Junior colleges—Directories; Physicians— Directories; United States—Directories;** etc.

Directories—Telephone. *See* names of cities with the subdivision *Telephone directories,* e.g. **Chicago (Ill.)—Telephone directories;** etc.

Directors and producers. *See* specific medium phrase heading, e.g. **Motion picture producers and directors;** etc.

Directory, French, 1795-1799. *See* **France— History—1789-1799, Revolution**

Dirigible balloons. *See* **Airships**

Disability insurance. *See* **Accident insurance; Health insurance**

Disability, Learning. *See* **Learning disabilities**

Disability, Reading. *See* **Reading disability**

Disabled. *See* **Handicapped**

Disadvantaged. *See* **Socially handicapped**

Disadvantaged children. *See* **Socially handicapped children**

Disarmament. *See* **Arms control**

Disaster preparedness. *See* **Disaster relief**

Disaster relief   363.3

See also **Civil defense; Food relief**

x Disaster preparedness; Emergency preparedness; Emergency relief

xx **Charities; Civil defense; Public welfare**

Disasters   904

See also types of disasters, e.g. **Accidents; Fires; Natural disasters; Railroads—Accidents; Shipwrecks;** etc.

x Catastrophes

xx **Accidents**

Disc players, Compact. *See* **Compact disc players**

Disciples, Twelve. *See* **Apostles**

Discipline. *See* **Punishment**

Discipline of children. *See* **Child rearing; School discipline**

Discipline, Self. *See* **Self-control**

Discography. *See* **Sound recordings;** and subjects and names of persons with the subdivision *Discography,* e.g. **Music—Discography; Shakespeare, William, 1564-1616—Discography;** etc., for lists or catalogs of sound recordings.

Discount stores   381; 658.8

x Stores

xx **Retail trade**

Discoverers. *See* **Discoveries (in geography); Explorers**

Discoveries and exploration. *See* **Discoveries (in geography)**

Discoveries (in geography)   910.9

See also **Explorers; Northeast Passage; Northwest Passage; Scientific expeditions; Voyages and travels;** also names of countries with the subdivisions *Description,* and *Exploring expeditions,* e.g. **United States—Description; United States—Exploring expeditions;** etc.; and names of places that were unsettled or sparsely settled and largely unknown to the rest of the world at the time of exploration, with the subdivision *Exploration,* e.g. **America—Exploration;** etc.

x Discoverers; Discoveries and exploration; Discoveries, Maritime; Exploration; Explorations; Maritime discoveries; Navigators

xx **Adventure and adventurers; Explorers; Geography; History; Voyages and travels**

Discoveries (in science). *See* **Inventions; Patents; Science**

Discoveries, Maritime. *See* **Discoveries (in geography)**

Discrimination   177; 305

Use for general materials on discrimination by race, religion, sex, age, social status, or other factors. Reverse discrimination is subsumed under **Discrimination** and headings beginning with the word **Discrimination.**

See also

Age discrimination	**Race discrimination**
Civil rights	**Segregation**
Hate crimes	**Sex discrimination**
Minorities	**Toleration**

Discrimination—*Continued*

    xx **Civil rights; Ethnic relations; Human relations; Minorities; Prejudices; Race relations; Segregation; Social problems; Social psychology; Toleration**

Discrimination in education   370.19

    Use same pattern for discrimination in other areas.

    See also **Segregation in education**

    x Education, Discrimination in

    xx **Race discrimination; Segregation in education**

Discrimination in employment   331.1

    See also **Affirmative action programs; Age and employment; Equal pay for equal work;** also names of groups of people with the subdivision *Employment,* e.g. **Blacks—Employment; Men—Employment; Women—Employment;** etc.

    x E.E.O.; EEO; Employment discrimination; Equal employment opportunity; Equal opportunity in employment; Fair employment practice; Job discrimination; Right to work

Discrimination in housing   363.5

    x Fair housing; Housing, Discrimination in; Open housing; Segregation in housing

Discrimination in public accommodations   305

    x Public accommodations, Discrimination in; Segregation in public accommodations

Discrimination, Racial.   *See* **Race discrimination**

Discrimination, Sex.   *See* **Sex discrimination**

Discs, Compact.   *See* **Compact discs**

Discs, Optical.   *See* **Optical storage devices**

Discs, Sound.   *See* **Sound recordings**

Discs, Video.   *See* **Videodiscs**

Discussion.   *See* **Conversation; Debates and debating; Negotiation**

Discussion groups   374

    x Forums (Discussions); Great books program; Group discussion; Panel discussions

    xx **Debates and debating**

Disease germs.   *See* **Bacteriology; Germ theory of disease**

Disease (Pathology).   *See* **Pathology**

Diseases   614.4; 616

    See also

AIDS (Disease)	**Influenza**
Chickenpox	**Mental illness**
Cold (Disease)	**Occupational diseases**
Epidemics	**Pathology**
Health	**Sick**
Infants—Diseases	

    also names of diseases and groups of diseases, e.g. **Diphtheria; Lyme disease; Communicable diseases;** etc.; and names of animals, classes of persons, and parts of the body with the subdivision *Diseases,* e.g. **Animals—Diseases; Children—Diseases; Lungs—Diseases; Skin—Diseases;** etc.

    x Illness; Sickness

    xx **Health; Medicine; Sick**

Diseases and pests.   *See* **Agricultural bacteriology; Agricultural pests; Fungi; Household pests; Insect pests; Parasites; Plant diseases;** and

Diseases and pests—*Continued*
      names of individual pests, e.g. **Locusts;**
      etc.; and names of crops, etc., with the sub-
      division *Diseases and pests,* e.g. **Fruit—**
      Diseases and pests; etc.
Diseases, Communicable. *See* **Communicable dis-**
      eases
Diseases, Contagious. *See* **Communicable diseases**
Diseases, Industrial. *See* **Occupational diseases**
Diseases, Infectious. *See* **Communicable diseases**
Diseases, Mental. *See* **Mental illness; Psychology,**
      Pathological
Diseases, Occupational. *See* **Occupational diseases**
Diseases of animals. *See* **Animals—Diseases**
Diseases of children. *See* **Children—Diseases**
Diseases of occupation. *See* **Occupational diseases**
Diseases of plants. *See* **Plant diseases**
Diseases of the blood. *See* **Blood—Diseases**
Diseases of women. *See* **Women—Diseases**
Diseases—Prevention. *See* **Preventive medicine**
Diseases—Treatment. *See* **Therapeutics**
Diseases, Tropical. *See* **Tropical medicine**
Dishes. *See* **Glassware; Porcelain; Pottery**
Dishonesty. *See* **Honesty**
Disinfection and disinfectants **614.4**
    See also **Antiseptics; Fumigation**
    x Germicides
    xx **Antiseptics; Bacteriology; Communicable dis-**
      eases; Fumigation; Hygiene; Pharmaceutical
      chemistry; Public health; Sanitation
Disney World (Fla.). *See* **Walt Disney World (Fla.)**
Disobedience. *See* **Obedience**
Displaced persons. *See* **Political refugees; Refu-**
      gees; and names of wars with the subdivi-
      sion *Refugees,* e.g. **World War, 1939-**
      1945—Refugees; etc.
Display terminals, Video. *See* **Video display termi-**
      nals
Disposal of medical waste. *See* **Medical wastes**
Disposal of refuse. *See* **Refuse and refuse disposal**
Disputes, Labor. *See* **Labor disputes**
Dissent **303.48; 361.2**
    x Nonconformity; Protest
    xx **Conformity**
Dissertations, Academic **378.2; 808**
    Use for materials about theses and dissertations.
    x Academic dissertations; Doctoral theses; The-
      ses
    xx **Colleges and universities**
Distillation **641.2; 663**
    See also **Alcohol; Essences and essential oils; Li-**
      quors and liqueurs
    x Stills
    xx **Alcohol; Liquors and liqueurs**
Distribution, Cooperative. *See* **Cooperation; Coop-**
      erative societies
Distribution (Economics). *See* **Commerce; Market-**
      ing
Distribution of animals and plants. *See* **Biogeogra-**
      phy
Distribution of wealth. *See* **Economics; Wealth**
District libraries. *See* **Regional libraries**
District nurses. *See* **Nurses**
District schools. *See* **Rural schools**

Districting (in city planning). *See* **Zoning**

Diversified corporations. *See* **Conglomerate corporations**

Dividends. *See* **Securities; Stocks**

Divination   133.3

> *See also*
>
> | | |
> |---|---|
> | **Astrology** | **Palmistry** |
> | **Clairvoyance** | **Prophecies (Occult sci-** |
> | **Dreams** | **ences)** |
> | **Fortune telling** | **Superstition** |
> | **Oracles** | |
>
> *x* Crystal gazing; Necromancy; Soothsaying
>
> *xx* **Clairvoyance; Occultism; Oracles; Prophecies (Occult sciences); Supernatural; Superstition**

Divine healing. *See* **Christian Science; Miracles; Spiritual healing**

Diving   797.2

> *See also* **Scuba diving; Skin diving**
>
> *xx* **Swimming; Water sports**

Diving, Scuba. *See* **Scuba diving**

Diving, Skin. *See* **Skin diving**

Diving, Submarine   627

> *See also* **Scuba diving; Skin diving; Underwater exploration**
>
> *x* Deep sea diving; Submarine diving
>
> *xx* **Oceanography—Research; Underwater exploration**

Divinity of Christ. *See* **Jesus Christ—Divinity**

Division of powers. *See* **Separation of powers**

Divorce   173; 306.89; 346.01

> *See also* **Children of divorced parents; Desertion and nonsupport; Marriage; Marriage—Annulment; Remarriage**
>
> *x* Separation (Law)
>
> *xx* **Domestic relations; Family; Marriage; Marriage—Annulment; Men—Social conditions; Social problems; Women—Social conditions**

Divorce counseling. *See* **Divorce mediation**

Divorce mediation   362.82

> *See also* **Child custody; Child support**
>
> *x* Divorce counseling; Mediation, Divorce
>
> *xx* **Marriage counseling**

DNA   574.87

> *See also* **Recombinant DNA**
>
> *x* D.N.A.; Deoxyribonucleic acid; Desoxyribonucleic acid
>
> *xx* **Cells; Heredity; Nucleic acids**

DNA cloning. *See* **Clones and cloning; Molecular cloning**

DNA fingerprinting. *See* **DNA Fingerprints**

DNA Fingerprints   614

> *x* DNA fingerprinting; DNA identification; DNA profiling; Genetic fingerprints; Genetic profiling
>
> *xx* **Genetics; Identification; Medical jurisprudence**

DNA identification. *See* **DNA Fingerprints**

DNA profiling. *See* **DNA Fingerprints**

DNA synthesizer. *See* **Genetic engineering, Automated**

Docks 386; 387.1; 627
    See also **Harbors**
  xx **Harbors; Hydraulic structures; Marinas**
Doctoral theses. *See* **Dissertations, Academic**
Doctors. *See* **Physicians**
Doctors' degrees. *See* **Academic degrees**
Doctrinal theology 230; 240
    See also **Liberation theology; Love (Theology);**
      Regeneration (Theology)
    x Christian doctrine; Dogmatic theology; Dog-
      matics; Theology, Doctrinal
  xx **Theology**
Doctrine of fairness (Broadcasting). *See* **Fairness**
      doctrine (Broadcasting)
Documentaries (Motion pictures). *See* **Documen-**
      tary films
Documentary films 070.1
    x Documentaries (Motion pictures); Motion pic-
      tures, Documentary; Nonfiction films
  xx **Motion pictures**
Documentation 025
    See also

Archives	**Classification—Books**
Bibliographic control	**Information services**
Bibliography	**Information systems**
Cataloging	**Library science**

    also subjects with the subdivision
      Documentation, e.g. **Agriculture—**
      Documentation; etc.
  xx **Information science; Information services**
Documents. *See* **Archives; Charters; Government**
      publications
Dog. *See* **Dogs**
Dog breeding. *See* **Dogs—Breeding**
Dog guides. *See* **Guide dogs**
Dogmatic theology. *See* **Doctrinal theology**
Dogmatics. *See* **Doctrinal theology**
Dogs 599.74; 636.7
    See also classes of dogs, e.g. **Guide dogs; Hear-**
      ing ear dogs; etc.; also names of specific
      breeds, e.g. **Collies;** etc.
    x Dog; Puppies
  xx **Pets**
Dogs—Breeding 636.7
    x Dog breeding
  xx **Breeding**
Dogs—Fiction E; Fic
  xx **Animals—Fiction**
Dogs for the blind. *See* **Guide dogs**
Dogs for the deaf. *See* **Hearing ear dogs**
Dogs in literature 809
  xx **Animals in literature**
Dogs—Psychology 636.7
  xx **Animal intelligence; Psychology, Comparative**
Dogs—Training 636.7
  xx **Animals—Training**
Dogs—War use 355.4
    x War use of dogs
  xx **Animals—War use**
Doll. *See* **Dolls**
Dollhouses 688.7
    x Miniature objects
  xx **Toys**

Dolls 688.7

   x Doll

   xx **Toys**

Domesday book 942.02

   x Doomsday book

Domestic animals 636

   Use for general materials on farm animals. Materials limited to animals as pets are entered under **Pets.** Materials on stock raising as an industry are entered under **Livestock.** Names of all animals are not included in this List but are to be added as needed.

   See also **Livestock; Working animals;** also names of domestic animals, e.g. **Cats; Cattle; Pets; Poultry; Reindeer;** etc.

   x Animal industry; Animals, Domestic; Beasts; Farm animals

   xx **Agriculture; Animals; Breeding; Livestock; Pets; Zoology, Economic**

Domestic animals—Diseases. *See* **Animals— Diseases**

Domestic appliances. *See* **Household appliances, Electric; Household equipment and supplies**

Domestic architecture. *See* **Architecture, Domestic**

Domestic arts. *See* **Home economics**

Domestic education. *See* **Home instruction**

Domestic finance. *See* **Budgets, Household; Personal finance**

Domestic relations 346.01

   See also **Desertion and nonsupport; Divorce; Family; Grandparent and child; Marriage; Parent and child; Visitation rights (Domestic relations)**

   x Family relations

   xx **Family; Marriage**

Domestic violence. *See* **Family violence**

Domestic workers. *See* **Household employees**

Dominicans. *See* **Dominicans (Religious order)**

Dominicans (Religious order) 271

   x Black Friars; Dominicans; Friars, Black; Friars Preachers; Jacobins (Dominicans); Mendicant orders; Preaching Friars; Saint Dominic, Order of; St. Dominic, Order of

   xx **Religious orders for men, Catholic**

Dominion of the sea. *See* **Sea power**

Dominions, British. *See* **Commonwealth of Nations**

Donation of organs, tissues, etc. 362.1

   See also **Transplantation of organs, tissues, etc.**

   x Anatomical gifts; Organ donation; Tissue donation

   xx **Gifts; Transplantation of organs, tissues, etc.**

Donations. *See* **Gifts**

Doomsday book. *See* **Domesday book**

Door to door selling. *See* **Peddlers and peddling**

Doors 721

   xx **Architecture—Details; Building; Carpentry**

Doping in horse racing. *See* **Drugs and sports**

Doping in sports. *See* **Drugs and sports**

Double employment. *See* **Supplementary employment**

Double stars. *See* **Stars**

Doubt. *See* **Belief and doubt**

Draft   355.2

   x Compulsory military service; Conscription, Military; Military draft; Military service, Compulsory; Military training, Universal; Selective service; Service, Compulsory military; Universal military training

  xx **Armies; Human resources; Military law**

Draft dodgers.   *See* **Draft resisters**

Draft evaders.   *See* **Draft resisters**

Draft resisters   355.2

   See also **Conscientious objectors; Military desertion**; also names of wars with the subdivision *Draft resisters,* e.g. **World War, 1939-1945—Draft resisters**; etc.

   x Draft dodgers; Draft evaders; Military service, Compulsory—Draft resisters

  xx **Conscientious objectors; Military desertion**

Drafting, Automatic.   *See* **Computer aided design; Computer graphics**

Drafting, Mechanical.   *See* **Mechanical drawing**

Dragons   398.24

  xx **Animals—Folklore; Folklore; Monsters; Mythical animals**

Drainage   631.6

   Use for materials on land drainage. Materials on house drainage are entered under **Drainage, House.**

   See also **Marshes; Sewerage**

   x Land drainage

  xx **Agricultural engineering; Civil engineering; Hydraulic engineering; Municipal engineering; Reclamation of land; Sanitary engineering; Sewerage; Soils**

Drainage, House   690

   See note under **Drainage.**

   See also **Plumbing; Sanitary engineering; Sewerage**

   x House drainage

  xx **Plumbing; Sanitation, Household**

Drama   808.2

   Use for general materials on drama. Materials on the history and criticism of drama as literature are entered under **Drama—History and criticism.** Materials on criticism of drama as presented on the stage are entered under **Dramatic criticism.** Materials on the presentation of plays are entered under **Acting; Amateur theater; Theater—Production and direction.** Materials on how to write plays are entered under **Drama—Technique.** Collections of plays are entered under **Drama—Collections; American drama—Collections; English drama—Collections;** etc.

   See also

Acting	**Folk drama**
American drama	**Indians of North America—Drama**
Ballet	
Children's plays	**Masks (Plays)**
College and school drama	**Morality plays**
Comedy	
Dramatic criticism	**Motion picture plays**
Dramatists	**Mysteries and miracle plays**
English drama	

Drama—*Continued*

<table>
<tr><td>One act plays</td><td>Radio plays</td></tr>
<tr><td>Opera</td><td>Religious drama</td></tr>
<tr><td>Pantomimes</td><td>Television plays</td></tr>
<tr><td>Passion plays</td><td>Theater</td></tr>
<tr><td>Plots (Drama, fiction, etc.)</td><td>Tragedy</td></tr>
<tr><td>Puppets and puppet plays</td><td></td></tr>
</table>

also names of special subjects, historical events, and famous persons with the subdivision *Drama,* e.g. **Easter—Drama; United States—History—1861-1865, Civil War—Drama; Napoleon I, Emperor of the French, 1769-1821—Drama;** etc.

x Stage

xx **Literature; Theater**

Drama—Collected works. *See* **Drama—Collections**

Drama—Collections   808.82; 812.008, etc.

Use for collections of plays by several authors.

See also **American drama—Collections; Children's plays; College and school drama—Collections; English drama—Collections**

x **Drama—Collected works; Plays**

Drama—History and criticism   809.2

Use for materials on criticism of drama as a literary form. Materials on criticism of drama as presented on the stage are entered under **Dramatic criticism.**

See also **American drama—History and criticism; English drama—History and criticism**

Drama in education   372.6

See also **Acting; Amateur theater; College and school drama; Religious drama; Theater**

xx **Acting; Amateur theater; College and school drama; School assembly programs**

Drama—Plots. *See* **Plots (Drama, fiction, etc.)**

Drama, Religious. *See* **Religious drama**

Drama—Technique   808.2

See also **Motion picture plays—Technique; Radio plays—Technique; Television plays—Technique**

x **Play writing; Playwriting**

xx **Authorship; Characters and characteristics in literature**

Dramatic art. *See* **Acting**

Dramatic criticism   792.9

Use for materials on criticism of drama as presented on the stage. Materials on criticism of drama as a literary form are entered under **Drama—History and criticism; American drama—History and criticism;** etc.

x Theater criticism

xx **Criticism; Drama; Theater**

Dramatic music. *See* **Musicals; Opera; Operetta**

Dramatic plots. *See* **Plots (Drama, fiction, etc.)**

Dramatists (May subdiv. geog. adjective form, e.g. **Dramatists, American;** etc.)   **809.2; 920**

Use for materials dealing largely with the personal lives of several playwrights. Materials dealing with their literary work are entered under **Drama—History and criticism; English drama—History and criticism;** etc.

x Playwrights; Writers

xx **Authors; Drama; Poets**

Dramatists, American 812.009; 920
    x American dramatists; United States—
        Dramatists
Drapery 684.3
    x Curtains
    xx **Interior design; Upholstery**
Draughts. *See* **Checkers**
Drawing (May subdiv. geog. adjective form, e.g.
        Drawing, American; etc.) 741; 743
    See also

Anatomy, Artistic	**Mechanical drawing**
Architectural drawing	**Painting**
Commercial art	**Pastel drawing**
Crayon drawing	**Pen drawing**
Figure drawing	**Pencil drawing**
Geometrical drawing	**Perspective**
Graphic methods	**Shades and shadows**
Illustration of books	**Topographical drawing**
Landscape drawing	

    x Drawings; Sketching
    xx **Art; Graphic arts; Illustration of books; Paint-
        ing; Perspective**
Drawing, American 741.973
    x American drawing; United States—Drawing
Drawing, Architectural. *See* **Architectural drawing**
Drawing, Automatic. *See* **Computer graphics**
Drawing, Computer. *See* **Computer art**
Drawing, Electronic. *See* **Computer art; Computer
    graphics**
Drawing materials. *See* **Artists' materials**
Drawings. *See* **Drawing**
Dreaming. *See* **Dreams**
Dreams 154.6
    See also **Fantasy; Psychoanalysis; Sleep**
    x Dreaming
    xx **Brain; Divination; Fortune telling; Mind and
        body; Parapsychology; Psychoanalysis; Psy-
        chophysiology; Sleep; Subconsciousness;
        Superstition; Visions**
Dredging 627
    xx **Civil engineering; Hydraulic engineering**
Dress. *See* **Clothing and dress**
Dress accessories 646
    xx **Clothing and dress**
Dressage. *See* **Horsemanship**
Dressing of ores. *See* **Ore dressing**
Dressmaking 646.4; 687
    See also **Needlework; Sewing; Tailoring**
    x Garment making
    xx **Clothing and dress; Fashion; Needlework;
        Sewing; Tailoring**
Dressmaking—Patterns 646.4; 687
Dried flowers. *See* **Flower drying**
Dried foods 641.4; 664
    See also **Dried milk; Freeze-dried foods**
    x Dehydrated foods; Food, Dehydrated; Food,
        Dried
    xx **Food—Preservation**
Dried milk 637
    x Dehydrated milk; Milk, Dried; Powdered
        milk
    xx **Dried foods; Milk**
Drifting of continents. *See* **Continental drift**

Drill and minor tactics   355.5

    See also **Military art and science**

    x Military drill; Minor tactics

    xx **Military art and science**

Drill (Nonmilitary)   613.7

    x Marches (Exercises)

    xx **Physical education**

Drilling and boring   621.9

    Use for materials dealing with workshop operations in metal, wood, etc. Materials relating to the operation of cutting holes in earth or rock are entered under **Boring.**

    x Boring (Metal, wood, etc.)

Drilling and boring (Earth and rocks).   *See* **Boring**

Drilling, Oil well.   *See* **Oil well drilling**

Drilling platforms   627

    x Artificial islands; Islands, Artificial; Offshore structures; Platforms, Drilling; Structures, Offshore

    xx **Ocean engineering; Oil well drilling, Submarine**

Drinking age (May subdiv. geog.)   **351.76; 363.4; 613.81**

    x Age, Drinking; Minimum drinking age

    xx **Teenagers—Alcohol use; Youth—Alcohol use**

Drinking and employees.   *See* **Employees—Alcohol use**

Drinking and teenagers.   *See* **Teenagers—Alcohol use**

Drinking and youth.   *See* **Youth—Alcohol use**

Drinking in the workplace.   *See* **Employees—Alcohol use**

Drinking of alcoholic beverages (May subdiv. geog.)   **178; 351.76; 363.4; 394.1; 613.81**

    Use for materials on drinking in its social aspects and as a social problem.

    See also **Alcoholism; Drunk driving; Temperance;** also classes of persons and ethnic groups with the subdivision *Alcohol use,* e.g. **Employees—Alcohol use; Youth—Alcohol use;** etc.

    x Alcohol consumption; Alcoholic beverage consumption; Consumption of alcoholic beverages; Drinking problem; Liquor problem; Social drinking

    xx **Alcoholic beverages; Alcoholism; Temperance**

Drinking problem.   *See* **Alcoholism; Drinking of alcoholic beverages**

Drinks.   *See* **Alcoholic beverages; Beverages; Liquors and liqueurs**

Driver education.   *See* **Automobile drivers—Education**

Drivers, Automobile.   *See* **Automobile drivers**

Driving under the influence of alcohol.   *See* **Drunk driving**

Driving while intoxicated.   *See* **Drunk driving**

Dromedaries.   *See* **Camels**

Drop forging.   *See* **Forging**

Dropouts   371.2

    See also **Educational counseling; School attendance**

    x College dropouts; Elementary school dropouts; High school dropouts; School drop-

Dropouts—*Continued*

outs; School withdrawals; Student dropouts; Teenage dropouts

xx **Educational counseling; School attendance; Students; Youth**

Droughts   551.57; 632

See also **Dust storms; Rain**

xx **Meteorology; Rain**

Drug abuse   362.29; 613.8; 616.86

Use for comprehensive materials on the general misuse of drugs. These may include aspirin, bromides, caffeine, sedatives, alcohol, LSD, marijuana, and narcotics, etc. Materials limited to addiction to hard drugs such as crack, heroin, etc., are entered under **Drug addiction.** Also see note at **Drug addiction.**

See also **Drug addicts; Hallucinogens;** also classes of people with the subdivision *Drug use,* e.g. **Criminals—Drug use; Employees—Drug use; Teenagers—Drug use; Youth—Drug use;** etc.; also types of drug abuse, e.g. **Alcoholism; Drug addiction;** etc.

x Addiction to drugs; Drug habit; Drug misuse; Drug use; Drugs—Abuse; Drugs—Misuse

xx **Crimes without victims; Substance abuse**

Drug abuse counseling   362.29; 613.8

See also **Drug addicts—Rehabilitation**

x Drug addiction counseling; Drug counseling; Narcotic addiction counseling

xx **Counseling**

Drug abuse education. *See* **Drug education**

Drug abuse—Physiological effect. *See* **Drugs—Physiological effect**

Drug abuse screening. *See* **Drug testing**

Drug abuse—Study and teaching. *See* **Drug education**

Drug abuse—Testing. *See* **Drug testing**

Drug abusing physicians. *See* **Physicians—Drug use**

Drug addicted physicians. *See* **Physicians—Drug use**

Drug addiction   362.29; 616.86

Use for materials on addiction to hard drugs, that is, those narcotics, stimulants, synthetic drugs, etc., capable of causing severe physical or psychological dependence in most users. Comprehensive materials and materials on the misuse of drugs in a broad sense, are entered under **Drug abuse.** Also see note at **Drug abuse.**

See also **Children of drug addicts; Drug addicts; Temperance;** also classes of people with the subdivision *Drug use,* e.g. **Criminals—Drug use; Employees—Drug use; Teenagers—Drug use; Youth—Drug use;** etc.

x Addiction to hard drugs; Drug habit; Hard drug addiction; Intoxication; Narcotic habit

xx **Drug abuse; Habit; Temperance**

Drug addiction counseling. *See* **Drug abuse counseling**

Drug addiction education. *See* **Drug education**

Drug addicts   362.29; 616.86

See also **Children of drug addicts;** also classes of

Drug addicts—*Continued*

    people with the subdivision *Drug use,* e.g. **Criminals—Drug use; Employees—Drug use; Youth—Drug use;** etc.

    x Addicts, Drug; Narcotic addicts

    xx **Drug abuse; Drug addiction**

Drug addicts' children. *See* **Children of drug addicts**

Drug addicts' infants. *See* **Children of drug addicts**

Drug addicts—Rehabilitation 362.29; 613.8; 616.86

    xx **Drug abuse counseling**

Drug counseling. *See* **Drug abuse counseling**

Drug-crime relationship. *See* **Drugs and crime**

Drug dealing. *See* **Drug traffic**

Drug education 362.29; 371.7; 613.8

    Use for materials on the study of drugs, including their source, abuse, chemical composition, and social, physical, and personal effects.

    x Drug abuse education; Drug abuse—Study and teaching; Drug addiction education

    xx **Health education**

Drug habit. *See* **Drug abuse; Drug addiction**

Drug misuse. *See* **Drug abuse**

Drug plants. *See* **Botany, Medical**

Drug pushers. *See* **Drug traffic**

Drug testing 344; 363.1

    Use for materials on testing to identify users and misusers of drugs. Materials on the adulteration of drugs and on the analysis of the composition of drugs are entered under **Drugs—Adulteration and analysis.**

    See also classes of people with the subdivision *Drug testing,* e.g. **Employees—Drug testing;** etc.

    x Drug abuse screening; Drug abuse—Testing; Screening for drug abuse; Testing for drug abuse

Drug testing in the workplace. *See* **Employees—Drug testing**

Drug therapy. *See* **Chemotherapy**

Drug trade, Illicit. *See* **Drug traffic**

Drug traffic 364.1

    x Drug dealing; Drug pushers; Drug trade, Illicit; Narcotic traffic; Smuggling of drugs; Trafficking in drugs; Trafficking in narcotics

    xx **Drugs and crime**

Drug use. *See* **Drug abuse;** and classes of people with the subdivision *Drug use,* e.g. **Criminals—Drug use; Employees—Drug use; Teenagers—Drug use; Youth—Drug use;** etc.

Drugs 615

    See also

Designer drugs	**Orphan drugs**
Drugs and crime	**Pharmacology**
Drugs and sports	**Poisons and poisoning**
Generic drugs	**Psychotropic drugs**
Materia medica	**Steroids**

    also classes of people with the subdivision *Drug use,* e.g. **Criminals—Drug use; Employees—Drug use; Teenagers—Drug use;**

Drugs—*Continued*
>> **Youth—Drug use;** etc.; and names of groups of drugs, e.g. **Amphetamines; Hallucinogens; Narcotics; Stimulants;** etc.; and names of individual drugs, e.g. **Crack (Drug); Marijuana;** etc.
> *x* Pharmaceuticals
> *xx* **Materia medica; Pharmacology; Pharmacy; Therapeutics**

Drugs—Abuse. *See* **Drug abuse**
Drugs—Adulteration and analysis   363.19
> *xx* **Consumer protection**
Drugs and crime   364.1
> Use for general materials on the interrelationship of drugs and crime. For materials restricted to the illicit drug trade, use **Drug traffic.** For materials on drug use by criminals, use **Criminals—Drug use.**
> *See also* **Criminals—Drug use; Drug traffic**
> *x* Crime and drugs; Crime and narcotics; Crime-drug relationship; Drug-crime relationship; Narcotics and crime
> *xx* **Crime; Criminals—Drug use; Drugs**

Drugs and criminals.   *See* **Criminals—Drug use**
Drugs and employees.   *See* **Employees—Drug use**
Drugs and sports   617.1; 796
> Use for general materials on the relationship of drugs and sports. Materials restricted to the use of drugs by athletes are entered under **Athletes—Drug use.**
> *See also* **Athletes—Drug use**
> *x* Doping in horse racing; Doping in sports; Sports and drugs
> *xx* **Drugs; Sports; Sports medicine**

Drugs and teenagers.   *See* **Teenagers—Drug use**
Drugs and youth.   *See* **Youth—Drug use**
Drugs—Chemistry.   *See* **Pharmaceutical chemistry**
Drugs, Designer.   *See* **Designer drugs**
Drugs—Generic substitution.   *See* **Generic drugs**
Drugs, Hallucinogenic.   *See* **Hallucinogens**
Drugs in the workplace.   *See* **Employees—Drug use**
Drugs—Misuse.   *See* **Drug abuse**
Drugs, Nonprescription.   *See* **Nonprescription drugs**
Drugs of abuse, Synthetic.   *See* **Designer drugs**
Drugs, Orphan.   *See* **Orphan drugs**
Drugs—Physiological effect   615; 616.86
> Use for materials limited to the effect of drugs on the functions of living organisms.
> *See also* names of drugs with the subdivision *Physiological effect,* e.g. **Opium—Physiological effect;** etc.
> *x* Drug abuse—Physiological effect
> *xx* **Pharmacology**
Drugs—Psychological aspects   615; 616.86
> *xx* **Psychology, Applied**
Drugs, Psychotropic.   *See* **Psychotropic drugs**
Druids and Druidism   299
> *xx* **Celts; Religions**
Drum   786.9
> *xx* **Musical instruments; Percussion instruments**
Drum majoring   784.9; 791.6
> *See also* **Baton twirling**
> *xx* **Bands (Music); Baton twirling**

Drunk driving   363.12; 364.1

  x Driving under the influence of alcohol; Driving while intoxicated

  xx **Drinking of alcoholic beverages; Traffic accidents**

Drunkards.   *See* **Alcoholics**

Drunkenness.   *See* **Alcoholism; Temperance**

Dry cleaning   646.6; 667

  x Clothing and dress—Dry cleaning

  xx **Cleaning**

Dry farming   631.5

  x Farming, Dry

  xx **Agriculture; Irrigation**

Dry goods.   *See* **Fabrics**

Dual career family   306.85

  x Families, Dual career; Two-career family; Working couples

  xx **Family**

Dual employment.   *See* **Supplementary employment**

Ducks   636.5

  xx **Poultry**

Ductless glands.   *See* **Endocrine glands**

Dueling   179; 394

  x Fighting

  xx **Manners and customs; Martial arts**

Dumps, Toxic.   *See* **Hazardous waste sites**

Dunes.   *See* **Sand dunes**

Dungeons.   *See* **Prisons**

Duplicate bridge.   *See* **Bridge (Game)**

Duplicating processes.   *See* **Copying processes and machines**

Dust, Radioactive.   *See* **Radioactive fallout**

Dust storms   551.55

  xx **Droughts; Erosion; Storms**

Dusting and spraying.   *See* **Spraying and dusting**

Duties.   *See* **Tariff; Taxation**

Duty   170

  See also **Conscience**

  xx **Ethics; Human behavior**

Dwarf trees   582.16; 635.9

  See also names of dwarf trees, e.g. **Bonsai;** etc.

  xx **Trees**

Dwarfism.   *See* **Growth disorders**

Dwellings.   *See* **Architecture, Domestic; Houses; Housing;** and classes of people with the subdivision *Housing,* e.g. **Physically handicapped—Housing;** etc.

Dyes and dyeing   646; 667; 746.6

  See also **Bleaching;** also types of dyeing, e.g. **Batik; Tie dyeing;** etc.

  xx **Bleaching; Chemistry, Technical; Cleaning; Color; Pigments; Textile chemistry; Textile industry; Wool**

Dying children.   *See* **Terminally ill children**

Dying patients.   *See* **Terminally ill**

Dynamics   531

  See also

Aerodynamics	**Matter**
Astrodynamics	**Motion**
Chaos (Science)	**Physics**
Force and energy	**Quantum theory**
Hydrodynamics	**Statics**
Kinematics	**Thermodynamics**

Dynamics—*Continued*

   x Kinetics

   xx **Force and energy; Mathematics; Mechanics;**
      Physics; Statics

Dynamite 662

   xx **Explosives**

Dynamos. *See* **Electric generators**

Dyslexia 371.91; 616.85

   xx **Reading disability**

Dyspepsia. *See* **Indigestion**

E.E.O. *See* **Discrimination in employment**

E-mail systems. *See* **Electronic mail systems**

E.R.A.'s. *See* **Equal rights amendments**

E.S.P. *See* **Extrasensory perception**

Eagles 598.9

   xx **Birds of prey**

Ear 611; 612.8

   See also **Hearing**

   xx **Deafness; Head; Hearing**

Early Christian literature 281

   Use for materials about writings of early Chris-
      tian authors to the time of Gregory the
      Great in the West and John of Damascus in
      the East. Collections of such writings are en-
      tered under this heading with the subdivi-
      sion *Collections.*

   See also **Church history—30(ca.)-600, Early**
      church

   x Christian literature—30(ca.)-600, Early; Chris-
      tian literature, Early

   xx **Church history—30(ca.)-600, Early church;**
      Latin literature; Literature; Literature, Me-
      dieval; Religious literature

Early church history. *See* **Church history—30(ca.)-**
      600, Early church

Early warning system, Ballistic missile. *See* **Ballis-**
      tic missile early warning system

Earth 525; 550

   Use for general materials on the whole planet.
      Materials limited to the structure and com-
      position of the earth and the physical
      changes it has undergone and is still under-
      going are entered under **Geology.**

   See also

Antarctic regions	**Geophysics**
Arctic regions	**Ice age**
Atmosphere	**Latitude**
Creation	**Longitude**
Earthquakes	**Meteorology**
Gaia hypothesis	**Ocean**
Geodesy	**Oceanography**
Geography	**Physical geography**
Geology	**Universe**

   x **World**

   xx **Creation; Geology; Physical geography; Solar**
      system; Universe

Earth—Age 551.7

Earth—Chemical composition. *See* **Geochemistry**

Earth—Crust 551.1

   See also **Plate tectonics**

Earth, Effect of man on. *See* **Man—Influence on**
      nature

Earth fills. *See* **Landfills**

Earth—Internal structure 551.1

Earth—Photographs from space 778.3
 xx **Space photography**
Earth sciences 550
  See also

Climate	**Geophysics**
Geochemistry	**Meteorology**
Geography	**Oceanography**
Geology	**Water**

   x Geoscience
   xx **Science**
Earth sheltered houses 690; 728
   x Houses, Earth sheltered; Houses, Underground; Underground houses
   xx **House construction; Houses; Underground architecture**
Earth—Space attack and defense. *See* **Space warfare**
Earthenware. *See* **Pottery**
Earthquake sea waves. *See* **Tsunamis**
Earthquakes (May subdiv. geog.) **551.2**
   See also subject headings for types of structures subject to earthquake forces with the subdivision *Earthquake effects,* e.g. **Buildings—Earthquake effects; Skyscrapers—Earthquake effects;** etc.
   x Seismography; Seismology
   xx **Earth; Geology; Natural disasters; Physical geography**
Earthquakes and building. *See* **Buildings—Earthquake effects**
Earthquakes—California 551.2
Earthquakes—United States 551.2
   x United States—Earthquakes
Earthwork. *See* **Soils (Engineering)**
Earthworks (Archeology). *See* **Excavations (Archeology)**
Earthworks (Art) 709.04
   x Landscape sculpture; Site oriented art
   xx **Art, Modern—1900-1999 (20th century)**
East. *See* **Asia**
East Africa 967.6
   Use for materials dealing collectively with the eastern region of the continent of Africa. Although used loosely, the term is usually used to include the areas now occupied by the countries of Burundi, Kenya, Rwanda, Tanzania, Uganda, and Somalia. Both the terms East Africa and Eastern Africa are sometimes used to cover the area extending from Sudan and Ethiopia in the north to the Zambizi River in the south, thereby including Malawi and Mozambique.
   See also **Northeast Africa**
   x Africa, East; Africa, Eastern; Eastern Africa
East and West 306; 909
   Use for materials on both acculturation and cultural conflict between Asian and Occidental civilizations.
   See also **Acculturation; Civilization, Asian; Civilization, Occidental**
   xx **Acculturation**
East Asia 950
   Use for materials on East Asia including China,

236

East Asia—*Continued*
> Japan, Korea, Taiwan, Hong Kong and Macao.
> *x* Asia, East; East (Far East); Far East; Orient
> *xx* **Asia**

East (Far East). *See* **East Asia**
East Germany. *See* **Germany (East)**
East Indians 954
> *See also* **Hindus**
> *x* Indians (of India)
> *xx* **Hindus**

East (Near East). *See* **Middle East**
Easter 263; 394.2
> *x* Religious festivals
> *xx* **Fasts and feasts; Holy Week; Lent**

Easter carols. *See* **Carols**
Easter—Drama 808.82; 812, etc.
> *xx* **Drama**

Easter egg decoration. *See* **Egg decoration**
Eastern Africa. *See* **East Africa**
Eastern churches 281
> *See also* **Orthodox Eastern Church**

Eastern Empire. *See* **Byzantine Empire**
Eastern Europe 947
> *x* Europe, Eastern

Eastern Seaboard. *See* **Atlantic States**
Easy and quick cookery. *See* **Quick and easy cookery**
Easy reading materials E
> *x* Beginning reading materials; Preprimers; Preschool reading materials; Primers
> *xx* **Children's literature; Reading materials**

Eating. *See* **Dinners and dining**
Eating customs 394.1
> *See also* **Eating disorders; Table etiquette**
> *x* Food customs; Food habits
> *xx* **Diet; Human behavior; Nutrition**

Eating disorders 616.3; 616.85
> *See also* **Bulimia**; also types of eating disorders, e.g. **Anorexia nervosa**; etc.
> *x* Appetite disorders; Ingestion disorders
> *xx* **Eating customs; Psychology, Pathological**

Eavesdropping 363.2
> *See also* **Wiretapping**
> *x* Bugging, Electronic; Electronic bugging; Electronic eavesdropping; Electronic listening devices; Listening devices; Surveillance, Electronic
> *xx* **Criminal investigation; Right of privacy; Wiretapping**

Eccentrics and eccentricities 920
> *x* Cranks
> *xx* **Curiosities and wonders; Personality**

Ecclesiastical antiquities. *See* **Christian antiquities**
Ecclesiastical architecture. *See* **Church architecture**
Ecclesiastical art. *See* **Christian art and symbolism**
Ecclesiastical biography. *See* **Christianity—Biography**
Ecclesiastical fasts and feasts. *See* **Fasts and feasts**; and names of special fasts and feasts, e.g. **Lent; Easter;** etc.
Ecclesiastical furniture. *See* **Church furniture**
Ecclesiastical history. *See* **Church history**

Ecclesiastical law   262.9
    See also **Tithes**
    x Canon law; Church law; Law, Ecclesiastical
    xx **Church—Government policy; Law**
Ecclesiastical rites and ceremonies.   *See* **Funeral
    rites and ceremonies; Liturgies; Lord's Sup-
    per; Rites and ceremonies; Sacraments**
Echo ranging.   *See* **Sonar**
Eclipses, Lunar   523.3
    x Lunar eclipses; Moon—Eclipses
    xx **Astronomy**
Eclipses, Solar   523.7
    x Solar eclipses; Sun—Eclipses
    xx **Astronomy**
Ecology   574.5
    See also **Adaptation (Biology); Biogeography;
    Botany—Ecology; Environmental protection;
    Food chains (Ecology); Gaia hypothesis;** also
    types of ecology, e.g. **Marine ecology;** etc.
    x Balance of nature; Biology—Ecology; Eco-
    systems
    xx **Environment**
Ecology, Human.   *See* **Human ecology**
Ecology, Marine.   *See* **Marine ecology**
Ecology, Social.   *See* **Human ecology**
Economic aspects.   *See* subjects with the subdivi-
    sion *Economic aspects,* e.g. **Agriculture—
    Economic aspects;** etc.
Economic assistance (May subdiv. geog. adjective
    form)   338.91
    Use for general materials on international eco-
    nomic aid given in the form of gifts, loans,
    relief grants, or technical assistance. Materi-
    als limited to the latter are entered under
    Technical assistance.
    See also **Developing countries; Reconstruction
    (1939-1951); Technical assistance; World
    War, 1939-1945—Civilian relief**
    x Aid to developing areas; Assistance to devel-
    oping areas; Foreign aid program
    xx **Developing countries; Economic policy; Inter-
    national cooperation; International eco-
    nomic relations; Reconstruction (1939-1951)**
Economic assistance, American   338.91; 361.6
    x American economic assistance; United
    States—Economic assistance
Economic assistance, Domestic   338.9
    See also **Community development; Government
    lending; Grants-in-aid; Poverty; Public
    works; Subsidies; Unemployed**
    x Anti-poverty programs; Antipoverty pro-
    grams; Poor relief
    xx **Economic policy; Grants-in-aid; Unemployed**
Economic botany.   *See* **Botany, Economic**
Economic conditions   330.9
    Use for general materials on some or all of the
    following: natural resources, business, com-
    merce, industry, labor, manufactures, finan-
    cial conditions; and for the history of the
    economic development of several countries.
    See also **Business cycles; Developing countries;
    Economic policy; Geography, Commercial;
    Labor supply; Natural resources; Quality of**

Economic conditions—*Continued*

life; also classes of people and names of countries, cities, areas, etc., with the subdivision *Economic conditions,* e.g. **Blacks—Economic conditions; United States—Economic conditions;** etc.

x Business depressions; Economic development; Economic history; Stabilization in industry; World economics

xx **Business; Economics; Geography, Commercial; Social conditions; Wealth**

Economic cycles. *See* **Business cycles**

Economic depressions. *See* **Depressions, Economic**

Economic development. *See* **Economic conditions**

Economic entomology. *See* **Beneficial insects; Insect pests**

Economic forecasting   338.5

See also **Business forecasting; Employment forecasting**

xx **Business cycles; Economics; Forecasting**

Economic geography. *See* **Geography, Commercial**

Economic geology. *See* **Geology, Economic**

Economic history. *See* **Economic conditions**

Economic mobilization. *See* **Industrial mobilization**

Economic planning. *See* **Economic policy**

Economic policy   338.9

Use for materials on the policy of government towards economic problems.

See also

Commercial policy	**policy**
Economic assistance	**International economic re-**
Economic assistance, Do-	**lations**
mestic	**Land reform**
Fiscal policy	**Municipal ownership**
Free trade and protection	**National security**
Government lending	**Sanctions (International**
Government ownership	**law)**
Human resources policy	**Social policy**
Industrial mobilization	**Subsidies**
Industrialization	**Tariff**
Industry—Government	**Technical assistance**

also names of countries and states with the subdivision *Economic policy,* e.g. **United States—Economic policy; Ohio—Economic policy;** etc.; and names of countries with the subdivision *Commercial policy,* e.g. **United States—Commercial policy;** etc.

x Economic planning; National planning; Planning, Economic; Planning, National; Welfare state; World economics

xx **Economic conditions; Economics; Industry—Government policy; National security; Social policy**

Economic relations, Foreign. *See* **International economic relations**

Economic sanctions. *See* **Sanctions (International law)**

Economic zones (Maritime law). *See* **Territorial waters**

Economic zoology. *See* **Zoology, Economic**

239

Economics   330

See also

Balance of trade	Income
Barter	Industry
Business	Labor
Capital	Land use
Capitalism	Money
Christianity and econom- ics	Monopolies Population
Commerce	Prices
Consumption (Economics)	Profit
Cooperation	Property
Cost of living	Public debts
Credit	Saving and thrift
Depressions, Economic	Socialism
Economic conditions	Statistics
Economic forecasting	Trusts, Industrial
Economic policy	Underground economy
Finance	Wages
Free trade and protection	Waste (Economics)
Government ownership	Wealth

   also subjects with the subdivision *Economic as-pects,* e.g. **Agriculture—Economic aspects;** etc.

   x Distribution of wealth; Political economy; Production

   xx **Social sciences**

Economics and Christianity. *See* **Christianity and economics**

Economics—History   330.1; 330.09

   Use for materials describing the development of economic theories. Materials on the economic conditions and development of countries are entered under **Economic conditions.**

Economics, Medical. *See* **Medical economics**

Economics of war. *See* **War—Economic aspects**

Economy. *See* **Saving and thrift**

Economy, Underground. *See* **Underground economy**

Ecosystems. *See* **Ecology**

Ectogenesis, Preimplantational. *See* **Fertilization in vitro**

Ecumenical councils. *See* **Councils and synods**

Ecumenical movement. *See* **Christian unity**

Eddas   839

   xx **Old Norse literature; Poetry; Scandinavian literature**

Edible plants   581.6

   x Food plants; Plants, Edible; Plants, Useful

   xx **Botany, Economic; Food; Plants**

Editions. *See* **Bibliography—Editions**

Editors and editing. *See* **Journalism; Journalists; Publishers and publishing**

Education (May subdiv. geog.)   **370**

   Subdivisions listed under this heading may be used under other education headings where applicable. All types of education are not included in this List but are to be added as needed.

   See also

Adult education	Audiovisual education
Area studies	Basic education

Education—*Continued*

Books and reading
Business education
Church and education
Classical education
Coeducation
Colleges and universities
Continuing education
Correspondence schools
  and courses
Culture
Educators
Elementary education
Evening and continuation
  schools
Fundamentalism and edu-
  cation
Home instruction
International education
Learning and scholarship
Learning, Psychology of
Libraries
Library education
Literacy
Mainstreaming in educa-
  tion
Military education
Moral education
Nature study
Naval education
Physical education
Professional education
Religious education
Scholarships, fellowships,
  etc.
Schools
Simulation games in edu-
  cation
Socialization
Special education
Study skills
Teachers
Teaching
Technical education
Vocational education
World War, 1939-1945—
  Education and the war

also names of classes of people and social and
  ethnic groups with the subdivision
  Education, e.g. **Automobile drivers—
  Education; Blacks—Education; Deaf—
  Education; Mentally handicapped children—
  Education;** etc.; subjects with the subdivi-
  sion *Study and teaching,* e.g. **Science—
  Study and teaching;** etc.; and headings be-
  ginning with the words **Education** and **Ed-
  ucational**

  x Instruction; Pedagogy
 xx **Civilization; Coeducation; Culture; Learning
  and scholarship; Schools; Teaching**

Education, Adult. *See* **Adult education**
Education—Aims and objectives 370.11
Education and church. *See* **Church and education**
Education and Fundamentalism. *See* **Fundamental-
  ism and education**
Education and radio. *See* **Radio in education**
Education and religion. *See* **Church and education**
Education and state. *See* **Education—Government
  policy**
Education and television. *See* **Television in educa-
  tion**
Education associations. *See* **Educational associa-
  tions**
Education at home. *See* **Home instruction**
Education—Automation. *See* **Computer assisted
  instruction**
Education, Bilingual. *See* **Bilingual education**
Education, Business. *See* **Business education**
Education, Character. *See* **Moral education**
Education, Christian. *See* **Christian education**
Education, Classical. *See* **Classical education**
Education, Compulsory. *See* **Compulsory education**
Education, Continuing. *See* **Continuing education**
Education—Curricula 375
  See also **Articulation (Education);** also types of
  education and schools with the subdivision

241

Education—Curricula—*Continued*
   Curricula, e.g. **Library education—
   Curricula; Colleges and universities—
   Curricula;** etc.
   x Core curriculum; Courses of study; Curricula
      (Courses of study); Schools—Curricula;
      Study, Courses of
Education—Data processing. *See* **Computer as-
   sisted instruction**
Education—Developing countries   370.9172
Education, Discrimination in. *See* **Discrimination
   in education**
Education, Elementary. *See* **Elementary education**
Education, Ethical. *See* **Moral education; Religious
   education**
Education—Experimental methods   371.3
   See also **Experimental schools;** also types of ex-
      perimental methods, e.g. **Nongraded
      schools; Open plan schools;** etc.
   x Activity schools; Experimental methods in ed-
      ucation; Progressive education; Teaching—
      Experimental methods
Education—Federal aid. *See* **Federal aid to educa-
   tion**
Education—Finance   371.2; 379.1
   See also **Federal aid to education; State aid to ed-
      ucation**
   x School finance; School taxes; Tuition
   xx **Finance**
Education for librarianship. *See* **Library education**
Education—Government policy   379.2
   See also **Federal aid to education; Scholarships,
      fellowships, etc.; State aid to education**
   x Education and state; Educational policy; State
      and education
Education, Higher. *See* **Higher education**
Education, Home. *See* **Home instruction**
Education, Industrial. *See* **Industrial arts educa-
   tion; Technical education**
Education—Integration. *See* **School integration**
Education, Intercultural. *See* **Intercultural educa-
   tion**
Education, International. *See* **International educa-
   tion**
Education, Medical. *See* **Medicine—Study and
   teaching**
Education, Military. *See* **Military education**
Education, Moral. *See* **Moral education**
Education, Multicultural. *See* **Intercultural educa-
   tion**
Education, Musical. *See* **Music—Study and teach-
   ing**
Education, Naval. *See* **Naval education**
Education, Nonformal. *See* **Free universities**
Education of adults. *See* **Adult education**
Education of children. *See* **Elementary education**
Education of criminals. *See* **Prisoners—Education**
Education of men. *See* **Men—Education**
Education of prisoners. *See* **Prisoners—Education**
Education of the blind. *See* **Blind—Education**
Education of the deaf. *See* **Deaf—Education**
Education of veterans. *See* **Veterans—Education**
Education of women. *See* **Women—Education**
Education of workers. *See* **Labor—Education**

Education—Personnel service. *See* **Educational counseling**

Education, Physical. *See* **Physical education**

Education, Preschool. *See* **Preschool education**

Education, Primary. *See* **Elementary education**

Education, Professional. *See* **Professional education**

Education, Religious. *See* **Religious education**

Education, Scientific. *See* **Science—Study and teaching**

Education, Secondary. *See* **Secondary education**

Education, Segregation in. *See* **Segregation in education**

Education, Special. *See* **Special education**

Education—State aid. *See* **State aid to education**

Education—Statistics   370

Education—Study and teaching   370.7

> Use for materials on the study and teaching of education as a science. Materials limited to the methods of training teachers are entered under **Teachers—Training.** Materials on the methods of teaching are entered under **Teaching.**
>
> *See also* **Teachers colleges; Teachers—Training**
>
> *x* Pedagogy

Education, Technical. *See* **Technical education**

Education, Theological. *See* **Religious education; Theology—Study and teaching**

Education—United States   370.973

> *x* United States—Education

Education, Vocational. *See* **Vocational education**

Educational achievement. *See* **Academic achievement**

Educational administration. *See* **Schools—Administration**

Educational associations   370.6

> *See also* **Parents' and teachers' associations**
>
> *x* Education associations
>
> *xx* **Societies; Teachers**

Educational consultants   370.7

> *xx* **Consultants**

Educational counseling   371.4

> Use for materials on the assistance given to students by schools, colleges, or universities in the selection of a program of studies suited to their abilities, interests, future plans, and general circumstances. Materials on the assistance given to students in understanding and coping with adjustment problems are entered under **School counseling.** Consider also **Vocational guidance.**
>
> *See also* **Dropouts; School counseling; School psychologists; Vocational guidance**
>
> *x* Academic advising; Education—Personnel service; Educational guidance; Guidance counseling, Educational; Personnel service in education; Student guidance; Students—Counseling
>
> *xx* **Counseling; Dropouts; School counseling; Vocational guidance**

Educational films. *See* **Libraries and motion pictures; Motion pictures in education**

Educational freedom. *See* **Academic freedom**

Educational gaming. *See* **Simulation games in education**

243

Educational guidance. *See* **Educational counseling**

Educational measurements. *See* **Educational tests and measurements**

Educational media. *See* **Teaching—Aids and devices**

Educational media centers. *See* **Instructional materials centers**

Educational policy. *See* **Education—Government policy**

Educational psychology 370.15

  See also

Apperception	**Memory**
Attention	**Mental tests**
Child psychology	**Perception**
Imagination	**Psychology, Applied**
Learning, Psychology of	**Thought and thinking**

  x Psychology, Educational

  xx **Child psychology; Psychology; Teaching**

Educational reports. *See* **School reports**

Educational simulation games. *See* **Simulation games in education**

Educational sociology 370.19

  x Social problems in education; Sociology, Educational

  xx **Sociology**

Educational surveys 370

  x School surveys

  xx **Social surveys**

Educational television. *See* **Public television; Television in education**

Educational tests and measurements 371.2

  See also **Ability—Testing; Colleges and universities—Entrance examinations; Examinations; Grading and marking (Education); Mental tests**

  x Educational measurements; Tests

  xx **Mental tests**

Educators 370.92; 920

  See also **Teachers**

  x College teachers; Faculty (Education)

  xx **Education; Teachers**

EEO. *See* **Discrimination in employment**

Efficiency, Household. *See* **Home economics**

Efficiency, Industrial 658

  Use for materials dealing with specific means of increasing efficiency and output in business and industries. Such materials include time and motion studies, and the application of psychological principles.

  See also

Executive ability	**Motion study**
Factory management	**Office management**
Job analysis	**Personnel management**
Labor productivity	**Time study**

  x Industrial efficiency

  xx **Business; Cost accounting; Engineering; Executive ability; Factory management; Industrial management; Industry; Management; Personnel management**

Egg decoration 745.59

  x Easter egg decoration; Eggshell craft

  xx **Decoration and ornament; Handicraft**

Eggs 636.5; 641

  See also **Birds—Eggs and nests**

Eggshell craft. *See* **Egg decoration**
Egypt 962
Egypt—Antiquities 932
   x Egyptology
Egypt—History 932; 962
   See also **Sinai Campaign, 1956**
Egypt—History—1970- 962.05
Egyptology. *See* **Egypt—Antiquities**
Eight-hour day. *See* **Hours of labor**
Eighteenth century 909.7
   See note under **Nineteenth century.**
   See also **Enlightenment**
   x 1700-1799 (18th century)
Elder abuse. *See* **Elderly abuse**
Elder care. *See* **Elderly—Care**
Elderly (May subdiv. geog.) **155.67; 305.26**
   See also **Aging; Libraries and the elderly; Retire-**
      ment income; Social work with the elderly
   x Aged; Older people; Senior citizens
   xx **Gerontology; Old age**
Elderly abuse 362.6
   x Abuse of the elderly; Abused aged; Battered
      elderly; Elder abuse; Elderly—
      Mistreatment; Elderly neglect; Gramslam-
      ming; Parent abuse
   xx **Family violence**
Elderly and libraries. *See* **Libraries and the elderly**
Elderly—Care 362.6
   Use for materials on the general care of the de-
      pendent elderly or for materials covering
      several types of care for the dependent el-
      derly. Materials on specific types of care for
      the elderly are entered under Elderly with
      subdivision for the specific type of care, e.g.
      Elderly—Home care; Elderly—Institutional
      care; Elderly—Medical care; etc.
   See also **Nursing homes**
   x Elder care; Elderly—Care and hygiene
Elderly—Care and hygiene. *See* **Elderly—Care; El-**
      derly—Health and hygiene
Elderly—Counseling of 362.6
   xx **Counseling**
Elderly—Diseases 618.97
   See also **Elderly—Health and hygiene**
   x Geriatrics
   xx **Elderly—Health and hygiene**
Elderly—Health and hygiene 618.97
   See also **Elderly—Diseases**
   x Elderly—Care and hygiene; Geriatrics
   xx **Elderly—Diseases**
Elderly—Home care 362.6
   xx **Home care services**
Elderly—Housing 362.6
   See also **Retirement communities**
   x Housing for the elderly
Elderly—Institutional care 362.6
   x Homes for the elderly; Old age homes
Elderly—Life skills guides 362.6; 646.7
   See also **Retirement**
   xx **Life skills; Retirement**
Elderly—Medical care 362.6; 618.97
   See also **Medicare**
   x Medical care for the elderly
   xx **Medical care**

Elderly—Mistreatment. *See* **Elderly abuse**
Elderly neglect. *See* **Elderly abuse**
Elderly—Recreation   790.084
   xx **Recreation**
Elderly—Societies   367
Elderly—United States   305.260973
   x United States—Elderly
Election (Theology). *See* **Predestination**
Electioneering. *See* **Politics, Practical**
Elections (May subdiv. geog.)   **324.6**
   See also

Campaign funds	**Referendum**
Equal time rule (Broad-	**Representative government**
casting)	**and representation**
Presidents—United	**Suffrage**
States—Election	**Voter registration**
Primaries	

   x Ballot; Franchise; Polls, Election; Voting
   xx **Politics, Practical; Primaries; Proportional**
        representation; Representative government
        and representation
Elections—Finance. *See* **Campaign funds**
Elections, Primary. *See* **Primaries**
Elections—United States   324.973
   x United States—Elections
Elections—United States—Finance. *See* **Campaign**
        funds—United States
Electoral college. *See* **Presidents—United States—**
        Election
Electric apparatus and appliances   621.3028; 644
   See also names of electric apparatus and appli-
        ances, e.g. **Burglar alarms; Electric batter-**
        ies; Electric generators; Electric lamps; etc.
   x Apparatus, Electric; Appliances, Electric; Elec-
        tric appliances
   xx **Electric engineering; Scientific apparatus and**
        instruments
Electric apparatus and appliances, Domestic. *See*
        Household appliances, Electric
Electric appliances. *See* **Electric apparatus and ap-**
        pliances; Household appliances, Electric
Electric automobiles   629.222
   See also **Automobiles—Engines**
   x Automobiles, Electric; Electric cars
   xx **Automobiles—Engines**
Electric batteries   621.31
   See also **Fuel cells; Solar batteries; Storage bat-**
        teries
   x Batteries, Electric; Cells, Electric
   xx **Electric apparatus and appliances; Electro-**
        chemistry; Storage batteries
Electric cars. *See* **Electric automobiles**
Electric circuits   621.319
   See also **Electronic circuits**
   x Circuits, Electric
Electric communication. *See* **Telecommunication**
Electric condensers. *See* **Condensers (Electricity)**
Electric conductors   621.319
   See also **Semiconductors; Shortwave radio; Su-**
        perconductors
   x Conductors, Electric
   xx **Electronics**
Electric controllers   629.8
   x Automatic control

Electric currents   537.6; 621.31
> *See also* **Electric measurements; Electric transformers**
> *x* Currents, Electric

Electric currents, Alternating   621.31
> *x* Alternating currents; Currents, Alternating

Electric distribution.   *See* **Electric lines; Electric power distribution**

Electric engineering   621.3
> *See also*

> | | |
> |---|---|
> | **Electric apparatus and appliances** | **Electric railroads** |
> | | **Electricity in mining** |
> | **Electric lighting** | **Radio** |
> | **Electric machinery** | **Telegraph** |
> | **Electric power distribution** | **Telephone** |

> *xx* **Engineering; Mechanical engineering**

Electric equipment of automobiles.   *See* **Automobiles—Electric equipment**

Electric eye.   *See* **Photoelectric cells**

Electric generators   621.31
> *x* Dynamos; Generators, Electric
> *xx* **Electric apparatus and appliances; Electric machinery**

Electric heating   621.402; 644; 697
> *x* Electricity in the home
> *xx* **Heating**

Electric household appliances.   *See* **Household appliances, Electric**

Electric industries   338.4
> *x* Electric utilities; Industries, Electric
> *xx* **Public utilities**

Electric lamps   621.32; 645
> *See also* **Electric lighting**
> *x* Incandescent lamps
> *xx* **Electric apparatus and appliances; Electric lighting; Lamps**

Electric light.   *See* **Electric lighting; Photometry; Phototherapy**

Electric lighting   621.32
> *See also* **Electric lamps**
> *x* Arc light; Electric light; Electricity in the home; Light, Electric
> *xx* **Electric engineering; Electric lamps; Electric wiring; Lighting**

Electric lighting, Fluorescent.   *See* **Fluorescent lighting**

Electric lines   621.319
> Use for materials on general transmission systems.
> *See also* **Electric wiring**
> *x* Electric distribution; Electric power transmission; Electric transmission; Electricity—Distribution; Power transmission, Electric; Transmission of power
> *xx* **Electric power distribution**

Electric machinery   621.31
> Use for discussions of more than one kind or class of machines. Materials dealing with smaller machines and appliances are entered under **Electric apparatus and appliances.**
> *See also* **Electric generators; Electric motors; Electric transformers**
> *xx* **Electric engineering; Machinery**

Electric machinery—Alternating current   621.319
> x Alternating current machinery

Electric machinery—Direct current   621.319
> x Direct current machinery

Electric measurements   621.37
> *See also* **Electric meters; Electric testing**
> x Measurements, Electric
> xx **Electric currents; Electric testing; Weights and measures**

Electric meters   621.37
> x Meters, Electric
> xx **Electric measurements**

Electric motors   621.4
> *See also* **Electric transformers**
> x Induction motors; Motors
> xx **Electric machinery**

Electric power   621.31
> xx **Energy resources; Power (Mechanics)**

Electric power distribution   621.319
> *See also* **Electric lines; Electric wiring**
> x Electric distribution; Electric power transmission; Electric transmission; Electricity—Distribution; Power transmission, Electric; Rural electrification; Transmission of power
> xx **Electric engineering; Power transmission**

Electric power failures   621.319
> x Blackouts, Electric power; Brownouts; Electric power interruptions; Power blackouts; Power failures

Electric power in mining. *See* **Electricity in mining**

Electric power interruptions. *See* **Electric power failures**

Electric power plants   621.31
> *See also* **Hydroelectric power plants**
> x Electric utilities; Power plants, Electric
> xx **Power plants**

Electric power transmission. *See* **Electric lines; Electric power distribution**

Electric railroads   385; 621.33; 625.1
> *See also* **Railroads—Electrification; Street railroads**
> x Interurban railroads; Railroads, Electric
> xx **Electric engineering; Public utilities; Railroads; Railroads—Electrification; Street railroads; Transportation**

Electric signs   621.32; 659.13
> *See also* **Neon tubes**
> x Signs (Advertising); Signs, Electric
> xx **Advertising; Signs and signboards**

Electric smelting. *See* **Electrometallurgy**

Electric switches. *See* **Electric switchgear**

Electric switchgear   621.31
> x Electric switches; Switches, Electric

Electric testing   621.37
> *See also* **Electric measurements**
> x Testing
> xx **Electric measurements**

Electric toys   688.7
> xx **Toys**

Electric transformers   621.31
> x Transformers, Electric
> xx **Electric currents; Electric machinery; Electric motors**

Electric transmission.   *See* **Electric lines; Electric power distribution**

Electric utilities.   *See* **Electric industries; Electric power plants; Public utilities**

Electric waves   537; 621.381
> *See also* **Electromagnetic waves; Microwaves; Shortwave radio**
> *x* Hertzian waves; Radio waves
> *xx* **Waves**

Electric welding   671.5
> *x* Arc welding; Resistance welding; Spot welding; Welding, Electric
> *xx* **Welding**

Electric wiring   621.319
> *See also* **Electric lighting; Telegraph; Telephone**
> *x* Wiring, Electric
> *xx* **Electric lines; Electric power distribution**

Electricity   537; 621.3
> *See also* **Electrons; Lightning; Magnetism; Radioactivity; Telegraph; Telephone; X rays;** also headings beginning with **Electric** and **Electro**
> *xx* **Magnetism; Physics**

Electricity—Distribution.   *See* **Electric lines; Electric power distribution**

Electricity in agriculture   333.79; 631.3
> Use same form for electricity in other endeavors, e.g. **Electricity in mining;** etc.
> *x* Electricity on the farm; Rural electrification
> *xx* **Agricultural engineering; Agricultural machinery**

Electricity in medicine.   *See* **Electrotherapeutics**

Electricity in mining   622
> *See also* **Mining engineering**
> *x* Electric power in mining; Mining, Electric
> *xx* **Electric engineering; Mining engineering**

Electricity in the home.   *See* **Electric heating; Electric lighting; Household appliances, Electric**

Electricity, Medical.   *See* **Electrotherapeutics**

Electricity on the farm.   *See* **Electricity in agriculture**

Electrification of railroads.   *See* **Railroads—Electrification**

Electrochemistry   541.3; 547.1; 660
> *See also* **Electric batteries; Electrometallurgy; Electroplating; Electrotyping; Fuel cells**
> *xx* **Chemistry, Physical and theoretical; Chemistry, Technical**

Electromagnetic waves   537
> *See also* **Gamma rays; Heat; Infrared radiation; Light; Microwaves; Ultraviolet rays; X rays**
> *x* Waves, Electromagnetic
> *xx* **Electric waves; Radiation**

Electromagnetism   621.34
> *See also* **Masers**
> *xx* **Magnetism**

Electromagnets   621.34
> *x* Magnet winding
> *xx* **Magnetism; Magnets**

Electrometallurgy   669
> *See also* **Electroplating; Electrotyping**
> *x* Electric smelting
> *xx* **Electrochemistry; Electroplating; Electrotyping; Metallurgy; Smelting**

Electron microscope and microscopy   502.8; 578
  xx **Microscope and microscopy**
Electron tubes.   *See* **Vacuum tubes**
Electronic apparatus and appliances   621.381
  See also **Electronic toys**; also names of electronic
    apparatus and appliances, e.g. **Computers;**
    Intercommunication systems; Video games;
    etc.
  x Apparatus, Electronic; Appliances, Electronic
  xx **Electronics; Scientific apparatus and instru-**
    ments
Electronic art.   *See* **Computer art; Video art**
Electronic brains.   *See* **Artificial intelligence; Com-**
    puters
Electronic bugging.   *See* **Eavesdropping**
Electronic bulletin boards.   *See* **Computer bulletin**
    boards
Electronic calculating machines.   *See* **Computers**
Electronic circuits   621.319; 621.3815
  xx **Electric circuits; Electronics**
Electronic computers.   *See* **Computers**
Electronic cottage.   *See* **Telecommuting**
Electronic data processing   004
  See also

Artificial intelligence	**Data transmission systems**
Computer assisted instruc-	**Database management**
tion	**Online data processing**
Computer bulletin boards	**Optical data processing**
Computer graphics	**Programming (Computers)**
Computer networks	**Programming languages**
Computer science	**(Computers)**
Computer systems	**System design**

    also subjects with the subdivision *Data process-*
      ing, e.g. **Banks and banking—Data pro-**
      cessing; etc.
  x Automatic data processing; Data processing
  xx **Computer science; Computers; Information**
    science; Information systems
Electronic data processing—Keyboarding.   *See* **Key-**
    boarding (Electronics)
Electronic drawing.   *See* **Computer art; Computer**
    graphics
Electronic eavesdropping.   *See* **Eavesdropping**
Electronic games.   *See* **Electronic toys; Video games**
Electronic listening devices.   *See* **Eavesdropping**
Electronic mail systems   383; 384.3
    Use for materials on the electronic transmission
      of letters, messages, etc., primarily through
      the use of computers and computer termi-
      nals.
  See also **Computer bulletin boards**
  x E-mail systems; Email systems; Mail systems,
    Electronic
  xx **Data transmission systems; Tele-**
    communication
Electronic marketing.   *See* **Telemarketing**
Electronic music   786.7
  See also **Computer music**
  x Music, Electronic; Synthesizer music; Tape re-
    corder music
  xx **Music**
Electronic musical instruments.   *See* **Musical in-**
    struments, Electronic

Electronic publishing   070.5; 686.2

Use for materials on the process of publishing in which data is entered on a word processor or computer terminal, submitted to an editor or publisher, and made available online or offline.

See also **Desktop publishing; Teletext systems**

x Online publishing; Publishing, Electronic

xx **Information services; Publishers and publishing; Telecommunication**

Electronic speech processing systems.   *See* **Speech processing systems**

Electronic spread sheets.   *See* **Electronic spreadsheets**

Electronic spreadsheets   005.3

x Electronic spread sheets; Spread sheets, Electronic; Spreadsheeting, Electronic; Spreadsheets, Electronic

xx **Business; Computer programs**

Electronic toys   688.7

See also **Computer games; Video games**

x Electronic games; Games, Electronic

xx **Electronic apparatus and appliances; Toys**

Electronics   537.5; 621.381

See also

Amplifiers (Electronics)	**Facsimile transmission**
Cybernetics	**High-fidelity sound systems**
Digital electronics	**tems**
Electric conductors	**Microelectronics**
Electronic apparatus and appliances	**Semiconductors**
	Superconductors
Electronic circuits	**Transistors**

xx **Electrons; Photoelectric cells; Vacuum tubes**

Electrons   539.7

See also **Electronics**

xx **Atoms; Electricity; Neutrons; Particles (Nuclear physics); Physics; Protons; Radioactivity**

Electroplating   671.7

See also **Electrometallurgy**

xx **Electrochemistry; Electrometallurgy; Metalwork**

Electrotherapeutics   615.8

See also **Radiotherapy**

x Electricity in medicine; Electricity, Medical; Medical electricity

xx **Massage; Physical therapy; Therapeutics**

Electrotyping   686.2

See also **Electrometallurgy**

xx **Electrochemistry; Electrometallurgy; Printing**

Elementary education   372

Use for general materials on education of children below the secondary school level.

See also **Creative activities; Exceptional children; Kindergarten; Montessori method of education; Nursery schools; Readiness for school**

x Children—Education; Education, Elementary; Education of children; Education, Primary; Grammar schools; Primary education

xx **Education**

Elementary particles (Physics).   *See* **Particles (Nuclear physics)**

Elementary school dropouts.   *See* **Dropouts**

Elementary school libraries   027.8

    See also **Children's libraries**

    x School libraries (Elementary school)

    xx **Children's libraries; School libraries**

Elements, Chemical.   *See* **Chemical elements**

Elephants   569; 599.6

    xx **Mammals**

Elevators   621.8

    x Lifts

    xx **Hoisting machinery**

Elite (Social sciences) (May subdiv. geog.)   **305.5**

    xx **Leadership; Power (Social sciences); Social
classes; Social groups**

Elizabeth II, Queen of Great Britain, 1926-   92; B

    xx **Kings, queens, rulers, etc.**

Elk Mountain (Wyo.)   978.7

    xx **Mountains**

Elocution.   *See* **Public speaking**

Elves.   *See* **Fairies**

Email systems.   *See* **Electronic mail systems**

Emancipation.   *See* **Freedom**

Emancipation of slaves.   *See* **Slavery; Slavery—
United States**

Emancipation of women.   *See* **Women—Civil rights**

Embarrassment.   *See* **Self-consciousness**

Embassies.   *See* **Diplomatic and consular service**

Emblems.   *See* **Decorations of honor; Heraldry; Insignia; Mottoes; Seals (Numismatics); Signs
and symbols**

Embracing.   *See* **Hugging**

Embroidery   746.44

    See also types of embroidery, e.g. **Beadwork;
Crewelwork; Needlepoint;** etc.

    xx **Decoration and ornament; Needlework; Sew-
ing**

Embryology   574.3; 612.6

    See also **Cells; Fertilization in vitro; Fetus; Fro-
zen embryos; Genetics; Protoplasm; Repro-
duction**

    x Development

    xx **Biology; Cells; Evolution; Protoplasm; Repro-
duction; Zoology**

Embryos, Frozen.   *See* **Frozen embryos**

Emergencies.   *See* **Accidents; First aid**

Emergency assistance.   *See* **Helping behavior**

Emergency medical technicians   610.69; 616.02

    x Emergency paramedics; EMTs (Medicine);
Paramedical personnel; Paramedics, Emergency

    xx **Allied health personnel**

Emergency medicine   616

    xx **Medicine**

Emergency paramedics.   *See* **Emergency medical
technicians**

Emergency preparedness.   *See* **Disaster relief**

Emergency relief.   *See* **Disaster relief**

Emergency survival.   *See* **Survival skills**

Emigration.   *See* **Immigration and emigration**

Eminent domain   333.1; 343

    x Condemnation of land; Expropriation; Land,
Condemnation of

    xx **Constitutional law; Land use; Property; Rail-
roads; Real estate**

Emotional stress.   *See* **Stress (Psychology)**

Emotionally disturbed children 155.4; 362.2; 371.94; 618.92

    See also **Juvenile delinquency; Mentally ill children**

    x Behavior problems (Children); Children, Emotionally disturbed; Maladjusted children; Problem children

    xx **Exceptional children**

Emotions 152.4

    See also

Attitude (Psychology)	**Love**
Bashfulness	**Pain**
Belief and doubt	**Pleasure**
Fear	**Prejudices**
Horror	**Self-confidence**
Joy and sorrow	**Sympathy**
Laughter	

    also names of other emotions

    x Feelings; Frustration; Passions

    xx **Psychology; Psychophysiology**

Emperors. *See* **Kings, queens, rulers, etc.; Roman emperors;** and names of emperors, e.g. **Nero, Emperor of Rome, 37-68;** etc.

Empiricism 146

    See also **Pragmatism**

    x Experience

    xx **Knowledge, Theory of; Philosophy; Pragmatism; Reality**

Employee absenteeism. *See* **Absenteeism (Labor)**

Employee benefits. *See* **Nonwage payments**

Employee drinking. *See* **Employees—Alcohol use**

Employee drug testing. *See* **Employees—Drug testing**

Employee health services. *See* **Occupational health services**

Employee morale 158.7; 658.3

    See also **Job satisfaction**

    xx **Absenteeism (Labor); Morale; Personnel management; Psychology, Applied; Work**

Employee sex in the workplace. *See* **Sex in the workplace**

Employees 331.11; 920

    See also classes of employees, e.g. **Office employees;** etc.

Employees—Alcohol use 331.25; 658.3

    x Alcohol and employees; Alcohol in the workplace; Drinking and employees; Drinking in the workplace; Employee drinking; Employees and alcohol

Employees and alcohol. *See* **Employees—Alcohol use**

Employees and drugs. *See* **Employees—Drug use**

Employees and narcotics. *See* **Employees—Drug use**

Employees and officials. *See* **Civil service;** and names of countries, cities, etc. and organizations with the subdivision *Officials and employees,* e.g. **Chicago (Ill.)—Officials and employees; United Nations—Officials and employees;** etc.

Employees, Clerical. *See* **Office employees**

Employees—Dismissal 331.25; 658.3

    xx **Job security; Personnel management**

Employees—Drug testing   331.25; 344; 658.3
   x Drug testing in the workplace; Employee drug
      testing
Employees—Drug use   331.25; 658.3
   x Drugs and employees; Drugs in the work-
      place; Employees and drugs; Employees and
      narcotics
Employees—Labor productivity   331.11
   xx **Labor productivity**
Employees—Production standards   331.11; 658.3
   xx **Production standards**
Employees—Rating   331.25; 658.3
   xx **Performance standards**
Employees' representation in management.   *See*
      Participative management
Employees—Training   331.25; 658.3
   See note under **Occupational training.**
   See also **Apprentices; Occupational retraining;**
      Technical education
   x Factories—Training departments; Factory
      schools; In-service training; Inservice train-
      ing; Training of employees
   xx **Apprentices; Occupational training; Personnel**
      management; Technical education; Voca-
      tional education
Employer-employee relations.   *See* **Industrial rela-**
      tions
Employers' liability.   *See* **Workers' compensation**
Employment   331.1
   See also **Human resources; Labor supply; Part-**
      time employment; Summer employment;
      Temporary employment; Unemployment; Vo-
      cational guidance; also names of groups of
      people with the subdivision *Employment,*
      e.g. **Blacks—Employment; Veterans—**
      Employment; etc.
   xx **Labor; Vocational guidance**
Employment agencies   331.12
   See also **Job hunting; Labor supply**
   x Jobs
   xx **Labor; Labor supply; Labor turnover; Person-**
      nel management; Recruiting of employees;
      Unemployment
Employment and age.   *See* **Age and employment**
Employment applications.   *See* **Applications for po-**
      sitions
Employment discrimination.   *See* **Discrimination in**
      employment
Employment forecasting   331.1
   See also **Labor supply**
   x Occupational forecasting
   xx **Economic forecasting; Labor supply**
Employment guidance.   *See* **Vocational guidance**
Employment management.   *See* **Personnel manage-**
      ment
Employment of children.   *See* **Children—**
      Employment
Employment of teenagers.   *See* **Teenagers—**
      Employment
Employment of veterans.   *See* **Veterans—**
      Employment
Employment of women.   *See* **Women—**
      Employment
Employment of youth.   *See* **Youth—Employment**

Employment, Part-time. *See* **Part-time employment**
Employment references. *See* **Applications for positions**
Employment security. *See* **Job security**
Employment, Supplementary. *See* **Supplementary employment**
Employment, Temporary. *See* **Temporary employment**
EMTs (Medicine). *See* **Emergency medical technicians**
Enamel and enameling   738.4
   x Porcelain enamels
   xx **Decoration and ornament; Decorative arts**
Encounter groups. *See* **Group relations training**
Encyclicals, Papal. *See* **Papal encyclicals**
Encyclopedias and dictionaries   030; 031, etc.; 403; 413, etc.
   See also **Classical dictionaries; Machine readable dictionaries; Picture dictionaries; Polyglot dictionaries;** also names of languages and subjects with the subdivision *Dictionaries,* e.g. **English language—Dictionaries; Biography—Dictionaries; Chemistry—Dictionaries; English literature—Dictionaries; United States—Biography—Dictionaries;** etc.
   x Cyclopedias; Dictionaries; Glossaries; Subject dictionaries
   xx **Reference books**
End of the earth. *See* **End of the world**
End of the world   001.9; 236; 291.2; 523.1
   Use for materials on the end of the world from an eschatological point of view including Judgment Day, signs, fulfillments of prophecies, etc., an astronomical point of view, or discussions of other possible causes.
   x End of the earth; World, End of the
   xx **Eschatology**
Endangered species   333.95; 574.5
   See also **Bison; Plant conservation; Rare animals; Rare plants; Wildlife conservation**
   x Threatened species; Vanishing species
   xx **Environmental protection; Nature conservation; Rare animals; Rare plants**
Endocrine glands   616.4
   See also **Hormones**
   x Ductless glands; Glands, Ductless
   xx **Endocrinology; Hormones**
Endocrinology   616.4
   See also **Endocrine glands; Hormones**
Endorphins   612.8; 615
   x Brain opioids; Opioids, Brain
   xx **Narcotics**
Endowed charities. *See* **Charities; Endowments**
Endowments   001.4; 361.6; 361.7
   See also **Charities; Scholarships, fellowships, etc.**
   x Endowed charities; Foundations (Endowments); Philanthropy
   xx **Charities**
Endurance, Physical. *See* **Physical fitness**
Energy. *See* **Energy resources; Force and energy**
Energy and state. *See* **Energy resources—Government policy**
Energy, Biomass. *See* **Biomass energy**

Energy conservation   333.791

    See also **Energy consumption; Energy resources—Government policy;** also types of energy conservation, e.g. **Recycling (Waste, etc.);** etc.

    x Conservation of energy; Conservation of power resources; Power resources conservation

    xx **Conservation of natural resources; Energy consumption; Energy resources**

Energy consumption   333.79

    See also **Energy conservation;** also subjects with the subdivision *Fuel consumption,* e.g. **Automobiles—Fuel consumption;** etc.

    x Consumption of energy

    xx **Energy conservation; Energy resources**

Energy conversion from waste.   *See* **Waste products as fuel**

Energy conversion, Microbial.   *See* **Biomass energy**

Energy development   333.79

    x Energy resources development; Power resources development

Energy policy.   *See* **Energy resources—Government policy**

Energy resources   333.79

    Materials on the physics and engineering aspects of power are entered under **Power (Mechanics).**

    See also

Biomass energy	**Renewable energy resources**
Electric power	
Energy conservation	**Solar energy**
Energy consumption	**Water power**
Fuel	**Wind power**
Ocean energy resources	

    x Energy; Power resources; Power supply

    xx **Natural resources; Power (Mechanics)**

Energy resources development.   *See* **Energy development**

Energy resources—Government policy   333.79; 351.82

    x Energy and state; Energy policy; State and energy

    xx **Energy conservation**

Energy resources, Ocean.   *See* **Ocean energy resources**

Energy resources, Renewable.   *See* **Renewable energy resources**

Energy technology.   *See* **Power (Mechanics)**

Enforcement of law.   *See* **Law enforcement**

Engineering   620

    All types of engineering are not included in this List but are to be added as needed.

    See also

Aeronautics	**Genetic engineering**
Agricultural engineering	**Highway engineering**
Building materials	**Human engineering**
Chemical engineering	**Hydraulic engineering**
Civil engineering	**Marine engineering**
Computer aided design	**Mechanical drawing**
Efficiency, Industrial	**Mechanics**
Electric engineering	**Military engineering**
Engineers	**Mining engineering**

Engineering—*Continued*

Minorities in engineering	Sanitary engineering
Municipal engineering	Steam engineering
Nuclear engineering	Structural engineering
Ocean engineering	Systems engineering
Railroad engineering	Traffic engineering
Reliability (Engineering)	Water supply engineering

    x Construction
    xx **Building; Industrial arts; Mechanics; Technology**

Engineering drawing. *See* **Mechanical drawing**
Engineering, Genetic. *See* **Genetic engineering**
Engineering instruments 620.0028
    x Instruments, Engineering
    xx **Scientific apparatus and instruments**
Engineering materials. *See* **Materials**
Engineering—Periodicals 620.005
    xx **Periodicals**
Engineering, Structural. *See* **Structural engineering**
Engineering—Study and teaching 620.007
    xx **Technical education**
Engineers 620.0092; 920
    See also **Inventors**
    xx **Engineering**
Engines 621.4
    See also

Airplanes—Engines	Heat engines
Automobiles—Engines	Marine engines
Diesel engines	Pumping machinery
Farm engines	Solar engines
Fire engines	Steam engines
Fuel	Turbines
Gas and oil engines	

    x Motors
    xx **Machinery; Mechanical engineering**
England 942
    Use with the subdivisions *Description; Industries; Intellectual life; Social life and customs* for works limited to England.
    xx **Great Britain**
England, Church of. *See* **Church of England**
England—History. *See* **Great Britain—History**
English as a foreign language. *See* **English as a second language**
English as a second language 420.7; 428
    See also **English language—Conversations and phrases**
    x English as a foreign language; English for foreigners; English language as a second language; English language—Study and teaching, Foreign; English language—Texts for foreigners
English authors. *See* **Authors, English**
English composition. *See* **English language—Composition and exercises**
English drama 822
    See also **Morality plays; Mysteries and miracle plays**
    xx **Drama; English literature**
English drama—Collected works. *See* **English drama—Collections**
English drama—Collections 822.008
    x English drama—Collected works
    xx **Drama—Collections**

English drama—History and criticism   822.009
   xx **Drama—History and criticism**
English essays   824; 824.008
     Use for collections of literary essays by several
       authors.
   xx **English literature; Essays**
English fiction   823; Fic
   x Fiction, English
   xx **English literature; Fiction**
English fiction—History and criticism   823.009
English for foreigners. *See* **English as a second lan-**
     guage; English language—Conversations
     and phrases
English grammar. *See* **English language—**
     Grammar
English history. *See* **Great Britain—History**
English language   420
     Subdivisions used under this heading may be
       used under other languages unless otherwise
       specified.
   xx **Language and languages**
English language—0-1100. *See* **Anglo-Saxon lan-**
     guage
English language—Acronyms. *See* **Acronyms**
English language—Americanisms. *See* **American-**
     isms
English language—Antonyms. *See* **English lan-**
     guage—Synonyms and antonyms
English language as a second language. *See* **English**
     as a second language
English language—Basal readers. *See* **Basal readers**
English language—Business English   428; 808
    Business English is a unique subdivision for
      English language. Use same pattern with
      unique subdivisions for other languages, e.g.
      Japanese language—Business Japanese;
      etc.
   See also **Business letters**
   x Business English
   xx **Business letters**
English language—Comparison   425
   x Comparison (English grammar); Grammatical
     comparison
English language—Composition and exercises   428;
   808
   See also **Rhetoric**
   x English composition
   xx **Rhetoric**
English language—Conversations and phrases   428
   x English for foreigners
   xx **English as a second language**
English language—Dialects   427
   See also **Americanisms**
English language—Dictionaries   423
     Dictionaries of English and another language are
       assigned the heading **English language—**
       Dictionaries—[name of second language],
       i.e. **English language—Dictionaries—**
       French; etc.
   See also **English language—Terms and phrases**
   xx **Encyclopedias and dictionaries; English lan-**
     guage—Terms and phrases

English language—Dictionaries—French 443
> Use for English-French dictionaries. French-English dictionaries are entered under **French language—Dictionaries—English.** Use both headings for an English-French and French-English dictionary.
>
> *See also* **French language—Dictionaries—English**
>
> *xx* **French language—Dictionaries—English**

English language—Errors 428

English language—Etymology 422
> *xx* **English language—History**

English language—Examinations 420.76

English language—Foreign words and phrases 422
> *x* Foreign language phrases

English language—Grammar 425
> *See also* **English language—Usage**
>
> *x* English grammar
>
> *xx* **Grammar**

English language—History 420.9
> *See also* **English language—Etymology**

English language—Homonyms 423

English language—Idioms 428
> *See also* **English language—Provincialisms; English language—Usage**
>
> *x* Idioms
>
> *xx* **English language—Provincialisms**

English language—Jargon 427
> *x* Jargon

English language—Old English, ca.450-1100. *See* **Anglo-Saxon language**

English language—Orthography. *See* **English language—Spelling**

English language—Phonetics. *See* **English language—Pronunciation**

English language—Phrases and terms. *See* **English language—Terms and phrases**

English language—Programmed instruction 420.7

English language—Pronunciation 421
> *See also* **Reading—Phonetic method**
>
> *x* English language—Phonetics
>
> *xx* **Phonetics**

English language—Provincialisms 427
> *See also* **English language—Idioms**
>
> *xx* **English language—Idioms**

English language—Punctuation. *See* **Punctuation**

English language—Reading materials. *See* **Reading materials**

English language—Rhetoric. *See* **Rhetoric**

English language—Rhyme 808.1
> *xx* **Rhyme**

English language—Slang 427

English language—Social aspects 420

English language—Spelling 421
> *See also* **Spellers; Spelling reform**
>
> *x* English language—Orthography

English language—Spelling reform. *See* **Spelling reform**

English language—Study and teaching 420.7

English language—Study and teaching, Foreign. *See* **English as a second language**

English language—Synonyms and antonyms 423
> *x* English language—Antonyms

English language—Terms and phrases   423; 427; 428

Use for general lists of words and phrases that are applicable to certain situations (curious expressions, public speaking phrases, etc.) rather than to a specific subject. If the list is limited to a special field, use the name of the subject with the subdivision *Dictionaries,* e.g. **Chemistry—Dictionaries;** etc.

See also **English language—Dictionaries**

x English language—Phrases and terms

xx **English language—Dictionaries**

English language—Texts for foreigners.   *See* **English as a second language**

English language—Usage   428

xx **English language—Grammar; English language—Idioms**

English language—Versification.   *See* **Versification**

English language—Vocabulary.   *See* **Vocabulary**

English letters   826; 826.008

xx **English literature; Letters**

English literature   820

Subdivisions used under this heading may be used under other literatures.

See also

Authors, English	**English prose literature**
English drama	**English wit and humor**
English essays	**Satire, English**
English fiction	**Speeches, addresses, etc.,**
English letters	**English**
English poetry	

xx **Literature**

English literature—0-1100.   *See* **Anglo-Saxon literature**

English literature—African authors.   *See* **African literature (English)**

English literature—Bibliography   016.82

English literature—Bio-bibliography   820.92

xx **Authors, English**

English literature—Collected works.   *See* **English literature—Collections**

English literature—Collections   820.8

Use for collections of poetry and prose by several authors. Collections of prose are entered under **English prose literature.** Collections of poetry are entered under **English poetry—Collections.**

See also **English poetry—Collections; English prose literature**

x Collections of literature; English literature—Collected works

xx **Literature—Collections**

English literature—Criticism.   *See* **English literature—History and criticism**

English literature—Dictionaries   820.3

See also **English literature—Indexes**

xx **Encyclopedias and dictionaries; English literature—Indexes**

English literature—Examinations   820.76

xx **English literature—Study and teaching**

English literature—History and criticism   820.9

x English literature—Criticism

xx **Criticism; History**

260

English literature—Indexes   016.82
    See also English literature—Dictionaries
    xx English literature—Dictionaries
English literature—Old English, ca. 450-1100.   *See*
       Anglo-Saxon literature
English literature—Outlines, syllabi, etc.   820.2
    See also English literature—Study and teaching
    xx English literature—Study and teaching; Liter-
       ature—Outlines, syllabi, etc.
English literature—Study and teaching   820.7
    See also English literature—Examinations; Eng-
       lish literature—Outlines, syllabi, etc.
    xx English literature—Outlines, syllabi, etc.
English newspapers   072
    xx Newspapers
English orations.   *See* Speeches, addresses, etc.,
       English
English periodicals   052
    xx Periodicals
English poetry   821
    xx English literature; Poetry
English poetry—Collected works.   *See* English poet-
       ry—Collections
English poetry—Collections   821.008
    x English poetry—Collected works
    xx English literature—Collections; Poetry—
       Collections
English poetry—History and criticism   821.009
    xx Criticism; Poetry—History and criticism
English prose literature   828
    Use for collections of prose writings that may in-
       clude several literary forms, such as essays,
       fiction, orations, etc.
    x Prose literature, English
    xx English literature; English literature—
       Collections
English satire.   *See* Satire, English
English speeches.   *See* Speeches, addresses, etc.,
       English
English wit and humor   827; 827.008; 827.009
    Use for collections of several authors. May be
       used also for materials about English wit
       and humor.
    xx English literature; Wit and humor
Engravers   760.92; 920
    See also Etchers; Lithographers
    xx Artists
Engraving (May subdiv. geog. adjective form, e.g.
       Engraving, American; etc.)   760; 765
    See also Etching; Gems; Linoleum block print-
       ing; Mezzotint engraving; Photoengraving;
       Wood engraving
    x Copper engraving; Engravings; Line engrav-
       ing; Steel engraving
    xx Art; Etching; Graphic arts; Illustration of
       books; Pictures
Engraving, American   760; 769
    x American engraving; United States—
       Engraving
Engravings.   *See* Engraving
Enhanced radiation weapons.   *See* Neutron weapons
Enigmas.   *See* Curiosities and wonders; Riddles
Enlarged texts for shared reading.   *See* Big books

Enlarging (Photography). *See* **Photography—Enlarging**

Enlightenment   190; 909.7; 940.2

    Use for materials on the philosophic movement of the 18th century marked by the questioning of traditional doctrines and values, naturalistic and individualistic tendencies, and an emphasis on the empirical method in science and the free use of reason.

  xx **Eighteenth century; Philosophy, Modern; Rationalism**

Enlistment. *See* names of armies and navies with the subdivision *Recruiting, enlistment, etc.,* e.g. **United States. Army—Recruiting, enlistment, etc.; United States. Navy—Recruiting, enlistment, etc.;** etc.

Ensembles (Mathematics). *See* **Set theory**

Ensigns. *See* **Flags**

Ensilage. *See* **Silage and silos**

Enteric fever. *See* **Typhoid fever**

Entertainers   791.092; 920

  See also **Fools and jesters;** also names of types of entertainers, e.g. **Actors; Clowns; Comedians; Dancers;** etc.

Entertaining   395; 642

    Use for materials dealing with the art and skill of entertaining and hospitality.

  See also **Amusements; Business entertaining; Dinners and dining; Games; Luncheons; Parties**

  x Guests; Hospitality

  xx **Amusements; Etiquette; Home economics**

Entertainments. *See* **Amusements; Christmas entertainments; Church entertainments; Skits**

Entomology. *See* **Insects**

Entomology, Economic. *See* **Beneficial insects; Insect pests**

Entomology, Medical. *See* **Insects as carriers of disease**

Entozoa. *See* **Parasites**

Entrance examinations for colleges. *See* **Colleges and universities—Entrance examinations**

Entrance requirements for colleges and universities. *See* **Colleges and universities—Entrance requirements;** and names of individual colleges and universities with the subdivision *Entrance requirements*

Entrepreneurs (May subdiv. geog.)   338.092; 920

  xx **Business people; Self-employed**

Entrepreneurship   338; 658.4

  x Business enterprises—Management

  xx **Business; Capitalism; Small business**

Environment   304.2; 333.7; 363.7

  See also **Ecology; Environmental protection;** also subjects with the subdivision *Environmental aspects,* e.g. **Nuclear power plants—Environmental aspects;** etc.

Environment and pesticides. *See* **Pesticides—Environmental aspects**

Environment and state. *See* **Environment—Government policy**

Environment—Government policy (May subdiv. geog.)   344; 351.82; 363.7

Environment—Government policy—*Continued*
> *See also* **Conservation of natural resources; Human ecology; Man—Influence on nature; Natural resources; Pollution**
> *x* Environment and state; Environmental policy; State and environment
> *xx* **Human ecology; Man—Influence on nature**

Environment—Government policy—United States 344; 353.0082; 363.7
> *x* American environmental policy; United States—Environmental policy

Environment, Space. *See* **Space environment**
Environmental aspects. *See* subjects with the subdivision *Environmental aspects,* e.g. **Nuclear power plants—Environmental aspects;** etc.

Environmental health 616.9
> *See also* **Air pollution; Occupational health and safety; Pollution; Water pollution;** also subjects with the subdivision *Environmental aspects,* e.g. **Nuclear power plants— Environmental aspects;** etc.
> *x* Health—Environmental aspects
> *xx* **Man—Influence of environment; Public health**

Environmental policy. *See* **Environment— Government policy**
Environmental pollution. *See* **Pollution**

Environmental protection 344; 363.7
> *See also* **Conservation of natural resources; Endangered species; Landscape protection; Pollution; Soil conservation; Wildlife conservation**
> *x* Environmentalism; Protection of environment
> *xx* **Ecology; Environment; Pollution**

Environmental radioactivity. *See* **Radioactive pollution**
Environmentalism. *See* **Environmental protection**

Enzymes 547.7; 574.19
> *See also* **Catalytic RNA; Fermentation**

Eolithic period. *See* **Stone Age**
Ephemerides. *See* **Nautical almanacs**

Epic poetry 808.81; 811, etc.
> *See also* **Romances**
> *xx* **Poetry**

Epidemics 614.4
> *See also* **Communicable diseases;** also names of contagious diseases, e.g. **AIDS (Disease);** etc.
> *x* Pestilences
> *xx* **Communicable diseases; Diseases; Public health**

Epigrams 808.88; 818, etc.
> *See also* **Proverbs; Quotations; Toasts**
> *x* Sayings
> *xx* **Proverbs; Wit and humor**

Epigraphy. *See* **Inscriptions**

Epilepsy 616.8
> *xx* **Nervous system—Diseases**

Episcopal Church 283
> Use for materials on the Episcopal Church in the United States after 1789. Materials on the Episcopal Church in the United States prior

Episcopal Church—*Continued*

　　to 1789 are entered under **Church of England—United States.**

　See also **Church of England—United States**

　x Protestant Episcopal Church in the U.S.A.

　xx **Church of England—United States**

Epistemology. *See* **Knowledge, Theory of**

Epitaphs 929

　x Burial; Graves

　xx **Biography; Cemeteries; Inscriptions; Tombs**

Epithets. *See* **Names; Nicknames**

Epizoa. *See* **Parasites**

Equal employment opportunity. *See* **Discrimination in employment**

Equal opportunity in employment. *See* **Discrimination in employment**

Equal pay for equal work 331.2; 658.3

　x Pay equity

　xx **Discrimination in employment; Wages; Women—Employment**

Equal rights amendments (May subdiv. geog.) **305.42; 323.4; 342**

　x Amendments, Equal rights; E.R.A.'s; ERAs

　xx **Constitutions; Sex discrimination**

Equal time rule (Broadcasting) 324.7; 342; 343

　Use for materials on the requirement that all qualified candidates for public office be granted equal broadcast time if one of the candidates is granted time.

　See also **Fairness doctrine (Broadcasting)**

　x Rule of equal time (Broadcasting)

　xx **Elections; Fairness doctrine (Broadcasting); Radio broadcasting; Television broadcasting; Television in politics**

Equality 323.42

　See also **Aristocracy; Democracy; Freedom; Individualism; Social classes; Socialism**

　x Inequality; Social equality

　xx **Democracy; Freedom; Socialism; Sociology**

Equations, Chemical. *See* **Chemical equations**

Equestrianism. *See* **Horsemanship**

Equipment and supplies. *See* appropriate subjects with the subdivision *Equipment and supplies,* e.g. **Sports—Equipment and supplies;** etc.

ERAs. *See* **Equal rights amendments**

Ergonomics. *See* **Human engineering**

Erosion 551.3

　See also **Dust storms; Soil conservation;** also types of erosion, e.g. **Soil erosion;** etc.

　xx **Soil conservation**

Erotic art 704.9

　x Art, Erotic; Sex in art

　xx **Erotica**

Erotic literature 808.8; 809

　x Literature, Erotic

　xx **Erotica**

Erotica 704.9; 809

　See also **Pornography;** also types of erotica, e.g. **Erotic art; Erotic literature;** etc.

　xx **Pornography**

Errors 001.9; 153.7; 165

　Use for materials on errors of judgment, errors

Errors—*Continued*

of observation, scientific errors, popular misconceptions, etc. Errors in language are entered under names of languages with the subdivision *Errors,* e.g. **English language—Errors;** etc.

See also **Superstition**

x Fallacies; Medical errors; Mistakes; Scientific errors

xx **Superstition**

Ersatz products. *See* **Substitute products**

Eruptions. *See* **Geysers; Volcanoes**

Escapes   365; 904

x Hostage escapes; Prison escapes

xx **Adventure and adventurers; Prisons**

Eschatology   236; 291.2

See also **Death; End of the world; Future life; Immortality; Millennium; Second Advent**

x Intermediate state

xx **Theology**

Eskimos. *See* **Inuit**

ESP. *See* **Extrasensory perception**

Esperanto   499

xx **Universal language**

Espionage (May subdiv. geog. adjective form) **327.12; 355.3**

See also **Spies**

xx **Intelligence service; Secret service; Subversive activities**

Espionage, American   327.1273; 355.3

x American espionage

Esquimaux. *See* **Inuit**

Essay   808.4

Use for materials on the appreciation of the essay and on writing the essay.

xx **Literature**

Essays   808.84

Use for collections of literary essays by authors of different nationalities. Collections of literary essays by American authors are entered under **American essays;** by English authors, under **English essays;** etc. Essays limited to a particular subject, by one or more authors, are entered under that subject.

See also **American essays; English essays**

x Collections of literature

xx **Literature—Collections**

Essences and essential oils   664; 668

See also **Flavoring essences; Perfumes**

x Aromatic plant products; Oils, Essential; Vegetable oils; Volatile oils

xx **Distillation; Oils and fats**

Estate planning   332.024; 343.05

See also **Inheritance and transfer tax; Insurance; Investments; Taxation**

xx **Personal finance**

Estate tax. *See* **Inheritance and transfer tax**

Esthetics. *See* **Aesthetics**

Estimates. *See* appropriate technical subjects with the subdivision *Estimates,* e.g. **Building—Estimates;** etc.

Estimation (Mathematics). *See* **Approximate computation**

Estrangement (Social psychology). *See* **Alienation (Social psychology)**

Etchers   769.92; 920
   xx **Artists; Engravers**
Etching   767
   See also **Engraving**
   x Etchings
   xx **Art; Engraving; Pictures**
Etchings. *See* **Etching**
Eternal life. *See* **Future life**
Eternal punishment. *See* **Hell**
Eternity   115
   Use for materials on the philosophical concept of eternity. Materials dealing with the character and form of a future life are entered under **Future life.**
   See also **Future life**
   xx **Future life**
Ethanol. *See* **Alcohol as fuel**
Ethical education. *See* **Moral education; Religious education**
Ethics (May subdiv. geog. adjective form, e.g. **Ethics, American;** etc.)   **170**
   See also

Charity	**Justice**
Conscience	**Loyalty**
Cruelty	**Moral education**
Duty	**Secularism**
Free will and determinism	**Sin**
Good and evil	**Social ethics**
Honesty	**Spiritual life**
Human behavior	**Stoics**
Jewish ethics	**Utilitarianism**
Joy and sorrow	**Values**

   also types of ethics, e.g. **Business ethics; Christian ethics; Professional ethics; Work ethics;** etc.; and subjects with the subdivision *Moral and religious aspects,* e.g. **Birth control—Moral and religious aspects;** etc.
   x Moral philosophy; Morality; Morals; Natural law; Philosophy, Moral
   xx **Human behavior; Philosophy**
Ethics, American   170.973
   x American ethics; United States—Ethics
Ethics, Biological. *See* **Bioethics**
Ethics, Business. *See* **Business ethics**
Ethics, Christian. *See* **Christian ethics**
Ethics, Jewish. *See* **Jewish ethics**
Ethics, Legal. *See* **Legal ethics**
Ethics, Medical. *See* **Medical ethics**
Ethics, Political. *See* **Political ethics**
Ethics, Professional. *See* **Professional ethics**
Ethics, Sexual. *See* **Sexual ethics**
Ethics, Social. *See* **Social ethics**
Ethics, Work. *See* **Work ethics**
Ethiopian-Italian War, 1935-1936. *See* **Italo-Ethiopian War, 1935-1936**
Ethnic groups   305.8
   Use for theoretical materials on groups of people who are bound together by common ties of ancestry and culture. Materials on several ethnic groups in a particular region or country are entered under **Ethnology** subdi-

Ethnic groups—*Continued*

vided geographically. Materials on individual ethnic groups are entered under the name of the group, e.g. **Mexican Americans;** etc.

See also **Ethnic relations; Minorities; Race relations**

x Groups, Ethnic

xx **Ethnology**

Ethnic psychology. *See* **Ethnopsychology**

Ethnic relations   305.8; 323.1

See also **Culture conflict; Discrimination; Intercultural education; Minorities; Race relations**

x Conflict, Ethnic; Relations among ethnic groups

xx **Acculturation; Ethnic groups; Ethnology; Minorities; Race relations; Social problems; Sociology**

Ethnography. *See* **Ethnology**

Ethnology (May subdiv. geog.)   **305.8; 572**

See note under **Ethnic groups.**

See also

Acculturation	**Folklore**
Anthropogeography	**Language and languages**
Anthropology	**Manners and customs**
Anthropometry	**Nonliterate folk society**
Archeology	**Nonliterate man**
Cannibalism	**Physical anthropology**
Civilization	**Prehistoric man**
Costume	**Race**
Ethnic groups	**Race relations**
Ethnic relations	**Sacrifice**
Ethnopsychology	**Totems and totemism**

also names of peoples, e.g. **Afrikaners; Australian aborigines; Blacks; Teutonic peoples;** etc.; and names of countries with the subdivision *Social life and customs,* e.g. **United States—Social life and customs;** etc.

x Aborigines; Cultural anthropology; Ethnography; Geographical distribution of people; Indigenous peoples; Native peoples; Races of people; Social anthropology

xx **Anthropology; Archeology; Civilization; Geography; History; Man; Science**

Ethnology—United States   305.813

See also names of individual ethnic groups, e.g. **Hispanic Americans; Indians of North America; Mexican Americans;** etc.

x United States—Ethnology; United States—Peoples

Ethnopsychology   155.8

See also **Culture conflict; National characteristics; Social psychology;** also names of racial or ethnic groups with the subdivision *Psychology,* e.g. **Indians of North America—Psychology;** etc.

x Cross cultural psychology; Ethnic psychology; Folk psychology; National psychology; Psychology, Ethnic; Psychology, National; Psychology, Racial; Race psychology

xx **Anthropology; Ethnology; National characteristics; Psychology; Social psychology; Sociology**

Ethyl alcohol fuel.   *See* **Alcohol as fuel**
Etiquette   395
>   *See also* **Courtesy; Dancing; Dating (Social customs); Dinners and dining; Entertaining; Letter writing; Manners and customs;** also types of etiquette as in phrases, e.g. **Table etiquette;** etc.; and names of countries with the subdivision *Social life and customs,* e.g. **United States—Social life and customs;** etc.
>   *x* Ceremonies; Manners; Politeness; Salutations
>   *xx* **Human behavior; Manners and customs**
Etymology.   *See* names of languages with the subdivision *Etymology,* e.g. **English language—Etymology;** etc.
Eucharist.   *See* **Lord's Supper**
Eugenics   363.9; 573.2
>   *See also* **Birth control; Heredity**
>   *xx* **Anthropology; Family; Genetics; Heredity; Population; Social problems**
Europe   940
>   *x* Europe, Western; Western Europe
Europe, Central.   *See* **Central Europe**
Europe, Eastern.   *See* **Eastern Europe**
Europe—History   940
Europe—History—0-476   936; 937
Europe—History—476-1492   940.1; 940.2
>   *See also* **Holy Roman Empire; Hundred Years' War, 1339-1453; Middle Ages—History**
>   *xx* **Middle Ages—History**
Europe—History—1492-1789   940.2
>   *See also* **Thirty Years' War, 1618-1648**
>   *xx* **Reformation**
Europe—History—1789-1900   940.2
>   *x* Europe—History—1800-1899 (19th century); Napoleonic Wars
Europe—History—1800-1899 (19th century).   *See* **Europe—History—1789-1900**
Europe—History—1900-1999 (20th century)   940.5
Europe—History—1914-1945   940.5
>   *See also* **World War, 1914-1918; World War, 1939-1945**
Europe—History—1945-   940.55
Europe—Politics and government   940
>   May be subdivided by period using the same subdivisions as under **Europe—History,** e.g. **Europe—Politics and government—1789-1900.**
>   *See also* **European federation**
Europe, Western.   *See* **Europe**
European Common Market.   *See* **European Economic Community**
European Economic Community   382
>   *x* Common market; European Common Market
European federation   341.24; 940
>   *x* Federation of Europe; Paneuropean federation; United States of Europe (proposed)
>   *xx* **Europe—Politics and government; Federal government; International organization**
European War, 1914-1918.   *See* **World War, 1914-1918**
European War, 1939-1945.   *See* **World War, 1939-1945**

Euthanasia   179

    See also **Right to die**

    x Death, Mercy; Killing, Mercy; Mercy killing;
        Right to life

    xx **Homicide; Medical ethics; Right to die**

Evacuation of civilians.   *See* names of wars with
        the subdivision *Evacuation of civilians,* e.g.
        **World War, 1939-1945—Evacuation of civil-
        ians;** etc.

Evaluation of literature.   *See* **Books and reading;
        Books and reading—Best books; Books—
        Reviews; Criticism; Literature—History and
        criticism**

Evangelism.   *See* **Evangelistic work**

Evangelism and politics.   *See* **Religion and politics**

Evangelistic healing.   *See* **Spiritual healing**

Evangelistic work   253

    See also **Conversion; Missions, Christian; Reviv-
        als**

    x Evangelism; Revival (Religion)

    xx **Church work; Missions, Christian; Revivals**

Evening and continuation schools   374

    See also **Adult education**

    x Continuation schools; Evening schools; Night
        schools

    xx **Adult education; Compulsory education; Con-
        tinuing education; Education; Public
        schools; Secondary education; Technical ed-
        ucation**

Evening schools.   *See* **Evening and continuation
        schools**

Evergreens   582.1; 635.9

    See also **Christmas trees**

    xx **Landscape gardening; Shrubs; Trees**

Everyday living skills.   *See* **Life skills**

Evidences of Christianity.   *See* **Apologetics**

Evidences of the Bible.   *See* **Bible—Evidences, au-
        thority, etc.**

Evil.   *See* **Good and evil**

Evil spirits.   *See* **Demonology**

Evolution   573.2; 575

    See also

    Adaptation (Biology)   ronment
    Anatomy, Comparative   **Man—Origin**
    Biology   **Mendel's law**
    Creation   **Natural selection**
    Embryology   **Religion and science**
    Heredity   **Social change**
    Life—Origin   **Variation (Biology)**
    Man—Influence of envi-

    x Darwinism; Development; Mutation (Biol-
        ogy); Origin of species

    xx **Biology; Creation; Genetics; Heredity; Man—
        Origin; Natural selection; Philosophy, Mod-
        ern; Religion and science; Variation (Biol-
        ogy); Zoology**

Evolution—Study and teaching   575.007

    See also **Creation—Study and teaching**

    xx **Creation—Study and teaching**

Ex libris.   *See* **Bookplates**

Ex-nuns   271; 305.43; 920

    x Catholic ex-nuns; Former nuns

    xx **Nuns**

Ex-priests   305.33; 920
    x Catholic ex-priests; Former priests
    xx **Catholic Church—Clergy; Priests**
Ex-service men. *See* **Veterans**
Examinations   371.2
    Use for general materials, such as discussions of
        the value of examinations, statistics, history,
        etc. Materials discussing the requirements
        for examinations in particular branches of
        study, or compilations of questions and an-
        swers for such examinations, are entered un-
        der the subject with the subdivision
        Examinations, e.g. **English language—**
        Examinations; etc.
    See also **Civil service—Examinations; Colleges**
        and universities—Entrance examinations;
        Colleges and universities—Entrance require-
        ments; Mental tests; also particular
        branches of study with the subdivision
        Examinations, e.g. **English language—**
        Examinations; Music—Examinations; etc.;
        and names of individual examinations, e.g.
        Graduate record examination; Scholastic ap-
        titude test; etc.
    x Achievement tests; Objective tests; Tests
    xx **Educational tests and measurements; Ques-**
        tions and answers; Teaching
Examinations—Design and construction   371.2
Excavation   624.1
    xx **Civil engineering; Tunnels**
Excavations (Archeology) (May subdiv. geog.)   930.1
    See also **Mounds and mound builders**
    x Earthworks (Archeology); Ruins
    xx **Archeology; Cities and towns, Ruined, extinct,**
        etc.; Mounds and mound builders
Excavations (Archeology)—United States   973
    x United States—Excavations (Archeology)
Exceptional children   155.45
    See also **Brain damaged children; Emotionally**
        disturbed children; Gifted children; Handi-
        capped children; Mainstreaming in educa-
        tion; Slow learning children; Wild children
    x Abnormal children; Children, Abnormal;
        Children, Exceptional
    xx **Children; Elementary education**
Exchange   332.4; 332.64
    See also **Commerce; Foreign exchange; Money;**
        Stock exchange
    xx **Commerce**
Exchange, Barter. *See* **Barter**
Exchange, Foreign. *See* **Foreign exchange**
Exchange of persons programs   370.19
    See also headings for exchange programs for
        classes of persons, e.g. **Teacher exchange;**
        etc.
    x Cultural exchange programs; Interchange of
        visitors; Specialists exchange programs; Vis-
        itors' exchange programs
    xx **Cultural relations; International cooperation**
Exchange of prisoners of war. *See* **Prisoners of war**
Exchange of teachers. *See* **Teacher exchange**
Exchange rates. *See* **Foreign exchange**
Executions. *See* **Capital punishment**

Executive ability   658.4
    See also **Efficiency, Industrial; Leadership**
    x Administrative ability
    xx **Ability; Efficiency, Industrial**
Executive departments.   *See* names of countries,
        states, etc. with the subdivision *Executive*
        departments, e.g. **United States—Executive**
        departments; etc.
Executive departments—Reorganization.   *See*
        names of countries, states, etc. with the sub-
        division *Executive departments—*
        Reorganization, e.g. **United States—**
        Executive departments—Reorganization;
        etc.
Executive investigations.   *See* **Governmental investi-**
        gations
Executive power (May subdiv. geog.)   **351**
    Use for materials that discuss the duties, rights
        and abuses of the highest administrative au-
        thority of a country, often as compared or
        contrasted with the legislative power.
    See also **Heads of state; Monarchy; Presidents;**
        Prime ministers; Separation of powers
    x Presidents—Powers and duties
    xx **Constitutional law; Political science; Presi-**
        dents
Executive power—United States   353
    x Presidents—United States—Power; United
        States—Executive power
Executors and administrators   346.05
    See also **Wills**
    x Administrators and executors
    xx **Inheritance and succession; Wills**
Exegesis, Biblical.   *See* **Bible—Criticism, interpreta-**
        tion, etc.
Exercise   613.7
    See also **Bodybuilding; Gymnastics; Hatha yoga;**
        Physical education; Physical fitness; Reduc-
        ing; also names of special exercises and
        physical activities, e.g. **Aerobics; Rowing;**
        Weight lifting; etc.
    xx **Health; Hygiene; Physical education**
Exercise addiction   616.85
    x Addiction to exercise; Compulsive exercising
    xx **Compulsive behavior**
Exercises, Aerobic.   *See* **Aerobics**
Exercises, problems, etc.   *See* subjects with the sub-
        division *Problems, exercises, etc.,* for com-
        pilations of practice problems or exercises
        for use in the study of a topic, e.g. **Chemis-**
        try—Problems, exercises, etc.; etc.
Exercises, Reducing.   *See* **Reducing**
Exhaustion.   *See* **Fatigue**
Exhibitions
    See also **Craft shows; Fairs; Fashion shows;**
        Flower shows; also subjects with the subdi-
        vision *Exhibitions,* e.g. **Art—Exhibitions;**
        Printing—Exhibitions; etc.; and names of
        exhibitions, e.g. **Expo 92 (Seville, Spain);**
        etc.
    x Exhibits; Expositions; Industrial exhibitions;
        International exhibitions; World's fairs
    xx **Fairs**
Exhibits.   *See* **Exhibitions**

Exiles. *See* **Refugees**

Existentialism 142

　　xx **Metaphysics; Phenomenology; Philosophy, Modern**

Exobiology. *See* **Life on other planets; Space biology**

Exorcism 133.4; 291.3

　　See also **Demoniac possession; Demonology; Witchcraft**

　　xx **Demoniac possession; Demonology; Superstition**

Expanding universe. *See* **Universe**

Expeditions, Antarctic and Arctic. *See* names of expeditions, e.g. **Byrd Antarctic Expedition;** etc.

Expeditions, Scientific. *See* **Scientific expeditions**

Experience. *See* **Empiricism**

Experimental farms. *See* **Agricultural experiment stations**

Experimental films 791.43

　　x Avant-garde films; Motion pictures, Experimental; Personal films; Underground films

　　xx **Motion pictures**

Experimental methods in education. *See* **Education—Experimental methods**

Experimental psychology. *See* **Psychophysiology**

Experimental schools 371

　　Use for materials on schools in which new teaching methods, organizations of subject matter, educational theories, personnel practices, etc., are tested.

　　See also **Open plan schools**

　　x Alternative schools; Free schools; Nonformal schools; Project schools; Schools, Nonformal

　　xx **Education—Experimental methods; Open plan schools**

Experimental theater 792

　　x Avant-garde theater

　　xx **Theater**

Experimental universities. *See* **Free universities**

Experimentation on animals. *See* **Animal experimentation**

Experiments, Scientific. *See* **Science—Experiments;** and particular branches of science with the subdivision *Experiments,* for discussions about experiments and instructions for carrying them out, e.g. **Chemistry—Experiments;** etc.

Exploration. *See* **Discoveries (in geography)**

Exploration, Space. *See* **Outer space—Exploration**

Exploration, Submarine. *See* **Underwater exploration**

Exploration, Underwater. *See* **Underwater exploration**

Explorations. *See* **Discoveries (in geography); Explorers;** and names of places discovered or explored with the subdivision *Exploration,* e.g. **America—Exploration;** etc.; and names of countries sponsoring exploring expeditions with the subdivision *Exploring expeditions,* e.g. **United States—Exploring expeditions;** etc.

Explorer (Artificial satellite)   629.46
  xx **Artificial satellites**
Explorers   910.92; 920
      See also **Discoveries (in geography); Travelers;**
        Voyages and travels; also names of places
        explored with the subdivision *Exploration,*
        e.g. **America—Exploration;** etc.; also
        names of countries with the subdivisions
        Description and *Exploring expeditions,* e.g.
        United States—Exploring expeditions; etc.;
        and names of individual explorers
    x Discoverers; Explorations; Navigators; Voyag-
        ers
    xx **Adventure and adventurers; Discoveries (in ge-**
        ography); Heroes and heroines; Travelers;
        Voyages and travels
Exploring expeditions. *See* names of countries
        sponsoring exploring expeditions with the
        subdivision *Exploring expeditions,* e.g.
        United States—Exploring expeditions; etc.;
        and names of expeditions, e.g. **Lewis and**
        Clark Expedition (1804-1806); etc.
Explosions   904
    xx **Accidents**
Explosives   363.3; 623.4; 662
      See also types of explosives and explosive de-
        vices, e.g. **Ammunition; Dynamite; Gunpow-**
        der; Torpedoes; etc.
    xx **Chemistry**
Expo 92 (Seville, Spain)   909.82
    x Seville (Spain). World's Fair, 1992; World's
        Fair (1992 : Seville, Spain)
    xx **Exhibitions; Fairs**
Exports. *See* **Commerce; Tariff**
Expositions. *See* **Exhibitions**
Express highways   388.1; 625.7
    x Freeways; Interstate highways; Limited access
        highways; Motorways; Parkways; Super-
        highways; Toll roads; Turnpikes (Modern)
    xx **Roads; Traffic engineering**
Express service   388
      See also **Pony express**
    xx **Railroads; Transportation**
Expressionism (Art)   759.06
      See also **Postimpressionism (Art)**
    xx **Painting; Postimpressionism (Art)**
Expropriation. *See* **Eminent domain**
Extended care facilities. *See* **Long-term care facili-**
        ties
Extension work, Agricultural. *See* **Agricultural ex-**
        tension work
Extermination of Jews (1933-1945). *See* **Holocaust,**
        Jewish (1933-1945)
Extermination of pests. *See* **Pests—Control**
Extinct animals   560
      See also **Prehistoric animals; Rare animals;** also
        names of extinct animals, e.g. **Mastodon;**
        etc.
    x Animals, Extinct
    xx **Fossils; Prehistoric animals; Rare animals;**
        Wildlife
Extinct cities. *See* **Cities and towns, Ruined, ex-**
        tinct, etc.
Extinct plants. *See* **Plants, Fossil**

Extracurricular activities.   *See* **Student activities**
Extragalactic nebulae.   *See* **Galaxies**
Extramarital relationships.   *See* **Adultery**
Extrasensory perception   133.8
>   *See also* **Clairvoyance; Telepathy**
>   *x* E.S.P.; ESP
>   *xx* **Parapsychology**
Extraterrestrial bases   629.44
>   Use for materials on bases established on natural
>   extraterrestrial bodies for specific functions
>   other than colonization. Materials on com-
>   munities established in space or on natural
>   extraterrestrial bodies are entered under
>   **Space colonies.** Materials on manned instal-
>   lations orbiting in space for specific func-
>   tions, such as servicing space ships, are en-
>   tered under **Space stations.**
>   *See also* **Space colonies**
>   *xx* **Space colonies**
Extraterrestrial beings   574.999
>   *x* Aliens from outer space; Interplanetary visi-
>   tors
>   *xx* **Life on other planets**
Extraterrestrial communication.   *See* **Interstellar**
communication
Extraterrestrial environment.   *See* **Space environ-**
ment
Extraterrestrial life.   *See* **Life on other planets**
Extravehicular activity (Space flight)   629.45
>   *x* Space vehicles—Extravehicular activity;
>   Space walk; Walking in space
>   *xx* **Space flight**
Extremism (Political science).   *See* **Radicals and**
radicalism; Right and left (Political science)
Extremities, Artificial.   *See* **Artificial limbs**
Eye   611; 612.8
>   *See also* **Optometry; Vision**
>   *xx* **Face; Head; Optometry; Vision**
Eyeglasses   617.7; 681
>   *See also* kinds of eyeglasses, e.g. **Contact lenses;**
>   etc.
>   *x* Spectacles
F.M. radio.   *See* **Radio frequency modulation**
Fables   398.2
>   Use as a form heading for these short tales in-
>   tended to teach moral lessons, often with
>   animals or inanimate objects speaking and
>   acting like human beings, and usually with
>   the lesson stated briefly at the ending. May
>   also be used for materials about fables.
>   *See also* **Animals—Fiction; Folklore; Parables**
>   *x* Tales
>   *xx* **Allegories; Fiction; Folklore; Legends; Litera-**
>   **ture; Parables**
Fabrics   677
>   *See also* names and types of fabrics, e.g. **Linen;**
>   **Nylon; Synthetic fabrics;** etc.
>   *x* Cloth; Dry goods; Textiles
>   *xx* **Decorative arts**
Fabrics, Synthetic.   *See* **Synthetic fabrics**
Face   611; 612
>   *See also* **Eye; Nose; Physiognomy**
>   *xx* **Head; Physiognomy**
Facetiae.   *See* **Anecdotes; Wit and humor**

Facsimile transmission   384.1; 621.382
   x Fax; Telefax
   xx **Data transmission systems; Electronics; Tele-**
      communication
Factories   725
   See also kinds of factories, e.g. **Mills and mill-**
      work; etc.; also headings beginning with the
      word **Factory**
   x Industrial plants; Mill and factory buildings;
      Plants, Industrial
   xx **Industrial buildings; Mills and millwork**
Factories—Management.   *See* **Factory management**
Factories—Training departments.   *See* **Employ-**
      ees—Training
Factory and trade waste.   *See* **Industrial wastes**
Factory management   658.5
   Use for materials on the technical aspects of
      manufacturing processes. Materials on gen-
      eral principles of management of industries
      are entered under **Industrial management.**
   See also
   Efficiency, Industrial   Participative management
   Job analysis   Personnel management
   Motion study   Supervisors
   Office management   Time study
   x Factories—Management; Production engi-
      neering; Shop management
   xx **Efficiency, Industrial; Industrial management;**
      Management; Personnel management
Factory schools.   *See* **Employees—Training**
Factory waste.   *See* **Industrial wastes**
Factory workers.   *See* **Labor**
Facts, Miscellaneous.   *See* **Curiosities and wonders**
Faculty (Education).   *See* **Colleges and universi-**
      ties—Faculty; Educators; Teachers
Faience.   *See* **Pottery**
Failure in business.   *See* **Bankruptcy; Business fail-**
      ures
Failure of banks.   *See* **Bank failures**
Failure to thrive syndrome.   *See* **Growth disorders**
Failures, Structural.   *See* **Structural failures**
Fair employment practice.   *See* **Discrimination in**
      employment
Fair housing.   *See* **Discrimination in housing**
Fair trade.   *See* **Unfair competition**
Fair trade (Tariff).   *See* **Free trade and protection**
Fair trial and free press.   *See* **Freedom of the press**
      and fair trial
Fair use (Copyright)   341.7
   xx **Copyright**
Fairies   398.21
   See also **Fairy tales**
   x Elves; Gnomes; Goblins
   xx **Folklore; Superstition**
Fairness doctrine (Broadcasting)   384.54; 384.55
   Use for materials on the requirement that, if one
      side of a controversial issue is aired, the
      other side must have the same opportunity.
   See also **Equal time rule (Broadcasting)**
   x Doctrine of fairness (Broadcasting)
   xx **Equal time rule (Broadcasting); Radio broad-**
      casting; Television broadcasting; Television
      in politics

Fairs 381; 607.4; 907.4

> Use for general materials on public showings
> that suggest a variety of kinds of display and
> entertainment, usually in an outdoor setting,
> sometimes for the promotion of sales and
> sometimes in competition for prizes of ex-
> cellence.

> *See also* **Exhibitions; Markets;** also names of
> fairs, e.g. **Expo 92 (Seville, Spain);** etc.

> *x* Bazaars; Trade fairs; World's fairs

> *xx* **Exhibitions; Markets**

**Fairy tales 398.21; 808.83; 813, etc.; 813.008, etc.
Fic**

> Use as a form heading for short, simple narra-
> tives, often of folk origin and usually in-
> tended for children, involving fantastic
> forces and magical beings such as dragons,
> elves, fairies, goblins, witches, and wizards.
> May also be used for materials about fairy
> tales.

> *See also* **Fantastic fiction; Folklore**

> *x* Children's stories; Stories; Tales

> *xx* **Children's literature; Fairies; Fantastic fiction;
> Fiction; Folklore; Legends; Literature**

Faith 234

> Use for materials on religious belief and doubt.
> Materials on belief and doubt from the
> philosophical standpoint are entered under
> **Belief and doubt.**

> *See also* **Agnosticism; Atheism; Hope; Skepti-
> cism; Truth**

> *x* Religious belief

> *xx* **Religion; Salvation; Spiritual life; Theology**

Faith, Confessions of. *See* **Creeds**

Faith cure. *See* **Spiritual healing**

Faith healing. *See* **Spiritual healing**

Faith—Psychology 200.1; 248; 253.5

> *xx* **Psychology, Religious**

Faithfulness. *See* **Loyalty**

Falconry 799.2

> *x* Hawking

> *xx* **Game and game birds; Hunting**

Fall. *See* **Autumn**

Fallacies. *See* **Errors; Logic**

Falling stars. *See* **Meteors**

Fallout, Radioactive. *See* **Radioactive fallout**

Fallout shelters. *See* **Air raid shelters**

False advertising. *See* **Deceptive advertising**

Falsehood. *See* **Truthfulness and falsehood**

Families, Dual career. *See* **Dual career family**

Families, Nonrelated. *See* **Shared housing**

Family (May subdiv. geog.) **306.85**

> Use for materials stressing the sociological con-
> cept and structure of the family. Materials
> stressing the everyday life, interaction, and
> relationships of family members are entered
> under **Family life.**

> *See also*

Birth order	**Dual career family**
Brothers and sisters	**Eugenics**
Clans	**Family life**
Divorce	**Family reunions**
Domestic relations	**Family size**

276

Family—*Continued*
  Farm family   Parent and child
  Grandparent and child   Single parent family
  Home   Stepfamily
  Husbands   Widowers
  Marriage   Widows
  Married people   Wives
    also names of members of the family, e.g. **Chil-
       dren; Fathers; Mothers;** etc.
  xx **Domestic relations; Family reunions; Home;
       Human relations; Marriage; Sociology**
Family budget. *See* **Budgets, Household**
Family devotions. *See* **Devotional exercises; Fami-
       ly—Religious life**
Family farms   338.1; 630
  See also **Farm family; Farm life**
  xx **Agriculture; Farm family; Farm life; Farms**
Family finance. *See* **Personal finance**
Family histories. *See* **Genealogy**
Family life   306.85; 392; 646.7
    See note under **Family.**
  x Family relations; Home life
  xx **Family**
Family life education   306.85; 362.82; 372.82
  See also **Home economics; Human relations;
       Marriage counseling; Sex education**
  xx **Human relations**
Family names. *See* **Personal names**
Family planning. *See* **Birth control**
Family prayers. *See* **Devotional exercises; Family—
       Religious life**
Family relations. *See* **Domestic relations; Family
       life**
Family—Religious life   249
  x Family devotions; Family prayers; Family
       worship
  xx **Religious life**
Family reunions   394.2
  See also **Family**
  x Reunions, Family
  xx **Family**
Family size   304.6
  See also **Birth control; Childlessness; Only child**
  xx **Birth control; Family**
Family social work. *See* **Social case work**
Family trees. *See* **Genealogy**
Family—United States   306.850973
Family violence   362.82
  See also **Child abuse; Elderly abuse; Husband
       abuse; Wife abuse**
  x Domestic violence; Household violence
  xx **Violence**
Family worship. *See* **Family—Religious life**
Famines (May subdiv. geog.)   **904**
  xx **Food supply; Starvation**
Famines—United States   363.80973; 973
  x United States—Famines
Famous people. *See* **Celebrities**
Fanaticism   152.4; 200.1; 303
  See also **Asceticism**
  x Intolerance
Fancy dress. *See* **Costume**
Fans   391
  xx **Costume**

Fantastic fiction   808.83; 809.3; 813, etc.; Fic
>   Use for collections of and materials on imagina-
>   tive fiction with strange settings, grotesque
>   or fanciful characters, and supernatural or
>   unnatural events or forces.
>   *See also* **Fairy tales; Science fiction**
>   *x* Fantasy (Fiction)
>   *xx* **Fairy tales; Fiction**

Fantasy   154.3
>   *See also* **Hallucinations and illusions**
>   *x* Day dreams
>   *xx* **Dreams; Imagination**

Fantasy (Fiction).   *See* **Fantastic fiction**

Far East.   *See* **East Asia**

Far north.   *See* **Arctic regions**

Farm animals.   *See* **Domestic animals; Livestock**

Farm buildings   631.2; 728
>   *See also* names of specific farm buildings, e.g.
>   **Barns;** etc.
>   *x* Architecture, Rural; Buildings, Farm; Rural
>   architecture
>   *xx* **Architecture; Architecture, Domestic; Build-
>   ings**

Farm corporations.   *See* **Agribusiness**

Farm credit.   *See* **Agricultural credit**

Farm crops.   *See* **Farm produce**

Farm engines   631.3
>   *See also* **Agricultural engineering; Tractors**
>   *xx* **Agricultural machinery; Engines; Gas and oil
>   engines; Steam engines**

Farm family   306.85
>   *See also* **Family farms; Farm life; Sociology, Ru-
>   ral**
>   *xx* **Family; Family farms; Farm life; Sociology,
>   Rural**

Farm implements.   *See* **Agricultural machinery**

Farm laborers.   *See* **Agricultural laborers**

Farm life (May subdiv. geog.)   306.3; 630
>   *See also* **Family farms; Farm family; Ranch life;
>   Sociology, Rural**
>   *x* Rural life
>   *xx* **Country life; Family farms; Farm family;
>   Farmers; Sociology, Rural**

Farm life—United States   306.3; 630
>   *x* United States—Farm life

Farm machinery.   *See* **Agricultural machinery**

Farm management   630
>   *See also* **Agriculture—Economic aspects**
>   *xx* **Agriculture—Economic aspects; Farms; Man-
>   agement**

Farm mechanics.   *See* **Agricultural engineering; Agricultural machinery**

Farm produce   338.1; 630; 631.5
>   *See also* names of farm products, e.g. **Hay;** etc.
>   *x* Agricultural products; Crops; Farm crops
>   *xx* **Food; Raw materials**

Farm produce—Marketing   338.1
>   *See also* **Agriculture—Economic aspects**
>   *x* Fruit—Marketing; Marketing of farm pro-
>   duce; Vegetables—Marketing
>   *xx* **Agriculture—Economic aspects; Marketing;
>   Prices**

Farm tenancy   333.5
>
> Use for materials on the economic and social as-
> pects of farm tenancy. Materials dealing
> with the legal aspects are entered under
> **Landlord and tenant.**
>
> *x* Agriculture—Tenant farming; Farming on
> shares; Sharecropping; Tenant farming
>
> *xx* **Farms; Land tenure; Landlord and tenant**

Farmers   630.92; 920
> *See also* **Farm life**
>
> *xx* **Agriculture; Country life**

Farmers' cooperatives.   *See* **Agriculture, Cooperative**

Farming.   *See* **Agriculture**

Farming corporations.   *See* **Agribusiness**

Farming, Dry.   *See* **Dry farming**

Farming on shares.   *See* **Farm tenancy**

Farms   333.76; 630; 636
> *See also* **Family farms; Farm management; Farm
> tenancy**
>
> *xx* **Agriculture; Land use; Real estate**

Farms, Experimental.   *See* **Agricultural experiment
stations**

Farriering.   *See* **Blacksmithing**

Fascism (May subdiv. geog.)   **320.5; 321.9; 355.6**
> Use for materials on the political philosophy,
> movement or regime that advocates a cen-
> tralized autocratic government, severe eco-
> nomic and social regimentation, and the ex-
> altation of nation and race over the
> individual. Materials on fascism in Ger-
> many during the Nazi regime are entered
> under **National socialism.**
>
> *See also* **National socialism**
>
> *x* Authoritarianism; Neo-fascism; Neo-nazism
>
> *xx* **National socialism; Totalitarianism**

Fascism—Germany   320.5; 943.086
> *See also* **National socialism**

Fascism—United States   320.5; 973.9
> *x* United States—Fascism

Fashion   391
> Use for materials describing the prevailing mode
> or style of dress. Descriptive and historical
> materials on the costume of particular coun-
> tries, periods, or peoples and materials on
> fancy dress and theatrical costumes are en-
> tered under **Costume.** Materials dealing
> with clothing from a practical standpoint,
> including the art of dress, are entered under
> **Clothing and dress.**
>
> *See also* **Clothing and dress; Costume; Dress-
> making; Tailoring**
>
> *x* Style in dress
>
> *xx* **Clothing and dress; Costume**

Fashion design   746.9
> *x* Costume design
>
> *xx* **Commercial art; Design**

Fashion models.   *See* **Models, Fashion**

Fashion shows   391.074; 659.1
> *xx* **Exhibitions**

Fashionable society.   *See* **Upper classes**

Fast breeder reactors.   *See* **Nuclear reactors**

Fast foods.   *See* **Convenience foods**

Faster reading.   *See* **Rapid reading**

Fasting   178
>   *See also* **Asceticism; Fasts and feasts; Hunger; Hunger strikes; Starvation**
>   *x* Abstinence
>   *xx* **Hunger; Starvation**

Fasts and feasts   263; 394.2
>   Use for materials on religious fasts and feasts in general and on Christian fasts and feasts. May be subdivided by religion, e.g. **Fasts and feasts—Judaism;** etc. Materials on secular festivals are entered under **Festivals.**
>   *See also* **Christmas; Easter; Festivals; Good Friday; Holidays; Lent; Thanksgiving Day;** also names of individual fasts and feasts
>   *x* Church festivals; Days; Ecclesiastical fasts and feasts; Feasts; Fiestas; Holy days; Religious festivals
>   *xx* **Fasting; Festivals; Holidays; Rites and ceremonies**

Fasts and feasts—Judaism   296.4
>   *See also* names of individual fasts and feasts, e.g. **Hanukkah; Passover; Yom Kippur;** etc.
>   *x* Festivals—Jews; Holidays, Jewish; Jewish holidays; Jews—Festivals
>   *xx* **Judaism**

Fat.   *See* **Oils and fats**
Fatally ill children.   *See* **Terminally ill children**
Fatally ill patients.   *See* **Terminally ill**

Fate and fatalism   149
>   *See also* **Free will and determinism; Predestination**
>   *x* Destiny; Fortune
>   *xx* **Philosophy**

Father and child   306.874
>   *See also* **Fathers and daughters; Fathers and sons**
>   *x* Child and father; Father-child relationship
>   *xx* **Parent and child**

Father-child relationship.   *See* **Father and child**

Fathers   306.8
>   *See also* **Teenage fathers; Unmarried fathers**
>   *xx* **Family; Homemakers; Men**

Fathers and daughters   306.874
>   *x* Daughters and fathers
>   *xx* **Father and child; Girls**

Fathers and sons   306.874
>   *x* Sons and fathers
>   *xx* **Boys; Father and child**

Fathers, Single parent.   *See* **Single parent family**

Fatigue   152.1; 612; 613.7
>   *See also* **Jet lag; Rest**
>   *x* Exhaustion; Weariness
>   *xx* **Physiology; Rest**

Fatness.   *See* **Obesity**
Fats.   *See* **Oils and fats**
Fauna.   *See* **Animals; Zoology**
Fawns.   *See* **Deer**
Fax.   *See* **Facsimile transmission**
Fayence.   *See* **Pottery**

Fear   152.4
>   *See also* **Horror; Phobias; Separation anxiety in children**
>   *x* Anxiety

Fear—*Continued*

    xx **Courage; Emotions; Nervous system—
       Diseases; Neuroses**

Feast of Dedication. *See* **Hanukkah**

Feast of Lights. *See* **Hanukkah**

Feasts. *See* **Fasts and feasts**

Fecundity. *See* **Fertility**

Federal aid to education 379.1

    Use same pattern for federal aid to other sub-
      jects.

    x Education—Federal aid

    xx **Colleges and universities—Finance; Educa-
       tion—Finance; Education—Government
       policy; Grants-in-aid**

Federal aid to libraries 021.8

    x Libraries—Federal aid

    xx **Grants-in-aid; Libraries—Government policy;
       Library finance**

Federal budget. *See* **Budget—United States**

Federal-city relations 351.09

    x City-federal relations; Federal-municipal rela-
      tions; Municipal-federal relations; Urban-
      federal relations

    xx **Federal government; Municipal government**

Federal courts. *See* **Courts—United States**

Federal debt. *See* **Public debts**

Federal debt—United States. *See* **Public debts—
    United States**

Federal government 351

    See also **Democracy; European federation; Feder-
      al-city relations; Federal-state relations;
      State governments**

    x Confederacies; Federalism

    xx **Constitutional law; Democracy; Political sci-
      ence; Republics; State governments**

Federal grants. *See* **Grants-in-aid**

Federal-Indian relations. *See* **Indians of North
    America—Government policy**

Federal libraries. *See* **Government libraries**

Federal-municipal relations. *See* **Federal-city rela-
    tions**

Federal Reserve banks 332.1

    xx **Banks and banking**

Federal revenue sharing. *See* **Revenue sharing**

Federal spending policy. *See* **United States—
    Appropriations and expenditures**

Federal-state relations 351.09; 353.9

    x State-federal relations

    xx **Federal government; State governments**

Federal-state tax relations. *See* **Intergovernmental
    tax relations**

Federalism. *See* **Federal government**

Federation, International. *See* **International organi-
    zation**

Federation of Europe. *See* **European federation**

Feedback control systems 629.8

    See also **Servomechanisms**

    xx **Automation**

Feedback (Psychology) 153.1

    See also **Biofeedback training**

    xx **Learning, Psychology of**

Feeding behavior in animals. *See* **Animals—Food**

Feeds   633.2; 633.3
>   *See also* **Forage plants; Hay; Root crops; Silage and silos;** also names of feeds, e.g. **Oats;** etc.
>   *x* Fodder
>   *xx* **Grasses; Hay; Root crops**

Feeling.   *See* **Perception; Touch**
Feelings.   *See* **Emotions**
Feet.   *See* **Foot**
Fellowships.   *See* **Scholarships, fellowships, etc.**
Felony.   *See* **Crime**
Female climacteric.   *See* **Menopause**
Female role.   *See* **Sex role**
Feminine psychology.   *See* **Women—Psychology**
Femininity of God   212; 231
>   *x* God—Femininity
>   *xx* **God**

Feminism   305.42; 323.3
>   *See also* **Women—Civil rights; Women's movement**
>   *x* Women—Rights; Women's rights
>   *xx* **Women—Civil rights; Women's movement**

Fencing   796.8
>   *x* Fighting
>   *xx* **Physical education**

Feral animals.   *See* **Wildlife**
Feral children.   *See* **Wild children**
Fermentation   547; 663
>   *See also* **Bacteriology; Wine and wine making; Yeast**
>   *xx* **Bacteriology; Chemistry; Enzymes; Wine and wine making**

Ferns   587; 635.9
>   *xx* **Plants**

Fertility   574.1; 591.1
>   Use for general materials on fertility in animals, including humans. Materials limited to fertility in humans are entered under **Fertility, Human.**
>   *See also* **Infertility**
>   *x* Fecundity
>   *xx* **Infertility; Reproduction**

Fertility control.   *See* **Birth control**
Fertility, Human   304.6; 612.6; 616.6
>   See note under **Fertility.**
>   *See also* **Birth control; Childlessness; Infertility; Population**
>   *x* Human fertility
>   *xx* **Birth control; Birthrate; Population**

Fertilization in vitro   176; 618.1; 636.089
>   *x* Ectogenesis, Preimplantational; Fertilization in vitro, Human; Fertilization, Laboratory; Fertilization, Test tube; In vitro fertilization; Laboratory fertilization; Preimplantational ectogenesis; Test tube babies; Test tube fertilization
>   *xx* **Embryology; Genetic engineering; Reproduction**

Fertilization in vitro, Human.   *See* **Fertilization in vitro**
Fertilization, Laboratory.   *See* **Fertilization in vitro**
Fertilization of plants   581.1
>   *x* Plants—Fertilization; Pollination

Fertilization of plants—*Continued*
    xx **Flowers; Insects; Plant breeding; Plant physiology; Plants**
Fertilization, Test tube. *See* **Fertilization in vitro**
Fertilizers and manures   **631.8; 668**
    See also **Compost; Lime; Nitrates; Phosphates; Potash**
    x Manures
    xx **Agricultural chemicals; Soils**
Festivals (May subdiv. geog.)   **394.2**
    See note under **Fasts and feasts.**
    See also **Fasts and feasts; Film festivals; Holidays; Pageants;** also names of types of festivals, e.g. **Craft shows; Music festivals;** etc.
    x Carnivals; Days; Fiestas
    xx **Fasts and feasts; Manners and customs; Pageants**
Festivals—Jews. *See* **Fasts and feasts—Judaism**
Festivals—United States   **394.2**
    x United States—Festivals
Fetal death. *See* **Abortion; Miscarriage**
Fetus   **574.3; 612.6**
    x Unborn child
    xx **Embryology; Reproduction**
Fetus—Growth retardation. *See* **Growth disorders**
Feudalism   **321**
    See also **Chivalry; Clans; Middle Ages; Peasantry**
    x Fiefs; Vassals
    xx **Chivalry; Civilization, Medieval; Land tenure; Land use; Middle Ages—History**
Fever   **616**
    See also **Body temperature;** also names of fevers, e.g. **Malaria;** etc.
    xx **Body temperature; Pathology**
Fiat money. *See* **Paper money**
Fiber content of food. *See* **Food—Fiber content**
Fiber glass. *See* **Glass fibers**
Fibers   **677**
    See also **Cotton; Flax; Hemp; Linen; Paper; Silk; Wool**
    x Textile fibers
Fibers, Glass. *See* **Glass fibers**
Fiction   **808.3**
    Use for fiction as a literary form.
    See also

Allegories	**Plots (Drama, fiction, etc.)**
Fables	**Romances**
Fairy tales	**Romanticism**
Folklore	**Short stories**
Humorous stories	**Short story**
Legends	**United States—Fiction**
Plot-your-own stories	

    also **American fiction; English fiction;** etc.; and persons, places and subjects with the subdivision *Fiction,* e.g. **Animals—Fiction; Slavery—United States—Fiction; Napoleon I, Emperor of the French, 1769-1821—Fiction; United States—Fiction;** etc.; and phrase headings that do not lend themselves to the subdivided format, e.g. **Fantastic fiction; Historical fiction; Love stories; Mystery and detective stories; Science fiction;** etc.

Fiction—*Continued*
    x Novels; Stories
    xx **Literature**
Fiction, American. *See* **American fiction**
Fiction, English. *See* **English fiction**
Fiction, Historical. *See* **Historical fiction**
Fiction—History and criticism 809.3
Fiction—Plots. *See* **Plots (Drama, fiction, etc.)**
Fiction—Technique 808.3
    xx **Authorship**
Fictitious animals. *See* **Mythical animals**
Fictitious names. *See* **Pseudonyms**
Fictitious places. *See* **Geographical myths**
Fiddle. *See* **Violin**
Fiefs. *See* **Feudalism; Land tenure**
Field athletics. *See* **Track athletics**
Field hockey 796.35
    x Hockey
Field hospitals. *See* **Medicine, Military; Military hospitals**
Field photography. *See* **Outdoor photography**
Field trips 069; 371.3
    x School excursions; School trips
Fiestas. *See* **Fasts and feasts; Festivals**
Fifteenth century 909.07; 909.08
    See note under **Nineteenth century.**
    x 1400-1499 (15th century)
    xx **Middle Ages; Renaissance**
Fifth column. *See* **Subversive activities; World War, 1939-1945—Collaborationists**
Fighting. *See* **Battles; Boxing; Bullfights; Dueling; Fencing; Gladiators; Military art and science; Naval art and science; Self-defense; Self-defense for women; War**
Figure drawing 743
    See also **Figure painting**
    x Human figure in art
    xx **Anatomy, Artistic; Drawing; Figure painting**
Figure painting 757
    See also **Figure drawing; Portrait painting**
    x Human figure in art
    xx **Anatomy, Artistic; Figure drawing; Painting; Portrait painting**
Figure skating. *See* **Ice skating; Roller skating**
Files and filing 025.3; 651.5
    See also **Indexing**
    x Alphabetizing; Filing systems
    xx **Indexing; Office management**
Filing systems. *See* **Files and filing**
Filling stations. *See* **Automobiles—Service stations**
Fills (Earthwork). *See* **Landfills**
Film adaptations 791.43
    x Adaptations; Adaptations, Film; Books, Filmed; Filmed books; Films from books; Literature—Film and video adaptations; Motion picture adaptations
    xx **Motion pictures**
Film direction. *See* **Motion pictures—Production and direction**
Film festivals 791.43
    x Motion picture festivals; Movie festivals
    xx **Festivals**
Film industry (Motion pictures). *See* **Motion picture industry**

Film production. *See* **Motion pictures—Production and direction**
Film projectors. *See* **Projectors**
Filmed books. *See* **Film adaptations**
Filmmaking. *See* **Motion pictures—Production and direction**
Filmography. *See* **Motion pictures;** and subjects and names of individuals with the subdivision *Filmography,* e.g. **Animals—Filmography; Shakespeare, William, 1564-1616—Filmography;** etc.
Films. *See* **Filmstrips; Microfilms; Motion pictures**
Films, Amateur. *See* **Amateur films**
Films from books. *See* **Film adaptations**
Filmstrips   371.3; 778.2
>   *See also* **Slides (Photography)**
>   *x* Films; Strip films
>   *xx* **Audiovisual materials; Photography; Slides (Photography)**
Finance (May subdiv. geog.)   **332; 336**
>   *See also*

Bankruptcy	**Internal revenue**
Banks and banking	**Investments**
Bonds	**Metropolitan finance**
Budget	**Monetary policy**
Capital	**Money**
Church finance	**Municipal finance**
Commerce	**Paper money**
Credit	**Personal finance**
Deficit financing	**Prices**
Fiscal policy	**Public debts**
Foreign exchange	**Securities**
Government lending	**Speculation**
Income	**Stock exchange**
Income tax	**Tariff**
Inflation (Finance)	**Taxation**
Insurance	**Wealth**
Interest (Economics)	

>   also subjects with the subdivision *Finance,* e.g. **Education—Finance;** etc.
>   *x* Finance, Public; Funds; Public finance
>   *xx* **Budget; Economics; Monetary policy**
Finance, Church. *See* **Church finance**
Finance, Household. *See* **Budgets, Household**
Finance, Municipal. *See* **Municipal finance**
Finance, Personal. *See* **Personal finance**
Finance, Public. *See* **Finance**
Finance—United States   336.73
>   *x* United States—Finance
Financial accounting. *See* **Accounting**
Financial planning, Personal. *See* **Personal finance**
Financiers. *See* **Capitalists and financiers**
Finding things. *See* **Lost and found possessions**
Fine arts. *See* **Arts**
Finger alphabet. *See* **Deaf—Means of communication**
Finger games. *See* **Finger play**
Finger marks. *See* **Fingerprints**
Finger painting   751.4
>   *x* Painting, Finger
>   *xx* **Child artists; Painting**
Finger play   796.1
>   *x* Finger games
>   *xx* **Play**

Finger pressure therapy. *See* **Acupressure**

Finger prints. *See* **Fingerprints**

Fingerprints 363.2

    x Finger marks; Finger prints

    xx **Anthropometry; Criminal investigation; Crimi-
nals—Identification; Identification**

Finishes and finishing. *See* **Lacquer and lacquering;
Paint; Painting, Industrial; Varnish and varnishing; Wood finishing**

Finno-Russian War, 1939-1940. *See* **Russo-Finnish
War, 1939-1940**

Fire 536

    See also **Combustion; Fires; Fuel; Heat; Heating**

    xx **Chemistry; Combustion; Heat**

Fire balls. *See* **Meteors**

Fire bombs. *See* **Incendiary bombs**

Fire departments 628.9

    x Fire stations

Fire engines 628.9

    xx **Engines; Fire fighting**

Fire fighters 363.3092; 920

    x Firemen and firewomen

Fire fighting 628.9

    See also **Fire engines**

    xx **Fire prevention; Fires**

Fire insurance 368.1

    See also **Fireproofing**

    x Insurance, Fire

    xx **Fires; Insurance**

Fire prevention (May subdiv. geog.) **363.37**

    See also **Fire fighting; Fireproofing;** also types of
institutions, buildings, industries, and vehicles with the subdivision *Fires and fire prevention,* e.g. **Nuclear power plants—Fires
and fire prevention;** etc.

    x Prevention of fire

    xx **Fires**

Fire stations. *See* **Fire departments**

Firearms 623.4; 739.7

    See also **Gunpowder; Ordnance; Shooting;** also
types of firearms, e.g. **Pistols; Rifles; Shotguns;** etc.

    x Guns; Small arms; Weapons and weaponry

    xx **Arms and armor; Shooting**

Firearms—Control. *See* **Firearms—Law and legislation**

Firearms industry 338.4; 683.4

    Use for materials on the small arms industry.
Materials on heavy firearms are entered under **Ordnance.**

    x Firearms industry and trade; Firearms trade;
Gunsmithing

    xx **Munitions**

Firearms industry and trade. *See* **Firearms industry**

Firearms—Law and legislation 344

    x Firearms—Control; Gun control; Guns—
Control

Firearms trade. *See* **Firearms industry**

Firemen and firewomen. *See* **Fire fighters**

Fireplaces 697; 749

    See also **Chimneys**

    xx **Architecture—Details; Heating; Space heaters**

Fireproofing 628.9; 693.8

    xx **Fire insurance; Fire prevention**

Fires (May subdiv. geog.) **363.37; 904**

See also **Fire fighting; Fire insurance; Fire prevention; Forest fires;** also types of institutions, buildings, industries, and vehicles with the subdivision *Fires and fire prevention,* e.g. **Nuclear power plants—Fires and fire prevention;** etc.

xx **Accidents; Disasters; Fire**

Fireworks **662**

First aid **616.02**

See also **Accidents; Artificial respiration; Bandages and bandaging; Cardiac resuscitation; Lifesaving**

x Emergencies; Injuries; Wounded, First aid to

xx **Accidents; Health self-care; Home accidents; Lifesaving; Medicine, Military; Military hospitals; Nursing; Rescue work; Sick**

First editions. *See* **Bibliography—First editions**

First generation children. *See* **Children of immigrants**

First ladies—United States. *See* **Presidents— United States—Spouses**

Firstborn child. *See* **Birth order**

Fiscal policy (May subdiv. geog.) **336.3**

See also **Monetary policy**

xx **Economic policy; Finance; Monetary policy**

Fiscal policy—United States **336.73**

x United States—Fiscal policy

Fish. *See* **Fishes**

Fish as food **641.3**

See also **Seafood**

xx **Fishes; Food; Seafood**

Fish culture **639.3**

See also **Aquariums**

x Fish farming; Fish hatcheries

xx **Aquaculture; Aquariums; Fishes**

Fish farming. *See* **Fish culture**

Fish hatcheries. *See* **Fish culture**

Fisheries (May subdiv. geog.) **338.3; 639.2**

Use for materials on the fishing industry.

See also **Pearlfisheries; Whaling**

x Fishing industry; Sea fisheries

xx **Fishes; Marine resources; Natural resources**

Fisheries—United States **338.3; 639.2**

x United States—Fisheries

Fishes (May subdiv. geog.) **597**

Names of all fishes are not included in this List but are to be added as needed.

See also **Aquariums; Fish as food; Fish culture; Fisheries; Fishing; Tropical fish;** also names of fishes, e.g. **Salmon;** etc.

x Fish; Ichthyology

xx **Marine animals; Vertebrates**

Fishes—Geographical distribution **597.09**

xx **Biogeography**

Fishes—Photography. *See* **Photography of fishes**

Fishes—United States **597.0973**

x United States—Fishes

Fishing (May subdiv. geog.) **799.1**

Use for materials on fishing as a sport. Materials on fishing as an industry are entered under **Fisheries.**

See also **Artificial flies;** also types of fishing, e.g.

Fishing—*Continued*

>> Fly casting; Spear fishing; Trout fishing; etc.

> *x* Angling
> *xx* **Fishes; Water sports**

Fishing—Equipment and supplies   799.1
> *x* Fishing tackle

Fishing flies.   *See* **Artificial flies**

Fishing industry.   *See* **Fisheries**

Fishing tackle.   *See* **Fishing—Equipment and supplies**

Fishing—United States   799.10973
> *x* United States—Fishing

Five-day work week.   *See* **Hours of labor**

Flags (May subdiv. geog.)   **929.9**
> *See also* **Signals and signaling**
> *x* Banners; Ensigns
> *xx* **Heraldry; Signals and signaling**

Flags—United States   929.9
> *x* American flag; United States—Flags

Flats.   *See* **Apartment houses**

Flatware, Silver.   *See* **Silverware**

Flavoring essences   664
> *xx* **Cookery; Essences and essential oils; Food**

Flax   633.5; 677
> *See also* **Linen**
> *xx* **Fibers; Linen; Yarn**

Flexible hours of labor.   *See* **Hours of labor**

Flexiplace.   *See* **Telecommuting**

Flexitime.   *See* **Hours of labor**

Flies   595.77
> *See also* names of flies, e.g. **Fruit flies;** etc.
> *x* Diptera; Fly; House flies
> *xx* **Household pests; Insects as carriers of disease; Pests**

Flies, Artificial.   *See* **Artificial flies**

Flight   629.132
> *See also* **Aeronautics**
> *x* Flying; Locomotion
> *xx* **Aeronautics**

Flight attendants.   *See* **Airlines—Flight attendants**

Flight to the moon.   *See* **Space flight to the moon**

Flight training.   *See* **Aeronautics—Study and teaching; Airplanes—Piloting**

Flights around the world.   *See* **Aeronautics—Flights**

Flint implements.   *See* **Stone implements**

Floating hospitals.   *See* **Hospital ships**

Floats (Parades).   *See* **Parades**

Flood control   627
> *See also* **Dams; Forest influences; Rivers**
> *x* Flood prevention; Floods—Control
> *xx* **Forest influences; Hydraulic engineering**

Flood prevention.   *See* **Flood control**

Floods (May subdiv. geog. by countries, states, cities, etc. and by rivers)   **551.48; 904**
> *See also* **Reclamation of land; Rivers**
> *xx* **Meteorology; Natural disasters; Rain; Rivers; Water**

Floods and forests.   *See* **Forest influences**

Floods—Control.   *See* **Flood control**

Floors   694; 721
> *xx* **Architecture—Details; Building; Carpentry**

Flora.   *See* **Botany; Plants**

Floral decoration.   *See* **Flower arrangement**

Floriculture. *See* **Flower gardening**
Florists' designs. *See* **Flower arrangement**
Flour   664
>   *See also* **Grain; Wheat**
>   *x* Breadstuffs
>   *xx* **Wheat**
Flour mills   664
>   *x* Grist mills; Milling (Flour)
>   *xx* **Mills and millwork**
Flow charts. *See* **Graphic methods; System analysis**
Flow charts (Computer science). *See* **Programming (Computers)**
Flowcharting. *See* **Graphic methods; System analysis**
Flowcharting (Computer science). *See* **Programming (Computers)**
Flower arrangement   745.92
>   Use for materials on the artistic arrangement of flowers, including decoration of houses, churches, etc. with flowers.
>   *x* Designs, Floral; Floral decoration; Florists' designs; Flowers—Arrangement
>   *xx* **Decoration and ornament; Flowers; Table setting and decoration**
Flower drying   745.92
>   *x* Dried flowers; Flowers, Drying
>   *xx* **Plants—Collection and preservation**
Flower gardening   635.9
>   Use for practical materials on the cultivation of flowering plants for either commercial or private purposes.
>   *See also*

Annuals (Plants)	**Ornamental plants**
Bulbs	**Perennials**
Flowers	**Plant breeding**
Greenhouses	**Plant propagation**
House plants	**Window gardening**

>   also names of flowers, e.g. **Roses;** etc.
>   *x* Floriculture
>   *xx* **Botany; Flowers; Gardening; Horticulture; Plants**
Flower painting and illustration   758
>   *x* Flowers in art
>   *xx* **Flowers; Painting; Plants in art**
Flower shows   635.9074
>   *x* Flowers—Exhibitions
>   *xx* **Exhibitions**
Flowers (May subdiv. geog.)   **582.13**
>   Use for general materials on the botanical characteristics of flowers, guides for studying and classifying them or for the study of flowers from the artistic point of view. Materials limited to the cultivation of flowers are entered under **Flower gardening.**
>   Names of all flowers are not included in this List but are to be added as needed, in the plural form, e.g. **Roses;** etc.
>   *See also*

Annuals (Plants)	tration
Fertilization of plants	**Perennials**
Flower arrangement	**State flowers**
Flower gardening	**Wild flowers**
Flower painting and illus-	**Window gardening**

289

Flowers—*Continued*

    also names of flowers, e.g. **Roses;** etc.

    xx **Botany; Flower gardening; Plants**

Flowers—Arrangement. *See* **Flower arrangement**

Flowers, Artificial. *See* **Artificial flowers**

Flowers, Drying. *See* **Flower drying**

Flowers—Exhibitions. *See* **Flower shows**

Flowers in art. *See* **Flower painting and illustration;**
    Plants in art

Flowers, State. *See* **State flowers**

Flowers—United States 582.13

    x United States—Flowers

Flowers, Wild. *See* **Wild flowers**

Flu. *See* **Influenza**

Fluid mechanics 532; 620.1

    Use for materials on the branch of mechanics
        dealing with the properties of liquids or
        gases, either at rest or in motion.

    See also **Gases; Hydraulic engineering; Hydrau-**
        lics; Hydrodynamics; Hydrostatics; Liquids

    x Hydromechanics

    xx **Mechanics**

Fluorescent lighting 621.32

    x Electric lighting, Fluorescent; Light, Electric

    xx **Lighting**

Fluoridation of water. *See* **Water—Fluoridation**

Flute 788.3

    xx **Wind instruments**

Fly. *See* **Flies**

Fly casting 799.1

    xx **Artificial flies; Fishing**

Flying. *See* **Flight**

Flying bombs. *See* **Guided missiles**

Flying saucers. *See* **Unidentified flying objects**

FM radio. *See* **Radio frequency modulation**

Foals. *See* **Horses; Ponies**

Fodder. *See* **Feeds**

Fog 551.57

    xx **Meteorology; Water**

Fog signals. *See* **Signals and signaling**

Foliage. *See* **Leaves**

Folk art (May subdiv. geog. or ethnic adjective form,
        e.g. **Folk art, American;** etc.) **745**

    Use for general and historical materials on peas-
        ant and popular art in the fields of decora-
        tive arts, music, dancing, theater, etc.

    See also **Arts and crafts movement; Decorative**
        arts; Handicraft

    x Peasant art

    xx **Art; Art and society; Decorative arts; Handi-**
        craft

Folk art, American 745.0973

    x American folk art; United States—Folk art

    xx **Art, American**

Folk dancing (May subdiv. geog. or ethnic adjective
        form, e.g. **Folk dancing, American;** etc.)
        793.3

    See also **Indians of North America—Dances;**
        Square dancing

    x National dances

    xx **Dancing; Folk music**

Folk dancing, American 793.3

    x American folk dancing; United States—Folk

Folk dancing, American—*Continued*
  dancing
  xx **Dancing—United States**
Folk drama 808.82; 812, etc.; 812.008, etc.
  See also **Puppets and puppet plays**
  x Folk plays
  xx **Drama**
Folk lore. *See* **Folklore**
Folk medicine 615.8
  x Folklore, Medical; Medical folklore
  xx **Medicine, Popular**
Folk music (May subdiv. geog.) **781.62**
  See also **Folk dancing**
  xx **Music**
Folk music—United States 781.62
  See also **Blues music; Country music**
  x American folk music; United States—Folk
    music
Folk plays. *See* **Folk drama**
Folk psychology. *See* **Ethnopsychology**
Folk society, Nonliterate. *See* **Nonliterate folk society**
Folk songs (May subdiv. geog. or ethnic adjective
    form, except for the U.S. and states and re-
    gions of the U.S. where the noun form is
    used, e.g. **Folk songs, French;** etc.; but
    **Folk songs—United States; Folk songs—
    Ohio;** etc.) **782.42162**
  See note under **Ballads.**
  See also **Ballads; Carols; Folklore; National
    songs**
  xx **Ballads; Folklore; National songs; Songs; Vo-
    cal music**
Folk songs, African. *See* **Songs, African**
Folk songs, American. *See* **Folk songs—United
    States**
Folk songs, Black (African). *See* **Songs, African**
Folk songs, Black (American). *See* **Black songs**
Folk songs—France. *See* **Folk songs, French**
Folk songs, French 782.4216200944
  x Folk songs—France; France—Folk songs;
    French folk songs
Folk songs—Ohio 782.42162009771
  x Ohio—Folk songs
Folk songs—United States 782.4216200973
  See also **Spirituals (Songs)**
  x American folk songs; Folk songs, American;
    United States—Folk songs
  xx **Songs, American**
Folk tales. *See* **Folklore**
Folklore (May subdiv. geog.) **398; 398.2**
  Use for general materials on folklore. May also
    be used as a form heading for a story or a
    collection of stories based on spoken rather
    than written traditions.
  See also

Chapbooks	**Ghosts**
Charms	**Graffiti**
Dragons	**Grail**
Fables	**Legends**
Fairies	**Monsters**
Fairy tales	**Mythology**
Folk songs	**Nursery rhymes**

Folklore—*Continued*

Proverbs
Sagas
Storytelling
Superstition

Tall tales
Tongue twisters
Witchcraft

also topics as themes in folklore and names of ethnic, national or occupational groups with the subdivision *Folklore,* e.g. **Animals—Folklore; Plants—Folklore; Weather—Folklore; Blacks—Folklore; Indians of North America—Folklore; Inuit—Folklore; Jews—Folklore;** etc.

x Folk lore; Folk tales; Tales; Traditions
xx **Ethnology; Fables; Fairy tales; Fiction; Folk songs; Legends; Manners and customs; Mythology; Storytelling; Superstition**

Folklore, Black. *See* **Blacks—Folklore**
Folklore, Inuit. *See* **Inuit—Folklore**
Folklore, Jewish. *See* **Jews—Folklore**
Folklore, Medical. *See* **Folk medicine**
Folklore—United States   398.0973
   x United States—Folklore
Folkways. *See* **Manners and customs**
Food   641; 641.3; 664
   See also

Beverages
Convenience foods
Cookery
Dinners and dining
Edible plants
Farm produce
Fish as food
Flavoring essences

Grain
Markets
Nutrition
Nuts
Seafood
Vegetarianism
Vitamins

also names of foods, e.g. **Bread; Fruit; Meat; Vegetables;** etc.; also types of food, e.g. **Animal food; Artificial foods; Dietetic foods; Natural foods;** etc.; and subjects with the subdivision *Food,* e.g. **Animals—Food; School children—Food;** etc.

x Gastronomy
xx **Cookery; Digestion; Dinners and dining; Home economics; Hygiene; Nutrition**
Food additives   641.4; 664
   x Additives, Food
   xx **Food—Analysis; Food—Preservation**
Food adulteration and inspection   363.19
   See also **Food—Law and legislation; Meat inspection; Milk supply**
   x Adulteration of food; Analysis of food; Food inspection; Inspection of food; Pure food
   xx **Consumer protection; Food—Law and legislation; Public health**
Food—Analysis   664
   See also **Food additives; Food—Composition**
   x Analysis of food; Chemistry of food; Food chemistry
   xx **Chemistry, Technical; Food—Composition**
Food, Artificial. *See* **Artificial foods**
Food assistance programs. *See* **Food relief**
Food, Canned. *See* **Canning and preserving**
Food chains (Ecology)   574.5
   xx **Animals—Food; Ecology**
Food chemistry. *See* **Food—Analysis; Food—Composition**

Food—Cholesterol content   641.1
  x Cholesterol content of food
  xx **Food—Composition**
Food—Composition   641.1; 664
  See also **Food—Analysis;** also **Food—
      Cholesterol content; Food—Fiber content;
      Food—Sodium content;** and similar head-
      ings
  x Chemistry of food; Food chemistry
  xx **Food—Analysis**
Food contamination   363.19
  x Contaminated food
Food control.   *See* **Food supply**
Food, Cost of.   *See* **Cost of living**
Food customs.   *See* **Eating customs**
Food, Dehydrated.   *See* **Dried foods**
Food, Dietetic.   *See* **Dietetic foods**
Food, Dried.   *See* **Dried foods**
Food—Fiber content   641.1
  x Dietary fiber; Fiber content of food; Roughage
  xx **Food—Composition**
Food for invalids.   *See* **Cookery for the sick**
Food for school children.   *See* **School children—
      Food**
Food, Freeze dried.   *See* **Freeze-dried foods**
Food, Frozen.   *See* **Frozen foods**
Food habits.   *See* **Eating customs**
Food inspection.   *See* **Food adulteration and inspec-
      tion**
Food—Labeling   363.19; 641.1
  x Food labels
Food labels.   *See* **Food—Labeling**
Food—Law and legislation   344
  See also **Food adulteration and inspection**
  x Food laws; Laws
  xx **Food adulteration and inspection; Law; Legis-
      lation**
Food laws.   *See* **Food—Law and legislation**
Food, Natural.   *See* **Natural foods**
Food plants.   *See* **Edible plants**
Food poisoning   615.9
  xx **Poisons and poisoning**
Food preparation.   *See* **Cookery**
Food—Preservation   641.4; 664
  See also **Canning and preserving; Cold storage;
      Dried foods; Food additives; Frozen foods;**
      also names of food with the subdivision
      Preservation, e.g. **Fruit—Preservation;** etc.
  x Preservation of food
Food relief (May subdiv. geog.)   **363.8**
  See also types of food relief, e.g. **Meals on
      wheels programs;** etc.; also names of wars
      with the subdivisions *Civilian relief* or *Food
      supply,* e.g. **World War, 1939-1945—
      Civilian relief; World War, 1939-1945—
      Food supply;** etc.
  x Food assistance programs
  xx **Charities; Disaster relief; Public welfare; Un-
      employed**
Food service   642; 647.95
      Use for materials on the preparation, delivery,
          and serving of ready-to-eat foods in large
          quantities outside of the home. For materi-

Food service—*Continued*

> als solely on the preparation of food in large
> quantities, use **Quantity cookery.**
>
> *See also* **Caterers and catering; Quantity cookery;
> Restaurants, bars, etc.**
>
> *x* Cookery for institutions; Mass feeding; Vol-
> ume feeding
>
> *xx* **Quantity cookery**

Food—Sodium content   641.1

> *x* Sodium content of food
>
> *xx* **Food—Composition**

Food supply   363.8

> Use for economic materials on the availability of
> food. For materials on the conservation of
> food in wartime, use the subdivision *Food
> supply* under the name of the war, e.g.
> **World War, 1939-1945—Food supply;** etc.
>
> *See also* **Agriculture; Aquaculture; Famines;
> Meat industry**
>
> *x* Food control
>
> *xx* **Agriculture**

Fools and jesters   791.092; 920

> *x* Court fools; Jesters
>
> *xx* **Comedians; Courts and courtiers; Entertainers**

Foot   611

> *x* Feet; Toes

Foot—Care and hygiene   617.5

> *xx* **Podiatry**

Football   796.332

> *See also* **Soccer**
>
> *xx* **College sports; Sports**

Football—Coaching   796.33207

> *xx* **Coaching (Athletics)**

Footwear. *See* **Shoes**

Forage plants   633.2

> *See also* **Grasses; Pastures; Silage and silos;** also
> names of specific forage plants, e.g. **Corn;
> Hay; Soybean;** etc.
>
> *xx* **Feeds; Grasses; Pastures; Plants**

Force and energy   531

> *See also* **Dynamics; Mechanics; Motion; Quan-
> tum theory**
>
> *x* Conservation of energy; Energy
>
> *xx* **Dynamics; Mechanics; Motion; Power (Me-
> chanics); Quantum theory**

Force pumps. *See* **Pumping machinery**

Forced indoctrination. *See* **Brainwashing**

Forced labor. *See* **Convict labor; Peonage; Slavery**

Ford automobile   629.222

> *xx* **Automobiles**

Forecasting   003

> *See also* types of forecasting, e.g. **Business fore-
> casting; Economic forecasting; Weather fore-
> casting;** etc.
>
> *x* Forecasts; Futurology; Predictions

Forecasts. *See* **Forecasting**

Foreign aid program. *See* **Economic assistance;
Military assistance; Technical assistance**

Foreign area studies. *See* **Area studies**

Foreign automobiles   629.222

> *See also* names of specific makes and models
>
> *x* Automobiles, Foreign; Foreign cars

Foreign cars. *See* **Foreign automobiles**

Foreign economic relations. *See* **International economic relations**

Foreign economic relations—United States. *See* **United States—Foreign economic relations**

Foreign exchange **332.4**
> *x* Cambristry; Exchange, Foreign; Exchange rates; International exchange
> *xx* **Banks and banking; Exchange; Finance; Money; Stock exchange**

Foreign investments **332.6**
> *x* International investment; Investments, Foreign
> *xx* **Multinational corporations**

Foreign language laboratories. *See* **Language laboratories**

Foreign language phrases. *See* **Languages, Modern—Conversations and phrases;** and names of languages with the subdivision *Conversations and phrases,* e.g. **French language—Conversations and phrases;** etc. Materials on foreign words and phrases incorporated into languages are entered under the names of languages with the subdivision *Foreign words and phrases,* e.g. **English language—Foreign words and phrases;** etc.

Foreign missions, Christian. *See* **Missions, Christian**

Foreign opinion. *See* names of countries with the subdivision *Foreign opinion,* or *Foreign opinion* subdivided geog. adjective form, e.g. **United States—Foreign opinion; United States—Foreign opinion, French;** etc.

Foreign policy. *See* names of countries with the subdivision *Foreign relations,* e.g. **United States—Foreign relations;** etc.

Foreign population. *See* **Immigration and emigration;** and names of countries with the subdivision *Immigration and emigration,* e.g. **United States—Immigration and emigration;** etc.; and names of countries, cities, etc. with the subdivision *Foreign population,* e.g. United States—Foreign population; Chicago (Ill.)—Foreign population; etc.

Foreign public opinion. *See* names of countries with the subdivision *Foreign opinion,* or *Foreign opinion* subdivided geog. adjective form, e.g. **United States—Foreign opinion; United States—Foreign opinion, French;** etc.

Foreign relations. *See* **International relations;** and names of countries with the subdivision *Foreign relations,* e.g. **United States— Foreign relations;** etc.

Foreign service. *See* **Diplomatic and consular service**

Foreign students **370.19**
> *x* College students, Foreign; Students, Foreign
> *xx* **Students**

Foreign study **370.19**
> *x* Overseas study; Study abroad; Study, Foreign; Study overseas

Foreign trade. *See* **Commerce**

Foreigners. *See* **Aliens; Citizenship; Naturalization;**

Foreigners—*Continued*
> and names of countries, cities, etc. with the
> subdivision *Foreign population,* e.g. **United
> States—Foreign population;** etc.

Foremen and foreladies. *See* **Supervisors**

Forenames. *See* **Personal names**

Forensic medicine. *See* **Medical jurisprudence**

Foreordination. *See* **Predestination**

Forest animals   591.52
> *See also* **Jungle animals**
> *xx* **Animals; Wildlife**

Forest conservation. *See* **Forests and forestry**

Forest fires   634.9
> *xx* **Fires**

Forest influences   574.5; 581.5
> *See also* **Botany—Ecology; Flood control; Forests
> and forestry; Rain**
> *x* Climate and forests; Floods and forests; For-
> ests and climate; Forests and floods; Forests
> and rainfall; Forests and water supply;
> Rainfall and forests
> *xx* **Climate; Flood control; Rain; Water supply**

Forest plants   581.5
> *xx* **Plants**

Forest products   634.9; 674
> *See also* **Gums and resins; Lumber and lumber-
> ing; Rubber; Wood**
> *xx* **Botany, Economic; Commercial products; Raw
> materials**

Forest reserves   719
> *See also* **Forests and forestry; National parks and
> reserves; Wilderness areas**
> *x* National forests; Public lands
> *xx* **National parks and reserves; Wildlife conser-
> vation**

Forestry. *See* **Forests and forestry**

Forests and climate. *See* **Forest influences**

Forests and floods. *See* **Forest influences**

Forests and forestry (May subdiv. geog.)   **574.5;
634.9**
> Use for general materials on forests and on for-
> est conservation. Consider also **Jungles** or
> **Rain forests.**
> *See also*

Christmas tree growing	**Reforestation**
Jungles	**Tree planting**
Lumber and lumbering	**Trees**
Pruning	**Wood**
Rain forests	

> also headings beginning with the word **Forest**
> *x* Arboriculture; Conservation of forests; Forest
> conservation; Forestry; Preservation of for-
> ests; Timber; Woods
> *xx* **Agriculture; Forest influences; Forest reserves;
> Natural resources; Trees; Wood**

**Forests and forestry—United States   574.5;
634.90973**
> *x* United States—Forests and forestry

Forests and rainfall. *See* **Forest influences**

Forests and water supply. *See* **Forest influences**

Forgery   332; 364.1
> *See also* **Counterfeits and counterfeiting**
> *xx* **Crime; Fraud; Impostors and imposture**

Forgery of works of art 702.8; 751.5
    See also **Literary forgeries**
    x Art forgeries; Art objects, Forgery of
    xx **Art**
Forging 671.3; 682
    See also **Blacksmithing; Ironwork; Welding**
    x Drop forging
    xx **Blacksmithing; Ironwork**
Form, Musical. *See* **Musical form**
Formal gardens. *See* **Gardens**
Former nuns. *See* **Ex-nuns**
Former priests. *See* **Ex-priests**
Formosa. *See* **Taiwan**
Formula translation (Computer language). *See*
        FORTRAN (Computer language)
Fortification 623
    See also **Military engineering;** also names of
        countries with the subdivision *Defenses,*
        e.g. **United States—Defenses;** etc.
    x Forts
    xx **Military art and science; Military engineering**
FORTRAN (Computer language) 005.13
    x Formula translation (Computer language);
        FORTRAN (Computer program language)
    xx **Programming languages (Computers)**
FORTRAN (Computer program language). *See*
        FORTRAN (Computer language)
Forts. *See* **Fortification**
Fortune. *See* **Fate and fatalism; Probabilities; Suc-**
    cess; Wealth
Fortune telling 133.3
    See also **Astrology; Clairvoyance; Dreams; Palm-**
    istry; Tarot
    xx **Amusements; Clairvoyance; Divination; Oc-**
    cultism; Prophecies (Occult sciences); Su-
    perstition
Fortunes. *See* **Income; Wealth**
Forums (Discussions). *See* **Discussion groups**
Fossil mammals. *See* **Mammals, Fossil**
Fossil plants. *See* **Plants, Fossil**
Fossil reptiles. *See* **Reptiles, Fossil**
Fossils 560
    See also **Extinct animals; Mammals, Fossil;**
    Plants, Fossil; Prehistoric animals; Reptiles,
    Fossil
    x Animals, Fossil; Paleontology
    xx **Geology, Stratigraphic; Natural history; Sci-**
    ence; Zoology
Foster grandparents 362.7
    xx **Voluntarism**
Foster home care 362.7
    See also **Adoption; Children—Institutional care;**
    Group homes
    x Child placing; Children—Placing out
    xx **Adoption; Child welfare; Children—**
    Institutional care; Group homes
Foundations 624.1
    See also **Basements; Compressed air; Concrete;**
    Masonry; Soils (Engineering); Walls
    xx **Architecture—Details; Building; Civil engi-**
    neering; Masonry; Structural engineering;
    Walls
Foundations (Endowments). *See* **Endowments**

Founding 671.2

Use for materials on the melting and casting of metals.

See also **Brass; Metalwork; Pattern making; Type and type founding**

x Casting; Foundry practice; Iron founding; Molding (Metal); Moulding (Metal)

xx **Metalwork; Pattern making**

Foundlings. *See* **Orphans**

Foundry practice. *See* **Founding**

Four-day work week. *See* **Hours of labor**

Four-H clubs. *See* **4-H clubs**

Fourteenth century 909.07

See note under **Nineteenth century.**

x 1300-1399 (14th century)

xx **Middle Ages**

Fourth dimension 516; 530.1

x Dimension, Fourth

xx **Mathematics; Space and time**

Fourth of July 394.2

x 4th of July; Independence Day (United States); July Fourth

xx **Holidays; United States—History—1775-1783, Revolution**

Fourth World. *See* **Developing countries**

Fractal geometry. *See* **Fractals**

Fractals 514; 516

Use for materials on shapes or mathematical sets that have fractional, i.e. irregular, dimensions as opposed to the regular dimensions of Euclidean geometry.

x Fractal geometry; Sets, Fractal; Sets of fractional dimension

xx **Geometry; Mathematical models; Set theory; Topology**

Fractions 513.2

xx **Arithmetic; Mathematics**

Fractures 617.1

xx **Bones; Wounds and injuries**

Framing of pictures. *See* **Picture frames and framing**

France 944

May be subdivided like U.S. except for *History.*

France—Folk songs. *See* **Folk songs, French**

France—History 944

France—History—0-1328 944

See also **Celts**

France—History—1328-1589, House of Valois 944

See also **Hundred Years' War, 1339-1453**

France—History—1589-1789, Bourbons 944

France—History—1789-1799, Revolution 944.04

x Directory, French, 1795-1799; French Revolution; Napoleonic Wars; Reign of Terror; Revolution, French; Terror, Reign of

France—History—1799-1815 944.05

France—History—1815-1914 944.06-944.08

France—History—1914-1940 944.081

France—History—1940-1945, German occupation 944.081

x German occupation of France, 1940-1945

France—History—1945-1958 944.082

France—History—1958-1969 944.083

France—History—1969- 944.083

Franchise. *See* **Citizenship; Elections; Suffrage**

Franciscans   271
    x Friars, Gray; Friars, Minor; Gray Friars; Grey
           Friars; Mendicant orders; Minorites; Saint
           Francis, Order of; St. Francis, Order of
    xx **Religious orders for men, Catholic**
Fraternities and sororities   371.8
    x College fraternities; College sororities; Greek
           letter societies; Sororities
    xx **Colleges and universities; Secret societies;**
           Students—Societies
Fraud   364.1
    See also **Forgery; Impostors and imposture;**
           Swindlers and swindling
    x Deceit; Ripoffs
    xx **Impostors and imposture; Swindlers and swin-**
           dling
Fraud, Computer. *See* **Computer crimes**
Fraud, Credit card. *See* **Credit card crimes**
Frauds, Literary. *See* **Literary forgeries**
Fraudulent advertising. *See* **Deceptive advertising**
Freaks. *See* **Monsters**
Free agency. *See* **Free will and determinism**
Free coinage. *See* **Monetary policy**
Free diving. *See* **Scuba diving; Skin diving**
Free fall. *See* **Weightlessness**
Free love   176; 306.7
    xx **Sexual ethics**
Free material   371.3
    x Giveaways
Free press. *See* **Freedom of the press**
Free press and fair trial. *See* **Freedom of the press**
           and fair trial
Free schools. *See* **Experimental schools**
Free speech   323.44
    See also **Freedom of information; Freedom of the**
           press; Libel and slander
    x Freedom of speech; Liberty of speech; Speech,
           Liberty of
    xx **Censorship; Civil rights; Freedom of assembly;**
           Freedom of information; Intellectual free-
           dom; Libel and slander
Free thought   211
    See also **Agnosticism; Bible—Evidences, author-**
           ity, etc.; Freedom of religion; Rationalism;
           Skepticism
    xx **Deism; Freedom of conscience; God; Rational-**
           ism
Free trade and protection   382
    See also **Balance of trade; Tariff**
    x Fair trade (Tariff); Protection; Tariff ques-
           tion—Free trade and protection
    xx **Commerce; Commercial policy; Economic pol-**
           icy; Economics; Tariff
Free universities   378
    See also **Colleges and universities—Entrance re-**
           quirements
    x Alternative universities; Colleges and univer-
           sities, Nonformal; Education, Nonformal;
           Experimental universities; Nonformal col-
           leges and universities; Open universities
    xx **Colleges and universities**
Free verse   808.1
    x Vers libre
    xx **Poetry**

Free will and determinism   123

    x Choice, Freedom of; Determinism and inde-
       terminism; Free agency; Freedom of choice;
       Freedom of the will; Indeterminism; Lib-
       erty of the will; Will

    xx **Ethics; Fate and fatalism; Philosophy; Predes-
       tination; Sin**

Freebooters.   *See* **Pirates**

Freedom   323.4

    Use for general or abstract materials on the
      power or condition of acting or choosing
      without compulsion or constraint.

    See also

Academic freedom	**Freedom of association**
Anarchism and anarchists	**Freedom of conscience**
Civil rights	**Freedom of movement**
Conformity	**Freedom of religion**
Equality	**Intellectual freedom**
Freedom of assembly	**Slavery**

    x Civil liberty; Emancipation; Liberty; Natural
      law; Personal freedom

    xx **Civil rights; Democracy; Equality; Political
      science**

Freedom, Academic.   *See* **Academic freedom**

Freedom marches—United States.   *See* **Blacks—
    Civil rights**

Freedom of assembly   323.4

    See also **Free speech; Freedom of association;
      Public meetings; Riots**

    x Assembly, Right of; Right of assembly

    xx **Civil rights; Freedom**

Freedom of association   323.4

    x Association, Freedom of; Right of association

    xx **Civil rights; Freedom; Freedom of assembly**

Freedom of choice.   *See* **Free will and determinism**

Freedom of choice movement.   *See* **Pro-choice
    movement**

Freedom of conscience   323.44

    See also **Conscientious objectors; Free thought;
      Freedom of religion; Public opinion**

    x Intolerance; Liberty of conscience

    xx **Church—Government policy; Conscience;
      Freedom; Freedom of religion; Toleration**

Freedom of information   323.44

    See also **Censorship; Free speech; Freedom of
      the press; Press—Government policy**

    x Information, Freedom of; Right to know

    xx **Censorship; Civil rights; Free speech; Free-
      dom of the press; Intellectual freedom**

Freedom of movement   323.4

    x Movement, Freedom of

    xx **Civil rights; Freedom**

Freedom of religion   261.7; 323.44

    Use for materials on the right or privilege of act-
      ing according to one's own view of religion
      without undue restraints or within reason-
      ably formulated and legally specified limits.

    See also **Church—Government policy; Freedom
      of conscience; Persecution**

    x Freedom of worship; Intolerance; Religious
      freedom; Religious liberty

    xx **Church—Government policy; Civil rights;
      Free thought; Freedom; Freedom of con-
      science; Persecution; Toleration**

Freedom of speech. *See* **Free speech**
Freedom of teaching. *See* **Academic freedom**
Freedom of the press   323.44
 See also **Books—Censorship; Freedom of information; Libel and slander; Press**
 x Free press; Liberty of the press; Press censorship
 xx **Censorship; Civil rights; Free speech; Freedom of information; Intellectual freedom; Journalism; Libel and slander; Newspapers; Periodicals; Press**
Freedom of the press and fair trial   323.42; 323.44; 342
 x Fair trial and free press; Free press and fair trial; Prejudicial publicity; Trial by publicity
 xx **Press**
Freedom of the will. *See* **Free will and determinism**
Freedom of worship. *See* **Freedom of religion**
Freelancers. *See* **Self-employed**
Freemasons   366
 x Masonic orders; Masons (Secret order)
 xx **Secret societies**
Freeways. *See* **Express highways**
Freeze-dried foods   641.4; 664
 x Food, Freeze dried
 xx **Dried foods**
Freezing. *See* **Cryobiology; Frost; Ice; Refrigeration**
Freezing of human bodies. *See* **Cryonics**
Freight and freightage   388
 See also **Aeronautics, Commercial; Railroads—Rates; Trucking**
 xx **Maritime law; Materials handling; Railroads; Railroads—Rates; Transportation**
French and Indian War. *See* **United States—History—1755-1763, French and Indian War**
French Canadian literature   840; C840
 May use same subdivisions and names of literary forms as for **English literature.**
 x Canadian literature, French; French literature—Canada
 xx **Canadian literature**
French Canadians   305.811; 971
 xx **Canadians**
French cookery. *See* **Cookery, French**
French Equatorial Africa. *See* **French-speaking Equatorial Africa**
French folk songs. *See* **Folk songs, French**
French foreign opinion—United States. *See* **United States—Foreign opinion, French**
French language   440
 May be subdivided like **English language.**
 xx **Romance languages**
French language—Conversations and phrases   448
 x Conversation in foreign languages; Foreign language phrases
French language—Dictionaries—English   443
 See note under **English language—Dictionaries—French.**
 See also **English language—Dictionaries—French**
 xx **English language—Dictionaries—French**
French language—Reading materials   448.6

301

French literature   840
    May use same subdivisions and names of literary forms as for **English literature.**
    xx **Literature; Romance literature**
French literature—Canada. *See* **French Canadian literature**
French literature—West Indian authors. *See* **West Indian literature (French)**
French poetry   841
    See also **Troubadours**
French Revolution. *See* **France—History—1789-1799, Revolution**
French-speaking Equatorial Africa   967
    Use for materials dealing collectively with the Central African Republic, Chad, Congo, and Gabon. The former name for the region was French Equatorial Africa.
    x Africa, French-speaking Equatorial; French Equatorial Africa
    xx **Central Africa**
French-speaking West Africa   966
    Use for materials dealing collectively with Benin, Burkina Faso, Guinea, Ivory Coast, Mali, Mauritania, Niger, Senegal, and Togo.
    x Africa, French-speaking West; French West Africa
    xx **West Africa**
French West Africa. *See* **French-speaking West Africa**
Frequency modulation, Radio. *See* **Radio frequency modulation**
Fresco painting. *See* **Mural painting and decoration**
Freshwater animals   591.92
    See also **Aquariums; Marine animals;** also names of fresh water animals, e.g. **Beavers;** etc.
    x Animals, Aquatic; Animals, Freshwater; Aquatic animals; Water animals
    xx **Animals; Freshwater biology; Marine animals; Wildlife**
Freshwater aquaculture. *See* **Aquaculture**
Freshwater biology   574.92
    See also **Aquariums; Freshwater animals; Freshwater plants; Marine biology**
    xx **Biology; Marine biology; Natural history**
Freshwater plants   581.92
    See also **Aquariums; Marine plants**
    x Aquatic plants; Water plants
    xx **Freshwater biology; Marine plants; Plants**
Friars, Black. *See* **Dominicans (Religious order)**
Friars, Gray. *See* **Franciscans**
Friars, Minor. *See* **Franciscans**
Friars Preachers. *See* **Dominicans (Religious order)**
Friends. *See* **Friendship**
Friends, Imaginary. *See* **Imaginary playmates**
Friends, Society of. *See* **Society of Friends**
Friendship   177
    See also **Imaginary playmates; Love**
    x Affection; Friends
    xx **Human behavior; Love; Social ethics**
Friesian cattle. *See* **Holstein-Friesian cattle**
Fringe benefits. *See* **Nonwage payments**
Frogmen and frogwomen. *See* **Scuba diving; Skin diving**

Frogs 597.8
>*x* Tadpoles
>*xx* **Amphibians**

Frontier and pioneer life (May subdiv. geog. by state and region) **978**
>*See also* **Cowhands; Indians of North America— Captivities; Overland journeys to the Pacific; Ranch life**
>*x* Border life; Pioneer life
>*xx* **Adventure and adventurers**

Frontiers. *See* **Boundaries;** and names of countries with the subdivision *Boundaries,* e.g. **United States—Boundaries;** etc.

Frost 551.57
>*See also* **Ice; Refrigeration**
>*x* Freezing
>*xx* **Meteorology; Water**

Frozen animal embryos. *See* **Frozen embryos**

Frozen embryos 176; 574.3; 612.6
>*x* Animal embryos, Frozen; Embryos, Frozen; Frozen animal embryos; Frozen human embryos; Human embryos, Frozen
>*xx* **Cryobiology; Embryology**

Frozen foods 641.4; 664
>*See also* **Ice cream, ices, etc.**
>*x* Food, Frozen
>*xx* **Food—Preservation**

Frozen human embryos. *See* **Frozen embryos**

Frozen stars. *See* **Black holes (Astronomy)**

Fruit 634; 641.3
>Names of all fruits are not included in this List but are to be added as needed, usually in the singular form, e.g. **Apple;** etc.
>*See also* **Fruit culture; Nuts;** also types of fruit, e.g. **Berries; Citrus fruit;** etc.; and names of fruits, e.g. **Apple;** etc.
>*xx* **Botany; Food**

Fruit—Canning. *See* **Fruit—Preservation**

Fruit culture 634
>*See also* **Berries; Grafting; Nurseries (Horticulture); Plant propagation; Pruning**
>*x* Arboriculture; Orchards
>*xx* **Agriculture; Fruit; Gardening; Horticulture; Trees**

Fruit—Diseases and pests 634
>*See also* **Spraying and dusting**
>*xx* **Agricultural bacteriology; Agricultural pests; Insect pests; Pests; Plant diseases**

Fruit flies 595.77
>*xx* **Flies**

Fruit—Marketing. *See* **Farm produce—Marketing**

Fruit—Preservation 641.4; 664
>*x* Fruit—Canning
>*xx* **Canning and preserving; Food—Preservation**

Frustration. *See* **Attitude (Psychology); Emotions**

Fuel 662; 665
>*See also* **Biomass energy; Heating;** also names of fuel, e.g. **Alcohol as fuel; Charcoal; Coal; Gas; Petroleum as fuel; Synthetic fuels; Wood;** etc.; and subjects with the subdivision *Fuel consumption,* e.g. **Automobiles— Fuel consumption;** etc.
>*xx* **Combustion; Energy resources; Engines; Fire;**

Fuel—*Continued*
   Heating; Home economics; Smoke prevention
Fuel cells   621.31
   xx **Electric batteries; Electrochemistry**
Fuel consumption.   *See* subjects with the subdivision *Fuel consumption,* e.g. **Automobiles—Fuel consumption;** etc.
Fuel, Liquid.   *See* **Gasoline; Petroleum as fuel**
Fuel oil.   *See* **Petroleum as fuel**
Fugue   784.18
   xx **Composition (Music); Counterpoint; Music—Theory; Musical form**
Fulfillment, Self.   *See* **Self-realization**
Fumigation   614.4; 648
   See also **Disinfection and disinfectants**
   xx **Communicable diseases; Disinfection and disinfectants; Insecticides**
Functional competencies.   *See* **Life skills**
Functional literacy   302.2; 374
   x Occupational literacy
   xx **Literacy**
Fund raising   361.7068; 658.15
   x Community chests; Money raising
Fundamental education.   *See* **Basic education**
Fundamental life skills.   *See* **Life skills**
Fundamental rights.   *See* **Civil rights; Human rights**
Fundamental theology.   *See* **Apologetics**
Fundamentalism   273
   Use for materials on the conservative interpretation of Christianity as opposed to Modernism.
   See also **Modernism**
   xx **Modernism**
Fundamentalism and education   377
   Use same form for fundamentalism and other subjects.
   See also **Christian education; Church schools; Creation—Study and teaching; Religion in the public schools**
   x Education and Fundamentalism
   xx **Christian education; Church and education; Church schools; Creation—Study and teaching; Education; Religion in the public schools**
Funding for the arts.   *See* **Art patronage; Arts—Government policy**
Funds.   *See* **Finance**
Funeral directors.   *See* **Undertakers and undertaking**
Funeral rites and ceremonies   393
   See also **Cremation**
   x Burial; Ecclesiastical rites and ceremonies; Graves; Mortuary customs; Mourning customs
   xx **Archeology; Cremation; Manners and customs; Rites and ceremonies**
Fungi   589.2
   See also **Bacteriology; Molds (Botany); Mushrooms; Plant diseases**
   x Diseases and pests; Mycology
   xx **Agricultural pests; Molds (Botany); Mushrooms; Pests**

Fungicides   632; 668
  See also **Spraying and dusting**
  x Germicides
  xx **Pesticides; Spraying and dusting**
Funicular railroads.   *See* **Cable railroads**
Funnies.   *See* **Comic books, strips, etc.**
Fur   675; 685
  See also **Hides and skins**
  xx **Hides and skins**
Fur seals.   *See* **Seals (Animals)**
Fur trade   338.3
  xx **Trapping**
Furbearing animals   636.088; 639
  See also names of furbearing animals, e.g. **Bea-**
    vers; etc.
  xx **Animals; Wildlife; Zoology, Economic**
Furnaces   697
  See also **Blast furnaces; Smelting**
  xx **Heating; Smoke prevention**
Furniture (May subdiv. geog. adjective form, e.g.
      Furniture, American; etc.)   **684.1; 749**
  See also

Built-in furniture	**Schools—Equipment and**
Cabinet work	**supplies**
Church furniture	**Upholstery**
Garden ornaments and fur-	**Veneers and veneering**
niture	**Wood carving**
Libraries—Equipment and	
supplies	

    also names of articles of furniture, e.g. **Chairs;**
      Mirrors; etc.
  xx **Art objects; Decoration and ornament; Decora-**
    tive arts; Home economics; Interior design;
    Manufactures; Upholstery; Woodwork
Furniture, American   684.100973; 749.213
  x American furniture; Colonial furniture (U.S.);
    Furniture, Colonial; United States—
    Furniture
Furniture, Built-in.   *See* **Built-in furniture**
Furniture, Colonial.   *See* **Furniture, American**
Furniture finishing   684.1; 749
  x Furniture—Refinishing; Furniture—
    Restoration; Refinishing furniture
Furniture—Refinishing.   *See* **Furniture finishing**
Furniture—Restoration.   *See* **Furniture finishing**
Future life   236
    Use for materials dealing with the character and
      form of a future existence. Materials dealing
      with the question of the endless existence of
      the soul are entered under **Immortality.**
      Materials on the philosophical concept of
      eternity are entered under **Eternity.**
  See also **Eternity; Heaven; Hell; Immortality;**
    Millennium; Soul; Spiritualism
  x Afterlife; Eternal life; Future punishment; Ha-
    des; Intermediate state; Life after death;
    Life, Future; Resurrection; Retribution
  xx **Death; Eschatology; Eternity; Immortality**
Future punishment.   *See* **Future life**
Future shock.   *See* **Culture conflict**
Futurism (Art)   759.06
  See also **Kinetic sculpture; Postimpressionism**
    (Art)
  xx **Art; Painting; Postimpressionism (Art)**
Futurology.   *See* **Forecasting**

G.I.'s. *See* **Soldiers—United States; Veterans—United States**

G.R.E. *See* **Graduate record examination**

Gaels. *See* **Celts**

Gaia concept. *See* **Gaia hypothesis**

Gaia hypothesis 550.1; 574.01

 Use for materials on the theory formulated by James Lovelock that various terrestrial life forms can act as a unified organism regulating earth's temperature, atmospheric conditions and other physical characteristics.

 x Gaia concept; Gaia principle; Gaia theory; Living earth theory

 xx **Atmosphere; Biology; Earth; Ecology; Life (Biology)**

Gaia principle. *See* **Gaia hypothesis**

Gaia theory. *See* **Gaia hypothesis**

Galaxies 523.1

 x Extragalactic nebulae; Nebulae, Extragalactic

 xx **Astronomy; Stars**

Gales. *See* **Winds**

Galleries, Art. *See* names of appropriate subjects with the subdivision *Museums,* e.g. **Art—Museums; World War, 1939-1945—Museums;** etc.; and names of galleries and museums

Gambling 175; 795

 See also **Compulsive gambling; Probabilities;** also types of gambling, e.g. **Card games; Horse racing; Lotteries;** etc.

 x Betting; Gaming

 xx **Crimes without victims**

Gambling, Compulsive. *See* **Compulsive gambling**

Game and game birds 636.6

 See also **Falconry; Game protection; Hunting; Shooting; Trapping;** also names of animals and birds, e.g. **Deer; Pheasants;** etc.

 x Wild fowl

 xx **Animals; Birds; Hunting; Trapping; Wildlife**

Game preserves 333.95

 xx **Hunting; Wildlife conservation**

Game protection 333.95; 636.9

 See also **Birds—Protection**

 x Game wardens; Protection of game

 xx **Birds—Protection; Game and game birds; Hunting; Wildlife conservation**

Game theory 519.3

 See also **Decision making; Simulation games in education**

 x Games, Theory of; Theory of games

 xx **Mathematical models; Mathematics; Probabilities**

Game wardens. *See* **Game protection**

Games 790

 See also

Amusements	**Kindergarten**
Children's parties	**Play**
Computer games	**Simulation games in edu-**
Indians of North Ameri-	**cation**
ca—Games	**Sports**

 also names of types of games and of individual games, e.g. **Ball games; Card games; Chess; Indoor games; Olympic games; Singing**

Games—*Continued*
        games; Tennis; Video games; Word games;
        etc.
    x Pastimes
    xx **Amusements; Entertaining; Physical educa-
        tion; Play; Recreation; Sports**
Games, Electronic. *See* **Electronic toys; Video
    games**
Games, Olympic. *See* **Olympic games**
Games, Theory of. *See* **Game theory**
Games, Video. *See* **Video games**
Gaming. *See* **Gambling**
Gaming, Educational. *See* **Simulation games in ed-
    ucation**
Gamma rays 537.5; 539.7
    xx **Electromagnetic waves; Radiation; X rays**
Gangs. *See* **Criminals; Juvenile delinquency**
Garage sales 381
    x Yard sales
    xx **Secondhand trade**
Garbage. *See* **Refuse and refuse disposal**
Garden design. *See* **Gardens—Design; Landscape
    gardening**
Garden furniture. *See* **Garden ornaments and furni-
    ture**
Garden ornaments and furniture 717
    See also **Sundials**
    x Garden furniture
    xx **Decoration and ornament; Furniture; Gardens;
        Landscape architecture**
Garden pests. *See* **Agricultural pests; Insect pests;
    Plant diseases**
Gardening 635
    Use for practical materials on the practical as-
        pects of the cultivation of flowers, fruits,
        vegetables, etc.
    See also

Bulbs	**Landscape gardening**
Climbing plants	**Nurseries (Horticulture)**
Flower gardening	**Organiculture**
Fruit culture	**Plant propagation**
Gardens	**Plants**
Gardens—Design	**Plants, Cultivated**
Grafting	**Pruning**
Greenhouses	**Vegetable gardening**
Grounds maintenance	**Weeds**
Horticulture	**Window gardening**
Indoor gardening	

    x Planting
    xx **Agriculture; Horticulture; Plants**
Gardening in space. *See* **Aeroponics**
Gardening in the shade 635
    x Gardens, Shade; Shade gardens; Shady gar-
        dens
Gardens (May subdiv. geog.) **635; 712**
    Use for general materials about the history of
        gardens, various types of gardens, etc. Mate-
        rials about the design or rearrangement of
        extensive gardens or estates are entered un-
        der **Landscape gardening.** Materials lim-
        ited to the cultivation of gardens are entered
        under **Gardening.**
    See also **Botanical gardens; Garden ornaments**

Gardens—*Continued*
>> **and furniture; Rock gardens**
> *x* Formal gardens
> *xx* **Gardening**

Gardens—Design **712**
> *See also* **Landscape gardening**
> *x* Garden design
> *xx* **Gardening; Landscape gardening**

Gardens, Miniature **635.9**
> *x* Miniature gardens; Miniature objects; Tray gardens
> *xx* **Indoor gardening; Terrariums**

Gardens, Shade. *See* **Gardening in the shade**
Garment making. *See* **Dressmaking; Tailoring**
Garments. *See* **Clothing and dress**
Garments, Leather. *See* **Leather garments**

Gas **665.7**
> *See also* **Coal tar products; Gases; Petroleum**
> *x* Coal gas; Illuminating gas
> *xx* **Coal tar products; Fuel; Public utilities**

Gas and oil engines **621.43**
> *See also* **Carburetors; Diesel engines; Farm engines;** also subjects with the subdivision *Engines,* e.g. **Airplanes—Engines; Automobiles—Engines;** etc.
> *x* Gas engines; Gasoline engines; Internal-combustion engines; Oil engines; Petroleum engines
> *xx* **Engines**

Gas companies. *See* **Public utilities**
Gas engines. *See* **Gas and oil engines**
Gas, Natural. *See* **Natural gas**
Gas stations. *See* **Automobiles—Service stations**

Gas turbines **621.43**
> *xx* **Turbines**

Gas warfare. *See* **Poisonous gases—War use**

Gases **530.4; 533**
> *See also* **Pneumatics; Poisonous gases;** also names of gases, e.g. **Nitrogen;** etc.
> *xx* **Fluid mechanics; Gas; Hydrostatics; Physics; Pneumatics**

Gases, Poisonous. *See* **Poisonous gases**
Gasification of coal. *See* **Coal gasification**

Gasohol **662**
> *xx* **Alcohol as fuel**

Gasoline **665.5**
> *x* Fuel, Liquid; Liquid fuel
> *xx* **Petroleum**

Gasoline engines. *See* **Gas and oil engines**
Gastronomy. *See* **Cookery; Dinners and dining; Food; Menus**
Gauchos. *See* **Cowhands**

Gay liberation movement **305.9**
> *xx* **Homosexuality**

Gay lifestyle. *See* **Homosexuality**

Gay men **305.38; 306.76**
> *x* Gays, Men; Homosexuals, Male

Gay women **305.48; 306.76**
> *x* Gays, Women; Homosexuals, Female; Lesbians

Gays, Men. *See* **Gay men**
Gays, Women. *See* **Gay women**

Gazetteers 910.3

See also **Geographic names**; also names of countries, states, etc. with the subdivision *Gazetteers*, e.g. **United States—Gazetteers**; etc.

xx **Geographic names**

Gearing 621.8

See also **Automobiles—Transmission devices; Mechanical movements**

x Bevel gearing; Cog wheels; Gears; Spiral gearing

xx **Machinery; Mechanical movements; Power transmission; Wheels**

Gears. *See* **Gearing**

Geese 636.5

x Goose

xx **Poultry; Water birds**

Gemini project 629.45

x Project Gemini

xx **Orbital rendezvous (Space flight); Space flight**

Gems 736

Use for materials on cut and polished precious stones treated from the point of view of art or antiquity. Materials on uncut stones treated from the mineralogical point of view are entered under **Precious stones.** Materials on gems in which the emphasis is on the setting are entered under **Jewelry.**

See also **Jewelry; Precious stones**

x Jewels

xx **Archeology; Art; Decoration and ornament; Engraving; Jewelry; Mineralogy; Precious stones**

Gemstones. *See* **Precious stones**

Gender identity. *See* **Sex role**

Gene machine. *See* **Genetic engineering, Automated**

Gene mapping. *See* **Genetic mapping**

Gene splicing. *See* **Genetic engineering; Recombinant DNA**

Gene therapy 616

Use for materials on therapeutic efforts involving the replacement or supplementation of genes in order to cure diseases caused by genetic defects.

x Therapy, Gene

xx **Genetic engineering; Therapeutics**

Gene transfer. *See* **Genetic engineering**

Genealogy 929

See also **Biography; Heraldry; Registers of births, etc.; Wills**; also names of families, e.g. **Lincoln family**; etc.

x Ancestry; Descent; Family histories; Family trees; Pedigrees

xx **Biography; Heraldry; History**

Generals 355.3092; 920

xx **Military personnel**

Generation. *See* **Reproduction**

Generation gap. *See* **Conflict of generations**

Generative organs. *See* **Reproductive system**

Generators, Electric. *See* **Electric generators**

Generic drugs 615

x Drugs—Generic substitution

xx **Drugs; Generic products**

Generic products   658.8
> *See also* **Generic drugs**
> *x* Products, Generic
> *xx* **Commercial products; Manufactures**
Genes.   *See* **Heredity**
Genetic aspects.   *See* names of diseases with the
> subdivision *Genetic aspects,* e.g. **Cancer—
> Genetic aspects;** etc.
Genetic code   574.87
> *xx* **Molecular biology**
Genetic counseling   616; 618
> *xx* **Medical genetics; Prenatal diagnosis**
Genetic engineering   660
> *See also* **Biotechnology; Clones and cloning; Fer-
> tilization in vitro; Gene therapy; Genetic en-
> gineering, Automated; Molecular cloning;
> Recombinant DNA**
> *x* Designed genetic change; Engineering, Ge-
> netic; Gene splicing; Gene transfer; Genetic
> intervention; Genetic surgery; Splicing of
> genes; Transgenics
> *xx* **Biotechnology; Engineering; Genetic recombi-
> nation**
Genetic engineering, Automated   660
> *x* Automated genetic engineering; DNA synthe-
> sizer; Gene machine
> *xx* **Genetic engineering**
Genetic engineering—Government policy   351.85
Genetic engineering—Social aspects   306.4
Genetic fingerprints.   *See* **DNA Fingerprints**
Genetic intervention.   *See* **Genetic engineering**
Genetic mapping   575.1
> *x* Chromosome mapping; Gene mapping; Ge-
> nome mapping
> *xx* **Genetics; Heredity**
Genetic profiling.   *See* **DNA Fingerprints**
Genetic recombination   574.87
> *See also* **Genetic engineering; Genetic transfor-
> mation; Recombinant DNA**
> *x* Recombination, Genetic
> *xx* **Chromosomes**
Genetic surgery.   *See* **Genetic engineering**
Genetic transformation   574.87
> *x* Transformation (Genetics)
> *xx* **Genetic recombination**
Genetics   573.2; 575.1
> Use for materials dealing with reproduction, he-
> redity, evolution and variation.
> *See also*

Adaptation (Biology)	**Evolution**
Behavior genetics	**Genetic mapping**
Breeding	**Heredity**
Chromosomes	**Medical genetics**
DNA Fingerprints	**Natural selection**
Eugenics	**Variation (Biology)**

> *xx* **Biology; Breeding; Embryology; Life (Biology);
> Mendel's law; Reproduction**
Genitalia.   *See* **Reproductive system**
Genius   153.9
> *See also* **Creation (Literary, artistic, etc.); Gifted
> children**
> *x* Talent
> *xx* **Psychology**
Genome mapping.   *See* **Genetic mapping**

Gentiles and Jews. *See* **Jews and Gentiles**

Geochemistry **551.9**

> *See also* **Geothermal resources**

> *x* Chemical geology; Earth—Chemical composition; Geological chemistry

> *xx* **Chemistry; Earth sciences; Petrology; Physical geography; Rocks**

Geodesy **526**

> *See also* **Latitude; Longitude; Surveying**

> *x* Degrees of latitude and longitude

> *xx* **Earth; Measurement; Surveying**

Geographic names (May subdiv. geog.) **910**

> *See also* **Gazetteers**

> *x* Names, Geographical; Place names

> *xx* **Gazetteers; Names**

Geographic names—United States **917.3**

> *x* Names, Geographical—United States; United States—Geographic names; United States—Names, Geographic

Geographical atlases. *See* **Atlases**

Geographical distribution of animals and plants. *See* **Biogeography; Plants—Geographical distribution;** and names of plants and animals with the subdivision *Geographical distribution,* e.g. **Fishes—Geographical distribution;** etc.

Geographical distribution of people. *See* **Anthropogeography; Ethnology**

Geographical myths **398.23**

> *x* Cities, Imaginary; Fictitious places; Imaginary places; Islands, Imaginary; Places, Imaginary

> *xx* **Mythology**

Geography **910**

> Use for general materials, frequently school materials, that describe the surface of the earth and its interrelationship with various peoples, animals, natural products and industries. For such materials limited to a particular place, use the subdivision *Geography* under the place. For general descriptive materials and travel materials limited to a particular place, use the subdivision *Description* under cities (except ancient cities), countries, states, regions, etc. Materials dealing with the physical features of the earth's surface and its atmosphere are entered under **Physical geography.**

> *See also*

Anthropogeography	**Ethnology**
Atlases	**Maps**
Biogeography	**Physical geography**
Boundaries	**Surveying**
Discoveries (in geography)	**Voyages and travels**

> also names of countries, states, etc., with the subdivisions *Description* and *Geography,* e.g. **United States—Description; United States—Geography;** etc.; and also sacred works with the subdivision *Geography,* e.g. **Bible—Geography;** etc.

> *x* Social studies

> *xx* **Earth; Earth sciences; World history**

311

Geography, Ancient 913

Use for materials on the geography of the ancient world in general.

See also names of modern countries with the subdivision *Historical geography,* e.g. **Greece—Historical geography;** etc.; and names of countries of antiquity with the subdivision **Geography,** e.g. *Rome—Geography;* etc.

x Ancient geography; Classical geography

xx **Geography, Historical; History, Ancient**

Geography, Biblical. *See* **Bible—Geography**

Geography, Commercial 330.9

See also **Economic conditions; Trade routes**

x Commercial geography; Economic geography; Geography, Economic; World economics

xx **Commerce; Commercial products; Economic conditions**

Geography—Dictionaries 910.3

Use for dictionaries of geographic terms. Materials listing names and descriptions of places are entered under **Gazetteers.**

Geography, Economic. *See* **Geography, Commercial**

Geography, Historical 911

Use for materials that discuss the extent of territory held by the states or nations at a given period of history. When limited to one country or region still existing in modern times, use the name of the place with the subdivision *Historical geography.* Under names of countries of antiquity use, instead, the subdivision *Geography.*

See also **Geography, Ancient;** also names of modern countries or regions with the subdivision *Historical geography,* e.g. **Greece—Historical geography; United States—Historical geography;** etc.; and names of ancient countries with the subdivision *Geography,* e.g. **Rome—Geography;** etc.

x Historical geography

xx **History**

Geography, Historical—Maps. *See* **Atlases, Historical**

Geography, Military. *See* **Military geography**

Geography, Physical. *See* **Physical geography**

Geography—Pictorial works. *See* **Views**

Geography, Political. *See* **Boundaries; Geopolitics**

Geography, Social. *See* **Anthropogeography**

Geological chemistry. *See* **Geochemistry**

Geological physics. *See* **Geophysics**

Geologists 551.092; 920

xx **Scientists**

Geology (May subdiv. geog.) **550**

See note under **Earth.**

See also

Astrogeology	**Glaciers**
Continental drift	**Mineralogy**
Continental shelf	**Mountains**
Coral reefs and islands	**Oceanography**
Earth	**Ore deposits**
Earthquakes	**Petrology**
Geysers	**Physical geography**

Geology—*Continued*

> **Rocks** **Volcanoes**
> **Submarine geology**
>> *x* Geoscience
>> *xx* **Earth; Earth sciences; Natural history; Petrology; Rocks; Science**

Geology, Dynamic. *See* **Geophysics**
Geology, Economic 553
> *See also*
> **Coal** **Petroleum geology**
> **Mines and mineral re-** **Quarries and quarrying**
> **sources** **Soils**
> **Natural gas** **Stone**
> **Ores**
>> also names of other geological products, e.g. **Asbestos; Gypsum;** etc.
>> *x* Economic geology

Geology, Historical. *See* **Geology, Stratigraphic**
Geology, Lunar. *See* **Lunar geology**
Geology—Maps 550.22
> *xx* **Maps**
Geology—Moon. *See* **Lunar geology**
Geology, Petroleum. *See* **Petroleum geology**
Geology, Stratigraphic 551.7
> *See also* **Fossils**
>> *x* Geology, Historical; Historical geology; Rocks—Age; Stratigraphic geology
Geology, Submarine. *See* **Submarine geology**
Geology—United States 557.3
> *x* United States—Geology
Geometric art. *See* **Art, Abstract**
Geometric patterns. *See* **Patterns (Mathematics)**
Geometrical drawing 516; 604.2
> *See also* **Geometry, Descriptive; Graphic methods; Mechanical drawing; Perspective**
>> *x* Mathematical drawing; Plans
>> *xx* **Drawing; Geometry; Mechanical drawing**
Geometry 516
> *See also* **Fractals; Geometrical drawing; Ratio and proportion; Square; Topology; Trigonometry; Volume (Cubic content)**
>> *x* Geometry, Plane; Geometry, Solid; Plane geometry; Solid geometry
>> *xx* **Mathematics**
Geometry, Analytic 516.3
> *x* Analytical geometry
Geometry, Descriptive 516
> *See also* **Perspective**
>> *x* Descriptive geometry
>> *xx* **Geometrical drawing**
Geometry, Plane. *See* **Geometry**
Geometry, Projective 516
> *x* Projective geometry
Geometry, Solid. *See* **Geometry**
Geophysics 550
> *See also* **Auroras; Meteorology; Oceanography; Plate tectonics**
>> *x* Geological physics; Geology, Dynamic; Physics, Terrestrial; Terrestrial physics
>> *xx* **Earth; Earth sciences; Physical geography; Physics; Space sciences**
Geopolitics 320.1; 327.101
> *See also* **Anthropogeography; Boundaries; World**

313

Geopolitics—*Continued*
>   **politics**
>   *x* Geography, Political
>   *xx* **Anthropogeography; Boundaries; International
>   relations; Political science; World politics**

Geoscience.   *See* **Earth sciences; Geology**
Geothermal resources   333.8
>   *See also* names of geothermal resources, e.g.
>   **Geysers;** etc.
>   *x* Natural steam energy; Thermal waters
>   *xx* **Geochemistry; Ocean energy resources; Re-
>   newable energy resources**

Geriatrics.   *See* **Elderly—Diseases; Elderly—
>   Health and hygiene**

Germ theory.   *See* **Life—Origin**
Germ theory of disease   616
>   *See also* **Bacteriology**
>   *x* Bacilli; Disease germs; Germs; Microbes
>   *xx* **Bacteriology; Communicable diseases**

Germ warfare.   *See* **Biological warfare**
German Democratic Republic.   *See* **Germany
>   (East)**

German Federal Republic.   *See* **Germany (West)**
German Hebrew.   *See* **Yiddish language**
German language   430
>   May be subdivided like **English language.**
German literature   830
>   May use same subdivisions and names of liter-
>   ary forms as for **English literature.**
German occupation of France, 1940-1945.   *See*
>   **France—History—1940-1945, German oc-
>   cupation**
German occupation of Netherlands, 1940-1945.   *See*
>   **Netherlands—History—1940-1945, German
>   occupation**
Germany   943
>   Use for materials discussing the pre-World War
>   II region and the country through World
>   War II and following reunification, as well
>   as materials on East and West Germany dis-
>   cussed collectively as occupied zones or
>   countries. Materials relevant only to the
>   eastern part of Germany from 1945 to 1990,
>   the Russian occupation zone, or the Ger-
>   man Democratic Republic are entered under
>   **Germany (East).** Materials relevant only to
>   the western part of Germany from 1945 to
>   1990, the United States, British, and French
>   occupation zones, or the German Federal
>   Republic are entered under **Germany
>   (West).**
>   May be subdivided like U.S. except for *History.*
>   *See also* **Germany (East); Germany (West)**
Germany (Democratic Republic).   *See* **Germany
>   (East)**
Germany (East)   943.1087
>   See note under **Germany.**
>   *x* East Germany; German Democratic Republic;
>   Germany (Democratic Republic)
>   *xx* **Germany**
Germany (Federal Republic).   *See* **Germany (West)**
Germany—History   943
Germany—History—0-1517   943
>   *See also* **Holy Roman Empire**

314

Germany—History—1517-1740 943
 See also **Thirty Years' War, 1618-1648**
Germany—History—1740-1815 943
 See also **Seven Years' War, 1756-1763**
Germany—History—1815-1866 943
Germany—History—1848-1849, Revolution 943
Germany—History—1866-1918 943.08
Germany—History—1918-1933 943.085
Germany—History—1933-1945 943.086
Germany—History—1945-1990 943.087
Germany—History—1990- 943.087
Germany (West) 943.087
 See note under **Germany.**
 x German Federal Republic; Germany (Federal
  Republic); West Germany
 xx **Germany**
Germicides. *See* **Disinfection and disinfectants;**
  Fungicides
Germination 581.1
 x Seeds—Germination
 xx **Plant physiology**
Germs. *See* **Bacteriology; Germ theory of disease;**
  Microorganisms
Gerontology 305.26; 362.6; 612.6
 See also **Aging; Elderly; Old age**
Gestalt psychology 150.19
 x Configuration (Psychology); Psychology,
  Structural; Structural psychology
 xx **Consciousness; Knowledge, Theory of; Percep-**
  tion; Psychology; Senses and sensation
Getting ready for bed. *See* **Bedtime**
Gettysburg (Pa.), Battle of, 1863 973.7
 xx **United States—History—1861-1865, Civil**
  War—Campaigns
Geysers 551.2
 x Eruptions; Thermal waters
 xx **Geology; Geothermal resources; Physical ge-**
  ography; Water
Ghettoes, Inner city. *See* **Inner cities**
Ghost stories. *See* **Ghosts—Fiction**
Ghost towns
 See also **Cities and towns, Ruined, extinct, etc.**
 x Abandoned towns
 xx **Cities and towns, Ruined, extinct, etc.**
Ghosts 133.1
 See also **Apparitions; Demonology; Hallucina-**
  tions and illusions; Parapsychology; Spiritu-
  alism; Superstition
 x Haunted houses; Phantoms; Poltergeists;
  Specters; Spirits
 xx **Apparitions; Folklore; Hallucinations and illu-**
  sions; Parapsychology; Spiritualism; Super-
  stition
Ghosts—Fiction Fic
 x Ghost stories
Giants 398.21
 See also **Growth disorders**
 xx **Growth disorders; Monsters; Mythical ani-**
  mals
Gift wrapping 745.54
 x Wrapping of gifts
 xx **Gifts; Packaging; Paper crafts**

Gifted children   155.45

See also **Child artists; Child authors**

x Bright children; Children, Gifted; Precocious children; Superior children; Talent

xx **Exceptional children; Genius**

Gifts

See also **Donation of organs, tissues, etc.; Gift wrapping**

x Bequests; Donations; Philanthropy; Presents

Gigantism.   *See* **Growth disorders**

Gipsies.   *See* **Gypsies**

Girl Scouts (May subdiv. geog.)   **369.463**

xx **Girls' clubs; Scouts and scouting**

Girls   155.43; 305.23

See also **Children; Fathers and daughters; Mothers and daughters; Teenagers; Young women**

xx **Children; Teenagers; Young women**

Girls' agricultural clubs.   *See* **4-H clubs; Agriculture—Societies; Girls' clubs**

Girls' clubs   369.46

See also **4-H clubs; Camp Fire Girls; Girl Scouts**

x Girls' agricultural clubs; Girls—Societies and clubs

xx **Clubs; Social settlements; Societies; Women—Societies**

Girls—Education   370.82; 376

Girls—Employment.   *See* **Children—Employment; Women—Employment**

Girls—Societies and clubs.   *See* **Girls' clubs**

Girls, Teenage.   *See* **Teenagers**

GIs.   *See* **Soldiers—United States; Veterans—United States**

Giveaways.   *See* **Free material**

Glacial epoch.   *See* **Ice age**

Glaciers   551.3

xx **Geology; Ice; Physical geography; Water**

Gladiators   796.8092; 920

x Fighting

Gladness.   *See* **Happiness**

Glands   591.1; 611; 612.4

Glands, Ductless.   *See* **Endocrine glands**

Glass   666

xx **Ceramics; Windows**

Glass construction   693

xx **Building materials**

Glass fibers   666

x Fiber glass; Fibers, Glass; Glass, Spun; Spun glass

Glass manufacture   666

xx **Ceramic industries**

Glass painting and staining   748.5

x Glass, Stained; Painted glass; Stained glass; Windows, Stained glass

xx **Decoration and ornament; Painting**

Glass, Spun.   *See* **Glass fibers**

Glass, Stained.   *See* **Glass painting and staining**

Glassware   642; 748.2

See also **Vases**

x Dishes

xx **Decorative arts; Tableware; Vases**

Glazes   666; 738.1

xx **Ceramics; Pottery**

Gliders (Aeronautics)   629.133
  x Aircraft; Sailplanes (Aeronautics)
  xx **Aeronautics; Airplanes**
Gliding and soaring   797.5
  x Air surfing; Hang gliding; Soaring flight
Global satellite communications systems.   *See* **Artificial satellites in telecommunication**
Global warming.   *See* **Greenhouse effect**
Globes   912
Glossaries.   *See* **Encyclopedias and dictionaries;** and names of languages or subjects with the subdivision *Dictionaries,* e.g. **English language—Dictionaries; Chemistry—Dictionaries;** etc.
Glue   668
  xx **Adhesives**
Glue sniffing.   *See* **Solvent abuse**
Gnomes.   *See* **Fairies**
Gnosticism   299
  xx **Church history—30(ca.)-600, Early church; Philosophy; Religions**
Go karts.   *See* **Karts and karting**
Goblins.   *See* **Fairies**
God (May subdiv. by religion)   **211; 212; 231**
  See also

Agnosticism	**Metaphysics**
Atheism	**Mythology**
Creation	**Natural theology**
Deism	**Rationalism**
Femininity of God	**Religion**
Free thought	**Theism**

  xx **Creation; Deism; Metaphysics; Philosophy; Religion; Theism**
God—Christianity   231
  Use same pattern for God in other religions.
  See also **Christianity; Holy Spirit; Jesus Christ; Providence and government of God; Theology; Trinity**
  xx **Christianity; Theology; Trinity**
God—Femininity.   *See* **Femininity of God**
Goddesses.   *See* **Gods and goddesses**
Gods and goddesses   291; 292
  See also **Mythology; Religions**
  x Deities; Goddesses
  xx **Mythology; Religions**
Gold   332.4; 549; 553.4; 669
  See also **Coinage; Gold mines and mining; Goldwork; Money**
  x Bimetallism; Bullion
  xx **Coinage; Metals; Monetary policy; Money; Precious metals**
Gold articles.   *See* **Goldwork**
Gold fish.   *See* **Goldfish**
Gold mines and mining   622
  See also **Prospecting**
  xx **Gold**
Gold plate.   *See* **Plate**
Gold rush.   *See* **California—Gold discoveries**
Gold work.   *See* **Goldwork**
Golden Gate Bridge (San Francisco, Calif.)   624; 979.4
  xx **Bridges**

Goldfish   597; 639.3
   x Gold fish
   xx **Aquariums**
Goldsmithing.   *See* **Goldwork**
Goldwork   739.2
   See also **Jewelry; Plate**
   x Gold articles; Gold work; Goldsmithing
   xx **Art metalwork; Gold; Jewelry; Metalwork**
Golf courses   796.352
   xx **Grounds maintenance**
Good and evil   170; 216; 241
   See also **Sin**
   x Evil
   xx **Ethics; Suffering; Theology**
Good Friday   263
   See also **Jesus Christ—Crucifixion**
   xx **Fasts and feasts; Holy Week; Jesus Christ—
      Crucifixion; Lent**
Good grooming.   *See* **Personal grooming**
Good Neighbor Policy.   *See* **Pan-Americanism**
Goose.   *See* **Geese**
Gorge-purge syndrome.   *See* **Bulimia**
Gospel music   781.71; 782.25
   See also **Spirituals (Songs)**
   x Music, Gospel; Revivals—Music
   xx **Black music; Church music; Popular music;
      Spirituals (Songs)**
Gossip   070.4; 177; 302.2
   xx **Journalism; Libel and slander**
Gothic architecture.   *See* **Architecture, Gothic**
Gothic fiction   Fic
   x Suspense fiction
Goths.   *See* **Teutonic peoples**
Gout   616.3
   See also **Arthritis**
Government.   *See* **Political science;** and names of
      countries, cities, etc. with the subdivision
      Politics and government, e.g. **United
      States—Politics and government;** etc.
Government and business.   *See* **Industry—
      Government policy**
Government and the press.   *See* **Press—
      Government policy**
Government buildings.   *See* **Public buildings**
Government by commission.   *See* **Municipal gov-
      ernment by commission**
Government, Comparative.   *See* **Comparative gov-
      ernment**
Government debts.   *See* **Public debts**
Government documents.   *See* **Government publica-
      tions**
Government employees.   *See* **Civil service;** and
      names of countries, cities, etc. and corporate
      bodies with the subdivision *Officials and
      employees,* e.g. **United States—Officials
      and employees; Chicago (Ill.)—Officials and
      employees; United Nations—Officials and
      employees;** etc.
Government housing.   *See* **Public housing**
Government investigations.   *See* **Governmental in-
      vestigations**

Government lending (May subdiv. geog.)   332.7;
    351.82
   xx **Economic assistance, Domestic; Economic pol-
        icy; Finance; Industry—Government policy;
        Loans**
Government libraries   027.5
   Use for materials on special libraries maintained
        by government funds.
   See also **National libraries; State libraries**
   x Federal libraries; Libraries, Governmental
   xx **Special libraries**
Government, Local. *See* **Local government**
Government, Mandatory. *See* **Mandates**
Government, Military. *See* **Military government**
Government, Municipal. *See* **Municipal govern-
    ment**
Government ownership   333.1; 338.9
   See also **Municipal ownership; Privatization;
        Railroads—Government policy**
   x Nationalization; Public ownership; Socializa-
        tion of industry; State ownership
   xx **Corporations; Economic policy; Economics;
        Industry—Government policy; Political sci-
        ence; Privatization; Socialism**
Government ownership of railroads. *See* **Rail-
    roads—Government policy**
Government policy. *See* subjects with the subdivi-
        sion *Government policy,* e.g. **Homeless peo-
        ple—Government policy; Industry—
        Government policy;** etc.
Government procurement. *See* **Government pur-
    chasing**
Government publications   011; 015; 025.17
   See also names of countries, cities, etc. with the
        subdivision *Government publications,* e.g.
        United States—Government publications;
        etc.
   x Documents; Government documents; Official
        publications; Public documents
Government purchasing (May subdiv. geog.)   351.71;
    352.1
   See also **Buy national policy**
   x Government procurement; Procurement,
        Government; Public procurement; Purchas-
        ing, Government
   xx **Buying**
Government records—Preservation. *See* **Archives**
Government regulation of commerce. *See* **Com-
    mercial policy; Interstate commerce; Tariff**
Government regulation of industry. *See* **Industry—
    Government policy**
Government regulation of railroads. *See* **Interstate
    commerce; Railroads—Government policy**
Government reorganization. *See* **United States—
    Executive departments—Reorganization**
Government, Resistance to   322.4
   See also **Hunger strikes; Insurgency; Passive re-
        sistance; Revolutions**
   x Civil disobedience; Resistance to government
   xx **Insurgency; Political crimes and offenses; Po-
        litical ethics; Political science; Revolutions**
Government service. *See* **Civil service**
Government spending policy. *See* **United States—
    Appropriations and expenditures**

Governmental investigations (May subdiv. geog.)
328; 351.9
> Use for materials on investigations initiated by the legislative, executive and judicial branches of the government.
> *x* Congressional investigations; Executive investigations; Government investigations; Investigations, Governmental; Judicial investigations; Legislative investigations
> *xx* **Justice, Administration of**

Governmental investigations—United States   328.3; 353.009
> *x* United States—Governmental investigations

Governments in exile. *See* **World War, 1939-1945—Governments in exile**

Governors   351.092; 920
> *xx* **State governments**

Graal. *See* **Grail**

Grace (Theology)   234
> *xx* **Conversion; Salvation; Theology**

Grade repetition. *See* **Promotion (School)**

Grade retention. *See* **Promotion (School)**

Grading and marking (Education)   371.2
> *See also* **Ability grouping in education; Promotion (School); School reports**
> *x* Grading and marking (Students); Marking (Students); Students—Grading and marking
> *xx* **Educational tests and measurements; School reports**

Grading and marking (Students). *See* **Grading and marking (Education)**

Graduate record examination   378.1
> *x* G.R.E.; GRE
> *xx* **Colleges and universities—Entrance examinations; Scholastic aptitude test**

Graduates, College. *See* **College graduates**

Graduation. *See* **Commencements**

Graffiti   001.55
> *xx* **Folklore; Inscriptions**

Graft in politics. *See* **Corruption in politics**

Grafting   631.5
> *xx* **Botany; Fruit culture; Gardening; Plant propagation; Trees**

Grail   398.22
> *See also* **Arthurian romances**
> *x* Graal; Holy Grail
> *xx* **Arthurian romances; Folklore; Legends**

Grain   633.1
> *See also* **Prepared cereals;** also names of cereal plants, e.g. **Corn; Wheat;** etc.
> *x* Breadstuffs; Cereals
> *xx* **Botany, Economic; Flour; Food**

Grammar   415
> *See also* **Language and languages; Philology, Comparative;** also names of languages with the subdivision *Grammar,* e.g. **English language—Grammar;** etc.
> *xx* **Language and languages**

Grammar schools. *See* **Elementary education; Public schools**

Grammatical comparison. *See* **English language—Comparison**

Gramslamming. *See* **Elderly abuse**

Grand opera. *See* **Opera**

Grandchild and grandparent.   *See* **Grandparent and child**

Grandparent and child   306.874
>   Use for materials on the interaction between grandparents and their grandchildren. For materials restricted to the legal right of grandparents to visit their grandchildren, use **Visitation rights (Domestic relations).**
>   *x* Child and grandparent; Children and grandparents; Grandchild and grandparent; Grandparent and grandchild; Grandparenting
>   *xx* **Children and adults; Domestic relations; Family; Human relations**

Grandparent and grandchild.   *See* **Grandparent and child**

Grandparenting.   *See* **Grandparent and child**

Grange   334
>   *xx* **Agriculture—Societies**

Granite   552
>   *xx* **Petrology; Rocks**

Grants.   *See* **Subsidies**

Grants-in-aid   338.9
>   Use for materials on grants of money made from a central government to a local government.
>   *See also* **Economic assistance, Domestic; Federal aid to education; Federal aid to libraries**
>   *x* Block grants; Federal grants
>   *xx* **Economic assistance, Domestic**

Grapes   634.8
>   *See also* **Wine and wine making**
>   *x* Vineyards
>   *xx* **Wine and wine making**

Graph theory   510; 511
>   *x* Graphs, Theory of; Theory of graphs
>   *xx* **Algebra; Mathematical analysis; Topology**

Graphic arts (May subdiv. geog. adjective form, e.g. **Graphic arts, American;** etc.)   **760**
>   *See also* types of graphic arts, e.g. **Drawing; Engraving; Painting; Printing; Prints;** etc.
>   *x* Art, Graphic; Arts, Graphic
>   *xx* **Art**

Graphic arts, American   760.0973
>   *x* American graphic arts; United States—Graphic arts

Graphic methods   001.4; 511
>   *See also* **Statistics—Graphic methods**
>   *x* Flow charts; Flowcharting; Graphs
>   *xx* **Drawing; Geometrical drawing; Mechanical drawing**

Graphics, Computer.   *See* **Computer graphics**

Graphite   549; 553.2
>   *x* Black lead
>   *xx* **Carbon**

Graphology   137
>   See note under **Writing.**
>   *xx* **Handwriting; Writing**

Graphs.   *See* **Graphic methods**

Graphs, Theory of.   *See* **Graph theory**

Grass (Drug).   *See* **Marijuana**

Grasses   584; 633.2
>   *See also* **Feeds; Forage plants; Grasslands; Hay; Pastures**

Grasses—*Continued*

   x Herbage

   xx **Botany, Economic; Forage plants; Hay; Lawns; Pastures**

Grasslands (May subdiv. geog.) **581.5**

   xx **Grasses**

Graves. *See* **Cemeteries; Epitaphs; Funeral rites and ceremonies; Mounds and mound builders; Tombs**

Graveyard of the Atlantic. *See* **Bermuda Triangle**

Graveyards. *See* **Cemeteries**

Gravitation 521; 531

   x Gravity

   xx **Physics**

Gravity. *See* **Gravitation**

Gravity free state. *See* **Weightlessness**

Gray Friars. *See* **Franciscans**

GRE. *See* **Graduate record examination**

Grease. *See* **Lubrication and lubricants; Oils and fats**

Great books program. *See* **Discussion groups**

Great Britain 941

   May be subdivided like U.S. except for *History.* For a list of subjects that may be used under either England or Great Britain, see **England.**

   See also **Commonwealth of Nations; England**

Great Britain—Antiquities 936

Great Britain—Colonies 325

   See also **Commonwealth of Nations**

   x British Empire

   xx **Colonies; Commonwealth of Nations**

Great Britain—History 941

   x England—History; English history

Great Britain—History—0-1066 941.01

   See also **Anglo-Saxons; Celts**

Great Britain—History—1066-1154, Norman period 941.02

   See also **Hastings (East Sussex, England), Battle of, 1066; Normans**

Great Britain—History—1154-1399, Plantagenets 941.03

Great Britain—History—1399-1485, Lancaster and York 941.04

   See also **Hundred Years' War, 1339-1453**

Great Britain—History—1455-1485, War of the Roses 941.04

   x Wars of the Roses, 1455-1485

Great Britain—History—1485-1603, Tudors 941.05

   See also **Spanish Armada, 1588**

Great Britain—History—1603-1714, Stuarts 941.06

Great Britain—History—1642-1660, Civil War and Commonwealth 941.06

   x Civil War—England; Commonwealth of England

Great Britain—History—1714-1837 941.07

Great Britain—History—1800-1899 (19th century) 941.081

   x Industrial revolution

Great Britain—History—1853-1856, Crimean War. *See* **Crimean War, 1853-1856**

Great Britain—History—1900-1999 (20th century) 941.082

Great Britain—History—1945-1952   941.085
Great Britain—History—1952-   941.085
Great Britain—Kings, queens, rulers, etc.   920;
    941.092
   xx **Kings, queens, rulers, etc.**
Great Britain—Prime ministers.   *See* **Prime minis-**
    ters—Great Britain
Greece   938; 949.5
Greece, Ancient.   *See* **Greece—History—0-323**
Greece—Antiquities   938
   See also **Delphi (Ancient city)**
   xx **Classical antiquities**
Greece—Biography   920.038; 920.0495
   x Classical biography
Greece—Civilization.   *See* **Civilization, Greek**
Greece—Description   914.95
   Use for descriptive materials on modern Greece,
    including materials for travelers. Descrip-
    tive materials on ancient Greece, including
    accounts by travelers in ancient times, are
    entered under **Greece—Description—0-323.**
   x Greece—Description and travel
Greece—Description—0-323   913.8
   Use for descriptive materials on ancient Greece
    including accounts by travelers of ancient
    times.
   x Ancient Greece—Description; Greece—
    Description and geography
Greece—Description and geography.   *See* **Greece—**
    Description—0-323; Greece—Historical ge-
    ography
Greece—Description and travel.   *See* **Greece—**
    Description
Greece—Geography   914.95
   Use for geographical materials on modern
    Greece.
   See also **Greece—Historical geography**
Greece—Historical geography   911; 913.8
   x Classical geography; Greece—Description and
    geography
   xx **Greece—Geography**
Greece—History   938; 949.5
Greece—History—0-323   938
   x Greece, Ancient
Greece—History—323-1453   949.5
   x Greece, Medieval
Greece—History—1453-   949.5
   x Greece, Modern
Greece—History—1967-1974   949.507
Greece—History—1974-   949.507
Greece, Medieval.   *See* **Greece—History—323-**
    1453
Greece, Modern.   *See* **Greece—History—1453-**
Greek antiquities.   *See* **Classical antiquities**
Greek architecture.   *See* **Architecture, Greek**
Greek art.   *See* **Art, Greek**
Greek Church.   *See* **Orthodox Eastern Church**
Greek civilization.   *See* **Civilization, Greek; Helle-**
    nism
Greek language   480
   Use for classical Greek. Modern Greek is en-
    tered under **Greek language, Modern.** May
    be subdivided like **English language.**

Greek language—*Continued*
    See also **Hellenism**
    x Classical languages
Greek language, Modern   489
    May be subdivided like **English language.**
    x Romaic language
Greek letter societies. *See* **Fraternities and sororities; Secret societies**
Greek literature 880
    May use same subdivisions and names of literary forms as for **English literature.**
    See also **Classical literature; Hellenism**
    xx **Classical literature**
Greek literature, Modern 889
    x Neo-Greek literature; Romaic literature
Greek mythology. *See* **Mythology, Classical**
Greek philosophy. *See* **Philosophy, Ancient**
Greek sculpture. *See* **Sculpture, Greek**
Greenbacks. *See* **Paper money**
Greenhouse effect 363.73; 551.5; 551.6
    x Atmospheric greenhouse effect; Carbon dioxide greenhouse effect; Global warming; Greenhouse effect, Atmospheric
    xx **Climate; Solar radiation**
Greenhouse effect, Atmospheric. *See* **Greenhouse effect**
Greenhouses 631.5
    x Hothouses
    xx **Flower gardening; Gardening; Horticulture**
Greenhouses, Window. *See* **Window gardening**
Greeting cards 741.6; 745.594
    x Cards, Greeting; Christmas cards
Gregorian chant. *See* **Chants (Plain, Gregorian, etc.)**
Grey Friars. *See* **Franciscans**
Grief. *See* **Joy and sorrow**
Grievance procedures (Public administration). *See* **Ombudsman**
Grill cookery. *See* **Barbecue cookery**
Grinding and polishing 621.9
    x Buffing; Polishing
Grippe. *See* **Influenza**
Grist mills. *See* **Flour mills**
Grocery trade 338.4
    See also **Supermarkets**
Grooming for men. *See* **Personal grooming**
Grooming for women. *See* **Personal grooming**
Grooming, Personal. *See* **Personal grooming**
Grottoes. *See* **Caves**
Ground cushion phenomena 629.3
    See also **Ground effect machines**
    x Air bearing lift
    xx **Aerodynamics; Pneumatics**
Ground effect machines 629.3
    See also **Helicopters; Vertically rising airplanes**
    x Air bearing vehicles; Air cushion vehicles; Ground proximity machines; Hovercraft; Surface effect machines
    xx **Ground cushion phenomena**
Ground proximity machines. *See* **Ground effect machines**
Grounds maintenance 712
    Use for materials on maintenance of public, in-

Grounds maintenance—*Continued*
>> dustrial, and institutional grounds and large estates.

>> *See also* **Golf courses; Roadside improvement**

>> *xx* **Gardening**

Group discussion. *See* **Discussion groups**

Group dynamics. *See* **Social groups**

Group health. *See* **Health insurance**

Group homes   362; 363.5
>> Use for materials on planned housing for groups of unrelated people needing supervision.

>> *See also* **Foster home care; Halfway houses**

>> *x* Community based residences; Group residences; Residential treatment centers

>> *xx* **Foster home care; Institutional care; Social work**

Group hospitalization. *See* **Hospitalization insurance**

Group insurance   368.3
>> Includes group life insurance. Materials on group insurance in other fields are entered under the specific heading, e.g. **Health insurance;** etc.

>> *x* Insurance, Group

>> *xx* **Life insurance**

Group living. *See* **Collective settlements**

Group medical practice. *See* **Medical practice**

Group medical practice, Prepaid. *See* **Health maintenance organizations**

Group medical service. *See* **Health insurance**

Group problem solving. *See* **Problem solving, Group**

Group relations training   616.89
>> *x* Encounter groups; Sensitivity training; T groups

>> *xx* **Human relations**

Group residences. *See* **Group homes**

Group theory   510; 512
>> *See also* **Algebra, Boolean**

>> *x* Groups, Theory of

>> *xx* **Algebra; Mathematics; Number theory**

Group travel. *See* **Travel**

Group values. *See* **Social values**

Group work, Social. *See* **Social group work**

Grouping by ability. *See* **Ability grouping in education**

Groups, Ethnic. *See* **Ethnic groups**

Groups, Social. *See* **Social groups**

Groups, Theory of. *See* **Group theory**

Growing of Christmas trees. *See* **Christmas tree growing**

Growth   155; 574.3; 612.6
>> *See also* subjects with the subdivision *Growth*, e.g. **Children—Growth; Cities and towns—Growth; Plants—Growth;** etc.

>> *xx* **Physiology**

Growth disorders   612.6
>> *See also* **Birth defects; Giants**

>> *x* Abnormal growth; Development; Dwarfism; Failure to thrive syndrome; Fetus—Growth retardation; Gigantism

>> *xx* **Birth defects; Giants; Metabolism**

Guaranteed annual income. *See* **Wages—Annual wage**

Guaranteed income. *See* **Wages—Annual wage**
Guerillas. *See* **Guerrillas**
Guerrilla warfare   355.02; 355.4
> Use for materials on the military aspects of ir-
> regular warfare. General and historical ma-
> terials are entered under **Guerrillas.**
> *x* Unconventional warfare
> *xx* **Insurgency; Military art and science; Tactics;
> War**
Guerrillas (May subdiv. geog.)   **356**
> Use for general and historical materials. For ma-
> terials on the military aspects of guerrilla
> warfare use **Guerrilla warfare.**
> *See also* **National liberation movements;** also in-
> dividual wars with the subdivision
> *Underground movements,* e.g. **World War,
> 1939-1945—Underground movements.**
> *x* Guerillas; Partisans
> *xx* **National liberation movements**
Guests. *See* **Entertaining**
Guidance. *See* **Counseling**
Guidance counseling, Educational. *See* **Educational
counseling**
Guidance counseling, School. *See* **School counsel-
ing**
Guidance, Vocational. *See* **Vocational guidance**
Guide dogs   636.7
> *x* Blind, Dogs for the; Dog guides; Dogs for the
> blind; Seeing eye dogs
> *xx* **Animals and the handicapped; Dogs**
Guide posts. *See* **Signs and signboards**
Guidebooks. *See* names of cities (except ancient
cities), countries, states, etc. with the subdi-
vision *Description—Guidebooks,* e.g. **Chi-
cago (Ill.)—Description—Guidebooks;
United States—Description—Guidebooks;**
etc.
Guided missiles   623.4
> *See also* types of missiles, e.g. **Antimissile mis-
> siles; Ballistic missiles;** etc.; also names of
> specific missiles, e.g. **Nike rocket;** etc.
> *x* Bombs, Flying; Flying bombs; Missiles,
> Guided
> *xx* **Bombs; Projectiles; Rocketry; Rockets (Aero-
> nautics)**
Guitar   787.87
> *xx* **Stringed instruments**
Guitar music   787.87
> *xx* **Instrumental music**
Gulf States (U.S.)   976
> *xx* **United States**
Gulf War, 1991-. *See* **Persian Gulf War, 1991-**
Gums and resins   547.7; 668
> *x* Resins; Rosin
> *xx* **Chemistry, Technical; Forest products; Plas-
> tics**
Gun control. *See* **Firearms—Law and legislation**
Gunning. *See* **Hunting; Shooting**
Gunpowder   623.4
> *See also* **Ammunition**
> *x* Powder, Smokeless; Smokeless powder
> *xx* **Ammunition; Explosives; Firearms**
Guns. *See* **Firearms; Ordnance; Rifles; Shotguns**

Guns—Control. *See* **Firearms—Law and legislation**

Gunsmithing. *See* **Firearms industry**

Gymnastics 613.7; 796.44

    See also **Acrobats and acrobatics; Physical education**

    x Calisthenics

    xx **Acrobats and acrobatics; Athletics; Exercise; Physical education; Sports**

Gynecology. *See* **Women—Diseases; Women—Health and hygiene**

Gypsies 305.891

    x Gipsies; Romanies

Gypsum 553.6

    x Plaster of paris

    xx **Geology, Economic**

Gyroscope 629.135; 681

    xx **Aeronautical instruments**

H.B.O. *See* **Home Box Office**

H bomb. *See* **Hydrogen bomb**

H.M.O.'s. *See* **Health maintenance organizations**

Habit 152.3

    See also **Drug addiction; Instinct; Tobacco habit**

    xx **Human behavior; Instinct; Psychology**

Habitations, Human. *See* **Architecture, Domestic; Houses; Housing**

Habitations of animals. *See* **Animals—Habitations**

Habits of animals. *See* **Animals—Behavior**

Hades. *See* **Future life; Hell**

Haiku 808.1; 808.81; 811.008, etc.

    xx **Poetry**

Hair and hairdressing 611; 646.7

    Includes materials on hairdressing and haircutting.

    See also **Wigs**

    x Coiffure; Hairdressing

    xx **Head**

Hairdressing. *See* **Hair and hairdressing**

Halftone process. *See* **Photoengraving**

Halfway houses 362; 365

    Use for materials on centers for formerly institutionalized individuals, such as mental patients or drug addicts, that are designed to facilitate their readjustment to private life.

    xx **Correctional institutions; Group homes**

Halley's comet 523.6

    xx **Comets**

Hallmarks

    See also **Plate**

    x Marks on plate

    xx **Plate**

Halloween 394.2

    x All Hallows' Eve

    xx **Manners and customs**

Hallucinations and illusions 616.85; 616.89

    See also **Apparitions; Ghosts; Magic; Optical illusions; Personality disorders**

    x Delusions; Illusions

    xx **Apparitions; Fantasy; Ghosts; Parapsychology; Personality disorders; Psychology, Pathological; Subconsciousness; Visions**

Hallucinogenic drugs. *See* **Hallucinogens**

Hallucinogenic plants. *See* **Hallucinogens**

Hallucinogens 615

See also **Marijuana;** also names of hallucinogens

x Consciousness expanding drugs; Drugs, Hallucinogenic; Hallucinogenic drugs; Hallucinogenic plants; Plants, Hallucinogenic

xx **Drug abuse; Drugs; Psychotropic drugs; Stimulants**

Ham radio stations. See **Amateur radio stations**

Hand shadows. See **Shadow pictures**

Hand weaving. See **Weaving**

Handbooks, manuals, etc. See general subjects with the subdivision *Handbooks, manuals, etc.,* e.g. **Photography—Handbooks, manuals, etc.;** etc.

Handedness. See **Left- and right-handedness**

Handguns. See **Pistols**

Handheld computers. See **Portable computers**

Handi-animals. See **Animals and the handicapped**

Handicapped 305.9; 362.4

See also **Mentally handicapped; Physically handicapped; Sick; Socially handicapped**

x Disabled

Handicapped and animals. See **Animals and the handicapped**

Handicapped and architecture. See **Architecture and the handicapped**

Handicapped children 362.7

See also **Brain damaged children; Hyperactive children; Mainstreaming in education; Mentally handicapped children; Physically handicapped children; Socially handicapped children**

x Abnormal children; Children, Abnormal

xx **Children; Exceptional children**

Handicraft 745.5; 746

Use for materials on creative work done by hand, sometimes with the aid of simple tools or machines. Consider also **Decoration and ornament** and **Decorative arts.**

See also

Arts and crafts movement	**Industrial arts**
Craft shows	**Industrial arts education**
Creative activities	**Nature craft**
Folk art	**Occupational therapy**
Hobbies	

also names of individual crafts, e.g. **Collage; Egg decoration; Leather work; Weaving;** etc.

x Crafts (Arts)

xx **Arts and crafts movement; Folk art; Hobbies; Occupational therapy**

Handling of materials. See **Materials handling**

Handwriting 652

See note under **Writing.**

See also **Calligraphy; Graphology; Writing; Writing of numerals**

x Copybooks; Penmanship

xx **Business education; Writing**

Hang gliding. See **Gliding and soaring**

Hanging. See **Capital punishment**

Hanukkah 296.4; 394.2

x Chanukah; Feast of Dedication; Feast of Lights; Lights, Feast of; Maccabbees, Feast of the

Hanukkah—*Continued*
　　xx **Fasts and feasts—Judaism**
Happiness 158
　　See also **Joy and sorrow; Pleasure**
　　x Gladness
　　xx **Joy and sorrow; Pleasure**
Harassment, Sexual. *See* **Sexual harassment**
Harbors (May subdiv. geog.) **386; 387.1; 627**
　　See also **Docks; Marinas; Pilots and pilotage**
　　x Ports
　　xx **Civil engineering; Docks; Hydraulic struc-
　　　　tures; Merchant marine; Navigation; Ship-
　　　　ping; Transportation**
Hard drug addiction. *See* **Drug addiction**
Hares. *See* **Rabbits**
Harlem Renaissance 810.9; 974.7
　　x New Negro Movement; Renaissance, Harlem
　　xx **American literature—Black authors; Black
　　　　art; Black music**
Harmful insects. *See* **Insect pests**
Harmony 781.2
　　xx **Composition (Music); Music; Music—Theory**
Harry S. Truman Library 026
　　xx **Presidents—United States—Archives**
Harvesting machinery 631.3
　　x Reapers
　　xx **Agricultural machinery**
Hashish. *See* **Marijuana**
**Hastings (East Sussex, England), Battle of, 1066
　　941.02**
　　xx **Great Britain—History—1066-1154, Norman
　　　　period**
Hate crimes 364
　　x Bias attacks; Bias crimes; Bigotry-motivated
　　　　crimes; Crimes of hate; Prejudice-
　　　　motivated crimes
　　xx **Crime; Discrimination; Violence**
Hatha yoga 613.7
　　See also **Yoga**
　　x Yoga exercises; Yoga, Hatha
　　xx **Exercise; Respiration; Yoga**
Hats 391; 646.5; 687
　　See also **Millinery**
　　xx **Clothing and dress; Costume; Millinery**
Haunted houses. *See* **Ghosts**
Hawking. *See* **Falconry**
Hay 633.2
　　See also **Feeds; Grasses;** also names of hay
　　　　crops, e.g. **Alfalfa;** etc.
　　xx **Farm produce; Feeds; Forage plants; Grasses**
Hay fever 616.2
　　xx **Allergy**
Hazardous materials. *See* **Hazardous substances**
Hazardous occupations 331.7
　　See also **Occupational diseases**
　　x Dangerous occupations; Injurious occupa-
　　　　tions; Occupations, Dangerous
　　xx **Accidents; Labor; Occupational diseases; Oc-
　　　　cupational health and safety**
Hazardous substances 363.17; 604.7
　　See also **Hazardous wastes; Poisons and poison-
　　　　ing**
　　x Dangerous materials; Hazardous materials;

Hazardous substances—*Continued*
> Inflammable substances; Toxic substances
> *xx* **Materials; Occupational health and safety**

Hazardous substances—Transportation 363.17;
> **604.7**

Hazardous waste disposal. *See* **Hazardous wastes**

Hazardous waste sites 363.72; 628.4
> *See also* **Love Canal Chemical Waste Landfill
> (Niagara Falls, N.Y.)**
> *x* Chemical landfills; Dumps, Toxic; Toxic
> dumps
> *xx* **Landfills**

Hazardous wastes 363.72
> *See also* **Medical wastes; Pollution**
> *x* Hazardous waste disposal; Toxic wastes;
> Wastes, Hazardous
> *xx* **Hazardous substances; Industrial wastes;
> Medical wastes; Pollution; Refuse and re-
> fuse disposal**

HBO. *See* **Home Box Office**

HDTV (Television). *See* **High definition television**

Head 611; 612
> *See also* **Brain; Ear; Eye; Face; Hair and hair-
> dressing; Nose; Phrenology**
> *xx* **Brain**

Heads of state (May subdiv. geog.) 351.003; 920
> *See also* **Dictators; Kings, queens, rulers, etc.;
> Presidents; Prime ministers**
> *x* Rulers; State, Heads of
> *xx* **Executive power; Statesmen**

Healing, Mental. *See* **Mental healing**

Healing, Spiritual. *See* **Spiritual healing**

Health 613
> Use for materials on physical, mental, and social
> well-being. Materials on personal body care
> are entered under **Hygiene.**
> *See also*

Diet	**Hygiene**
Diseases	**Longevity**
Exercise	**Mental health**
Health education	**Physical fitness**
Health self-care	**Rest**
Holistic medicine	**Sleep**

> also parts of the body with the subdivision *Care
> and hygiene,* e.g. **Foot—Care and hygiene;**
> etc.; and classes of people and ethnic groups
> with the subdivision *Health and hygiene,*
> e.g. **Women—Health and hygiene;** etc.
> *x* Personal health
> *xx* **Diseases; Holistic medicine; Hygiene; Medi-
> cine; Physiology; Preventive medicine**

Health and hygiene. *See* classes of people and eth-
> nic groups with the subdivision *Health and
> hygiene,* e.g. **Women—Health and hygiene;**
> etc.; and parts of the body with the subdivi-
> sion *Care and hygiene,* e.g. **Foot—Care and
> hygiene; Skin—Care and hygiene;** etc.

Health boards 614.06
> *x* Boards of health; Public health boards
> *xx* **Public health**

Health care. *See* **Medical care**

Health care, Self. *See* **Health self-care**

Health clubs. *See* **Health resorts, spas, etc.**

Health counseling   362.1; 613
   xx Counseling; Health education
Health education   372.3; 613.07
   See also Drug education; Health counseling;
      School hygiene
   x Health—Study and teaching; Hygiene—Study
      and teaching
   xx Children—Health and hygiene; Health; Phys-
      ical education
Health—Environmental aspects.   *See* Environmen-
    tal health
Health foods.   *See* Natural foods
Health, Industrial.   *See* Occupational health and
    safety
Health insurance   368.3
   See also Health maintenance organizations; Hos-
      pitalization insurance; Workers' compensa-
      tion
   x Disability insurance; Group health; Group
      medical service; Health plans, Prepaid; In-
      surance, Disability; Insurance, Health; In-
      surance, Sickness; Medical care, Prepaid;
      Medical service, Prepaid; Prepaid health
      plans; Prepaid medical care; Sickness insur-
      ance; Socialized medicine
  xx Insurance
Health maintenance organizations   368.3; 610.6
   x Comprehensive health care organizations;
      Group medical practice, Prepaid; H.M.O.'s;
      HMOs; Prepaid group medical practice
  xx Health insurance; Medical care
Health, Mental.   *See* Mental health
Health of infants.   *See* Infants—Health and hygiene
Health plans, Prepaid.   *See* Health insurance
Health, Public.   *See* Public health
Health resorts, spas, etc.   613
   See also Summer resorts; Winter resorts
   x Health clubs; Physical fitness centers; Resorts;
      Sanatoriums; Spas; Watering places
  xx Hydrotherapy; Medicine; Sick; Summer re-
      sorts; Travel; Winter resorts
Health self-care   613; 616
   See also First aid; Holistic medicine; Medicine,
      Popular; Nutrition; Physical fitness
   x Health care, Self; Medical self-care; Self-care,
      Health; Self-care, Medical; Self-
      examination, Medical; Self health care; Self-
      help medical care; Self-medication
  xx Alternative medicine; Health; Holistic medi-
      cine; Medical care; Medicine, Popular
Health—Study and teaching.   *See* Health education
Healths, Drinking of.   *See* Toasts
Hearing   152.1; 612.8
   See also Deafness; Ear
   x Acoustics
  xx Deafness; Ear; Senses and sensation; Sound
Hearing aids   617.8
   See also Hearing ear dogs
  xx Deafness
Hearing ear dogs   636.7
   x Deaf, Dogs for; Dogs for the deaf
  xx Animals and the handicapped; Deaf; Dogs;
      Hearing aids
Hearing impaired.   *See* Deaf

Heart   591.1; 611; 612.1
  See also **Artificial heart; Blood—Circulation**
  xx **Cardiovascular system; Human anatomy;**
       Physiology
Heart attack. *See* **Heart—Diseases**
Heart—Diseases   616.1
  x Angina pectoris; Cardiac diseases; Coronary
       heart diseases; Heart attack
Heart—Diseases—Prevention   616.1
Heart resuscitation. *See* **Cardiac resuscitation**
Heart—Surgery   617.4
  x Open heart surgery
  xx **Surgery**
Heart—Surgery—Nursing   610.73; 617.4
  xx **Nursing**
Heart—Transplantation   617.4
  xx **Transplantation of organs, tissues, etc.**
Heat   536
  See also **Combustion; Fire; Steam; Temperature;**
       Thermodynamics; Thermometers
  xx **Combustion; Electromagnetic waves; Fire;**
       Temperature; Thermodynamics
Heat—Conduction   536
Heat engines   621.43
  See also **Steam engines; Thermodynamics**
  x Hot air engines
  xx **Engines; Thermodynamics**
Heat insulating materials. *See* **Insulation (Heat)**
Heat pumps   621.4
  xx **Pumping machinery; Thermodynamics**
Heat—Transmission   536
Heathenism. *See* **Paganism**
Heating   644; 697
  See also

Chimneys	**Oil burners**
Electric heating	**Radiant heating**
Fireplaces	**Solar heating**
Fuel	**Space heaters**
Furnaces	**Steam heating**
Hot air heating	**Stoves**
Hot water heating	**Ventilation**
Insulation (Heat)	

    also subjects with the subdivision *Heating and*
       ventilation, e.g. **Houses—Heating and ven-**
       tilation; etc.
  xx **Fire; Fuel; Home economics; Ventilation**
Heaven   236
  See also **Angels**
  xx **Death; Future life**
Heavy water. *See* **Deuterium oxide**
Hebrew language   492.4
    May be subdivided like **English language.**
    See also **Yiddish language**
  x Jewish language; Jews—Language
Hebrew literature   892.4
    May use same subdivisions and names of liter-
       ary forms as for **English literature.**
    See also **Bible; Cabala; Jewish literature; Talmud**
  x Jews—Literature
  xx **Jewish literature**
Hebrews. *See* **Jews**
Heirs. *See* **Inheritance and succession**

Helicopters   387.7; 629.133
 x Aircraft
 xx **Aeronautics; Airplanes; Ground effect machines**
Helicopters—Piloting   629.132
 xx **Airplanes—Piloting**
Heliports   387.7
 xx **Airports**
Helium   546
 xx **Radioactivity**
Hell   236
 x Eternal punishment; Hades; Retribution
 xx **Death; Future life**
Hellenism   938; 939
 x Greek civilization
 xx **Civilization, Greek; Greek language; Greek literature; Humanism**
Helpful insects.   *See* **Beneficial insects**
Helpfulness.   *See* **Helping behavior**
Helping behavior   158
 See also **Counseling**
 x Assistance in emergencies; Behavior, Helping; Emergency assistance; Helpfulness
 xx **Human behavior; Human relations**
Hemp   633.5; 677
 See also **Marijuana; Rope**
 xx **Fibers; Linen; Rope**
Heraldry   929.6
 See also

Chivalry	**Knights and knighthood**
Decorations of honor	**Mottoes**
Flags	**Nobility**
Genealogy	**Seals (Numismatics)**
Insignia	

 x Arms, Coats of; Coats of arms; Crests; Devices (Heraldry); Emblems; Pedigrees
 xx **Archeology; Biography; Chivalry; Decorations of honor; Genealogy; Knights and knighthood; Nobility; Signs and symbols; Symbolism**
Herbage.   *See* **Grasses**
Herbal medicine.   *See* **Botany, Medical**
Herbals.   *See* **Botany, Medical; Herbs; Materia medica**
Herbaria.   *See* **Plants—Collection and preservation**
Herbicides   632; 668
 See also **Plants; Spraying and dusting;** also names of herbicides, e.g. **Agent Orange;** etc.
 x Defoliants; Weed killers; Weedicides
 xx **Agricultural chemicals; Pesticides; Plants; Spraying and dusting**
Herbs   635
 x Herbals
Herbs, Medical.   *See* **Botany, Medical**
Hereditary diseases.   *See* **Medical genetics**
Hereditary succession.   *See* **Inheritance and succession**
Heredity   575.1
 See also

Blood groups	**Eugenics**
Chromosomes	**Evolution**
DNA	**Genetic mapping**

Heredity—*Continued*
    Mendel's law   Variation (Biology)
    Natural selection
       x Ancestry; Descent; Genes; Inheritance (Biology)
      xx **Biology; Breeding; Children; Eugenics; Evolution; Genetics; Man; Mendel's law; Natural selection; Sociology**
Heredity of diseases. *See* **Medical genetics**
Hereford cattle   636.2
    xx **Beef cattle**
Hermeneutics, Biblical. *See* **Bible—Criticism, interpretation, etc.**
Hermetic art and philosophy. *See* **Alchemy; Astrology; Occultism**
Hermits   920
    x Recluses
    xx **Religious orders; Saints**
Heroes and heroines   920
    See also **Courage; Explorers; Martyrs; Mythology; Saints**
    x Heroines; Heroism
    xx **Adventure and adventurers; Courage; Mythology**
Heroin   362.29; 615
    xx **Morphine; Narcotics**
Heroines. *See* **Heroes and heroines; Women—Biography; Women in the Bible**
Heroism. *See* **Courage; Heroes and heroines**
Hertzian waves. *See* **Electric waves**
Hi-fi systems. *See* **High-fidelity sound systems**
Hibernation of animals. *See* **Animals—Hibernation**
Hidden treasure. *See* **Buried treasure**
Hides and skins   636.088; 675
    See also **Fur; Leather; Tanning**
    x Animal products; Pelts; Skins
    xx **Fur; Leather; Tanning**
Hieroglyphics   411
    Use for materials on that form of picture writing which is distinguished by conventionalized pictures used chiefly to represent meanings that seem arbitrary and are seldom obvious, such as the pictographic styles used in ancient Egypt, Crete, Central America, and Mexico.
    See also **Picture writing; Rosetta stone inscription**
    xx **Inscriptions; Picture writing; Writing**
High blood pressure. *See* **Hypertension**
High definition television   621.388
    x HDTV (Television)
    xx **Television**
High-fidelity sound systems   621.389
    See also **Stereophonic sound systems**
    x Hi-fi systems
    xx **Electronics; Sound—Recording and reproducing**
High-frequency radio. *See* **Shortwave radio**
High rise buildings. *See* **Skyscrapers**
High school dropouts. *See* **Dropouts**
High school education. *See* **Secondary education**

High school libraries   027.8
> *See also* **Young adults' library services**
>
> *x* Junior high school libraries; School libraries
>   (High school); Secondary school libraries
>
> *xx* **School libraries; Young adults' library services**

High school life.   *See* **High school students**

High school students   373
> *x* High school life; High schools—Students
>
> *xx* **Students**

High school yearbooks.   *See* **School yearbooks**

High schools (May subdiv. geog.)   373
> *See also* **Commencements; Junior high schools;**
>   **Secondary education**
>
> *x* Secondary schools
>
> *xx* **Public schools; Secondary education**

High schools, Junior.   *See* **Junior high schools**

High schools, Rural.   *See* **Rural schools**

High schools—Students.   *See* **High school students**

High society.   *See* **Upper classes**

High speed aerodynamics.   *See* **Aerodynamics, Su-**
     personic

High speed aeronautics   629.132
> *See also* **Aerodynamics, Supersonic; Aerothermo-**
>   **dynamics; Rocket planes; Rockets (Aeronau-**
>   **tics)**
>
> *x* Aeronautics, High speed
>
> *xx* **Aeronautics**

High tech.   *See* **Technology**

High technology.   *See* **Technology**

High treason.   *See* **Treason**

High-yield junk bonds.   *See* **Junk bonds**

Higher criticism.   *See* **Bible—Criticism, interpreta-**
     tion, etc.

Higher education   378
> Use for general consideration of education above
>   the secondary level, i.e. for materials on col-
>   lege education, professional education, etc.
>   Use for materials not specific enough to be
>   entered under **Colleges and universities.**
>
> *See also* **Adult education; Classical education;**
>   **Colleges and universities; Junior colleges;**
>   **Professional education; Technical education;**
>   **University extension**
>
> *x* Education, Higher
>
> *xx* **Colleges and universities**

Highjacking of airplanes.   *See* **Hijacking of air-**
     planes

Highland clans.   *See* **Clans**

Highland costume.   *See* **Tartans**

Highway accidents.   *See* **Traffic accidents**

Highway beautification.   *See* **Roadside improvement**

Highway construction.   *See* **Roads**

Highway engineering   625.7
> *See also* **Roads; Traffic engineering**
>
> *x* Road engineering
>
> *xx* **Civil engineering; Engineering; Roads**

Highway transportation.   *See* **Transportation, High-**
     way

Highwaymen.   *See* **Robbers and outlaws**

Highways.   *See* **Roads**

Hijacking of airplanes   364.1
> Use same form for the hijacking of other modes
>   of transportation.

Hijacking of airplanes—*Continued*

    x Aeronautics, Commercial—Hijacking; Air piracy; Airlines—Hijacking; Airplane hijacking; Airplanes—Hijacking; Highjacking of airplanes; Sky hijacking; Skyjacking

    xx **Offenses against public safety**

Hiking   796.5

    See also **Direction sense; Orienteering;** also names of forms of hiking, e.g. **Backpacking; Walking;** etc.

    xx **Outdoor life; Walking**

Hillbilly music. *See* **Country music**

Hindoos. *See* **Hindus**

Hinduism   294.5

    See also **Brahmanism; Caste; Vedas; Yoga**

    xx **Brahmanism; Religions**

Hindus   294.5092; 305.891

    See also **East Indians**

    x Hindoos

    xx **East Indians**

Hippies (May subdiv. geog.)   **306**

    x Yippies

    xx **Bohemianism**

Hippies—United States   306

    x United States—Hippies

Hire-purchase plan. *See* **Instalment plan**

Hispanic Americans   305.868

    Use for materials on United States citizens of Latin American descent. Materials on citizens of Latin American countries are entered under **Latin Americans.**

    See also names of groups of U.S. citizens from specific countries, e.g. **Mexican Americans;** etc.

    x Latinos (U.S.)

    xx **Ethnology—United States**

Hispano-American War, 1898. *See* **United States—History—1898, War of 1898**

Historians (May subdiv. geog. adjective form)   **907; 920**

    See also **Archeologists**

    x Writers

    xx **Historiography; History**

Historians, American   907; 920

    x American historians; United States—Historians

Historic buildings (May subdiv. geog.)   **363.6; 720.9**

    See also **Literary landmarks;** also types of historic buildings, e.g. **Castles; Churches; Temples; Theaters;** etc.

    x Buildings, Historic; Historic houses; Houses, Historic

    xx **Architecture; Buildings; Historic sites; Monuments**

Historic buildings—Chicago (Ill.)   720.9773; 977.3

    x Chicago (Ill.)—Historic buildings

Historic buildings—Ohio   720.9771; 977.1

    x Ohio—Historic buildings

Historic buildings—United States   720.973; 973

    x United States—Historic buildings

    xx **Architecture, Colonial**

Historic houses. *See* **Historic buildings**

Historic sites (May subdiv. geog.)　**363.6**
　　See also **Historic buildings**
　　x Historical sites
　　xx **Archeology; History**
Historical atlases.　*See* **Atlases, Historical**
Historical chronology.　*See* **Chronology, Historical**
Historical dictionaries.　*See* **History—Dictionaries**
Historical fiction　808.3; 809.3
　　Use for materials about historical fiction. Histor-
　　　ical novels are entered under the names of
　　　historical topics, events, and characters with
　　　the subdivision *Fiction.*
　　See also names of historical events and charac-
　　　ters with the subdivision *Fiction,* e.g. **Slav-
　　　ery—United States—Fiction; United
　　　States—History—1861-1865, Civil War—
　　　Fiction; Napoleon I, Emperor of the French,
　　　1769-1821—Fiction;** etc.
　　x Fiction, Historical
　　xx **Fiction; History**
Historical geography.　*See* **Atlases, Historical; Ge-
　　　ography, Historical;** and names of modern
　　　countries or regions with the subdivision
　　　Historical geography, e.g. **Greece—
　　　Historical geography; United States—
　　　Historical geography;** etc.; and names of
　　　ancient countries with the subdivision
　　　Geography, e.g. **Rome—Geography;** etc.
Historical geology.　*See* **Geology, Stratigraphic**
Historical materialism.　*See* **Dialectical materialism**
Historical records—Preservation.　*See* **Archives**
Historical sites.　*See* **Historic sites**
Historical societies.　*See* **History—Societies**
Historiography　907
　　See note under **History.**
　　See also **Historians;** also subjects with the subdi-
　　　vision *Historiography,* e.g. **Philosophy—
　　　Historiography; United States—History—
　　　Historiography;** etc.
　　x History—Criticism; History—Historiography
History　900
　　Use for general materials on history as a science.
　　　This includes the principles of history, the
　　　influence of various factors on history and
　　　the relation of the science of history to other
　　　subjects. Materials on the interpretation and
　　　meaning of history, the course of events and
　　　their resulting consequences, are entered un-
　　　der **History—Philosophy.** Materials lim-
　　　ited to the study and criticism of sources of
　　　history, methods of historical research, and
　　　the writing of history are entered under
　　　Historiography.
　　See also

Anthropogeography	**Ethnology**
Archeology	**Genealogy**
Biography	**Geography, Historical**
Chronology	**Historians**
Church history	**Historic sites**
Civilization	**Historical fiction**
Colonization	**Kings, queens, rulers, etc.**
Constitutional history	**Man**
Discoveries (in geography)	**Massacres**

History—*Continued*

Military history	**Political science**
Naval history	**Seals (Numismatics)**
Numismatics	**World history**
Oral history	

also headings beginning with the word **History;** and names of countries, states, etc. with the subdivisions *Antiquities; Foreign relations; History; Politics and government.* The history of a subject is entered under the name of the subject with the subdivision *History,* or, for literature, film, and music headings, *History and criticism,* e.g. **Art—History; English language—History; English literature—History and criticism; Music—History and criticism;** etc.

x Social studies

History, Ancient   930

See also **Archeology; Bible; Civilization, Ancient; Classical dictionaries; Geography, Ancient; Inscriptions; Numismatics;** also names of ancient peoples, e.g. **Hittites;** etc,; and names of countries of antiquity

x Ancient history

xx **World history**

History—Atlases.   *See* **Atlases, Historical**

History, Biblical.   *See* **Bible—History of biblical events**

History—Chronology.   *See* **Chronology, Historical**

History, Church.   *See* **Church history**

History, Constitutional.   *See* **Constitutional history**

History—Criticism.   *See* **Historiography**

History—Dictionaries   903

x Historical dictionaries

History—Historiography.   *See* **Historiography**

History, Local.   *See* names of countries, states, etc. with the subdivision *History, Local,* e.g. **United States—History, Local;** etc.

History, Medieval.   *See* **Middle Ages—History**

History, Military.   *See* **Military history;** and names of countries with the subdivision *History, Military,* e.g. **United States—History, Military;** etc.

History, Modern   909.08

Use for materials covering the period after 1453.
See also **Civilization, Modern; Reformation; Renaissance**

x Modern history

xx **Civilization, Modern; World history**

History, Modern—1800-1899 (19th century)   909.81

See also **Nineteenth century**

History, Modern—1900-1999 (20th century)   909.82

See also **Twentieth century; World War, 1914-1918; World War, 1939-1945**

History, Modern—1945-   909.82

History, Modern—Study and teaching   907

See also **Current events**

History, Natural.   *See* **Natural history**

History, Naval.   *See* **Naval history;** and names of countries with the subdivision *History, Naval,* e.g. **United States—History, Naval;** etc.

History, Oral.   *See* **Oral history**

History—Periodicals   905

History—Philosophy   901
    See note under **History.**
    See also **Civilization**
    x Philosophy of history
    xx **Philosophy**
History—Societies   906
    See also **United States—History—Societies**
    x Historical societies
History—Sources   900
    Use only for documents, records and other source materials upon which narrative history is based.
    See also **Archives; Charters;** also names of countries, states, etc. with the subdivision *History—Sources,* e.g. **United States—History—Sources;** etc.; and names of periods of history and names of wars with the subdivision *Sources,* e.g. **United States—History—1861-1865, Civil War—Sources; World War, 1939-1945—Sources;** etc.
History, Universal. *See* **World history**
Histrionics. *See* **Acting; Theater**
Hittites   939
    xx **History, Ancient**
HIV disease. *See* **AIDS (Disease)**
HMOs. *See* **Health maintenance organizations**
Hoaxes. *See* **Impostors and imposture**
Hobbies   790.1
    See also **Collectors and collecting; Handicraft;** also names of hobbies
    x Avocations; Recreations
    xx **Amusements; Handicraft; Leisure; Recreation**
Hoboes. *See* **Tramps**
Hockey. *See* **Field hockey; Ice hockey**
Hogs. *See* **Pigs**
Hoisting machinery   621.8
    See also types of hoisting machinery, e.g. **Conveying machinery; Cranes, derricks, etc.; Elevators;** etc.
    x Lifts
    xx **Conveying machinery; Machinery**
Holiday decorations   394.2; 745.4
    x Decorations, Holiday
    xx **Decoration and ornament**
Holidays   394.2
    See also

Christmas	**Memorial Day**
Fasts and feasts	**Thanksgiving Day**
Lincoln's Birthday	**Vacations**
Martin Luther King Day	**Veterans Day**

    also names of holidays, e.g. **Fourth of July; Valentine's Day;** etc.
    x Anniversaries; Days; Legal holidays; National holidays
    xx **Fasts and feasts; Festivals; Manners and customs; Vacations**
Holidays, Jewish. *See* **Fasts and feasts—Judaism**
Holistic health. *See* **Holistic medicine**
Holistic medicine   150; 615
    See also **Health; Health self-care; Mind and body**
    x Holistic health; Humanistic medicine; Wholistic medicine

Holistic medicine—*Continued*
  xx **Alternative medicine; Health; Health self-care; Medicine; Mind and body**
Holland. *See* **Netherlands**
Holocaust, Jewish (1933-1945) **940.54; 943.086**
  Use for materials on the period of persecution and extermination of European Jews by National Socialist, or Nazi, Germany that began with Adolf Hitler's rise to power in 1933.
  See also **World War, 1939-1945—Jews;** also names of concentration camps
  x Destruction of Jews (1933-1945); Extermination of Jews (1933-1945); Jewish holocaust (1933-1945)
  xx **Antisemitism; Jews—Persecutions; World War, 1939-1945—Jews**
Holography **774**
  See also **Three dimensional photography**
  x Laser photography; Lensless photography; Photography, Laser; Photography, Lensless
  xx **Laser recording; Three dimensional photography**
Holstein-Friesian cattle **636.2**
  x Friesian cattle
  xx **Dairy cattle**
Holy days. *See* **Fasts and feasts**
Holy Ghost. *See* **Holy Spirit**
Holy Grail. *See* **Grail**
Holy Office. *See* **Inquisition**
Holy Roman Empire **943**
  xx **Europe—History—476-1492; Germany—History—0-1517; Middle Ages—History**
Holy Scriptures. *See* **Bible**
Holy See. *See* **Papacy; Popes**
Holy Spirit **231**
  See also **Trinity**
  x Holy Ghost; Spirit, Holy
  xx **God—Christianity; Theology; Trinity**
Holy Week **263**
  See also **Easter; Good Friday**
  xx **Lent**
Home **306.8; 640**
  See also **Family; Home economics; Marriage**
  xx **Family; Marriage**
Home accidents **363.13**
  See also **First aid**
  xx **Accidents**
Home and school **371.1**
  See also **Parent-teacher relationships; Parents' and teachers' associations**
  x School and home
  xx **Parent-teacher relationships; Parents' and teachers' associations**
Home Box Office **384.55**
  x H.B.O.; HBO
  xx **Cable television; Subscription television**
Home business **650**
  See also **Telecommuting**
  x At-home employment; Cottage industry; Home labor; Work at home; Working at home
  xx **Business; Self-employed; Small business**
Home buying. *See* **Houses—Buying and selling**

Home care services   362.1

   See also **Home nursing;** also classes of people
      with the subdivision *Home care,* e.g. **El-
      derly—Home care;** etc.

   x Home health care; Home medical care; Re-
      spite care

   xx **Medical care**

Home computers   621.39

   x Household data processing; Personal comput-
      ers

   xx **Computers; Microcomputers; Minicomputers;**
      Telecommuting

Home construction.   *See* **House construction**

Home decoration.   *See* **Interior design**

Home delivered meals.   *See* **Meals on wheels programs**

Home designs.   *See* **Architecture, Domestic—
   Designs and plans**

Home economics   640

   See also

Consumer education	**Household employees**
Cookery	**Household pests**
Cost of living	**Interior design**
Dairying	**Laundry**
Entertaining	**Mobile home living**
Food	**Sewing**
Fuel	**Shopping**
Furniture	**Storage in the home**
Heating	**Ventilation**
House cleaning	

   x Domestic arts; Efficiency, Household; Home-
      making; Household management; House-
      keeping

   xx **Family life education; Home**

Home economics—Accounting.   *See* **Budgets,
   Household**

Home economics—Equipment and supplies.   *See*
   Household equipment and supplies

Home education.   *See* **Correspondence schools and
   courses; Home instruction; Self-culture**

Home health care.   *See* **Home care services**

Home instruction   649

   See also **Child development; Child rearing; Par-
      enting; Tutors and tutoring**

   x Domestic education; Education at home; Edu-
      cation, Home; Home education; Home
      teaching; Instruction, Home; Teaching at
      home

   xx **Child development; Child rearing; Education;
      Parenting; Teaching**

Home labor.   *See* **Home business; Telecommuting**

Home life.   *See* **Family life**

Home loans.   *See* **Mortgages**

Home medical care.   *See* **Home care services**

Home missions, Christian.   *See* **Missions, Christian**

Home movies.   *See* **Amateur films**

Home nursing   649.8

   See also **Sick**

   xx **Home care services; Nursing; Sick**

Home purchase.   *See* **Houses—Buying and selling**

Home remodeling.   *See* **Houses—Remodeling**

Home repairing.   *See* **Houses—Maintenance and
   repair**

Home sharing.   *See* **Shared housing**

Home storage. *See* **Storage in the home**
Home study courses. *See* **Correspondence schools
    and courses; Self-culture**
Home teaching. *See* **Home instruction**
Home video cameras. *See* **Camcorders**
Home video movies. *See* **Amateur films**
Home video systems   384.55; 621.388; 778.59
    See also **Camcorders; Videotape recorders and re-
        cording; Videotapes**
    xx **Television**
Home work (Employment). *See* **Telecommuting**
Homeless people   305.5; 362.5
    See also **Homelessness; Refugees; Runaway
        adults; Runaway children; Runaway teen-
        agers; Tramps**
    x Street people
    xx **Homelessness; Poor**
Homeless people—Government policy   362.5
Homelessness   305.5; 362.5
    See also **Homeless people**
    xx **Homeless people; Housing; Poverty; Social
        problems**
Homemakers   306.85; 640
    See also **Fathers; Mothers**
    x Househusbands; Housewives
Homemaking. *See* **Home economics**
Homeopathy   615.5
    xx **Alternative medicine; Pharmacy**
Homes. *See* **Houses**
Homes for the elderly. *See* **Elderly—Institutional
    care**
Homes (Institutions). *See* **Charities; Institutional
    care; Orphanages;** and classes of people
    with the subdivision *Institutional care,* e.g.
    **Blind—Institutional care; Children—
    Institutional care; Deaf—Institutional care;**
    etc.
Homes, Mobile. *See* **Mobile homes**
Homework (Employment). *See* **Telecommuting**
Homicide   364.1
    See also **Assassination; Capital punishment; Eu-
        thanasia; Suicide; Trials (Homicide)**
    x Manslaughter; Murder
    xx **Crime; Criminal law; Offenses against the
        person; Suicide**
Homicide trials. *See* **Trials (Homicide)**
Homonyms. *See* names of languages with the sub-
    division *Homonyms,* e.g. **English lan-
    guage—Homonyms;** etc.
Homosexuality   306.76
    See also **Gay liberation movement; Lesbianism**
    x Gay lifestyle
    xx **Sexual behavior**
Homosexuals, Female. *See* **Gay women**
Homosexuals, Male. *See* **Gay men**
Honesty   179
    See also **Truthfulness and falsehood**
    x Dishonesty
    xx **Ethics; Human behavior; Truthfulness and
        falsehood**
Honey   638; 641.3
    See also **Bees**
    xx **Bees**
Honor system. *See* **Student government**

Honorary degrees. *See* **Academic degrees**
Hooked rugs   746.7
   x Rugs, Hooked
Hoover Dam (Ariz. and Nev.)   627
   x Boulder Dam (Ariz. and Nev.); Colorado River—Hoover Dam
   xx **Dams**
Hope   179; 241
   xx **Faith**
Hormones   574.19; 612.4
   See also **Endocrine glands; Steroids**
   xx **Endocrine glands; Endocrinology**
Hornbooks   028.5; 372.4
Horology. *See* **Clocks and watches; Sundials**
Horoscopes   133.5
   xx **Astrology**
Horror   152.4
   xx **Emotions; Fear**
Horror—Fiction   Fic
   x Horror stories
Horror stories. *See* **Horror—Fiction**
Horse. *See* **Horses**
Horse breeding. *See* **Horses—Breeding**
Horse racing   798.4
   See also **Horsemanship**
   x Racing
   xx **Gambling; Horsemanship**
Horse riding. *See* **Horsemanship**
Horseback riding. *See* **Horsemanship**
Horsebreaking. *See* **Horses—Training**
Horsemanship   798.2
   See also **Horse racing; Horses—Breeding; Horses—Training; Rodeos**
   x Coaching; Dressage; Equestrianism; Horse riding; Horseback riding; Riding
   xx **Horse racing; Rodeos**
Horses   599.72; 636.1
   See also **Ponies**
   x Foals; Horse
Horses—Breeding   636.1
   x Horse breeding
   xx **Breeding; Horsemanship**
Horses—Diseases   636.089
Horses—Training   636.1
   x Horsebreaking
   xx **Animals—Training; Horsemanship**
Horseshoeing. *See* **Blacksmithing**
Horticulture   635
   Use for materials on the scientific and economic aspects of the cultivation of flowers, fruits, vegetables, etc.
   See also

Aeroponics	**Hydroponics**
Flower gardening	**Landscape gardening**
Fruit culture	**Organiculture**
Gardening	**Vegetable gardening**
Greenhouses	

   xx **Agriculture; Gardening; Plants**
Hosiery   391; 687
   x Stockings
   xx **Clothing and dress; Textile industry**
Hospices   362.1
   xx **Hospitals; Social medicine; Terminal care**

Hospital libraries 027.6
   x Libraries, Hospital
   xx **Libraries**
Hospital ships 362.1; 623.8
   x Floating hospitals
   xx **Hospitals; Ships**
Hospital wastes. *See* **Medical wastes**
Hospitality. *See* **Entertaining**
Hospitalization insurance 368.3
   x Group hospitalization; Insurance, Hospitalization
   xx **Health insurance**
Hospitals (May subdiv. geog.) 362.1
   See also

Children's hospitals	**Medical centers**
Hospices	**Military hospitals**
Hospital ships	**Nursing**
Life support systems	**Nursing homes**
(Medical environment)	**Psychiatric hospitals**
Long-term care facilities	

   also names of hospitals
   x Infirmaries; Institutions, Charitable and philanthropic; Sanatoriums
   xx **Charities, Medical; Institutional care; Medical centers; Medicine; Nursing; Public health; Public welfare; Sick**
Hospitals, Military. *See* **Military hospitals**
Hospitals—United States 362.1
   x United States—Hospitals
Hostage escapes. *See* **Escapes**
Hostage negotiation
   xx **Hostages; Negotiation**
Hostages (May subdiv. geog. adjective form) 920
   See also **Hostage negotiation**
   xx **Terrorism**
Hostages, American (May subdiv. geog. except U.S.) 920
   x American hostages; United States—Hostages
Hostages, American—Iran 920
   See also **Iran hostage crisis, 1979-1981**
Hostels, Youth. *See* **Youth hostels**
Hostesses, Airline. *See* **Airlines—Flight attendants**
Hot air engines. *See* **Heat engines**
Hot air heating 697
   x Warm air heating
   xx **Heating**
Hot water heating 697
   xx **Heating**
Hotels, motels, etc. (May subdiv. geog.) 647.94; 728
   x Auto courts; Bed and breakfast accommodations; Boarding houses; Inns; Lodging houses; Motels; Motor courts; Rooming houses; Tourist accommodations
Hotels, motels, etc.—United States 647.9473; 728
   x United States—Hotels, motels, etc.
Hothouses. *See* **Greenhouses**
Hotlines (Telephone counseling) 361.3; 362.2
   See also **Crisis centers**
   x Crisis counseling; Crisis intervention telephone service; Switchboard hotlines; Telephone counseling
   xx **Counseling; Crisis centers; Human relations; Information services; Social work**

Hours of labor   331.2
> *See also* **Absenteeism (Labor); Children—**
> **Employment; Part-time employment**
> *x* Alternative work schedules; Compressed work
> week; Eight-hour day; Five-day work week;
> Flexible hours of labor; Flexitime; Four-day
> work week; Labor, Hours of; Overtime;
> Working day; Working hours
> *xx* **Children—Employment; Labor**

Hours (Time).   *See* **Chronology**
House boats.   *See* **Houseboats**
House buying.   *See* **Houses—Buying and selling**
House cleaning   648
> *xx* **Cleaning; Home economics; Sanitation,**
> **Household**

House construction   690
> *See also* **Houses;** also special kinds of house con-
> struction, e.g. **Earth sheltered houses; Log**
> **cabins and houses; Prefabricated houses;**
> etc.
> *x* Building, House; Construction, House; Home
> construction; Residential construction
> *xx* **Architecture, Domestic; Building**

House decoration.   *See* **Interior design**
House drainage.   *See* **Drainage, House**
House flies.   *See* **Flies**
House furnishing.   *See* **Interior design**
House of Representatives (U.S.).   *See* **United**
> **States. Congress. House**

House painting   698
> *xx* **Painting, Industrial**

House plans.   *See* **Architecture, Domestic—Designs**
> **and plans**

House plants   635.9
> *See also* **Indoor gardening**
> *xx* **Flower gardening; Indoor gardening; Plants;**
> **Plants, Cultivated; Window gardening**

House purchase.   *See* **Houses—Buying and selling**
House repairing.   *See* **Houses—Maintenance and**
> **repair**

House sanitation.   *See* **Sanitation, Household**
House selling.   *See* **Houses—Buying and selling**
House trailers.   *See* **Mobile homes; Travel trailers**
> **and campers**

Houseboats   728.7
> *x* House boats
> *xx* **Boats and boating**

Household appliances.   *See* **Household equipment**
> **and supplies**

Household appliances, Electric   643
> *See also* names of specific appliances
> *x* Appliances, Electric; Domestic appliances;
> Electric apparatus and appliances, Domes-
> tic; Electric appliances; Electric household
> appliances; Electricity in the home; Labor
> saving devices, Household
> *xx* **Household equipment and supplies**

Household budget.   *See* **Budgets, Household**
Household data processing.   *See* **Home computers**
Household employees   640
> *x* Domestic workers; Housemaids; Servants
> *xx* **Home economics; Labor**

Household equipment and supplies   643; 683

   See also **Household appliances, Electric**

   x Cooking utensils; Domestic appliances; Home
      economics—Equipment and supplies;
      Household appliances; Implements, uten-
      sils, etc.; Kitchen utensils; Labor saving de-
      vices, Household; Utensils, Kitchen

Household finances.   *See* **Budgets, Household; Cost
   of living**

Household management.   *See* **Home economics**

Household moving.   *See* **Moving, Household**

Household pests   648

   See also names of pests, e.g. **Flies;** etc.

   x Diseases and pests; Vermin

   xx **Home economics; Insect pests; Pests; Sanita-
      tion, Household**

Household sanitation.   *See* **Sanitation, Household**

Household violence.   *See* **Family violence**

Househusbands.   *See* **Homemakers**

Housekeeping.   *See* **Home economics**

Housemaids.   *See* **Household employees**

Houses   728

   Use for general materials on houses.

   See also **Apartment houses; Building; Housing;
      Solar homes; Tenement houses;** also types of
      houses, e.g. **Earth sheltered houses; Log
      cabins and houses; Prefabricated houses;**
      etc.; and parts of the house, e.g. **Kitchens;**
      etc.

   x Cottages; Dwellings; Habitations, Human;
      Homes; Residences; Summer homes

   xx **Architecture, Domestic; House construction**

Houses—Buying and selling   333.33

   x Home buying; Home purchase; House buying;
      House purchase; House selling

   xx **Real estate business**

Houses, Earth sheltered.   *See* **Earth sheltered
   houses**

Houses—Heating and ventilation   644; 697

   xx **Heating**

Houses, Historic.   *See* **Historic buildings**

Houses, Log.   *See* **Log cabins and houses**

Houses—Maintenance and repair   643

   x Home repairing; House repairing

   xx **Buildings—Maintenance and repair**

Houses of animals.   *See* **Animals—Habitations**

Houses, Prefabricated.   *See* **Prefabricated houses**

Houses—Remodeling   643

   x Home remodeling; Remodeling of houses

Houses, Underground.   *See* **Earth sheltered houses**

Housewives.   *See* **Homemakers**

Housing   307.3; 363.5

   Use for materials on the social and economic aspects of the housing problem.

   See also

Apartment houses	**Public housing**
City planning	**Shared housing**
Homelessness	**Tenement houses**
Mobile homes	**Timesharing (Real estate)**

   also subjects with the subdivision *Housing,* e.g.

      **Blacks—Housing; Physically handicapped—
      Housing;** etc.

   x Dwellings; Habitations, Human

Housing—*Continued*
    xx **City planning; Houses; Landlord and tenant;
        Social problems; Tenement houses; Welfare
        work in industry**
Housing, Black. *See* **Blacks—Housing**
Housing, Discrimination in. *See* **Discrimination in
    housing**
Housing for the elderly. *See* **Elderly—Housing**
Housing for the physically handicapped. *See* **Phys-
    ically handicapped—Housing**
Housing loans. *See* **Mortgages**
Housing projects, Government. *See* **Public housing**
Houston Astros (Baseball team)   796.357
    x Astros (Baseball team); Houston (Tex.). Base-
        ball Club (National League)
    xx **Baseball clubs**
Houston (Tex.). Baseball Club (National
    League). *See* **Houston Astros (Baseball
    team)**
Hovercraft. *See* **Ground effect machines**
How-to-stop-smoking programs. *See* **Smoking ces-
    sation programs**
Hudson River (N.Y. and N.J.)—Bridges. *See*
    Bridges—Hudson River (N.Y. and N.J.)
Hugging   158; 302.2; 395; E
    x Embracing; Hugs
    xx **Manners and customs; Nonverbal communica-
        tion; Touch**
Hugs. *See* **Hugging**
Huguenots   284
    See also **Saint Bartholomew's Day, Massacre of,
        1572**
    xx **Christianity; Reformation**
Hull House   361.4
    xx **Social settlements**
Human abnormalities. *See* **Birth defects**
Human anatomy   611
    See also names of organs and regions of the
        body, e.g. **Heart;** etc.
    x Anatomy, Human; Body, Human; Human
        body
    xx **Anatomy**
Human anatomy—Atlases   611
    xx **Atlases**
Human anatomy in art. *See* **Anatomy, Artistic;
    Nude in art**
Human behavior   150; 302
    See also

Aggressiveness (Psychol- **ogy)**	**Honesty**
	Human relations
Behavior modification	**Justice**
Behaviorism	**Life skills**
Cannibalism	**Lifestyles**
Charity	**Love**
Courage	**Loyalty**
Courtesy	**Obedience**
Duty	**Patience**
Eating customs	**Patriotism**
Ethics	**Punctuality**
Etiquette	**Self-respect**
Friendship	**Social adjustment**
Habit	**Spiritual life**
Helping behavior	**Sportsmanship**

Human behavior—*Continued*

Sympathy   **Truthfulness and false-**
Temperance   **hood**

   x Behavior; Conduct of life; Morals; Personal
      conduct; Social behavior

   xx **Character; Ethics; Human relations; Life**
      skills; Psychology; Social sciences

Human body. *See* **Human anatomy; Physiology**

Human cold storage. *See* **Cryonics**

Human ecology 304.2

   See also **Anthropogeography; Environment—**
      Government policy; Man—Influence of envi-
      ronment; Man—Influence on nature; Popu-
      lation; Survival skills

   x Ecology, Human; Ecology, Social; Social ecol-
      ogy

   xx **Environment—Government policy; Sociology**

Human embryos, Frozen. *See* **Frozen embryos**

Human engineering 620.8

   Use for materials on engineering design as re-
      lated to human anatomical, physiological
      and psychological capabilities and limita-
      tions.

   See also **Life support systems (Space environ-**
      ment)

   x Biomechanics; Ergonomics

   xx **Engineering; Industrial design; Industrial**
      management; Machinery—Design and con-
      struction; Psychology, Applied; Psycho-
      physiology

Human fertility. *See* **Fertility, Human**

Human figure in art. *See* **Anatomy, Artistic; Figure**
      drawing; Figure painting; Nude in art

Human life education. *See* **Sex education**

Human race. *See* **Anthropology; Man**

Human records. *See* **World records**

Human relations 158; 302

   Use for materials that deal with the integration
      of people so that they can live and work to-
      gether with psychological, social, and eco-
      nomic satisfaction.

   See also

Conflict of generations	**Life skills**
Discrimination	**Personal space**
Family	**Personnel management**
Family life education	**Prejudices**
Grandparent and child	**Psychology, Applied**
Group relations training	**Social adjustment**
Helping behavior	**Social values**
Hotlines (Telephone coun-	**Teacher-student relation-**
seling)	**ships**
Human behavior	**Toleration**
Intercultural education	**Transactional analysis**
Interfaith relations	

   also interpersonal relations between individuals
      or groups of individuals, e.g. **Jews and Gen-**
      tiles; Landlord and tenant; Parent and child;
      etc.

   x Interpersonal relations

   xx **Family life education; Human behavior; Life**
      skills; Psychology, Applied; Social psychol-
      ogy

Human resource management. *See* **Personnel man-**
      agement

Human resources   331.11

   See also **Draft; Labor supply; Military service, Voluntary; Unemployment;** also names of wars with the subdivision *Human resources,* e.g. **World War, 1939-1945—Human resources;** etc.

   x Man power; Manpower; Woman power

   xx **Employment; Labor supply**

Human resources development. *See* **Human resources policy**

Human resources policy   331.11

   See also **Labor supply; Occupational retraining; Occupational training; Vocational education**

   x Human resources development; Manpower policy

   xx **Economic policy; Labor supply**

Human rights   323; 341.4

   Use for materials on the rights of persons regardless of their legal, socioeconomic or cultural status and as recognized by the international community. For materials on citizens' rights as established by law and protected by constitution, use **Civil rights.**

   See also **Civil rights**

   x Basic rights; Civil rights (International law); Fundamental rights; Rights, Human; Rights of man

Human survival skills. *See* **Survival skills**

Human values. *See* **Values**

Humane treatment of animals. *See* **Animal welfare**

Humanism   001.2; 880

   Use for materials on culture founded on the study of the classics, sometimes narrowly for Greek and Roman scholarship.

   See also **Classical education; Hellenism; Humanities; Learning and scholarship; Renaissance**

   xx **Classical education; Culture; Learning and scholarship; Literature; Philosophy; Renaissance**

Humanism—1900-1999 (20th century)   144

   Use for materials on any intellectual, philosophical or religious movement or system that is centered in people rather than in nature, the supernatural, or the absolute.

Humanistic medicine. *See* **Holistic medicine**

Humanitarians. *See* **Philanthropists**

Humanities   001.3

   See also **Classical education;** also such subjects as **Art; Literature; Music; Philosophy;** etc.

   xx **Classical education; Humanism**

Humanities and science. *See* **Science and the humanities**

Humanity, Religion of. *See* **Positivism**

Humans in space. *See* **Space flight**

Humidity   551.57

   x Air, Moisture of; Atmospheric humidity; Relative humidity

   xx **Meteorology; Weather**

Humor. *See* **Wit and humor;** and subjects with the subdivision *Humor,* e.g. **World War, 1939-1945—Humor;** etc.

Humorists   809.7; 920

   xx **Wit and humor**

Humorous pictures. *See* **Cartoons and caricatures; Comic books, strips, etc.**

Humorous poetry   808.81; 811, etc.
> *See also* **Limericks; Nonsense verses**
> *xx* **Poetry; Wit and humor**

Humorous stories   813, etc.; E; Fic
> *x* Stories
> *xx* **Fiction; Wit and humor**

Hundred Years' War, 1339-1453   944
> *x* 100 years' war
> *xx* **Europe—History—476-1492; France—History—1328-1589, House of Valois; Great Britain—History—1399-1485, Lancaster and York**

Hungary—History   943.9

Hungary—History—1956, Revolution   943.905

Hunger   363.8
> *See also* **Fasting; Starvation**
> *xx* **Fasting; Starvation**

Hunger strikes   303.6
> *x* Strikes, Hunger
> *xx* **Fasting; Government, Resistance to; Nonviolence; Passive resistance; Protests, demonstrations, etc.**

Hunting (May subdiv. geog.)   **799.2**
> *See also* **Decoys (Hunting); Game and game birds; Game preserves; Game protection;** also types of hunting, e.g. **Falconry; Shooting; Tracking and trailing; Trapping; Whaling;** etc.
> *x* Gunning
> *xx* **Game and game birds; Shooting; Trapping**

Hunting, Job. *See* **Job hunting**

Hunting—United States   799.2973
> *x* United States—Hunting

Hurricanes (May subdiv. geog.)   **551.55**
> Use for cyclonic storms originating in the region of the West Indies.
> *See also* **Typhoons**
> *xx* **Cyclones; Meteorology; Storms; Typhoons; Winds**

Husband abuse   362.82
> *x* Abuse of husbands; Battered husbands; Battered men; Husband battering; Husband beating
> *xx* **Family violence**

Husband battering. *See* **Husband abuse**

Husband beating. *See* **Husband abuse**

Husbands   306.872
> *See also* **Widowers**
> *x* Married men; Spouses
> *xx* **Family; Marriage; Married people; Men**

Husbands, Runaway. *See* **Runaway adults**

Hybridization. *See* **Plant breeding**

Hydraulic cement. *See* **Cement**

Hydraulic engineering   627
> *See also*

Boring	**Hydrodynamics**
Drainage	**Hydrostatics**
Dredging	**Irrigation**
Flood control	**Pumping machinery**
Hydraulic structures	**Reclamation of land**
Hydraulics	**Rivers**

Hydraulic engineering—*Continued*

Turbines   Water supply engineering

Water   Wells

  xx Civil engineering; Engineering; Fluid mechanics; Hydraulics; Rivers; Water; Water
power; Water supply engineering

Hydraulic machinery   621.2

  See also Turbines

  xx Machinery; Water power

Hydraulic structures   627

  See also Pipelines; also types of hydraulic structures, e.g. Aqueducts; Canals; Dams; Docks;
Harbors; Reservoirs; etc.

  xx Hydraulic engineering; Structural engineering

Hydraulics   621.2; 627

  Use for materials on technical applications of
the theory of hydrodynamics.

  See also Hydraulic engineering; Hydrodynamics;
Hydrostatics; Water; Water power

  x Water flow

  xx Fluid mechanics; Hydraulic engineering; Liquids; Mechanics; Physics

Hydrodynamics   532

  Use for materials on the theory of the motion
and action of fluids. Materials on the experimental investigation and technical application of this theory are entered under Hydraulics.

  See also Hydrostatics; Viscosity; Waves

  xx Dynamics; Fluid mechanics; Hydraulic engineering; Hydraulics; Liquids; Mechanics

Hydroelectric power.   *See* Water power

Hydroelectric power plants   621.31

  x Power plants, Hydroelectric

  xx Electric power plants; Water power; Water resources development

Hydrofoil boats   623.8

Hydrogen   546

  xx Chemical elements

Hydrogen bomb   623.4

  See also Atomic bomb; Radioactive fallout

  x H bomb; Thermonuclear bomb

  xx Atomic bomb; Bombs; Nuclear warfare; Nuclear weapons

Hydrogen nucleus.   *See* Protons

Hydrology.   *See* Water

Hydromechanics.   *See* Fluid mechanics

Hydropathy.   *See* Hydrotherapy

Hydrophobia.   *See* Rabies

Hydroponics   631.5

  x Agriculture, Soilless; Chemiculture; Plants—
Soilless culture; Soilless agriculture; Water
farming

  xx Horticulture

Hydrostatics   532

  See also Gases

  xx Fluid mechanics; Hydraulic engineering; Hydraulics; Hydrodynamics; Liquids; Mechanics; Physics; Statics

Hydrotherapy   615.8

  See also Baths; Health resorts, spas, etc.

  x Hydropathy; Water cure

  xx Baths; Physical therapy; Therapeutics; Water

Hygiene 613
See also

Baths	**Military health**
Diet	**Personal grooming**
Disinfection and disinfec-	**Physical education**
tants	**Rest**
Exercise	**Sanitation**
Food	**School hygiene**
Health	**Sleep**
Mental health	**Ventilation**

also parts of the body with the subdivision *Care and hygiene,* e.g. **Foot—Care and hygiene;** etc.; and classes of people and ethnic groups with the subdivision *Health and hygiene,* e.g. **Women—Health and hygiene;** etc.

x Body care; Personal cleanliness; Personal hygiene

xx **Cleanliness; Health; Medicine; Preventive medicine; Sanitation**

Hygiene, Industrial. *See* **Occupational health and safety**

Hygiene, Mental. *See* **Mental health**

Hygiene, Military. *See* **Military health**

Hygiene, Public. *See* **Public health**

Hygiene, School. *See* **School hygiene**

Hygiene, Sexual. *See* **Sexual hygiene**

Hygiene, Social. *See* **Prostitution; Public health; Sexual hygiene**

Hygiene—Study and teaching. *See* **Health education**

Hygiene, Tropical. *See* **Tropical medicine**

Hymenoptera. *See* **Ants; Bees; Wasps**

Hymnology. *See* **Hymns**

Hymns 245; 264; 782.27

See also **Carols; Church music; Religious poetry; Spirituals (Songs)**

x Hymnology; Psalmody

xx **Church music; Devotional literature; Liturgies; Poetry; Religious poetry; Songs; Vocal music**

Hyperactive children 155.4; 618.92

See also **Hyperactivity**

x Children, Hyperactive; Hyperkinetic children; Overactive children

xx **Handicapped children; Hyperactivity**

Hyperactivity 152.3

See also **Hyperactive children**

x Hyperkinesia; Overactivity

xx **Hyperactive children**

Hyperkinesia. *See* **Hyperactivity**

Hyperkinetic children. *See* **Hyperactive children**

Hypertension 616.1

x High blood pressure

xx **Blood pressure**

Hypnotism 154.7

See also **Mental suggestion; Mind and body; Personality disorders; Psychoanalysis; Subconsciousness; Therapeutics, Suggestive**

x Animal magnetism; Autosuggestion; Mesmerism

xx **Mental healing; Mental suggestion; Mind and body; Personality disorders; Psychoanalysis; Psychophysiology; Subconsciousness; Therapeutics, Suggestive**

352

I.B.M. 7090 (Computer). *See* **IBM 7090 (Computer)**

I.C.B.M. *See* **Intercontinental ballistic missiles**

I.Q. tests. *See* **Mental tests**

I.R.A.'s (Pensions). *See* **Individual retirement accounts**

I.S.B.D. *See* **International Standard Bibliographic Description**

I.S.B.N. *See* **International Standard Book Numbers**

I.S.S.N. *See* **International Standard Serial Numbers**

IBM 7090 (Computer)   621.39
>   *x* I.B.M. 7090 (Computer)
>   *xx* **Computers**

ICBM. *See* **Intercontinental ballistic missiles**

Ice   551.3
>   *See also* **Glaciers; Icebergs**
>   *x* Freezing
>   *xx* **Cold; Frost; Physical geography; Water**

Ice age   551.7
>   *x* Glacial epoch
>   *xx* **Earth**

Ice boats. *See* **Iceboats**

Ice cream, ices, etc.   637; 641.8
>   *See also* **Confectionery**
>   *x* Ices
>   *xx* **Desserts; Frozen foods**

Ice (Drug)   362.29; 615
>   *xx* **Designer drugs; Methamphetamine**

Ice hockey   796.962
>   *x* Hockey
>   *xx* **Winter sports**

Ice manufacture. *See* **Refrigeration**

Ice skating   796.91
>   *x* Figure skating; Skating
>   *xx* **Winter sports**

Ice sports. *See* **Winter sports**

Icebergs   551.3
>   *xx* **Ice; Ocean; Physical geography**

Iceboats   623.8
>   *x* Ice boats
>   *xx* **Boats and boating**

Icelandic language   439
>   *xx* **Scandinavian languages**

Icelandic language—0-1500. *See* **Old Norse language**

Icelandic literature   839
>   *See also* **Old Norse literature**
>   *xx* **Scandinavian literature**

Ices. *See* **Ice cream, ices, etc.**

Ichthyology. *See* **Fishes**

Iconography. *See* **Art; Christian art and symbolism; Portraits; Religious art and symbolism**

Ideal states. *See* **Utopias**

Idealism   141
>   *See also* **Materialism; Realism; Transcendentalism**
>   *xx* **Materialism; Philosophy; Positivism; Realism; Transcendentalism**

Identification
>   *See also* **DNA Fingerprints; Fingerprints;** also subjects with the subdivision *Identification,* e.g. **Airplanes—Identification; Criminals—Identification;** etc.

Identity. *See* **Individuality; Personality**

353

Idioms. *See* names of languages with the subdivision *Idioms,* e.g. **English language—Idioms;** etc.

Illegal aliens   323.6; 325; 342
   See also **Sanctuary movement**
   x Aliens, Illegal; Underground aliens; Undocumented aliens
   xx **Aliens; Immigration and emigration; Sanctuary movement; Underground economy**

Illegitimacy   346.01; 362.7
   See also **Unmarried fathers; Unmarried mothers**
   x Bastardy; Children, Illegitimate
   xx **Social problems**

Illiteracy. *See* **Literacy**

Illiterate societies. *See* **Nonliterate folk society**

Illness. *See* **Diseases**

Illuminated manuscripts. *See* **Illumination of books and manuscripts**

Illuminating gas. *See* **Gas**

Illumination. *See* **Lighting**

Illumination of books and manuscripts   096; 745.6
   See also **Initials**
   x Illuminated manuscripts; Manuscripts, Illuminated; Miniatures (Illumination of books and manuscripts); Ornamental alphabets
   xx **Alphabets; Art; Art, Medieval; Books; Christian art and symbolism; Decoration and ornament; Illustration of books; Initials; Manuscripts**

Illusions. *See* **Hallucinations and illusions; Optical illusions**

Illustration of books   741.6
   See also **Caldecott Medal books; Drawing; Engraving; Illumination of books and manuscripts; Photomechanical processes; Picture books for children**
   x Book illustration
   xx **Art; Books; Color printing; Decoration and ornament; Drawing; Picture books for children**

Illustrations. *See* subjects with the subdivision *Pictorial works,* e.g. **Animals—Pictorial works; United States—History—1861-1865, Civil War—Pictorial works;** etc.

Illustrations, Humorous. *See* **Cartoons and caricatures**

Illustrators (May subdiv. geog. adjective form, e.g. **Illustrators, American;** etc.)   **741.6092; 920**
   xx **Artists**

Illustrators, American   741.6092; 920
   x American illustrators; United States—Illustrators

Images, National. *See* **National characteristics**

Imaginary animals. *See* **Mythical animals**

Imaginary friends. *See* **Imaginary playmates**

Imaginary places. *See* **Geographical myths**

Imaginary playmates   155.4; E
   x Friends, Imaginary; Imaginary friends; Invisible playmates; Make-believe playmates; Playmates, Imaginary
   xx **Friendship; Imagination; Play**

Imagination   153.3
   See also **Creation (Literary, artistic, etc.); Fan-**

Imagination—*Continued*

tasy; **Imaginary playmates**

xx **Educational psychology; Intellect; Psychology**

Imaging, Magnetic resonance. *See* **Magnetic resonance imaging**

Immersion, Baptismal. *See* **Baptism**

Immigrants. *See* **Immigration and emigration**

Immigration and emigration 325

Use for materials on migration from one country to another. Materials on the movement of population within a country for permanent settlement are entered under **Migration, Internal.**

See also **Aliens; Anthropogeography; Children of immigrants; Colonization; Illegal aliens; Naturalization; Refugees;** also names of countries with the subdivision *Immigration and emigration,* e.g. **United States—Immigration and emigration;** etc.; names of countries, cities, etc. with the subdivision *Foreign population,* e.g. **United States—Foreign population;** etc.; and names of nationality groups, e.g. **Mexican Americans; Mexicans—United States;** etc.

x Emigration; Foreign population; Immigrants; Migration; Population, Foreign

xx **Colonies; Colonization; Race relations; Social problems; Sociology**

Immortality 129

Use for materials dealing with the question of the endless existence of the soul. Materials dealing with the character and form of a future existence are entered under **Future life.**

See also **Future life**

x Life after death

xx **Eschatology; Future life; Soul; Theology**

Immunity 574.2; 591.2; 616.07

See also **Allergy; Communicable diseases; Vaccination**

xx **Bacteriology; Communicable diseases; Pathology; Preventive medicine; Vaccination**

Immunization. *See* **Vaccination**

Impeachments 351.9

See also **Recall (Political science)**

xx **Justice, Administration of**

Imperialism 325

See also **Colonies; Colonization;** also names of countries with the subdivision *Foreign relations,* e.g. **United States—Foreign relations;** etc.

x Colonialism

xx **Political science**

Implements, utensils, etc. *See* **Agricultural machinery; Household equipment and supplies; Stone implements; Tools**

Imports. *See* **Commerce; Tariff**

Impostors and imposture 364.1

See also **Counterfeits and counterfeiting; Forgery; Fraud; Quacks and quackery; Swindlers and swindling**

x Charlatans; Hoaxes; Pretenders

xx **Fraud; Swindlers and swindling**

Impregnation, Artificial. *See* **Artificial insemination**

Impressionism (Art)   759.05
> *See also* **Postimpressionism (Art)**
> *x* Neo-impressionism (Art)
> *xx* **Art, Modern—1800-1899 (19th century);
>   Painting; Postimpressionism (Art)**

Imprisonment. *See* **Prisons**

In-service training. *See* **Employees—Training;
        Librarians—In-service training**

In vitro fertilization. *See* **Fertilization in vitro**

Inaudible sound. *See* **Ultrasonics**

Incandescent lamps. *See* **Electric lamps**

Incas   980.004
> *xx* **Indians of South America**

Incendiary bombs   623.4
> *x* Bombs, Incendiary; Fire bombs
> *xx* **Bombs; Incendiary weapons**

Incendiary weapons   623.4
> *See also* **Incendiary bombs**
> *xx* **Chemical warfare**

Incentive (Psychology). *See* **Motivation (Psychol-
        ogy)**

Incest   306.877; 616.85
> *See also* **Child molesting**
> *xx* **Sex crimes**

Incineration. *See* **Cremation; Refuse and refuse dis-
        posal**

Income   331.2; 339.3
> *See also* **Capital; Profit; Retirement income;
>   Wages—Annual wage**
> *x* Fortunes
> *xx* **Economics; Finance; Profit; Property; Wealth**

Income tax   336.24
> *See also* **Tax credits**
> *x* Direct taxation; Payroll taxes; Taxation of in-
>   come
> *xx* **Finance; Internal revenue; Taxation; Wealth**

Income, Untaxed. *See* **Underground economy**

Indentured servants. *See* **Contract labor**

Independence Day (United States). *See* **Fourth of
        July**

Independent schools. *See* **Private schools**

Independent study   371.3
> Use for materials on individual study that may
>   be directed or assisted by instructional staff
>   through periodic consultations.
> *xx* **Study skills; Tutors and tutoring**

Indeterminism. *See* **Free will and determinism**

Index librorum prohibitorum. *See* **Books—
        Censorship; Catholic literature**

Indexes   016
> *See also* **Subject headings;** also subjects with the
>   subdivision *Indexes,* e.g. **Newspapers—
>   Indexes; Periodicals—Indexes; Short sto-
>   ries—Indexes;** etc.
> *xx* **Bibliography**

Indexing   025.3
> *See also* **Cataloging; Files and filing**
> *xx* **Bibliographic control; Bibliography; Catalog-
>   ing; Files and filing**

India rubber. *See* **Rubber**

Indian languages (North American). *See* **Indians of
        North America—Languages**

Indian literature (American). *See* **American litera-
        ture—American Indian authors**

Indian literature (East Indian).   *See* **Indic literature**
Indian literature (North American Indian).   *See* **Indians of North America—Literature**
Indian reservations.   *See* **Indians of North America—Reservations**
Indians   970.004
> Use for general materials on the Indians of the Western Hemisphere. Names of all peoples and linguistic families are not included in this List but are to be added as needed.
> May be subdivided topically like **Indians of North America.**
> *See also* **Indians of Central America; Indians of Mexico; Indians of North America; Indians of South America; Indians of the West Indies**
> *x* American Indians; Amerindians
Indians of Canada.   *See* **Indians of North America—Canada**
Indians of Central America (May subdiv. geog. by countries or regions of Central America, e.g. **Indians of Central America—Guatemala;** etc.)   **972.8004**
> May be subdivided topically like **Indians of North America.**
> *See also* **Mayas**
> *x* American Indians; Amerindians
> *xx* **Indians**
Indians of Central America—Guatemala   972.81004
Indians (of India).   *See* **East Indians**
Indians of Mexico (May subdiv. geog. by states of Mexico, e.g. **Indians of Mexico—Yucatan;** etc.)   **972.004**
> May be subdivided topically like **Indians of North America.**
> *See also* **Aztecs; Mayas**
> *x* American Indians; Amerindians
> *xx* **Indians**
Indians of North America (May subdiv. geog. by Canada, its provinces or regions or by the United States, its states or regions, e.g. **Indians of North America—British Columbia; Indians of North America—Massachusetts;** etc.)   **970.004**
> Names of all peoples and linguistic families are not included in this List but are to be added as needed, e.g. **Navajo Indians;** etc.
> Topical subdivisions used under this heading may also be used under names of peoples and linguistic families.
> *See also* **Cliff dwellers and cliff dwellings; Mounds and mound builders;** also names of peoples and linguistic families, e.g. **Navajo Indians;** etc.
> *x* American Indians; Amerindians; Native Americans; Native peoples; North American Indians; Pre-Columbian Americans; Precolumbian Americans
> *xx* **Ethnology—United States; Indians**
Indians of North America—Amusements.   *See* **Indians of North America—Games; Indians of North America—Social life and customs**

Indians of North America—Antiquities   970.004
   See also **Mounds and mound builders**
   xx **Antiquities; United States—Antiquities**
Indians of North America—Architecture   720.97;
   970.004
   xx **Architecture**
Indians of North America—Art   704; 709.01
   x Art, Indian
   xx **Art**
Indians of North America—Canada   971.004
   x Canadian Indians; Indians of Canada
Indians of North America—Captivities   970.004
   xx **Frontier and pioneer life**
Indians of North America—Children   305.23;
   970.004
   xx **Children**
Indians of North America—Chronology   970.004
   xx **Chronology**
Indians of North America—Civilization and culture
   970.004
Indians of North America—Claims   970.004
   x Indians of North America—Land claims; Indians of North America—Legal status,
   laws, etc.
Indians of North America—Costume and adornment
   970.004
Indians of North America—Customs.   *See* **Indians
   of North America—Social life and customs**
Indians of North America—Dances   793.3; 970.004
   xx **Folk dancing; Indians of North America—
   Religion; Indians of North America—Social
   life and customs**
Indians of North America—Drama   812, etc.
   xx **Drama**
Indians of North America—Economic conditions
   970.004
Indians of North America—Education   371.97;
   970.004
   x Indians of North America—Schools
Indians of North America—Ethnology   305.897
Indians of North America—Fiction   Fic
Indians of North America—Folklore   398
   Use for materials about the folklore of North
   American Indians. Collections of North
   American Indian legends, myths, tales, etc.
   are entered under **Indians of North America—Legends.**
   See also **Indians of North America—Legends**
   x Indians of North America—Mythology
   xx **Folklore; Indians of North America—Legends**
Indians of North America—Games   790.1; 970.004
   x Indians of North America—Amusements; Indians of North America—Recreations; Indians of North America—Sports
   xx **Games; Indians of North America—Social life
   and customs**
Indians of North America—Government policy
   323.1; 970.5
   x Federal-Indian relations; Indians of North
   America—Legal status, laws, etc.
Indians of North America—History   970.004
   See also **Indians of North America—Wars**
Indians of North America—Industries   338.4; 680;
   970.004

Indians of North America—Land claims. *See* **Indians of North America—Claims**
Indians of North America—Languages 497
See also **Indians of North America—Sign language;** also names of individual languages, e.g. **Navajo language;** etc.
x Indian languages (North American)
Indians of North America—Legal status, laws, etc. *See* **Indians of North America—Claims; Indians of North America—Government policy**
Indians of North America—Legends 398.2
Use for collections of North American Indian legends, myths, tales, etc. Materials about the folklore of North American Indians are entered under **Indians of North America—Folklore.**
See also **Indians of North America—Folklore**
x Indians of North America—Mythology; Legends, Indian
xx **Indians of North America—Folklore**
Indians of North America—Literature 897
Use for literature written in the Indian languages. For literature written in the English language use **American literature—American Indian authors.**
x Indian literature (North American Indian)
xx **Literature**
Indians of North America—Missions, Christian 266
x Missions, Indian
Indians of North America—Music. *See* **Indians of North America—Songs and music**
Indians of North America—Mythology. *See* **Indians of North America—Folklore; Indians of North America—Legends; Indians of North America—Religion**
Indians of North America—Names 929.4
Indians of North America—Origin 970.004
Indians of North America—Poetry 811, etc.
xx **Poetry**
Indians of North America—Psychology 155.8
xx **Ethnopsychology**
Indians of North America—Recreations. *See* **Indians of North America—Games**
Indians of North America—Religion 299
See also **Indians of North America—Dances; Totems and totemism**
x Indians of North America—Mythology; Mythology, Indian
xx **Mythology; Religion**
Indians of North America—Reservations 333.1
x Indian reservations; Reservations, Indian
Indians of North America—Rites and ceremonies 291.3; 970.004
xx **Rites and ceremonies**
Indians of North America—Schools. *See* **Indians of North America—Education**
Indians of North America—Sign language 419
xx **Indians of North America—Languages; Sign language**
Indians of North America—Silverwork 739.2
xx **Silverwork**

359

Indians of North America—Social conditions
970.004
xx Social conditions
Indians of North America—Social life and customs
970.004
See also **Indians of North America—Dances; Indians of North America—Games**
x Indians of North America—Amusements; Indians of North America—Customs
xx **Manners and customs**
Indians of North America—Songs and music
780.89
x Indians of North America—Music; Music, Indian
Indians of North America—Sports. *See* **Indians of North America—Games**
Indians of North America—Wars 970.004
See also **Black Hawk War, 1832; King Philip's War, 1675-1676; Pontiac's Conspiracy, 1763-1765; United States—History—1689-1697, King William's War; United States—History—1755-1763, French and Indian War**
xx **Indians of North America—History**
Indians of South America (May subdiv. geog. by country, e.g. **Indians of South America—Peru;** etc.) **980**
May be subdivided topically like **Indians of North America.**
See also **Incas**
x American Indians; Amerindians
xx **Indians**
Indians of South America—Peru 985
Indians of the West Indies 972.9004
May be subdivided topically like **Indians of North America.**
x American Indians; Amerindians
xx **Indians**
Indic literature 891
x Indian literature (East Indian)
Indigenous peoples. *See* **Ethnology**
Indigestion 616.3
x Dyspepsia
xx **Digestion**
Individual retirement accounts 332.024
x I.R.A.'s (Pensions); IRAs (Pensions)
xx **Pensions; Retirement income**
Individualism 141; 302.5; 330.1
See also **Communism; Socialism**
xx **Equality; Socialism; Sociology**
Individuality 155.2
See also **Conformity; Personality; Self**
x Identity
xx **Conformity; Consciousness; Personality; Psychology**
Individualized instruction 371.3
Use for materials on the adaptation of instruction to meet individual needs within the group.
xx **Open plan schools; Slow learning children; Tutors and tutoring**
Indochina 959
Use for the area comprising Laos, Cambodia, and Vietnam.

Indoctrination, Forced. *See* **Brainwashing**
Indoor games 793
　　See also **Amusements**
　　xx **Amusements; Games**
Indoor gardening 635.9
　　See also **Aquariums; Gardens, Miniature; House**
　　　　plants; Terrariums; Window gardening
　　xx **Gardening; House plants**
Induction coils 537.6; 621.319
　　See also **Condensers (Electricity)**
Induction (Logic). *See* **Logic**
Induction motors. *See* **Electric motors**
Industrial alcohol. *See* **Alcohol, Denatured**
Industrial arbitration. *See* **Arbitration, Industrial**
Industrial arts 600
　　See also **Engineering; Technology;** also names of
　　　　specific industries, arts, trades, e.g. **Book-**
　　　　binding; Printing; Shipbuilding; etc.; and
　　　　names of countries, cities, etc. with the sub-
　　　　division *Industries,* e.g. **United States—**
　　　　Industries; etc.
　　x Arts, Useful; Mechanic arts; Trades; Useful
　　　　arts
　　xx **Handicraft; Technology**
Industrial arts education 607
　　See also **Technical education**
　　x Education, Industrial; Industrial education;
　　　　Industrial schools; Manual training
　　xx **Handicraft; Technical education; Vocational**
　　　　education
Industrial arts shops. *See* **School shops**
Industrial buildings 725
　　See also **Factories; Office buildings; Skyscrapers**
　　x Buildings, Industrial
　　xx **Architecture; Buildings**
Industrial chemistry. *See* **Chemical engineering;**
　　　　Chemical industry; Chemistry, Technical
Industrial combinations. *See* **Trusts, Industrial**
Industrial conciliation. *See* **Arbitration, Industrial**
Industrial councils. *See* **Participative management**
Industrial design 745.2
　　See also **Human engineering; Systems engineer-**
　　　　ing
　　x Art, Applied; Design, Industrial
Industrial diseases. *See* **Occupational diseases**
Industrial disputes. *See* **Labor disputes**
Industrial drawing. *See* **Mechanical drawing**
Industrial education. *See* **Industrial arts education;**
　　　　Technical education
Industrial efficiency. *See* **Efficiency, Industrial**
Industrial engineering. *See* **Industrial management**
Industrial exhibitions. *See* **Exhibitions**
Industrial health. *See* **Occupational health and**
　　　　safety
Industrial insurance 368.3
　　Use for materials on insurance as carried on by
　　　　companies whose agents collect the premi-
　　　　ums from policy holders in small weekly
　　　　payments.
　　x Insurance, Industrial
　　xx **Labor; Life insurance; Saving and thrift**
Industrial libraries. *See* **Corporate libraries**
Industrial management 658
　　Use for general materials on the application of
　　　　the principles of management to industries,
　　　　including problems of production, market-
　　　　ing, financial control, office management,
　　　　etc. Materials limited to the technical as-
　　　　pects of manufacturing processes are entered
　　　　under **Factory management.**

Industrial management—*Continued*

   See also

Business	**Materials handling**
Buying	**Occupational health and**
Efficiency, Industrial	**safety**
Factory management	**Office management**
Human engineering	**Personnel management**
Industrial relations	**Production standards**
Job analysis	**Sales management**
Machinery	**Welfare work in industry**
Marketing	

   x Business administration; Business enter-
      prises—Management; Corporations—
      Management; Industrial engineering; Indus-
      trial organization; Industry—Organization,
      control, etc.; Management, Industrial

  xx **Business; Industry; Management**

Industrial materials. *See* **Materials**

Industrial mergers. *See* **Corporate mergers and ac-**
     quisitions; Railroads—Consolidation;
     Trusts, Industrial

Industrial mobilization   355.2

   Use for materials dealing with industrial and la-
     bor policies and programs for defense mobi-
     lization.

   See also **Munitions**

   x Defenses, National; Economic mobilization;
      Industry and war; Mobilization, Industrial;
      National defenses

  xx **Armaments; Economic policy; Military art and**
     science; War—Economic aspects

Industrial organization. *See* **Industrial management**

Industrial painting. *See* **Painting, Industrial**

Industrial plants. *See* **Factories**

Industrial psychology. *See* **Psychology, Applied**

Industrial relations   331

   Use for general materials on employer-employee
     relations. Materials on problems of person-
     nel and relations from the employer's point
     of view are entered under **Personnel man-**
     agement.

   See also

Arbitration, Industrial	**Labor unions**
Collective bargaining	**Participative management**
Labor contract	**Personnel management**
Labor disputes	**Strikes and lockouts**

   x Capital and labor; Employer-employee rela-
      tions; Labor and capital; Labor-
      management relations; Labor relations

  xx **Industrial management; Labor**

Industrial revolution. *See* **Great Britain—**
     History—1800-1899 (19th century); Indus-
     try—History

Industrial robots   629.8

   x Robots, Industrial; Working robots

  xx **Machinery in industry; Robotics**

Industrial safety. *See* **Occupational health and**
     safety

Industrial schools. *See* **Industrial arts education;**
     Technical education

Industrial secrets. *See* **Trade secrets**

Industrial trusts. *See* **Trusts, Industrial**

Industrial uses of space. *See* **Space industrialization**

Industrial wastes   363.72; 628.4
    See also **Hazardous wastes; Pollution; Refuse
        and refuse disposal; Waste products; Water
        pollution**
    x Factory and trade waste; Factory waste; Trade
        waste; Waste disposal; Wastes, Industrial
    xx **Pollution; Refuse and refuse disposal; Waste
        products; Water pollution**
Industrial workers. *See* **Labor**
Industrialization   338
    Use for general materials only. Materials on the
        industrialization of individual countries, re-
        gions, etc. are entered under the name of
        country, city, etc. with the subdivision
        Industries.
    See also **Developing countries; Modernization;
        Space industrialization; Technical assistance**
    xx **Economic policy; Industry; Modernization;
        Technical assistance**
Industries. *See* **Industry;** and names of industries,
        e.g. **Steel industry;** etc.; and names of
        countries, cities, etc. with the subdivision
        Industries, e.g. **United States—Industries;**
        etc.
Industries, Electric. *See* **Electric industries**
Industries, Service. *See* **Service industries**
Industry   338
    Use for general materials on manufacturing and
        mechanical activities. Names of all individ-
        ual industries are not included in this List
        but are to be added as needed, e.g. **Steel in-
        dustry;** etc.
    See also

Business failures	**Industrialization**
Business people	**Machinery in industry**
Efficiency, Industrial	**Manufactures**
Industrial management	**Steel industry**

    x Industries; Production
    xx **Civilization; Economics**
Industry and state. *See* **Industry—Government pol-
        icy**
Industry and war. *See* **Industrial mobilization;
        War—Economic aspects**
Industry—Government policy (May subdiv. geog.)
        338.9; 351.82
    See also

Agriculture—Government	**Public service commis-**
policy	**sions**
Economic policy	**Railroads—Government**
Government lending	**policy**
Government ownership	**Subsidies**
Public interest	

    x Business and government; Government and
        business; Government regulation of indus-
        try; Industry and state; Industry—
        Organization, control, etc.; Laissez faire;
        Socialization of industry; State and indus-
        try; State regulation of industry
    xx **Economic policy; Socialism**
**Industry—Government policy—United States
        353.0082**
    x United States—Industry—Government policy
Industry—History   338.09
    x Industrial revolution

Industry—Organization, control, etc. *See* **Indus-trial management; Industry—Government policy**

Inebriates. *See* **Alcoholics**

Inequality. *See* **Equality**

Infallibility of the Pope. *See* **Popes—Infallibility**

Infant care. *See* **Infants—Care**

Infantile paralysis. *See* **Poliomyelitis**

Infants   155.42; 305.23; 362.7; 618.92

> Use for materials about children in the earliest period of life, usually the first two years only.
>
> *See also* **Children**
>
> *x* Babies
>
> *xx* **Children**

Infants and strangers. *See* **Children and strangers**

Infants—Birth defects. *See* **Birth defects**

Infants—Care   649

> *See also* **Babysitting**
>
> *x* Baby care; Infant care; Infants—Care and hygiene
>
> *xx* **Child care**

Infants—Care and hygiene. *See* **Infants—Care; Infants—Health and hygiene**

Infants—Clothing   646; 649

Infants—Diseases   618.92

> *See also* **Infants—Health and hygiene**
>
> *x* Pediatrics
>
> *xx* **Diseases; Infants—Health and hygiene**

Infants—Education. *See* **Preschool education**

Infants—Health and hygiene   613; 618.92

> *See also* **Infants—Diseases**
>
> *x* Health of infants; Infants—Care and hygiene; Infants—Hygiene; Pediatrics
>
> *xx* **Infants—Diseases**

Infants—Hygiene. *See* **Infants—Health and hygiene**

Infants—Nutrition   641.1; 649

> *See also* **Breast feeding**

Infants, Sale of. *See* **Adoption—Corrupt practices**

Infection and infectious diseases. *See* **Communicable diseases**

Infectious wastes. *See* **Medical wastes**

Infertility   616.6

> Use for materials on infertility in humans and in animals.
>
> *See also* **Fertility; Sterilization (Birth control)**
>
> *x* Sterility in animals; Sterility in humans
>
> *xx* **Childlessness; Fertility; Fertility, Human; Sterilization (Birth control)**

Infidelity, Marital. *See* **Adultery**

Infirmaries. *See* **Hospitals**

Inflammable substances. *See* **Hazardous substances**

Inflation (Finance)   332.4

> *See also* **Monetary policy; Paper money; Wage-price policy**
>
> *xx* **Finance; Monetary policy**

Influenza   616.2

> *See also* **Vaccination**
>
> *x* Flu; Grippe
>
> *xx* **Cold (Disease); Communicable diseases; Diseases; Vaccination**

Information centers. *See* **Information services**

Information, Freedom of. *See* **Freedom of information**

Information networks   004.6

    See also **Computer networks;** also types of information networks, e.g. **Library information networks;** etc.

    x Automated information networks; Networks, Information; Telereference

    xx **Data transmission systems; Information services; Information systems**

Information science   020

    See also **Documentation; Electronic data processing; Information services; Information systems; Library science**

    xx **Communication**

Information services   020

    See also

Archives	**Libraries**
Documentation	**Machine readable biblio-**
Electronic publishing	**graphic data**
Hotlines (Telephone coun-	**Reference services (Li-**
seling)	**braries)**
Information networks	**Research**
Information systems	

    also special subjects or organizations with the subdivision *Information services,* e.g. **Business—Information services; United Nations—Information services;** etc.

    x Information centers

    xx **Documentation; Information science; Libraries; Research**

Information storage and retrieval systems. *See* **Information systems**

Information systems   025.04

    See also

Database management	**graphic data**
Electronic data processing	**Management information**
Information networks	**systems**
Libraries—Automation	**Teletext systems**
Machine readable biblio-	**Videotex systems**

    x Automatic information retrieval; Computer-based information systems; Data processing; Data storage and retrieval systems; Information storage and retrieval systems; Punched card systems

    xx **Bibliographic control; Bibliography; Computers; Documentation; Information science; Information services; Libraries—Automation**

Information systems—Management   025.04

    Use for materials on the management of information systems.

    xx **Management**

Infrared radiation   535.01; 621.36

    xx **Electromagnetic waves; Radiation**

Ingestion disorders. *See* **Eating disorders**

Inhalation abuse of solvents. *See* **Solvent abuse**

Inheritance and succession   346.05

    See also **Executors and administrators; Inheritance and transfer tax; Land tenure; Wills**

    x Bequests; Heirs; Hereditary succession; Intestacy; Legacies; Succession, Intestate

    xx **Parent and child; Wealth; Wills**

Inheritance and transfer tax   343.05
>   *x* Estate tax; Taxation of legacies; Transfer tax
>   *xx* **Estate planning; Inheritance and succession; Internal revenue; Taxation**

Inheritance (Biology).   *See* **Heredity**

Initialisms.   *See* **Acronyms**

Initials   745.6
>   *See also* **Alphabets; Illumination of books and manuscripts; Lettering; Monograms; Printing—Specimens; Type and type founding**
>   *xx* **Alphabets; Illumination of books and manuscripts; Lettering; Monograms; Type and type founding**

Initiative and referendum.   *See* **Referendum**

Injunctions   331.89
>   *See also* **Strikes and lockouts**
>   *xx* **Constitutional law; Labor unions; Strikes and lockouts**

Injuries.   *See* **Accidents; First aid; Wounds and injuries**

Injurious insects.   *See* **Insect pests**

Injurious occupations.   *See* **Hazardous occupations**

Ink drawing.   *See* **Pen drawing**

Inland navigation   386
>   *See also* **Canals; Lakes; Rivers**
>   *x* Navigation, Inland
>   *xx* **Canals; Navigation; Rivers; Shipping; Transportation; Water resources development; Waterways**

Inner cities   307.76; 362.5
>   Use for materials on densely populated, usually deteriorating, central areas of large cities, inhabited predominantly by the poor, often of a specific ethnic group, and for materials on the social and economic problems of these areas.
>   *x* Central cities; Ghettoes, Inner city; Inner city ghettoes; Inner city problems
>   *xx* **Cities and towns**

Inner city ghettoes.   *See* **Inner cities**

Inner city problems.   *See* **Inner cities**

Inns.   *See* **Hotels, motels, etc.**

Innuit.   *See* **Inuit**

Inoculation.   *See* **Vaccination**

Inorganic chemistry.   *See* **Chemistry, Inorganic**

Input equipment (Computers).   *See* **Computer peripherals**

Inquisition (May subdiv. geog.)   **272**
>   *x* Holy Office
>   *xx* **Catholic Church; Church history—600-1500, Middle Ages**

Insane.   *See* **Mentally ill**

Insane—Hospitals.   *See* **Mentally ill—Institutional care; Psychiatric hospitals**

Insanity.   *See* **Mental illness—Jurisprudence**

Insanity defense   345
>   *x* Insanity plea
>   *xx* **Criminal law; Mental illness—Jurisprudence**

Insanity plea.   *See* **Insanity defense**

Inscriptions   411
>   *See also* **Brasses; Epitaphs; Graffiti; Hieroglyphics; Seals (Numismatics)**
>   *x* Epigraphy
>   *xx* **Archeology; History, Ancient**

Insect pests 632
  See also **Aeronautics in agriculture; Agricultural pests; Beneficial insects; Household pests; Insects as carriers of disease; Veterinary medicine;** also names of insect pests, e.g. **Locusts;** etc.; and names of crops, plants, trees, etc., with the subdivision *Diseases and pests,* e.g. **Fruit—Diseases and pests;** etc.
  x Destructive insects; Diseases and pests; Economic entomology; Entomology, Economic; Garden pests; Harmful insects; Injurious insects; Insects, Injurious and beneficial
  xx **Aeronautics in agriculture; Agricultural pests; Beneficial insects; Insects; Parasites; Pests; Veterinary medicine; Zoology, Economic**
Insecticides 632; 668
  See also **Fumigation; Spraying and dusting;** also names of insecticides, e.g. **D.D.T. (Insecticide);** etc.
  xx **Agricultural chemicals; Pesticides; Spraying and dusting**
Insecticides—Toxicology 615.9
  xx **Poisons and poisoning**
Insects 595.7
  See also **Beneficial insects; Fertilization of plants; Insect pests;** also names of insects, e.g. **Ants; Bees; Butterflies; Moths; Wasps;** etc.
  x Entomology
  xx **Invertebrates**
Insects as carriers of disease 614.4
  See also **Flies; Lyme disease; Mosquitoes**
  x Entomology, Medical; Medical entomology
  xx **Communicable diseases; Insect pests; Lyme disease**
Insects, Injurious and beneficial. *See* **Beneficial insects; Insect pests**
Insemination, Artificial. *See* **Artificial insemination**
Inservice training. *See* **Employees—Training; Librarians—In-service training**
Insider trading 346; 364.1
  x Securities trading, Insider; Stocks—Insider trading
  xx **Commercial law; Securities; Stock exchange**
Insignia 929
  See also **Decorations of honor; Medals;** also armies and navies and other appropriate subjects with the subdivision *Insignia* or *Medals, badges, decorations, etc.,* e.g. **Colleges and universities—Insignia; United States. Army—Insignia; United States. Army—Medals, badges, decorations, etc.; United States. Navy—Insignia; United States. Navy—Medals, badges, decorations, etc.;** etc.
  x Badges of honor; Devices (Heraldry); Emblems
  xx **Decorations of honor; Heraldry; Medals**
Insolvency. *See* **Bankruptcy**
Insomnia 616.8
  See also **Sleep**
  x Sleeplessness; Wakefulness
  xx **Sleep**

Inspection of food. *See* **Food adulteration and inspection**
Inspection of meat. *See* **Meat inspection**
Inspection of schools. *See* **School supervision; Schools—Administration**
Inspiration. *See* **Creation (Literary, artistic, etc.)**
Inspiration, Biblical. *See* **Bible—Inspiration**
Instalment plan   658.8
  x Hire-purchase plan
  xx **Business; Buying; Consumer credit; Credit**
Instinct   152.3; 156
  See also **Animal intelligence; Habit; Psychology, Comparative**
  x Animal instinct
  xx **Animal intelligence; Animals—Behavior; Habit; Psychology; Psychology, Comparative**
Institutional care   361
  See also **Group homes; Hospitals; Nursing homes; Orphanages;** also classes of people with the subdivision *Institutional care,* e.g. **Blind—Institutional care; Children—Institutional care; Mentally ill—Institutional care;** etc.
  x Asylums; Benevolent institutions; Charitable institutions; Homes (Institutions)
  xx **Charities; Charities, Medical; Public welfare**
Institutions, Charitable and philanthropic. *See* **Charities; Hospitals**
Instruction. *See* **Education; Teaching**
Instruction, Home. *See* **Home instruction**
Instructional materials. *See* **Teaching—Aids and devices**
Instructional materials centers   027.7
  See also **School libraries**
  x Audiovisual materials centers; Curriculum materials centers; Educational media centers; Learning resource centers; Media centers (Education); Multimedia centers; School media centers
  xx **Libraries**
Instructional supervision. *See* **School supervision**
Instrument flying   629.132
  xx **Aeronautical instruments; Airplanes—Piloting**
Instrumental music   784
  See also **Musical instruments;** also types of instrumental music, e.g. **Band music; Chamber music; Dance music; Guitar music; Orchestral music; Piano music;** etc.
  x Music, Instrumental
  xx **Music; Musical instruments**
Instrumentation and orchestration   781.3; 784.13
  See also **Musical instruments**
  x Orchestration
  xx **Bands (Music); Composition (Music); Music; Musical instruments; Orchestra**
Instruments, Aeronautical. *See* **Aeronautical instruments**
Instruments, Astronautical. *See* **Astronautical instruments**
Instruments, Astronomical. *See* **Astronomical instruments**
Instruments, Engineering. *See* **Engineering instruments**

Instruments, Measuring. *See* **Measuring instruments**

Instruments, Meteorological. *See* **Meteorological instruments**

Instruments, Musical. *See* **Musical instruments**

Instruments, Negotiable. *See* **Negotiable instruments**

Instruments, Scientific. *See* **Scientific apparatus and instruments**

Insulation (Heat) 693.8; 697
> *x* Heat insulating materials; Thermal insulation
> *xx* **Heating**

Insulation (Sound). *See* **Soundproofing**

Insults. *See* **Invective**

Insurance 368
> All types of insurance are not included in this List but are to be added as needed, e.g. **Automobile insurance;** etc.
>
> *See also*

Automobile insurance	**Malpractice insurance**
Casualty insurance	**Marine insurance**
Fire insurance	**Saving and thrift**
Health insurance	**Unemployment insurance**
Life insurance	

> *x* Underwriting
> *xx* **Estate planning; Finance; Personal finance**

Insurance, Accident. *See* **Accident insurance**

Insurance, Automobile. *See* **Automobile insurance**

Insurance, Casualty. *See* **Casualty insurance**

Insurance, Disability. *See* **Accident insurance; Health insurance**

Insurance, Fire. *See* **Fire insurance**

Insurance, Group. *See* **Group insurance**

Insurance, Health. *See* **Health insurance**

Insurance, Hospitalization. *See* **Hospitalization insurance**

Insurance, Industrial. *See* **Industrial insurance**

Insurance, Life. *See* **Life insurance**

Insurance, Malpractice. *See* **Malpractice insurance**

Insurance, Marine. *See* **Marine insurance**

Insurance, Old age. *See* **Old age pensions**

Insurance, Professional liability. *See* **Malpractice insurance**

Insurance, Sickness. *See* **Health insurance**

Insurance, Social. *See* **Social security**

Insurance, State and compulsory. *See* **Social security**

Insurance, Unemployment. *See* **Unemployment insurance**

Insurance, Workers'. *See* **Social security**

Insurance, Workers' compensation. *See* **Workers' compensation**

Insurgency (May subdiv. geog.) 322.4; 355.02
> *See also* **Government, Resistance to; Guerrilla warfare; Internal security; Subversive activities; Terrorism**
> *x* Rebellions
> *xx* **Government, Resistance to; Internal security; Revolutions**

Integrated churches. *See* **Church and race relations**

Integrated language arts (Holistic). *See* **Whole language**

Integrated schools. *See* **School integration**

Integration in education. *See* **Articulation (Education); School integration; Segregation in education**

Integration, Racial. *See* **Blacks—Integration; Race relations**

Intellect   153.4
   See also

Creation (Literary, artistic, etc.)	**Mental tests**
	Perception
Imagination	**Reason**
Knowledge, Theory of	**Reasoning**
Logic	**Senses and sensation**
Memory	**Thought and thinking**

   x Intelligence; Mind; Understanding
   xx **Knowledge, Theory of; Psychology; Reasoning; Thought and thinking**

Intellectual cooperation   370.19
   See also **Congresses and conventions; Cultural relations; International education**
   x Cooperation, Intellectual
   xx **International cooperation; International education**

Intellectual freedom   323.44
   See also **Academic freedom; Censorship; Free speech; Freedom of information; Freedom of the press**
   xx **Freedom**

Intellectual life. *See* **Culture; Learning and scholarship;** and particular classes of people and names of countries, cities, etc. with the subdivision *Intellectual life,* e.g. **Blacks—Intellectual life; United States—Intellectual life;** etc.

Intellectual property. *See* **Copyright; Inventions; Patents**

Intellectuals (May subdiv. geog.)   **305.5**
   See also particular classes of people and names of countries, cities, etc. with the subdivision *Intellectual life,* e.g. **Blacks—Intellectual life; United States—Intellectual life;** etc.
   x Intelligentsia
   xx **Professions**

Intelligence. *See* **Intellect**

Intelligence agents. *See* **Spies**

Intelligence, Artificial. *See* **Artificial intelligence**

Intelligence of animals. *See* **Animal intelligence**

Intelligence service (May subdiv. geog.)   **327.12; 355.3**
   Use for materials on a government agency that is engaged in obtaining information, usually about an enemy, but sometimes about an ally or a neutral country, and also in blocking the attempts by foreign agents to gain information about one's own national secrets. Some intelligence services are used for covert political action, such as aerial and space reconnaissance, electronic eavesdropping, and the employment of secret agents.
   See also **Espionage; Secret service**
   x Counterespionage; Counterintelligence
   xx **Secret service**

Intelligence service—United States   327.1273; 355.3
   x United States—Intelligence service

Intelligence tests. *See* **Mental tests**

Intelligentsia. *See* **Intellectuals**
Intemperance. *See* **Alcoholism; Temperance**
Inter-American relations. *See* **Pan-Americanism**
Interactive CD technology. *See* **CD-I technology**
Interactive videotex. *See* **Videotex systems**
Interchange of teachers. *See* **Teacher exchange**
Interchange of visitors. *See* **Exchange of persons programs**
Intercollegiate athletics. *See* **Athletics; College sports**
Intercommunication systems   621.38; 651.7
>   *See also* **Closed-circuit television; Microwave communication systems**
>   *x* Interoffice communication systems; Loud-speakers
>   *xx* **Electronic apparatus and appliances; Sound— Recording and reproducing; Tele-communication**

Intercontinental ballistic missiles   623.4
>   *See also* names of specific ICBM missiles, e.g. **Atlas (Missile);** etc.
>   *x* I.C.B.M.; ICBM
>   *xx* **Ballistic missiles**

Intercultural education   370.19
>   Use for materials dealing with the eradication of racial and religious prejudices by showing the nature and effects of race, creed and immigrant cultures.
>   *See also* **Bilingual education; International education**
>   *x* Education, Intercultural; Education, Multicultural; Multicultural education
>   *xx* **Acculturation; Ethnic relations; Human relations; International education; Race relations**

Intercultural relations. *See* **Cultural relations**
Intercultural studies. *See* **Cross cultural studies**
Interest centers approach to teaching. *See* **Open plan schools**
Interest (Economics)   332.8
>   *xx* **Banks and banking; Business arithmetic; Capital; Finance; Loans**

Interest groups. *See* **Lobbying and lobbyists**
Interfaces, Computer. *See* **Computer interfaces**
Interfaith marriage   261.8; 306.84
>   *x* Intermarriage, Religious; Marriage, Mixed; Mixed marriage
>   *xx* **Intermarriage**

Interfaith relations   261; 262.2
>   *xx* **Christian unity; Human relations**
Intergovernmental tax relations   336.1
>   *See also* **Revenue sharing**
>   *x* Federal-state tax relations; State-local tax relations; Tax relations, Intergovernmental; Tax sharing
>   *xx* **Taxation**

Interior decoration. *See* **Interior design**
Interior design   747
>   Use for materials on the art and techniques of planning and supervising the design and execution of architectural interiors and their furnishings.

Interior design—*Continued*
    See also

Bedspreads	**Paper hanging**
Carpets	**Quilts**
Drapery	**Rugs**
Furniture	**Tapestry**
Mural painting and deco-	**Upholstery**
ration	**Wallpaper**

    x Arts, Decorative; Decoration, Interior; De-
       sign, Interior; Home decoration; House dec-
       oration; House furnishing; Interior decora-
       tion
    xx **Art; Decoration and ornament; Decorative**
       arts; Design; Home economics
Interlibrary loans. *See* **Library circulation**
Interlocking signals. *See* **Railroads—Signaling**
Intermarriage   306.84
    Use for materials that discuss collectively mar-
       riage between persons of different religions,
       religious denominations, races, and ethnic
       groups.
    See also **Interfaith marriage; Interracial marriage**
    x Marriage, Mixed; Mixed marriage
    xx **Marriage**
Intermarriage, Racial. *See* **Interracial marriage**
Intermarriage, Religious. *See* **Interfaith marriage**
Intermediate state. *See* **Eschatology; Future life**
Internal-combustion engines. *See* **Gas and oil en-**
    gines
Internal revenue   336.2
    See also **Income tax; Inheritance and transfer tax**
    x Revenue, Internal
    xx **Finance; Taxation**
Internal revenue law   343.04
    x Law, Internal revenue
    xx **Law**
Internal security (May subdiv. geog.)   **351.74; 363.2**
    See also **Insurgency; Subversive activities**
    x Loyalty oaths; Security, Internal
    xx **Insurgency; Subversive activities**
Internal security—United States   353.0074;
    363.20973
    x United States—Internal security
International agencies   060
    See also names of individual agencies
    x Associations, International; International as-
       sociations; International organizations
    xx **International cooperation**
International arbitration. *See* **Arbitration, Interna-**
    tional
International associations. *See* **International agen-**
    cies
International business enterprises. *See* **Multina-**
    tional corporations
International conferences. *See* **Congresses and con-**
    ventions
International cooperation   327.1; 341.7
    Use for general materials on international coop-
       erative activities, with or without the partic-
       ipation of governments.
    See also

Arbitration, International	**tions**
Congresses and conven-	**Cultural relations**

International cooperation—*Continued*

Economic assistance
Exchange of persons pro- grams
Intellectual cooperation
International agencies
International education
International organization

International police
League of Nations
Reconstruction (1939- 1951)
Technical assistance
United Nations

also subjects with the subdivision *International cooperation,* e.g. **Astronautics— International cooperation;** etc.

x Cooperation, International

xx **Cooperation; International education; International law; International organization; International relations; Reconstruction (1939- 1951)**

International copyright. *See* **Copyright**

International economic relations   382

See also **Balance of payments; Commercial policy; Economic assistance; Multinational corporations; Sanctions (International law); Technical assistance**

x Economic relations, Foreign; Foreign economic relations

xx **Economic policy; International relations**

International education   370.19

Use for materials on education for international understanding, world citizenship, etc.

See also **Comparative librarianship; Intellectual cooperation; Intercultural education; International cooperation; Teacher exchange**

x Education, International

xx **Education; Intellectual cooperation; Intercultural education; International cooperation**

International exchange. *See* **Foreign exchange**

International exhibitions. *See* **Exhibitions**

International federation. *See* **International organization**

International investment. *See* **Foreign investments**

International language. *See* **Universal language**

International law   341

See also

Aliens
Arbitration, International
Asylum
Boundaries
International cooperation
International organization
International relations
Intervention (International law)
Mandates
Maritime law
Military law

Naturalization
Neutrality
Pirates
Political refugees
Privateering
Salvage
Sanctions (International law)
Slave trade
Space law
Treaties
War

x Law, International; Law of nations; Nations, Law of; Natural law

xx **International organization; International relations; Law; War**

International mediation. *See* **Arbitration, International**

International organization   341.2

Use for materials on plans leading towards political organization of nations.

International organization—*Continued*
    See also **European federation; International cooperation; International law; International police; Mandates; World politics;** also names of specific organizations, e.g. **United Nations;** etc.
    x Federation, International; International federation; Organization, International; World government; World organization
    xx **Congresses and conventions; International cooperation; International law; International relations; Security, International; World politics**
International organizations. *See* **International agencies**
International police   **341**
    x Interpol; Police, International
    xx **International cooperation; International organization; International relations; Security, International**
International politics. *See* **World politics**
International relations   **327; 341.3**
    Use for materials on the theory of international relations. Historical accounts are entered under **World politics; Europe—Politics and government;** etc. Materials limited to diplomatic relations between two countries are entered under the name of each country with the subdivision *Foreign relations* further subdivided by the name of the reverse place, i.e. **United States—Foreign relations—Iran** and also **Iran—Foreign relations—Iran.**
    See also

Arbitration, International	**International law**
Arms control	**International organization**
Boundaries	**International police**
Catholic Church—	**Mandates**
Relations (Diplomatic)	**Monroe Doctrine**
Cultural relations	**Munitions**
Diplomacy	**National security**
Diplomatic and consular	**Nationalism**
service	**Neutrality**
Diplomats	**Peace**
Geopolitics	**Political refugees**
International cooperation	**Security, International**
International economic re-	**Treaties**
lations	**World politics**

    also names of countries with the subdivision *Foreign relations,* e.g. **United States—Foreign relations;** etc.
    x Foreign relations
    xx **International law; National security; World politics**
International security. *See* **Security, International**
International space cooperation. *See* **Astronautics—International cooperation**
International Standard Bibliographic Description   **025.3**
    x I.S.B.D; ISBD
International Standard Book Numbers   **070.5**
    x I.S.B.N.; ISBN
    xx **Publishers' standard book numbers**

International Standard Serial Numbers   070.5
  x I.S.S.N.; ISSN
International trade. *See* **Commerce**
Internationalism. *See* **Nationalism**
Internment camps. *See* **Concentration camps**
Interoffice communication systems. *See* **Intercommunication systems**
Interpersonal relations. *See* **Human relations**
Interplanetary communication. *See* **Interstellar communication**
Interplanetary visitors. *See* **Extraterrestrial beings**
Interplanetary voyages   629.45
  See also **Outer space—Exploration; Rockets (Aeronautics); Space flight**
  x Interstellar travel; Outer space travel; People in space; Space travel
  xx **Astronautics; Space flight**
Interplanetary warfare. *See* **Space warfare**
Interpol. *See* **International police**
Interpreting and translating. *See* **Translating and interpreting**
Interpretive dance. *See* **Modern dance**
Interracial adoption   362.7
  x Adoption, Interracial
  xx **Adoption; Race relations**
Interracial marriage   306.84
  x Intermarriage, Racial; Marriage, Interracial; Mixed marriage; Racial intermarriage
  xx **Intermarriage**
Interracial relations. *See* **Race relations**
Interscholastic sports. *See* **School sports**
Interstate commerce   381
  See note under **Commerce.**
  See also **Railroads—Government policy; Restraint of trade**
  x Commerce, Interstate; Government regulation of commerce; Government regulation of railroads
  xx **Commerce; Railroads—Government policy; Railroads—Rates; Restraint of trade; Trusts, Industrial**
Interstate highways. *See* **Express highways**
Interstellar communication   621.38
  See also **Astronautics—Communication systems; Radio astronomy**
  x Extraterrestrial communication; Interplanetary communication; Outer space—Communication; Space communication; Space telecommunication
  xx **Life on other planets; Telecommunication**
Interstellar travel. *See* **Interplanetary voyages**
Interstellar warfare. *See* **Space warfare**
Interurban railroads. *See* **Electric railroads; Street railroads**
Intervention (International law)   341.5
  See also **Monroe Doctrine; Neutrality**
  x Military intervention
  xx **International law; Neutrality; War**
Interviewing   158
  See also **Counseling; Psychology, Applied; Talk shows**
  xx **Applications for positions; Counseling; Psychology, Applied; Social psychology**

Interviewing (Journalism). *See* **Journalism; Reporters and reporting**

Interviews, Parent-teacher. *See* **Parent-teacher conferences**

Intestacy. *See* **Inheritance and succession**

Intolerance. *See* **Fanaticism; Freedom of conscience; Freedom of religion; Toleration**

Intoxicants. *See* **Alcohol; Alcoholic beverages; Cocaine; Liquors and liqueurs; Stimulants**

Intoxication. *See* **Alcoholism; Drug addiction; Temperance**

Intuition **153.4**

    See also **Perception; Reality**

    xx **Knowledge, Theory of; Perception; Philosophy; Psychology; Rationalism**

Inuit **970.004**

    In 1977 the Inuit Circumpolar Conference, representing Eskimos from Alaska, Canada, and Greenland, met in Barrow, Alaska, and officially adopted Inuit as a designation for all Eskimos. The Canadian government has also adopted Inuit as the official term for all Eskimo peoples in Canada. The Sears List adopted this form with the 12th edition. However, Inuit is sometimes used to refer to only some Eskimo peoples, and the term Eskimos is then used for the larger group. Libraries may want to establish policy on the use of this heading based upon local needs.

    x Eskimos; Esquimaux; Innuit

Inuit—Folklore **398**

    x Folklore, Inuit

Invalid cookery. *See* **Cookery for the sick; Diet therapy**

Invalids. *See* **Physically handicapped; Sick**

Invasion of privacy. *See* **Right of privacy**

Invective **808.88**

    x Abuse, Verbal; Insults; Verbal abuse

    xx **Satire**

Inventions **608**

    See also **Creation (Literary, artistic, etc.); Inventors; Patents**

    x Discoveries (in science); Intellectual property

    xx **Civilization; Inventors; Machinery; Patents; Technology**

Inventors **609.2; 920**

    See also **Inventions**

    xx **Engineers; Inventions**

Inventory control **658.7**

    x Stock control

    xx **Management; Retail trade**

Invertebrates **592**

    See also **Corals; Crustacea; Insects; Mollusks; Protozoa; Sponges; Worms**

    xx **Zoology**

Investigations, Governmental. *See* **Governmental investigations**

Investment in real estate. *See* **Real estate investment**

Investment trusts **332.63**

    x Mutual funds

    xx **Banks and banking; Trust companies**

Investments 332.6
> *See also*
> **Annuities**
> **Bonds**
> **Mortgages**
> **Real estate investment**
> **Saving and thrift**
> **Savings and loan associa-**
> tions
> **Securities**
> **Speculation**
> **Stock exchange**
> **Stocks**
> *xx* **Banks and banking; Capital; Estate planning; Finance; Loans; Personal finance; Saving and thrift; Securities; Speculation; Stock exchange; Stocks**

Investments, Foreign. *See* **Foreign investments**
Invincible Armada. *See* **Spanish Armada, 1588**
Invisible playmates. *See* **Imaginary playmates**
IQ tests. *See* **Mental tests**
Iran 935; 955
> *x* Persia

Iran-Contra Affair, 1985- 973.927
> *x* Contra-Iran Affair, 1985-; Iran-Contra Arms Scandal, 1985-; Irangate, 1985-
> *xx* **Corruption in politics; Military assistance, American; United States—Politics and government**

Iran-Contra Arms Scandal, 1985-. *See* **Iran-Contra Affair, 1985-**
Iran—Foreign relations—United States 327.55073
> *See also* **Iran hostage crisis, 1979-1981**
Iran—History—1941-1979 955.05
Iran—History—1979- 955.05
Iran hostage crisis, 1979-1981 327.73055; 327.55073; 955
> *x* Iranian seizure of American embassy
> *xx* **Hostages, American—Iran; Iran—Foreign relations—United States; United States—Foreign relations—Iran**

Irangate, 1985-. *See* **Iran-Contra Affair, 1985-**
Iranian seizure of American embassy. *See* **Iran hostage crisis, 1979-1981**
Iraq—History—1990, Invasion of Kuwait. *See* **Kuwait—History—1990, Iraqi Invasion**
Iraq—History—1991- , Persian Gulf War. *See* **Persian Gulf War, 1991-**
Iraq-Kuwait Crisis, 1990. *See* **Kuwait—History—1990, Iraqi Invasion; Persian Gulf War, 1991-**
IRAs (Pensions). *See* **Individual retirement accounts**
Iron 669; 672
> *See also* **Building, Iron and steel; Iron ores; Ironwork**
> *xx* **Steel**
Iron Age 930.1
> *See also* **Archeology; Bronze Age**
> *x* Prehistory
> *xx* **Archeology; Bronze Age**
Iron and steel building. *See* **Building, Iron and steel**
Iron curtain countries. *See* **Communist countries**
Iron founding. *See* **Founding**
Iron industry 338.2
> *See also* **Ironwork; Steel industry**
> *x* Iron industry and trade; Iron trade
> *xx* **Steel industry**

Iron industry and trade.   *See* **Iron industry**
Iron ores   549
   xx **Iron; Ore deposits; Ores**
Iron trade.   *See* **Iron industry**
Ironing.   *See* **Laundry**
Ironwork   672; 682; 739.4
   See also **Blacksmithing; Forging; Steel industry;**
      Welding
   x Wrought iron work
   xx **Decoration and ornament; Forging; Iron; Iron**
      industry; Metalwork
Irreversible coma.   *See* **Brain death**
Irrigation (May subdiv. geog.)   **333.91; 627; 631.5**
   See also **Dams; Dry farming; Reclamation of**
      land; Water rights; Windmills
   xx **Agricultural engineering; Civil engineering;**
      Hydraulic engineering; Reclamation of land;
      Reservoirs; Soils; Water resources develop-
      ment; Water supply
Irrigation—United States   333.91; 627; 631.5
   x United States—Irrigation
ISBD.   *See* **International Standard Bibliographic**
      Description
ISBN.   *See* **International Standard Book Numbers**
Islam   297
   Use for materials on the religion. Materials on
      the believers in this religion are entered un-
      der **Muslims.**
   See also **Bahai Faith; Koran; Mosques**
   x Islamism; Mohammedanism; Moslemism;
      Muhammedanism; Muslimism
   xx **Religions**
Islamic art.   *See* **Art, Islamic**
Islamic countries   956
   See also **Arab countries**
   x Muslim countries
Islamism.   *See* **Islam**
Islands   551.4
   See also **Coral reefs and islands; Oceania;** also
      names of islands and groups of islands, e.g.
      Cuba; Islands of the Pacific; etc.
Islands, Artificial.   *See* **Drilling platforms**
Islands, Imaginary.   *See* **Geographical myths**
Islands of the Pacific   990
   Use for comprehensive materials on all the is-
      lands of the Pacific Ocean. Materials re-
      stricted to comprehensive treatment of the
      island groups of Melanesia, Micronesia, and
      Polynesia are entered under **Oceania.**
   See also **Oceania**
   x Pacific Islands; Pacific Ocean Islands
   xx **Islands**
Isotopes   539
   See also **Radioisotopes**
Israel   956.94
   xx **Middle East**
Israel-Arab relations.   *See* **Jewish-Arab relations**
Israel-Arab War, 1948-1949   956.04
   x Arab-Israel War, 1948-1949
Israel-Arab War, 1956.   *See* **Sinai Campaign, 1956**
Israel-Arab War, 1967   956.04
   x Arab-Israel War, 1967; Six Day War, 1967

Israel-Arab War, 1973 956.04
>   *x* Arab-Israel War, 1973; Yom Kippur War, 1973

Israel—Collective settlements. *See* **Collective settlements—Israel**

Israeli-Arab relations. *See* **Jewish-Arab relations**

Israeli intervention in Lebanon, 1982-1984. *See* **Lebanon—History—1982-1984, Israeli intervention**

Israelis 305.892; 920; 956.94
>   *xx* **Jews**

Israelites. *See* **Jews**

ISSN. *See* **International Standard Serial Numbers**

Italo-Ethiopian War, 1935-1936 963
>   *x* Ethiopian-Italian War, 1935-1936

Italy 945
>   May be subdivided like U.S. except for *History.*

Italy—History 945
Italy—History—0-1559 945
Italy—History—1559-1789 945
Italy—History—1789-1815 945
Italy—History—1815-1914 945; 945.09
Italy—History—1914-1945 945.091
Italy—History—1945-1976 945.092
Italy—History—1976- 945.092

Ivory 679
>   *x* Animal products

Jacobins (Dominicans). *See* **Dominicans (Religious order)**

Jails. *See* **Prisons**

Japan 952
Japan—History 952
Japan—History—0-1868 952
Japan—History—1868-1945 952.03
Japan—History—1945-1952, Allied occupation 952.04
>   *xx* **Military occupation; World War, 1939-1945—Occupied territories**

Japan—History—1952- 952.04

Japanese color prints. *See* **Color prints, Japanese**

Japanese language 495.6
>   May be subdivided like **English language.**

Japanese language—Business Japanese 495.6
>   *Business Japanese* is a unique subdivision for **Japanese language.**
>   *See also* **Business letters**
>   *x* Business Japanese
>   *xx* **Business letters**

Japanese paper folding. *See* **Origami**

Japanese prints. *See* **Color prints, Japanese**

Jargon. *See* subjects with the subdivision *Jargon,* e.g. **English language—Jargon;** etc.

Jargon, Computer. *See* **Computer science—Dictionaries**

Jazz ensembles 784.4

Jazz music 781.65; 782.42165
>   *See also* **Blues music**
>   *xx* **Blues music; Dance music; Music**

Jestbooks. *See* **Chapbooks**

Jesters. *See* **Fools and jesters**

Jesuits 271
>   *x* Jesus, Society of; Society of Jesus
>   *xx* **Religious orders for men, Catholic**

Jesus Christ 232

    See also **Atonement—Christianity; Christianity;**
        Lord's Supper; Second Advent; Trinity

    x Christ; Christology

    xx **Christianity; God—Christianity; Trinity**

Jesus Christ—Art 704.9

    See also **Bible—Pictorial works; Christian art**
        and symbolism; Mary, Blessed Virgin,
        Saint—Art

    x Jesus Christ—Iconography; Jesus Christ in art

    xx **Christian art and symbolism; Mary, Blessed**
        Virgin, Saint—Art

Jesus Christ—Atonement. *See* **Atonement—**
    Christianity

Jesus Christ—Biography 232.9

    See also **Jesus Christ—Crucifixion; Jesus**
        Christ—Historicity; Jesus Christ—Nativity

Jesus Christ—Birth. *See* **Jesus Christ—Nativity**

Jesus Christ—Crucifixion 232.96

    See also **Good Friday**

    x Crucifixion of Christ

    xx **Good Friday; Jesus Christ—Biography**

Jesus Christ—Divinity 232

    See also **Trinity; Unitarianism**

    x Divinity of Christ

    xx **Unitarianism**

Jesus Christ—Drama 808.82; 812, etc.

    See also **Passion plays**

Jesus Christ—Historicity 232.9

    xx **Jesus Christ—Biography**

Jesus Christ—Iconography. *See* **Jesus Christ—Art**

Jesus Christ in art. *See* **Jesus Christ—Art**

Jesus Christ—Last Supper. *See* **Lord's Supper**

Jesus Christ—Messiahship 232

Jesus Christ—Nativity 232.92

    See also **Christmas**

    x Jesus Christ—Birth; Nativity of Christ

    xx **Christmas; Jesus Christ—Biography**

Jesus Christ—Parables 226.8

    xx **Bible—Parables; Parables**

Jesus Christ—Prayers 232.9

    See also **Lord's prayer**

Jesus Christ—Prophecies 232

    xx **Bible—Prophecies**

Jesus Christ—Resurrection 232.9

    x Resurrection

Jesus Christ—Second Advent. *See* **Second Advent**

Jesus Christ—Sermon on the mount. *See* **Sermon**
    on the mount

Jesus Christ—Teachings 232.9

    x Teachings of Jesus

Jesus, Society of. *See* **Jesuits**

Jet lag 616.9

    xx **Aviation medicine; Biological rhythms; Fa-**
    tigue

Jet planes 629.133

    See also **Short take off and landing aircraft**

    x Airplanes, Jet propelled

Jet propulsion 621.43; 629.47

    See also **Rockets (Aeronautics)**

    xx **Airplanes—Engines; Rockets (Aeronautics)**

Jewelry 739.27

    See note under **Gems.**

Jewelry—*Continued*
> *See also* **Gems; Goldwork; Silverwork;** also
> names of specific jewelry
> *x* Costume jewelry; Jewels
> *xx* **Art metalwork; Decoration and ornament;**
> **Decorative arts; Gems; Goldwork; Metal-**
> **work; Silver; Silverwork**

Jewels. *See* **Gems; Jewelry; Precious stones**
Jewish-Arab relations   956
> *See also* **Lebanon—History—1982-1984, Israeli**
> **intervention**
> *x* Arab-Jewish relations; Israel-Arab relations;
> Israeli-Arab relations; Palestine problem,
> 1917-
> *xx* **Palestinian Arabs**

Jewish civilization. *See* **Jews—Civilization**
Jewish ethics   296.3
> Use same form for ethics of other religious
> groups, e.g. **Christian ethics;** etc.
> *x* Ethics, Jewish
> *xx* **Ethics**

Jewish holidays. *See* **Fasts and feasts—Judaism**
Jewish holocaust (1933-1945). *See* **Holocaust, Jew-**
> **ish (1933-1945)**
Jewish language. *See* **Hebrew language; Yiddish**
> **language**
Jewish legends. *See* **Legends, Jewish**
Jewish literature   839; 892.4
> *See also* **Bible; Cabala; Hebrew literature; Tal-**
> **mud; Yiddish literature**
> *x* Jews—Literature
> *xx* **Hebrew literature**

Jewish religion. *See* **Judaism**
Jews (May subdiv. geog.)   **305.892; 909**
> *See also* **Israelis**
> *x* Hebrews; Israelites
> *xx* **Church history; Judaism**
Jews and Gentiles   305.6
> *See also* **Antisemitism**
> *x* Gentiles and Jews; Jews—Relations with
> Gentiles
> *xx* **Human relations**

Jews—Antiquities   933
Jews—Civilization   909
> *x* Civilization, Jewish; Jewish civilization

Jews—Customs. *See* **Jews—Social life and customs**
Jews—Economic conditions   305.892; 330.9
Jews—Festivals. *See* **Fasts and feasts—Judaism**
Jews—Folklore   398
> *x* Folklore, Jewish

Jews—Language. *See* **Hebrew language; Yiddish**
> **language**
Jews—Legends. *See* **Legends, Jewish**
Jews—Literature. *See* **Hebrew literature; Jewish**
> **literature**
Jews—Persecutions   909; 933
> *See also* **Holocaust, Jewish (1933-1945); World**
> **War, 1939-1945—Jews—Rescue**
> *xx* **Antisemitism; Persecution**

Jews—Political activity   909; 956.94
Jews—Relations with Gentiles. *See* **Jews and Gen-**
> **tiles**
Jews—Religion. *See* **Judaism**

Jews—Restoration 956.94
> Use for materials dealing with the belief that the Jews, in fulfillment of Biblical prophecy, would some day return to Palestine.
> *See also* **Zionism**
> *xx* **Zionism**

Jews—Rites and ceremonies. *See* **Judaism—Customs and practices**

Jews—Ritual. *See* **Judaism—Liturgy**

Jews—Social conditions 305.892; 909
> Use for materials relating to social conditions of the Jews themselves. Materials on the relation of the Jews to non-Jews are entered under **Jews and Gentiles.**
> *xx* **Social conditions**

Jews—Social life and customs 305.892
> *x* Customs, Social; Jews—Customs; Social customs; Social life and customs
> *xx* **Manners and customs**

Job analysis 658.3
> *See also* **Motion study; Time study**
> *x* Personnel classification
> *xx* **Efficiency, Industrial; Factory management; Industrial management; Occupations; Personnel management; Wages**

Job applications. *See* **Applications for positions**

Job discrimination. *See* **Discrimination in employment**

Job hunting 650.14
> *See also* **Applications for positions; Résumés (Employment)**
> *x* Hunting, Job; Job searching
> *xx* **Employment agencies; Vocational guidance**

Job performance standards. *See* **Performance standards**

Job placement guidance. *See* **Vocational guidance**

Job résumés. *See* **Résumés (Employment)**

Job retraining. *See* **Occupational retraining**

Job satisfaction 650.1; 658.3
> *See also* **Burn out (Psychology)**
> *x* Satisfaction in work; Work satisfaction
> *xx* **Attitude (Psychology); Employee morale; Personnel management; Work**

Job searching. *See* **Job hunting**

Job security 331.25; 650.1; 658.3
> *See also* **Employees—Dismissal**
> *x* Employment security; Security, Job
> *xx* **Personnel management**

Job sharing 331.2; 658.3
> *x* Sharing of jobs
> *xx* **Part-time employment**

Job stress 158.7; 658.3
> *See also* **Burn out (Psychology)**
> *x* Occupational stress; On the job stress; Organizational stress; Work stress
> *xx* **Stress (Physiology)**

Job training. *See* **Occupational training**

Jobless people. *See* **Unemployed**

Joblessness. *See* **Unemployment**

Jobs. *See* **Employment agencies; Occupations; Professions**

Jogging 613.7
> *xx* **Running**

Joint custody of children. *See* **Child custody**

Joke books. *See* **Jokes**
Jokes   808.7; 808.88; 818, etc.
>   *See also* **Practical jokes**
>   *x* Joke books
>   *xx* **Wit and humor**
Journalism   070.4
>   Use for materials dealing with writing for the periodical press and with the editing of this writing, or for materials on journalism as an occupation. Materials limited to the history, organization and management of newspapers are entered under **Newspapers.** Journalism in a particular field is entered under **Journalism** with adjective modifier, e.g. **Journalism, Scientific;** etc.
>   *See also*

Broadcast journalism	**Newspapers**
College and school jour-	**Periodicals**
nalism	**Photojournalism**
Freedom of the press	**Press**
Gossip	**Reporters and reporting**
Libel and slander	

>   *x* Editors and editing; Interviewing (Journalism); Writing (Authorship)
>   *xx* **Authorship; Broadcast journalism; Literature; Newspapers; Periodicals; Reporters and reporting**
Journalism—Objectivity   070.4
>   *x* Slanted journalism
Journalism, Scientific   070.4
>   *x* Scientific journalism
Journalistic photography. *See* **Photojournalism**
Journalists   070.92; 920
>   *x* Columnists; Editors and editing; Writers
Journals. *See* **Periodicals**
Journals (Machinery). *See* **Bearings (Machinery)**
Journeys. *See* **Voyages and travels;** and names of cities (except ancient cities), countries, regions, etc. with the subdivision *Description,* e.g. **United States—Description;** etc.
Joy and sorrow   152.4
>   *See also* **Happiness; Pleasure**
>   *x* Affliction; Grief; Sorrow
>   *xx* **Emotions; Ethics; Happiness; Suffering**
Judaeo-German. *See* **Yiddish language**
Judaism   296
>   *See also*

Atonement—Judaism	**Rabbis**
Cabala	**Sabbath**
Fasts and feasts—Judaism	**Synagogues**
Jews	**Talmud**

>   *x* Jewish religion; Jews—Religion
>   *xx* **Religions**
Judaism—Customs and practices   296.4
>   *See also* **Judaism—Liturgy**
>   *x* Jews—Rites and ceremonies
>   *xx* **Rites and ceremonies**
Judaism—Liturgy   296.4
>   *x* Jews—Ritual
>   *xx* **Judaism—Customs and practices; Liturgies**
Judges   347.092; 920
>   *See also* **Courts; Women judges**
>   *x* Chief justices
>   *xx* **Courts; Lawyers**

Judicial investigations. *See* **Governmental investigations**

Judiciary. *See* **Courts**

Judo 796.8

    See also **Karate**

    xx **Physical education; Self-defense; Wrestling**

Juggling 793.8

    See also **Magic**

    x Legerdemain; Sleight of hand

    xx **Amusements; Magic; Tricks**

July Fourth. *See* **Fourth of July**

Jungle animals 591.52

    xx **Animals; Forest animals; Wildlife**

Jungles 634.9

    Use for materials on impenetrable thickets of second-growth vegetation replacing tropical rain forest that has been disturbed or degraded. Consider also **Rain forests.**

    x Selvas; Tropical jungles

    xx **Forests and forestry; Rain forests; Tropics**

Junior colleges 378.1

    x Community colleges

    xx **Colleges and universities; Higher education**

Junior colleges—Directories 378.1

    xx **Directories**

Junior high school libraries. *See* **High school libraries**

Junior high schools 373.2

    x High schools, Junior; Secondary schools

    xx **High schools; Public schools; Secondary education**

Junk. *See* **Waste products**

Junk bonds 332.63

    x High-yield junk bonds

    xx **Bonds**

Junk in space. *See* **Space debris**

Jurisprudence. *See* **Law**

Jurisprudence, Medical. *See* **Medical jurisprudence**

Jurists. *See* **Lawyers**

Jury 345; 347

    x Trial by jury

    xx **Courts; Criminal law**

Justice 340

    xx **Ethics; Human behavior; Law**

Justice, Administration of 351.8

    See also **Courts; Crime; Governmental investigations; Impeachments**

    x Administration of justice

    xx **Courts; Crime**

Juvenile courts 345

    See also **Probation**

    x Children's courts

    xx **Courts; Juvenile delinquency; Probation; Reformatories**

Juvenile delinquency 364.3

    See also **Child welfare; Juvenile courts; Juvenile prostitution; Reformatories; School violence; Teenagers—Drug use; Youth—Drug use**

    x Children, Delinquent; Delinquency, Juvenile; Delinquents; Gangs

    xx **Child welfare; Crime; Emotionally disturbed children; Reformatories; Social problems; Teenagers—Drug use; Youth—Drug use**

Juvenile delinquency—Case studies 364.3

Juvenile literature. *See* **Children's literature**

Juvenile prostitution 176; 306.74; 362.7; 363.4; 364.1

 x Adolescent prostitution; Child prostitution; Children and prostitution; Prostitution, Juvenile; Teenage prostitution

 xx **Child abuse; Juvenile delinquency; Prostitution**

K.K.K. *See* **Ku Klux Klan (1865-1876); Ku Klux Klan (1915-)**

Kabbala. *See* **Cabala**

Kamuti. *See* **Bonsai**

Karate 796.8

 xx **Judo; Self-defense**

Kart racing. *See* **Karts and karting**

Karting. *See* **Karts and karting**

Karts and karting 796.7

 Use for materials on miniature, lightweight, low-slung, four-wheeled racing or recreational motorcars that can be driven at speeds of up to 60 mph.

 x Carts (Midget cars); Go karts; Kart racing; Karting; Karts (Midget cars); Midget cars

 xx **Automobile racing**

Karts (Midget cars). *See* **Karts and karting**

Keyboarding (Electronics) 004.7; 652.5

 See also **Typewriting**

 x Computer keyboarding; Data processing, Electronic—Keyboarding; Electronic data processing—Keyboarding; Word processor keyboarding

 xx **Business education; Office practice; Typewriting**

Keyboards (Electronics) 004.7

 x Computer keyboards; Word processor keyboards

 xx **Computer peripherals; Office equipment and supplies**

Keyboards (Musical instruments) 786

 xx **Organ; Piano**

Keys. *See* **Locks and keys**

Kibbutz. *See* **Collective settlements—Israel**

Kidnapping 364.1

 x Abduction

 xx **Criminal law; Offenses against the person**

Kidnapping, Parental. *See* **Parental kidnapping**

Killing, Mercy. *See* **Euthanasia**

Kindergarten 372.21

 See also **Creative activities; Montessori method of education; Preschool education**

 xx **Children; Elementary education; Games; Nursery schools; Preschool education; Schools; Teaching**

Kinematics 531

 See also **Mechanical movements; Mechanics; Motion**

 xx **Dynamics; Mechanics; Motion**

Kinetic art 701; 709.04

 See also **Kinetic sculpture**

 x Art in motion; Art, Kinetic

 xx **Art, Modern—1900-1999 (20th century)**

Kinetic sculpture 731; 735

 See also **Mobiles (Sculpture)**

Kinetic sculpture—*Continued*

   x Sculpture in motion; Sculpture, Kinetic

   xx **Futurism (Art); Kinetic art**

Kinetics. *See* **Dynamics; Motion**

King, Martin Luther, holiday. *See* **Martin Luther King Day**

King Philip's War, 1675-1676 973.2

   x United States—History—1675-1676, King Philip's War

   xx **Indians of North America—Wars; United States—History—1600-1775, Colonial period**

King William's War, 1689-1697. *See* **United States—History—1689-1697, King William's War**

Kings, queens, rulers, etc. 920

   See also **Courts and courtiers; Dictators; Presidents; Roman emperors;** also names of countries with the subdivision *Kings, queens, rulers, etc.,* e.g. **Great Britain—Kings, queens, rulers, etc.;** also names of individual kings, queens, and rulers, e.g. **Elizabeth II, Queen of Great Britain, 1926- ;** etc.

   x Emperors; Monarchs; Queens; Royalty; Rulers; Sovereigns

   xx **Courts and courtiers; Heads of state; History; Monarchy; Political science**

Kitchen gardens. *See* **Vegetable gardening**

Kitchen utensils. *See* **Household equipment and supplies**

Kitchens 643

   xx **Houses**

Kites 629.133; 796.1

   xx **Aeronautics**

Kittens. *See* **Cats**

Kneetop computers. *See* **Portable computers**

Knighthood. *See* **Knights and knighthood**

Knights and knighthood 394; 940.1

   See also **Chivalry; Heraldry**

   x Knighthood

   xx **Chivalry; Heraldry; Middle Ages; Nobility**

Knights of the Round Table. *See* **Arthurian romances**

Knitting 746.43

Knots and splices 623.88

   x Splicing

   xx **Navigation; Rope**

Knowledge, Theory of 001.01; 121

   Use for materials dealing with the origin, nature, methods and limits of human knowledge.

   See also

Apperception	**Perception**
Belief and doubt	**Pragmatism**
Empiricism	**Rationalism**
Gestalt psychology	**Reality**
Intellect	**Senses and sensation**
Intuition	**Truth**

   x Cognition; Epistemology; Understanding

   xx **Apperception; Consciousness; Intellect; Logic; Metaphysics; Philosophy; Reality; Truth**

Kodak camera 771.3

   xx **Cameras**

Koran 297

    x Alkoran; Qur'an

    xx **Islam; Sacred books**

Korea 951.9

    Use for materials on Korea as a whole before
1948 when two separate republics were established.

    See also **Korea (North); Korea (South)**

Korea (Democratic People's Republic). *See* **Korea
(North)**

Korea (North) 951.93

    Use for materials on the Democratic People's
Republic of Korea, established in 1948.

    x Korea (Democratic People's Republic); North
Korea

    xx **Korea**

Korea (Republic). *See* **Korea (South)**

Korea (South) 951.95

    Use for materials on the Republic of Korea, es-
tablished in 1948.

    x Korea (Republic); South Korea

    xx **Korea**

Korean War, 1950-1953 951.904

Ku Klux Klan (1865-1876) 322.4

    x K.K.K.

    xx **Reconstruction (1865-1876)**

Ku Klux Klan (1915-) 322.4

    x K.K.K.

Kuwait—History—1990, Iraqi Invasion 953.67

    Use for materials limited to the Iraqi invasion of
Kuwait. Comprehensive materials on the
subsequent war that include discussion of
the Iraqi invasion as a prelude to the war
are entered under **Persian Gulf War, 1991-.**

    x Iraq—History—1990, Invasion of Kuwait;
Iraq-Kuwait Crisis, 1990

Kuwait—History—1991- , Persian Gulf War. *See*
Persian Gulf War, 1991-

Labor (May subdiv. geog.) **331**

    Use for materials on the collective human activi-
ties involved in the production and distribution of goods and services in an economy.
These services are performed by workers for
wages as distinguished from those performed by entrepreneurs for profits. Also
use for materials on the group of workers
who render these services for wages. Materials on the physical or mental exertion of individuals to produce or accomplish something are entered under **Work.**

    See also

Apprentices	**Hazardous occupations**
Arbitration, Industrial	**Hours of labor**
Capitalism	**Household employees**
Children—Employment	**Industrial insurance**
Church and labor	**Industrial relations**
Collective bargaining	**Labor unions**
Communism	**Libraries and labor**
Contract labor	**Machinery in industry**
Convict labor	**Men—Employment**
Cost of living	**Migrant labor**
Employment	**Occupational diseases**
Employment agencies	**Occupations**

Labor—*Continued*

Open and closed shop
Part-time employment
Peasantry
Peonage
Proletariat
Slavery
Socialism
Strikes and lockouts
Supplementary employment

Teenagers—Employment
Unemployed
Wages
Welfare work in industry
Women—Employment
Work
Work ethics
World War, 1939-1945—
    Human resources
Youth—Employment

also names of classes of laborers, e.g. **Agricultural laborers; Miners;** etc.; and headings beginning with the word **Labor.**

x Blue collar workers; Factory workers; Industrial workers; Labor and laboring classes; Labor movement; Laborers; Manual workers; Skilled workers; Unskilled workers; Working class

xx **Economics; Social classes; Social conditions; Socialism; Sociology; Work**

Labor absenteeism. *See* **Absenteeism (Labor)**
Labor—Accidents 363.1; 658.3
Labor and capital. *See* **Industrial relations**
Labor and laboring classes. *See* **Labor**
Labor and libraries. *See* **Libraries and labor**
Labor and the church. *See* **Church and labor**
Labor arbitration. *See* **Arbitration, Industrial**
Labor (Childbirth). *See* **Childbirth**
Labor contract 331.1; 331.89
Use for materials dealing with agreements between employer and employee in which the latter agrees to perform work in return for compensation from the former.
See also **Collective bargaining; Open and closed shop; Wages**
x Collective labor agreements; Trade agreements (Labor)
xx **Collective bargaining; Contracts; Industrial relations**
Labor disputes 331.89
See also **Arbitration, Industrial; Collective bargaining; Strikes and lockouts**
x Disputes, Labor; Industrial disputes
xx **Industrial relations**
Labor—Education 331.25
x Education of workers
Labor force. *See* **Labor supply**
Labor, Hours of. *See* **Hours of labor**
Labor—Housing 363.5
Labor—Insurance. *See* **Old age pensions; Social security; Unemployment insurance**
Labor-management relations. *See* **Industrial relations**
Labor market. *See* **Labor supply**
Labor, Migratory. *See* **Migrant labor**
Labor movement. *See* **Labor**
Labor negotiations. *See* **Arbitration, Industrial; Collective bargaining**
Labor organizations. *See* **Labor unions**
Labor output. *See* **Labor productivity**
Labor participation in management. *See* **Participative management**

Labor productivity   331.11

   See also **Machinery in industry; Production standards;** also subjects with the subdivision *Labor productivity,* e.g. **Employees—Labor productivity;** etc.

   x Labor output; Productivity of labor

   xx **Efficiency, Industrial; Machinery in industry**

Labor relations. *See* **Industrial relations**

Labor saving devices, Household. *See* **Household appliances, Electric; Household equipment and supplies**

Labor supply   331.11

   See also

Children—Employment	**Teenagers—Employment**
Employment agencies	**Unemployed**
Employment forecasting	**Unemployment**
Human resources	**Women—Employment**
Human resources policy	**World War, 1939-1945—**
Men—Employment	**Human resources**
Occupational retraining	**Youth—Employment**

   x Labor force; Labor market

   xx **Economic conditions; Employment; Employment agencies; Employment forecasting; Human resources; Human resources policy; Unemployed**

Labor turnover   331.12

   See also **Employment agencies**

   xx **Personnel management**

Labor unions (May subdiv. geog.)   **331.88**

   See also **Arbitration, Industrial; Collective bargaining; Injunctions; Open and closed shop; Sabotage; Strikes and lockouts;** also names of types of unions and names of individual labor unions, e.g. **Librarians' unions; United Steelworkers of America;** etc.

   x Labor organizations; Organized labor; Trade unions; Unions, Labor

   xx **Collective bargaining; Cooperation; Industrial relations; Labor; Socialism; Societies; Strikes and lockouts**

Labor unions—United States   331.880973

   x American labor unions; United States—Labor unions

Labor—United States   331.0973

   x United States—Labor

Laboratories, Language. *See* **Language laboratories**

Laboratories, Space. *See* **Space stations**

Laboratory animal experimentation. *See* **Animal experimentation**

Laboratory animal welfare. *See* **Animal welfare**

Laboratory fertilization. *See* **Fertilization in vitro**

Laboratory manuals. *See* scientific and technical subjects with the subdivision *Laboratory manuals,* for workbooks containing concise background information and directions for performing work, including experiments, in the laboratory, e.g. **Chemistry—Laboratory manuals;** etc.

Laborers. *See* **Labor;** and names of classes of laborers, e.g. **Agricultural laborers; Miners;** etc.

Lace and lace making   746.2

   xx **Crocheting; Needlework; Weaving**

Lacquer and lacquering 667
   See also **Varnish and varnishing**
   x Finishes and finishing
   xx **Decorative arts; Varnish and varnishing;
       Wood finishing**
Laissez faire. *See* **Industry—Government policy**
Laity 262
   May be subdivided by religious denomination.
   See also **Lay ministry**
   x Laymen
   xx **Lay ministry**
Laity—Catholic Church 262
   x Catholic laity
Lakes (May subdiv. geog. country and state) **551.48**
   See also names of lakes
   xx **Inland navigation; Physical geography; Water;
       Waterways**
Lakes—United States 551.48
   x United States—Lakes
Lamaze method of childbirth. *See* **Natural child-
       birth**
Lambs. *See* **Sheep**
Lamps 621.32; 749
   See also **Electric lamps**
   xx **Lighting**
Land. *See* **Land use**
Land, Condemnation of. *See* **Eminent domain**
Land drainage. *See* **Drainage**
Land question. *See* **Land tenure**
Land, Reclamation of. *See* **Reclamation of land**
Land reform (May subdiv. geog.) **333.3**
   See also **Agriculture—Government policy; Land
       tenure**
   x Agrarian reform; Reform, Agrarian
   xx **Agriculture—Government policy; Economic
       policy; Land use; Social policy**
Land settlement (May subdiv. geog.) **304.8; 325**
   See also **Colonization; Migration, Internal**
   x Resettlement; Settlement of land
   xx **Colonies; Migration, Internal**
Land settlement—United States 304.8; 325.73
   x United States—Land settlement
Land surveying. *See* **Surveying**
Land tenure 333.3
   Use for general and historical discussions on sys-
       tems of holding land.
   See also **Farm tenancy; Feudalism; Landlord and
       tenant; Peasantry; Real estate**
   x Agrarian question; Fiefs; Land question; Ten-
       ure of land
   xx **Agriculture; Agriculture—Economic aspects;
       Inheritance and succession; Land reform;
       Land use; Peasantry; Real estate**
Land use 333
   Use for general materials that cover such topics
       as types of land, the utilization, distribution
       and development of land, and the economic
       factors affecting the value of land. Materials
       dealing only with ownership of land are en-
       tered under **Real estate.**
   See also **Eminent domain; Farms; Feudalism;
       Land reform; Land tenure; Real estate; Rec-
       lamation of land**

Land use—*Continued*

   x Land

   xx **Agriculture; Economics**

Landfills   363.72; 628.3; 628.4

   Use for materials on places for waste disposal in which waste is buried in layers of earth in low ground.

   See also **Hazardous waste sites**; also names of landfills, e.g. **Love Canal Chemical Waste Landfill (Niagara Falls, N.Y.)**; etc.

   x Earth fills; Fills (Earthwork); Sanitary landfills

Landlord and tenant   333.5; 346.04

   Use for materials on the legal relationships between landlord and tenant.

   See also **Apartment houses; Farm tenancy; Housing**

   x Tenant and landlord

   xx **Commercial law; Human relations; Land tenure; Real estate**

Landmarks, Literary.   *See* **Literary landmarks**

Landmarks, Preservation of.   *See* **Natural monuments**

Landscape architecture   712

   Use for materials on modifying or arranging the features of a landscape, urban area, etc. for aesthetic or pragmatic purposes.

   See also **Garden ornaments and furniture; Landscape gardening; Landscape protection; Parks; Patios; Roadside improvement**

   x Landscape design

   xx **Landscape gardening; Landscape protection**

Landscape design.   *See* **Landscape architecture**

Landscape drawing   743

   See also **Landscape painting**

   xx **Drawing; Landscape painting**

Landscape gardening   712

   Use for materials on the designing or arrangement of extensive gardens, estates, etc.

   See also **Evergreens; Gardens—Design; Landscape architecture; Ornamental plants; Shrubs; Trees**

   x Garden design; Planting

   xx **Gardening; Gardens—Design; Horticulture; Landscape architecture; Shrubs; Trees**

Landscape painting   758

   See also **Landscape drawing**

   xx **Landscape drawing; Painting**

Landscape protection   333.73

   See also **Landscape architecture; Natural monuments; Regional planning**

   x Beautification of landscape; Natural beauty conservation; Preservation of natural scenery; Protection of natural scenery; Scenery

   xx **Environmental protection; Landscape architecture; Nature conservation; Regional planning**

Landscape sculpture.   *See* **Earthworks (Art)**

Language and languages   400

   Use for general materials on the history, philosophy, origin, etc. of language. Comparative studies of languages are entered under **Philology, Comparative.**

Language and languages—*Continued*
　　See also
Bilingualism　　　　　　**Semantics**
Conversation　　　　　　**Sign language**
Grammar　　　　　　　　**Sociolinguistics**
Literature　　　　　　　**Speech**
Philology, Comparative　**Translating and interpret-**
Phonetics　　　　　　　　**ing**
Programming languages　**Verbal learning**
(Computers)　　　　　　**Voice**
Rhetoric　　　　　　　　**Writing**
Russian language
　　also names of languages or groups of cognate
　　　　languages, e.g. **English language;** etc.; also
　　　　classes of people with the subdivision
　　　　Language, e.g. **Children—Language;** etc.
　　x Comparative linguistics; Linguistics; Philology
　　xx **Anthropology; Communication; Ethnology;**
　　　　Grammar; Philology, Comparative; Speech
Language and languages—Business language.　*See*
　　names of languages with unique language
　　　subdivisions, e.g. **English language—**
　　　Business English; Japanese language—
　　　Business Japanese; etc.
Language and languages—Comparative
　　philology.　*See* **Philology, Comparative**
Language and society.　*See* **Sociolinguistics**
Language arts　372.6; 400
　　See also **Creative writing; Literature; Reading;**
　　　Speech; Whole language; Writing
　　x Communication arts
　　xx **Communication**
Language arts (Holistic).　*See* **Whole language**
Language arts—Patterning　372.6
　　x Patterns (Language arts); Reading—
　　　Patterning; Writing—Patterning
Language games.　*See* **Literary recreations**
Language, International.　*See* **Universal language**
Language laboratories　407
　　See also **Languages, Modern—Study and teach-**
　　　ing
　　x Foreign language laboratories; Laboratories,
　　　Language
　　xx **Languages, Modern—Study and teaching**
Language, Universal.　*See* **Universal language**
Languages, Modern　410
　　Use for materials dealing collectively with living
　　　literary languages.
　　May be subdivided like **English language.**
　　x Modern languages
Languages, Modern—Conversations and phrases
　　418
　　x Conversation in foreign languages; Foreign
　　　language phrases
Languages, Modern—Study and teaching　418
　　See also **Language laboratories**
　　xx **Language laboratories**
Languages—Vocabulary.　*See* **Vocabulary**
Lantern projection.　*See* **Projectors**
Lantern slides.　*See* **Slides (Photography)**
Laptop computers.　*See* **Portable computers**
Large and small.　*See* **Size and shape**

Large print books 028
   See also **Big books**
   x Books for sight saving; Books—Large print;
      Large type books; Sight saving books
   xx **Big books; Blind—Books and reading**
Large type books. *See* **Large print books**
Laser-beam recording. *See* **Laser recording**
Laser disc players. *See* **Compact disc players**
Laser photography. *See* **Holography**
Laser recording 621.36; 621.38
   See also **Holography; Optical storage devices**
   x Laser-beam recording; Recording, Laser
   xx **Lasers; Optical storage devices**
Lasers 621.36
   See also **Laser recording**
   x Light amplification by stimulated emission of
      radiation; Masers, Optical; Optical masers
   xx **Light**
Lasers in aeronautics 629.13
   Use same form for lasers in other subjects.
   xx **Aeronautics**
Last Supper. *See* **Lord's Supper**
Latchkey children 306.874; 362.7; 640
   Use for materials on children who carry
      doorkeys to let themselves into the house on
      returning from school because the parents
      are at work.
   x Children, Latchkey
   xx **Children of working parents**
Lateness. *See* **Punctuality**
Lathe work. *See* **Lathes; Turning**
Lathes 621.9
   See also **Turning**
   x Lathe work
   xx **Turning; Woodworking machinery**
Latin America 980
   Use for materials discussing collectively the area
      and/or countries south of the Rio Grande,
      as well as all or parts of three or more of the
      regions that make up Latin America, i.e.
      Mexico, Central America, South America,
      and the West Indies. **Latin America** may
      also be used as the collective geographic
      heading and subdivision for the Spanish-
      speaking countries of Latin America.
   See also **Pan-Americanism; South America**; also
      names of individual Latin American coun-
      tries
   x Spanish America
   xx **America**
Latin America—Politics and government 980
   x Politics
Latin American literature 860
   Use for materials on French, Portuguese, and/or
      Spanish literature of Latin American coun-
      tries.
   May use same subdivisions and names of liter-
      ary forms as for **English literature.**
   See also **Brazilian literature; Mexican literature**
   x South American literature
   xx **Literature; Spanish literature**
Latin Americans 920; 980
   Use for materials on citizens of Latin American
      countries. Materials on United States citi-

Latin Americans—*Continued*
　　zens of Latin American descent are entered
　　under **Hispanic Americans.**
Latin language　470
　　May be subdivided like **English language.**
　　See also **Romance languages**
　　x Classical languages
Latin literature　870
　　May use same subdivisions and names of liter-
　　ary forms as for **English literature.**
　　See also **Classical literature; Early Christian lit-**
　　erature
　　x Roman literature
　　xx **Classical literature**
Latinos (U.S.).　*See* **Hispanic Americans**
Latitude　526; 527
　　x Degrees of latitude and longitude
　　xx **Earth; Geodesy; Nautical astronomy**
Latter-day Saints.　*See* **Church of Jesus Christ of**
　　Latter-day Saints
Laughter　152.4
　　See also **Wit and humor**
　　xx **Emotions**
Launching of satellites.　*See* **Artificial satellites—**
　　Launching
Laundry　648
　　x Ironing; Washing
　　xx **Cleaning; Home economics; Sanitation,**
　　Household
Law (May subdiv. geog.)　**340**
　　See also

Courts	**Litigation**
Justice	**Medical jurisprudence**
Lawyers	**Police**
Legal ethics	**Water rights**
Legislation	

　　also special branches of law, e.g. **Administrative**
　　law; Commercial law; Constitutional law;
　　Corporation law; Criminal law; Ecclesiasti-
　　cal law; Internal revenue law; International
　　law; Maritime law; Military law; Space law;
　　etc. For laws on special subjects see names
　　of subjects with the subdivision *Law and*
　　legislation, e.g. **Automobiles—Law and leg-**
　　islation; Food—Law and legislation; etc.
　　x Jurisprudence; Laws; Statutes
　　xx **Legislation; Political science**
Law, Administrative.　*See* **Administrative law**
Law, Business.　*See* **Commercial law**
Law, Commercial.　*See* **Commercial law**
Law, Constitutional.　*See* **Constitutional law**
Law, Corporation.　*See* **Corporation law**
Law, Criminal.　*See* **Criminal law**
Law, Ecclesiastical.　*See* **Ecclesiastical law**
Law enforcement　363.2
　　See also **Police**
　　x Enforcement of law
Law, Internal revenue.　*See* **Internal revenue law**
Law, International.　*See* **International law**
Law, Maritime.　*See* **Maritime law**
Law, Military.　*See* **Military law**
Law of nations.　*See* **International law**
Law of the sea.　*See* **Maritime law**

Law reform 340
   x Legal reform
Law, Space. *See* **Space law**
Law suits. *See* **Litigation**
Law—United States 349.73
   x United States—Law
Law—Vocational guidance 340.023
   xx **Professions; Vocational guidance**
Lawn tennis. *See* **Tennis**
Lawns 716
   See also **Grasses**
Laws. *See* **Law; Legislation;** and subjects with the
     subdivision *Law and legislation,* e.g. **Auto-**
     mobiles—Law and legislation; Food—Law
     and legislation; etc.
Lawsuits. *See* **Litigation**
Lawyers 340.092; 920
   See also **Judges; Legal ethics**
   x Attorneys; Bar; Barristers; Jurists; Legal pro-
     fession
   xx **Law**
Lay ministry 253
   See also **Laity**
   x Volunteers in church work
   xx **Church work; Laity**
Laymen. *See* **Laity**
Layout and typography. *See* **Printing**
LBOs (Corporations). *See* **Leveraged buyouts**
LD (Disease). *See* **Lyme disease**
Lead poisoning 615.9
   x Lead—Toxicology
   xx **Occupational diseases; Poisons and poisoning**
Lead—Toxicology. *See* **Lead poisoning**
Leadership 158
   See also **Elite (Social sciences)**
   xx **Ability; Executive ability; Social groups; Suc-**
     cess
League of Nations 341.22
   xx **Arbitration, International; International coop-**
     eration; Peace; World War, 1914-1918—
     Peace
League of Nations—Mandatory system. *See* **Man-**
     dates
Learned societies. *See* **Societies**
Learning and scholarship 001.2
   See also **Culture; Education; Humanism; Profes-**
     sional education; Research
   x Intellectual life; Scholarship
   xx **Civilization; Culture; Education; Humanism;**
     Research
Learning, Art of. *See* **Study skills**
Learning center approach to teaching. *See* **Open**
     plan schools
Learning, Concept. *See* **Concept learning**
Learning disabilities 153.1; 370.15; 371.9; 616.85
   See also types of learning disabilities, e.g. **Read-**
     ing disability; etc.
   x Disability, Learning; Learning disorders
   xx **Learning, Psychology of; Slow learning chil-**
     dren
Learning disorders. *See* **Learning disabilities**

Learning, Psychology of 153.1
> *See also*
>> **Behavior modification**   **Feedback (Psychology)**
>> **Biofeedback training**   **Learning disabilities**
>> **Brainwashing**   **Reading comprehension**
>> **Concept learning**   **Verbal learning**
>
> *x* Psychology of learning
> *xx* **Animal intelligence; Child psychology; Education; Educational psychology; Memory**

Learning resource centers. *See* **Instructional materials centers**

Learning, Verbal. *See* **Verbal learning**

Lease and rental services 333.5
> *x* Lease services; Rental services

Lease services. *See* **Lease and rental services**

Leather 675
> *See also* **Hides and skins; Tanning**
> *xx* **Hides and skins; Tanning**

Leather garments 685
> *x* Clothing, Leather; Garments, Leather; Skin garments
> *xx* **Clothing and dress; Leather work**

Leather industry 338.4
> *See also* **Bookbinding; Shoe industry**
> *x* Leather industry and trade; Leather trade

Leather industry and trade. *See* **Leather industry**

Leather trade. *See* **Leather industry**

Leather work 745.53
> *See also* **Leather garments**
> *xx* **Decoration and ornament; Decorative arts; Handicraft**

Leaves 581
> *x* Foliage
> *xx* **Botany; Trees**

Lebanon 956.92

Lebanon—History 956.92

Lebanon—History—1975-1976, Civil War 956.9204

Lebanon—History—1982-1984, Israeli intervention 956.05
> *x* Israeli intervention in Lebanon, 1982-1984
> *xx* **Jewish-Arab relations**

Lectures and lecturing 808.5
> Use for general materials on the art of lecturing, effectiveness of the lecture method, announcements of lectures, etc. Collections of lectures on several subjects are entered under **Speeches, addresses, etc.** Lectures on one topic are entered under that subject.
> *See also* **Radio addresses, debates, etc.**
> *x* Addresses; Speaking
> *xx* **Public speaking; Rhetoric; Speeches, addresses, etc.; Teaching**

Left and right E
> Use for mostly children's materials on left and right as indications of location or direction. Materials on political views or attitudes are entered under **Right and left (Political science).** Materials on the physical characteristics of favoring one hand or the other are entered under **Left- and right-handedness.**
> *x* Right and left

Left- and right-handedness 152.3
>See note under **Left and right.**
>*x* Handedness; Right- and left-handedness
>*xx* **Psychophysiology**

Left (Political science). *See* **Right and left (Political science)**

Legacies. *See* **Inheritance and succession; Wills**

Legal aid 362.5
>*See also* types of legal aid, e.g. **Legal assistance to the poor;** etc.
>*x* Charities, Legal

Legal assistance to the poor 362.5
>*x* Legal representative of the poor; Legal service for the poor; Poor—Legal assistance
>*xx* **Legal aid; Public welfare**

Legal ethics 174; 340
>*x* Ethics, Legal
>*xx* **Law; Lawyers; Professional ethics**

Legal holidays. *See* **Holidays**

Legal medicine. *See* **Medical jurisprudence**

Legal profession. *See* **Lawyers**

Legal reform. *See* **Law reform**

Legal representative of the poor. *See* **Legal assistance to the poor**

Legal responsibility. *See* **Liability (Law)**

Legal service for the poor. *See* **Legal assistance to the poor**

Legal tender. *See* **Paper money**

Legations. *See* **Diplomatic and consular service**

Legends (May subdiv. geog. noun form, e.g. **Legends—United States;** etc., or, where country subdivision is not applicable, use ethnic or religious subdivision, adjective form, e.g. **Legends, Jewish;** etc.) **398.2**
>Use for tales coming down from the past, especially those relating to actual events or persons. Collections of tales written between the eleventh and fourteenth centuries and dealing with the age of chivalry or the supernatural are entered under **Romances.**
>*See also*

Fables	**Mythology**
Fairy tales	**Romances**
Folklore	**Saints**
Grail	**Tall tales**

>*x* Stories; Tales; Traditions
>*xx* **Fiction; Folklore; Literature; Saints**

Legends, Celtic 398.2
>*x* Celtic legends

Legends, Indian. *See* **Indians of North America—Legends**

Legends, Jewish 296.1; 398.2
>Use for collections of and materials about Jewish legends.
>*x* Jewish legends; Jews—Legends

Legends, Norse 398.2
>*x* Norse legends

Legends—United States 398.20973; 973
>*x* United States—Legends

Legerdemain. *See* **Juggling; Magic**

Legislation 328
>Use for materials on the theory of lawmaking and descriptions of the preparation and en-

Legislation—*Continued*
    actment of laws.
    See also **Law; Legislative bodies; Parliamentary practice;** also subjects with the subdivision *Law and legislation,* e.g. **Automobiles—Law and legislation; Food—Law and legislation;** etc.
    x Laws
    xx **Constitutional law; Law; Political science**
Legislation, Direct. *See* **Referendum**
Legislative bodies 328.3
    Use for descriptions and histories of law making bodies, discussions of one-house legislatures, etc.
    See also **Parliamentary practice; Right and left (Political science);** also names of individual legislative bodies, e.g. **United States. Congress;** etc.
    x Parliaments; Unicameral legislatures
    xx **Constitutional law; Legislation; Representative government and representation**
Legislative investigations. *See* **Governmental investigations**
Legislative reapportionment. *See* **Apportionment (Election law)**
Leisure 790.01
    See also **Hobbies; Recreation; Retirement; Time management**
LEM. *See* **Lunar excursion module**
Lending. *See* **Loans**
Lending of library materials. *See* **Library circulation**
Lenses 535
    See also types of lenses, e.g. **Contact lenses;** etc.
Lensless photography. *See* **Holography**
Lent 263
    See also **Easter; Good Friday; Holy Week**
    xx **Fasts and feasts**
Lepidoptera. *See* **Butterflies; Moths**
Lesbianism 306.76
    xx **Homosexuality**
Lesbians. *See* **Gay women**
Less developed countries. *See* **Developing countries**
Letter-sound association. *See* **Reading—Phonetic method**
Letter writing 808.6
    Use for materials on composition, forms, and etiquette of correspondence. Materials limited to business correspondence are entered under **Business letters.** Collections of literary letters are entered under **Letters.**
    See also **Business letters**
    x Correspondence; Salutations
    xx **Etiquette; Rhetoric; Style, Literary**
Lettering 745.6
    See also **Alphabets; Initials; Monograms; Sign painting**
    x Ornamental alphabets
    xx **Alphabets; Decoration and ornament; Initials; Mechanical drawing; Painting, Industrial; Sign painting**

Letters   808.86
>   See note under **Letter writing.**
>   *See also* **American letters; English letters**
>   *x* Correspondence
>   *xx* **Literature—Collections**

Letters of credit.   *See* **Credit; Negotiable instruments**

Letters of marque.   *See* **Privateering**

Letters of recommendation.   *See* **Applications for positions**

Letters of the alphabet.   *See* **Alphabet**

Leukemia   616.99
>   *xx* **Blood—Diseases; Cancer**

Levant.   *See* **Middle East**

Leveraged buyouts   338.8; 658.1
>   *x* Buyouts, Leveraged; LBOs (Corporations);
>   Management buyouts
>   *xx* **Corporate mergers and acquisitions**

Lewis and Clark Expedition (1804-1806)   973.4
>   *x* Exploring expeditions
>   *xx* **United States—Exploring expeditions; United States—History—1783-1809**

Liability (Law)   346
>   *See also* **Malpractice**
>   *x* Accountability; Legal responsibility; Responsibility, Legal
>   *xx* **Contracts**

Liability, Professional.   *See* **Malpractice**

Libel and slander   346.03
>   *See also* **Free speech; Freedom of the press; Gossip; Right of privacy**
>   *x* Character assassination; Defamation; Slander (Law)
>   *xx* **Free speech; Freedom of the press; Journalism**

Liberalism   320.5
>   *See also* **Right and left (Political science)**
>   *xx* **Right and left (Political science)**

Liberation movements, National.   *See* **National liberation movements**

Liberation theology   261.8
>   Use for materials on the Christian theological movement that argues for the total liberation of humanity and supports causes of social justice.
>   *x* Theology of liberation
>   *xx* **Church and social problems; Doctrinal theology; Sociology, Christian**

Liberty.   *See* **Freedom**

Liberty of conscience.   *See* **Freedom of conscience**

Liberty of speech.   *See* **Free speech**

Liberty of the press.   *See* **Freedom of the press**

Liberty of the will.   *See* **Free will and determinism**

Librarians   020.92; 920
>   *See also* **Black librarians; Library technicians**

Librarians, Black.   *See* **Black librarians**

Librarians—Collective bargaining.   *See* **Collective bargaining—Librarians**

Librarians—Education.   *See* **Library education**

Librarians—In-service training   023
>   *x* In-service training; Inservice training
>   *xx* **Library education**

Librarians—Professional ethics   174
>   *xx* **Professional ethics**

Librarians—Rating   023
   xx **Performance standards**
Librarians—Recruiting   023
   xx **Recruiting of employees**
Librarians—Training.   *See* **Library education**
Librarians' unions   331.88
   x Library unions
   xx **Labor unions**
Librarianship.   *See* **Library science**
Librarianship, Comparative.   *See* **Comparative librarianship**
Libraries (May subdiv. geog.)   027
     See also special types of libraries, e.g. **Academic libraries; Archives; Business libraries; Church libraries; Hospital libraries; Information services; Instructional materials centers; Music libraries; Public libraries; School libraries; High school libraries; Special libraries;** names of individual libraries, e.g. **Library of Congress;** etc.; and headings beginning with the words **Libraries** and **Library.**
   xx **Archives; Books; Books and reading; Education; Information services**
Libraries—Acquisitions   025.2
    See also **Book selection**
   x Acquisitions (Libraries); Book buying (Libraries); Libraries—Order department; Library acquisitions
   xx **Libraries—Collection development; Library technical processes**
Libraries—Administration   025.1
    See also **Libraries—Trustees; Library finance**
   x Administration; Library administration; Library policies
Libraries—Advertising.   *See* **Advertising—Libraries**
Libraries and Blacks   027.6
   x Blacks and libraries; Library services to Blacks
   xx **Blacks; Reader services (Libraries)**
Libraries and children.   *See* **Children's libraries**
Libraries and community   021.2
   Use same form for libraries and other subjects
   See also **Public relations—Libraries**
   x Community and libraries
Libraries and labor   027.6
   x Labor and libraries; Library services to labor
   xx **Labor; Reader services (Libraries)**
Libraries and motion pictures   021
   x Educational films; Motion pictures and libraries
   xx **Library services; Motion pictures in education**
Libraries and pictures   021
   xx **Pictures**
Libraries and readers.   *See* **Reader services (Libraries)**
Libraries and schools   021
    See also **Children's libraries; Children's literature; Libraries and students; School libraries**
   x Schools and libraries
   xx **Children's libraries; Children's literature; School libraries; Schools**
Libraries and state.   *See* **Libraries—Government policy**

Libraries and students 027.62
    x Students and libraries
    xx **Libraries and schools**
Libraries and the elderly 027.6
    x Elderly and libraries; Library services to the
        elderly
    xx **Elderly; Reader services (Libraries)**
Libraries and young adults. *See* **Young adults' li-
    brary services**
Libraries—Automation 025.04
    See also **Information systems; Machine readable
        bibliographic data; Online catalogs;** also
        names of projects and systems, e.g. **MARC
        system;** etc.
    x Library automation
    xx **Automation; Information systems; Online cat-
        alogs**
Libraries—Boards of trustees. *See* **Libraries—
    Trustees**
Libraries, Business. *See* **Business libraries**
Libraries—Catalogs. *See* **Library catalogs**
Libraries—Censorship 025.2
Libraries—Centralization 021.6
    x Library systems
Libraries, Children's. *See* **Children's libraries**
Libraries, Church. *See* **Church libraries**
Libraries—Circulation, loans. *See* **Library circula-
    tion**
Libraries—Classification. *See* **Classification—
    Books**
Libraries—Collection development 025.2
    See also **Book selection; Libraries—Acquisitions**
    x Collection development (Libraries)
    xx **Library technical processes**
Libraries—Collective bargaining. *See* **Collective
    bargaining—Librarians**
Libraries, College. *See* **Academic libraries**
Libraries, Company. *See* **Corporate libraries**
Libraries—Cooperation. *See* **Library cooperation**
Libraries, Corporate. *See* **Corporate libraries**
Libraries, County. *See* **County libraries**
Libraries—Equipment and supplies 022
    x Library equipment and supplies; Library sup-
        plies
    xx **Furniture**
Libraries—Federal aid. *See* **Federal aid to libraries**
Libraries—Finance. *See* **Library finance**
Libraries—Government policy 021.8; 351.85
    See also **Federal aid to libraries; State aid to li-
        braries**
    x Libraries and state
Libraries, Governmental. *See* **Government libraries**
Libraries, Hospital. *See* **Hospital libraries**
Libraries, Industrial. *See* **Corporate libraries**
Libraries—Law and legislation 344
    x Library laws; Library legislation
Libraries—Lighting 022
    xx **Lighting**
Libraries, Music. *See* **Music libraries**
Libraries, National. *See* **National libraries**
Libraries—Order department. *See* **Libraries—
    Acquisitions**
Libraries, Presidential. *See* **Presidents—United
    States—Archives**

Libraries, Public. *See* **Public libraries**
Libraries—Public relations. *See* **Public relations—Libraries**
Libraries, Regional. *See* **Regional libraries**
Libraries, School. *See* **School libraries**
Libraries, Special. *See* **Special libraries**
Libraries—Special collections 026
> May be subdivided by subject or form, e.g. **Libraries—Special collections—Science fiction; Libraries—Special collections—Videotapes;** etc.
> *x* Special collections in libraries
Libraries—Standards 020
Libraries, State. *See* **State libraries**
Libraries—State aid. *See* **State aid to libraries**
Libraries—Statistics 020
Libraries—Technical services. *See* **Library technical processes**
Libraries—Trustees 021.8
> *x* Libraries—Boards of trustees; Library boards; Library trustees
> *xx* **Libraries—Administration**
Libraries—United States 027.073
> *x* United States—Libraries
Libraries, University. *See* **Academic libraries**
Libraries, Young adults'. *See* **Young adults' library services**
Library acquisitions. *See* **Libraries—Acquisitions**
Library administration. *See* **Libraries—Administration**
Library advertising. *See* **Advertising—Libraries**
Library architecture 727
> *x* Buildings, Library; Library buildings
> *xx* **Architecture**
Library assistants. *See* **Library technicians**
Library automation. *See* **Libraries—Automation**
Library boards. *See* **Libraries—Trustees**
Library buildings. *See* **Library architecture**
Library catalogs 017; 025.3
> *See also* types of library catalogs, e.g. **Catalogs, Book; Catalogs, Card; Catalogs, Classified; Catalogs, Subject; Library catalogs on microfilm; Online catalogs;** etc.
> *x* Catalogs; Catalogs, Library; Libraries—Catalogs
Library catalogs on microfilm 025.3
> *x* Catalogs, COM; Catalogs on microfilm; COM catalogs
> *xx* **Library catalogs; Microfilms**
Library circulation 025.6
> *x* Book lending; Circulation of library materials; Interlibrary loans; Lending of library materials; Libraries—Circulation, loans
> *xx* **Library services**
Library classification. *See* **Classification—Books**
Library clerks. *See* **Library technicians**
Library consortia. *See* **Library cooperation; Library information networks**
Library cooperation 021.6
> *See also* **Library information networks**
> *x* Consortia, Library; Cooperation, Library; Libraries—Cooperation; Library consortia

Library education   020.7
   Use for materials on the education of librarians. Materials dealing with the instruction of readers in library use are entered under **Library instruction.**
   See also **Librarians—In-service training; Library schools**
   x Education for librarianship; Librarians— Education; Librarians—Training; Library science—Study and teaching
   xx **Education; Professional education**
Library education—Audiovisual aids   020.7
   xx **Audiovisual education; Audiovisual materials**
Library education—Curricula   020.7
   x Core curriculum; Courses of study; Curricula (Courses of study); Schools—Curricula; Study, Courses of
   xx **Education—Curricula**
Library equipment and supplies.   *See* **Libraries— Equipment and supplies**
Library extension   021.6
   See also **Bookmobiles; County libraries**
Library finance   025.1
   See also **Federal aid to libraries; State aid to libraries**
   x Libraries—Finance
   xx **Libraries—Administration**
Library information networks   021.6
   x Consortia, Library; Library consortia; Library networks; Library systems; Networks, Library
   xx **Data transmission systems; Information networks; Library cooperation**
Library instruction   025.5
   Use for materials dealing with the instruction of readers in library use. Materials on the education of librarians are entered under **Library education.**
   x Library orientation; Library skills; Library user orientation
   xx **Reader services (Libraries)**
Library laws.   *See* **Libraries—Law and legislation**
Library legislation.   *See* **Libraries—Law and legislation**
Library materials.   *See* **Library resources**
Library materials—Preservation.   *See* **Library resources—Conservation and restoration**
Library networks.   *See* **Library information networks**
Library of Congress   027.573
   x United States. Library of Congress
   xx **Libraries**
Library orientation.   *See* **Library instruction**
Library policies.   *See* **Libraries—Administration**
Library processing.   *See* **Library technical processes**
Library reference services.   *See* **Reference services (Libraries)**
Library resources   021
   x Library materials
Library resources—Conservation and restoration 025.8
   x Books—Preservation; Library materials— Preservation; Preservation of library resources

Library schools   020.7

  xx **Library education**

Library science   020

      Use for general materials on the knowledge and skill necessary for the organization and administration of libraries. Materials about services offered by libraries to patrons are entered under **Library services.**

      See also **Bibliography; Cataloging; Classification—Books; Comparative librarianship; Library services; Library surveys; Library technical processes;** also headings beginning with the words **Libraries** and **Library**

  x Librarianship

  xx **Bibliography; Documentation; Information science**

Library science—Study and teaching.   *See* **Library education**

Library services   025.5

      See note under **Library science.**

      See also **Libraries and motion pictures; Library circulation; Reader services (Libraries)**

  xx **Library science**

Library services to Blacks.   *See* **Libraries and Blacks**

Library services to children.   *See* **Children's libraries**

Library services to labor.   *See* **Libraries and labor**

Library services to teenagers.   *See* **Young adults' library services**

Library services to the elderly.   *See* **Libraries and the elderly**

Library services to young adults.   *See* **Young adults' library services**

Library skills.   *See* **Library instruction**

Library supplies.   *See* **Libraries—Equipment and supplies**

Library surveys   020

  x Surveys

  xx **Library science**

Library systems.   *See* **Libraries—Centralization; Library information networks**

Library technical processes   025

      Use for materials on the activities and processes concerned with the acquisition, organization, and preparation of library materials for use.

      See also **Cataloging; Classification—Books; Libraries—Acquisitions; Libraries—Collection development**

  x Centralized processing (Libraries); Libraries—Technical services; Library processing; Processing (Libraries); Technical services (Libraries)

  xx **Library science**

Library technicians   020.92; 920

  x Library assistants; Library clerks; Paraprofessional librarians

  xx **Librarians; Paraprofessions and paraprofessionals**

Library trustees.   *See* **Libraries—Trustees**

Library unions.   *See* **Librarians' unions**

Library user orientation.   *See* **Library instruction**

Librettos   780; 780.26
   See also **Operas—Stories, plots, etc.**; also musical forms with the subdivision *Librettos,*
      e.g. **Operas—Librettos**; etc.
Lie detectors and detection   363.2
   x Polygraph
   xx **Criminal investigation; Medical jurisprudence;
      Truthfulness and falsehood**
Life   128
   See also **Death**
Life after death.   *See* **Future life; Immortality**
Life (Biology)   574; 577
   See also

Biology	**Middle age**
Gaia hypothesis	**Old age**
Genetics	**Protoplasm**
Longevity	**Reproduction**

   xx **Biology**
Life care communities.   *See* **Retirement communities**
Life, Christian.   *See* **Christian life**
Life expectancy.   *See* **Longevity**
Life, Future.   *See* **Future life**
Life histories.   *See* names of countries, cities, etc.
      and subjects with the subdivision
      Biography, e.g. **Musicians—Biography**;
      etc.
Life insurance   368.3
   See also **Annuities; Group insurance; Industrial
      insurance; Probabilities**
   x Insurance, Life
   xx **Annuities; Insurance**
Life on other planets   574.999
   Use for materials on the question of life in outer
      space and for materials on life indigenous to
      outer space. For materials on the biology of
      man or other earth life while in outer space,
      use **Space biology.**
   See also **Extraterrestrial beings; Interstellar communication**
   x Astrobiology; Exobiology; Extraterrestrial life;
      Planets, Life on other
   xx **Astronomy; Planets; Space biology; Universe**
Life—Origin   113
   x Germ theory; Origin of life
   xx **Evolution**
Life quality.   *See* **Quality of life**
Life saving.   *See* **Lifesaving**
Life sciences   570
   See also **Agriculture; Biology; Medicine**
   x Biosciences
   xx **Science**
Life sciences ethics.   *See* **Bioethics**
Life skills   158; 640
   Use for materials on skills needed by an individual to exist in modern society, including
      skills related to education, employment, finance, etc.
   See also **Human behavior; Human relations; Survival skills**; also types and groups of persons
      with the subdivision *Life skills guides,* e.g.
      Elderly—Life skills guides; etc.
   x Basic life skills; Competencies, Functional;

Life skills—*Continued*
>> Coping behavior; Everyday living skills;
>> Functional competencies; Fundamental life
>> skills; Personal life skills; Skills, Life
>> *xx* **Human behavior; Human relations; Success**

Life span prolongation. *See* **Longevity**
Life, Spiritual. *See* **Spiritual life**
Life styles. *See* **Lifestyles**
Life support systems (Medical environment) 362.1
>> *xx* **Hospitals; Terminal care**
Life support systems (Space environment) 629.47
>> *See also* **Apollo project; Astronauts—Clothing;**
>> **Space ships**
>> *xx* **Human engineering; Space medicine**
Life support systems (Submarine environment) 627
Lifelong education. *See* **Adult education; Continu-**
>> **ing education**
Lifesaving 363.1
>> *See also* **First aid**
>> *x* Life saving
>> *xx* **First aid; Rescue work**
Lifestyles 306
>> Use for the distinctive way of life or manner of
>> living characteristic of an individual or
>> groups of people.
>> *See also* names of lifestyles, e.g. **Counter cul-**
>> **ture; Unmarried couples;** etc.
>> *x* Alternative lifestyle; Life styles
>> *xx* **Human behavior; Quality of life**
Lifts. *See* **Elevators; Hoisting machinery**
Light 535
>> *See also*

Color	**Radiation**
Lasers	**Radioactivity**
Optics	**Refraction**
Phosphorescence	**Spectrum analysis**
Photometry	**X rays**

>> *xx* **Electromagnetic waves; Optics; Photometry;**
>> **Physics; Radiation; Spectrum analysis; Vi-**
>> **bration; Waves**

Light amplification by stimulated emission of
>> radiation. *See* **Lasers**
Light and shade. *See* **Shades and shadows**
Light, Electric. *See* **Electric lighting; Fluorescent**
>> **lighting; Photometry; Phototherapy**
Light production in animals. *See* **Bioluminescence**
Light ships. *See* **Lightships**
Light—Therapeutic use. *See* **Phototherapy**
Lighthouses 387.1; 623.89; 627
>> *See also* **Lightships**
>> *xx* **Navigation**
Lighting (May subdiv. geog.) **621.32**
>> *See also* **Candles; Electric lighting; Fluorescent**
>> **lighting; Lamps;** also subjects with the sub-
>> division *Lighting,* e.g. **Libraries—Lighting;**
>> **Streets—Lighting;** etc.
>> *x* Illumination
Lightning 551.5
>> *xx* **Electricity; Meteorology; Thunderstorms**
Lights, Feast of. *See* **Hanukkah**
Lightships 623.89; 627
>> *x* Light ships
>> *xx* **Lighthouses**
Limbs, Artificial. *See* **Artificial limbs**

Lime   631.8; 666
 See also Cement
 xx Fertilizers and manures
Limericks   808.81; 811, etc.
 See also Nonsense verses
 x Rhymes
 xx Humorous poetry; Nonsense verses
Limitation of armament.   See Arms control
Limited access highways.   See Express highways
Lincoln, Abraham, 1809-1865   92; B
 xx Presidents—United States
Lincoln Day.   See Lincoln's Birthday
Lincoln family   920; 929
 xx Genealogy
Lincoln's Birthday   394.2
 x Lincoln Day
 xx Holidays
Line engraving.   See Engraving
Linear algebras.   See Algebras, Linear
Linear system theory.   See System analysis
Linen   677
 See also Flax; Hemp
 xx Fabrics; Fibers; Flax
Linguistics.   See Language and languages
Linoleum block printing   761
 x Block printing
 xx Color prints; Engraving
Linotype   686.2
 xx Printing; Type and type founding; Typesetting
Lip reading.   See Deaf—Means of communication
Liquefaction of coal.   See Coal liquefaction
Liqueurs.   See Liquors and liqueurs
Liquid fuel.   See Gasoline; Petroleum as fuel
Liquids   532
 See also Hydraulics; Hydrodynamics; Hydrostat-
 ics
 xx Fluid mechanics; Physics
Liquor industry   338.4
 xx Alcohol
Liquor problem.   See Alcoholism; Drinking of alco-
 holic beverages
Liquors and liqueurs   641.2; 663
 See also Distillation; also names of specific li-
 quors and liqueurs
 x Cordials (Liquor); Drinks; Intoxicants; Li-
 queurs; Spirits, Alcoholic
 xx Alcohol; Alcoholic beverages; Beverages; Dis-
 tillation; Stimulants
Listening   152.1
 See also Attention
 xx Attention
Listening devices.   See Eavesdropping
Literacy (May subdiv. geog.)   302.2; 379.2
 See also Computer literacy; Functional literacy;
 Visual literacy
 x Illiteracy
 xx Education
Literacy, Computer.   See Computer literacy
Literacy, Visual.   See Visual literacy
Literary awards.   See Literary prizes
Literary characters.   See Characters and character-
 istics in literature
Literary criticism.   See Criticism; Literature—
 History and criticism

Literary forgeries 098

    x Frauds, Literary

    xx **Forgery of works of art**

Literary landmarks (May subdiv. geog.) **809; 810.9, etc.**

    x Authors—Homes and haunts; Landmarks, Literary

    xx **Historic buildings; Literature—History and criticism**

Literary landmarks—United States 810.9

    x United States—Literary landmarks

Literary prizes 807.9

    See also **Literature—Competitions;** also names of awards, e.g. **Caldecott Medal books; Newbery Medal books;** etc.

    x Awards, Literary; Book awards; Book prizes; Literary awards; Literature—Prizes; Prizes, Literary

    xx **Rewards (Prizes, etc.)**

Literary property. *See* **Copyright**

Literary recreations 793.73

    See also **Charades; Plot-your-own stories; Riddles; Word games**

    x Language games; Recreations, Literary

    xx **Amusements**

Literary style. *See* **Style, Literary**

Literature 800

    Use for materials on literature in general, not limited to history, philosophy, or any one aspect.

    See also

Authorship	**Indians of North America—Literature**
Ballads	
Biography (as a literary form)	**Journalism**
	Latin American literature
Books	**Legends**
Canadian literature	**Music and literature**
Catholic literature	**Parody**
Chapbooks	**Plots (Drama, fiction, etc.)**
Children's literature	**Poetry**
Classical literature	**Religious literature**
Criticism	**Romanticism**
Devotional literature	**Sagas**
Drama	**Satire**
Early Christian literature	**Short story**
Essay	**Speeches, addresses, etc.**
Fables	**Style, Literary**
Fairy tales	**Wit and humor**
Fiction	**World War, 1939-1945—**
Humanism	**Literature and the war**

    also names of literatures, e.g. **English literature; French literature;** etc.; and subjects and themes in literature, e.g. **Bible in literature; Blacks in literature; Characters and characteristics in literature; Children in literature; Realism in literature; Symbolism in literature; Women in literature;** etc.

    x Belles lettres

    xx **Books; Books and reading; Humanities; Language and languages; Language arts**

Literature and communism. *See* **Communism and literature**

Literature and music. *See* **Music and literature**

Literature—Bio-bibliography 809.2
  See also **Authors**
  xx **Authors**
Literature, Classical. *See* **Classical literature**
Literature—Collected works. *See* **Literature—
  Collections**
Literature—Collections 808.8
  See also **Essays; Letters; Parodies; Quotations;
  Romances; Short stories;** also names of liter-
  atures and names of literary forms with the
  subdivision *Collections,* e.g. **English litera-
  ture—Collections; Poetry—Collections;** etc.
  x Collections of literature; Literature—Collected
  works; Literature—Selections
Literature, Comparative 809
  x Comparative literature
  xx **Philology, Comparative**
Literature—Competitions 807.9
  xx **Contests; Literary prizes**
Literature—Criticism. *See* **Literature—History and
  criticism**
Literature—Dictionaries 803
  See also **Literature—Indexes**
  xx **Literature—Indexes**
Literature, Erotic. *See* **Erotic literature**
Literature—Evaluation. *See* **Books and reading;
  Books and reading—Best books; Books—
  Reviews; Criticism; Literature—History and
  criticism**
Literature—Film and video adaptations. *See* **Film
  adaptations; Television adaptations**
Literature—History and criticism 809
  See also **Authors; Criticism; Literary landmarks**
  x Appraisal of books; Books—Appraisal; Evalu-
  ation of literature; Literary criticism; Liter-
  ature—Criticism; Literature—Evaluation
  xx **Authors; Style, Literary**
Literature—Indexes 016.8
  See also **Literature—Dictionaries**
  xx **Literature—Dictionaries**
Literature, Medieval 809
  May use same subdivisions as for **Literature.**
  See also **Early Christian literature**
  x Medieval literature
  xx **Middle Ages; Renaissance**
Literature—Outlines, syllabi, etc. 802
  See also **English literature—Outlines, syllabi,
  etc.**
Literature—Prizes. *See* **Literary prizes**
Literature—Selections. *See* **Literature—Collections**
Literature—Stories, plots, etc. 802
  Use for collections of stories, plots, etc. Materi-
  als dealing with the construction and analy-
  sis of plots as a literary technique are en-
  tered under **Plots (Drama, fiction, etc.).**
Literatures of the Soviet Union. *See* **Soviet
  Union—Literatures**
Lithographers 763.092; 920
  xx **Engravers**
Lithography 686.2; 763; 764
  See also **Offset printing**
  xx **Color printing; Prints**
Lithoprinting. *See* **Offset printing**

Litigation 347

See also **Arbitration and award**

  x Actions and defenses; Civil law suits; Defense
      (Law); Law suits; Lawsuits; Personal actions
      (Law); Suing (Law); Suits (Law)

  xx **Arbitration and award; Law**

Littering. *See* **Refuse and refuse disposal**

Little league baseball 796.357

  xx **Baseball**

Little theater movement 792

  x Community theater; Theater—Little theater
      movement

  xx **Amateur theater; Theater**

Liturgies 264; 291.3

Use for general materials on the forms of
    prayers, rituals, and ceremonies used in
    public worship, including the theological
    and historical study of liturgies.

See also **Hymns; Mass;** also names of individual
    religions and denominations with the subdi-
    vision *Liturgy,* e.g. **Catholic Church—
    Liturgy; Judaism—Liturgy;** etc.

  x Church service books; Ecclesiastical rites and
      ceremonies; Ritual; Service books (Liturgy)

  xx **Church music; Devotional literature; Theology**

Live poliovirus vaccine. *See* **Poliomyelitis vaccine**

Livestock 636

Use for materials on breeds of livestock and on
    stock raising as an industry. General de-
    scriptions of farm and other domestic ani-
    mals are entered under **Domestic animals.**

See also **Dairying; Domestic animals; Livestock
    judging; Veterinary medicine;** also names of
    livestock, e.g. **Cattle; Sheep;** etc.

  x Animal husbandry; Animal industry; Farm
      animals; Stock and stock breeding; Stock
      raising

  xx **Domestic animals**

Livestock—Breeding 636.08

  xx **Breeding**

Livestock judging 636

  x Stock judging

  xx **Livestock**

Living, Cost of. *See* **Cost of living**

Living earth theory. *See* **Gaia hypothesis**

Living, Standard of. *See* **Standard of living**

Living together. *See* **Unmarried couples**

Living wills. *See* **Right to die**

Lizards 597.95

  xx **Reptiles**

Loan associations. *See* **Savings and loan associa-
    tions**

Loan funds, Student. *See* **Student loan funds**

Loans 332.7

See also

Credit unions	**Personal loans**
Government lending	**Public debts**
Interest (Economics)	**Savings and loan associa-**
Investments	**tions**
Mortgages	

  x Borrowing money; Lending

  xx **Credit**

Loans, Personal. *See* **Personal loans**

Lobbying and lobbyists   328.3
> *See also* **Corruption in politics;** also names of
> special lobbying and pressure groups
>
> *x* Interest groups; Lobbyists; PAC's; Political ac-
> tion committees; Pressure groups
>
> *xx* **Corruption in politics; Politics, Practical**

Lobbyists.   *See* **Lobbying and lobbyists**

Lobsters   595.3
> *xx* **Crustacea; Shellfish**

Local government   352
> Use for materials about local government of dis-
> tricts, counties, townships, etc. Materials
> about county government only are entered
> under **County government;** materials about
> city government are entered under **Munici-
> pal government.**
>
> *See also* **Cities and towns; County government;
> Metropolitan government; Municipal govern-
> ment; Public administration; State-local re-
> lations; Villages**
>
> *x* Government, Local; Town meeting; Township
> government
>
> *xx* **Administrative law; Community organization;
> Political science; Villages**

Local history.   *See* names of countries, states, etc.
> with the subdivision *History, Local,* e.g.
> **United States—History, Local;** etc.

Local-state relations.   *See* **State-local relations**

Local traffic.   *See* **City traffic**

Local transit (May subdiv. geog.)   **388.4**
> Use for materials on the transit systems of urban
> areas, such as bus lines, subways, etc. and
> for materials on general local transportation
> in urban areas, including private transporta-
> tion, streets, roads, etc. Consider also
> **Transportation.**
>
> *See also* **Buses; Street railroads; Subways**
>
> *x* City transit; Mass transit; Municipal transit;
> Public transit; Rapid transit; Transit sys-
> tems; Urban transportation
>
> *xx* **Traffic engineering; Transportation**

Localism.   *See* **Sectionalism (United States)**

Localisms.   *See* names of languages with the subdi-
> vision *Provincialisms,* e.g. **English lan-
> guage—Provincialisms;** etc.

Lockouts.   *See* **Strikes and lockouts**

Locks and keys   683
> *x* Keys
>
> *xx* **Burglary protection**

Locomotion.   *See* **Aeronautics; Animal locomotion;
> Automobiles; Boats and boating; Flight;
> Navigation; Transportation; Walking**

Locomotives   625.2
> *x* Railroads—Rolling stock; Rolling stock
>
> *xx* **Machinery; Steam engines**

Locomotives—Models   625.1
> *xx* **Machinery—Models**

Locusts   595.7; 632
> *xx* **Insect pests**

Locusts, Seventeen-year.   *See* **Cicadas**

Lodging houses.   *See* **Hotels, motels, etc.**

Log cabins and houses   728
> *x* Cabins; Houses, Log
>
> *xx* **House construction; Houses**

Logarithms 513.2
> *See also* **Slide rule**
> *xx* **Algebra; Mathematics—Tables; Trigonometry—Tables**

Logging. *See* **Lumber and lumbering**
Logic 160
> *See also* **Critical thinking; Knowledge, Theory of; Probabilities; Reasoning; Thought and thinking**
> *x* Argumentation; Deduction (Logic); Dialectics; Fallacies; Induction (Logic)
> *xx* **Intellect; Philosophy; Reasoning; Science—Methodology; Thought and thinking**

Logic, Symbolic and mathematical 511.3
> *See also* **Algebra, Boolean; Set theory**
> *xx* **Mathematics; Set theory**

Long distance running. *See* **Marathon running**
Long distance swimming. *See* **Marathon swimming**
Long life. *See* **Longevity**
Long-term care facilities 362.1
> *See also* **Nursing homes**
> *x* Extended care facilities
> *xx* **Hospitals; Medical care**

Longevity 613
> *See also* **Aging; Middle age; Old age**
> *x* Life expectancy; Life span prolongation; Long life
> *xx* **Death; Health; Life (Biology); Middle age; Old age**

Longitude 526; 527
> *See also* **Time**
> *x* Degrees of latitude and longitude
> *xx* **Earth; Geodesy; Nautical astronomy**

Looking glasses. *See* **Mirrors**
Looms 677; 746
> *xx* **Weaving**

Loran 621.384
> *xx* **Navigation**

Lord's Day. *See* **Sabbath**
Lord's prayer 226.9; 242
> *xx* **Jesus Christ—Prayers**

Lord's Supper 232.9; 264
> *See also* **Mass**
> *x* Communion; Ecclesiastical rites and ceremonies; Eucharist; Jesus Christ—Last Supper; Last Supper
> *xx* **Jesus Christ; Mass; Sacraments**

Losing things. *See* **Lost and found possessions**
Lost and found possessions E; Fic
> *x* Finding things; Losing things; Lost pets; Possessions, Lost and found

Lost children. *See* **Missing children**
Lost pets. *See* **Lost and found possessions**
Lotteries 336.1
> *xx* **Gambling**

Loudspeakers. *See* **Intercommunication systems**
Louisiana Purchase 973.4; 976.3
> *xx* **United States—History—1783-1809**

Love 152.4; 177; 306.7
> *See also* **Dating (Social customs); Friendship; Marriage**
> *x* Affection
> *xx* **Dating (Social customs); Emotions; Friendship; Human behavior**

Love Canal Chemical Waste Landfill (Niagara Falls, N.Y.) 363.72
    xx **Hazardous waste sites; Landfills**
Love poetry 808.81; 811.008, etc.
    x Poetry of love
    xx **Poetry**
Love stories 808.83; 813, etc.
    x Romance novels; Romances (Love stories); Romantic fiction; Romantic stories
    xx **Fiction**
Love stories—Technique 808.3
    x Technique
    xx **Authorship**
Love (Theology) 231
    xx **Charity; Doctrinal theology**
Low income housing. *See* **Public housing**
Low sodium diet. *See* **Salt free diet**
Low temperature biology. *See* **Cryobiology**
Low temperatures 536; 621.5
    See also **Cold; Cryobiology; Refrigeration**
    x Cryogenics; Temperatures, Low
    xx **Cold; Refrigeration; Temperature**
Loyalists, American. *See* **American Loyalists**
Loyalty 172
    See also **Patriotism**
    x Faithfulness
    xx **Ethics; Human behavior**
Loyalty oaths. *See* **Internal security**
Lubrication and lubricants 621.8
    See also **Bearings (Machinery); Oils and fats**
    x Grease
    xx **Bearings (Machinery); Machinery; Oils and fats**
Lullabies 782.42
    x Cradle songs; Slumber songs
    xx **Bedtime; Children's poetry; Children's songs; Songs**
Lumber and lumbering 634.9; 674
    Use for materials on cut timber, its preparation for construction and building purposes, and uses of various kinds of lumber.
    x Logging; Timber
    xx **Forest products; Forests and forestry; Trees; Wood**
Luminescence. *See* **Phosphorescence**
Luminescence, Animal. *See* **Bioluminescence**
Lunar bases 629.45
    x Moon bases
Lunar cars. *See* **Moon cars**
Lunar eclipses. *See* **Eclipses, Lunar**
Lunar excursion module 629.45
    x LEM; Lunar module
    xx **Space vehicles**
Lunar expeditions. *See* **Space flight to the moon**
Lunar exploration. *See* **Moon—Exploration**
Lunar geology 559.9
    See also **Lunar petrology; Lunar soil**
    x Geology, Lunar; Geology—Moon; Moon—Geology
    xx **Astrogeology**
Lunar module. *See* **Lunar excursion module**
Lunar petrology 552; 552.0999
    x Lunar rocks; Moon rocks; Rocks, Moon
    xx **Lunar geology; Petrology**

Lunar photography 778.3
>*See also* **Moon—Photographs**
>*x* Moon photography
>*xx* **Space photography**

Lunar probes 629.43
>*See also* names of space projects, e.g. **Project Ranger;** etc.
>*x* Moon probes
>*xx* **Space probes**

Lunar rocks. *See* **Lunar petrology**

Lunar rover vehicles. *See* **Moon cars**

Lunar soil 523.3; 552.0999; 631.4
>*See also* **Moon—Surface**
>*x* Moon soil; Soils, Lunar
>*xx* **Lunar geology; Moon—Surface**

Lunar surface. *See* **Moon—Surface**

Lunar surface radio communication. *See* **Radio in astronautics**

Lunar surface vehicles. *See* **Moon cars**

Lunch rooms. *See* **Restaurants, bars, etc.**

Luncheons 642
>*xx* **Caterers and catering; Cookery; Entertaining; Menus**

Lungs 611; 612.2
>*See also* **Respiration**

Lungs—Diseases 616.2
>*See also* names of lung diseases, e.g. **Pneumonia; Tuberculosis;** etc.

Lying. *See* **Truthfulness and falsehood**

Lyme disease 616.9
>*See also* **Insects as carriers of disease; Ticks**
>*x* LD (Disease)
>*xx* **Diseases; Insects as carriers of disease; Ticks**

Lymphatic system 596; 612.4; 616.4
>*xx* **Physiology**

Lynching 364.1
>*See also* **Vigilance committees**
>*xx* **Crime**

Lyricists 782.0092; 920
>*x* Songwriters
>*xx* **Poets**

M.I.A.'s. *See* **Missing in action**

Maccabbees, Feast of the. *See* **Hanukkah**

Machine design. *See* **Machinery—Design and construction**

Machine intelligence. *See* **Artificial intelligence**

Machine language. *See* **Programming languages (Computers)**

Machine readable bibliographic data 025.3
>*See also* names of projects or systems, e.g. **MARC system;** etc.
>*x* Bibliographic data in machine readable form; Cataloging data in machine readable form; Computer stored cataloging data
>*xx* **Cataloging; Information services; Information systems; Libraries—Automation**

Machine readable catalog system. *See* **MARC system**

Machine readable dictionaries 423, etc.
>*x* Dictionaries, Machine readable
>*xx* **Encyclopedias and dictionaries**

Machine shop practice 670.42
>*x* Shop practice

Machine shops   670.42
   x Shops, Machine
Machine tools   621.9
   See also names of machine tools, e.g. **Planing machines;** etc.
   xx **Machinery; Milling machines; Tools**
Machine translating. *See* **Translating and interpreting**
Machinery   621.8
   See also

Agricultural machinery	**Lubrication and lubricants**
Bearings (Machinery)	**Machine tools**
Belts and belting	**Mechanical drawing**
Conveying machinery	**Mechanics**
Electric machinery	**Metalworking machinery**
Engines	**Milling machines**
Gearing	**Patents**
Hoisting machinery	**Power transmission**
Hydraulic machinery	**Steam engines**
Inventions	**Woodworking machinery**
Locomotives	

   x Machines
   xx **Industrial management; Manufactures; Mechanical engineering; Mechanics; Mills and millwork; Power (Mechanics); Power transmission; Technology; Tools**
Machinery, Automatic. *See* **Automation**
Machinery—Construction. *See* **Machinery—Design and construction**
Machinery—Design. *See* **Machinery—Design and construction**
Machinery—Design and construction   621.8
   See also **Human engineering; Machinery—Models**
   x Machine design; Machinery—Construction; Machinery—Design
Machinery—Drawing. *See* **Mechanical drawing**
Machinery in industry   338
   Use for materials on the social and economic aspects of mechanization in the industrial world, the machine age, etc.
   See also **Automation; Industrial robots; Labor productivity**
   xx **Industry; Labor; Labor productivity; Technology and civilization**
Machinery—Models   621.8
   See also **Airplanes—Models; Automobiles—Models; Locomotives—Models; Motorboats—Models; Railroads—Models; Ships—Models**
   x Mechanical models; Models, Mechanical
   xx **Machinery—Design and construction**
Machines. *See* **Machinery**
Madonna. *See* **Mary, Blessed Virgin, Saint**
Magazines. *See* **Periodicals**
Maghreb. *See* **North Africa**
Magic   793.8
   Use for materials dealing with modern ("Parlor") magic, legerdemain, etc., as entertainment. Materials on the supernatural not connected with magic tricks are entered under **Occultism.**
   See also **Card tricks; Juggling; Occultism; Sym-**

Magic—*Continued*
        bolism of numbers; Tricks
    x Conjuring; Legerdemain; Magic tricks; Sleight
       of hand
  xx **Amusements; Hallucinations and illusions;**
       Juggling; Occultism; Tricks
Magic tricks. *See* **Magic**
Magna Carta   342; 942.03
Magnet schools   370.19; 371.9
    Use for materials on schools offering special
       courses not available in the regular school
       curriculum and designed to attract students
       without reference to the usual attendance
       zone rules. Magnet schools are often used as
       an aid to voluntary school desegregation.
    x Schools, Magnet
  xx **Public schools; School integration**
Magnet winding. *See* **Electromagnets**
Magnetic needle. *See* **Compass**
Magnetic recorders and recording   621.382
    Use for general materials on audio, computer,
       and video recording on a magnetizable me-
       dium.
    See also **Sound recordings; Videotape recorders**
      and recording
    x Cassette recorders and recording; Recorders,
       Tape; Tape recorders
  xx **Sound—Recording and reproducing; Sound re-**
      cordings
Magnetic resonance accelerator. *See* **Cyclotron**
Magnetic resonance imaging   616.07
    x Clinical magnetic resonance imaging; Diag-
       nostic magnetic resonance imaging; Imag-
       ing, Magnetic resonance; NMR imaging;
       Nuclear magnetic resonance imaging
Magnetism   538
    See also **Compass; Electricity; Electromagnetism;**
      Electromagnets; Magnets
  xx **Electricity; Physics**
Magnets   538; 621.34
    See also **Electromagnets**
  xx **Magnetism**
Mail-order business   658.8; 659.13
  xx **Advertising; Business; Direct selling; Selling**
Mail service. *See* **Postal service**
Mail systems, Electronic. *See* **Electronic mail sys-**
    tems
Mainstreaming in education   371.9
    See also **Special education**
  xx **Education; Exceptional children; Handicapped**
    children; Special education
Maintenance and repair. *See* **Buildings—**
       Maintenance and repair; and names of ma-
       chines, instruments, etc. with the subdivi-
       sion *Maintenance and repair,* e.g. **Automo-**
       biles—Maintenance and repair; etc.
Maize. *See* **Corn**
Make-believe playmates. *See* **Imaginary playmates**
Makeup (Cosmetics). *See* **Cosmetics**
Makeup, Theatrical   791.43; 791.45; 792
    x Theatrical makeup
  xx **Cosmetics; Costume**
Making-choices stories. *See* **Plot-your-own stories**

Maladjusted children. *See* **Emotionally disturbed children**

Maladjustment (Psychology). *See* **Adjustment (Psychology)**

Malaria 616.9
  x Ague
  xx Fever

Male change of life. *See* **Male climacteric**

Male climacteric 612.6
  x Change of life in men; Climacteric, Male; Male change of life; Male menopause; Menopause, Male
  xx **Aging**

Male menopause. *See* **Male climacteric**

Male role. *See* **Sex role**

Malfeasance in office. *See* **Misconduct in office**

Malformations, Congenital. *See* **Birth defects**

Malignant tumors. *See* **Cancer**

Malls, Shopping. *See* **Shopping centers and malls**

Malnutrition 616.3
  See also **Starvation**
  xx **Nutrition; Starvation**

Malpractice 346.03
  See also names of professional people with the subdivision *Malpractice,* e.g. **Physicians—Malpractice;** etc.
  x Liability, Professional; Professional liability; Professions—Tort liability; Tort liability of professions
  xx **Liability (Law)**

Malpractice insurance 368.5
  x Insurance, Malpractice; Insurance, Professional liability; Professional liability insurance
  xx **Insurance**

Mammals 599
  See also groups of mammals, e.g. **Carnivores; Marine mammals; Primates;** etc.; also names of mammals, e.g. **Bats; Elephants;** etc.
  xx **Animals; Vertebrates; Zoology**

Mammals, Fossil 569
  See also names of extinct animals, e.g. **Mastodon;** etc.
  x Fossil mammals
  xx **Fossils**

Mammals, Marine. *See* **Marine mammals**

Man 572; 573
  Use this heading only in its generic meaning.
  See also **Anthropology; Anthropometry; Creation; Ethnology; Heredity**
  x Human race
  xx **Anthropology; Creation; History**

Man—Antiquity. *See* **Man—Origin**

Man—Color 572; 573
  xx **Color**

Man in space. *See* **Space flight**

Man—Influence of environment 304.2; 573
  See also **Environmental health; Survival skills; Weightlessness**
  x Acclimatization; Altitude, Influence of
  xx **Adaptation (Biology); Anthropogeography; Evolution; Human ecology**

Man—Influence on nature   304.2; 363.7

   See also **Environment—Government policy; Pol-
      lution**

   x Earth, Effect of man on; Nature, Effect of man
      on

   xx **Environment—Government policy; Human
      ecology**

Man, Nonliterate.   *See* **Nonliterate man**

Man—Origin   573.2

   See also **Anatomy, Comparative; Evolution; Pre-
      historic man**

   x Antiquity of man; Man—Antiquity; Origin of
      man

   xx **Anatomy, Comparative; Evolution; Physical
      anthropology; Prehistoric man; Religion and
      science**

Man power.   *See* **Human resources**

Man, Prehistoric.   *See* **Prehistoric man**

Man, Primitive.   *See* **Nonliterate man**

Man (Theology)   218; 233

   See also **Soul**

   xx **Theology**

Management   658

   Use for general materials on the principles of
      management in factories, industries, shops,
      etc. Materials on the application of such
      principles are entered under the specific
      headings such as those listed below. Add
      others as needed.

   See also

Crisis management	**Inventory control**
Efficiency, Industrial	**Office management**
Factory management	**Personnel management**
Farm management	**Sales management**
Industrial management	**Time management**

   also subjects with the subdivision *Management,*
      e.g. **Information systems—Management;
      Natural resources—Management;** etc.;
      types of industries, industrial plants and
      processes, names of government agencies,
      special activities, etc.; and types of institu-
      tions and names of individual institutions
      with the subdivision *Administration,* e.g.
      **Libraries—Administration; Schools—
      Administration;** etc.

   x Administration; Management, Scientific; Or-
      ganization and management; Scientific
      management

Management buyouts.   *See* **Leveraged buyouts**

Management—Employee participation.   *See* **Partic-
      ipative management**

Management, Industrial.   *See* **Industrial manage-
      ment**

Management information systems   658.4

   x Computer-based information systems; MIS
      (Information systems)

   xx **Information systems**

Management, Sales.   *See* **Sales management**

Management, Scientific.   *See* **Management**

Managers.   *See* **Supervisors**

Mandates   321

   x Government, Mandatory; League of Na-
      tions—Mandatory system

Mandates—*Continued*
  xx International law; International organization;
        International relations; World War, 1914-
        1918—Territorial questions
Mania. *See* Manic-depressive psychoses
Manic depression. *See* Manic-depressive psychoses
Manic-depressive psychoses 616.89
  See also Depression, Mental
  x Mania; Manic depression; Melancholia
  xx Depression, Mental; Mental illness
Manikins (Fashion models). *See* Models, Fashion
Manipulative materials 371.3078
      Use for works on educational materials designed
        to be handled or touched by students as well
        as for the materials themselves.
  See also Patterns (Mathematics); Perception
  x Tactile materials
  xx Audiovisual materials; Patterns (Mathemat-
        ics); Perception; Teaching—Aids and de-
        vices
Manned space flight. *See* Space flight
Manned space flight—Rescue work. *See* Space res-
        cue operations
Manned undersea research stations. *See* Undersea
        research stations
Mannequins (Fashion models). *See* Models, Fash-
        ion
Manners. *See* Courtesy; Etiquette
Manners and customs 390
  See also

April Fools' Day	Funeral rites and ceremo-
Bohemianism	nies
Caste	Halloween
Chivalry	Holidays
Clothing and dress	Hugging
Costume	Marriage customs and
Courts and courtiers	rites
Dating (Social customs)	Popular culture
Dueling	Rites and ceremonies
Etiquette	Social classes
Festivals	Travel
Folklore	

      also names of ethnic groups, countries, cities,
        etc., with the subdivision *Social life and cus-
        toms,* e.g. Indians of North America—
        Social life and customs; Jews—Social life
        and customs; United States—Social life and
        customs; etc.
  x Ceremonies; Customs, Social; Folkways; So-
        cial customs; Social life and customs; Tra-
        ditions
  xx Civilization; Ethnology; Etiquette; Rites and
        ceremonies
Manpower. *See* Human resources
Manpower policy. *See* Human resources policy
Manslaughter. *See* Homicide
Manual training. *See* Industrial arts education
Manual workers. *See* Labor
Manufactures 338.4; 670
  See also

Brand name products	Patents
Generic products	Prices
Machinery	Trademarks
Mills and millwork	Waste products

419

Manufactures—*Continued*

also names of articles manufactured, e.g. **Furniture;** etc.; and names of industries, e.g. **Paper industry;** etc.; also names of countries, cities, etc., with the subdivision *Industries,* e.g. **Chicago (Ill.)—Industries;** etc.

x Consumer goods; Consumer products

xx **Business; Commercial products; Industry; Technology**

Manufactures—Defects. *See* **Product recall**

Manufactures recall. *See* **Product recall**

Manufacturing in space. *See* **Space industrialization**

Manures. *See* **Fertilizers and manures**

Manuscripts 091

See also **Autographs; Charters; Illumination of books and manuscripts**

xx **Archives; Autographs; Bibliography; Books; Charters**

Manuscripts, Illuminated. *See* **Illumination of books and manuscripts**

Manuscripts—Prices. *See* **Books—Prices**

Map drawing 526.022

See also **Topographical drawing**

x Cartography; Chartography; Plans

xx **Topographical drawing**

Maple sugar 641.3; 664

xx **Sugar**

Maps 912

Use for general materials about maps and their history. Materials on the methods of map making and the mapping of areas are entered under **Map drawing.** Geographical atlases of world coverage are entered under **Atlases.**

See also **Atlases; Automobiles—Road guides; Charts;** also types of maps, e.g. **Road maps;** etc.; also subjects with the subdivision *Maps,* e.g. **Geology—Maps;** etc.; and names of countries, cities, etc. with the subdivision *Maps,* e.g. **United States—Maps; Chicago (Ill.)—Maps;** etc.

x Cartography; Chartography; Plans

xx **Charts; Geography**

Maps, Historical. *See* **Atlases, Historical**

Maps, Military. *See* **Military geography**

Maps, Road. *See* **Road maps**

Marathon running 796.42

x Long distance running

xx **Running**

Marathon swimming 797.2

x Long distance swimming

xx **Swimming**

Marble 553.5

xx **Petrology; Stone**

MARC project. *See* **MARC system**

MARC system 025

x Machine readable catalog system; MARC project; Project MARC

xx **Bibliographic control; Libraries—Automation; Machine readable bibliographic data**

Marches (Demonstrations). *See* **Protests, demonstrations, etc.**

Marches (Exercises). *See* **Drill (Nonmilitary)**

Marches for Black civil rights—United States. *See*
    Blacks—Civil rights
Marches (Music)   783.18
  xx **Military music**
Margarine   641.3; 664
  x Butter, Artificial; Oleomargarine
  xx **Butter**
Mariculture. *See* **Aquaculture**
Marihuana. *See* **Marijuana**
Marijuana   362.29; 613.8; 615; 633.7
  x Cannabis; Grass (Drug); Hashish; Marihuana;
    Pot (Drug)
  xx **Hallucinogens; Hemp; Narcotics; Smoking**
Marinas   387.1
  See also **Docks**
  x Yacht basins
  xx **Boats and boating; Harbors; Yachts and
    yachting**
Marine animals   591.92
  See also **Corals; Fishes; Freshwater animals;
    Marine mammals**
  x Animals, Aquatic; Animals, Marine; Animals,
    Sea; Aquatic animals; Marine fauna; Ma-
    rine zoology; Sea animals; Water animals
  xx **Animals; Freshwater animals; Marine biology;
    Wildlife**
Marine aquaculture. *See* **Aquaculture**
Marine aquariums   597.0074; 599.5; 639.3
  See also names of specific marine aquariums,
    e.g. **Marineland (Fla.);** etc.
  x Aquariums, Saltwater; Oceanariums; Salt wa-
    ter aquariums; Sea water aquariums
  xx **Aquariums**
Marine architecture. *See* **Naval architecture; Ship-
  building**
Marine biology   574.92
  See also **Freshwater biology; Marine animals;
    Marine ecology; Marine plants; Marine re-
    sources; Ocean bottom**
  x Biological oceanography; Biology, Marine;
    Ocean life
  xx **Biology; Freshwater biology; Natural history;
    Oceanography; Underwater exploration**
Marine disasters. *See* **Shipwrecks**
Marine ecology   574.5
  x Biological oceanography; Ecology, Marine
  xx **Ecology; Marine biology**
Marine engineering   623.8
  Use for materials on engineering as applied to
    ships and their machinery.
  x Naval engineering
  xx **Civil engineering; Engineering; Mechanical
    engineering; Naval architecture; Naval art
    and science; Steam navigation**
Marine engines   623.8
  xx **Engines; Shipbuilding; Steam engines**
Marine fauna. *See* **Marine animals**
Marine flora. *See* **Marine plants**
Marine geology. *See* **Submarine geology**
Marine insurance   368.2
  x Insurance, Marine
  xx **Commerce; Insurance; Maritime law; Mer-
    chant marine; Shipping**
Marine law. *See* **Maritime law**

421

Marine mammals   599.5

 See also names of marine mammals, e.g. **Seals (Animals); Whales;** etc.

 x Mammals, Marine

 xx **Mammals; Marine animals**

Marine mineral resources   553

 See also **Ocean mining**

 x Mineral resources, Marine; Ocean mineral resources

 xx **Marine resources; Mines and mineral resources; Ocean bottom; Ocean energy resources**

Marine painting   758

 x Sea in art; Seascapes; Ships in art

 xx **Painting**

Marine plants   581.92

 See also **Algae; Freshwater plants**

 x Aquatic plants; Marine flora; Water plants

 xx **Freshwater plants; Marine biology**

Marine pollution   363.73

 See also types of water pollution, e.g. **Oil pollution of rivers, harbors, etc.; Oil spills;** etc.

 x Ocean pollution; Offshore water pollution; Sea pollution

 xx **Pollution**

Marine resources   333.91; 574.92

 See also **Aquaculture; Fisheries; Marine mineral resources; Ocean energy resources; Ocean engineering; Seafood**

 x Ocean—Economic aspects; Ocean resources; Resources, Marine; Sea resources

 xx **Commercial products; Marine biology; Natural resources; Oceanography**

Marine transportation. *See* **Shipping**

Marine zoology. *See* **Marine animals**

Marineland (Fla.)   597.0074; 599.5; 639.3

 xx **Marine aquariums**

Mariners. *See* **Sailors**

Mariner's compass. *See* **Compass**

Marionettes. *See* **Puppets and puppet plays**

Marital counseling. *See* **Marriage counseling**

Marital infidelity. *See* **Adultery**

Maritime discoveries. *See* **Discoveries (in geography)**

Maritime law   341; 343

 See also **Commercial law; Freight and freightage; Marine insurance; Merchant marine; Pirates; Salvage; Territorial waters**

 x Law, Maritime; Law of the sea; Marine law; Merchant marine—Law and legislation; Naval law; Navigation—Law and legislation; Sea laws

 xx **Commercial law; International law; Law; Shipping; Territorial waters**

Market gardening. *See* **Vegetable gardening**

Market surveys   658.8

 See also **Public opinion polls**

 xx **Public opinion polls**

Marketing   380.1; 658.8

 Use for materials on the principles and methods involved in the distribution of merchandise from producer to consumer.

 See also **Direct selling; Sales management; Tele-**

Marketing—*Continued*
>> **marketing;** also subjects with the subdivision *Marketing,* e.g. **Farm produce— Marketing;** etc.

    x Distribution (Economics); Merchandising

    xx **Advertising; Business; Industrial management; Selling**

Marketing (Home economics). *See* **Shopping**

Marketing of farm produce. *See* **Farm produce— Marketing**

Markets (May subdiv. geog.) **380.1; 658.8**

    See also **Fairs**

    xx **Business; Cities and towns; Commerce; Fairs; Food**

Marking (Students). *See* **Grading and marking (Education)**

Marks on plate. *See* **Hallmarks**

Marks, Potters'. *See* **Pottery—Marks**

Marriage 173; 306.81; 346.01

    See also

Childlessness	**Marriage contracts**
Divorce	**Marriage counseling**
Domestic relations	**Married people**
Family	**Remarriage**
Home	**Weddings**
Husbands	**Wives**
Intermarriage	

    x Matrimony

    xx **Divorce; Domestic relations; Family; Home; Love; Sacraments**

Marriage—Annulment 262.9; 346.01

    See also **Divorce**

    x Annulment of marriage

    xx **Divorce**

Marriage contracts 306.81; 346.01

    x Antenuptial contracts; Premarital contracts; Prenuptial contracts

    xx **Marriage**

Marriage counseling 362.82

    See also **Divorce mediation**

    x Marital counseling; Premarital counseling

    xx **Counseling; Family life education; Marriage**

Marriage customs and rites 392

    x Bridal customs

    xx **Manners and customs; Rites and ceremonies; Weddings**

Marriage, Interracial. *See* **Interracial marriage**

Marriage, Mixed. *See* **Interfaith marriage; Intermarriage**

Marriage, Open ended. *See* **Unmarried couples**

Marriage registers. *See* **Registers of births, etc.**

Marriage statistics. *See* **Vital statistics**

Married men. *See* **Husbands**

Married people 306.872

    See also **Husbands; Wives**

    x Couples, Married; Married persons; People, Married

    xx **Family; Marriage**

Married persons. *See* **Married people**

Married women. *See* **Wives**

Mars (Planet) 523.4

    See also **Mars probes**

Mars (Planet)—Exploration 629.43

    xx **Planets—Exploration**

Mars (Planet)—Geology   559.9
  xx **Astrogeology**
Mars (Planet)—Photographs   523.4; 778.3
Mars probes   629.43
  x Martian probes
  xx **Mars (Planet); Space probes**
Marshall Plan.   *See* **Reconstruction (1939-1951)**
Marshes   333.91; 551.4
  See also **Swamp animals**
  x Bogs; Swamps
  xx **Drainage; Reclamation of land**
Martial arts   796.8
  See also **Archery; Dueling; Self-defense; Self-**
    defense for women
  xx **Athletics; Self-defense; Self-defense for**
    women
Martian probes.   *See* **Mars probes**
Martin Luther King Day   394.2
  x King, Martin Luther, holiday
  xx **Holidays**
Martyrs   272.092; 920
  See also **Persecution; Saints**
  xx **Church history; Heroes and heroines; Persecu-**
    tion; Saints
Marxism.   *See* **Communism; Socialism**
Mary, Blessed Virgin, Saint   232.91
  x Blessed Virgin Mary; Madonna; Virgin Mary
Mary, Blessed Virgin, Saint—Art   704.9
  See also **Jesus Christ—Art**
  xx **Christian art and symbolism; Jesus Christ—**
    Art
Masculine psychology.   *See* **Men—Psychology**
Masers   621.381
  x Microwave amplification by stimulated emis-
    sion of radiation
  xx **Amplifiers (Electronics); Electromagnetism;**
    Microwaves
Masers, Optical.   *See* **Lasers**
Masks (Facial)   391
Masks (Plays)   808.82; 812, etc.
  x Masques (Plays)
  xx **Drama; Pageants; Theater**
Masks (Sculpture)   731
  x Death masks
  xx **Sculpture**
Masonic orders.   *See* **Freemasons**
Masonry   693
  See also

Bricklaying	**Foundations**
Bridges	**Plaster and plastering**
Cement	**Stonecutting**
Concrete	**Walls**

  xx **Bricklaying; Building; Civil engineering;**
    Foundations; Stone; Walls
Masons (Secret order).   *See* **Freemasons**
Masques (Plays).   *See* **Masks (Plays)**
Mass   264
  See also **Lord's Supper**
  xx **Liturgies; Lord's Supper**
Mass communication.   *See* **Communication; Mass**
    media; Telecommunication
Mass feeding.   *See* **Food service**

424

Mass media   302.23
   See also **Motion pictures; Newspapers; Periodicals; Popular culture; Radio broadcasting; Television broadcasting**
   x Mass communication; Media
   xx **Communication**
Mass psychology.   *See* **Social psychology**
Mass spectra.   *See* **Mass spectrometry**
Mass spectrometry   543; 547.3
   x Mass spectra; Mass spectrum analysis
   xx **Spectrum analysis**
Mass spectrum analysis.   *See* **Mass spectrometry**
Mass transit.   *See* **Local transit**
Massacres (May subdiv. geog.)   179; 900
   See also names of individual massacres, e.g. **Saint Bartholomew's Day, Massacre of, 1572;** etc.
   xx **Atrocities; History; Persecution**
Massage   615.8
   See also **Acupressure; Chiropractic; Electrotherapeutics; Osteopathy**
   xx **Osteopathy; Physical therapy**
Mastodon   569
   xx **Extinct animals; Mammals, Fossil**
Mate selection in animals.   *See* **Animal courtship**
Materia medica   615
   See also **Anesthetics; Drugs; Pharmacology; Pharmacy; Poisons and poisoning;** also names of classes of drugs and individual drugs, e.g. **Narcotics;** etc.
   x Herbals; Pharmacopoeias
   xx **Drugs; Medicine; Pharmaceutical chemistry; Pharmacy; Therapeutics**
Materialism   146
   See also **Idealism; Realism**
   xx **Idealism; Philosophy; Positivism; Realism**
Materials   620.1
   Use for comprehensive discussions on materials of engineering and industry.
   See also **Strength of materials;** also types of materials, e.g. **Building materials; Hazardous substances; Raw materials;** etc.; and scientific and technical disciplines and types of equipment and construction with the subdivision *Materials,* e.g. **Airplanes—Materials;** etc.
   x Engineering materials; Industrial materials; Strategic materials
Materials handling   388; 658.7
   See also **Conveying machinery; Freight and freightage; Trucks**
   x Handling of materials; Mechanical handling
   xx **Industrial management; Trucks**
Materials, Strength of.   *See* **Strength of materials**
Maternity.   *See* **Mothers**
Mathematical analysis   515
   See also **Algebra; Algebras, Linear; Calculus; Graph theory; Numerical analysis; Programming (Computers)**
   x Analysis (Mathematics)
Mathematical drawing.   *See* **Geometrical drawing; Mechanical drawing**

Mathematical models 511
> *See also* **Fractals; Game theory; Programming (Computers); System analysis;** also subjects with the subdivision *Mathematical models,* e.g. **Pollution—Mathematical models;** etc.
> *x* Models, Mathematical

Mathematical notation 510
> Use for materials on the system of graphic symbols used in mathematics as well as for materials on the process or method of setting these down.
> *See also* **Type and type founding**
> *x* Mathematical symbols; Mathematics—Notation; Mathematics—Symbols; Notation, Mathematical; Symbols, Mathematical
> *xx* **Type and type founding**

Mathematical readiness 372.7
> *x* Arithmetical readiness; Mathematics readiness; Number readiness; Readiness for mathematics
> *xx* **Arithmetic—Study and teaching; Mathematics—Study and teaching**

Mathematical recreations 793.7
> *See also* **Number games**
> *x* Recreations, Mathematical
> *xx* **Amusements; Puzzles; Scientific recreations**

Mathematical sets. *See* **Set theory**
Mathematical symbols. *See* **Mathematical notation**

Mathematicians 510.92; 920
> *xx* **Scientists**

Mathematics 510
> *See also*

Algebra	**Group theory**
Arithmetic	**Logic, Symbolic and mathematical**
Binary system (Mathematics)	**Measurement**
Biomathematics	**Number theory**
Calculus	**Numerals**
Dynamics	**Numeration**
Fourth dimension	**Patterns (Mathematics)**
Fractions	**Set theory**
Game theory	**Trigonometry**
Geometry	

> also subjects with the subdivision *Mathematics,* e.g. **Astronomy—Mathematics;** etc.
> *xx* **Science**

Mathematics—Computer assisted instruction 372.7; 510.7
> *xx* **Computer assisted instruction**

Mathematics—Notation. *See* **Mathematical notation**

Mathematics readiness. *See* **Mathematical readiness**

Mathematics—Study and teaching 372.7; 510.7
> *See also* **Mathematical readiness**

Mathematics—Symbols. *See* **Mathematical notation**

Mathematics—Tables 510
> *See also* **Logarithms; Trigonometry—Tables**
> *x* Mathematics—Tables, etc.; Ready reckoners

Mathematics—Tables, etc. *See* **Mathematics—Tables**

Mating behavior. *See* **Animal courtship; Sexual behavior in animals**

Matrimony. *See* **Marriage**
Matter   530; 530.4
   xx **Dynamics; Physics**
Mausoleums. *See* **Tombs**
Maxims. *See* **Proverbs**
Mayas   972.004
   xx **Indians of Central America; Indians of Mexico**
Meal planning. *See* **Menus; Nutrition**
Meals. *See* **Dinners and dining;** and types of meals, e.g. **Breakfasts;** etc.
Meals for astronauts. *See* **Astronauts—Food**
Meals for school children. *See* **School children—Food**
Meals on wheels programs   363.8
   Use for materials on programs that deliver meals to the homebound.
   x Home delivered meals
   xx **Food relief**
Measurement   389; 530.8
   See also **Geodesy; Measuring instruments; Surveying; Volume (Cubic content); Weights and measures;** also subjects with the subdivision *Measurement,* e.g. **Air pollution—Measurement;** etc.
   x Mensuration; Metrology
   xx **Mathematics; Weights and measures**
Measurements, Electric. *See* **Electric measurements**
Measures. *See* **Weights and measures**
Measuring instruments   389; 681
   See also **Slide rule**
   x Instruments, Measuring
   xx **Measurement; Weights and measures**
Meat   641.3; 664
   See also types of meat, e.g. **Beef;** etc.
   xx **Food**
Meat-eating animals. *See* **Carnivores**
Meat industry   338.1
   See also **Cold storage; Meat inspection**
   x Meat industry and trade; Meat packing industry; Meat trade; Packing industry; Stockyards
   xx **Food supply**
Meat industry and trade. *See* **Meat industry**
Meat inspection   363.19
   x Inspection of meat
   xx **Food adulteration and inspection; Meat industry; Public health**
Meat packing industry. *See* **Meat industry**
Meat trade. *See* **Meat industry**
Mechanic arts. *See* **Industrial arts**
Mechanical brains. *See* **Computers; Cybernetics**
Mechanical drawing   604.2
   See also **Architectural drawing; Geometrical drawing; Graphic methods; Lettering**
   x Drafting, Mechanical; Engineering drawing; Industrial drawing; Machinery—Drawing; Mathematical drawing; Plans; Structural drafting
   xx **Drawing; Engineering; Geometrical drawing; Machinery; Pattern making**
Mechanical engineering   620.1
   See note under **Applied mechanics.**

Mechanical engineering—*Continued*

   See also

Electric engineering	**Power (Mechanics)**
Engines	**Power transmission**
Machinery	**Robotics**
Marine engineering	**Steam engineering**
Mechanical movements	

   xx **Civil engineering; Steam engineering**

Mechanical handling. *See* **Materials handling**

Mechanical models. *See* **Machinery—Models**

Mechanical movements   531

   See also **Gearing; Robots**

   x Mechanisms (Machinery)

   xx **Gearing; Kinematics; Mechanical engineering; Mechanics; Motion**

Mechanical musical instruments. *See* **Musical instruments, Mechanical**

Mechanical painting. *See* **Painting, Industrial**

Mechanical speech recognition. *See* **Automatic speech recognition**

Mechanical stokers. *See* **Stokers, Mechanical**

Mechanical translating. *See* **Translating and interpreting**

Mechanics   530; 531

   See also

Dynamics	**Motion**
Engineering	**Power (Mechanics)**
Fluid mechanics	**Statics**
Force and energy	**Steam engines**
Hydraulics	**Strains and stresses**
Hydrodynamics	**Strength of materials**
Hydrostatics	**Vibration**
Kinematics	**Viscosity**
Machinery	**Wave mechanics**
Mechanical movements	

   xx **Engineering; Force and energy; Kinematics; Machinery; Motion; Physics**

Mechanics, Applied. *See* **Applied mechanics**

Mechanics (Persons)   920

Mechanisms (Machinery). *See* **Mechanical movements**

Medallions. *See* **Medals**

Medals   355.1; 737

   See also **Decorations of honor; Insignia; Numismatics;** also names of military services and other appropriate subjects with the subdivision *Medals, badges, decorations, etc.,* e.g. **United States. Army—Medals, badges, decorations, etc.; United States. Navy—Medals, badges, decorations, etc.;** etc.; and names of specific medals

   x Badges of honor; Medallions

   xx **Decorations of honor; Insignia; Numismatics**

Media. *See* **Mass media**

Media centers (Education). *See* **Instructional materials centers**

Mediation. *See* **Arbitration and award**

Mediation, Divorce. *See* **Divorce mediation**

Mediation, Industrial. *See* **Arbitration, Industrial**

Mediation, International. *See* **Arbitration, International**

Medicaid   368.4

   x Medical care for the poor; Medical care, State

   xx **Poor—Medical care**

Medical appointments and schedules. *See* **Medical practice**

Medical botany. *See* **Botany, Medical**

Medical care   362.1

See also **Charities, Medical; Health maintenance organizations; Health self-care; Home care services; Long-term care facilities; Occupational health services; Sports medicine;** also classes of people with the subdivision *Medical care,* e.g. **Elderly—Medical care;** etc.

x Care, Medical; Health care; Medical service

xx **Public health**

Medical care—Costs   362.1

x Cost of medical care; Medical service, Cost of; Medicine—Cost of medical care

xx **Medical economics**

Medical care for the elderly. *See* **Elderly—Medical care; Medicare**

Medical care for the poor. *See* **Medicaid; Poor—Medical care**

Medical care—Moral and religious aspects. *See* **Medical ethics**

Medical care, Prepaid. *See* **Health insurance**

Medical care—Social aspects. *See* **Social medicine**

Medical care, State. *See* **Medicaid; Medicare**

Medical centers   362.1

See also **Hospitals; Medicine—Study and teaching**

xx **Hospitals**

Medical charities. *See* **Charities, Medical**

Medical chemistry. *See* **Clinical chemistry**

Medical colleges. *See* **Medicine—Study and teaching**

Medical consultation. *See* **Medical practice**

Medical diagnosis. *See* **Diagnosis**

Medical economics   338.4

Use for comprehensive materials on the economic aspects of medical service from the point of view of both the practitioner and the public. Materials on special aspects of medical economics are entered under specific headings, e.g. **Medical care—Costs;** etc.

See also **Medical care—Costs**

x Economics, Medical

Medical education. *See* **Medicine—Study and teaching**

Medical electricity. *See* **Electrotherapeutics**

Medical entomology. *See* **Insects as carriers of disease**

Medical errors. *See* **Errors; Physicians—Malpractice**

Medical ethics   174

See also **Euthanasia; Physicians—Malpractice; Right to die; Social medicine**

x Ethics, Medical; Medical care—Moral and religious aspects; Medicine—Moral and religious aspects

xx **Bioethics; Professional ethics; Social medicine**

Medical folklore. *See* **Folk medicine**

Medical genetics   611; 616

See also **Birth defects; Genetic counseling;** also

429

Medical genetics—*Continued*
    names of diseases with the subdivision
    Genetic aspects, e.g. **Cancer—Genetic aspects;** etc.
    x Clinical genetics; Congenital diseases; Hereditary diseases; Heredity of diseases
    xx **Genetics; Pathology**
Medical jurisprudence   614
    Use for materials dealing with the application of
    medical knowledge to questions of law. Materials that include laws, or discussion of
    those laws affecting medicine and the medical profession, are entered under **Medicine—Law and legislation.**
    See also **DNA Fingerprints; Lie detectors and detection; Medicine—Law and legislation; Poisons and poisoning; Suicide;** also subjects
    with the subdivision *Jurisprudence,* e.g.
    Mental illness—Jurisprudence; etc.
    x Forensic medicine; Jurisprudence, Medical;
    Legal medicine; Medicine, Legal
    xx **Criminal investigation; Criminal law; Law;
    Medicine—Law and legislation; Medicine,
    State**
Medical law and legislation.   *See* **Medicine—Law
    and legislation**
Medical malpractice.   *See* names of groups of people in the medical field with the subdivision
    Malpractice, e.g. **Physicians—Malpractice;**
    etc.
Medical missions.   *See* **Missions, Medical**
Medical offices.   *See* **Medical practice**
Medical partnership.   *See* **Medical practice**
Medical photography   621.36; 778.3
    x Photography, Medical
    xx **Photography—Scientific applications**
Medical practice   610.6
    x Clinics; Group medical practice; Medical appointments and schedules; Medical consultation; Medical offices; Medical partnership; Medicine—Practice
    xx **Medicine**
Medical profession.   *See* **Medicine; Physicians; Surgeons**
Medical research.   *See* **Medicine—Research**
Medical self-care.   *See* **Health self-care**
Medical service.   *See* **Medical care**
Medical service, Cost of.   *See* **Medical care—Costs**
Medical service, Prepaid.   *See* **Health insurance**
Medical sociology.   *See* **Social medicine**
Medical technologists   610.69
    xx **Allied health personnel**
Medical technology   610.28
    xx **Medicine**
Medical transplantation.   *See* **Transplantation of organs, tissues, etc.**
Medical waste disposal.   *See* **Medical wastes**
Medical wastes   363.72
    See also **Hazardous wastes**
    x Disposal of medical waste; Hospital wastes;
    Infectious wastes; Medical waste disposal;
    Waste disposal; Wastes, Medical
    xx **Hazardous wastes; Refuse and refuse disposal**

Medicare   368.4

    x Medical care for the elderly; Medical care,
        State

    xx **Elderly—Medical care**

Medicinal chemistry. *See* **Pharmaceutical chemis-
      try**

Medicinal plants. *See* **Botany, Medical**

Medicine (May subdiv. geog.) **610**

    All types of medicine are not included in this
        List but are to be added as needed.

    See also

Acupuncture	**Medical practice**
Alternative medicine	**Medical technology**
Anatomy	**Mind and body**
Aviation medicine	**Missions, Medical**
Bacteriology	**Nursing**
Biochemistry	**Pathology**
Botany, Medical	**Pharmacology**
Chiropractic	**Pharmacy**
Diagnosis	**Physiology**
Diseases	**Preventive medicine**
Emergency medicine	**Quacks and quackery**
Health	**Sports medicine**
Health resorts, spas, etc.	**Submarine medicine**
Holistic medicine	**Surgery**
Hospitals	**Therapeutics**
Hygiene	**Tropical medicine**
Materia medica	

    also names of diseases and groups of diseases,
        e.g. **AIDS (Disease); Fever; Nervous sys-
        tem—Diseases;** etc.; and headings begin-
        ning with the word **Medical**

    x Medical profession

    xx **Life sciences; Pathology; Therapeutics**

Medicine and religion   615.8

    See also **Christian Science; Mental healing; Spir-
      itual healing**

    x Religion and medicine

Medicine, Atomic. *See* **Nuclear medicine**

Medicine, Aviation. *See* **Aviation medicine**

Medicine—Biography   610.92; 920

Medicine—Cost of medical care. *See* **Medical
      care—Costs**

Medicine, Dental. *See* **Dentistry; Teeth—Diseases**

Medicine—Law and legislation   344

    See note under **Medical jurisprudence.**

    See also **Medical jurisprudence; Physicians—
      Malpractice; Right to die**

    x Medical law and legislation

    xx **Medical jurisprudence**

Medicine, Legal. *See* **Medical jurisprudence**

Medicine, Military   616.9

    See also **Armies—Medical care; First aid; Mili-
      tary health; Military hospitals;** also names
      of wars with the subdivision *Medical care,*
      e.g. **World War, 1939-1945—Medical care;**
      etc.

    x Field hospitals; Military medicine

    xx **Armies—Medical care; Military health**

Medicine—Miscellanea   610.2

    xx **Curiosities and wonders**

Medicine—Moral and religious aspects. *See* **Medi-
      cal ethics**

Medicine, Nuclear. *See* **Nuclear medicine**

Medicine, Pediatric.   *See* **Children—Diseases**
Medicine—Physiological effect.   *See* **Pharmacology**
Medicine, Popular   616.02
> Use for medical books written for the layman.
> *See also* **Folk medicine; Health self-care**
> *xx* **Health self-care**
Medicine—Practice.   *See* **Medical practice**
Medicine, Preventive.   *See* **Preventive medicine**
Medicine, Psychosomatic   616.08
> *x* Psychosomatic medicine
> *xx* **Mind and body; Neuroses; Psychoanalysis;**
> **Psychology, Pathological**
Medicine—Research   610.7
> *x* Medical research
> *xx* **Research**
Medicine, Social.   *See* **Social medicine**
Medicine—Social aspects.   *See* **Social medicine**
Medicine, Socialized.   *See* **Medicine, State**
Medicine, State   614
> Use for general materials on the relations of the
> state to medicine, public health, medical leg-
> islation, examinations of physicians by state
> boards, etc.
> *See also* **Charities, Medical; Medical jurispru-**
> **dence; Public health**
> *x* Medicine, Socialized; National health service;
> Socialized medicine; State medicine
Medicine—Study and teaching   610.7
> *x* Education, Medical; Medical colleges; Medical
> education
> *xx* **Medical centers; Professional education;**
> **Schools; Vocational education**
Medicine, Submarine.   *See* **Submarine medicine**
Medicine, Tropical.   *See* **Tropical medicine**
Medicine—United States   610.973
> *x* United States—Medicine
Medicine, Veterinary.   *See* **Veterinary medicine**
Medieval architecture.   *See* **Architecture, Medieval**
Medieval art.   *See* **Art, Medieval**
Medieval church history.   *See* **Church history—**
> **600-1500, Middle Ages**
Medieval civilization.   *See* **Civilization, Medieval**
Medieval history.   *See* **Middle Ages—History**
Medieval literature.   *See* **Literature, Medieval**
Medieval philosophy.   *See* **Philosophy, Medieval**
Meditation   291.4; 296.7
> Use for materials on the act or process of medi-
> tating.
> *See also* **Transcendental meditation**
> *xx* **Devotional exercises; Spiritual life**
Meditations   242; 291.4; 296.7
> Use as a form heading for actual discourses writ-
> ten to express the author's reflections or to
> serve as a guide to contemplation.
> *xx* **Devotional literature; Prayers**
Meetings, Public.   *See* **Public meetings**
Melancholia.   *See* **Depression, Mental; Manic-**
> **depressive psychoses**
Memoirs.   *See* **Autobiographies; Biography**
Memorial Day   394.2
> *x* Days; Decoration Day
> *xx* **Holidays**

Memory 153.1
   See also **Attention; Learning, Psychology of**
   x Mnemonics
   xx **Brain; Educational psychology; Intellect; Psychology; Psychophysiology; Thought and thinking**
Men 305.31
   See also **Fathers; Husbands; Single men; Widowers; Young men**
Men actors. *See* **Actors**
Men—Biography 920
   xx **Biography**
Men—Civil rights 305.32
   See also **Men's liberation movement**
   xx **Civil rights; Sex discrimination**
Men—Clothing. *See* **Men's clothing**
Men—Clubs. *See* **Men—Societies**
Men—Diseases 616.0081
Men—Education 370.81
   See also **Coeducation**
   x Education of men
   xx **Coeducation**
Men—Employment 331.11
   xx **Discrimination in employment; Labor; Labor supply**
Men in business. *See* **Businessmen**
Men—Psychology 155.3
   x Masculine psychology
Men, Single. *See* **Single men**
Men—Social conditions 305.32
   See also **Divorce; Men—Societies; Men's liberation movement**
Men—Societies 367
   See also **Boys' clubs**
   x Men—Clubs; Men's clubs; Men's organizations
   xx **Clubs; Men—Social conditions; Societies**
Mendel's law 575.1
   See also **Genetics; Heredity**
   xx **Breeding; Evolution; Heredity; Variation (Biology)**
Mendicancy. *See* **Begging**
Mendicant orders. *See* **Dominicans (Religious order); Franciscans**
Mennonites 289.7
   See also **Amish**
   xx **Baptists**
Menopause 618.1
   x Change of life in women; Climacteric, Female; Female climacteric
   xx **Aging**
Menopause, Male. *See* **Male climacteric**
Men's clothing 646; 687
   x Clothing, Men's; Men—Clothing
   xx **Clothing and dress**
Men's clubs. *See* **Men—Societies**
Men's liberation movement 305.32
   xx **Men—Civil rights; Men—Social conditions**
Men's organizations. *See* **Men—Societies**
Menstruation 612.6
   See also **Premenstrual syndrome**
   xx **Reproduction**
Mensuration. *See* **Measurement**
Mental arithmetic. *See* **Arithmetic, Mental**

Mental deficiency. *See* **Mental retardation**
Mental depression. *See* **Depression, Mental**
Mental diseases. *See* **Mental illness; Psychology, Pathological**
Mental healing   615.8
> Use for materials on psychic or psychological means to treat illness. Materials on the use of faith, prayer, or religious means to treat illness are entered under **Spiritual healing.**
> *See also*

Christian Science	**Psychotherapy**
Hypnotism	**Spiritual healing**
Mental suggestion	**Subconsciousness**
Mind and body	**Therapeutics, Suggestive**

> *x* Healing, Mental; Mind cure; Psychic healing
> *xx* **Christian Science; Medicine and religion; Mental suggestion; Mind and body; Psychotherapy; Spiritual healing; Subconsciousness; Therapeutics, Suggestive**

Mental health   362.2
> *See also*

Burn out (Psychology)	**Occupational therapy**
Mental illness	**Psychology, Pathological**
Mental retardation	**Psychophysiology**
Mind and body	**Worry**

> *x* Health, Mental; Hygiene, Mental; Mental hygiene
> *xx* **Health; Hygiene; Mental illness; Mind and body**

Mental hospitals. *See* **Mentally ill—Institutional care; Psychiatric hospitals**
Mental hygiene. *See* **Mental health**
Mental illness   362.2; 616.8
> See note under **Psychiatry.**
> *See also* **Mental health; Mental retardation;** also names of specific illnesses, e.g. **Manic-depressive psychoses;** etc.
> *x* Diseases, Mental; Mental diseases; Psychoses
> *xx* **Diseases; Mental health; Psychiatry; Psychology, Pathological**

Mental illness—Jurisprudence   344
> Use for materials on the legal aspects of mental disorders.
> *See also* **Insanity defense**
> *x* Insanity
> *xx* **Medical jurisprudence**

Mental institutions. *See* **Mentally ill—Institutional care**
Mental retardation   362.3; 616.85
> *x* Mental deficiency
> *xx* **Mental health; Mental illness**

Mental suggestion   131; 154.7; 615.8
> *See also* **Brainwashing; Hypnotism; Mental healing; Therapeutics, Suggestive**
> *x* Autosuggestion; Suggestion, Mental
> *xx* **Hypnotism; Mental healing; Mind and body; Parapsychology; Subconsciousness; Therapeutics, Suggestive**

Mental telepathy. *See* **Telepathy**
Mental tests   153.9; 371.2
> *See also* **Ability—Testing; Educational tests and measurements**
> *x* I.Q. tests; Intelligence tests; IQ tests; Objec-

Mental tests—*Continued*
> tive tests; Psychological tests; Tests
> *xx* **Child psychology; Educational psychology; Educational tests and measurements; Examinations; Intellect; Psychophysiology**

Mentally depressed. *See* **Depression, Mental**
Mentally deranged. *See* **Mentally ill**
Mentally handicapped   362.2; 362.3
> *x* Mentally retarded
> *xx* **Handicapped**

Mentally handicapped children   155.45; 362.2; 362.3
> *See also* **Slow learning children**
> *x* Children, Retarded; Mentally retarded children; Retarded children
> *xx* **Child psychiatry; Handicapped children; Mentally ill children; Slow learning children**

Mentally handicapped children—Education   371.92
> *xx* **Education; Special education**

Mentally ill   616.8
> *x* Insane; Mentally deranged; Psychotics
> *xx* **Psychiatry**

Mentally ill children   155.4; 362.2; 616.89
> *See also* **Mentally handicapped children**
> *x* Psychotic children
> *xx* **Child psychiatry; Emotionally disturbed children**

Mentally ill—Institutional care   362.2
> *See also* **Psychiatric hospitals**
> *x* Asylums; Charitable institutions; Insane—Hospitals; Mental hospitals; Mental institutions
> *xx* **Institutional care**

Mentally retarded. *See* **Mentally handicapped**
Mentally retarded children. *See* **Mentally handicapped children**
Menus   642
> *See also* **Breakfasts; Caterers and catering; Dinners and dining; Luncheons**
> *x* Bills of fare; Gastronomy; Meal planning
> *xx* **Caterers and catering; Cookery; Diet; Dinners and dining**

Menus for space flight. *See* **Astronauts—Food**
Mercantile law. *See* **Commercial law**
Mercantile marine. *See* **Merchant marine**
Mercenary soldiers   355.3
> *xx* **Military personnel; Soldiers**

Merchandise. *See* **Commercial products**
Merchandising. *See* **Marketing; Retail trade**
Merchant marine (May subdiv. geog.)   **387.5**
> *See also* **Harbors; Marine insurance; Shipping**
> *x* Mercantile marine
> *xx* **Maritime law; Sailors; Shipping; Ships; Transportation**

Merchant marine—Law and legislation. *See* **Maritime law**
Merchant marine—United States   387.50973
> *x* United States—Merchant marine

Merchants   920
> *xx* **Business; Business people; Commerce**

Mercury   546
> *x* Quicksilver

Mercy killing. *See* **Euthanasia**
Merger of corporations. *See* **Corporate mergers and acquisitions**

Mergers, Industrial. *See* **Railroads—Consolidation; Trusts, Industrial**

Mermaids and mermen   398.21
xx **Mythical animals**

Mesmerism. *See* **Hypnotism**

Messages to Congress. *See* **Presidents—United States—Messages**

Messiness. *See* **Cleanliness**

Metabolism   574.1
See also **Growth disorders; Nutrition**
xx **Biochemistry; Nutrition**

Metal work. *See* **Metalwork**

Metallography   669
Use for materials on the science of metal structures and alloys, especially the study of such structures visually, with the microscope. Materials dealing with the science and art of extracting metals from their ores, refining and preparing them for use, are entered under **Metallurgy.**
x Analysis, Microscopic; Micrographic analysis; Microscopic analysis
xx **Metals; Microscope and microscopy**

Metallurgy   669
See note under **Metallography.**
See also **Alloys; Chemical engineering; Chemistry, Technical; Electrometallurgy; Metals; Smelting**
xx **Alloys; Chemical engineering; Ores; Smelting**

Metals   546; 549
See also **Alloys; Aluminum; Metallography; Mineralogy; Precious metals; Solder and soldering;** also names of metals, e.g. **Gold;** etc.
xx **Chemistry, Inorganic; Metallurgy; Ores**

Metals, Transmutation of. *See* **Alchemy; Transmutation (Chemistry)**

Metalwork   671; 739
See also

Architectural metalwork	**Jewelry**
Art metalwork	**Plate metalwork**
Bronzes	**Sheet metalwork**
Copperwork	**Silverwork**
Dies (Metalworking)	**Solder and soldering**
Electroplating	**Steel**
Founding	**Tinwork**
Goldwork	**Welding**
Ironwork	

x Metal work
xx **Decoration and ornament; Founding**

Metalwork, Architectural. *See* **Architectural metalwork**

Metalwork, Art. *See* **Art metalwork**

Metalworking machinery   621.9
xx **Machinery**

Metamorphic rocks. *See* **Rocks**

Metaphysics   110
See also **Existentialism; God; Knowledge, Theory of; Universe**
xx **God; Philosophy**

Meteorites   523.5
xx **Astronomy; Meteors**

Meteorological instruments   551.5
See also names of meteorological instruments,

Meteorological instruments—*Continued*
  e.g. **Barometers; Thermometers;** etc.
  x Instruments, Meteorological
  xx **Scientific apparatus and instruments**
Meteorological observatories. *See* **Meteorology—
  Observatories**
Meteorological satellites   629.46
  See also names of satellites, e.g. **Tiros (Meteo-
    rological satellite);** etc.
  x Weather satellites
  xx **Artificial satellites**
Meteorology   551.5
  See note under **Climate.**
  See also

Air	**Rainbow**
Atmosphere	**Seasons**
Auroras	**Snow**
Climate	**Solar radiation**
Clouds	**Storms**
Cyclones	**Sunspots**
Droughts	**Thunderstorms**
Floods	**Tornadoes**
Fog	**Weather**
Frost	**Weather control**
Humidity	**Weather—Folklore**
Hurricanes	**Weather forecasting**
Lightning	**Winds**
Rain	

  xx **Atmosphere; Climate; Earth; Earth sciences;
    Geophysics; Physical geography; Rain; Sci-
    ence; Storms; Weather**
Meteorology in aeronautics   629.132
  x Aeronautics, Meteorology in
  xx **Aeronautics; Weather forecasting**
Meteorology—Observatories   551.5028
  x Meteorological observatories; Observatories,
    Meteorological; Weather stations
Meteorology—Tables   551.5
  x Meteorology—Tables, etc.
Meteorology—Tables, etc. *See* **Meteorology—
  Tables**
Meteors   523.5
  See also **Meteorites**
  x Falling stars; Fire balls; Shooting stars; Stars,
    Falling
  xx **Astronomy; Solar system; Stars**
Meter. *See* **Musical meter and rhythm; Versifica-
  tion**
Meters, Electric. *See* **Electric meters**
Meth (Drug). *See* **Methamphetamine**
Methamphetamine   362.29; 615
  See also **Ice (Drug)**
  x Meth (Drug); Speed (Drug)
  xx **Amphetamines**
Method of study. *See* **Study skills**
Methodology. *See* special subjects with the subdi-
  vision *Methodology,* e.g. **Science—
  Methodology;** etc.
Metric system   389; 530.8
  xx **Weights and measures**
Metrical romances. *See* **Romances**
Metrology. *See* **Measurement; Weights and mea-
  sures**

Metropolitan areas   307.76

See also **Urban renewal;** also names of metropolitan areas, e.g. **Chicago metropolitan area (Ill.);** etc.

x Suburban areas; Urban areas

xx **Cities and towns—Growth**

Metropolitan finance   336

xx **Finance; Municipal finance**

Metropolitan government   352

See also **Municipal government;** also names of metropolitan areas with the subdivision *Politics and government,* e.g. **Chicago metropolitan area (Ill.)—Politics and government;** etc.

xx **Local government; Municipal government**

Metropolitan planning.   *See* **Regional planning**

Mexican Americans   305.868

Use for materials on American citizens of Mexican descent. Materials on noncitizens from Mexico are entered under **Mexicans— United States.** Use these same patterns for other ethnic groups in the U.S. and other countries.

See also **Mexicans—United States**

x Chicanos

xx **Ethnology—United States; Hispanic Americans; Immigration and emigration; Mexicans—United States; Minorities; United States—Foreign population; United States—Immigration and emigration**

Mexican literature   860; M860

May use same subdivisions and names of literary forms as for **English literature.**

xx **Latin American literature**

Mexican War, 1845-1848.   *See* **United States— History—1845-1848, War with Mexico**

Mexicans (May subdiv. geog.)   305.868; 920; 972

Mexicans—United States   305.868

See note under **Mexican Americans.**

See also **Mexican Americans**

xx **Aliens; Immigration and emigration; Mexican Americans; Minorities; United States— Foreign population; United States— Immigration and emigration**

Mexico—Presidents.   *See* **Presidents—Mexico**

Mezzotint engraving   766

xx **Engraving**

MIA's.   *See* **Missing in action**

Mice   599.32; 636.088

x Mouse

Microbes.   *See* **Bacteriology; Germ theory of disease; Microorganisms; Viruses**

Microbial energy conversion.   *See* **Biomass energy**

Microbiology   576

See also **Bacteriology; Biotechnology; Microorganisms; Microscope and microscopy;** also subjects with the subdivision *Microbiology,* e.g. **Air—Microbiology;** etc.

xx **Biology; Microorganisms; Microscope and microscopy**

Microchemistry   540

xx **Chemistry; Microscope and microscopy**

Microcomputers   004.16; 621.39

Use for materials on small, usually desk-top-sized computers whose central processing units may consist of a single integrated circuit type chip. Most microcomputers include a keyboard terminal and disk drives for floppy disks; some may include a video display terminal and a printer. Consider also **Minicomputers.**

See also **Home computers; Microprocessors; Portable computers**

x **Computers**

Microelectronics   621.381

x Microminiature electronic equipment; Microminiaturization (Electronics)

xx **Electronics; Semiconductors**

Microfilming. *See* **Microphotography**

Microfilms   686.4

See also **Library catalogs on microfilm**

x Films

xx **Microforms**

Microforms   001.55; 686.4

See also types of microforms, e.g. **Microfilms;** etc.

x Micropublications

xx **Microphotography**

Micrographic analysis. *See* **Metallography; Microscope and microscopy**

Microminiature electronic equipment. *See* **Microelectronics**

Microminiaturization (Electronics). *See* **Microelectronics**

Microorganisms   576

See also **Bacteriology; Microbiology; Microscope and microscopy; Protozoa; Viruses**

x Germs; Microbes; Microscopic organisms

xx **Bacteriology; Microbiology; Microscope and microscopy**

Microphotography   686.4

Use for materials dealing with the photographing of objects of any size upon a microscopic or very small scale.

See also **Microforms**

x Microfilming

xx **Photography**

Microprocessors   004.16

Use for materials on the central processing units of microcomputers.

xx **Microcomputers**

Micropublications. *See* **Microforms**

Microscope and microscopy   502.8; 578

See also **Electron microscope and microscopy; Metallography; Microbiology; Microchemistry; Microorganisms**

x Analysis, Microscopic; Micrographic analysis; Microscopic analysis

xx **Microbiology; Microorganisms**

Microscopic analysis. *See* **Metallography; Microscope and microscopy**

Microscopic organisms. *See* **Microorganisms**

Microwave amplification by stimulated emission of radiation. *See* **Masers**

Microwave communication systems   621.381
>   *See also* **Closed-circuit television**
>   *xx* **Intercommunication systems; Shortwave radio; Telecommunication; Television**

Microwave cookery   641.5; 641.7
>   *x* Cookery, Microwave
>   *xx* **Cookery**

Microwaves   537.5
>   *See also* **Masers**
>   *xx* **Electric waves; Electromagnetic waves; Short-wave radio**

Mid-career changes.   *See* **Career changes**

Middle age   305.24
>   *See also* **Age and employment; Aging; Longevity; Old age**
>   *x* Age
>   *xx* **Life (Biology); Longevity**

Middle Ages   909.07
>   *See also*

Architecture, Medieval	**Fourteenth century**
Art, Medieval	**Knights and knighthood**
Chivalry	**Literature, Medieval**
Church history—600-	**Philosophy, Medieval**
1500, Middle Ages	**Renaissance**
Civilization, Medieval	**Thirteenth century**
Fifteenth century	

>   *x* Dark Ages
>   *xx* **Civilization, Medieval; Feudalism; Renaissance**

Middle Ages—History   909.07; 940.1
>   *See also* **Civilization, Medieval; Crusades; Europe—History—476-1492; Feudalism; Holy Roman Empire; Monasticism**
>   *x* History, Medieval; Medieval history
>   *xx* **Europe—History—476-1492; World history**

Middle Atlantic States.   *See* **Atlantic States**

Middle child.   *See* **Birth order**

Middle classes   305.5
>   *x* Bourgeoisie; Middle-income class
>   *xx* **Social classes**

Middle East   956
>   Use for materials on the region consisting of Asia west of Pakistan, Northeastern Africa, and occasionally including Greece and Pakistan. For materials dealing collectively with the Arabic-speaking countries of Asia and Africa, or of Asia only, use **Arab countries.**
>   *See also* **Arab countries; Israel**
>   *x* East (Near East); Levant; Near East; Orient
>   *xx* **Asia**

Middle East—Strategic aspects   956
>   *xx* **Military geography; Strategy**

Middle East War, 1991-.   *See* **Persian Gulf War, 1991-**

Middle-income class.   *See* **Middle classes**

Middle West   977
>   *See also* **Old Northwest**
>   *x* Central States; Midwest; North Central States
>   *xx* **Mississippi River Valley; Old Northwest; United States**

Mideast War, 1991-.   *See* **Persian Gulf War, 1991-**

Midget cars.   *See* **Karts and karting**

Midwest.   *See* **Middle West**

Midwifery.   *See* **Childbirth**

Migrant labor   331.5; 362.85

Use for materials dealing with casual or seasonal workers who move from place to place in search of employment. Materials on the movement of population within a country for permanent settlement are entered under **Migration, Internal.**

x Labor, Migratory; Migratory workers

xx **Agricultural laborers; Labor**

Migration. *See* **Immigration and emigration**

Migration, Internal   304.8

See note under **Migrant labor.**

See also **Cities and towns—Growth; Land settlement**

xx **Colonization; Land settlement; Population**

Migration of animals. *See* **Animals—Migration**

Migration of birds. *See* **Birds—Migration**

Migratory workers. *See* **Migrant labor**

Milch cattle. *See* **Dairy cattle**

Military aeronautics. *See* **Aeronautics, Military**

Military aid. *See* **Military assistance**

Military air bases. *See* **Air bases**

Military airplanes. *See* **Airplanes, Military**

Military art and science   355

See also

Aeronautics, Military	**Guerrilla warfare**
Armaments	**Industrial mobilization**
Armed forces	**Military hospitals**
Armies	**Military personnel**
Arms and armor	**Naval art and science**
Arms control	**Ordnance**
Battles	**Poisonous gases—War use**
Biological warfare	**Psychological warfare**
Camouflage (Military science)	**Signals and signaling**
	Spies
Camps (Military)	**Strategy**
Chemical warfare	**Tactics**
Civil defense	**Transportation, Military**
Drill and minor tactics	**War**
Fortification	

also headings beginning with the word **Military**

x Army; Fighting; Military power; Military science

xx **Armies; Drill and minor tactics; Military personnel; Naval art and science; Strategy; War**

Military art and science—Study and teaching. *See* **Military education**

Military assistance (May subdiv. geog. adjective form)   **355**

x Arms aid; Arms sales; Foreign aid program; Military aid; Mutual defense assistance program

Military assistance, American   355

See also **Iran-Contra Affair, 1985-**

x American military assistance

Military atrocities. *See* names of wars with the subdivision *Atrocities,* e.g. **World War, 1939-1945—Atrocities;** etc.; and names of specific atrocities

Military biography. *See* names of armies and navies with the subdivision *Biography,* e.g. **United States. Army—Biography; United States. Navy—Biography;** etc.

Military camps. *See* **Camps (Military)**
Military costume. *See* **Uniforms, Military**
Military courts. *See* **Courts martial and courts of inquiry**
Military crimes. *See* **Military offenses**
Military desertion (May subdiv. geog.) 343
> *See also* **Draft resisters;** also names of wars with the subdivision *Desertions,* e.g. **World War, 1939-1945—Desertions;** etc.
> *x* Army desertion; Defectors, Military; Desertion; Desertion, Military
> *xx* **Draft resisters; Military offenses**
Military desertion—United States 343
> *x* United States. Army—Desertions
Military draft. *See* **Draft**
Military drill. *See* **Drill and minor tactics**
Military education 355.1; 355.5
> *See also* **Military training camps;** also names of military schools, e.g. **United States Military Academy;** etc.
> *x* Army schools; Education, Military; Military art and science—Study and teaching; Military training; Schools, Military
> *xx* **Education**
Military engineering 623
> *See also* **Fortification;** also names of wars with the subdivision *Engineering and construction,* e.g. **World War, 1939-1945—Engineering and construction;** etc.
> *xx* **Civil engineering; Engineering; Fortification**
Military forces. *See* **Armies; Navies;** and names of countries with the subdivision *Armed forces,* e.g. **United States—Armed forces;** etc.
Military geography 355.4
> *See also* areas of the world with the subdivision *Strategic aspects,* e.g. **Middle East—Strategic aspects;** etc.
> *x* Geography, Military; Maps, Military
Military government (May subdiv. geog.) 341.6; 355.4
> *x* Government, Military
> *xx* **Military occupation; Public administration**
Military health 613.6
> *See also* **Armies—Medical care; Medicine, Military;** also names of wars with the subdivision *Health aspects* or *Medical care,* e.g. **World War, 1939-1945—Health aspects; World War, 1939-1945—Medical care;** etc.
> *x* Hygiene, Military; Soldiers—Hygiene
> *xx* **Armies—Medical care; Hygiene; Medicine, Military; Sanitation**
Military history 355
> *See also* **Battles; Military policy; Naval history;** also names of countries with the subhead *Army* or the subdivision *History, Military,* e.g. **United States. Army; United States—History, Military;** and names of wars, battles, sieges, etc.
> *x* History, Military; Wars
> *xx* **History; Naval history**
Military hospitals 355.7
> *See also* **First aid;** also names of wars with the subdivision *Medical care,* e.g. **World War,**

Military hospitals—*Continued*
>   **1939-1945—Medical care;** etc.
>   *x* Field hospitals; Hospitals, Military; Veterans—Hospitals
>   *xx* **Hospitals; Medicine, Military; Military art and science; Veterans**

Military intervention. *See* **Intervention (International law)**

Military law   343
>   *See also* **Courts martial and courts of inquiry; Draft; Military offenses; Veterans—Legal status, laws, etc.**
>   *x* Articles of war; Law, Military; War, Articles of
>   *xx* **Courts martial and courts of inquiry; International law; Law; War**

Military life. *See* **Military personnel;** and names of countries with the subdivision *Armed forces* or the subheads *Army* or *Navy;* etc., with the subdivision *Military life,* e.g. **United States—Armed forces—Military life; United States. Army—Military life;** etc.

Military medicine. *See* **Medicine, Military**

Military motorization. *See* **Transportation, Military**

Military music   781.5
>   *See also* **Band music; Marches (Music);** also names of wars with the subdivision *Songs and music,* e.g. **World War, 1939-1945—Songs and music;** etc.
>   *x* Music, Military
>   *xx* **Music**

Military occupation   341.6; 355.4
>   *See also* **Military government; World War, 1939-1945—Occupied territories;** also names of occupied countries with the subdivision *History—1940-1945, German occupation; History—1945- , Allied occupation,* e.g. **Netherlands—History—1940-1945, German occupation; Japan—History—1945-1952, Allied occupation;** etc.
>   *x* Occupation, Military; Occupied territory

Military offenses (May subdiv. geog.)   343
>   *See also* names of military offenses, e.g. **Military desertion;** etc.
>   *x* Crimes, Military; Military crimes; Naval offenses; Offenses, Military
>   *xx* **Criminal law; Military law**

Military offenses—United States   343
>   *x* United States. Army—Crimes and misdemeanors; United States—Military offenses

Military pensions. *See* **Pensions, Military**

Military personnel   355.3
>   *See also*

Admirals	**Navies**
Armies	**Sailors**
Generals	**Soldiers**
Mercenary soldiers	**Veterans**

>   **Military art and science**
>   also names of countries with the subdivision *Armed forces* or the subheads *Army* or *Navy,* etc., with the subdivision *Military life,* e.g. **United States—Armed forces—**

Military personnel—*Continued*
> **Military life; United States. Army—**
> **Military life;** etc.
>> *x* Military life; Servicemen; Servicewomen
>> *xx* **Armed forces; Military art and science; Veterans; War**

Military personnel missing in action. *See* **Missing in action**

Military personnel—United States 355.30973
> *x* United States—Military personnel

Military policy 355
> *See also* **National security;** also names of countries with the subdivision *Military policy,*
>> e.g. **United States—Military policy;** etc.
> *x* Defense policy
> *xx* **Military history; National security**

Military posts 355.7
> *x* Army posts

Military power. *See* **Armies; Arms control; Military art and science; Navies; Sea power**

Military science. *See* **Military art and science**

Military service, Compulsory. *See* **Draft**

Military service, Compulsory—Draft resisters. *See* **Draft resisters**

Military service, Voluntary 355.2
> *x* Volunteer military service
> *xx* **Armed forces; Human resources**

Military signaling. *See* **Signals and signaling**

Military strategy. *See* **Strategy**

Military tactics. *See* **Tactics**

Military training. *See* **Military education**

Military training camps 355.7
> *x* Students' military training camps; Training camps, Military
> *xx* **Military education**

Military training, Universal. *See* **Draft**

Military transportation. *See* **Transportation, Military**

Military uniforms. *See* **Uniforms, Military**

Military vehicles. *See* **Vehicles, Military**

Militia. *See* names of countries and states with the subdivision *Militia,* e.g. **United States— Militia;** etc.

Milk 637; 641.3
> *See also* **Butter; Cheese; Dried milk**
> *xx* **Dairy products; Dairying**

Milk—Analysis 637; 641.3

Milk, Dried. *See* **Dried milk**

Milk supply 338.1
> *xx* **Food adulteration and inspection; Public health**

Mill and factory buildings. *See* **Factories**

Millennialism. *See* **Millennium**

Millennium 236
> *See also* **Second Advent**
> *x* Millennialism
> *xx* **Eschatology; Future life; Second Advent**

Millikan rays. *See* **Cosmic rays**

Millinery 646.5; 687
> *See also* **Hats**
> *xx* **Costume; Hats**

Milling (Flour). *See* **Flour mills**

Milling machines 621.9
    See also **Machine tools**
    xx **Machinery**
Millionaires 920
    See also **Wealth**
    xx **Capitalists and financiers; Wealth**
Mills and millwork 670.42
    See also **Factories; Machinery;** also names of
        types of mills, e.g. **Flour mills;** etc.
    xx **Factories; Manufactures; Technology**
Mime 792.3
    See also **Pantomimes**
    xx **Acting; Pantomimes**
Mind. *See* **Intellect; Psychology**
Mind and body 150
    See also

Biofeedback training	**Personality disorders**
Consciousness	**Phrenology**
Dreams	**Psychoanalysis**
Holistic medicine	**Psychology, Pathological**
Hypnotism	**Psychophysiology**
Medicine, Psychosomatic	**Sleep**
Mental healing	**Spiritual healing**
Mental health	**Subconsciousness**
Mental suggestion	**Temperament**
Nervous system	

    x Body and mind; Mind cure
    xx **Brain; Holistic medicine; Hypnotism; Medicine; Mental healing; Mental health; Parapsychology; Philosophy; Phrenology; Psychoanalysis; Psychophysiology; Subconsciousness**
Mind control. *See* **Brainwashing**
Mind cure. *See* **Christian Science; Mental healing; Mind and body**
Mind reading. *See* **Telepathy**
Mine surveying 622.028
    xx **Mining engineering; Prospecting; Surveying**
Mineral industries. *See* **Mines and mineral resources**
Mineral lands. *See* **Mines and mineral resources**
Mineral resources. *See* **Mines and mineral resources**
Mineral resources, Marine. *See* **Marine mineral resources**
Mineralogy 549
    See also **Gems; Petrology; Phosphorescence; Precious stones;** also names of minerals, e.g. **Quartz;** etc.
    x Minerals
    xx **Crystallography; Geology; Metals; Mines and mineral resources; Natural history; Ores; Petrology; Rocks; Science**
Minerals. *See* **Mineralogy; Mines and mineral resources;** and names of minerals, e.g. **Quartz;** etc.
Miners 622.092; 920
    See also types of miners, e.g. **Coal miners;** etc.
    x Laborers
    xx **Labor**
Mines and mineral resources (May subdiv. geog.)
    333.8; 338.2
    Use for general descriptive materials and for

Mines and mineral resources—*Continued*
> technical and economic materials on mining, metallurgy and minerals of economic value.
> *See also* **Marine mineral resources; Mineralogy; Mining engineering; Precious metals; Prospecting;** also specific types of mines and mining, e.g. **Coal mines and mining;** etc.
> *x* Mineral industries; Mineral lands; Mineral resources; Minerals; Mining
> *xx* **Geology, Economic; Natural resources; Ores; Raw materials**

Mines and mineral resources—United States 333.8; 338.2
> *x* United States—Mines and mineral resources

Mingles housing. *See* **Shared housing**

Miniature computers. *See* **Minicomputers**

Miniature gardens. *See* **Gardens, Miniature**

Miniature objects. *See* names of miniature objects, e.g. **Dollhouses; Gardens, Miniature; Models and model making; Toys;** etc.; and names of objects with the subdivision *Models,* e.g. **Airplanes—Models;** etc.

Miniature painting 757
> *See also* **Portrait painting**
> *x* Miniatures (Portraits)
> *xx* **Painting; Portrait painting**

Miniatures (Illumination of books and manuscripts). *See* **Illumination of books and manuscripts**

Miniatures (Portraits). *See* **Miniature painting**

Minibikes 629.227
> *xx* **Bicycles and bicycling; Motorcycles**

Minicomputers 004.16; 621.39
> Use for materials on computers larger than microcomputers, but smaller than mainframes. Consider also **Microcomputers.**
> *See also* **Home computers**
> *x* Miniature computers
> *xx* **Computers**

Minimum drinking age. *See* **Drinking age**

Minimum wage. *See* **Wages—Minimum wage**

Mining. *See* **Mines and mineral resources; Mining engineering**

Mining, Electric. *See* **Electricity in mining**

Mining engineering 622
> *See also* **Boring; Electricity in mining; Mine surveying; Ocean mining**
> *x* Mining
> *xx* **Civil engineering; Coal mines and mining; Electricity in mining; Engineering; Mines and mineral resources**

Mining, Ocean. *See* **Ocean mining**

Ministers (Diplomatic agents). *See* **Diplomats**

Ministers of state. *See* **Cabinet officers**

Ministers of the gospel. *See* **Clergy**

Ministry (May subdiv. by religion or denomination, adjective form) **253**
> *x* Clergy—Office

Ministry, Christian 253
> *x* Christian ministry

Minor arts. *See* **Decorative arts**

Minor tactics. *See* **Drill and minor tactics**

Minorites. *See* **Franciscans**

Minorities   305.8; 323.1
　　　See also **Discrimination; Ethnic relations; Na-
　　　　tionalism; Race relations; Segregation;** also
　　　　names of peoples living within a country,
　　　　state, or city dominated by another nation-
　　　　ality, e.g. **Mexican Americans; Mexicans—
　　　　United States;** etc.; and names of countries
　　　　with the subdivisions *Foreign population*
　　　　and *Race relations,* e.g. **United States—
　　　　Foreign population; United States—Race re-
　　　　lations;** etc.
　　　x Minority groups
　　　xx **Discrimination; Ethnic groups; Ethnic rela-
　　　　tions; Nationalism; Segregation**
Minorities in broadcasting   384.5; 791.4
　　　Use same form for minorities in other industries
　　　　or fields of endeavor.
　　　x Minority groups in broadcasting
　　　xx **Broadcasting**
Minorities in engineering   620
　　　x Minority groups in engineering
　　　xx **Engineering**
Minority groups.   *See* **Minorities**
Minority groups in broadcasting.   *See* **Minorities in
　　　broadcasting**
Minority groups in engineering.   *See* **Minorities in
　　　engineering**
Minstrels   791.092; 920
　　　See also **Troubadours**
　　　xx **Poets**
Mints   332.4
　　　See also **Coinage**
　　　xx **Coinage; Money**
Miracle plays.   *See* **Mysteries and miracle plays**
Miracles   231
　　　See also **Supernatural**
　　　x Bible—Miracles; Divine healing
　　　xx **Apparitions; Shrines; Spiritual healing; Super-
　　　　natural**
Miracles—Christianity   231.7
　　　x Bible. N.T.—Miracles
　　　xx **Christianity; Church history**
Mirrors   748.8
　　　x Looking glasses
　　　xx **Furniture**
MIS (Information systems).   *See* **Management in-
　　　formation systems**
Miscarriage   618.3
　　　x Abortion, Spontaneous; Fetal death; Sponta-
　　　　neous abortion
　　　xx **Pregnancy**
Miscellanea.   *See* subjects with the subdivision
　　　　Miscellanea, e.g. **Medicine—Miscellanea;**
　　　　etc.
Miscellaneous facts.   *See* **Curiosities and wonders**
Misconduct in office   351.9
　　　See also **Corruption in politics; Police—Corrupt
　　　　practices;** also names of specific incidents
　　　　and offenses, e.g. **Watergate Affair, 1972-
　　　　1974;** etc.
　　　x Malfeasance in office; Official misconduct
　　　xx **Conflict of interests; Corruption in politics;
　　　　Criminal law**
Misdemeanors (Law).   *See* **Criminal law**

Misleading advertising. *See* **Deceptive advertising**
Misrepresentation in advertising. *See* **Deceptive advertising**
Missiles, Ballistic. *See* **Ballistic missiles**
Missiles, Guided. *See* **Guided missiles**
Missing children 363.2
    See also **Runaway children**
    x Lost children
    xx **Children; Criminal investigation; Missing persons**
Missing in action
    See also names of wars with the subdivision
    Missing in action, e.g. **World War, 1939-1945—Missing in action;** etc.
    x M.I.A.'s; MIA's; Military personnel missing in action
    xx **Prisoners of war; Soldiers**
Missing persons (May subdiv. geog.) 363.2
    See also **Missing children; Runaway teenagers**
    xx **Criminal investigation**
Missionaries, Christian 920
    xx **Missions, Christian**
Missions, Christian 266
    See also **Evangelistic work; Missionaries, Christian; Salvation Army;** also names of churches, denominations, religious orders, etc. with the subdivision *Missions,* e.g. **Catholic Church—Missions;** etc.
    x Christian missions; Foreign missions, Christian; Home missions, Christian
    xx **Christianity; Church history; Church work; Evangelistic work**
Missions, Indian. *See* **Indians of North America—Missions, Christian**
Missions, Medical 362.1
    x Medical missions
    xx **Medicine**
Mississippi River Valley 977
    See also **Middle West**
    x Mississippi Valley
    xx **United States**
Mississippi River Valley—History 977
    x New France—History
Mississippi Valley. *See* **Mississippi River Valley**
Mistakes. *See* **Errors**
Mixed marriage. *See* **Interfaith marriage; Intermarriage; Interracial marriage**
Mnemonics. *See* **Memory**
Mobile home living 728.7
    See also **Van life**
    xx **Home economics; Mobile homes**
Mobile home parks 647
    xx **Trailer parks**
Mobile homes 629.226; 643; 728.7
    See also **Mobile home living**
    x Homes, Mobile; House trailers; Motor homes; Trailers, Home
    xx **Housing; Travel trailers and campers**
Mobiles (Sculpture) 731
    xx **Kinetic sculpture; Sculpture**
Mobilization, Industrial. *See* **Industrial mobilization**
Mobs. *See* **Crowds; Riots**
Model airplanes. *See* **Airplanes—Models**

Model cars. *See* **Automobiles—Models**
Modeling   731.4; 738.1
 See also **Sculpture—Technique; Soap sculpture**
 x Clay modeling
 xx **Clay; Sculpture; Sculpture—Technique**
Models. *See* **Models and model making;** and
  names of objects with the subdivision
  Models, e.g. **Airplanes—Models;** etc.
Models and model making   688
 See also names of objects with the subdivision
  Models, e.g. **Airplanes—Models; Ships—**
  Models; etc.
 x Miniature objects; Models
Models, Fashion   659.1
 x Fashion models; Manikins (Fashion models);
  Mannequins (Fashion models); Style mani-
  kins
Models, Mathematical. *See* **Mathematical models**
Models, Mechanical. *See* **Machinery—Models**
Modern architecture. *See* **Architecture, Modern**
Modern art. *See* **Art, Modern**
Modern church history. *See* **Church history—**
  1500- , Modern period
Modern civilization. *See* **Civilization, Modern**
Modern dance   792.8
 x Interpretive dance
 xx **Dancing**
Modern history. *See* **History, Modern**
Modern languages. *See* **Languages, Modern**
Modern painting. *See* **Painting, Modern**
Modern philosophy. *See* **Philosophy, Modern**
Modern sculpture. *See* **Sculpture, Modern**
Modernism   230
 Use for materials on the movement in the Prot-
  estant churches that applies modern critical
  methods to biblical study and the history of
  dogma, and emphasizes the spiritual and
  ethical side of Christianity rather than his-
  toric dogmas and creeds.
 See also **Fundamentalism**
 xx **Fundamentalism**
Modernization   303.44
 Use for materials on the process of change in a
  society or social institution in which the
  most recent styles, ideas, or usages are ac-
  quired or adapted.
 See also **Industrialization**
 x Development
 xx **Industrialization; Social change**
Mohammedan art. *See* **Art, Islamic**
Mohammedanism. *See* **Islam**
Mohammedans. *See* **Muslims**
Mold (Botany). *See* **Molds (Botany)**
Molding (Metal). *See* **Founding**
Molds (Botany)   589.2
 See also **Fungi**
 x Mold (Botany)
 xx **Fungi**
Molecular biochemistry. *See* **Molecular biology**
Molecular biology   574.8
 See also **Genetic code**
 x Biology, Molecular; Molecular biochemistry;
  Molecular biophysics
 xx **Biochemistry; Biophysics**

Molecular biophysics. *See* **Molecular biology**
Molecular cloning   174; 574.87
    x Cloning, Molecular; DNA cloning
    xx **Clones and cloning; Genetic engineering**
Molecular physiology. *See* **Biophysics**
Molecules   539; 541
    xx **Chemistry, Physical and theoretical**
Molesting of children. *See* **Child molesting**
Mollusks   594
    See also **Shells**
    xx **Invertebrates; Shellfish; Shells**
Monarchs. *See* **Kings, queens, rulers, etc.**
Monarchy   321; 321.8
    See also **Democracy; Kings, queens, rulers, etc.**
    x Sovereigns
    xx **Constitutional history; Constitutional law; De-**
        mocracy; Executive power; Political science
Monasteries (May subdiv. geog.)   **255; 271; 726**
    See also **Abbeys; Convents; Monasticism**
    x Cloisters
    xx **Abbeys; Convents; Monasticism**
Monastic orders. *See* **Religious orders**
Monasticism   255; 271
    See also **Monasteries; Religious life; Religious**
        orders
    xx **Civilization, Medieval; Middle Ages—**
        History; Monasteries
Monetary policy (May subdiv. geog.)   **332.4**
    See also **Finance; Fiscal policy; Gold; Inflation**
        (Finance); Money; Silver
    x Bimetallism; Currency devaluation; Devalua-
        tion of currency; Free coinage
    xx **Coinage; Finance; Fiscal policy; Inflation (Fi-**
        nance); Money
Monetary policy—United States   332.4
    x United States—Monetary policy
Money   332.4
    Use for materials on currency as a medium of
        exchange or measure of value.
    See also

Banks and banking	**Credit**
Barter	**Foreign exchange**
Capital	**Gold**
Children's allowances	**Mints**
Coinage	**Monetary policy**
Coins	**Paper money**
Counterfeits and counter-	**Silver**
feiting	**Wealth**

    x Bullion; Currency; Specie; Standard of value
    xx **Banks and banking; Coinage; Economics; Ex-**
        change; Finance; Gold; Monetary policy;
        Silver; Wealth
Money, Paper. *See* **Paper money**
Money raising. *See* **Fund raising**
Moneymaking projects for children   332.024; 650.1
    See also **Children's allowances**
    x Children's moneymaking projects
    xx **Children—Employment; Children's allow-**
        ances
Monkeys   599.8
    xx **Animals; Primates**
Monkeys—Behavior   599.8
    x Monkeys—Habits and behavior
    xx **Animals—Behavior**

Monkeys—Habits and behavior. *See* **Monkeys—Behavior**
Monks 255; 271
   xx **Religious orders for men**
Monograms 745.6
   See also **Initials**
   x Ciphers (Lettering)
   xx **Alphabets; Decoration and ornament; Initials; Lettering**
Monologues with music 808.2; 808.82; 812, etc.
   x Declamations, Musical; Narration with music; Recitations with music
Monoplanes. *See* **Airplanes**
Monopolies 338.8
   See also **Competition; Corporation law; Railroads—Consolidation; Restraint of trade; Trusts, Industrial**
   xx **Commerce; Competition; Economics; Restraint of trade; Trusts, Industrial**
Monorail railroads 385; 625.1
   x Railroads, Single rail; Single rail railroads
   xx **Railroads**
Monroe Doctrine 327.73
   xx **International relations; Intervention (International law); Pan-Americanism; United States—Foreign relations**
Monsters 001.9; 398.2
   See also **Birth defects; Dragons; Giants; Yeti**
   x Freaks; Monstrosities
   xx **Animals—Folklore; Birth defects; Curiosities and wonders; Folklore**
Monstrosities. *See* **Monsters**
Montessori method of education 371.33; 372.1
   xx **Elementary education; Kindergarten; Teaching**
Months 529
   See also names of individual months
   xx **Calendars; Chronology**
Monumental brasses. *See* **Brasses**
Monuments (May subdiv. geog.) 725
   See also **Historic buildings; Obelisks; Pyramids; Tombs**
   x Statues
   xx **Architecture; Sculpture**
Monuments, Natural. *See* **Natural monuments**
Moon 523.3
   See also **Tides**
   xx **Astronomy; Solar system**
Moon bases. *See* **Lunar bases**
Moon cars 629.2
   x Lunar cars; Lunar rover vehicles; Lunar surface vehicles
Moon—Eclipses. *See* **Eclipses, Lunar**
Moon—Exploration 629.45
   x Lunar exploration
   xx **Space flight to the moon**
Moon—Geology. *See* **Lunar geology**
Moon (in religion, folklore, etc.). *See* **Moon worship**
Moon—Maps 523.3022
Moon—Photographs 523.3; 778.3
   xx **Lunar photography**
Moon—Photographs from space 523.2; 778.3
   xx **Space photography**
Moon photography. *See* **Lunar photography**

Moon probes. *See* **Lunar probes**
Moon rocks. *See* **Lunar petrology**
Moon soil. *See* **Lunar soil**
Moon—Surface   523.3
   See also **Lunar soil**
   x Lunar surface
   xx **Lunar soil**
Moon, Voyages to. *See* **Space flight to the moon**
Moon worship   291.2
   x Moon (in religion, folklore, etc.)
   xx **Religion**
Moonlighting. *See* **Supplementary employment**
Moors   305.892; 909
   xx **Arabs**
Moral and religious aspects. *See* subjects with the
      subdivision *Moral and religious aspects,*
      e.g. **Birth control—Moral and religious as-**
      pects; etc.
Moral conditions   900
   See also names of countries, cities, etc. with the
      subdivision *Moral conditions,* e.g. **United**
      States—Moral conditions; etc.
   x Morals
   xx **Social conditions**
Moral education   370.11
   See also **Religious education**
   x Character education; Education, Character;
      Education, Ethical; Education, Moral; Ethi-
      cal education
   xx **Education; Ethics; Religious education**
Moral philosophy. *See* **Ethics**
Moral theology, Christian. *See* **Christian ethics**
Morale   152.4
   See also **Psychological warfare;** also types of mo-
      rale, e.g. **Employee morale;** etc.
   xx **Courage**
Moralities. *See* **Morality plays**
Morality. *See* **Ethics**
Morality plays   792.1; 808.82; 812, etc.
   See also **Mysteries and miracle plays**
   x Moralities
   xx **Drama; English drama; Mysteries and miracle**
      plays; Religious drama; Theater
Morals. *See* **Ethics; Human behavior; Moral condi-**
      tions
Moravians   284
   x United Brethren
Mormon Church. *See* **Church of Jesus Christ of**
      Latter-day Saints
Mormons   289.3
   See also **Church of Jesus Christ of Latter-day**
      Saints
Morphine   362.29; 615
   See also **Heroin; Opium**
   xx **Narcotics; Opium**
Morphology. *See* **Anatomy; Anatomy, Comparative;**
      Biology; Botany—Anatomy
Morse code. *See* **Cipher and telegraph codes**
Mortality   304.6
   See also **Death**
   x Burial statistics; Death rate; Mortuary statis-
      tics
   xx **Death; Population; Vital statistics**

Mortar 666; 691

    xx **Adhesives; Plaster and plastering**

Mortgage loans. *See* **Mortgages**

Mortgages 332.63; 332.7

    See also **Agricultural credit**

    x Chattel mortgages; Home loans; Housing
         loans; Mortgage loans

    xx **Commercial law; Contracts; Credit; Invest-
         ments; Loans; Personal loans; Real estate;
         Securities**

Morticians. *See* **Undertakers and undertaking**

Mortuary customs. *See* **Cremation; Funeral rites
         and ceremonies**

Mortuary statistics. *See* **Mortality; Vital statistics**

Mosaics 729; 738.5; 748.5

    See also **Mural painting and decoration**

    xx **Decoration and ornament; Decorative arts;
         Mural painting and decoration**

Moslem art. *See* **Art, Islamic**

Moslemism. *See* **Islam**

Moslems. *See* **Muslims**

Mosques 726

    xx **Architecture; Architecture, Asian; Church ar-
         chitecture; Islam; Temples**

Mosquitoes 595.77

    x Diptera

    xx **Insects as carriers of disease**

Mosquitoes—Control 595.77; 614.4

    xx **Pests—Control**

Mosses 588

    xx **Plants**

Motels. *See* **Hotels, motels, etc.**

Mother and child 306.874

    See also **Mothers and daughters; Mothers and
         sons**

    x Child and mother; Mother-child relationship

    xx **Parent and child**

Mother-child relationship. *See* **Mother and child**

Mothers 306.874

    See also **Surrogate mothers; Teenage mothers;
         Unmarried mothers**

    x Maternity

    xx **Family; Homemakers; Women**

Mothers and daughters 305.4; 306.874

    x Daughters and mothers

    xx **Girls; Mother and child**

Mothers and sons 306.874

    x Sons and mothers

    xx **Boys; Mother and child**

Mothers' pensions 362.82

    See also **Child welfare**

    xx **Child welfare; Pensions**

Mothers, Single parent. *See* **Single parent family**

Moths 595.78

    See also **Butterflies; Caterpillars; Silkworms**

    x Cocoons; Lepidoptera

    xx **Butterflies; Insects**

Motion 531

    See also **Force and energy; Kinematics; Mechani-
         cal movements; Mechanics; Speed**

    x Kinetics

    xx **Dynamics; Force and energy; Kinematics; Me-
         chanics**

Motion picture actors. *See* **Actors**

Motion picture adaptations. *See* **Film adaptations**
Motion picture cameras 778.5
 See also **Amateur films**
 x Movie cameras
 xx **Amateur films; Cameras; Motion picture photography**
Motion picture cartoons. *See* **Animated films**
Motion picture direction. *See* **Motion pictures—Production and direction**
Motion picture festivals. *See* **Film festivals**
Motion picture industry (May subdiv. geog.) **384; 791.43**
 See also **Blacks in the motion picture industry; Women in the motion picture industry**
 x Film industry (Motion pictures)
Motion picture photography 778.5
 See also **Amateur films; Motion picture cameras**
 x Cinematography; Photography—Motion pictures
 xx **Photography**
Motion picture plays 808.82; 812, etc.
 Use as a form heading for actual screen scripts.
 x Photoplays; Scenarios; Screen plays
 xx **Drama**
Motion picture plays—Technique 808.2
 x Motion pictures—Play writing; Play writing; Playwriting
 xx **Drama—Technique**
Motion picture producers and directors 791.43; 920
 x Directors and producers; Producers and directors
Motion picture production. *See* **Motion pictures—Production and direction**
Motion picture projectors. *See* **Projectors**
Motion pictures (May subdiv. geog.) **384; 791.43**
 Use for general materials on motion pictures themselves, including motion pictures as an art form, etc. For materials on motion pictures produced by the motion picture industry of an individual country or on the motion pictures shown in an individual country, subdivide geographically, e.g. **Motion pictures—United States.**
 See also

Animals in motion pictures	producing
Blacks in motion pictures	**Videotapes**
Documentary films	**Women in motion pictures**
Experimental films	**World War, 1939-1945—**
Film adaptations	**Motion pictures and the**
Silent films	**war**
Sound—Recording and re-	

 also names of individual motion pictures
 x Cinema; Filmography; Films; Movies; Moving pictures; Talking pictures
 xx **Amusements; Audiovisual materials; Mass media; Theater**
Motion pictures, Amateur. *See* **Amateur films**
Motion pictures, American. *See* **Motion pictures—United States**
Motion pictures and children 305.23; 649; 791.43
 Use for materials dealing with the effect of motion pictures on children and youth.
 Use same form for motion pictures and other

Motion pictures and children—*Continued*
>subjects.
>*See also* **Television and children**
>*x* Children and motion pictures
>*xx* **Children; Television and children**

Motion pictures and libraries. *See* **Libraries and motion pictures**

Motion pictures—Biography   791.43092; 920

Motion pictures—Catalogs   016.79143

Motion pictures—Censorship   791.43
>*xx* **Censorship**

Motion pictures, Documentary. *See* **Documentary films**

Motion pictures, Experimental. *See* **Experimental films**

Motion pictures in education   371.3; 791.43
>Use same form for motion pictures as used in other subjects.
>*See also* **Libraries and motion pictures**
>*x* Educational films
>*xx* **Audiovisual education; Teaching—Aids and devices**

Motion pictures—Moral and religious aspects 791.43

Motion pictures—Play writing. *See* **Motion picture plays—Technique**

Motion pictures—Production and direction   384; 791.43
>*x* Direction (Motion pictures); Film direction; Film production; Filmmaking; Motion picture direction; Motion picture production
>*xx* **Theater—Production and direction**

Motion pictures, Silent. *See* **Silent films**

Motion pictures—Television adaptations. *See* **Television adaptations**

Motion pictures—United States   791.430973
>Use for materials on motion pictures produced by the motion picture industry of the United States or on motion pictures shown in the United States.
>*x* American films; American motion pictures; Motion pictures, American

Motion study   658.5
>*See also* **Time study**
>*xx* **Efficiency, Industrial; Factory management; Job analysis; Personnel management; Production standards; Time study**

Motivation (Psychology)   153.8
>*See also* **Burn out (Psychology); Wishes**
>*x* Incentive (Psychology)
>*xx* **Psychology**

Motor boats. *See* **Motorboats**

Motor buses. *See* **Buses**

Motor cars. *See* **Automobiles**

Motor coordination. *See* **Movement education**

Motor courts. *See* **Hotels, motels, etc.**

Motor cycles. *See* **Motorcycles**

Motor homes. *See* **Mobile homes**

Motor trucks. *See* **Trucks**

Motorboat racing. *See* **Boat racing**

Motorboats   623.8
>*x* Motor boats; Outboard motorboats; Power boats
>*xx* **Boats and boating**

Motorboats—Models 623.8
   xx **Machinery—Models**
Motorcycles 629.227
    See also **Minibikes;** also specific makes and
      models of motorcycles
    x Cycles, Motor; Cycling; Motor cycles; Motor-
      cycling
   xx **Bicycles and bicycling**
Motorcycling. *See* **Motorcycles**
Motoring. *See* **Automobiles—Touring**
Motorization, Military. *See* **Transportation, Mili-
    tary**
Motors. *See* **Electric motors; Engines**
Motorways. *See* **Express highways**
Mottoes 808.88; 818.008, etc.
   x Emblems
   xx **Heraldry**
Moulding (Metal). *See* **Founding**
Mounds and mound builders 930.1; 970.004
    See also **Excavations (Archeology)**
   x Barrows; Burial; Graves
   xx **Archeology; Excavations (Archeology); Indi-
    ans of North America; Indians of North
    America—Antiquities; Tombs**
Mountain animals. *See* **Alpine animals**
Mountain climbing. *See* **Mountaineering**
Mountain life 307.72
   xx **Country life**
Mountain plants. *See* **Alpine plants**
Mountaineering 796.5
   x Mountain climbing; Rock climbing
   xx **Mountains; Outdoor life**
Mountains (May subdiv. geog.) **551.4**
    Names of all mountain ranges and mountains
      are not included in this List but are to be
      added as needed.
    See also **Mountaineering; Volcanoes;** also names
      of mountain ranges, e.g. **Rocky Mountains;**
      etc.; and names of mountains, e.g. **Elk
      Mountain (Wyo.);** etc.
   xx **Geology; Physical geography**
Mourning customs. *See* **Funeral rites and ceremo-
    nies**
Mouse. *See* **Mice**
Movable books. *See* **Toy and movable books**
Movement education 152.3; 153.7; 372.86
   x Creative movement; Motor coordination
   xx **Physical education**
Movement, Freedom of. *See* **Freedom of movement**
Movements of animals. *See* **Animal locomotion**
Movie cameras. *See* **Motion picture cameras**
Movie festivals. *See* **Film festivals**
Movies. *See* **Motion pictures**
Moving, Household 648
   x Household moving
Moving pictures. *See* **Motion pictures**
Muhammedanism. *See* **Islam**
Muhammedans. *See* **Muslims**
Multiage grouping. *See* **Nongraded schools**
Multicultural education. *See* **Intercultural educa-
    tion**
Multilingual dictionaries. *See* **Polyglot dictionaries**
Multilingual glossaries, phrase books, etc. *See*
    Polyglot dictionaries

Multimedia centers. *See* **Instructional materials centers**

Multimedia materials. *See* **Audiovisual materials**

Multinational corporations   338.8; 658
> *See also* **Foreign investments**
> *x* Business enterprises, International; Business—International aspects; Corporations, International; Corporations, Multinational; International business enterprises
> *xx* **Commerce; Corporations; International economic relations**

Multiple birth   618.2
> *See also* names of multiple births, e.g. **Twins;** etc.
> *x* Birth, Multiple
> *xx* **Childbirth**

Multiple plot stories. *See* **Plot-your-own stories**

Multiplication   513.2
> *xx* **Arithmetic**

Mummies   393
> *x* Burial
> *xx* **Archeology**

Municipal administration. *See* **Municipal government**

Municipal art. *See* **Art, Municipal**

Municipal employees. *See* **Civil service; Municipal government;** and names of cities with the subdivision *Officials and employees,* e.g. **Chicago (Ill.)—Officials and employees;** etc.

Municipal engineering   628
> *See also* **Drainage; Refuse and refuse disposal; Sanitary engineering; Sewerage; Street cleaning; Water supply**
> *xx* **Engineering; Public works; Sanitary engineering**

Municipal-federal relations. *See* **Federal-city relations**

Municipal finance   352.1
> *See also* **Metropolitan finance**
> *x* Finance, Municipal
> *xx* **Finance; Municipal government**

Municipal government (May subdiv. geog.)   **320.8; 352**
> Use for materials on the government of cities in general and, when subdivided by country, for general consideration of municipal government of countries, or regions. Materials on the government of individual cities, towns, or areas are entered under the name of the city, town, or area with the subdivision *Politics and government.*
> *See also* **Cities and towns; Federal-city relations; Metropolitan government; Municipal finance; Public administration; State-local relations;** also names of cities with the subdivision *Politics and government,* e.g. **Chicago (Ill.)—Politics and government;** etc.
> *x* City government; Government, Municipal; Municipal administration; Municipal employees; Municipalities
> *xx* **Local government; Metropolitan government; Political science**

Municipal government by city manager   320.8; 352
  x City manager; Commission government with
     city manager
Municipal government by commission   320.8; 352
  x Commission government; Government by
     commission
Municipal government—United States   320.8; 352
  x United States—Municipal government
Municipal improvements.   *See* **Art, Municipal; Cit-
     ies and towns—Civic improvement;** and
     names of cities with the subdivision *Public
     works,* e.g. **Chicago (Ill.)—Public works;**
     etc.
Municipal ownership   338.9; 352
  x Public ownership
  xx **Corporations; Economic policy; Government
     ownership**
Municipal planning.   *See* **City planning**
Municipal transit.   *See* **Local transit**
Municipalities.   *See* **Cities and towns; Municipal
     government**
Munitions   338.4; 623.4
  See note under **Armaments.**
  See also **Arms race; Firearms industry; Space
     weapons;** also names of wars with the subdi-
     vision *Equipment and supplies,* e.g. **World
     War, 1939-1945—Equipment and supplies;**
     etc.
  x Arms sales
  xx **Armaments; Industrial mobilization; Interna-
     tional relations; War; War—Economic as-
     pects**
Muppets.   *See* **Puppets and puppet plays**
Mural painting and decoration   729; 751.7
  See also **Cave drawings; Mosaics; Rock draw-
     ings, paintings, and engravings**
  x Fresco painting; Wall decoration; Wall paint-
     ing
  xx **Decoration and ornament; Interior design;
     Mosaics; Painting; Walls**
Murder.   *See* **Homicide**
Murder trials.   *See* **Trials (Homicide)**
Muscles   611; 612.7
  xx **Musculoskeletal system; Physiology**
Muscular system.   *See* **Musculoskeletal system**
Musculoskeletal system   611; 612.7
  See also **Bones; Muscles**
  x Muscular system
  xx **Anatomy; Physiology**
Museums (May subdiv. geog.)   069; 708
  See also appropriate subjects, names of wars
     and corporate bodies with the subdivision
     Museums, e.g. **Art—Museums; World
     War, 1939-1945—Museums;** etc.; and
     names of galleries and museums
Museums and schools   069
  x Schools and museums
  xx **Schools**
Museums—Ohio   708.171
  x Ohio—Museums
Museums—United States   708.13
  x United States—Museums

Mushrooms   589.2; 635
> *See also* **Fungi**
> *x* Toadstools
> *xx* **Fungi**

Music (May subdiv. geog. adjective form, e.g. **Music, American;** etc.)   **780**
> All types of music are not included in this List but are to be added as needed for vocal or instrumental, classical or popular, solo or group music.
>
> *See also*

Chamber music	**Jazz music**
Church music	**Military music**
Composition (Music)	**Musicians**
Computer music	**Orchestral music**
Concerts	**Organ music**
Dance music	**Piano music**
Electronic music	**Popular music**
Folk music	**Radio and music**
Harmony	**Rock music**
Instrumental music	**Romanticism**
Instrumentation and or-	**Sound**
chestration	**Vocal music**

> also subjects with the subdivision *Songs and music,* e.g. **Cowhands—Songs and music; Surfing—Songs and music;** etc.; and headings beginning with the words **Music** and **Musical**
> *xx* **Humanities**

Music—Acoustics and physics   781.2
> *See also* **Sound**
> *x* Acoustics
> *xx* **Music—Theory; Physics; Sound**

Music, American   780.973
> *See also* **Black songs; Spirituals (Songs)**
> *x* American music; United States—Music

Music—Analysis, appreciation   781.1
> *x* Appreciation of music; Music appreciation; Musical appreciation

Music and literature   780
> *x* Literature and music; Music and poetry; Poetry and music
> *xx* **Literature**

Music and poetry. *See* **Music and literature**
Music and radio. *See* **Radio and music**
Music—Anecdotes   780
> *x* Music—Anecdotes, facetiae, satire, etc.
> *xx* **Anecdotes**

Music—Anecdotes, facetiae, satire, etc. *See* **Music—Anecdotes; Music—Humor**
Music appreciation. *See* **Music—Analysis, appreciation**
Music, Black. *See* **Black music**
Music box   786.6
> *xx* **Musical instruments, Mechanical**

Music—Cataloging. *See* **Cataloging—Music**
Music, Choral. *See* **Choral music**
Music—Composition. *See* **Composition (Music)**
Music, Computer. *See* **Computer music**
Music conductors. *See* **Conductors (Music)**
Music—Discography   016.78
Music, Dramatic. *See* **Opera; Operetta**
Music education. *See* **Music—Study and teaching**
Music, Electronic. *See* **Electronic music**

Music—Examinations 780.76
   x Music—Examinations, questions, etc.
   xx **Examinations**
Music—Examinations, questions, etc. *See* **Music— Examinations**
Music festivals 780.79
   x Musical festivals
   xx **Concerts; Festivals**
Music, Gospel. *See* **Gospel music**
Music—History and criticism 780.9
   x Musical criticism
   xx **Criticism; History**
Music—Humor 780
   x Music—Anecdotes, facetiae, satire, etc.
   xx **Wit and humor**
Music, Indian. *See* **Indians of North America— Songs and music**
Music, Influence of. *See* **Music—Psychological aspects**
Music—Instruction and study. *See* **Music—Study and teaching**
Music, Instrumental. *See* **Instrumental music**
Music libraries 026
   x Libraries, Music
   xx **Libraries; Special libraries**
Music, Military. *See* **Military music**
Music—Notation. *See* **Musical notation**
Music, Popular (Songs, etc.). *See* **Popular music**
Music—Psychological aspects 781
   x Music, Influence of; Psychology of music
   xx **Psychology**
Music, Rock. *See* **Rock music**
Music, Sacred. *See* **Church music**
Music—Study and teaching 780.7
   See also **Composition (Music); Conducting; Musical form**
   x Education, Musical; Music education; Music—Instruction and study; Musical education; Musical instruction; School music
Music—Theory 781
   See also **Composition (Music); Counterpoint; Fugue; Harmony; Music—Acoustics and physics; Musical form; Musical meter and rhythm**
Music videos 384.55; 778.59
   x Videos, Music
   xx **Television programs; Videodiscs; Videotapes**
Music, Vocal. *See* **Vocal music**
Musical ability 780.7
   x Musical talent; Talent
   xx **Ability**
Musical accompaniment 781.47
   x Accompaniment, Musical
   xx **Composition (Music)**
Musical appreciation. *See* **Music—Analysis, appreciation**
Musical comedies. *See* **Musicals**
Musical composition. *See* **Composition (Music)**
Musical criticism. *See* **Music—History and criticism**
Musical education. *See* **Music—Study and teaching**
Musical festivals. *See* **Music festivals**

460

Musical form   784.18
>   *See also* names of specific types of musical
>   forms, e.g. **Concerto; Fugue; Opera; Oper-**
>   **etta; Sonata; Symphony;** etc. Add names of
>   musical forms as needed for the music itself,
>   e.g. **Concertos; Suites;** etc.
>   *x* Form, Musical
>   *xx* **Music—Study and teaching; Music—Theory**

Musical instruction.   *See* **Music—Study and teach-**
        ing
Musical instruments   784.19
>   *See also* **Instrumental music; Instrumentation**
>   **and orchestration; Orchestra; Tuning;** also
>   groups of instruments, e.g. **Percussion in-**
>   **struments; Stringed instruments; Wind in-**
>   **struments;** etc.; and names of specific musi-
>   cal instruments, e.g. **Drum; Organ;** etc.
>   *x* Instruments, Musical
>   *xx* **Instrumental music; Instrumentation and or-**
>   **chestration**

Musical instruments, Electronic   786.7
>   *See also* **Synthesizer (Musical instrument)**
>   *x* Electronic musical instruments

Musical instruments, Mechanical   786.6
>   *See also* names of instruments, e.g. **Music box;**
>   etc.
>   *x* Mechanical musical instruments

Musical meter and rhythm   781.2
>   *x* Meter
>   *xx* **Music—Theory; Rhythm**

Musical notation   780.1
>   *x* Music—Notation; Notation, Music

Musical revues, comedies, etc.   *See* **Musicals**
Musical talent.   *See* **Musical ability**
Musicals   782.1; 792.6
>   *See also* **Operetta**
>   *x* Dramatic music; Musical comedies; Musical
>   revues, comedies, etc.
>   *xx* **Operetta**

Musicians (May subdiv. geog. adjective form)
        780.92; 920
>   *See also* **Violinists, violoncellists, etc.;** also types
>   of musicians, e.g. **Composers; Conductors**
>   **(Music); Organists; Pianists; Singers; Vio-**
>   **linists, Violoncellists, etc.;** etc.; and names
>   of musicians
>   *xx* **Music**

Musicians, American   780.92; 920
>   *x* American musicians; United States—
>   Musicians

Musicians—Biography   780.92; 920
>   *xx* **Biography**

Musicians, Black.   *See* **Black musicians**
Musicians—Portraits   780.92
>   *xx* **Portraits**

Muslim countries.   *See* **Islamic countries**
Muslimism.   *See* **Islam**
Muslims (May subdiv. geog.)   **297**
>   *x* Mohammedans; Moslems; Muhammedans;
>   Mussulmans

Muslims, Black.   *See* **Black Muslims**
Muslims—United States   297.0973
>   *See also* **Black Muslims**
>   *x* United States—Muslims

461

Mussulmans. *See* **Muslims**

Mutation (Biology). *See* **Evolution; Variation (Biology)**

Mutual defense assistance program. *See* **Military assistance**

Mutual funds. *See* **Investment trusts**

Mycology. *See* **Fungi**

Myotherapy. *See* **Acupressure**

Mysteries and miracle plays 808.82; 812, etc.
    See also **Morality plays**
    x Bible plays; Miracle plays
    xx **Bible—Drama; Drama; English drama; Morality plays; Pageants; Passion plays; Religious drama; Theater**

Mystery and detective stories 808.83; 813, etc.; Fic
    May be used for single novels as well as for collections of stories.
    x Detective stories; Stories
    xx **Fiction**

Mysticism 149; 248.2
    See also **Cabala; Religious art and symbolism; Spiritual life; Symbolism of numbers; Theosophy**
    xx **Philosophy; Religion; Theology**

Mythical animals 398.24; Fic
    See also **Animals—Folklore;** also names of mythical animals, e.g. **Dragons; Giants; Mermaids and mermen; Vampires;** etc.
    x Animal lore; Animals, Fictitious; Animals, Imaginary; Animals, Mythical; Creatures, Imaginary; Fictitious animals; Imaginary animals
    xx **Animals—Folklore; Mythology**

Mythology (May use ethnic or geog. subdiv. adjective form) **291.1**
    See also

Art and mythology	**Indians of North America—Religion**
Folklore	
Geographical myths	**Mythical animals**
Gods and goddesses	**Symbolism**
Heroes and heroines	**Totems and totemism**

    x Myths
    xx **Creation; Folklore; God; Gods and goddesses; Heroes and heroines; Legends; Religion; Religions**

Mythology, Classical 292.1
    x Classical mythology; Greek mythology; Roman mythology
    xx **Classical antiquities**

Mythology in art. *See* **Art and mythology**

Mythology, Indian. *See* **Indians of North America—Religion**

Myths. *See* **Mythology**

N.A.T.O. *See* **North Atlantic Treaty Organization**

Names 929.4
    See also types of names, e.g. **Code names; Geographic names; Personal names; Pseudonyms;** etc.
    x Epithets; Nomenclature; Proper names; Terminology

Names, Fictitious. *See* **Pseudonyms**

Names, Geographical. *See* **Geographic names**

Names, Geographical—United States. *See* **Geographic names—United States**

Names, Personal. *See* **Personal names**
Names, Personal—Scottish. *See* **Personal names, Scottish**
Names, Personal—United States. *See* **Personal names—United States**
Names—Pronunciation 421
   x Pronunciation
Napoleon I, Emperor of the French, 1769-1821—Drama 808.82; 812, etc.
Napoleon I, Emperor of the French, 1769-1821—Fiction 813, etc.
Napoleonic Wars. *See* **Europe—History—1789-1900; France—History—1789-1799, Revolution**
Narcotic addiction counseling. *See* **Drug abuse counseling**
Narcotic addicts. *See* **Drug addicts**
Narcotic habit. *See* **Drug addiction**
Narcotic traffic. *See* **Drug traffic**
Narcotics 178; 394.1; 615
   See also **Cocaine; Endorphins; Opium; Stimulants;** also names of specific narcotics, e.g. **Heroin; Marijuana; Morphine;** etc.
   x Opiates; Soporifics
   xx **Drugs; Materia medica; Stimulants; Therapeutics**
Narcotics and crime. *See* **Drugs and crime**
Narcotics and criminals. *See* **Criminals—Drug use**
Narcotics and teenagers. *See* **Teenagers—Drug use**
Narcotics and youth. *See* **Youth—Drug use**
Narration with music. *See* **Monologues with music**
Nation of Islam. *See* **Black Muslims**
National anthems. *See* **National songs**
National book week 021.7
   x Book week, National
   xx **Books and reading**
National characteristics (May subdiv. geog. adjective form)
   See also **Ethnopsychology**
   x Characteristics, National; Images, National; National images; National psychology; Psychology, National
   xx **Anthropology; Ethnopsychology; Nationalism; Social psychology**
National characteristics, American 306.0973; 973
   x American characteristics; American national characteristics; United States—National characteristics
National consciousness. *See* **Nationalism**
National dances. *See* **Folk dancing**
National debts. *See* **Public debts**
National defenses. *See* **Industrial mobilization;** and names of countries with the subdivision *Defenses,* e.g. **United States—Defenses;** etc.
National forests. *See* **Forest reserves**
National Guard (U.S.). *See* **United States. National Guard**
National health service. *See* **Medicine, State**
National holidays. *See* **Holidays;** and names of national holidays, e.g. **Memorial Day;** etc.
National hymns. *See* **National songs**
National images. *See* **National characteristics**
National interest. *See* **Public interest**

National liberation movements (May subdiv. geog. except U.S.) **320.5**

　See also **Guerrillas;** also names of specific groups

　x Liberation movements, National

　xx **Colonies; Guerrillas; Nationalism; Revolutions**

National libraries　027.5

　Use for materials on libraries, maintained by government funds, that serve the nation as a whole, particularly in the function of collection and preservation of a nation's publications.

　x Libraries, National

　xx **Government libraries**

National monuments.　*See* **National parks and reserves; Natural monuments**

National parks and reserves (May subdiv. geog.) **363.6; 719**

　See also **Forest reserves; Natural monuments; Wilderness areas;** also names of national parks, e.g. **Yosemite National Park (Calif.);** etc.

　x National monuments; Public lands

　xx **Conservation of natural resources; Forest reserves; Parks; Wildlife conservation**

National parks and reserves—United States　719; 917.3

　x United States—National parks and reserves

National planning.　*See* **Economic policy; Social policy;** and names of countries with the subdivision *Economic policy* or *Social policy,* e.g. **United States—Economic policy; United States—Social policy;** etc.; and appropriate topical subjects with the subdivision *Government policy,* e.g. **Environment—Government policy;** etc.

National psychology.　*See* **Ethnopsychology; National characteristics**

National resources.　*See* **Natural resources;** and names of countries with the subdivision *Economic conditions,* e.g. **United States—Economic conditions;** etc.

National security　350; 355

　See also **Economic policy; International relations; Military policy;** also names of countries with the subdivision *National security,* e.g. **United States—National security;** etc.

　xx **Economic policy; International relations; Military policy**

National socialism　320.5; 335.6

　Use for materials limited to fascism in Germany during the Nazi regime.

　See also **Fascism; Neo-Nazis; Socialism**

　x Nazism

　xx **Fascism; Fascism—Germany; Neo-Nazis; Socialism; Totalitarianism; World War, 1939-1945—Causes**

National songs (May subdiv. geog. adjective form) **782.42**

　See also **Folk songs; Patriotic poetry; War songs**

　x Anthems, National; National anthems; National hymns; Patriotic songs; Songs, National

　xx **Folk songs; Songs**

National songs, American   782.420973
  x American national songs; United States—
        National songs
  xx **Songs, American**
Nationalism (May subdiv. geog.)   **320.5**
  See also **Minorities; National characteristics;**
        National liberation movements; Patriotism
  x Internationalism; National consciousness; Re-
        gionalism
  xx **International relations; Minorities; Patriotism;**
        Political science
Nationalism, Black. *See* **Black nationalism**
Nationalism—United States   320.5
Nationalist China. *See* **Taiwan**
Nationality (Citizenship). *See* **Citizenship**
Nationalization. *See* **Government ownership**
Nationalization of railroads. *See* **Railroads—**
        Government policy
Nations, Law of. *See* **International law**
Native Americans. *See* **Indians of North America**
Native peoples. *See* **Ethnology; Indians of North**
        America
Nativity of Christ. *See* **Jesus Christ—Nativity**
NATO. *See* **North Atlantic Treaty Organization**
Natural beauty conservation. *See* **Landscape pro-**
        tection
Natural Bridge (Va.)   975.5
  xx **Natural monuments**
Natural childbirth   618.4
  x Childbirth, Natural; Lamaze method of child-
        birth
  xx **Childbirth**
Natural disasters (May subdiv. geog.)   **904**
  See also **Storms; Tsunamis;** also types of natural
        disasters, e.g. **Earthquakes; Floods;** etc.
  xx **Disasters**
Natural disasters—United States   973
  x United States—Natural disasters
Natural food cookery. *See* **Cookery—Natural foods**
Natural foods   641.3
  See also **Cookery—Natural foods**
  x Food, Natural; Health foods; Organically
        grown foods
  xx **Cookery—Natural foods; Food**
Natural gas   665.5; 665.7
  See also **Boring**
  x Gas, Natural
  xx **Geology, Economic; Wells**
Natural history (May subdiv. geog.)   **508**
  Use for popular materials describing animals,
        plants, minerals and nature in general. Ma-
        terials on the study of animals and plants,
        especially by amateurs, are entered under
        Nature study.
  See also

Aquariums	**Freshwater biology**
Biogeography	**Geology**
Biology	**Marine biology**
Botany	**Mineralogy**
Fossils	**Zoology**

  x Animal lore; History, Natural
  xx **Animals; Biology; Science; Zoology**
Natural history, Biblical. *See* **Bible—Natural his-**
        tory

Natural history—Outdoor guides. *See* **Nature study**
Natural history—United States 508.73
  x United States—Natural history
Natural law. *See* **Ethics; Freedom; International law**
Natural monuments (May subdiv. geog.) **719**
  Use for general materials on natural objects of historic or scientific interest such as caves, cliffs, and natural bridges, and for those created as national monuments by presidential proclamation.
  See also **Wilderness areas;** also names of natural monuments, e.g. **Natural Bridge (Va.);** etc.
  x Landmarks, Preservation of; Monuments, Natural; National monuments; Preservation of natural scenery; Protection of natural scenery
  xx **Landscape protection; National parks and reserves; Nature conservation**
Natural monuments—United States 719; 917.3
  x United States—Natural monuments
Natural parents. *See* **Birthparents**
Natural pesticides 668
  xx **Pesticides**
Natural religion. *See* **Natural theology**
Natural resources (May subdiv. geog.) **333.7**
  See also **Conservation of natural resources; Fisheries; Reclamation of land;** also names of natural resources, e.g. **Energy resources; Forests and forestry; Marine resources; Mines and mineral resources;** etc.
  x National resources; Resources, Natural
  xx **Economic conditions; Environment— Government policy; Wildlife conservation**
Natural resources—Management 333.7
  xx **Management**
Natural resources—United States 333.7
  See also **United States—Economic conditions**
  x United States—Natural resources
Natural selection 575.01
  See also **Evolution; Heredity**
  x Selection, Natural; Survival of the fittest
  xx **Evolution; Genetics; Heredity; Variation (Biology)**
Natural steam energy. *See* **Geothermal resources**
Natural theology 210
  Use for materials dealing with the knowledge of God's existence obtained by observing the visible processes of nature.
  See also **Creation; Religion and science**
  x Natural religion; Theology, Natural
  xx **Apologetics; God; Religion; Religion and science; Theology**
Natural therapy. *See* **Naturopathy**
Naturalism in literature. *See* **Realism in literature**
Naturalists 508.092; 920
  See also names of types of naturalists, e.g. **Biologists; Botanists;** etc.
  xx **Scientists**
Naturalization 323.6
  See also **Aliens; Citizenship**
  x Foreigners
  xx **Aliens; Americanization; Citizenship; Immi-**

Naturalization—*Continued*
>> gration and emigration; International law;
>> Suffrage

Nature conservation   333.7
> *See also* **Endangered species; Landscape protection; Natural monuments; Plant conservation; Wildlife conservation**
> *x* Conservation of nature; Nature protection; Preservation of natural scenery; Protection of natural scenery
> *xx* **Conservation of natural resources**

Nature craft   745.5
> Use for materials on crafts using objects found in nature, e.g., eggshells, feathers, flowers, leaves, nuts, sand, seeds, shells, twigs, vegetables, etc.
> *x* Naturecraft
> *xx* **Handicraft**

Nature, Effect of man on.   *See* **Man—Influence on nature**

Nature in literature   809
> *See also* **Animals in literature; Birds in literature; Nature in poetry**

Nature in poetry   809.1
> *x* Nature poetry; Poetry of nature
> *xx* **Nature in literature; Poetry**

Nature photography   778.9
> *See also* **Outdoor photography; Photography of animals; Photography of birds; Photography of fishes; Photography of plants**
> *x* Photography of nature
> *xx* **Nature study; Outdoor photography; Photography**

Nature poetry.   *See* **Nature in poetry**

Nature protection.   *See* **Nature conservation**

Nature study (May subdiv. geog.)   **372.3; 508**
> See note under **Natural history.**
> *See also* **Animals—Behavior; Botany; Nature photography; Zoology**
> *x* Natural history—Outdoor guides
> *xx* **Animals—Behavior; Education; Outdoor life; Science—Study and teaching**

Nature study—United States   508.73
> *x* United States—Nature study

Naturecraft.   *See* **Nature craft**

Naturopathy   615.5
> *See also* **Chiropractic**
> *x* Natural therapy
> *xx* **Alternative medicine; Chiropractic; Therapeutics**

Nautical almanacs   528
> *x* Ephemerides
> *xx* **Almanacs; Navigation**

Nautical astronomy   527
> *See also* **Latitude; Longitude; Navigation**
> *x* Astronomy, Nautical
> *xx* **Astronomy; Navigation**

Navaho Indians.   *See* **Navajo Indians**

Navaho language.   *See* **Navajo language**

Navajo Indians   970.004
> *x* Navaho Indians
> *xx* **Indians of North America**

Navajo language 497

   x Navaho language

   xx **Indians of North America—Languages**

Naval administration. *See* **Naval art and science;**
       and names of countries with the subhead
       Navy, e.g. **United States. Navy;** etc.

Naval aeronautics. *See* **Aeronautics, Military**

Naval air bases. *See* **Air bases**

Naval airplanes. *See* **Airplanes, Military**

Naval architecture 623.8

   See also **Boatbuilding; Marine engineering; Ship-
      building; Ships; Steamboats; Warships**

   x Architecture, Naval; Marine architecture

   xx **Architecture; Shipbuilding**

Naval art and science 359

   See also

Camouflage (Military science)	Sailors
	Sea power
Marine engineering	Shipbuilding
Military art and science	Signals and signaling
Navies	Strategy
Navigation	Submarine warfare
Navy yards and naval stations	Submarines
	Torpedoes
Privateering	Warships

   x Fighting; Naval administration; Naval sci-
      ence; Naval warfare; Navy

   xx **Military art and science; Navies; Navigation;
      Strategy; War**

Naval art and science—Study and teaching. *See*
      Naval education

Naval bases. *See* **Navy yards and naval stations**

Naval battles 359.4; 904

   See also **Battles; Naval history;** also names of
      countries with the subdivision *History, Na-
      val,* e.g. **United States—History, Naval;**
      etc.; names of wars with the subdivision
      Naval operations, e.g. **World War, 1939-
      1945—Naval operations;** etc.; and names of
      naval battles

   x Naval warfare

   xx **Battles; Sea power**

Naval biography. *See* names of navies with the
      subdivision *Biography,* e.g. **United States.
      Navy—Biography;** etc.

Naval education 359.5

   x Education, Naval; Naval art and science—
      Study and teaching; Naval schools

   xx **Education**

Naval engineering. *See* **Marine engineering**

Naval history 359.409

   See also **Military history; Pirates; Privateering;
      Sea power;** also names of countries with the
      subhead *Navy* or the subdivision *History,
      Naval,* e.g. **United States. Navy; United
      States—History, Naval;** etc.

   x History, Naval; Wars

   xx **History; Military history; Naval battles; Sea
      power**

Naval law. *See* **Maritime law**

Naval offenses. *See* **Military offenses**

Naval pensions. *See* **Pensions, Military**

Naval personnel. *See* **Sailors**

Naval power. *See* **Sea power**

Naval schools. *See* **Naval education**
Naval science. *See* **Naval art and science**
Naval shipyards. *See* **Navy yards and naval stations**
Naval signaling. *See* **Signals and signaling**
Naval strategy. *See* **Strategy**
Naval uniforms. *See* **Uniforms, Military**
Naval warfare. *See* **Naval art and science; Naval
battles; Submarine warfare;** and names of
wars with the subdivision *Naval operations,*
e.g. **World War, 1939-1945—Naval opera-
tions;** etc.
Navies   359.3
See also **Admirals; Armies; Arms control; Naval
art and science; Sailors; Sea power; Warships;** also names of countries with the subhead *Navy,* e.g. **United States. Navy;** etc.
x Military forces; Military power; Navy
xx **Armaments; Armed forces; Armies; Military
personnel; Naval art and science; Sea power;
Ships; War; Warships**
Navigation   527; 623.89
See also

Compass	**Orienteering**
Harbors	**Pilot guides**
Inland navigation	**Pilots and pilotage**
Knots and splices	**Radar**
Lighthouses	**Sailing**
Loran	**Shipwrecks**
Nautical almanacs	**Signals and signaling**
Nautical astronomy	**Steam navigation**
Naval art and science	**Tides**
Ocean currents	**Winds**

x Locomotion; Seamanship
xx **Direction sense; Nautical astronomy; Naval
art and science; Oceanography; Pilots and
pilotage; Sailing; Ships; Steam navigation**
Navigation, Aerial. *See* **Navigation (Aeronautics)**
Navigation (Aeronautics)   629.132
See also **Airplanes—Piloting; Radio in aeronau-
tics**
x Aerial navigation; Aeronautics—Navigation;
Air navigation; Navigation, Aerial
xx **Aeronautics**
Navigation (Astronautics)   629.45
See also **Astronautical instruments; Space flight;
Space vehicles—Piloting**
x Astronavigation; Space navigation
xx **Astrodynamics; Astronautics; Space flight**
Navigation, Inland. *See* **Inland navigation**
Navigation—Law and legislation. *See* **Maritime
law**
Navigation, Steam. *See* **Steam navigation**
Navigators. *See* **Discoveries (in geography); Ex-
plorers; Sailors**
Navy. *See* **Naval art and science; Navies; Sea
power;** and names of countries with the
subhead *Navy,* e.g. **United States. Navy;**
etc.
Navy Sealab project. *See* **Sealab project**
Navy yards and naval stations   359.7
x Naval bases; Naval shipyards
xx **Naval art and science**
Nazism. *See* **National socialism**
Near East. *See* **Middle East**

Neatness. *See* **Cleanliness**
Nebulae, Extragalactic. *See* **Galaxies**
Necrologies. *See* **Obituaries**
Necromancy. *See* **Divination; Witchcraft**
Needlepoint 746.2
> *x* Canvas embroidery
> *xx* **Embroidery; Needlework**
Needlework 746.4
> *See also* types of needlework, e.g. **Dressmaking; Embroidery; Lace and lace making; Needle-point; Sewing; Tapestry;** etc.
> *xx* **Decoration and ornament; Decorative arts; Dressmaking; Sewing**
Negotiable instruments 332.4; 332.7
> *See also* **Bonds**
> *x* Bills and notes; Bills of credit; Commercial paper; Instruments, Negotiable; Letters of credit
> *xx* **Banks and banking; Commercial law; Contracts; Credit**
Negotiation 158; 302.3
> *See also* **Arbitration, Industrial; Collective bargaining; Hostage negotiation**
> *x* Bargaining; Discussion
> *xx* **Psychology, Applied**
Negritude. *See* **Blacks—Race identity**
Negroes. *See* **Blacks**
Neighborhood. *See* **Community life**
Neighborhood centers. *See* **Social settlements**
Neighborhood development. *See* **Community development**
Neighborhood schools. *See* **Schools**
Neo-fascism. *See* **Fascism**
Neo-Greek literature. *See* **Greek literature, Modern**
Neo-impressionism (Art). *See* **Impressionism (Art)**
Neo-Latin languages. *See* **Romance languages**
Neo-Nazis 320.5
> Use for materials on political groups whose social beliefs or political agendas are reminiscent of those of Hitler's Nazis.
> *See also* **National socialism**
> *xx* **National socialism**
Neo-nazism. *See* **Fascism**
Neolithic period. *See* **Stone Age**
Neon tubes 621.32
> *xx* **Electric signs**
Nero, Emperor of Rome, 37-68 92; B
> *xx* **Roman emperors**
Nerves 611; 612.8
> *See also* **Nervous system**
> *xx* **Nervous system**
Nerves—Diseases. *See* **Nervous system—Diseases**
Nervous breakdown. *See* **Neurasthenia**
Nervous exhaustion. *See* **Neurasthenia**
Nervous prostration. *See* **Neurasthenia**
Nervous system 611; 612.8
> *See also* **Brain; Nerves; Psychology, Pathological; Psychophysiology**
> *x* Neurology
> *xx* **Anatomy; Brain; Mind and body; Nerves; Physiology**
Nervous system—Diseases 616.8
> *See also* **Epilepsy; Fear; Neurasthenia; Worry**
> *x* Nerves—Diseases; Neuropathology

Nests. *See* **Birds—Eggs and nests**
Netherlands   949.2
   x Holland
Netherlands—History   949.2
**Netherlands—History—1940-1945, German occupa-
      tion   949.207**
   x German occupation of Netherlands, 1940-
      1945
   xx **Military occupation; World War, 1939-1945—
      Occupied territories**
Network theory. *See* **System analysis**
Networks, Computer. *See* **Computer networks**
Networks, Information. *See* **Information networks**
Networks, Library. *See* **Library information net-
      works**
Neurasthenia   616.8
   x Nervous breakdown; Nervous exhaustion;
      Nervous prostration
   xx **Nervous system—Diseases**
Neurology. *See* **Nervous system**
Neuropathology. *See* **Nervous system—Diseases**
Neuroses   616.8
   See also **Depression, Mental; Fear; Medicine,
      Psychosomatic; Phobias**
   xx **Psychology, Pathological**
Neutrality   327.1; 341.6
   See also **Intervention (International law);** also
      names of countries with the subdivision
      Neutrality, e.g. **United States—Neutrality;**
      etc.
   x Nonalignment
   xx **International law; International relations; In-
      tervention (International law); Security, In-
      ternational**
Neutron bombs   623.4
   xx **Bombs; Neutron weapons**
Neutron weapons   623.4
   See also **Neutron bombs**
   x Enhanced radiation weapons; Weapons, En-
      hanced radiation; Weapons, Neutron
   xx **Nuclear weapons**
Neutrons   539.7
   See also **Atoms; Electrons; Protons**
   xx **Particles (Nuclear physics); Quantum theory**
New Age movement   131; 133; 291; 299
   Use for materials on the group of post-1970 cults
      and organizations influenced by Eastern and
      Native American religions, by occult beliefs
      and practices, mysticism, etc., and employ-
      ing techniques, such as meditation, to en-
      hance consciousness and develop human
      potential.
   x Aquarian Age movement
   xx **Cults; Occultism; Social movements**
New birth (Theology). *See* **Regeneration (Theology)**
New England   974
   xx **United States**
New France—History. *See* **Canada—History—0-
      1763 (New France); Mississippi River Val-
      ley—History**
New left. *See* **Right and left (Political science)**
New nations. *See* **States, New**
New Negro Movement. *See* **Harlem Renaissance**
New Testament. *See* **Bible. N.T.**

New words. *See* **Words, New**
Newbery Medal books   028.5
   xx **Children's literature; Literary prizes**
News agencies   070.4
   x News services; Wire agencies
   xx **Press**
News broadcasting. *See* **Broadcast journalism**
News photography. *See* **Photojournalism**
News services. *See* **News agencies**
Newspaper advertising   659.13
   Use for materials discussing advertising in news-
      papers. Materials discussing advertising of
      newspapers are entered under **Advertis-
      ing—Newspapers.**
   x Advertising, Newspaper
   xx **Newspapers**
Newspaper clippings. *See* **Clippings (Books, news-
      papers, etc.)**
Newspaper work. *See* **Reporters and reporting**
Newspapers   070
   See note under **Journalism.**
   See also **Clippings (Books, newspapers, etc.);
      Freedom of the press; Journalism; Newspa-
      per advertising; Periodicals; Press; Report-
      ers and reporting; also American newspa-
      pers; English newspapers;** etc.; and names
      of individual newspapers
   xx **Journalism; Mass media; Periodicals; Press;
      Serial publications**
Newspapers—Advertising. *See* **Advertising—
      Newspapers**
Newspapers—Indexes   070.1
   xx **Indexes**
Nicene Creed   238
   xx **Creeds**
Nicknames   929.4
   x Epithets; Sobriquets; Soubriquets
   xx **Personal names**
Night   529
   See also **Bedtime; Day**
   xx **Chronology; Day; Time**
Night schools. *See* **Evening and continuation
      schools**
Nike rocket   623.4
   xx **Guided missiles**
Nineteenth century   909.81
   Use for general materials covering progress and
      development during this period in one or in
      several countries.
   x 1800-1899 (19th century)
   xx **History, Modern—1800-1899 (19th century)**
Nitrates   546; 661
   xx **Fertilizers and manures**
Nitrogen   546; 665
   xx **Gases**
NMR imaging. *See* **Magnetic resonance imaging**
No fault automobile insurance. *See* **Automobile in-
      surance**
Nobel prizes   001.4; 807.9
   xx **Rewards (Prizes, etc.)**
Nobility   305.5; 929.7
   See also **Aristocracy; Heraldry; Knights and
      knighthood**

Nobility—*Continued*

   x Baronage; Peerage

   xx **Aristocracy; Heraldry; Social classes**

Noise   534

   See also subjects with the subdivision *Noise,*
       e.g. **Airplanes—Noise;** etc.

   xx **Public health; Sound**

Noise pollution   363.7

   See also subjects with the subdivision *Noise,*
       e.g. **Airplanes—Noise;** etc.

   xx **Pollution**

Nomads   304.2; 306.08

   x Pastoral peoples

   xx **Nonliterate folk society**

Nomenclature. *See* **Names;** and scientific and
      technical subjects with the subdivision
      Terminology, e.g. **Botany—Terminology;**
      etc.

Nomination of presidents. *See* **Presidents—United
      States—Nomination**

Non-proliferation of nuclear weapons. *See* **Arms
      control**

Non-promotion (School). *See* **Promotion (School)**

Non-victim crimes. *See* **Crimes without victims**

Non-wage payments. *See* **Nonwage payments**

Nonalignment. *See* **Neutrality**

Nonbook materials. *See* **Audiovisual materials**

Noncitizens. *See* **Aliens**

Nonconformity. *See* **Conformity; Counter culture;
      Dissent**

Nondenominational churches. *See* **Community
      churches**

Nonfamily households. *See* **Shared housing**

Nonfiction films. *See* **Documentary films**

Nonformal colleges and universities. *See* **Free uni-
      versities**

Nonformal schools. *See* **Experimental schools**

Nonfossil fuels. *See* **Synthetic fuels**

Nongraded schools   371.2

   x Multiage grouping; Schools, Nongraded;
      Schools, Ungraded; Ungraded schools

   xx **Ability grouping in education; Education—
      Experimental methods**

Noninstitutional churches   289.9

   x Avant-garde churches; Churches, Avant-garde;
      Churches, Noninstitutional

Nonlinguistic communication. *See* **Nonverbal com-
      munication**

Nonliterate folk society   305.8; 306

   See also **Nomads; Nonliterate man**

   x Folk society, Nonliterate; Illiterate societies;
      Preliterate society; Primitive society; Soci-
      ety, Nonliterate folk; Society, Primitive

   xx **Civilization; Ethnology; Sociology**

Nonliterate man   306

   x Man, Nonliterate; Man, Primitive; Preliterate
      man; Primitive man

   xx **Ethnology; Nonliterate folk society**

Nonmarital relations. *See* **Unmarried couples**

Nonnationals. *See* **Aliens**

Nonnutritive sweeteners. *See* **Sugar substitutes**

Nonobjective art. *See* **Art, Abstract**

Nonprescription drugs   615
>   *x* Drugs, Nonprescription; Over-the-counter
>   drugs; Patent medicines

Nonprint materials.   *See* **Audiovisual materials**

Nonprofitable drugs.   *See* **Orphan drugs**

Nonpublic schools.   *See* **Church schools; Private
    schools**

Nonrelated families.   *See* **Shared housing**

Nonsense verses   808.81; 811, etc.
>   *See also* **Limericks; Tongue twisters**
>   *x* Rhymes
>   *xx* **Children's poetry; Humorous poetry; Limer-
>   icks; Poetry—Collections; Wit and humor**

Nonsupport.   *See* **Desertion and nonsupport**

Nonverbal communication   302.2
>   *See also* **Deaf—Means of communication; Hug-
>   ging; Personal space;** also types of nonver-
>   bal communication, e.g. **Body language;**
>   etc.
>   *x* Nonlinguistic communication
>   *xx* **Communication; Deaf—Means of communica-
>   tion**

Nonvictim crimes.   *See* **Crimes without victims**

Nonviolence   172; 322.4
>   *See also* **Hunger strikes; Pacifism; Passive resis-
>   tance**
>   *xx* **Pacifism; Passive resistance**

Nonviolent noncooperation.   *See* **Passive resistance**

Nonwage payments   331.25
>   *x* Employee benefits; Fringe benefits; Non-wage
>   payments
>   *xx* **Wages**

Nonword stories.   *See* **Stories without words**

Nordic peoples.   *See* **Teutonic peoples**

Normal schools.   *See* **Teachers colleges**

Normandy (France), Attack on, 1944   940.54
>   *x* D Day

Normans   941.02
>   *See also* **Vikings**
>   *xx* **Great Britain—History—1066-1154, Norman
>   period; Vikings**

Norse languages.   *See* **Old Norse language; Scandi-
    navian languages**

Norse legends.   *See* **Legends, Norse**

Norse literature.   *See* **Old Norse literature; Scandi-
    navian literature**

Norsemen.   *See* **Vikings**

North Africa   961
>   Use for materials dealing collectively with Mo-
>   rocco, Algeria, Tunisia, and Libya.
>   *x* Africa, North; Barbary States; Maghreb

North America   970
>   *See also* **Pacific Northwest**
>   *xx* **America**

North America—Exploration.   *See* **America—
    Exploration**

North American Indians.   *See* **Indians of North
    America**

North Atlantic Treaty Organization   341.24
>   *x* N.A.T.O.; NATO

North Central States.   *See* **Middle West**

North Korea.   *See* **Korea (North)**

North Pole   910.9163; 998
> *See also* **Arctic regions**
> *x* Polar expeditions
> *xx* **Arctic regions; Polar regions**

Northeast Africa   960
> Use for materials dealing collectively with Sudan, Ethiopia, Somalia, and Djibouti.
> *x* Africa, Northeast
> *xx* **East Africa**

Northeast Passage   998
> *xx* **Arctic regions; Discoveries (in geography); Voyages and travels**

Northern lights.   *See* **Auroras**

Northmen.   *See* **Vikings**

Northwest Africa   964
> Use for materials dealing collectively with the area extending eastward from Morocco, Western Sahara, and Mauritania to include Libya and Chad. Northwest Africa includes the political entities of Morocco, Western Sahara, Mauritania, Algeria, Mali, Tunisia, Libya, Niger, and Chad.
> *x* Africa, Northwest

Northwest, Canadian   971.2
> *x* Canada, Northwest; Canadian Northwest
> *xx* **Canada**

Northwest coast of North America   979.5
> *x* Northwest, Pacific coast; Pacific Northwest coast

Northwest, Old.   *See* **Old Northwest**

Northwest, Pacific.   *See* **Pacific Northwest**

Northwest, Pacific coast.   *See* **Northwest coast of North America**

Northwest Passage   971.9
> *xx* **America—Exploration; Arctic regions; Discoveries (in geography); Voyages and travels**

Northwest Territory.   *See* **Old Northwest**

Norwegian language   439.8
> May be subdivided like **English language.**
> *See also* **Danish language**
> *xx* **Scandinavian languages**

Norwegian language—0-1350.   *See* **Old Norse language**

Norwegian literature   839.8
> May use same subdivisions and names of literary forms as for **English literature.**
> *xx* **Scandinavian literature**

Nose   611; 612.2
> *xx* **Face; Head; Smell**

Notation, Mathematical.   *See* **Mathematical notation**

Notation, Music.   *See* **Musical notation**

Novelists (May subdiv. geog. adjective form)   809.3; 920
> *xx* **Authors**

Novelists, American   813.009; 920
> *x* American novelists; United States—Novelists

Novels.   *See* **Fiction**

Novels—Plots.   *See* **Plots (Drama, fiction, etc.)**

Nuclear bomb shelters.   *See* **Air raid shelters**

Nuclear energy   539.7; 621.48
> *See also* **Nuclear engineering; Nuclear industry; Nuclear power plants; Nuclear propulsion;**

Nuclear energy—*Continued*
> **Nuclear reactors**
> *x* Atomic energy; Atomic power; Nuclear power
> *xx* **Atomic theory; Nuclear physics; Nuclear power plants**

Nuclear engineering   621.48
> *See also* **Nuclear reactors; Radioactive waste disposal; Radioisotopes**
> *xx* **Engineering; Nuclear energy; Nuclear physics**

Nuclear freeze movement. *See* **Antinuclear movement**

Nuclear industry   621.48
> *x* Atomic industry
> *xx* **Nuclear energy**

Nuclear magnetic resonance imaging. *See* **Magnetic resonance imaging**

Nuclear medicine   616.9
> *x* Atomic medicine; Medicine, Atomic; Medicine, Nuclear
> *xx* **Radiation—Physiological effect**

Nuclear particles. *See* **Particles (Nuclear physics)**

Nuclear physics   539.7
> *See also*

Chemistry, Physical and theoretical	**Nuclear reactors**
	Particles (Nuclear physics)
Cosmic rays	**Radioactivity**
Cyclotron	**Radiobiology**
Nuclear energy	**Transmutation (Chemistry)**
Nuclear engineering	

> *x* Atomic nuclei; Physics, Nuclear
> *xx* **Atoms; Chemistry, Physical and theoretical; Physics; Radioactivity**

Nuclear pollution. *See* **Radioactive pollution**

Nuclear power. *See* **Nuclear energy**

Nuclear power plants   621.48
> *See also* **Antinuclear movement; Nuclear energy**
> *x* Atomic power plants; Power plants, Atomic
> *xx* **Antinuclear movement; Nuclear energy; Power plants**

Nuclear power plants—Environmental aspects   333.792; 621.48
> *See also* **Radioactive waste disposal**
> *xx* **Environment; Environmental health**

Nuclear power plants—Fires and fire prevention   363.37; 621.48
> *xx* **Fire prevention; Fires**

Nuclear power plants—Security measures   621.48
> *xx* **Burglary protection**

Nuclear propulsion   621.48; 629.47
> *See also* **Nuclear reactors;** also specific applications, e.g. **Nuclear submarines;** etc.
> *x* Atomic powered vehicles
> *xx* **Nuclear energy**

Nuclear reactors   621.48
> *x* Atomic piles; Breeder reactors; Fast breeder reactors; Reactors (Nuclear physics)
> *xx* **Nuclear energy; Nuclear engineering; Nuclear physics; Nuclear propulsion**

Nuclear submarines   623.8
> *x* Atomic submarines; Submarines, Nuclear
> *xx* **Nuclear propulsion; Submarines**

Nuclear test ban. *See* **Arms control**

476

Nuclear warfare 355

See also **Atomic bomb; Hydrogen bomb; Nuclear weapons**

x Atomic warfare

Nuclear waste disposal. *See* **Radioactive waste disposal**

Nuclear weapons 355.8; 623.4

See also **Antinuclear movement; Hydrogen bomb;** also names of nuclear weapons, e.g. **Atomic bomb; Ballistic missiles; Neutron weapons;** etc.

x Atomic weapons; Weapons, Atomic; Weapons, Nuclear

xx **Nuclear warfare; Ordnance**

Nuclear weapons and disarmament. *See* **Arms control**

Nucleic acids 547.7; 574.87

See also **DNA; RNA**

x Polynucleotides

Nucleons. *See* **Particles (Nuclear physics)**

Nude in art 704.9

See also **Anatomy, Artistic**

x Human anatomy in art; Human figure in art

xx **Art**

Number concept 119; 155.4; 372.7

See note under **Numeration.**

xx **Apperception; Psychology**

Number games 793.7

xx **Arithmetic—Study and teaching; Counting; Mathematical recreations**

Number patterns. *See* **Patterns (Mathematics)**

Number readiness. *See* **Mathematical readiness**

Number symbolism. *See* **Symbolism of numbers**

Number systems. *See* **Numeration**

Number theory 510.1

See also **Group theory; Numeration**

x Numbers, Theory of; Theory of numbers

xx **Algebra; Mathematics; Set theory**

Numbers, Theory of. *See* **Number theory**

Numeral formation. *See* **Writing of numerals**

Numeral writing. *See* **Writing of numerals**

Numerals 513

See also **Symbolism of numbers; Writing of numerals;** also names of individual numbers, e.g. **Three (The number);** etc.

xx **Mathematics**

Numerals, Writing of. *See* **Writing of numerals**

Numeration 513.5

Use for materials on systems of numeration and for the theory of numeration. Works on the psychology of numeration are entered under **Number concept.** Materials on counting, including counting books, are entered under **Counting.**

See also **Counting;** also systems of numeration, e.g. **Binary system (Mathematics); Decimal system;** etc.

x Number systems

xx **Arithmetic; Counting; Mathematics; Number theory**

Numerical analysis 515

See also **Approximate computation**

xx **Mathematical analysis**

Numerology. *See* **Symbolism of numbers**

Numismatics 737

Use for materials on coins, paper money, medals, and tokens considered as works of art, as historical specimens, or as aids to the study of history, archeology, etc.

See also **Coins; Medals; Seals (Numismatics)**

xx **Archeology; Coins; History; History, Ancient; Medals**

Nunneries. *See* **Convents**

Nuns 255; 271; 920

See also **Ex-nuns**

x Sisters (in religious orders, congregations, etc.)

xx **Religious orders for women**

Nurse clinicians. *See* **Nurse practitioners**

Nurse practitioners 610.73092; 920

x Nurse clinicians

xx **Allied health personnel; Nurses**

Nurseries, Day. *See* **Child care centers**

Nurseries (Horticulture) 635

See also **Plant propagation**

xx **Fruit culture; Gardening; Trees**

Nursery rhymes 398.8

x Poetry for children; Rhymes

xx **Children's poetry; Children's songs; Folklore**

Nursery schools 372.21

See also **Child care centers; Kindergarten; Preschool education**

xx **Child care centers; Elementary education; Preschool education**

Nurses 610.73092; 920

See also types of nurses, e.g. **Nurse practitioners; Practical nurses; School nurses;** etc.

x District nurses; Trained nurses

Nursing 610.73; 649.8

See also **Cookery for the sick; First aid; Hospitals; Sick;** also types of nursing, e.g. **Home nursing; Practical nursing;** etc.; and diseases and medical procedures with the subdivision *Nursing,* e.g. **Cancer—Nursing; Heart—Surgery—Nursing;** etc.

xx **Hospitals; Medicine; Sick; Therapeutics**

Nursing homes 362.1

xx **Elderly—Care; Hospitals; Institutional care; Long-term care facilities**

Nursing (Infant feeding). *See* **Breast feeding**

Nutrition 641.1

See also **Diet; Digestion; Eating customs; Food; Malnutrition; Metabolism; Vitamins;** also subjects with the subdivision *Nutrition,* e.g. **Astronauts—Nutrition; Children—Nutrition; Plants—Nutrition;** etc.

x Meal planning

xx **Diet; Digestion; Food; Health self-care; Metabolism; Physiology; Therapeutics**

Nuts 634

Names of all nuts are not included in this List but are to be added as needed, in the singular form, e.g. **Pecan;** etc.

See also names of nuts, e.g. **Pecan;** etc.

xx **Food; Fruit; Seeds; Trees**

Nylon 677

xx **Fabrics; Synthetic fabrics**

Oak 583

xx **Trees; Wood**

Oats 633.1
   xx **Feeds**
Obedience 179
   x Disobedience
   xx **Human behavior**
Obelisks 721
   xx **Archeology; Architecture; Monuments; Pyramids**
Obesity 613.2; 616.3
   x Corpulence; Fatness; Overweight
Obesity—Control. *See* **Reducing**
Obituaries 920
   x Death notices; Necrologies
   xx **Biography**
Objective tests. *See* **Examinations; Mental tests**
Obscene materials. *See* **Pornography**
Obscenity (Law) 344; 345
   See also **Pornography**
Observatories, Astronomical. *See* **Astronomical observatories**
Observatories, Meteorological. *See* **Meteorology—Observatories**
Obstetrics. *See* **Childbirth**
Occidental civilization. *See* **Civilization, Occidental**
Occult sciences. *See* **Occultism**
Occult, The. *See* **Occultism**
Occultism 133
   See also

Alchemy	**Oracles**
Astrology	**Palmistry**
Cabala	**Parapsychology**
Clairvoyance	**Prophecies (Occult sci-**
Demonology	**ences)**
Divination	**Spiritualism**
Fortune telling	**Superstition**
Magic	**Witchcraft**
New Age movement	

   x Hermetic art and philosophy; Occult sciences; Occult, The; Sorcery
   xx **Demonology; Magic; Parapsychology; Religions; Supernatural; Superstition; Witchcraft**
Occupation, Military. *See* **Military occupation**
Occupational crimes. *See* **White collar crimes**
Occupational diseases 616.9
   See also **Hazardous occupations; Lead poisoning; Occupational health services; Workers' compensation**
   x Diseases, Industrial; Diseases, Occupational; Diseases of occupation; Industrial diseases; Occupations—Diseases
   xx **Diseases; Hazardous occupations; Labor; Occupational health and safety; Public health**
Occupational forecasting. *See* **Employment forecasting**
Occupational guidance. *See* **Vocational guidance**
Occupational health and safety 363.11; 658.3
   See also **Burn out (Psychology); Hazardous occupations; Hazardous substances; Occupational diseases**
   x Health, Industrial; Hygiene, Industrial; Industrial health; Industrial safety; Safety, Industrial

Occupational health and safety—*Continued*
  xx **Environmental health; Industrial management; Public health**
Occupational health services   362.1; 613.6; 658.3
  Use for materials on health services for employees, usually provided at the place of work.
  x Employee health services
  xx **Medical care; Occupational diseases**
Occupational literacy. *See* **Functional literacy**
Occupational retraining   331.25
  See note under **Occupational training.**
  x Job retraining; Retraining, Occupational
  xx **Employees—Training; Human resources policy; Labor supply; Occupational training; Technical education; Unemployed; Vocational education**
Occupational stress. *See* **Job stress**
Occupational therapy   615.8
  See also **Handicraft**
  xx **Handicraft; Mental health; Physical therapy; Physically handicapped—Rehabilitation; Therapeutics**
Occupational training   331.25; 331.7
  Use for materials on teaching people a skill after formal education. Materials on teaching a skill during the educational process are entered under **Vocational education.** Materials discussing on-the-job training are entered under **Employees—Training.** Materials on retraining are entered under **Occupational retraining.**
  See also **Employees—Training; Occupational retraining**
  x Job training; Training, Occupational; Training, Vocational; Vocational training
  xx **Human resources policy; Technical education; Vocational education**
Occupations   331.7
  Use for descriptions and lists of occupations.
  See also **Job analysis; Paraprofessions and paraprofessionals; Professions; Vocational guidance;** also names of countries, cities, etc. with the subdivision *Occupations,* e.g. **United States—Occupations; Chicago (Ill.) —Occupations;** etc.; and names of occupations
  x Careers; Jobs; Trades; Vocations
  xx **Business; Labor; Professions; Vocational guidance**
Occupations, Dangerous. *See* **Hazardous occupations**
Occupations—Diseases. *See* **Occupational diseases**
Occupied territory. *See* **Military occupation**
Ocean   551.46
  See also **Icebergs; Oceanography; Seashore;** also names of oceans and seas, e.g. **Atlantic Ocean;** etc.
  x Oceans; Sea
  xx **Earth; Physical geography; Water**
Ocean bottom   551.46
  See also **Marine mineral resources**
  x Ocean floor; Sea bed
  xx **Marine biology; Oceanography; Submarine geology**

Ocean cables. *See* **Cables, Submarine**
Ocean currents 551.47
  x Currents, Ocean
  xx **Navigation; Oceanography; Physical geogra-
    phy**
Ocean—Economic aspects. *See* **Marine resources;
    Shipping**
Ocean energy resources 333.91
  See also **Geothermal resources; Marine mineral
    resources**
  x Energy resources, Ocean
  xx **Energy resources; Marine resources; Ocean
    engineering**
Ocean engineering 627
  Use for materials on engineering beneath the
    surface of the ocean.
  See also **Drilling platforms; Ocean energy re-
    sources; Ocean mining; Oil well drilling,
    Submarine**
  x Deep sea engineering; Submarine engineering;
    Undersea engineering
  xx **Engineering; Marine resources; Oceanography**
Ocean farming. *See* **Aquaculture**
Ocean floor. *See* **Ocean bottom**
Ocean life. *See* **Marine biology**
Ocean mineral resources. *See* **Marine mineral re-
    sources**
Ocean mining 622
  x Deep sea mining; Mining, Ocean
  xx **Marine mineral resources; Mining engineer-
    ing; Ocean engineering**
Ocean pollution. *See* **Marine pollution**
Ocean resources. *See* **Marine resources**
Ocean routes. *See* **Trade routes**
Ocean transportation. *See* **Shipping**
Ocean travel 910.4
  See also **Ships; Steamboats; Yachts and yachting**
  x Cruises; Sea travel
  xx **Transportation; Travel; Voyages and travels**
Ocean waves 551.47
  See also **Tsunamis**
  x Breakers; Sea waves; Surf; Swell; Tidal waves
  xx **Oceanography; Waves**
Oceanariums. *See* **Marine aquariums**
Oceanauts. *See* **Aquanauts**
Oceania 995
  Use for comprehensive materials on the lands
    and area of the central and southern Pacific
    Ocean, including Micronesia, Melanesia,
    and Polynesia. Comprehensive works on all
    the islands of the Pacific Ocean are entered
    under **Islands of the Pacific.**
  x South Pacific region; South Sea Islands; South
    Seas; Southwest Pacific region
  xx **Islands; Islands of the Pacific**
Oceanographic research. *See* **Oceanography—
    Research**
Oceanographic submersibles. *See* **Submersibles**
Oceanography (May subdiv. geog. area, e.g. **Ocean-
    ography—Atlantic Ocean;** etc.) **551.46**
  See also

Marine biology	**Navigation**
Marine resources	**Ocean bottom**

Oceanography—*Continued*

Ocean currents	**Submarine geology**
Ocean engineering	**Tides**
Ocean waves	

> *x* Deep sea technology; Oceanology; Undersea technology
>
> *xx* **Earth; Earth sciences; Geology; Geophysics; Ocean**

Oceanography—Atlantic Ocean   551.46

Oceanography—Computer programs   551.46

> *xx* **Computer programs**

Oceanography—Research   551.46

> *See also* **Bathyscaphe; Diving, Submarine; Skin diving; Submersibles; Undersea research stations; Underwater exploration**
>
> *x* Oceanographic research

Oceanology. *See* **Oceanography**

Oceans. *See* **Ocean**

Oddities. *See* **Curiosities and wonders**

Offenses against public safety   364.1

> *See also* names of specific offenses, e.g. **Hijacking of airplanes; Riots; Sabotage;** etc.
>
> *x* Crimes against public safety; Public safety, Crimes against
>
> *xx* **Criminal law**

Offenses against the person   364.1

> *See also* names of specific offenses, e.g. **Assassination; Homicide; Kidnapping; Rape;** etc.
>
> *x* Abuse of persons; Crimes against the person; Persons, Crimes against
>
> *xx* **Crime; Criminal law**

Offenses, Military. *See* **Military offenses**

Office buildings (May subdiv. geog.)   **725**

> *See also* **Skyscrapers**
>
> *x* Buildings, Office
>
> *xx* **Industrial buildings**

Office employees   331.7; 651.3

> *See also* **Office practice; Sales personnel**
>
> *x* Clerical employees; Clerks; Commercial employees; Employees, Clerical
>
> *xx* **Employees; Office practice; Sales personnel**

Office equipment and supplies   651

> *See also* types of office equipment and supplies, e.g. **Calculators; Keyboards (Electronics); Typewriters;** etc.
>
> *x* Business machines; Office machines; Office supplies
>
> *xx* **Bookkeeping; Office management**

Office machines. *See* **Office equipment and supplies**

Office management   651.3

> *See also* **Files and filing; Office equipment and supplies; Office practice; Personnel management; Secretaries; Word processing**
>
> *x* Office procedures
>
> *xx* **Business; Efficiency, Industrial; Factory management; Industrial management; Management; Personnel management**

Office practice   651.3

> *See also* **Keyboarding (Electronics); Office employees; Shorthand; Typewriting; Word processing**
>
> *x* Secretarial practice
>
> *xx* **Office employees; Office management**

Office procedures. *See* **Office management**
Office romance. *See* **Sex in the workplace**
Office supplies. *See* **Office equipment and supplies**
Office, Tenure of. *See* **Civil service**
Office work—Training. *See* **Business education**
Official misconduct. *See* **Misconduct in office**
Official publications. *See* **Government publications;** and names of countries, cities, etc. with the subdivision *Government publications,* e.g. **United States—Government publications;** etc.
Officials. *See* **Civil service;** and names of countries, cities, etc. and corporate bodies with the subdivision *Officials and employees,* e.g. **United States—Officials and employees; Chicago (Ill.)—Officials and employees; United Nations—Officials and employees;** etc.
Offset printing   686.2
   x Lithoprinting; Printing, Offset
   xx **Lithography; Printing**
Offshore oil well drilling. *See* **Oil well drilling, Submarine**
Offshore structures. *See* **Drilling platforms**
Offshore water pollution. *See* **Marine pollution**
Ohio   977.1
   Subdivisions have been given under this subject to serve as a guide to the subdivisions that may be used under the name of any state of the United States or province of Canada. The subdivisions under **United States** may be consulted as a guide for formulating other references that may be needed.
Ohio—Antiquities   977.1
Ohio—Bibliography   015.771; 016.9771
Ohio—Bio-bibliography   012
Ohio—Biography   920.0771
Ohio—Biography—Dictionaries   920.0771
Ohio—Biography—Portraits   920.0771
Ohio—Boundaries   977.1
Ohio—Census   317.71
Ohio—Church history   277.71
Ohio—Civilization   977.1
Ohio—Climate   551.69771
Ohio—Commerce   381
Ohio—Constitution   342.771
   xx **State constitutions**
Ohio—Constitutional history   342.771
Ohio—Cookery. *See* **Cookery—Ohio**
Ohio—Description   917.71
   x Ohio—Description and travel; Ohio—Travel
Ohio—Description and travel. *See* **Ohio—Description**
Ohio—Description—Guidebooks   917.71
Ohio—Description—Views   917.71
Ohio—Directories   917.710025
   Use for lists of names and addresses. Lists of names without addresses are entered under **Ohio—Registers.**
   See also **Ohio—Registers**
   xx **Ohio—Registers**
Ohio—Economic conditions   330.9771
Ohio—Economic policy   338.9771
   xx **Economic policy**

Ohio—Executive departments 353.9771
Ohio—Folk songs. *See* **Folk songs—Ohio**
Ohio—Foreign population 325.771
Ohio—Gazetteers 917.71
Ohio—Government publications 015.771
Ohio—Historic buildings. *See* **Historic buildings—
  Ohio**
Ohio—History 977.1
Ohio—History, Local 977.1
Ohio—History—Societies 977.106
Ohio—History—Sources 977.1
Ohio—Industries 338.09771
  x Ohio—Manufactures
Ohio—Intellectual life 977.1
Ohio—Manufactures. *See* **Ohio—Industries**
Ohio—Maps 912.771
Ohio—Militia 355.3
Ohio—Moral conditions 977.1
Ohio—Museums. *See* **Museums—Ohio**
Ohio—Occupations 331.7
Ohio—Officials and employees 353.9771004
Ohio—Politics and government 977.1
  xx **State governments**
Ohio—Population 304.609771
Ohio—Public buildings 725.09771
  x Public buildings—Ohio
Ohio—Public lands 333.109771
Ohio—Public works 353.97710086
Ohio—Race relations 305.8009771
Ohio—Registers 917.710025
    Use for lists of names without addresses. Lists of
      names that include addresses are entered
      under **Ohio—Directories.**
    See also **Ohio—Directories**
    xx **Ohio—Directories**
Ohio—Religion 277.71
Ohio—Rural conditions 307.7209771
Ohio—Social conditions 977.1
Ohio—Social life and customs 977.1
Ohio—Social policy 361.6; 977.1
  x State planning
Ohio—Statistics 317.71
Ohio—Travel. *See* **Ohio—Description**
Oil. *See* **Oils and fats; Petroleum**
Oil burners 697
  xx **Heating; Petroleum as fuel**
Oil engines. *See* **Gas and oil engines**
Oil fuel. *See* **Petroleum as fuel**
Oil painting. *See* **Painting**
Oil pollution of rivers, harbors, etc. 363.73
  x Rivers—Pollution
  xx **Marine pollution; Oil pollution of water; Oil
    spills**
Oil pollution of water 363.73; 628.1
  See also **Oil pollution of rivers, harbors, etc.**
  x Petroleum pollution of water; Water—Oil pol-
    lution
  xx **Oil spills; Water pollution**
Oil spills 363.73
  See also **Oil pollution of rivers, harbors, etc.; Oil
    pollution of water**
  xx **Marine pollution**

Oil well drilling 622
> *See also* **Oil wells—Blowouts**
> *x* Drilling, Oil well; Petroleum—Well boring;
>> Well drilling, Oil

Oil well drilling, Submarine 622
> *See also* **Drilling platforms**
> *x* Deep sea drilling (Petroleum); Offshore oil
>> well drilling; Submarine oil well drilling;
>> Underwater drill (Petroleum)
> *xx* **Ocean engineering**

Oil wells 622

Oil wells—Blowouts 622
> *x* Blowouts, Oil well
> *xx* **Oil well drilling**

Oils and fats 665
> *See also* **Essences and essential oils; Lubrication**
>> **and lubricants; Petroleum**
> *x* Animal oils; Fat; Fats; Grease; Oil; Vegetable
>> oils
> *xx* **Coal tar products; Lubrication and lubricants**

Oils, Essential. *See* **Essences and essential oils**

Old age 305.26
> *See also* **Age and employment; Aging; Elderly;**
>> **Longevity; Retirement**
> *x* Age
> *xx* **Gerontology; Life (Biology); Longevity; Mid-**
>> **dle age; Physiology**

Old age homes. *See* **Elderly—Institutional care**

Old age pensions 331.25; 368.4
> *x* Insurance, Old age; Labor—Insurance
> *xx* **Pensions; Retirement income; Saving and**
>> **thrift; Social security**

Old English language. *See* **Anglo-Saxon language**

Old English literature. *See* **Anglo-Saxon literature**

Old Icelandic language. *See* **Old Norse language**

Old Norse language 439
> *See also* **Scandinavian languages**
> *x* Icelandic language—0-1500; Norse languages;
>> Norwegian language—0-1350; Old Icelandic
>> language; Old Norwegian language
> *xx* **Scandinavian languages**

Old Norse literature 839
> *See also* **Eddas; Sagas; Scandinavian literature**
> *x* Norse literature
> *xx* **Icelandic literature; Scandinavian literature**

Old Northwest 977
> Use for materials on the region between the
>> Ohio and Mississippi rivers and the Great
>> Lakes.
> *See also* **Middle West**
> *x* Northwest, Old; Northwest Territory
> *xx* **Middle West; United States**

Old Norwegian language. *See* **Old Norse language**

Old Southwest 976
> Use for materials on that section of the United
>> States that comprised the southwestern part
>> before the cessions of land from Mexico fol-
>> lowing the Mexican War. It included Louisi-
>> ana, Texas, Arkansas, Tennessee, Kentucky
>> and Missouri.
> *x* Southwest, Old
> *xx* **United States**

Old Testament. *See* **Bible. O.T.**

Older people. *See* **Elderly**

Oldest child. *See* **Birth order**
Oleomargarine. *See* **Margarine**
Olympic games   796.48; 796.98
  See also **Special Olympics**
    x Games, Olympic
    xx **Athletics; Contests; Games; Sports**
Olympics, Special. *See* **Special Olympics**
Ombudsman (May subdiv. geog.)   **328.3; 342; 351.9**
    x Citizen's defender; Grievance procedures
        (Public administration)
    xx **Administrative law; Public interest**
On the job stress. *See* **Job stress**
One act plays   808.82; 812, etc.
    x Plays; Short plays
    xx **Amateur theater; Drama**
One parent family. *See* **Single parent family**
Online catalogs   025.3
  See also **Libraries—Automation**
    x Catalogs, Online; Online public access cata-
        logs; OPACs (Online public access catalogs)
    xx **Libraries—Automation; Library catalogs**
Online data processing   004
  See also **Computer bulletin boards**
    xx **Electronic data processing**
Online public access catalogs. *See* **Online catalogs**
Online publishing. *See* **Electronic publishing**
Online reference services. *See* **Reference services
    (Libraries)**
Only child   155.44; 306.874
    x Single child
    xx **Children; Family size**
OPACs (Online public access catalogs). *See* **Online
    catalogs**
Opaque projectors. *See* **Projectors**
Open and closed shop   331.88
    x Closed shop; Right to work; Union shop
    xx **Labor; Labor contract; Labor unions**
Open classroom approach to teaching. *See* **Open
    plan schools**
Open education. *See* **Open plan schools**
Open ended marriage. *See* **Unmarried couples**
Open heart surgery. *See* **Heart—Surgery**
Open housing. *See* **Discrimination in housing**
Open plan schools   371.3
    Use for materials on schools without interior
        walls.
  See also **Experimental schools; Individualized in-
    struction**
    x Interest centers approach to teaching; Learn-
        ing center approach to teaching; Open class-
        room approach to teaching; Open education
    xx **Education—Experimental methods; Experi-
        mental schools**
Open universities. *See* **Free universities**
Opera   782.1; 792.5
  See also **Ballet; Operetta**
    x Comic opera; Dramatic music; Grand opera;
        Music, Dramatic
    xx **Drama; Musical form; Theater**
Opera houses. *See* **Theaters**
Operas   782.1
    xx **Vocal music**
Operas—Librettos   782.1026
    xx **Librettos**

486

Operas—Stories, plots, etc. 782.1026
  x Stories
  xx **Librettos; Plots (Drama, fiction, etc.)**
Operating systems (Computers). *See* **Computer operating systems**
Operation Desert Shield. *See* **Persian Gulf War, 1991-**
Operation Desert Storm. *See* **Persian Gulf War, 1991-**
Operation Pluto. *See* **Cuba—History—1961, Invasion**
Operations research 658.5
  See also **Systems engineering**
  xx **Research; System theory; Systems engineering**
Operations, Surgical. *See* **Surgery**
Operetta 782.1; 792.5
  See also **Musicals**
  x Comic opera; Dramatic music; Music, Dramatic
  xx **Musical form; Musicals; Opera; Vocal music**
Opiates. *See* **Narcotics**
Opinion polls. *See* **Public opinion polls**
Opinion, Public. *See* **Public opinion**
Opioids, Brain. *See* **Endorphins**
Opium 615
  See also **Morphine**
  xx **Morphine; Narcotics**
Opium—Physiological effect 615
  xx **Drugs—Physiological effect**
Optical data processing 006.4; 621.36; 621.39; 651.8
  x Visual data processing
  xx **Bionics; Electronic data processing**
Optical discs. *See* **Optical storage devices**
Optical illusions 152.14
  x Illusions
  xx **Hallucinations and illusions; Psychophysiology; Vision**
Optical masers. *See* **Lasers**
Optical storage devices 004.5; 621.39
  Use for materials on data storage devices in which data (audio, digital, or video) are optically encoded and that permit playing back through a mechanical system or a laser system.
  See also **CD-I technology; CD-ROM; Compact discs; Laser recording; Videodiscs**
  x Discs, Optical; Optical discs
  xx **Computer storage devices; Laser recording; Optics**
Optics 535; 621.36
  See also

Color	**Radiation**
Light	**Refraction**
Optical storage devices	**Space optics**
Perspective	**Spectrum analysis**
Phosphorescence	**Vision**
Photometry	

  xx **Light; Photometry; Physics**

Optometry 617.7
  See also **Eye**
  xx **Eye**

Oracles   133.3

    See also **Divination**

    xx **Divination; Occultism; Prophecies (Occult sciences)**

Oral arithmetic.   *See* **Arithmetic, Mental**

Oral history   900

    Use for materials on recording the oral recollections of events by persons. Use appropriate subject headings for the content of the recollections.

    x History, Oral

    xx **History**

Orange   634

    xx **Citrus fruit; Trees**

Orations.   *See* **Speeches, addresses, etc.**

Oratorios   782.23

    xx **Church music; Vocal music**

Oratory.   *See* **Public speaking**

Orbital debris.   *See* **Space debris**

Orbital laboratories.   *See* **Space stations**

Orbital rendezvous (Space flight)   629.45

    See also names of projects, e.g. **Apollo project; Gemini project;** etc.; also names of space ships

    x Rendezvous in space; Space orbital rendezvous

    xx **Space flight; Space ships; Space stations**

Orbiting vehicles.   *See* **Artificial satellites; Space stations**

Orchards.   *See* **Fruit culture**

Orchestra   784.2

    See also **Bands (Music); Conducting; Conductors (Music); Instrumentation and orchestration; Orchestral music;** also names of types of orchestras

    xx **Bands (Music); Conducting; Musical instruments**

Orchestral music   784.2

    See also types of orchestral music, e.g. **Chamber music; Concertos; Quintets; Sonatas; String orchestra music; Suites; Symphonies;** etc.

    xx **Instrumental music; Music; Orchestra**

Orchestration.   *See* **Instrumentation and orchestration**

Orders, Monastic.   *See* **Religious orders**

Ordination   262

    xx **Rites and ceremonies; Sacraments**

Ordination of men   262

Ordination of women   262

Ordnance   355.8; 623.4

    See also names of general and specific military ordnance, e.g. **Bombs; Nuclear weapons; Projectiles;** etc.; also names of armies with the subdivision *Ordnance and ordnance stores,* e.g. **United States. Army—Ordnance and ordnance stores;** etc.

    x Cannon; Guns

    xx **Armaments; Arms and armor; Artillery; Firearms; Military art and science; Projectiles**

Ore deposits   553

    See also **Ores;** also names of ores, e.g. **Iron ores;** etc.

    xx **Geology; Ores**

Ore dressing   622
    x Dressing of ores
    xx **Smelting**
Oregon country.   *See* **Pacific Northwest**
Oregon Trail   978
    xx **Overland journeys to the Pacific; United**
        States
Ores   553
    See also **Metallurgy; Metals; Mineralogy; Mines**
        and mineral resources; Ore deposits; also
        names of ores, e.g. **Iron ores;** etc.
    xx **Geology, Economic; Ore deposits**
Organ   786.5
    See also **Keyboards (Musical instruments)**
    x Pipe organ
    xx **Musical instruments**
Organ donation.   *See* **Donation of organs, tissues,**
    etc.
Organ music   786.5
    xx **Church music; Music**
Organ preservation (Anatomy).   *See* **Preservation of**
    organs, tissues, etc.
Organ transplantation.   *See* **Transplantation of or-**
    gans, tissues, etc.
Organic art.   *See* **Art, Abstract**
Organic chemistry.   *See* **Chemistry, Organic**
Organic farming.   *See* **Organiculture**
Organic gardening.   *See* **Organiculture**
Organic waste as fuel.   *See* **Waste products as fuel**
Organically grown foods.   *See* **Natural foods**
Organiculture   631.5; 635.9
    x Organic farming; Organic gardening
    xx **Agriculture; Gardening; Horticulture**
Organists   786.5092; 920
    xx **Musicians**
Organization and management.   *See* **Management**
Organization, International.   *See* **International orga-**
    nization
Organizational stress.   *See* **Job stress**
Organizations.   *See* **Associations**
Organized crime   364.1
    See also types of organized crime, e.g. **Racke-**
        teering; etc.
    x Crime syndicates
    xx **Crime**
Organized labor.   *See* **Labor unions**
Organs (Anatomy)—Preservation.   *See* **Preservation**
    of organs, tissues, etc.
Organs, Artificial.   *See* **Artificial organs**
Orient.   *See* **Asia; East Asia; Middle East**
Oriental architecture.   *See* **Architecture, Asian**
Oriental art.   *See* **Art, Asian**
Oriental civilization.   *See* **Civilization, Asian**
Oriental rugs   746.7
    Use for materials on handwoven or hand-
        knotted one-piece rugs made in the Orient.
    x Persian rugs; Rugs, Oriental
    xx **Rugs**
Orientation.   *See* **Direction sense**
Orienteering   796.5
    Use for materials on the cross-country sport in
        which competitors using maps and com-
        passes proceed on foot to checkpoints

Orienteering—*Continued*
    through unknown terrain.
    See also **Direction sense**
    x Racing
    xx **Direction sense; Hiking; Navigation; Running;**
      Sports
Origami   745.54
    x Japanese paper folding; Paper folding, Japanese
    xx **Paper crafts**
Origin of life.   *See* **Life—Origin**
Origin of man.   *See* **Man—Origin**
Origin of species.   *See* **Evolution**
Ornament.   *See* **Decoration and ornament**
Ornamental alphabets.   *See* **Illumination of books**
    and manuscripts; Lettering
Ornamental plants   635.9; 715
    x Plants, Ornamental
    xx **Flower gardening; Landscape gardening;**
      Plants, Cultivated; Shrubs
Ornithology.   *See* **Birds**
Orphan drugs   615
    Use for materials on drugs that appear to be useful for the treatment of rare disorders but owing to their limited commercial value have difficulty in finding funding for research and marketing.
    x Drugs, Orphan; Nonprofitable drugs
    xx **Drugs**
Orphanages (May subdiv. geog.)   **362.7**
    See also **Child welfare**
    x Charitable institutions; Homes (Institutions)
    xx **Charities; Child welfare; Children—**
      Institutional care; Institutional care; Public
      welfare
Orphans   362.7
    See also **Abandoned children; Adopted children**
    x Foundlings
    xx **Abandoned children; Adopted children; Children**
Orthodox Eastern Church   281.9
    x Greek Church
    xx **Eastern churches**
Orthodox Eastern Church, Russian   281.9
    x Russian Church
Orthography.   *See* **Spelling reform;** and names of
    languages with the subdivision *Spelling,* e.g.
    English language—Spelling; etc.
Orthopedic surgery.   *See* **Orthopedics**
Orthopedics   617.3
    See also **Physically handicapped**
    x Orthopedic surgery; Surgery, Orthopedic
    xx **Physically handicapped; Surgery**
Osteology.   *See* **Bones**
Osteopathy   615.5
    See also **Chiropractic; Massage**
    xx **Alternative medicine; Massage**
Ostrogoths.   *See* **Teutonic peoples**
Out-of-work people.   *See* **Unemployed**
Outboard motorboats.   *See* **Motorboats**
Outdoor cookery   641.5; 641.7
    See also **Barbecue cookery**
    x Camp cooking; Cookery, Outdoor
    xx **Camping; Cookery**

Outdoor education. *See* **Outdoor life**
Outdoor life   796.5
>   *See also* types of outdoor education, life and ac-
>   tivities, e.g. **Camping; Country life; Hiking;**
>   **Mountaineering; Nature study; Sports; Wil-**
>   **derness survival;** etc.
>   *x* Outdoor education; Rural life
>   *xx* **Camping; Country life; Sports**
Outdoor photography   778.7
>   *See also* **Nature photography**
>   *x* Field photography; Photography, Outdoor
>   *xx* **Nature photography; Photography**
Outdoor recreation   796
>   *See also* **Parks; Recreational vehicles;** also types
>   of outdoor recreation, e.g. **Camping;** etc.
>   *xx* **Recreation**
Outdoor survival. *See* **Wilderness survival**
Outer space   523.1
>   *See also* **Space environment; Space warfare**
>   *x* Space, Outer
>   *xx* **Astronautics; Astronomy; Space sciences**
Outer space and civilization. *See* **Astronautics and**
>   **civilization**
Outer space—Colonies. *See* **Space colonies**
Outer space—Communication. *See* **Interstellar**
>   **communication**
Outer space—Exploration   629.4
>   *See also* **Planets—Exploration; Space probes**
>   *x* Exploration, Space; Space exploration (As-
>   tronautics); Space research
>   *xx* **Interplanetary voyages; Space flight**
Outer space—Pollution. *See* **Space debris**
Outer space travel. *See* **Interplanetary voyages**
Outlaws. *See* **Robbers and outlaws**
Outlines, syllabi, etc. *See* general subjects with the
>   subdivision *Outlines, syllabi, etc.,* e.g. **Eng-**
>   **lish literature—Outlines, syllabi, etc.;** etc.
Output equipment (Computers). *See* **Computer pe-**
>   **ripherals**
Output standards. *See* **Production standards**
Over-the-counter drugs. *See* **Nonprescription drugs**
Overactive children. *See* **Hyperactive children**
Overactivity. *See* **Hyperactivity**
Overland journeys to the Pacific   978
>   Use for materials on the pioneers' crossing of the
>   American continent toward the Pacific by
>   foot, horseback, wagon, etc.
>   *See also* **Oregon Trail; West (U.S.)—Exploration**
>   *x* Transcontinental journeys (American conti-
>   nent)
>   *xx* **Frontier and pioneer life; Voyages and travels;**
>   **West (U.S.)—Exploration**
Overseas study. *See* **Foreign study**
Oversized books for shared reading. *See* **Big books**
Overtime. *See* **Hours of labor; Wages**
Overweight. *See* **Obesity**
Overweight—Control. *See* **Reducing**
Ownership. *See* **Property**
Oxyacetylene welding. *See* **Welding**
Oxygen   546; 547
>   *See also* **Ozone**
Oysters, Pearl. *See* **Pearlfisheries**
Ozone   665
>   *xx* **Oxygen**

Ozone layer   363.73; 551.5
  x Ozonosphere; Stratospheric ozone
  xx **Stratosphere**
Ozonosphere.   *See* **Ozone layer**
P.O.W.'s.   *See* **Prisoners of war**
P.T.A.'s.   *See* **Parents' and teachers' associations**
Pacific cable.   *See* **Cables, Submarine**
Pacific Islands.   *See* **Islands of the Pacific**
Pacific Northwest   979.5
  Use for materials on the old Oregon country,
    comprising the present states of Oregon,
    Washington and Idaho, parts of Montana
    and Wyoming, and the province of British
    Columbia.
  x Northwest, Pacific; Oregon country
  xx **North America; West (U.S.)**
Pacific Northwest coast.   *See* **Northwest coast of
    North America**
Pacific Ocean Islands.   *See* **Islands of the Pacific**
Pacific States   979
  xx **West (U.S.)**
Pacifism   341.7
  See also **Conscientious objectors; Nonviolence**
  x Peace movements
  xx **Conscientious objectors; Nonviolence; Peace;
    War and religion**
Pack transportation.   *See* **Backpacking**
Packaged houses.   *See* **Prefabricated houses**
Packaging   658.5; 658.7; 658.8
  See also types of packaging and packaging mate-
    rials, e.g. **Aluminum foil; Boxes; Gift wrap-
    ping;** etc.
  xx **Advertising; Retail trade**
Packing industry.   *See* **Meat industry**
PAC's.   *See* **Lobbying and lobbyists**
Paganism   291
  x Heathenism
  xx **Christianity and other religions; Religions**
Pageants   394; 791.6
  See also **Festivals; Masks (Plays); Mysteries and
    miracle plays**
  xx **Acting; Festivals**
Pain   152.1; 612.8
  See also **Anesthetics; Pleasure; Suffering**
  xx **Diagnosis; Emotions; Pleasure; Psychophys-
    iology; Senses and sensation; Suffering**
Paint   645; 667
  See also **Corrosion and anticorrosives; Pigments**
  x Finishes and finishing
  xx **Corrosion and anticorrosives; Painting, Indus-
    trial; Pigments**
Paint sniffing.   *See* **Solvent abuse**
Painted glass.   *See* **Glass painting and staining**
Painters (May subdiv. geog. adjective form)   **759;
    920**
  See also **Artists;** also names of individual paint-
    ers
  xx **Artists**
Painters, American   759.13; 920
  x American painters; United States—Painters
Painters' materials.   *See* **Artists' materials**
Painting (May subdiv. geog. adjective form)   **750**
  Names of all types of painting are not included
    in this List but are to be added as needed.

Painting—*Continued*
   See also

Animal painting and illustration
China painting
Color
Composition (Art)
Cubism
Drawing
Expressionism (Art)
Figure painting
Finger painting
Flower painting and illustration
Futurism (Art)
Glass painting and staining
Impressionism (Art)
Landscape painting
Marine painting
Miniature painting
Mural painting and decoration
Perspective
Portrait painting
Postimpressionism (Art)
Scene painting
Stencil work
Textile painting
Watercolor painting

   x Oil painting; Paintings
   xx **Aesthetics; Art; Composition (Art); Decoration and ornament; Drawing; Graphic arts; Pictures**

Painting, Abstract. *See* **Art, Abstract**
Painting, American 759.13
   x American painting; United States—Painting
Painting books. *See* **Coloring books**
Painting—Color reproductions. *See* **Color prints**
Painting—Conservation and restoration 751.6
   x Conservation of works of art, books, etc.
Painting, Decorative. *See* **Decoration and ornament**
Painting, Dutch 759.492
Painting, Finger. *See* **Finger painting**
Painting, Industrial 698
   See also **House painting; Lettering; Paint; Sign painting; Varnish and varnishing; Wood finishing**
   x Finishes and finishing; Industrial painting; Mechanical painting; Painting, Mechanical
Painting, Mechanical. *See* **Painting, Industrial**
Painting, Modern 759.06
   x Modern painting
Painting, Modern—1800-1899 (19th century) 759.05
Painting, Modern—1900-1999 (20th century) 759.06
Painting, Religious. *See* **Religious art and symbolism**
Painting, Romanesque 759.02
   x Romanesque painting
   xx **Art, Romanesque**
Painting—Technique 751.4
   x Technique
Paintings. *See* **Painting**
Pair system. *See* **Binary system (Mathematics)**
Palaces (May subdiv. geog.) **728.8**
   xx **Architecture**
Paleobiogeography. *See* **Biogeography**
Paleobotany. *See* **Plants, Fossil**
Paleolithic period. *See* **Stone Age**
Paleontology. *See* **Fossils**
Palestine problem, 1917-. *See* **Jewish-Arab relations**
Palestinian Arabs 305.892; 956.94
   See also **Jewish-Arab relations**
   x Arabs—Palestine

Palmistry 133.6
  xx **Divination; Fortune telling; Occultism**
Palsy, Cerebral. *See* **Cerebral palsy**
Pamphlets 025.17
  See also **Chapbooks**
Pan-Africanism 320.5; 327
  x African relations
  xx **Africa**
Pan-Americanism 320.5; 327
  Use for materials on the theory and policy of co-
    operation and mutual cultural understand-
    ing among the countries of America.
  See also **America—Politics and government;
    Monroe Doctrine**
  x Good Neighbor Policy; Inter-American rela-
    tions
  xx **America—Politics and government; Latin
    America**
Pan-Arabism 320.5
  x Panarabism
  xx **Arab countries—Politics and government**
Panama Canal 972.87
  xx **Canals**
Panarabism. *See* **Pan-Arabism**
Panel discussions. *See* **Discussion groups**
Panel heating. *See* **Radiant heating**
Paneuropean federation. *See* **European federation**
Panhandling. *See* **Begging**
Panics, Economic. *See* **Depressions, Economic**
Pantomimes 792.3
  See also **Mime; Shadow pantomimes and plays**
  xx **Acting; Amateur theater; Ballet; Drama;
    Mime; Theater**
Papacy 262
  See also **Popes**
  x Holy See
  xx **Catholic Church; Church history; Popes**
Papal encyclicals 262.9
  x Encyclicals, Papal
Paper 676
  See also **Papermaking**
  xx **Fibers**
Paper airplanes. *See* **Airplanes—Models**
Paper bound books. *See* **Paperback books**
Paper crafts 731; 736; 745.54
  See also **Gift wrapping;** also names of paper
    crafts, e.g. **Decoupage; Origami;** etc.
  x Paper folding; Paper sculpture; Paper work;
    Papier-maché
Paper folding. *See* **Paper crafts**
Paper folding, Japanese. *See* **Origami**
Paper hanging 698
  See also **Wallpaper**
  xx **Interior design; Wallpaper**
Paper industry 338.4; 676
  See also **Book industries**
  x Paper making and trade; Paper trade; Paper-
    making industry
  xx **Book industries; Manufactures**
Paper making and trade. *See* **Paper industry;
    Papermaking**
Paper manufacture. *See* **Papermaking**

Paper money   332.4

   x Bills of credit; Fiat money; Greenbacks; Legal tender; Money, Paper

   xx **Finance; Inflation (Finance); Money**

Paper sculpture. *See* **Paper crafts**

Paper trade. *See* **Paper industry**

Paper work. *See* **Paper crafts**

Paperback books   070.5

   x Books, Paperback; Paper bound books

   xx **Bibliography—Editions; Books; Publishers and publishing**

Papermaking   676

   x Paper making and trade; Paper manufacture

   xx **Paper**

Papermaking industry. *See* **Paper industry**

Papier-maché. *See* **Paper crafts**

Parables   808

   See also **Allegories; Bible—Parables; Fables; Jesus Christ—Parables**

   xx **Allegories; Fables**

Parachute troops   356

   See also names of armies with the subdivision *Parachute troops,* e.g. **United States. Army—Parachute troops;** etc.

   x Paratroops

   xx **Aeronautics, Military; Parachutes**

Parachutes   623; 629.134

   See also **Parachute troops**

   xx **Aeronautics**

Parades   791.6

   x Floats (Parades); Processions

Paralysis, Anterior spinal. *See* **Poliomyelitis**

Paralysis, Cerebral. *See* **Cerebral palsy**

Paralysis, Infantile. *See* **Poliomyelitis**

Paralysis, Spastic. *See* **Cerebral palsy**

Paramedical personnel. *See* **Allied health personnel; Emergency medical technicians**

Paramedics, Emergency. *See* **Emergency medical technicians**

Paranormal phenomena. *See* **Parapsychology**

Paraphilia. *See* **Sexual deviation**

Paraprofessional librarians. *See* **Library technicians**

Paraprofessions and paraprofessionals   331.7

   See also names of paraprofessions and paraprofessional personnel, e.g. **Library technicians;** etc.

   xx **Occupations; Professions; Vocational guidance**

Parapsychology   133

   Use for materials on investigations of phenomena that appear to be contrary to physical laws and beyond the normal sense perceptions.

   See also

Apparitions	**Mind and body**
Clairvoyance	**Occultism**
Dreams	**Personality disorders**
Extrasensory perception	**Psychokinesis**
Ghosts	**Spiritualism**
Hallucinations and illusions	**Subconsciousness**
	Telepathy
Mental suggestion	

   x Paranormal phenomena; Psi (Parapsychology); Psychic phenomena; Psychical research

Parapsychology—*Continued*

   xx **Ghosts; Occultism; Psychology; Research; Spiritualism; Supernatural**

Parasites   574.5; 581.5; 591.52

   See also **Bacteriology; Insect pests; Ticks**

   x Animal parasites; Diseases and pests; Entozoa; Epizoa

   xx **Pests**

Parasols. *See* **Umbrellas and parasols**

Paratroops. *See* **Parachute troops**

Parcel post. *See* **Postal service**

Pardon   364.6

   See also **Amnesty**

   xx **Amnesty; Criminal justice, Administration of; Parole**

Parent abuse. *See* **Elderly abuse**

Parent and child   306.874

   Use for materials on the psychological and social interaction between parents and their minor children. Materials on the skills, attributes and attitudes needed for parenthood are entered under **Parenting**. Materials on the principles and techniques of raising children are entered under **Child rearing**. For materials restricted to the legal right of parents to visit their children in situations of separation, divorce, etc., use **Visitation rights (Domestic relations)**.

   See also

Adult children of alcoholics	Children of immigrants
Child abuse	Children of working parents
Child custody	Conflict of generations
Child rearing	Father and child
Children of alcoholics	Inheritance and succession
Children of divorced parents	Mother and child
Children of drug addicts	Parenting

   x Child and parent

   xx **Children and adults; Conflict of generations; Domestic relations; Family; Human relations**

Parent-teacher associations. *See* **Parents' and teachers' associations**

Parent-teacher conferences   371.1

   x Conferences, Parent-teacher; Interviews, Parent-teacher; Teacher-parent conferences

   xx **Parent-teacher relationships**

Parent-teacher relationships   370.19

   See also **Home and school; Parent-teacher conferences; Parents' and teachers' associations**

   x Parents and teachers; Teacher-parent relationships; Teachers and parents

   xx **Home and school**

Parental behavior. *See* **Parenting**

Parental custody. *See* **Child custody**

Parental kidnapping   362.82; 364.1

   x Child snatching by parents; Childnapping; Custody kidnapping; Kidnapping, Parental

   xx **Child custody**

Parenting   306.874; 649

   See note under **Parent and child.**

Parenting—*Continued*
    See also **Child rearing; Home instruction**
    x Parental behavior
    xx **Child rearing; Home instruction; Parent and child**
Parenting, Part-time   306.874; 649
    See also **Children of divorced parents; Single parent family**
    x Part-time parenting
    xx **Children of divorced parents**
Parents and teachers. *See* **Parent-teacher relationships**
Parents' and teachers' associations   370.19
    See also **Home and school**
    x P.T.A.'s; Parent-teacher associations; PTAs
    xx **Community and school; Educational associations; Home and school; Parent-teacher relationships; Societies**
Parents, Biological. *See* **Birthparents**
Parents, Single. *See* **Single parent family**
Parents, Teenage. *See* **Teenage fathers; Teenage mothers**
Parents, Unmarried. *See* **Unmarried fathers; Unmarried mothers**
Parents without partners. *See* **Single parent family**
Parish libraries. *See* **Church libraries**
Parish registers. *See* **Registers of births, etc.**
Parks (May subdiv. geog.)   363.6; 712
    See also **Amusement parks; Botanical gardens; National parks and reserves; Playgrounds; Zoos**
    xx **Cities and towns; Landscape architecture; Outdoor recreation; Playgrounds**
Parks—United States   363.6; 712; 917.3
    x United States—Parks
Parkways. *See* **Express highways**
Parliamentary government. *See* **Representative government and representation**
Parliamentary practice   060.4
    x Rules of order
    xx **Debates and debating; Legislation; Legislative bodies; Public meetings**
Parliaments. *See* **Legislative bodies**
Parochial schools. *See* **Church schools**
Parodies 808.87; 817, etc.; 817.008, etc.
    Use for collections of parodies. Materials on the literary form of parody, that is, satirical or humorous imitation of a serious piece of literature, are entered under **Parody.**
    See also names of prominent authors with the subdivision *Parodies, travesties, etc.,* e.g. **Shakespeare, William, 1564-1616—Parodies, travesties, etc.;** etc.
    x Travesties
    xx **Literature—Collections**
Parody 808.7
    Use for materials about the literary form of parody, that is, satirical or humorous imitation of a serious piece of literature. Collections of parodies are entered under **Parodies.**
    x Comic literature
    xx **Literature; Satire; Wit and humor**

Parole   364.6

    See also **Pardon; Probation**

    xx **Corrections; Crime; Criminal justice, Administration of; Probation; Social case work**

Part-time employment   331.2

    See also **Job sharing; Supplementary employment**

    x Alternative work schedules; Employment, Part-time

    xx **Employment; Hours of labor; Labor**

Part-time parenting.   *See* **Parenting, Part-time**

Participative management   331.89; 658.3

    See also **Collective bargaining**

    x Consultative management; Employees' representation in management; Industrial councils; Labor participation in management; Management—Employee participation; Workers' participation in management; Workshop councils

    xx **Collective bargaining; Factory management; Industrial relations; Personnel management**

Particles (Nuclear physics)   539.7

    See also names of particles, e.g. **Electrons; Neutrons; Protons; Quarks;** etc.

    x Elementary particles (Physics); Nuclear particles; Nucleons

    xx **Nuclear physics**

Parties   793.2

    See also types of parties, e.g. **Children's parties; Showers (Parties);** etc.

    xx **Entertaining**

Parties, Political.   *See* **Political parties**

Partisans.   *See* **Guerrillas**

Passion plays   792.1

    See also **Mysteries and miracle plays**

    xx **Drama; Jesus Christ—Drama; Religious drama; Theater**

Passions.   *See* **Emotions**

Passive resistance   172; 322.4

    See also **Boycott; Hunger strikes; Nonviolence**

    x Civil disobedience; Nonviolent noncooperation

    xx **Government, Resistance to; Nonviolence**

Passover   296.4; 394.2

    x Pesach

    xx **Fasts and feasts—Judaism**

Pastel drawing   741.2

    See also **Crayon drawing**

    xx **Crayon drawing; Drawing; Portrait painting**

Pastimes.   *See* **Amusements; Games; Recreation**

Pastoral peoples.   *See* **Nomads**

Pastoral psychiatry.   *See* **Psychology, Pastoral**

Pastoral psychology.   *See* **Psychology, Pastoral**

Pastoral theology.   *See* **Pastoral work**

Pastoral work   253

    See also **Church work; Clergy; Preaching; Psychology, Pastoral**

    x Pastoral theology; Theology, Pastoral

Pastors.   *See* **Clergy; Priests**

Pastry   641.8

    xx **Baking; Cookery**

Pastures   333.74

    See also **Forage plants; Grasses**

    xx **Agriculture; Cattle; Forage plants; Grasses**

Patchwork quilts. *See* **Quilts**
Patent medicines. *See* **Nonprescription drugs**
Patents   608
    See also **Inventions; Trademarks**
    x Discoveries (in science); Intellectual property
    xx **Inventions; Machinery; Manufactures; Trademarks**
Pathological botany. *See* **Plant diseases**
Pathological psychology. *See* **Psychology, Pathological**
Pathology   616.07
    See also

Bacteriology	**Medical genetics**
Birth defects	**Medicine**
Diagnosis	**Preventive medicine**
Fever	**Therapeutics**
Immunity	

    x Disease (Pathology)
    xx **Diagnosis; Diseases; Medicine; Preventive medicine**
Pathology, Vegetable. *See* **Plant diseases**
Patience   152.4; 179
    xx **Human behavior**
Patience (Game). *See* **Solitaire (Game)**
Patients. *See* **Sick**
Patios   643
    x Decks (Domestic architecture)
    xx **Landscape architecture**
Patriotic poetry   808.81; 811.008, etc.
    xx **National songs; Poetry—Collections**
Patriotic songs. *See* **National songs**
Patriotism   172
    See also **Nationalism**
    xx **Citizenship; Human behavior; Loyalty; Nationalism**
Patronage of the arts. *See* **Art patronage**
Pattern making   671.2
    See also **Design; Founding; Mechanical drawing**
    xx **Design; Founding**
Patterns for crafts. *See* appropriate subjects with the subdivision *Patterns,* e.g. **Dressmaking—Patterns;** etc.
Patterns (Language arts). *See* **Language arts—Patterning**
Patterns (Mathematics)   372.7
    See also **Manipulative materials**
    x Geometric patterns; Number patterns
    xx **Manipulative materials; Mathematics**
Pauperism. *See* **Poverty**
Pavements   625.8
    See also **Roads; Streets**
    xx **Cement; Concrete; Roads; Streets**
Pay equity. *See* **Equal pay for equal work**
Pay television, Cable. *See* **Cable television**
Pay television, Subscription. *See* **Subscription television**
Payroll taxes. *See* **Income tax; Unemployment insurance**
Peace   172; 327.1; 341.7
    See also **Arbitration, International; Arms control; League of Nations; Pacifism; Security, International; War;** also names of wars with the subdivision *Peace,* e.g. **World War, 1939-**

499

Peace—*Continued*
    1945—Peace; etc.
    xx **Arbitration, International; Arms control; International relations; Reconstruction (1914-1939); Security, International; War**
Peace keeping forces. *See* **United Nations—Armed forces**
Peace movements. *See* **Pacifism**
Peacocks 598.6
    x Peafowl; Peahens
    xx **Birds**
Peafowl. *See* **Peacocks**
Peahens. *See* **Peacocks**
Pearl Harbor (Oahu, Hawaii), Attack on, 1941 940.54
    xx **World War, 1939-1945—Campaigns**
Pearlfisheries 338.3; 639
    x Oysters, Pearl
    xx **Fisheries**
Peasant art. *See* **Folk art**
Peasantry 305.5; 307.72
    See also **Agricultural laborers; Land tenure; Sociology, Rural**
    x Rural life
    xx **Agricultural laborers; Feudalism; Labor; Land tenure; Sociology, Rural**
Pecan 634
    xx **Nuts; Trees**
Pedagogy. *See* **Education; Education—Study and teaching; Teaching**
Peddlers and peddling 658.8
    x Door to door selling
    xx **Direct selling; Sales personnel**
Pediatric psychiatry. *See* **Child psychiatry**
Pediatrics. *See* **Children—Diseases; Children—Health and hygiene; Infants—Diseases; Infants—Health and hygiene**
Pedigrees. *See* **Genealogy; Heraldry**
Peer counseling 158; 361.3
    x Peer counseling in rehabilitation; Peer counseling of students; Peer group counseling; Rehabilitation peer counseling; Student to student counseling
    xx **Counseling**
Peer counseling in rehabilitation. *See* **Peer counseling**
Peer counseling of students. *See* **Peer counseling**
Peer group counseling. *See* **Peer counseling**
Peer group influence. *See* **Peer pressure**
Peer pressure 303.3; 364.2
    x Peer group influence
    xx **Socialization**
Peerage. *See* **Nobility**
Pelts. *See* **Hides and skins**
Pen drawing 741.2
    x Ink drawing
    xx **Drawing**
Pen names. *See* **Pseudonyms**
Penal codes. *See* **Criminal law**
Penal colonies 365
    x Convicts
    xx **Colonies; Colonization; Criminals; Prisons; Punishment**

Penal institutions. *See* **Correctional institutions; Prisons; Reformatories**

Penal law. *See* **Criminal law**

Penal reform. *See* **Prison reform**

Pencil drawing 741.2
   xx **Drawing**

Penicillin 615
   xx **Antibiotics**

Peninsulas (May subdiv. geog.) **551.4**
   See also names of peninsulas, e.g. **Arabian Peninsula;** etc.

Penitentiaries. *See* **Prisons**

Penmanship. *See* **Handwriting**

Pennsylvania Dutch 974.8
   x Pennsylvania Germans

Pennsylvania Germans. *See* **Pennsylvania Dutch**

Penology. *See* **Corrections; Punishment**

Pensions 331.25; 350.5; 351.5
   See also **Individual retirement accounts; Mothers' pensions; Old age pensions; Social security**
   x Compensation
   xx **Annuities; Retirement income**

Pensions, Military 355.1
   See also **Veterans**
   x Bonus, Soldiers'; Military pensions; Naval pensions; Pensions, Naval; Soldiers' bonus; War pensions
   xx **Veterans**

Pensions, Naval. *See* **Pensions, Military**

Peonage 306.3; 331.5
   See also **Contract labor; Convict labor**
   x Compulsory labor; Forced labor; Servitude
   xx **Contract labor; Convict labor; Labor; Slavery**

People in space. *See* **Interplanetary voyages; Space flight**

People, Married. *See* **Married people**

People, Single. *See* **Single people**

People's banks. *See* **Banks and banking, Cooperative**

People's democracies. *See* **Communist countries**

People's Republic of China. *See* **China**

Pep pills. *See* **Amphetamines**

Percentage 513.2
   xx **Arithmetic**

Perception 152.1; 153.7
   See also **Apperception; Concepts; Consciousness; Gestalt psychology; Intuition; Manipulative materials;** also types of concepts and images, e.g. **Size and shape;** etc.
   x Feeling
   xx **Apperception; Educational psychology; Intellect; Intuition; Knowledge, Theory of; Manipulative materials; Psychology; Thought and thinking**

Percussion instruments 786.8
   See also **Piano;** also names of percussion instruments, e.g. **Drum;** etc.
   xx **Musical instruments**

Perennials 635.9
   xx **Flower gardening; Flowers**

Perfectionism (Personality trait) 155.2
   x Self-expectations, Perfectionist
   xx **Personality**

Performance standards   658.5
>   *See also* subjects and classes of people with the
>   subdivision *Rating,* e.g. **Bonds—Rating;
>   Employees—Rating; Librarians—Rating;**
>   etc.
>   *x* Job performance standards; Rating; Work per-
>   formance standards

Performing arts   790.2
>   *See also* **Centers for the performing arts; The-
>   ater;** also art forms performed on stage or
>   screen, e.g. **Ballet; Dancing;** etc.
>   *x* Show business

Perfumes   391; 668
>   *xx* **Cosmetics; Essences and essential oils**

Periodic law   541.2
>   *xx* **Chemical elements; Chemistry, Physical and
>   theoretical**

Periodicals   050
>   *See also* **Chapbooks; Freedom of the press; Jour-
>   nalism; Newspapers;** also **American periodi-
>   cals; English periodicals; Press;** etc.; and
>   general subjects with the subdivision
>   *Periodicals,* e.g. **Engineering—Periodicals;**
>   etc.; and names of individual periodicals
>   *x* Journals; Magazines
>   *xx* **Journalism; Mass media; Newspapers; Press;
>   Serial publications**

Periodicals—Indexes   050
>   *xx* **Indexes**

Periodicity   574.1
>   *See also* **Biological rhythms; Rhythm; Time**
>   *x* Cycles
>   *xx* **Rhythm; Time**

Permanent education. *See* **Continuing education**

Persecution   272
>   *See also* **Freedom of religion; Jews—
>   Persecutions; Martyrs; Massacres**
>   *x* Christians—Persecutions
>   *xx* **Atrocities; Church history; Freedom of reli-
>   gion; Martyrs**

Persia. *See* **Iran**

Persian Gulf War, 1991-   956.704
>   Use for comprehensive materials on the war.
>   Materials limited to the Iraqi invasion of
>   Kuwait are entered under **Kuwait—History—
>   1990, Iraqi Invasion.**
>   *x* Desert Shield Operation; Desert Storm Opera-
>   tion; Gulf War, 1991-; Iraq—History—
>   1991- , Persian Gulf War; Iraq-Kuwait Cri-
>   sis, 1990-; Kuwait—History—1991- , Per-
>   sian Gulf War; Middle East War, 1991-;
>   Mideast War, 1991-; Operation Desert
>   Shield; Operation Desert Storm; United
>   States—History—1991- , Persian Gulf War

Persian rugs. *See* **Oriental rugs**
Personal actions (Law). *See* **Litigation**
Personal appearance. *See* **Personal grooming**
Personal cleanliness. *See* **Hygiene**
Personal computers. *See* **Home computers**
Personal conduct. *See* **Human behavior**
Personal development. *See* **Personality; Success**
Personal films. *See* **Amateur films; Experimental
       films**

Personal finance   332.024

    See also **Budgets, Household; Children's allowances; Consumer credit; Estate planning; Insurance; Investments; Saving and thrift**

    x Budgets, Personal; Domestic finance; Family finance; Finance, Personal; Financial planning, Personal

  xx **Finance**

Personal freedom. *See* **Freedom**

Personal grooming   646.7

    x Beauty, Personal; Good grooming; Grooming for men; Grooming for women; Grooming, Personal; Personal appearance

  xx **Hygiene**

Personal health. *See* **Health**

Personal hygiene. *See* **Hygiene**

Personal life skills. *See* **Life skills**

Personal loans   332.7

  Use for materials on loans to individuals for personal rather than business uses.

    See also **Banks and banking, Cooperative; Credit unions; Mortgages; Savings and loan associations**

    x Consumer loans; Loans, Personal; Small loans

  xx **Consumer credit; Loans**

Personal names (May subdiv. geog. or by ethnic adjective, e.g. **Personal names—United States; Personal names, Scottish;** etc.) **929.4**

    See also **Nicknames; Pseudonyms**

    x Christian names; Family names; Forenames; Names, Personal; Surnames

  xx **Names**

Personal names, Scottish   929.4

    x Names, Personal—Scottish; Scottish personal names

Personal names—United States   929.40973

    x American personal names; Names, Personal—United States; United States—Names, Personal; United States—Personal names

Personal narratives. *See* **Autobiographies; Biography;** and subjects with the subdivision *Biography* or *Correspondence,* and names of events and wars with the subdivision *Personal narratives,* e.g. **World War, 1939-1945—Personal narratives;** etc., for collective or individual eyewitness reports or autobiographical accounts of these events and wars.

Personal space   153.6; 302.2

  Use for materials on the sense of physical space required for psychological comfort.

    x Space, Personal

  xx **Human relations; Nonverbal communication; Space and time**

Personal time management. *See* **Time management**

Personality   155.2

    See also **Character; Eccentrics and eccentricities; Individuality; Perfectionism (Personality trait); Self; Soul**

    x Identity; Personal development

  xx **Consciousness; Individuality; Psychology; Soul**

503

Personality disorders   616.85
    See also **Hallucinations and illusions; Hypnotism**
    xx **Hallucinations and illusions; Hypnotism;**
        Mind and body; Parapsychology; Psychol-
        ogy, Pathological; Subconsciousness
Personnel administration.   *See* **Personnel manage-**
        ment
Personnel classification.   *See* **Job analysis**
Personnel management   658.3
    Use for materials dealing with problems of per-
        sonnel in factories, business, etc., hiring and
        dismissing employees, and general questions
        of the relationship between officials and em-
        ployees.
    See also

Absenteeism (Labor)	**Job analysis**
Affirmative action pro-	**Job satisfaction**
grams	**Job security**
Applications for positions	**Labor turnover**
Counseling	**Motion study**
Efficiency, Industrial	**Office management**
Employee morale	**Participative management**
Employees—Dismissal	**Recruiting of employees**
Employees—Training	**Supervisors**
Employment agencies	**Time study**
Factory management	

    x Career development; Employment manage-
        ment; Human resource management; Per-
        sonnel administration; Supervision of em-
        ployees
    xx **Efficiency, Industrial; Factory management;**
        Human relations; Industrial management;
        Industrial relations; Management; Office
        management
Personnel service in education.   *See* **Educational**
        counseling
Persons, Care of.   *See* classes of dependent persons
        with the subdivisions *Care* or *Home care*
        or *Institutional care,* e.g. **Infants—Care;**
        Elderly—Home care; Mentally ill—
        Institutional care; etc.
Persons, Crimes against.   *See* **Offenses against the**
        person
Persons, Single.   *See* **Single people**
Perspective   701
    See also **Drawing**
    x Architectural perspective
    xx **Drawing; Geometrical drawing; Geometry, De-**
        scriptive; Optics; Painting
Persuasion (Rhetoric).   *See* **Public speaking; Rheto-**
        ric
Perversion, Sexual.   *See* **Sexual deviation**
Pesach.   *See* **Passover**
Pest control.   *See* **Pests—Control**
Pesticide pollution.   *See* **Pesticides—Environmental**
        aspects
Pesticides   632; 668
    See also **Fungicides; Herbicides; Insecticides;**
        Natural pesticides
    xx **Agricultural chemicals; Pests—Control; Poi-**
        sons and poisoning
Pesticides and wildlife   574.5
    x Wildlife and pesticides

Pesticides and wildlife—*Continued*
  xx **Pesticides—Environmental aspects; Wildlife
    conservation**
Pesticides—Environmental aspects   363.7; 632
  See also **Pesticides and wildlife**
  x Environment and pesticides; Pesticide pollu-
    tion
  xx **Pollution**
Pestilences.   *See* **Epidemics**
Pests   574.6; 632
  Use for materials on detrimental or annoying
    plants or animals.
  See also types of pests, e.g. **Agricultural pests;
    Fungi; Household pests; Insect pests; Para-
    sites;** etc.; also names of crops, trees, etc.
    with the subdivision *Diseases and pests,* e.g.
    Fruit—Diseases and pests; etc.; and names
    of pests, e.g. **Flies;** etc.
  x Vermin
  xx **Zoology, Economic**
Pests—Biological control   632
  x Agricultural pests—Biological control; Biolog-
    ical control of pests
Pests—Control   363.7; 628.9; 632
  See also **Pesticides;** also names of specific pests
    with the subdivision *Control,* e.g. **Mosqui-
    toes—Control;** etc.
  x Extermination of pests; Pest control; Pests—
    Extermination
  xx **Agricultural pests; Zoology, Economic**
Pests—Extermination.   *See* **Pests—Control**
Pet-facilitated psychotherapy.   *See* **Pet therapy**
Pet therapy   158; 362.2; 615.5
  x Animal-facilitated therapy; Animals, Visiting;
    Companion-animal partnership; Pet-
    facilitated psychotherapy; Visiting animals
  xx **Animals and the handicapped; Therapeutics**
Petrochemicals   661
  x Petroleum chemicals
  xx **Chemicals**
Petroglyphs.   *See* **Rock drawings, paintings, and en-
    gravings**
Petroleum (May subdiv. geog.)   553.2; 665.5
  See also **Boring; Coal tar products; Gasoline**
  x Coal oil; Crude oil; Oil
  xx **Gas; Oils and fats; Wells**
Petroleum as fuel   338.4; 665.5
  See also **Oil burners**
  x Fuel, Liquid; Fuel oil; Liquid fuel; Oil fuel
  xx **Fuel**
Petroleum chemicals.   *See* **Petrochemicals**
Petroleum engines.   *See* **Gas and oil engines**
Petroleum geology   553.2
  x Geology, Petroleum
  xx **Geology, Economic; Prospecting**
Petroleum industry   338.2
  x Petroleum industry and trade; Petroleum
    trade
Petroleum industry and trade.   *See* **Petroleum in-
    dustry**
Petroleum—Pipelines   338.2; 665.5
  x Pipelines, Petroleum
Petroleum pollution of water.   *See* **Oil pollution of
    water**

Petroleum trade. *See* **Petroleum industry**
Petroleum—United States   553.2; 665.5
> *x* United States—Petroleum
Petroleum—Well boring. *See* **Oil well drilling**
Petrology   552
> *See also* **Crystallography; Geochemistry; Geol-
> ogy; Lunar petrology; Mineralogy; Rocks;
> Stone;** also varieties of rocks, e.g. **Granite;
> Marble;** etc.
> *xx* **Geology; Mineralogy; Rocks; Science; Stone**
Pets   636.088
> *See also* **Domestic animals;** also names of ani-
> mals, e.g. **Cats; Dogs;** etc.
> *xx* **Animals; Domestic animals**
Pets and the handicapped. *See* **Animals and the
> handicapped**
Petting zoos   590.74
> *x* Animals—Petting zoos
> *xx* **Zoos**
Pewter   673
> *xx* **Alloys; Plate; Tin**
Phantoms. *See* **Apparitions; Ghosts**
Pharmaceutical chemistry   615
> *See also* **Disinfection and disinfectants; Materia
> medica; Pharmacy; Poisons and poisoning;
> Therapeutics**
> *x* Chemistry, Medical and pharmaceutical;
> Chemistry, Pharmaceutical; Drugs—
> Chemistry; Medicinal chemistry
> *xx* **Chemistry; Pharmacy; Therapeutics**
Pharmaceuticals. *See* **Drugs**
Pharmacodynamics. *See* **Pharmacology**
Pharmacology   615
> Use for materials on the action and properties of
> drugs in general. For materials limited to
> the effect of drugs on the functions of living
> organisms, use **Drugs—Physiological effect.**
> *See also* **Chemotherapy; Drugs; Drugs—
> Physiological effect; Pharmacy**
> *x* Medicine—Physiological effect; Pharmacody-
> namics
> *xx* **Drugs; Materia medica; Medicine; Pharmacy**
Pharmacopoeias. *See* **Materia medica**
Pharmacotherapy. *See* **Chemotherapy**
Pharmacy   615
> Use for materials on the art or practice of pre-
> paring, preserving, and dispensing drugs.
> *See also* **Botany, Medical; Drugs; Homeopathy;
> Materia medica; Pharmaceutical chemistry;
> Pharmacology**
> *xx* Chemistry; Materia medica; Medicine; Phar-
> maceutical chemistry; Pharmacology
Pheasants   598.6; 636.5
> *xx* **Game and game birds**
Phenomenology   142
> *See also* **Existentialism**
> *xx* **Philosophy, Modern**
Philanthropists   361.7092; 920
> *x* Altruists; Humanitarians
Philanthropy. *See* **Charities; Charity organization;
> Endowments; Gifts; Social work**
Philately. *See* **Postage stamps—Collectors and col-
> lecting**

Philology. *See* **Language and languages; Philology, Comparative**

Philology, Comparative 410

Use for comparative studies of languages. General materials on the history, philosophy, origin, etc. of languages are entered under **Language and languages.**

See also **Language and languages; Literature, Comparative**

x Comparative linguistics; Comparative philology; Language and languages—Comparative philology; Philology

xx **Grammar; Language and languages**

Philosophers (May subdiv. geog. adjective form) **180.92; 190.92; 920**

Philosophers, American 191.092; 920

x American philosophers; United States—Philosophers

Philosophers' stone. *See* **Alchemy**

Philosophy (May subdiv. geog. adjective form) **100**

See also

Belief and doubt	**Mind and body**
Empiricism	**Mysticism**
Ethics	**Positivism**
Fate and fatalism	**Pragmatism**
Free will and determinism	**Psychology**
Gnosticism	**Rationalism**
God	**Realism**
Humanism	**Reality**
Idealism	**Skepticism**
Intuition	**Soul**
Knowledge, Theory of	**Theism**
Logic	**Transcendentalism**
Materialism	**Truth**
Metaphysics	**Universe**

also subjects with the subdivision *Philosophy,* e.g. **History—Philosophy;** etc.

xx **Humanities**

Philosophy, American 191

x American philosophy; United States—Philosophy

Philosophy, Ancient 180

See also **Stoics**

x Ancient philosophy; Greek philosophy; Philosophy, Greek; Philosophy, Roman; Roman philosophy

Philosophy and religion 210

See also **Religion—Philosophy**

x Religion and philosophy

xx **Religion—Philosophy**

Philosophy, Greek. *See* **Philosophy, Ancient**

Philosophy, Hindu 181

See also **Yoga**

Philosophy—Historiography 109

xx **Historiography**

Philosophy, Medieval 189

x Medieval philosophy

xx **Middle Ages**

Philosophy, Modern 190

See also **Enlightenment; Evolution; Existentialism; Phenomenology**

x Modern philosophy

Philosophy, Moral. *See* **Ethics**

Philosophy of history. *See* **History—Philosophy**

Philosophy of religion. *See* **Religion—Philosophy**
Philosophy, Roman. *See* **Philosophy, Ancient**
Phobias   616.85
   xx **Fear; Neuroses**
Phonetic spelling. *See* **Spelling reform**
Phonetics   414
      See also **Reading—Phonetic method; Speech;**
            Voice; also names of languages with the sub-
            division *Pronunciation,* e.g. **English lan-**
            guage—Pronunciation; etc.
      x Phonics; Phonology
      xx **Language and languages; Reading—Phonetic**
            method; Sound; Speech; Voice
Phonics. *See* **Phonetics; Reading—Phonetic**
         method
Phonograph   621.389
      See also **Compact disc players; Sound—**
            Recording and reproducing
Phonograph records. *See* **Sound recordings**
Phonology. *See* **Phonetics;** and names of languages
         with the subdivision *Pronunciation,* e.g.
         English language—Pronunciation; etc.
Phosphates   546; 553.6; 631.8
   xx **Fertilizers and manures**
Phosphorescence   535; 574.19
      See also **Bioluminescence**
      x Luminescence
      xx **Light; Mineralogy; Optics; Radiation; Radio-**
            activity
Photo journalism. *See* **Photojournalism**
Photocopying machines. *See* **Copying processes**
         and machines
Photoelectric cells   537.5; 621.3815
      See also **Electronics**
      x Electric eye
Photoengraving   686.2
      See also **Photomechanical processes**
      x Halftone process
      xx **Engraving; Photomechanical processes**
Photographic chemistry   771
      Use for materials on the chemical processes em-
         ployed in photography.
      See also **Photography—Processing**
      x Chemistry, Photographic
      xx **Chemistry**
Photographic film. *See* **Photography—Film**
Photographic slides. *See* **Slides (Photography)**
Photographic supplies. *See* **Photography—**
         Equipment and supplies
Photography   770
      See also

Aerial photography	**Photography, Artistic**
Astronomical photography	**Photojournalism**
Cameras	**Photomechanical pro-**
Color photography	**cesses**
Commercial photography	**Slides (Photography)**
Filmstrips	**Space photography**
Microphotography	**Telephotography**
Motion picture photogra-	**Three dimensional photog-**
phy	**raphy**
Nature photography	**Underwater photography**
Outdoor photography	

Photography, Aerial. *See* **Aerial photography**

Photography—Aesthetics. *See* **Photography, Artistic**
Photography, Artistic   770; 779
x Artistic photography; Photography—
Aesthetics
xx **Art; Photography**
Photography, Astronomical. *See* **Astronomical pho-
tography**
Photography, Color. *See* **Color photography**
Photography, Commercial. *See* **Commercial pho-
tography**
Photography—Darkroom technique. *See* **Photogra-
phy—Processing**
Photography—Developing and developers   771
xx **Photography—Processing**
Photography—Enlarging   771
x Enlarging (Photography)
Photography—Equipment and supplies   771
See also **Cameras**
x Photographic supplies
Photography—Film   771
x Photographic film
Photography—Handbooks, manuals, etc.   770.2
Photography in astronautics. *See* **Space photogra-
phy**
Photography, Journalistic. *See* **Photojournalism**
Photography, Laser. *See* **Holography**
Photography, Lensless. *See* **Holography**
Photography—Lighting   771; 778.7
Photography, Medical. *See* **Medical photography**
Photography—Motion pictures. *See* **Motion picture
photography**
Photography of animals   778.9
Use for materials on the technique and accounts
of photographing animals. Materials consist-
ing of photographs and pictures of animals
are entered under **Animals—Pictorial
works.**
See also **Animal painting and illustration; Animals—Pictorial works**
x Animal photography; Animals—Photography
xx **Animal painting and illustration; Animals—
Pictorial works; Nature photography**
Photography of birds   778.9
Use same form for photography of other subjects.
x Bird photography; Birds—Photography
xx **Nature photography**
Photography of fishes   778.9
x Fishes—Photography
xx **Nature photography**
Photography of nature. *See* **Nature photography**
Photography of plants   778.9
x Plants—Photography
xx **Nature photography**
Photography, Outdoor. *See* **Outdoor photography**
Photography—Portraits   778.9; 779
xx **Portraits**
Photography—Printing processes   771
xx **Photography—Processing**
Photography—Processing   771
See also names of special techniques, e.g. **Photography—Developing and developers; Pho-**

Photography—Processing—*Continued*
   tography—**Printing processes;** etc.
   x Darkroom technique in photography; Photog-
       raphy—Darkroom technique
   xx **Photographic chemistry**
Photography—Retouching   771
   x Retouching (Photography)
Photography—Scientific applications   778.3
   See also specific applications, e.g. **Medical pho-
       tography;** etc.
Photography, Space.   *See* **Space photography**
Photography, Stereoscopic.   *See* **Three dimensional
       photography**
Photography, Submarine.   *See* **Underwater photog-
       raphy**
Photojournalism   070.4; 779
   x Journalistic photography; News photography;
       Photo journalism; Photography, Journalis-
       tic
   xx **Commercial photography; Journalism; Pho-
       tography**
Photomechanical processes   686.2
   See also types of photomechanical processes,
       e.g. **Photoengraving;** etc.
   xx **Illustration of books; Photoengraving; Photog-
       raphy**
Photometry   535
   See also **Color; Light; Optics**
   x Electric light; Light, Electric
   xx **Light; Optics**
Photoplays.   *See* **Motion picture plays**
Photosynthesis   581.1
   xx **Plants**
Phototherapy   615.8
   See also **Radiotherapy; Ultraviolet rays**
   x Electric light; Light, Electric; Light—
       Therapeutic use
   xx **Physical therapy; Radiotherapy; Therapeutics**
Photovoltaic power generation   621.3815
   See also **Solar batteries**
   x Solar cells
   xx **Solar energy**
Phrenology   139
   See also **Mind and body; Physiognomy**
   xx **Brain; Head; Mind and body; Physiognomy;
       Psychology**
Physical anthropology   573
   See also **Man—Origin**
   x Anthropology, Physical; Biological anthropol-
       ogy; Somatology
   xx **Anthropology; Ethnology**
Physical chemistry.   *See* **Chemistry, Physical and
       theoretical**
Physical culture.   *See* **Physical education**
Physical education   613.7
   See also

Athletics	**Health education**
Coaching (Athletics)	**Movement education**
Drill (Nonmilitary)	**Physical fitness**
Exercise	**Posture**
Games	**Sports**
Gymnastics	

   also names of kinds of exercises, e.g. **Fencing;**

Physical education—*Continued*
    Judo; etc.
    x Calisthenics; Education, Physical; Physical
        culture; Physical training
    xx **Athletics; Education; Exercise; Gymnastics;
        Hygiene; Sports**
Physical education—Medical aspects. *See* **Sports
    medicine**
Physical fitness 613.7
    See also **Bodybuilding**
    x Endurance, Physical; Physical stamina; Stam-
        ina, Physical
    xx **Exercise; Health; Health self-care; Physical
        education**
Physical fitness centers. *See* **Health resorts, spas,
    etc.**
Physical geography (May subdiv. geog.) **910**
    Use for materials dealing with the physical fea-
        tures of the earth's surface and its atmo-
        sphere. For general materials, frequently
        school materials, describing the surface of
        the earth and its interrelationship with vari-
        ous peoples, animals, natural products and
        industries, use **Geography.**
    See also

Climate	**Lakes**
Earth	**Meteorology**
Earthquakes	**Mountains**
Geochemistry	**Ocean**
Geophysics	**Ocean currents**
Geysers	**Rivers**
Glaciers	**Tides**
Ice	**Volcanoes**
Icebergs	**Winds**

    x Geography, Physical; Physiography
    xx **Earth; Geography; Geology**
Physical geography—United States 917.3
    x United States—Physical geography
Physical stamina. *See* **Physical fitness**
Physical therapy 615.8
    Use for general materials on the treatment of
        disability, injury or disease through exercise,
        heat, water, body manipulation, massage,
        etc.
    See also types of therapy, e.g. **Baths; Electro-
        therapeutics; Hydrotherapy; Massage;
        Occupational therapy; Phototherapy;
        Radiotherapy;** etc.
    x Physiotherapy
    xx **Therapeutics**
Physical training. *See* **Physical education**
Physically handicapped 362.4
    See also **Orthopedics;** also names of the physi-
        cally handicapped, e.g. **Blind; Deaf;** etc.
    x Crippled people; Invalids
    xx **Handicapped; Orthopedics**
**Physically handicapped children 155.45; 362.4;
    362.7**
    x Children, Crippled; Crippled children
    xx **Handicapped children**
Physically handicapped—Housing 362.4
    x Housing for the physically handicapped
    xx **Housing**

Physically handicapped—Rehabilitation 362.4
   See also **Occupational therapy**
Physicians 610.69; 920
   See also **Women physicians;** also names of specialists, e.g. **Radiologists; Surgeons;** etc.
   x Doctors; Medical profession
   xx **Surgeons**
Physicians—Directories 610.69
   xx **Directories**
Physicians—Drug use 362.29; 610.69
   x Drug abusing physicians; Drug addicted physicians
Physicians—Malpractice 346.03
   x Medical errors; Medical malpractice; Physicians—Tort liability
   xx **Malpractice; Medical ethics; Medicine—Law and legislation**
Physicians—Tort liability. *See* **Physicians— Malpractice**
Physicists 920
   xx **Scientists**
Physics 530
   See also

Astrophysics	**Matter**
Biophysics	**Mechanics**
Chemistry, Physical and theoretical	**Music—Acoustics and physics**
Dynamics	**Nuclear physics**
Electricity	**Optics**
Electrons	**Pneumatics**
Gases	**Quantum theory**
Geophysics	**Radiation**
Gravitation	**Radioactivity**
Hydraulics	**Relativity (Physics)**
Hydrostatics	**Solids**
Light	**Sound**
Liquids	**Statics**
Magnetism	**Thermodynamics**

   xx **Dynamics; Science**
Physics, Astronomical. *See* **Astrophysics**
Physics, Biological. *See* **Biophysics**
Physics, Nuclear. *See* **Nuclear physics**
Physics, Terrestrial. *See* **Geophysics**
Physiognomy 138
   See also **Face; Phrenology**
   xx **Face; Phrenology; Psychology**
Physiography. *See* **Physical geography**
Physiological chemistry. *See* **Biochemistry**
Physiological effect. *See* appropriate subjects with the subdivision *Physiological effect,* e.g. **Alcohol—Physiological effect; Opium— Physiological effect;** etc.
Physiological psychology. *See* **Psychophysiology**
Physiological stress. *See* **Stress (Physiology)**
Physiology 574.1; 612
   See also

Anatomy	**Growth**
Blood	**Health**
Body temperature	**Lymphatic system**
Bones	**Muscles**
Cells	**Musculoskeletal system**
Digestion	**Nervous system**
Fatigue	**Nutrition**

Physiology—*Continued*
> Old age   Respiration
> Psychophysiology   Senses and sensation
> Reproduction
>> also names of organs of the body, e.g. **Heart;**
>> etc.
>> *x* Body, Human; Human body
>> *xx* **Anatomy; Biology; Medicine; Science**

Physiology, Comparative 574.1
>> *x* Comparative physiology

Physiology, Molecular. *See* **Biophysics**
Physiology of plants. *See* **Plant physiology**
Physiotherapy. *See* **Physical therapy**
Physique. *See* **Bodybuilding**
Phytogeography. *See* **Plants—Geographical distri-
>> bution**

Pianists 786.2092; 920
>> *xx* **Musicians**

Piano 786.2
>> *See also* **Keyboards (Musical instruments)**
>> *xx* **Percussion instruments**

Piano music 786.2
>> *xx* **Instrumental music; Music**

Piano—Tuning 786.2
>> *xx* **Tuning**

Picketing. *See* **Strikes and lockouts**
Pickling. *See* **Canning and preserving**
Pickup campers. *See* **Travel trailers and campers**
Pictographs. *See* **Picture writing**
Pictorial works. *See* **Pictures;** and subjects, names
>> of ancient cities, and named entities, such as
>> individual parks, structures, etc. with the
>> subdivision *Pictorial works,* e.g. **Animals—
>> Pictorial works; United States—History—
>> 1861-1865, Civil War—Pictorial works; Yo-
>> semite National Park (Calif.)—Pictorial
>> works;** etc.; also names of cities (except an-
>> cient cities), states, countries, etc., with the
>> subdivision *Description—Views,* e.g. **Chi-
>> cago (Ill.)—Description—Views; United
>> States—Description—Views;** etc.; also
>> names of persons or groups of persons with,
>> as appropriate, the subdivisions *Cartoons
>> and caricatures; Pictorial works;* or
>> *Portraits.*

Picture books for children   E
>> *See also* **Coloring books; Illustration of books;
>> Stories without words; Toy and movable
>> books**
>> *xx* **Children's literature; Illustration of books**

Picture books for children, Wordless. *See* **Stories
>> without words**

Picture dictionaries 423.1; 433.1, etc.
>> *x* Dictionaries, Picture; Word books
>> *xx* **Encyclopedias and dictionaries**

Picture frames and framing 749
>> *x* Framing of pictures

Picture galleries. *See* **Art—Museums**
Picture postcards. *See* **Postcards**
Picture posters. *See* **Posters**
Picture telephone. *See* **Video telephone**
Picture writing 411
>> Use for materials on the recording of events or

Picture writing—*Continued*

the expression of messages by pictures representing actions or facts.

See also **Cave drawings; Hieroglyphics; Rock drawings, paintings, and engravings**

x Pictographs

xx **Hieroglyphics; Writing**

Pictures   025.17; 759; 769; 779

Use for general materials on the study and use of pictures; also for miscellaneous collections of pictures.

See also **Cartoons and caricatures; Engraving; Etching; Libraries and pictures; Painting; Portraits;** also subjects, names of ancient cities, and named entities, such as individual parks, structures, etc. with the subdivision *Pictorial works,* e.g. **Animals— Pictorial works; United States—History— 1861-1865, Civil War—Pictorial works; Yosemite National Park (Calif.)—Pictorial works;** etc.; also names of cities (except ancient cities), states, countries, etc., with the subdivision *Description—Views,* e.g. **Chicago (Ill.)—Description—Views; United States—Description—Views;** etc.; also names of persons or groups of persons with, as appropriate, the subdivisions *Cartoons and caricatures; Pictorial works;* or *Portraits.*

x Pictorial works

xx **Art**

Pictures, Humorous. *See* **Cartoons and caricatures**

Pigments   667; 751.2

See also **Dyes and dyeing; Paint**

xx **Paint**

Pigs   636.4

x Hogs; Swine

Pilgrims and pilgrimages   248.4

See also **Saints; Shrines**

xx **Shrines; Voyages and travels**

Pilgrims (New England colonists)   974.4

xx **Puritans; United States—History—1600- 1775, Colonial period**

Pilot guides   623.88

x Coast pilot guides

xx **Navigation; Pilots and pilotage**

Piloting (Aeronautics). *See* types of aircraft with the subdivision *Piloting,* e.g. **Airplanes— Piloting;** etc.

Piloting (Astronautics). *See* **Space vehicles— Piloting**

Piloting (Ships). *See* **Pilots and pilotage**

Pilots, Airplane. *See* **Air pilots**

Pilots and pilotage   623.88

See also **Navigation; Pilot guides**

x Piloting (Ships); Pilots, Ship; Ship pilots

xx **Harbors; Navigation; Sailors**

Pilots, Ship. *See* **Pilots and pilotage**

Pimples (Acne). *See* **Acne**

Ping-pong   796.34

x Table tennis

Pioneer life. *See* **Frontier and pioneer life**

Pipe fitting 696
  See also **Plumbing**
  x Steam fitting
  xx **Plumbing**
Pipe lines. *See* **Pipelines**
Pipe organ. *See* **Organ**
Pipelines 621.8
  See also special subjects with the subdivision
      Pipelines, e.g. **Petroleum—Pipelines;** etc.
  x Pipe lines
  xx **Hydraulic structures; Transportation**
Pipelines, Petroleum. *See* **Petroleum—Pipelines**
Pipes, Tobacco. *See* **Tobacco pipes**
Pirates 364.1; 910.4
  See also **Privateering; United States—History—**
      1801-1805, Tripolitan War
  x Barbary corsairs; Buccaneers; Corsairs; Free-
      booters
  xx **Criminals; International law; Maritime law;**
      Naval history
Pistols 683
  x Handguns
  xx **Firearms**
Pity. *See* **Sympathy**
Place names. *See* **Geographic names**
Places, Imaginary. *See* **Geographical myths**
Places of retirement. *See* **Retirement communities**
Plague 616.9
  x Black death; Bubonic plague
Plain chant. *See* **Chants (Plain, Gregorian, etc.)**
Plainsong. *See* **Chants (Plain, Gregorian, etc.)**
Plane geometry. *See* **Geometry**
Plane trigonometry. *See* **Trigonometry**
Planetariums 520.74
  xx **Astronomy**
Planets 523.4
  See also **Life on other planets; Solar system;**
      Stars; also names of planets, e.g. **Saturn**
      (Planet); etc.
  xx **Astronomy; Solar system; Stars**
Planets—Exploration 523.4
  See also names of planets with the subdivision
      Exploration, e.g. **Mars (Planet)—**
      Exploration; etc.
  xx **Outer space—Exploration**
Planets, Life on other. *See* **Life on other planets**
Planing machines 621.9
  xx **Machine tools**
Planned parenthood. *See* **Birth control**
Planning, City. *See* **City planning**
Planning, Economic. *See* **Economic policy;** and
      names of countries, states, etc. with the sub-
      division *Economic policy,* e.g. **United**
      States—Economic policy; etc.
Planning, National. *See* **Economic policy; Social**
      policy; and names of countries with the
      subdivision *Economic policy* or *Social pol-*
      icy, e.g. **United States—Economic policy;**
      United States—Social policy; etc.; and ap-
      propriate topical subjects with the subdivi-
      sion *Government policy,* e.g. **Environ-**
      ment—Government policy; etc.
Planning, Regional. *See* **Regional planning**

Plans. *See* **Architectural drawing; Geometrical
drawing; Map drawing; Maps; Mechanical
drawing**
Plant anatomy. *See* **Botany—Anatomy**
Plant breeding   581.1; 631.5
Use for materials on that form of plant propagation that aims to improve plants, as by selection after controlled mating, etc.
See also **Fertilization of plants; Plant propagation**
x Hybridization
xx **Agriculture; Breeding; Flower gardening;
Plant propagation**
Plant chemistry. *See* **Botanical chemistry; Plants—
Analysis**
Plant conservation   333.95; 639.9
See also **Rare plants; Scarecrows**
x Conservation of plants; Plants—
Conservation; Protection of plants; Wild
flowers—Conservation
xx **Botany, Economic; Conservation of natural resources; Endangered species; Nature conservation; Rare plants**
Plant diseases   581.2; 632
See also names of crops, etc., with the subdivision *Diseases and pests,* e.g. **Fruit—
Diseases and pests;** etc.
x Botany—Pathology; Diseases and pests; Diseases of plants; Garden pests; Pathological
botany; Pathology, Vegetable; Plant pathology; Plants—Diseases; Vegetable pathology
xx **Agricultural pests; Fungi**
Plant distribution. *See* **Plants—Geographical dis-
tribution**
Plant introduction   581.5
x Acclimatization
xx **Botany, Economic**
Plant lore. *See* **Plants—Folklore**
Plant names, Popular   581
See note under **Botany—Terminology.**
See also **Botany—Terminology; Plants—Folklore**
x Botany—Nomenclature
xx **Botany—Terminology**
Plant names, Scientific. *See* **Botany—Terminology**
Plant nutrition. *See* **Plants—Nutrition**
Plant pathology. *See* **Plant diseases**
Plant physiology   581.1
See also **Fertilization of plants; Germination;
Plants—Growth; Plants—Nutrition**
x Botany—Physiology; Physiology of plants
xx **Botany**
Plant propagation   581.1; 631.5
Use for materials on the continuance or multi-
plication of plants by successive production.
Materials dealing with methods adopted to
secure new and improved varieties are en-
tered under **Plant breeding.**
See also **Grafting; Plant breeding; Seeds**
x Plants—Propagation; Propagation of plants
xx **Flower gardening; Fruit culture; Gardening;
Nurseries (Horticulture); Plant breeding**
Plantation life   307.72
Planting. *See* **Agriculture; Gardening; Landscape
gardening; Tree planting**

Plants (May subdiv. geog.) **581**
    See also

Edible plants	**Herbicides**
Fertilization of plants	**Horticulture**
Flower gardening	**Photosynthesis**
Forest plants	**Rare plants**
Gardening	

      also names of types of plants, e.g. **Alpine plants;**
        Climbing plants; Desert plants; Flowers;
        Forage plants; Freshwater plants; House
        plants; etc.; also names of individual plants,
        e.g. **Ferns; Mosses;** etc.; and headings be-
        ginning with the words **Plant** and **Plants**
    x Flora; Vegetable kingdom
    xx **Botany; Gardening; Herbicides; Trees**
Plants—Analysis 581.19
    x Plant chemistry; Plants—Chemical analysis
    xx **Botanical chemistry**
Plants—Anatomy. *See* **Botany—Anatomy**
Plants—Chemical analysis. *See* **Plants—Analysis**
Plants—Collection and preservation 579
    See also **Flower drying**
    x Botanical specimens—Collection and preser-
      vation; Herbaria; Preservation of botanical
      specimens; Specimens, Preservation of
    xx **Collectors and collecting**
Plants—Conservation. *See* **Plant conservation**
Plants, Cultivated (May subdiv. geog.) **581.6; 631.5**
    See also **Annuals (Plants); House plants; Orna-**
        mental plants
    xx **Gardening**
Plants, Cultivated—United States 581.6; 631.5
    x United States—Plants, Cultivated
Plants—Diseases. *See* **Plant diseases**
Plants—Ecology. *See* **Botany—Ecology**
Plants, Edible. *See* **Edible plants**
Plants—Effect of poisons on 581.2
    See note under **Poisons and poisoning.**
    xx **Poisons and poisoning**
Plants, Extinct. *See* **Plants, Fossil**
Plants—Fertilization. *See* **Fertilization of plants**
Plants—Folklore 398.24
    x Plant lore
    xx **Folklore; Plant names, Popular**
Plants, Fossil 561
    x Botany, Fossil; Extinct plants; Fossil plants;
      Paleobotany; Plants, Extinct
    xx **Botany; Fossils**
Plants—Geographical distribution 581.9
    Use for materials on the geographical relation-
      ships of plants.
    x Geographical distribution of animals and
      plants; Phytogeography; Plant distribution
    xx **Biogeography**
Plants—Growth 581.3
    xx **Plant physiology**
Plants, Hallucinogenic. *See* **Hallucinogens**
Plants in art 704.9
    See also **Flower painting and illustration**
    x Flowers in art; Trees in art
    xx **Decoration and ornament**
Plants, Industrial. *See* **Factories**
Plants, Medicinal. *See* **Botany, Medical**

Plants—Nutrition   581.1; 631.5
   x Plant nutrition
   xx **Nutrition; Plant physiology**
Plants, Ornamental. *See* **Ornamental plants**
Plants—Photography. *See* **Photography of plants**
Plants, Poisonous. *See* **Poisonous plants**
Plants—Propagation. *See* **Plant propagation**
Plants—Soilless culture. *See* **Aeroponics; Hydro-**
      ponics
Plants—United States   581.973
   x Botany—United States; United States—Plants
Plants, Useful. *See* **Botany, Economic; Edible**
      plants
Plaster and plastering   693
   See also **Cement; Concrete; Mortar; Stucco**
   x Plastering
   xx **Masonry**
Plaster casts   731.4
   x Casting; Casts, Plaster
   xx **Sculpture**
Plaster of paris. *See* **Gypsum**
Plastering. *See* **Plaster and plastering**
Plastic industries. *See* **Plastics industry**
Plastic materials. *See* **Plastics**
Plastic surgery   617.9
   x Cosmetic surgery; Surgery, Cosmetic; Surgery,
      Plastic
   xx **Surgery; Transplantation of organs, tissues,**
      etc.
Plastics   668.4
   See also **Chemistry, Organic—Synthesis; Gums**
      and resins; Synthetic products; Synthetic
      rubber; also names of specific plastics
   x Plastic materials
   xx **Chemistry, Organic—Synthesis; Polymers and**
      polymerization; Synthetic products
Plastics industry   338.4; 668.4
   x Plastic industries; Plastics trade
   xx **Chemical industry**
Plastics trade. *See* **Plastics industry**
Plate   739.2
   See also **Hallmarks; Pewter; Sheffield plate**
   x Gold plate
   xx **Goldwork; Hallmarks; Silverwork**
Plate metalwork   671.8
   xx **Metalwork; Sheet metalwork**
Plate tectonics   551.1
   See also **Continental drift; Submarine geology**
   xx **Continental drift; Earth—Crust; Geophysics;**
      Submarine geology
Platforms, Drilling. *See* **Drilling platforms**
Play   790
   See also **Amusements; Finger play; Games;**
      Imaginary playmates; Recreation; Sports
   xx **Amusements; Children; Games; Recreation**
Play centers. *See* **Community centers; Playgrounds**
Play direction (Theater). *See* **Theater—Production**
      and direction
Play production. *See* **Amateur theater; Theater—**
      Production and direction
Play writing. *See* **Drama—Technique; Motion pic-**
      ture plays—Technique; Radio plays—
      Technique; Television plays—Technique
Players, Compact disc. *See* **Compact disc players**

Playgrounds   796.06

  See also **Community centers; Parks**

  x Play centers; Public playgrounds; School play-
    grounds

  xx **Child welfare; Children; Community centers;
    Parks; Recreation; Social settlements**

Playhouses. *See* **Theaters**

Playing cards. *See* **Card games**

Playmates, Imaginary. *See* **Imaginary playmates**

Plays. *See* **Drama—Collections; One act plays**

Plays, Bible. *See* **Bible—Drama**

Plays, Christmas. *See* **Christmas—Drama**

Plays, College. *See* **College and school drama—
    Collections**

Plays for children. *See* **Children's plays**

Playwrights. *See* **Dramatists**

Playwriting. *See* **Drama—Technique; Motion pic-
    ture plays—Technique; Radio plays—
    Technique; Television plays—Technique**

Pleasure   152.4

  See also **Happiness; Pain**

  xx **Emotions; Happiness; Joy and sorrow; Pain;
    Senses and sensation**

Plot-your-own stories   E; Fic

  x Choose-your-own story plots; Making-choices
    stories; Multiple plot stories; Which-way
    stories

  xx **Children's literature; Fiction; Literary recre-
    ations**

Plots (Drama, fiction, etc.)   808

  Use for materials dealing with the construction
    and analysis of plots as a literary technique.
    Collections of plots are entered under **Liter-
    ature—Stories, plots, etc.**

  See also literary or musical forms with the sub-
    division *Stories, plots, etc.,* e.g. **Ballets—
    Stories, plots, etc.; Operas—Stories, plots,
    etc.;** etc.

  x Drama—Plots; Dramatic plots; Fiction—
    Plots; Novels—Plots; Scenarios

  xx **Authorship; Characters and characteristics in
    literature; Drama; Fiction; Literature**

Plows   631.3

  xx **Agricultural machinery**

Plumbing   696

  See also **Drainage, House; Pipe fitting; Sanitary
    engineering; Sanitation, Household; Sewer-
    age; Solder and soldering**

  xx **Drainage, House; Pipe fitting; Sanitation,
    Household**

Pluto operation. *See* **Cuba—History—1961, Inva-
    sion**

Plywood   674

  xx **Wood**

PMS (Gynecology). *See* **Premenstrual syndrome**

Pneumatic transmission. *See* **Compressed air**

Pneumatics   533; 621.5

  See also **Aerodynamics; Compressed air; Gases;
    Ground cushion phenomena; Sound**

  xx **Gases; Physics**

Pneumonia   616.2

  xx **Lungs—Diseases**

Pocket calculators. *See* **Calculators**

Podiatry   617.5
> *See also* **Foot—Care and hygiene**
> *x* Chiropody

Poetics   808.1
> Use for materials on the art and technique of poetry. General materials on the appreciation, philosophy, etc. of poetry are entered under **Poetry.**
> *See also* **Rhyme; Rhythm; Versification**
> *x* Poetry—Technique

Poetry   809.1
> See note under **Poetics.**
> Names of all types of poetry are not included in this List but are to be added as needed.
> *See also*

American poetry	**Free verse**
Ballads	**Haiku**
Children's poetry	**Humorous poetry**
Eddas	**Hymns**
English poetry	**Love poetry**
Epic poetry	**Nature in poetry**

> also subjects with the subdivision *Poetry,* e.g. **Animals—Poetry; Bunker Hill (Boston, Mass.), Battle of, 1775—Poetry; Chicago (Ill.)—Poetry; Indians of North America—Poetry; Shakespeare, William, 1564-1616—Poetry;** etc.
> *x* Poetry—Philosophy
> *xx* **Aesthetics; Literature; Versification**

Poetry and music. *See* **Music and literature**

Poetry—Collected works. *See* **Poetry—Collections**

Poetry—Collections   808.81; 811.08, etc.
> *See also*

American poetry— Collections	**Nonsense verses**
	Patriotic poetry
Children's poetry	**Religious poetry**
Christmas—Poetry	**Sea poetry**
English poetry— Collections	**Songs**
	War poetry

> *x* Collections of literature; Poetry—Collected works; Poetry—Selections; Rhymes
> *xx* **Literature—Collections**

Poetry for children. *See* **Children's poetry; Nursery rhymes**

Poetry—History and criticism   809.1
> *See also* **American poetry—History and criticism; English poetry—History and criticism**

Poetry of love. *See* **Love poetry**

Poetry of nature. *See* **Nature in poetry**

Poetry—Philosophy. *See* **Poetry**

Poetry—Selections. *See* **Poetry—Collections**

Poetry—Technique. *See* **Poetics**

Poets (May subdiv. geog. adjective form) **809.1; 920**
> Use for materials dealing with the personal lives of several poets. Materials about their literary productions are entered under **Poetry—History and criticism; English poetry—History and criticism;** etc.
> *See also* **Dramatists; Lyricists; Minstrels; Troubadours**
> *xx* **Authors**

Poets, American   811.009; 920
> *x* American poets; United States—Poets

Point Four program. *See* **Reconstruction (1939-1951)**

Poison ivy   583

   xx **Poisonous plants**

Poisonous animals   591.6

   See also names of poisonous animals, e.g. **Rattlesnakes;** etc.

   xx **Animals; Dangerous animals; Poisons and poisoning; Zoology**

Poisonous gases   363.17; 363.7

   See also **Radon**

   x Asphyxiating gases; Gases, Poisonous

   xx **Gases; Poisons and poisoning**

Poisonous gases—War use   623.4

   See also **World War, 1914-1918—Gas warfare**

   x Gas warfare

   xx **Air defenses; Chemical warfare; Military art and science**

Poisonous plants   581.6

   See also names of poisonous plants, e.g. **Poison ivy;** etc.

   x Plants, Poisonous

   xx **Botany, Economic; Poisons and poisoning**

Poisonous substances. *See* **Poisons and poisoning**

Poisons and poisoning   615.9

   Materials on the poisonous effect of chemical substances on man and animals are entered under the names of substances with the subdivision *Toxicology,* e.g. **Insecticides—Toxicology;** etc. The heading **Lead poisoning** is an exception. Materials on the effect of poisons on plants are entered under **Plants—Effect of poisons on.**

   See also **Food poisoning; Lead poisoning; Pesticides; Plants—Effect of poisons on; Poisonous animals; Poisonous gases; Poisonous plants;** also subjects with the subdivision *Toxicology,* e.g. **Insecticides—Toxicology;** etc.

   x Poisonous substances; Toxic substances; Toxicology

   xx **Accidents; Chemistry; Criminal law; Drugs; Hazardous substances; Materia medica; Medical jurisprudence; Pharmaceutical chemistry**

Polar expeditions. *See* **North Pole; Polar regions; Scientific expeditions; South Pole**

Polar lights. *See* **Auroras**

Polar regions   998

   Use for materials dealing with both the Antarctic and Arctic regions.

   See also **Antarctic regions; Arctic regions; North Pole; South Pole**

   x Polar expeditions

Police (May subdiv. geog.)   363.2

   See also **Animals in police work; Crime; Criminal investigation; Detectives; Secret service; State police**

   x Police officers; Policemen; Policewomen; Women police

   xx **Crime; Criminal investigation; Detectives; Law; Law enforcement**

Police brutality. *See* **Police—Complaints against**

Police—Complaints against 363.2
   x Complaints against police; Police brutality
Police—Corrupt practices 363.2
   x Corruption, Police; Police corruption
   xx **Misconduct in office**
Police corruption. *See* **Police—Corrupt practices**
Police, International. *See* **International police**
Police officers. *See* **Police**
Police, State. *See* **State police**
Police—United States 363.20973
   x United States—Police
Policemen. *See* **Police**
Policewomen. *See* **Police**
Polio. *See* **Poliomyelitis**
Poliomyelitis 616.8
   x Infantile paralysis; Paralysis, Anterior spinal;
      Paralysis, Infantile; Polio; Spinal paralysis,
      Anterior
Poliomyelitis vaccine 614.4; 615
   x Live poliovirus vaccine; Sabin vaccine; Salk
      vaccine
Polishing. *See* **Grinding and polishing**
Politeness. *See* **Courtesy; Etiquette**
Political action committees. *See* **Lobbying and lob-
      byists**
Political assessments. *See* **Campaign funds**
Political asylum. *See* **Asylum**
Political behavior. *See* **Political psychology**
Political boundaries. *See* **Boundaries**
Political conventions 324.5
   See also **Political parties; Primaries**
   x Conventions, Political
   xx **Political parties; Political science**
Political corruption. *See* **Corruption in politics**
Political crimes and offenses 364.1
   See also

   Anarchism and anarchists   **Government, Resistance to**
   Assassination   **Political prisoners**
   Concentration camps   **Terrorism**
   Corruption in politics   **Treason**

   x Crimes, Political; Sedition
   xx **Political ethics; Subversive activities**
Political defectors. *See* **Defectors**
Political economy. *See* **Economics**
Political ethics 172
   See also **Citizenship; Conflict of interests; Cor-
      ruption in politics; Government, Resistance
      to; Political crimes and offenses**
   x Ethics, Political
   xx **Political science; Social ethics**
Political geography. *See* **Boundaries**
Political participation. *See* **Politics, Practical;** and
      classes of people with the subdivision
      Political activity, e.g. **College students—
      Political activity; Women—Political activity;**
      etc.
Political parties (May subdiv. geog.) 324.2
   See also **Political conventions; Politics, Practical;
      Right and left (Political science); Third par-
      ties (United States politics);** also names of
      parties, e.g. **Democratic Party (U.S.); Re-
      publican Party (U.S.);** etc.
   x Parties, Political
   xx **Political conventions; Political science**

Political parties—Finance. *See* **Campaign funds**
Political prisoners   365
    x Prisoners, Political
    xx **Political crimes and offenses; Prisoners**
Political psychology   302
    See also **Propaganda; Public opinion**
    x Political behavior; Politics, Practical—
        Psychological aspects; Psychology, Political
    xx **Political science; Psychology; Social psychol-
        ogy**
Political refugees   325
    See also **Defectors;** also names of wars with the
        subdivision *Refugees,* e.g. **World War,
        1939-1945—Refugees;** etc.
    x Displaced persons; Refugees, Political
    xx **Asylum; International law; International rela-
        tions**
Political scandals. *See* **Corruption in politics**
Political science   320
    Use for materials on the discipline of political
        science. Materials dealing with political pro-
        cesses in general, such as electioneering, po-
        litical machines, etc., are entered under
        Politics, Practical. Materials on the politi-
        cal processes of particular regions, countries,
        cities, etc. are entered under the place
        names with the subdivision *Politics and gov-
        ernment,* e.g. **United States—Politics and
        government;** etc.
    See also

Anarchism and anarchists	**Nationalism**
Aristocracy	**Political conventions**
Bureaucracy	**Political ethics**
Citizenship	**Political parties**
Civil rights	**Political psychology**
Civil service	**Politics, Practical**
Communism	**Power (Social sciences)**
Comparative government	**Public administration**
Constitutional history	**Representative government**
Constitutional law	**and representation**
Constitutions	**Republics**
Democracy	**Revolutions**
Executive power	**Right and left (Political**
Federal government	**science)**
Freedom	**Separation of powers**
Geopolitics	**Socialism**
Government ownership	**State constitutions**
Government, Resistance to	**State governments**
Imperialism	**State rights**
Kings, queens, rulers, etc.	**State, The**
Law	**Suffrage**
Legislation	**Taxation**
Local government	**Utopias**
Monarchy	**World politics**
Municipal government	

    also names of countries, cities, etc. with the sub-
        division *Politics and government,* e.g.
        United States—Politics and government;
        etc.
    x Administration; Civics; Civil government;
        Commonwealth, The; Government; Politics
    xx **Constitutional history; Constitutional law;
        History; Social sciences; State, The**
Political violence. *See* **Terrorism**

Politicians (May subdiv. geog.)   324.2092; 920; 923
> *See also* **Diplomats; Statesmen; Women politicians**
> *xx* **Statesmen**

Politicians, American.   *See* **Politicians—United States**

Politicians—United States   324.2092; 920
> *x* American politicians; Politicians, American; United States—Politicians

Politics.   *See* **Political science; Politics, Practical;** and names of continents, areas, countries, states, counties, and cities with the subdivision *Politics and government,* e.g. **Asia— Politics and government; Latin America— Politics and government; United States— Politics and government; Chicago (Ill.)— Politics and government;** etc.

Politics and business.   *See* **Business and politics**

Politics and Christianity.   *See* **Christianity and politics**

Politics and religion.   *See* **Religion and politics**

Politics and students.   *See* **Students—Political activity**

Politics—Corrupt practices.   *See* **Corruption in politics**

Politics, Practical   324.2; 324.7
> Use for materials dealing with practical politics in general, such as electioneering, political machines, etc. Materials on the science of politics are entered under **Political science.**
> *See also*

Business and politics	**Elections**
Campaign funds	**Lobbying and lobbyists**
Campaign literature	**Primaries**
Corruption in politics	**Television in politics**

> also names of countries, cities, etc. with the subdivision *Politics and government,* e.g. **United States—Politics and government;** etc.; also classes of people with the subdivision *Political activity,* e.g. **College students—Political activity; Women—Political activity;** etc.; and headings beginning with the word **Political**
> *x* Campaigns, Political; Electioneering; Political participation; Politics; Practical politics
> *xx* **Political parties; Political science**

Politics, Practical—Psychological aspects.   *See* **Political psychology**

Pollination.   *See* **Fertilization of plants**

Polls, Election.   *See* **Elections**

Polls, Public opinion.   *See* **Public opinion polls**

Pollution   304.2; 363.73
> *See also* **Environmental protection; Industrial wastes; Pollution control industry; Refuse and refuse disposal; Space debris;** also types of pollution, e.g. **Air pollution; Hazardous wastes; Marine pollution; Noise pollution; Pesticides—Environmental aspects; Radioactive pollution; Water pollution;** etc.
> *x* Chemical pollution; Contamination of environment; Environmental pollution
> *xx* **Environment—Government policy; Environmental health; Environmental protection;**

Pollution—*Continued*

    Hazardous wastes; Industrial wastes; Man—Influence on nature; Public health; Refuse and refuse disposal; Sanitary engineering; Sanitation

Pollution control. *See* **Pollution control industry**

Pollution control devices (Motor vehicles). *See* **Automobiles—Pollution control devices**

Pollution control industry   338.4; 363.73

    See also **Automobiles—Pollution control devices; Recycling (Waste, etc.); Refuse and refuse disposal**

    x Pollution control; Pollution—Prevention

    xx **Pollution; Refuse and refuse disposal**

Pollution—Mathematical models   304.2; 363.73

    xx **Mathematical models**

Pollution of air. *See* **Air pollution**

Pollution of water. *See* **Water pollution**

Pollution—Prevention. *See* **Pollution control industry**

Pollution, Radioactive. *See* **Radioactive pollution**

Pollution, Space. *See* **Space debris**

Poltergeists. *See* **Ghosts**

Polyglot dictionaries   413

    x Dictionaries, Multilingual; Dictionaries, Polyglot; Multilingual dictionaries; Multilingual glossaries, phrase books, etc.; Polyglot glossaries, phrase books, etc.

    xx **Encyclopedias and dictionaries**

Polyglot glossaries, phrase books, etc. *See* **Polyglot dictionaries**

Polygraph. *See* **Lie detectors and detection**

Polymers and polymerization   541.3; 547.7; 668.9

    See also types of polymers, e.g. **Plastics;** etc.

    xx **Chemistry, Organic—Synthesis; Chemistry, Physical and theoretical**

Polynucleotides. *See* **Nucleic acids**

Ponds   551.48

    xx **Water**

Ponies   636.1

    x Foals

    xx **Horses**

Pontiac's Conspiracy, 1763-1765   973.2

    xx **Indians of North America—Wars; United States—History—1600-1775, Colonial period; United States—History—1755-1763, French and Indian War**

Pony express   383

    xx **Express service; Postal service**

Poor (May subdiv. geog.)   305.5; 362.5

    See also **Homeless people; Tramps; Unemployed**

    xx **Poverty; Public welfare**

Poor—Legal assistance. *See* **Legal assistance to the poor**

Poor—Medical care   362.6; 368.4

    See also **Medicaid**

    x Medical care for the poor

Poor relief. *See* **Charities; Economic assistance, Domestic; Public welfare**

Pop-up books. *See* **Toy and movable books**

Popes   262; 920

    See also **Papacy**

    x Holy See

    xx **Church history; Papacy**

Popes—Infallibility 262

   x Infallibility of the Pope

Popes—Temporal power 262

   See also **Church—Government policy**

   x Temporal power of the Pope

   xx **Church—Government policy; Church history—600-1500, Middle Ages**

Popes—Voyages and travels 262

   xx **Voyages and travels**

Popular culture 306.4

   Use for materials on literature, art, and music, etc. produced for the general public.

   See also names of countries, cities, etc. with the subdivision *Popular culture,* e.g. **United States—Popular culture;** etc.

   x Culture, Popular

   xx **Civilization; Communication; Culture; Manners and customs; Mass media; Recreation**

Popular government. *See* **Democracy**

Popular music 781.64; 782.42164

   See also **Gospel music; Rap music;** also names of types of popular music, e.g. **Blues music; Country music; Rock music;** etc.

   x Music, Popular (Songs, etc.); Popular songs; Songs, Popular

   xx **Dance music; Music; Songs**

Popular music—Writing and publishing 070.5; 781.3

   x Song writing

   xx **Composition (Music)**

Popular songs. *See* **Popular music**

Popularity 158

Population 304.6; 363.9

   See also

Birth control	**Eugenics**
Birthrate	**Fertility, Human**
Census	**Migration, Internal**
Cities and towns—Growth	**Mortality**

   also names of countries, cities, etc. with the subdivision *Population,* e.g. **United States—Population; Chicago (Ill.)—Population;** etc.

   xx **Birthrate; Economics; Fertility, Human; Human ecology; Sociology; Vital statistics**

Population, Foreign. *See* **Immigration and emigration;** and names of countries with the subdivision *Immigration and emigration,* e.g. **United States—Immigration and emigration;** etc.; and names of countries, cities, etc. with the subdivision *Foreign population,* e.g. **Chicago (Ill.)—Foreign population; United States—Foreign population;** etc.

Porcelain 738.2

   See note under **Ceramics.**

   See also **China painting;** also names of varieties of porcelain

   x China (Porcelain); Chinaware; Dishes

   xx **Decorative arts; Pottery**

Porcelain enamels. *See* **Enamel and enameling**

Porcelain painting. *See* **China painting**

Pornography 176; 363.4

   See also **Erotica**

   x Obscene materials

   xx **Erotica; Obscenity (Law)**

Portable computers   004.16
    x Computers, Portable; Handheld computers;
        Kneetop computers; Laptop computers
    xx **Microcomputers**
Portrait painting   757
    See also **Crayon drawing; Figure painting; Min-**
        iature painting; Pastel drawing
    xx **Figure painting; Miniature painting; Painting**
Portraits   704.9; 757
    See also **Cartoons and caricatures; Photogra-**
        phy—Portraits; also headings for collective
        and individual biography and classes of peo-
        ple with the subdivision *Portraits,* e.g.
        United States—Biography—Portraits; Mu-
        sicians—Portraits; Shakespeare, William,
        1564-1616—Portraits; etc.
    x Iconography
    xx **Art; Biography; Pictures**
Ports.   *See* **Harbors**
Portuguese literature   869
    See also **Brazilian literature**
    xx **Brazilian literature**
Position analysis.   *See* **Topology**
Positivism   146
    See also **Agnosticism; Idealism; Materialism;**
        Pragmatism; Realism
    x Humanity, Religion of; Religion of humanity
    xx **Agnosticism; Deism; Philosophy; Rationalism;**
        Realism
Possessions, Lost and found.   *See* **Lost and found**
    possessions
Post cards.   *See* **Postcards**
Post-impressionism.   *See* **Postimpressionism (Art)**
Post office.   *See* **Postal service**
Postage stamps   383; 769.56
    x Stamps, Postage
Postage stamps—Collectors and collecting   769.56
    x Collectibles; Collections of objects; Philately
    xx **Collectors and collecting**
Postal cards.   *See* **Postcards**
Postal delivery code.   *See* **Zip code**
Postal service (May subdiv. geog.)   **351.0087; 383**
    See also **Air mail service; Pony express; Zip code**
    x Mail service; Parcel post; Post office
    xx **Communication; Transportation**
Postal service—United States   353.0087; 383
    x United States—Mail; United States—Postal
        service
Postcards   383; 741.6
    Use for materials on cards sold by post offices
        with stamps printed on them as well as for
        materials on commercially printed cards
        usually having a picture printed on one side
        and sold without stamps.
    x Picture postcards; Post cards; Postal cards
Postcards—Collectors and collecting   790.1
Posters   741.6
    See also **Signs and signboards**
    x Advertising, Pictorial; Picture posters
    xx **Advertising; Commercial art; Signs and sign-**
        boards
Postimpressionism (Art)   709.03
    See also **Cubism; Expressionism (Art); Futurism**

Postimpressionism—*Continued*
    (Art); **Impressionism (Art); Surrealism**
    x Post-impressionism
    xx **Art, Modern—1800-1899 (19th century); Cubism; Expressionism (Art); Futurism (Art); Impressionism (Art); Painting**
Posture   613.7
    xx **Physical education**
Pot (Drug).   *See* **Marijuana**
Potash   631.8; 668
    xx **Fertilizers and manures**
Potatoes   635; 641.3
    xx **Vegetables**
Potters   738.092; 920
    xx **Artists**
Pottery (May subdiv. geog. adjective form, e.g. **Pottery, American;** etc.)   **666; 738**
    See note under **Ceramics.**
    See also **Glazes; Porcelain; Terra cotta; Tiles; Vases**
    x Crockery; Dishes; Earthenware; Faience; Fayence; Stoneware
    xx **Archeology; Art objects; Ceramics; Clay industries; Decoration and ornament; Decorative arts; Tableware; Vases**
Pottery, American   738.0973
    x American pottery; United States—Pottery
Pottery—Marks   738
    x Marks, Potters'
Poultry   636.5
    See also names of domesticated birds, e.g. **Ducks; Geese; Turkeys;** etc.
    xx **Domestic animals**
Poverty   305.5; 362.5
    See also **Charities; Homelessness; Poor; Public welfare; Subsistence economy;** also names of countries with the subdivisions *Economic conditions* and *Social conditions,* e.g. **United States—Economic conditions; United States—Social conditions;** etc.
    x Destitution; Pauperism
    xx **Economic assistance, Domestic; Subsistence economy; Wealth**
Powder, Smokeless. *See* **Gunpowder**
Powdered milk.   *See* **Dried milk**
Power blackouts. *See* **Electric power failures**
Power boats. *See* **Motorboats**
Power failures. *See* **Electric power failures**
Power (Mechanics)   531; 621
    See note under **Energy resources.**
    See also

Compressed air	**Power transmission**
Electric power	**Steam**
Energy resources	**Water power**
Force and energy	**Wind power**
Machinery	

    x Energy technology
    xx **Mechanical engineering; Mechanics; Steam engineering**
Power plants   621.4
    See also types of power plants, e.g. **Electric power plants; Nuclear power plants; Steam power plants;** etc.
    x Power stations

Power plants, Atomic. *See* **Nuclear power plants**
Power plants, Electric. *See* **Electric power plants**
Power plants, Hydroelectric. *See* **Hydroelectric power plants**
Power plants, Steam. *See* **Steam power plants**
Power politics. *See* **Balance of power; World politics—1945-1965; World politics—1965-**
Power resources. *See* **Energy resources**
Power resources conservation. *See* **Energy conservation**
Power resources development. *See* **Energy development**
Power (Social sciences) 303.3
  See also **Elite (Social sciences)**
  xx **Political science**
Power stations. *See* **Power plants**
Power supply. *See* **Energy resources**
Power tools 621.9
  xx **Tools**
Power transmission 621.8
  See also **Belts and belting; Cables; Electric power distribution; Gearing; Machinery**
  x Transmission of power
  xx **Belts and belting; Machinery; Mechanical engineering; Power (Mechanics)**
Power transmission, Electric. *See* **Electric lines; Electric power distribution**
Powerlifting. *See* **Weight lifting**
Powers, Separation of. *See* **Separation of powers**
POWs. *See* **Prisoners of war**
Practical jokes 818, etc.
  x Pranks
  xx **Jokes; Wit and humor**
Practical nurses 610.73; 920
  xx **Nurses**
Practical nursing 610.73; 649.8
  xx **Nursing**
Practical politics. *See* **Politics, Practical**
Practice teaching. *See* **Student teaching**
Pragmatism 144
  See also **Empiricism; Reality; Truth; Utilitarianism**
  xx **Empiricism; Knowledge, Theory of; Philosophy; Positivism; Realism; Reality; Truth; Utilitarianism**
Pranks. *See* **Practical jokes**
Prayer 242
  See also **Devotional exercises; Prayers**
  x Devotion
  xx **Devotional exercises; Prayers; Worship**
Prayers 242; 264
  See also **Meditations; Prayer**
  x Collects; Theology, Devotional
  xx **Prayer**
Prayers in the public schools. *See* **Religion in the public schools**
Pre-Columbian Americans. *See* **Indians of North America**
Preachers. *See* **Clergy**
Preaching 251
  See also **Sermons**
  x Speaking
  xx **Pastoral work; Public speaking; Rhetoric; Sermons**

Preaching Friars. *See* **Dominicans (Religious order)**
Precious metals   549; 553.8
>   *See also* **Gold; Silver**
>   *xx* **Metals; Mines and mineral resources**
Precious stones   549; 553.8
>   Use for mineralogical and technological materi-
>   als on uncut stones. Materials on cut and
>   polished precious stones treated from the
>   point of view of art or antiquity are entered
>   under **Gems.** Materials on gems in which
>   the emphasis is on the setting are entered
>   under **Jewelry.**
>   *See also* **Gems;** also names of precious stones,
>   e.g. **Diamonds;** etc.
>   *x* Gemstones; Jewels; Stones, Precious
>   *xx* **Gems; Mineralogy**
Precipitation forecasting. *See* **Weather forecasting**
Precipitation (Meteorology). *See* **Rain; Snow**
Precocious children. *See* **Gifted children**
Precolumbian Americans. *See* **Indians of North
    America**
Predestination   234
>   *See also* **Free will and determinism**
>   *x* Election (Theology); Foreordination
>   *xx* **Calvinism; Fate and fatalism; Theology**
Predictions. *See* **Forecasting; Prophecies (Occult
    sciences)**
Prefabricated buildings   693
>   *See also* **Prefabricated houses**
>   *x* Buildings, Prefabricated
>   *xx* **Buildings**
Prefabricated houses   693; 728
>   *x* Demountable houses; Houses, Prefabricated;
>   Packaged houses
>   *xx* **Architecture, Domestic; House construction;
>   Houses; Prefabricated buildings**
Pregnancy   599; 612.6; 618.2
>   *See also* **Childbirth; Miscarriage; Prenatal care**
>   *xx* **Childbirth; Reproduction**
Pregnancy, Adolescent. *See* **Teenage pregnancy**
Pregnancy, Teenage. *See* **Teenage pregnancy**
Pregnancy, Termination of. *See* **Abortion**
Prehistoric animals   560
>   *See also* **Dinosaurs; Extinct animals**
>   *x* Animals, Prehistoric
>   *xx* **Animals; Extinct animals; Fossils**
Prehistoric art. *See* **Art, Prehistoric**
Prehistoric man   573.3
>   *See also* **Bronze Age; Cave dwellers; Man—
>   Origin;** also names of prehistoric people,
>   e.g. **Cro-Magnons;** etc.; and names of
>   countries, cities, etc. with the subdivision
>   *Antiquities,* e.g. **United States—
>   Antiquities;** etc.
>   *x* Man, Prehistoric
>   *xx* **Antiquities; Archeology; Civilization, Ancient;
>   Ethnology; Man—Origin; Stone Age**
Prehistory. *See* **Archeology; Bronze Age; Iron Age;
    Stone Age;** and names of countries, cities,
    etc. with the subdivision *Antiquities,* e.g.
    United States—Antiquities; etc.
Preimplantational ectogenesis. *See* **Fertilization in
    vitro**
Prejudice-motivated crimes. *See* **Hate crimes**

Prejudices   152.4; 177; 303.3
> *See also* **Discrimination;** also types of prejudice,
> e.g. **Antisemitism; Racism; Sexism;** etc.
> *x* Antipathies; Bias (Psychology); Bigotry
> *xx* **Attitude (Psychology); Emotions; Human rela-
> tions; Race awareness**

Prejudicial publicity. *See* **Freedom of the press and
fair trial**

Preliterate man. *See* **Nonliterate man**

Preliterate society. *See* **Nonliterate folk society**

Premarital contracts. *See* **Marriage contracts**

Premarital counseling. *See* **Marriage counseling**

Premenstrual syndrome   618.1
> *x* PMS (Gynecology); Premenstrual tension;
> Tension, Premenstrual
> *xx* **Menstruation**

Premenstrual tension. *See* **Premenstrual syndrome**

Premiers. *See* **Prime ministers**

Prenatal care   618.2
> *xx* **Pregnancy**

Prenatal diagnosis   618.3
> *See also* **Amniocentesis; Genetic counseling**
> *xx* **Diagnosis**

Prenuptial contracts. *See* **Marriage contracts**

Prepaid group medical practice. *See* **Health maintenance organizations**

Prepaid health plans. *See* **Health insurance**

Prepaid medical care. *See* **Health insurance**

Prepared cereals   641.3; 664
> *x* Breakfast cereals; Cereals, Prepared
> *xx* **Grain**

Preprimers. *See* **Easy reading materials**

Presbyterian Church   285

Preschool children. *See* **Children**

Preschool education   372.21
> *See also* **Kindergarten; Nursery schools; Readi-
> ness for school**
> *x* Children—Education; Education, Preschool;
> Infants—Education
> *xx* **Kindergarten; Nursery schools**

Preschool reading materials. *See* **Easy reading materials**

Presents. *See* **Gifts**

Preservation of antiquities. *See* **Antiquities—
Collection and preservation**

Preservation of botanical specimens. *See* **Plants—
Collection and preservation**

Preservation of buildings. *See* **Architecture—
Conservation and restoration**

Preservation of food. *See* **Food—Preservation**

Preservation of forests. *See* **Forests and forestry**

Preservation of historical records. *See* **Archives**

Preservation of library resources. *See* **Library resources—Conservation and restoration**

Preservation of natural resources. *See* **Conservation
of natural resources**

Preservation of natural scenery. *See* **Landscape
protection; Natural monuments; Nature conservation; Wilderness areas**

Preservation of organs, tissues, etc.   617.9
> *See also* **Transplantation of organs, tissues, etc.**
> *x* Organ preservation (Anatomy); Organs (Anat-
> omy)—Preservation

Preservation of specimens. *See* **Taxidermy**

Preservation of wildlife. *See* **Wildlife conservation**

Preservation of wood. *See* **Wood—Preservation**

Preservation of works of art. *See* subjects with the
 subdivision *Conservation and restoration,*
 e.g. **Painting—Conservation and restoration;** etc.

Preservation of zoological specimens. *See* **Zoological specimens—Collection and preservation**

Preserving. *See* **Canning and preserving**

Presidential aides. *See* **Presidents—United
 States—Staff**

Presidential campaigns—United States. *See* **Presidents—United States—Election**

Presidential libraries. *See* **Presidents—United
 States—Archives**

Presidents (May subdiv. geog.) **351.003; 920**
 See also **Executive power; Presidents—United
 States; Vice-presidents;** also names of presidents
 xx **Executive power; Heads of state; Kings,
 queens, rulers, etc.**

Presidents—Mexico 920; 972
 x Mexico—Presidents

Presidents—Powers and duties. *See* **Executive
 power**

Presidents—United States 353.03; 920
 When applicable, the subdivisions under this
 heading may be used under names of presidents, prime ministers, and other rulers.
 See also names of presidents, e.g. **Lincoln,
 Abraham, 1809-1865;** etc.
 x United States—Presidents
 xx **Presidents**

Presidents—United States—Appointment 353.03

Presidents—United States—Archives 026
 See also names of libraries, e.g. **Harry S. Truman Library;** etc.
 x Libraries, Presidential; Presidential libraries;
 Presidents—United States—Libraries

**Presidents—United States—Assassination 364.1;
 973**
 xx **Assassination; Presidents—United States—
 Death and burial**

Presidents—United States—Burial. *See* **Presidents—United States—Death and burial**

Presidents—United States—Children 920

**Presidents—United States—Death and burial 393;
 973**
 See also **Presidents—United States—
 Assassination**
 x Presidents—United States—Burial; Presidents—United States—Funeral and memorial services; Presidents—United States—
 Memorial services

Presidents—United States—Election (May subdiv.
 by date) **324.973**
 x Campaigns, Presidential—United States; Electoral college; Presidential campaigns—
 United States
 xx **Elections**

Presidents—United States—Family 920

Presidents—United States—Fathers 920

Presidents—United States—Friends and associates
920
Presidents—United States—Funeral and memorial
services. *See* **Presidents—United States—
Death and burial**
Presidents—United States—Health   353.03; 920
x Presidents—United States—Illness
Presidents—United States—Homes   728
Presidents—United States—Illness. *See* **Presi-
dents—United States—Health**
**Presidents—United States—Impeachment   353.03;
353.009**
Presidents—United States—Inability. *See* **Presi-
dents—United States—Succession**
**Presidents—United States—Inaugural addresses
353.03**
xx **Presidents—United States—Inauguration;
Speeches, addresses, etc.**
Presidents—United States—Inauguration   353.03
See also **Presidents—United States—Inaugural
addresses**
Presidents—United States—Libraries. *See* **Presi-
dents—United States—Archives**
Presidents—United States—Medals   353.03
Presidents—United States—Memorial services. *See*
**Presidents—United States—Death and
burial**
Presidents—United States—Messages   353.03
x Messages to Congress; Presidents—United
States—State of the Union message; State
of the Union messages
Presidents—United States—Mothers   920
Presidents—United States—Nomination   324.50973
x Nomination of presidents
Presidents—United States—Portraits   973
Presidents—United States—Power. *See* **Executive
power—United States**
**Presidents—United States—Press relations   070.4;
353.03**
Presidents—United States—Protection   353.03
Presidents—United States—Quotations   818
xx **Quotations**
**Presidents—United States—Relations with Congress
328.73; 353.03**
Presidents—United States—Religion   920
Presidents—United States—Resignation   353.03
Presidents—United States—Sports   920
Presidents—United States—Spouses   920
x First ladies—United States; Presidents'
wives—United States; Wives of presidents—United States
xx **Women—United States**
Presidents—United States—Staff   353.03
x Presidential aides
xx **United States—Executive departments**
Presidents—United States—State of the Union
message. *See* **Presidents—United States—
Messages**
**Presidents—United States—Succession   342;
353.03**
x Presidents—United States—Inability
Presidents—United States—Tombs   917.3
**Presidents—United States—Voyages and travels
353.03; 910**

Presidents' wives—United States. *See* **Presidents—United States—Spouses**

Press 070

> *See also* **Broadcast journalism; Freedom of the press; Freedom of the press and fair trial; News agencies; Newspapers; Periodicals; Underground press**
>
> *xx* **Freedom of the press; Journalism; Newspapers; Periodicals; Propaganda; Public opinion; Publicity**

Press and government. *See* **Press—Government policy**

Press censorship. *See* **Freedom of the press**

Press clippings. *See* **Clippings (Books, newspapers, etc.)**

Press—Government policy 323.44

> *x* Government and the press; Press and government
>
> *xx* **Freedom of information; Reporters and reporting**

Press, Underground. *See* **Underground press**

Press working of metal. *See* **Sheet metalwork**

Pressure groups. *See* **Lobbying and lobbyists**

Pressure suits. *See* **Astronauts—Clothing**

Pretenders. *See* **Impostors and imposture**

Prevention of accidents. *See* **Accidents—Prevention**

Prevention of crime. *See* **Crime prevention**

Prevention of cruelty to animals. *See* **Animal welfare**

Prevention of disease. *See* **Preventive medicine;** and names of diseases and medical conditions with the subdivision *Prevention,* e.g. **AIDS (Disease)—Prevention;** etc.

Prevention of fire. *See* **Fire prevention**

Prevention of smoke. *See* **Smoke prevention**

Preventive medicine 616

> *See also* **Health; Hygiene; Immunity; Pathology; Public health;** also names of diseases with the subdivision *Prevention,* e.g. **Heart—Diseases—Prevention;** etc.
>
> *x* Diseases—Prevention; Medicine, Preventive; Prevention of disease
>
> *xx* **Medicine; Pathology; Public health**

Price controls. *See* **Wage-price policy**

Price indexes, Consumer. *See* **Consumer price indexes**

Price-wage policy. *See* **Wage-price policy**

Prices 338.5

> *See also* **Consumer price indexes; Cost of living; Farm produce—Marketing; Wage-price policy; Wages;** also subjects with the subdivision *Prices,* e.g. **Art—Prices; Books—Prices;** etc.
>
> *xx* **Commerce; Consumption (Economics); Cost of living; Economics; Finance; Manufactures; Wages**

Priests 253; 253.092; 920

> *See also* **Ex-priests;** also names of church denominations with the subdivision *Clergy,* e.g. **Catholic Church—Clergy;** etc.
>
> *x* Pastors
>
> *xx* **Clergy**

Primaries 324.5

> *See also* **Elections**
>
> *x* Direct primaries; Elections, Primary
>
> *xx* **Elections; Political conventions; Politics, Practical; Representative government and representation**

Primary education. *See* **Elementary education**

Primates 599.8

> *See also* **Sasquatch; Yeti;** also names of individual primates, e.g. **Monkeys;** etc.
>
> *xx* **Animals; Mammals**

Primates—Behavior 599.8

> *x* Primates—Habits and behavior
>
> *xx* **Animals—Behavior**

Primates—Habits and behavior. *See* **Primates—Behavior**

Prime ministers (May subdiv. geog.) **351.003; 920**

> *x* Premiers
>
> *xx* **Cabinet officers; Executive power; Heads of state**

Prime ministers—Great Britain 351.003; 920

> *x* Great Britain—Prime ministers

Primers. *See* **Easy reading materials**

Primitive Christianity. *See* **Church history—30(ca.)-600, Early church**

Primitive man. *See* **Nonliterate man**

Primitive society. *See* **Nonliterate folk society**

Princes and princesses 920

> *x* Royalty

Printing 686.2

> *See also*

Advertising layout and typography	**Linotype**
	Offset printing
Books	**Proofreading**
Color printing	**Type and type founding**
Electrotyping	**Typesetting**

> *x* Layout and typography; Typography
>
> *xx* **Bibliography; Book industries; Books; Graphic arts; Industrial arts; Publishers and publishing; Typesetting**

Printing—Exhibitions 686.2074

> *See also* **Book industries—Exhibitions**
>
> *x* Books—Exhibitions
>
> *xx* **Book industries—Exhibitions; Exhibitions**

Printing, Offset. *See* **Offset printing**

Printing—Specimens 686.2

> *See also* **Type and type founding**
>
> *x* Type specimens
>
> *xx* **Advertising; Initials; Type and type founding**

Printing—Style manuals 686.02

> *See also* **Authorship—Handbooks, manuals, etc.**
>
> *x* Style manuals
>
> *xx* **Authorship—Handbooks, manuals, etc.**

Printing, Textile. *See* **Textile printing**

Prints (May subdiv. geog. adjective form) **769**

> *See also* **Lithography**
>
> *xx* **Graphic arts**

Prints, American 769.973

> *x* American prints; United States—Prints

Prison escapes. *See* **Escapes**

Prison labor. *See* **Convict labor**

Prison reform 365

> *x* Penal reform

Prison schools. *See* **Prisoners—Education**

Prisoners 365

See also **Political prisoners**

x Convicts

xx **Criminals; Prisons**

Prisoners—Education 365

x Education of criminals; Education of prisoners; Prison schools

xx **Adult education; Prisons**

Prisoners of war (May subdiv. geog. adjective form)
341.6; 355.7

See also **Concentration camps; Missing in action;**
also names of wars with the subdivision
Prisoners and prisons, e.g. **World War,**
1939-1945—Prisoners and prisons; etc.

x Exchange of prisoners of war; P.O.W.'s;
POWs

xx **Concentration camps**

Prisoners of war, American 341.6; 355.7

x American prisoners of war

Prisoners, Political. *See* **Political prisoners**

Prisons (May subdiv. geog.) 365

See also

Convict labor	**Prisoners**
Crime	**Prisoners—Education**
Criminal law	**Probation**
Escapes	**Reformatories**
Penal colonies	

also names of prisons

x Dungeons; Imprisonment; Jails; Penal institutions; Penitentiaries

xx **Convict labor; Correctional institutions;**
Crime; Criminal justice, Administration of;
Punishment

Prisons—United States 365

x United States—Prisons

Privacy, Right of. *See* **Right of privacy**

Private art collections. *See* names of original owners of private collections with the subdivision *Art collections.*

Private funding of the arts. *See* **Art patronage**

Private schools 371; 372; 373.2

See also **Church schools; Public schools, En-**
dowed (Great Britain)

x Boarding schools; Independent schools; Nonpublic schools; Secondary schools

xx **Secondary education**

Private theater. *See* **Amateur theater**

Privateering 341

x Letters of marque

xx **International law; Naval art and science; Na-**
val history; Pirates

Privatisation. *See* **Privatization**

Privatization 338.9

Use for materials on the transfer of public assets
and service functions to the private sector.

See also **Government ownership**

x Denationalization; Privatisation

xx **Government ownership**

Prize fighting. *See* **Boxing**

Prizes, Literary. *See* **Literary prizes**

Prizes (Rewards). *See* **Rewards (Prizes, etc.)**

Pro-abortion movement. *See* **Pro-choice movement**

Pro-choice movement 179; 363.4

    x Abortion rights movement; Freedom of
      choice movement; Pro-abortion movement;
      Right to choose movement

    xx **Abortion—Moral and religious aspects; Birth
      control—Moral and religious aspects; So-
      cial movements; Women—Civil rights**

Pro-life movement 179; 363.4

    x Anti-abortion movement; Antiabortion move-
      ment; Right-to-life movement (Anti-
      abortion movement)

    xx **Abortion—Moral and religious aspects; Birth
      control—Moral and religious aspects; So-
      cial movements; Women—Civil rights**

Probabilities 519.2

    See also **Average; Game theory; Reliability (En-
      gineering); Sampling (Statistics)**

    x Certainty; Fortune; Statistical inference

    xx **Algebra; Gambling; Life insurance; Logic; Sta-
      tistics**

Probation 364.6

    See also **Juvenile courts; Parole**

    x Reform of criminals; Suspended sentence

    xx **Corrections; Criminal law; Juvenile courts;
      Parole; Prisons; Punishment; Reformato-
      ries; Social case work**

Probes, Space. *See* **Space probes**

Problem children. *See* **Emotionally disturbed chil-
    dren**

Problem drinking. *See* **Alcoholism**

Problem solving 510.76

    See also **Crisis management; Critical thinking;
      Decision making**

    x Solution achievement

    xx **Decision making**

Problem solving, Group 153.4

    x Brain storming; Group problem solving;
      Think tanks

    xx **Social groups**

Problems, exercises, etc. *See* subjects with the sub-
    division *Problems, exercises, etc.,* for com-
    pilations of practice problems or exercises
    for use in the study of a topic, e.g. **Chemis-
    try—Problems, exercises, etc.;** etc.

Processing (Libraries). *See* **Library technical pro-
    cesses**

Processions. *See* **Parades**

Procurement, Government. *See* **Government pur-
    chasing**

Producers and directors. *See* **Motion picture pro-
    ducers and directors**

Product recall 658.5

    x Commercial products recall; Manufactures—
      Defects; Manufactures recall; Recall of
      products

    xx **Consumer protection**

Product safety 363.19; 658.5

    x Commercial products—Safety measures

    xx **Consumer protection**

Production. *See* **Economics; Industry**

Production engineering. *See* **Factory management**

Production standards 658.5

    See also **Motion study; Time study;** also subjects

Production standards—*Continued*
> with the subdivision *Production standards,*
> e.g. **Employees—Production standards;** etc.
>
> *x* Output standards; Standards of output; Time
> production standards; Work standards
>
> *xx* **Industrial management; Labor productivity**

Productivity of labor. *See* **Labor productivity**
Products, Brand name. *See* **Brand name products**
Products, Commercial. *See* **Commercial products**
Products, Dairy. *See* **Dairy products**
Products, Generic. *See* **Generic products**
Products, Waste. *See* **Waste products**
Professional associations. *See* **Trade and profes-**
> **sional associations**

Professional education   378.1
> *See also* **Colleges and universities; Library educa-**
> **tion; Technical education; Vocational educa-**
> **tion;** also names of professions with the sub-
> division *Study and teaching,* e.g.
> **Medicine—Study and teaching;** etc.
>
> *x* Education, Professional
>
> *xx* **Education; Higher education; Learning and**
> **scholarship; Technical education; Voca-**
> **tional education**

Professional ethics   174
> *See also* **Business ethics; Legal ethics; Medical**
> **ethics;** also names of professions with the
> subdivision *Professional ethics,* e.g. **Librar-**
> **ians—Professional ethics;** etc.
>
> *x* Ethics, Professional
>
> *xx* **Ethics**

Professional liability. *See* **Malpractice**
Professional liability insurance. *See* **Malpractice**
> **insurance**

Professional sports   796
> *See also* names of specific sports
>
> *xx* **Sports**

Professions   331.7
> *See also* **College graduates; Intellectuals; Occu-**
> **pations; Paraprofessions and paraprofession-**
> **als; Vocational guidance;** also names of pro-
> fessions with the subdivision *Vocational*
> *guidance,* e.g. **Law—Vocational guidance;**
> etc.
>
> *x* Careers; Jobs; Vocations
>
> *xx* **Occupations; Self-employed; Vocational guid-**
> **ance**

Professions—Tort liability. *See* **Malpractice**
Professors. *See* **Teachers**
Profit   338.5; 658.15
> *See also* **Capitalism; Income**
>
> *xx* **Business; Capital; Economics; Income; Wealth**

Profit sharing   331.2; 658.3
> *See also* **Cooperation**
>
> *xx* **Commerce; Cooperation; Wages**

Programmed instruction   371.3
> *See also* **Computer assisted instruction; Teaching**
> **machines;** also subjects with the subdivision
> *Programmed instruction,* e.g. **English lan-**
> **guage—Programmed instruction;** etc.
>
> *x* Programmed textbooks
>
> *xx* **Teaching—Aids and devices**

Programmed textbooks. *See* **Programmed instruc-**
> **tion**

Programming (Computers)   005.1

   See also **Computer programs; Computer software; Programming languages (Computers);** also subjects with the subdivision *Computer programs,* e.g. **Oceanography—Computer programs;** etc.

   x Computer programming; Computers— Programming; Flow charts (Computer science); Flowcharting (Computer science)

   xx **Computer software; Electronic data processing; Mathematical analysis; Mathematical models**

Programming languages (Computers)   005.13

   See also specific languages, e.g. **FORTRAN (Computer language);** etc.

   x Autocodes; Automatic programming languages; Computer program languages; Machine language

   xx **Computer software; Electronic data processing; Language and languages; Programming (Computers)**

Programs, Computer.   *See* **Computer programs**

Programs, Radio.   *See* **Radio programs**

Programs, School assembly.   *See* **School assembly programs**

Programs, Television.   *See* **Television programs**

Programs, Utility (Computer programs).   *See* **Utilities (Computer programs)**

Progress   303.44

   See also **Civilization; Science and civilization; Social change; War and civilization**

   xx **Civilization**

Progressive education.   *See* **Education— Experimental methods**

Prohibited books.   *See* **Books—Censorship**

Prohibition   344

   Use for materials dealing with the legal prohibition of liquor traffic and liquor manufacture.

   See also **Temperance**

   xx **Temperance**

Project Apollo.   *See* **Apollo project**

Project Gemini.   *See* **Gemini project**

Project MARC.   *See* **MARC system**

Project method in teaching   371.3

   xx **Teaching**

Project Ranger   629.43

   x Ranger project

   xx **Lunar probes**

Project schools.   *See* **Experimental schools**

Project Sealab.   *See* **Sealab project**

Project Telstar.   *See* **Telstar project**

Project Voyager   629.43

   x Voyager project

   xx **Astronautics—United States**

Projectiles   623.4

   See also **Ammunition; Bombs; Guided missiles; Ordnance; Rockets (Aeronautics)**

   x Bullets; Shells (Projectiles)

   xx **Ordnance**

Projective geometry.   *See* **Geometry, Projective**

Projectors 778.2

    x Film projectors; Lantern projection; Motion picture projectors; Opaque projectors; Slide projectors

Proletariat 305.5

    xx **Labor; Socialism**

Proliferation of arms. *See* **Arms race**

Promotion in school. *See* **Promotion (School)**

Promotion (School) 371.2

    x Grade repetition; Grade retention; Non-promotion (School); Promotion in school; Retention, Grade; School grade retention; School promotion; Student promotion

    xx **Grading and marking (Education)**

Promptness. *See* **Punctuality**

Pronunciation. *See* **Names—Pronunciation;** and names of languages with the subdivision *Pronunciation*, e.g. **English language—Pronunciation;** etc.

Proofreading 070.5; 686.2

    xx **Printing**

Propaganda (May subdiv. geog. adjective form) 303.3; 327.1

    See also **Advertising; Press; Psychological warfare; World War, 1939-1945—Propaganda**

    xx **Advertising; Political psychology; Public opinion; Publicity**

Propaganda, American 303.3; 327.1

    x American propaganda; United States—Propaganda

Propagation of plants. *See* **Plant propagation**

Propellers, Aerial 629.134

    x Airplanes—Propellers

    xx **Airplanes**

Proper names. *See* **Names**

Property 330.1

    See also **Eminent domain; Income; Real estate; Wealth**

    x Ownership

    xx **Economics; Wealth**

Property, Literary. *See* **Copyright**

Property, Real. *See* **Real estate**

Prophecies (Bible). *See* **Bible—Prophecies**

Prophecies (Occult sciences) 133.3

    See also **Astrology; Divination; Fortune telling; Oracles**

    x Predictions

    xx **Divination; Occultism; Supernatural**

Prophets 221.9; 920

Proportion (Architecture). *See* **Architecture—Composition, proportion, etc.**

Proportional representation 328.3

    See also **Elections**

    x Representation, Proportional; Voting, Cumulative

    xx **Constitutional law; Representative government and representation**

Prose literature, American. *See* **American prose literature**

Prose literature, English. *See* **English prose literature**

Prosody. *See* **Versification**

Prospecting   622
   See also **Mine surveying; Petroleum geology**
   xx **Gold mines and mining; Mines and mineral
        resources; Silver mines and mining**
Prosthesis.   *See* **Artificial limbs; Artificial organs**
Prostitution   176; 306.74; 363.4; 364.1
   See also **Juvenile prostitution; Sexually transmit-
        ted diseases**
   x Hygiene, Social; Social hygiene; Vice
   xx **Crime; Sexual ethics; Sexual hygiene; Social
        problems; Women—Social conditions**
Prostitution, Juvenile.   *See* **Juvenile prostitution**
Protection.   *See* **Free trade and protection**
Protection against burglary.   *See* **Burglary protec-
        tion**
Protection of animals.   *See* **Animal welfare**
Protection of birds.   *See* **Birds—Protection**
Protection of children.   *See* **Child welfare**
Protection of environment.   *See* **Environmental pro-
        tection**
Protection of game.   *See* **Game protection**
Protection of natural scenery.   *See* **Landscape pro-
        tection; Natural monuments; Nature conser-
        vation; Wilderness areas**
Protection of plants.   *See* **Plant conservation**
Protection of wildlife.   *See* **Wildlife conservation**
Proteins   547.7
   xx **Biochemistry**
Protest.   *See* **Dissent**
Protest marches and rallies.   *See* **Protests, demon-
        strations, etc.**
Protest movements (War).   *See* names of wars with
        the subdivision *Protests, demonstrations,
        etc.,* e.g. **World War, 1939-1945—Protests,
        demonstrations, etc.;** etc.
Protestant churches   280
   See also **Protestantism**
   xx **Church history; Protestantism**
Protestant Episcopal Church in the U.S.A.   *See*
        Episcopal Church
Protestant Reformation.   *See* **Reformation**
Protestantism   280
   See also **Protestant churches; Reformation**
   xx **Christianity; Church history; Protestant
        churches; Reformation**
Protests, demonstrations, etc. (May subdiv. geog.)
        322.4; 361.2
   Use for materials on public gatherings, marches,
        etc., organized for nonviolent protest even
        though incidental disturbances or rioting
        may occur.
   See also **Hunger strikes; Riots; Youth movement;**
        also wars with the subdivision *Protests,
        demonstrations, etc.,* e.g. **World War, 1939-
        1945—Protests, demonstrations, etc.;** etc.
   x Demonstrations (Protest); Marches (Demon-
        strations); Protest marches and rallies; Pub-
        lic demonstrations; Rallies (Protest)
   xx **Crowds; Public meetings; Riots**
Protests, demonstrations, etc.—Chicago (Ill.)
        322.409773
   x Chicago (Ill.)—Protests, demonstrations, etc.

Protests, demonstrations, etc.—United States
322.40973; 361.2
  x United States—Protests, demonstrations, etc.
Protons 539.7
  See also Atoms; Electrons
  x Hydrogen nucleus
  xx Neutrons; Particles (Nuclear physics)
Protoplasm 574.8
  See also Cells; Embryology
  xx Biology; Cells; Embryology; Life (Biology)
Protozoa 593
  xx Cells; Invertebrates; Microorganisms
Proverbs 398.9
  See also Epigrams
  x Adages; Maxims; Sayings
  xx Epigrams; Folklore; Quotations
Providence and government of God 214; 231
  xx God—Christianity; Theology
Provincialism. *See* Sectionalism (United States)
Provincialisms. *See* names of languages with the
      subdivision *Provincialisms,* e.g. **English
      language—Provincialisms;** etc.
Pruning 631.5
  xx Forests and forestry; Fruit culture; Gardening;
      Trees
Psalmody. *See* Church music; Hymns
Pseudonyms 929.4
  x Anonyms; Fictitious names; Names, Ficti-
      tious; Pen names
  xx Authors; Names; Personal names
Psi (Parapsychology). *See* Parapsychology
Psychiatric hospitals 362.2
  x Insane—Hospitals; Mental hospitals
  xx Hospitals; Mentally ill—Institutional care
Psychiatrists 920; 926
  x Psychopathologists
  xx Psychologists
Psychiatry 616.89
      Use for materials on clinical aspects of mental
      disorders, including therapy. Popular mate-
      rials and materials on regional or social as-
      pects of mental disorders are entered under
      Mental illness. Systematic descriptions of
      mental disorders are entered under **Psy-
      chology, Pathological.**
  See also Adolescent psychiatry; Child psychiatry;
      Mental illness; Mentally ill; Psychology,
      Pathological; Psychotherapy
  xx Psychology, Pathological
Psychiatry, Adolescent. *See* Adolescent psychiatry
Psychiatry, Child. *See* Child psychiatry
Psychic healing. *See* Mental healing
Psychic phenomena. *See* Parapsychology
Psychical research. *See* Parapsychology
Psychoactive drugs. *See* Psychotropic drugs
Psychoanalysis 616.89
  See also

Dreams	**Psychology**
Hypnotism	**Psychology, Pathological**
Medicine, Psychosomatic	**Psychophysiology**
Mind and body	**Subconsciousness**

  xx Dreams; Hypnotism; Mind and body; Psy-
      chology; Psychology, Pathological;
      Psychophysiology; Subconsciousness

Psychogenetics. *See* **Behavior genetics**
Psychokinesis   133.8
   x Telekinesis
   xx **Parapsychology; Spiritualism**
Psychological aspects. *See* topical subjects with the
      subdivision *Psychological aspects,* e.g.
      **Drugs—Psychological aspects; World War,
      1939-1945—Psychological aspects;** etc.
Psychological stress. *See* **Stress (Psychology)**
Psychological tests. *See* **Mental tests**
Psychological warfare   355.3
   Use for materials dealing with the methods used
      to undermine the morale of the civilian
      population and the military forces of an en-
      emy country.
   See also **Brainwashing;** also names of wars with
      the subdivision *Psychological aspects,* e.g.
      **World War, 1939-1945—Psychological as-
      pects;** etc.
   x Cold war; War of nerves
   xx **Military art and science; Morale; Propaganda;
      Psychology, Applied; War**
Psychologists   150.92; 920
   See also **Psychiatrists**
Psychologists, School. *See* **School psychologists**
Psychology   150
   See also

Adjustment (Psychology)	**Instinct**
Adolescent psychology	**Intellect**
Aggressiveness (Psychol-	**Intuition**
ogy)	**Memory**
Apperception	**Motivation (Psychology)**
Assertiveness (Psychology)	**Number concept**
Attention	**Parapsychology**
Attitude (Psychology)	**Perception**
Behavior genetics	**Personality**
Behaviorism	**Phrenology**
Child psychology	**Physiognomy**
Choice (Psychology)	**Political psychology**
Consciousness	**Psychoanalysis**
Educational psychology	**Reasoning**
Emotions	**Self-acceptance**
Ethnopsychology	**Senses and sensation**
Genius	**Social psychology**
Gestalt psychology	**Stress (Psychology)**
Habit	**Subconsciousness**
Human behavior	**Temperament**
Imagination	**Thought and thinking**
Individuality	**Values**

      also subdivision *Biography—Psychology* under
      names of individual literary authors, e.g.
      **Shakespeare, William, 1564-1616—
      Biography—Psychology;** also subdivision
      Psychology under titles of individual sacred
      works, and under religions, religious topics,
      names of animals, classes of persons, ethnic
      groups, and names of other individual per-
      sons, e.g. **Christianity—Psychology;
      Faith—Psychology; Dogs—Psychology; In-
      dians of North America—Psychology;** etc;
      and the subdivision *Psychological aspects*
      under topical subjects for works that discuss
      the influence of particular situations, condi-

Psychology—*Continued*

tions, activities, environments, or objects on the mental condition or personality of the individual, e.g. **Color—Psychological aspects; Music—Psychological aspects;** etc.

x Mind

xx **Brain; Philosophy; Psychoanalysis; Soul**

Psychology, Abnormal. *See* **Psychology, Pathological**

Psychology, Adolescent. *See* **Adolescent psychology**

Psychology, Applied 158

See also

Behavior modification	**Interviewing**
Counseling	**Negotiation**
Employee morale	**Psychological warfare**
Human engineering	**Psychology, Pastoral**
Human relations	

also subjects with the subdivision *Psychological aspects,* e.g. **Drugs—Psychological aspects;** etc.

x Applied psychology; Industrial psychology; Psychology, Industrial; Psychology, Practical

xx **Educational psychology; Human relations; Interviewing; Psychology, Religious; Public relations; Social psychology**

Psychology, Biblical. *See* **Bible—Psychology**

Psychology, Child. *See* **Child psychology**

Psychology, Comparative 156

See also **Animal intelligence; Instinct; Sociobiology;** also names of animals with the subdivision *Psychology,* e.g. **Dogs—Psychology;** etc.

x Animal psychology; Comparative psychology

xx **Animal intelligence; Instinct; Zoology**

Psychology, Criminal. *See* **Criminal psychology**

Psychology, Educational. *See* **Educational psychology**

Psychology, Ethnic. *See* **Ethnopsychology**

Psychology, Experimental. *See* **Psychophysiology**

Psychology, Industrial. *See* **Psychology, Applied**

Psychology, Medical. *See* **Psychology, Pathological**

Psychology, National. *See* **Ethnopsychology; National characteristics**

Psychology of color. *See* **Color—Psychological aspects**

Psychology of learning. *See* **Learning, Psychology of**

Psychology of music. *See* **Music—Psychological aspects**

Psychology, Pastoral 253.5

Use for materials on the application of psychology and psychiatry by the clergy to the spiritual problems of individuals.

x Pastoral psychiatry; Pastoral psychology

xx **Christian ethics; Church work; Pastoral work; Psychology, Applied; Psychology, Religious; Therapeutics, Suggestive**

Psychology, Pathological 616.89

See note under **Psychiatry.**

See also

Compulsive behavior	**Depression, Mental**
Criminal psychology	**Eating disorders**

Psychology, Pathological—*Continued*

Hallucinations and illusions	**Personality disorders**
	Psychiatry
Medicine, Psychosomatic	**Psychoanalysis**
Mental illness	**Subconsciousness**
Neuroses	

  x Abnormal psychology; Diseases, Mental;
    Mental diseases; Pathological psychology;
    Psychology, Abnormal; Psychology, Medical; Psychopathology; Psychopathy

  xx **Criminal psychology; Mental health; Mind and body; Nervous system; Psychiatry; Psychoanalysis**

Psychology, Physiological. *See* **Psychophysiology**
Psychology, Political. *See* **Political psychology**
Psychology, Practical. *See* **Psychology, Applied**
Psychology, Racial. *See* **Ethnopsychology**
Psychology, Religious **200.1; 253.5**

  See also **Psychology, Applied; Psychology, Pastoral;** also titles of individual sacred works and names of religions or religious topics with the subdivision *Psychology,* e.g. **Christianity—Psychology; Faith—Psychology;** etc.

  x Religious psychology
  xx **Religion**

Psychology, Social. *See* **Social psychology**
Psychology, Structural. *See* **Gestalt psychology**
Psychopathologists. *See* **Psychiatrists**
Psychopathology. *See* **Psychology, Pathological**
Psychopathy. *See* **Psychology, Pathological**
Psychopharmaceuticals. *See* **Psychotropic drugs**
Psychophysics. *See* **Psychophysiology**
Psychophysiology **152**

  Use for materials on the relationship between psychological and physiological processes.

  See also

Behaviorism	**Mental tests**
Color sense	**Mind and body**
Dreams	**Optical illusions**
Emotions	**Pain**
Human engineering	**Psychoanalysis**
Hypnotism	**Senses and sensation**
Left- and right-handedness	**Sleep**
Memory	**Temperament**

  x Experimental psychology; Physiological psychology; Psychology, Experimental; Psychology, Physiological; Psychophysics

  xx **Mental health; Mind and body; Nervous system; Physiology; Psychoanalysis**

Psychoses. *See* **Mental illness**
Psychosomatic medicine. *See* **Medicine, Psychosomatic**
Psychotherapy **616.89**

  See also **Biofeedback training; Mental healing; Sex therapy; Therapeutics, Suggestive; Transactional analysis**

  xx **Mental healing; Psychiatry; Therapeutics, Suggestive**

Psychotic children. *See* **Mentally ill children**
Psychotics. *See* **Mentally ill**
Psychotropic drugs **615**

  Use for comprehensive materials on the group of

Psychotropic drugs—*Continued*
>   drugs that act on the central nervous system to affect behavior, mental activity or perception, including the antipsychotic drugs, antidepressants, hallucinogenic agents, and tranquilizers
>   *See also* **Cocaine; Hallucinogens**
>   *x* Drugs, Psychotropic; Psychoactive drugs; Psychopharmaceuticals
>   *xx* **Drugs**

PTAs. *See* **Parents' and teachers' associations**

Public accommodations, Discrimination in. *See* **Discrimination in public accommodations**

Public administration   350
>   Use for general materials on the principles and techniques involved in the conduct of public business. Materials limited to the governmental process of a particular country, state, etc. are entered under the name of the area with the subdivision *Politics and government.*
>   *See also* **Administrative law; Bureaucracy; Civil service; Military government;** also names of countries, cities, etc. with the subdivision *Politics and government,* e.g. **United States—Politics and government;** etc.
>   *x* Administration
>   *xx* **Administrative law; Local government; Municipal government; Political science**

Public assistance. *See* **Public welfare**

Public buildings   350.86; 725
>   *See also* names of cities, states, etc. with the subdivision *Public buildings,* e.g. **Chicago (Ill.)—Public buildings;** etc.; and names of countries with the subdivision *Public buildings* for that government's public buildings located within the country, as well as for embassies, consulates, and other public buildings of that country in foreign locations, e.g. **United States—Public buildings;** etc.
>   *x* Buildings, Public; Government buildings
>   *xx* **Architecture; Art, Municipal; Public works**

Public buildings, American. *See* **United States—Public buildings**

Public buildings—Chicago (Ill.). *See* **Chicago (Ill.)—Public buildings**

Public buildings—Ohio. *See* **Ohio—Public buildings**

Public buildings—United States. *See* **United States—Public buildings**

Public charities. *See* **Public welfare**

Public debts (May subdiv. geog.)   **336.3**
>   Use for materials on government debts.
>   *See also* **Bonds; Deficit financing;** also names of wars with the subdivision *Finance,* e.g. **World War, 1939-1945—Finance;** etc.
>   *x* Debts, Government; Debts, Public; Federal debt; Government debts; National debts; State debts; War debts
>   *xx* **Bonds; Credit; Deficit financing; Economics; Finance; Loans**

Public debts—United States 336.3

   x Federal debt—United States; United States—
     Public debts

Public demonstrations. *See* **Protests, demonstra-**
     tions, etc.

Public documents. *See* **Government publications**

Public figures. *See* **Celebrities**

Public finance. *See* **Finance**

Public health (May subdiv. geog.) 362.1; 614

   See also

Cemeteries	Noise
Charities, Medical	Occupational diseases
Communicable diseases	Occupational health and
Community health services	safety
Cremation	Pollution
Disinfection and disinfec-	Preventive medicine
tants	Refuse and refuse disposal
Environmental health	Sanitary engineering
Epidemics	Sanitation
Food adulteration and in-	School hygiene
spection	Sewage disposal
Health boards	Social medicine
Hospitals	Street cleaning
Meat inspection	Vaccination
Medical care	Water pollution
Milk supply	Water supply

   x Health, Public; Hygiene, Public; Hygiene, So-
     cial; Social hygiene

   xx Medicine, State; Preventive medicine; Sanita-
     tion; Social problems

Public health boards. *See* **Health boards**

Public health—United States 362.10973; 614

   x United States—Public health

Public housing (May subdiv. geog.) 363.5

   x Government housing; Housing projects, Gov-
     ernment; Low income housing

   xx **Housing**

Public interest 172; 320.01; 344

   See also **Ombudsman; Whistle blowing**

   x National interest

   xx **Industry—Government policy; State, The**

Public lands. *See* **Forest reserves; National parks**
     and reserves; and names of countries,
     states, etc. with the subdivision *Public*
     lands, e.g. **United States—Public lands;**
     etc.

Public libraries (May subdiv. geog.) 027.4

   See also **County libraries; Regional libraries**

   x Libraries, Public

   xx **Libraries**

Public meetings 302.3

   See also **Parliamentary practice; Protests, dem-**
     onstrations, etc.

   x Meetings, Public

   xx **Freedom of assembly**

Public opinion 303.3

   See also **Attitude (Psychology); Press; Propa-**
     ganda; Public relations; Publicity; also sub-
     jects with the subdivision *Public opinion,*
     e.g. **World War, 1939-1945—Public opin-**
     ion; etc.; and names of countries with the
     subdivision *Foreign opinion* for materials
     dealing with foreign public opinion about

Public opinion—*Continued*
>> the country, e.g. **United States—Foreign opinion;** etc.
> *x* Opinion, Public
> *xx* **Attitude (Psychology); Freedom of conscience; Political psychology; Public relations**

Public opinion polls   303.3
> *See also* **Market surveys**
> *x* Opinion polls; Polls, Public opinion; Straw votes
> *xx* **Market surveys**

Public ownership.   *See* **Government ownership; Municipal ownership**

Public playgrounds.   *See* **Playgrounds**

Public procurement.   *See* **Government purchasing**

Public records—Preservation.   *See* **Archives**

Public relations   659.2
> May be subdivided by topic, e.g. **Public relations—Libraries;** etc.
> *See also* **Advertising; Business entertaining; Customer relations; Psychology, Applied; Public opinion; Publicity**
> *xx* **Advertising; Public opinion; Publicity**

Public relations—Libraries   021.7
> *x* Libraries—Public relations
> *xx* **Libraries and community**

Public safety, Crimes against.   *See* **Offenses against public safety**

Public schools (May subdiv. geog.)   **371**
> Use for materials on preschool, elementary, and secondary schools supported by state and local government. Materials on British privately endowed schools known as "public schools" are entered under **Public schools, Endowed (Great Britain).**
> *See also* **Evening and continuation schools; High schools; Junior high schools; Magnet schools; Rural schools; Schools; Summer schools;** also headings beginning with the word **School**
> *x* Common schools; Grammar schools; Secondary schools
> *xx* **Schools; Secondary education**

Public schools and religion.   *See* **Religion in the public schools**

Public schools, Endowed (Great Britain)   373.2; 373.42
> See note under **Public schools.**
> *xx* **Private schools**

Public schools—United States   371; 379.73
> *x* United States—Public schools

Public service commissions   350
> Use for materials on bodies appointed to regulate or control public utilities.
> *x* Public utility commissions
> *xx* **Corporation law; Corporations; Industry—Government policy**

Public service corporations.   *See* **Public utilities**

Public shelters.   *See* **Air raid shelters**

Public speaking   808.5
> *See also* **Acting; Debates and debating; Lectures and lecturing; Preaching; Voice**
> *x* Elocution; Oratory; Persuasion (Rhetoric);

Public speaking—*Continued*
    Speaking
    xx **Voice**
Public television   384.55
    Use for materials on non-commercial television,
        publicly owned and operated, that presents
        educational, cultural, and public service pro-
        grams.
    x Educational television; Television, Public
    xx **Television broadcasting**
Public transit.   *See* **Local transit**
Public utilities   343.09; 351.87; 363.6
    See also

Corporation law	**Railroads—Government**
Corporations	**policy**
Electric industries	**Street railroads**
Electric railroads	**Telegraph**
Gas	**Telephone**
Railroads	**Water supply**

    x Electric utilities; Gas companies; Public ser-
        vice corporations; Utilities, Public
    xx **Corporation law; Corporations**
Public utility commissions.   *See* **Public service com-
        missions**
Public welfare   361.6
    Use for materials on tax-supported welfare activ-
        ities. Materials on privately supported wel-
        fare activities are entered under **Charities.**
        Materials on the methods employed in wel-
        fare work, public or private, are entered un-
        der **Social work.**
    See also

Charities	**Legal assistance to the**
Child welfare	**poor**
Children's hospitals	**Orphanages**
Disaster relief	**Poor**
Food relief	**Social medicine**
Hospitals	**Unemployed**
Institutional care	

    x Charities, Public; Poor relief; Public assis-
        tance; Public charities; Relief, Public; Social
        welfare; Welfare state; Welfare work
    xx **Charities; Poverty; Social work**
Public works   350.86; 363
    See also **Municipal engineering; Public buildings;**
        also names of countries, cities, etc. with the
        subdivision *Public works,* e.g. **United**
        States—Public works; Chicago (Ill.)—
        Public works; etc.
    xx **Civil engineering; Economic assistance, Do-
        mestic**
Public worship   264
    x Church attendance
    xx **Worship**
Publicity   659
    See also **Advertising; Press; Propaganda; Public
        relations**
    xx **Advertising; Public opinion; Public relations**
Publishers and authors.   *See* **Authors and publish-
        ers**

Publishers and publishing 070.5
See also

Authors and publishers	**Electronic publishing**
Book industries	**Paperback books**
Books	**Printing**
Booksellers and booksell-	**Publishers' standard book**
ing	**numbers**
Catalogs, Publishers'	**Serial publications**
Copyright	

    x Book trade; Editors and editing; Publishing
    xx **Book industries; Books; Booksellers and book-**
        selling; Copyright
Publishers' catalogs. *See* **Catalogs, Publishers'**
Publishers' standard book numbers 070.5
    See also **International Standard Book Numbers**
    x Book numbers, Publishers' standard; Standard
        book numbers
    xx **Publishers and publishing**
Publishing. *See* **Publishers and publishing**
Publishing, Electronic. *See* **Electronic publishing**
Pugilism. *See* **Boxing**
Pulmonary resuscitation. *See* **Artificial respiration**
Pulsars 523.8
    x Pulsating radio sources
    xx **Astronomy**
Pulsating radio sources. *See* **Pulsars**
Pumping iron. *See* **Weight lifting**
Pumping machinery 621.6
    See also types of pumping machinery, e.g. **Heat**
        pumps; etc.
    x Force pumps; Pumps; Steam pumps
    xx **Engines; Hydraulic engineering**
Pumps. *See* **Pumping machinery**
Punch and Judy. *See* **Puppets and puppet plays**
Punched card systems. *See* **Information systems**
Punctuality E
    x Lateness; Promptness; Tardiness
    xx **Human behavior; Time**
Punctuation 411; 421, etc.
    x English language—Punctuation
    xx **Rhetoric**
Punishment 364.6
    See also **Capital punishment; Crime; Criminal**
        law; Penal colonies; Prisons; Probation; Re-
        formatories
    x Discipline; Penology
    xx **Corrections; Crime; Criminal justice, Adminis-**
        tration of; Criminal law
Punishment in schools. *See* **School discipline**
Puns and punning 808.88; 818, etc.
    xx **Wit and humor**
Pupil-teacher relationships. *See* **Teacher-student**
    relationships
Puppets and puppet plays 791.5
    See also **Shadow pantomimes and plays**
    x Marionettes; Muppets; Punch and Judy
    xx **Drama; Folk drama; Theater**
Puppies. *See* **Dogs**
Purchase tax. *See* **Sales tax**
Purchasing. *See* **Buying; Shopping**
Purchasing, Government. *See* **Government pur-**
    chasing
Pure food. *See* **Food adulteration and inspection**
Purification of water. *See* **Water—Purification**

Puritans   285; 920
>   *See also* **Calvinism; Church of England—United States; Congregationalism; Pilgrims (New England colonists)**
>   *xx* **Calvinism; Church of England—United States; Congregationalism; United States—History—1600-1775, Colonial period**

Puzzles   793.73
>   *See also* **Crossword puzzles; Mathematical recreations; Riddles**
>   *xx* **Amusements; Riddles**

Pyramids   722
>   *See also* **Obelisks**
>   *xx* **Archeology; Architecture, Ancient; Monuments**

Quacks and quackery   615.8
>   *xx* **Impostors and imposture; Medicine; Swindlers and swindling**

Quakers.   *See* **Society of Friends**

Qualitative analysis.   *See* **Chemistry, Analytic**

Quality control   519.8; 658.5
>   *See also* specific industries with the subdivision *Quality control,* e.g. **Steel industry—Quality control;** etc.
>   *xx* **Reliability (Engineering); Sampling (Statistics)**

Quality of life   303.3
>   Use for materials on the combination of objective standards and subjective attitudes, by which individuals and groups assess their life situations.
>   *See also* **Lifestyles; Social values; Standard of living**
>   *x* Life quality
>   *xx* **Economic conditions; Social conditions; Social values**

Quantitative analysis.   *See* **Chemistry, Analytic**

Quantity cookery   641.5
>   Use for general materials solely on the preparation of food in large quantities. For materials on the preparation, delivery, and serving of ready-to-eat foods in large quantities outside of the home, use **Food service.**
>   *See also* **Food service**
>   *x* Cookery for large numbers; Cookery, Quantity
>   *xx* **Cookery; Food service**

Quantum mechanics.   *See* **Quantum theory**

Quantum theory   530.1
>   *See also*

Atomic theory	**Radiation**
Chemistry, Physical and theoretical	**Relativity (Physics)**
	Thermodynamics
Force and energy	**Wave mechanics**
Neutrons	

>   *x* Quantum mechanics
>   *xx* **Atomic theory; Chemistry, Physical and theoretical; Dynamics; Force and energy; Physics; Radiation; Relativity (Physics); Thermodynamics**

Quarantine.   *See* **Communicable diseases**

Quarks   539.7
>   *xx* **Particles (Nuclear physics)**

Quarries and quarrying 622
   See also **Stone**
   x Stone quarries
   xx **Geology, Economic; Stone**
Quartz 549
   x Rock crystal
   xx **Mineralogy**
Quasars 523.1
   x Quasi-stellar radio sources
   xx **Astronomy; Radio astronomy**
Quasi-stellar radio sources. *See* **Quasars**
Québec (Province) 971.4
Québec (Province)—History 971.4
Québec (Province)—History—Autonomy and independence movements 971.4
   x Québec (Province)—Separatist movement; Separatist movement in Québec (Province)
   xx **Canada—English-French relations**
Québec (Province)—Separatist movement. *See* **Québec (Province)—History—Autonomy and independence movements**
Queens. *See* **Kings, queens, rulers, etc.**
Queries. *See* **Questions and answers**
Questions and answers 793.73
   Use for informal quizzes of miscellany. Informal quizzes on a particular subject are entered under the subject with the subdivision *Miscellanea.* For materials on formal examinations, use **Examinations.** Examination questions on a particular subject are entered under the subject with the subdivision *Examinations,* e.g. **Music—Examinations;** etc. Compilations of practice problems or exercises for use in the study of a topic are entered under the topic with the subdivision *Problems, exercises, etc.,* e.g. **Chemistry— Problems, exercises, etc.;** etc.
   See also **Examinations;** also subjects with the subdivision *Miscellanea,* e.g. **Medicine— Miscellanea;** etc.
   x Answers to questions; Queries; Quizzes
Quick and easy cookery 641.5
   Use for materials on the art of cooking, as well as for materials consisting of collections of recipes emphasizing economy of preparation time and the use of readily available ingredients.
   x Convenience cookery; Easy and quick cookery; Quick-meal cookery; Time saving cookery
   xx **Cookery**
Quick-meal cookery. *See* **Quick and easy cookery**
Quicksilver. *See* **Mercury**
Quilt designing. *See* **Quilts—Design**
Quilting 746.46
Quilts 746.9
   x Coverlets; Patchwork quilts
   xx **Interior design**
Quilts—Design 746.9
   x Quilt designing
Quintets 785
   xx **Orchestral music**
Quislings. *See* **World War, 1939-1945— Collaborationists**

552

Quit-smoking programs. *See* **Smoking cessation programs**

Quizzes. *See* **Questions and answers**

Qumran texts. *See* **Dead Sea scrolls**

Quotations 080; 808.88

See also **Proverbs;** also subjects and names of people with the subdivision *Quotations,* e.g. **Presidents—United States—Quotations;** etc.

x Sayings

xx **Epigrams; Literature—Collections**

Qur'an. *See* **Koran**

R.V.'s. *See* **Recreational vehicles**

Rabbis 296.6; 920

xx **Clergy; Judaism**

Rabbits 599.32; 636

x Bunnies; Bunny rabbits; Hares

Rabies 616.9; 636.089

x Hydrophobia

Race 572

xx **Ethnology**

Race awareness 305.8

See also **Blacks—Race identity; Prejudices; Racism**

xx **Race relations**

Race discrimination 305.8

Use for materials on the restriction or denial of rights, privileges, or choice because of race. Materials on prejudicial attitudes about particular groups because of their race are entered under **Racism.**

See also types of discrimination, e.g. **Discrimination in education;** etc.

x Discrimination, Racial; Racial discrimination

xx **Discrimination; Race relations; Racism; Social problems**

Race identity. *See* names of races with the subdivision *Race identity,* e.g. **Blacks—Race identity;** etc.

Race prejudice. *See* **Racism**

Race problems. *See* **Race relations**

Race psychology. *See* **Ethnopsychology**

Race relations 305.8

Use for materials on the contact and interaction between racial groups.

See also

Culture conflict	**Intercultural education**
Discrimination	**Interracial adoption**
Ethnic relations	**Race awareness**
Immigration and emigration	**Race discrimination**
	Racism

also names of countries, cities, etc., with the subdivision *Race relations,* e.g. **United States—Race relations; Chicago (Ill.)—Race relations; South Africa—Race relations;** etc.

x Integration, Racial; Interracial relations; Race problems

xx **Acculturation; Ethnic groups; Ethnic relations; Ethnology; Minorities; Social problems; Sociology**

Race relations and the church. *See* **Church and race relations**

Races of people. *See* **Ethnology**

Racial balance in schools. *See* **Busing (School integration); School integration; Segregation in education**

Racial bias. *See* **Racism**

Racial discrimination. *See* **Race discrimination**

Racial identity. *See* names of races with the subdivision *Race identity,* e.g. **Blacks—Race identity;** etc.

Racial intermarriage. *See* **Interracial marriage**

Racing. *See* **Orienteering;** and names of types of racing, e.g. **Automobile racing; Bicycle racing; Boat racing; Horse racing; Soap box derbies;** etc.

Racism   305.8; 320.5
> See note under **Race discrimination.**
> *See also* **Race discrimination**
> *x* Race prejudice; Racial bias
> *xx* **Attitude (Psychology); Prejudices; Race awareness; Race relations**

Racketeering   364.1
> *x* Crime syndicates
> *xx* **Crime; Organized crime**

Radar   621.3848
> *xx* **Navigation; Radio; Remote sensing**

Radar defense networks   623
> *See also* **Ballistic missile early warning system**
> *x* Defenses, Radar
> *xx* **Air defenses**

Radiant heating   697
> *x* Panel heating
> *xx* **Heating**

Radiation   539.2
> *See also*

Cosmic rays	**Radioactivity**
Electromagnetic waves	**Radium**
Gamma rays	**Sound**
Infrared radiation	**Spectrum analysis**
Light	**Ultraviolet rays**
Phosphorescence	**X rays**
Quantum theory	

> *xx* **Light; Optics; Physics; Quantum theory; Waves**

Radiation biology. *See* **Radiobiology**

Radiation—Physiological effect   612
> *See also* **Atomic bomb—Physiological effect; Nuclear medicine**
> *xx* **Atomic bomb—Physiological effect**

Radiation—Safety measures   363.1; 612

Radiation, Solar. *See* **Solar radiation**

Radiation therapy. *See* **Radiotherapy**

Radicals and radicalism   320.5
> *x* Extremism (Political science)
> *xx* **Revolutions; Right and left (Political science)**

Radio   621.384
> *See also* **Radar; Sound—Recording and reproducing**
> *x* Wireless
> *xx* **Electric engineering; Telecommunication**

Radio addresses, debates, etc.   384.54; 808.5; 808.85
> *x* Radio lectures
> *xx* **Debates and debating; Lectures and lecturing; Radio broadcasting; Radio scripts**

Radio advertising   659.14
   x Advertising, Radio; Commercials, Radio; Radio commercials
   xx **Advertising; Radio broadcasting**
Radio and music   780; 781.5
   Use same form for radio and other subjects.
   x Music and radio
   xx **Music**
Radio apparatus industry.   *See* **Radio supplies industry**
Radio astronomy   522
   See also names of celestial radio sources, e.g. **Quasars;** etc.
   xx **Astronomy; Interstellar communication**
Radio authorship   808
   See also **Radio plays—Technique; Radio scripts**
   x Radio script writing; Radio writing
   xx **Authorship; Radio broadcasting; Radio scripts**
Radio broadcasting   384.54
   See also **Equal time rule (Broadcasting); Fairness doctrine (Broadcasting); Radio addresses, debates, etc.; Radio advertising; Radio authorship; Radio programs**
   x Radio industry
   xx **Broadcasting; Mass media**
Radio chemistry.   *See* **Radiochemistry**
Radio commercials.   *See* **Radio advertising**
Radio drama.   *See* **Radio plays**
Radio—Equipment and supplies   621.384028
   See also **Radio—Receivers and reception; Radio supplies industry**
   xx **Radio supplies industry**
Radio equipment industry.   *See* **Radio supplies industry**
Radio frequency modulation   621.384
   See also **Shortwave radio**
   x F.M. radio; FM radio; Frequency modulation, Radio
Radio in aeronautics   629.135
   Use same form for radio in other subjects.
   x Aeronautics, Radio in
   xx **Aeronautics; Navigation (Aeronautics)**
Radio in astronautics   629.4
   x Lunar surface radio communication
   xx **Astronautics—Communication systems**
Radio in education   371.3
   x Education and radio
   xx **Audiovisual education; Teaching—Aids and devices**
Radio industry.   *See* **Radio broadcasting**
Radio industry and trade.   *See* **Radio supplies industry**
Radio journalism.   *See* **Broadcast journalism**
Radio lectures.   *See* **Radio addresses, debates, etc.**
Radio news.   *See* **Broadcast journalism**
Radio operators   621.3841
Radio plays   808.82; 809.2; 812, etc.
   Use for individual radio plays, for collections of plays, and for works about them. Works on how to write radio plays are entered under **Radio plays—Technique.**
   x Radio drama; Scenarios
   xx **Drama; Radio programs; Radio scripts**

Radio plays—Technique   808.2
    See also **Television plays—Technique**
    x Play writing; Playwriting
    xx **Drama—Technique; Radio authorship; Television plays—Technique**
Radio programs   384.54
    See also types of programs and specific programs, e.g. **Radio plays; Talk shows;** etc.
    x Programs, Radio
    xx **Radio broadcasting**
Radio—Receivers and reception   621.384
    x Radio reception; Radios
    xx **Radio—Equipment and supplies**
Radio reception.   *See* **Radio—Receivers and reception**
Radio—Repairing   621.384
    x Radio servicing
    xx **Repairing**
Radio script writing.   *See* **Radio authorship**
Radio scripts   808.8; 818, etc.
    See also **Radio addresses, debates, etc.; Radio authorship; Radio plays; Television scripts**
    xx **Radio authorship; Television scripts**
Radio servicing.   *See* **Radio—Repairing**
Radio, Shortwave.   *See* **Shortwave radio**
Radio stations   384.54
    See also names of radio stations
Radio stations, Amateur.   *See* **Amateur radio stations**
Radio supplies industry   338.4
    See also **Radio—Equipment and supplies**
    x Radio apparatus industry; Radio equipment industry; Radio industry and trade
    xx **Radio—Equipment and supplies**
Radio waves.   *See* **Electric waves**
Radio writing.   *See* **Radio authorship**
Radioactive fallout   539.7
    x Dust, Radioactive; Fallout, Radioactive
    xx **Atomic bomb; Hydrogen bomb; Radioactive pollution**
Radioactive isotopes.   *See* **Radioisotopes**
Radioactive pollution   363.17; 363.73; 621.48
    See also **Radioactive fallout; Radioactive waste disposal**
    x Environmental radioactivity; Nuclear pollution; Pollution, Radioactive
    xx **Pollution; Radioactive waste disposal; Radioactivity**
Radioactive substances.   *See* **Radioactivity**
Radioactive waste disposal   363.72; 621.48
    See also **Radioactive pollution**
    x Nuclear waste disposal; Waste disposal
    xx **Nuclear engineering; Nuclear power plants—Environmental aspects; Radioactive pollution; Radioactivity; Refuse and refuse disposal**
Radioactivity   539.7
    See also

Cosmic rays	**Radioactive pollution**
Electrons	**Radioactive waste disposal**
Helium	**Radiobiology**
Nuclear physics	**Radiochemistry**
Phosphorescence	**Radiotherapy**

Radioactivity—*Continued*

Radium	**Uranium**
Radon	
Transmutation (Chemistry)	**X rays**

   x Radioactive substances
   xx **Electricity; Light; Nuclear physics; Physics; Radiation; Radium; Radon**
Radiobiology 574.19
   x Radiation biology
   xx **Biology; Biophysics; Nuclear physics; Radioactivity**
Radiocarbon dating 539.7
   x Carbon 14 dating; Dating, Radiocarbon
   xx **Archeology**
Radiochemistry 541.3
   x Radio chemistry
   xx **Chemistry, Physical and theoretical; Radioactivity**
Radiography. *See* **X rays**
Radioisotopes 621.48
   x Radioactive isotopes
   xx **Isotopes; Nuclear engineering**
Radiologists 920
   x Roentgenologists
   xx **Physicians; Radiotherapy; X rays**
Radios. *See* **Radio—Receivers and reception**
Radiotherapy 615.8
   See also **Phototherapy; Radiologists; Radium; Ultraviolet rays; X rays**
   x Radiation therapy
   xx **Electrotherapeutics; Phototherapy; Physical therapy; Radioactivity; Radium; Therapeutics; X rays**
Radium 546; 661; 669
   See also **Radioactivity; Radiotherapy**
   xx **Radiation; Radioactivity; Radiotherapy**
Radium emanation. *See* **Radon**
Radon 363.73; 546
   See also **Radioactivity**
   x Radium emanation
   xx **Poisonous gases; Radioactivity**
Railroad accidents. *See* **Railroads—Accidents**
Railroad construction. *See* **Railroad engineering**
Railroad engineering 625.1
   x Railroad construction
   xx **Civil engineering; Engineering; Railroads**
Railroad fares. *See* **Railroads—Rates**
Railroad mergers. *See* **Railroads—Consolidation**
Railroad rates. *See* **Railroads—Rates**
Railroad workers. *See* **Railroads—Employees**
Railroads (May subdiv. geog.) **385; 625.1**
   See also

Electric railroads	**Monorail railroads**
Eminent domain	**Railroad engineering**
Express service	**Street railroads**
Freight and freightage	**Subways**

   also names of individual railroads
   x Railways; Trains, Railroad
   xx **Public utilities; Transportation**
Railroads—Accidents 363.12
   See also **Railroads—Safety appliances; Railroads—Signaling**
   x Collisions, Railroad; Derailments; Railroad

Rain—*Continued*
   x Precipitation (Meteorology); Rain and rainfall;
       Rainfall
   xx **Climate; Droughts; Forest influences; Meteo-
       rology; Storms; Water; Weather**
Rain, Acid.   *See* **Acid rain**
Rain and rainfall.   *See* **Rain**
Rain forests (May subdiv. geog.)   **574.5; 634.9**
   Use for materials on forests of broad-leaved,
       mainly evergreen trees found in continually
       moist climates in the tropics, subtropics,
       and some parts of the temperate zones.
       Consider also **Jungles.**
   See also **Jungles**
   x Tropical rain forests
   xx **Forests and forestry**
Rain making.   *See* **Weather control**
Rainbow   551.5
   See also **Refraction**
   xx **Meteorology**
Rainfall.   *See* **Rain**
Rainfall and forests.   *See* **Forest influences**
Rallies (Protest).   *See* **Protests, demonstrations, etc.**
Ranch life   307.72; 636
   See also **Cowhands**
   xx **Farm life; Frontier and pioneer life**
Random access memories (Data processing).   *See*
       Computer storage devices
Random access storage devices (Data
       processing).   *See* **Computer storage devices**
Random sampling.   *See* **Sampling (Statistics)**
Ranger project.   *See* **Project Ranger**
Rank.   *See* **Social classes**
Rap music   782.42164
   x Rap songs; Rappin' (Music); Rapping (Music)
   xx **Black music; Popular music**
Rap songs.   *See* **Rap music**
Rape   364.1
   x Assault, Criminal; Criminal assault
   xx **Offenses against the person; Sex crimes**
Rapid reading   372.4
   x Accelerated reading; Faster reading; Speed
       reading
   xx **Reading—Remedial teaching**
Rapid transit.   *See* **Local transit**
Rappin' (Music).   *See* **Rap music**
Rapping (Music).   *See* **Rap music**
Rare animals   591
   See also **Endangered species; Extinct animals;
       Wildlife conservation;** also names of specific
       animals, e.g. **Bison;** etc.
   x Animals, Rare
   xx **Animals; Endangered species; Extinct ani-
       mals; Wildlife; Wildlife conservation**
Rare books   090
   x Book rarities; Books, Rare
   xx **Bibliography—Editions**
Rare plants   581
   See also **Endangered species; Plant conservation**
   xx **Endangered species; Plant conservation;
       Plants**
Rating.   *See* **Performance standards;** and subjects
       and classes of people with the subdivision

Rating—*Continued*

  Rating, e.g. **Bonds—Rating; Employees—Rating;** etc.

Ratio and proportion 513.2

  xx **Arithmetic; Geometry**

Rationalism 149; 211

  See also

Agnosticism	**Intuition**
Atheism	**Positivism**
Belief and doubt	**Realism**
Deism	**Reason**
Enlightenment	**Skepticism**
Free thought	**Theism**

  xx **Agnosticism; Atheism; Belief and doubt; Deism; Free thought; God; Knowledge, Theory of; Philosophy; Realism; Religion; Secularism**

Rattlesnakes 597.96

  xx **Poisonous animals; Snakes**

Raw materials 333

  See also **Farm produce; Forest products; Mines and mineral resources**

  xx **Commercial products; Materials**

Rayon 677

  x Acetate silk; Artificial silk; Silk, Artificial

  xx **Synthetic fabrics; Synthetic products**

Rays, Roentgen. *See* **X rays**

Rays, Ultra-violet. *See* **Ultraviolet rays**

Reaction (Political science). *See* **Right and left (Political science)**

Reactions, Chemical. *See* **Chemical reactions**

Reactors (Nuclear physics). *See* **Nuclear reactors**

Reader services (Libraries) 025.5

  Use for materials on that part of library service devoted to the provision of assistance, advice, etc. to library users. Reader services are usually in tandem with technical services.

  Materials on library services for specific types of library users or on services for users involved in specific activities are entered under specific headings, e.g. **Libraries and the elderly.**

  See also **Libraries and Blacks; Libraries and labor; Libraries and the elderly; Library instruction; Reference services (Libraries)**

  x Libraries and readers

  xx **Library services**

Readers. *See* **Reading materials**

Readers' theater 792

  Use for materials on oral interpretation before an audience, of scripts that are read aloud rather than memorized.

  x Chamber theater; Story theater

  xx **Amateur theater; Theater**

Readiness for mathematics. *See* **Mathematical readiness**

Readiness for reading. *See* **Reading readiness**

Readiness for school 372

  Use for materials on the prerequisite abilities, such as degree of psychosocial maturity, previous experience, cognition, physical abilities, etc., to learning in a school setting.

Readiness for school—*Continued*
   x School readiness
   xx **Elementary education; Preschool education**
Reading   372.4
   Use for materials on methods of teaching read-
      ing, and general materials on the art of read-
      ing. Materials on teaching slow readers are
      entered under **Reading—Remedial teach-**
      ing. Materials on the cultural or informa-
      tional aspects of reading and general discus-
      sions of books are entered under **Books and**
      reading.
   See also **Books and reading; Reading—Phonetic**
      method; Reading readiness; Whole language
   x Children's reading; Reading—Study and
      teaching; Word skills
   xx **Language arts**
Reading clinics.   *See* **Reading—Remedial teaching**
Reading comprehension   372.4
   xx **Learning, Psychology of; Verbal learning**
Reading disability   371.91
   See also names of specific reading disabilities,
      e.g. **Dyslexia;** etc.
   x Disability, Reading; Reading retardation; Re-
      tarded readers
   xx **Learning disabilities**
Reading interests.   *See* **Books and reading**
Reading interests of children.   *See* **Children—**
      Books and reading
Reading materials   372.4
   Use for materials in English. For readers in
      other languages, use the language with the
      subdivision *Reading materials,* e.g. **French**
      language—Reading materials; etc.
   See also **Basal readers; Big books; Easy reading**
      materials; Readings and recitations
   x English language—Reading materials; Readers
   xx **Children's literature**
Reading—Patterning.   *See* **Language arts—**
      Patterning
Reading—Phonetic method   372.4
   See also **Phonetics**
   x Letter-sound association; Phonics
   xx **English language—Pronunciation; Phonetics;**
      Reading
Reading readiness   372.4
   x Readiness for reading
   xx **Reading**
Reading—Remedial teaching   372.4
   See also **Rapid reading**
   x Reading clinics; Remedial reading
Reading retardation.   *See* **Reading disability**
Reading—Study and teaching.   *See* **Reading**
Readings and recitations   808.85
   x Recitations and readings; Speakers (Recitation
      books)
   xx **Reading materials; School assembly programs**
Ready reckoners.   *See* **Mathematics—Tables**
Real estate   333.3
   Use for general materials on real property in the
      legal sense, i.e., ownership of land and
      buildings as opposed to personal property.
      Materials limited to the buying and selling

Real estate—*Continued*
>> of real property are entered under **Real estate business.** General materials on land without the ownership aspects are entered under **Land use.** Materials on the assessment of property are entered under **Taxation.**
>> *See also* **Eminent domain; Farms; Land tenure; Landlord and tenant; Mortgages; Real estate business**
>> *x* Property, Real; Real property; Realty
>> *xx* **Land tenure; Land use; Property**

Real estate business 333.33; 346.04
>> See note under **Real estate.**
>> *See also* **Houses—Buying and selling**
>> *xx* **Business; Real estate**

Real estate investment 332.63
>> *x* Investment in real estate; Real property investment
>> *xx* **Investments; Speculation**

Real estate investment—Taxation 343.05
>> *xx* **Taxation**

Real estate timesharing. *See* **Timesharing (Real estate)**

Real property. *See* **Real estate**

Real property investment. *See* **Real estate investment**

Realism 149
>> *See also* **Idealism; Materialism; Positivism; Pragmatism; Rationalism**
>> *xx* **Idealism; Materialism; Philosophy; Positivism; Rationalism**

Realism in literature 809
>> *See also* **Romanticism**
>> *x* Naturalism in literature
>> *xx* **Literature; Romanticism**

Reality 111
>> *See also* **Empiricism; Knowledge, Theory of; Pragmatism**
>> *xx* **Intuition; Knowledge, Theory of; Philosophy; Pragmatism; Truth**

Realty. *See* **Real estate**

Reapers. *See* **Harvesting machinery**

Reapportionment (Election law). *See* **Apportionment (Election law)**

Reason 160
>> *See also* **Reasoning**
>> *xx* **Intellect; Rationalism**

Reasoning 153.4; 160
>> *See also* **Critical thinking; Intellect; Logic**
>> *xx* **Intellect; Logic; Psychology; Reason; Thought and thinking**

Rebates (Railroads). *See* **Railroads—Rates**

Rebellions. *See* **Insurgency; Revolutions**

Rebels (Social psychology). *See* **Alienation (Social psychology)**

Rebirth. *See* **Reincarnation**

Rebuses. *See* **Riddles**

Recall of products. *See* **Product recall**

Recall (Political science) 324.6
>> *xx* **Impeachments; Representative government and representation**

Recessions, Economic. *See* **Depressions, Economic**

Recipes. *See* **Cookery**

Reciprocity. *See* **Commercial policy**

Recitations and readings. *See* **Readings and recitations**

Recitations with music. *See* **Monologues with music**

Reclamation of land   627; 631.6

    Use for general materials on reclamation, including drainage and irrigation.

    See also **Drainage; Irrigation; Marshes; Sand dunes**

    x Clearing of land; Land, Reclamation of

    xx **Agriculture; Civil engineering; Floods; Hydraulic engineering; Irrigation; Land use; Natural resources; Soils**

Recluses. *See* **Hermits**

Recombinant DNA   574.87

    x Gene splicing

    xx **DNA; Genetic engineering; Genetic recombination**

Recombination, Genetic. *See* **Genetic recombination**

Recommendations for positions. *See* **Applications for positions**

Reconnaissance, Aerial. *See* **Aerial reconnaissance**

Reconstruction (1865-1876)   973.8

    See also **Ku Klux Klan (1865-1876)**

    x Carpetbag rule; United States—History—1861-1865, Civil War—Reconstruction

    xx **United States—History—1865-1898**

Reconstruction (1914-1939)   940.3

    See also **Peace; Veterans—Education; Veterans—Employment; World War, 1914-1918—Economic aspects**

    x World War, 1914-1918—Reconstruction

Reconstruction (1939-1951) (May subdiv. geog. except U.S.)   **940.53**

    See also **Economic assistance; International cooperation; Veterans—Education; Veterans—Employment; World War, 1939-1945—Civilian relief; World War, 1939-1945—Economic aspects; World War, 1939-1945—Reparations**

    x Marshall Plan; Point Four program; World War, 1939-1945—Reconstruction

    xx **Economic assistance; International cooperation; World War, 1939-1945—Economic aspects**

Recorders, Tape. *See* **Magnetic recorders and recording**

Recording, Laser. *See* **Laser recording**

Recordings, Sound. *See* **Sound recordings**

Records, Human. *See* **World records**

Records of achievement. *See* **World records**

Records of births, etc. *See* **Registers of births, etc.; Vital statistics**

Records, Phonograph. *See* **Sound recordings**

Records—Preservation. *See* **Archives**

Records, World. *See* **World records**

Recovery of space vehicles. *See* **Space vehicles—Recovery**

Recovery of waste products. *See* **Recycling (Waste, etc.); Salvage (Waste, etc.)**

Recreation (May subdiv. geog.)   **790**

    Use for materials on the psychological and social aspects of recreation and for materials on organized recreational projects.

Recreation—*Continued*
  See also
  Amusements   **Play**
  Community centers   **Playgrounds**
  Games   **Popular culture**
  Hobbies   **Sports**
  Outdoor recreation **Vacations**
    also classes of people with the subdivision
        Recreation, e.g. **Elderly—Recreation;** etc.
    x Pastimes; Relaxation
    xx **Amusements; Leisure; Play**
Recreation centers. *See* **Community centers**
Recreational vehicles   629.226
    See also types of recreational vehicles, e.g.
        Travel trailers and campers; etc.
    x R.V.'s; RVs; Vehicles, Recreational
    xx **Outdoor recreation; Vehicles**
Recreations. *See* **Hobbies**
Recreations, Literary. *See* **Literary recreations**
Recreations, Mathematical. *See* **Mathematical rec-
    reations**
Recreations, Scientific. *See* **Scientific recreations**
Recruiting and enlistment. *See* names of armies
        and navies with the subdivision *Recruiting,
        enlistment, etc.,* e.g. **United States. Army—
        Recruiting, enlistment, etc.; United States.
        Navy—Recruiting, enlistment, etc.;** etc.
Recruiting of employees   658.3
    See also **Employment agencies;** also names of oc-
        cupations and professions with the subdivi-
        sion *Recruiting,* e.g. **Librarians—
        Recruiting;** etc.
    xx **Personnel management**
Rectors. *See* **Clergy**
Recurrent education. *See* **Continuing education**
Recycling (Waste, etc.)   628.4
    Use for materials on the processing of waste pa-
        per, cans, bottles, etc. Materials on the recy-
        cling or reuse of specific waste products are
        entered under the products with the subdivi-
        sion *Recycling.* Materials on reclaiming and
        reusing equipment or parts are entered un-
        der **Salvage (Waste, etc.).**
    See also **Refuse and refuse disposal; Salvage
        (Waste, etc.); Waste products;** also subjects
        with the subdivision *Recycling,* e.g. **Alumi-
        num—Recycling;** etc.
    x Conversion of waste products; Recovery of
        waste products; Reuse of waste; Utilization
        of waste; Waste products—Recycling;
        Waste reclamation
    xx **Energy conservation; Pollution control indus-
        try; Refuse and refuse disposal; Salvage
        (Waste, etc.); Waste products**
Red   535.6; 752
    xx **Color**
Redemption. *See* **Salvation**
Reducing   613.2
    See also **Diet**
    x Body weight control; Dieting; Diets, Reduc-
        ing; Exercises, Reducing; Obesity—Control;
        Overweight—Control; Weight control
    xx **Diet; Exercise**

Reference books   028.7

See also **Books and reading—Best books; Encyclopedias and dictionaries**

xx **Books and reading**

Reference services (Libraries)   025.5

Use for materials on activities designed to make information available to library users; includes direct personal assistance.

x Library reference services; Online reference services; Reference work (Libraries)

xx **Information services; Reader services (Libraries)**

Reference work (Libraries). *See* **Reference services (Libraries)**

Referendum   328.2

x Direct legislation; Initiative and referendum; Legislation, Direct

xx **Constitutional law; Democracy; Elections; Representative government and representation**

Refinishing furniture. *See* **Furniture finishing**

Reforestation   634.9

See also **Tree planting**

xx **Forests and forestry; Tree planting**

Reform, Agrarian. *See* **Land reform**

Reform of criminals. *See* **Criminals; Probation; Reformatories**

Reform schools. *See* **Reformatories**

Reform, Social. *See* **Social problems**

Reformation   270.6

See also **Calvinism; Europe—History—1492-1789; Protestantism; Sixteenth century;** also names of religious sects, e.g. **Huguenots;** etc.

x Anti-Reformation; Antireformation; Church history—1517-1648, Reformation; Counter-Reformation; Counterreformation; Protestant Reformation

xx **Christianity; Church history; History, Modern; Protestantism; Sixteenth century**

Reformatories   365

See also **Juvenile courts; Juvenile delinquency; Probation**

x Penal institutions; Reform of criminals; Reform schools

xx **Children—Institutional care; Correctional institutions; Crime; Juvenile delinquency; Prisons; Punishment**

Reformers   920

Use for materials about political, social, religious, etc., reformers.

Refraction   535

x Dioptrics

xx **Light; Optics; Rainbow**

Refrigeration   621.5

See also **Air conditioning; Cold storage; Low temperatures**

x Cooling appliances; Freezing; Ice manufacture; Refrigeration and refrigerating machinery; Refrigerators

xx **Air conditioning; Cold storage; Frost; Low temperatures**

Refrigeration and refrigerating machinery. *See* **Refrigeration**

Refrigerators. *See* **Refrigeration**
Refugees (May subdiv. geog. or ethnic adjective
      form, e.g. **Refugees, Vietnamese; Refugees,**
      Arab; etc.) **325; 341.4**
    x Displaced persons; Exiles
    xx **Aliens; Homeless people; Immigration and**
      emigration
Refugees, Arab 325
    x Arab refugees
Refugees, Political. *See* **Political refugees**
Refugees, Vietnamese 325
    x Vietnamese refugees
Refuges, Wildlife. *See* **Wildlife refuges**
Refuse and refuse disposal 363.72; 628.4
    See also

Hazardous wastes	**Recycling (Waste, etc.)**
Industrial wastes	**Salvage (Waste, etc.)**
Medical wastes	**Sewage disposal**
Pollution	**Street cleaning**
Pollution control industry	**Waste products**
Radioactive waste disposal	**Water pollution**

    x Disposal of refuse; Garbage; Incineration; Lit-
      tering; Solid waste disposal; Waste disposal
    xx **Industrial wastes; Municipal engineering; Pol-**
      lution; Pollution control industry; Public
      health; Recycling (Waste, etc.); Salvage
      (Waste, etc.); Sanitary engineering; Sanita-
      tion; Street cleaning; Waste products; Water
      pollution
Regattas. *See* **Rowing; Yachts and yachting**
Regeneration (Christianity) 234; 248.2
    x Born again Christians; Christian new birth;
      Christian regeneration
    xx **Regeneration (Theology)**
Regeneration (Theology) 234
    See also **Conversion; Regeneration (Christianity);**
    Salvation
    x New birth (Theology)
    xx **Baptism; Conversion; Doctrinal theology; Sal-**
      vation
Regional libraries 027.4
    Use for materials on public libraries serving a
      group of communities, several counties, or
      other regions.
    See also **County libraries**
    x District libraries; Libraries, Regional
    xx **Public libraries**
Regional planning (May subdiv. geog.) **711**
    See also **City planning; Landscape protection;**
    Social surveys
    x County planning; Metropolitan planning;
      Planning, Regional; State planning
    xx **Landscape protection**
Regionalism. *See* **Nationalism; Sectionalism**
    (United States)
Registers of births, etc. 929
    See also **Vital statistics; Wills**
    x Birth records; Births, Registers of; Burial sta-
      tistics; Deaths, Registers of; Marriage regis-
      ters; Parish registers; Records of births, etc.;
      Vital records
    xx **Genealogy; Vital statistics**
Registers of persons. *See* names of countries, cities,

Registers of persons—*Continued*
    etc. and names of colleges, universities, etc.
    with the subdivision *Registers,* e.g. **United
    States—Registers; United States Military
    Academy—Registers;** etc.
Registration of voters. *See* **Voter registration**
Rehabilitation. *See* groups of people with the sub-
    division *Rehabilitation,* e.g. **Drug ad-
    dicts—Rehabilitation; Physically handi-
    capped—Rehabilitation;** etc.
Rehabilitation peer counseling. *See* **Peer counsel-
    ing**
Reign of Terror. *See* **France—History—1789-1799,
    Revolution**
Reincarnation   129
    See also **Soul**
    x Rebirth
    xx **Soul; Theosophy**
Reindeer   599.73; 636.2
    xx **Deer; Domestic animals**
Reinforced concrete   691
    x Concrete, Reinforced
    xx **Building materials; Concrete**
Relations among ethnic groups. *See* **Ethnic rela-
    tions**
Relative humidity. *See* **Humidity**
Relativity (Physics)   530.1
    See also **Quantum theory; Space and time**
    xx **Physics; Quantum theory**
Relaxation. *See* **Recreation; Rest**
Reliability (Engineering)   620
    See also **Quality control; Structural failures**
    x Reliability of equipment; Systems reliability;
    Testing
    xx **Engineering; Probabilities; Systems engineer-
    ing**
Reliability of equipment. *See* **Reliability (Engi-
    neering)**
Relief, Public. *See* **Public welfare**
Religion   200
    See also

Agnosticism	**Religions**
Ancestor worship	**Religious awakening**
Atheism	**Revelation**
Belief and doubt	**Sacrifice**
Deism	**Skepticism**
Faith	**Spiritual life**
God	**Sun worship**
Moon worship	**Supernatural**
Mysticism	**Superstition**
Mythology	**Theism**
Natural theology	**Theology**
Psychology, Religious	**Worship**
Rationalism	

    also names of peoples, ethnic groups, countries,
    states, etc. with the subdivision *Religion,*
    e.g. **Indians of North America—Religion;
    Blacks—Religion; United States—Religion;**
    etc.; and headings beginning with the words
    Religion and **Religious**
    xx **God; Religions; Theology**
Religion and art. *See* **Art and religion**
Religion and communism. *See* **Communism and
    religion**

Religion and education. *See* **Church and education**
Religion and literature. *See* **Religion in literature**
Religion and medicine. *See* **Medicine and religion**
Religion and philosophy. *See* **Philosophy and religion**
Religion and politics   261.7
>*See also* **Christianity and politics**
>*x* Evangelism and politics; Politics and religion
Religion and science   215
>*See also* **Bible and science; Creation; Evolution; Man—Origin; Natural theology**
>*x* Science and religion
>*xx* **Apologetics; Evolution; Natural theology; Theology**
Religion and social problems. *See* **Church and social problems**
Religion and state. *See* **Church—Government policy**
Religion and war. *See* **War and religion**
Religion in literature   809
>*See also* **Bible in literature**
>*x* Religion and literature
>*xx* **Bible in literature**
Religion in the public schools   377
>*See also* **Fundamentalism and education**
>*x* Bible in the schools; Prayers in the public schools; Public schools and religion; Schools—Prayers
>*xx* **Church and education; Church—Government policy; Fundamentalism and education; Religious education**
Religion of humanity. *See* **Positivism**
Religion—Philosophy   200.1
>*See also* **Philosophy and religion**
>*x* Philosophy of religion
>*xx* **Philosophy and religion**
Religion—Study and teaching. *See* **Religious education; Theology—Study and teaching**
Religions   200
>All religions are not included in this List but are to be added as needed.
>*See also*

Bahai Faith	**Islam**
Brahmanism	**Judaism**
Buddhism	**Mythology**
Christianity	**Occultism**
Confucianism	**Paganism**
Cults	**Religion**
Druids and Druidism	**Sects**
Gnosticism	**Shinto**
Gods and goddesses	**Taoism**
Hinduism	**Theosophy**

>*x* Comparative religion
>*xx* **Civilization; Gods and goddesses; Religion**
Religions—Biography   200.92; 920
>*See also* names of religions with the subdivision *Biography,* e.g. **Christianity—Biography;** etc.
>*x* Religious biography
>*xx* **Biography**
Religious art. *See* **Art, Medieval; Church architecture; Religious art and symbolism**

Religious art and symbolism 704.9
  See also **Art and religion; Christian art and symbolism**
  x Iconography; Painting, Religious; Religious art; Religious painting; Religious symbolism; Sacred art; Sculpture, Religious
  xx **Archeology; Art; Art and religion; Mysticism; Symbolism**
Religious awakening 200; 269
  Use for materials on a renewal of interest in religion.
  x Awakening, Religious
  xx **Religion**
Religious belief. *See* **Faith**
Religious biography. *See* **Christianity—Biography; Religions—Biography**
Religious ceremonies. *See* **Rites and ceremonies**
Religious cults. *See* **Cults**
Religious denominations. *See* **Sects;** and names of particular denominations and sects, e.g. **Presbyterian Church;** etc.
Religious drama 792.12; 808.82; 812, etc.
  See also **Bible—Drama; Christmas—Drama; Morality plays; Mysteries and miracle plays; Passion plays**
  x Drama, Religious
  xx **Drama; Drama in education; Religious literature**
Religious education 268; 377
  See note under **Church and education.**
  See also **Christian education; Moral education; Religion in the public schools; Sunday schools; Theology—Study and teaching**
  x Education, Ethical; Education, Religious; Education, Theological; Ethical education; Religion—Study and teaching
  xx **Education; Moral education; Theology—Study and teaching**
Religious festivals. *See* **Fasts and feasts;** and names of festivals, e.g. **Christmas; Easter;** etc.
Religious freedom. *See* **Freedom of religion**
Religious history. *See* **Church history**
Religious liberty. *See* **Freedom of religion**
Religious life 248
  See also **Celibacy;** also classes of people with the subdivision *Religious life,* e.g. **Family—Religious life;** etc.
  xx **Monasticism; Religious orders**
Religious life (Christian). *See* **Christian life**
Religious literature 800
  See also **Bible as literature; Religious drama; Religious poetry; Sacred books;** also names of religious and denominational literatures, e.g. **Catholic literature; Early Christian literature;** etc.
  xx **Bible as literature; Literature**
Religious music. *See* **Church music**
Religious orders 255; 271
  See also **Asceticism; Celibacy; Hermits; Religious life**
  x Monastic orders; Orders, Monastic
  xx **Monasticism**

569

Religious orders for men (May subdiv. by religion or denomination)   **255; 271**
   See also **Monks**
Religious orders for men, Catholic   271
   See also names of specific orders, e.g. **Dominicans (Religious order); Franciscans; Jesuits;** etc.
Religious orders for women (May subdiv. by religion or denomination)   **255; 271**
   See also **Nuns**
   x Sisterhoods
   xx **Convents**
Religious poetry   808.81; 811, etc.; 811.008, etc.
   See also names of specific orders
Religious painting.   *See* **Religious art and symbolism**
Religious poetry   808.81; 811.008, etc.; 811, etc.
   See also **Carols; Hymns**
   xx **Hymns; Poetry—Collections; Religious literature**
Religious psychology.   *See* **Psychology, Religious**
Religious symbolism.   *See* **Religious art and symbolism**
Remarriage   306.84
   xx **Divorce; Marriage**
Remedial reading.   *See* **Reading—Remedial teaching**
Remodeling of buildings.   *See* **Buildings—Remodeling**
Remodeling of houses.   *See* **Houses—Remodeling**
Remote sensing   621.36
   See also **Aerial reconnaissance; Radar; Space optics**
   x Sensing, Remote; Terrain sensing, Remote
   xx **Aerial photography; Space optics**
Renaissance   940.2
   See also

Architecture, Renaissance	**Humanism**
Art, Renaissance	**Literature, Medieval**
Civilization, Medieval	**Middle Ages**
Fifteenth century	**Sixteenth century**

   x Revival of letters
   xx **Civilization, Modern; History, Modern; Humanism; Middle Ages**
Renaissance, Harlem.   *See* **Harlem Renaissance**
Rendezvous in space.   *See* **Orbital rendezvous (Space flight)**
Renewable energy resources   333.79
   See also **Geothermal resources;** also names of renewable resources, e.g. **Solar energy; Water power; Wind power;** etc.
   x Alternate energy resources; Alternative energy resources; Energy resources, Renewable
   xx **Energy resources**
Rental services.   *See* **Lease and rental services**
Reorganization of administrative agencies.   *See* **United States—Executive departments—Reorganization**
Repairing   620
   See also **Buildings—Maintenance and repair;** also names of machines, instruments, etc. that require maintenance with the subdivision *Maintenance and repair,* e.g. **Automo-**

Repairing—*Continued*

    biles—**Maintenance and repair;** and names of subjects that need no maintenance with the subdivision *Repairing,* e.g. **Radio—Repairing;** etc.

Reparations (World War, 1939-1945). *See* **World War, 1939-1945—Reparations**

Report writing   808

    See also **School reports**

    x Reports—Preparation; Research paper writing; Term paper writing

    xx **Authorship**

Reporters and reporting   070.4

    See also **Journalism; Press—Government policy**

    x Interviewing (Journalism); Newspaper work

    xx **Journalism; Newspapers**

Reports—Preparation. *See* **Report writing**

Reports, Teachers'. *See* **School reports**

Representation. *See* **Representative government and representation**

Representation, Proportional. *See* **Proportional representation**

Representative government and representation   321.8

    See also

Apportionment (Election law)	**Proportional representation**
Constitutions	**Recall (Political science)**
Democracy	**Referendum**
Elections	**Republics**
Legislative bodies	**Suffrage**
Primaries	

    x Parliamentary government; Representation; Self-government

    xx **Constitutional history; Constitutional law; Democracy; Elections; Political science; Republics; Suffrage**

Representatives, House of (U.S.). *See* **United States. Congress. House**

Reprints. *See* **Bibliography—Editions**

Reproduction   574.1; 612.6

    See also

Artificial insemination	**Genetics**
Cells	**Menstruation**
Embryology	**Pregnancy**
Fertility	**Reproductive system**
Fertilization in vitro	**Sex (Biology)**
Fetus	

    x Generation

    xx **Biology; Embryology; Life (Biology); Physiology; Reproductive system; Sex (Biology)**

Reproduction processes. *See* **Copying processes and machines**

Reproductive behavior. *See* **Sexual behavior in animals**

Reproductive organs. *See* **Reproductive system**

Reproductive system   574.1; 611; 612.6

    See also **Reproduction; Transsexuality**

    x Generative organs; Genitalia; Reproductive organs; Sex organs

    xx **Reproduction; Sex (Biology)**

Reprography. *See* **Copying processes and machines**

Reptiles 597.9
> See also **Crocodiles; Lizards; Snakes; Turtles**
> *xx* **Vertebrates**

Reptiles, Fossil 567.9
> See also names of fossil reptiles, e.g. **Dinosaurs;**
> etc.
> *x* Fossil reptiles
> *xx* **Fossils**

Republic of China, 1949-. *See* **Taiwan**

Republic of South Africa. *See* **South Africa**

Republican Party (U.S.) 324.2734
> *xx* **Political parties**

Republics 321.8
> See also **Democracy; Federal government; Repre-**
> **sentative government and representation**
> *x* Commonwealth, The
> *xx* **Constitutional history; Constitutional law; De-**
> **mocracy; Political science; Representative**
> **government and representation**

Rescue of Jews, 1939-1945. *See* **World War, 1939-**
> **1945—Jews—Rescue**

Rescue operations, Space. *See* **Space rescue opera-**
> **tions**

Rescue work 363.1
> See also **First aid; Lifesaving; Space rescue oper-**
> **ations**
> *x* Search and rescue operations
> *xx* **Civil defense**

Research 001.4
> See also **Animal experimentation; Information**
> **services; Learning and scholarship; Opera-**
> **tions research; Parapsychology;** also subjects
> with the subdivision *Research,* e.g. **Agri-**
> **culture—Research; Medicine—Research;**
> etc.
> *xx* **Information services; Learning and scholar-**
> **ship**

Research paper writing. *See* **Report writing**

Reservations, Indian. *See* **Indians of North Ameri-**
> **ca—Reservations**

Reservoirs 627; 628.1
> See also **Irrigation; Water supply**
> *xx* **Hydraulic structures; Water supply**

Resettlement. *See* **Land settlement**

Residences. *See* **Architecture, Domestic; Houses**

Residential construction. *See* **House construction**

Residential security. *See* **Burglary protection**

Residential treatment centers. *See* **Group homes**

Resins. *See* **Gums and resins**

Resistance of materials. *See* **Strength of materials**

Resistance to government. *See* **Government, Resis-**
> **tance to**

Resistance welding. *See* **Electric welding**

Resorts. *See* types of resorts, e.g. **Health resorts,**
> **spas, etc.; Summer resorts; Winter resorts;**
> etc.

Resource management. *See* **Conservation of natural**
> **resources**

Resources, Marine. *See* **Marine resources**

Resources, Natural. *See* **Natural resources**

Respiration 574.1; 612.2
> See also **Aerobics; Hatha yoga; Respiratory sys-**
> **tem**

Respiration—*Continued*
    x Breathing
    xx **Lungs; Physiology; Singing; Voice**
Respiration, Artificial. *See* **Artificial respiration**
Respiratory organs. *See* **Respiratory system**
Respiratory system   **591.1; 611; 612.2**
    x Respiratory organs
    xx **Respiration**
Respite care. *See* **Home care services**
Responsibility, Legal. *See* **Liability (Law)**
Rest   **613.7**
    See also **Fatigue; Sleep**
    x Relaxation
    xx **Fatigue; Health; Hygiene**
Restaurants, bars, etc. (May subdiv. geog.)   **647.95**
    See also **Coffeehouses**
    x Bars and restaurants; Cafeterias; Coffee shops;
       Diners; Lunch rooms; Saloons; Taverns;
       Tea rooms; Tearooms
    xx **Food service**
Restoration of automobiles. *See* **Automobiles—Restoration**
Restoration of buildings. *See* **Architecture—Conservation and restoration**
Restoration of works of art. *See* subjects with the
    subdivision *Conservation and restoration,*
    e.g. **Painting—Conservation and restoration;** etc.
Restraint of trade   **338.6**
    See also **Interstate commerce; Monopolies; Trusts, Industrial; Unfair competition**
    x Combinations in restraint of trade; Restrictive
       trade practices; Trade, Restraint of
    xx **Commerce; Commercial law; Interstate commerce; Monopolies; Trusts, Industrial; Unfair competition**
Restrictive trade practices. *See* **Restraint of trade**
Résumés (Employment)   **331.1**
    x Job résumés
    xx **Applications for positions; Job hunting**
Resurrection. *See* **Future life; Jesus Christ—Resurrection**
Resuscitation, Heart. *See* **Cardiac resuscitation**
Resuscitation, Pulmonary. *See* **Artificial respiration**
Retail sales tax. *See* **Sales tax**
Retail trade   **381; 658.8**
    See also

Advertising	**Packaging**
Chain stores	**Sales personnel**
Department stores	**Selling**
Direct selling	**Shopping centers and**
Discount stores	**malls**
Inventory control	**Supermarkets**

    x Merchandising; Stores
    xx **Commerce**
Retarded children. *See* **Mentally handicapped children; Slow learning children**
Retarded readers. *See* **Reading disability**
Retention, Grade. *See* **Promotion (School)**
Retirement   **305.26; 306.3**
    See also **Elderly—Life skills guides**
    xx **Elderly—Life skills guides; Leisure; Old age**

Retirement communities 307.7
   x Life care communities; Places of retirement;
      Retirement places
   xx Elderly—Housing
Retirement income 351.5; 368.4
   See also Annuities; Individual retirement ac-
      counts; Old age pensions; Pensions
   xx Elderly; Income
Retirement places. *See* Retirement communities
Retouching (Photography). *See* Photography—
   Retouching
Retraining, Occupational. *See* Occupational re-
   training
Retribution. *See* Future life; Hell
Reunions, Family. *See* Family reunions
Reusable space vehicles. *See* Space shuttles
Reuse of waste. *See* Recycling (Waste, etc.); Sal-
   vage (Waste, etc.)
Revelation 231
   xx Religion; Supernatural; Theology
Revenue. *See* Tariff; Taxation
Revenue, Internal. *See* Internal revenue
Revenue sharing 336; 336.1; 336.2
   Use for materials on the practice of returning a
      percentage of federal tax money to state and
      local governments for locally directed and
      controlled public service programs.
   x Federal revenue sharing; Tax sharing
   xx Intergovernmental tax relations
Reviews. *See* subjects with the subdivision
      Reviews, e.g. Books—Reviews; etc.
Revival of letters. *See* Renaissance
Revival (Religion). *See* Evangelistic work; Revivals
Revivals 269
   See also Evangelistic work
   x Revival (Religion)
   xx Christian life; Church history; Church work;
      Evangelistic work
Revivals—Music. *See* Gospel music
Revolution, American. *See* United States—
   History—1775-1783, Revolution
Revolution, French. *See* France—History—1789-
   1799, Revolution
Revolution, Russian. *See* Soviet Union—History—
   1917-1921, Revolution
Revolutions 303.6
   See also Government, Resistance to; Insurgency;
      National liberation movements; Radicals and
      radicalism; Terrorism; also names of coun-
      tries with the subdivision *History—[dates],
      Revolution,* e.g. France—History—1789-
      1799, Revolution; Hungary—History—1956,
      Revolution; Soviet Union—History—1917-
      1921, Revolution; United States—History—
      1775-1783, Revolution; etc.
   x Coups d'état; Rebellions; Sedition
   xx Government, Resistance to; Political science
Rewards (Prizes, etc.) 001.4
   See also Contests; Literary prizes; also names of
      awards and prizes, e.g. Nobel prizes; etc.
   x Awards; Competitions; Prizes (Rewards)
   xx Contests
Rh factor. *See* Blood groups

Rhetoric   808
See also

Criticism	**Preaching**
Debates and debating	**Punctuation**
Lectures and lecturing	**Satire**
Letter writing	**Style, Literary**

also names of languages with the subdivision *Composition and exercises,* e.g. **English language—Composition and exercises;** etc.

x Composition (Rhetoric); English language—Rhetoric; Persuasion (Rhetoric); Speaking

xx **English language—Composition and exercises; Language and languages; Style, Literary**

Rheumatism   616.7
See also **Arthritis**

Rhyme   808.1
See also **Rhythm; Stories in rhyme;** also names of languages with the subdivision *Rhyme,* e.g. **English language—Rhyme;** etc.

xx **Poetics; Versification**

Rhymes.   *See* **Limericks; Nonsense verses; Nursery rhymes; Poetry—Collections**

Rhythm   808.1
See also **Musical meter and rhythm; Periodicity; Versification**

xx **Aesthetics; Periodicity; Poetics; Rhyme**

Ribonucleic acid.   *See* **RNA**

Ribose nucleic acid.   *See* **RNA**

Ribozymes.   *See* **Catalytic RNA**

Riches.   *See* **Wealth**

Riddles   398.6; 793.73; 818, etc.
Use for riddles as folklore, riddles as games, or for riddles written by specific authors.

See also **Charades; Puzzles**

x Conundrums; Enigmas; Rebuses

xx **Amusements; Literary recreations; Puzzles**

Ride sharing.   *See* **Car pools**

Riding.   *See* **Horsemanship**

Rifles   799
x Carbines; Guns

xx **Arms and armor; Firearms**

Right and left.   *See* **Left and right**

Right- and left-handedness.   *See* **Left- and right-handedness**

Right and left (Political science)   320.5
Use for general materials on political views or attitudes, i.e. conservative, traditional, liberal, radical, etc. Materials on the physical characteristics of favoring one hand or the other are entered under **Left- and right-handedness.** Materials on left and right as indications of location or direction are entered under **Left and right.**

See also **Conservatism; Liberalism; Radicals and radicalism**

x Extremism (Political science); Left (Political science); New left; Reaction (Political science); Right (Political science)

xx **Conservatism; Legislative bodies; Liberalism; Political parties; Political science**

Right of assembly.   *See* **Freedom of assembly**

Right of association.   *See* **Freedom of association**

Right of asylum.   *See* **Asylum**

Right of privacy 323.44
>*See also* **Computer crimes; Eavesdropping; Trade secrets; Wiretapping**
>
>*x* Invasion of privacy; Privacy, Right of
>
>*xx* **Civil rights; Computer crimes; Libel and slander**

Right (Political science). *See* **Right and left (Political science)**

Right to choose movement. *See* **Pro-choice movement**

Right to die 179
>*See also* **Euthanasia; Suicide**
>
>*x* Death, Right of; Death with dignity; Living wills; Wills, Living
>
>*xx* **Death; Euthanasia; Medical ethics; Medicine—Law and legislation; Suicide**

Right to know. *See* **Freedom of information**

Right to life. *See* **Euthanasia**

Right-to-life movement (Anti-abortion movement). *See* **Pro-life movement**

Right to work. *See* **Discrimination in employment; Open and closed shop**

Rights, Civil. *See* **Civil rights**

Rights, Human. *See* **Human rights**

Rights of animals. *See* **Animal rights**

Rights of man. *See* **Human rights**

Rights of women. *See* **Women—Civil rights**

Riot control 303.6
>*x* Riots—Control
>
>*xx* **Crowds**

Riots (May subdiv. geog.) 303.6
>*See also* **Crowds; Protests, demonstrations, etc.;** also names of institutions with the subdivision *Riots;* also names of specific riots
>
>*x* Civil disorders; Mobs
>
>*xx* **Crime; Freedom of assembly; Offenses against public safety; Protests, demonstrations, etc.**

Riots—Control. *See* **Riot control**

Ripoffs. *See* **Fraud**

Rites and ceremonies (May subdiv. geog.) 390
>*See also*

Baptism	**Marriage customs and**
Fasts and feasts	**rites**
Funeral rites and ceremo-	**Ordination**
nies	**Sacraments**
Manners and customs	**Secret societies**

>also classes of people and ethnic groups with the subdivision *Rites and ceremonies,* e.g. **Indians of North America—Rites and ceremonies;** etc.; also names of individual religions and denominations with the subdivisions *Liturgy* and *Customs and practices,* e.g. **Catholic Church—Liturgy; Judaism—Customs and practices;** etc.
>
>*x* Ceremonies; Ecclesiastical rites and ceremonies; Religious ceremonies; Ritual; Traditions
>
>*xx* **Manners and customs**

Ritual. *See* **Liturgies; Rites and ceremonies**

River animals. *See* **Stream animals**

River pollution. *See* **Water pollution**

Rivers   551.48
See also

Dams	**Stream animals**
Floods	**Water pollution**
Hydraulic engineering	**Water power**
Inland navigation	**Water rights**

also names of rivers

xx **Civil engineering; Flood control; Floods; Hydraulic engineering; Inland navigation; Physical geography; Water; Waterways**

Rivers—Pollution.   *See* **Oil pollution of rivers, harbors, etc.**

RNA   574.87
See also **Catalytic RNA**
x Ribonucleic acid; Ribose nucleic acid
xx **Nucleic acids**

RNA, Catalytic.   *See* **Catalytic RNA**

Road construction.   *See* **Roads**

Road engineering.   *See* **Highway engineering**

Road maps   912
See also **Automobiles—Road guides;** also names of countries, areas, states, cities, etc. with the subdivision *Maps,* e.g. **United States—Maps; Chicago (Ill.)—Maps;** etc.
x Maps, Road; Roads—Maps
xx **Automobiles—Road guides; Maps**

Road signs.   *See* **Signs and signboards**

Roads   388.1; 625.7
See also **Express highways; Highway engineering; Pavements; Roadside improvement; Soils (Engineering); Street cleaning; Streets**
x Construction of roads; Highway construction; Highways; Road construction; Thoroughfares
xx **Civil engineering; Highway engineering; Pavements; Streets; Transportation**

Roads—Maps.   *See* **Road maps**

Roadside improvement   713
x Highway beautification
xx **Grounds maintenance; Landscape architecture; Roads**

Robbers and outlaws   364.3
x Bandits; Brigands; Burglars; Highwaymen; Outlaws; Thieves
xx **Criminals**

Robins   598.8
xx **Birds**

Robotics   629.8
Use for materials on the construction, maintenance, and automatic operation of robots.
See also **Industrial robots; Robots**
xx **Mechanical engineering**

Robots   629.8
Use for materials on completely self-controlled electronic, electric, or mechanical devices that perform functions ordinarily ascribed to human beings or that operate with what appears to be almost human intelligence.
x Androids; Automata
xx **Mechanical movements; Robotics**

Robots, Industrial.   *See* **Industrial robots**

Rochdale system.   *See* **Cooperation**

Rock and roll music.   *See* **Rock music**

Rock climbing.   *See* **Mountaineering**

Rock crystal. *See* **Quartz**
Rock drawings, paintings, and engravings   411; 743; 759.01
  See also **Cave drawings**
  x Petroglyphs; Rock engravings; Rock paintings
  xx **Archeology; Art; Art, Prehistoric; Cave drawings; Mural painting and decoration; Picture writing**
Rock engravings. *See* **Rock drawings, paintings, and engravings**
Rock gardens   635.9
  xx **Gardens**
Rock music   781.66; 782.42166
  x Music, Rock; Rock and roll music
  xx **Dance music; Music; Popular music**
Rock paintings. *See* **Rock drawings, paintings, and engravings**
Rock tombs. *See* **Tombs**
Rocket airplanes. *See* **Rocket planes**
Rocket flight. *See* **Space flight**
Rocket planes   629.133
  See also names of rocket planes, e.g. **X-15 (Rocket aircraft);** etc.
  x Airplanes, Rocket propelled; Rocket airplanes
  xx **High speed aeronautics; Space ships**
Rocketry   621.43
  See also **Guided missiles; Rockets (Aeronautics); Space ships; Space vehicles**
  xx **Aeronautics; Astronautics**
Rockets (Aeronautics)   629.133
  See also **Artificial satellites—Launching; Jet propulsion;** also names of types of rockets, e.g. **Ballistic missiles; Guided missiles;** etc.; and names of specific rockets
  x Aerial rockets
  xx **Aeronautics; High speed aeronautics; Interplanetary voyages; Jet propulsion; Projectiles; Rocketry**
Rocks   552
  See also **Crystallography; Geochemistry; Geology; Mineralogy; Petrology; Stone;** also varieties of rock, e.g. **Granite;** etc.
  x Crystalline rocks; Metamorphic rocks
  xx **Geology; Petrology; Stone**
Rocks—Age. *See* **Geology, Stratigraphic**
Rocks, Moon. *See* **Lunar petrology**
Rocky Mountains   978
  xx **Mountains**
Rodeos   791.8
  See also **Horsemanship**
  xx **Cowhands; Horsemanship; Sports**
Roentgen rays. *See* **X rays**
Roentgenologists. *See* **Radiologists**
Role conflict   302; 302.5
  Use for materials on the conflict within one person who is being called upon to fulfil two or more competing roles.
  See also **Sex role**
  xx **Social conflict; Social role**
Role playing   302
  xx **Social role**
Role, Social. *See* **Social role**
Roller skating   796.2
  x Figure skating; Skating

Rolling stock. *See* **Locomotives**
Romaic language. *See* **Greek language, Modern**
Romaic literature. *See* **Greek literature, Modern**
Roman antiquities. *See* **Classical antiquities;**
        Rome—Antiquities
Roman architecture. *See* **Architecture, Roman**
Roman art. *See* **Art, Roman**
Roman Catholic Church. *See* **Catholic Church**
Roman emperors   920
    See also names of Roman emperors, e.g.
        Nero, Emperor of Rome, 37-68; etc.
    x Emperors; Sovereigns
    xx **Kings, queens, rulers, etc.**
Roman Empire. *See* **Rome**
Roman literature. *See* **Latin literature**
Roman mythology. *See* **Mythology, Classical**
Roman philosophy. *See* **Philosophy, Ancient**
Romance languages   440
    See also names of languages belonging to the
        Romance group, e.g. **French language;** etc.
    x Neo-Latin languages
    xx **Latin language**
Romance literature   840
    See also names of literatures belonging to the
        Romance group, e.g. **French literature;** etc.
Romance novels. *See* **Love stories**
Romances   808.8; 820.8, etc.
    Use for collections of medieval tales dealing
        with the age of chivalry or the supernatural.
        They may be either metrical or prose ver-
        sions and may or may not have a factual ba-
        sis.
    See also **Arthurian romances;** also names of his-
        toric persons with the subdivision
        Romances
    x Chivalry—Romances; Metrical romances;
        Stories
    xx **Chivalry; Epic poetry; Fiction; Legends; Liter-**
        ature—Collections
Romances (Love stories). *See* **Love stories**
Romanesque architecture. *See* **Architecture, Ro-**
        manesque
Romanesque art. *See* **Art, Romanesque**
Romanesque painting. *See* **Painting, Romanesque**
Romanies. *See* **Gypsies**
Romantic fiction. *See* **Love stories**
Romantic stories. *See* **Love stories**
Romanticism   141; 709.03; 809
    See also **Realism in literature**
    xx **Aesthetics; Fiction; Literature; Music; Real-**
        ism in literature
Rome   937
    Use for materials about the Roman Empire. Ma-
        terials dealing with the modern city of
        Rome are entered under **Rome (Italy).**
    x Roman Empire
Rome—Antiquities   937
    x Roman antiquities
    xx **Classical antiquities**
Rome—Biography   920.037
    x Classical biography

Rome—Description   913.7; 937
> Use for descriptive materials on the Roman Empire including accounts by travelers of ancient times.
>
> *x* Rome—Description and geography

Rome—Description and geography.   *See* **Rome—Description; Rome—Geography**

Rome—Geography   913.7
> Use for geographic materials on ancient Rome.
>
> *x* Classical geography; Rome—Description and geography

Rome—History   937

Rome (Italy)   945
> See note under **Rome.**

Rome (Italy)—Description   914.5

Rome (Italy)—History   945

Roofs   695
> *xx* **Architecture—Details; Building; Building, Iron and steel; Carpentry**

Rooming houses.   *See* **Hotels, motels, etc.**

Root crops   633; 635
> *See also* **Feeds**
>
> *xx* **Feeds; Vegetables**

Rope   623.88; 677
> *See also* **Cables; Hemp; Knots and splices**
>
> *xx* **Hemp**

Roses   635.9
> *xx* **Flower gardening; Flowers**

Rosetta stone inscription   493
> *xx* **Hieroglyphics**

Rosin.   *See* **Gums and resins**

Rotating memory devices (Data processing).   *See* **Computer storage devices**

Rotation of crops.   *See* **Crop rotation**

Roughage.   *See* **Food—Fiber content**

Round stage.   *See* **Arena theater**

Routes of trade.   *See* **Trade routes**

Routines, Utility (Computer programs).   *See* **Utilities (Computer programs)**

Rowing   797.1
> *x* Regattas; Sculling
>
> *xx* **Athletics; Boats and boating; College sports; Exercise; Water sports**

Royalty.   *See* **Kings, queens, rulers, etc.; Princes and princesses**

Rubber   678
> *x* India rubber
>
> *xx* **Forest products**

Rubber, Artificial.   *See* **Synthetic rubber**

Rubber sheet geometry.   *See* **Topology**

Rubber, Synthetic.   *See* **Synthetic rubber**

Rubber tires.   *See* **Tires**

Rugs   645; 677; 746.7
> Use for materials on one-piece floor coverings, such as woven fabrics, animal skins, etc. Materials on heavy woven or felted fabrics used as floor coverings, usually covering large areas, are entered under **Carpets.**
>
> *See also* **Carpets; Oriental rugs**
>
> *xx* **Carpets; Decorative arts; Interior design**

Rugs, Hooked.   *See* **Hooked rugs**

Rugs, Oriental.   *See* **Oriental rugs**

Ruins.   *See* **Archeology; Cities and towns, Ruined,**

Ruins—*Continued*

    extinct, etc.; **Excavations (Archeology)**; and names of ancient cities, e.g. **Delphi (Ancient city)**; also names of cities (except ancient cities), countries, regions, etc. with the subdivision *Antiquities,* e.g. **Rome— Antiquities**; etc.

Rule of equal time (Broadcasting). *See* **Equal time rule (Broadcasting)**

Rulers. *See* **Heads of state; Kings, queens, rulers, etc.;** and names of individual rulers

Rules of order. *See* **Parliamentary practice**

Runaway adults   173; 306.88
    x Adults, Runaway; Desertion; Husbands, Runaway; Wives, Runaway
    xx **Desertion and nonsupport; Homeless people**

Runaway children   362.7
    xx **Children; Homeless people; Missing children**

Runaway teenagers   362.7
    xx **Homeless people; Missing persons; Teenagers**

Running   796.42
    See also **Jogging; Marathon running; Orienteering**
    xx **Track athletics**

Rural architecture. *See* **Architecture, Domestic; Farm buildings**

Rural churches   254
    x Church work, Rural; Churches, Country; Churches, Rural; Country churches
    xx **Church work**

Rural conditions. *See* names of countries, states, etc. with the subdivision *Rural conditions,* e.g. **United States—Rural conditions; Ohio—Rural conditions**; etc.

Rural credit. *See* **Agricultural credit**

Rural electrification. *See* **Electric power distribution; Electricity in agriculture**

Rural high schools. *See* **Rural schools**

Rural life. *See* **Country life; Farm life; Outdoor life; Peasantry**

Rural schools   371
    x Country schools; District schools; High schools, Rural; Rural high schools
    xx **Public schools; Schools**

Rural sociology. *See* **Sociology, Rural**

Russia. *See* **Soviet Union**

Russian Church. *See* **Orthodox Eastern Church, Russian**

Russian communism. *See* **Communism—Soviet Union**

Russian intervention in Czechoslovakia. *See* **Czechoslovakia—History—1968-1989**

Russian language   491.7
    May be subdivided like **English language.**
    xx **Language and languages**

Russian literature   891.7
    Use for materials discussing literature in the Russian language, which is the principal state and cultural language of the Soviet Union. Materials discussing several of the literatures of the Soviet Union are entered under **Soviet Union—Literatures.**
    May use same subdivisions and names of literary forms as for **English literature.**

Russian revolution. *See* **Soviet Union—History—
1917-1921, Revolution**
Russian satellite countries. *See* **Communist countries**
Russians (May subdiv. geog.) **920; 947**
Use for materials on the dominant Slavic-
speaking Great Russian ethnic group of the
Soviet Union. For materials on the citizens
of the Soviet Union as a whole, use **Soviets
(People).**
xx **Soviet Union**
Russo-Finnish War, 1939-1940   948.97
x Finno-Russian War, 1939-1940; Soviet
Union—History—1939-1940, War with
Finland
Russo-Turkish War, 1853-1856. *See* **Crimean War,
1853-1856**
Rust. *See* **Corrosion and anticorrosives**
Rustless coatings. *See* **Corrosion and anticorrosives**
RVs. *See* **Recreational vehicles**
S.A.T. *See* **Scholastic aptitude test**
S.S.T.'s. *See* **Supersonic transport planes**
Sabbath   263; 296.4
x Lord's Day
xx **Judaism**
Sabin vaccine. *See* **Poliomyelitis vaccine**
Sabotage   331.89; 364.1
xx **Labor unions; Offenses against public safety;
Strikes and lockouts; Subversive activities;
Terrorism**
Sacraments   234; 265
See also **Baptism; Lord's Supper; Marriage; Or-
dination**
x Ecclesiastical rites and ceremonies
xx **Rites and ceremonies; Theology**
Sacred art. *See* **Christian art and symbolism; Reli-
gious art and symbolism**
Sacred books   291.8
See also names of sacred books, e.g. **Bible; Ko-
ran; Vedas;** etc.
x Books, Sacred
xx **Religious literature**
Sacred music. *See* **Church music**
Sacred numbers. *See* **Symbolism of numbers**
Sacrifice   291.3
See also **Atonement—Christianity**
xx **Ethnology; Religion; Theology; Worship**
Safe sex in AIDS prevention   613.9; 616.97
Use for materials on sexual activities in which
measures are taken to reduce the risk of
passing on or contracting AIDS.
xx **AIDS (Disease)—Prevention; Sexual hygiene**
Safety appliances   363.19; 620.8
See also **Accidents—Prevention;** also subjects
with the subdivision *Safety appliances,* e.g.
Railroads—Safety appliances; etc.
x Safety devices; Safety equipment
xx **Accidents—Prevention**
Safety devices. *See* **Safety appliances**
Safety education   371.7
See also **Accidents—Prevention**
xx **Accidents—Prevention**
Safety equipment. *See* **Safety appliances**

Safety, Industrial. *See* **Occupational health and safety**

Safety measures. *See* **Accidents—Prevention;** and subjects with the subdivision *Safety measures,* e.g. **Aeronautics—Safety measures;** etc.

Sagas 398.22; 839

    xx **Folklore; Literature; Old Norse literature; Scandinavian literature**

Sailboarding. *See* **Windsurfing**

Sailing 623.88; 797.1

    See also **Boats and boating; Navigation; Windsurfing; Yachts and yachting**

    xx **Boats and boating; Navigation; Ships; Water sports; Yachts and yachting**

Sailors 623.88092; 920

    See also **Merchant marine; Pilots and pilotage; Seafaring life;** also names of navies, e.g. **United States. Navy;** etc.

    x Mariners; Naval personnel; Navigators; Sailors' life; Sea life; Seamen

    xx **Military personnel; Naval art and science; Navies; Seafaring life; Voyages and travels**

Sailors' life. *See* **Sailors; Seafaring life**

Sailors' song. *See* **Sea songs**

Sailplanes (Aeronautics). *See* **Gliders (Aeronautics)**

Saint Bartholomew's Day, Massacre of, 1572 940.2; 944

    xx **Huguenots; Massacres**

Saint Dominic, Order of. *See* **Dominicans (Religious order)**

Saint Francis, Order of. *See* **Franciscans**

Saint Valentine's Day. *See* **Valentine's Day**

Saints 920

    See also **Hermits; Legends; Martyrs; Shrines;** also names of saints of different religions, e.g. **Christian saints;** etc.; and names of individual saints

    xx **Heroes and heroines; Legends; Martyrs; Pilgrims and pilgrimages; Shrines**

Salads 641.8

    xx **Cookery**

Salamanders 597.6

    xx **Amphibians**

Sale of infants. *See* **Adoption—Corrupt practices**

Sales, Auction. *See* **Auctions**

Sales management 658.8

    x Management, Sales

    xx **Industrial management; Management; Marketing; Selling**

Sales personnel 658.85

    See also **Booksellers and bookselling; Office employees; Peddlers and peddling**

    x Agents, Sales; Clerks (Retail trade); Salesmen; Saleswomen; Traveling sales personnel

    xx **Office employees; Retail trade**

Sales tax 336.2

    x Purchase tax; Retail sales tax; Taxation of sales

    xx **Taxation**

Salesmanship. *See* **Selling**

Salesmen. *See* **Sales personnel**

Saleswomen. *See* **Sales personnel**

Saline water. *See* **Sea water**

Salk vaccine. *See* **Poliomyelitis vaccine**

Salmon 597

  xx **Fishes**

Saloons. *See* **Restaurants, bars, etc.**

Salt free diet 613.2

  x Low sodium diet

  xx **Cookery for the sick; Diet; Diet in disease**

Salt water. *See* **Sea water**

Salt water aquariums. *See* **Marine aquariums**

Salutations. *See* **Etiquette; Letter writing**

Salvage 387.5; 627

  See also **Shipwrecks; Skin diving**

  xx **International law; Maritime law; Shipwrecks**

Salvage (Waste, etc.) 628.4

  See note under **Recycling (Waste, etc.).**

  See also **Recycling (Waste, etc.); Refuse and refuse disposal; Waste products; Waste products as fuel**

  x Conversion of waste products; Recovery of waste products; Reuse of waste; Solid waste disposal; Utilization of waste; Waste products—Recycling; Waste reclamation

  xx **Recycling (Waste, etc.); Refuse and refuse disposal; Waste products**

Salvation 234

  See also **Atonement—Christianity; Faith; Grace (Theology); Regeneration (Theology); Sanctification; Sin**

  x Redemption

  xx **Regeneration (Theology)**

Salvation Army 287.9

  xx **Missions, Christian**

Sampling (Statistics) 519.5

  See also **Quality control**

  x Random sampling

  xx **Probabilities; Statistics**

Sanatoriums. *See* **Health resorts, spas, etc.; Hospitals**

Sanctification 234

  xx **Salvation; Spiritual life; Theology**

Sanctions (International law) 341.5

  x Economic sanctions

  xx **Economic policy; International economic relations; International law**

Sanctuaries, Wildlife. *See* **Wildlife refuges**

Sanctuary (Law). *See* **Asylum**

Sanctuary movement 261.8

  Use for materials on the network of religious congregations, cities, etc., in the United States that shelters refugees.

  See also **Illegal aliens**

  x Sanctuary movement (Refugee aid)

  xx **Asylum; Church and social problems; Illegal aliens; Social movements**

Sanctuary movement (Refugee aid). *See* **Sanctuary movement**

Sand dunes 551.3

  x Dunes

  xx **Reclamation of land; Seashore**

Sandwiches 641.8

  xx **Cookery**

Sanitary affairs. *See* **Sanitary engineering; Sanitation**

Sanitary engineering   628
See also

Drainage
Municipal engineering
Pollution
Refuse and refuse disposal
Sanitation

Sewerage
Soils—Bacteriology
Street cleaning
Water supply

   x Sanitary affairs
   xx Building; Civil engineering; Drainage, House;
      Engineering; Municipal engineering;
      Plumbing; Public health; Sanitation
Sanitary landfills.   *See* **Landfills**
Sanitation   363.72; 648
See also

Cemeteries
Cremation
Disinfection and disinfec-
   tants
Hygiene
Military health
Pollution
Public health

Refuse and refuse disposal
Sanitary engineering
School hygiene
Ventilation
Water—Purification
Water supply
World War, 1939-1945—
   Health aspects

   x Sanitary affairs
   xx Cleanliness; Hygiene; Public health; Sanitary
      engineering
Sanitation, Household   648
   See also **Drainage, House; House cleaning;**
      Household pests; Laundry; Plumbing; Venti-
      lation
   x House sanitation; Household sanitation
   xx **Plumbing**
Santa Claus   394.2
   xx **Christmas**
Sasquatch   001.9
   x Big foot; Bigfoot
   xx **Primates**
SAT.   *See* **Scholastic aptitude test**
Satan.   *See* **Devil**
Satellite communication systems.   *See* **Artificial**
      satellites in telecommunication
Satellites, Artificial.   *See* **Artificial satellites**
Satire (May subdiv. geog. adjective form, e.g. **Satire,**
      English; etc.)   **808.7; 808.87**
   See also **Invective; Parody**
   x Comic literature
   xx **Literature; Rhetoric; Wit and humor**
Satire, American   817; 817.008
   x American satire
   xx **American literature**
Satire, English   827; 827.008
   x English satire
   xx **English literature**
Satisfaction in work.   *See* **Job satisfaction**
Saturn (Planet)   523.4
   xx **Planets; Solar system**
Saucers, Flying.   *See* **Unidentified flying objects**
Saving and thrift   332.024
   See also **Cost of living; Industrial insurance; In-**
      vestments; Old age pensions; Savings and
      loan associations
   x Economy; Thrift
   xx **Cost of living; Economics; Insurance; Invest-**
      ments; Personal finance; Success

Savings and loan associations   332.3
  x Building and loan associations; Cooperative
       building associations; Loan associations
  xx **Banks and banking; Cooperation; Cooperative
       societies; Investments; Loans; Personal
       loans; Saving and thrift**
Savings banks. *See* **Banks and banking**
Saws   621.9
  xx **Carpentry—Tools; Tools**
Saxons. *See* **Anglo-Saxons; Teutonic peoples**
Sayings. *See* **Epigrams; Proverbs; Quotations**
Scandinavian civilization. *See* **Civilization, Scandi-
       navian**
Scandinavian languages   439
  See also **Danish language; Icelandic language;
       Norwegian language; Old Norse language;
       Swedish language**
  x Norse languages
  xx **Old Norse language**
Scandinavian literature   839.7; 839.8
  See also **Danish literature; Eddas; Icelandic liter-
       ature; Norwegian literature; Old Norse liter-
       ature; Sagas; Swedish literature**
  x Norse literature
  xx **Old Norse literature**
Scandinavians   920; 948
  Use for materials on the people of Scandinavia
       since the 10th century. Materials on the
       early Scandinavians are entered under **Vi-
       kings.**
  See also **Vikings**
Scarecrows   632; E
  x Bird repelling devices
  xx **Plant conservation**
Scenarios. *See* **Motion picture plays; Plots (Drama,
       fiction, etc.); Radio plays; Television plays**
Scene painting   751.7
  xx **Painting; Theaters—Stage setting and scenery**
Scenery. *See* **Landscape protection; Views;** and
       names of cities (except ancient cities), coun-
       tries, states, etc. with the subdivision
       Description—Views, e.g. **Chicago (Ill.)—
       Description—Views; United States—
       Description—Views;** etc.; and names of an-
       cient cities and named entities, such as indi-
       vidual parks, structures, etc. with the subdi-
       vision *Pictorial works.*
Scenery (Stage). *See* **Theaters—Stage setting and
       scenery**
Scepticism. *See* **Skepticism**
Scholarship. *See* **Learning and scholarship**
Scholarships, fellowships, etc.   371.2; 378.3
  See also **Student loan funds**
  x Fellowships; Student aid
  xx **Colleges and universities; Education; Educa-
       tion—Government policy; Endowments;
       Student loan funds**
Scholastic achievement. *See* **Academic achievement**
Scholastic aptitude test   378.1
  See also **Graduate record examination**
  x S.A.T.; SAT
  xx **Colleges and universities—Entrance examina-
       tions; Examinations**

School administration and organization. *See* **Schools—Administration**
School age fathers. *See* **Teenage fathers**
School age mothers. *See* **Teenage mothers**
School and community. *See* **Community and school**
School and home. *See* **Home and school**
School architecture. *See* **School buildings**
School assembly programs 372; 373

> Use for general materials on school entertainments, literary and otherwise, assembly programs, etc. Collections of prose and poetry for public speaking are entered under **Readings and recitations.**

> *See also* **Commencements; Drama in education; Readings and recitations;** also names of days observed, e.g. **Memorial Day;** etc.

> *x* Assembly programs, School; Programs, School assembly; School entertainments; Schools—Exercises and recreations; Schools—Opening exercises

> *xx* **Student activities**

School attendance 371.2

> *See also* **Children—Employment; Compulsory education; Dropouts**

> *x* Absence from school; Absenteeism (School); Attendance, School; Compulsory school attendance; School enrollment; Truancy (Schools)

> *xx* **Compulsory education; Dropouts**

School boards 379.1

> *x* Boards of education

> *xx* **Schools—Administration**

School books. *See* **Textbooks**
School buildings 727

> *x* Buildings, School; School architecture; School houses; Schoolhouses

> *xx* **Architecture; Buildings; Schools**

School buildings as recreation centers. *See* **Community centers**
School busing. *See* **Busing (School integration); School children—Transportation**
School children 370.19

> *xx* **Children; Students**

School children—Food 371.7

> *x* Food for school children; Meals for school children; School lunches

> *xx* **Children—Food; Diet; Food**

School children—Transportation 371.8

> *See also* **Busing (School integration)**

> *x* School busing

> *xx* **Transportation**

School clubs. *See* **Students—Societies**
School counseling 371.4

> Use for materials on the assistance given to students by schools, colleges, or universities in understanding and coping with adjustment problems. Materials on the assistance given to students in the selection of a program of studies are entered under **Educational counseling.**

> *See also* **Educational counseling**

> *x* Guidance counseling, School

> *xx* **Counseling; Educational counseling**

School desegregation. *See* **School integration**

School discipline   371.5
> *See also* **Classroom management; Student government**
> *x* Discipline of children; Punishment in schools
> *xx* **Schools—Administration; Teaching**

School drama.   *See* **College and school drama**

School dropouts.   *See* **Dropouts**

School enrollment.   *See* **School attendance**

School entertainments.   *See* **School assembly programs**

School excursions.   *See* **Field trips**

School fiction.   *See* **School stories**

School finance.   *See* **Education—Finance**

School furniture.   *See* **Schools—Equipment and supplies**

School grade retention.   *See* **Promotion (School)**

School houses.   *See* **School buildings**

School hygiene   371.7
> *x* Hygiene, School
> *xx* **Children—Health and hygiene; Health education; Hygiene; Public health; Sanitation**

School inspection.   *See* **School supervision; Schools—Administration**

School integration   370.19
> *See also* **Busing (School integration); Magnet schools; Segregation in education**
> *x* Desegregated schools; Desegregation in education; Education—Integration; Integrated schools; Integration in education; Racial balance in schools; School desegregation
> *xx* **Blacks—Education; Blacks—Integration; Segregation in education**

School journalism.   *See* **College and school journalism**

School libraries   027.8
> *See also* **Children's libraries; Children's literature; Elementary school libraries; High school libraries; Libraries and schools**
> *x* Libraries, School
> *xx* **Instructional materials centers; Libraries; Libraries and schools**

School libraries (Elementary school).   *See* **Elementary school libraries**

School libraries (High school).   *See* **High school libraries**

School life.   *See* **Students**

School lunches.   *See* **School children—Food**

School management.   *See* **Schools—Administration**

School media centers.   *See* **Instructional materials centers**

School music.   *See* **Music—Study and teaching; School songbooks; Singing**

School newspapers.   *See* **College and school journalism**

School nurses   371.7
> *xx* **Children—Health and hygiene; Nurses**

School organization.   *See* **Schools—Administration**

School playgrounds.   *See* **Playgrounds**

School plays.   *See* **Children's plays; College and school drama—Collections**

School principals.   *See* **School superintendents and principals**

School promotion.   *See* **Promotion (School)**

School prose.   *See* **Children's writings**

School psychologists   371.4
    x Psychologists, School
    xx **Educational counseling**
School readiness.   *See* **Readiness for school**
School reports   371.2
    See also **Grading and marking (Education)**
    x Educational reports; Reports, Teachers';
        Teachers' reports
    xx **Grading and marking (Education); Report**
        writing
School shops   373.2
    x Industrial arts shops
    xx **Technical education**
School songbooks   782.42
    See also **Children's songs**
    x School music; Songbooks, School
    xx **Songbooks; Songs**
School sports   371.8
    See also **Coaching (Athletics); College sports**
    x Interscholastic sports
    xx **Sports; Student activities**
School stories   808.83; 813, etc.; Fic
    x School fiction; Schools—Fiction; Stories
School superintendents and principals   371.2
    See also **School supervision**
    x School principals; Superintendents of schools
    xx **School supervision; Schools—Administration;**
        Teachers; Teaching
School supervision   371.1
    Use for materials on the supervision of instruc-
        tion. Materials on the administrative duties
        of an educator are entered under **Schools—**
        Administration.
    See also **School superintendents and principals**
    x Inspection of schools; Instructional supervi-
        sion; School inspection; Supervision of
        schools
    xx **School superintendents and principals;**
        Schools—Administration; Teaching
School surveys.   *See* **Educational surveys**
School taxes.   *See* **Education—Finance**
School teaching.   *See* **Teaching**
School trips.   *See* **Field trips**
School vandalism.   *See* **School violence**
School verse.   *See* **Children's writings**
School violence   371.5
    x School vandalism; Student violence
    xx **Juvenile delinquency; Violence**
School withdrawals.   *See* **Dropouts**
School yearbooks   371.8
    x College yearbooks; High school yearbooks; Se-
        nior yearbooks; Senior yearbooks; Stu-
        dents—Yearbooks; Yearbooks, Student
Schoolboy fathers.   *See* **Teenage fathers**
Schoolgirl mothers.   *See* **Teenage mothers**
Schoolhouses.   *See* **School buildings**
Schools (May subdiv. geog.)   371
    See also **Business schools; Education; Libraries**
        and schools; Museums and schools; School
        buildings; Summer schools; Summer
        schools, Religious; also types of schools, e.g.
        Church schools; Colleges and universities;
        Kindergarten; Public schools; Rural schools;

Schools—*Continued*
　　　etc.; also subjects with the subdivision *Study and teaching,* e.g. **Medicine—Study and teaching;** etc.; headings beginning with the word **School;** and names of individual schools
　　x Community schools; Neighborhood schools
　　xx **Education; Public schools**
Schools—Administration　371.2
　　See note under **School supervision.**
　　See also

Articulation (Education)	**School supervision**
School boards	**Schools—Centralization**
School discipline	**Schools—Decentralization**
School superintendents and principals	**Student government**
	Teaching

　　x Educational administration; Inspection of schools; School administration and organization; School inspection; School management; School organization; Schools—Management and organization
Schools and libraries.　*See* **Libraries and schools**
Schools and museums.　*See* **Museums and schools**
Schools as social centers.　*See* **Community centers**
Schools, Business.　*See* **Business schools**
Schools—Centralization　379.1
　　x Centralization of schools; Consolidation of schools
　　xx **Schools—Administration**
Schools—Curricula.　*See* **Education—Curricula;** and types of education and schools with the subdivision *Curricula,* e.g. **Library education—Curricula; Colleges and universities—Curricula;** etc.
Schools—Decentralization　379.1
　　x Decentralization of schools
　　xx **Schools—Administration**
Schools—Equipment and supplies　371.6
　　x School furniture
　　xx **Furniture**
Schools—Exercises and recreations.　*See* **School assembly programs**
Schools—Fiction.　*See* **School stories**
Schools, Magnet.　*See* **Magnet schools**
Schools—Management and organization.　*See* **Schools—Administration**
Schools, Military.　*See* **Military education**
Schools, Nonformal.　*See* **Experimental schools**
Schools, Nongraded.　*See* **Nongraded schools**
Schools—Opening exercises.　*See* **School assembly programs**
Schools, Parochial.　*See* **Church schools**
Schools—Prayers.　*See* **Religion in the public schools**
Schools, Ungraded.　*See* **Nongraded schools**
Schools—United States　371
　　x United States—Schools
Science (May subdiv. geog.)　**500**
　　See also

Astronomy	**Chemistry**
Biology	**Computer science**
Botany	**Crystallography**
Chaos (Science)	**Earth sciences**

Science—*Continued*

Ethnology	Natural history
Fossils	Petrology
Geology	Physics
Life sciences	Physiology
Mathematics	Space sciences
Meteorology	Zoology
Mineralogy	

    also headings beginning with the word **Scientific**
   x Discoveries (in science)

Science and civilization 306.4
   x Civilization and science; Science and society
   xx **Civilization; Progress**

Science and religion. *See* **Religion and science**
Science and society. *See* **Science and civilization**
Science and space. *See* **Space sciences**
Science and state. *See* **Science—Government policy**
Science and the Bible. *See* **Bible and science**
Science and the humanities 001.3
   x Humanities and science
Science—Exhibitions 507.4
   x Science fairs
Science—Experiments 507
   See also particular branches of science with the
      subdivision *Experiments,* e.g. **Chemistry—**
      Experiments; etc.
   x Experiments, Scientific; Scientific experiments
Science fairs. *See* **Science—Exhibitions**
Science fiction 808.83; 809.3; 813, etc.; Fic
   Use for collections of and materials on imagina-
      tive fiction with a scientific factor, usually
      involving scientific speculation, but limited
      to the conceivably possible. May be used for
      science fiction as realized in various media,
      including films, comic strips, etc.
   x Stories
   xx **Fantastic fiction; Fiction**
Science—Government policy 351.85
   x Science and state; Science policy; State and
      science
Science—Methodology 501
   See also **Logic**
   x Scientific method
Science policy. *See* **Science—Government policy**
Science—Societies 506
   x Scientific societies
Science—Study and teaching 507
   See also **Nature study**
   x Education, Scientific; Scientific education
   xx **Education; Teaching**
Science—United States 509.73
   x American science; United States—Science
Scientific apparatus and instruments 502.8
   See also names of groups of instruments, e.g.
      Aeronautical instruments; Astronomical in-
      struments; Chemical apparatus; Electric ap-
      paratus and appliances; Electronic apparatus
      and appliances; Engineering instruments;
      Meteorological instruments; etc.; also
      names of specific instruments
   x Apparatus, Scientific; Instruments, Scientific;
      Scientific instruments
Scientific education. *See* **Science—Study and**
   teaching

Scientific errors. *See* **Errors**
Scientific expeditions   508
    See also names of regions explored, e.g. **Antarc-
       tic regions; Arctic regions;** etc.; and names
       of expeditions
    x Expeditions, Scientific; Polar expeditions
    xx **Discoveries (in geography); Voyages and trav-
       els**
Scientific experiments. *See* **Science—Experiments;**
       and particular branches of science with the
       subdivision *Experiments,* e.g. **Chemistry—
       Experiments;** etc.
Scientific instruments. *See* **Scientific apparatus and
       instruments**
Scientific journalism. *See* **Journalism, Scientific**
Scientific management. *See* **Management**
Scientific method. *See* special subjects with the
       subdivision *Methodology,* e.g. **Science—
       Methodology;** etc.
Scientific recreations   793.8
    See also **Mathematical recreations**
    x Recreations, Scientific
    xx **Amusements**
Scientific societies. *See* **Science—Societies**
Scientific writing. *See* **Technical writing**
Scientists   509.2; 920
    See also types of scientists, e.g. **Astronomers;
       Chemists; Geologists; Mathematicians; Nat-
       uralists; Physicists;** etc.; and names of indi-
       vidual scientists
Scottish clans. *See* **Clans**
Scottish personal names. *See* **Personal names,
       Scottish**
Scottish tartans. *See* **Tartans**
Scouts and scouting   369.4
    See also **Boy Scouts; Girl Scouts**
Screen plays. *See* **Motion picture plays**
Screen printing. *See* **Silk screen printing**
Screening for drug abuse. *See* **Drug testing**
Scriptures, Holy. *See* **Bible**
Scuba diving   797.2
    Use for materials on free diving with the aid of
       self-contained underwater breathing appara-
       tus.
    x Diving, Scuba; Free diving; Frogmen and
       frogwomen
    xx **Diving; Diving, Submarine; Skin diving**
Sculling. *See* **Rowing**
Sculptors (May subdiv. geog. adjective form, e.g.
       Sculptors, American; etc.)   **730.92; 920**
    xx **Artists**
Sculptors, American   730.92; 920
    x American sculptors; United States—Sculptors
Sculpture (May subdiv. geog. adjective form, e.g.
       Sculpture, Greek; etc.)   **730**
    See also types of sculpture, e.g. **Brasses;
       Bronzes; Masks (Sculpture); Mobiles
       (Sculpture); Modeling; Monuments; Plaster
       casts; Soap sculpture; Wood carving;** etc.
    x Statues
    xx **Aesthetics; Art; Decoration and ornament**
Sculpture, American   730.973
    x American sculpture; United States—Sculpture

Sculpture, Greek 730.938; 730.9495
   x Greek sculpture
Sculpture in motion. *See* **Kinetic sculpture**
Sculpture, Kinetic. *See* **Kinetic sculpture**
Sculpture, Modern 735
   x Modern sculpture
Sculpture, Modern—1900-1999 (20th century) 735
Sculpture, Religious. *See* **Religious art and symbolism**
   ism
Sculpture—Technique 731.4
   See also **Modeling**
   xx **Modeling**
SDI (Ballistic missile defense system). *See* **Strategic Defense Initiative**
   gic Defense Initiative
Sea. *See* **Ocean**
Sea animals. *See* **Marine animals**
Sea bed. *See* **Ocean bottom**
Sea farming. *See* **Aquaculture**
Sea fisheries. *See* **Fisheries**
Sea food. *See* **Seafood**
Sea in art. *See* **Marine painting**
Sea laboratories. *See* **Undersea research stations**
Sea laws. *See* **Maritime law**
Sea life. *See* **Sailors; Seafaring life;** and names of
   countries with the subhead *Navy,* e.g.
   United States. Navy; etc.
Sea lions. *See* **Seals (Animals)**
Sea mosses. *See* **Algae**
Sea poetry 808.81; 811, etc.; 811.008, etc.
   See also **Sea songs**
   xx **Poetry—Collections**
Sea pollution. *See* **Marine pollution**
Sea power 359
   See also **Arms control; Naval battles; Naval history; Navies; Warships;** also names of countries with the subhead *Navy* or the subdivision *History, Naval,* e.g. **United States. Navy; United States—History, Naval;** etc.
   x Dominion of the sea; Military power; Naval power; Navy
   xx **Arms control; Naval art and science; Naval history; Navies**
Sea resources. *See* **Marine resources**
Sea routes. *See* **Trade routes**
Sea shells. *See* **Shells**
Sea-shore. *See* **Seashore**
Sea songs 782.42
   x Chanties; Sailors' song
   xx **Sea poetry; Songs**
Sea stories 808.83; 813, etc.
   x Stories
   xx **Adventure and adventurers**
Sea transportation. *See* **Shipping**
Sea travel. *See* **Ocean travel**
Sea water 551.4
   x Saline water; Salt water
   xx **Water**
Sea water aquariums. *See* **Marine aquariums**
Sea water conversion 628.1
   x Conversion of saline water; Demineralization of salt water; Desalination of water; Desalting of water
   xx **Water—Purification**
Sea waves. *See* **Ocean waves**

Seafaring life 910.4

  See also **Sailors**

  x Sailors' life; Sea life

  xx **Adventure and adventurers; Sailors; Voyages
        and travels**

Seafood 641.3

  See also **Fish as food;** also names of marine fish,
        shellfish, etc., used as food

  x Sea food

  xx **Fish as food; Food; Marine resources**

Sealab project 551.46

  x Navy Sealab project; Project Sealab; United
        States. Navy—Sealab project

  xx **Undersea research stations**

Seals (Animals) 599.74

  x Fur seals; Sea lions

  xx **Marine mammals**

Seals (Numismatics) 737

  x Emblems; Signets

  xx **Heraldry; History; Inscriptions; Numismatics**

Seamanship. *See* **Navigation**

Seamen. *See* **Sailors**

Search and rescue operations. *See* **Rescue work**

Seascapes. *See* **Marine painting**

Seashore 551.4

  See also **Beaches; Sand dunes**

  x Sea-shore

  xx **Ocean**

Seasons 508; 525

  See also names of the seasons, e.g. **Autumn;**
        etc.

  xx **Astronomy; Climate; Meteorology**

Seaweeds. *See* **Algae**

Secession. *See* **State rights; United States—
        History—1861-1865, Civil War—Causes**

Second Advent 236

  See also **Millennium**

  x Jesus Christ—Second Advent; Second coming
        of Christ

  xx **Eschatology; Jesus Christ; Millennium**

Second coming of Christ. *See* **Second Advent**

Second hand trade. *See* **Secondhand trade**

Second job. *See* **Supplementary employment**

Secondary education 373

  A more inclusive subject than **High schools.**

  See also **Adult education; Evening and continua-
        tion schools; High schools; Junior high
        schools; Private schools; Public schools**

  x Education, Secondary; High school education;
        Secondary schools

  xx **High schools**

Secondary employment. *See* **Supplementary em-
        ployment**

Secondary school libraries. *See* **High school li-
        braries**

Secondary schools. *See* **High schools; Junior high
        schools; Private schools; Public schools;
        Secondary education**

Secondhand trade 381

  See also types of secondhand trade, e.g. **Garage
        sales;** etc.

  x Second hand trade; Used merchandise

  xx **Selling**

Secret service (May subdiv. geog.)   **327.12; 355.3**
Use for materials on a governmental service of a secret nature.
See also **Detectives; Espionage; Intelligence service; Spies;** also names of wars with the subdivision *Secret service,* e.g. **World War, 1939-1945—Secret service;** etc.
xx **Detectives; Intelligence service; Police; Spies**
Secret service—United States   353.0074
x United States—Secret service
Secret societies   366; 371.8
See also **Fraternities and sororities;** also names of secret societies, e.g. **Freemasons;** etc.
x Greek letter societies
xx **Rites and ceremonies; Societies**
Secret writing.   *See* **Cryptography**
Secretarial practice.   *See* **Office practice**
Secretaries   651.3
xx **Business education; Office management**
Secrets, Trade.   *See* **Trade secrets**
Sectionalism (U.S.).   *See* **Sectionalism (United States)**
Sectionalism (United States)   917.3; 973
x Localism; Provincialism; Regionalism; Sectionalism (U.S.)
Sects   280; 291.9; 296.8
See also **Cults; Shakers;** also names of churches and sects
x Church denominations; Denominations, Religious; Religious denominations
xx **Church history; Cults; Religions**
Secularism   211
See also **Atheism; Rationalism**
xx **Ethics; Theology; Utilitarianism**
Securities   332.6
See also **Insider trading;** also types of securities, e.g. **Bonds; Investments; Mortgages; Stocks;** etc.
x Capitalization (Finance); Dividends
xx **Finance; Investments; Speculation; Stock exchange**
Securities exchange.   *See* **Stock exchange**
Securities trading, Insider.   *See* **Insider trading**
Security, Internal.   *See* **Internal security**
Security, International   327.1; 341.7
See also **Arbitration, International; Arms control; International organization; International police; Neutrality; Peace**
x Collective security; International security
xx **Arms control; International relations; Peace**
Security, Job.   *See* **Job security**
Security measures.   *See* subjects with the subdivision *Security measures,* e.g. **Nuclear power plants—Security measures;** etc.
Security, Social.   *See* **Social security**
Sedition.   *See* **Political crimes and offenses; Revolutions**
Seeds   582
See also **Nuts**
xx **Botany; Plant propagation**
Seeds—Germination.   *See* **Germination**
Seeing eye dogs.   *See* **Guide dogs**

Segregation 305.8

    See also **Apartheid; Discrimination; Minorities;**
      also names of groups of people with the sub-
      division *Segregation,* e.g. **Blacks—**
      Segregation; etc.

    x Desegregation

    xx **Discrimination; Minorities**

Segregation in education 370.19

    See also **Busing (School integration); Discrimina-**
      tion in education; School integration

    x Education, Segregation in; Integration in edu-
      cation; Racial balance in schools

    xx **Blacks—Education; Blacks—Segregation;**
      Discrimination in education; School integra-
      tion

Segregation in housing. *See* **Discrimination in**
      housing

Segregation in public accommodations. *See* **Dis-**
      crimination in public accommodations

Seismic sea waves. *See* **Tsunamis**

Seismography. *See* **Earthquakes**

Seismology. *See* **Earthquakes**

Selection, Artificial. *See* **Breeding**

Selection, Natural. *See* **Natural selection**

Selective service. *See* **Draft**

Self 126; 155.2

    xx **Consciousness; Individuality; Personality**

Self-acceptance 155.2

    x Self-love (Psychology)

    xx **Psychology**

Self-actualization. *See* **Self-realization**

Self-assurance. *See* **Self-confidence; Self-reliance**

Self-awareness. *See* **Self-perception**

Self-care, Health. *See* **Health self-care**

Self-care, Medical. *See* **Health self-care**

Self-concept. *See* **Self-perception**

Self-confidence 155.2

    See also **Assertiveness (Psychology); Self-**
      reliance

    x Confidence, Self; Self-assurance

    xx **Assertiveness (Psychology); Emotions; Self-**
      reliance

Self-consciousness 155.2

    x Embarrassment

Self-control 153.8

    x Control of self; Discipline, Self; Self-
      discipline; Self-mastery; Will power;
      Willpower

Self-culture 371.3; 374

    x Home education; Home study courses; Self-
      development; Self-education; Self-
      improvement; Self-instruction; Teach your-
      self courses

    xx **Culture; Study skills**

Self-defense 613.6; 796.8

    See also **Boxing; Judo; Karate; Martial arts**

    x Fighting

    xx **Martial arts**

Self-defense for women 613.6; 796.8

    See also **Martial arts**

    x Fighting; Women—Self-defense; Women's
      self-defense

    xx **Martial arts**

Self-defense in animals. *See* **Animal defenses**

Self-development. *See* **Self-culture**
Self-discipline. *See* **Self-control**
Self-education. *See* **Self-culture**
Self-employed 331.12
> *See also* **Entrepreneurs; Home business; Professions; Small business**
> *x* Freelancers
Self-employed women 331.4
> *x* Women, Self-employed
> *xx* **Women—Employment**
Self-esteem. *See* **Self-respect**
Self-examination, Medical. *See* **Health self-care**
Self-expectations, Perfectionist. *See* **Perfectionism (Personality trait)**
Self-fulfillment. *See* **Self-realization**
Self-government. *See* **Democracy; Representative government and representation**
Self-government (in education). *See* **Student government**
Self health care. *See* **Health self-care**
Self-help medical care. *See* **Health self-care**
Self-improvement. *See* **Self-culture**
Self-instruction. *See* **Correspondence schools and courses; Self-culture;** and names of subjects with the subdivision *Programmed instruction,* e.g. **English language—Programmed instruction;** etc.
Self-love (Psychology). *See* **Self-acceptance; Self-respect**
Self-mastery. *See* **Self-control**
Self-medication. *See* **Health self-care**
Self-perception 155.2
> *x* Self-awareness; Self-concept
Self-protection in animals. *See* **Animal defenses**
Self-realization 155.2; 158
> *See also* **Success**
> *x* Fulfillment, Self; Self-actualization; Self-fulfillment
> *xx* **Success**
Self-reliance 179
> *See also* **Self-confidence; Survival skills**
> *x* Self-assurance
> *xx* **Self-confidence; Survival skills**
Self-respect 155.2
> *x* Self-esteem; Self-love (Psychology)
> *xx* **Human behavior**
Self-starvation. *See* **Anorexia nervosa**
Selling 658.85
> *See also* **Advertising; Booksellers and bookselling; Direct selling; Mail-order business; Marketing; Sales management; Secondhand trade**
> *x* Salesmanship
> *xx* **Advertising; Business; Department stores; Retail trade**
Selling of infants. *See* **Adoption—Corrupt practices**
Selvas. *See* **Jungles**
Semantics 121; 401; 412
> Use for materials on the historical and psychological study of meanings in language and changes in those meanings.
> *See also* **Semiotics; Words, New**
> *xx* **Language and languages; Semiotics**

Semiconductors   621.3815
> *See also* **Microelectronics; Transistors**
> *xx* **Electric conductors; Electronics**

Semiotics   001.51; 302.2; 401
> Use for materials on the study of signs and symbols, especially the relationship between written and spoken signs (words, phrases, utterances) and whatever it is they stand for.
> *See also* **Semantics; Signs and symbols; Visual literacy**
> *xx* **Semantics; Signs and symbols**

Semitic peoples   305.892
> *xx* **Anthropology**

Senate (U.S.).   *See* **United States. Congress. Senate**

Senescence.   *See* **Aging**

Senior citizens.   *See* **Elderly**

Senior yearbooks.   *See* **School yearbooks**

Sense of direction.   *See* **Direction sense**

Senses and sensation   152.1; 612.8
> *See also*

Color sense	**Smell**
Gestalt psychology	**Taste**
Hearing	**Touch**
Pain	**Vision**
Pleasure	

> *xx* **Intellect; Knowledge, Theory of; Physiology; Psychology; Psychophysiology**

Sensing, Remote.   *See* **Remote sensing**

Sensitivity training.   *See* **Group relations training**

Separate development (Race relations).   *See* **Apartheid**

Separation anxiety in children   155.4
> *xx* **Child psychology; Fear; Stress (Psychology)**

Separation (Law).   *See* **Divorce**

Separation of powers (May subdiv. geog.)   **342; 351**
> *x* Division of powers; Powers, Separation of
> *xx* **Constitutional law; Executive power; Political science**

Separation of powers—United States   342
> *x* United States—Separation of powers

Separatism, Black.   *See* **Black nationalism**

Separatist movement in Québec (Province).   *See* **Québec (Province)—History—Autonomy and independence movements**

Sepulchers.   *See* **Tombs**

Sepulchral brasses.   *See* **Brasses**

Serial publications   050
> Use for general materials on publications in any medium issued in successive parts bearing numerical or chronological designations and intended to be continued indefinitely.
> *See also* **Books; Newspapers; Periodicals**
> *xx* **Bibliography; Books; Publishers and publishing**

Serigraphy.   *See* **Silk screen printing**

Sermon on the mount   226.9
> *x* Jesus Christ—Sermon on the mount

Sermons   251; 252
> *See also* **Preaching**
> *xx* **Preaching**

Serpents.   *See* **Snakes**

Servants.   *See* **Household employees**

Service books (Liturgy).   *See* **Liturgies**

Service, Compulsory military.   *See* **Draft**

Service, Customer. *See* **Customer service**
Service dogs. *See* **Animals and the handicapped**
Service (in industry). *See* **Customer service**
Service industries   338.4
>   Use for general materials on service industries.
>   Names of all individual service industries
>   are not included in this List but may be
>   added as needed.
>   *See also* **Undertakers and undertaking**
>   *x* Industries, Service
Service stations, Automobile. *See* **Automobiles—
>   Service stations**
Servicemen. *See* **Military personnel**
Services, Customer. *See* **Customer service**
Servicewomen. *See* **Military personnel**
Servitude. *See* **Peonage; Slavery**
Servomechanisms   629.8
>   *x* Automatic control
>   *xx* **Automation; Feedback control systems**
Set theory   511.3
>   *See also* **Algebra, Boolean; Arithmetic; Fractals;
>   Logic, Symbolic and mathematical; Number
>   theory; Topology**
>   *x* Aggregates; Classes (Mathematics); Ensembles
>   (Mathematics); Mathematical sets; Sets
>   (Mathematics)
>   *xx* **Logic, Symbolic and mathematical; Mathe-
>   matics**
Sets, Fractal. *See* **Fractals**
Sets (Mathematics). *See* **Set theory**
Sets of fractional dimension. *See* **Fractals**
Settlement of land. *See* **Land settlement**
Settlements, Social. *See* **Social settlements**
Seven Years' War, 1756-1763   940.2
>   *xx* **Germany—History—1740-1815**
Seventeen-year locusts. *See* **Cicadas**
Seventeenth century   909.08
>   See note under **Nineteenth century.**
>   *x* 1600-1699 (17th century)
Seville (Spain). World's Fair, 1992. *See* **Expo 92
>   (Seville, Spain)**
Sewage disposal   628.3
>   *See also* **Water pollution**
>   *x* Waste disposal
>   *xx* **Public health; Refuse and refuse disposal; Wa-
>   ter pollution**
Sewerage   628
>   *See also* **Drainage**
>   *x* Sewers
>   *xx* **Drainage; Drainage, House; Municipal engi-
>   neering; Plumbing; Sanitary engineering**
Sewers. *See* **Sewerage**
Sewing   646.2; 646.4
>   *See also* **Dressmaking; Embroidery; Needlework**
>   *xx* **Dressmaking; Home economics; Needlework**
Sex. *See* **Sexual behavior**
Sex bias. *See* **Sexism**
Sex (Biology)   574.3; 612.6
>   Use for materials on the physiological traits that
>   distinguish the males and females of a spe-
>   cies.
>   *See also* **Androgyny; Reproduction; Reproductive
>   system; Sexual disorders;** also headings be-

Sex (Biology)—*Continued*
    ginning with the word **Sexual**
  xx **Biology; Reproduction**
Sex change. *See* **Transsexuality**
Sex crimes   364.1
    See also names of sex crimes, e.g. **Child molesting; Incest; Rape;** etc.
  x Crimes, Sex; Sexual crimes
  xx **Crime; Sexual behavior**
Sex customs. *See* **Sexual behavior**
Sex differences (Psychology)   155.3
    See also **Androgyny; Sex discrimination; Sex role; Sexual behavior**
  xx **Androgyny; Sex discrimination; Sexual behavior**
Sex discrimination   305.3
    Use for materials on the restriction or denial of rights, privileges, or choice because of one's sex. Materials on prejudicial attitudes toward people because of their sex are entered under **Sexism.**
    See also **Equal rights amendments; Men—Civil rights; Sex differences (Psychology); Women—Civil rights**
  x Discrimination, Sex
  xx **Discrimination; Sex differences (Psychology); Sexism**
Sex disorders. *See* **Sexual disorders**
Sex education   372.3; 613.907; 649
    See also **Sexual hygiene**
  x Human life education; Sex instruction
  xx **Family life education; Sexual hygiene**
Sex in art. *See* **Erotic art**
Sex in business. *See* **Sex in the workplace**
Sex in the office. *See* **Sex in the workplace**
Sex in the workplace   306.7; 658
    See also **Sexual harassment**
  x Employee sex in the workplace; Office romance; Sex in business; Sex in the office
  xx **Sexual harassment; Work**
Sex instruction. *See* **Sex education**
Sex organs. *See* **Reproductive system**
Sex (Psychology). *See* **Sexual behavior**
Sex role   305.3
    Use for materials on the patterns of attitudes and behavior that are regarded as appropriate to one sex rather than the other.
    See also **Androgyny; Sexism; Transsexuality**
  x Female role; Gender identity; Male role
  xx **Androgyny; Role conflict; Sex differences (Psychology); Social role**
Sex therapy   616.6; 616.85
    See also **Sexual disorders**
  xx **Psychotherapy; Sexual disorders**
Sexism   305.3
    See note under **Sex discrimination.**
    See also **Sex discrimination**
  x Sex bias
  xx **Attitude (Psychology); Prejudices; Sex role; Sexual behavior**

Sexual behavior   155.3
   See also
   Androgyny   **Sexual behavior in animals**
   Homosexuality   **Sexual deviation**
   Sex crimes   **Sexual disorders**
   Sex differences (Psychol-   **Sexual ethics**
      ogy)   **Sexual harassment**
   Sexism
      also classes and groups of people with the subdivision *Sexual behavior,* e.g. **College students—Sexual behavior;** etc.
   x Behavior, Sexual; Sex; Sex customs; Sex (Psychology); Sexuality
   xx **Sex differences (Psychology); Sexual disorders; Sexual ethics**
Sexual behavior in animals   591.56
   See also **Animal courtship**
   x Animals—Sexual behavior; Breeding behavior; Mating behavior; Reproductive behavior
   xx **Animals—Behavior; Sexual behavior**
Sexual crimes. *See* **Sex crimes**
Sexual deviation   306.7; 616.85
   x Deviation, Sexual; Paraphilia; Perversion, Sexual; Sexual perversion
   xx **Sexual behavior; Sexual disorders**
Sexual disorders   616.6; 616.85
   See also **Sex therapy; Sexual behavior; Sexual deviation**
   x Sex disorders
   xx **Sex (Biology); Sex therapy; Sexual behavior**
Sexual ethics   176
   See also
   Adultery   **Prostitution**
   Artificial insemination,   **Sexual behavior**
      Human   **Sexual hygiene**
   Birth control   **Unmarried couples**
   Free love
   x Ethics, Sexual
   xx **Sexual behavior; Social ethics**
Sexual harassment   331.13; 344; 370.19
   Use for materials on unsolicited and unwelcome sexual behavior that interferes with study, work or everyday activities and creates an intimidating or offensive environment.
   See also **Sex in the workplace;** also types of sexual harassment, e.g. **Child molesting;** etc.
   x Harassment, Sexual
   xx **Sex in the workplace; Sexual behavior**
Sexual hygiene   613.9
   See also **AIDS (Disease)—Prevention; Birth control; Prostitution; Safe sex in AIDS prevention; Sex education; Sexually transmitted diseases**
   x Hygiene, Sexual; Hygiene, Social; Social hygiene
   xx **AIDS (Disease)—Prevention; Sex education; Sexual ethics; Sexually transmitted diseases**
Sexual perversion. *See* **Sexual deviation**
Sexuality. *See* **Sexual behavior**
Sexually transmitted diseases   616.95
   See also **Sexual hygiene;** also names of sexually transmitted diseases, e.g. **AIDS (Disease);**

Sexually transmitted diseases—*Continued*
  Syphilis; etc.
  x V.D.; VD; Venereal diseases
  xx **Communicable diseases; Prostitution; Sexual hygiene**
Shade gardens. *See* **Gardening in the shade**
Shades and shadows 741.2
  x Light and shade; Shadows
  xx **Drawing**
Shadow pantomimes and plays 791.5
  xx **Amateur theater; Pantomimes; Puppets and puppet plays; Shadow pictures; Theater**
Shadow pictures 793
  See also **Shadow pantomimes and plays**
  x Hand shadows; Shadowplay
  xx **Amusements**
Shadowplay. *See* **Shadow pictures**
Shadows. *See* **Shades and shadows**
Shady gardens. *See* **Gardening in the shade**
Shaft sinking. *See* **Boring**
Shakers 289
  xx **Sects**
Shakespeare in fiction, drama, poetry, etc. *See* **Shakespeare, William, 1564-1616—Drama; Shakespeare, William, 1564-1616—Fiction; Shakespeare, William, 1564-1616—Poetry**
Shakespeare, William, 1564-1616 822.3
  When applicable, the following subdivisions may be used for other voluminous authors, e.g. **Dante; Goethe;** etc. The following subjects are to be used for materials about Shakespeare and about his writings. The texts of his plays, etc., are not given subject headings.
Shakespeare, William, 1564-1616—Adaptations 822.3
  x Shakespeare, William, 1564-1616—Paraphrases
Shakespeare, William, 1564-1616—Anniversaries 822.3
Shakespeare, William, 1564-1616—Authorship 822.3
  x Bacon-Shakespeare controversy
Shakespeare, William, 1564-1616—Bibliography 016.8223
Shakespeare, William, 1564-1616—Biography 92; B
Shakespeare, William, 1564-1616—Biography—Psychology 92; B
  x Shakespeare, William, 1564-1616—Psychological studies
Shakespeare, William, 1564-1616—Characters 822.3
  xx **Characters and characteristics in literature**
Shakespeare, William, 1564-1616—Comedies 822.3
  Use for criticism, etc., of the comedies, not for the texts of the plays.
Shakespeare, William, 1564-1616—Concordances 822.303
  x Shakespeare, William, 1564-1616—Indexes
  xx **Shakespeare, William, 1564-1616—Dictionaries**

Shakespeare, William, 1564-1616—Contemporary England 822.3; 942.05

Shakespeare, William, 1564-1616—Criticism, interpretation, etc. 822.3

Use for criticism of the works in general; criticism of the comedies is entered under **Shakespeare, William, 1564-1616—Comedies**; criticism of the tragedies under **Shakespeare, William, 1564-1616—Tragedies**; criticism of an individual play is entered under **Shakespeare, William, 1564-1616,** followed by the title of the play. Materials limited to criticism of the sonnets are entered under **Shakespeare, William, 1564-1616—Sonnets.**

x Shakespeare, William, 1564-1616—Psychological studies

xx **Criticism**

Shakespeare, William, 1564-1616—Dictionaries 822.303

See also **Shakespeare, William, 1564-1616—Concordances**

x Shakespeare, William, 1564-1616—Indexes

Shakespeare, William, 1564-1616—Discography 016.8223

Shakespeare, William, 1564-1616—Drama 812, etc.

x Shakespeare in fiction, drama, poetry, etc.

Shakespeare, William, 1564-1616—Dramatic production 822.3

x Shakespeare, William, 1564-1616—Stage setting and scenery

Shakespeare, William, 1564-1616—Fiction 813, etc.; **Fic**

x Shakespeare in fiction, drama, poetry, etc.

Shakespeare, William, 1564-1616—Filmography 016.8223

Shakespeare, William, 1564-1616—Histories 822.3

Use for criticism, etc., of the histories, not for the texts of the plays.

Shakespeare, William, 1564-1616—Indexes. *See* **Shakespeare, William, 1564-1616—Concordances; Shakespeare, William, 1564-1616—Dictionaries**

Shakespeare, William, 1564-1616—Influence 822.3

Use for materials on Shakespeare's impact on national literatures, literary movements and on specific persons.

Shakespeare, William, 1564-1616—Knowledge 822.3

Use for materials on Shakespeare's knowledge or treatment of specific subjects.

May be subdivided by subject, e.g. **Shakespeare, William, 1564-1616—Knowledge—Animals;** etc.

Shakespeare, William, 1564-1616—Music. *See* **Shakespeare, William, 1564-1616—Songs and music**

Shakespeare, William, 1564-1616—Paraphrases. *See* **Shakespeare, William, 1564-1616—Adaptations**

Shakespeare, William, 1564-1616—Parodies, travesties, etc. 822.3

Shakespeare, William, 1564-1616—Poetry   811, etc.
   x Shakespeare in fiction, drama, poetry, etc.
Shakespeare, William, 1564-1616—Portraits
   822.3022
Shakespeare, William, 1564-1616—Psychological
   studies. *See* **Shakespeare, William, 1564-**
   1616—Biography—Psychology; Shake-
   speare, William, 1564-1616—Criticism, in-
   terpretation, etc.
Shakespeare, William, 1564-1616—Quotations
   822.3
Shakespeare, William, 1564-1616—Religion and eth-
   ics   822.3
Shakespeare, William, 1564-1616—Songs and music
   822.3
   x Shakespeare, William, 1564-1616—Music
Shakespeare, William, 1564-1616—Sonnets   822.3
   Use for criticism, etc., of the sonnets, not for the
   texts of the sonnets.
Shakespeare, William, 1564-1616—Stage history
   792; 822.3
   xx **Theater**
Shakespeare, William, 1564-1616—Stage setting and
   scenery. *See* **Shakespeare, William, 1564-**
   1616—Dramatic production
Shakespeare, William, 1564-1616—Style. *See*
   Shakespeare, William, 1564-1616—
   Technique
Shakespeare, William, 1564-1616—Technique
   822.3
   x Shakespeare, William, 1564-1616—Style
Shakespeare, William, 1564-1616—Tragedies
   822.3
   Use for criticism, etc., of the tragedies, not for
   the texts of the plays
Shape. *See* **Size and shape**
Shapes. *See* names of geometric shapes, e.g.
   Square; etc.
Sharecropping. *See* **Farm tenancy**
Shared custody. *See* **Child custody**
Shared housing   363.5
   Use for materials on individuals who share
   housing because of economic necessity,
   loneliness, etc.
   See also **Unmarried couples**
   x Families, Nonrelated; Home sharing; Mingles
   housing; Nonfamily households; Non-
   related families
   xx **Housing**
Shared reading books. *See* **Big books**
Shares of stock. *See* **Stocks**
Sharing of jobs. *See* **Job sharing**
Sheep   599.73; 636.3
   x Lambs
   xx **Livestock**
Sheet metalwork   671.8
   See also **Plate metalwork**
   x Press working of metal
   xx **Metalwork**
Sheffield plate   739.2
   xx **Plate**
Shellfish   594; 595.3; 641.3
   See also **Crabs; Crustacea; Lobsters; Mollusks**

Shells 564; 594
> *See also* **Mollusks**
> *x* Conchology; Sea shells
> *xx* **Mollusks**

Shells (Projectiles). *See* **Projectiles**

Shelterbelts. *See* **Windbreaks**

Shelters, Air raid. *See* **Air raid shelters**

Shelters, Animal. *See* **Animal shelters**

Shinto 299
> *xx* **Religions**

Ship building. *See* **Shipbuilding**

Ship models. *See* **Ships—Models**

Ship pilots. *See* **Pilots and pilotage**

Shipbuilding 623.8
> *See also* **Boatbuilding; Marine engines; Naval architecture; Ships; Ships—Models; Steamboats**
> *x* Architecture, Naval; Marine architecture; Ship building; Ships—Construction
> *xx* **Boatbuilding; Industrial arts; Naval architecture; Naval art and science**

Shipping (May subdiv. geog.) **386; 387**
> *See also* **Harbors; Inland navigation; Marine insurance; Maritime law; Merchant marine; Territorial waters**
> *x* Marine transportation; Ocean—Economic aspects; Ocean transportation; Sea transportation; Water transportation
> *xx* **Merchant marine; Transportation**

Shipping—United States 387.00973
> *x* United States—Shipping

Ships 387.2; 623.8
> *See also* **Boats and boating; Hospital ships; Merchant marine; Navies; Navigation; Sailing;** also types of ships and vessels, e.g. **Clipper ships; Steamboats; Submarines; Warships; Yachts and yachting;** etc.; and names of individual ships
> *x* Vessels (Ships)
> *xx* **Boats and boating; Naval architecture; Ocean travel; Shipbuilding**

Ships—Construction. *See* **Shipbuilding**

Ships in art. *See* **Marine painting**

Ships—Models 623.8
> *x* Ship models
> *xx* **Machinery—Models; Models and model making; Shipbuilding**

Shipwrecks 910.4
> *See also* **Salvage; Survival (after airplane accidents, shipwrecks, etc.);** also names of wrecked ships
> *x* Marine disasters; Wrecks
> *xx* **Accidents; Adventure and adventurers; Disasters; Navigation; Salvage; Voyages and travels**

Shoe industry 338.4; 685
> *xx* **Leather industry; Shoes**

Shoes 391; 646; 685
> *See also* **Shoe industry**
> *x* Boots; Footwear
> *xx* **Clothing and dress**

Shooting 799.3
> Use for materials on the use of firearms. Materi-

Shooting—*Continued*

    als on shooting game are entered under **Hunting.**

    See also **Archery; Decoys (Hunting); Firearms; Hunting**

    x Gunning

    xx **Firearms; Game and game birds; Hunting**

Shooting stars. *See* **Meteors**

Shop management. *See* **Factory management**

Shop practice. *See* **Machine shop practice**

Shop windows. *See* **Show windows**

Shoppers' guides. *See* **Consumer education; Shopping**

Shopping 640.73

    Use for materials on buying by the consumer. Materials on buying by government agencies and by commercial and industrial enterprises are entered under **Buying.**

    See also **Buying; Consumer education; Consumers**

    x Buyers' guides; Marketing (Home economics); Purchasing; Shoppers' guides

    xx **Buying; Consumer education; Home economics**

Shopping centers and malls 658.8

    x Malls, Shopping; Shopping malls

    xx **Retail trade**

Shopping malls. *See* **Shopping centers and malls**

Shops, Machine. *See* **Machine shops**

Short plays. *See* **One act plays**

Short stories 808.83; 813, etc.; Fic

    May be used for collections of short stories by one author as well as for collections by several authors. Materials on the technique of writing short stories are entered under **Short story.**

    x Collections of literature; Stories

    xx **Fiction; Literature—Collections**

Short stories—Indexes 016.80883

    xx **Indexes**

Short story 808.3

    Use for materials on the technique of short story writing. Collections of stories are entered under **Short stories.**

    See also **Storytelling**

    xx **Authorship; Fiction; Literature; Storytelling**

Short take off and landing aircraft 629.133

    x STOL aircraft

    xx **Jet planes**

Shorthand 653

    See also **Abbreviations**

    x Stenography

    xx **Abbreviations; Business education; Office practice; Writing**

Shortwave radio 621.3841

    See also **Amateur radio stations; Citizens band radio; Microwave communication systems; Microwaves**

    x High-frequency radio; Radio, Shortwave; U. H.F. radio; UHF radio; Ultrahigh frequency radio

    xx **Electric conductors; Electric waves; Radio frequency modulation**

Shotguns   799
   x Guns
   xx **Firearms**
Show business.   *See* **Performing arts**
Show windows   659.1
   x Shop windows; Window dressing
   xx **Advertising; Decoration and ornament; Windows**
Showers (Parties)   793.2
   xx **Parties**
Shows, Craft.   *See* **Craft shows**
Shrines (May subdiv. geog.)   **291.3; 726**
   See also **Miracles; Pilgrims and pilgrimages; Saints; Tombs**
   xx **Pilgrims and pilgrimages; Saints**
Shrubs   582.1; 635.9
   See also **Evergreens; Landscape gardening; Ornamental plants**
   xx **Botany; Landscape gardening; Trees**
Shuttles, Space.   *See* **Space shuttles**
Shyness.   *See* **Bashfulness**
Sibling sequence.   *See* **Birth order**
Siblings.   *See* **Brothers and sisters**
Sick   362.1
   See also

Church work with the sick	**Home nursing**
Cookery for the sick	**Hospitals**
Diseases	**Nursing**
First aid	**Terminally ill**
Health resorts, spas, etc.	

   x Invalids; Patients
   xx **Diseases; Handicapped; Home nursing; Nursing**
Sickness.   *See* **Diseases**
Sickness insurance.   *See* **Health insurance**
Sidereal system.   *See* **Stars**
Sieges.   *See* **Battles**
Sight.   *See* **Vision**
Sight saving books.   *See* **Large print books**
Sign boards.   *See* **Signs and signboards**
Sign language   419
   See also **Deaf—Means of communication; Indians of North America—Sign language; Signs and symbols**
   x Deaf—Sign language
   xx **Deaf—Means of communication; Language and languages; Signs and symbols**
Sign painting   667
   See also **Alphabets; Lettering; Signs and signboards**
   xx **Advertising; Lettering; Painting, Industrial; Signs and signboards**
Signals and signaling   384
   See also **Flags; Railroads—Signaling; Sonar**
   x Coastal signals; Fog signals; Military signaling; Naval signaling
   xx **Communication; Flags; Military art and science; Naval art and science; Navigation; Signs and symbols**
Signboards.   *See* **Signs and signboards**
Signets.   *See* **Seals (Numismatics)**
Signs (Advertising).   *See* **Electric signs; Signs and signboards**

Signs and signboards 659.13
>*See also* **Electric signs; Posters; Sign painting**
>*x* Billboards; Guide posts; Road signs; Sign
>>boards; Signboards; Signs (Advertising)
>*xx* **Advertising; Posters; Sign painting**

Signs and symbols 302.2; 419
>*See also*

Abbreviations	**Semiotics**
Ciphers	**Sign language**
Cryptography	**Signals and signaling**
Heraldry	**Symbolism**

>*x* Emblems; Symbols
>*xx* **Abbreviations; Semiotics; Sign language; Sym-**
>>**bolism**

Signs, Electric. *See* **Electric signs**

Silage and silos 633.2
>*x* Ensilage; Silos
>*xx* **Feeds; Forage plants**

Silent films 791.43
>Use for materials on films made in the early
>>days of the motion picture industry before
>>the development of films with sound.
>*x* Motion pictures, Silent; Silent motion pictures
>*xx* **Motion pictures**

Silent motion pictures. *See* **Silent films**

Silk 677
>*See also* **Silkworms**
>*xx* **Fibers**

Silk, Artificial. *See* **Rayon**

Silk screen printing 764
>*x* Screen printing; Serigraphy
>*xx* **Color printing; Stencil work; Textile printing**

Silkworms 638
>*x* Cocoons
>*xx* **Beneficial insects; Moths; Silk**

Silos. *See* **Silage and silos**

Silver 332.4; 669
>*See also* **Coinage; Jewelry; Money; Silverware;**
>>**Silverwork**
>*x* Bimetallism; Bullion
>*xx* **Coinage; Monetary policy; Money; Precious**
>>**metals**

Silver articles. *See* **Silverwork**

Silver mines and mining 622
>*See also* **Prospecting**

Silver work. *See* **Silverwork**

Silversmithing. *See* **Silverwork**

Silverware 642; 739.2
>*x* Flatware, Silver
>*xx* **Decorative arts; Silver; Silverwork; Tableware**

Silverwork 739.2
>*See also* **Indians of North America—Silverwork;**
>>**Jewelry; Plate; Silverware**
>*x* Silver articles; Silver work; Silversmithing
>*xx* **Art metalwork; Jewelry; Metalwork; Silver**

Simulation games in education 371.3
>*x* Educational gaming; Educational simulation
>>games; Gaming, Educational
>*xx* **Education; Game theory; Games**

Sin 170; 231; 241
>*See also* **Free will and determinism**
>*xx* **Christian ethics; Ethics; Good and evil; Salva-**
>>**tion; Theology**

Sinai Campaign, 1956 956
  x Anglo-French intervention in Egypt, 1956;
    Arab-Israel War, 1956; Israel-Arab War,
    1956
  xx **Egypt—History**
Singers 782.0092; 920
  xx **Musicians**
Singing 782; 783
  See also **Choirs (Music); Respiration; Song-
    books; Vocal music; Voice**
  x School music; Vocal culture; Voice culture
  xx **Choirs (Music); Vocal music; Voice**
Singing games 796.1
  xx **Games**
Singing societies. *See* **Choral societies**
Single child. *See* **Only child**
Single men 155.6; 305.38
  See also **Widowers**
  x Men, Single; Unmarried men
  xx **Men; Single people**
Single parent family 306.85
  Use for materials on households in which a par-
    ent living without a partner is rearing chil-
    dren. Also use for materials on members of
    such a household. For materials focusing on
    parents who were not married at the time of
    the birth of their progeny, use **Unmarried
    fathers; Unmarried mothers.**
  See also **Children of divorced parents; Unmarried
    fathers; Unmarried mothers; Widowers;
    Widows**
  x Children of single parents; Fathers, Single par-
    ent; Mothers, Single parent; One parent
    family; Parents, Single; Parents without
    partners; Single parents
  xx **Family; Parenting, Part-time; Unmarried fa-
    thers; Unmarried mothers; Widowers; Wid-
    ows**
Single parents. *See* **Single parent family**
Single people 155.6; 305.9
  See also **Single men; Single women; Unmarried
    couples**
  x People, Single; Persons, Single; Unmarried
    people
Single rail railroads. *See* **Monorail railroads**
Single women 155.6; 305.48
  See also **Widows**
  x Unmarried women; Women, Single
  xx **Single people; Women**
Sirius 523.8
  xx **Stars**
Sisterhoods. *See* **Religious orders for women**
Sisters and brothers. *See* **Brothers and sisters**
Sisters (in religious orders, congregations, etc.). *See*
    Nuns
Sit-down strikes. *See* **Strikes and lockouts**
Site oriented art. *See* **Earthworks (Art)**
Sitters (Babysitters). *See* **Babysitters**
Six Day War, 1967. *See* **Israel-Arab War, 1967**
Sixteenth century 909.08
  See note under **Nineteenth century.**
  See also **Reformation**
  x 1500-1599 (16th century)
  xx **Reformation; Renaissance**

Size and shape   516

See also names of geometric shapes, e.g.
        Square; etc.
    x Large and small; Shape; Small and large
    xx **Concepts; Perception**
Skating.   See **Ice skating; Roller skating**
Skeletal remains.   See **Anthropometry**
Skeleton   591.4; 611

Use for materials on the human or animal skeleton.

See also **Bones**
    xx **Bones**
Skepticism   149; 211

See also **Agnosticism; Belief and doubt; Truth**
    x Scepticism; Unbelief
    xx **Agnosticism; Atheism; Belief and doubt;**
        Faith; Free thought; Philosophy; Rationalism; Religion; Truth
Sketching.   See **Drawing**
Skiing, Snow.   See **Skis and skiing**
Skiing, Water.   See **Water skiing**
Skilled workers.   See **Labor**
Skills, Life.   See **Life skills**
Skin   611; 612.7
Skin—Care and hygiene   616.5; 646.7
Skin—Diseases   616.5

See also names of skin diseases, e.g. **Acne;** etc.
    x Dermatitis
    xx **Diseases**
Skin diving   797.2

Use for free diving with masks, fins, and snorkel.

See also **Scuba diving; Undersea research stations; Underwater exploration**
    x Diving, Skin; Free diving; Frogmen and frogwomen; Snorkeling; Underwater swimming
    xx **Diving; Diving, Submarine; Oceanography—Research; Salvage; Underwater exploration; Water sports**
Skin garments.   See **Leather garments**
Skins.   See **Hides and skins**
Skis and skiing   796.93

See also **Water skiing**
    x Skiing, Snow
    xx **Winter sports**
Skits   791
    x Entertainments
Sky   520; 551.5
    xx **Astronomy; Atmosphere**
Sky diving.   See **Skydiving**
Sky hijacking.   See **Hijacking of airplanes**
Sky laboratories.   See **Space stations**
Skydiving   797.5
    x Sky diving
    xx **Aeronautical sports**
Skyjacking.   See **Hijacking of airplanes**
Skyscrapers   690; 725
    x High rise buildings
    xx **Architecture; Building, Iron and steel; Industrial buildings; Office buildings**
Skyscrapers—Earthquake effects   690; 725
    xx **Earthquakes**
Slander (Law).   See **Libel and slander**

Slang. *See* subjects with the subdivision *Slang,* e.g.
    English language—Slang; etc.
Slanted journalism. *See* **Journalism—Objectivity**
Slave trade   341; 345; 380.1
    xx **International law; Slavery; Slavery—United
        States**
Slavery (May subdiv. geog.)   177; 306.3; 326; 342
    See also **Peonage; Slave trade**
    x Abolition of slavery; Antislavery; Compulsory
        labor; Emancipation of slaves; Forced la-
        bor; Servitude
    xx **Contract labor; Freedom; Labor; Sociology**
Slavery—United States   306.3; 326.0973
    See also **Abolitionists; Blacks; Slave trade;
        Southern States—History; State rights; Un-
        derground railroad**
    x Emancipation of slaves
    xx **Blacks; Southern States—History; Under-
        ground railroad; United States—History—
        1861-1865, Civil War**
Slavery—United States—Fiction   Fic
    x Stories
    xx **Fiction; Historical fiction**
Sleds and sledding   796.9
    xx **Winter sports**
Sleep   154.6; 613.7
    See also **Bedtime; Dreams; Insomnia**
    xx **Brain; Dreams; Health; Hygiene; Insomnia;
        Mind and body; Psychophysiology; Rest;
        Subconsciousness**
Sleeplessness. *See* **Insomnia**
Sleight of hand. *See* **Juggling; Magic**
Slide projectors. *See* **Projectors**
Slide rule   510.28
    xx **Calculators; Logarithms; Measuring instru-
        ments**
Slides (Photography)   778.2
    See also **Filmstrips**
    x Color slides; Lantern slides; Photographic
        slides
    xx **Filmstrips; Photography**
Slow learning children   155.4; 371.92
    Use for materials on children who have between
        average and mentally deficient intelligence
        and whose social behavior is less than age
        level standards.
    See also **Individualized instruction; Learning dis-
        abilities; Mentally handicapped children**
    x Children, Retarded; Retarded children
    xx **Exceptional children; Mentally handicapped
        children**
Slum clearance. *See* **Urban renewal**
Slumber songs. *See* **Lullabies**
Small and large. *See* **Size and shape**
Small arms. *See* **Firearms**
Small business   338.6; 658.02
    Use for materials on small independent enter-
        prises as contrasted with "big business."
    See also **Entrepreneurship; Home business**
    x Business, Small
    xx **Business; Self-employed**
Small loans. *See* **Personal loans**

Smell   152.1
>   *See also* Nose
>   *xx* **Senses and sensation**
Smelting   669
>   *See also* **Blast furnaces; Electrometallurgy; Metallurgy; Ore dressing**
>   *xx* **Furnaces; Metallurgy**
Smoke-ending programs.   *See* **Smoking cessation programs**
Smoke prevention   363.73; 628.5
>   *See also* **Fuel; Furnaces**
>   *x* Prevention of smoke
Smoke stacks.   *See* **Chimneys**
Smokeless powder.   *See* **Gunpowder**
Smoking   178; 613.85
>   *See also* **Cigarettes; Cigars; Marijuana; Tobacco; Tobacco habit; Tobacco pipes**
>   *xx* **Tobacco**
Smoking cessation programs   613.85
>   *x* How-to-stop-smoking programs; Quit-smoking programs; Smoke-ending programs
>   *xx* **Tobacco habit**
Smuggling   364.1
>   *x* Contraband trade
>   *xx* **Crime; Tariff**
Smuggling of drugs.   *See* **Drug traffic**
Snakes   597.96
>   *See also* names of specific snakes, e.g. **Rattlesnakes;** etc.
>   *x* Serpents; Vipers
>   *xx* **Reptiles**
Snorkeling.   *See* **Skin diving**
Snow   551.57
>   *x* Precipitation (Meteorology)
>   *xx* **Meteorology; Rain; Storms; Water; Weather**
Snowmobiles   629.22
>   *xx* **All terrain vehicles; Vehicles**
Soap   668
>   *See also* **Detergents, Synthetic**
>   *xx* **Cleaning; Cleaning compounds**
Soap box derbies   796.6
>   *x* Racing
Soap carving.   *See* **Soap sculpture**
Soap sculpture   736
>   *x* Soap carving
>   *xx* **Modeling; Sculpture**
Soaring flight.   *See* **Gliding and soaring**
Sobriquets.   *See* **Nicknames**
Soccer   796.334
>   *xx* **Ball games; College sports; Football**
Social action   302
>   *See also* **Social work;** also subjects with the subdivision *Citizen participation,* e.g. **City planning—United States—Citizen participation;** etc.
>   *x* Action, Social; Activism, Social
>   *xx* **Social policy; Social problems; Social work**
Social adjustment   158; 303.3
>   *See also* **Socially handicapped**
>   *x* Adjustment, Social
>   *xx* **Human behavior; Human relations; Social psychology**
Social alienation.   *See* **Alienation (Social psychology)**

Social anthropology. *See* **Ethnology**
Social aspects. *See* subjects with the subdivision
     Social aspects, e.g. **Genetic engineering—**
     Social aspects; etc.
Social behavior. *See* **Human behavior**
Social case work   361.3
    See also **Counseling; Parole; Probation**
    x Case work, Social; Family social work
    xx **Counseling; Social work**
Social change   303.4; 909
    See also **Community development; Moderniza-**
      tion; Sociobiology; Urbanization
    x Change, Social; Cultural change; Social evolu-
      tion
    xx **Anthropology; Evolution; Progress; Social sci-**
      ences; Sociology
Social classes   305.5; 323.3
    See also **Aristocracy; Class consciousness; Elite**
      (Social sciences); Labor; Middle classes;
      Nobility; Upper classes
    x Class distinction; Rank; Social distinctions
    xx **Caste; Equality; Manners and customs; Social**
      conflict; Sociology
Social conditions   909
    Use for general materials relating to several or
      all of the following topics: labor, poverty,
      education, health, housing, recreation,
      moral conditions.
    See also

Cost of living	**Social movements**
Counter culture	**Social problems**
Economic conditions	**Social surveys**
Labor	**Standard of living**
Moral conditions	**Urbanization**
Quality of life	

    also names of groups of people and names of
      countries, cities, etc. with the subdivision
      Social conditions, e.g. **Indians of North**
      America—Social conditions; Jews—Social
      conditions; Blacks—Social conditions;
      United States—Social conditions; Chicago
      (Ill.)—Social conditions; etc.
    x Social history
    xx **Social ethics; Sociology**
Social conflict   303.6
    See also **Conflict of generations; Role conflict;**
      Social classes
    x Class conflict; Class struggle; Conflict, Social
    xx **Social psychology; Sociology**
Social conformity. *See* **Conformity**
Social customs. *See* **Manners and customs;** and
      names of ethnic groups, countries, cities,
      etc. with the subdivision *Social life and cus-*
      toms, e.g. **Indians of North America—**
      Social life and customs; Jews—Social life
      and customs; United States—Social life and
      customs; etc.
Social democracy. *See* **Socialism**
Social distinctions. *See* **Social classes**
Social drinking. *See* **Drinking of alcoholic bever-**
     ages
Social ecology. *See* **Human ecology**
Social equality. *See* **Equality**

Social ethics   177
See also
Bioethics   Political ethics
Citizenship   Sexual ethics
Crime   Social conditions
Friendship   Social problems
   x Ethics, Social
   xx **Ethics; Social problems**
Social evolution.   *See* **Social change**
Social group work   361.4; 362
   x Group work, Social
   xx **Associations; Clubs; Social work**
Social groups   302.3
   See also **Elite (Social sciences); Leadership;
      Problem solving, Group; Social psychology;
      Social values**
   x Group dynamics; Groups, Social
   xx **Sociology**
Social history.   *See* **Social conditions**
Social hygiene.   *See* **Prostitution; Public health;
      Sexual hygiene**
Social insurance.   *See* **Social security**
Social learning.   *See* **Socialization**
Social life and customs.   *See* **Manners and customs;**
      and names of ethnic groups, countries, cit-
      ies, etc. with the subdivision *Social life and
      customs,* e.g. **Indians of North America—
      Social life and customs; Jews—Social life
      and customs; United States—Social life and
      customs;** etc.
Social medicine (May subdiv. geog.)   362.1
      Use for materials on the study of social, genetic,
      and environmental influences on human
      disease and disability, as well as the promo-
      tion of health measures to protect both the
      individual and the community.
   See also **Hospices; Medical ethics**
   x Medical care—Social aspects; Medical sociol-
      ogy; Medicine, Social; Medicine—Social as-
      pects
   xx **Medical ethics; Public health; Public welfare;
      Sociology**
Social movements   303.4
      Names of all social movements are not included
      in this List but may be added as needed.
   See also **Anti-apartheid movement; Antinuclear
      movement; New Age movement; Pro-choice
      movement; Pro-life movement; Sanctuary
      movement; Survivalism**
   xx **Social conditions; Social problems; Social psy-
      chology**
Social planning.   *See* **Social policy**
Social policy   361.6
   See also **Economic policy; Land reform; Social
      action;** also names of countries, cities, etc.
      with the subdivision *Social policy,* e.g.
      United States—Social policy; etc.
   x National planning; Planning, National; Social
      planning; State planning
   xx **Economic policy**

Social problems 361.1

See also

Charities	Juvenile delinquency
Children—Employment	Prostitution
Community centers	Public health
Crime	Race discrimination
Discrimination	Race relations
Divorce	Social action
Ethnic relations	Social ethics
Eugenics	Social movements
Homelessness	Social surveys
Housing	Standard of living
Illegitimacy	Substance abuse
Immigration and emigra-tion	Suicide
	Unemployed

   x Reform, Social; Social reform; Social welfare

  xx **Social conditions; Social ethics; Sociology**

Social problems and the church.   *See* **Church and social problems**

Social problems in education.   *See* **Educational sociology**

Social psychology 302

See also

Alienation (Social psychology)	Interviewing
	National characteristics
Attitude (Psychology)	Political psychology
Class consciousness	Psychology, Applied
Crowds	Social adjustment
Discrimination	Social conflict
Ethnopsychology	Social movements
Human relations	Violence

   x Mass psychology; Psychology, Social

  xx **Crowds; Ethnopsychology; Psychology; Social groups; Sociology**

Social reform.   *See* **Social problems**

Social role 302

   See also **Role conflict; Role playing; Sex role**

   x Role, Social

Social sciences 300

   Use for general and comprehensive materials dealing with the various branches of the social sciences, such as sociology, political science, economics, etc.

   See also **Cross cultural studies; Economics; Human behavior; Political science; Social change; Sociology**

   x Social studies

Social security 368.4

   See also **Old age pensions; Workers' compensation**

   x Insurance, Social; Insurance, State and compulsory; Insurance, Workers'; Labor—Insurance; Security, Social; Social insurance; State and insurance

  xx **Pensions**

Social service.   *See* **Social work**

Social settlements 361.7; 362.5

   See also **Boys' clubs; Community centers; Girls' clubs; Playgrounds;** also names of settlements, e.g. **Hull House;** etc.

   x Church settlements; Neighborhood centers; Settlements, Social

  xx **Charities; Social work; Welfare work in industry**

Social studies. *See* **Geography; History; Social sciences**

Social surveys (May subdiv. geog.) **301**
> Use for materials on the methods employed in conducting surveys of social and economic conditions of communities and also for surveys of individual regions or cities. In the latter case a second heading may be used for the name of a region or city followed by the subdivision *Social conditions.*
>
> *See also* **Educational surveys**
>
> *x* Community surveys; Surveys
>
> *xx* **City planning; Regional planning; Social conditions; Social problems; Sociology**

Social surveys—United States 301
> *x* United States—Social surveys

Social values 303.3
> Use for materials on the principles and standards of human interaction within a particular group.
>
> *See also* **Quality of life**
>
> *x* Group values
>
> *xx* **Conformity; Human relations; Quality of life; Social groups; Values**

Social welfare. *See* **Charities; Public welfare; Social problems; Social work**

Social work 361.3
> Use for materials on the methods employed in welfare work, public or private. Materials on privately supported welfare activities are entered under **Charities.** Materials on tax-supported welfare activities are entered under **Public welfare.**
>
> *See also*

Charities	**Public welfare**
Community organization	**Social action**
Crisis centers	**Social case work**
Group homes	**Social group work**
Hotlines (Telephone counseling)	**Social settlements**
	Welfare work in industry

> *x* Philanthropy; Social service; Social welfare; Welfare work
>
> *xx* **Social action**

Social work with the elderly 362.6
> Use same form for social work with other classes of people.
>
> *xx* **Elderly**

Socialism (May subdiv. geog.) **320.5; 335**
> *See also*

Capitalism	**policy**
Communism	**Labor**
Dialectical materialism	**Labor unions**
Equality	**National socialism**
Government ownership	**Proletariat**
Individualism	**Utopias**
Industry—Government	

> *x* Collectivism; Marxism; Social democracy
>
> *xx* **Capitalism; Communism; Cooperation; Economics; Equality; Individualism; Labor; National socialism; Political science; Sociology**

Socialism—United States 320.5; 335.00973
> *x* United States—Socialism

Socialization   303.3

Use for materials on the process by which individuals acquire group values and learn to function effectively in society.

See also **Peer pressure**

x Children—Socialization; Social learning

xx **Acculturation; Child rearing; Education; Sociology**

Socialization of industry.   *See* **Government ownership; Industry—Government policy**

Socialized medicine.   *See* **Charities, Medical; Health insurance; Medicine, State**

Socially handicapped   362

x Culturally deprived; Culturally handicapped; Disadvantaged; Underprivileged

xx **Handicapped; Social adjustment**

Socially handicapped children   362.7

x Culturally deprived children; Culturally handicapped children; Disadvantaged children; Underprivileged children

xx **Handicapped children**

Socials.   *See* **Church entertainments**

Societies   060

Use for general materials about societies, etc. The headings enumerated below represent various types of societies and associations. Add others as needed. Materials about, and publications of, societies devoted to specific subjects are entered under the subject with the subdivision *Societies,* e.g. **Agriculture—Societies;** etc.

See also

Associations	**Labor unions**
Boys' clubs	**Men—Societies**
Choral societies	**Parents' and teachers' as-**
Clubs	**sociations**
Cooperative societies	**Secret societies**
Educational associations	**Women—Societies**
Girls' clubs	

also general subjects with the subdivision *Societies,* e.g. **Agriculture—Societies;** etc.; and names of individual societies

x Learned societies

xx **Associations; Clubs**

Societies, Cooperative.   *See* **Cooperative societies**

Society and art.   *See* **Art and society**

Society and language.   *See* **Sociolinguistics**

Society, Nonliterate folk.   *See* **Nonliterate folk society**

Society of Friends   289.6

x Friends, Society of; Quakers

xx **Congregationalism**

Society of Jesus.   *See* **Jesuits**

Society, Primitive.   *See* **Nonliterate folk society**

Society, Upper.   *See* **Upper classes**

Sociobiology   304.2; 304.5

Use for materials on the biological basis of social behavior, especially as transmitted genetically.

x Biology—Social aspects; Biosociology

xx **Psychology, Comparative; Social change**

Sociolinguistics   306.4

Use for materials on the study of the social as-

Sociolinguistics—*Continued*

pects of language, particularly linguistic behavior as determined by sociocultural factors.

x Language and society; Society and language;
Sociology and language

xx **Language and languages; Sociology**

Sociology (May subdiv. by religion adjective form,
e.g. **Sociology, Christian;** etc.) **301**

Use for systematic studies on the structure of society. General materials dealing with sociology, political science, economics, etc. are entered under **Social sciences.**

See also

Aristocracy	**Population**
Cities and towns	**Race relations**
Civilization	**Slavery**
Communism	**Social change**
Educational sociology	**Social classes**
Equality	**Social conditions**
Ethnic relations	**Social conflict**
Ethnopsychology	**Social groups**
Family	**Social medicine**
Heredity	**Social problems**
Human ecology	**Social psychology**
Immigration and emigra-	**Social surveys**
tion	**Socialism**
Individualism	**Socialization**
Labor	**Sociolinguistics**
Nonliterate folk society	**Unemployed**

xx **Social sciences**

Sociology and language. *See* **Sociolinguistics**

Sociology, Christian 261

See note under **Church and social problems.**

See also **Christianity and economics; Liberation
theology**

x Christian sociology

xx **Church and social problems**

Sociology, Educational. *See* **Educational sociology**

Sociology, Rural 307.72

Use for materials on the discipline of rural sociology and the theory of social organization
in rural areas. Materials on the rural conditions of particular regions, countries, cities,
etc. are entered under the place with the
subdivision *Rural conditions.* Descriptive,
popular and literary materials on living in
the country are entered under **Country life.**

See also **Country life; Farm family; Farm life;
Peasantry; Urbanization;** also names of
countries, states, etc. with the subdivision
Rural conditions, e.g. **United States—Rural
conditions;** etc.

x Rural sociology

xx **Country life; Farm family; Farm life; Peasantry**

Sociology, Urban 307.76

See also **Cities and towns; City life; Urban renewal; Urbanization**

x Urban sociology

xx **Cities and towns**

Sodium content of food. *See* **Food—Sodium content**

618

Softball　796.357
　　xx　**Baseball**
Software, Computer.　*See*　**Computer software**
Software viruses.　*See*　**Computer viruses**
Soil conservation　631.4
　　See also　**Erosion; Soil erosion**
　　x　Conservation of the soil
　　xx　**Conservation of natural resources; Environmental protection; Erosion; Soil erosion**
Soil erosion　631.4
　　See also　**Soil conservation**
　　x　Top soil loss
　　xx　**Erosion; Soil conservation**
Soil fertility.　*See*　**Soils**
Soil mechanics.　*See*　**Soils (Engineering)**
Soilless agriculture.　*See*　**Aeroponics; Hydroponics**
Soils　631.4
　　See also

Agricultural chemistry	**Fertilizers and manures**
Clay	**Irrigation**
Compost	**Reclamation of land**
Drainage	**Soils (Engineering)**

　　also headings beginning with the word　**Soil**
　　x　Soil fertility
　　xx　**Agricultural chemistry; Agriculture; Geology, Economic**
Soils—Bacteriology　631.4
　　See also　**Agricultural bacteriology**
　　xx　**Agricultural bacteriology; Sanitary engineering**
Soils (Engineering)　620.1
　　x　Earthwork; Soil mechanics
　　xx　**Foundations; Roads; Soils; Structural engineering**
Soils, Lunar.　*See*　**Lunar soil**
Solar batteries　621.31
　　x　Batteries, Solar; Solar cells; Sun powered batteries
　　xx　**Electric batteries; Photovoltaic power generation; Solar radiation**
Solar cells.　*See*　**Photovoltaic power generation; Solar batteries**
Solar eclipses.　*See*　**Eclipses, Solar**
Solar energy　621.47
　　See also　**Photovoltaic power generation; Solar engines; Solar heating**
　　x　Solar power
　　xx　**Energy resources; Renewable energy resources; Solar radiation; Sun**
Solar engines　621.47
　　xx　**Engines; Solar energy**
Solar heat.　*See*　**Solar heating**
Solar heating　621.47; 697
　　See also　names of applications, e.g.　**Solar homes; etc.**
　　x　Solar heat
　　xx　**Heating; Solar energy**
Solar homes　697; 728
　　xx　**Architecture, Domestic; Houses; Solar heating**
Solar physics.　*See*　**Sun**
Solar power.　*See*　**Solar energy**
Solar radiation　621.47
　　See also　**Greenhouse effect; Solar batteries; Solar energy; Sunspots**

Solar radiation—*Continued*
  x Radiation, Solar; Sun—Radiation
  xx **Meteorology; Space environment**
Solar system   523.2
    See also **Comets; Earth; Meteors; Moon; Plan-**
        ets; Sun; also names of planets, e.g. **Saturn**
        (Planet); etc.
  xx **Astronomy; Planets; Stars; Sun**
Solder and soldering   671.5
    See also **Alloys; Welding**
    x Brazing
  xx **Metals; Metalwork; Plumbing; Welding**
Soldiers (May subdiv. geog.)   **355.0092; 920**
    See also **Mercenary soldiers; Missing in action;**
        also names of countries with the subdivision
        Army—Military life, e.g. **United States.**
        Army—Military life; etc.
    x Army life; Soldiers' life
  xx **Armies; Military personnel**
Soldiers' bonus. *See* **Pensions, Military**
Soldiers' handbooks. *See* **United States. Army—**
        Handbooks, manuals, etc.
Soldiers—Hygiene. *See* **Military health**
Soldiers' life. *See* **Soldiers;** and names of countries
        with the subdivision *Army—Military life,*
        e.g. **United States. Army—Military life;**
        etc.
Soldiers' songs. *See* **War songs**
Soldiers—United States   355.0092; 920
    x G.I.'s; GIs; United States—Soldiers
Solid geometry. *See* **Geometry**
Solid waste disposal. *See* **Refuse and refuse dis-**
        posal; Salvage (Waste, etc.)
Solids   530.4; 531; 541
  xx **Chemistry, Physical and theoretical; Physics**
Solitaire (Game)   795.4
    x Patience (Game)
Solution achievement. *See* **Problem solving**
Solvent abuse   362.29
    x Aerosol sniffing; Glue sniffing; Inhalation
        abuse of solvents; Paint sniffing
  xx **Substance abuse**
Somatology. *See* **Physical anthropology**
Sonar   621.389
    x Echo ranging; Sound navigation
  xx **Signals and signaling**
Sonata   784.18
  xx **Musical form**
Sonatas   784.18
  xx **Orchestral music**
Song books. *See* **Songbooks**
Song writing. *See* **Composition (Music); Popular**
        music—Writing and publishing
Songbooks   782.42
    Use for general collections of songs, largely secu-
        lar in content, arranged principally for
        mixed voices and scored on two staves, as
        in their sacred counterpart, the hymnals.
    See also **School songbooks**
    x Community songbooks; Song books
  xx **Singing; Songs**
Songbooks, School. *See* **School songbooks**
Songs (May subdiv. geog. adjective form, e.g. **Songs,**
        American; etc.)   **782.42**
    Use for collections of songs that include both
        words and music, and for materials about
        songs. Collections of songs that contain the
        words but not the music are entered under
        Poetry—Collections.
    Names of all types of songs are not included in
        this List but are to be added as needed.

Songs—*Continued*
See also

Ballads	Popular music
Black songs	School songbooks
Carols	Sea songs
Children's songs	Songbooks
Folk songs	State songs
Hymns	Students' songs
Lullabies	War songs
National songs	

also general subjects, names of classes of persons, and of schools, colleges, etc. with the subdivision *Songs and music,* e.g. **Cowhands—Songs and music; Surfing—Songs and music; United States Military Academy—Songs and music;** etc.; and names of individual songs

xx **Poetry—Collections; Vocal music**

Songs, African   782.42096
   x African songs; Folk songs, African; Folk songs, Black (African)

Songs, American   782.420973
   See also **Black songs; Folk songs—United States; National songs, American**
   x American songs; United States—Songs

Songs for children.   *See* **Children's songs**
Songs, National.   *See* **National songs**
Songs, Popular.   *See* **Popular music**
Songwriters.   *See* **Composers; Lyricists**
Sons and fathers.   *See* **Fathers and sons**
Sons and mothers.   *See* **Mothers and sons**
Soothsaying.   *See* **Divination**
Soporifics.   *See* **Narcotics**
Sorcery.   *See* **Occultism; Witchcraft**
Sororities.   *See* **Fraternities and sororities**
Sorrow.   *See* **Joy and sorrow**
Soubriquets.   *See* **Nicknames**

Soul   128; 233
   See also **Immortality; Personality; Psychology; Reincarnation; Spiritual life**
   x Spirit
   xx **Future life; Man (Theology); Personality; Philosophy; Reincarnation**

Sound   534; 620.2
   See also

Architectural acoustics	Noise
Computer sound process-ing	Phonetics
	Soundproofing
Hearing	Sounds
Music—Acoustics and physics	Ultrasonics
	Vibration

   x Acoustics
   xx **Music; Music—Acoustics and physics; Physics; Pneumatics; Radiation**

Sound effects   534; 620.2
Sound insulation.   *See* **Soundproofing**
Sound navigation.   *See* **Sonar**
Sound processing, Computer.   *See* **Computer sound processing**
Sound recording.   *See* **Sound—Recording and reproducing**
Sound—Recording and reproducing   621.389
   See also **Compact disc players; High-fidelity**

Sound—Recording and reproducing—*Continued*
    sound systems; Intercommunication systems;
    Stereophonic sound systems; also methods
    of recording, e.g. **Magnetic recorders and
    recording;** etc.
  x Sound recording
  xx **Motion pictures; Phonograph; Radio**
Sound recordings   621.389; 780.26
    Use for materials on all types of sound record-
        ings including cylinders, discs, films, tapes,
        and wires.
    See also **Compact discs; Magnetic recorders and
        recording; Talking books**
  x Audio cassettes; Audiotapes; Cassette tapes,
        Audio; Compact discs, Audio; Discography;
        Discs, Sound; Phonograph records; Record-
        ings, Sound; Records, Phonograph; Tape re-
        cordings, Audio
  xx **Audiovisual materials; Magnetic recorders and
        recording**
Sound waves   534; 620.2
    See also **Ultrasonic waves**
  xx **Vibration; Waves**
Soundproofing   693.8
  x Insulation (Sound); Sound insulation
  xx **Architectural acoustics; Sound**
Sounds   534; 620.2
  xx **Sound**
Soups   641.8
  xx **Cookery**
South Africa   968
  x Africa, South; Republic of South Africa;
        Union of South Africa
South Africa—History   968
South Africa—Race relations   305.800968; 968
    See also **Anti-apartheid movement; Apartheid**
  xx **Race relations**
South African Dutch. *See* **Afrikaners**
South Africans, Afrikaans-speaking. *See* **Afrikaners**
South America   980
  xx **America; Latin America**
South America—Exploration. *See* **America—
        Exploration**
South American literature. *See* **Latin American lit-
        erature**
South Atlantic States. *See* **Atlantic States**
South Korea. *See* **Korea (South)**
South Pacific region. *See* **Oceania**
South Pole   998
    See also **Antarctic regions**
  x Polar expeditions
  xx **Antarctic regions; Polar regions**
South Sea Islands. *See* **Oceania**
South Seas. *See* **Oceania**
South (U.S.). *See* **Southern States**
Southeast Asia   959
    Use for materials on Southeast Asia including
        Burma, Thailand, Malaysia, Singapore, In-
        donesia, Vietnam, Cambodia, Laos, and the
        Philippines
  x Asia, Southeast
Southern Africa   968
    Use for materials dealing collectively with the

Southern Africa—*Continued*
area south of the countries of Zaire and
Tanzania. Southern Africa includes the po-
litical entities of Angola, Botswana, Como-
ros, Lesotho, Madagascar, Malawi, Mozam-
bique, Namibia, South Africa, Swaziland,
Zambia, and Zimbabwe. Materials on the
Republic of South Africa are entered under
South Africa.
  x Africa, Southern
Southern literature. *See* **American literature—**
    Southern States
Southern States 975
  x South (U.S.)
  xx **United States**
Southern States—Cookery. *See* **Cookery—**
    Southern States
Southern States—History 975
  See also **Slavery—United States**
  xx **Slavery—United States; United States—**
    History
Southwest, New. *See* **Southwestern States**
Southwest, Old. *See* **Old Southwest**
Southwest Pacific region. *See* **Oceania**
Southwestern States 979
  Use for materials on that part of the United
    States that corresponds roughly with the old
    Spanish province of New Mexico, including
    the present Arizona, New Mexico, southern
    Colorado, Utah, Nevada, and California.
  x Southwest, New
  xx **United States**
Sovereigns. *See* **Kings, queens, rulers, etc.; Monar-**
    chy; Roman emperors
Soviet artificial satellites. *See* **Artificial satellites,**
    Soviet
Soviet bloc. *See* **Communist countries**
Soviet intervention in Czechoslovakia. *See*
    Czechoslovakia—History—1968-1989
Soviet literatures. *See* **Soviet Union—Literatures**
Soviet people. *See* **Soviets (People)**
Soviet Union 947
  Materials on the Russian empire or the Union of
    Soviet Socialist Republics are entered under
    Soviet Union, regardless of time period. Ap-
    propriate period subdivisions may be
    added. Materials on the citizens of the So-
    viet Union are entered under **Soviets (Peo-**
    ple). For materials on the individual ethnic
    groups of the Soviet Union, use the name of
    the group, e.g. **Russians.**
  The adjective **Soviet** is used to refer to the So-
    viet Union as a whole, e.g. **Artificial satel-**
    lites, Soviet; etc. For materials on topics
    pertaining to individual republics, nationali-
    ties, or ethnic groups of the Soviet Union,
    use the appropriate qualifier, e.g., **Russian**
    language.
  See also **Russians; Soviets (People)**
  x Russia; U.S.S.R.; Union of Soviet Socialist
    Republics; USSR
Soviet Union—Communism. *See* **Communism—**
    Soviet Union
Soviet Union—History 947

Soviet Union—History—1905, Revolution   947.08
Soviet Union—History—1917-   947.084
Soviet Union—History—1917-1921, Revolution
      947.084
   x Revolution, Russian; Russian revolution
Soviet Union—History—1925-1953   947.084
Soviet Union—History—1939-1940, War with
      Finland.   *See* **Russo-Finnish War, 1939-
      1940**
Soviet Union—History—1953-   947.085
Soviet Union—History—1953-1985   947.085
Soviet Union—History—1985-   947.085
Soviet Union—Literatures   890
   Use for materials discussing several of the litera-
      tures of the Soviet Union. Materials discuss-
      ing literature in the Russian language, which
      is the principal state and cultural language
      of the Soviet Union, are entered under **Rus-
      sian literature.**
   x Literatures of the Soviet Union; Soviet litera-
      tures
Soviets (People)   947
   Use for materials on the citizens of the Soviet
      Union as a whole. For materials on the indi-
      vidual ethnic groups of the Soviet Union,
      use the name for the ethnic group, e.g. **Rus-
      sians;** etc.
   x Soviet people
   xx **Soviet Union**
Soybean   633.3
   xx **Forage plants**
Space age.   *See* **Astronautics and civilization**
Space and time   115
   See also **Fourth dimension; Personal space**
   x Time and space
   xx **Relativity (Physics)**
Space-based weapons.   *See* **Space weapons**
Space biology   574.19; 612
   Use for materials on the biology of man or other
      earth life while in outer space. Materials on
      the question of life on other planets and ma-
      terials on life indigenous to outer space are
      entered under **Life on other planets.**
   See also **Life on other planets; Space medicine**
   x Astrobiology; Bioastronautics; Cosmobiology;
      Exobiology
   xx **Biology; Space sciences**
Space chemistry   523
   x Cosmic chemistry; Cosmochemistry
   xx **Chemistry**
Space colonies   999
   Use for materials on communities established in
      space or on natural extraterrestrial bodies.
      Materials on bases established on natural
      extraterrestrial bodies for specific functions
      other than colonization are entered under
      Extraterrestrial bases. Materials on
      manned installations orbiting in space for
      specific functions, such as servicing space
      ships, are entered under **Space stations.**
   See also **Extraterrestrial bases**
   x Colonies, Space; Communities, Space; Outer
      space—Colonies

Space colonies—*Continued*

    xx **Astronautics and civilization; Extraterrestrial bases**

Space commercialization. *See* **Space industrialization**

Space communication. *See* **Astronautics—Communication systems; Interstellar communication**

Space craft. *See* **Space vehicles**

Space debris **629.4**

    x Debris, Space; Junk in space; Orbital debris; Outer space—Pollution; Pollution, Space; Space pollution

    xx **Pollution; Space environment**

Space environment **629.4**

    See also **Cosmic rays; Solar radiation; Space debris**

    x Environment, Space; Extraterrestrial environment; Space weather

    xx **Astronomy; Outer space**

Space exploration (Astronautics). *See* **Outer space—Exploration**

Space flight **629.4**

    See also

Astrodynamics	**Navigation (Astronautics)**
Astronauts	**Orbital rendezvous (Space**
Extravehicular activity	**flight)**
(Space flight)	**Outer space—Exploration**
Interplanetary voyages	**Space medicine**

    also names of projects, e.g. **Gemini project;** etc.

    x Humans in space; Man in space; Manned space flight; People in space; Rocket flight; Space flight, Manned; Space travel

    xx **Aeronautics—Flights; Astrodynamics; Astronautics; Interplanetary voyages; Navigation (Astronautics); Space medicine**

Space flight—Law and legislation. *See* **Space law**

Space flight, Manned. *See* **Space flight**

Space flight to the moon **629.45**

    Use same form for space flight to other planets.

    See also **Apollo project; Moon—Exploration**

    x Flight to the moon; Lunar expeditions; Moon, Voyages to; Voyages to the moon

    xx **Astronautics**

Space gardening. *See* **Aeroponics**

Space heaters **644**

    See also **Fireplaces; Stoves**

    xx **Heating**

Space industrial processing. *See* **Space industrialization**

Space industrialization **629.44**

    x Commercial endeavors in space; Industrial uses of space; Manufacturing in space; Space commercialization; Space industrial processing; Space manufacturing; Space stations—Industrial applications

    xx **Industrialization**

Space laboratories. *See* **Space stations**

Space law **341.4**

    See also **Airspace law**

    x Aerospace law; Artificial satellites—Law and legislation; Astronautics—Law and legislation; Law, Space; Space flight—Law and

Space law—*Continued*

legislation; Space stations—Law and legislation

  xx **Astronautics and civilization; International law; Law**

Space manufacturing. *See* **Space industrialization**

Space medicine 616.9

See also **Aviation medicine; Life support systems (Space environment); Space flight; Weightlessness**

  x Aerospace medicine; Bioastronautics

  xx **Aviation medicine; Space biology; Space flight; Space sciences**

Space navigation. *See* **Navigation (Astronautics)**

Space nutrition. *See* **Astronauts—Nutrition**

Space optics 535

See also **Astronautical instruments; Astronomical instruments; Remote sensing**

  xx **Optics; Remote sensing; Space sciences**

Space orbital rendezvous. *See* **Orbital rendezvous (Space flight)**

Space, Outer. *See* **Outer space**

Space, Personal. *See* **Personal space**

Space photography 778.3

See also **Lunar photography;** also objects with the subdivision *Photographs from space,* e.g. **Earth—Photographs from space; Moon—Photographs from space;** etc.

  x Astronautics, Photography in; Photography in astronautics; Photography, Space

  xx **Photography**

Space platforms. *See* **Space stations**

Space pollution. *See* **Space debris**

Space power. *See* **Astronautics and civilization**

Space probes 629.43

Use only for space exploration by remote control from earth.

See also types of probes, e.g. **Lunar probes; Mars probes;** etc.; also names of space vehicles and space projects, e.g. **Project Voyager;** etc.

  x Probes, Space

  xx **Outer space—Exploration; Space vehicles**

Space rescue operations 629.45

  x Manned space flight—Rescue work; Rescue operations, Space; Space ships—Rescue work

  xx **Rescue work**

Space research. *See* **Outer space—Exploration; Space sciences**

Space rockets. *See* **Space vehicles**

Space sciences 500.5

Use for general materials and for scientific results of space exploration and scientific applications of space flight.

See also **Astronautics; Astronomy; Geophysics; Outer space; Space biology; Space medicine; Space optics**

  x Science and space; Space research

  xx **Astronautics; Astronomy; Science**

Space sciences—International cooperation 500.5

Space ships 629.45

Use for materials limited to space vehicles with

Space ships—*Continued*

people on board. Comprehensive materials on spacecraft are entered under **Space vehicles.**

See also **Orbital rendezvous (Space flight); Rocket planes**

xx **Astronautics; Life support systems (Space environment); Rocketry; Space vehicles**

Space ships—Accidents. *See* **Astronautics—Accidents**

Space ships—Pilots. *See* **Astronauts**

Space ships—Rescue work. *See* **Space rescue operations**

Space shuttles   629.44

Use for materials on vehicles used to transport equipment and personnel to a space station.

See also names of individual space shuttles, e.g. **Challenger (Space shuttle);** etc.

x Reusable space vehicles; Shuttles, Space; Space vehicles, Reusable

xx **Space vehicles**

Space stations   629.44

Use for materials on manned installations orbiting in space for specific functions, such as servicing space ships. Materials on bases established on natural extraterrestrial bodies for specific functions other than colonization are entered under **Extraterrestrial bases.** For materials on communities established in space or on natural extraterrestrial bodies, use **Space colonies.**

See also **Orbital rendezvous (Space flight)**

x Laboratories, Space; Orbital laboratories; Orbiting vehicles; Sky laboratories; Space laboratories; Space platforms

xx **Artificial satellites; Astronautics; Space vehicles**

Space stations—Industrial applications. *See* **Space industrialization**

Space stations—Law and legislation. *See* **Space law**

Space suits. *See* **Astronauts—Clothing**

Space telecommunication. *See* **Interstellar communication**

Space television. *See* **Television in astronautics**

Space travel. *See* **Interplanetary voyages; Space flight**

Space vehicles   629.47

Use for comprehensive materials on spacecraft. Materials limited to space vehicles with people on board are entered under **Space ships.**

See also **Artificial satellites; Astronautics; Lunar excursion module; Space probes; Space ships; Space shuttles; Space stations**

x Space craft; Space rockets; Spacecraft

xx **Artificial satellites; Astronautics; Rocketry**

Space vehicles—Accidents. *See* **Astronautics—Accidents**

Space vehicles—Extravehicular activity. *See* **Extravehicular activity (Space flight)**

Space vehicles—Guidance systems   629.47

Space vehicles—Instruments. *See* **Astronautical instruments**

Space vehicles—Piloting 629.45
  x Piloting (Astronautics)
  xx **Astronauts; Navigation (Astronautics)**
Space vehicles—Propulsion systems 629.47
Space vehicles—Recovery 629.4
  x Recovery of space vehicles
Space vehicles, Reusable. *See* **Space shuttles**
Space vehicles—Thermodynamics 629.47
  xx **Thermodynamics**
Space vehicles—Tracking 629.4
  x Tracking of satellites
Space walk. *See* **Extravehicular activity (Space flight)**
Space warfare 358
    Use for materials on interplanetary warfare, attacks on earth from outer space, and warfare among the nations of earth in outer space.
    See also **Space weapons; Strategic Defense Initiative**
  x Earth—Space attack and defense; Interplanetary warfare; Interstellar warfare; Space wars; War, Space; Warfare, Space
  xx **Outer space**
Space wars. *See* **Space warfare**
Space weapons 358
    See also **Strategic Defense Initiative**
  x Space-based weapons; Star Wars weapons; Weapons, Space
  xx **Munitions; Space warfare; Strategic Defense Initiative**
Space weather. *See* **Space environment**
Spacecraft. *See* **Space vehicles**
Spain 946
    May be subdivided like United States except for *History.*
Spain—History 946
    See also **Spanish Armada, 1588**
Spain—History—1898, War of 1898. *See* **United States—History—1898, War of 1898**
Spain—History—1936-1939, Civil War 946.081
Spain—History—1939-1975 946.082
Spain—History—1975- 946.083
Spanish America. *See* **Latin America**
Spanish-American War, 1898. *See* **United States—History—1898, War of 1898**
Spanish Armada, 1588 942.05; 946
  x Armada, 1588; Invincible Armada
  xx **Great Britain—History—1485-1603, Tudors; Spain—History**
Spanish language 460
    May be subdivided like **English language.**
Spanish literature 860
    May use same subdivisions and names of literary forms as for **English literature.**
    See also **Latin American literature**
Sparring. *See* **Boxing**
Spas. *See* **Health resorts, spas, etc.**
Spastic paralysis. *See* **Cerebral palsy**
Speakers (Recitation books). *See* **Readings and recitations**
Speaking. *See* **Debates and debating; Lectures and lecturing; Preaching; Public speaking; Rhetoric; Voice**
Speaking choirs. *See* **Choral speaking**

Spear fishing 799.1

  xx **Fishing**

Special collections in libraries. *See* **Libraries—Special collections**

Special education 371.9

  See also **Mainstreaming in education;** also classes of exceptional children with the subdivision *Education,* e.g. **Mentally handicapped children—Education;** etc.

  x Education, Special

  xx **Education; Mainstreaming in education**

Special libraries 026; 027.6

  Use for materials on libraries covering specialized subjects, containing special format materials, or serving a specialized clientele.

  See also types of special libraries, e.g. **Business libraries; Corporate libraries; Government libraries; Music libraries;** etc.

  x Libraries, Special

  xx **Libraries**

Special Olympics 796.01

  x Olympics, Special

  xx **Olympic games; Sports for the handicapped**

Specialists exchange programs. *See* **Exchange of persons programs**

Specie. *See* **Money**

Specimens, Preservation of. *See* **Plants—Collection and preservation; Taxidermy; Zoological specimens—Collection and preservation;** and names of natural specimens with the subdivision *Collection and preservation,* e.g. **Birds—Collection and preservation;** etc.

Spectacles. *See* **Eyeglasses**

Specters. *See* **Apparitions; Ghosts**

Spectra. *See* **Spectrum analysis**

Spectrochemical analysis. *See* **Spectrum analysis**

Spectrochemistry. *See* **Spectrum analysis**

Spectroscopy. *See* **Spectrum analysis**

Spectrum analysis 535.8

  See also **Light; Mass spectrometry**

  x Analysis, Spectrum; Spectra; Spectrochemical analysis; Spectrochemistry; Spectroscopy

  xx **Astronomy; Astrophysics; Chemistry; Light; Optics; Radiation; Sun**

Speculation 332.64

  See also **Investments; Real estate investment; Securities; Stock exchange**

  xx **Finance; Investments; Stock exchange**

Speech 302.2; 372.6; 410; 612.7

  See also **Language and languages; Phonetics; Speech processing systems; Speech therapy; Voice**

  xx **Language and languages; Language arts; Phonetics; Voice**

Speech correction. *See* **Speech therapy**

Speech disorders 616.85

  x Defective speech; Speech pathology; Stammering; Stuttering

Speech, Liberty of. *See* **Free speech**

Speech pathology. *See* **Speech disorders**

Speech processing systems 006.5

  See also **Automatic speech recognition; Computer sound processing**

629

Speech processing systems—*Continued*
> *x* Computer speech processing systems; Electronic speech processing systems; Speech scramblers; Speech synthesis
> *xx* **Computer sound processing; Speech; Telecommunication**

Speech recognition, Automatic. *See* **Automatic speech recognition**

Speech scramblers. *See* **Speech processing systems**

Speech synthesis. *See* **Speech processing systems**

Speech therapy   616.85
> *x* Speech correction
> *xx* **Speech**

Speeches, addresses, etc. (May subdiv. geog. adjective form, e.g. **Speeches, addresses, etc., American;** etc.)   **808.85; 815.008, etc.**
> *See also* **After dinner speeches; Lectures and lecturing; Presidents—United States—Inaugural addresses; Toasts**
> *x* Addresses; Orations
> *xx* **Literature**

Speeches, addresses, etc., American   815; 815.008
> *x* American orations; American speeches
> *xx* **American literature**

Speeches, addresses, etc., English   825; 825.008
> *x* English orations; English speeches
> *xx* **English literature**

Speed   531
> *x* Velocity
> *xx* **Motion**

Speed (Drug). *See* **Methamphetamine**

Speed reading. *See* **Rapid reading**

Speed, Supersonic. *See* **Aerodynamics, Supersonic**

Speleology. *See* **Caves**

Spellers   421
> *xx* **English language—Spelling**

Spelling. *See* names of languages with the subdivision *Spelling,* e.g. **English language—Spelling;** etc.

Spelling reform   421
> *x* English language—Spelling reform; Orthography; Phonetic spelling
> *xx* **English language—Spelling**

Spells. *See* **Charms**

Spherical trigonometry. *See* **Trigonometry**

Spices   641.3
> *See also* names of spices

Spiders   595.4
> *x* Arachnida

Spies   327.12; 355.3
> *See also* **Secret service**
> *x* Intelligence agents
> *xx* **Espionage; Military art and science; Secret service; Subversive activities**

Spinal paralysis, Anterior. *See* **Poliomyelitis**

Spinning   677; 746.1
> *xx* **Textile industry**

Spiral gearing. *See* **Gearing**

Spires   726
> *x* Steeples
> *xx* **Architecture; Church architecture**

Spirit. *See* **Soul**

Spirit, Holy. *See* **Holy Spirit**

Spiritism. *See* **Spiritualism**

Spirits. *See* **Angels; Apparitions; Demonology; Ghosts; Spiritualism; Witchcraft**

Spirits, Alcoholic. *See* **Liquors and liqueurs**

Spiritual healing   615.8

Use for materials on the use of faith, prayer, or religious means to treat illness. Materials on psychic or psychological means to treat illness are entered under **Mental healing.**

See also **Christian Science; Mental healing; Miracles; Therapeutics, Suggestive**

x Divine healing; Evangelistic healing; Faith cure; Faith healing; Healing, Spiritual

xx **Christian Science; Medicine and religion; Mental healing; Mind and body; Subconsciousness; Therapeutics, Suggestive**

Spiritual life   248

See also **Faith; Meditation; Sanctification**

x Life, Spiritual

xx **Ethics; Human behavior; Mysticism; Religion; Soul; Theology**

Spiritualism   133.9

See also **Apparitions; Clairvoyance; Ghosts; Parapsychology; Psychokinesis**

x Spiritism; Spirits

xx **Apparitions; Future life; Ghosts; Occultism; Parapsychology; Supernatural**

Spirituals (Songs)   782.25

See also **Black songs; Gospel music**

xx **Black songs; Folk songs—United States; Gospel music; Hymns; Music, American**

Splicing. *See* **Knots and splices**

Splicing of genes. *See* **Genetic engineering**

Spoils system. *See* **Corruption in politics**

Sponges   593.4

xx **Invertebrates**

Spontaneous abortion. *See* **Miscarriage**

Spontaneous combustion. *See* **Combustion**

Sports (May subdiv. geog.)   **796**

See also

Aeronautical sports	**Orienteering**
Amusements	**Outdoor life**
Athletics	**Physical education**
Coaching (Athletics)	**Professional sports**
College sports	**Rodeos**
Drugs and sports	**School sports**
Games	**Sportsmanship**
Gymnastics	**Water sports**
Olympic games	**Winter sports**

also names of sports, e.g. **Baseball; Basketball; Football;** etc.; and names of competitions

xx **Amusements; Athletics; Games; Outdoor life; Physical education; Play; Recreation**

Sports and drugs. *See* **Drugs and sports**

Sports cars   629.222

See also names of specific sports cars

xx **Automobiles**

Sports coaching. *See* **Coaching (Athletics)**

Sports—Corrupt practices   796

x Cheating in sports; Corruption in sports; Sports scandals

Sports—Equipment and supplies   796.028

Sports for the handicapped   796.01

See also **Special Olympics**

Sports—Medical aspects. *See* **Sports medicine**

Sports medicine   613.7; 617.1
    See also **Drugs and sports**
    x Athletic medicine; Physical education—
        Medical aspects; Sports—Medical aspects
    xx **Medical care; Medicine**
Sports scandals. *See* **Sports—Corrupt practices**
Sportsmanship   175
    xx **Human behavior; Sports**
Spot welding. *See* **Electric welding**
Spouses. *See* **Husbands; Wives**
Spraying and dusting   632
    See also **Aeronautics in agriculture; Fungicides;**
        Herbicides; Insecticides
    x Dusting and spraying
    xx **Agricultural pests; Fruit—Diseases and pests;**
        Fungicides; Herbicides; Insecticides
Spread sheets, Electronic. *See* **Electronic spread-**
    sheets
Spreadsheeting, Electronic. *See* **Electronic spread-**
    sheets
Spreadsheets, Electronic. *See* **Electronic spread-**
    sheets
Spun glass. *See* **Glass fibers**
Sputniks. *See* **Artificial satellites, Soviet**
Square   516
    xx **Geometry; Size and shape**
Square dancing   793.3
    xx **Folk dancing**
Square root   513.2
    xx **Arithmetic**
Squirrels   599.32
    See also **Chipmunks**
SSTs. *See* **Supersonic transport planes**
St. Dominic, Order of. *See* **Dominicans (Religious**
    order)
St. Francis, Order of. *See* **Franciscans**
St. Valentine's Day. *See* **Valentine's Day**
Stabilization in industry. *See* **Business cycles; Eco-**
    nomic conditions
Stage. *See* **Acting; Actors; Drama; Theater**
Stage lighting   792
    x Television—Stage lighting; Theaters—Stage
        lighting
Stage scenery. *See* **Theaters—Stage setting and**
    scenery
Stage setting. *See* **Theaters—Stage setting and**
    scenery
Stagecoaches. *See* **Carriages and carts**
Stained glass. *See* **Glass painting and staining**
Stamina, Physical. *See* **Physical fitness**
Stammering. *See* **Speech disorders**
Stamps, Postage. *See* **Postage stamps**
Standard book numbers. *See* **Publishers' standard**
    book numbers
Standard of living   339.4
    See also **Cost of living**
    x Living, Standard of
    xx **Quality of life; Social conditions; Social prob-**
        lems; Wealth
Standard of value. *See* **Money**
Standard time. *See* **Time**
Standards of output. *See* **Production standards**
Star Wars (Ballistic missile defense system). *See*
    Strategic Defense Initiative

Star Wars weapons. *See* **Space weapons**

Stars **523.8**

    See also

    Astrology   **Meteors**

    Astronomy   **Planets**

    Astrophysics   **Solar system**

    Black holes (Astronomy)   **Supernovas**

    Galaxies

      also names of groups of stars and specific stars,
        e.g. **Sirius;** etc.

    x Constellations; Double stars; Sidereal system

    xx **Astronomy; Planets**

Stars—Atlases **523.8022**

    x Astronomy—Atlases; Atlases, Astronomical

    xx **Atlases**

Stars, Falling. *See* **Meteors**

Starvation **363.8**

    See also **Famines; Fasting; Hunger; Malnutrition**

    xx **Fasting; Hunger; Malnutrition**

Starvation, Self-imposed. *See* **Anorexia nervosa**

State aid to education **379**

    x Education—State aid

    xx **Education—Finance; Education—Government
      policy**

State aid to libraries **021.8**

    x Libraries—State aid

    xx **Libraries—Government policy; Library fi-
      nance**

State and agriculture. *See* **Agriculture—
      Government policy**

State and church. *See* **Church—Government policy**

State and education. *See* **Education—Government
      policy**

State and energy. *See* **Energy resources—
      Government policy**

State and environment. *See* **Environment—
      Government policy**

State and industry. *See* **Industry—Government pol-
      icy**

State and insurance. *See* **Social security**

State and railroads. *See* **Railroads—Government
      policy**

State and science. *See* **Science—Government policy**

State and the arts. *See* **Arts—Government policy**

State birds **598**

    xx **Birds**

State church. *See* **Church—Government policy**

State constitutions **342**

    See also **State governments;** also names of states
      with the subdivision *Constitution,* e.g.
      Ohio—Constitution; etc.

    x Constitutions, State

    xx **Constitutions; Political science; State govern-
      ments**

State debts. *See* **Public debts**

State encouragement of the arts. *See* **Arts—
      Government policy**

State-federal relations. *See* **Federal-state relations**

State flowers **582**

    Use same form for other state symbols.

    x Flowers, State

    xx **Flowers**

State governments 353.9

Use for general materials on state government, that is, the government of the administrative divisions of countries organized on a federal basis. Materials on the government of a particular state are entered under the name of the state with the subdivision *Politics and government.*

See also **Federal government; Federal-state relations; Governors; State constitutions; State-local relations;** also names of states with the subdivision *Politics and government,* e.g. **Ohio—Politics and government;** etc.

x United States—State governments

xx **Federal government; Political science; State constitutions**

State, Heads of. *See* **Heads of state**

State libraries 027.5

Use for materials on government libraries, maintained by state funds, that preserve state records and publications for use by state officials and residents.

x Libraries, State

xx **Government libraries**

State-local relations 342; 351.09

x City-state relations; Local-state relations

xx **Local government; Municipal government; State governments**

State-local tax relations. *See* **Intergovernmental tax relations**

State medicine. *See* **Medicine, State**

State of the Union messages. *See* **Presidents—United States—Messages**

State ownership. *See* **Government ownership**

State ownership of railroads. *See* **Railroads—Government policy**

State planning. *See* **Regional planning; Social policy;** and names of states with the subdivision *Economic policy* or *Social policy,* e.g. **Ohio—Economic policy; Ohio—Social policy;** etc.

State police 352.2

x Police, State

xx **Police**

State regulation of industry. *See* **Industry—Government policy**

State rights 320.1; 342

x Secession; States' rights

xx **Political science; Slavery—United States**

State songs 782.42

xx **Songs**

State, The 320.1

See also **Political science; Public interest**

x Administration; Commonwealth, The; Welfare state

xx **Political science**

States, New 321

x New nations

xx **Developing countries**

States' rights. *See* **State rights**

Statesmen (May subdiv. geog.) **920; 923**

See also **Diplomats; Heads of state; Politicians**

xx **Diplomats; Politicians**

Statics 531
  See also **Dynamics; Hydrostatics; Strains and
    stresses**
  xx **Dynamics; Mechanics; Physics**
Statistical inference. *See* **Probabilities**
Statistics 310
  Use for materials on the theory and methods of
    statistics.
  See also **Average; Census; Probabilities; Sam-
    pling (Statistics); Vital statistics;** also gen-
    eral subjects and names of countries, cities,
    etc. with the subdivision *Statistics,* e.g. **Ag-
    riculture—Statistics; United States—
    Statistics; Chicago (Ill.)—Statistics;** etc.
  xx **Economics**
Statistics—Graphic methods 001.4
  x Diagrams, Statistical
  xx **Graphic methods**
Statues. *See* **Monuments; Sculpture**
Statutes. *See* **Law**
Steam 536
  xx **Heat; Power (Mechanics); Water**
Steam engineering 621.1
  See also **Mechanical engineering; Power (Me-
    chanics); Steam engines; Steam navigation;
    Steam power plants**
  xx **Engineering; Mechanical engineering**
Steam engines 621.1
  See also **Condensers (Steam); Farm engines; Lo-
    comotives; Marine engines; Steam turbines**
  xx **Engines; Heat engines; Machinery; Mechan-
    ics; Steam engineering**
Steam fitting. *See* **Pipe fitting**
Steam heating 697
  xx **Heating**
Steam navigation 386; 387; 623.8
  See also **Marine engineering; Navigation; Steam
    turbines; Steamboats**
  x Navigation, Steam
  xx **Navigation; Steam engineering; Steamboats;
    Transportation**
Steam power plants 621.1
  x Power plants, Steam
  xx **Power plants; Steam engineering**
Steam pumps. *See* **Pumping machinery**
Steam turbines 621.1
  xx **Steam engines; Steam navigation; Turbines**
Steamboats 387.2
  See also **Steam navigation**
  x Steamships
  xx **Boats and boating; Naval architecture; Ocean
    travel; Shipbuilding; Ships; Steam naviga-
    tion**
Steamships. *See* **Steamboats**
Steel 669; 672
  See also **Building, Iron and steel; Iron;** also head-
    ings beginning with the word **Steel**
  xx **Metalwork**
Steel construction. *See* **Building, Iron and steel;
    Steel, Structural**
Steel engraving. *See* **Engraving**
Steel industry 338.4; 672
  See also **Iron industry**

Steel industry—*Continued*
 x Steel industry and trade; Steel trade
 xx **Industry; Iron industry; Ironwork**
Steel industry and trade. *See* **Steel industry**
Steel industry—Quality control 338.4; 672
 xx **Quality control**
Steel, Structural 691
 See also **Building, Iron and steel**
 x Steel construction; Structural steel
 xx **Building, Iron and steel; Building materials;**
  Civil engineering
Steel trade. *See* **Steel industry**
Steeples. *See* **Spires**
Steers. *See* **Beef cattle**
Stencil work 686.2
 See also **Silk screen printing**
 xx **Decoration and ornament; Painting**
Stenography. *See* **Shorthand**
Step-family. *See* **Stepfamily**
Stepfamilies. *See* **Stepfamily**
Stepfamily 306.85
 x Blended family; Step-family; Stepfamilies
 xx **Family**
Stereo photography. *See* **Three dimensional pho-**
  tography
Stereophonic sound systems 621.389
 xx **High-fidelity sound systems; Sound—**
  Recording and reproducing
Stereophotography. *See* **Three dimensional photog-**
  raphy
Stereoscopic photography. *See* **Three dimensional**
  photography
Sterility in animals. *See* **Infertility**
Sterility in humans. *See* **Infertility**
Sterilization (Birth control) 613.9
 See also **Infertility; Vasectomy**
 xx **Birth control; Infertility**
Steroids 574.19; 612
 See also **Athletes—Drug use**
 x Anabolic steroids
 xx **Athletes—Drug use; Biochemistry; Drugs;**
  Hormones
Stewardesses, Airline. *See* **Airlines—Flight atten-**
  dants
Stewards, Airline. *See* **Airlines—Flight attendants**
Stills. *See* **Distillation**
Stimulants 613.8; 615
 See also **Cocaine; Hallucinogens; Liquors and li-**
  queurs; Narcotics; also names of groups of
  stimulants, e.g. **Amphetamines;** etc.; and
  names of individual stimulants, e.g. **Alco-**
  hol; etc.
 x Intoxicants
 xx **Narcotics; Temperance; Therapeutics**
Stock and stock breeding. *See* **Livestock**
Stock control. *See* **Inventory control**
Stock exchange 332.6
 See also

Bonds	**Speculation**
Foreign exchange	**Stocks**
Insider trading	**Wall Street (New York,**
Investments	**N.Y.)**
Securities	

Stock exchange—*Continued*
> *x* Securities exchange; Stock market
> *xx* **Commerce; Exchange; Finance; Investments; Speculation; Stocks**

Stock judging. *See* **Livestock judging**
Stock market. *See* **Stock exchange**
Stock raising. *See* **Livestock**
Stockings. *See* **Hosiery**
Stocks 332.6
> *See also* **Bonds; Corporations; Investments; Stock exchange**
> *x* Dividends; Shares of stock
> *xx* **Bonds; Commerce; Investments; Securities; Stock exchange**

Stocks—Insider trading. *See* **Insider trading**
Stockyards. *See* **Meat industry**
Stoics 188
> *xx* **Ethics; Philosophy, Ancient**
Stokers, Mechanical 621.1
> *x* Mechanical stokers
STOL aircraft. *See* **Short take off and landing aircraft**
Stomach 612.3
> *See also* **Digestion**
Stone 552; 553.5; 693
> *See also* **Masonry; Petrology; Quarries and quarrying; Rocks; Stonecutting;** also names of stones, e.g. **Marble;** etc.
> *xx* **Building materials; Geology, Economic; Petrology; Quarries and quarrying; Rocks**
Stone Age 930
> *See also* **Archeology; Prehistoric man; Stone implements**
> *x* Eolithic period; Neolithic period; Paleolithic period; Prehistory
> *xx* **Archeology**
Stone-cutting. *See* **Stonecutting**
Stone implements 930
> *x* Flint implements; Implements, utensils, etc.
> *xx* **Archeology; Stone Age**
Stone quarries. *See* **Quarries and quarrying**
Stonecutting 693
> *x* Stone-cutting
> *xx* **Masonry; Stone**
Stones, Precious. *See* **Precious stones**
Stoneware. *See* **Pottery**
Storage batteries 621.31
> *See also* **Electric batteries**
> *x* Batteries, Electric
> *xx* **Electric batteries**
Storage devices, Computer. *See* **Computer storage devices**
Storage in the home 643; 648; 684.1
> *x* Home storage
> *xx* **Home economics**
Stores. *See* **Chain stores; Cooperative societies; Department stores; Discount stores; Retail trade; Supermarkets**
Stories. *See* **Anecdotes; Fairy tales; Fiction; Legends; Romances; Stories in rhyme; Stories without words; Storytelling;** and literary and musical forms with the subdivision *Stories, plots, etc.,* e.g. **Ballets—Stories, plots, etc.;**

Stories—*Continued*

    Operas—Stories, plots, etc.; etc.; also subjects with the subdivision *Fiction,* e.g. **Slavery—United States—Fiction;** etc.; and phrase headings that do not lend themselves to the subdivided form, e.g. **Bible stories; Humorous stories; Mystery and detective stories; School stories; Science fiction; Sea stories; Short stories;** etc.

Stories in rhyme   E; Fic
    x Stories
    xx **Rhyme**

Stories without words   E
    x Nonword stories; Picture books for children, Wordless; Stories; Wordless stories
    xx **Picture books for children**

Storms (May subdiv. geog.)   **551.55**
    Use for materials on storms in general.
    See also

Blizzards	**Snow**
Cyclones	**Thunderstorms**
Dust storms	**Tornadoes**
Hurricanes	**Typhoons**
Meteorology	**Winds**
Rain	

    also kinds of storms
    xx **Meteorology; Natural disasters; Rain; Weather; Winds**

Story theater. *See* **Readers' theater**

Storytelling   **027.62; 372.64**
    See also **Folklore; Short story**
    x Stories
    xx **Children's literature; Folklore; Short story**

Storytelling—Collections   **808.85**
    Use for collections of stories compiled primarily for oral presentation.
    x Collected works; Collections of literature

Stoves   **697**
    xx **Heating; Space heaters**

Strain (Psychology). *See* **Stress (Psychology)**

Strains and stresses   **531; 620.1; 624.1**
    See also **Strength of materials**
    x Architectural engineering; Stresses
    xx **Architecture; Mechanics; Statics; Strength of materials; Structures, Theory of**

Strangers and children. *See* **Children and strangers**

Strategic Defense Initiative   **358.1**
    See also **Space weapons**
    x SDI (Ballistic missile defense system); Star Wars (Ballistic missile defense system)
    xx **Space warfare; Space weapons; United States—Defenses; United States—Military policy**

Strategic materials. *See* **Materials**

Strategy   **355.4**
    See also **Armies; Military art and science; Naval art and science; Tactics;** also countries and areas of the world with the subdivision *Strategic aspects,* e.g. **Middle East—Strategic aspects;** etc.
    x Military strategy; Naval strategy
    xx **Military art and science; Naval art and science; War**

Stratigraphic geology. *See* **Geology, Stratigraphic**

Stratosphere   551.5
    See also **Ozone layer**
    xx **Upper atmosphere**
Stratospheric ozone.   *See* **Ozone layer**
Straw votes.   *See* **Public opinion polls**
Strawberries   634
    xx **Berries**
Stream animals   591.52
    x River animals
    xx **Animals; Rivers; Wildlife**
Streamlining.   *See* **Aerodynamics**
Street cars.   *See* **Street railroads**
Street cleaning   363.72; 628.4
    See also **Refuse and refuse disposal**
    xx **Cleaning; Municipal engineering; Public
        health; Refuse and refuse disposal; Roads;
        Sanitary engineering; Streets**
Street lighting.   *See* **Streets—Lighting**
Street people.   *See* **Homeless people**
Street railroads   388.4; 625.6
    See also **Cable railroads; Electric railroads; Sub-
        ways**
    x Interurban railroads; Railroads, Street; Street
        cars; Trams; Trolley cars
    xx **Cable railroads; Electric railroads; Local tran-
        sit; Public utilities; Railroads; Transporta-
        tion**
Street traffic.   *See* **City traffic; Traffic engineering;
        Traffic regulations**
Streets (May subdiv. geog.)   **388.4; 625.7**
    See also **City traffic; Pavements; Roads; Street
        cleaning**
    x Alleys; Avenues; Boulevards; Thoroughfares
    xx **Cities and towns; Civil engineering; Pave-
        ments; Roads; Transportation**
Streets—Chicago (Ill.)   977.3
    x Chicago (Ill.)—Streets
Streets—Lighting   628.9
    x Cities and towns—Lighting; Street lighting
    xx **Lighting**
Streets—New York (N.Y.)   974.7
    See also **Wall Street (New York, N.Y.)**
    xx **Wall Street (New York, N.Y.)**
Strength of materials   620.1
    See also **Building materials; Strains and stresses;**
        also special materials and forms with the
        subdivision *Testing,* e.g. **Concrete—
        Testing;** etc.
    x Architectural engineering; Materials, Strength
        of; Resistance of materials; Testing
    xx **Architecture; Building; Building, Iron and
        steel; Building materials; Civil engineering;
        Materials; Mechanics; Strains and stresses;
        Structures, Theory of**
Strength training.   *See* **Weight lifting**
Stress (Physiology)   612; 616.8
    See also **Job stress**
    x Physiological stress; Tension (Physiology)
Stress (Psychology)   155.9; 616.89
    See also **Burn out (Psychology); Separation anxi-
        ety in children**
    x Anxiety; Emotional stress; Psychological
        stress; Strain (Psychology); Tension (Psy-
        chology)

Stress (Psychology)—*Continued*
  xx **Psychology**
Stresses. *See* **Strains and stresses**
Strikes and lockouts (May subdiv. geog.) **331.89**
    May also subdivide by industry or occupation
      and then geographically.
    See also **Arbitration, Industrial; Collective bar-**
      gaining; Injunctions; Labor unions; Sabotage
    x Lockouts; Picketing; Sit-down strikes; Work
      stoppages
    xx **Arbitration, Industrial; Collective bargaining;**
      Industrial relations; Injunctions; Labor; La-
      bor disputes; Labor unions
Strikes and lockouts—Automobile industry—United
    States 331.89
Strikes and lockouts—United States 331.89
    x United States—Strikes and lockouts
Strikes, Hunger. *See* **Hunger strikes**
String orchestra music 784.7
  xx **Orchestral music**
Stringed instruments 787
    See also **Violoncello;** also names of stringed in-
      struments, e.g. **Guitar; Violin;** etc.
    x Bowed instruments
    xx **Musical instruments**
Strip films. *See* **Filmstrips**
Structural botany. *See* **Botany—Anatomy**
Structural drafting. *See* **Mechanical drawing**
Structural engineering 624.1
    See also **Building; Foundations; Hydraulic struc-**
      tures; Soils (Engineering); Structures, The-
      ory of
    x Engineering, Structural
    xx **Architecture; Building materials; Civil engi-**
      neering; Engineering; Structures, Theory of
Structural failures 624.1
    See also types of structural failures, e.g. **Build-**
      ing failures; etc.
    x Collapse of structures; Failures, Structural
    xx **Reliability (Engineering)**
Structural materials. *See* **Building materials**
Structural psychology. *See* **Gestalt psychology**
Structural steel. *See* **Steel, Structural**
Structures, Offshore. *See* **Drilling platforms**
Structures, Theory of 624
    See also **Building; Strains and stresses; Strength**
      of materials; Structural engineering
    x Architectural engineering; Theory of struc-
      tures
    xx **Building, Iron and steel; Structural engineer-**
      ing
Stucco 693
    xx **Building materials; Decoration and ornament;**
      Plaster and plastering
Student activities 371.8
    See also **After school programs; College and**
      school drama; College and school journal-
      ism; School assembly programs; School
      sports
    x Extracurricular activities
Student aid. *See* **Scholarships, fellowships, etc.;**
      Student loan funds
Student busing. *See* **Busing (School integration)**

Student clubs. *See* **Students—Societies**
Student councils. *See* **Student government**
Student customs. *See* **Student life**
Student dropouts. *See* **Dropouts**
Student evaluation of teachers 371.1
    x Student rating of teachers; Teachers, Student
       rating of
Student government 371.5
    x Honor system; Self-government (in educa-
       tion); Student councils; Student self-
       government
    xx **School discipline; Schools—Administration**
Student guidance. *See* **Educational counseling**
Student life 371.8
    x Student customs
    xx **Students**
Student loan funds 371.2; 378.3
    See also **Scholarships, fellowships, etc.**
    x Loan funds, Student; Student aid
    xx **Scholarships, fellowships, etc.**
Student movement. *See* **Youth movement**
Student promotion. *See* **Promotion (School)**
Student protests, demonstrations, etc. *See* **Stu-
       dents—Political activity; Youth movement**
Student rating of teachers. *See* **Student evaluation
       of teachers**
Student revolt. *See* **Students—Political activity;
       Youth movement**
Student self-government. *See* **Student government**
Student societies. *See* **Students—Societies**
Student-teacher interaction. *See* **Teacher-student
       relationships**
Student teaching 371.1
    x Practice teaching; Teachers—Practice teaching
    xx **Teachers—Training; Teaching**
Student to student counseling. *See* **Peer counseling**
Student violence. *See* **School violence**
Student yearbooks. *See* **School yearbooks**
Students (May subdiv. geog.) **371.8**
    See also **Dropouts; Foreign students; School chil-
       dren; Student life;** also types of students, e.g.
       College students; High school students; etc.;
       also headings beginning with the words
       College and **School**
    x School life
Students and libraries. *See* **Libraries and students**
Students—Counseling. *See* **Educational counseling**
Students, Foreign. *See* **Foreign students**
Students—Grading and marking. *See* **Grading and
       marking (Education)**
Students' military training camps. *See* **Military
       training camps**
Students—Political activity 324; 371.8
    x Politics and students; Student protests, dem-
       onstrations, etc.; Student revolt
    xx **Youth movement**
Students—Societies 371.8
    See also **Fraternities and sororities**
    x School clubs; Student clubs; Student societies
Students' songs 782.42
    x College songs
    xx **Songs**
Students—United States 371.8
    x United States—Students

Students—Yearbooks. *See* **School yearbooks**
Study abroad. *See* **Foreign study**
Study, Courses of. *See* **Education—Curricula;** and
   types of education and schools with the sub-
   division *Curricula,* e.g. **Library educa-**
   tion—Curricula; Colleges and universities—
   Curricula; etc.
Study, Foreign. *See* **Foreign study**
Study, Method of. *See* **Study skills**
Study overseas. *See* **Foreign study**
Study skills   371.3
  See also **Independent study; Self-culture;** also
   subjects with the subdivision *Study and*
   teaching, e.g. **Art—Study and teaching;**
   etc.
  x Learning, Art of; Method of study; Study,
   Method of
  xx **Education; Teaching**
Stunt flying   797.5
  x Aerobatic flying; Aerobatics
  xx **Airplanes—Piloting**
Stunt men and women   791.4
  xx **Acrobats and acrobatics**
Stuttering. *See* **Speech disorders**
Style in dress. *See* **Costume; Fashion**
Style, Literary   808; 809
  See also **Criticism; Letter writing; Literature—**
   History and criticism; Rhetoric
  x Literary style
  xx **Criticism; Literature; Rhetoric**
Style manikins. *See* **Models, Fashion**
Style manuals. *See* **Printing—Style manuals**
Sub-Saharan Africa   960
  x Africa, Sub-Saharan; Black Africa
Subconsciousness   127; 154.2
  See also

Consciousness	**Mind and body**
Dreams	**Personality disorders**
Hallucinations and illu-	**Psychoanalysis**
sions	**Sleep**
Hypnotism	**Spiritual healing**
Mental healing	**Telepathy**
Mental suggestion	

  xx **Consciousness; Hypnotism; Mental healing;**
   Mind and body; Parapsychology; Psycho-
   analysis; Psychology; Psychology, Patholog-
   ical; Therapeutics, Suggestive
Subculture. *See* **Counter culture**
Subgravity state. *See* **Weightlessness**
Subject dictionaries. *See* **Encyclopedias and dictio-**
   naries
Subject headings   025.4
  See also **Classification—Books**
  x Thesauri
  xx **Cataloging; Catalogs, Subject; Indexes**
Submarine boats. *See* **Submarines; Submersibles**
Submarine cables. *See* **Cables, Submarine**
Submarine diving. *See* **Diving, Submarine**
Submarine engineering. *See* **Ocean engineering**
Submarine exploration. *See* **Underwater explora-**
   tion
Submarine geology   551.46
  See also **Ocean bottom; Plate tectonics**

Submarine geology—*Continued*
  x Geology, Submarine; Marine geology; Underwater geology
  xx **Geology; Oceanography; Plate tectonics**
Submarine medicine   616.9
  x Medicine, Submarine; Underwater medicine; Underwater physiology
  xx **Medicine**
Submarine oil well drilling.   *See* **Oil well drilling, Submarine**
Submarine photography.   *See* **Underwater photography**
Submarine research stations.   *See* **Undersea research stations**
Submarine telegraph.   *See* **Cables, Submarine**
Submarine vehicles.   *See* **Submersibles**
Submarine warfare   359.4
  See also **Submarines; Torpedoes; World War, 1939-1945—Naval operations—Submarine**
  x Naval warfare; Warfare, Submarine
  xx **Naval art and science; War**
Submarines   359.3; 623.8
  Use for materials on submarines only. Materials on other underwater craft are entered under **Submersibles.**
  See also **Nuclear submarines**
  x Boats, Submarine; Submarine boats; U boats
  xx **Boats and boating; Naval art and science; Ships; Submarine warfare; Submersibles; Warships**
Submarines, Nuclear.   *See* **Nuclear submarines**
Submersibles   623.8
  See note under **Submarines.**
  See also types of submersibles, e.g. **Bathyscaphe; Submarines; Undersea research stations;** etc.
  x Boats, Submarine; Deep diving vehicles; Deep sea vehicles; Deep submergence vehicles; Oceanographic submersibles; Submarine boats; Submarine vehicles; Undersea vehicles; Underwater exploration devices
  xx **Oceanography—Research; Underwater exploration**
Subscription television   384.55
  See also **Home Box Office**
  x Pay television, Subscription; Television, Subscription
  xx **Television broadcasting**
Subsidies   338.9
  See also headings beginning with **Federal aid to. . .**
  x Bounties; Grants; Subventions
  xx **Economic assistance, Domestic; Economic policy; Industry—Government policy**
Subsistence economy   331.2; 339.4
  See also **Barter; Poverty**
  xx **Cost of living; Poverty**
Substance abuse   362.2; 616.86
  See also **Alcoholism; Drug abuse; Solvent abuse; Tobacco habit**
  x Abuse of substances; Addiction; Addiction to substances; Addictive behavior
  xx **Social problems**

Substitute products

    See also **Synthetic products;** also types of substitute products, e.g. **Sugar substitutes;** etc.

    x Ersatz products

    xx **Commercial products; Synthetic products; Waste products**

Subterranean economy. *See* **Underground economy**

Subtraction 513.2

    xx **Arithmetic**

Suburban areas. *See* **Metropolitan areas**

Suburban homes. *See* **Architecture, Domestic**

Suburban life 307.74

    See also names of cities with the subdivision *Suburbs and environs,* e.g. **Chicago (Ill.)— Suburbs and environs;** etc.

Subventions. *See* **Subsidies**

Subversive activities 322.4; 327.12

    See also **Espionage; Internal security; Political crimes and offenses; Sabotage; Spies; Terrorism**

    x Fifth column

    xx **Insurgency; Internal security**

Subways 388.4

    x Railroads, Underground; Underground railroads

    xx **Civil engineering; Local transit; Railroads; Street railroads; Transportation; Tunnels**

Success 158

    See also **Ability; Academic achievement; Leadership; Life skills; Saving and thrift; Self-realization**

    x Fortune; Personal development

    xx **Business ethics; Self-realization; Wealth**

Succession, Intestate. *See* **Inheritance and succession**

Suffering 152.1; 214

    See also **Good and evil; Joy and sorrow; Pain**

    xx **Pain**

Suffrage 324.6

    See also **Naturalization; Representative government and representation; Voter registration;** also classes of people with the subdivision *Suffrage,* e.g. **Blacks—Suffrage; Women— Suffrage;** etc.

    x Franchise; Voting

    xx **Citizenship; Constitutional law; Democracy; Elections; Political science; Representative government and representation**

Suffragettes. *See* **Women—Suffrage**

Sugar 641.3; 664

    See also **Syrups;** also types of sugar, e.g. **Maple sugar;** etc.

Sugar substitutes 641.3; 664

    x Artificial sweeteners; Nonnutritive sweeteners

    xx **Substitute products**

Suggestion, Mental. *See* **Mental suggestion**

Suggestive therapeutics. *See* **Therapeutics, Suggestive**

Suicide 179; 362.2

    See also **Homicide; Right to die**

    xx **Homicide; Medical jurisprudence; Right to die; Social problems**

Suing (Law). *See* **Litigation**

Suites 784.18
> *xx* **Musical form; Orchestral music**

Suits (Law). *See* **Litigation**

Sulfa drugs. *See* **Sulfonamides**

Sulfonamides 615
> *x* Sulfa drugs

Sulfur. *See* **Sulphur**

Sulphur 546; 553.6; 661
> *x* Sulfur

Summer camps. *See* **Camps**

Summer employment 331.1
> *See also* **Teenagers—Employment; Youth—Employment**
>
> *xx* **Employment; Teenagers—Employment; Youth—Employment**

Summer homes. *See* **Architecture, Domestic; Houses**

Summer resorts
> *See also* **Health resorts, spas, etc.**
>
> *x* Resorts
>
> *xx* **Health resorts, spas, etc.**

Summer schools 371.2
> *x* Vacation schools
>
> *xx* **Public schools; Schools**

Summer schools, Religious 377
> *x* Bible classes; Vacation church schools; Vacation schools, Religious
>
> *xx* **Schools**

Sun 523.7
> *See also* **Solar energy; Solar system; Spectrum analysis; Sunspots**
>
> *x* Solar physics
>
> *xx* **Astronomy; Solar system**

Sun-dials. *See* **Sundials**

Sun—Eclipses. *See* **Eclipses, Solar**

Sun (in religion, folklore, etc.). *See* **Sun worship**

Sun powered batteries. *See* **Solar batteries**

Sun—Radiation. *See* **Solar radiation**

Sun-spots. *See* **Sunspots**

Sun worship 291.2
> *x* Sun (in religion, folklore, etc.)
>
> *xx* **Religion**

Sunday schools 268
> *See also* **Bible—Study**
>
> *x* Bible classes
>
> *xx* **Church work; Religious education**

Sundials 681.1
> *x* Horology; Sun-dials
>
> *xx* **Clocks and watches; Garden ornaments and furniture; Time**

Sunken cities. *See* **Cities and towns, Ruined, extinct, etc.**

Sunken treasure. *See* **Buried treasure**

Sunspots 523.7
> *x* Sun-spots
>
> *xx* **Meteorology; Solar radiation; Sun**

Super markets. *See* **Supermarkets**

Supercomputers 004.1
> Use for materials on extraordinarily powerful computers with a capability of hundreds of millions of floating-point operations per second, and having word length in the order of 64 bits and main memory size measured in

645

Supercomputers—*Continued*
    millions of words.
  xx **Computers**
Superconducting materials. *See* **Superconductors**
Superconductive devices. *See* **Superconductors**
Superconductors   537.6; 621.3
  x Superconducting materials; Superconductive
    devices
  xx **Electric conductors; Electronics**
Superhighways. *See* **Express highways**
Superintendents of schools. *See* **School superintendents and principals**
Superior children. *See* **Gifted children**
Supermarkets   658.8
  x Stores; Super markets
  xx **Grocery trade; Retail trade**
Supernatural   133; 398.2
  See also

Divination	**Prophecies (Occult sciences)**
Miracles	**Revelation**
Occultism	**Spiritualism**
Parapsychology	**Superstition**

  xx **Miracles; Religion**
Supernovae. *See* **Supernovas**
Supernovas   523.8
  x Supernovae
  xx **Stars**
Supersonic aerodynamics. *See* **Aerodynamics, Supersonic**
Supersonic airliners. *See* **Supersonic transport planes**
Supersonic transport planes   629.133
  x S.S.T.'s; SSTs; Supersonic airliners
Supersonic waves. *See* **Ultrasonic waves**
Supersonics. *See* **Ultrasonics**
Superstition   001.9; 398
  See also

Alchemy	**Exorcism**
Apparitions	**Fairies**
Astrology	**Folklore**
Charms	**Fortune telling**
Demonology	**Ghosts**
Divination	**Occultism**
Dreams	**Vampires**
Errors	**Witchcraft**

  x Delusions; Traditions
  xx **Demonology; Divination; Errors; Folklore; Ghosts; Occultism; Religion; Supernatural**
Supervision of employees. *See* **Personnel management**
Supervision of schools. *See* **School supervision**
Supervisors   331.7
  x Foremen and foreladies; Managers
  xx **Factory management; Personnel management**
Supplementary employment   331.1
  x Double employment; Dual employment; Employment, Supplementary; Moonlighting; Second job; Secondary employment
  xx **Labor; Part-time employment**
Support of children. *See* **Child support**
Supreme Court—United States. *See* **United States. Supreme Court**
Surf. *See* **Ocean waves**

Surf riding. *See* **Surfing**
Surface effect machines. *See* **Ground effect machines**
Surfing   **797.3**
   x Surf riding
   xx **Water sports**
Surfing—Songs and music   **782.42**
   xx **Music; Songs**
Surgeons   **610.69; 617.092; 920**
   See also **Physicians**
   x Medical profession
   xx **Physicians**
Surgery   **617**
   See also **Anesthetics; Antiseptics; Cryosurgery; Orthopedics; Plastic surgery; Transplantation of organs, tissues, etc.; Vivisection;** also names of diseases and names of organs and regions of the body with the subdivision *Surgery,* e.g. **Cancer—Surgery; Heart—Surgery;** etc.
   x Operations, Surgical
   xx **Medicine**
Surgery, Cosmetic. *See* **Plastic surgery**
Surgery, Orthopedic. *See* **Orthopedics**
Surgery, Plastic. *See* **Plastic surgery**
Surgical transplantation. *See* **Transplantation of organs, tissues, etc.**
Surnames. *See* **Personal names**
Surrealism   **709.04; 759.06**
   xx **Art; Postimpressionism (Art)**
Surrogate mothers   **176; 306.874; 346**
   xx **Mothers**
Surveillance, Electronic. *See* **Eavesdropping**
Surveying   **526.9**
   See also **Geodesy; Mine surveying; Topographical drawing**
   x Land surveying
   xx **Civil engineering; Geodesy; Geography; Measurement**
Surveys. *See* types of surveys, e.g. **Educational surveys; Library surveys; Social surveys;** etc.
Survival (after airplane accidents, shipwrecks, etc.)   **613.6**
   See also **Wilderness survival**
   x Castaways
   xx **Aeronautics—Accidents; Shipwrecks**
Survival of the fittest. *See* **Natural selection**
Survival skills   **613.6**
   Use for materials on skills needed to survive in a hazardous environment, usually stressing self-reliance and economic self-sufficiency.
   See also **Self-reliance;** also types of survival, e.g. **Wilderness survival;** etc.
   x Emergency survival; Human survival skills
   xx **Civil defense; Human ecology; Life skills; Man—Influence of environment; Self-reliance**
Survivalism   **320.5; 613.6**
   x Survivalist movements
   xx **Social movements**
Survivalist movements. *See* **Survivalism**
Suspended sentence. *See* **Probation**
Suspense fiction. *See* **Gothic fiction**
Suspension bridges. *See* **Bridges**

Swamp animals   591.52
　　xx **Animals; Marshes; Wildlife**
Swamps.   *See* **Marshes**
Swedish language   439.7
　　May be subdivided like **English language.**
　　xx **Scandinavian languages**
Swedish literature   839.7
　　May use same subdivisions and names of liter-
　　　　ary forms as for **English literature.**
　　xx **Scandinavian literature**
Swell.   *See* **Ocean waves**
Swimming   797.2
　　See also **Diving; Marathon swimming; Synchro-
　　　　nized swimming**
　　xx **Water sports**
Swimming pools   690; 725; 797.2
Swindlers and swindling   364.1
　　See also **Counterfeits and counterfeiting; Credit
　　　　card crimes; Fraud; Impostors and impos-
　　　　ture; Quacks and quackery**
　　x Con artists; Con game; Confidence game
　　xx **Crime; Criminals; Fraud; Impostors and im-
　　　　posture**
Swine.   *See* **Pigs**
Switchboard hotlines.   *See* **Hotlines (Telephone
　　　　counseling)**
Switches, Electric.   *See* **Electric switchgear**
Symbiosis.   *See* **Botany—Ecology**
Symbolic numbers.   *See* **Symbolism of numbers**
Symbolism   291.3; 704.9
　　See also **Heraldry; Signs and symbols;** also types
　　　　of symbolism in religions, e.g. **Christian art
　　　　and symbolism; Religious art and symbol-
　　　　ism;** etc.
　　xx **Art; Mythology; Signs and symbols**
Symbolism in literature   809
　　Use same form for symbolism in other subjects.
　　See also **Allegories**
　　xx **Literature**
Symbolism of numbers   133.3
　　See also **Cabala; Three (The number)**
　　x Number symbolism; Numerology; Sacred
　　　　numbers; Symbolic numbers
　　xx **Cabala; Christian art and symbolism; Magic;
　　　　Mysticism; Numerals**
Symbols.   *See* **Abbreviations; Signs and symbols**
Symbols, Mathematical.   *See* **Mathematical nota-
　　　　tion**
Sympathy   152.4
　　See also **Bereavement**
　　x Compassion; Consolation; Pity
　　xx **Bereavement; Emotions; Human behavior**
Symphonic poems   784.2
Symphonies   784.2
　　Use for musical scores.
　　xx **Orchestral music**
Symphony   784.18
　　Use for materials on the symphony as a musical
　　　　form.
　　xx **Musical form**
Symptoms.   *See* **Diagnosis**
Synagogues (May subdiv. geog.)   **726**
　　xx **Architecture; Judaism**

Synchronized swimming   797.2
   x Ballet, Water; Water ballet
   xx **Swimming**
Synfuels.   *See* **Synthetic fuels**
Synods.   *See* **Councils and synods**
Synonyms.   *See* names of languages with the subdivision *Synonyms and antonyms,* e.g. **English language—Synonyms and antonyms;** etc.
Synthesizer music.   *See* **Electronic music**
Synthesizer (Musical instrument)   786.7
   xx **Musical instruments, Electronic**
Synthetic chemistry.   *See* **Chemistry, Organic—Synthesis**
Synthetic detergents.   *See* **Detergents, Synthetic**
Synthetic drugs of abuse.   *See* **Designer drugs**
Synthetic fabrics   677
   See also names of synthetic fabrics, e.g. **Nylon; Rayon;** etc.
   x Fabrics, Synthetic
   xx **Fabrics; Synthetic products**
Synthetic foods.   *See* **Artificial foods**
Synthetic fuels   662
   x Artificial fuels; Nonfossil fuels; Synfuels
   xx **Fuel; Synthetic products**
Synthetic products   677; 678
   See also **Substitute products;** also names of types of synthetic products and names of specific products, e.g. **Artificial foods; Plastics; Rayon; Synthetic fabrics; Synthetic fuels; Synthetic rubber;** etc.
   xx **Chemistry, Organic—Synthesis; Chemistry, Technical; Plastics; Substitute products**
Synthetic rubber   678
   x Rubber, Artificial; Rubber, Synthetic
   xx **Plastics; Synthetic products**
Syphilis   616.95
   xx **Sexually transmitted diseases**
Syrups   641.3
   xx **Sugar**
System analysis   003; 004.2; 658.4
   See also **System design; Systems engineering**
   x Flow charts; Flowcharting; Linear system theory; Network theory; Systems analysis
   xx **Cybernetics; Mathematical models; System theory**
System design   003; 004.2; 621.39
   x Design, System; Systems design
   xx **Electronic data processing; System analysis**
System engineering.   *See* **Systems engineering**
System theory   003
   See also **Chaos (Science); Cybernetics; Operations research; System analysis; Systems engineering**
   x Systems, Theory of; Theory of systems
Systems analysis.   *See* **System analysis**
Systems, Database management.   *See* **Database management**
Systems design.   *See* **System design**
Systems engineering   620
   See also **Bionics; Operations research; Reliability (Engineering)**
   x System engineering

Systems engineering—*Continued*
  xx **Automation; Cybernetics; Engineering; Industrial design; Operations research; System analysis; System theory**
Systems reliability. *See* **Reliability (Engineering)**
Systems, Theory of. *See* **System theory**
T groups. *See* **Group relations training**
T.I.R.O.S. (Meteorological satellite). *See* **Tiros (Meteorological satellite)**
T.V. *See* **Television**
Table decoration. *See* **Table setting and decoration**
Table etiquette 395
  xx **Eating customs; Etiquette**
Table setting and decoration 642
  See also **Flower arrangement; Tableware**
  x Table decoration
  xx **Decoration and ornament**
Table talk. *See* **Conversation**
Table tennis. *See* **Ping-pong**
Tables (Systematic lists). *See* scientific and economic subjects with the subdivision *Tables,* e.g. **Trigonometry—Tables;** etc.
Tableware 642; 738; 739; 748.2
  See also **Glassware; Pottery; Silverware**
  xx **Table setting and decoration**
Tactics 355.4
  See also **Biological warfare; Guerrilla warfare**
  x Military tactics
  xx **Military art and science; Strategy**
Tactile materials. *See* **Manipulative materials**
Tadpoles. *See* **Frogs**
Tailoring 646.4; 687
  See also **Dressmaking; Uniforms, Military**
  x Garment making
  xx **Clothing and dress; Clothing trade; Dressmaking; Fashion**
Taiwan 951.24
  Use for materials discussing the post-1948 Republic of China or the island of Taiwan, regardless of time period. Materials discussing mainland China or the People's Republic of China, regardless of time period, are entered under **China.**
  Appropriate period subdivisions may be added as needed.
  x China (Republic of China, 1949-); Formosa; Nationalist China; Republic of China, 1949-
Takeovers, Corporate. *See* **Corporate mergers and acquisitions**
Talent. *See* **Genius; Gifted children; Musical ability**
Tales. *See* **Fables; Fairy tales; Folklore; Legends**
Talismans. *See* **Charms**
Talk shows 791.44; 791.45
  xx **Interviewing; Radio programs; Television programs**
Talking. *See* **Conversation**
Talking books 027.6
  x Books, Talking; Cassette books
  xx **Blind—Books and reading; Sound recordings**
Talking pictures. *See* **Motion pictures**
Tall tales 398.2; 808.83; 813, etc.; Fic
  xx **Folklore; Legends; Wit and humor**

Talmud 296.1
  xx **Hebrew literature; Jewish literature; Judaism**
Tanks (Military science) 355
  x Armored cars (Tanks); Cars, Armored (Tanks)
Tanning 675
  See also **Hides and skins; Leather**
  xx **Chemistry, Technical; Hides and skins;
      Leather**
Taoism 299
  xx **Religions**
Tap dancing 792.7
  See also **Clog dancing**
  xx **Dancing**
Tape recorder music. *See* **Electronic music**
Tape recorders. *See* **Magnetic recorders and re-
      cording**
Tape recordings, Audio. *See* **Sound recordings**
Tape recordings, Video. *See* **Videotapes**
Tapestry 746.3
  xx **Decoration and ornament; Decorative arts; In-
      terior design; Needlework**
Tardiness. *See* **Punctuality**
Tariff (May subdiv. geog.) 336.2; 382
  See also **Balance of trade; Free trade and protec-
      tion; Smuggling**
  x Custom duties; Customs (Tariff); Duties; Ex-
      ports; Government regulation of commerce;
      Imports; Revenue
  xx **Commerce; Commercial policy; Economic pol-
      icy; Finance; Free trade and protection;
      Taxation; Trusts, Industrial**
Tariff question—Free trade and protection. *See*
      Free trade and protection
Tariff—United States 336.2; 382
  x United States—Tariff
Tarot 133.3; 795.4
  Use for materials on the cards and the game.
  xx **Card games; Fortune telling**
Tartans 391
  x Highland costume; Scottish tartans
  xx **Clans**
Taste 152.1
  xx **Senses and sensation**
Taste (Aesthetics). *See* **Aesthetics**
Taverns. *See* **Restaurants, bars, etc.**
Tax credits 336.2
  xx **Income tax**
Tax relations, Intergovernmental. *See* **Intergovern-
      mental tax relations**
Tax sharing. *See* **Intergovernmental tax relations;
      Revenue sharing**
Taxation (May subdiv. geog.) 336.2
  See also

Assessment	**relations**
Income tax	**Internal revenue**
Inheritance and transfer	**Sales tax**
tax	**Tariff**
Intergovernmental tax	**Tithes**

  also subjects with the subdivision *Taxation,* e.g.
      Real estate investment—Taxation; etc.
  x Direct taxation; Duties; Revenue; Taxes
  xx **Assessment; Estate planning; Finance; Politi-
      cal science**
Taxation of income. *See* **Income tax**

651

Taxation of legacies. *See* **Inheritance and transfer tax**

Taxation of sales. *See* **Sales tax**

Taxation—United States   336.200973

    x United States—Taxation

Taxes. *See* **Taxation**

Taxidermy   579

    See also **Zoological specimens—Collection and preservation;** also names of specimens with the subdivision *Collection and preservation,* e.g. **Birds—Collection and preservation;** etc.

    x Preservation of specimens; Specimens, Preservation of

    xx **Zoological specimens—Collection and preservation**

Tea rooms. *See* **Restaurants, bars, etc.**

Teach yourself courses. *See* **Self-culture**

Teacher exchange   370.19

    x Exchange of teachers; Interchange of teachers; Teachers, Exchange of; Teachers, Interchange of

    xx **Exchange of persons programs; International education**

Teacher-parent conferences. *See* **Parent-teacher conferences**

Teacher-parent relationships. *See* **Parent-teacher relationships**

Teacher-student relationships   371.1; 378.1

    x Pupil-teacher relationships; Student-teacher interaction

    xx **Children and adults; Human relations; Teaching**

Teacher training. *See* **Teachers colleges; Teachers—Training**

Teachers   371.1; 920

    See also **Educational associations; Educators; School superintendents and principals; Teaching**

    x College teachers; Faculty (Education); Professors

    xx **Education; Educators**

Teachers and parents. *See* **Parent-teacher relationships**

Teachers colleges   378.1

    Use for general and historical materials about teachers colleges. Materials dealing with their educational functions are entered under **Teachers—Training.**

    See also **Teachers—Training;** also names of teachers colleges

    x Normal schools; Teacher training; Training colleges for teachers

    xx **Colleges and universities; Education—Study and teaching; Teachers—Training**

Teachers, Exchange of. *See* **Teacher exchange**

Teachers' institutes. *See* **Teachers' workshops**

Teachers, Interchange of. *See* **Teacher exchange**

Teachers—Practice teaching. *See* **Student teaching**

Teachers' reports. *See* **School reports**

Teachers, Student rating of. *See* **Student evaluation of teachers**

652

Teachers—Training 371.1
Use for materials dealing with the history and
methods of training teachers, including the
educational functions of teachers colleges.
Materials on the study of education as a science are entered under **Education—Study
and teaching.**
See also **Student teaching; Teachers colleges;
Teachers' workshops**
x Teacher training
xx **Education—Study and teaching; Teachers colleges; Teaching**
Teachers' workshops 371.1
x Teachers' institutes; Workshops, Teachers'
xx **Teachers—Training**
Teaching 371.1
Use for materials on the art and method of
teaching.
See also

Classroom management	**School superintendents**
Education	**and principals**
Educational psychology	**School supervision**
Examinations	**Student teaching**
Home instruction	**Study skills**
Kindergarten	**Teacher-student relation-**
Lectures and lecturing	**ships**
Montessori method of edu-	**Teachers—Training**
cation	**Teaching teams**
Project method in teaching	**Tutors and tutoring**
School discipline	

also subjects with the subdivision *Study and
teaching,* e.g. **Science—Study and teaching;**
etc.
x Instruction; Pedagogy; School teaching
xx **Education; Schools—Administration; Teachers**
Teaching—Aids and devices 371.3
See also

Audiovisual materials	**Programmed instruction**
Bulletin boards	**Radio in education**
Manipulative materials	**Teaching machines**
Motion pictures in educa-	**Television in education**
tion	

x Educational media; Instructional materials;
Teaching materials
Teaching at home. *See* **Home instruction**
Teaching, Computer. *See* **Computer assisted in-
struction**
Teaching—Data processing. *See* **Computer assisted
instruction**
Teaching—Experimental methods. *See* **Educa-
tion—Experimental methods**
Teaching, Freedom of. *See* **Academic freedom**
Teaching machines 371.3
x Automatic teaching; Tutorial machines
xx **Programmed instruction; Teaching—Aids and
devices**
Teaching materials. *See* **Teaching—Aids and de-
vices**
Teaching teams 371.1
x Team teaching
xx **Teaching**
Teachings of Jesus. *See* **Jesus Christ—Teachings**
Team teaching. *See* **Teaching teams**

653

Tearooms. *See* **Restaurants, bars, etc.**
Technical assistance (May subdiv. geog. adjective
        form) **338.91; 361.6**
        See note under **Economic assistance.**
        See also **Community development; Developing
            countries; Industrialization**
        x Aid to developing areas; Assistance to devel-
            oping areas; Foreign aid program
        xx **Community development; Developing coun-
            tries; Economic assistance; Economic policy;
            Industrialization; International cooperation;
            International economic relations**
Technical assistance, American **338.91; 361.6**
        x American technical assistance; United
            States—Technical assistance
Technical chemistry. *See* **Chemistry, Technical**
Technical education **370.11; 373.2; 374**
        See also

Apprentices	**Industrial arts education**
Correspondence schools	**Occupational retraining**
and courses	**Occupational training**
Employees—Training	**Professional education**
Evening and continuation	**School shops**
schools	**Vocational education**

        also technical subjects with the subdivision
            Study and teaching, e.g. **Engineering—
            Study and teaching;** etc.
        x Education, Industrial; Education, Technical;
            Industrial education; Industrial schools;
            Technical schools; Trade schools
        xx **Education; Employees—Training; Higher edu-
            cation; Industrial arts education; Profes-
            sional education; Technology; Vocational
            education**
Technical schools. *See* **Technical education**
Technical service. *See* **Customer service**
Technical services (Libraries). *See* **Library techni-
            cal processes**
Technical terms. *See* **Technology—Dictionaries**
Technical writing **808**
        x Scientific writing
        xx **Authorship; Technology—Language**
Technique. *See* subjects with the subdivision
            Technique, e.g. **Fiction—Technique; Love
            stories—Technique; Painting—Technique;**
            etc.
Technology **600**
        See also

Building	**Machinery**
Chemistry, Technical	**Manufactures**
Engineering	**Mills and millwork**
Industrial arts	**Technical education**
Inventions	

        x Applied science; Arts, Useful; High tech; High
            technology; Useful arts
        xx **Industrial arts**
Technology and civilization **303.4**
        Use same form for technology and other subjects
        See also **Computers and civilization; Machinery
            in industry**
        x Civilization and technology
        xx **Civilization**
Technology—Dictionaries **603**
        x Technical terms

654

Technology—Language 601; 603
    See also **Technical writing**
Teen age. *See* **Adolescence**
Teen-agers. *See* **Teenagers**
Teenage consumers. *See* **Young consumers**
Teenage drinking. *See* **Teenagers—Alcohol use**
Teenage dropouts. *See* **Dropouts**
Teenage fathers 305.23; 362.7
    See note under **Unmarried fathers.**
    x Adolescent fathers; Parents, Teenage; School
        age fathers; Schoolboy fathers; Teenage par-
        ents
    xx **Fathers**
Teenage mothers 305.23; 362.7; 362.83
    See note under **Unmarried mothers.**
    See also **Teenage pregnancy**
    x Adolescent mothers; Parents, Teenage; School
        age mothers; Schoolgirl mothers; Teenage
        parents
    xx **Mothers; Teenage pregnancy**
Teenage parents. *See* **Teenage fathers; Teenage**
    mothers
Teenage pregnancy 362.7; 618.2
    See also **Teenage mothers**
    x Adolescent pregnancy; Pregnancy, Adolescent;
        Pregnancy, Teenage
    xx **Teenage mothers**
Teenage prostitution. *See* **Juvenile prostitution**
Teenagers (May subdiv. geog.) **305.23**
    Use for materials about teen youth. For materi-
        als on the time of life extending from thir-
        teen to twenty-five years, as well as on peo-
        ple in that general age range, use **Youth.**
        For materials limited to people in the gen-
        eral age range of eighteen through twenty-
        five years of age, use **Young men; Young**
        women. Materials on the process or state of
        growing up are entered under **Adolescence.**
    See also **Boys; Girls; Runaway teenagers**
    x Adolescents; Boys, Teenage; Girls, Teenage;
        Teen-agers; Teens
    xx **Boys; Girls; Youth**
Teenagers—Alcohol use 362.29; 613.81; 616.86
    See also **Drinking age**
    x Alcohol and teenagers; Drinking and teen-
        agers; Teenage drinking; Teenagers and al-
        cohol
Teenagers and alcohol. *See* **Teenagers—Alcohol**
    use
Teenagers and drugs. *See* **Teenagers—Drug use**
Teenagers and narcotics. *See* **Teenagers—Drug use**
Teenagers—Attitudes 155.5; 305.23
    xx **Attitude (Psychology)**
Teenagers—Development. *See* **Adolescence**
Teenagers—Drug use 362.29; 613.8; 616.86
    See also **Juvenile delinquency**
    x Drugs and teenagers; Narcotics and teenagers;
        Teenagers and drugs; Teenagers and narcot-
        ics
    xx **Juvenile delinquency; Youth—Drug use**
Teenagers—Employment 331.3
    See also **Summer employment**
    x Child labor; Employment of teenagers

Teenagers—Employment—*Continued*
  xx **Age and employment; Labor; Labor supply;
      Summer employment; Youth—Employment**
Teenagers' library services. *See* **Young adults' library services**
Teenagers—Literature. *See* **Young adults' literature**
Teenagers, Psychiatry of. *See* **Adolescent psychiatry**
Teenagers—Psychology. *See* **Adolescent psychology**
Teenagers—Religious life   248.8
  xx **Youth—Religious life**
Teenagers—United States   305.23
  x American teenagers; United States—Teenagers
  xx **Youth—United States**
Teens. *See* **Teenagers**
Teeth   611; 612.3; 617.6
  See also **Dentistry**
  x Anatomy, Dental
  xx **Dentistry**
Teeth—Diseases   617.6
  See also **Water—Fluoridation**
  x Medicine, Dental
Telecommunication   384; 621.38
  See also

Artificial satellites in telecommunication	**tems**
Broadcasting	**Interstellar communication**
Cables, Submarine	**Microwave communication systems**
Computer networks	**Radio**
Data transmission systems	**Speech processing systems**
Electronic mail systems	**Telecommuting**
Electronic publishing	**Telegraph**
Facsimile transmission	**Telephone**
Intercommunication sys-	**Television**

  also subjects with the subdivision
      Communication systems, e.g. **Astronautics—Communication systems;** etc.
  x Electric communication; Mass communication
  xx **Communication**
Telecommuting   331.2
  Use for materials on employment at home with computers, word processors, etc., connected to a central work site, permitting employees to substitute telecommunications for transportation.
  See also **Home computers**
  x Alternate work sites; At-home employment; Cottage industry, Electronic; Electronic cottage; Flexiplace; Home labor; Home work (Employment); Homework (Employment); Work at home; Working at home
  xx **Automation; Home business; Telecommunication**
Teleconferencing   384; 658.4
  x Conference calls (Teleconferencing); Telephone—Conference calls
  xx **Telephone**
Telefax. *See* **Facsimile transmission**
Telegraph   384.1; 621.383
  See also **Cables, Submarine; Cipher and telegraph codes**

656

Telegraph—*Continued*

 xx **Electric engineering; Electric wiring; Electricity; Public utilities; Telecommunication**

Telegraph codes. *See* **Cipher and telegraph codes**

Telegraph, Submarine. *See* **Cables, Submarine**

Telekinesis. *See* **Psychokinesis**

Telemarketing 381; 658.8

 Use for materials on the use of electronic media as a form of marketing that bypasses retail outlets in the advertising and selling of goods.

 x Electronic marketing

 xx **Direct selling; Marketing**

Telepathy 133.8

 See also **Clairvoyance**

 x Mental telepathy; Mind reading; Thought transference

 xx **Clairvoyance; Extrasensory perception; Parapsychology; Subconsciousness**

Telephone 384.6; 621.385

 See also **Teleconferencing; Video telephone**

 xx **Electric engineering; Electric wiring; Electricity; Public utilities; Telecommunication**

Telephone—Conference calls. *See* **Teleconferencing**

Telephone counseling. *See* **Hotlines (Telephone counseling)**

Telephone directories. *See* names of cities with the subdivision *Telephone directories,* e.g. **Chicago (Ill.)—Telephone directories;** etc.

Telephotography 778.3

 xx **Photography**

Teleprocessing networks. *See* **Computer networks**

Telereference. *See* **Information networks; Teletext systems; Videotex systems**

Telescope 522

 xx **Astronomical instruments**

Teletext systems 004.692; 384.3

 Use for materials on the one-way transmission of computer-based data, such as weather forecasts or stock quotations, from a central source to a television set.

 See also **Videotex systems**

 x Telereference

 xx **Data transmission systems; Electronic publishing; Information systems; Television broadcasting; Videotex systems**

Television 302.23; 384.55; 621.388

 See also

Closed caption television	**systems**
Closed-circuit television	**Video art**
Color television	**Video telephone**
High definition television	**Videodiscs**
Home video systems	**Videotapes**
Microwave communication	

 x T.V.; TV

 xx **Telecommunication**

Television actors. *See* **Actors**

Television adaptations 791.45

 x Adaptations; Adaptations, Television; Literature—Film and video adaptations; Motion pictures—Television adaptations

 xx **Television plays; Television programs; Television scripts**

Television advertising   659.14
   x Advertising, Television; Commercials, Television; Television commercials
   xx **Advertising; Television broadcasting**
Television and children   305.23; 384.55; 791.45
   Use for materials dealing with the effect of television on children.
   Use same form for television and other subjects.
   See also **Motion pictures and children**
   x Children and television
   xx **Children; Motion pictures and children**
Television and infrared observation satellite.   *See*
      Tiros (Meteorological satellite)
Television and youth   305.23; 384.55; 791.45
   x Youth and television
   xx **Youth**
Television apparatus industry.   *See* **Television supplies industry**
Television authorship   808
   See also **Television plays—Technique**
   x Television writing
   xx **Authorship**
Television broadcasting   384.55
   See also

Cable television	**Television advertising**
Equal time rule (Broadcasting)	**Television in education**
	Television in politics
Fairness doctrine (Broadcasting)	**Television programs**
	Television scripts
Public television	**Videotape recorders and**
Subscription television	**recording**
Teletext systems	**Videotex systems**

   x Television industry
   xx **Broadcasting; Mass media**
Television broadcasting—Vocational guidance 384.55
   xx **Vocational guidance**
Television, Cable.   *See* **Cable television**
Television—Censorship   384.55
   xx **Censorship**
Television, Closed-circuit.   *See* **Closed-circuit television**
Television, Color.   *See* **Color television**
Television commercials.   *See* **Television advertising**
Television drama.   *See* **Television plays**
Television—Equipment and supplies   621.388
   See also **Television—Receivers and reception; Television supplies industry; Videodisc players; Videotape recorders and recording**
Television equipment industry.   *See* **Television supplies industry**
Television games.   *See* **Video games**
Television in astronautics   621.388; 629.47
   x Space television; Television, Space
   xx **Astronautics—Communication systems**
Television in education   371.33
   Use same pattern for television in other subjects.
   See also **Closed-circuit television**
   x Education and television; Educational television
   xx **Audiovisual education; Closed-circuit television; Teaching—Aids and devices; Television broadcasting**

Television in politics   324.7
See also Equal time rule (Broadcasting); Fairness doctrine (Broadcasting)
xx Politics, Practical; Television broadcasting
Television industry.   See Television broadcasting; Television supplies industry
Television journalism.   See Broadcast journalism
Television news.   See Broadcast journalism
Television plays   808.82; 812, etc.
Use for individual television plays, for collections of plays and for materials about them. Materials on how to write television plays are entered under Television plays—Technique.
See also Television adaptations
x Scenarios; Television drama
xx Drama; Television programs; Television scripts
Television plays—Technique   808.2
See also Radio plays—Technique
x Play writing; Playwriting
xx Drama—Technique; Radio plays—Technique; Television authorship
Television—Production and direction   384.55; 791.45
Television programs   791.45
See also Television adaptations; also types of television programs and specific programs, e.g. Music videos; Talk shows; Television plays; etc.
x Programs, Television
xx Television broadcasting
Television, Public.   See Public television
Television—Receivers and reception   621.388
See also Video games
x Television reception; Television sets
xx Television—Equipment and supplies
Television reception.   See Television—Receivers and reception
Television—Repairing   621.388
Television scripts   791.45
See also Radio scripts; Television adaptations; Television plays
xx Radio scripts; Television broadcasting
Television sets.   See Television—Receivers and reception
Television, Space.   See Television in astronautics
Television—Stage lighting.   See Stage lighting
Television stations   384.55
Television, Subscription.   See Subscription television
Television supplies industry   338.4; 384.55
x Television apparatus industry; Television equipment industry; Television industry
xx Television—Equipment and supplies
Television writing.   See Television authorship
Telstar project   621.382
x Bell System Telstar satellite; Project Telstar
xx Artificial satellites in telecommunication
Temperament   155.2
See also Character
xx Character; Mind and body; Psychology; Psychophysiology

Temperance 178; 241; 613.81
>Use for general materials on the temperance
>question and the temperance movement.
>*See also* **Alcohol—Physiological effect; Alcohol-
>ism; Drinking of alcoholic beverages; Drug
>addiction; Prohibition; Stimulants**
>*x* Abstinence; Drunkenness; Intemperance; In-
>toxication; Total abstinence
>*xx* **Alcoholism; Drinking of alcoholic beverages;
>Drug addiction; Human behavior; Prohibi-
>tion**

Temperature 536
>*See also* **Heat; Low temperatures; Thermometers**
>*xx* **Heat; Thermometers**

Temperature, Animal and human. *See* **Body temperature**

Temperature, Body. *See* **Body temperature**

Temperatures, Low. *See* **Low temperatures**

Temples (May subdiv. geog.) 726
>*See also* **Mosques**
>*xx* **Archeology; Architecture; Architecture, An-
>cient; Architecture, Asian; Church architec-
>ture**

Temporal power of the Pope. *See* **Popes—
Temporal power**

Temporary employment 331.2
>*x* Employment, Temporary
>*xx* **Employment**

Ten commandments 222
>*x* Commandments, Ten; Decalogue

Tenant and landlord. *See* **Landlord and tenant**

Tenant farming. *See* **Farm tenancy**

Tenement houses 363.5
>*See also* **City planning; Housing**
>*xx* **Cities and towns; Houses; Housing**

Tennis 796.342
>*x* Lawn tennis
>*xx* **Games**

Tennis—Tournaments 796.342
>*xx* **Contests**

Tenpins. *See* **Bowling**

Tension (Physiology). *See* **Stress (Physiology)**

Tension, Premenstrual. *See* **Premenstrual syndrome**

Tension (Psychology). *See* **Stress (Psychology)**

Tents 796.54
>*xx* **Camping**

Tenure of land. *See* **Land tenure**

Tenure of office. *See* **Civil service**

Term paper writing. *See* **Report writing**

Terminal care 362.1; 649.8
>*See also* **Death; Hospices; Life support systems
>(Medical environment); Terminally ill; Ter-
>minally ill children**
>*x* Care of the dying
>*xx* **Death**

Terminally ill 362.1; 649.8
>*See also* **Death; Terminally ill children**
>*x* Dying patients; Fatally ill patients
>*xx* **Death; Sick; Terminal care**

Terminally ill children 362.1; 649.8
>*x* Dying children; Fatally ill children
>*xx* **Terminal care; Terminally ill**

Terminals, Computer. *See* **Computer terminals**

Termination of pregnancy. *See* **Abortion**

Terminology. *See* **Names;** and subjects with the
　　　subdivision *Terminology,* e.g. **Botany—**
　　　Terminology; etc.

Terns   598.3
　　xx **Water birds**

Terra cotta   620.1; 693
　　xx **Building materials; Decoration and ornament;**
　　　Pottery

Terrain sensing, Remote. *See* **Remote sensing**

Terrapins. *See* **Turtles**

Terrariums   635.9
　　See also **Gardens, Miniature**
　　x Vivariums
　　xx **Indoor gardening**

Terrestrial physics. *See* **Geophysics**

Territorial waters (May subdiv. geog.)   **341.4**
　　See also **Continental shelf; Maritime law**
　　x 3 mile limit; 200 mile limit; Economic zones
　　　(Maritime law); Three mile limit; Two hun-
　　　dred mile limit
　　xx **Continental shelf; Maritime law; Shipping**

Territorial waters—United States   341.4
　　x United States—Territorial waters

Terror, Reign of. *See* **France—History—1789-**
　　　1799, Revolution

Terrorism (May subdiv. geog.)   **322.4**
　　See also **Hostages; Sabotage**
　　x Political violence
　　xx **Anarchism and anarchists; Assassination; In-**
　　　surgency; Political crimes and offenses; Rev-
　　　olutions; Subversive activities

Terrorism—United States   303.6; 322.4
　　x United States—Terrorism

Test pilots. *See* **Air pilots; Airplanes—Testing**

Test tube babies. *See* **Fertilization in vitro**

Test tube fertilization. *See* **Fertilization in vitro**

Testing. *See* **Electric testing; Reliability (Engineer-**
　　　ing); Strength of materials; and things
　　　tested with the subdivision *Testing,* e.g.
　　　Ability—Testing; Airplanes—Testing; Con-
　　　crete—Testing; etc; and classes of people
　　　with the subdivision *Drug testing,* e.g. **Em-**
　　　ployees—Drug testing; etc.

Testing for drug abuse. *See* **Drug testing**

Tests. *See* **Educational tests and measurements;**
　　　Examinations; Mental tests

Teutonic peoples   305.83
　　See also **Anglo-Saxons**
　　x Goths; Nordic peoples; Ostrogoths; Saxons;
　　　Visigoths
　　xx **Ethnology**

Textbooks   371.3
　　Use for materials about textbooks, not for text-
　　　books of a subject. The latter are entered
　　　under the name of subject only, e.g. **Arith-**
　　　metic; Geography; etc.
　　x School books

Textile chemistry   677
　　See also **Dyes and dyeing**
　　x Chemistry, Textile
　　xx **Chemistry, Technical; Textile industry**

Textile design   746
    See also Textile painting
    xx Commercial art; Decoration and ornament;
        Design
Textile fibers.   *See* Fibers
Textile industry   677
    See also

Bleaching	Textile chemistry
Cotton manufacture	Textile printing
Dyes and dyeing	Weaving
Spinning	Yarn

    also names of articles manufactured, e.g Car-
        pets; Hosiery; etc
    xx Weaving
Textile painting   746.6
    xx Painting; Textile design
Textile printing   746.6
    See also Silk screen printing
    x Block printing; Printing, Textile
    xx Textile industry
Textiles.   *See* Fabrics
Thanksgiving Day   394.2
    xx Fasts and feasts; Holidays
Theater (May subdiv. geog.)   792
    Use for materials dealing with drama as acted on
        the stage, and with the historical, moral, and
        religious aspects of the theater. Materials
        dealing with drama from a literary point of
        view are entered under Drama; American
        drama; English drama; etc.
    See also

Acting	plays
Actors	Opera
Amateur theater	Pantomimes
Arena theater	Passion plays
Ballet	Puppets and puppet plays
Children's plays	Readers' theater
Drama	Shadow pantomimes and
Dramatic criticism	plays
Experimental theater	Shakespeare, William,
Little theater movement	1564-1616—Stage his-
Masks (Plays)	tory
Morality plays	Theaters
Motion pictures	Vaudeville
Mysteries and miracle	

    also names of wars with the subdivision *Theater
        and the war,* e.g. World War, 1939-1945—
        Theater and the war; etc.
    x Histrionics; Stage
    xx Acting; Actors; Amusements; Drama; Drama
        in education; Performing arts
Theater, Amateur.   *See* Amateur theater
Theater criticism.   *See* Dramatic criticism
Theater-in-the-round.   *See* Arena theater
Theater—Little theater movement.   *See* Little the-
    ater movement
Theater—Production and direction   792
    See also Motion pictures—Production and direc-
        tion
    x Direction (Theater); Play direction (Theater);
        Play production
Theater—United States   792.0973
    x United States—Theater

662

Theaters (May subdiv. geog.)   **725**
>   Use for materials dealing only with theater
>   buildings, their architecture, construction,
>   decoration, sanitation, etc.
>   *x* Opera houses; Playhouses
>   *xx* **Architecture; Centers for the performing arts;**
>   **Theater**
Theaters—Stage lighting.   *See* **Stage lighting**
Theaters—Stage setting and scenery   792
>   *See also* **Scene painting**
>   *x* Scenery (Stage); Stage scenery; Stage setting;
>   Theatrical scenery
Theatrical costume.   *See* **Costume**
Theatrical makeup.   *See* **Makeup, Theatrical**
Theatrical scenery.   *See* **Theaters—Stage setting**
>   **and scenery**
Theatricals, College.   *See* **College and school drama**
Thefts, Art.   *See* **Art thefts**
Theism   211
>   *See also* **Atheism; Christianity; Deism; God**
>   *xx* **Atheism; Deism; God; Philosophy; Rational-**
>   **ism; Religion; Theology**
Theme parks.   *See* **Amusement parks**
Theological education.   *See* **Theology—Study and**
>   **teaching**
Theology   230; 291
>   *See also*

Atheism	**Mysticism**
Baptism	**Natural theology**
Christianity	**Predestination**
Church	**Providence and govern-**
Conversion	**ment of God**
Creeds	**Religion**
Deism	**Religion and science**
Doctrinal theology	**Revelation**
Eschatology	**Sacraments**
Faith	**Sacrifice**
God—Christianity	**Sanctification**
Good and evil	**Secularism**
Grace (Theology)	**Sin**
Holy Spirit	**Spiritual life**
Immortality	**Theism**
Liturgies	**Trinity**
Man (Theology)	**Worship**

>   *xx* **Christianity; Creation; God—Christianity; Re-**
>   **ligion**
Theology, Devotional.   *See* **Devotional exercises;**
>   **Prayers**
Theology, Doctrinal.   *See* **Doctrinal theology**
Theology, Natural.   *See* **Natural theology**
Theology of liberation.   *See* **Liberation theology**
Theology, Pastoral.   *See* **Pastoral work**
Theology—Philosophy.   *See* **Christianity—**
>   **Philosophy**
Theology—Study and teaching   230; 291
>   *See also* **Catechisms; Christian education;**
>   **Church and education; Religious education**
>   *x* Education, Theological; Religion—Study and
>   teaching; Theological education
>   *xx* **Christian education; Church and education;**
>   **Religious education**
Theoretical chemistry.   *See* **Chemistry, Physical**
>   **and theoretical**
Theory of games.   *See* **Game theory**

Theory of graphs. *See* **Graph theory**
Theory of numbers. *See* **Number theory**
Theory of structures. *See* **Structures, Theory of**
Theory of systems. *See* **System theory**
Theosophy 299
   See also **Reincarnation; Yoga**
   xx **Mysticism; Religions**
Therapeutic systems. *See* **Alternative medicine**
Therapeutics 615.5
   See also

Antiseptics	**Naturopathy**
Diet in disease	**Nursing**
Drugs	**Nutrition**
Electrotherapeutics	**Pharmaceutical chemistry**
Gene therapy	**Stimulants**
Materia medica	**X rays**
Medicine	

     also names of diseases and groups of diseases,
        e.g. **AIDS (Disease); Fever; Nervous sys-**
        tem—Diseases; etc.; names of food with the
        subdivision *Therapeutic use,* e.g. **Corn—**
        Therapeutic use; etc.; names of drugs, e.g.
        Narcotics; etc.; and names of types of ther-
        apy, e.g. **Diet therapy; Hydrotherapy; Occu-**
        pational therapy; Pet therapy; Phototherapy;
        Physical therapy; Radiotherapy; etc.
   x Diseases—Treatment; Therapy; Treatment of
       diseases
   xx **Medicine; Pathology; Pharmaceutical chemis-**
       try
Therapeutics, Suggestive 615.8
   See also **Hypnotism; Mental healing; Mental**
       suggestion; Psychology, Pastoral; Psycho-
       therapy; Spiritual healing; Subconsciousness
   x Suggestive therapeutics
   xx **Hypnotism; Mental healing; Mental sugges-**
       tion; Psychotherapy; Spiritual healing
Therapy. *See* **Therapeutics**
Therapy, Gene. *See* **Gene therapy**
Thermal insulation. *See* **Insulation (Heat)**
Thermal waters. *See* **Geothermal resources; Gey-**
   sers
Thermoaerodynamics. *See* **Aerothermodynamics**
Thermodynamics 536
   See also **Aerothermodynamics; Heat; Heat en-**
       gines; Heat pumps; Quantum theory; also
       subjects with the subdivision
       Thermodynamics, e.g. **Space vehicles—**
       Thermodynamics; etc.
   xx **Chemistry, Physical and theoretical; Dynam-**
       ics; Heat; Heat engines; Physics; Quantum
       theory
Thermometers 536
   See also **Temperature**
   x Thermometers and thermometry; Thermome-
       try
   xx **Heat; Meteorological instruments; Tempera-**
       ture
Thermometers and thermometry. *See* **Thermome-**
   ters
Thermometry. *See* **Thermometers**
Thermonuclear bomb. *See* **Hydrogen bomb**
Thesauri. *See* **Subject headings;** and names of lan-

Thesauri—*Continued*
  guages with the subdivision *Synonyms and antonyms,* e.g. **English language— Synonyms and antonyms;** etc.
Theses. *See* **Dissertations, Academic**
Thieves. *See* **Robbers and outlaws**
Think tanks. *See* **Problem solving, Group**
Thinking. *See* **Thought and thinking**
Third parties (U.S. politics). *See* **Third parties (United States politics)**
Third parties (United States politics) 324.2
  x Third parties (U.S. politics)
  xx **Political parties; United States—Politics and government**
Third World. *See* **Developing countries**
Third World War. *See* **World War III**
Thirteenth century 909.07
  See note under **Nineteenth century.**
  x 1200-1299 (13th century)
  xx **Middle Ages**
Thirty Years' War, 1618-1648 909.08; 940.2
  xx **Europe—History—1492-1789; Germany— History—1517-1740**
Thoroughfares. *See* **Roads; Streets**
Thought and thinking 153.4
  See also **Attention; Critical thinking; Intellect; Logic; Memory; Perception; Reasoning**
  x Thinking
  xx **Educational psychology; Intellect; Logic; Psychology**
Thought control. *See* **Brainwashing**
Thought transference. *See* **Telepathy**
Threatened species. *See* **Endangered species**
Three dimensional photography 778.4
  See also **Holography**
  x 3-D photography; 3D photography; Photography, Stereoscopic; Stereo photography; Stereophotography; Stereoscopic photography
  xx **Holography; Photography**
Three mile limit. *See* **Territorial waters**
Three (The number) 513
  xx **Numerals; Symbolism of numbers**
Thrift. *See* **Saving and thrift**
Throat 611; 612; 617.5
  See also **Voice**
Thunderstorms 551.55
  See also **Lightning**
  xx **Meteorology; Storms**
Tiananmen Square Incident, China, 1989. *See* **China—History—1989, Tiananmen Square Incident**
Tiananmen Square Massacre, China. *See* **China— History—1989, Tiananmen Square Incident**
Ticks 595.4
  See also **Lyme disease**
  x Arachnida
  xx **Lyme disease; Parasites**
Tidal waves. *See* **Ocean waves**
Tidal waves, Seismic. *See* **Tsunamis**
Tides 551.47
  xx **Astronomy; Moon; Navigation; Oceanography; Physical geography**
Tie dyeing 667
  xx **Dyes and dyeing**

Tien-an men Incident, China, 1989. *See* **China—History—1989, Tiananmen Square Incident**

Tien-an men Massacre, 1989. *See* **China—History—1989, Tiananmen Square Incident**

Tiles   620.1; 693; 738.6
   xx **Bricks; Building materials; Ceramics; Clay industries; Pottery**

Timber. *See* **Forests and forestry; Lumber and lumbering; Trees; Wood**

Time   529
   See also

Calendars	**Night**
Chronology	**Periodicity**
Clocks and watches	**Punctuality**
Day	**Sundials**

   x Standard time
   xx **Longitude; Periodicity**

Time and space. *See* **Space and time**

Time management   640; 650.1
   x Allocation of time; Personal time management; Time—Organization; Time, Use of; Use of time
   xx **Leisure; Management**

Time—Organization. *See* **Time management**

Time production standards. *See* **Production standards**

Time saving cookery. *See* **Quick and easy cookery**

Time sharing (Real estate). *See* **Timesharing (Real estate)**

Time study   658.5
   See also **Motion study**
   xx **Efficiency, Industrial; Factory management; Job analysis; Motion study; Personnel management; Production standards**

Time, Use of. *See* **Time management**

Timesharing (Real estate)   333.3; 333.5; 643
   x Condominium timesharing; Real estate timesharing; Time sharing (Real estate); Vacation home timesharing
   xx **Condominiums; Housing**

Tin   669
   See also **Pewter**

Tinsmithing. *See* **Tinwork**

Tinwork   671
   x Tinsmithing
   xx **Metalwork**

Tires   678
   x Rubber tires
   xx **Wheels**

Tiros (Meteorological satellite)   551.6
   x T.I.R.O.S. (Meteorological satellite); Television and infrared observation satellite
   xx **Meteorological satellites**

Tissue donation. *See* **Donation of organs, tissues, etc.**

Tissues—Transplantation. *See* **Transplantation of organs, tissues, etc.**

Tithes   254.8
   xx **Church finance; Ecclesiastical law; Taxation**

Toadstools. *See* **Mushrooms**

Toasts   808.5; 808.85
   See also **After dinner speeches**
   x Healths, Drinking of

Toasts—*Continued*
> *xx* After dinner speeches; Epigrams; Speeches, addresses, etc.

Tobacco 633.7
> *See also* Smoking
> *xx* Smoking

Tobacco habit 178; 613.85; 616.86
> *See also* Smoking cessation programs
> *xx* Habit; Smoking; Substance abuse

Tobacco pipes 688
> *x* Pipes, Tobacco
> *xx* Smoking

Toes. *See* **Foot**

Toilet preparations. *See* **Cosmetics**

Toilet training 649
> *x* Training, Toilet
> *xx* Child rearing

Toleration 179; 323
> *See also* Academic freedom; Discrimination; Freedom of conscience; Freedom of religion
> *x* Bigotry; Intolerance
> *xx* Discrimination; Human relations

Toll roads. *See* **Express highways**

Tombs (May subdiv. geog.) **726**
> *See also* Brasses; Catacombs; Cemeteries; Epitaphs; Mounds and mound builders
> *x* Burial; Graves; Mausoleums; Rock tombs; Sepulchers; Vaults (Sepulchral)
> *xx* Archeology; Architecture; Cemeteries; Monuments; Shrines

Tomography 616.07; 621.36
> *x* CAT (Computerized axial tomography); CAT scan; Computerized tomography; CT (Computerized tomography)
> *xx* X rays

Tongue twisters 818
> *xx* Children's poetry; Folklore; Nonsense verses

Tools 621.9
> *See also* Agricultural machinery; Carpentry—Tools; Machine tools; Machinery; Power tools; also names of specific tools, e.g Saws; etc.
> *x* Implements, utensils, etc.

Top soil loss. *See* **Soil erosion**

Topographical drawing 526.022
> *See also* Map drawing
> *xx* Drawing; Map drawing; Surveying

Topology 514
> *See also* Algebras, Linear; Fractals; Graph theory
> *x* Analysis situs; Position analysis; Rubber sheet geometry
> *xx* Algebras, Linear; Geometry; Set theory

Tories, American. *See* **American Loyalists**

Tornadoes (May subdiv. geog.) **551.55**
> *x* Twisters (Tornadoes)
> *xx* Meteorology; Storms; Winds

Torpedoes 623.4
> *xx* Explosives; Naval art and science; Submarine warfare

Tort liability of professions. *See* **Malpractice**

Tortoises. *See* **Turtles**

Total abstinence. *See* **Temperance**

Totalitarianism   321.9
   See also **Communism; Dictators; Fascism; National socialism**
   x Authoritarianism
Totems and totemism   299
   xx **Ethnology; Indians of North America—Religion; Mythology**
Touch   152.1; 612
   See also **Hugging**
   x Feeling
   xx **Senses and sensation**
Tourism.   *See* **Tourist trade**
Tourist accommodations.   *See* **Hotels, motels, etc.; Youth hostels**
Tourist trade   910.2
   See also **Travel**
   x Tourism
   xx **Travel**
Tournaments.   *See* subjects with the subdivision *Tournaments,* e.g. **Tennis—Tournaments;** etc.
Town life.   *See* **City life**
Town meeting.   *See* **Local government**
Town planning.   *See* **City planning**
Towns.   *See* **Cities and towns**
Township government.   *See* **Local government**
Toxic dumps.   *See* **Hazardous waste sites**
Toxic substances.   *See* **Hazardous substances; Poisons and poisoning**
Toxic wastes.   *See* **Hazardous wastes**
Toxicology.   *See* **Poisons and poisoning**
Toy and movable books   E
   x Movable books; Pop-up books
   xx **Picture books for children**
Toys   688.7
   See also names of kinds of toys, e.g. **Dollhouses; Dolls; Electric toys; Electronic toys;** etc.
   x Miniature objects
   xx **Amusements**
Track and field.   *See* **Track athletics**
Track athletics   796.42
   See also names of specific track sports, e.g. **Running;** etc.
   x Field athletics; Track and field
   xx **Athletics; College sports**
Tracking and trailing   799.2
   See also **Animal tracks**
   x Trailing
   xx **Animals—Behavior; Hunting**
Tracking of satellites.   *See* **Artificial satellites—Tracking; Space vehicles—Tracking**
Tracks of animals.   *See* **Animal tracks**
Traction engines.   *See* **Tractors**
Tractors   629.225; 631.3
   x Traction engines
   xx **Agricultural machinery; Farm engines**
Trade.   *See* **Business; Commerce**
Trade agreements (Labor).   *See* **Arbitration, Industrial; Labor contract**
Trade and professional associations   380.1; 650
   Use for materials on business or professional organizations whose aim is the protection or

Trade and professional associations—*Continued*
    advancement of their common interests
    without regard to the relations of employer
    and employee.
  x Professional associations
  xx **Associations**
Trade, Balance of. *See* **Balance of trade**
Trade barriers. *See* **Commercial policy**
Trade, Boards of. *See* **Chambers of commerce**
Trade fairs. *See* **Fairs**
Trade marks. *See* **Trademarks**
Trade, Restraint of. *See* **Restraint of trade**
Trade routes   387
  x Ocean routes; Routes of trade; Sea routes
  xx **Commerce; Geography, Commercial; Trans-
    portation**
Trade schools. *See* **Technical education**
Trade secrets   346.04; 658.4
  x Business secrets; Commercial secrets; Indus-
    trial secrets; Secrets, Trade
  xx **Right of privacy; Unfair competition**
Trade unions. *See* **Labor unions**
Trade waste. *See* **Industrial wastes; Waste products**
Trademarks   341.7
  See also **Brand name products; Patents**
  x Company symbols; Corporate symbols; Trade
    marks
  xx **Brand name products; Commerce; Manufac-
    tures; Patents**
Trades. *See* **Industrial arts; Occupations**
Traditions. *See* **Folklore; Legends; Manners and
    customs; Rites and ceremonies; Superstition**
Traffic accidents   363.12
  See also **Drunk driving**
  x Automobile accidents; Automobiles—
    Accidents; Highway accidents
  xx **Accidents; Traffic regulations**
Traffic, City. *See* **City traffic**
Traffic control. *See* **Traffic engineering**
Traffic engineering   388.4
    Use for materials on the planning of the flow of
    traffic and related topics, largely as they
    concern street transportation in cities and
    metropolitan areas.
  See also **Car pools; City traffic; Express high-
    ways; Local transit**
  x Street traffic; Traffic control; Traffic regula-
    tion
  xx **Engineering; Highway engineering; Transpor-
    tation**
Traffic regulation. *See* **Traffic engineering**
Traffic regulations   388.4
  See also **Automobiles—Law and legislation;
    Traffic accidents**
  x Street traffic
  xx **Automobiles—Law and legislation; Transpor-
    tation**
Trafficking in drugs. *See* **Drug traffic**
Trafficking in narcotics. *See* **Drug traffic**
Tragedy   792.1
  xx **Drama**
Trailer parks   796.54
  See also **Mobile home parks**
  xx **Campgrounds**

Trailers. *See* **Automobiles—Trailers; Travel trailers and campers**

Trailers, Home. *See* **Mobile homes**

Trailing. *See* **Tracking and trailing**

Train wrecks. *See* **Railroads—Accidents**

Trained nurses. *See* **Nurses**

Training camps, Military. *See* **Military training camps**

Training colleges for teachers. *See* **Teachers colleges**

Training, Occupational. *See* **Occupational training**

Training of animals. *See* **Animals—Training**

Training of children. *See* **Child rearing**

Training of employees. *See* **Employees—Training**

Training, Toilet. *See* **Toilet training**

Training, Vocational. *See* **Occupational training**

Trains, Railroad. *See* **Railroads**

Tramps   305.5

   Use for materials on persons who travel about from place to place living on occasional jobs or gifts of money and food.

   See also **Begging; Unemployed**

   x Hoboes; Vagabonds; Vagrants

   xx **Begging; Homeless people; Poor; Unemployed**

Trams. *See* **Street railroads**

Transactional analysis   158

   xx **Human relations; Psychotherapy**

Transatlantic flights. *See* **Aeronautics—Flights**

Transcendental meditation   158

   xx **Meditation**

Transcendentalism   141

   See also **Idealism**

   xx **Idealism; Philosophy**

Transcontinental journeys (American continent). *See* **Overland journeys to the Pacific**

Transcultural studies. *See* **Cross cultural studies**

Transexuality. *See* **Transsexuality**

Transfer tax. *See* **Inheritance and transfer tax**

Transformation (Genetics). *See* **Genetic transformation**

Transformers, Electric. *See* **Electric transformers**

Transgenics. *See* **Genetic engineering**

Transistor amplifiers   621.3815

   x Amplifiers, Transistor; Audio amplifiers, Transistor; Transistor audio amplifiers

   xx **Amplifiers (Electronics); Transistors**

Transistor audio amplifiers. *See* **Transistor amplifiers**

Transistors   621.3815

   See also **Transistor amplifiers**

   xx **Electronics; Semiconductors**

Transit systems. *See* **Local transit**

Translating and interpreting   418

   x Interpreting and translating; Machine translating; Mechanical translating

   xx **Language and languages**

Transmission of data. *See* **Data transmission systems**

Transmission of power. *See* **Electric lines; Electric power distribution; Power transmission**

Transmissions, Automobile. *See* **Automobiles—Transmission devices**

670

Transmutation (Chemistry)   546; 547

Use for modern discussions on the transmutation of metals. Materials dealing with the medieval attempts to transmute baser metals into gold are entered under **Alchemy.**

See also **Cyclotron**

x Metals, Transmutation of; Transmutation of metals

xx **Alchemy; Atoms; Nuclear physics; Radioactivity**

Transmutation of metals.   *See* **Alchemy; Transmutation (Chemistry)**

Transplantation of organs, tissues, etc.   617.9

See also **Donation of organs, tissues, etc.; Plastic surgery;** also names of organs of the body with the subdivision *Transplantation,* e.g. **Heart—Transplantation;** etc.

x Medical transplantation; Organ transplantation; Surgical transplantation; Tissues—Transplantation

xx **Donation of organs, tissues, etc.; Preservation of organs, tissues, etc.; Surgery**

Transplantation of organs, tissues, etc.—Moral and religious aspects   174

xx **Bioethics**

Transportation   380

Use for general materials on the transportation of persons or goods.

See also

Aeronautics, Commercial	**Postal service**
Bridges	**Railroads**
Canals	**Roads**
Car pools	**Shipping**
Commerce	**Steam navigation**
Electric railroads	**Street railroads**
Express service	**Streets**
Freight and freightage	**Subways**
Harbors	**Trade routes**
Inland navigation	**Traffic engineering**
Local transit	**Traffic regulations**
Merchant marine	**Trucking**
Ocean travel	**Vehicles**
Pipelines	**Waterways**

also subjects with the subdivision *Transportation,* e.g. **School children—Transportation; World War, 1939-1945—Transportation;** etc.

x Locomotion

xx **Commerce**

Transportation, Highway   388.3

See also **Automobiles; Buses; Trucks**

x Highway transportation

Transportation, Military   355.8

See also **Vehicles, Military**

x Military motorization; Military transportation; Motorization, Military

xx **Military art and science**

Transsexuality   305.3; 616.85

x Change of sex; Sex change; Transexuality

xx **Reproductive system; Sex role**

Trapping   639

See also **Fur trade; Game and game birds; Hunting**

xx **Game and game birds; Hunting**

671

Travel 910.2

Use for materials on the art of travel, advice, enjoyment, etc. Descriptions of actual voyages are entered under **Voyages and travels** or under names of places with the subdivision *Description.* Assign the heading for the name of an ancient city or town, without further subdivision, for accounts by travelers in ancient times, e.g. **Delphi (Ancient city);** etc.

See also **Automobiles—Touring; Health resorts, spas, etc.; Ocean travel; Tourist trade; Voyages and travels; Voyages around the world;** also names of cities (except ancient cities), countries, states, etc., with the subdivision *Description,* e.g. **United States— Description;** etc.

x Group travel

xx **Manners and customs; Tourist trade; Voyages and travels**

Travel trailers and campers 629.226; 796.7

See also **Mobile homes; Vans**

x Campers and trailers; House trailers; Pickup campers; Trailers

xx **Automobiles—Trailers; Camping; Recreational vehicles**

Travelers (May subdiv. geog. adjective form, e.g. **Travelers, American;** etc.) **910.92; 920**

See also **Explorers**

x Voyagers

xx **Explorers; Voyages and travels**

Travelers, American 910.92; 920

x American travelers; United States—Travelers

Traveling sales personnel. *See* **Sales personnel**

Travels. *See* **Voyages and travels;** and names of cities (except ancient cities), countries, states, etc., with the subdivision *Description,* e.g. **United States—Description;** etc.; and names of ancient cities or towns, without further subdivision, for accounts of those places by travelers in ancient times, e.g. **Delphi (Ancient city);** etc.

Travesties. *See* **Parodies**

Tray gardens. *See* **Gardens, Miniature**

Treason 364.1

x Collaborationists; High treason

xx **Crime; Political crimes and offenses**

Treasure trove. *See* **Buried treasure**

Treaties 341; 341.3

See also **Arbitration, International;** also names of countries with the subdivision *Foreign relations—Treaties,* e.g. **United States— Foreign relations—Treaties;** etc.; and names of wars with the subdivision *Treaties,* e.g. **World War, 1939-1945— Treaties;** etc.

xx **Congresses and conventions; Diplomacy; International law; International relations**

Treatment of diseases. *See* **Therapeutics**

Tree planting 635.9

See also **Reforestation; Trees; Windbreaks**

x Planting

xx **Forests and forestry; Reforestation; Trees**

Trees (May subdiv. geog.) **582.16; 635.9**

Use for materials on the structure, care, characteristics and use of trees.

Names of all trees are not included in this List but are to be added as needed, in the singular form, e.g. **Oak;** etc.

Trees—*Continued*
   See also

Apple	**Lumber and lumbering**
Christmas tree growing	**Nurseries (Horticulture)**
Christmas trees	**Nuts**
Dwarf trees	**Orange**
Evergreens	**Pecan**
Forests and forestry	**Plants**
Fruit culture	**Pruning**
Grafting	**Shrubs**
Landscape gardening	**Tree planting**
Leaves	**Wood**

   also names of trees, e.g. **Oak;** etc.
   x Arboriculture; Timber
   xx **Botany; Forests and forestry; Landscape gar-
      dening; Tree planting**
Trees in art. *See* **Plants in art**
Trees—United States   582.160973
   x United States—Trees
Trent Affair, 1861   973.7
   xx **United States—History—1861-1865, Civil
      War**
Trial by jury. *See* **Jury**
Trial by publicity. *See* **Freedom of the press and
      fair trial**
Trial marriage. *See* **Unmarried couples**
Trials   345; 347
   May be subdivided by topic, e.g. **Trials (Homi-
      cide);** etc.
   See also **Courts martial and courts of inquiry;
      Crime**
   xx **Crime; Criminal law**
Trials (Homicide)   345
   x Homicide trials; Murder trials; Trials (Mur-
      der)
   xx **Homicide**
Trials (Murder). *See* **Trials (Homicide)**
Tricks   793.5
   See also **Card tricks; Juggling; Magic**
   xx **Magic**
Tricycles   629.227; 796.6
   x Cycling; Trikes
   xx **Bicycles and bicycling**
Trigonometry   516.24
   x Plane trigonometry; Spherical trigonometry
   xx **Geometry; Mathematics**
Trigonometry—Tables   516.24
   See also **Logarithms**
   x Trigonometry—Tables, etc.
   xx **Mathematics—Tables**
Trigonometry—Tables, etc. *See* **Trigonometry—
      Tables**
Trikes. *See* **Tricycles**
Trinity   231
   See also **God—Christianity; Holy Spirit; Jesus
      Christ**
   xx **God—Christianity; Holy Spirit; Jesus Christ;
      Jesus Christ—Divinity; Theology; Unitari-
      anism**
Tripoline War. *See* **United States—History—1801-
      1805, Tripolitan War**
Trivia. *See* **Curiosities and wonders**
Trolley cars. *See* **Street railroads**
Tropical diseases. *See* **Tropical medicine**

Tropical fish   597; 639.3
xx Fishes
Tropical jungles.   *See* **Jungles**
Tropical medicine   614
See also names of tropical diseases, e.g. **Yellow fever;** etc.
x Diseases, Tropical; Hygiene, Tropical; Medicine, Tropical; Tropical diseases
xx **Medicine; Tropics**
Tropical rain forests.   *See* **Rain forests**
Tropics   910.913
See also **Jungles; Tropical medicine;** also subjects with the subdivision *Tropics,* e.g. **Agriculture—Tropics;** etc.
Troubadours   791.092; 920
xx **French poetry; Minstrels; Poets**
Trout fishing   799.1
xx **Fishing**
Truancy (Schools).   *See* **School attendance**
Truck farming.   *See* **Vegetable gardening**
Truck freight.   *See* **Trucking**
Trucking   388.3
x Truck freight
xx **Freight and freightage; Transportation**
Trucks   629.224
See also **Materials handling;** also names of specific makes and models
x Automobile trucks; Motor trucks
xx **Automobiles; Materials handling; Transportation, Highway**
Trust companies   338.8; 658
See also **Banks and banking; Investment trusts**
x Companies, Trust
xx **Banks and banking; Business; Corporations**
Trusts, Industrial   338.8; 658.1
See also

Antitrust law	**Monopolies**
Capitalism	**Railroads—Consolidation**
Competition	**Restraint of trade**
Corporations	**Tariff**
Interstate commerce	

x Business combinations; Cartels; Combinations, Industrial; Industrial combinations; Industrial mergers; Industrial trusts; Mergers, Industrial
xx **Capital; Commerce; Competition; Corporation law; Corporations; Economics; Monopolies; Restraint of trade**
Trusts, Industrial—Law and legislation.   *See* **Antitrust law**
Truth   111
See also **Agnosticism; Knowledge, Theory of; Pragmatism; Reality; Skepticism; Truthfulness and falsehood**
x Certainty
xx **Belief and doubt; Faith; Knowledge, Theory of; Philosophy; Pragmatism; Skepticism**
Truth in advertising.   *See* **Deceptive advertising**
Truthfulness and falsehood   177
See also **Honesty; Lie detectors and detection**
x Credibility; Falsehood; Lying; Untruth
xx **Honesty; Human behavior; Truth**

Tsunamis 551.47
>
> Use for materials on unusually large sea waves generated by earthquakes or undersea volcanic eruptions.
>
> *x* Earthquake sea waves; Seismic sea waves; Tidal waves, Seismic
>
> *xx* **Natural disasters; Ocean waves**

Tuberculosis 616.9
>
> *xx* **Lungs—Diseases**

Tugboats 623.8

Tuition. *See* **College costs; Colleges and universities—Finance; Education—Finance**

Tumbling 796.47
>
> *xx* **Acrobats and acrobatics**

Tumors 616.99
>
> *See also* **Cancer**

Tuning 784.192
>
> *See also* names of instruments with the subdivision *Tuning,* e.g. **Piano—Tuning;** etc.
>
> *xx* **Musical instruments**

Tunnels 624.1
>
> *See also* **Boring; Excavation; Subways**
>
> *xx* **Civil engineering**

Turbines 621.2; 621.406
>
> *See also* **Gas turbines; Steam turbines**
>
> *xx* **Engines; Hydraulic engineering; Hydraulic machinery; Wheels**

Turkeys 636.5
>
> *xx* **Poultry**

Turncoats. *See* **Defectors**

Turning 621.9
>
> *See also* **Lathes; Woodwork**
>
> *x* Lathe work; Wood turning
>
> *xx* **Carpentry; Lathes; Woodwork**

Turnpikes (Modern). *See* **Express highways**

Turtles 597.92
>
> *x* Terrapins; Tortoises
>
> *xx* **Reptiles**

Tutorial machines. *See* **Teaching machines**

Tutors and tutoring 371.3
>
> Use for materials on instruction provided to an individual or small group by a professional teacher, peer, or individual with appropriate training or experience.
>
> *See also* **Independent study; Individualized instruction**
>
> *xx* **Home instruction; Teaching**

TV. *See* **Television**

Twentieth century 909.82
>
> See note under **Nineteenth century.**
>
> *x* 1900-1999 (20th century)
>
> *xx* **History, Modern—1900-1999 (20th century)**

Twenty-first century 909.83
>
> *x* 2000-2099 (21st century)

Twins 155.44; 306.875
>
> *See also* **Brothers and sisters**
>
> *xx* **Brothers and sisters; Multiple birth**

Twisters (Tornadoes). *See* **Tornadoes**

Two-career family. *See* **Dual career family**

Two hundred mile limit. *See* **Territorial waters**

Type and type founding 686.2
>
> *See also* **Advertising layout and typography; Initials; Linotype; Mathematical notation;**

Type and type founding—*Continued*
  Printing—Specimens; Typesetting
  xx **Founding; Initials; Mathematical notation;
    Printing; Printing—Specimens; Typesetting**
Type specimens. *See* **Printing—Specimens**
Typesetting 686.2
  See also **Linotype; Printing; Type and type
    founding**
  x Composition (Printing)
  xx **Printing; Type and type founding**
Typewriters 652.3; 681
  xx **Office equipment and supplies**
Typewriting 652.3
  See also **Keyboarding (Electronics)**
  xx **Business education; Keyboarding (Electron-
    ics); Office practice; Writing**
Typhoid fever 616.9
  x Enteric fever
Typhoons 551.55
  Use for cyclonic storms originating in the region
    of the China Seas and the Philippines.
  See also **Hurricanes**
  xx **Hurricanes; Storms; Winds**
Typography. *See* **Printing**
U boats. *See* **Submarines**
U.F.O.'s. *See* **Unidentified flying objects**
U.H.F. radio. *See* **Shortwave radio**
U.N. *See* **United Nations**
U.S. *See* **United States**
U.S.A. *See* **United States**
U.S.M.A. *See* **United States Military Academy**
U.S.S.R. *See* **Soviet Union**
UFOs. *See* **Unidentified flying objects**
UHF radio. *See* **Shortwave radio**
Ultrahigh frequency radio. *See* **Shortwave radio**
Ultrasonic waves 534.5
  x Supersonic waves; Waves, Ultrasonic
  xx **Sound waves; Ultrasonics**
Ultrasonics 534.5
  See also **Ultrasonic waves**
  x Inaudible sound; Supersonics
  xx **Sound**
Ultraviolet rays 535.01; 621.36
  x Rays, Ultra-violet
  xx **Electromagnetic waves; Phototherapy; Radia-
    tion; Radiotherapy**
Umbrellas and parasols 391; 685
  x Parasols
UN. *See* **United Nations**
Unbelief. *See* **Skepticism**
Unborn child. *See* **Fetus**
Unconventional warfare. *See* **Guerrilla warfare**
Undenominational churches. *See* **Community
  churches**
Under water exploration. *See* **Underwater explora-
  tion**
Underdeveloped areas. *See* **Developing countries**
Undergraduates. *See* **College students**
Underground aliens. *See* **Illegal aliens**
Underground, Anticommunist. *See* **Anticommunist
  movements**
Underground architecture 624.1; 690; 720
  See also **Basements; Earth sheltered houses**

Underground architecture—*Continued*
   x Underground design
   xx **Architecture**
Underground design. *See* **Underground architecture**
Underground economy 381
   See also **Barter; Illegal aliens**
   x Economy, Underground; Income, Untaxed;
      Subterranean economy
   xx **Economics**
Underground films. *See* **Experimental films**
Underground houses. *See* **Earth sheltered houses**
Underground literature 809
   See also **Underground press**
Underground movements (World War,
      1939-1945). *See* **World War, 1939-1945—**
      Underground movements
Underground press 070.4
   x Alternative press; Press, Underground
   xx **Press; Underground literature**
Underground railroad 326
   See also **Slavery—United States**
   xx **Slavery—United States**
Underground railroads. *See* **Subways**
Underprivileged. *See* **Socially handicapped**
Underprivileged children. *See* **Socially handi-**
   capped children
Undersea engineering. *See* **Ocean engineering**
Undersea exploration. *See* **Underwater exploration**
Undersea research habitats. *See* **Undersea research**
   stations
Undersea research stations 551.46
   See also **Aquanauts;** also names of special re-
      search projects and stations, e.g. **Sealab**
      project; etc.
   x Manned undersea research stations; Sea labo-
      ratories; Submarine research stations; Un-
      dersea research habitats; Underwater re-
      search stations
   xx **Oceanography—Research; Skin diving; Sub-**
      mersibles; Underwater exploration
Undersea technology. *See* **Oceanography**
Undersea vehicles. *See* **Submersibles**
Understanding. *See* **Intellect; Knowledge, Theory of**
Undertakers and undertaking 393
   x Funeral directors; Morticians
   xx **Service industries**
Underwater drill (Petroleum). *See* **Oil well drilling,**
   Submarine
Underwater exploration 551.46; 627
   See also **Aquanauts; Diving, Submarine; Marine**
      biology; Skin diving; Submersibles; Under-
      sea research stations
   x Exploration, Submarine; Exploration, Under-
      water; Submarine exploration; Under water
      exploration; Undersea exploration
   xx **Adventure and adventurers; Diving, Subma-**
      rine; Oceanography—Research; Skin diving
Underwater exploration devices. *See* **Submersibles**
Underwater geology. *See* **Submarine geology**
Underwater medicine. *See* **Submarine medicine**
Underwater photography 778.7
   x Deep-sea Photography; Photography, Subma-
      rine; Submarine photography
   xx **Photography**

Underwater physiology. *See* **Submarine medicine**
Underwater research stations. *See* **Undersea research stations**
Underwater swimming. *See* **Skin diving**
Underwriting. *See* **Insurance**
Undocumented aliens. *See* **Illegal aliens**
Unemployed 331.13
>*See also* **Economic assistance, Domestic; Food relief; Labor supply; Occupational retraining; Tramps**
>*x* Jobless people; Out-of-work people
>*xx* **Charities; Economic assistance, Domestic; Labor; Labor supply; Poor; Public welfare; Social problems; Sociology; Tramps; Unemployment**
Unemployment 331.13
>*See also* **Employment agencies; Unemployed**
>*x* Joblessness
>*xx* **Employment; Human resources; Labor supply**
Unemployment insurance 368.4
>*x* Insurance, Unemployment; Labor—Insurance; Payroll taxes
>*xx* **Insurance**
Unfair competition 338.6
>*See also* **Restraint of trade; Trade secrets**
>*x* Competition, Unfair; Fair trade; Unfair trade practices
>*xx* **Commercial law; Restraint of trade**
Unfair trade practices. *See* **Unfair competition**
Ungraded schools. *See* **Nongraded schools**
Unicameral legislatures. *See* **Legislative bodies**
Unidentified flying objects 001.9
>*x* Flying saucers; Saucers, Flying; U.F.O.'s; UFOs
>*xx* **Aeronautics; Astronautics**
Uniforms, Military 355.1; 355.8
>*x* Costume, Military; Military costume; Military uniforms; Naval uniforms; Uniforms, Naval
>*xx* **Costume; Tailoring**
Uniforms, Naval. *See* **Uniforms, Military**
Union churches. *See* **Community churches**
Union of South Africa. *See* **South Africa**
Union of Soviet Socialist Republics. *See* **Soviet Union**
Union shop. *See* **Open and closed shop**
Unions, Labor. *See* **Labor unions**
Unisexuality. *See* **Androgyny**
Unison speaking. *See* **Choral speaking**
Unitarianism 289.1
>*See also* **Jesus Christ—Divinity; Trinity**
>*xx* **Congregationalism; Jesus Christ—Divinity**
United Brethren. *See* **Moravians**
United Nations 341.23
>*x* U.N.; UN
>*xx* **Arbitration, International; International cooperation; International organization**
United Nations—Armed forces 341.23
>*x* Peace keeping forces
United Nations—Finance 341.23
United Nations—Information services 341.23
>*xx* **Information services**
United Nations—Officials and employees 341.23
>*x* Employees and officials; Officials

The subject subdivisions under this heading may be used under the name of any country or region, with the exception of the period divisions of history. For subdivisions that may be used under names of states, see **Ohio;** under names of cities, see **Chicago (Ill.).**

Most of these subdivisions are examples of the directions given in the general references under various headings throughout the List. *See* references are supplied more liberally than any library may need but they were included here in order to show what subjects are given geographic treatment, not only as a subdivision under the name of a country, but also as a heading subdivided by the country or by national adjective.

Corporate entries, that is, those official bodies that may be used as author entries and as subjects, are included only when they have been used as examples or as references, or when they are subdivided by subject. Corporate entries are distinguished by the use of a period between parts instead of a dash, e.g. **United States. Army.**

See also **Americans;** also names of regions of the United States and groups of states, e.g. **Atlantic States; Gulf States (U.S.); Middle West; Mississippi River Valley; New England; Old Northwest; Old Southwest; Oregon Trail; Pacific Northwest; Southern States; Southwestern States; West (U.S.);** etc.; and headings beginning with the word **American.**

x U.S.; U.S.A.; US; USA

United States—Actors. *See* **Actors, American**

United States—Agriculture. *See* **Agriculture—United States**

United States—Air pollution. *See* **Air pollution—United States**

United States—Animals. *See* **Animals—United States**

United States—Antiques. *See* **Antiques—United States**

United States—Antiquities   973

See also **Indians of North America—Antiquities**

United States—Appropriations and expenditures   353.0072

x Federal spending policy; Government spending policy

xx **Budget—United States**

United States—Architecture. *See* **Architecture, American**

United States—Archives. *See* **Archives—United States**

United States—Armed forces   355

See also official names and branches of the armed forces, e.g. **United States. Army; United States. Navy;** etc.

United States—Armed forces—Military life   355.1

xx **Military personnel**

United States. Army 355
    Subdivisions used under this subject may be
        used under armies of other countries.
    See also **United States Military Academy**
    xx **Armies; Military history; United States—
        Armed forces**
**United States. Army—Appointments and retirements
    355.1**
    x United States. Army—Retirements
United States. Army—Biography 920
United States. Army—Chaplains 355.3; 920
    xx **Chaplains**
United States. Army—Crimes and
        misdemeanors. *See* **Military offenses—
        United States**
United States. Army—Demobilization 355.2
United States. Army—Desertions. *See* **Military de-
        sertion—United States**
United States. Army—Enlistment. *See* **United
        States. Army—Recruiting, enlistment, etc.**
United States. Army—Examinations 355.1
    x Army tests
**United States. Army—Handbooks, manuals, etc.
    355**
    x Soldiers' handbooks; United States. Army—
        Officers' handbooks; United States.
        Army—Soldiers' handbooks
United States. Army—Insignia 355.1
    xx **Insignia**
**United States. Army—Medals, badges, decorations,
    etc. 355.1**
    xx **Insignia; Medals**
United States. Army—Military life 355.1
    xx **Military personnel; Soldiers**
United States. Army—Music. *See* **United States.
        Army—Songs and music**
United States. Army—Officers 355.3
United States. Army—Officers' handbooks. *See*
        **United States. Army—Handbooks, manuals,
        etc.**
**United States. Army—Ordnance and ordnance stores
    355.8**
    xx **Ordnance**
United States. Army—Parachute troops 356
    x United States—Parachute troops
    xx **Parachute troops**
**United States. Army—Recruiting, enlistment, etc.
    355.2**
    x United States. Army—Enlistment
United States. Army—Retirements. *See* **United
        States. Army—Appointments and retire-
        ments**
United States. Army—Soldiers' handbooks. *See*
        **United States. Army—Handbooks, manuals,
        etc.**
United States. Army—Songs and music 782.42
    x United States. Army—Music
United States—Art. *See* **Art, American**
United States—Artificial satellites. *See* **Artificial
        satellites, American**
United States—Artists. *See* **Artists, American**
United States—Astronautics. *See* **Astronautics—
        United States**
United States—Atlases. *See* **United States—Maps**

United States—Authors. *See* **Authors, American**

United States—Ballads. *See* **Ballads, American**

United States—Banks and banking. *See* **Banks and banking—United States**

United States—Bibliography 015.73; 016.973
   xx **Bibliography**

United States—Bicentennial celebrations. *See* **American Revolution Bicentennial, 1776-1976**

United States—Biculturalism. *See* **Biculturalism—United States**

United States—Bilingualism. *See* **Bilingualism—United States**

United States—Bio-bibliography 012
   x Bio-bibliography

United States—Biography 920.073
   xx **Biography**

United States—Biography—Dictionaries 920.073
   xx **Biography—Dictionaries; Encyclopedias and dictionaries**

United States—Biography—Portraits 920.073
   x United States—History—Portraits
   xx **Portraits**

United States—Birds. *See* **Birds—United States**

United States—Boundaries 973
   xx **Boundaries**

United States—Budget. *See* **Budget—United States**

United States—Campaign funds. *See* **Campaign funds—United States**

United States—Capital punishment. *See* **Capital punishment—United States**

United States—Cathedrals. *See* **Cathedrals—United States**

United States—Catholic Church. *See* **Catholic Church—United States**

United States—Catholics. *See* **Catholics—United States**

United States—Census 317.3; 353.0081
   xx **Census**

United States—Centennial celebrations, etc. 353.0085
   See also **American Revolution Bicentennial, 1776-1976**

United States—Children. *See* **Children—United States**

United States—Children—Employment. *See* **Children—Employment—United States**

United States—Christmas. *See* **Christmas—United States**

United States—Church—Government policy. *See* **Church—Government policy—United States**

United States—Church history 277.3
   See also **United States—Religion**
   x United States—Religious history
   xx **Church history; United States—Religion**

United States—Church of England. *See* **Church of England—United States**

United States—Churches. *See* **Churches—United States**

United States—Cities and towns. *See* **Cities and towns—United States**

United States—City planning. *See* **City planning—United States**

United States—Civil defense   363.3
  xx Civil defense
United States—Civil service. *See* Civil service—
    United States
United States—Civilization   973
  See also Americana
  x American civilization
  xx Civilization
United States—Civilization—1960-1970   973.92
United States—Civilization—1970-   973.92
United States—Civilization—Foreign influences
    973
United States—Climate   551.6973
  xx Climate; Weather
United States—Collective settlements. *See* Collec-
    tive settlements—United States
United States—Colleges and universities. *See* Col-
    leges and universities—United States
United States—Colonies   325; 973
  x United States—Insular possessions; United
    States—Territories and possessions
  xx Colonies
United States—Commerce   380.1
  xx Commerce
United States—Commercial policy   380.1; 381.3;
    382
  xx Commercial policy; Economic policy
United States—Communism. *See* Communism—
    United States
United States—Composers. *See* Composers, Amer-
    ican
United States. Congress   328.73
  x Congress (U.S.)
  xx Legislative bodies
United States. Congress. House   328.73
  x House of Representatives (U.S.); Representa-
    tives, House of (U.S.)
United States. Congress. Senate   328.73
  x Senate (U.S.)
United States—Constitution   342.73; 973.3
  x American Constitution; Constitution (U.S.)
  xx Constitutions
United States—Constitutional history   342.73
  xx Constitutional history; United States—
    History; United States—History—1783-
    1809
United States—Constitutional law   342.73
  xx Constitutional law
United States—Consular service. *See* United
    States—Diplomatic and consular service
United States—Country life. *See* Country life—
    United States
United States—Courts. *See* Courts—United States
United States—Crime. *See* Crime—United States
United States—Dancing. *See* Dancing—United
    States
United States—Declaration of independence   973.3
  x Declaration of independence (U.S.)
United States—Decoration and ornament. *See*
    Decoration and ornament, American
United States—Decorative arts. *See* Decorative
    arts—United States

United States—Defenses 355.4
See also Strategic Defense Initiative
xx Fortification
United States—Description 917.3
x United States—Description and travel;
United States—Travel
xx Discoveries (in geography); Geography;
Travel; Voyages and travels
United States—Description and travel. See United
States—Description
United States—Description and travel—Views. See
United States—Description—Views
United States—Description—Guidebooks 917.3
x United States—Guidebooks
United States—Description—Maps. See United
States—Maps
United States—Description—Views 917.3022
x United States—Description and travel—
Views
xx Pictures; Views
United States—Diplomatic and consular service
327.73; 353.0089
x United States—Consular service
xx Diplomatic and consular service
United States—Diplomatic and consular
service—Buildings. See United States—
Public buildings
United States—Directories 917.30025
Use for lists of names and addresses. Lists of
names without addresses are entered under
United States—Registers.
See also United States—Registers
xx Directories; United States—Registers
United States—Discovery and exploration. See
America—Exploration; West (U.S.)—
Exploration
United States—Dramatists. See Dramatists, Amer-
ican
United States—Drawing. See Drawing, American
United States—Earthquakes. See Earthquakes—
United States
United States—Economic assistance. See Eco-
nomic assistance, American
United States—Economic conditions 330.973
May be subdivided by period using the subdivi-
sions under United States—History, e.g.
United States—Economic conditions—1600-
1775, Colonial period; etc.
x United States—History, Economic; United
States—Natural resources
xx Economic conditions; Natural resources—
United States; Poverty
United States—Economic policy 338.973
xx Economic policy
United States—Education. See Education—United
States
United States—Elderly. See Elderly—United
States
United States—Elections. See Elections—United
States
United States—Emigration. See United States—
Immigration and emigration
United States—Employees. See United States—
Officials and employees

United States—Engraving. *See* **Engraving, American**

United States—Environmental policy. *See* **Environment—Government policy—United States**

United States—Ethics. *See* **Ethics, American**

United States—Ethnology. *See* **Ethnology—United States**

United States—European War, 1914-1918. *See* **World War, 1914-1918—United States**

United States—Excavations (Archeology). *See* **Excavations (Archeology)—United States**

United States—Executive departments 353.03
  See also **Presidents—United States—Staff**

United States—Executive departments—Reorganization 353.03
  x Administrative agencies—Reorganization; Government reorganization; Reorganization of administrative agencies

United States—Executive power. *See* **Executive power—United States**

United States—Exploration. *See* **America—Exploration; United States—Exploring expeditions; West (U.S.)—Exploration**

United States—Exploring expeditions 508.73; 973
  Use for materials on explorations sponsored by the United States. Materials on early exploration in territory that became a part of the United States are entered under **America—Exploration.**
  See also names of expeditions, e.g. **Lewis and Clark Expedition (1804-1806);** etc.
  x American exploring expeditions; United States—Exploration
  xx **America—Exploration; Explorers**

United States—Famines. *See* **Famines—United States**

United States—Farm life. *See* **Farm life—United States**

United States—Fascism. *See* **Fascism—United States**

United States—Festivals. *See* **Festivals—United States**

United States—Fiction Fic
  xx **Fiction**

United States—Finance. *See* **Finance—United States**

United States—Fiscal policy. *See* **Fiscal policy—United States**

United States—Fisheries. *See* **Fisheries—United States**

United States—Fishes. *See* **Fishes—United States**

United States—Fishing. *See* **Fishing—United States**

United States—Flags. *See* **Flags—United States**

United States—Flowers. *See* **Flowers—United States**

United States—Folk art. *See* **Folk art, American**

United States—Folk dancing. *See* **Folk dancing, American**

United States—Folk music. *See* **Folk music—United States**

United States—Folk songs. *See* **Folk songs—United States**

United States—Folklore. *See* **Folklore—United States**

United States—Foreign economic relations 337.73
  x Foreign economic relations—United States

United States—Foreign opinion (May subdiv. geog. adjective form) **303.3; 973**
  Use for materials on foreign public opinion about the United States.
  x Anti-Americanism; Antiamericanism; United States—Foreign public opinion
  xx **Public opinion**

United States—Foreign opinion, French 303.3; 973
  Use for materials on French public opinion about the United States.
  x French foreign opinion—United States; United States—Foreign public opinion, French

United States—Foreign policy. *See* **United States—Foreign relations**

United States—Foreign population 325.73
  See also **United States—Immigration and emigration;** also **Mexican Americans; Mexicans—United States;** and similar headings
  x Foreign population; Population, Foreign
  xx **Americanization; Immigration and emigration; Minorities; United States—Immigration and emigration**

United States—Foreign public opinion. *See* **United States—Foreign opinion**

United States—Foreign public opinion, French. *See* **United States—Foreign opinion, French**

United States—Foreign relations (May subdiv. geog.) **327.73**
  When further subdividing geographically, provide an additional subject entry with the two places in reversed positions, i.e. **United States—Foreign relations—Iran** and also **Iran—Foreign relations—United States.**
  See also **Monroe Doctrine; United States—Neutrality**
  x United States—Foreign policy
  xx **Diplomacy; Imperialism; International relations; United States—Neutrality; World politics**

United States—Foreign relations—Iran 327.73055
  See also **Iran hostage crisis, 1979-1981**

United States—Foreign relations—Treaties 327.73; 341.3
  x United States—Treaties
  xx **Treaties**

United States—Forests and forestry. *See* **Forests and forestry—United States**

United States—Furniture. *See* **Furniture, American**

United States—Gazetteers 917.3
  xx **Gazetteers**

United States—Geographic names. *See* **Geographic names—United States**

United States—Geography 917.3
  xx **Geography**

United States—Geology. *See* **Geology—United States**

United States—Government. *See* **United States—Politics and government**

United States—Government buildings. *See* **United States—Public buildings**

United States—Government employees. *See* **United States—Officials and employees**

United States—Government publications 015.73; 025.17

   x United States—Public documents

   xx **Government publications**

United States—Governmental investigations. *See* **Governmental investigations—United States**

United States—Graphic arts. *See* **Graphic arts, American**

United States—Guidebooks. *See* **United States—Description—Guidebooks**

United States—Hippies. *See* **Hippies—United States**

United States—Historians. *See* **Historians, American**

United States—Historic buildings. *See* **Historic buildings—United States**

United States—Historical geography 911

   xx **Geography, Historical**

United States—Historical geography—Maps 911

   xx **United States—Maps**

United States—History 973

   See also **Americana; Southern States—History; United States—Constitutional history**

   x American history

United States—History—1600-1775, Colonial period 973.2

   Use for the period from the earliest permanent English settlements on the Atlantic coast to the American Revolution, i.e. 1600-1775. Materials dealing with the period of discovery are entered under **America—Exploration.**

   See also **Bacon's Rebellion, 1676; King Philip's War, 1675-1676; Pilgrims (New England colonists); Pontiac's Conspiracy, 1763-1765; Puritans; United States—History—1689-1697, King William's War; United States—History—1755-1763, French and Indian War**

   x American colonies; Colonial history (U.S.)

United States—History—1675-1676, King Philip's War. *See* **King Philip's War, 1675-1676**

United States—History—1689-1697, King William's War 973.2

   x King William's War, 1689-1697

   xx **Indians of North America—Wars; United States—History—1600-1775, Colonial period**

United States—History—1755-1763, French and Indian War 973.2

   See also **Pontiac's Conspiracy, 1763-1765**

   x French and Indian War

   xx **Indians of North America—Wars; United States—History—1600-1775, Colonial period**

United States—History—1775-1783, Revolution 973.3

   May be subdivided like **United States—History—1861-1865, Civil War.**

United States—History—1775-1783,
      Revolution—*Continued*
    See also **American Loyalists; Canadian Invasion,
      1775-1776; Fourth of July**
    x American Revolution; Revolution, American;
      War of the American Revolution
United States—History—1775-1783, Revolution—
      Centennial celebrations, etc. *See* **American
      Revolution Bicentennial, 1776-1976**
United States—History—1783-1809   973.3; 973.4
    See also **Lewis and Clark Expedition (1804-
      1806); Louisiana Purchase; United States—
      Constitutional history**
    x Confederation of American colonies
United States—History—1783-1865   973.3-973.7
United States—History—1801-1805, Tripolitan War
      973.4
    x Tripoline War
    xx **Pirates**
United States—History—1812-1815, War of 1812
      973.5
    x War of 1812
United States—History—1815-1861   973.5; 973.6
    See also **Black Hawk War, 1832**
United States—History—1845-1848, War with Mex-
      ico   973.6
    x Mexican War, 1845-1848
United States—History—1861-1865, Civil War
      973.7
    See also **Confederate States of America; Slav-
      ery—United States; Trent Affair, 1861**
    x American Civil War; Civil War—United
      States; War of Secession (U.S.)
United States—History—1861-1865, Civil War—
      Biography   920; 973.7092
United States—History—1861-1865, Civil War—
      Campaigns   973.7
    See also names of battles, e.g. **Gettysburg (Pa.),
      Battle of, 1863;** etc.
United States—History—1861-1865, Civil War—
      Causes   973.7
    x Secession
United States—History—1861-1865, Civil War—
      Centennial celebrations, etc.   973.7
United States—History—1861-1865, Civil War—
      Drama   808.82; 812, etc.
    xx **Drama**
United States—History—1861-1865, Civil War—
      Fiction   Fic
    xx **Historical fiction**
United States—History—1861-1865, Civil War—
      Health aspects   973.7
United States—History—1861-1865, Civil War—
      Medical care   973.7
United States—History—1861-1865, Civil War—
      Naval operations   973.7
United States—History—1861-1865, Civil War—
      Personal narratives   973.7
    Use for collective or individual eyewitness re-
    ports or autobiographical accounts that re-
    late experiences of persons in connection
    with the war. Accounts limited to a special
    topic are entered under the specific subject.

United States—History—1861-1865, Civil War—
      Pictorial works 973.7022
United States—History—1861-1865, Civil War—
      Prisoners and prisons 973.7
United States—History—1861-1865, Civil
      War—Reconstruction. *See* **Reconstruction**
      (1865-1876)
United States—History—1861-1865, Civil War—
      Sources 973.7
  xx **History—Sources**
United States—History—1865-1898 973.8
  See also **Reconstruction (1865-1876)**
United States—History—1898-1919 973.9; 973.91
United States—History—1898, War of 1898 973.8
  x American-Spanish War, 1898; Hispano-
      American War, 1898; Spain—History—
      1898, War of 1898; Spanish-American War,
      1898
United States—History—1900-1999 (20th century)
      973.9
United States—History—1914-1918, European
      War. *See* **World War, 1914-1918—United**
      States
United States—History—1914-1918, World
      War. *See* **World War, 1914-1918—United**
      States
United States—History—1919-1933 973.91
United States—History—1933-1945 973.917
United States—History—1939-1945, World
      War. *See* **World War, 1939-1945—United**
      States
United States—History—1945- 973.92
United States—History—1945-1953 973.918
United States—History—1953-1961 973.921
United States—History—1961-1974
      973.922-973.924
  See also **Watergate Affair, 1972-1974**
United States—History—1974-1989
      973.925-973.927
United States—History—1989- 973.928
United States—History—1991- , Persian Gulf
      War. *See* **Persian Gulf War, 1991-**
United States—History—Bibliography 016.973
United States—History—Chronology 973
  xx **Chronology, Historical**
United States—History—Dictionaries 973.03
United States—History—Drama 808.82; 812, etc.
United States—History, Economic. *See* **United**
      States—Economic conditions
United States—History—Examinations 973.076
  See also **United States—History—Study and**
      teaching
  x United States—History—Examinations, ques-
      tions, etc.
  xx **United States—History—Study and teaching**
United States—History—Examinations, questions,
      etc. *See* **United States—History—**
      Examinations
United States—History—Fiction Fic
United States—History—Historiography 973.07
  xx **Historiography**
United States—History, Local 973

United States—History, Military   355.00973
   x United States—Military history
   xx **Military history**
United States—History, Naval   359.00973
   x United States—Naval history
   xx **Naval battles; Naval history; Sea power**
United States—History—Outlines, syllabi, etc.
   973.02
   xx **United States—History—Study and teaching**
United States—History—Periodicals   973.05
United States—History—Poetry   808.81; 811, etc.;
   811.008, etc.
United States—History, Political.   *See* **United
   States—Politics and government**
United States—History—Portraits.   *See* **United
   States—Biography—Portraits**
United States—History—Societies   973.06
   xx **History—Societies**
United States—History—Sources   973
   xx **History—Sources**
United States—History—Study and teaching
   973.07
   See also **United States—History—Examinations;
   United States—History—Outlines, syllabi,
   etc.**
   xx **United States—History—Examinations**
United States—Hospitals.   *See* **Hospitals—United
   States**
United States—Hostages.   *See* **Hostages, American**
United States—Hotels, motels, etc.   *See* **Hotels,
   motels, etc.—United States**
United States—Hunting.   *See* **Hunting—United
   States**
United States—Illustrators.   *See* **Illustrators, Amer-
   ican**
United States—Immigration and emigration   325;
   325.73
   See also **United States—Foreign population;** also
   names of nationality groups, e.g. **Mexican
   Americans; Mexicans—United States;** etc.
   x United States—Emigration
   xx **Americanization; Colonization; Immigration
   and emigration; United States—Foreign
   population**
United States—Industries   338.0973; 658; 670
   x United States—Manufactures
   xx **Industrial arts**
United States—Industry—Government policy.   *See*
   **Industry—Government policy—United
   States**
United States—Insular possessions.   *See* **United
   States—Colonies**
United States—Intellectual life   973
United States—Intelligence service.   *See* **Intelli-
   gence service—United States**
United States—Internal security.   *See* **Internal se-
   curity—United States**
United States—Irrigation.   *See* **Irrigation—United
   States**
United States—Labor.   *See* **Labor—United States**
United States—Labor unions.   *See* **Labor unions—
   United States**
United States—Lakes.   *See* **Lakes—United States**

United States—Land settlement. *See* **Land settlement—United States**

United States—Law. *See* **Law—United States**

United States—Legends. *See* **Legends—United States**

United States—Libraries. *See* **Libraries—United States**

United States. Library of Congress. *See* **Library of Congress**

United States—Literary landmarks. *See* **Literary landmarks—United States**

United States—Literature. *See* **American literature**

United States—Mail. *See* **Postal service—United States**

United States—Manners and customs. *See* **United States—Social life and customs**

United States—Manufactures. *See* **United States—Industries**

United States—Maps 912.73
> *See also* **United States—Historical geography—Maps**
>   *x* United States—Atlases; United States—Description—Maps
> *xx* **Atlases; Maps; Road maps**

United States—Medicine. *See* **Medicine—United States**

United States—Merchant marine. *See* **Merchant marine—United States**

United States Military Academy 355.0071
>   *x* U.S.M.A; USMA; West Point (Military academy)
> *xx* **United States. Army**

United States Military Academy—Registers 355.0071

United States Military Academy—Songs and music 782.42

United States—Military history. *See* **United States—History, Military**

United States—Military offenses. *See* **Military offenses—United States**

United States—Military personnel. *See* **Military personnel—United States**

United States—Military policy 355
> *See also* **Strategic Defense Initiative**
> *xx* **Military policy**

United States—Militia 355.3
> *See also* **United States. National Guard**

United States—Mines and mineral resources. *See* **Mines and mineral resources—United States**

United States—Monetary policy. *See* **Monetary policy—United States**

United States—Moral conditions 973
> *xx* **Moral conditions**

United States—Municipal government. *See* **Municipal government—United States**

United States—Museums. *See* **Museums—United States**

United States—Music. *See* **Music, American**

United States—Musicians. *See* **Musicians, American**

United States—Muslims. *See* **Muslims—United States**

United States—Names, Geographic. *See* **Geographic names—United States**

United States—Names, Personal. *See* **Personal names—United States**

United States—National characteristics. *See* **National characteristics, American**

United States. National Guard   355.3
  x National Guard (U.S.)
  xx **United States—Militia**

United States—National parks and reserves. *See* **National parks and reserves—United States**

United States—National security   355
  xx **National security**

United States—National songs. *See* **National songs, American**

United States—Natural disasters. *See* **Natural disasters—United States**

United States—Natural history. *See* **Natural history—United States**

United States—Natural monuments. *See* **Natural monuments—United States**

United States—Natural resources. *See* **Natural resources—United States; United States—Economic conditions**

United States—Nature study. *See* **Nature study—United States**

United States—Naval history. *See* **United States—History, Naval**

United States. Navy   359
  Subdivisions used under this subject may be used under navies of other countries.
  xx **Naval history; Navies; Sailors; Sea power; United States—Armed forces; Warships**

United States. Navy—Biography   920

United States. Navy—Enlistment. *See* **United States. Navy—Recruiting, enlistment, etc.**

United States. Navy—Handbooks, manuals, etc. 359
  x United States. Navy—Officers' handbooks

United States. Navy—Insignia   359.1
  xx **Insignia**

United States. Navy—Medals, badges, decorations, etc.   359.1
  xx **Insignia; Medals**

United States. Navy—Officers   359.3

United States. Navy—Officers' handbooks. *See* **United States. Navy—Handbooks, manuals, etc.**

United States. Navy—Recruiting, enlistment, etc. 359.2
  x United States. Navy—Enlistment

United States. Navy—Sealab project. *See* **Sealab project**

United States—Neutrality   327.73
  See also **United States—Foreign relations**
  xx **Neutrality; United States—Foreign relations**

United States—Novelists. *See* **Novelists, American**

United States—Occupations   331.700973
  xx **Occupations**

United States of Europe (proposed). *See* **European federation**

United States—Officials and employees   353.001
  See also **Civil service—United States**

United States—Officials and employees—Continued

   x United States—Employees; United States—
      Government employees

  xx **Civil service—United States**

United States—Painters. *See* **Painters, American**

United States—Painting. *See* **Painting, American**

United States—Parachute troops. *See* **United
    States. Army—Parachute troops**

United States—Parks. *See* **Parks—United States**

United States—Peoples. *See* **Ethnology—United
    States**

United States—Personal names. *See* **Personal
    names—United States**

United States—Petroleum. *See* **Petroleum—United
    States**

United States—Philosophers. *See* **Philosophers,
    American**

United States—Philosophy. *See* **Philosophy, Amer-
    ican**

United States—Physical geography. *See* **Physical
    geography—United States**

United States—Plants. *See* **Plants—United States**

United States—Plants, Cultivated. *See* **Plants, Cul-
    tivated—United States**

United States—Poets. *See* **Poets, American**

United States—Police. *See* **Police—United States**

United States—Politicians. *See* **Politicians—
    United States**

United States—Politics and government 973

   May be subdivided by period using the subdivi-
    sions under **United States—History,** e.g.
    **United States—Politics and government—
    1600-1775, Colonial period;** etc.

   See also **Iran-Contra Affair, 1985-; Third parties
    (United States politics)**

   x American government; American politics;
    Civics; Civil government; Politics; United
    States—Government; United States—
    History, Political

  xx **Comparative government; Political science;
    Politics, Practical; Public administration;
    World politics**

United States—Popular culture 973

   See also **Americana**

  xx **Popular culture**

United States—Population 304.6; 317.3

  xx **Population**

United States—Postal service. *See* **Postal service—
    United States**

United States—Pottery. *See* **Pottery, American**

United States—Presidents. *See* **Presidents—United
    States**

United States—Prints. *See* **Prints, American**

United States—Prisons. *See* **Prisons—United
    States**

United States—Propaganda. *See* **Propaganda,
    American**

United States—Protests, demonstrations, etc. *See*
    **Protests, demonstrations, etc.—United
    States**

**United States—Public buildings 353.0086;
    725.0973**

   Use for materials on U.S. federal government

United States—Public buildings—*Continued*
buildings located in or outside of the United
States, as well as for materials on U.S em-
bassy or consulate buildings abroad.
x Public buildings, American; Public build-
ings—United States; United States—
Diplomatic and consular service—
Buildings; United States—Government
buildings
United States—Public debts. *See* **Public debts—
United States**
United States—Public documents. *See* **United
States—Government publications**
United States—Public health. *See* **Public health—
United States**
United States—Public lands   333.10973
United States—Public schools. *See* **Public
schools—United States**
United States—Public works   353.0086; 363.0973
xx **Public works**
United States—Race relations   305.800973
See also **Black Muslims**
xx **Anthropology; Minorities; Race relations**
United States—Registers   917.30025
Use for lists of names without addresses. Lists of
names that include addresses are entered
under **United States—Directories.**
See also **United States—Directories**
xx **United States—Directories**
United States—Religion   277.3
See also **United States—Church history**
xx **Religion; United States—Church history**
United States—Religious history. *See* **United
States—Church history**
United States—Rural conditions   307.720973
x Rural conditions
xx **Sociology, Rural**
United States—Schools. *See* **Schools—United
States**
United States—Science. *See* **Science—United
States**
United States—Sculptors. *See* **Sculptors, American**
United States—Sculpture. *See* **Sculpture, American**
United States—Secret service. *See* **Secret service—
United States**
United States—Separation of powers. *See* **Separa-
tion of powers—United States**
United States—Shipping. *See* **Shipping—United
States**
United States—Social conditions   973
xx **Poverty; Social conditions**
United States—Social life and customs   973
x Customs, Social; Social customs; Social life
and customs; United States—Manners and
customs
xx **Ethnology; Manners and customs**
United States—Social policy   361.6; 973
x National planning; Planning, National
xx **Social policy**
United States—Social surveys. *See* **Social surveys—United States**
United States—Socialism. *See* **Socialism—United
States**

693

United States—Soldiers. *See* **Soldiers—United States**

United States—Songs. *See* **Songs, American**

United States—State governments. *See* **State governments**

United States—Statistics   317.3
   xx **Statistics**

United States—Strikes and lockouts. *See* **Strikes and lockouts—United States**

United States—Students. *See* **Students—United States**

United States. Supreme Court   347
   x Supreme Court—United States

United States. Supreme Court—Biography   920

United States—Tariff. *See* **Tariff—United States**

United States—Taxation. *See* **Taxation—United States**

United States—Technical assistance. *See* **Technical assistance, American**

United States—Teenagers. *See* **Teenagers—United States**

United States—Territorial expansion   973

United States—Territorial waters. *See* **Territorial waters—United States**

United States—Territories and possessions. *See* **United States—Colonies**

United States—Terrorism. *See* **Terrorism—United States**

United States—Theater. *See* **Theater—United States**

United States—Travel. *See* **United States—Description**

United States—Travelers. *See* **Travelers, American**

United States—Treaties. *See* **United States—Foreign relations—Treaties**

United States—Trees. *See* **Trees—United States**

United States—Universities. *See* **Colleges and universities—United States**

United States—Urban renewal. *See* **Urban renewal—United States**

United States—Veterans. *See* **Veterans—United States**

United States—Vice-presidents. *See* **Vice-presidents—United States**

United States—Women. *See* **Women—United States**

United States—World War, 1914-1918. *See* **World War, 1914-1918—United States**

United States—World War, 1939-1945. *See* **World War, 1939-1945—United States**

United States—Youth. *See* **Youth—United States**

United Steelworkers of America   331.88
   xx **Labor unions**

Universal bibliographic control. *See* **Bibliographic control**

Universal history. *See* **World history**

Universal language   401
   See also **Esperanto**
   x International language; Language, International; Language, Universal; World language

Universal military training. *See* **Draft**

Universe   113; 523.1

   See also **Astronomy; Creation; Earth; Life on
      other planets**
   x Big bang theory; Cosmogony; Cosmography;
      Cosmology; Expanding universe
   xx **Creation; Earth; Metaphysics; Philosophy**
Universities.   *See* **Colleges and universities**
University degrees.   *See* **Academic degrees**
University extension   378.1
   See also **Adult education; Correspondence
      schools and courses**
   xx **Colleges and universities; Higher education**
University graduates.   *See* **College graduates**
University libraries.   *See* **Academic libraries**
University students.   *See* **College students**
Unmarried couples   306.7
   x Cohabitation; Common law marriage; Living
      together; Marriage, Open ended; Nonmari-
      tal relations; Open ended marriage; Trial
      marriage; Unmarried people
   xx **Lifestyles; Sexual ethics; Shared housing; Sin-
      gle people**
Unmarried fathers   306.85; 362.82
   Use for materials on fathers who at the time of
      childbirth were not married to the child's
      mother. For materials focusing on fathers
      rearing children without a partner in the
      household, use **Single parent family.** For
      materials focusing on fathers who are teen-
      agers, use **Teenage fathers.**
   See also **Single parent family**
   x Parents, Unmarried; Unwed fathers
   xx **Child welfare; Fathers; Illegitimacy; Single
      parent family**
Unmarried men.   *See* **Single men**
Unmarried mothers   306.85; 362.83
   Use for materials on mothers who at the time of
      giving birth were not married to the child's
      father. For materials focusing on mothers
      rearing children without a partner in the
      household, use **Single parent family.** For
      materials focusing on mothers who are teen-
      agers, use **Teenage mothers.**
   See also **Single parent family**
   x Parents, Unmarried; Unwed mothers
   xx **Child welfare; Illegitimacy; Mothers; Single
      parent family**
Unmarried people.   *See* **Single people; Unmarried
   couples**
Unmarried women.   *See* **Single women**
Unskilled workers.   *See* **Labor**
Untruth.   *See* **Truthfulness and falsehood**
Unwed fathers.   *See* **Unmarried fathers**
Unwed mothers.   *See* **Unmarried mothers**
Upholstery   684.1
   See also **Drapery; Furniture**
   xx **Furniture; Interior design**
Upper atmosphere   551.5
   See also **Stratosphere**
   x Atmosphere, Upper
Upper classes   305.5
   x Fashionable society; High society; Society,
      Upper
   xx **Aristocracy; Social classes**

Uranium 669

   xx **Radioactivity**

Urban areas. *See* **Cities and towns; Metropolitan areas**

Urban development. *See* **Cities and towns—Growth; Urbanization**

Urban-federal relations. *See* **Federal-city relations**

Urban life. *See* **City life**

Urban planning. *See* **City planning**

Urban renewal (May subdiv. geog.) **307.3**

   Use for materials on urban redevelopment and the economic, sociological, and political factors involved. Architectural and engineering aspects are entered under **City planning.**

   See also **City planning; Community development; Community organization**

   x Slum clearance

   xx **City planning; Community organization; Metropolitan areas; Sociology, Urban**

Urban renewal—Chicago (Ill.) 307.3

   x Chicago (Ill.)—Urban renewal

Urban renewal—United States 307.3

   x United States—Urban renewal

Urban sociology. *See* **Sociology, Urban**

Urban traffic. *See* **City traffic**

Urban transportation. *See* **Local transit**

Urbanization (May subdiv. geog.) **307.76**

   Use for materials on the process of acquiring urban characteristics or on the state of becoming urbanized.

   x Cities and towns, Movement to; Urban development

   xx **Cities and towns; Social change; Social conditions; Sociology, Rural; Sociology, Urban**

US. *See* **United States**

USA. *See* **United States**

Use of time. *See* **Time management**

Used merchandise. *See* **Secondhand trade**

Useful arts. *See* **Industrial arts; Technology**

Useful insects. *See* **Beneficial insects**

USMA. *See* **United States Military Academy**

USSR. *See* **Soviet Union**

Utensils, Kitchen. *See* **Household equipment and supplies**

Utilitarianism 144

   See also **Pragmatism; Secularism**

   xx **Ethics; Pragmatism**

Utilities (Computer programs) 005.4

   Use for materials on software used to perform standard computer system operations such as sorting data, searching for viruses, copying data from one file to another, etc.

   x Computer utility programs; Computers—Utility programs; Programs, Utility (Computer programs); Routines, Utility (Computer programs); Utility programs (Computer programs); Utility routines (Computer programs)

   xx **Computer programs**

Utilities, Public. *See* **Public utilities**

Utility programs (Computer programs). *See* **Utilities (Computer programs)**

Utility routines (Computer programs). *See* **Utilities (Computer programs)**

Utilization of waste. *See* **Recycling (Waste, etc.);
        Salvage (Waste, etc.)**
Utopias   321
    x Ideal states
    xx **Political science; Socialism**
V.C.R.'s. *See* **Videotape recorders and recording**
V.D. *See* **Sexually transmitted diseases**
V.T.O.L.'s. *See* **Vertically rising airplanes**
Vacation church schools. *See* **Summer schools, Re-
        ligious**
Vacation home timesharing. *See* **Timesharing
        (Real estate)**
Vacation schools. *See* **Summer schools**
Vacation schools, Religious. *See* **Summer schools,
        Religious**
Vacations   331.25; 658.3
    See also **Holidays**
    xx **Holidays; Recreation**
Vaccination   614.4
    See also **Immunity; Influenza**
    x Immunization; Inoculation
    xx **Communicable diseases; Immunity; Influenza;
        Public health**
Vacuum tubes   537.5; 621.3815
    See also **Cathode ray tubes; Electronics**
    x Electron tubes
    xx **X rays**
Vagabonds. *See* **Tramps**
Vagrants. *See* **Tramps**
Valentine's Day   394.2
    x Saint Valentine's Day; St. Valentine's Day
    xx **Holidays**
Valuation   338.5
        Use for general materials only. Materials on val-
        uation of special classes of property are en-
        tered under the class, e.g. **Real estate;** etc.
        Materials on valuation for taxing purposes
        are entered under **Assessment.**
    x Appraisal; Capitalization (Finance)
    xx **Assessment**
Values   121; 170; 303.3
        Use for materials on moral and aesthetic values.
    See also **Social values**
    x Axiology; Human values; Worth
    xx **Aesthetics; Ethics; Psychology**
Vampires   398.21
    xx **Mythical animals; Superstition**
Van life   728.7
    x Vanning; Vans—Social aspects
    xx **Mobile home living; Vans**
Van pools. *See* **Car pools**
Vanishing species. *See* **Endangered species**
Vanning. *See* **Van life**
Vans   728.7
    See also **Van life**
    xx **Travel trailers and campers**
Vans—Social aspects. *See* **Van life**
Variation (Biology)   575.2
    See also **Adaptation (Biology); Evolution; Men-
        del's law; Natural selection**
    x Mutation (Biology)
    xx **Biology; Botany; Evolution; Genetics; Hered-
        ity; Zoology**

Varnish and varnishing 667; 698

    See also **Lacquer and lacquering**

    x Finishes and finishing

    xx **Lacquer and lacquering; Painting, Industrial;**
       Wood finishing

Varsity sports. *See* **College sports**

Vascular system. *See* **Cardiovascular system**

Vasectomy 613.9

    xx **Sterilization (Birth control)**

Vases 666; 731; 738.3

    See also **Glassware; Pottery**

    xx **Glassware; Pottery**

Vassals. *See* **Feudalism**

Vatican City 945.6

    Use for materials discussing the independent pa-
    pal state of Vatican City, consisting of the
    Vatican Palace, Saint Peter's Basilica, Saint
    Peter's Square, the Vatican Gardens, etc.,
    and certain palaces and churches that are
    not located within Vatican City but are un-
    der its jurisdiction.

Vatican City—Foreign relations. *See* **Catholic**
    Church—Relations (Diplomatic)

Vatican Council (2nd : 1962-1965) 262

    xx **Councils and synods**

Vaudeville 792.7

    xx **Amusements; Theater**

Vaults (Sepulchral). *See* **Tombs**

VCRs. *See* **Videotape recorders and recording**

VD. *See* **Sexually transmitted diseases**

VDTs. *See* **Video display terminals**

Vedas 294.5

    xx **Hinduism; Sacred books**

Vegetable anatomy. *See* **Botany—Anatomy**

Vegetable gardening 635

    See also **Vegetables**

    x Kitchen gardens; Market gardening; Truck
      farming

    xx **Gardening; Horticulture; Vegetables**

Vegetable kingdom. *See* **Botany; Plants**

Vegetable oils. *See* **Essences and essential oils;**
    Oils and fats

Vegetable pathology. *See* **Plant diseases**

Vegetables 635; 641.3

    Names of all vegetables are not included in this
    List but are to be added as needed, e.g. **Cel-**
    ery; Potatoes; etc.

    See also **Cookery—Vegetables; Root crops; Vege-**
    table gardening; Vegetarianism; also names
    of vegetables, e.g. **Celery; Potatoes;** etc.

    xx **Botany; Food; Vegetable gardening**

Vegetables—Canning. *See* **Vegetables—**
    Preservation

Vegetables—Marketing. *See* **Farm produce—**
    Marketing

Vegetables—Preservation 641.4

    x Vegetables—Canning

    xx **Canning and preserving**

Vegetarian cookery 641.5

    See also **Cookery—Vegetables**

    x Cookery, Vegetarian

    xx **Cookery**

Vegetarianism 613.2

    xx **Diet; Food; Vegetables**

Vehicles   629.2
> *See also* types of vehicles and individual vehicles, e.g. **All terrain vehicles; Automobiles; Recreational vehicles; Snowmobiles;** etc.
> *xx* **Transportation**

Vehicles, Military   355.8
> *x* Army vehicles; Military vehicles
> *xx* **Transportation, Military**

Vehicles, Recreational.   *See* **Recreational vehicles**

Velocity.   *See* **Speed**

Veneers and veneering   674; 698
> *xx* **Cabinet work; Furniture**

Venereal diseases.   *See* **Sexually transmitted diseases**

Ventilation   697
> *See also* **Air conditioning; Chimneys; Heating**
> *xx* **Air; Air conditioning; Heating; Home economics; Hygiene; Sanitation; Sanitation, Household**

Ventriloquism   793.8
> *xx* **Amusements; Voice**

Verbal abuse.   *See* **Invective**

Verbal learning   153.1; 370.15
> Use for materials on the process of learning and understanding written or spoken language, ranging from learning to associate two nonsense syllables to solving problems presented in verbal terms.
> *See also* **Reading comprehension**
> *x* Learning, Verbal
> *xx* **Language and languages; Learning, Psychology of**

Vermin.   *See* **Household pests; Pests**

Vers libre.   *See* **Free verse**

Versification   808.1
> *See also* **Poetry; Rhyme**
> *x* English language—Versification; Meter; Prosody
> *xx* **Authorship; Poetics; Rhythm**

Vertebrates   596
> *See also* **Amphibians; Birds; Fishes; Mammals; Reptiles**
> *xx* **Animals; Zoology**

Vertical take off airplanes.   *See* **Vertically rising airplanes**

Vertically rising airplanes   629.133
> *x* Airplanes, Vertically rising; V.T.O.L.'s; Vertical take off airplanes; VTOLs
> *xx* **Airplanes; Ground effect machines**

Vessels (Ships).   *See* **Ships**

Veterans (May subdiv. geog.)   **305.9; 351.81; 362.86; 920**
> *See also* **Military hospitals; Military personnel; Pensions, Military**
> *x* Ex-service men; War veterans
> *xx* **Military personnel; Pensions, Military**

Veterans Day   394.2
> *x* Armistice Day
> *xx* **Holidays**

Veterans—Education   362.86
> *x* Education of veterans
> *xx* **Reconstruction (1914-1939); Reconstruction (1939-1951)**

Veterans—Employment 331.5
  x Employment of veterans
  xx **Employment; Reconstruction (1914-1939); Reconstruction (1939-1951)**
Veterans—Hospitals. *See* **Military hospitals**
Veterans—Law and legislation. *See* **Veterans—Legal status, laws, etc.**
Veterans—Legal status, laws, etc. 343
  x Veterans—Law and legislation
  xx **Military law**
Veterans—United States 353.0081; 920
  x G.I.'s; GIs; United States—Veterans
Veterinary medicine 636.089
  See also **Animals—Diseases; Insect pests;** also
    names of animals with the subdivision
    Diseases, e.g. **Cattle—Diseases;** etc.
  x Medicine, Veterinary
  xx **Insect pests; Livestock**
Viaducts. *See* **Bridges**
Vibration 531; 620.3
  See also **Light; Sound waves; Waves**
  xx **Mechanics; Sound**
Vicarious atonement. *See* **Atonement—Christianity**
Vice. *See* **Crime;** and names of specific vices, e.g.
    Gambling; Prostitution; etc.
Vice-presidents (May subdiv. geog.) **351.003; 920**
  xx **Presidents**
Vice-presidents—United States 353.03; 920
  x United States—Vice-presidents
Victimless crimes. *See* **Crimes without victims**
Victims of atomic bombings. *See* **Atomic bomb victims**
Victims of crime 362.88
  See also **Abused women**
  x Crime victims
  xx **Crime**
Video art 700; 791.45
  Use for materials on works of art created with
    the use of television and videorecording
    technology.
  x Art, Electronic; Art, Video; Electronic art
  xx **Art; Art, Modern—1900-1999 (20th century);
    Television; Videotape recorders and recording**
Video cameras, Home. *See* **Camcorders**
Video cassette recorders and recording. *See* **Videotape recorders and recording**
Video cassettes. *See* **Videotapes**
Video disc players. *See* **Videodisc players**
Video discs. *See* **Videodiscs**
Video display terminals 004.7
  x CRT display terminals; Display terminals,
    Video; VDTs
  xx **Computer peripherals; Computer terminals**
Video games 688.7; 794.8
  Use for materials on electronic games played by
    means of images on a video screen.
  x Electronic games; Games, Electronic; Games,
    Video; Television games
  xx **Electronic toys; Games; Television—Receivers
    and reception**
Video recordings. *See* **Videodiscs; Videotapes**
Video recordings, Closed caption. *See* **Closed caption video recordings**

Video recordings for the hearing impaired. *See* **Closed caption video recordings**

Video tapes. *See* **Videotapes**

Video telephone 384.6; 621.386
 x Picture telephone; Videophone
 xx **Data transmission systems; Telephone; Television**

Videocassettes. *See* **Videotapes**

Videodisc players 384.55; 621.388
 Use for materials on electronic units resembling a record player that play back pictures and sound from prerecorded discs onto a television receiver.
 x Video disc players
 xx **Television—Equipment and supplies**

Videodiscs 384.55; 621.388
 Use for materials on plastic discs that play back optically encoded, prerecorded sound and pictures through a television receiver.
 See also **Closed caption video recordings; Music videos**
 x Discs, Video; Video discs; Video recordings
 xx **Audiovisual materials; Optical storage devices; Television**

Videophone. *See* **Video telephone**

Videorecorders. *See* **Videotape recorders and recording**

Videos, Music. *See* **Music videos**

Videotape recorders and recording 384.55; 621.388; 778.59
 Use for materials on electromechanical devices that make possible the electronic recording and playback of video or video and audio materials on magnetic tape.
 See also **Camcorders; Video art; Videotapes**
 x V.C.R.'s; VCRs; Video cassette recorders and recording; Videorecorders
 xx **Camcorders; Home video systems; Magnetic recorders and recording; Television broadcasting; Television—Equipment and supplies**

Videotapes 384.55; 778.59
 Use for materials dealing with magnetic tapes on which video or video and audio material are recorded and reproduced by the videotape recorder.
 See also **Closed caption video recordings; Music videos**
 x Cassette tape recordings, Video; Tape recordings, Video; Video cassettes; Video recordings; Video tapes; Videocassettes
 xx **Audiovisual materials; Home video systems; Motion pictures; Television; Videotape recorders and recording**

Videotex systems 004.69; 384.3
 Use for materials on the transmission of computer-based data from a central source to a television set or personal computer allowing for two-way interactions, such as with home shopping or home banking.
 See also **Teletext systems**
 x Interactive videotex; Telereference; Viewdata systems

Videotex systems—*Continued*
    xx **Data transmission systems; Information systems; Teletext systems; Television broadcasting**
Vietnam War, 1961-1975   959.704
    May use appropriate subdivisions under **World War, 1939-1945.**
    x Vietnamese War, 1961-1975
Vietnamese refugees. *See* **Refugees, Vietnamese**
Vietnamese War, 1961-1975. *See* **Vietnam War, 1961-1975**
Viewdata systems. *See* **Videotex systems**
Views   910.22
    Use for collections of pictures of many places.
    See also names of cities (except ancient cities), countries, states, etc. with the subdivision *Description—Views,* e.g. **Chicago (Ill.)—Description—Views; United States—Description—Views;** etc.; and names of ancient cities and named entities, such as individual parks, structures, etc. with the subdivision *Pictorial works.*
    x Geography—Pictorial works; Scenery
Vigilance committees   364.1; 364.4
    xx **Crime; Criminal law; Lynching**
Vikings   948
    Use for materials on early Scandinavian people. Materials on the people since the 10th century are entered under **Scandinavians.**
    See also **Normans**
    x Norsemen; Northmen
    xx **Normans; Scandinavians**
Villages   307.76
    See also **Community development; Local government**
    xx **Cities and towns; Local government**
Villas. *See* **Architecture, Domestic**
Vines. *See* **Climbing plants**
Vineyards. *See* **Grapes**
Violence   303.6
    See also **Hate crimes;** also types of violence, e.g. **Family violence; School violence;** etc.
    xx **Aggressiveness (Psychology); Social psychology**
Violin   787.2
    x Fiddle
    xx **Stringed instruments**
Violin music   787.2
Violinists, violoncellists, etc.   787.2092; 920
    x Violoncellists
    xx **Musicians**
Violoncellists. *See* **Violinists, violoncellists, etc.**
Violoncello   787.4
    x Cello
    xx **Stringed instruments**
Vipers. *See* **Snakes**
Virgin Mary. *See* **Mary, Blessed Virgin, Saint**
Viruses   576
    See also **Chickenpox**
    x Microbes
    xx **Microorganisms**
Viruses, Computer. *See* **Computer viruses**
Visceral learning. *See* **Biofeedback training**

Viscosity   532; 620.1
   xx **Hydrodynamics; Mechanics**
Visigoths.   *See* **Teutonic peoples**
Vision   152.14; 591.1; 612.8; 617.7
   See also **Color sense; Eye; Optical illusions**
   x Sight
   xx **Eye; Optics; Senses and sensation**
Vision disorders   362.4; 617.7
   See also **Blind; Color blindness**
   x Defective vision
Visions   133.8
   See also **Apparitions; Dreams; Hallucinations
     and illusions**
   xx **Apparitions**
Visitation rights (Domestic relations)   306.8
   Use for materials on the legal right of parents or
     grandparents to visit their children or grand-
     children in situations of separation, divorce,
     etc.
   xx **Domestic relations**
Visiting animals.   *See* **Pet therapy**
Visitors' exchange programs.   *See* **Exchange of per-
   sons programs**
Visual data processing.   *See* **Optical data processing**
Visual instruction.   *See* **Audiovisual education**
Visual literacy   153; 707
   Use for materials on the ability to interpret and
     evaluate visual objects and symbols, such as
     television, motion pictures, art works, etc.
   x Literacy, Visual
   xx **Arts; Literacy; Semiotics**
Vital records.   *See* **Registers of births, etc.**
Vital statistics   304.6; 310
   See also **Census; Cities and towns—Growth;
     Mortality; Population; Registers of births,
     etc.**
   x Burial statistics; Death rate; Marriage statis-
     tics; Mortuary statistics; Records of births,
     etc.
   xx **Registers of births, etc.; Statistics**
Vitamins   574.1; 615; 641.1
   xx **Food; Nutrition**
Vivariums.   *See* **Terrariums**
Vivisection   179
   xx **Animal experimentation; Surgery**
Vocabulary   418; 428, etc.
   See also **Words, New**
   x English language—Vocabulary; Languages—
     Vocabulary; Words
Vocal culture.   *See* **Singing; Voice**
Vocal music   782
   See also

Cantatas	**Operas**
Carols	**Operetta**
Choral music	**Oratorios**
Folk songs	**Singing**
Hymns	**Songs**

   x Music, Vocal

   xx **Music; Singing**

Vocation, Choice of.   *See* **Vocational guidance**

Vocational education   370.11; 373.246; 374

   See note under **Occupational training.**

Vocational education—*Continued*

See also

Blind—Education
Deaf—Education
Employees—Training
Industrial arts education
Occupational retraining
Occupational training
Professional education
Technical education
Vocational guidance

also names of industries, professions, etc. with the subdivision *Study and teaching,* e.g. **Agriculture—Study and teaching; Medicine—Study and teaching;** etc.

x Career education; Education, Vocational

xx **Education; Human resources policy; Professional education; Technical education**

Vocational guidance   331.7; 371.4

Use for materials on the activities and programs designed to help people plan, choose, and succeed in their careers. Consider also **Educational counseling.**

See also

Blind—Education
Career changes
Deaf—Education
Educational counseling
Employment
Job hunting
Occupations
Paraprofessions and paraprofessionals
Professions

also fields of knowledge and industries and trades with the subdivision *Vocational guidance,* e.g. **Law—Vocational guidance; Television broadcasting—Vocational guidance;** etc.

x Career counseling; Career development; Career guidance; Choice of profession, occupation, vocation, etc.; Employment guidance; Guidance, Vocational; Job placement guidance; Occupational guidance; Vocation, Choice of

xx **Counseling; Educational counseling; Employment; Occupations; Professions; Vocational education**

Vocational training.   *See* **Occupational training**

Vocations.   *See* **Occupations; Professions**

Voice   783

See also **Automatic speech recognition; Phonetics; Public speaking; Respiration; Singing; Speech; Ventriloquism**

x Speaking; Vocal culture; Voice culture

xx **Language and languages; Phonetics; Public speaking; Singing; Speech; Throat**

Voice culture.   *See* **Singing; Voice**

Volatile oils.   *See* **Essences and essential oils**

Volcanoes (May subdiv. geog.)   **551.2**

See also names of volcanoes

x Eruptions

xx **Geology; Mountains; Physical geography**

Volleyball   796.325

Volume (Cubic content)   389; 530.8

x Cubic measurement

xx **Geometry; Measurement; Weights and measures**

Volume feeding.   *See* **Food service**

Voluntarism   361.7; 361.8

See also **Associations; Charities; Foster grandparents;** also names of volunteer programs,

Voluntarism—*Continued*
> e.g. **Meals on wheels programs;** etc.
> *x* Volunteer work; Volunteering; Volunteerism;
> Volunteers
> *xx* **Associations; Charities**

Voluntary associations. *See* **Associations**
Volunteer military service. *See* **Military service, Voluntary**
Volunteer work. *See* **Voluntarism**
Volunteering. *See* **Voluntarism**
Volunteerism. *See* **Voluntarism**
Volunteers. *See* **Voluntarism**
Volunteers in church work. *See* **Lay ministry**
Voter registration   324.6
> *x* Registration of voters
> *xx* **Elections; Suffrage**

Voting. *See* **Elections; Suffrage**
Voting, Cumulative. *See* **Proportional representation**
Voyager project. *See* **Project Voyager**
Voyagers. *See* **Explorers; Travelers**
Voyages and travels   910.4
> *See also*

Adventure and adventurers	**Sailors**
Aeronautics—Flights	**Scientific expeditions**
Discoveries (in geography)	**Seafaring life**
Explorers	**Shipwrecks**
Northeast Passage	**Travel**
Northwest Passage	**Travelers**
Ocean travel	**Voyages around the world**
Overland journeys to the	**Whaling**
Pacific	**Yachts and yachting**
Pilgrims and pilgrimages	

> also names of cities (except ancient cities), coun-
> tries, continents, etc., with the subdivision
> *Description,* e.g. **United States—
> Description;** etc.; also names of regions, e.g.
> **Antarctic regions;** etc., and names of indi-
> vidual ships; and classes of people and indi-
> viduals with the subdivision *Voyages and
> travels,* e.g. **Popes—Voyages and travels;**
> etc.; also names of countries with the subdi-
> vision *Exploring expeditions,* e.g. **United
> States—Exploring expeditions;** etc.; and
> names of places that were unsettled or
> sparsely settled and largely unknown to the
> rest of the world at the time of exploration,
> with the subdivision *Exploration,* e.g.
> **America—Exploration;** etc.
> *x* Journeys; Travels
> *xx* **Adventure and adventurers; Discoveries (in ge-
> ography); Explorers; Geography; Travel**

Voyages around the world   910.4
> *x* Circumnavigation
> *xx* **Travel; Voyages and travels**

Voyages to the moon. *See* **Space flight to the moon**
VTOLs. *See* **Vertically rising airplanes**
Wage-price controls. *See* **Wage-price policy**
Wage-price policy   339.2
> *x* Price controls; Price-wage policy; Wage-price
> controls
> *xx* **Inflation (Finance); Prices; Wages**

Wages   331.2; 658.3
    See also Cost of living; Equal pay for equal work;
        Job analysis; Nonwage payments; Prices;
        Profit sharing; Wage-price policy
    x Compensation; Overtime
    xx Cost of living; Economics; Labor; Labor con-
        tract; Prices
Wages—Annual wage   331.2
    x Annual income; Annual wage plans; Guaran-
        teed annual income; Guaranteed income
    xx Income
Wages—Minimum wage   331.2
    x Minimum wage
Wagons.   *See* Carriages and carts
Waiters and waitresses   642
    x Waitresses
Waitresses.   *See* Waiters and waitresses
Wakefulness.   *See* Insomnia
Walking   796.5
    See also Hiking
    x Locomotion
    xx Hiking
Walking in space.   *See* Extravehicular activity
    (Space flight)
Wall decoration.   *See* Mural painting and decora-
    tion
Wall painting.   *See* Mural painting and decoration
Wall Street (New York, N.Y.)   332.6
    Use for materials on the activities of Wall Street
        as a financial district. Historical and de-
        scriptive materials on Wall Street as a street
        are entered under Streets—New York
        (N.Y.).
    See also Streets—New York (N.Y.)
    xx Stock exchange; Streets—New York (N.Y.)
Wallpaper   676
    See also Paper hanging
    xx Interior design; Paper hanging
Walls   694; 721
    See also Foundations; Masonry; Mural painting
        and decoration
    xx Building; Carpentry; Civil engineering; Foun-
        dations; Masonry
Walt Disney World (Fla.)   791.06
    x Disney World (Fla.)
    xx Amusement parks
War   172; 303.6; 355.02
    See also

Aeronautics, Military	Military law
Armies	Military personnel
Arms control	Munitions
Battles	Naval art and science
Chemical warfare	Navies
Guerrilla warfare	Peace
International law	Psychological warfare
Intervention (International	Strategy
law)	Submarine warfare
Military art and science	World War III

    also names of wars, battles, etc., e.g. United
        States—History—1861-1865, Civil War;
        Gettysburg (Pa.), Battle of, 1863; etc.
    x Fighting; Wars
    xx Armies; International law; Military art and
        science; Peace

War and civilization   172; 303.4
>Use same form for war with other subjects.
>*x* Civilization and war
>*xx* **Civilization; Progress**

War and industry.   *See* **War—Economic aspects**

War and religion   201; 261.8
>*See also* **Conscientious objectors; Pacifism; World War, 1939-1945—Moral and religious aspects**
>*x* Christianity and war; Church and war; Religion and war

War, Articles of.   *See* **Military law**

War crime trials   341.6
>*xx* **World War, 1939-1945—Atrocities**

War crimes.   *See* names of wars with the subdivision *Atrocities,* e.g. **World War, 1939-1945—Atrocities;** etc.; and names of specific atrocities

War debts.   *See* **Public debts;** and names of wars with the subdivision *Finance,* e.g. **World War, 1939-1945—Finance;** etc.

War—Economic aspects   303.6
>Use for materials discussing the economic causes of war and the effect of war on industry and trade.
>*See also* **Industrial mobilization; Munitions; World War, 1939-1945—Human resources;** also names of wars with the subdivision *Economic aspects,* e.g. **World War, 1939-1945—Economic aspects;** etc.
>*x* Economics of war; Industry and war; War and industry

War of 1812.   *See* **United States—History—1812-1815, War of 1812**

War of 1914.   *See* **World War, 1914-1918**

War of 1939-1945.   *See* **World War, 1939-1945**

War of nerves.   *See* **Psychological warfare**

War of Secession (U.S.).   *See* **United States—History—1861-1865, Civil War**

War of the American Revolution.   *See* **United States—History—1775-1783, Revolution**

War pensions.   *See* **Pensions, Military**

War poetry   808.81; 811, etc.; 811.008, etc.
>*See also* **War songs;** also names of wars with the subdivision *Poetry,* e.g. **World War, 1939-1945—Poetry;** etc.
>*xx* **Poetry—Collections; War songs**

War protest movements.   *See* names of wars with the subdivision *Protests, demonstrations, etc.,* e.g. **World War, 1939-1945—Protests, demonstrations, etc.;** etc.

War ships.   *See* **Warships**

War songs   782.42
>*See also* **War poetry; World War, 1939-1945—Songs and music**
>*x* Battle songs; Soldiers' songs
>*xx* **National songs; Songs; War poetry**

War, Space.   *See* **Space warfare**

War use of animals.   *See* **Animals—War use**

War use of dogs.   *See* **Dogs—War use**

War veterans.   *See* **Veterans**

War work.   *See* names of wars with the subdivision *War work,* e.g. **World War, 1939-1945—War work;** etc.

Warfare, Space. *See* **Space warfare**
Warfare, Submarine. *See* **Submarine warfare**
Warm air heating. *See* **Hot air heating**
Wars. *See* **Military history; Naval history; War;**
and names of wars, e.g. **World War, 1939-**
1945; etc.
Wars of the Roses, 1455-1485. *See* **Great Britain—**
History—1455-1485, War of the Roses
Warships   359.3; 623.8
See also **Aircraft carriers; Navies; Submarines;**
also names of countries with the subhead
Navy, e.g. **United States. Navy;** etc.; and
names of individual warships
x Battle ships; Battleships; War ships
xx **Naval architecture; Naval art and science; Na-**
vies; Sea power; Ships
Washing. *See* **Laundry**
Wasps   595.79
x Hymenoptera
xx **Insects**
Waste as fuel. *See* **Waste products as fuel**
Waste disposal. *See* **Industrial wastes; Medical**
wastes; Radioactive waste disposal; Refuse
and refuse disposal; Sewage disposal; Waste
products
Waste (Economics)   339.4
xx **Economics**
Waste products   628.4
See also **Industrial wastes; Recycling (Waste,**
etc.); Refuse and refuse disposal; Salvage
(Waste, etc.); Substitute products
x By-products; Junk; Products, Waste; Trade
waste; Waste disposal
xx **Chemistry, Technical; Industrial wastes; Man-**
ufactures; Recycling (Waste, etc.); Refuse
and refuse disposal; Salvage (Waste, etc.)
Waste products as fuel   333.79; 662; 665
See also **Biomass energy**
x Energy conversion from waste; Organic waste
as fuel; Waste as fuel
xx **Biomass energy; Salvage (Waste, etc.)**
Waste products—Recycling. *See* **Recycling (Waste,**
etc.); Salvage (Waste, etc.)
Waste reclamation. *See* **Recycling (Waste, etc.);**
Salvage (Waste, etc.)
Wastes, Hazardous. *See* **Hazardous wastes**
Wastes, Industrial. *See* **Industrial wastes**
Wastes, Medical. *See* **Medical wastes**
Watches. *See* **Clocks and watches**
Water   551.4; 553.7
See also

Floods	**Lakes**
Fog	**Ocean**
Frost	**Ponds**
Geysers	**Rain**
Glaciers	**Rivers**
Hydraulic engineering	**Sea water**
Hydrotherapy	**Snow**
Ice	**Steam**

x Hydrology
xx **Earth sciences; Hydraulic engineering; Hy-**
draulics
Water—Analysis   546; 628.1
xx **Chemistry, Analytic; Water pollution**

Water animals. *See* **Freshwater animals; Marine animals**
Water ballet. *See* **Synchronized swimming**
Water birds   598.29
   See also **Geese;** also names of water birds, e.g. **Terns;** etc.
   x Aquatic birds; Birds, Aquatic; Water fowl; Wild fowl
   xx **Birds**
Water color painting. *See* **Watercolor painting**
Water colors. *See* **Watercolor painting**
Water conduits. *See* **Aqueducts**
Water conservation   333.91
   See also **Water supply**
   x Conservation of water
   xx **Water supply**
Water cure. *See* **Hydrotherapy**
Water—Detergent pollution. *See* **Detergent pollution of rivers, lakes, etc.**
Water farming. *See* **Hydroponics**
Water flow. *See* **Hydraulics**
Water—Fluoridation   628.1
   x Fluoridation of water
   xx **Teeth—Diseases**
Water fowl. *See* **Water birds**
Water—Heavy water. *See* **Deuterium oxide**
Water—Oil pollution. *See* **Oil pollution of water**
Water plants. *See* **Freshwater plants; Marine plants**
Water pollution   363.73; 628.1
   See also **Acid rain; Industrial wastes; Refuse and refuse disposal; Sewage disposal; Water—Analysis; Water supply;** also types of pollution, e.g. **Detergent pollution of rivers, lakes, etc.; Oil pollution of water;** etc.
   x Pollution of water; River pollution
   xx **Environmental health; Industrial wastes; Pollution; Public health; Refuse and refuse disposal; Rivers; Sewage disposal; Water supply**
Water power   333.9; 621.2
   See also **Dams; Hydraulic engineering; Hydraulic machinery; Hydroelectric power plants**
   x Hydroelectric power
   xx **Energy resources; Hydraulics; Power (Mechanics); Renewable energy resources; Rivers; Water resources development**
Water—Purification   628.1
   See also **Sea water conversion**
   x Purification of water
   xx **Sanitation; Water supply**
Water resources development   333.9
   See also **Hydroelectric power plants; Inland navigation; Irrigation; Water power; Water supply**
Water rights   333.91; 346.04
   xx **Irrigation; Law; Rivers**
Water skiing   797.3
   x Skiing, Water
   xx **Skis and skiing; Water sports**
Water sports   797
   See also

Boats and boating	**Diving**
Canoes and canoeing	**Fishing**

Water sports—*Continued*

Rowing	**Swimming**
Sailing	**Water skiing**
Skin diving	**Yachts and yachting**
Surfing	

    also names of other water sports

    x Aquatic sports

    xx **Sports**

Water supply (May subdiv. geog.)   363.6; 628.1

    See also

Aqueducts	**Water conservation**
Dams	**Water pollution**
Forest influences	**Water—Purification**
Irrigation	**Wells**
Reservoirs	

    x Waterworks

    xx **Civil engineering; Municipal engineering;
        Public health; Public utilities; Reservoirs;
        Sanitary engineering; Sanitation; Water
        conservation; Water pollution; Water re-
        sources development; Wells**

Water supply engineering   628.1

    See also **Boring; Hydraulic engineering**

    xx **Civil engineering; Engineering; Hydraulic en-
        gineering**

Water transportation. *See* **Shipping**

Watercolor painting   751.42

    x Water color painting; Water colors; Watercol-
       ors

    xx **Painting**

Watercolors. *See* **Watercolor painting**

Watergate Affair, 1972-1974   351.9; 973.924

    xx **Corruption in politics; Misconduct in office;
        United States—History—1961-1974**

Watering places. *See* **Health resorts, spas, etc.**

Waterways   386

    Use for general materials on rivers, lakes, and
       canals as highways for transportation or
       commerce.

    See also **Canals; Inland navigation; Lakes; Rivers**

    xx **Transportation**

Waterworks. *See* **Water supply**

Wave mechanics   530.1

    xx **Mechanics; Quantum theory; Waves**

Waves   551.47

    See also **Electric waves; Light; Ocean waves; Ra-
       diation; Sound waves; Wave mechanics**

    xx **Hydrodynamics; Vibration**

Waves, Electromagnetic. *See* **Electromagnetic
    waves**

Waves, Ultrasonic. *See* **Ultrasonic waves**

Wealth   330.1

    See also

Capital	**Money**
Capitalists and financiers	**Poverty**
Economic conditions	**Profit**
Income	**Property**
Income tax	**Standard of living**
Inheritance and succession	**Success**
Millionaires	

    x Distribution of wealth; Fortune; Fortunes;
       Riches

    xx **Capital; Economics; Finance; Millionaires;
        Money; Property**

Weapons and weaponry. *See* **Arms and armor; Firearms**
Weapons, Atomic. *See* **Nuclear weapons**
Weapons, Enhanced radiation. *See* **Neutron weapons**
Weapons, Neutron. *See* **Neutron weapons**
Weapons, Nuclear. *See* **Nuclear weapons**
Weapons, Space. *See* **Space weapons**
Weariness. *See* **Fatigue**
Weather 551.6
See note under **Climate.**
See also

Climate	**Storms**
Humidity	**Weather control**
Meteorology	**Weather forecasting**
Rain	**Winds**
Snow	

also names of countries, cities, etc. with the subdivision *Climate,* e.g. **United States—Climate;** etc.
xx **Climate; Meteorology**
Weather control 551.68
x Artificial weather control; Cloud seeding; Rain making; Weather modification
xx **Meteorology; Weather**
Weather—Folklore 551.6
x Weather lore
xx **Folklore; Meteorology; Weather forecasting**
Weather forecasting 551.6
See also **Meteorology in aeronautics; Weather—Folklore**
x Precipitation forecasting
xx **Forecasting; Meteorology; Weather**
Weather lore. *See* **Weather—Folklore**
Weather modification. *See* **Weather control**
Weather satellites. *See* **Meteorological satellites**
Weather stations. *See* **Meteorology—Observatories**
Weaving 746.1; 746.4
See also **Basket making; Beadwork; Lace and lace making; Looms; Textile industry;** also names of woven articles, e.g. **Carpets;** etc.
x Hand weaving
xx **Carpets; Handicraft; Textile industry**
Weddings 392
See also **Marriage customs and rites**
xx **Marriage**
Weed killers. *See* **Herbicides**
Weedicides. *See* **Herbicides**
Weeds 632
xx **Agricultural pests; Botany; Botany, Economic; Gardening**
Week 529
xx **Calendars; Chronology**
Weight control. *See* **Reducing**
Weight lifting 613.7; 796.41
See also **Bodybuilding**
x Bodybuilding (Weight lifting); Powerlifting; Pumping iron; Strength training; Weight training; Weightlifting
xx **Athletics; Bodybuilding; Exercise**
Weight training. *See* **Weight lifting**
Weightlessness 531
x Free fall; Gravity free state; Subgravity state;

Weightlessness—*Continued*
> Zero gravity
> *xx* **Man—Influence of environment; Space medicine**

Weightlifting. *See* **Weight lifting**
Weights and measures 389
> *See also* **Decimal system; Electric measurements; Measurement; Measuring instruments; Metric system; Volume (Cubic content)**
> *x* Cambistry; Measures; Metrology
> *xx* **Measurement**

Welding 671
> *See also* **Electric welding; Solder and soldering**
> *x* Oxyacetylene welding
> *xx* **Blacksmithing; Forging; Ironwork; Metalwork; Solder and soldering**

Welding, Electric. *See* **Electric welding**
Welfare agencies. *See* **Charities**
Welfare state. *See* **Economic policy; Public welfare; State, The**
Welfare work. *See* **Charities; Public welfare; Social work**
Welfare work in industry 658.3
> *See also* **Counseling; Housing; Social settlements**
> *xx* **Industrial management; Labor; Social work**

Well boring. *See* **Boring**
Well drilling, Oil. *See* **Oil well drilling**
Wells 551.49; 628.1
> *See also* **Boring; Natural gas; Petroleum; Water supply**
> *x* Artesian wells
> *xx* **Boring; Hydraulic engineering; Water supply**

West Africa 966
> Use for materials dealing collectively with the southern half of the western bulge of the African continent. The area is defined on the north by the Sahara and on the south and west by the Atlantic Ocean. The term is used loosely, but includes Benin, Burkina Faso, Cameroon, Gambia, Ghana, Guinea, Guinea-Bissau, Ivory Coast, Liberia, Nigeria, Senegal, Sierra Leone, and Togo. Sometimes, additional countries of the Sahel (Mali, Mauritania, and Niger) are also included.
> *See also* **French-speaking West Africa**
> *x* Africa, West

West Germany. *See* **Germany (West)**
West Indian literature (French) 840
> *x* French literature—West Indian authors

West Point (Military academy). *See* **United States Military Academy**
West (U.S.) 978
> Use for the region west of the Mississippi River.
> *See also* **Pacific Northwest; Pacific States;** also names of individual states in this region
> *x* Western States
> *xx* **United States**

West (U.S.)—Exploration 978
> *See also* **Overland journeys to the Pacific**
> *x* United States—Discovery and exploration; United States—Exploration
> *xx* **America—Exploration; Overland journeys to the Pacific**

Western and country music. *See* **Country music**
Western civilization. *See* **Civilization, Occidental**
Western Europe. *See* **Europe**
Western States. *See* **West (U.S.)**
Westminster Abbey 726
> *xx* **Abbeys**
Whales 599.5
> *xx* **Marine mammals**
Whaling 639.2
> *xx* **Fisheries; Hunting; Voyages and travels**
Wheat 633.1
> *See also* **Flour**
> *x* Breadstuffs
> *xx* **Flour; Grain**
Wheels 621.8; 629.2
> *See also* **Gearing; Tires; Turbines**
> *x* Car wheels
Which-way stories. *See* **Plot-your-own stories**
Whistle blowing 174; 351.9; 352
> Use for materials on the practice of calling pub-
> lic attention to corruption, mismanagement,
> or waste in government, business, the mili-
> tary, etc.
> *x* Blowing the whistle; Whistleblowing
> *xx* **Corruption in politics; Public interest**
Whistleblowing. *See* **Whistle blowing**
White collar crimes 364.1
> Use for comprehensive materials on crimes such
> as fraud, embezzlement, stealing of com-
> pany property, etc., committed by business
> persons and professionals in the course of
> their work.
> *x* Crimes, White collar; Occupational crimes
> *xx* **Crime**
Whittling. *See* **Wood carving**
Whole language 372.6
> Use for materials on the integration of listening,
> speaking, writing, and reading skills in
> meaningful situations in which children par-
> ticipate actively.
> *x* Integrated language arts (Holistic); Language
> arts (Holistic)
> *xx* **Language arts; Reading; Writing**
Wholistic medicine. *See* **Holistic medicine**
Widowers 305.38; 306.88
> *See also* **Single parent family**
> *xx* **Family; Husbands; Men; Single men; Single
> parent family**
Widows 305.48; 306.88
> *See also* **Single parent family**
> *xx* **Family; Single parent family; Single women;
> Wives; Women**
Wife abuse 362.82
> *See also* **Abused women**
> *x* Abuse of wives; Battering of wives; Wife bat-
> tering; Wife beating
> *xx* **Abused women; Family violence**
Wife battering. *See* **Wife abuse**
Wife beating. *See* **Wife abuse**
Wigs 391
> *xx* **Costume; Hair and hairdressing**
Wild animals. *See* **Animals; Wildlife**

Wild children 155.45

Use for materials on children who have been raised by animals or have lived their formative years in the wild without contact with human society

x Feral children; Wolf children

xx **Exceptional children**

Wild flowers 582.13

x Flowers, Wild; Wildflowers

xx **Flowers**

Wild flowers—Conservation. *See* **Plant conservation**

Wild fowl. *See* **Game and game birds; Water birds**

Wilderness areas 333.78

x Preservation of natural scenery; Protection of natural scenery

xx **Forest reserves; National parks and reserves; Natural monuments**

Wilderness survival 613.6; 796.5

x Bush survival; Outdoor survival

xx **Camping; Outdoor life; Survival (after airplane accidents, shipwrecks, etc.); Survival skills**

Wildflowers. *See* **Wild flowers**

Wildlife (May subdiv. geog.) 333.95; 639

Names of all categories of wildlife are not included in this List but are to be added as needed.

See also

Alpine animals	**Game and game birds**
Dangerous animals	**Jungle animals**
Desert animals	**Marine animals**
Extinct animals	**Rare animals**
Forest animals	**Stream animals**
Freshwater animals	**Swamp animals**
Furbearing animals	

x Feral animals; Wild animals

xx **Animals**

Wildlife and pesticides. *See* **Pesticides and wildlife**

Wildlife conservation 639.9

See also

Birds—Protection	serves
Forest reserves	**Natural resources**
Game preserves	**Pesticides and wildlife**
Game protection	**Rare animals**
National parks and re-	**Wildlife refuges**

x Conservation of wildlife; Preservation of wildlife; Protection of wildlife

xx **Conservation of natural resources; Endangered species; Environmental protection; Nature conservation; Rare animals; Zoology, Economic**

Wildlife refuges 639.9

See also names of specific refuges

x Refuges, Wildlife; Sanctuaries, Wildlife; Wildlife sanctuaries

xx **Wildlife conservation**

Wildlife sanctuaries. *See* **Wildlife refuges**

Will. *See* **Brainwashing; Free will and determinism**

Will power. *See* **Self-control**

Willpower. *See* **Self-control**

Wills 346

See also **Executors and administrators; Inheritance and succession**

Wills—*Continued*

　　x Bequests; Legacies
　　xx **Executors and administrators; Genealogy; Inheritance and succession; Registers of births, etc.**

Wills, Living. *See* **Right to die**

Wind. *See* **Winds**

Wind instruments 788
　　See also **Bands (Music);** also names of wind instruments, e.g. **Flute;** etc.
　　x Brass instruments; Woodwind instruments
　　xx **Bands (Music); Musical instruments**

Wind power 621.4
　　See also **Windmills**
　　xx **Energy resources; Power (Mechanics); Renewable energy resources; Windmills**

Windbreaks 634.9
　　x Shelterbelts
　　xx **Tree planting**

Windmills 621.4
　　See also **Wind power**
　　xx **Irrigation; Wind power**

Window dressing. *See* **Show windows**

Window gardening 635.9
　　See also **House plants**
　　x Greenhouses, Window; Window greenhouses; Windowbox gardening; Windowsill gardening
　　xx **Flower gardening; Flowers; Gardening; Indoor gardening**

Window greenhouses. *See* **Window gardening**

Windowbox gardening. *See* **Window gardening**

Windows 721
　　See also **Glass; Show windows**
　　xx **Architecture—Details; Building**

Windows, Stained glass. *See* **Glass painting and staining**

Windowsill gardening. *See* **Window gardening**

Winds 551.5
　　See also **Cyclones; Hurricanes; Storms; Tornadoes; Typhoons**
　　x Gales; Wind
　　xx **Meteorology; Navigation; Physical geography; Storms; Weather**

Windsurfing 797.3
　　x Board sailing; Sailboarding
　　xx **Sailing**

Wine and wine making (May subdiv. geog.) **664**
　　See also **Fermentation; Grapes**
　　xx **Alcoholic beverages; Fermentation; Grapes**

Winter resorts 613; 796.9
　　See also **Health resorts, spas, etc.**
　　x Resorts
　　xx **Health resorts, spas, etc.**

Winter sports 796.9
　　See also names of winter sports, e.g. **Ice hockey; Ice skating; Skis and skiing; Sleds and sledding;** etc.
　　x Ice sports
　　xx **Sports**

Wire agencies. *See* **News agencies**

Wireless. *See* **Radio**

Wiretapping 363.2

  See also **Eavesdropping**

  xx **Criminal investigation; Eavesdropping; Right of privacy**

Wiring, Electric. *See* **Electric wiring**

Wishes 153.8

  xx **Motivation (Psychology)**

Wit and humor 808.7; 808.87

  See also

Anecdotes	Nonsense verses
Chapbooks	Parody
Comedy	Practical jokes
Epigrams	Puns and punning
Humorists	Satire
Humorous poetry	Tall tales
Humorous stories	World War, 1939-1945—
Jokes	Humor

  also **American wit and humor; English wit and humor;** etc.; and subjects with the subdivision *Humor,* e.g. **Music—Humor;** etc.

  x Facetiae; Humor

  xx **Anecdotes; Laughter; Literature**

Witchcraft 133.4

  See also **Charms; Demonology; Occultism; Witches**

  x Black art (Magic); Black magic (Witchcraft); Delusions; Necromancy; Sorcery; Spirits; Wizardry

  xx **Demonology; Exorcism; Folklore; Occultism; Superstition**

Witches 133.4

  x Covens

  xx **Witchcraft**

Witnesses 345; 347

  x Cross-examination

Wives 306.872

  Use for materials on wives in general and for materials on the legal status of married women.

  See also **Abused women; Widows**

  x Married women; Spouses

  xx **Abused women; Family; Marriage; Married people; Women**

Wives of presidents—United States. *See* **Presidents—United States—Spouses**

Wives, Runaway. *See* **Runaway adults**

Wizardry. *See* **Witchcraft**

Wolf children. *See* **Wild children**

Woman. *See* **Women**

Woman power. *See* **Human resources**

Women (May subdiv. geog.) 305.4

  See also

Abused women	Wives
Black women	World War, 1939-1945—
Mothers	Women
Single women	Young women
Widows	

  also headings beginning with the words **Women** and **Women's**

  x Woman

Women actors. *See* **Actors**

Women air pilots 629.132

  xx **Air pilots**

Women artists   704

Use same form for the attainments of women in other occupations and professions, e.g. **Women physicians;** etc.

xx **Artists; Women—Employment**

Women authors   809; 920

See also **American literature—Women authors**

xx **Authors**

Women—Biography   920

x Heroines

xx **Biography**

Women, Black.   *See* **Black women**

Women—Civil rights   323.3; 342

See also **Feminism; Pro-choice movement; Pro-life movement; Women—Suffrage; Women's movement**

x Emancipation of women; Rights of women; Women—Emancipation; Women—Equal rights; Women's rights

xx **Civil rights; Feminism; Sex discrimination; Women—Suffrage**

Women—Clothing.   *See* **Women's clothing**

Women—Clubs.   *See* **Women—Societies**

Women—Diseases   616.0082; 618.1

See also **Women—Health and hygiene**

x Diseases of women; Gynecology

xx **Women—Health and hygiene**

Women—Dress.   *See* **Women's clothing**

Women—Education   376

See also **Coeducation**

x Education of women

xx **Coeducation**

Women—Emancipation.   *See* **Women—Civil rights**

Women—Employment   331.4

See also **Equal pay for equal work; Self-employed women;** also **Women artists; Women physicians** and similar headings

x Employment of women; Girls—Employment; Women—Occupations; Working women

xx **Discrimination in employment; Labor; Labor supply**

Women—Enfranchisement.   *See* **Women—Suffrage**

Women—Equal rights.   *See* **Women—Civil rights**

Women—Health and hygiene   613

See also **Women—Diseases**

x Gynecology; Women—Hygiene

xx **Women—Diseases**

Women—Hygiene.   *See* **Women—Health and hygiene**

Women in art   704.9

Use for materials on women depicted in works of art. Materials on the attainments of women in the area of art are entered under **Women artists.**

xx **Art**

Women in business.   *See* **Businesswomen**

Women in literature   809

Use for materials on the theme of women in works of literature. Materials on the attainments of women in the area of literature are entered under **Women authors.**

xx **Characters and characteristics in literature; Literature**

Women in motion pictures 791.43
    Use for materials discussing the portrayal of
        women in motion pictures. Materials dis-
        cussing all aspects of women's involvement
        in motion pictures are entered under
        Women in the motion picture industry.
   xx **Motion pictures**
Women in the Bible 220.8
   x Bible—Women; Heroines
   xx **Bible—Biography**
Women in the motion picture industry 791.43
   See note under **Women in motion pictures.**
   xx **Motion picture industry**
Women judges 347.092; 920
   xx **Judges**
Women—Occupations. *See* **Women—Employment**
Women physicians 610.69
   xx **Physicians; Women—Employment**
Women police. *See* **Police**
Women—Political activity 324
   See also **Women politicians**
   xx **Politics, Practical**
Women politicians 920
   xx **Politicians; Women—Political activity**
Women—Psychology 155.3
   x Feminine psychology
Women—Rights. *See* **Feminism**
Women—Self-defense. *See* **Self-defense for women**
Women, Self-employed. *See* **Self-employed women**
Women, Single. *See* **Single women**
Women—Social conditions 305.42
   See also **Divorce; Prostitution; Women—**
      Societies; Women's movement
Women—Societies 367
   See also **Girls' clubs**
   x Women—Clubs; Women's clubs; Women's
      organizations
   xx **Clubs; Societies; Women—Social conditions**
Women—Suffrage 324.6
   See also **Women—Civil rights**
   x Suffragettes; Women—Enfranchisement
   xx **Suffrage; Women—Civil rights**
Women—United States 305.40973
   See also **Presidents—United States—Spouses**
   x United States—Women
Women's clothing 646
   x Women—Clothing; Women—Dress
   xx **Clothing and dress**
Women's clubs. *See* **Women—Societies**
Women's liberation movement. *See* **Women's**
   movement
Women's movement 305.42; 323.3
   See also **Feminism**
   x Women's liberation movement
   xx **Feminism; Women—Civil rights; Women—**
      Social conditions
Women's organizations. *See* **Women—Societies**
Women's rights. *See* **Feminism; Women—Civil**
   rights
Women's self-defense. *See* **Self-defense for women**
Wonders. *See* **Curiosities and wonders**
Wood 674
   Use for materials on the chemical and physical

Wood—*Continued*

    properties of different kinds of wood and how they are used.

    See also **Forests and forestry; Lumber and lumbering; Plywood; Woodwork;** also kinds of wood, e.g. **Oak;** etc.

    x Timber

    xx **Building materials; Forest products; Forests and forestry; Fuel; Trees**

Wood block printing. *See* **Wood engraving; Woodcuts**

Wood carving 736

    x Carving, Wood; Whittling

    xx **Decoration and ornament; Furniture; Sculpture; Woodwork**

Wood engraving 761

    x Block printing; Wood block printing

    xx **Engraving**

Wood finishing 684; 698

    See also **Lacquer and lacquering; Varnish and varnishing**

    x Finishes and finishing

    xx **Painting, Industrial**

Wood—Preservation 674

    x Preservation of wood

Wood turning. *See* **Turning**

Woodcuts 761

    x Block printing; Wood block printing

Woods. *See* **Forests and forestry**

Woodwind instruments. *See* **Wind instruments**

Woodwork 684

    See also **Cabinet work; Carpentry; Furniture; Turning; Wood carving**

    xx **Architecture—Details; Cabinet work; Carpentry; Decorative arts; Turning; Wood**

Woodworking machinery 621.9; 684

    See also special kinds of machines, e.g. **Lathes;** etc.

    xx **Machinery**

Wool 677

    See also **Dyes and dyeing; Yarn**

    x Animal products

    xx **Fibers; Yarn**

Word books. *See* **Picture dictionaries**

Word games 793.73

    See also names of specific word games, e.g. **Crossword puzzles;** etc.

    xx **Games; Literary recreations**

Word processing 652.5

    xx **Office management; Office practice**

Word processor keyboarding. *See* **Keyboarding (Electronics)**

Word processor keyboards. *See* **Keyboards (Electronics)**

Word skills. *See* **Reading**

Wordless stories. *See* **Stories without words**

Words. *See* **Vocabulary**

Words, New 422

    x Coinage of words; New words

    xx **Semantics; Vocabulary**

Work 331.1

    Use for materials on the physical or mental exertion of individuals to produce or accomplish

Work—*Continued*

something. Materials on the collective human activities involved in the production and distribution of goods and services in an economy, as well as materials on the group of workers who render these services for wages, are entered under **Labor.**

See also **Employee morale; Job satisfaction; Labor; Sex in the workplace; Work ethics**

xx **Labor**

Work addiction. *See* **Workaholism**

Work at home. *See* **Home business; Telecommuting**

Work ethics   174

x Ethics, Work

xx **Ethics; Labor; Work**

Work performance standards. *See* **Performance standards**

Work satisfaction. *See* **Job satisfaction**

Work standards. *See* **Production standards**

Work stoppages. *See* **Strikes and lockouts**

Work stress. *See* **Job stress**

Workaholic syndrome. *See* **Workaholism**

Workaholism   155.2; 616.85

x Addiction to work; Compulsive working; Work addiction; Workaholic syndrome; Working, Compulsive

xx **Compulsive behavior**

Workers' compensation   368.4

x Compensation; Employers' liability; Insurance, Workers' compensation; Workmen's compensation

xx **Accident insurance; Health insurance; Occupational diseases; Social security**

Workers' participation in management. *See* **Participative management**

Working animals   636.088

See also headings for animals in specific working situations, e.g. **Animals—War use; Animals in police work; Dogs—War use;** etc.

x Animals, Working

xx **Animals; Domestic animals; Zoology, Economic**

Working at home. *See* **Home business; Telecommuting**

Working children. *See* **Children—Employment**

Working class. *See* **Labor**

Working, Compulsive. *See* **Workaholism**

Working couples. *See* **Dual career family**

Working day. *See* **Hours of labor**

Working hours. *See* **Hours of labor**

Working parents, Children of. *See* **Children of working parents**

Working robots. *See* **Industrial robots**

Working women. *See* **Women—Employment**

Workmen's compensation. *See* **Workers' compensation**

Workshop councils. *See* **Participative management**

Workshops, Teachers'. *See* **Teachers' workshops**

World. *See* **Earth**

World economics. *See* **Commercial policy; Economic conditions; Economic policy; Geography, Commercial**

World, End of the. *See* **End of the world**

World government. *See* **International organization**
World history   909
> *See also* **Geography; History, Ancient; History,
> Modern; Middle Ages—History**
> *x* History, Universal; Universal history
> *xx* **History**
World language. *See* **Universal language**
World organization. *See* **International organization**
World politics   909
> See note under **International relations.**
> *See also* **Geopolitics; International organization;
> International relations; World War, 1914-
> 1918; World War, 1939-1945; World War
> III;** also names of countries with the subdi-
> visions *Foreign relations* and *Politics and
> government,* e.g. **United States—Foreign
> relations; United States—Politics and gov-
> ernment;** etc.
> *x* International politics
> *xx* **Geopolitics; International organization; Inter-
> national relations; Political science**
World politics—1945-1965   909.82
> *x* Cold war; Power politics
World politics—1965-   909.82
> *x* Power politics
World records   030
> *x* Human records; Records, Human; Records of
> achievement; Records, World; World's re-
> cords
> *xx* **Curiosities and wonders**
World War, 1914-1918 (May subdiv. geog.)   **940.3;
940.4**
> May be subdivided like **World War, 1939-1945.**
> Here are listed references applicable only to
> this war.
> *x* European War, 1914-1918; War of 1914
> *xx* **Europe—History—1914-1945; History, Mod-
> ern—1900-1999 (20th century); World poli-
> tics**
World War, 1914-1918—Economic aspects   940.3
> *xx* **Reconstruction (1914-1939)**
World War, 1914-1918—Gas warfare   940.4
> *xx* **Poisonous gases—War use**
World War, 1914-1918—Peace   940.3
> *See also* **League of Nations**
World War, 1914-1918—Reconstruction. *See* **Re-
construction (1914-1939)**
**World War, 1914-1918—Territorial questions
940.3**
> *See also* **Mandates**
**World War, 1914-1918—United States   940.3;
940.4; 973.91**
> *x* United States—European War, 1914-1918;
> United States—History—1914-1918, Euro-
> pean War; United States—History—1914-
> 1918, World War; United States—World
> War, 1914-1918
World War, 1939-1945 (May subdiv. geog.)   **940.53;
940.54**
> Subdivisions used under this heading may be
> used under other wars.
> *See also* names of battles, sieges, etc., e.g. **Ar-
> dennes, Battle of the, 1944-1945; Pearl Har-**

World War, 1939-1945—*Continued*
        bor (Oahu, Hawaii), Attack on, 1941; etc.
   x European War, 1939-1945; War of 1939-1945
   xx **Europe—History—1914-1945; History, Modern—1900-1999 (20th century); World politics**
World War, 1939-1945—Aerial operations 940.54
   x World War, 1939-1945—Battles, sieges, etc.
   xx **Aeronautics, Military**
World War, 1939-1945—Amphibious operations 940.54
   xx **World War, 1939-1945—Naval operations**
World War, 1939-1945—Antiwar movements. *See* **World War, 1939-1945—Protests, demonstrations, etc.**
World War, 1939-1945—Armistices 940.53
World War, 1939-1945—Arms. *See* **World War, 1939-1945—Equipment and supplies**
World War, 1939-1945—Art and the war 940.53
   x World War, 1939-1945—Iconography; World War, 1939-1945, in art
   xx **Art**
World War, 1939-1945—Atrocities 940.54
   See also **War crime trials;** also names of specific atrocities and crimes
World War, 1939-1945—Battles, sieges, etc. *See* **World War, 1939-1945—Aerial operations; World War, 1939-1945—Campaigns; World War, 1939-1945—Naval operations**
World War, 1939-1945—Biography 920
World War, 1939-1945—Blacks 940.53; 940.54
World War, 1939-1945—Blockades 940.54
World War, 1939-1945—Campaigns (May subdiv. geog.) **940.54**
   See also **Pearl Harbor (Oahu, Hawaii), Attack on, 1941;** also names of battles, campaigns, sieges, etc., **Ardennes, Battle of the, 1944-1945; Pearl Harbor, (Oahu, Hawaii), Attack on, 1941;** etc.
   x World War, 1939-1945—Battles, sieges, etc.
World War, 1939-1945—Cartoons and caricatures 940.53
   x World War, 1939-1945—Humor, caricatures, etc.
   xx **Cartoons and caricatures**
World War, 1939-1945—Causes 940.53
   See also **National socialism**
World War, 1939-1945—Censorship 940.54
World War, 1939-1945—Charities. *See* **World War, 1939-1945—Civilian relief; World War, 1939-1945—War work**
World War, 1939-1945—Chemical warfare 940.54
   xx **Chemical warfare**
World War, 1939-1945—Children 940.53
   xx **Children**
World War, 1939-1945—Civilian evacuation. *See* **World War, 1939-1945—Evacuation of civilians**
World War, 1939-1945—Civilian relief 940.54
   See also **World War, 1939-1945—Refugees**
   x World War, 1939-1945—Charities
   xx **Charities; Economic assistance; Food relief; Reconstruction (1939-1951); World War,**

World War, 1939-1945—Civilian relief—*Continued*
    1939-1945—Food supply; World War,
    1939-1945—Medical care; World War,
    1939-1945—Refugees; World War, 1939-
    1945—War work
World War, 1939-1945—Collaborationists   940.53
  x Fifth column; Quislings
  xx **World War, 1939-1945—Occupied territories**
World War, 1939-1945—Congresses   940.53
  xx **Congresses and conventions**
World War, 1939-1945—Conscientious objectors
    940.53
  See also **World War, 1939-1945—Draft resisters**
  xx **Conscientious objectors; World War, 1939-
    1945—Protests, demonstrations, etc.**
World War, 1939-1945—Correspondents. *See*
    World War, 1939-1945—Journalists
World War, 1939-1945—Desertions   940.54
  xx **Military desertion**
World War, 1939-1945—Destruction and pillage
    940.54
World War, 1939-1945—Diplomatic history   940.53
  See also **World War, 1939-1945—Governments
    in exile**
World War, 1939-1945—Displaced persons. *See*
    World War, 1939-1945—Refugees
World War, 1939-1945—Draft resisters   940.54
  xx **Draft resisters; World War, 1939-1945—
    Conscientious objectors**
World War, 1939-1945—Economic aspects   940.53
  Use for materials dealing with the economic
    causes of the war and the effect of the war
    on commerce and industry.
  See also **Reconstruction (1939-1951); World
    War, 1939-1945—Finance; World War,
    1939-1945—Human resources; World War,
    1939-1945—Reparations**
  xx **Reconstruction (1939-1951); War—Economic
    aspects**
World War, 1939-1945—Education and the war
    940.53
  xx **Education**
World War, 1939-1945—Engineering and construc-
    tion   940.54
  xx **Military engineering**
World War, 1939-1945—Equipment and supplies
    940.54
  x World War, 1939-1945—Arms; World War,
    1939-1945—Military supplies; World War,
    1939-1945—Munitions; World War, 1939-
    1945—Ordnance; World War, 1939-1945—
    Supplies; World War, 1939-1945—
    Weapons
  xx **Munitions**
World War, 1939-1945—Evacuation of civilians
    940.54
  x Civilian evacuation; World War, 1939-1945—
    Civilian evacuation
  xx **Civil defense; World War, 1939-1945—
    Refugees**
World War, 1939-1945—Fiction   Fic
World War, 1939-1945—Finance   940.53
  Use for materials on the cost and financing of

World War, 1939-1945—Finance—*Continued*
the war, including war debts, and the effect
of the war on financial systems, including
inflation.
xx **Public debts; World War, 1939-1945—**
Economic aspects
World War, 1939-1945—Food question. *See*
World War, 1939-1945—Food supply
World War, 1939-1945—Food supply   940.53
See also **World War, 1939-1945—Civilian relief**
x World War, 1939-1945—Food question
xx **Food relief**
World War, 1939-1945—Forced repatriation   940.53
See also **World War, 1939-1945—Refugees**
xx **World War, 1939-1945—Prisoners and pris-**
ons; World War, 1939-1945—Refugees
World War, 1939-1945—Governments in exile
940.53
x Governments in exile
xx **World War, 1939-1945—Diplomatic history**
World War, 1939-1945—Guerrillas. *See* **World**
War, 1939-1945—Underground movements
World War, 1939-1945—Health aspects   940.54
xx **Military health; Sanitation**
World War, 1939-1945—Hospitals. *See* **World**
War, 1939-1945—Medical care
World War, 1939-1945—Human resources   940.54
xx **Armies; Human resources; Labor; Labor sup-**
ply; War—Economic aspects; World War,
1939-1945—Economic aspects
World War, 1939-1945—Humor   940.53
x World War, 1939-1945—Humor, caricatures,
etc.
xx **Wit and humor**
World War, 1939-1945—Humor, caricatures,
etc. *See* **World War, 1939-1945—**
Cartoons and caricatures; World War, 1939-
1945—Humor
World War, 1939-1945—Iconography. *See* **World**
War, 1939-1945—Art and the war
World War, 1939-1945, in art. *See* **World War,**
1939-1945—Art and the war
World War, 1939-1945, in literature. *See* **World**
War, 1939-1945—Literature and the war
World War, 1939-1945, in motion pictures. *See*
World War, 1939-1945—Motion pictures
and the war
World War, 1939-1945—Influence   940.53
World War, 1939-1945—Jews   940.53
See also **Holocaust, Jewish (1933-1945)**
xx **Holocaust, Jewish (1933-1945)**
World War, 1939-1945—Jews—Rescue   940.54
x Rescue of Jews, 1939-1945
xx **Jews—Persecutions**
World War, 1939-1945—Journalists   940.54
x World War, 1939-1945—Correspondents;
World War, 1939-1945—War correspon-
dents
World War, 1939-1945—Literature and the war
809; 810, etc.; 940.53
x World War, 1939-1945, in literature
xx **Literature**
World War, 1939-1945—Maps   940.53022

724

World War, 1939-1945—Medical care   940.54
See also World War, 1939-1945—Civilian relief
x World War, 1939-1945—Hospitals
xx Armies—Medical care; Medicine, Military;
Military health; Military hospitals
World War, 1939-1945—Military supplies.   See
World War, 1939-1945—Equipment and
supplies
World War, 1939-1945—Missing in action   940.54
xx Missing in action; World War, 1939-1945—
Prisoners and prisons
World War, 1939-1945—Moral and religious aspects
940.53; 940.54
x World War, 1939-1945—Religious aspects
xx War and religion
World War, 1939-1945—Motion pictures and the war
791.43; 940.53
x World War, 1939-1945, in motion pictures
xx Motion pictures
World War, 1939-1945—Munitions.   See World
War, 1939-1945—Equipment and supplies
World War, 1939-1945—Museums   940.54
xx Museums
World War, 1939-1945—Naval operations   940.54
See also World War, 1939-1945—Amphibious
operations
x World War, 1939-1945—Battles, sieges, etc.
xx Naval battles
World War, 1939-1945—Naval operations—
Submarine   940.54
x World War, 1939-1945—Submarine operations
xx Submarine warfare
World War, 1939-1945—Occupied territories
940.54
Use for general treatment of the subject. For oc-
cupation of specific countries, use the name
of the country with the subdivision
History—1940-1945, German occupation or
History— 1945- , Allied occupation, e.g.
Netherlands—History—1940-1945, German
occupation; Japan—History—1945-1952,
Allied occupation; etc.
See also Japan—History—1945-1952, Allied oc-
cupation; World War, 1939-1945—
Collaborationists; World War, 1939-1945—
Underground movements; also names of
countries with the subdivision
History—1940-1945, German occupation,
e.g. Netherlands—History—1940-1945,
German occupation; etc.
xx Military occupation; World War, 1939-1945—
Territorial questions
World War, 1939-1945—Ordnance.   See World
War, 1939-1945—Equipment and supplies
World War, 1939-1945—Peace   940.53
xx Peace
World War, 1939-1945—Personal narratives
940.53; 940.54
Use for collective or individual eyewitness reports or autobiographical accounts that re-
late experiences of persons in connection
with the war.
xx Autobiographies; Biography

725

World War, 1939-1945—Pictorial works 940.53022
World War, 1939-1945—Poetry 808.81; 811, etc.
  xx War poetry
World War, 1939-1945—Prisoners and prisons
    940.54
  See also World War, 1939-1945—Forced repatri-
    ation; World War, 1939-1945—Missing in
    action
  xx Concentration camps; Prisoners of war
World War, 1939-1945—Propaganda 940.54
  xx Propaganda
World War, 1939-1945—Protests, demonstrations,
    etc. 940.53
  See also World War, 1939-1945—Conscientious
    objectors
  x World War, 1939-1945—Antiwar movements
World War, 1939-1945—Psychological aspects
    940.53
  xx Psychological warfare
World War, 1939-1945—Public opinion 940.53
  xx Public opinion
World War, 1939-1945—Railroads. *See* World
    War, 1939-1945—Transportation
World War, 1939-1945—Reconstruction. *See* Re-
    construction (1939-1951)
World War, 1939-1945—Refugees 940.53
  See also World War, 1939-1945—Civilian relief;
    World War, 1939-1945—Evacuation of civil-
    ians; World War, 1939-1945—Forced repa-
    triation
  x World War, 1939-1945—Displaced persons
  xx Political refugees; World War, 1939-1945—
    Civilian relief; World War, 1939-1945—
    Forced repatriation
World War, 1939-1945—Regimental histories
    940.54
World War, 1939-1945—Religious aspects. *See*
    World War, 1939-1945—Moral and reli-
    gious aspects
World War, 1939-1945—Reparations 940.53
  x Reparations (World War, 1939-1945)
  xx Reconstruction (1939-1951); World War,
    1939-1945—Economic aspects
World War, 1939-1945—Resistance
    movements. *See* World War, 1939-
    1945—Underground movements
World War, 1939-1945—Secret service 940.54
  xx Secret service
World War, 1939-1945—Social aspects 940.53
World War, 1939-1945—Social work. *See* World
    War, 1939-1945—War work
World War, 1939-1945—Songs and music 782.42
  xx Military music; War songs
World War, 1939-1945—Sources 940.53
  xx History—Sources
World War, 1939-1945—Submarine
    operations. *See* World War, 1939-1945—
    Naval operations—Submarine
World War, 1939-1945—Supplies. *See* World War,
    1939-1945—Equipment and supplies
World War, 1939-1945—Territorial questions
    940.53
  See also World War, 1939-1945—Occupied terri-

World War, 1939-1945—Territorial questions—*Continued*
     tories
     xx **Boundaries**
World War, 1939-1945—Theater and the war   792;
     940.53
     xx **Theater**
World War, 1939-1945—Transportation   940.54
     x World War, 1939-1945—Railroads
     xx **Transportation**
World War, 1939-1945—Treaties   940.53
     xx **Treaties**
World War, 1939-1945—Underground movements
     940.54
     x Underground movements (World War, 1939-
          1945); World War, 1939-1945—Guerrillas;
          World War, 1939-1945—Resistance movements
     xx **World War, 1939-1945—Occupied territories**
World War, 1939-1945—United States   940.53;
     940.54; 973.917
     x United States—History—1939-1945, World
          War; United States—World War, 1939-
          1945
World War, 1939-1945—War correspondents. *See*
     World War, 1939-1945—Journalists
World War, 1939-1945—War work   940.53
     See also **World War, 1939-1945—Civilian relief**
     x World War, 1939-1945—Charities; World
          War, 1939-1945—Social work
World War, 1939-1945—Weapons. *See* **World**
     War, 1939-1945—Equipment and supplies
World War, 1939-1945—Women   940.54
     xx **Women**
World War III   355
     x Third World War
     xx **War; World politics**
World's Fair (1992 : Seville, Spain). *See* **Expo 92**
     (Seville, Spain)
World's fairs. *See* **Exhibitions; Fairs**
World's records. *See* **World records**
Worms   595.1
     xx **Invertebrates**
Worms, Computer. *See* **Computer viruses**
Worry   152.4
     x Anxiety
     xx **Mental health; Nervous system—Diseases**
Worship   248.3; 264; 291.3
     See also **Devotional exercises; Prayer; Public**
          worship; Sacrifice
     x Devotion
     xx **Religion; Theology**
Worth. *See* **Values**
Wounded, First aid to. *See* **First aid**
Wounds and injuries   617.1
     See also **Fractures**
     x Injuries
     xx **Accidents**
Wrapping of gifts. *See* **Gift wrapping**
Wrecks. *See* **Shipwrecks;** and subjects with the
          subdivision *Accidents,* e.g. **Railroads—**
          Accidents; etc.
Wrestling   796.8
     See also **Judo**

Writers. *See* **Authors;** and classes of writers, e.g.
Dramatists; Historians; Journalists; etc.
Writing   411
Use for general materials on the history and art
of writing and on elegant handwriting. Prac-
tical guides are entered under **Handwriting.**
Materials on handwriting as an expression
of the writer's character are entered under
Graphology.
See also

Abbreviations	**Handwriting**
Alphabet	**Hieroglyphics**
Autographs	**Picture writing**
Calligraphy	**Shorthand**
Ciphers	**Typewriting**
Cryptography	**Whole language**
Graphology	**Writing of numerals**

xx **Alphabet; Ciphers; Communication; Handwriting; Language and languages; Language
arts**
Writing (Authorship). *See* **Authorship; Creative
writing; Journalism**
Writing of numerals   513
x Numeral formation; Numeral writing; Numerals, Writing of
xx **Handwriting; Numerals; Writing**
Writing—Patterning. *See* **Language arts—
Patterning**
Wrought iron work. *See* **Ironwork**
X-15 (Rocket aircraft)   629.133
xx **Rocket planes**
X rays   539.7
See also **Gamma rays; Radiologists; Radiotherapy; Tomography; Vacuum tubes**
x Radiography; Rays, Roentgen; Roentgen rays
xx **Electricity; Electromagnetic waves; Light; Ra-
diation; Radioactivity; Radiotherapy; Thera-
peutics**
Xerography   686.4
xx **Copying processes and machines**
Yacht basins. *See* **Marinas**
Yacht racing. *See* **Boat racing**
Yachts and yachting   797.1
See also **Marinas; Sailing**
x Regattas
xx **Boatbuilding; Boats and boating; Ocean travel;
Sailing; Ships; Voyages and travels; Water
sports**
Yard sales. *See* **Garage sales**
Yarn   677
See also **Cotton; Flax; Wool**
xx **Textile industry; Wool**
Yearbooks. *See* subjects with the subdivision
Periodicals, e.g. **Engineering—Periodicals;**
etc.
Yearbooks, Student. *See* **School yearbooks**
Yeast   641.3
xx **Fermentation**
Yellow fever   616.9
xx **Tropical medicine**
Yeti   001.9
x Abominable snowman
xx **Monsters; Primates**

Yiddish language 437
> May be subdivided like **English language.**
>
> *x* German Hebrew; Jewish language; Jews—
> Language; Judaeo-German
>
> *xx* **Hebrew language**

Yiddish literature 839
> May use same subdivisions and names of literary forms as for **English literature.**
>
> *xx* **Jewish literature**

Yippies. *See* **Hippies**

Yoga 181; 613.7
> *See also* **Hatha yoga**
>
> *xx* **Hatha yoga; Hinduism; Philosophy, Hindu;
> Theosophy**

Yoga exercises. *See* **Hatha yoga**

Yoga, Hatha. *See* **Hatha yoga**

Yom Kippur 296.4
> *x* Atonement, Day of; Day of Atonement
>
> *xx* **Fasts and feasts—Judaism**

Yom Kippur War, 1973. *See* **Israel-Arab War,
1973**

Yosemite National Park (Calif.) 719; 979.4
> *xx* **National parks and reserves**

Yosemite National Park (Calif.)—Pictorial works
979.4

Young adults' library services 027.62
> *See also* **Children's libraries; High school libraries; Young adults' literature**
>
> *x* Libraries and young adults; Libraries, Young
> adults'; Library services to teenagers; Library services to young adults; Teenagers'
> library services; Young people's libraries
>
> *xx* **Children's libraries; High school libraries;
> Young adults' literature**

Young adults' literature 028.5
> *See also* **Young adults' library services**
>
> *x* Teenagers—Literature
>
> *xx* **Young adults' library services**

Young consumers 640.73; 658.8
> *x* Children as consumers; Teenage consumers;
> Youth market
>
> *xx* **Consumers**

Young men 305.23; 305.31
> Use for materials on men in the general age
> range of eighteen through twenty-five years.
> Materials on the time of life between thirteen and twenty-five, as well as on people in
> that greater age range are entered under
> **Youth.**
>
> *See also* **Boys**
>
> *xx* **Boys; Men; Youth**

Young people. *See* **Youth**

Young people's libraries. *See* **Young adults' library
services**

Young persons. *See* **Youth**

Young women 305.23; 305.4
> Use for materials on women in the general age
> range of eighteen through twenty-five years.
> Materials on the time of life between thirteen and twenty-five, as well as on people in
> that greater age range are entered under
> **Youth.**
>
> *See also* **Girls**
>
> *xx* **Girls; Women; Youth**

Youngest child. *See* **Birth order**

Youth (May subdiv. geog.)   **305.23**
>
> Use for materials on the time of life between thirteen and twenty-five years, as well as on people in this general age range. For materials limited to teen youth, use **Teenagers.** For materials limited to people in the general age range of eighteen through twenty-five years of age, use **Young men; Young women.** Materials on the process or state of growing up are entered under **Adolescence.**
>
> *See also* **Church work with youth; Dropouts; Teenagers; Television and youth; Young men; Young women**
>
> *x* Young people; Young persons

Youth—Alcohol use   613.81; 616.86
> *See also* **Drinking age**
> *x* Alcohol and youth; Drinking and youth

Youth and drugs. *See* **Youth—Drug use**

Youth and narcotics. *See* **Youth—Drug use**

Youth and television. *See* **Television and youth**

Youth—Drug use   613.8; 616.86
> *See also* **Juvenile delinquency; Teenagers—Drug use**
> *x* Drugs and youth; Narcotics and youth; Youth and drugs; Youth and narcotics
> *xx* **Juvenile delinquency**

Youth—Employment   331.3
> *See also* **Summer employment; Teenagers—Employment**
> *x* Child labor; Employment of youth
> *xx* **Age and employment; Labor; Labor supply; Summer employment**

Youth hostels   647.94
> *x* Hostels, Youth; Tourist accommodations

Youth market. *See* **Young consumers**

Youth movement (May subdiv. geog.)   **322.4**
> *See also* **Students—Political activity**
> *x* Student movement; Student protests, demonstrations, etc.; Student revolt
> *xx* **Protests, demonstrations, etc.**

Youth—Religious life   268
> *See also* **Teenagers—Religious life**

Youth—United States   305.230973
> *See also* **Teenagers—United States**
> *x* American youth; United States—Youth

Zen Buddhism   294.3
> *xx* **Buddhism**

Zeppelins. *See* **Airships**

Zero gravity. *See* **Weightlessness**

Zinc   669
> *See also* **Brass**

Zionism   320.5
> *See also* **Jews—Restoration**
> *xx* **Jews—Restoration**

Zip code (May subdiv. geog.)   **383; 912**
> *x* Postal delivery code
> *xx* **Postal service**

Zodiac   133.5; 523
> *xx* **Astronomy**

Zoning   346.04; 352.9
> *x* City planning—Zone system; Districting (in city planning)
> *xx* **City planning**

Zoogeography. *See* **Biogeography**

Zoological gardens. *See* **Zoos**
Zoological specimens—Collection and preservation
  579
    See also **Taxidermy;** also names of specimens
  with the subdivision *Collection and preser-*
  vation, e.g. **Birds—Collection and preserva-**
  tion; etc.
    x Collections of natural specimens; Preservation
  of zoological specimens; Specimens, Preservation of
  xx **Collectors and collecting; Taxidermy**
Zoology 590; 591
    See also

Anatomy, Comparative	**Natural history**
Animals	**Poisonous animals**
Embryology	**Psychology, Comparative**
Evolution	**Variation (Biology)**
Fossils	

    also names of divisions, classes, etc. of the ani-
  mal kingdom, e.g. **Invertebrates; Verte-**
  brates; Birds; Mammals; etc.; and names of
  animals
    x Animal kingdom; Animal physiology; Fauna
  xx **Animals; Biology; Natural history; Nature**
  study; Science
Zoology, Economic 591.6
    Use for general materials on animals injurious
  and beneficial to man and to agriculture,
  and for materials on the extermination of
  wild animals, venomous snakes, etc.
    See also

Agricultural pests	**Pests**
Beneficial insects	**Pests—Control**
Domestic animals	**Wildlife conservation**
Furbearing animals	**Working animals**
Insect pests	

    x Animals, Useful and harmful; Biology, Eco-
  nomic; Economic zoology
Zoology of the Bible. *See* **Bible—Natural history**
Zoology—United States. *See* **Animals—United**
  States
Zoos 590.74
    See also **Petting zoos;** also names of zoos
    x Zoological gardens
  xx **Animals; Parks**